LATE ANTIQUITY

HARVARD
UNIVERSITY
PRESS
REFERENCE
LIBRARY

Research Assistants

Michael Gaddis
Jennifer Hevelone-Harper
Megan Reid
Kevin Uhalde

LATE ANTIQUITY

A GUIDE TO THE POSTCLASSICAL WORLD

G. W. BOWERSOCK

PETER BROWN

OLEG GRABAR

Editors

The Belknap Press of Harvard University Press

Cambridge, Massachusetts, and London, England · 1999

Library of Congress Cataloging-in-Publication Data

Late antiquity : a guide to the postclassical world / G. W. Bowersock,
    Peter Brown, Oleg Grabar, editors.
        p.   cm. — (Harvard University Press reference library)
    Includes bibliographical references and index.
    ISBN 0-674-51173-5 (alk. paper)
    1. Classical dictionaries.
    I. Bowersock, G. W. (Glen Warren), 1936–   .
    II. Brown, Peter Robert Lamont.   III. Grabar, Oleg.
    IV. Series.
  DE5.L29   1999
938'.003—dc21   99-25639

CONTENTS

INTRODUCTION

In the year 250 C.E., the most populous and long-settled regions of western Eurasia, which stretched in a great arc from the Atlantic coasts of France, Portugal, and Morocco across the Mediterranean, the Balkans, and the Middle East as far as Afghanistan, were subject to the control of two—and only two—immense imperial systems: the Roman empire and the Sassanian empire of Persia. Over five hundred years later, around 800 C.E., the populations of the same area still lived largely in the shadow of empire. The Roman empire was still there. From Calabria, across the southern Balkans, and deep into Anatolia, the territories of what we call, by a modern misnomer redolent of ill-informed contempt, the "Byzantine" empire, had been ruled continuously for over eight hundred years by the direct successors of Emperor Augustus. In Rome itself, the pope was still a "Roman." Every document emanating from the papal chancery was dated by the regnal date of the Roman emperor who reigned at Constantinople and by the *Indictio,* a fifteen-year tax cycle that had started in 312.

In 800, also, from Central Asia to the plateau of Castile, an Islamic caliphate, created at headlong speed by the Arab conquests of the 7th century, had gained stability by settling back into the habits of the ancient empires it had replaced. The tax system of the Islamic empire continued with little break the practices of the Roman and Sassanian states. Its coins were *denarii, dinar*s. The system of post-horses and of governmental information on which its extended rule depended was called after its Roman predecessor *veredus, al-barīd.* Its most significant enemy was still known, in Arabic, as the empire of *Rum*—the empire of Rome in the east, centered on Constantinople.

For all the startling and self-conscious novelty of their religion, the early Muslim conquerors of the Middle East found themselves heirs to a past of extraordinary density. This past piled up around them in every city they had occupied. The first great public mosque was created, at the Umayyad capital at Damascus, by the simple and dramatic expedient of embracing, in a single enclosure made of porticoes sheathed in shimmering east Roman mosaics, the former temple precinct of Jupiter/Haddad and its recent Christian rival, the shrine of St. John the Baptist. A thousand years of unbroken urban history, and the history of two religions, were thus encased in a new, Muslim place of worship. In 762, the center of what would become the medieval Islamic caliphate was created by the founding of Baghdad. Baghdad stood on ground heavy with the past. It lay upriver from the ruins of the former Sassanian capital of Ctesiphon. These ruins were dominated by the Taq-i Kesra, the immense shell of the Sassanian Palace Arch ascribed to Khosro I Anushirvan (530–579). The awesome height and apparent indestructibility of that great arch of brick was a permanent reminder of an ancient, pre-Islamic style of rule, indelibly associated with the memory of Khosro, the contemporary and rival of the east Roman emperor Justinian (527–565)—himself no mean creator of enduring legacies, the builder of the Hagia Sophia and the definitive codifier of the laws of Rome.

Only at the western tip of Eurasia, in what we call western Europe, did it seem as if the long summer's afternoon of empire had begun to fade. Yet from Ireland to the upper Danube, the clergy shared a common Catholicism, first formed in the Christian Roman empire of Constantine and Theodosius I. Even on the outer periphery of Europe, the clergy still thought of themselves as part of a wider world embraced by great empires. To enter the library of Iona, on the southwest coast of Scotland, and to consult its books was to share in a sacred geography of Christendom that still stretched along the entire length of the old Roman empire and beyond: it included not only Jerusalem and the Holy Places, but also Alexandria, Damascus, Edessa, and memories of Christian martyrs yet farther to the east, in Mesopotamia and northern Iraq.

Although alternately decried and romanticized by scholars of the 18th and 19th centuries as pure "barbarians," the ruling classes of the postimperial kingdoms of the west had, in fact, inherited a basically Roman sense of social order and a Roman penchant for extended empire. Power still wore a Roman face. The acclamation of the Frankish king, Charlemagne, by the Roman people and by the pope as "their" emperor, in 800 (and the deadly seriousness with which Charlemagne accepted the compliment) was yet another case of a successful state-builder from a once peripheral region easing himself into the comfortable seat provided by half a millennium of empire. Charlemagne's contemporary, Caliph Hārūn al-Rashīd, viewed the indestructible arch of Khosro with much the same mixture of awe and proud entitlement as did Charlemagne when faced with a Rome heavy with pagan and Christian memories. They were both, each in his own distinctive way, inheritors of a remarkable Age of Empires.

We should not take this for granted. Back in 250 it was far from certain that an Age of Empires lay in the immediate future. Torn by civil war and largely unprepared for large-scale mobilization, the Roman empire seemed doomed to disintegrate. Nor could anyone have foretold that the Sassanian dynasty, which emerged so rapidly from Fars in the 220s, would eventually mold the sub-kingdoms of the Iranian plateau and Mesopotamia into the formidable world power of the age of Khosro Anushirvan, and in so doing would provide a model of empire as enduring, for the populations of Islamic Asia, as was the myth of Rome for the Christians of western Europe. By the end of the 7th century, it seemed as if the Arab conquerors would destroy themselves through reckless civil wars within fifty years of their conquests. Yet none of these possible events happened. In each case, the immediate future lay not with chaos but with the reassertion of strong, extended empires. The reformed Roman empire of Diocletian and Constantine was the most formidably governed state ever created in the ancient world. It survived largely intact in its eastern regions until 640. The consolidation of the Iranian territories under the Sassanian King of Kings involved a similar, if less clearly documented achievement. After a period of civil wars, the Islamic caliphate emerged, under the Abbasid dynasty at Baghdad, to form what has rightly been called the last great empire of antiquity. As a result, the populations of western Eurasia (even those of western Europe) could look back, in the year 800, to find their horizon blocked by the massive outlines of great empires, frequently overhauled since 250 yet still irreplaceable.

But there was more to it than that. Today, as Jews, Zoroastrians, Christians, and Muslims, millions of persons are the direct heirs of religions either born or refashioned in late antiquity. Some religions took the form in which they are still recognizable—as was the case with the Jews—within communities bounded by the Roman and the Sassanian empires. Others grasped the fact of empire with spectacular results. Zoroastrians look back to the age of the Sassanians as the time of the restoration of their orthodoxy and of the formation of their religious literature. The Christians embraced with zeal the Christian Roman empire of Constantine and his successors. The Muslims created rapidly, from the remnants of the Roman and the Sassanian states, an empire of their own.

This, very briefly, is what we mean when we talk of "late antiquity." *Late Antiquity: A Guide to the Postclassical World* has been put together on the frank assumption that the time has come for scholars, students, and the educated public in general to treat the period between around 250 and 800 as a distinctive and quite decisive period of history that stands on its own. It is not, as it once was for Edward Gibbon, a subject of obsessive fascination only as the story of the unraveling of a once glorious and "higher" state of civilization. It was not a period of irrevocable Decline and Fall; nor was it merely a violent and hurried prelude to better things. It cannot be treated as a corpse to be dragged quickly offstage so that the next great act of the drama of the Middle Ages should begin—with the emergence of Catholic Europe and the creation of the Arabic civilization associated with the golden age of medieval Islam.

Not only did late antiquity last for over half a millennium; much of what was created in that period still runs in our veins. It is, for instance, from late antiquity, and not from any earlier period of Roman history, that we have inherited the codifications of Roman law that are the root of the judicial systems of so many states in Europe and the Americas. The forms of Judaism associated with the emergence of the rabbinate and the codification of the Talmud emerged from late antique Roman Palestine and from the distinctive society of Sassanian Mesopotamia. The basic structures and dogmatic formulations of the Christian church, both in Latin Catholicism and in the many forms of eastern Christianity, came from this time, as did the first, triumphant expression of the Muslim faith. Even our access to the earlier classics of the ancient world, in Latin and Greek, was made possible only through the copying activities of late antique Christians and their early medieval successors, locked in an endless, unresolved dialogue with their own pagan past.

Compared with the solid, almost unseen ground-course of institutions and ideas created in late antiquity that still lie at the foundations of our own world, the earlier classical period of the ancient world has a surreal, almost weightless quality about it. It is the Dream Time of western civilization. It can act as a never failing source of inspiration. But we cannot claim to come from that classical world alone, for whole segments of the modern world had no place in it. These emerged, rather, in the period between 250 and 800: a Europe in which the non-Roman north and the Roman south came to be joined in a common Catholic Christianity; a Greek-speaking world that stood at the western pole of a widely extended federation of Christian communities which ranged from Georgia to Ethiopia, and from Mesopotamia to Kerala and western China; a Middle East in which Constantinople/Istanbul and Baghdad were founded (in 324 and in 762) and have remained among the most emotionally charged cities of Asia; a paganism that lived on, no longer in temples, but in austere philosophical systems that summed up an ancient wisdom which continued to fascinate and to repel Christians, Jews, and Muslims for centuries to come; a Middle East in which Islam had, by 800, become an overwhelming presence. Nothing like this was to be seen before 250. These developments belong to late antiquity. If we do not like what we see in late antiquity, it is often because the ideas and the structures that first emerged at that time are still with us. They have the power to move or to repel us even today. The period which has bequeathed to us such living legacies deserves attention in its own right.

This Guide will also attempt to treat as a single whole the vast geographic space covered by the Roman and the Sassanian empires. And even this extensive space must be seen as no more than a vivid cluster of settlements set in a yet wider world. For, in this period, societies as far apart as Scandinavia and the Hadramawt, Saharan Africa and western China were touched by events along that great arc of imperially governed societies and interacted decisively, at crucial moments, with those societies.

Above all, *Late Antiquity* was written so that readers should have no doubt as to the advances in scholarship that have enabled scholars for the first time to treat, with even-handed erudition, the very different regions of western Europe, the eastern empire, the Sassanian empire, and the early caliphate, as well as the many more distant societies that were implicated in the overall development of the late antique period.

For if there is one thing which this Guide would wish to bring about, it is that its readers should begin the 21st century with fewer artificial barriers in their minds, erected between periods and regions which have proved, in the light of modern research, to be more continuous with each other than we had once thought. For instance, we go out of our way to encourage readers to join the history of the later Roman empire in the east with the subsequent evolution of the first centuries of Islam. We also encourage the reader to stand on both sides of the political frontiers of the empires of that time. For if they do this, they will be able better to appreciate the all-important process of symbiosis that led to the creation, and to the eventual triumph over the traditional empires, of new societies, created in the "war zones" of the Rhine and the Danube, of Sassanian Central Asia and of the steppelands of Syria and Iraq.

With this Guide in hand, we hope that the interested reader will travel, with sufficient basic information, from the world of Constantine to the seemingly very different world of the Damascus of 'Abd al-Malik—and may be surprised to see that not everything had changed. We wish our readers to make a habit of crossing the political frontier that separated late Roman Syria from the busy world of Sassanian Iraq, and of traveling to the steppes of Central Asia and eastern Europe to take up an unexpected viewpoint upon the Roman empire.

Late Antiquity exists to encourage the reader to make such leaps across time and space. In the same way, it hopes to remind the students of religion and of the history of ideas of the unexpected, long-term consequences of many of the better-known achievements of the period. They will find, for instance, that texts of Greek philosophy, science, and medicine written at the beginning of our period will, by the end of it, be circulating in more copies in Syriac and Arabic than in their Greek original. They will be struck by the tenacity and by the long-term implications of the philosophical and theological issues debated in the period. Such themes can be appreciated only when seen in the long term, as they endure and change over many centuries and in very different environments. Not least of the surprises in store for the reader will be the extent to which religious groups, who throughout this period made a point of distinguishing themselves from each other with singular ferocity, continued, in fact, to be drawn together by the mute force of common intellectual preoccupations and, even when they fought most fiercely (by attacking the cult sites of their rivals), by the oceanic weight of shared notions of the sacred. Whether they liked each other or not, they remained not only "Christians," "Jews," and "pagans," "orthodox" and "heretics," "clergy" and "laity": they breathed the same heavy air of a common civilization—that of late antiquity.

Travel of this kind is calculated to broaden the mind. It is also the aim of this Guide to enable its readers to compare regions which have often been kept apart by the barriers erected by separate disciplines. Students of well-known topics in much-studied regions—for instance, those interested in the Christianization of western Europe—will here be reminded of the working out of analogous processes in other parts of the Christian world. To take one example, the recent remarkable increase of archaeological discoveries in the countries of the Middle East adds a new dimension to such study. It is now possible to compare phenomena well known to the student of the postimperial west, such as the explosion of church building in the cities of Merovingian Gaul, with evidence for a similar explosion among the Christian communities of the Middle East. Fifteen late antique churches, mainly from the 6th century, have been discovered in Jerash (Jordan) alone. The splendid mosaics recently uncovered at

Mefaa, modern Umm ar-Rasas (also in Jordan) have made us all sit up and take notice. These are recognizably late antique productions. They contain scenes that lovingly depict the classical facades of neighboring cities. Yet they were laid down in 718 C.E., that is, by exact contemporaries of the Venerable Bede. They were the work of Christians who had already lived for almost eighty years as subjects of the Islamic empire. It is in such small details, unavailable to us until only a few decades ago, that we can gain, through comparison across widely separated regions, a sense of scale and of the pace of a worldwide phenomenon, such as the establishment and survival of the Christian church in its many regions.

It is for this reason, also, that the Guide has paid so much attention to recent archaeological discoveries. Through these it is now possible to grasp an entire world no longer in its broad outlines, through the magisterial sweep of narratives such as Edward Gibbon's *Decline and Fall of the Roman Empire* or, as in a magnificent bird's eye view, through A. H. M. Jones's *The Later Roman Empire,* but rather in the accumulation of vivid details on the ground. An entire landscape has filled up with the traces of villages and unpretentious bathhouses, with the jolly mosaics of the petty gentry and with hundreds of little churches and synagogues dedicated by pious notables. Scattered across the entire sweep of the late antique Mediterranean and the Middle East, these recently discovered remains remind us that late antiquity did, indeed, happen. We are dealing with a distinctive civilization, whose density and sheer tenacity, on a humble level that we had hitherto barely suspected, demands some form of overall treatment.

This is what we hope that *Late Antiquity* will do. The reader, however, should know that it is a guide. It is not an encyclopedia, a dictionary, or a lexicon. Dr. Samuel Johnson, with becoming irony, once defined a lexicographer as "a harmless drudge." Neither in our contributors nor in our readers have we expected such tame qualities. In the essays with which the volume begins, we have not wished to sacrifice the vividness of a personal introduction to selected themes to the harmless drudgery of a comprehensive survey. The essays are meant to provoke thought. They are not there to repeat, under the guise of providing comprehensive information, the narrative stereotypes that have weighed particularly heavily on our interpretation of the period. It is the frank intention of the authors of these essays to encourage readers to travel further in new directions. For it is their opinion that new directions have, indeed, been opened up for the period of late antiquity in a manner which would barely have been thinkable only a century ago; and that these directions point firmly away from many commonly accepted stereotypes of the period.

Last but not least, the editors have always considered that the purpose of this Guide was to provide as wide a range of information as possible on the late antique period. But it was never our intention that it should be all-inclusive. We have, indeed, attempted to cast our net wide. But an Irishman's definition of a net remains true: it is "a lot of holes tied together with string." No editor can long contemplate a venture such as our own without being painfully aware, also, of those holes.

What matters, in this case, is that we have been freed from the need to tell all. It has long been recognized that the late antique period stands at the crossroads of many histories. The great highroads of many well-established disciplines traverse our period: dictionaries of the classical world end in late antiquity, dictionaries of Judaism and Christianity inevitably pass through it, dictionaries of Islam, Byzantium, and the Middle Ages make it their starting point. As a result, we can refer the reader to those many exhaustive dictionaries, encyclopedias, and lexicons that deal competently with themes that are central to late antiquity. None of these specialized works of reference covers the late antique period in all its aspects. But what they do cover, they cover with such thoroughness as to make it unnecessary and positively counter-productive to our enterprise to reproduce what they already contain. To take an obvious example: those interested in the history of the Christian church are urged to turn to works such as *The Oxford Dictionary of the Christian Church*, the *Dictionnaire de Spiritualité*, the *Prosopographie chrétienne* (which has already produced one precious volume for Africa), the *Reallexikon für Antike und Christentum* and, now, to *The Coptic Encyclopedia*—to mention only a few—to find in them the many Christian figures that do not appear in our own Guide. Our reason for failure to include such persons is blunt, and we hope that it will prove acceptable: given that the Christian church has received abundant specialized treatment in this period, and is likely to continue to do so, we concluded that too many saintly men and women, too many bishops and too many heretics would have meant too few villages, too few recently discovered mosaics, altogether too little emphasis on the continuity of the humdrum, profane life of the majority of "worldly" persons of whom we now have evidence and about whom we have seldom spoken at sufficient length.

The same can be said of almost every theme on which we touch. Our Guide is there to point the way. It is not there to act as a substitute for the many well-established reference works that touch upon this period. The contributors to the essays and to every article have done their best to provide up-to-date bibliography. The index will enable the reader to follow subjects, places, and persons that are not dealt with explicitly in the essays or in the articles. We think that, in the end, the reader who uses this Guide with enterprise and patience will find more solid string in its net than he or she had first thought, and fewer holes. And for those in whom we trust this Guide has instilled a salutary zest for further information, we need only point out *The Oxford Dictionary of Byzantium*, the *Prosopography of the Later Roman Empire*, and the new edition of *The Oxford Classical Dictionary*, not to mention *The Encyclopedia Judaica*, the *Encyclopedia of Islam*, and the *Reallexikon für germanische Altertumskunde*, among many other reliable and largely up-to-date works of reference. If this Guide inspires, in those who read it, a wish to continue to study the distinctive period of late antiquity in its many aspects, to follow the directions into new territory to which it points, eventually to add to the areas sketched inevitably so briefly in its pages and to attempt, by their own further efforts, to remedy its omissions, then the editors will consider that this volume will have served its purpose.

Atlantic Ocean

Russian Steppe

Sea of Azov

Black Sea

Dnepr

Dnestr

Prut

Carpathian Mountains

Cherson

Sinope

Kelkit

Sivas

Aleppo

Emesa

Tripoli

Damascus

CAPPADOCIA

Anatolia

CILICIA

Taurus Mtns.

Adana

ISAURIA

Antioch

Famagusta

Gaza

Cyprus

Nessana

Petra

Alia

Red Sea

Madaba

Malfar

Constantinople

Chalcedon

Nicaea

Ankara

GALATIA

Iconium

Antalya

Tiberias

Caesarea

Jerusalem

Cairo

EGYPT

Nile

Thebes

NUBIA

Aphroditopolis

Alexandria

Nitria

THRACE

Balkan Mtns.

Transylvanian Alps

Danube

Vardar

DACIA

Philippopolis

MACEDONIA

Thessalonica

EPIRUS

Smyrna

Ephesus

Aphrodisias

Aegean Sea

Athens

Daphne

Corinth

Crete

Mediterranean Sea

CYRENAICA

Cyrene

Dinaric Alps

Adriatic Sea

Durazzo

Ionian Sea

PANNONIA

NORICUM

Aquileia

Venice

Ravenna

Po

LOMBARDY

Milan

Apennine Mtns.

Rome

Naples

Tyrrhenian Sea

Messina

Sicily

Syracuse

Sardinia

Corsica

Mediterranean Sea

Carthage

AFRICA PROCONSULARIS

TRIPOLITANIA

Sahara Desert

Alps

Rhine

Trier

Aachen

Pars

Loire

Tours

AQUITAINE

Bordeaux

Garonne

BURGUNDY

Lyon

Rhone

Arles

Marseilles

Narbonne

Pyrenees Mtns.

Barcelona

Ebro

Balearic Islands

Valencia

Duero

Toledo

Tagus

Cordoba

Guadiana

Tangiers

MAURETANIA

Atlas Mountains

miles

0   100   200   300   400   500

Cartography by Philip Schwartzberg, Meridian Mapping

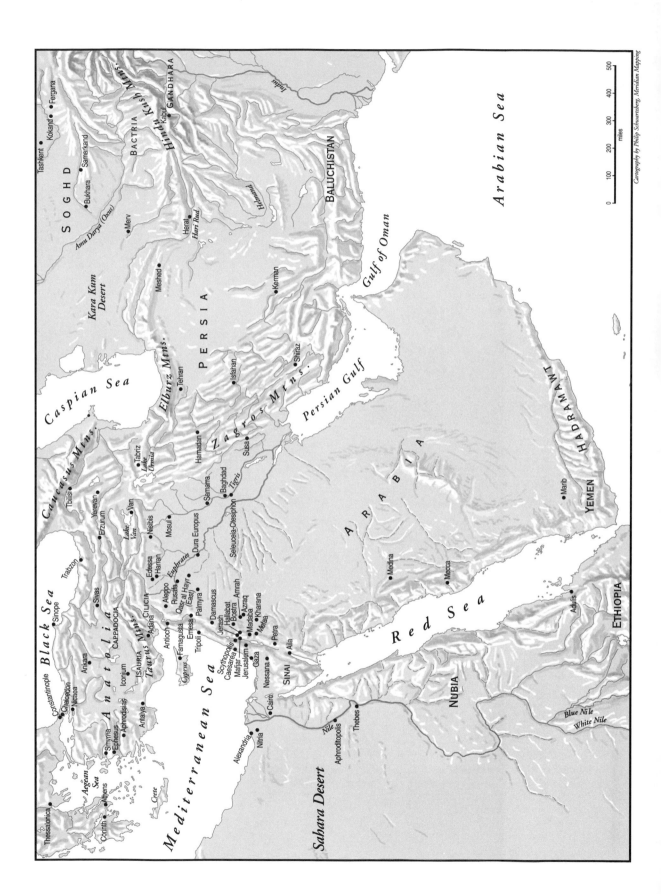

Tashkent • • Fergana
• Kokand
SOGHD • Samarkand
• Bukhara
BACTRIA
Hindu Kush Mtns. GANDHARA
Kabul •
BALUCHISTAN

Amu Darya (Oxus) *Indus*

Kara Kum
Desert
• Merv
Herat •
Hari Rud *Helmand*

• Meshed

PERSIA

Caspian Sea
• Kerman
Elburz Mtns.
Tehran •

• Isfahan
• Tabriz
Lake
Urmia
Zagros Mtns.
• Hamadan • Shiraz
• Susa

Caucasus Mtns.
• Tbilisi
• Yerevan Persian Gulf
• Erzurum
Lake Van • Van
• Nisibis
Samarra •
Baghdad • *Tigris*
• Mosul
Seleucia-Ctesiphon •

Gulf of Oman

HADRAMAWT

A R A B I A

• Marib
YEMEN

Black Sea
• Sinope
• Trabzon
• Sivas
CAPPADOCIA
Edessa •
Harran •
Euphrates
Dura Europus •

Arabian Sea

Anatolia
• Ankara
ISAURIA Mtns.
Taurus Mtns.
• Iconium
CILICIA
• Adana
Aleppo •
Rusafa •
Qasr al Hayr
(East) •
Palmyra •

Constantinople •
Chalcedon •
Nicaea •
Antioch •
Famagusta •
Cyprus
Emesa •
Tripoli •
Damascus •
Jerash •
Hallabat •
Bostra •
Azraq •
Kharana •

• Aphrodisias
• Antalya
Scythopolis •
Caesarea •
Mafjar •
Jerusalem •
Gaza •
Madaba •
Mshatta •
Petra •
Ella •

• Smyrna
• Ephesus
• Nessana
SINAI

Red Sea

• Medina

• Mecca

Thessalonica •
Aegean
Sea
• Athens
Crete

Cairo •
Nitria •
Alexandria •

Mediterranean Sea

• Corinth

Sahara Desert
Aphroditopolis •
Thebes •

NUBIA

Nile

ETHIOPIA
Adulis •

Blue Nile
White Nile

Cartography by Philip Schwartzberg, Meridian Mapping

miles
0 100 200 300 400 500

LATE ANTIQUITY

Remaking the Past

Averil Cameron

In his poem on the war against Count Gildo in North Africa, the late 4th century Latin poet Claudian depicts Roma, the personification of the city, as aged and unkempt, "feeble her voice, slow her step, her eyes deep buried. Her cheeks were sunken and hunger had wasted her limbs. Scarce can her weak shoulders support her unpolished shield. Her ill-fitting helmet shows her grey hairs and the spear she carries is a mass of rust."[1] His contemporary Quintus Aurelius Symmachus depicted Rome in similar guise, pleading with the emperor for toleration for pagans, while the Christian poet Prudentius reversed the trope and portrayed Roma rejuvenated by Christianity.

There was no nostalgia for the past here. Romantic ruins and decayed grandeur held no magic for this generation; indeed, Emperor Constantius II, who visited Rome in 357, and the historian Ammianus Marcellinus, who was at work on his Latin history there in the 380s, were as overcome by Rome's present majesty as by her great past.[2] Not for men such as these the self-conscious lament for past greatness or the fascination with antique decline familiar to us from Edward Gibbon's *History of the Decline and Fall of the Roman Empire,* or from 18th century pictures such as Fuseli's *The Artist Moved by the Grandeur of Ancient Ruins* (1778–1779), which shows a seated figure mourning beside the colossal hand and foot that remain from the monumental statue of Constantine the Great set up after his victory over Maxentius and his entry into Rome.[3] By the 7th and 8th centuries, Constantine the Great had passed from history into orthodox sainthood, his chief function in Byzantine legend being his commemoration with his mother Helena as the founder of Constantinople and finder of the True Cross; in the west, Rome laid claim to his Christian identity by means of the legend of his baptism by Pope Sylvester.[4] This is no romanticizing of the past, but rather its practical adaptation to the needs of the present. If the men and women of late antiquity did not romanticize the past, nor were they conscious of a sense of modernity. Rather, they wished devoutly to connect with a past which they still saw as part of their own experience and their own world. This could easily lead to incongruity in modern eyes; but it puzzles us far more than it did contemporaries to find, for example, fragments of classical masonry or sculpture built in to new constructions which we tend to find inferior.[5] The past was very real to the men and women of late antiquity: as they saw it, it had not so much to be remade as to be reasserted.

The past was so real that it was the subject of intense competition. For Eusebius of Caesarea (d. 339), the apologist of Constantine the Great, and for other Christian writers, it had above all to be wrested from the grip of pagans. According to Eusebius, the great oracles, the sources of ancient knowledge, were silent and the pagan shrines the home only of "dead idols." So much for centuries of tradition. But in fact the most prestigious oracular shrines were far from dead, and Eusebius's views were set out in direct challenge to the recent arguments of the great Neoplatonic philosopher and scholar Porphyry, expressed in his work *On Philosophy from Oracles,* which demonstrated through a collection of oracles that oriental, Jewish, and indeed Christian divine revelation had all been encompassed in the sayings of the gods.[6] Just as crucial for Eusebius, the greatest biblical scholar of his generation, was the question of the date of Moses; his Christian conception of history required a progression from the Mosaic law, through the development of Greek philosophy, represented above all by Plato, toward the attainment of the *pax Augusta* which alone provided the necessary setting for the coming of Christ and the spread of Christianity. Eusebius had set out these ideas most fully in his *Preparation for the Gospel,* an apologetic positioning of Christian revelation in the context of world history. Here too Porphyry, also the author of *Against the Christians,* a dangerously influential attack on Christianity (Emperor Constantine later ordered copies to be burnt), was Eusebius's chief target.

The *Preparation* asserted the primacy of Moses over Plato, the Jewish law over Greek philosophy, more particularly in its contemporary Neoplatonic manifestation in the teachings of Porphyry. In the *Life of Constantine,* a panegyrical defense of the emperor, Eusebius went much further than he had done in book nine of the *Ecclesiastical History* in presenting Constantine himself as the new Moses, bringing his people from the slavery of persecution and paganism to the new dispensation of Christianity, and—as Eusebius also claimed in the *Oration* he wrote for Constantine's thirtieth anniversary in 335–36—establishing a Christian kingdom on earth that was a true likeness of God's kingdom in heaven. In the heat of victory the emperor had made Porphyry the subject of public condemnation, but even so Eusebius's optimistic assertions were far from convincing pagan intellectuals. As so often, the optimism publicly expressed by both sides betrays the intense anxiety which was privately felt. Just one among many revealing indications of that is the scornful portrayal of Constantine by Julian, the son of his half-brother and a convert from Christianity to paganism, in Julian's *Caesares;* far from being the triumphant new Moses of Eusebius, Julian's Constantine is a pitiful suppliant in heaven unable to find a god willing to befriend him.

The need to claim the past for one's own in no way diminished. A curious work by Epiphanius, bishop of Salamis (Constantia) in Cyprus, known as the *Panarion* or "Medicine Chest" (376 C.E.), presents a catalogue of heresies starting with a chronological survey of religious belief in world history, from the Bible to Christian heresy. There are two schemes: in one, heresy was preceded by the sins of adultery, rebellion, and idolatry, which originated from the Fall, while in the other, four great periods of heresy succeeded each other from Adam onward: barbarism, Scythian superstition, Hellenism, and Judaism. Epiphanius's catalogue is not of course a history, but rather a formalist treatise, in which, indeed, the number of heresies is explicitly made to fit the eighty concubines in the Song of Songs (6:8). It is an odd work to modern eyes. Yet Epiphanius was a leading controversialist of his generation, and the work answered to burning contemporary concerns.[7]

The *Panarion* also displays the difficulty which Christian scholars experienced in their attempts to deal with biblical texts. The later 4th century saw a series of such efforts, focusing on the accounts of creation in the Book of Genesis. Basil of Caesarea composed a *Hexaemeron*, a series of sermons on the six days of creation. Their purpose was, in the words of a recent writer, to present a "complete cosmology," which would give "an account of humanity's place in that world, and of humanity's destiny."[8] For Christians, the two aims were inseparable, for Christianity saw itself as a religion grounded in history; consequently, not just the Scriptures but the whole of history had to be expounded in Christian terms. This rereading of history also implied human psychology; it called forth from Basil a "translucent overlay of different planes of perception: the self, the world and the drama of God's action."[9] But a detailed exegesis of Genesis was also required. Augustine attempted to expound its meaning in several of his major works, including the *Confessions* and the *City of God*.[10] He also composed twelve books of commentary on its literal meaning, the *De Genesi ad litteram* (from 401 C.E.). Then as now, others gave the text a fundamentalist interpretation, and Augustine too wrote with an eye to the Neoplatonist view that the world was uncreated. The debate on creation between Christians and Neoplatonists was still continuing in the 6th century, when the Alexandrian John Philoponus wrote a work in which he argued against the views of Proclus on the subject, and a mysterious Cosmas Indicopleustes, "the sailor to India," composed a prose *Christian Topography* arguing against Aristotle for a flat earth with the damned below and heaven above; illustrations from the 9th century and later indicate that Cosmas's work included pictures of this hierarchical arrangement, which took the Ark of the Covenant as their model.[11] Augustine's approach to creation and to time was of course more sophisticated: Plato's *Timaeus*, with its account of creation, was a work read by both Christians and Neoplatonists and offered Augustine some possibility of a middle ground. Yet God must be seen to have created the world.

The Scriptures, above all Genesis, provided more than a guide to the history of the world and a template for anthropological understanding. The advent of sin and its effects in history pervade Augustine's *City of God*, and this consideration of sin led him and others to ask a whole variety of further questions about the past, for instance whether angels existed before the creation of the world.[12] Especially in the late 4th century, Genesis also became the fundamental text for expounding male and female relations, the "tunics of skins" of Gen. 3:21 a token for some interpreters of the fact that human sexuality followed only after and as a consequence of the Fall.[13] But as human history, and human anthropology, were thus mapped onto the biblical story of Paradise lost, so the present was offered as a series of reenactments of Scriptural history, Constantine as Moses, holy men and women as Job. Scripture provided both a past and a living present. Even the conservative genre of imperial panegyric eventually wove images from the Hebrew Bible into its texture, and the victories of Heraclius over the Persians in the early 7th century led to his being hailed in poetry and depicted in visual art as the new David.[14] Heraclius is likened also to Elijah and Moses, and his court poet, George of Pisidia, also returned to the theme of the creation as an image of imperial renewal in a long poem also known as the *Hexaemeron*, written soon after Heraclius's victory over the Persians in 628 and his restoration of the True Cross to Jerusalem in 630.[15]

The Scriptures, then, presented both an opportunity and a challenge in late antiquity. They provided vocabulary, imagery, and subject matter for poets; models for holy men and women; and ways of understanding humanity and the world. But they required exegesis, and this could be difficult and risky. Sometimes "saving the text" resulted in interpretations which now seem fanciful and undisciplined in the extreme. But no one in late antiquity would have understood the post 19th century view of the story of the creation and Fall as "profound religious myths, illuminating our human situation."[16]

It was not only Christians in late antiquity who were remaking their past or using mythology in order to do so. The same inventive Epiphanius, author of the *Panarion*, gives us some information about a cult of Kore's giving birth to Aion ("time") in late 4th century Alexandria.[17] Aion is known at an earlier date from an inscription at Eleusis, a relief at Aphrodisias and a cosmological mosaic at Mérida in Spain, and from the 4th century from mosaics at New Paphos in Cyprus. But by the 4th century, in Egypt at least, Aion had taken on the new role of god of the mysteries, sprung from a virgin birth. In the Cyprus mosaic he is associated with the myth of Cassiopeia, in a composition including the infancy of Dionysus, themes also found at Apamea.[18] Domestic textiles surviving from Egypt show the popularity of mythological and especially Dionysiac themes as decoration even into the Islamic period. Paganism in late antiquity, especially of the more intellectual kind, was vigorous and productive, and knew how to take its cue from Christianity. It was not only Christians, for instance, who made pilgrimages: Neoplatonists, too, sought for origins, and went looking for sacred springs and streams in remote places.[19]

One way of shaping and making sense of the past in accordance with contemporary ideas was, paradoxically, via the routes of prophecy, eschatology, and millennialism. Again, one is confronted by a powerful sense of rivalry and competition. An industry grew up in oracles: in the 3rd century, the thirteenth Sibylline Oracle (the very name lent an aura of antiquity and mystery) interpreted the wars and invasions in the east in that period in oracular terms,[20] while the so-called Chaldaean Oracles popularized by Iamblichus claimed to convey messages from the soul of Plato himself. The net was cast wide: a late 5th century collection of oracular utterances known today as the Tübingen Theosophy survives as part of a Christian polemical work, and corresponds in some part with a famous inscription from the city of Oenoanda in Lycia.[21] Though oracles by their essence were anonymous, no less a person than the Emperor Constantine cited the Sibylline Oracles and Virgil's Fourth Eclogue to Christian purpose in his *Oration to the Saints*.[22] Even as late as the 7th century a collection of pagan oracles was circulating in Syria.

The appeal to tradition was another way of staking a claim in the past. Church fathers like Basil of Caesarea sought authority in the notion of an unbroken tradition handed down since the early days of the church. More recent tradition could be held to lie in councils, above all those recognized as ecumenical. By the 6th and 7th century, lists of councils, with their canons, had become a standard way of claiming authority in doctrinal matters. John Scholasticus and Eutychius, rival patriarchs of Constantinople in the late 6th century, drew up competing lists of conciliar decisions to support their opposing positions. During the period of the iconoclast controversy in Byzantium, from 726 to 843, the nature and meaning of "tradition" were vigorously debated; icons were held by their defenders to represent "unwritten tradition," which, it was claimed, had equal authority with the written tradition of Scriptures, the Fathers, and the councils. Like the drafting of their acts, the identification of authoritative councils was also a matter of contest; the iconoclasts held their own Council at Hieria in 754, the proceedings of which have survived only in the long quotations contained for the purpose of refutation in the Acts of the (iconophile) Second Council of Nicaea of 787.[23] After the ending of iconoclasm, the visual depiction of the ecumenical councils in Byzantine churches was one of the ways of asserting the triumph of tradition and authority which was how the iconophiles saw their victory.[24]

But citation of councils was only one of the means by which competing groups within the church had sought to claim the authority of the past. Handbooks, lists of approved citations from Scripture or from the Fathers, commentaries on the Scriptures are only a few of the methods they used.[25] Once the church had gone down the route of trying to define the nature of God in formulas that must be generally agreed, the inevitable result was intense competition and rivalry, in which every participant and every group resorted separately to the authority of tradition. The ultimate futility of the search can be seen in the progressive appeal to God as mystery, beyond human knowing;[26] nevertheless, neither the attempt nor the appeal to authority was abandoned. Not only Christians appealed to tradition. Proclus and other Neoplatonists saw Plato as offering a kind of sacred text.[27] Reading Plato constituted true spiritual life; the dialogues contained the truth about the gods, and this knowledge was handed down by the succession of heads of the Academy, the Platonic school *par excellence*. A program of Neoplatonic studies presented the dialogues in progression of difficulty. And the succession of heads of the Academy was accompanied by appeals to divine inspiration, as with Proclus, whom Marinus depicts as the recipient of signs that he should take on the mantle and preserve the heritage of Athena in her own city of Athens.[28]

Athens shared with all other cities in late antiquity a changing urban environment. It had suffered from Herul attack in the 3rd century, was probably sacked by Alaric in 395–96, and was to undergo invasion again by the Slavs and Avars who raided Greece at the end of the 6th century.[29] But church building came late to Athens, and even in the early 5th century a substantial amount of secular building and restoration took place, which according to a recent excavator "respected the traditional character of the city."[30] It included restoration of the Library of Hadrian and the so-called Palace of the Giants, probably in fact a large villa; additions to the Theater of Dionysus; and restorations of a sundial, the so-called House of Proclus, and several other villas and private and public baths. A late Roman villa at Cenchreae, the port of Corinth, was adorned in the 4th century with representations of antique philosophers, like the seven Sages at Apamea in Syria in the same period. The Empress Eudocia, whose husband was Theodosius II, was an Athenian, said to be the daughter of a sophist and a Christian convert; she had pretensions to classical learning (she wrote rather bad poetry), presented herself as a patron of building in the Holy Land, and may have provided the incentive for some of this 5th century building in Athens.[31]

No doubt Athens was a special case; nevertheless, the majority of city-dwellers in late antiquity still lived among manifestations of the past in the built and visual environment. The porticoed houses of the rich in late antiquity continued in use into the 6th century, even though the stones of the forum might be used without embarrassment for church-building. In Carthage, the Vandal aristocracy on the eve of the Byzantine reconquest by Belisarius in the 530s prided itself on the culture it had taken over from its Roman subjects; passable Latin epigrams celebrated the houses and lifestyle of the Vandal nobles, and the circus remained in use into the Byzantine period. In what is now Jordan, the 6th century was a period of economic vitality, and some Christian communities were still commissioning fine Hellenizing mosaics late into the 8th. But in Constantinople the fire which accompanied the so-called Nika revolt in 532 destroyed not only the original Great Church but also the classical statuary which had adorned the Baths of Zeuxippus and the Senate House. An Egyptian poet, Christodorus of Coptus, had written a long (416 lines) Greek hexameter poem in praise of the Zeuxippus statues.[32] The *spina* around which the chariots raced in the Hippodrome continued to display some of the most famous statues of antiquity, including the reclining Herakles of Lysippus, until they were looted in the Fourth Crusade. But already by the 8th century the city had shrunk to a shadow of its former self, and the remaining classical statuary was only half-understood, or indeed the object of superstitious fear by reason of its pagan associations.[33] By now there was little sound secular education to be had, even in the capital; fascination with the past had replaced actual knowledge, just as the historical Constantine had given way to the Constantine of legend, the saintly founder of Christian Constantinople.

This legendary past was embellished in the imagination in a variety of ways.

An exotic growth of story steadily came to overlay the historical record. Unsatisfactory gaps in the Gospel record were filled in by an abundant mass of apocryphal detail: the infancy of the Virgin and her Dormition and Assumption into heaven, Christ's descent into Hades, the journeyings of the apostles and their contests with pagan disputants like Simon Magus, or the exploits of Thecla, the virgin follower of St. Paul—as vivid and real a model as any real-life person for late antique Christian women like Macrina, the sister of Basil of Caesarea and Gregory of Nyssa. The powerful but apocryphal idea of the finding of the True Cross by Constantine's mother Helena gave rise to a tangle of further stories, among them the entirely legendary tale of the baptism of Constantine by Sylvester, the bishop of Rome.[34] The legends of Constantine lead us, perhaps, into a more recognizably medieval atmosphere, but the apocryphal stories came into being early, and some of them had immense popularity during late antiquity. From the 5th and 6th centuries onward, in particular, the very abundance of their versions and translations indicates how widespread was their influence. Some of their themes were taken into visual art, especially the scenes from the life of the Virgin and the typically Byzantine portrayal of the Resurrection ("Anastasis"), with Christ throwing open the gates of Hell, bringing up Adam, surrounded by the figures of the dead being raised, with the keys and chains of Hell scattered around. Greek homilies, many of them preserved without the name of the author, developed these scenes in dramatic dialogues between Pilate and the Jews, or Hades and Satan, and in the 6th century Romanos, the great poet and deacon of Hagia Sophia, wove similar dialogues between Mary and the Archangel into the texture of his elaborate *kontakia* for performance in the Great Church.[35] The past was open to the poetic and the religious imagination. Even as more severe and scholastic authors were attempting to control the past by marshalling conciliar decisions, or, as John of Damascus did in the 8th century, listing the forms of orthodox belief in a comprehensive synthesis, a flowering of legend, homiletic, and poetry covered the bare bones of Scripture with human detail and unbridled embellishment.

In such a context, and under the influence of a powerful desire for local heroes and heroines, it was easy to conjure up new martyrs to add to the historical record. Many of these were claimed as victims of the Great Persecution under Diocletian or the earlier 3rd century persecutions. Among them were the Forty Martyrs of Sebasteia in the Pontos—according to Basil of Caesarea, whose homily is the earliest testimony, all of them soldiers who froze to death for their Christian faith when they were condemned to stand naked all night in an icy lake; the story was to become so popular that it became one of the commonest motifs in Byzantine art.[36] In the late 4th century the Spanish poet Prudentius composed the *Peristephanon*, a collection of Latin hymns in Horatian style and meter, in which he celebrated the local female martyr Eulalia; he was not the only Latin author to experiment with hymns, but his are the most accomplished to survive, and earned him the description "the Christian Virgil and Horace" from the classical scholar Bentley.[37] Other martyrs appear for the first time in Prudentius's collection, including Emeterius and Chelidonius, the Eighteen Martyrs of Saragossa and St. Cassian of Imola, a schoolteacher killed by his own pupils; Lawrence and Vincent, on the other hand, were already popular saints when Prudentius wrote about them. Lawrence was the subject of inscriptions put up by Pope Damasus and of an account by Ambrose of Milan, even if the "Acta" of the saint are themselves later, and Vincent was the subject of five sermons by Augustine. Yet another category is that of the early fictional or apocryphal figures like Thecla, subject of the late 2nd century *Acts of Paul and Thecla,* who acquire shrines and increasingly elaborate legends; Thecla's shrine at Seleucia in Isauria (Meriemlik in southern Turkey) was one of the largest of such complexes, with extensive hostel accommodation for visitors. It was visited and described by Egeria on her journey in the 380s, and the large basilica was rebuilt on a grand scale by the Emperor Zeno in the 5th century. The Greek *Life and Miracles of Thecla,* also of the 5th century, was therefore an understandable and desirable addition to the available materials about the saint.[38]

By these means, the past became populated with heroic figures capable of marvelous deeds. The "invention" (quite literally, "finding") of relics of such saints, whether for a new church or as the focal point of a town or a shrine, was simply another way of connecting with the saints of the past, of rendering the past more real. In the 6th century a pilgrim to the Holy Land from Piacenza recorded that when he came to Cana in Galilee, he reclined on the very couch where Jesus had attended the famous wedding; he then did what so many others have done since in other such places—he carved on it the names of his family.[39] The bones of martyrs, eagerly transported across the empire, conveyed the same exciting feeling of closeness to the past. Constantine had to make do with being placed in his mausoleum at Constantinople surrounded by twelve empty sarcophagi representing the apostles, but his son Constantius managed to find the bones of Timothy, Luke, and Andrew and bring them to the capital.[40] Likewise Ambrose of Milan immediately appropriated for the city's basilica the relics of SS. Gervasius and Protasius conveniently found in a different shrine nearby. Peter Brown has written of the sense of closeness, and the link with the past, which Paulinus of Nola experienced through the honors he paid to St. Felix.[41] Relics provided a sense of supernatural protection in the present; but they also linked the present and the past.

The most prestigious of relics, but also the most elusive, were those associated with Christ himself. Constantinople claimed Mary's girdle and her robe, Ephesus her last dwelling place. In the late 6th century the pilgrim from Piacenza saw a cloth at Memphis in Egypt which bore the features of Christ, and in the 7th century Arculf, another western pilgrim, saw his burial cloth in Jerusalem.[42] Eusebius in the early 4th century already knew that the city of Edessa in northern Mesopotamia boasted of a letter written by Jesus to King Abgar, and Egeria saw it when she visited Edessa in the 380s. But a written document was not enough: a miraculous image was also produced, impressed directly from Christ's face onto a cloth, and thus "not made by human hands."[43] Other such images existed in the late 6th century, but this one had a longer history. By the 8th century it was known in the west, and it was cited during iconoclasm as proof that pictures had divine approval, and that they represented the unwritten but authentic tradition to be set beside the written one of the Scriptures and the Fathers. The culmination of the story came in 944, when the Edessan image itself, now known as the "Mandylion," was brought to Constantinople and solemnly ensconced in the imperial palace chapel. It was destined to become the model for reproductions of the Holy Face of Christ in Byzantine and later churches even up to the present century. But significantly, reproductions were not enough; a new narrative of origins was produced, which combined a variety of early stories about how the image had come into being and been found and preserved at Edessa.[44] Once again the past was retold to fit the present.

Religious images—icons, mosaics, frescoes, or works in other media—also retold the past. Their authority was challenged by the iconoclasts in favor of the Eucharist and the symbol of the Cross. But iconoclasm did not last, and its end (represented by the iconophiles as a major victory) was an endorsement of the truth claims of religious narrative art. For even though the formal cycles characteristic of later Byzantine figural church decoration were by no means yet established,[45] nevertheless, icons were held not merely to symbolize but actually to reveal the truth, and as such to make plain the sacred past.[46] They revealed it as much as did the councils, the Scriptures, and tradition; and in so doing they affirmed orthodox belief.[47] The past was not only rewritten, it was revealed in pictures.

The physical remains of the sacred past were also sought elsewhere, above all in what is tellingly referred to as "the Holy Land."[48] The late 4th century pilgrim Egeria traveled to the east, book in hand; the Bible provided the text and the guidebook. But she also found human guides ready to point out what she should see. On her first sighting of Mt. Sinai, she was told by her guides, she should say a prayer; in this valley the children of Israel made their golden calf, and waited for Moses to come down from the mountain. There were already holy men living in cells around a church at the foot of the mountain, who could show the way, and a little church on the very top, where Egeria and her party listened to the reading of the story of Moses from the Bible and received communion.[49] The Burning Bush was growing in "a very pretty garden" in front of a church, much as today it grows beside the *katholikon* of the Monastery of St. Catherine, and Egeria was shown the spot where Moses unloosed his sandals, again with a reading of the appropriate passage in Exodus. This pattern was repeated as the journey continued, and Egeria's own account is full of her close knowledge of the Hebrew Bible and her enthusiasm to fit what she saw to the biblical text. On the way to Mt. Nebo, Egeria identifies the plain where the children of Israel wept for Moses, where Joshua the son of Nun was filled with the spirit of wisdom when Moses died, and "where Moses wrote the Book of Deuteronomy" and blessed all the Israelites individually before he died.

Egeria may not have possessed the highest level of culture, to judge from her style of writing, but she was an enthusiast. She already had copies at home of the letter sent by Abgar of Edessa to Jesus and the latter's reply, when she was given further copies by the local bishop; nor was she anyone's fool, noticing at once that the new text was not only preferable, as coming from Edessa itself, but was in fact longer.[50] The praise given to Egeria in a letter to fellow monks by a certain Galician monk called Valerius in the 7th century is entirely justified. He describes her approach to the task before her very well: "First with great industry she perused all the books of the Old and New Testaments, and discovered all their descriptions of the wonders of the world; and its regions, provinces, cities, mountains and deserts. Then in eager haste (though it was to take many years) she set out with God's help to explore them."

By Egeria's day the idea of a Christian Holy Land was well established; Jerome, Paula, Melania the Elder, and other prominent persons went there to found monastic communities and live in proximity to the holy places. It had not always been so. Another of Eusebius's works, the *Onomasticon*, paved the way for the identification of Scriptural sites. But it was Constantine who invented the notion of Christian archaeology in the Holy Land with the excavation of the sites of Golgotha and the tomb of Christ. The aim was to go down below the Hadrianic levels of Aelia Capitolina and reveal the city as it had been in the time of Christ. The workmen demolished a pagan temple built on the spot, and the emperor ordered all the rubble and stones to be cleared away from the site, and for the site to be excavated to a great depth. Then, "as stage by stage the underground was exposed, at last against all expectation the revered and all-hallowed Martyrion of the Savior's resurrection was itself revealed, and the cave, the holy of holies, took on the appearance of a representation of the Saviour's return to life."[51] Even Eusebius's contorted prose, and the many difficulties surrounding this account, cannot hide the sense of excitement in the writing. This piece of excavation was followed by others: the Church of the Nativity at Bethlehem and a church on the Mount of Olives were both built over and around caves, and there was a further church at Mamre, where Abraham met with the angels. In due course the building of the Holy Sepulcher complex (which was also described in detail by Egeria) produced the greatest relic of all, the True Cross, soon to be joined by such objects as the *titulus* (inscription) from the cross of Christ, the crosses of the two thieves, the crown of thorns, the sponge, and the lance used to pierce Jesus's side.[52] Pilgrimage took off in the 4th century, and Egeria was one among many who sought to make the sites of sacred history their own.[53] The emotion with which these holy places became vested can be experienced nowhere more profoundly than in the laments after the loss of Jerusalem to the Persians in 614 composed by Sophronius, monk of St. Theodosius and future patriarch of the city; or in the heartfelt sermon written on his first Christmas by the same Sophronius after he became patriarch in 634, when he found Bethlehem, the place of Christ's birth, in the hands of "Saracens" and out of reach of his flock.[54] In late antiquity the Christian Holy Land was won and lost, reclaimed by Constantine and his mother in the 320s and lost first to the Persians and then to the Arabs in the 7th century. Both sets of events required extraordinary feats of historical reorientation.

The Sassanians had their own annals of the dynasty.[55] And when Muhammad received his revelations they included long disquisitions on the past of the peoples of the Book, the descent from Abraham, and the line of prophets of whom Muhammad was the final example and culmination. Like Christianity, Islam found a way of incorporating the Hebrew Bible to its own advantage. Jesus, too, was recognized as a prophet; he could perform miracles, and his mother was honored as a virgin, but he did not die on the cross, and certainly was not God incarnate. Muhammad's task was to correct history as well as to fulfill it by announcing the final revelation. The debt of Islam to Judaism and to Christianity is profound, but it did not continue those religions so much as reinterpret them. The process took some time; in the meantime the religious culture of the Middle East presented the appearance of a patchwork of interpretations and memories by three religions with a shared past (which is not to discount either the surviving traces of paganism or the different varieties of Christianity). One technique employed in the Qur'ān, as in the Bible, was genealogy: the genealogy of Mary, for example, was a theme shared in Muslim scholarship and in the Christian-Jewish debates,[56] and the descent of the children of Israel became a major issue. In the west, too, genealogy was a powerful tool in the formation of a Gothic history and Gothic self-understanding.[57] The writers of Gothic history created a historical past and a written history for the Goths out of materials which included the existing social memory.[58]

Those who sought to understand history from within the context of the Roman empire faced different, though often related, problems. In his *Histories against the Pagans,* Orosius tried to make sense of the fact that disaster could strike an apparently Christian empire by placing the sack of Rome by Alaric in 410 in a long context of disasters which had happened before the *tempora christiana.* Augustine's view expressed in the *City of God* was more complex and more profound, but not essentially different: Rome before Christianity had been fundamentally flawed, the missing element a proper respect for God. Augustine was less interested here to absorb Old Testament history into his own long view than to wrestle with the Roman, non-Christian past, and to ask wherein lay Rome's greatness; the answer he came up with was not encouraging. But Augustine was hardly typical; for most, the past represented by the Hebrew Bible was indeed gradually incorporated into general historical understanding.

Some writers, indeed, were resistant, and went on composing secular histories without recourse to the Scriptures or to sacred time. As late as the 6th century it was still possible to write in this way, taking studious care to preserve conventions set a thousand years before. But the task became more difficult, and the attempt was eventually abandoned. In the late 4th century Ammianus Marcellinus was the author of a Latin history which in its sweep and sheer energy rivals any of the works of the classical historians, and he was followed by a line of historians writing in Greek, of whom Procopius of Caesarea was the best and the last. But there was no Byzantine narrative history of the Arab conquests, and the Persian wars of Heraclius have to be pieced together from poetic and religiously inspired sources.[59] In late antiquity, and even through to the late Byzantine period, the yearly calendar with its representations of the months and seasons continued to carry a heavy traditional symbolism; a mosaic from the Villa of the Falconer at Argos of around 500 displays a cycle of months with their attributes that can be paralleled in manuscript illustration as late as the Empire of Trebizond in the 14th century.[60] But already the more explicitly pagan elements of earlier imagery of the months had given place to the more neutral theme of the labors of the months, and the familiar symbolism of the seasons had long been adapted to a Christian purpose. In his Latin panegyric on the accession of Justin II (565 C.E.), Corippus applies to the Hippodrome the symbolism of the annually revolving seasons and the sun god with his four-horse chariot. He adds the cautious reminder that "when the maker of the sun decided to let himself be seen beneath the sun, and when God took the shape of humankind from a virgin, then the games of the sun were abolished, and honors and games were offered to the Roman emperors, and the pleasant amusements of the circus to New Rome";[61] but the disclaimer licenses him to associate the accession of the new emperor with the rising of the sun and the perpetual renewal of the phoenix, another symbol of *renovatio* that had been appropriated for Christian use since the 4th century, when the image was applied to Constantine by Eusebius.

Historical time, that is, linear time, was by and large transformed into religious time. Augustine struggled to understand time; "What is time? Who can explain this easily and briefly? Who can comprehend this even in thought so as to articulate the answer in words?"[62] He was sure, though, that it must have begun with creation. So were the writers of the chronicles, who now self-confidently began to take as their starting point nothing less than the creation of the world. If a chronicle did not begin with creation, it was only because it was a continuation of an earlier one which did; thus Marcellinus the *comes,* writing in Latin in 6th century Constantinople, begins by recalling the wonderful work by Eusebius which covered the period from the creation of the world to Emperor Constantine, and its Latin continuation by Jerome up to the time of Emperor Valens (d. 378).[63] The date of creation was a matter of dispute, being variously counted as 5500, 5508, or (by Eusebius and Jerome) 5200 B.C.E., but the point was to continue the tradition of harmonizing scriptural events with Greek and Roman history, and for the more recent period to weave together secular and religious material. Marcellinus took official lists, such as lists of consuls, and material that apparently came from city annals of Constantinople, and expanded it with the aid of a limited range of other authorities.[64] His chronicle was continued in turn by another author, just as he had consciously continued that of Jerome. But the chroniclers' perception also pointed to the future: linear time implied not only the beginning but also the end of the world. The Second Coming would be preceded by the rule of Antichrist and the end of things; history could be divided according to the prophecy of the four successive kingdoms contained in the Book of Daniel, and the last things could be expected at a date which would allow an interpretation of the history of the world as corresponding in millennial terms to the six days of creation.[65] Speculation as to exactly when and how this would occur varied. It intensified as the year which might notionally represent 6000 years since creation approached, and particularly so in the context of the wars against the Persians and then against the Arabs. As always, the actual date was successively adjusted to accommodate the world's stubborn refusal to end. The claim that Jewish prophecy had in truth been fulfilled in Christianity was reiterated with more and more urgency, both in written texts and in visual art; Jews are shown as routed, and Christian imagery to have appropriated and subsumed that of the Tabernacle. (It was a small step, given this scenario, for iconophile art and texts to represent the iconoclasts in the guise of Jews.)[66]

In Islam, which inherited the linear conception of history, the progression was that of revelation. Previous prophets, of whom Jesus was one, had served to prepare the way for the final revelation and for Muhammad, the final prophet; the peoples of the Book had their place in history, and were worthy of respect—certainly they were to be placed far above pagans and idolaters—but their revelation was at best partial and therefore inferior. The shadow of impending judgment extended to all.

Faced with so powerfully coherent a view, historians found it hard to maintain a secular approach to the past. Christians found various ways in which to exert a claim over the classical culture which long remained the main staple of education for the elite. Indeed, among the 7th century liturgical and documentary papyri found in the remote outpost of Nessana on the Egyptian border are texts of Virgil. Attempts to come to terms with this literary heritage included Christian experiments with classical form, among which one of the quainter attempts is the Christian "cento" on creation and the life of Jesus, which was put together by an upper-class woman called Proba in the 4th century from lines taken from Virgil's *Aeneid;* portrayed in the vocabulary and persona of *pius Aeneas,* this is a heroicized Jesus who would fail to convince most Christians. Corippus's use of the Virgilian model for his eight-book hexameter poem on the campaigns of John Troglita in North Africa in the 540s was somewhat more appropriate. Others also tried the experiment of putting Christian material into classical dress: the Greek paraphrase of the Gospel according to John by the learned 5th century poet Nonnus was one example, and in Latin, biblical epic became a respectable genre. Claudian, another major Latin poet of the late 4th century, and an Egyptian, like so many of the poets of the period, was the author of a short poem on the Savior, but preferred to keep Christian themes and vocabulary out of his major works, choosing even in his eulogy of Serena, the pious wife of Stilicho, to draw instead on the conventional apparatus of classical mythology.[67] Generations of Christians struggled to reconcile the literary culture they had learned with their Christian faith. Many of their accommodations were facile. But others, like Tertullian in the 2nd century, who had asked, "What had Athens to do with Jerusalem?" or Augustine in the 5th, who was still wrestling with the question, saw the issue in bleaker terms; Augustine's answer, in the *City of God,* was long in coming and gloomy in its message. His "great and arduous work"[68] devoted ten of its twenty-two books to the demonstration that the literary and philosophical culture of Augustine's youth, to which he had given his best efforts and his loyalties, must finally be rejected. "Your" Virgil, the Virgil of the pagans, is contrasted with "our" Scriptures, and the edifice of Platonism, which Augustine recognizes as having come nearest to that of Christianity, is seen to be, in Peter Brown's words, "a magnificent failure."[69]

But even a rejected pagan past could be put to use. A work that proved to be fundamental in providing the model for subsequent saints' lives, the *Life of Antony* (d. 356) by Athanasius, makes much of its hero's rejection of worldly education and sophisticated learning; Antony's speech to pagans, as well as his response to the receipt of an imperial letter, are meant to teach the superiority of faith and holiness over learning and secular authority.[70] Yet the text itself deployed literary models borrowed from pagan lives, and pointed the way for virtually all subsequent hagiographic literature to base itself on the categories of the classical encomium. The Christian holy man or woman described in hagiographic literature was henceforth presented in the mode prescribed for the classical writers of encomia by the rhetorical handbooks.[71]

Nor were emperors exempt from this treatment; it was applied to Constantine by Eusebius, and continued to provide the basic categories of the qualities of the Christian emperor.[72] Till late in the Byzantine period, emperors were judged and their reigns interpreted in the light of expectations derived from the twin sources of the traditional Roman imperial virtues and the Christian framework, onto which the former had been grafted by Eusebius and his successors. Inevitably emperors themselves also accepted these categories, and presented themselves in their official pronouncements and writings simultaneously as heirs to the Romans and as pious Christian *basileis*.[73] In what was surely one of the greatest achievements of late antiquity, Justinian brought about the codification of the whole of existing Roman law, and legislated how law was to be taught and the legal profession recruited henceforth. His preambles present him in the guise of restorer, his work of codification as a *renovatio*. But his reign was fraught with ambiguities. While in the works of Procopius we find both praise and condemnation, John Lydus, a contemporary and a conservative, saw the emperor as a restorer, and placed the blame on his ministers when things went wrong; the contradictions led Edward Gibbon to the negative verdict that Justinian's proclaimed restoration of Roman law was no such thing.[74] Gibbon's final verdict on Justinian as lawmaker reads: "the government of Justinian united the evils of liberty and servitude; and the Romans were oppressed at the same time by the multiplicity of their laws and the arbitrary will of their master." John Lydus complained of the decline of Latin in his day, and indeed Justinian's own laws were commonly issued in Greek. But while Greek did indeed take the place of Latin in official use from the reign of Heraclius (610–641), emperors continued to see themselves as following in the Roman tradition, and Byzantines called themselves by the name "Romans" for centuries.

It would be wrong, however, to suggest uniformity. Gregory of Tours, the historian of the Franks, begins his history by asserting his own Christian faith and doctrinal correctness; part of the proof of that probity is, "for the sake of those who are losing hope as they see the end of the world coming nearer and nearer," to explain in chronicle fashion the history of the world since creation.[75] His predecessors in this enterprise are named as Eusebius, Jerome, Orosius, and Victorius. Signs, portents, and wonders articulate Gregory's work and point to the approaching end, and the bloody history of the Merovingian dynasty marks the "beginning of our sorrows," when internal strife and disorder were destroying the Frankish people and the kingdom.[76] The work ends with a computation of the years that have elapsed since the creation: 5792,[77] perilously close to the 6000 after which the world would end. Gregory precedes this computation with a list of all the bishops of Tours, and of his own works.

Yet life in Merovingian Gaul also preserved some of the qualities of the elite lifestyle of the late Roman upper class, and a courtly piety developed among women in royal circles and elsewhere. Gregory's friend and contemporary, the poet Venantius Fortunatus, who ended his life as bishop of Tours, conducted a delicate literary friendship with Queen Radegund and the ladies of the convent at Poitiers, punctuated by elegant poems and gifts of fruit and delicacies.[78] Despite the praise of the Byzantine historian Agathias, when he wrote about the Franks in the late 6th century,[79] the Merovingian royal dynasty was prone to plots and violence; nevertheless, it created a kingdom in which, for all Gregory of Tours's complaints about the decline of the liberal arts, the court and the administration continued until the later 7th century to act as a focus and stimulus for the kind of social and governmental literacy familiar from the later Roman empire.[80] Even in the 7th century, it was still possible at times to think of a united Mediterranean, linked by common ties of religion and learning. Greek culture, in the persons of monks and ecclesiastics, spread to Italy and Sicily; there was a series of Greek popes; and Archbishop Theodore of Canterbury, himself from the east, founded a scriptorium for the copying of Greek texts and was a participant in the theological disputes which occupied the minds of 7th century eastern churchmen.[81]

The project of remaking the past during late antiquity demanded great imaginative effort and ingenuity. Successive generations of Christians struggled either to weave together the strands of their classical and their biblical inheritance or to assert the primacy of the latter over the former. Their attitudes toward Jews sharpened; the Hebrew Bible, and especially the prophets, were now to be read as foretelling Christianity, the Tabernacle and the Mosaic law as superseded by the new dispensation. Already in the 4th century Eusebius had portrayed Constantine, the new Moses, as building a tabernacle for himself while on campaign, and in the 8th century Bede in his Northumbrian monastery composed three homilies and three works of biblical exegesis on the themes of the Tabernacle and the Temple. The Temple, the cherubim, the Ark, and manna were all read as prototypes of Christian religious images, proof against any suspicion that the latter might be the cause of idolatry. Dealing with the classical past presented other problems: it could be approached on the level of literary culture, attacked as false and demonic for its pagan associations, or neutralized by being absorbed into the Christian chronological framework which started with creation and placed world history in successive phases thereafter. Islam marked the past as different, as the "age of ignorance" for the idolatrous pagan past, or as containing only partial, if legitimate, revelation in the cases of Judaism and Christianity. Moreover, the past was assigned a meaning and a purpose; it pointed the way toward full revelation, which in turn pointed toward the end of the world. Much effort and labor went into this remaking of the past: first the scholarly labor of commentary and chronicle and, especially from the 6th century onward, encyclopedic labor which sought to define a total and comprehensive definition of Christian knowledge; and second the labor of imagination, which filled every gap in the record with a rich texture of story and legend.

The sheer energy of late antiquity is breathtaking. Every inch of the past received attention, and many topics and many texts were the subject of volumes of exegesis and comment. Nor were texts enough: the story was told, and thus its truth fixed, in pictures and other forms of visual art. It was this very exuberance and invention which the reforming iconoclasts attempted unsuccessfully to curb.

We see in late antiquity a mass of experimentation, new ways being tried and new adjustments made. The process of myth-making and development of new identities inevitably implied the shaping of the past according to current preoccupations. Like the medieval west, Byzantium was also engaged in this process. Byzantine society has often been seen as static and unchanging, "theocratic" and without the possibility of dissent. But all recent research demonstrates that this was far from the case in practice: we have been taken in by the Byzantines themselves, who liked to emphasize their own traditionalism. Both east and west continued to engage in the reshaping of the past. The contemporary sense of the approaching end of the world lent itself to infinite procrastination and renegotiation as the projected day came closer.[82] The early medieval west was characterized by diversity, not uniformity.[83] The final collapse of iconoclasm gave rise in the east to a burst of artistic and cultural activity, from manuscript decoration to literary works. In both east and west, state and church, the two poles of authority, were in constant tension with each other.[84] Conversion continued to be a main preoccupation in both east and west. Faced by a huge loss of territory, including Jerusalem and the Holy Land, Byzantium turned its attention to the peoples of the north, peoples like the Slavs and the Bulgars who were still pagan. The outcome of the struggle between church and state was as yet uncertain; and within the diminished empire of the 8th century the relation of the present to the past was still a topic of tension and struggle. During late antiquity the past had been remade, but it had been remade in many different ways, and the effort continued.

Notes

1. Claudian, *De bello Gildonico* 1.21–25, Loeb trans.; see Alan Cameron, *Claudian* (Oxford, 1970), 365–366.

2. Ammianus Marcellinus, 16.10.1ff.; see John Matthews, *The Roman Empire of Ammianus* (London, 1989).

3. See David Lowenthal, *The Past Is a Foreign Country* (Cambridge, 1955), 155.

4. Some of the legends of Constantine are translated in S. C. Lieu, *From Constantine to Julian: Pagan and Byzantine Views. A Source History* (London, 1996).

5. The difficult question of an apparently changing aesthetic sensitivity is the subject

of an interesting discussion by Jas Elsner, *Art and the Roman Viewer: The Transformation of Art from the Pagan World to Christianity* (Cambridge, Eng., 1995).

6. For a major discussion of Eusebius's apologetic work and his biblical scholarship see T. D. Barnes, *Constantine and Eusebius* (Cambridge, Mass., 1981). Contrary to Eusebius's claims, oracular shrines were in full function in the reign of Constantine and after, and were supported by many other forms of pagan divination: see R. Lane Fox, *Pagans and Christians in the Mediterranean World from the Second Century A.D. to the Conversion of Constantine* (Harmondsworth, 1986); P. Athanassiadi, "Dreams, Theurgy, and Freelance Divination: The Testimony of Iamblichus," *Journal of Roman Studies* 83 (1993): 114–130; "Persecution and Response in Late Paganism: The Evidence of Damascius," *Journal of Hellenic Studies* 113 (1993): 1–29.

7. See Elizabeth A. Clark, *The Origenist Controversy: The Cultural Construction of an Early Christian Debate* (Princeton, 1992).

8. Philip Rousseau, *Basil of Caesarea* (Berkeley, 1994), 320.

9. Ibid., 325.

10. *Confessions* 11–12; *De civ.Dei* 11.

11. See Herbert Kessler, "Gazing at the Future: The *Parousia* Miniature in Vatican gr. 699," in Christopher Moss and Katherine Kiefer, eds., *Byzantine East, Latin West: Art-Historical Studies in Honor of Kurt Weitzmann* (Princeton, 1996), 365–371. Kessler describes the miniature in question (fol. 89r) as "one of the earliest representations of the Last Judgment" (365).

12. *De civ.Dei* 11.32.

13. See Elaine Pagels, *Adam, Eve, and the Serpent* (New York and London, 1988); Peter Brown, *The Body and Society: Men, Women, and Sexual Renunciation in Early Christianity* (New York, 1988).

14. *Exp. Pers.* 2.2.113; for the Heraclian "David plates," part of a silver treasure found on Cyprus at the site of the Byzantine town of Lambousa, see K. Weitzmann, *The Age of Spirituality: Late Antique and Early Christian Art, Third to Seventh Century* (New York, 1979), nos. 425–433.

15. *PG* 92.1161–1754; see Mary Whitby, "The Devil in Disguise: The End of George of Pisidia's *Hexaemeron* Reconsidered," *Journal of Hellenic Studies* 115 (1995): 115–129; "A New Image for a New Age: George of Pisidia on the Emperor Heraclius," in E. Dabrowa, ed., *The Roman and Byzantine Army in the Near East* (Cracow, 1994), 197–225.

16. John Hick, in John Hick, ed., *The Myth of God Incarnate* (London, 1977), 184.

17. *Panarion* 51.22.10; see G. W. Bowersock, *Hellenism in Late Antiquity* (Cambridge, Eng., 1990), 22–28.

18. See Bowersock, *Hellenism*, 49–52.

19. See M. Tardieu, *Les paysages reliques: Routes et haltes syriennes d'Isidore à Simplicius* (Louvain and Paris, 1990).

20. See David S. Potter, *Prophecy and History in the Crisis of the Roman Empire: A Historical Commentary on the Thirteenth Sibylline Oracle* (Oxford, 1990).

21. Potter, *Prophecy*, 351–355, and see also Stephen Mitchell, *Anatolia: Land, Men, and Gods in Asia Minor II. The Rise of the Church* (Oxford, 1993), 43–44, in the context of a very interesting discussion of the linked developments in pagan, Christian, and Jewish theology.

22. *Or.* 18–21.

23. For the uses (and sometimes the fabrication) of texts at these councils see P. Van den Ven, "La patristique et l'hagiographie au concile de Nicée en 787," *Byzantion* 25–27 (1955–1957): 325–362; and see Cyril Mango, "The Availability of Books in the Byzantine Empire, A.D. 750–850," in *Byzantine Books and Bookmen* (Washington, D.C., 1975), 29–45.

24. Councils in visual art: C. Walter, "Le souvenir du IIe Concile de Nicée dans

l'iconographie byzantine," in F. Boespflug and N. Lossky, eds., *Nicée II, 787–1987: Douze siècles d'images religieuses* (Paris, 1987), 163–183.

25. Averil Cameron, "Texts as Weapons: Polemic in the Byzantine Dark Ages," in Alan K. Bowman and Greg Woolf, eds., *Literacy and Power in the Ancient World* (Cambridge, 1994), 198–215; "Ascetic Closure and the End of Antiquity," in Vincent L. Wimbush and Richard Valantasis, eds., *Asceticism* (New York, 1995), 147–161.

26. See Frances Young in Hick, ed., *The Myth of God Incarnate*, 13–47, 28–29; for the expression of Christianity in terms of mystery and paradox, which pulled against the totalizing thrust of theological discourse, see Averil Cameron, *Christianity and the Rhetoric of Empire* (Berkeley, 1991), chap. 5.

27. Proclus, *Platonic Theology* 1.4.

28. Marinus, *Vit.Procli* 10.

29. See Paavo Castrén, ed., *Post-Herulian Athens* (Helsinki, 1994) (for Alaric see p. 9); Alison Frantz, *The Athenian Agora XXIV: Late Antiquity, A.D. 267–700* (Princeton, 1988), 93.

30. Ibid., 9.

31. Socrates, *Hist.eccl.* 7.21; see Julia Burman, in Castrén, *Post-Herulian Athens*, 63–87; Alan Cameron, "The Empress and the Poet: Paganism and Politics at the Court of Theodosius II," in John J. Winkler and Gordon Williams, eds., *Later Greek Literature* (Cambridge, 1982), 217–289.

32. *Anth.Pal.* II.

33. Gilbert Dagron, *Constantinople imaginaire: Étude sur le recueil du Patria* (Paris, 1984); Averil Cameron and Judith Herrin et al., eds., *Constantinople in the Eighth Century: The Parastaseis Syntomoi Chronikai* (Leiden, 1984); Cyril Mango, "Antique Statuary and the Byzantine Beholder," *Dumbarton Oaks Papers* 17 (1963): 53–75; Liz James, "'Pray Not To Fall into Temptation and Be on Your Guard': Pagan Statues in Christian Constantinople," *Gesta* 35.1 (1996): 12–20.

34. See Lieu, *From Constantine to Julian*, 27.

35. Anna Kartsonis, *Anastasis: The Making of an Image* (Princeton, 1986). Dramatic dialogues: Averil Cameron, "Disputations, Polemical Literature, and the Formation of Opinion in the Early Byzantine Period," in G. J. Reinink and H. L. J. Vanstiphout, eds., *Dispute Poems and Dialogues in the Ancient and Mediaeval Near East* (Leuven, 1991), 91–108.

36. Henry Maguire, *Art and Eloquence in Byzantium* (Princeton, 1981), 36–42; Basil, *PG* 31.508–540.

37. Anne-Marie Palmer, *Prudentius on the Martyrs* (Oxford, 1989), 98.

38. Gilbert Dagron, ed., *Vie et miracles de Sainte Thècle* (Brussels, 1978); F. Hild and H. Hellenkemper, *Kilikien und Isaurien* (Vienna, 1990), 441–443; S. Hill, *The Early Byzantine Churches of Cilicia and Isauria* (Aldershot, 1966), 208–234.

39. *Itin.Anton.* 4.

40. See Cyril Mango, "Constantine's Mausoleum and the Translation of Relics," *Byzantinische Zeitschrift* 83 (1990): 51–62, repr. in Mango, *Studies on Constantinople* (Aldershot, 1993), V, with Addendum.

41. Peter Brown, *The Cult of the Saints* (Chicago, 1981), 53–57; cf. 36–39 on Ambrose.

42. See E. Kitzinger, "The Cult of Images before Iconoclasm," *Dumbarton Oaks Papers* 8 (1954): 85–150; Memphis: *Itin.Anton.* 4: *pallium linteum in quo est effigies Salvatoris*.

43. See Averil Cameron, "The History of the Image of Edessa: The Telling of a Story," *Okeanos: Essays Presented to I. Ševčenko* (Cambridge, Mass., 1983), 80–94; the first reference to the image as "not made by human hands" is in the *Ecclesiastical History* of Evagrius Scholasticus, written in the 590s (*Hist.eccl.* 4.27).

44. *Narratio de imagine edessena, PG* 113: 421–454.

45. Liz James, "Monks, Monastic Art, the Sanctoral Cycle, and the Middle Byzantine Church," in Margaret Mullett and Anthony Kirby, eds., *The Theotokos Evergetis and Eleventh-Century Monasticism* (Belfast, 1994), 162–175.

46. This is the argument of Hans Belting, *Likeness and Presence: A History of the Image before the Era of Art* (Chicago, 1994).

47. The bibliography is large: see especially J.-M. Sansterre, "La parole, le texte et l'image selon les auteurs byzantins des époques iconoclastes et posticonoclaste," in *Testo e Immagine nell'alto medioevo, 15–21 aprile 1993* (Spoleto, 1994), 197–243.

48. On the development of the idea of the Christian "Holy Land," see Robert L. Wilken, *The Land Called Holy: Palestine in Christian History and Thought* (New Haven, 1992).

49. John Wilkinson, trans., *Egeria's Travels*, rev. ed. (Warminster, 1981), 96, 105, 117, 175.

50. The process is vividly described in book 3 of Eusebius's *Life of Constantine;* for the history of the site and scholarly investigation to date see the comprehensive account by Martin Biddle, "The Tomb of Christ: Sources, Methods, and a New Approach," in Kenneth Painter, ed., *"Churches Built in Ancient Times": Recent Studies in Early Christian Archaeology* (London, 1994), 73–147.

51. *Vit.Const.* 3.28.

52. Three crosses and the nails: Socrates, *Hist.eccl.* 1.17 (5th century).

53. See in particular E. D. Hunt, *Holy Land Pilgrimage in the Later Roman Empire A.D. 312–460* (Oxford, 1982); R. Ousterhout, ed., *The Blessings of Pilgrimage* (Urbana, Ill., 1990).

54. Ed. H. Usener, "Das Weihnachtspredigt des Sophronios," *Rheinisches Museum für Philologie*, n.s. 41 (1886): 500–516.

55. Discussion of this *Book of the Lords,* traces of which survive in the later Persian *Shāhnāma* of Firdausi and Arabic chronicle of al-Tabarī: Zeev Rubin, "The reforms of Khusro Anūshirwān," in Averil Cameron, ed., *The Byzantine and Early Islamic Near East I: States, Resources, and Armies* (Princeton, 1995), 227–297. In the late 6th century Agathias claims to have drawn on these *Annals* in the sections of his *History* where he recounts the history of the Sassanians (*Hist.* 2.23–27; 4.24–30; cf. 2.27.4–8; 4.30.2–5).

56. See Averil Cameron, "Byzantines and Jews: Recent Work on Early Byzantium," *Byzantine and Modern Greek Studies* 20 (1996).

57. See Peter Heather, "Cassiodorus and the Rise of the Amals: Genealogy and the Goths under Hun Domination," *Journal of Roman Studies* 79 (1989): 103–128.

58. For the historians, see Walter Goffart, *The Narrators of Barbarian History (A.D. 550–800): Jordanes, Gregory of Tours, Bede, and Paul the Deacon* (Princeton, 1988); James Fentress and Chris Wickham, *Social Memory* (Oxford, 1992), contains a chapter on the medieval west (144–172).

59. See Michael Whitby, "Greek Historical Writing after Procopius: Variety and Vitality," in Averil Cameron and Lawrence I. Conrad, eds., *The Byzantine and Early Islamic Near East I: Problems in the Literary Source Material* (Princeton, 1992), 25–80.

60. See G. Åkerström-Hougen, *The Calendar and Hunting Mosaics of the Villa of the Falconer in Argos: A Study in Early Byzantine Iconography* (Stockholm, 1974), esp. 83–85.

61. Corippus, *Iust.* 1.340–44.

62. *Confessions* 11.17, trans. Chadwick.

63. Marcellinus, *Chron.*, praef.

64. See Brian Croke, *The Chronicle of Marcellinus: Translation and Commentary* (Sydney, 1995); another well-known (Greek) 6th century chronicle is that of John Malalas, for which see the translation by Elizabeth Jeffreys, Michael Jeffreys, and Roger Scott et al., *The Chronicle of John Malalas* (Melbourne, 1986), and Elizabeth Jeffreys et al., eds., *Studies in John Malalas* (Sydney, 1990).

65. See Paul Magdalino, "The History of the Future and Its Uses: Prophecy, Policy, and Propaganda," in Roderick Beaton and Charlotte Roueché, eds., *The Making of Byzantine History: Studies Dedicated to Donald M. Nicol* (Aldershot, 1993), 3–34.

66. See Averil Cameron, "Byzantines and Jews."

67. *Carm.min.* 32. De Salvatore, ed. J. B. Hall., cf. 30, Laus Serenae.

68. *De civ.Dei* I, *praef.*, 8.

69. Peter Brown, *Augustine of Hippo* (London, 1967), 306–307.

70. Athanasius, *Vit.Ant.* 74–80, 81.

71. See Cameron, *Christianity and the Rhetoric of Empire,* chaps. 2 and 3.

72. From the surviving collection of twelve Latin imperial panegyrics, several deal with Constantine and their content, and the categories they apply are closely paralleled in Eusebius's Greek *Vita Constantiniana:* see C. E. V. Nixon and Barbara Saylor Rogers, eds., *In Praise of Later Roman Emperors: The Panegyrici Latini* (Berkeley, 1994).

73. The combination persisted: see Margaret Mullett, "The Imperial Vocabulary of Alexios I Komnenos," in Margaret Mullett and Dion Smythe, eds., *Alexios I Komnenos: Papers* (Belfast, 1996), 359–397. One of Eusebius's most influential successors was Agapetos the deacon, author of a "Mirror for Princes" in the 6th century (*PG* 86.1, 1163–1186): see P. Henry III, "A Mirror for Justinian: The *Ekthesis* of Agapetus Diaconus," *Greek, Roman, and Byzantine Studies* 8 (1967): 281–308.

74. *Renovatio:* see Michael Maas, "Roman History and Christian Ideology in Justinianic Reform Legislation," *Dumbarton Oaks Papers* 40 (1986): 17–31; John Lydus on Justinian: cf. *Mag.* 2.28; 3.69; see Michael Maas, *John Lydus and the Roman Past* (London, 1992), esp. chap. 6. Edward Gibbon, *History of the Decline and Fall of the Roman Empire,* ed. J. B. Bury, IV (London, 1901), chap. 44.

75. *Hist.* 1, *praef.* (trans. Thorpe).

76. *Hist.* 5, *praef.*

77. *Hist.* 10.31.

78. Peter Brown, *The Rise of Western Christendom: Triumph and Diversity (A.D. 200–1000)* (Oxford, 1996), 151–153.

79. Agathias, *Hist.* 1.2–5; II.14.8–14.

80. *Hist.* 1, *praef.;* cf. Ian Wood, "Administration, Law, and Culture in Merovingian Gaul," in Rosamond McKitterick, ed., *The Uses of Literacy in Mediaeval Europe* (Cambridge, 1990), 63–81; Ian Wood, *The Merovingian Kingdoms 450–751* (London, 1994).

81. Michael Lapidge, ed., *Archbishop Theodore: Commemorative Studies on His Life and Influence* (Cambridge, 1995); Jane Stevenson, *The Laterculus Malalianus and the School of Archbishop Theodore* (Cambridge, 1995); Bernard Bischoff and Michael Lapidge, *Biblical Commentaries from the Canterbury School of Theodore and Hadrian* (Cambridge, 1994).

82. See Magdalino, "The History of the Future."

83. See Brown, *Rise of Western Christendom,* Part II: "Divergent Legacies: A.D. 500–750."

84. See Gilbert Dagron, *Empereur et prêtre: Étude sur le "césaropapisme" byzantin* (Paris, 1996).

Sacred Landscapes

Béatrice Caseau

In 201, when the newly arrived Roman legionaries decided to build a military camp at Gholaia (Bu Njem, Libya), in the province of Tripolitania, their first move was to consecrate the place to divine beings. Their immediate concern was to conciliate the deity presiding over that precise spot, the genius of Gholaia.[1] The Romans, although they brought their own deities with them, did not want to vex local gods ruling this part of the universe. They installed their own gods inside the camp, along with the genius of Gholaia. Around the camp, the Romans also built or maintained a circle of temples dedicated to romanized African gods—such as Jupiter Hammon, overseer of caravan routes—acknowledging the competence and power of these gods. Indeed, in the Roman mind, it was the duty of human beings to honor and not to offend those divine beings who had some power over a region.

This sacralization of the land could be undone either through an elaborate ritual of deconsecration or, more violently, through desecration. After the departure of the Roman legion from Gholaia around 260, the local inhabitants, now freed from Roman domination, took their revenge on the gods of the invaders. They carefully desecrated the religious spaces inside the Roman camp and destroyed the cult statues. This gesture was meant to prove the weakness of the Roman gods, already demonstrated by the retreat of the army. It was also a gesture of fear. By destroying the cult statues of Victory and Fortune, these people were making sure that the goddesses would not have any means of harming them.

This episode of consecration and desecration of a Roman camp in the 3rd century reveals two possible attitudes toward divine beings: one encompassing and accumulative, that seeks the protection of and attempts to avoid the wrath of all sorts of divine beings; the other a deliberate choice of one or more deities accompanied by the rejection of all others. The Roman legion had chosen the syncretistic attitude by incorporating African gods into their Roman pantheon.

The local inhabitants of Gholaia chose the second option. Their iconoclasm was selective: they continued to worship Jupiter Hammon in the temple built by the Romans into the 4th and 5th centuries, but rejected those goddesses whose cult had been organized inside the camp for Roman legionaries. Their iconoclasm was directed against foreign deities whose cult was closely connected to the military domination by their former Roman rulers.

The phenomenon of sacralization includes the dedication of something or somebody to a divine being. Space, in particular, can be transformed into or revealed as a place of interaction between human beings and gods. Dedicating a space to a deity creates a nodal point of communication, ensuring the benevolence of that divine being over a region or over a group of persons. Not only space and objects but also time can become sacred, through the organization of a religious calendar. People also can be consecrated to a divine being. The rituals of sacralization range from public and solemn ceremonies, such as the dedication of a city, to small private offerings, like the burning of incense.

The notion of desacralization is more complex: it encompasses both the return of sacred things to a profane use, such as the secularization of religious buildings, and desecration, that is, a violent breach of the rules of behavior toward sacred things or persons. Defilement of shrines, sacrilege, and willful destruction fall in this category.

In the late antique period we can watch the processes of sacralization and desacralization as different religions came into contact and competed with each other. By altering the spatial and temporal rhythms of a community, sacralization also profoundly affected many other aspects of life and thus made cohabitation between different religious groups difficult. Defining sacredness in each religion required the setting of the boundaries of licit and illicit behavior, as well as restricting access to some categories of persons. What was impure for one religion was not for another; what was considered impious by some was perceived as pious by others. Episodes of public religious persecution and private religious violence were recorded during this long period of time. Religious communities desecrated sacred buildings or cult objects belonging to competing religious groups. Civil authorities often preferred one specific religion and wished to restrict the public display of other less favored religions. If the Roman and Sassanian empires could not control individual minds, they could nevertheless persecute religious communities and control their religious buildings. More than once, Roman authorities ordered the confiscation or the destruction of Christian religious buildings and sacred books.

At the same time, on the eastern border of the Roman empire the Sassanians, who had made Zoroastrianism the official religion of their empire, were also persecuting the Christian minority within their borders—especially members of the Sassanian aristocracy who converted to this faith, known to be the favored religion of their powerful Roman neighbor. When Christianity became the official religion in the Roman empire, the pagan forms of sacralization were gradually outlawed by church and state authorities. Pagan religious buildings and objects were desacralized and sometimes desecrated, while the land and the people were undergoing a new Christian sacralization. The intense sacralization of space during the centuries that saw the establishment of numerous pagan cults was superseded by the no less intense sacralization of space by Christianity.

Despite thriving economies in many provinces of the Roman world, members of a religious community no longer sought to impress by building secular public structures as their ancestors had done; instead, from the 4th to the 6th century money was poured into constructing churches and synagogues. In some regions, such as Palestine, it is possible to follow the spread of two competing religious groups, the Jews and the Christians, as they built splendid synagogues and churches that shared many similar architectural features.[2] The transformation of the Roman empire into a Christian state eventually led to restricted freedom for Jews and non-orthodox Christians. Although Judaism was a legal cult, Jewish proselytism and the building of new synagogues or the adornment of old ones were forbidden by law during the 5th century. This legal restriction on constructing religious buildings was also imposed by Islamic authorities on Jews, Christians, and Zoroastrians when the Muslim Arabs came to rule the Middle East. Under their influence, Christian, Jewish, and Zoroastrian sacred sites slowly vanished during the Middle Ages, to be replaced by shining new mosques, which are now the landmarks of Islamic cities.

Religious buildings attested to the vitality of a community and its right to practice its religion and publicize its cult. This is why they were targeted by imperial authorities who wished to control the religious affiliation of the population they ruled. By taking a journey through the late antique landscape, from the 3rd to the 8th century, it is possible to visualize the effects of sacralization and desacralization at different times. How did the religious buildings of the different communities fit into the fabric of ancient cities? How did they relate to existing religious buildings? Was the sacralization of a space valid only for a specific religious community, or could it be recaptured by another?

The competition for converts as well as for highly visible or conveniently located sacred spaces can be tracked in the conversion of buildings from one religion to another. Monumental new shrines were erected next to the derelict religious buildings of an ancient cult. Avoidance of ancient religious centers and the deliberate creation of new sanctuaries, located far away, was another tactic. The shift in religious preferences of the people and of the rulers over this long period of time, resulting in successive waves of sacralization and desacralization, should not be isolated from other relevant factors. Economic and demographic changes such as the decline of urban life, the loss of population after the plague of the 6th century, and catastrophes—natural and manmade, earthquakes and wars—transformed the sacred landscape.

A visitor to the Roman world at the end of the 3rd century would have been overwhelmed by the presence of temples, altars, and images of gods and goddesses. Whether in town or in the countryside, shrines consecrated to the gods were ubiquitous. They were often the first visible buildings of a distant city, gleaming on top of an acropolis. In any new city, reports Libanius (*Oration* 30.5), shrines were the first buildings erected, immediately after the walls. Splendid entrances to majestic temples opened on the main streets. Statues of gods and goddesses, adorned with garlands and fragrant with the offerings of incense, were to be found in numerous parts of the cities: they embellished not only temples, but crossroads, theaters, baths, and forums.

The gods were offered sacrifices in exchange for their benevolence and protection of the city or the house. In each house, space was devoted to propitiating the deities of the household. Often this was a simple patch of earth, while shrines, or even miniature temples, adorned more opulent houses.[3] Inhabited space was religiously consecrated space in a broader sense: prescribed religious rites modeled after the mythical foundation of Rome set the limits of each Roman city, consecrating the inner space of the city to the gods. When the city of Constantinople was established, in 324, the new limits of the city, three times bigger than Byzantium, were duly consecrated following the traditional rites of inauguration.

A stroll in the countryside would also reveal an intense sacralization of space. Cities were surrounded by temples, fields were limited by consecrated "boundary marks," and major estates had rural shrines where peasants thanked the deities for the harvest by offering them first fruits, flowers, and incense. Numbers of these *sacella*, little sacred spots in the countryside, were donated by wealthy landlords, along with a statue of a divinity and an altar for the offerings.

The sacralization of the landscape proceeded either from a sense of the numinous in natural spots or from a deliberate attempt to attract the benevolence of the deities. Some places were felt to have been elected by the gods and goddesses, who made them holy. Seneca evokes this source of sacralization in a letter to a friend: "If you have ever come on a dense wood of ancient trees that have risen to an exceptional height, shutting out all sight of the sky with one thick screen of branches upon another, the loftiness of the forest, the seclusion of the spot, your sense of wonderment at finding so deep and unbroken a gloom out of doors, will persuade you of the presence of a deity" (Seneca, *Letters* 41.5, trans. R. Campbell). Sites of natural beauty such as springs, hills, caves, and groves were often seen as numinous.[4] A sacred geography was thus created, grounded in the mythology of the deities' birthplaces, travels, and adventures. To honor the gods and goddesses in these locations, offerings were deposited and enclosures, altars, and temples were built. Some expanded into major sanctuaries such as those at Delphi or Aegae. Others remained natural holy spots, where food offerings or votive ribbons tied to a tree indicated that this was a place of worship.

A space could also be made sacred through the deliberate dedication of a piece of land to a deity. To propitiate specific gods, Roman magistrates and generals vowed to build temples to them.[5] The ritual of dedication transferred land to the deities, but only the ritual of *consecratio,* performed on public land in the name of the *populus,* transformed this dedicated land into a *res sacra,* a public sacred space where violent or damaging behavior would be a sacrilege *(sacrilegium).* Damage done to private shrines was not considered a sacrilege, yet they were to be approached with respect, for the sake of piety. They too were dedicated to the gods and therefore sacralized. Thus the Romans distinguished two different types of religious spaces: one closely connected to the state, where sacrifices funded by the state were offered for the prosperity of the Roman people, and one private, where sacrifices were offered in the name and with the money of private persons or groups of persons. The Roman empire officially approved and sponsored a number of cults which were celebrated at public festivals. Yet the pontiffs, state priests responsible for imperially sponsored cults, also supervised private cults, ruled by the *ius divinum*. The emperor, as *pontifex maximus,* was at the top of the priestly hierarchy. His duty was to preside over official religious ceremonies and to offer sacrifices for the sake of the empire. He also supervised the temples and authorized and patronized the erection of new shrines and the restoration or embellishment of old ones. Wherever he went, he was expected to offer sacrifices to the gods. When the city of Alexandria heard of Caracalla's impending arrival in 215, large public sacrifices were organized for his reception: "All kinds of musical instruments were set up everywhere and produced a variety of sounds. Clouds of perfume and incense of all sorts presented a sweet odor at the city gates. As soon as Antoninus entered the city with his whole army, he went up to the temple, where he made a large number of sacrifices and laid quantities of incense on the altars" (Herodian 4.8.7–8, trans. C. R. Whittaker).

Rather than imagining a homogenous pagan world before Christianization, we should picture flourishing cultic centers, the loci of major festivals, as well as a number of more or less deserted shrines left to decay.[6] While some cults were popular at the end of the 3rd century, others had lost their appeal and declined. The maintenance of religious buildings relied on public money for public and civic cults and on generous worshipers for private cults, but cities as well as private donors could decide which temples they preferred to restore, embellish, or build anew. The Mithraea, for example, were private religious buildings. Although Mithraea were still being maintained in some areas in the 4th century, their often decayed state in Gaul, Germany, and Britain reveals both the crisis that struck these regions in the 3rd century and the slow decline of Mithraism.[7]

Sacralization was not therefore a continuous phenomenon everywhere. It tended to be cumulative, creating holy spaces that remained holy even if the buildings were left in decay. Yet even this sacralization could fade away if no one cared to maintain the sacred enclosure any longer. It is therefore important to keep in mind the very real diversity in status and success of the numerous cults in the late antique Roman world.

Common features in the buildings and in the rituals of sacrifice nevertheless gave some unity to the pagan cultic centers of the late Roman world. Cities had undergone drastic changes during the High Empire: from Gaul to Arabia, lavish temples to Jupiter or Zeus, to Rome, and to the imperial cult were built on prominent sites in the provincial cities. They added a Roman aspect to cities that already had a long history. At Jerash (Gerasa), for example, the major Hellenistic cultic center disappeared when it was rebuilt into monumental Roman temples dedicated to Zeus.[8] Throughout the Roman empire, local cults were maintained following an *interpretatio romana,* while oriental cults were introduced to Rome and the western provinces.[9] The addition of new cults and festivals to the city of Rome can be traced by comparing 1st century religious calendars with that of 354, which records the state-supported public festivals celebrated at Rome.[10] Those festivals, which included processions, sacrifices, and banquets as well as games and spectacles, were major social events.[11] The numerous new festivals reveal the vitality and flexibility of late antique paganism.[12] Yet this flexibility had limits. Although in general Roman rulers confirmed the existing privileges of an ancient sanctuary when they conquered a region, and also welcomed numerous oriental cults into Rome, not every new cult was legally recognized.[13] After the expulsion of Christians from the synagogues, Christianity no longer enjoyed the legal protection that was granted to Judaism as a *religio licita*. Starting with Nero in 64 C.E., Roman emperors began to persecute the devotees of this new cult. The simple fact of professing Christianity could lead to death, if one were denounced to the Roman authorities, as the rescript of Emperor Trajan to Pliny the Younger reveals. Another religious group, the Manichees, disciples of Mani (216–276), a man from Persia who claimed to be an apostle of Jesus, was also persecuted for introducing into the Roman empire a "superstitious doctrine" based on principles opposed to those of the Romans' ancient religion.[14] The standard punishment for individuals who were denounced as belonging to either group and who refused to renounce their religion was capital punishment and confiscation of their goods.

Religion in the pagan Roman world had a civic and consensual dimension. The religious skyline of cities was very often dominated by the imperial cult. Some participation in civic cults was mandatory to preserve the *pax deorum* and to show political loyalty to the Roman rulers. The latter took on a renewed importance with the political crisis of the 3rd century. In 250, Emperor Decius ordered a general sacrifice for his sake. Those who could not produce the *libellus* proving that they had offered the sacrifice were thrown into jail. The sacralization of imperial power, already well established through the temples devoted to the imperial cult, found a renewed expression in the sacralization of living emperors under the tetrarchs. Diocletian and his colleagues considered themselves *dis geniti* and *deorum creatores,* to whom *adoratio* should be offered. In pagan houses as well as in temples of the imperial cult, the *genius* of the emperor was to be honored for the *natalis Caesaris,* birthday of the emperor; for the *natalis imperii,* anniversary of his accession to power; and for the health of the imperial family, at the *vota publica* each year, and at the *vota quinquennalia.* The tetrarchs resented Christians' refusal to offer sacrifices for the emperors. After isolated cases of Christian soldiers who were martyred for their refusal to offer a sacrifice, a general persecution was launched against the Christians in 303. Their churches were to be destroyed, their leaders arrested, their sacred books burned, and their sacred vessels confiscated. In 304, when a general sacrifice was ordered, those who refused to perform it were to be put to death or condemned to the mines. It was the longest and the most destructive of the persecutions against the Christians. It was enforced with such efficacy in the east, and so thoroughly destroyed Christian meeting places, that we hardly know anything about their style and characteristics. What most enraged the emperors and their officials was the Christians' belief that contact with pagan sacrifices was polluting. In 308 Maximinus Daia, to punish the quite numerous Christian population, ordered food sold in the markets to be sprinkled with libations or blood from the sacrifices.[15] A petition against the Christians addressed to the emperors by the provincial assembly of Lycia-Pamphylia in 312 reveals that pagans felt threatened by their refusal to participate in pagan festivals, including those of the imperial cult: "all should take part in the worship of the gods your kinsmen on behalf of your eternal and imperishable kingship. Such an action [forcing Christians to participate] will be most beneficial to all your people, as is obvious."[16]

Even when they were not deliberately persecuted, those who wanted to avoid contact with what they considered a reprehensible cult found it difficult to avoid its observances, because sacrifices were offered not only on altars inside the temple's precincts but also in private houses and in public spaces. Jews and Christians shared the same aversion to pagan sacrifices, based on strict biblical prohibition against taking part in them. Treatises were written to help Jews and Christians sort out licit from polluting contact with the pagan way of life. At stake was their participation in the social life of the Roman world. One of the arguments that Tertullian, a 3rd century African Christian, developed to forbid the marriage of a Christian woman with a pagan concerns the intense sacralization of pagan life: "The maiden of God lives with foreign *lares;* in their midst, she will be tormented by the vapor of incense each time the demons are honored, each solemn festivity in honor of the emperors, each beginning of the year, each beginning of the month" (*Ad uxorem,* 6.1). Even an invitation to a banquet in a pagan house meant that a Christian would be exposed to sacrifices. Banquets included prayers and offerings to the gods, in particular to the protective deities of the household, the *lares.* The church authorities frowned on any involvement of Christians in pagan religious festivals. Some gestures, such as the exchange of gifts with neighbors and patrons for the religious festival of the Kalends, or the running in the streets of Rome for the *Lupercalia,* were seen by many Christians as traditional activities rather than participation in pagan worship, and bishops had a hard time trying to enforce a complete withdrawal from these social aspects of pagan festivals.[17] The bishops' criticism of the theater is also linked to the traditional association of spectacles with pagan festivals and with the lewdness of some of the mime and pantomime performances.[18]

Jewish sources such as the Mishnah or Talmudic treatises *Avodah Zarah* reveal that the same kind of questions were raised by the Jewish rabbis. Was it an act of idolatry to go to the theater or to the baths, both places where statues of the gods were often presented with sacrifices? The answer attributed to the Jewish patriarch Gamaliel asserts that it is an act of idolatry to go to the theater if sacrifices take place there; otherwise it is just foolishness (Tosefta 2.5–6). It is not an act of idolatry to go to the baths of the Gentiles as long as the statues displayed there—that of Aphrodite often stood at the entrance—are simply meant to adorn the place (Mishnah, *Avodah Zarah* 3.4).

One of the last echoes of this debate could still be heard in the preaching of Jacob of Serugh, an early 6th century bishop in Syria. He complains about the theater as a place where the stories of the gods are publicized and some forms of sacrifice are still performed: "[the actor] mimes the stories of the gods, and burns perfumes at the plays, in order that he may do great honor to tales which are true for him. If this is not so, why then does he burn incense at that time to the Fortune of anything? All this pertains to paganism."[19]

Even if pious Christians avoided public spectacles and all forms of festivities tinged with pagan rites, the risk of pollution by contact with sacrificial offerings was still significant for anyone mixing with pagans on an everyday basis. In a letter to Augustine, Publicola reveals how difficult it still was in 398 for a pious Christian to avoid all contact with pagan sacrality. He voices his concern by asking the bishop: "Is it lawful for a Christian to use wheat or beans from the threshing-floor, wine or oil from the press, if, with his knowledge, some part of what has been taken thence was offered in sacrifice to a false god? . . . May a Christian drink at a fountain or well into which anything from a sacrifice has been cast? . . . May a Christian use baths in places in which sacrifice is offered to images?" Publicola had reason to be concerned, for the meat found at the butcher's could very well come from sacrifices offered to the gods, and the food at the market could come from temple estates. Images of the gods in public buildings did receive garlands and fragrant offerings from worshipers.

This fear of pollution and prohibition against participating in idolatrous sacrifices had far-reaching consequences. It not only condemned a religion and the way of life that accompanied it, but it also required the complete desacralization of a world. Maximus, bishop of Turin in the early 5th century, preached that Christian landowners should desacralize everything on their property: "Idolatry is a great evil. It pollutes those who practice it. It pollutes the inhabitants of the region. It pollutes those who look on. The peasant's offering defiles the lord of the land. He cannot not be polluted when he eats food gathered by sacrilegious hands, brought forth by earth stained with blood, stored in foul barns . . . There is nothing free from evil where everything is steeped in evil."[20]

Yet it is possible to find numerous examples of peaceful cohabitation without much religious concern. One also finds acknowledgment by Christians that works of art produced for pagan cults or inspired by mythology possessed beauty. And the continued value of an education based on classical pagan authors was widely recognized. Yet the ruins of despoiled theaters, not to mention defaced temples, attest to the quite thorough desacralization of the pagan Roman empire in the 5th and 6th centuries.[21] Starting with the Roman state, desacralization spread to pagan religious monuments and cultic objects and, at the same time, to cities, where inhumation of the dead took place inside the consecrated boundaries.

Because the approval of the gods was necessary for any acts involving the community, prescribed rituals were followed in dutifully giving to the gods the offerings and prayers that they were entitled to receive. Sacrifices and festivals were paid for by public funds because they were offered for the benefit of the entire community. The emperor, as *pontifex maximus,* was designated to offer sacrifices for the sake of the empire. At the local level, magistrates assumed religious responsibilities. If they were Christians, they were caught between their civic duty to perform sacrifices for the sake of the community and their religion's proscription. When Christians were still a minority in the town councils, Christian magistrates could find someone to replace them to perform the sacrifices, but who could replace a Christian emperor?

Although he is depicted as offering a sacrifice on the arch dedicated to him by the Senate in Rome, Constantine, the first emperor to adopt Christianity, shied away from performing the sacrifices traditionally offered on the Capitoline. If we are to believe Zosimus, who wrote in the 6th century with a definite hostility toward Christianity, Constantine agreed to participate in the festivities to placate his soldiers, but nevertheless refused to perform the sacrifices (*Hist.eccl.* 2.29.5). With the exception of Julian, all the following emperors were also Christians, whose religious affiliation led them first to withdraw their participation from state-funded sacrifices. Then, as the population in the empire became increasingly Christian, the emperors ordered the end of all sacrifices.

The strict interdiction of all pagan sacrifices at the end of the 4th century, which sapped the consensual and public aspect of the Roman religion and desacralized the Roman state, followed a series of intermediate steps.[22] In 325, a small city in Phrygia, Orcistus, was granted a dispensation from taxes used to fund civic pagan cults. In 333, Constantine authorized the inhabitants of a group of towns in Umbria to build a temple of the Gens Flavia, with the restriction that the building "should not be polluted by the deceits of any contagious superstition"—which means he agreed to an imperial cult only if no sacrifices were performed.[23] By the middle of the century, orders were given to close the temples and sacrifices were forbidden,[24] though these laws suffered numerous exceptions and were not enforced everywhere.[25] In February 391, a law addressed to the praetorian prefect, Albinus, specified: "No person shall pollute himself with sacrificial animals, no person shall slaughter an innocent victim; no person shall approach the shrines, shall wander through the temples" (*C.Th.* 16.10.10). The prohibition was extended the following year to domestic and rural cults, forbidding burning incense, lighting candles in honor of the *lares,* hanging garlands on sacred trees, and making offerings on improvised turf altars (*C.Th.* 16.10.12). This was the official end of public as well as private forms of pagan sacrifices.[26]

One of these measures in particular was symbolic of the deliberate desacralization of the state: the removal of the altar to Victory placed in the Roman Senate. If there was a place where religious piety and the fate of the republic had been combined, and where the juridical-religious system of the Roman world had been created, it was the Senate in Rome. Senators offered incense and libations on the altar of Victory. On their accession, emperors took an oath of loyalty on it. Removing this altar was a symbolically charged gesture, a rupture with the pagan understanding that the virtuous piety of the Romans toward the gods had entitled them to conquer an empire. This altar of Victory, removed under Constantius in 357, was restored, perhaps by Julian, and remained in the Curia until the emperor Gratian ordered its removal in 382. The plea of a group of pagan senators led by Symmachus has come down to us in the form of a *relatio*, a petition, addressed to the emperor. Symmachus movingly referred to the "religious institutions that had served the state well for so long," to the love of tradition and to the powerful symbol of Victory, at a time when the Goths were a real threat to the empire. For Symmachus and his friends, no prosperity or protection would be granted by the gods if they did not receive sacrifices funded by public taxes. The measures taken by Gratian completely cut out the public funding of pagan ceremonies. He even ordered the imperial treasury to confiscate properties bequeathed to the priesthoods and to the temples. Gratian's decree that "public funding was denied to a religion no longer that of the state" was the crux of the problem. Shall our seat of government be no longer holy? exclaimed Symmachus in dismay. Symmachus was drawing the emperor's attention toward a very real change. The Curia had lost its sacrality for many of the senators who were Christians and who protested against Symmachus's petition to the emperor. It is easy for us, knowing the outcome, to assume that Symmachus was wasting his time. The worried letter from Ambrose to the emperor proves that this assumption would be wrong. Yet Symmachus, aware of the idolatrous implications of sacrifices for the Christians and of their revulsion for them, himself proposed desacralization of the statue of Victory: "If she cannot be honored as a god, at least let her name be honored."[27] This is precisely what happened. The statue remained in the Curia as a secular symbol of the state, held in honor but no longer offered sacrifices.

The desacralization of the Roman state and the conviction that sacrifices were a source of pollution led the Christian emperors to order the closing of the temples. It was the only way to make sure that the interdiction of pagan sacrifices would be respected. Yet the temples were significant structures in the cities, often occupying the most prominent sites. Leaving them as deserted shells was impractical. The legislation concerning the fate of these buildings left room for very diverse treatments of both the temples and their contents. Some temples were desacralized by the removal of their cultic statue, then closed and left to decay. Others received a harsher treatment: they were not only desacralized but desecrated. Many temples, damaged either by natural causes or by human action, were used as stone quarries, their *spolia* adorning other buildings, including churches. Finally, some temples, usually after a time of desacralization and abandonment, came back into use either as secular buildings or as Christian churches.

The first cases of desacralization of temples may have occurred early in the 4th century, sponsored by *curiales* (town councilmen) in cities where the majority of the population was already Christian.[28] Town councils and provincial magistrates could indeed decide what to do with public religious buildings, such as whether to repair them. Failing to repair old or damaged temples amounted to de facto condemnation of the buildings. Yet until the end of the 4th century, and apart from rural and private temples, the destruction of temples was carried out under imperial orders, in accordance with legal procedure.

Official consent of the governor and the emperor was required to deconsecrate and remove public temples.[29] As *pontifex maximus,* the emperor had the right to direct the removal as well as the construction of a temple.

Constantine used that power after the defeat of Licinius. He ordered the confiscation of precious objects from the temples in the east and the destruction of specific sanctuaries. Some of the temples Constantine chose to destroy were located on biblical sites, especially those associated with the life of Christ. Other temples were destroyed because they were offensive to new standards of morality, like the temple of Aphrodite at Aphaca in Phoenicia where ritual prostitution was practiced, or because they were a locus of anti-Christian polemics and had encouraged the previous emperors to persecute the Christians.[30] The temple at Aegeae in Cilicia falls in this last category. Dedicated to the "Savior god" of healing Aesculapius, who was perceived as a dangerous competitor of Christ, its fame had been publicized in the *Life of Apollonius of Tyana.* A pagan wonder-worker, Apollonius shared many features with Christ, including a godlike ability to resurrect the dead, and he had been exalted as superior to Christ during the great persecution. The destruction of the building ordered by Constantine did not eradicate the cult, but the faithful in search of a cure had to leave without the traditional night's stay in the temple. A priest was still present under the reign of Julian, and is reported to have asked the apostate emperor to order the restitution of the columns of the temple, which the Christians had removed to build a church.[31]

The complete demolition of the Roman temple which stood on the supposed site of Christ's crucifixion and tomb in Jerusalem is linked to the emerging interest in all the places where Christ had set foot.[32] In that case, not only was the temple razed but the stones and even the soil, perceived as defiled by the pagan sacrifices, were removed, until "the most holy cave," identified as the hallowed place where the resurrection had taken place, appeared. Constantine ordered that the place be purified and that a "house of prayer worthy of God" be built on "a scale of rich and imperial costliness."[33] Along with a church on the supposed site of the nativity at Bethlehem and a church on the Mount of Olives commemorating Christ's ascension, the Church of the Holy Sepulcher, for which no expense was spared by Constantine, contributed to the creation of the Holy Land.[34] These edifices also supported new notions of the inherent holiness of places and objects touched by Christ—a holiness made palpable by miracles, as the identification of the True Cross by its miraculous healing powers made plain.[35]

As these examples show, the destruction of temples ordered by Constantine, though very sporadic, was still precise in its targets. It did not entail a general destruction of temples, yet it created a precedent. At the end of the 4th century and even more in the 5th century, the destruction of temples, sometimes in the hands of imperial authorities, sometimes totally out of their hands, became so common as to worry those who wished to preserve the monumentality of the Roman cities.[36]

Legislation on this matter was not consistent. Emperors authorized the destruction of rural temples devoid of artistic value, especially if the work could be done without causing turmoil (*C.Th.* 16.10.16; 399). They also allowed stones from the destroyed buildings to be quarried, especially for use in building roads, bridges, or city walls (*C.Th.* 15.1.36; 397), but they repeatedly tried to curb the destruction and spoliation of sound public monuments in cities. The imperial edicts distinguished among temples, altars, and idols. City temples had to be protected against vandalism and unauthorized looting, for they contributed to the monumentality of the cities and could be turned to secular use. But their altars had to be destroyed because they had been defiled with sacrifices. The idols could be desacralized unless they were still openly worshiped. In that case, they too should be destroyed. This last clause is very interesting. It is likely that violent desecration of temples, with destruction of the statues or of the temple itself, happened mainly in places where a strong pagan party organized resistance in the face of the imperial edicts and a growing Christian community. The combination of zealous missionary bishops preaching against idolatry and a social order still dominated by pagans often led to violent clashes around pagan statues or temples.

Determined bishops like Porphyry of Gaza asked for edicts authorizing the demolition of specific temples and the deposition of idols.[37] When Porphyry arrived as the new bishop of Gaza in 395, the Christian community was a minority kept at bay by the pagan-dominated town council. It may have counted less than 300 souls, relative to an estimated population of 15,000 to 20,000 pagans and Jews. The church of Gaza was also rather poor, with only one basilica inside the city and two churches located outside the city walls. Bishop Porphyry was determined to change that situation, and he used his connections at Constantinople to win the emperor to his cause. He first sent one of his deacons to gain the support of the bishop, John Chrysostom, who helped him obtain an audience with Eutropius, one of the influential eunuchs at the court. The deacon triumphantly returned in 398 with an imperial edict ordering the closing of the temples at Gaza. To obtain the more problematic permission to destroy the famous temple of Marnas, Porphyry himself went to the capital. He gained the confidence of Empress Eudocia, and although Emperor Arcadius pointed out that the city was duly paying its taxes and should not be disturbed, in 402 Porphyry finally brought back an imperial edict not only allowing the destruction of the temples of Gaza by imperial troops but also endowing the church of Gaza. To further humiliate the pagans, he used the precious slabs of marble taken from the temple as pavement for the street now leading to the church named after its main donor, Empress Eudocia. Mark the Deacon points to the deliberate defiling of the marble slabs, placing them where they would be trodden upon by men, women, and animals.

Temple destruction was a costly process that required manpower, so the only temples that were completely razed were those on which the army worked. The vast majority of temples were probably left to decay.[38] Sacred caves, springs, and trees, which could not be destroyed, remained the last refuge for pagan piety, a fact attested by medieval church councils.[39] Private missions were sometimes organized to destroy temples in a specific region, but in the face of so many temples, their effect was rather negligible, in spite of the assertion by

Libanius that the countryside around Antioch had lost its soul through the destruction of rural shrines stormed by Christian monks (*Oration* 30.9). Theodoret, bishop of Cyrrhus, records the organization of an expedition against some Phoenician temples by John Chrysostom: "John got together certain monks who were fired with divine zeal, armed them with imperial edicts and dispatched them against the idols' shrines. The money which was acquired to pay the craftsmen and their assistants who were engaged in the work of destruction was not taken by John from imperial resources, but he persuaded certain wealthy and faithful women to make liberal contributions, pointing out to them how great would be the blessing their generosity would win" (*Hist.eccl.* 5.29). Temple bashing had become a meritorious act.[40] Episodes of temple destruction or idol-smashing became an expected element in male saints' careers. Such activities were even projected back onto the martyrs of the early church, who in later accounts of their lives were shown smashing idols or burning pagan sacred books. It is possible to demonstrate that monks and bishops with a monastic background, fired with a mission to fight demons, could have a stronger inclination toward temple destruction than others.[41] Yet the desacralization of the pagan religious buildings and the ending of idol worship was applauded by the vast majority of bishops and monks. A council of African bishops held in Carthage in 419 agreed to ask the emperors to order the destruction of idols and of remaining temples. The shrines and altars which had once sacralized the land were now scorned as polluting the earth, and the statues of the deities worshiped there became the first target of that mopping-up operation.

Many pagans believed that the statues of the gods rendered the deities present in the minds of those who passed by. They were more than art objects, even if they could be recognized and valued for their beauty and grace: they were portents of the sacred, potentially inhabited by the deities they represented. Christians often shared the pagan belief that deities inhabited their sculptured images, a belief that pagan priests sometimes reinforced through hidden mechanisms which made these statues move.[42] Yet, for Christians, the deities living in the statues were now identified with demons.[43] Some Christians even viewed idols as dangerous objects, in which devils lay in waiting, willing and able to harm pious Christians.[44]

When, around 480, a group of Christians discovered a hidden pagan shrine filled with idols at Menouthis, not far from Alexandria, stories circulated that the profanation of their statues would be punished by the offended deities and that the Christians who had agreed to guard the sanctuary during the night would not be alive the next day (Zacharias Scholasticus, *Life of Severus*). Christian monks settling in an abandoned pagan enclosure expected the demonic pagan deity to give them trouble. For example, after finding a buried bronze idol during the construction of Benedict of Nursia's monastery on the hill dedicated to Apollo at Monte Cassino, around 530, the monks were so scared that they attributed the collapse of a wall that killed a young monk to the action of the disturbed demon (Gregory the Great, *Dialogues* 2.10.1–2). An episode in the *Life* of the patriarch Eutychius illustrates that even flat images could be dangerous: the vengeful Artemis bites a poor mosaicist who had been paid to remove the image of the goddess and replace it with a Christian motif when the room of a house was transformed into a chapel.[45]

For many Christians influenced by these beliefs, the safest action regarding the statues was their utter destruction. The belief that deities could act through their representations explains the thoroughgoing mutilation of many statues or bas-reliefs. Rufinus of Aquileia describes the Alexandrian Christians' efforts to be as thorough as possible in their destruction of images of Sarapis after the main cult statue located in the famous temple had been chopped up and the parts publicly burned in different parts of the city. The images of Sarapis and other deities omnipresent on walls, doorposts, and windows of private houses were effaced throughout the city.[46] Archaeological traces of this iconoclastic behavior have been found in the Allat temple at Palmyra and in the Mithraea of Saarebourg, Macwiller, and Koenigshofen, to cite just a few examples from different regions. At Palmyra, the head of the goddess Allat-Athena was knocked off the torso, the facial features were then scrupulously obliterated, and the statue was ultimately hacked into pieces which were discovered scattered on the floor of the temple.[47] In the Mithraea, cultic reliefs had been hammered into hundreds of pieces.[48] Such actions were not necessarily the work of a minority of overzealous monks, or of fearful uneducated Christians. When Justinian ordered the transformation of the Isis temple into a Christian church, precautions were taken to exorcise the place. The temple's treasures of gold and silver were carried away to be melted down at Constantinople, while the images of the deities were carefully scratched and chiseled away (this work was done by the army). The sign of the cross and exorcistic inscriptions were carved on the lintel and the columns to protect the building: on the north pylon, one of the crosses was positioned to obliterate the goddess's head.[49] Those among the Christians who destroyed pagan statues believed that the biblical exhortations ordering the children of Israel to throw down idols and reduce them into dust (Deut. 7:5) were meant to guide them in dealing with pagan cult statues.

Yet another attitude toward pagan statues also came to be adopted by Christians, one of appreciation for the artistic value of the statues and their adornment of gardens, villas, and public spaces. Constantine epitomizes the complex attitude of many late antique Christians toward pagan shrines and works of art.[50] He was the first emperor inclined toward Christianity to order both the complete destruction of some pagan temples and the collection of beautiful pagan statues to adorn his capital, Constantinople. Eusebius of Caesarea, in the *Life of Constantine,* found it difficult to reconcile the two attitudes in the same person: he attempted to assert that Constantine had collected those sculptures for the purpose of ridicule. Yet the destruction of specific temples to promote Christianity and fill up the imperial treasury was not irreconcilable with the collection of secularized statues chosen for their size and beauty. Displayed in the public spaces of the new city bearing his name, these masterpieces proclaimed his imperial glory and power to the world. For him, as later for Constantius (*C.Th.* 16.10.3), the traditions that celebrated the grandeur of Rome should be preserved, for they also celebrated the might of Rome's emperors.

Masterpieces of statuary and monumental temples should be preserved—in a desacralized form—for the enjoyment of Roman Christians, who had a different understanding of history from their pagan ancestors but shared their civic pride.

This civic pride is revealed in the inscriptions that some *curiales* put up after transferring statues from the desacralized temples to open public spaces. They were proud of the beauty of their cities and wished not only to preserve it but also to contribute to it.[51] For them as for the Christian poet Prudentius, the statues, once desacralized, were perfectly harmless and enhanced the monumental centers of the cities (Prudentius, *Peristephanon* 2.481–484; *Contra Symmachum* 499–505)

Some well-connected Christians even took the opportunity offered by the desacralization of the temples to gather important art collections for themselves. In the 5th century, under the reign of Theodosius II, at a time when Christianity was dominant at the court of the emperor, a member of that court had masterpieces imported from different sanctuaries that had been officially closed. He could not have collected the Phidian statue of Zeus from Olympia, a statue of Aphrodite from Cnidos, and other valuable works of art without the full consent and help of the emperor.[52] The mosaics discovered in numerous villas dating from that period also reveal a taste for mythological subjects; the presence of pagan deities did not seem in the least to bother their Christian owners.[53] It is possible that this relaxed attitude toward pagan art was a privilege of the well-to-do. In a rather poor villa outside the walls of Antioch, a collection of figures of emperors and deities, mostly replicas of well-known statues, was found buried.[54] Many ancient statues were discovered piled up in wells or in pits, which indicates that some statues had either become an embarrassment for the owners or were in need of protection from zealous Christians.

In a Roman house at Carthage, the entrance to an underground room was concealed under early 5th century mosaics. In that room, behind a hastily constructed wall, archaeologists were surprised to find a collection of cult statues. Beautiful marble images of Venus, Jupiter, and Demeter had been carefully hidden in that remote room, possibly awaiting the return of better times. Jean-Charles Picard has suggested that Caecilius Honoratus, the owner of the house at that time, had gathered these objects not only to save them from iconoclasts but also to sacralize his house and attract to himself and his family the beneficial powers of the divine beings.[55] In Athens, on the other hand, some statues were buried in humiliating fashion, such as one found face-down under the threshold of a late antique house. The house, once owned by an amateur of pagan art or a person inclined toward pagan cults, was occupied by devout Christians at the time of the burial.[56]

Christian attitudes toward pagan cult statues and spaces were very diverse during this period. The violent and destructive behavior of the Egyptian abbot Shenoute of Athribis/Atripe (ca. 335–451) becomes understandable in a world where Christians feared demons. If we are to believe Shenoute's biographer, the abbot dreamed of freeing the world from demonic powers by searching temples and private homes for idols to smash. The protective or admiring attitude toward the same sort of image held by a wealthy *curialis,* ready to follow in the footsteps of his fathers and adorn a public building with the statues, is also perfectly understandable in its context. Indifference and disdainful abandonment of pagan cultic spaces and objects were also common. Each of these attitudes contributed to the eventual desacralization of the pagan world. Religious motives evidently played a major role in the action against pagan temples and idols, yet they do not alone account for the destruction of temples. Tense relationships between the two main religious communities (as in Gaza), a sense of pollution, or the fear that the beauty of a temple could entice Christians to take part in sacrifices (as in Baalbek) could lead to destructive behavior, as could the very profane desire of ambitious magistrates to avail themselves of cheap and beautiful building material in order to place their name on a new building (as in Rome). A new world was created with the ruins of the old one. Religious change was accompanied by a wider change in the perception and use of space.

Even with their temples closed and their religious festivals partially secularized, cities remained religiously consecrated ground. One consequence of this dedication of inhabited space to the gods was the prohibition against burying the dead inside the city walls. Christians had developed a different attitude than pagans and Jews toward the dead. Their martyrs' dead bodies, far from being perceived as polluting, were approached with veneration, for the saints were deemed to be alive and present at God's side, interceding for the faithful who placed their trust in them. Such ideas were horrendous to pagans and Jews (not to mention Zoroastrians), who considered that contact with the dead created impurity that barred one from performing religious duties. Rather than an obstacle to sacrality, the dead bodies of the saints were considered by Christians a locus of sacrality and became the most common means of making space sacred.

This new attitude required a shift of attitude toward the dead that happened only gradually. St. Thecla would not hear of having bodies buried in her shrine. Some Christians, such as Gregory of Nyssa in the 4th century, did not approve of the disinterment of dead bodies presumed to belong to saints. During the reign of Julian tensions were caused by Christians' religious attitude toward the dead. Julian's edict on funerals, in 363, ordered that burial rites take place at night, "for the persons happening upon a funeral are filled frequently with disgust, supposing a bad omen; for others proceeding to the temples, it is not meet and right to enter until they have washed from themselves the pollution. It is not proper after such a sight to approach the gods, who are the cause of life and are, of all things, most unfavorably disposed toward dissolution."[57] Christian funerary processions had become a nuisance for the polytheists who wanted to worship in their temples. In a rich suburb of Antioch, at Daphne, an incident caused by the attention Christians paid to their holy dead powerfully reveals the difficult cohabitation of Christians and pagans. It was claimed that the oracle of the temple of Apollo had ceased to speak because the god was repulsed by the presence of the remains of St. Babylas buried nearby. Julian, in an effort to please the priests, ordered the removal of the saint's sarcophagus from that area of the temple.

Christians were often suspected of not respecting the religious dedication of urban space. Pagans justly feared that Christians would unlawfully bury martyrs inside their churches. Some complaints must have reached the emperors because, in 381, a law promulgated by Gratian, Valentinian II, and Theodosius I tried to curb this development: "All bodies that are contained in urns or sarcophagi and are kept above the ground shall be carried and placed outside the city, that they may present an example of humanity and leave the homes of the citizens their sanctity." Although written by Christian emperors, the law reminded everyone that Roman cities still sat upon religiously consecrated ground that was not to be polluted by the dead, and that burial of bodies was not allowed in the shrines of the martyrs. The law ultimately did not stop this practice, but it did make it possible for pagan believers to defend the religious purity of their cities for a short time. Such conflicts between Christians and pagans over sacred ground are still in evidence at the end of the 4th century. Around 396, in the city of Gaza, a riot started when some pagans thought that Christians were bringing a dead body into the city.

This was a battle the pagans were to lose: from the 5th century onward, the dead began to make their triumphal entrance into the cities. It started with saints, the "very special dead," who were formally installed in churches located inside the city walls during the 4th century.[58] It then continued with the remains of privileged Christians, such as clerics and generous patrons of the churches, who wished to be buried close to the saints. Finally the tombs of ordinary Christians slowly but steadily appeared inside the cities.

The Christian lack of respect for this fundamental element of pagan sacralization is well illustrated by the case of Constantinople. Although the new capital had probably received formal pagan rites at its foundation in 324, its new walls included former cemeteries. They were covered with earth and the rule requiring the dead to be buried outside the city was still enforced during the 4th century. Yet, as the walls were extended under Theodosius II, burial of the dead outside the city walls became more expensive and the space between the two walls was used for burial. By that time the city had closed and desacralized its temples and become a Christian city. It was now a metropolis not in the least concerned with the pollution brought by dead bodies and it gladly welcomed corporeal relics into city churches. An ivory plaque of the 5th or 6th century, now in Trier, depicts a procession of relics triumphantly carried by the bishop while censers are swinging on their passage. The whole community gathered to celebrate this coming of heavenly patronage in the city.[59] The presence of the saints' bodies was considered a blessing and a protection for the city.

In about a century, a total revolution had happened. That which had defiled the space in the eyes of pagans sacralized it in the eyes of Christians. Prudentius, at the dawn of the 5th century, could write about Rome's famous relics of Paul and Peter: "Tiber separates the bones of the two and both its banks are consecrated as it flows between the hallowed tombs" (*Peristephanon* 12.29, trans.

H. J. Thompson). For Christians, Rome was made sacred by its famous martyrs. Cities less favored with local martyrs "invited" saints to reside with the Christian community. Bishops such as Gaudentius of Brescia or Vitricius of Rouen gathered relics as they journeyed to communities more richly endowed with saints than their own. The practice of moving and parceling out the remains of the saints became very common. As a result, a city as unfavored with local saints as Rouen in 396 could boast: "our habitation is now among a legion of Saints and the renowned powers of the Heavens."[60]

A visitor to the Roman world in the 380s would still have been impressed by the temples of the pagan world. He would have found the monumental city center quite intact and would have searched in vain for Christian buildings in the midst of pagan temples. The city had been offered Christian basilicas by the generous Constantine, yet they were not to be seen near the Fora, nor on the Capitoline or Palatine hills.

Arriving at Ephesus, by sea or by road, he would have been impressed by the huge pagan religious complexes, and by the bathhouses and other public monuments which gave character to the cities of the east. In Ephesus at that time the churches were very much in the shadow of these impressive buildings. Returning half a century later by sea, he would have noted major changes. The huge baths and the gymnasium complex on the harbor were still dominant, and the biggest church in the city was very tiny next to them, but the largest temple—probably the Olympeum, built in honor of Hadrian, that had proudly shone on top of the hill facing the sea—had been pulled down, its stones ground and burned for lime. No longer would he have found the temples of Domitian or Isis, for they had been destroyed and their stones reused elsewhere. On the site of what may have been a Sarapeum now stood a church. Temples damaged by earthquakes had not been repaired but rather had been used as stone quarries. Similarly, the slightly earthquake-damaged statues of Artemis were no longer visible: they had been carefully buried underground. A church council organized in Ephesus in 441 to defend the title of Mary as Theotokos, Mother of God, was held in a large church dedicated to her, possibly built into the southern portico of the now destroyed Olympeum. On a hill overlooking the road leading to the city, an impressive Christian basilica dedicated to St. John dominated the landscape. Down the hill, the world-renowned temple of Artemis lay closed and abandoned. Had this visitor journeyed to the city in the 380s and again in the 440s, he would have felt like one of the Seven Sleepers of Ephesus, who woke from their slumbers to walk in a city they could hardly recognize.

The stories of Rome and of Ephesus are not uncommon. About twenty churches have been identified in Ephesus, and in each case that excavation has reached the level before the construction of the church, a public building or a temple has been found. This is the major difference with Rome. Numerous churches were built in Rome in the course of the 4th and 5th centuries, yet the city did not transform its temples or public buildings into churches. Only in the late 6th century do we hear of a chapel built in the imperial palace on the

Palatine. In the early 7th century we know of a public temple, the Pantheon, that was transformed into a church with due imperial authorization. The difference between the two cities reveals the growing power of the bishops of Ephesus, who were able to control the town council and use public sites for their religious buildings. In Rome, the resistance of a pagan aristocracy, along with the symbolic aura of most public buildings of the Roman Fora, kept the powerful church of Rome from having much effect on the central areas of the city. By the 6th century, the Christianization of space was accomplished. In the depiction of cities, churches were landmarks as important as city walls and porticoed streets, as the 6th century mosaic depicting the Holy Land discovered in a church at Madaba attests.

The late 5th and the 6th centuries were a time of intense church building.[61] In Palestine and Arabia, for example, over 350 churches have been discovered, most of them built during the 6th century. Bishops, who had gained a leading position in the town councils, often chose to spend money on building or beautifying churches. As a result, Jerash had 15 churches; Caesarea, 10.[62] Attention shifted from civil buildings to private and religious buildings. Private individuals built oratories, and small communities gathered money to erect or adorn new churches. Umm al-Jîmal, a big village, but still only a village, had 15 churches, mostly private oratories large enough to welcome only the local residents.[63] Money was also poured into monastic complexes and other religious buildings or objects, as the beautiful ecclesiastical silver treasures discovered in the region reveal.[64] In Justinian's time, the emperor, the bishops, and the wealthy citizens shared the same enthusiasm for religious buildings.

In Syria and Palestine, most cities went through intense rebuilding. Social and judicial activities shifted to sites untrammeled by pagan cult associations. Sections of the cities were deliberately abandoned, in particular those linked to pagan shrines. New active city centers emerged, often around the bishop's cathedral. The erections of churches, *xenodochia* (inns), and monasteries Christianized the cityscape. By the 6th century, in many of the prosperous cities of Syria, churches competed in size and splendor with former temples.

In Apamea, for example, the cathedral complex grew to cover 12,000 square meters. The city had chosen to move away from the area of the major temples. Around 384 the majestic temple of Zeus Belios was first desecrated and damaged, possibly by an expedition against it organized by Bishop Marcellus. This partial destruction was followed by a more insulting desecration: it was used as a dump in the 5th century. During the 6th century this ignominious treatment was followed by sealing off access to the abandoned sanctuary. The road leading from the *cardo* (main transverse street) to the temple and the once-thriving agora was blocked by latrines.[65]

In Jerash, the temples were partially reused. The city had two major cultic centers, one devoted to Zeus, the other to Artemis. At the end of the 5th century, the temple of Zeus was partially demolished and its stones used to adorn nearby churches. The vaulted corridors of its lower terrace were transformed into Christian shrines and dwellings, possibly for a monastic community.[66] The temple of Artemis, once a splendid monument, also served as a quarry. One of the frieze blocks from the temple embellished the door of the Theodore church, dated to 496. Church building reached its peak at the time when whole sections of the pagan city were destroyed or abandoned. Building materials ranging from ordinary stones to beautiful colored marbles were accessible and cheap. The 6th century church of Bishop Isaiah was built with columns taken from the *decumanus,* whose northern part went out of use in the 5th century.[67] A new geography of the sacred, composed of numerous Christian sanctuaries—from simple chapels to imposing basilicas—was emerging in a transformed city landscape.

The Christian sacralization of space was not as old as Christianity itself. For the first two or three centuries, Christians met in private houses, which were not sacred buildings. Christianity emerged in Jewish circles and drew its religious life from Jewish traditions. The first disciples of Christ used to pray every day in the Temple of Jerusalem until its destruction by the Romans in 70 C.E. Ejected from the Jewish synagogues, they set up their own religious meeting places on the model of the synagogues.

Before the year 70, the Jews had two types of religious buildings: the Temple at Jerusalem and the synagogues. The synagogues were houses of the congregation, where prayer, learning, and communal social events took place. They were not buildings dedicated to God, in that God did not live in them in the way that a pagan deity lived in his or her temple. Not being sacred in itself, a synagogue could be sold or moved to another location when necessary, although during late antiquity Jewish synagogues recaptured some of the Temple's sacrality.[68] The one sacred place where the *shekhinah,* the divine presence, always resided was the Holy of Holies in the Temple of Jerusalem. (At least this was true for the first Temple; and it was argued about for the Herodian Temple.) It was in the Temple that sacrifices were offered to God. Although their Temple had been defiled and replaced by a pagan temple, the Jews never lost the sense of the sacrality of the Temple platform on Mount Moriah. They repeatedly attempted to have the Temple rebuilt, at first under Julian, who granted them permission to do so, and then under the Persian occupation in the early 7th century. For Christians, the destruction of the Temple was the fulfillment of a prophecy and the visible proof of God's displeasure with the Jews for rejecting Christ. It mattered to Christians that the Temple area be left unoccupied. As a result, they did not try to build a church on the Temple platform, though they very probably used the stones of the Roman temple for their own building purposes in the 4th century. In 638, when the Arabs arrived in Jerusalem, they found the platform filled with stones and rubbish.

For Christians, the Temple had been replaced by Christ, and its sacrifices by spiritual worship. They no longer had an official sacred space. The Jerusalem community had dispersed to Pella and elsewhere in the Roman world. Although Christians believed Jerusalem would be the place of the *parousia,* the second coming, there is no indication that Christians chose to consider Jerusalem a sacred place during the first four centuries of Christianity. The location of their religious buildings, like the synagogues', depended on the opportune donation of a house or part of a house for the needs of the community. The only excavated example of a group of rooms obviously remodeled to suit the needs of the Christian community is the so-called house-church at Dura-Europos, abandoned after the city's destruction by the Sassanians in 256.[69] This house, located not far from the city walls, was in the same street as a synagogue and a Mithraeum. During the 3rd century, two rooms located at the back of the house, away from the entrance, were transformed and used only for religious ceremonies.

At one point, probably in the 3rd century, the development of Christian communities began to require the erection of specific buildings for worship, vast enough to welcome the faithful. The first Christian basilicas were built on sites that were not in themselves sacred, but had been determined by the donation of land by converts. This rule still applied in the later centuries: donations of land were the most common origin of churches. From the discourse of the early Christian apologists, very insistent on the fact that God cannot be circumscribed in a space and that Christians are very different from pagans in respect to temples and altars, we can deduce that the Christians were not interested in creating sacred spaces, let alone a sacred geography.[70] Indeed, if the Christian communities adopted a model for their religious spaces, it was that of synagogues rather than pagan temples. Like synagogues, early churches were houses of the congregation rather than houses of God, but they were religious buildings, already called basilicas during the persecution of Diocletian.[71] These churches owned movable goods, such as precious vessels and books that they had to surrender during persecutions.[72]

The reluctance that Christians felt at having to give up vessels used for the Eucharist to the Roman magistrates is an indication that some form of sacralization was taking place in the pre-Constantinian basilicas. The vessel used for the Eucharist was no longer used also for profane purposes. The table around which Christians shared *agapē* had become an altar, even if it was a portable one. The location of the church was not sacred, but the celebration of the Eucharist sacralized the church. It was a place of theophany, where decent and respectful behavior was expected.

Until the 6th century the celebration of the Eucharist was the only thing required to dedicate a church. The Christian ceremony of the Eucharist was surrounded with solemnity and splendor, as the long list of objects donated to adorn the altars of the Roman churches founded by Constantine attests. Nothing was spared to beautify the area of the church where Christ made himself available in the bread and the wine: magnificent candelabra holding a myriad of oil lamps, standing censers perfuming the sanctuary, colored marbles, and shimmering mosaics all contributed to attract attention toward the altar. The organization of space inside the basilicas also reveals that there was a gradual increase in sacredness from the door to the sanctuary. The sacred rites of the Eucharist were open only to fully baptized Christians. The catechumens were kept at the back of the church, along with the penitents, and escorted to the doors after the sermon. The sanctuary was reserved for clerics, while the rest of the faithful shared the nave.

The long-lasting defensiveness of Christian apologists against sacred spaces of a pagan kind was still echoed in the 4th and early 5th centuries. Christianity sacralized people, not objects: the true dwelling place of God was the heart of the baptized Christian, not his or her church, and holiness resided in the whole community of Christians rather than in the stones permeated with their prayers (Augustine, *Sermon* 337). Yet the belief that God had sent his son to walk on this earth and the theological debates about the nature of Christ made physical traces of his incarnation and humanity all the more important. The sacralization of the Holy Land transformed the sacred geography of Christianity from one of a relative uniformity, where God could be worshiped anywhere and the sacrifice of the Eucharist could be shared by Christians all over the world, to one incorporating the notion of privileged holy space and of local sanctity.

Persecutions greatly contributed to the creation of a specific Christian way to sacralize space. They deprived Christians of their religious buildings and killed many of the faithful, leaving Christian communities to express their faith through the mourning of their dead at the tombs of their martyrs. Many of the Christians' gestures and attitudes toward the martyrs were similar to those offered by the pagans to their dead. But they differed with the pagans in imagining for their martyrs an eternal bliss in the company of God, and an eternal loving concern for the Christians left behind. The welcoming of the saints to heaven gave the martyrs a privileged position as intercessors. Brothers and sisters in humanity, they also belonged to the court of God and could intercede for the faithful.

Early in the 4th century, around 305, the church of Cirta had a house in the *area martyrum* that it used for its meetings.[73] This is an early attestation of construction linked to the tombs of the martyrs, which created numerous basilicas around Roman cities.[74] In Rome, Constantine provided funds to build magnificent basilicas in honor of the most prominent Christian martyrs, Paul and Peter. During the 4th and 5th centuries, other basilicas were built in the different cemeteries where the martyrs rested in peace. By engraving poems near the tombs of fifteen unknown saints whose days were added to the church festal calendar, Pope Damasus created a wreath of oratories around the city, defining an *urbs sacra* surrounded by martyrs.[75]

The two springs of holiness, the Eucharist and the martyrs, were from now on combined to create a specifically Christian way of sacralizing space and time. In the 4th century, the location of the *martyria* was dictated by the location of the tombs, but the habit of disinterring the saints gave many other areas a chance to enjoy the protection and blessings of relics. The saints were distributed or sold in bits and pieces until only the dust collecting on their tombs and reliquaries was left to sell.[76] Relics make sacredness transportable, as even tiny fragments could protect their owners and link them to the inhabitants of paradise. Caution had to be exerted by church authorities before welcoming the cult of a new saint. Martin of Tours stopped a group of Christians from offering veneration at a tomb which was, according to Martin, that of a brigand, not of a saint. Sure signs of sanctity such as the smell of sweet perfume emanating from an opened tomb or miracles that contact with saintly relics produced were now dutifully recorded in books of miracles or saints' lives to justify the ecclesiastical recognition of a cult.

A fundamental idea in the cult of martyrs was that holiness was contagious. The sweet perfume coming from St. Stephen's sarcophagus had healing powers, for it came from paradise. Because Stephen was in heaven and yet still in contact with his body, the healing perfume of divinity emanated from his bones.[77] This holy contagion could be extended: in Syria, reliquaries were made with holes allowing oil to be poured on the holy bones, which was gathered at the other end to produce blessings for the pilgrims.[78] Most of the time, contact with just the place was enough to invoke the power of relics; even the fragrant oil that was burned before the tombs of saints became invested with holiness and was carried away by pilgrims in *ampullae*.[79] The success of a shrine can be established by the number of its *ampullae* distributed through the Roman world.

Celebrations of the discovery of relics and their processions filled up the Christian festal calendar as they did Christian chapels. Both time and space were made sacred through the idea that the saints are particularly available when and where they are honored. Many of the miracles performed by St. Martin at Tours happened during his festivals. It is clearly in the interest of Bishop Gregory of Tours to publicize such events in order to attract pilgrims to the shrine of St. Martin. The *virtus* and goodwill of the saint are localized in time as well as in space: Martin was believed more likely to hear the prayers of the faithful near his tomb at the date of his festival.

Bishop Perpetuus (458/9–488/9) also understood the power of festivals for gathering Christian pilgrims, mostly from neighboring regions, in the city of Tours, around the bishop. For the pilgrims Perpetuus had a basilica rebuilt in honor of St. Martin. A new festival was created celebrating the dedication of the new church. The date, July 4, conveniently occurred during a month with no festival, far from the other festival in honor of St. Martin, November 11. Both festivals were major events: pilgrims came two to three days before and stayed one or two days after the festival. As the holiness of the tomb had spread to the building and the immediate area, so the holiness of the saint's festival also spread to the days before and after.[80]

These practices changed the notion of space for Christians. As they traveled to the shrines of the saints, they created a sacred geography. The location of churches where the saints were buried went from being neutral to being sacred. There was nothing cosmically determined about this sacredness. It was acquired through contact, linked to the saint's relics and to the consecration of the Host on the altar. A removal of reliquaries and altars could desacralize a church and the site on which it was built. Contrary to pagan natural holy sites, and with the exception of the sites linked to Christ's life, Christian sacred geography was movable.[81]

Christian sacrality also became dispersed and private. Innumerable fragments of the remains of the saints circulated widely, often in the possession of individual owners. Images of the saints sold to the faithful were invested with the protective power of the saints, as the stories in hagiographies make plain.[82] By performing miracles, icons proved that they were not mere images but were the resting place of the saints. This dispersion of sacrality, now movable and portable, and no longer confined to the altar or to the churches, allowed a very individualistic approach to the sacred. From the major monastic sanctuaries such as that of the two saints known as Simeon Stylites or that of St. Menas, relics and icons could be bought to protect persons and houses. This privatization of the sacred created inequalities. While the powerful or well-connected, such as Queen Radegund in Poitiers or Bishop John the Almsgiver in Alexandria, could avail themselves of a piece of the Holy Cross, the less fortunate had to hope that less prestigious relics or images would still offer some protection. The protection saints were deemed to grant to the faithful and the resources they could bring to churches explains why they began to be transported from their original resting places. The first centuries of the Middle Ages saw an increase in the traffic of relics. It became a standard practice both in the west and in Byzantium to deposit relics before dedicating a new church. As precious relics were bought, exchanged, or even stolen, the sacred geography of the Christian world was constantly being redefined.[83]

The increasing attention devoted to relics and the belief in their power to protect the faithful explain the shock felt by the Christian world when the holy city of Jerusalem and the relic of the Cross were captured by the Persians in 614.[84] The conquest by the Persians of the eastern provinces of the Byzantine empire led not only to the destruction of numerous cities but also to a spiritual crisis among Byzantine Christians. Stories circulated relating the desecration of the churches of the Holy Land, the massacres of Christians, and the cruelty of the Jews. How could God let fire-worshipers defeat the Christians? Had he abandoned the Holy Land to Zoroastrian Persians and to their Jewish allies to punish the Christians for their sins? The Monophysites and the Chalcedonians believed that the theological error of the opposite camp had attracted onto them the wrath of God. They did not question the power of the saints. Heraclius had an icon of the Virgin attached to the mast of the ship that took him from Carthage to Constantinople to conquer the imperial title. When in 626 Avars and Persians besieged the city of Constantinople, the patriarch Sergius had icons of the Virgin mounted on the doors of the city and carried in processions on the walls, in the hope that they would create an invisible protective barrier against the enemy. The eventual retreat of the enemies was ascribed to the active protection of the city by the Virgin. By the early 630s, Emperor Heraclius had reconquered the lost lands and negotiated the return of the relic of the Cross to Byzantine hands. This victorious return of the Byzantines in Syria and the Holy Land, accompanied by theological compromises to unify the Christians and forced baptism of the Jews, was short-lived, for in 634 Muslim Arabs invaded Syria. The army of this new religious group overpowered the Byzantine and Sassanian rulers of the Middle East, and came to control a vast region populated mostly by Christians, Jews, and Zoroastrians. Muslims were only a tiny minority, but as rulers they transformed the religious life of the communities under their power.

In Arabia, the Prophet Muhammad treated the pagans, Jews, and Christians he encountered differently. Pagans were offered a choice of death or conversion to Islam. The pagan Arabs had created *ḥaram* territories, areas in which the neighboring tribes agreed that no blood should be shed, no trees cut, no farming done. These areas also provided a right of asylum. Mecca in the 6th century was very much a pagan stronghold, with a temple where idols were worshiped. The takeover of that shrine by Muhammad in 630 and his destruction of the numerous idols inside the temple combines a Judeo-Christian aversion for idols with a wish for the continuity of an important Arabic sacred space. Muhammad kept not only the sanctuary and the black stone, but also the rules of behavior which prevailed around sacred spaces in pre-Islamic Arabia. This continuity was justified by the reconstruction of the history of the holy site as having been originally built by Abraham, a true worshiper of the one God, and later misused by polytheists until the Prophet reestablished monotheism.[85]

Christians and Jews had a special status because the Prophet recognized their religions as revealed by God. If they did not want to convert, they usually could keep their life in exchange for tribute. At Medina, however, the Prophet had encountered the resistance of three Jewish tribes. He offered the choice of conversion or exile to two of the tribes, conversion or death to the other.[86] After each conquest, relations with the non-Muslims were regulated by negotiated agreements. At the oasis of Khaybar, after the victory of the Prophet, the Jews were allowed to keep their lives and their land, but would have to hand over one-half of their produce to the Muslims. For the Christians of Najran, settlement included the payment of a tribute by the Christians, who were also to welcome the Prophet's representatives and provide them with supplies in time of war. They could otherwise practice their religion and run their own affairs. This arrangement was abrogated when Caliph 'Umar ibn al-Khattab (634–644) ordered the expulsion of Christians and Jews from the Arab peninsula.

Under 'Umar's reign, Syria, Palestine, Mesopotamia, western Iran, and Egypt came under Muslim rule. As Palestinian and Syrian cities opened their gates or were conquered, treaties were concluded which secured the life and property of the citizens, as well as their right to keep some if not all of their religious buildings, in exchange for taxes and services. The Muslims were mostly interested in the wealth of these regions and many Christians belonging to the Monophysite and Nestorian churches found that the change of rulers also meant the end of persecution.

In the conquest of the Sassanian empire, the Muslim armies came in contact with Zoroastrians. The Sassanian rulers had followed a form of Zoroastrianism closely associated with their structures of power.[87] They worshiped in fire temples.[88] In Mesopotamia, the Muslims took over the Sassanian state's properties, including the fire temples, which they desacralized. The disappearance of the main fire temples did not mean the end of the religion, whose cult continued domestically. Yet the religion did lose its main centers of worship and its public festivals.[89] Eventually Zoroastrianism came to be identified with the third religion recognized in the Qur'ān. As a result, the status of Zoroastrians became quite similar to that of Jews or Christians.[90]

As the Muslims settled in the conquered lands, they started to assert their religious presence through the building of mosques where the male Muslims gathered for prayer. Instruction and legal functions also took place in mosques.[91] Unlike churches, mosques were not consecrated buildings. Indeed, at first they were not always buildings. Early mosques, such as those dated to the end of the 7th century or the early 8th century discovered in the Negev, were simple stone enclosures, often located on a hilltop, facing south toward Mecca and adorned with a protruding prayer niche, the *miḥrāb*. These mosques served nearby settlements and accompanied the dispersal of Arab tribes.[92]

These mosques consisted mainly of a hall to allow as many persons to gather as necessary, yet the space was not randomly organized. Even in very early mosques, the *qibla*—the direction of Mecca—gave an orientation to the enclosure. This sacred direction was soon marked by the *miḥrāb*. Sometimes a simple niche, sometimes surrounded by columns and richly adorned, the *miḥrāb* gave a focus to the prayer inside the mosques. It was eventually invested with sacrality. The process of sacralization started for mosques as it had for churches and synagogues. Rules of behavior that were at first mainly dictated by common sense, such as the removal of shoes or the prohibition of spitting, became charged with religious meaning. They were marks of respect for God and by extension for the place where prayers were offered to him. Three major sanctuaries, Muslim *ḥaram,* are mentioned in the Qur'ān: Mecca, Medina, and what has been identified as Jerusalem. These were the historical holy places of Islam, sacralized by the Prophet. As the navel of the earth, Mecca added a cosmological sanctity, akin to that of Jerusalem, to its historical role in the Prophet's life. The sacralization of these holy places progressed with time, as stories proved their holiness. Sanctity could also arise in other Muslim cities: Damascus was revealed to be the place where the house of Noah stood before the flood, and Aleppo was identified as a site visited by Abraham.[93]

In newly founded cities such as Basra, Kufa, or Fustat, the mosque was set up in the center of the city, but in ancient Byzantine or Sassanian cities the Muslims had to find a place for their mosques in already built cities. The location of these new religious buildings was in part determined by the availability of space, as well as by a wish to secure a central and convenient location for the rulers' religion. Like the Christians in the late 4th century, the Muslims could avoid the monuments of the old religions and build anew; or they could try to capture some of the attraction of the old shrines by building their mosques next to them. Or they could take over the holy places of the old religions and eventually replace their buildings.

When the Muslim armies arrived in Palestine and in Syria, they must have been overwhelmed by the number and splendor of Christian churches, and to a lesser extent of Jewish synagogues.[94] Churches glittering with marbles and mosaics caught the eye in cities as well as in villages. In the countryside monastic sites dotted the landscape, some with huge complexes such as Qalat Seman, some with very simple dwellings such as the hermits' caves of the Judean desert. A traveler such as Arculf, who came from Gaul to the Holy Land and Constantinople in 670, commented admiringly on the beautiful churches that he was able to visit along his pilgrimage route. He is the first pilgrim from the lands of the former western empire to report a mosque in Jerusalem. The building, which he appropriately called a house of prayers, did not impress him. Like many other mosques in that region, it was a very simple and unadorned structure built on open ground. In the conquered lands, early mosques were usually new and very simple buildings, easily distinguished from pagan temples, Jewish synagogues, and Christian churches.[95] Muslim authorities were concerned about the effect such beautiful buildings could have on their flock.

Early Muslims did not hesitate to visit and even pray in Christian churches.[96] Some Christian saints' shrines in particular attracted them. The shrine of St. Sergius at Resafa-Sergiopolis was an important pilgrimage center, which received numerous donations from Muslims that made possible the erection of beautiful churches in the city. St. Sergius had even received gifts from the Sassanian Zoroastrian king Khosro II, in thanksgiving for the child his Christian wife had prayed to the saint for. The cult of St. Sergius was particularly popular among the Ghassanids, an Arab tribe converted to Christianity in the 4th century, whose princes had established their residence in Resafa. They may have been connected with the erection in the 7th century of a mosque attached to the Christian cathedral, with the hope of benefiting from the cult of St. Sergius by attracting pilgrims to the mosque and to the new religion. The mosque was built north of the cathedral in the pilgrims' courtyard. Two passageways were built between the courtyard, now reduced in size but still in use, and the mosque, creating an architectural unity between the two religious spaces. Thilo Ulbert, in charge of the excavations at Resafa, explains the choice of this location by the enduring veneration of St. Sergius among the nomads of the region.[97] The mosque was built with the stones of a nearby Christian basilica dating from the 6th century and apparently destroyed by an earthquake before its final dedication. If the presence of the mosque next to the Christian basilica can be interpreted as a sign of the tolerance of early Umayyads for Christianity, it also shows a wish to occupy a religious site very much in favor among the local Arab population with a prestigious building belonging to the new religion.

In the Negev, the location of some early mosques indicates a wish to supersede the stele cult as well as Christianity. At Shivta, for example, the building of the mosque blocked a road which led from the village to a Christian church. The curved *miḥrāb* was built so close to the Christian baptistery as to bar one of its entrances.[98] Such competition is also clearly at play in the decision of the Umayyad caliph 'Abd al-Malik to build the Dome of the Rock on the Temple Mount higher than the Anastasis church, and to take over the church of St. John the Baptist in Damascus.[99]

In the 4th century Damascus was called the true city of the god (Julian, *Ep.*

24), for it worshiped Jupiter in splendid ceremonies staged by a temple renowned for its wealth and beauty, on the site of a shrine dating back to the Iron Age—in fact the biggest temple that is known in Syria. The temple was protected and separated from the city by two walls. The first contained a wide area inside which a market, the property of the temple, developed. The second wall surrounded the most sacred area, where only purified visitors could enter, and contained the altar and the temple itself. Its central location and its market made of the Jupiter temple a focus of city life. To cross the city from east to west, one had to go through the temple market. Although the site of the temple was very ancient, some of the temple walls were still under construction until the 3rd century. An extension of the market was built in the first half of the 4th century with temple funds. When the temple was closed along with the other pagan temples, at the end of the 4th century under the reign of Theodosius I, its site was very quickly transformed by Christians. The temple was destroyed and its stones were probably used to build a Christian basilica on a different site inside the *temenos* (sacred enclosure).[100] The Christian community of Damascus had lost two churches, burned by Jews during the reign of Julian if we accept Ambrose of Milan's testimony. This community, then, very certainly wished to assert itself with the support of the imperial authorities. What better way to do that than to occupy this central area of the city? The Christian cathedral was an impressive building. It was built on the south wall of the *temenos* and used its door, now Christianized with an invocation to the Trinity, as the main entrance. It deliberately turned its back on the desecrated temple courtyard where sacrifices had taken place.

It is only during the 5th century, when the memory of the sacrifices had begun to wane, that the cathedral was rebuilt to open onto the courtyard. The Christian basilica was dedicated to St. John the Baptist, whose relics had been dispersed under the reign of Julian. Once again the brief episode of Julian's reign and its religious turmoil seem to have played a major role in the self-assertion of the Christian community in Damascus. At the dawn of the 7th century, the city of Damascus was taken twice by the Arabs. The first time, in 634, a treaty granted the citizens their life, property, and churches. But after the Byzantine defeat at Yarmuk in 636, the city was taken again and the conditions of the Muslim rulers were less favorable to the Christians. One tradition reports that only fourteen of the forty-two churches remained at the disposal of the Christian community.[101] The Muslim conquerors also decided that the central area where the temple had been and where the Christian basilica now stood in splendor should be the site for their mosque. A mosque was built in the courtyard of the *temenos,* which Arculf saw around 670.[102] Another ancient tradition, possibly influenced by the situation in cities such as Homs, reports that the Christian church was divided into two buildings with different doors. The Christians kept only the western part of the building and lost the altar area. The eastern part was desacralized as a Christian church and transformed into a mosque with direct communication to the palace of the governor.

Finally, the sharing of the religious heart of the city was no longer admitted by the Muslim rulers who had made Damascus their capital. In 705 Caliph al-Walīd decided to evict the Christians. A new splendid mosque was to be built in this area and the remains of the previous religions erased.[103] The antique square towers were transformed into minarets. Oleg Grabar has noted that minarets were first built in Christian cities and were absent from mosques of the major Iraqi cities. Their function was not only to call the Muslims to prayer but also to assert the victorious presence of Islam in the center of Christian cities.[104] So, in Damascus, competition for a highly visible and central spot of the city led to a succession of religions inside the same sacred area, marked each time by the physical elimination of previous sacred buildings whose stones were often simply reused. The place retained its continuous sacrality. The right of asylum that the temple had probably enjoyed under the Seleucids was granted to the same area of the *temenos* in the 5th century, possibly at the time of the extension of the church. Under Muslim rule, this area held the ancient right of asylum under the name of Djairoun, in which *jer* means to be the guest of the God. Ibn Baṭṭūṭa saw men who lived in the shadow of the mosque, never leaving the enclosure and constantly praying.[105] In his *Cosmography* written around 1300, the compiler Dimishqi marveled at what was for him a sanctuary of four thousand years. The mosque, he noted, was originally a temple to Jupiter. He even added an episode to that long story: the Jews had transformed Jupiter's temple into a prayer house before the Christians changed it into a church and the Muslims into a mosque. Dimishqi had no doubt that he could in that place, and in that building, recapture the religious history of the human race and assert the one true religion that finally overcame the others, Islam.

Like rivers that create currents when they meet the sea, the religions in competition in the Roman and Persian worlds altered the societies they encountered. In regions like Syria and Palestine the currents were the strongest. First the sounds and perfumes of pagan processions had filled the streets of Syrian cities; then the music of Christian hymns and the odor of incense sanctified the urban space as Christians went in procession from one sanctuary to another; finally their voices were silenced by the chanting of the muezzin calling the Muslims to prayer from the minarets which dominated the ancient cities.

These two major religious changes within five centuries took different forms. Pagan sanctuaries were officially closed and their rites forbidden by Christian authorities of late Rome, while when the Muslims came to power they allowed Christians and Jews to practice their religions as long as they were silent and discreet. Yet Christians were often not allowed to repair their religious buildings, let alone build new ones, after the 8th century. The effect of these two religious shifts on the landscape can therefore be compared. With each new wave, religious buildings, once sacred sites visited by the faithful, collapsed in decay, while others were created to sacralize the land and the life of the faithful in a new manner. The Syrian and Palestinian landscape is dotted with ruins of abandoned temples, churches, and synagogues. Other religious buildings were officially desacralized and used for profane purposes. Still others were considered highly charged holy places and were transformed from temples to churches to mosques, such as in Damascus.

The 8th century was a turning point in the relationship between the Muslims and the *dhimmīs* (subject peoples). In Palestine, churches show traces of deliberate destruction of mosaics, particularly human and animal figures. We know that ʿUmar II (d. 720) had ordered that representations of crosses be destroyed.[106] Caliph Yazid II (720–724) ordered the destruction of statues, according to an Arab source of the 10th century, and of Christian images representing living creatures, if we follow Byzantine sources.[107] A study of the damaged mosaics suggests that they were destroyed not by violent Muslims intruders, but most probably by Christians themselves.[108] Whether this attitude was the result of Islamic pressure or arose from an inner and independent conviction that the representation of human and animal figures was ungodly remains an open and debatable question.[109] This period was marked by a tightening of the rules concerning the *dhimmīs*. A ruling of ʿUmar II (717–720) excluded non-Muslims from government administration unless they were willing to convert. The family of John of Damascus had been involved with tax collecting for many generations, under Persian, Byzantine, and now Muslim rulers. When he heard of the new ruling, John resigned and became a monk at St. Sabas in Palestine. This unfavorable evolution of the status of the *dhimmīs*, protected yet second-class citizens, clearly appears in the writings of the "Abbasid jurists," where numerous prohibitions, including restrictions on religious freedom and other new vexations, are noted.[110] No new churches or synagogues were to be erected, no proselytizing or public ceremonies were allowed. Authorization was required for the restoration of damaged religious buildings. Whether or not the prohibitions and vexations were enforced depended on the policies of the caliphs or the local emirs.

Archaeological evidence shows that until the middle of the 8th century Christians in Palestine still built or embellished churches. The same mosaicists worked for the Christian community in churches and for the new rulers in palaces.[111] Compared with the desacralization of pagan temples in the course of the 4th and 5th centuries, the desacralization of churches and synagogues was not caused primarily by the conversion of the population to the new religion— the evidence for massive conversion to Islam is rather later[112]—nor was it imposed by Umayyad caliphs or by violent actions on the part of individual Muslims. The abandonment of religious buildings, which is very noticeable throughout these regions in the course of the 7th and the 8th centuries, was due to a combination of causes, human (such as invasions, mostly the Persian invasion) and natural (such as earthquakes). Most likely the depopulation and impoverishment of the congregations explain why buildings were not repaired.[113] The same desacralization of Christian buildings happened in regions where no earthquakes damaged the churches. In Egypt, the taxes that the *dhimmīs* had to pay to the Muslim state eventually led to a real impoverishment of the Christian communities. At Philae, the Isis temple transformed into a Christian shrine under Justinian had remained a simple chapel, for the Christian community had other churches, notably a cathedral, also at Philae. Only after the Arabic invasion did the declining Christian community adopt the sturdy temple as its regular church, which probably indicates a lack of means or authorization to repair its other churches.[114]

Earthquakes in the Middle East, such as the terrible one of 746/7, caused the destruction of many buildings, among them numerous churches which were never rebuilt. One example reveals how an earthquake could follow a period of declining means combined with a gradual loss of respect to wipe out a magnificent church. The most majestic church in Pella, probably the cathedral, was built around 400 with columns and stones from a monumental temple.[115] The church was erected in the busy civic center of Pella, a prominent site in the city, highly visible to travelers coming from the Jordan valley. The building was refurbished in the 6th century. It was restored after the departure of the Persians in the early 7th century, and its final embellishments were a new monumental entrance, consisting of a majestic staircase and a large arch, along with new apartments for the clergy. The staircase enhanced the grandeur of the entrance to the building and served as a stage for solemn processions of the Christian community. Yet little more than a century later the atrium was being used to stable animals—as the discovery of the bones of camels who died in the earthquake of 747 reveals. In the city conquered by the Muslims in 635, the Christian community had lost its prosperity as well as its political power. After the earthquakes of 658–660, the grand portal was sealed. At that time, Christian processions were forbidden and Christians were allowed to practice their cult only inside their churches, as discreetly as possible. The loss of respect for the sacred building by a growing non-Christian population is attested by the fate of the other church entrances; during this time they were either sealed or reduced in size, probably to prevent animals from wandering into the atrium and the sanctuary. Finally, after the 717 earthquake, the partially collapsed church must have been deconsecrated and its interior furnishings, including the altar, removed. The fallen stones, tiles, and marble paving were taken away to repair other buildings. The rest of the church collapsed during the earthquake of 747, which destroyed most of the city of Pella. The fate of the once magnificent church of Pella was shared by many churches, synagogues, and Zoroastrian temples located in Muslim lands.

In the Byzantine world, it is also possible to see the 8th century as a turning point. As the Byzantine empire was still in shock from the amputation of its richest provinces, Egypt and Syria, as well as that of the nearby province of Illyricum, the Byzantine population turned its attention to saints, who seemed to be the only powers able to protect them. They did not consider the emergence of Islam, which they believed was only another Christian heresy, to be the cause of their empire's defeat. Rather, they assumed that the shrinking of the empire resulted from their own sins. Particularly under scrutiny were the remaining "pagan" or idolatrous practices, which could have angered God.[116] In 692, the Trullan Synod denounced a number of them. In the early 8th century, voices were raised by bishops in Asia Minor against the veneration of icons. Yet it was the deliberate policy of two emperors, Leo III (717–741) and Constantine V (741–775), who wanted to focus all energy on the figure of the emperor in order to save the empire, which created the destructive iconoclast movement.[117] The intense sacralization of painted images, which focused attention away from the altar and the Eucharist, was suddenly condemned as idolatry, opening a debate concerning the *locus* of the sacred. This reaction against the dispersal of Christian sacrality was combined with a political agenda of centralization of powers: Leo III replaced the image of Christ on coins with his own portrait. In 730 he ordered the destruction of all icons in the Byzantine empire. Only crosses were allowed, because they were symbols rather than images. By 787, when Empress Irene decided to restore the veneration of icons, a different Byzantine empire had emerged. Whole regions had seen their urban centers destroyed or depopulated.[118] Moreover, the late antique ceremonial modes of sacralizing space and time had changed to more discreet and inward-looking forms. Instead of huge basilicas with atria where large processions took place, the Byzantines now built more centripetal churches on a modest scale. In the new liturgies, processional movements were reduced to symbolic steps inside the churches.[119]

In the west, the 8th century is marked by the rise of the Carolingian rulers in Francia, changes in the political geography in many other countries, and the threat of the Islamic empire, which reached Spain and Sicily either through raiding or through conquest. Yet from a religious point of view, there was overall continuity from the 5th to the 8th century. The church domesticated the landscape through an intense sacralization of the land. In Rome, the number of churches, monasteries, and religious institutions rose to some 200 around 800 C.E., in a city whose population had sharply declined since the 4th century.[120] Churches large and small, hermits' cells and imposing monasteries, holy wells and monumental crosses studded the inhabited landscape. Kings maintained the tradition of church patronage in urban centers in order to demonstrate their public standing above other aristocratic families. In Metz, church building depended on the royal patronage of the Merovingian kings of Austrasia after they chose the city as their major urban base after 560. Six known churches, possibly fifteen in all, were built on their order. By 700 the citizens of Metz could hear the psalms sung in thirty churches or so.[121]

These numbers, however, conceal the deep transformation that occurred in early medieval kingdoms. Organized around their kings and their aristocracies, these Christian societies invested mostly in private religious buildings and in family monasteries set up on their lands. As the urban population diminished, some suburban sanctuaries were slowly abandoned. Even in Rome, a city marked by the continuity of its sacred spaces, the insecurity caused by Saracen raids led to the removal of relics from the catacombs in the 8th century and a withdrawal of religious activity from the once thriving cemeterial basilicas. Finally, as the sacred geography of the former Roman provinces adapted to the new medieval societies, the religious conquest of new lands started. East of the

Rhine and north of the Danube there were still pagans to convert, pagan shrines to desecrate, and new Christian sanctuaries to consecrate with perfumed oil and incense.

Notes

1. René Rebuffat, "Divinités de l'oued Kebir (Tripolitaine)," in Attilio Mastino, *L'Africa romana: Atti del VII convegno di studio* (Sassari, 1990), 119–159. An inscription on an altar records the consecration of the camp to the local genius (150).

2. Michael Avi-Yonah, "The Mosaic of Mopsuestia—Church or Synagogue?" in Lee I. Levine, ed., *Ancient Synagogues Revealed* (Jerusalem, 1981), 186–190.

3. David G. Orr, "Roman Domestic Religion: The Evidence of the Household Shrines," *ANRW* 16.2.1557–1591; J. T. Baker, *Living and Working with the Gods: Studies of Evidence for Private Religion and Its Material Environment in the City of Ostia (100–500 AD)* (Amsterdam, 1994).

4. Henri Fugier, *Recherches sur l'expression du sacré dans la langue latine* (Paris, 1963), 71–88.

5. E. M. Orlin, *Temples, Religion and Politics in the Roman Republic* (Leiden, 1997).

6. Susan E. Alcock, "Minding the Gap in Hellenistic and Roman Greece," in Susan E. Alcock and Robin Osborne, eds., *Placing the Gods: Sanctuaries and Sacred Space in Ancient Greece* (Oxford, 1994), 247–261.

7. Eberhard Sauer, *The End of Paganism in the North-Western Provinces of the Roman Empire: The Example of the Mithras Cult* (London, 1996).

8. Fawzi Zayadine, ed., *Jerash Archaeological Project (1981–1983)* (Amman, 1986).

9. Martin Henig and A. C. King, *Pagan Gods and Shrines of the Roman Empire* (Oxford, 1986); Françoise Dunand, *Le culte d'Isis dans le bassin oriental de la Méditerranée*, vol. 2 (Leiden, 1973); Robert Turcan, *The Cults of the Roman Empire* (Oxford, 1996).

10. Such a comparison is offered for *ludi* and festivals in Michele R. Salzman, *On Roman Time: The Codex-Calendar of 354 and the Rhythms of Urban Life in Late Antiquity* (Berkeley, 1990), 121–125.

11. Wonderful descriptions of the colorful and lively processions can be read in Greek novels; see B. P. Reardon, ed., *Collected Ancient Greek Novels* (Berkeley, 1989). On the imperial cult festivals, see Simon R. F. Price, *Rituals and Power: The Roman Imperial Cult in Asia Minor* (Cambridge, Eng., 1984).

12. J. H. W. G. Liebeschuetz, *Continuity and Change in Roman Religion* (Oxford, 1979).

13. K. J. Rigsby, *Asylia: Territorial Inviolability in the Hellenistic World* (Berkeley, 1996).

14. S. N. C. Lieu, *Manichaeism in the Later Roman Empire and Medieval China: A Historical Survey* (Manchester, 1985).

15. Eusebius, *Hist.eccl.* 9.5.

16. *CIL* 3.12132, trans. in Simon R. F. Price, *Rituals and Power: The Roman Imperial Cult in Asia Minor* (Cambridge, Eng., 1984), 124.

17. Gelasius, *Lettre contre les Lupercales et dix-huit messes du sacramentaire léonien* (Paris, 1959); Augustine, *Sermon Dolbeau 26*, in François Dolbeau, ed., *Vingt-Six Sermons au peuple d'Afrique* (Paris, 1996), 345–417.

18. O. Pasquato, *Gli spettacoli in S. Giovanni Crisostomo: Paganesimo e cristianesimo ad Antiochia e Costantinopoli nel IV secolo* (Rome, 1976); Timothy Barnes,

"Christians and the Theater," in W. J. Slater, ed., *Roman Theater and Society*, E. Togo Salmon Papers 1 (Ann Arbor, 1996), 161–180; Richard Lim, "Consensus and Dissensus on Public Spectacles in Early Byzantium," in L. Garland, ed., *Conformity and Non-Conformity in Byzantium, Byzantinische Forschungen* 24 (1997): 159–179.

19. C. Moss, "Jacob of Serugh's Homilies on the Spectacles," in *Le Museon* 48 (1935): 87–112, trans. at 106.

20. Maximus of Turin, *Sermon* 107, trans. in J. N. Hillgarth, *Christianity and Paganism, 350–750: The Conversion of Western Europe* (Philadelphia, 1986), 55.

21. Dietrich Claude, *Die byzantinische Stadt im 6. Jahrhundert* (Munich, 1969), 74–76.

22. A number of the texts relevant to the ending of pagan cults can be found in English translation in Brian Croke and Jill Harries, *Religious Conflict in Fourth-Century Rome: A Documentary Study* (Sydney, 1982). See also Pierre Chuvin, *A Chronicle of the Last Pagans* (Cambridge, Mass., 1990). For a very different view of Constantine's policy toward pagans, see Timothy D. Barnes, *Constantine and Eusebius* (Cambridge, Mass., 1981).

23. Jean Gascou, "Le rescrit d'Hispellum," in *Mélanges de l'Ecole française de Rome* 79 (1967): 609–659.

24. *C.Th.* 16.10.4 [346; 354; 356]; 16.10.6 [Feb. 356]: death penalty for anyone performing a sacrifice.

25. *C.Th.* 16.10.8 [Nov. 382] to the Dux of Osroëne: "We decree that the temple shall be continually open . . . In order that this temple may be seen by the assemblages of the city and by frequent crowds, Your Experience shall preserve all celebrations of festivities . . . but in such a way that the performance of sacrifices forbidden therein may not be supposed to be permitted under the pretext of such access to the temple" (trans. Pharr). In 357, during his visit to Rome, Emperor Constantius consecrated a temple to Apollo (*CIL* 6.45 = Dessau 3222). At the end of the 4th century, but before 391, altars to the gods were restored in Sardis and sacrifices offered by a "vicar of Asia" and a "governor of Lydia" (Pierre Chuvin, *Chronicle of the Last Pagans*, 48). On restoration of temples in the west at the end of the 4th century, see H. Bloch, "The Pagan Revival in the West at the End of the Fourth Century," in Arnaldo Momigliano, ed., *The Conflict between Paganism and Christianity in the Fourth Century* (Oxford, 1963), 193–218; André Chastagnol, "La restauration du temple d'Isis au Portus Romae sous le règne de Gratien," in *Hommage à Marcel Renard* (Brussels, 1969), 135–144, repr. in *L'Italie et l'Afrique au Bas-Empire, Scripta Varia* (Lille, 1987); Claude Lepelley, *Les cités de l'Afrique romaine au Bas Empire* (Paris, 1979), 347–351.

26. It was obviously very difficult to enforce the closing of the temples and even more the suppression of sacrifices, especially those made in the privacy of an individual's house; for an archaeological record of private sacrifices, see Arja Karivieri, "The 'House of Proclus' on the Southern Slope of the Acropolis: A Contribution," in Paavo Castren, ed., *Post Herulian Athens: Aspects of Life and Culture in Athens, A.D. 267–529* (Helsinki, 1994), 115–139. Certain cults were hard to kill. In 417, Isiac cults were still being honored in Gaul (Rutilius Namatianus, 1.371–376). Individuals worshiping and sacrificing to the goddess are still attested in the late 6th century: see Michel Tardieu, *Les paysages reliques: Routes et haltes syriennes d'Isidore à Simplicius* (Louvain, 1990); Glen W. Bowersock, *Hellenism in Late Antiquity* (Ann Arbor, 1990). However, sacrifice was now conducted in private in clandestine temples or secret chambers: see Zacharias Scholasticus, *Life of Severus*, ed. and trans. M. A. Kugener, *PO* 2: 20–35.

27. Symmachus, *Relatio* 3, in R. Barrow, *Prefect and Emperor: The Relationes of Symmachus A.D. 384* (Oxford, 1973).

28. Stephen Mitchell, *Anatolia: Land, Men and Gods in Asia Minor*, vol. 2: *The Rise of the Church* (Oxford, 1993).

29. In the year 112, Pliny the Younger, then a governor, wrote to Emperor Trajan concerning a temple obstructing the building of the new forum in Nicomedia. He had religious scruples about authorizing its removal. Trajan answered directing him to remove the temple to another site (Pliny, *Ep.* 10, 50).

30. Robin Lane Fox, *Pagans and Christians* (New York, 1989), 671–672.

31. Louis Robert, "De Cilicie à Messine et à Plymouth avec deux inscriptions grecques errantes," in *Journal des Savants* (1973): 161–211; see esp. 185–192.

32. The notion of physical contact is crucial for understanding the creation of holy places and eventually of the Holy Land, an idea expressed quite literally by Eusebius in a sentence explaining the construction of a shrine on the Mount of Olives, which he identified as the place where the Ascension took place: "There stood in truth . . . the feet of our Lord and Savior, Himself the Word of God" (*Demonstratio evangelica* 6.18.23). On this new notion, see Peter W. L. Walker, *Holy City, Holy Places? Christian Attitudes to Jerusalem and the Holy Land in the Fourth Century* (Oxford, 1990), 206.

33. Eusebius, *Vit.Const.* 3.28–29.

34. Robert L. Wilken, *The Land Called Holy: Palestine in Christian History and Thought* (New Haven, 1992); Francis E. Peters, *Jerusalem: The Holy City in the Eyes of Chroniclers, Visitors, Pilgrims, and Prophets from the Days of Abraham to the Beginnings of Modern Times* (Princeton, 1985); Hagith Sivan, "Pilgrimage, Monasticism, and the Emergence of Christian Palestine in the 4th Century," in Robert Ousterhout, ed., *The Blessings of Pilgrimage* (Chicago, 1990), 54–65.

35. Jan W. Drijvers, *Helena Augusta: The Mother of Constantine the Great and the Legends of Her Finding of the True Cross* (Leiden, 1992); A. Frolow, *La relique de la vraie croi: Recherches sur le développement d'un culte* (Paris, 1961).

36. Claude Lepelley, "The Survival and Fall of the Classical City in Late Roman Africa," in John Rich, ed., *The City in Late Antiquity* (London, 1992), 50–76; Cristina La Rocca, "Public Buildings and Urban Change in Northern Italy in the Early Mediaeval Period," ibid., 161–180.

37. Henri Grégoire and M. A. Kugener, ed. and trans., *Marc Le Diacre: Vie de Porphyre évêque de Gaza* (Paris, 1930). On Gaza, see Frank Trombley, *Hellenic Religion and Christianization, c. 370–529*, vol. 1 (Leiden, 1993); Carol A. M. Glucker, *The City of Gaza in the Roman and Byzantine Periods* (Oxford, 1987); Raymond Van Dam, "From Paganism to Christianity at Late Antique Gaza," in *Viator* 16 (1985): 1–20; Garth Fowden, "Bishops and Temples in the Eastern Roman Empire A.D. 320–435," *Journal of Theological Studies*, n.s. 29.1 (April 1978): 53–78.

38. For Greece: Jean-Marie Spieser, "La christianisation des sanctuaires païens en Grèce," in *Neue Forschungen in Griechischen Heiligtümern*, ed. U. Jantzen (Tübingen, 1976), 309–320. Highly charged parts of a temple could be deliberately attacked, like the *aduton* in the temple of Apollo at Delphi: see Vincent Déroche, "Delphes: La christianisation d'un sanctuaire païen," in *Actes du XIe congrès international d'archéologie chrétienne*, vol. 3 (Rome, 1989), 2713–23. For central Gaul, see Bailey Young, "Que restait-il de l'ancien paysage religieux à l'époque de Grégoire de Tours?" in Nancy Gauthier and Henri Galinié, eds., *Grégoire de Tours et l'espace gaulois*, Suppl. 13 to *Revue archéologique du centre de la France* (1997).

39. Canons of the Trullan Synod in 692.

40. Compare with the early church: T. C. G. Thornton, "The Destruction of Idols: Sinful or Meritorious?" *Journal of Theological Studies*, n.s. 37 (1986): 121–124.

41. W. H. C. Frend, "Monks and the End of Greco-Roman Paganism," in *L'intolleranza cristiana nei confronti dei pagani*, in P. F. Beatrice, ed., *Cristianesimo nella storia* 11:3 (1990): 469–484. On Libanius's accusations of widespread destruction of rural temples at the hand of monks, see François Paschoud, "L'intolérance chrétienne vue et jugée par les païens," ibid., 27–54, and Peter Brown, *Authority and the Sacred* (Cambridge, Eng., 1995): 545–577.

42. Françoise Thélamon, "Destruction du paganisme et construction du Royaume de Dieu d'après Rufin et Augustin," in *Cristianesimo nella storia* 11:3 (1990): 523–544.

43. Sabina MacCormack, "Loca Sancta: The Organization of Sacred Topography in Late Antiquity," in Ousterhout, *The Blessings of Pilgrimage,* 14; for the identification of pagan gods with demons, see Jean-Marie Vermander, "La polémique des Apologistes latins contre les dieux du paganisme," *Recherches Augustiniennes* 17 (1982): 3–128.

44. Even in 8th century Constantinople, extraordinary stories circulated about the antique pagan statues' malevolence toward Christians: see *Constantinople in the Early Eighth Century: The Parastaseis syntomoi chronikai,* ed. Averil Cameron and Judith Herrin in conjunction with Alan Cameron, Robin Cormack, and Charlotte Roueché (Leiden, 1984); Gilbert Dagron, *Constantinople imaginaire: Etudes sur le recueil des "Patria"* (Paris, 1984).

45. Eustratios, *Life of Eutychius* 53, PG 86.2333D, cited in Cyril Mango, "L'attitude byzantine à l'égard des antiquités gréco-romaines," in *Byzance et les images,* ed. Jannic Durand (Paris, 1994), 97–120.

46. Rufinus, *Ecclesiastical History,* 2.29; Françoise Thélamon, *Païens et Chrétiens au IVe siècle: L'apport de l'Histoire ecclésiastique de Rufin d'Aquilée* (Paris, 1981), 267; Christopher Haas, *Alexandria in Late Antiquity: Topography and Social Conflict* (Baltimore, 1997), 159–169.

47. Barbara Gassowska, "Maternus Cynegius, praefectus Praetorio Orientis and the Destruction of the Allat Temple in Palmyra," in *Archeologia* 33 (1982): 114–115.

48. Robert Turcan, *Mithra et le Mithraicisme* (Paris, 1993), 119.

49. The temple, located in the south of Egypt, had remained open long after the official closing of pagan temples, to placate the tumultuous pagan Blemmyes who came to worship Isis in that sanctuary; see Roger S. Bagnall, *Egypt in Late Antiquity* (Princeton, 1993), 147 and 251. The peace treaty being broken, Justinian ordered the closing of the temple and its transformation into a church; see Pierre Nautin, "La conversion du temple de Philae en église chrétienne," in *Cahiers Archéologiques* 17 (1967): 1–43.

50. Helen Saradi-Mendelovici, "Christian Attitudes toward Pagan Monuments in Late Antiquity and Their Legacy in Later Byzantine Centuries," in *Dumbarton Oaks Papers* 44 (1990): 47–59.

51. Claude Lepelley, "Le Musée des statues divines: La volonté de sauvegarder le patrimoine artistique païen à l'époque théodosienne," *Cahiers archéologiques* 42 (1994): 5–15.

52. Marlia Mundell Mango, "Art Collecting in Byzantium," *Etudes balkaniques* 2 (1995): 137–160.

53. Michele Piccirillo, *Mosaics of Jordan* (Amman, 1993); Katherine Dunbabin, *Mosaics of Roman North Africa: Studies in Iconography and Patronage* (Oxford, 1978); R. Wilson, *Piazza Armerina* (Austin, 1983).

54. Dericksen M. Brinkerhoff, *A Collection of Sculpture in Classical and Early Christian Antioch* (New York, 1970).

55. Jean-Charles Picard, *La Carthage de Saint Augustin* (Paris, 1965), 98–107.

56. Jean-Pierre Sodini, "L'habitat urbain en Grèce à la veille des invasions," in *Villes et peuplement dans l'Illyricum protobyzantin* (Rome, 1984), 341–397.

57. Allan C. Johnson, Paul R. Coleman-Norton, and Frank Card Bourne, eds., *Ancient Roman Statutes* (Austin, 1961), 249–250.

58. Peter Brown, *The Cult of the Saints: Its Rise and Function in Latin Christianity* (Chicago, 1981).

59. Kenneth G. Holum, "The Trier Ivory, Adventus Ceremonial and the Relics of Saint Stephen," *Dumbarton Oaks Papers* 33 (1979): 113–133. The author interprets the scene as the welcoming of the relics of St. Stephen by Empress Pulcheria in 421. For another interpretation, see S. Spain, "The Translation of Relics Ivory, Trier," *Dumbarton Oaks Papers* 31 (1977): 279–304.

60. Vitricius of Rouen, *De laude Sanctorum* 1, *PL* 20.433A, cited in Hillgarth, *Christianity and Paganism*, 23.

61. Neil Christie and Simon T. Loseby, *Towns in Transition: Urban Evolution in Late Antiquity and the Early Middle Ages* (Aldershot, 1996).

62. Alan Walmsley, "Byzantine Palestine and Arabia: Urban Prosperity in Late Antiquity," ibid., 126–158.

63. Bert de Vries, "Jordan's Churches: Their Urban Context in Late Antiquity," *Biblical Archaeologist* 51 (1988): 222–226.

64. Hugh Kennedy, "The Last Century of Byzantine Syria," *Byzantinische Forschungen* 10 (1985): 141–183.

65. Jean-Charles Balty, paper delivered at a conference on Apamea at the École Normale Supérieure, May 21, 1996. A publication on the temple is forthcoming.

66. Jacques Seigne, "Jerash: Le sanctuaire de Zeus et ses abords," *Contribution française à l'Archéologie Jordanienne* (Amman, 1989), 40–48.

67. Fawzi Zayadine, "The Jerash Project for Excavation and Restoration: A Synopsis with Special Reference to the Work of the Department of Antiquities," in *Jerash Archaeological Project, 1981–1983,* ed. F. Zayadine (Amman, 1986), 11–12.

68. Steven Fine, "From Meeting House to Sacred Realm: Holiness and the Ancient Synagogue," in Fine, ed., *Sacred Realm: The Emergence of the Synagogue in the Ancient World* (New York and Oxford, 1996); Joan R. Branham, "Vicarious Sacrality: Temple Space in Ancient Synagogues," in D. Urman and Paul V. M. Flesher, eds., *Ancient Synagogues: A Historical Analysis and Archaeological Discovery* (Leiden, 1995), 319–346.

69. Annabel J. Wharton, *Refiguring the Post Classical City: Dura Europos, Jerash, Jerusalem and Ravenna* (Cambridge, Eng., 1995).

70. C.Cels. 8.17–20; Origen, *The Letter of Barnabas,* 16; Joan E. Taylor, *Christians and the Holy Places: The Myth of Jewish-Christian Origins* (Oxford, 1993); Robert Markus, "How on Earth Could Places Become Holy? Origins of the Christian Idea of Holy Places," *Journal of Early Christian Studies* 2:3 (1994): 257–271.

71. In the *Acta purgationis Felicis Abthugnitani,* a pagan *duumvir,* coming back to his city in 303, reports the destruction of two Christian basilicas at Furnos and Zama (*Acta purgationis Felicis Abthugnitani,* ed. C. Ziwsa, *CSEL* 26, 199).

72. In a city such as Carthage, the church's treasure consisted of gold and silver vessels (*Optatus Milevitani* 1.17, ed. C. Ziwsa, *CSEL* 26, 19).

73. Bishop Silvanus was elected there; see Yvette Duval, *Auprès des saints, corps et ame: L'inhumation "ad sanctos" dans la chrétienté d'Orient et d'Occident du IIIe au VIIe siècle* (Paris, 1988), 54.

74. Michel-Yves Perrin, "Le nouveau style missionnaire: La conquête de l'espace et du temps," in Jean-Marie Mayeur et al., eds., *Histoire du christianisme des origines à nos jours* (Paris, 1995), 584–621; André Grabar, *Martyrium: Recherches sur le culte des reliques et l'art chrétien* (Paris, 1943–1946).

75. Charles Pietri, "Le temps de la semaine à Rome et dans l'Italie," in *Le temps chrétien de la fin de l'Antiquité au Moyen Age, IIIe–XIIIe siècles* (Paris, 1984), 63–81.

76. E. D. Hunt, "The Traffic in Relics: Some Late Roman Evidence," in S. Hackel, *The Byzantine Saint* (Birmingham, 1981), 171–179.

77. *Epistula Luciani,* 2, *PL* 41.809; commented on in Brown, *Cults of the Saints,* 91–92.

78. Pauline Donceel-Voûte, *Les pavements des églises byzantines de Syrie et du Liban: Décor, archéologie et liturgie* (Louvain-La-Neuve, 1988), 534; Gary Vikan, *Byzantine Pilgrimage Art* (Washington, D.C., 1982).

79. In Monza, the cathedral owns a collection of these *ampullae,* which contained oils that had burned in front of sixty different tombs of martyrs buried in Rome. See André Grabar, *Ampoules de Terre Sainte* (Paris, 1958); Nicole Herrmann-Mascard, *Les reliques des saints: Formation coutumière d'un droit* (Paris, 1975), 47–48.

80. Luce Pietri, "Calendrier liturgique et temps vécu: L'exemple de Tours au VIe siècle," in *Le Temps Chrétien*, 129–141.

81. Church councils and civil legislation tried to enforce the notion of the irrevocability of church dedication. Once sacralized, a space could not be used for profane purposes.

82. Hans Belting, *Likeness and Presence: A History of the Image before the Era of Art,* trans. Edmund Jephcott (Chicago, 1994).

83. Patrick Geary, *Furta Sacra: Theft of Relics in the Central Middle Ages* (Princeton, 1990).

84. Bernard Flusin, *Saint Anastase le Perse et l'histoire de la Palestine au début du VIIe siècle* (Paris, 1992).

85. Francis E. Peters, *The Hajj: The Muslim Pilgrimage to Mecca and the Holy Places* (Princeton, 1994).

86. Bernard Lewis, *The Jews of Islam* (Princeton, 1984).

87. Carol Bier, "Piety and Power in Early Sasanian Art," in Eiko Matsushima, ed., *Official Cult and Popular Religion in the Ancient Near East* (Heidelberg, 1993).

88. Mary Boyce, *A History of Zoroastrianism,* vol. 3 (Leiden, 1991); Klaus Schippmann, *Die iranischen Feuerheiligtümer* (Berlin, 1971); Paul Bernard, "Le temple du dieu Oxus à Takht-i Sangin en Bactriane: Temple du feu ou pas?" in *Studia Iranica* 23 (1994): 81–121.

89. Michael Morony, *Iraq after the Muslim Conquest* (Princeton, 1984), 121; Eshan Yarshater, *The Cambridge History of Iran,* vol. 3 (Cambridge, 1983).

90. Jamsheed K. Choksy, "Zoroastrians in Muslim Iran: Selected Problems of Coexistence and Interaction during the Early Medieval Period," *Iranian Studies* 20 (1987): 17–30, and "Conflict, Coexistence, and Cooperation: Muslims and Zoroastrians in Eastern Iran during the Medieval Period," *The Muslim World* 80 (1990): 213–233.

91. Annemarie Schimmel, *Deciphering the Signs of God: A Phenomenological Approach to Islam* (Albany, 1994).

92. G. Avni, "Early Mosques in the Negev Highlands: New Archaeological Evidence on Islamic Penetration of Southern Palestine," *Bulletin of the American Schools of Oriental Research* 294 (1994): 83–100.

93. Gustave E. von Grunebaum, "The Sacred Character of Islamic Cities," in *Islam and Medieval Hellenism: Social and Cultural Perspectives* (London, 1976).

94. Oleg Grabar, *The Formation of Islamic Art* (New Haven, 1973; rev. ed. 1987).

95. Oleg Grabar, "La grande mosquée de Damas et les origines architecturales de la Mosquée," in *Synthronon: Art et Archéologie de la fin de l'Antiquité et du Moyen Age* (Paris, 1968), 107–114, at 108; Geoffrey King, C. J. Lenzen, and Gary O. Rollefson, "Survey of Byzantine and Islamic Sites of Jordan: Second Season Report, 1981," *Annual of the Department of Antiquities* 27 (1983): 399–405; Antonio Almagro, "Building Patterns in Umayyad Architecture in Jordan," in Muna Zaghloul et al., eds., *Studies in the History and Archaeology of Jordan IV* (Amman and Lyon, 1992), 351–356.

96. Suliman Bashear, "Qibla Musharriqa and Early Muslim Prayer in Churches," *The Muslim World* 81 (1991): 268–282.

97. Thilo Ulbert, "Resafa-Sergiupolis: Archäologische Forschungen in der Nordsyrischen Pilgerstadt," in *Syrien von den Aposteln zu den Kalifen,* ed. E. M. Ruprechtsberger (Linz, 1993), 112–127.

98. G. Avni, "Early Mosques," 83–100.

99. Oleg Grabar, *The Shape of the Holy: Early Islamic Jerusalem* (Princeton, 1996).

100. Michel Gawlikowski, "Les temples de Syrie à l'époque hellénistique et romaine," in *Archéologie et histoire de la Syrie, 2: La Syrie de l'époque achéménide à l'avènement de l'Islam,* ed. Jean-Marie Dentzer and Winfried Orthmann (Saarbrücken, 1989), 334.

101. Joseph Nasrallah, "De la cathédrale de Damas à la mosquée Omayyade," in *La*

Syrie de Byzance à l'Islam, VIIe–VIIIe siècles, ed. Pierre Canivet and Jean-Paul Rey-Coquais (Damascus, 1992).

102. Lucien Golvin, *Essai sur l'architecture religieuse musulmane, 2: L'art religieux des Umayyades de Syrie* (Paris, 1971).

103. Oleg Grabar, "La grande mosquée de Damas et les origines architecturales de la Mosquée," in *Synthronon: Art et Archéologie de la fin de l'Antiquité et du Moyen Age* (Paris, 1968), 107–114.

104. Oleg Grabar, "Islam and Byzantium," *Dumbarton Oaks Papers* 18 (1964): 74.

105. René Dussaud, "Le temple de Jupiter Damascénien et ses transformations aux époques chrétienne et musulmane," *Syria* 3 (1922): 219–250.

106. Abu Yusuf Ya'qub, *Le livre de l'impôt foncier,* tr. E. Fagnan (Paris, 1921), 196.

107. Texts gathered by André Grabar, *L'iconoclasme byzantin: Le dossier archéologique* (Paris, 1984), 128–129.

108. Robert Schick, *The Christian Communities of Palestine from Byzantine to Islamic Rule: A Historical and Archaeological Study* (Princeton, 1995).

109. G. R. D. King, "Islam, Iconoclasm, and the Declaration of Doctrine," *Bulletin of the School of Oriental and African Studies* 48 (1985): 267–277.

110. Anne-Marie Eddé et al., *Communautés chrétiennes en Pays d'Islam du début du VIIe siècle au milieu du XIe siècle* (Paris, 1997).

111. Michele Piccirillo, "The Umayyad Churches of Jordan," *Annual of the Department of Antiquities of Jordan* 28 (1994): 333–341.

112. Richard W. Bulliet, *Conversion to Islam in the Medieval Period* (Cambridge, Eng., 1979).

113. When the Muslims arrived in cities such as Hama, they found empty houses, the result of depopulation as well as desertion in face of the enemy; see Hugh Kennedy, "The Last Century of Byzantine Syria: A Reinterpretation," *Byzantinische Forschungen* 10 (1985): 141–183. The decline of the population and of the general prosperity in the second half of the 6th century, notably after the plague, is a matter of discussion: see Mark Whittow, "Ruling the Late Roman and Early Byzantine City: A Continuous History," *Past and Present* 129 (1990): 3–29.

114. Nautin, "La conversion du temple de Philae."

115. Robert H. Smith and Leslie P. Day, *Pella of the Decapolis, vol. 2, Final Report on the College of Wooster Excavations in Area IX, The Civic Complex, 1979–1985* (Wooster, Ohio, 1989).

116. Patricia Crone, "Islam, Judeo-Christianity and Byzantine Iconoclasm," *Jerusalem Studies in Arabic and Islam* 2 (1980): 59–95.

117. Gilbert Dagron, "Le christianisme byzantin du VIIe au milieu du XIe siècle," in *Histoire du Christianisme des origines à nos jours,* ed. Jean-Marie Mayeur et al., vol. 4: *Evêques, moines et empereurs (610–1054),* ed. Gilbert Dagron et al. (Paris, 1993).

118. For an evaluation of the destruction of early Christian basilicas and of the few new buildings in the 7th and 8th centuries, see Cyril Mango, *Byzantine Architecture* (London, 1979).

119. Robert F. Taft, *The Byzantine Rite: A Short History* (Collegeville, Minn., 1992); Thomas F. Mathews, *The Early Churches of Constantinople: Architecture and Liturgy* (University Park, Pa., 1971); Natalia B. Tetariatnikov, *The Liturgical Planning of Byzantine Churches in Cappadocia* (Rome, 1996).

120. Louis Reekmans, "L'implantation monumentale chrétienne dans le paysage urbain de Rome de 300 à 850," *Actes du XIe Congrès international d'archéologie chrétienne* 2 (1989): 861–915.

121. Guy Halsall, "Towns, Societies and Ideas: The Not-so-strange Case of Late Roman and Early Merovingian Metz," in Christie and Loseby, *Towns in Transition,* 235–261.

Philosophical Tradition and the Self

Henry Chadwick

Neither classical Greek nor Latin had a word meaning "self" approximating the senses in which that term has come to be used in philosophical discussions since the time of Descartes in the 17th century. Nevertheless there were discussions especially in late antiquity which anticipate propositions heard in more recent times, and the Neoplatonists in particular explored ways and means of investigating the subject, not least because they had an interest in restating the mind-body problem in terms of a Platonic dualism. They wanted to put distance between Platonism (received by them as authoritative truth) and both the materialist accounts of the soul characteristic of Stoicism and the Aristotelian middle position that the soul which gives life and form to the physical body cannot be thought of as existing apart from it and having sovereign independence, though it is not a physical substance.

In late antiquity the logical works of Aristotle's *Organon* were read, and in Alexander of Aphrodisias in Caria, about 200, the master found a learned and very intelligent advocate whose writings on the subject were known to the Neoplatonists. In the interest of showing Aristotle to be in harmony with Plato, they produced voluminous commentaries on his logic, metaphysics, and ethics. Nevertheless Aristotle was largely a philosopher's philosopher, read by an educated elite, but not widely or popularly studied. Nemesius, the cultivated and widely read bishop of Emesa at the end of the 4th century, admired Aristotle's achievements.

Stoicism found influential expositors in Epictetus and Emperor Marcus Aurelius. Galen recorded attending good lectures by a disciple of a Stoic named Philopator. Philopator's book arguing that belief in fate was compatible with free will left Nemesius unimpressed. In the Latin-speaking world Seneca, in the Greek world Epictetus, enjoyed considerable popularity and influence. Writing in 248, Origen observed that Plato's dialogues were not found to be easy reading and that the discourses of Epictetus (written up by his disciple and admirer

Arrian) were much more likely to be read and enjoyed. Stoic logic and ethics long remained influential in a way that the school's physics and metaphysics did not. Yet while in the early Roman empire of the 1st and 2nd centuries Stoic teachers ranked high in the popularity stakes, from the 3rd century onward Platonism became more and more dominant. In the Latin west of the second half of the 4th century, the legacy of Plotinus teaching in Rome and of Porphyry living in Sicily ensured that the new lease of life given to Platonic studies by Plotinus created a widespread Platonizing culture no less general than in the Greek east. Moreover, that educated Christians in Rome or Alexandria found much in the Platonic tradition with which they felt a deep sympathy helped to underpin their generalized assumption that Platonic ideas provided a good background for an appropriate way of life. This Christian sympathy was not welcome to the pagan tradition, within which part of the popularity of Platonism came from its potential to provide an alternative and rival to the rising power of Christianity. Just as within the boundaries of the church the most intense controversies were between those who stood closest to each other, so also Christians such as Gregory of Nyssa or Augustine of Hippo could be particularly sharp in their negativity toward pagan philosophers—and vice versa. But the understanding of the mind-body problem on both sides of this kind of divide was really remarkably similar.

Accordingly the modern reader looking for a coherent account of the self in the writers of this period of antiquity needs to be willing to make some mental adjustment. The ancients were not students of neuroscience and did not comprehend the extremely intricate workings of the brain. They had long known the mind to be all-important in the human constitution, and acutely argued about freedom, responsibility, deliberation, intention, conscience, even consciousness.

One must not forget that although they had read neither Descartes nor Foucault they nevertheless had something to say. Embryonic elements of the theme of the self can be traced in classical authors. The dominance of Platonism among both Christian and non-Christian provided a milieu in which the soul or mind (nous) or self became a major topic with wide areas of agreement and common terminology. One pervasively influential text was the *First Alcibiades* of Plato in which, starting from the Delphic recommendation "Know thyself," the real nature of man is defined as the soul's making use of the body as an instrument (and therefore secondary). The knowing of oneself is the very first principle of philosophy, the self-understanding which determines a person's way of life, and is therefore also the ultimate ground of religious awareness. It is a widely diffused axiom that the purified soul is a mirror image of the divine, found for example in the apostle Paul (2 Cor. 3:18) or the Sentences of Sextus (450) in the 2nd century. The apostle's aspiration was to know the divine "as he himself is known" (1 Cor. 13:12). In the Coptic *Gospel of Thomas III* the world is declared by Jesus to be unworthy of the person who achieves self-discovery, and through self-knowledge comes repose (anapausis). Realizing oneself to be one of the elect is the gnostic message giving meaning and dignity to an otherwise dull and probably miserable existence. There are ethical consequences. In

Poimandres, first tract in the corpus of Hermetic writings, this self-recognition entails awareness that the sexual drive is the cause of death (*CH* 1.18), and thereby the soul's elevation is weighed down. Bodily sensation has to be left behind (*CH* 13.10).

Porphyry, biographer and editor of Plotinus, began the *Life* of his master with the famous sentence that Plotinus always seemed ashamed of being in the body. His concern was with the soul which, true to Plato, he saw as being midway between the inferior flesh and the superior incorporeal mind. Moral choices are therefore decisions whether to follow the higher reason or lower bodily appetite. The self (for which Plotinus uses the word *autos*) therefore has levels and power of movement. But the true self is divine and the body no more than its temporary instrument (IV 7.1.20ff.). Naturally the union of soul with body makes for interaction between them. When ashamed we blush, when terrified we go white with fear. Conversely there are pressures which the body can put upon the soul, drawing it downward toward material satisfactions. But the soul's true home is in that higher realm which is not governed by the determinism of fate. Self-knowledge is synonymous with the soul's being identical in being *(homoousios)* with mind (IV 4.28.56; IV 7.10.19). Thereby salvation is the divinizing of the soul, a mystical union comparable to the merging of two torches (I 6.9.18ff.) "in the measure possible to the human soul" (2.9.9.45ff.). The route by which one returns to true being is self-knowledge (VI 5.7), and is a restoration of the unity from which the soul has fallen into multiplicity and has been torn apart in a "scattering" (VI 6.1.5). As the soul moves toward the good, it recovers freedom, which is a liberation from the constraints of the body (VI 8.6–7). Plotinus noted explicitly that in his doctrine of the soul's retaining its divine nature "undescended" he was departing from the normal view of the Platonic schools (IV 8.8.1). Origen (*Prin.* 3.4) shows that the idea was not new with Plotinus.

Iamblichus came to think Plotinus mistaken to suppose that a higher part of the soul does not descend to the body; the entire soul is responsible (Proclus, *In Tim.* 3.334.3–8). It retains choice, and descent is not to a determinist world. Plotinus's language was felt by some among his Neoplatonist successors to have offered a brilliant interpretation of Plato's *Parmenides,* taking the three hypotheses of that dialogue to speak of the One, *nous,* and soul, but nevertheless to have bequeathed some difficult problems. Iamblichus, contemporary with Emperor Constantine the Great, thought the language about the relation between *nous* and soul to be confused and confusing: Was it correct to say that the soul becomes "identical in being" with *nous,* and if so, does that imply that in *nous* itself there are higher and lower levels? It seemed easier to hold that soul is in principle distinct from *nous* and on an inferior level of being. Then again, the Plotinian soul comes from and rises to such exalted heights as to force the questions how and why it could ever have descended to occupy the body, and how it could make gravely mistaken moral decisions so as to sin. Iamblichus's critique of Plotinus on these points does not survive independently of Proclus's summary in his commentary on Plato's *Timaeus* (3.231.245, and especially 333f. Diehl) and a fragment of Iamblichus "On the Soul" preserved in Stobaeus

(1.365–66 Wachsmuth). Proclus warmly concurred with Iamblichus that it must be impossible to assert that "our soul" can be placed on an equality with the gods, identical in being *(homoousios)* with divine souls and on the same level with mind and indeed the One itself, leaving the lower world wholly behind it and by virtue of the union becoming "established." Plotinus's notion that at least the higher part of the human soul remains in the sphere of the noetic realm is impossible to reconcile with the sin and wretchedness of the human condition. It could even be questioned whether the human soul has inherent immortality.

In Plotinus's doctrine of the soul it was important for him to affirm an intimate original link between soul and *nous*. He had to say that *nous* is the sun but soul is the sunlight. Above all, this connection with the *nous* was not destroyed or lost when soul became embodied (IV 3.11–12). For as fire and air remain what they are without the mixture changing their natures, so also is the presence of soul to the body (IV 3.22), and hence Plato was correct in *Timaeus* (36d–e) when he put the body in the soul, not the soul in the body.

In the Platonic tradition there was a tenacious belief that the body is a drag and a hindrance. It penetrated the Wisdom of Solomon that "the perishable body weighs down the soul" (9:15). In *Phaedo* (65a, 66c) the body's unremitting need for food, the diseases which beset it, passions, desires, and fears, the body's love of money "which causes all wars," all add up to a major distraction from philosophical thinking. Plato anticipated the Neoplatonists here in writing of the need for the soul to "collect and bring itself together" from the separate parts of the body (67c).

Plotinus had no hesitation in labeling the body as an evil on the ground of its materiality, whereas the incorporeal soul is free of evil (I 8.4.1ff.). The temporal successiveness of bodily existence—"one thing after another"—created by our physical needs and external circumstances "drags the soul in all directions" (IV 4.17). In the *Republic* (10.603c–d) Plato observed that human beings can hold contradictory opinions at the same time, and that the strife is not merely between one person and another, but within the same person's mind.

Plotinus and the Neoplatonists did not doubt that in the soul or self there is a continuity which makes possible the act of remembering. At the same time, if asked whether this self is multiple or a single entity in a constant state, the answer would certainly have been that amid the distractions of this present physical life, with all the materialist suggestions coming to the soul from the body, the soul's experience is one of alarming multiplicity, and that coherence or unity is the goal to which the study of philosophy can help to guide. In *Phaedo* 78c Plato had based an argument for immortality on the axiom that the nature of the soul is to be a single entity, and that entities composed of a diversity of elements eventually disintegrate and come to destruction; they cannot then be eternal. The argument recurs in the tenth book of the *Republic* (609–610).

Plotinus's answer to the problems of multiplicity and radical diversity in the concerns of the soul is to declare that the soul needs to turn in on itself. Among the complexity of forces pulling the soul in different directions (IV 4.36.9), the soul which has descended from a higher realm rediscovers itself by a return. The self needs to get back to the dynamic source of its being and so to move from an inferior actuality to a higher potentiality. The "true self" is what at its best the soul aspires to be. And that means to return to what it once was, before the body beset and besieged it with distractions. It is, however, axiomatic for Plotinus that if the soul's prayer is answered, that is not a special intervention of universal providence but explicable on the principle of "cosmic sympathy." The soul should not ask for help or grace from higher realms. The calling is to rediscover the presence of the divine already present within the soul.

A century after Plotinus's time the pagan writer Eunapius commented that this philosopher was very hard to comprehend. The language of Plotinus is often sufficiently obscure to have a discouraging effect on would-be readers. It becomes more comprehensible when placed in its historical setting in the mid 3rd century. It should be added that gratitude to his clever biographer and editor Porphyry (who in the view of Eunapius had done much to bring light into dark places) is modified by his bizarre rearrangement of the order of Plotinus's discourses. He was capable of splitting up discourses, sometimes even in the middle of a sentence, and arranged the text into six groups of nine chapters each (hence the entirely non-Plotinian title *Enneads*). Porphyry lived in an age when it could readily be taken for granted that aesthetic or philosophical truth had ultimately a numerological basis. Six was a perfect number.[1] At least it is clear that Aristotle's sharp criticisms of Plato found in Plotinus an eloquent challenger. Aristotle's negative criticism of the Platonic doctrine of the soul began from the utter rejection of the notion that a higher element wholly independent of the body constitutes everything of significance about a human being.

In the 2nd century Aristotle's critique of Plato had been restated and gravely debated. Its force is apparent both in the strenuousness of Plotinus's answers and in those areas where he found it necessary to compromise with so acute a philosophic mind. Plotinus was committed to the defense and restatement of the Platonic system, and could not countenance the dangerous commonsense opinion that the definition of human being must include the body. For him the self is surely more than meets the eye when one contemplates a living man or woman.

Plotinus was able to concede that in an important sense an empirical description of a human being includes both body and soul, soul being the living vitality with powers of choice, deliberation, inward discomfort at the memory of wrong choices, and often awkward emotional experiences of fear, grief, desire, envy, and jealousy. But Plotinus demanded recognition of a higher self, an intellect or *nous* which is no physical thing at all, and is even to be distinguished from the psychological experiences of a human subject. The ordinary embodied soul has powers, some of which are exalted and admirable, others inferior. But all such powers are to be described as the soul's possessions rather than its being. It has them and uses them. Beyond and above them, however, lies something which is more than the skills acquired by a good liberal education. This is the true self.

Being sure that Plato was in essentials right and that if and when his words need correction one should not draw attention to that fact,[2] Plotinus affirmed that the soul has a heavenly and indeed divine origin, but has fallen to be incarcerated in the material body. Nevertheless something crucially important in its transcendent condition has survived, an "undescended" soul which shares in the eternity and immutability of the divine, very different from the time-conditioned existence of the composite empirical being that walks and talks, eats and sleeps, loves and hates, and is ravaged by despair and anguish as successive hopes are dashed.

This higher soul is untroubled by any tie to bodily life. In *Theaetetus* (176a–b) Plato had spoken of flight or escape from this earthly habitat, where we are troubled by pain and seduced by pleasure. Plotinus was surrounded by gnostics, even in his own lecture room, and was vehemently resistant to suggestions that this visible material order was the consequence of some super- or pre-cosmic smudge on the part of an incompetent creator. Some gnostics coupled incompetence with malevolence. His anger against gnostic estimates of the cosmos moved him to his most powerful and eloquent statement, in 2.9. The material body deserves to be properly cared for and not rubbished. The composite human being should regard it with a certain detachment. Plotinus uses the paradoxical analogy of an actor who plays his part but, in his view wisely, does not become totally engrossed with it and identified with his theatrical role (III 2.15–18). However, the body is to the soul a necessary and useful instrument—like a lyre. A good man knows himself to be other than his body and is at any time free to abandon it (I 4.16.17–29). The cultivation of detachment makes possible a gradual purification which is also an awakening of the soul to its true destiny.

Plotinus discusses but is never totally clear about the relationship between the soul that uses the body as tool and the higher soul which aspires to union with the universal soul, which is the third primary hypostasis of the entire cosmic order. What he is perfectly certain about is that mind is not a physical thing, and accounts of it which make it physical end curiously by leaving the mental processes out of the story. He was sure there is something mental about the mind.

The empirical composite human being continually experiences not only fear, desire, pain, grief, and envy but also the relentless sensations of change, destroying any sense of self-sufficiency. How seldom people find satisfaction when they obtain their desires. By contrast the higher soul is self-sufficient and "remains what it always is" (I 12.25). The higher soul and the inferior reflection of it tied to the body are related in the way that in Platonism the intelligible and sensible worlds are related. So the undescended soul is truer in its being. "Intellect transcends us"; everywhere it is one and the same, and each of us has the whole of it (I 1.8.3). Accordingly, the most exalted powers of the composite soul-and-body are a reflection or image of the higher ideal self, which is happily free of all the ills that flesh is heir to and sheds its light upon the lower soul (I 1.10.11). This ideal or true self is the god within, and to wake up to this degree of self-realization is to achieve some identity with the divine, even if the experience of mystical union is never, in this life, more than transient. The embodied soul is in a median position between body and mind *(nous)*, and its destiny is decided by whichever of the two it turns toward. Plotinus (and the Neoplatonic tradition generally) therefore thought of the body as a cause of differentiation and division, while the soul's potential for union with *nous* led to a restoration of unity.

A problem in Plotinus's language is apparent, namely that although he uses strong terms to distinguish soul from *nous*, the characteristics and functions of the two overlap. In part this difficulty interconnects with the wider question how far a concept of individuality can fit Platonic ideas or forms. The Neoplatonists speak as if all souls participate in one common soulness, and separateness or individuality is entirely a matter of body. Providentially (Nemesius and others say), faces are distinct to prevent confusion. But do all differences lie in accidents rather than substance?

Since Celsus in the late 2nd century Platonist critics of Christianity had particularly objected to the notion that after death the souls of the redeemed enjoy union with a resurrected body, a retention of individuality which contradicts any idea of the soul's being absorbed into a greater and amorphous whole or into some kind of Nirvana. The Neoplatonists found themselves divided by speculation about the individuality of souls hereafter. Damascius understood Numenius of Apamea (mid 2nd century) to hold that immortality and participation in the intelligible world extend from the rational soul to the animate body. A less than lucid paragraph in Plotinus (IV 7.14) concludes with the proposition that "nothing of reality perishes." It was widely held among the Neoplatonists that after death the soul possesses a "vehicle," which in the view of (e.g.) Syrianus must be more than temporary and therefore is everlasting. Porphyry himself ascribed immortality only to the rational soul, but denied that this entailed the destruction of the soul's vehicle and irrational functions. So runs the report of Damascius in his commentary on *Phaedo*. The Christians who discuss these problems feared Platonic language about the inherent immortality of the soul because it was inextricably associated with belief in reincarnation and that, in turn, with belief in the eternity of the cosmos, whereas they understood the creation and the end of the world to be unrepeatable, not part of a fatalistic cycle of repetition. On the other hand, Christians could find a sympathetic chord struck in Plotinus's doctrine (V 1.1.6f.) that the initial fall of souls was an act of audacious self-assertion, delighting in the exercise of independence.

Plotinus saw two routes by which the soul is enabled to ascend. The first is to contemplate the world accessible to the five bodily senses and to realize both its beauty and its impermanence. In this process the soul can discern a higher realm belonging to the world-soul, serene and untroubled. The second route is by an interior contemplation leading to the awareness that the higher, indeed eternal world is already present within the truest and deepest self. This process of interior contemplation is also one of moral purification because the body's concerns are being set aside. And this setting aside of the physical means great restraint in food and drink and other bodily pleasures, with complete abstinence from sexual activity.

Porphyry's *Life of Plotinus* depicts not only the sage's ascetic austerity but also his contact with the supernatural. During the six years of Porphyry's study with him, Plotinus had four experiences of ecstatic elevation to "a condition of good feeling," or joy, in union with the highest—admittedly transient, but for those moments liberated from passion and even from being a separate individual mind (VI 7.35.42–45), beyond time and space. The experience is like the melting down which separates gold from the dross (I 6.5.53). Plotinus's language here and in several other passages bequeathed a vocabulary for describing what later writers would call mystical union or beatific vision. Already in Plotinus it is called union with the One (also God), or vision. Following Plato's *Symposium,* he can use strongly erotic terms for his ecstatic experience. To touch the supreme good is a source of joy beyond the power of human words. This vision is on no account to be thought of as physical. God is everywhere because he is nowhere. In the *Enneads* the journey to this union ("not by carriage or ship," a phrase which captured Augustine's imagination) entails a gradual transformation of one's being and is achieved by stages, but ends in an ultimate bliss portrayed in the exalted imagery of earthly love; only there is no notion of the Absolute's reciprocating.

Plotinus was both a schoolman committed to expounding an authoritative Plato and also, like Aristotle, an investigator of difficulties *(aporiai)*. His solutions were not necessarily watertight and consistent, especially on such speculative issues as the relationship between the soul qua third hypostasis after the One, and *nous,* the world-soul mentioned in Plato, and the share that individual souls might have in either or both. Plotinus III 9.1, containing a disconnected series of notes, could easily leave a reader bewildered on the question whether or not the divine Creator is *nous* or soul.

There were other problems on which Platonists were divided among themselves, particularly the destiny of the human soul after this life. Would there be reincarnation and, if so, could it really be true, as Platonic dialogues suggested, that the rational soul could be reincarnated in animal bodies? or should Platonic language be glossed to have a demythologized sense, for instance that evil persons will be reincarnated as humans who behave like pigs or indeed other more fearsome creatures? In *City of God* (10.30) Augustine understood Porphyry to be decisively against the notion that the rational soul is capable of being reincarnated in irrational animals. Texts of Porphyry himself (e.g., on vegetarianism, *De abstinentia* 2.31f.) are hesitant. He either committed himself to no such denial or he simply contradicted himself.

Another debate was whether language about Hades and punishment hereafter should be taken literally or figuratively. Plato certainly regarded the myths of Hades as incorporating truth. The 2nd century Platonist Celsus mocked Christian talk of hell, but disowned the least intention to cast doubt on the judgment of the dead. Porphyry too was decisive for realism and literalism (e.g., *Sententiae* 29), hesitating only about the location of Hades. Porphyry held to the permanent return of the soul to its divine home (Augustine, *City of God* 10.30); Plotinus thought the highest part of the soul could not again fall. Iamblichus thought a fall was possible, but did not in fact occur. Damascius judged it impossible for a soul to remain forever either in the world of intellect or, unredeemed, in Tartarus, the destiny of the apparently incurable. For all in Hades there would be purification. Expounding *Phaedo* 114b–c, Damascius concluded that sinless and godly souls have tenuous spiritual bodies hereafter, the philosophic have luminous bodies at a higher level, while those purified return bodiless to the supramundane region.

By unremitting industry Porphyry was to become among the most influential of 3rd century writers. In the retrospect of the mid 6th century, Simplicius (*In cat.* p. 2.5 Kalbfleisch) called him "the person responsible for all our good things." He regarded himself as Plotinus's best pupil, not only author of Plotinus's *Life* and (three decades after Plotinus's death) editor of his discourses, but also a singularly clear-headed expositor of Aristotle's logical works. A Platonist who thought most of Aristotle to be correct, he became an influential advocate of the conciliatory opinion that, with one or two exceptions such as the reality of universals, Plato and Aristotle could be massaged to speak with a single voice on all essentials. His motives in presenting this last thesis were likely to have included the need to rebuff arguments from Skeptical or Christian sources that the disagreements among the warring philosophical schools of the past altogether discredited any claims they might have to provide reliable guidance. At one stage of his life he was considerably interested in Christianity but the diversities in the Bible persuaded him that allegorists such as Origen were unjustifiably embalming embarrassing texts with explanatory unction. On the eve of the Great Persecution of the church in 303 he composed a sharply negative critique of the Christian Bible. Among the numerous Christian authors mobilized to reply to him, Eusebius, the learned bishop of Palestinian Caesarea, was moved to give quotations of his works a fairly prominent place in his "Preparation of the Gospel," the main thesis of which was that he could find in pagan philosophers themselves witnesses to the truths of faith.

Porphyry did not consider Christians mistaken to think divine power had given holy books to help souls to salvation. Their error was to use the wrong inspired books. The oracles that for Porphyry truly revealed the divine way of salvation were either those of Apollo or the Chaldaean Oracles composed in the pagan interest late in the 2nd century. A special work on "The Philosophy To Be Derived from Oracles," written before he came under Plotinus's spell, developed the theme of the guidance these inspired texts can give for the soul's health and for the purification of the self.

Porphyry's concern to present Plotinus's teaching to a wide public led him to produce a little book of "Pointers toward the Intelligibles" *(Sententiae),* beginning with terse maxims on the superiority of mental concepts to physical facts but going on to include quite long statements of high spirituality and ethics. The argument is repetitive; Porphyry evidently did not expect his readers to grasp the inferiority of the material world unless he said it many times. The debt to Plotinus is very large. One paragraph (32) outlines the frugal ascetic way of self-purification on the path to union with the ground of our being: the irrational passions have to be suppressed, pleasure is to be forgone, with the proviso that it is allowable as a natural concomitant of wholly necessary acts.

Food and drink may be allowed to the extent necessary for good health, but sexual activity is unnecessary and disallowed (except that there is no responsibility in conscience for seminal emissions in sleep).

The *Life* of Plotinus portrays an elderly man practicing intense mental concentration and deliberate abstinence from meat and baths, and reducing hours of sleep by taking little food. In spirit he was already living in the divine realm, and was the recipient of special illumination and inspiration. His discourses came from the gods; he "loved the god with all his soul" (23). He had a firm belief that he was under the direction of a guardian *daimon* ("daemon," 10 and 22), and had inward power to frustrate the black magic deployed against him by a professional rival (10). When speaking, his face was radiant with light (13.5–7). He was endowed with second sight and could discern the hidden thoughts of those he met, enabling him to realize that Porphyry was on the verge of committing suicide (11).

The first sentence on Plotinus's sense of shame at being in a physical body is more than an observation about Plotinus's psychology or inhibitions about sex. For Porphyry it is a basic principle of a sound doctrine of the soul that "everything physical is to be fled from," *omne corpus fugiendum* in Augustine's lapidary version (*City of God* 10.29 and often). Augustine observes further that in Porphyry's eyes this basic principle of Platonic spirituality was the central ground on which Christian estimates of the body-soul relationship are to be rejected. Augustine himself was nevertheless clear that "we ascend to God not in body but by a likeness to him which is incorporeal" (9.18). Porphyry's personal belief surprised him by being so very close to his own. But Augustine found him—and was glad to find him—hopelessly inconsistent, juxtaposing beliefs that no doubt came to him by authority, as he understood it, but could not really be reconciled. Above all, his continual genuflections to the Chaldaean Oracles (10.32) and his defense of theurgy and the traditional rites of the old gods (e.g., *De abstinentia* 2.33–34) did not easily go with his affirmations that the way of ascent for the soul to union with *nous* is by philosophical reflection, not by theurgy, which he judged incapable of purifying the "intellectual soul" (*City of God* 10.27).

Despite the ascetic model of his hero Plotinus, in his sixties Porphyry married. His eye had fallen upon a well-to-do widow, Marcella, encumbered with children but a strong admirer of his considerable learning. A late and not very trustworthy text says that she was Jewish and came from Palestinian Caesarea. Soon after the wedding Porphyry was called away on a long journey "by the affairs of the Greeks," a phrase suggesting that he was consulted about the persecution of the church unleashed early in 303. He was extremely well informed about the Christian Bible, and the same untrustworthy text says that at one time he had been associated with the Christian church, which is not at all impossible. The biography of Plotinus can be read as a veiled attack on the history of Jesus in the gospels. His wife looked to him as her guide in "the way of salvation," and to assist her spiritual progress during his unhappy absence he wrote her a striking letter of considerable length which survives in a single manuscript at Milan. His advice took the form of a chain of religious and moral aphorisms, some Epicurean, but the majority Neopythagorean, these latter also attested in other collections. One of these Pythagorean maxims runs, "The real ego is not this tangible person accessible to the senses, but that which is furthest removed from the body, without color and shape, untouchable by hands, capable of being grasped only by the mind *(dianoia)*." Marcella's true teacher is within herself, and by concentrating on inward purity she will find Porphyry himself close to her day and night as in continence she gathers her disintegrated and distracted self. She should reckon that every good act has God for its author; evil acts we do ourselves and God is not responsible.

The Pythagorean aphorisms contained warnings that "it is impossible for one person to love both God and bodily pleasure or money" (14). Marcella should be reserved, not uttering even the truth about God to people corrupted by mere opinion. Indeed to be giving honor to God the sage does not need to break silence. God is pleased by works of devotion, not by sacrifices and participation in cults, whose worshipers may be very evil people. Nevertheless "the greatest fruit of piety is to honor God in accordance with ancestral customs," at the same time remembering that "God's temple is the mind within you," and that the four essentials are faith, truth, love, and hope (24). The quartet of virtues echoes the Chaldaean Oracles, on which Porphyry wrote a lost commentary.

The aphorisms which Porphyry found congenial for his wife's edification were also highly estimated by a Christian who about the end of the 2nd century made an adaptation of the collection for use in the church. The "Sentences of Sextus" became immensely popular among Christians, as Origen in 248 expressly testified, and the Latin translation by Rufinus of Aquileia enjoyed a large circulation. The collection was a Christianizing of an originally Neopythagorean text. Sextus wanted a believer (his word to replace "sage") to realize the noble dignity to which he or she is called. In the hierarchy of the cosmos the believer is next to God. Only by this realization can the Delphic command "Know thyself" be fulfilled. The mind within is the mirror of God, and so the soul is to be "ever with God." Bodily appetites may be satisfied only to the extent necessary to maintain health, which is the meaning of Jesus's saying that one should render to the world the things of the world, while the soul renders to God the things that are God's. But the body is the door of temptation. A man and his wife should compete to see which of them can most suppress the sexual impulse. Castration would be better than sexual incontinence. Meat-eating is allowable, but vegetarianism is more congruous with the higher life. Private property is incompatible with the ideal of universal brotherhood in the one family of God. Love of money is a snare; the desire to possess was never yet quenched by acquisition. Indispensable to the good life is almsgiving to the destitute and to orphans. The dignity of the true self depends on the practicalities of the moral life.

Porphyry's letter to Marcella is so close in spirit to the kind of Christian spirituality found in Clement of Alexandria and later ascetic texts that it is no wonder to find later pagan Neoplatonists regarding his writings with mixed feelings. In correspondence with Iamblichus he put a series of awkward questions about polytheistic ritual. Following a lead given by the Chaldaean

Oracles, Iamblichus and others in the Neoplatonic tradition fused Plotinus's highly philosophical path, bringing the self to realize God within the mind, with a zealous justification of the rites for the old gods, under the name of theurgy. The term *theourgia* is ambivalent in meaning, signifying both human rites to persuade (or according to the Chaldaean Oracles to compel) the gods, and also the willing cooperation of the gods in bringing about certain effects. Insofar as the rites are understood to compel divine powers, theurgy is hard to distinguish from magic—white in polytheistic eyes, black in the view of monotheists. Theurgy depended for its credibility on the general ancient belief that between the various constituent parts of the cosmos there is a hidden sympathy. The argument could be used by a disbeliever in astrology to explain why the forecasts of some horoscopes turn out to be correct (Augustine, *Confessions* 4.3.5).

Porphyry's defense of theurgy was embarrassed. Iamblichus, who settled at Apamea in Syria, had no hesitations or blushes. Iamblichus's defense of theurgy coheres with his generally more pessimistic estimate of the capacities of the human soul as compared with Plotinus's and Porphyry's. Whereas his predecessors wrote as if the soul possessed innate powers to rise to union with *nous* or even the One, Iamblichus took a more somber view, and therefore thought fragile souls needed propping up with old cultic rites.

In the *Republic* (10.600b) Plato had written of the Pythagorean life as a known frugal lifestyle. Iamblichus wrote an impressive, repetitive work on this way of living, insisting on Pythagorean respect for the traditional rites in the temples, with the correct white vestments and the right images. "The fruit of piety is faith in the gods" (148). With this goes an austere way of life which reads as conscious rivalry to incipient Christian monasticism. Requirements are little food or sleep, no meat or wine, contempt for money or fame, control of the opposing powers within the body (69, 229), chastisements to check self-indulgence and greed, and property held in community (168, 257). There are Pythagorean hermits in the desert (253). The rule on sex is that a woman who has slept with her husband can go to temples the same day, but never if she has slept with someone else (55, 132). A procreative intention is also indispensable (210). It is presupposed that the majority of adherents to the old religion are women (54–56). The goal is purification of *nous* and soul together (68–70). In the 2nd century Lucian observed that Pythagoreans were generally regarded as superhuman (*Vit.Auct.* 2).

The notion that formulas and rites and amulets could compel the gods seemed very difficult to Porphyry in his questions to Iamblichus. Nevertheless he could concede that theurgy could bring some degree of purification to the soul, even if it could not actually achieve a return to God. Augustine (*City of God* 10.9) thought Porphyry wavered between superstition and philosophy, granting with embarrassment that a kind of magic, though without influence on the *nous* of intelligible realities, does something for the inferior soul, putting it into a prepared state for angelic and divine visions; but he goes on to say that the spirit powers influenced by these rites are inferior daemons inhabiting the lower air. Even Porphyry thought it strange that the rites of the gods needed herbs or stones, special forms of words and gestures, and celestial observations of the configurations of the stars. Iamblichus, who was certainly much impressed by the Egyptian hermetic tradition, seemed to Porphyry to have gone altogether too Egyptian.

To Iamblichus, on the other hand, Porphyry was capable of expounding Platonic dialogues in a sense which was neither Platonic nor true and manifested barbarian arrogance—this last phrase, Emperor Julian's and Iamblichus's label for Christianity, suggests that he regarded Porphyry as influenced by Christian notions and terminology.[3] His skeptical questions were playing the Christians' game for them (*De mysteriis* 10.2). There are also places where Iamblichus judged Porphyry's doctrine of the soul to be unrealistically exalted and his doctrine of inferior deities and daemons too pessimistic and perhaps akin to gnosticism. Proclus's commentary on *Timaeus* frequently records Iamblichus's criticisms of Porphyry, some of which reflect the judgment that Porphyry was too detached toward religious practice. For pagans like Eunapius, Iamblichus was supreme as a holy man, able to work miracles to call up spirits from the vasty deep, credited with powers of levitation (which he modestly disowned). Marinus's funerary panegyric on Proclus (d. 485) is no less rich in anecdotes of his hero's powers as a thaumaturge. Damascius once marked a clear line between the philosophers Plotinus and Porphyry and the "hieratics," Iamblichus and Proclus.

No Neoplatonist was so prolific in writing as Proclus, who, after studying in Alexandria, became head of the richly endowed academy in Athens. His commentaries on Plato's *Timaeus*, *Republic*, *Cratylus*, and *First Alcibiades* contain major restatements of the general Neoplatonic theses. In his large but unfinished six-book "Platonic Theology" he especially set out the theological exegesis of the *Parmenides*.

Proclus's commentary on the *First Alcibiades* (edited by L. G. Westerink, 1954; English trans. by William O'Neill, 1965) expounds the dialogue as a proper introduction to all Platonic dialogues and indeed to philosophy generally. He presupposes that in between Plato and Plotinus philosophers did not get many things right. The exchanges between Socrates and Alcibiades are treated as an elaborate allegory of the role of higher reason in moderating and healing the soul of an amiable but highly undisciplined person of considerable influence. Plato's dialogue meditates on the Delphic command "Know thyself." The primary task of philosophy is to make such self-knowledge possible. Throughout the commentary Proclus's discussion revolves around the question, What is the true self? On the one hand the mind's experience is marked by multiplicity, pulled in many diverse and contradictory directions and finding concentration hopelessly problematic as attention is captured by irrational pleasures and bodily appetites (245f.). Time for reflection on philosophy needs to be set free from the tugs of many loves (44f.—a phrase strikingly reminiscent of Augustine in the garden at Milan, *Confessions* 8.11.26). The soul, as in Plato and Plotinus, is in a middle position between mind and body (116, 226). The body exerts a downward pressure on the soul and would bring the soul to "the region of dissimilarity" (Plato, *Politicus* 273d, cited by Plotinus I 8.13.15f. and Augustine, *Confessions* 7.10.16).

Nevertheless, the soul's choices, which determine who we are, are freely made (144) and capable of being trained into good habits (224f.). The soul is self-moved. Irrational decisions result from the emotions, rooted in the world of matter (233), responsible for the incoherence and disconnectedness of experience (57), tearing us apart like the Titans (104). Each human individual has a restraining guardian daemon, one of a semi-divine order of spirits in six ranks watching over the souls as they descend and ascend (71ff.), but this daemon is not to be identified with the rational soul (73).

Proclus rejects both those who think the soul part of the physical organism and those who claim that soul is part of divine being (226). The ascending soul has the capacity to be united with higher intellect or *nous*. Therefore the physical body is no more than the instrument being used by the soul (73), and only a strong dualism of soul and body can underpin the belief that it is never right to pursue private advantage at the expense of what is just (294, 315), or can justify the courageous confidence that death is no evil (332).

The soul's upward ascent begins from a freely chosen decision to contemplate itself (17). It is axiomatic that while the first mover or *nous* is unmoved and physical entities are moved by external pressures, the soul in its intermediate existence is self-moved and so has the power to revert to itself. Soul is incorporeal and in principle independent of the body. The key to ascent is the power of self-consciousness. When the self authentically knows itself, it also sees the divine (20) and enters into a relationship of love (51).

The priestly rituals or theurgy of the traditional gods are means of elevating the soul to the level of and to union with *nous*. For Proclus, Iamblichus was right about theurgy. Its power is greater than all human knowledge attained by philosophical thinking (*Theol. Plat.* 1.25), able not only to thrill the ascending soul but also to be a means of divination. Cosmic sympathy pervading the realm of nature explains how what appears as (white) magic can assist the soul to be one with the highest. Syrianus of Alexandria and Proclus his pupil appear to have retained usage of the term "theurgy" for a transcendent mental experience in which, on the far side of the rituals of the old gods, the mind is carried up to an ecstatic knowledge of God.[4] Iamblichus in *On the Mysteries* had written of divine epiphanies and visions granted through theurgy (2.9, 3.6).

Proclus was saddened by the negative attitudes of the "atheists," i.e. the Christians, who in his time had become a majority. They denied the very existence of the gods. Yet they said things marked by moderation and even divine inspiration (*In Alcib.* 264). This last concession is remarkable when one considers in Proclus's writings a number of veiled allusions to the Christians indicating ice-cold hatred for them. In his eyes they were a cultural and intellectual Black Death. But then the Christians made no secret of their belief that whatever merits there were in Neoplatonic religious philosophy (which might be deemed considerable), theurgy with the old rites was black rather than white magic, an invocation of spirits which, as one could see in the pages of Porphyry, were essentially inferior and malevolent, longing for their nostrils to be titillated by the blood and smoke of animal sacrifices, and needing to be placated if they were not to make life unpleasant.

Iamblichus's criticism of Porphyry's doctrine of the soul centered on the vulnerable notion that the true self is always constant and unchanging by virtue of its participation in the higher realm of divine entities. This, however, bequeathed a problem for his successors: If the soul is mutable and changeable, in what sense can it be said to remain the same throughout its existence? Can the soul undergo substantial changes and still retain its identity? The issue troubled Damascius, the last head of the Platonic Academy at Athens. During his tenure Justinian discontinued its large endowments, in part perhaps because of its militantly anti-Christian stance (529), in part because, after an undistinguished period of mediocre successors to Proclus after his death in 485, the Athenian school began to enjoy a dangerous revival led by Damascius and Simplicius. The closing of the school did not bring Neoplatonist teaching to an end. Damascius and Simplicius temporarily traveled to the Persian court, but soon found it better to return to the eastern Roman empire (exactly where is not known) and to continue working much more privately.

Damascius judged it necessary to grant that the soul can undergo considerable changes in its moral and spiritual life. Soul is not to be thought of as serene and secure, always gifted with divine illumination. For soul is not an order of being that remains ever attentive to the will of the gods without a touch of neglect or satiety. Soul is capable of going down a long way into the inferior realm of matter and the flux of "becoming," of the passions and inferior daemons. In a somber estimate of the depravity to which soul is vulnerable, Damascius can say that the very being of the soul is altered when matter and the daemonic spirits get a hold. And yet identity remains because free choice makes soul responsible for its actions. Damascius felt harassed by Justinian's Christianity. Nevertheless his estimate of human nature was remarkably close to the kind of language found in Augustine of Hippo or in some passages of Cyril of Alexandria.

The Platonic account of the relationship between soul and body and the dominance of Platonism generally among educated people of both east and west in late antiquity created problems for the Christians. They were committed to belief that the human body was made by the supreme Creator and, whatever problems it might cause, must be good. At the same time the Christians were also disinclined to think that the soul or *psyche* in its natural state, at least since Adam's Fall, was readily capable of knowing its Maker as it should. The natural order needed elevation by divine grace. The apostle Paul spoke of *psyche* as being on a lower level than spirit or *pneuma* (1 Cor. 2:14). *Psyche* is the natural order of creation but flawed by human sinfulness; *pneuma* is the point at which humanity can touch the divine. And in 1 Cor. 15:44 the *psyche* can rise to the level of *pneuma* in the life to come. To remain at the level of natural creation is not necessarily a permanent condition.

Third century Alexandria produced in Origen a commentator and theologian who was highly competent in his grasp of the classical Greek philosophers. There are Stoic and Epicurean doctrines which first become intelligible when his discussions of them are considered. He knew his Plato intimately. He built on foundations already outlined by two predecessors, Philo and Clement. Philo understood the two accounts of creation in Genesis 1 and 2 to signify that the first and primary creation was spiritual, the second earthly and bodily. So there is an inferior soul giving vitality to the body, as to animals or plants, and a higher soul which is divine and has pride of place in the divine plan. (Paul in 1 Cor. 15:46 opposes the interpretations that the spiritual creation preceded the physical.) In Philo, as mind ascends to God it comes to see the body to be an evil, presumably by comparison (*Leg. Alleg.* 3.71). The fall of souls began when they became sated with the divine goodness (*Heres* 240) so that they neglected to love God. Some souls fell further than others (*Gig.* 12). To know oneself is to realize one's weakness and dependence on God (*Spec. Leg.* 1.263ff. and 293). God gives the soul illumination and grace, drawing souls up toward Being (*Plant.* 21). No ascent is possible without divine aid (*Migr.* 170f.). A real self-knowledge is self-despair (*Somn.* 1.60), a realization of the nothingness of created thoughts in comparison with the transcendent uncreated mind (*Congr. erud.* 107). But deep self-knowledge is impossible for the individual soul (*Leg. Alleg.* 1.91). Because mind has the capacity to know something of God it is necessarily incorporeal (*Somn.* 1.30f.). But all things human, including the soul, are unstable and mutable (*Somn.* 1.192).

Most of these themes recur in Origen, who particularly took over the idea of degrees or levels of soul both in descent and in possible ascent. The notion that souls fell in consequence of satiety he found congenial. That souls fell varying distances from heaven helped to explain the diversity of humanity. Though all human beings have mind, soul, and body, the quality of each individual differs (*Or.* 24.2). The human soul, being in God's image, possessing powers of reasoning, memory, imagination, and reception of impressions from the five senses, differs in kind from the soul or life principle in animals (*C.Cels.* 4.83). Therefore it cannot be true that all souls have the same "form" *(eidos)*, a universal soulness in which all living things and angels share.

Origen thought it would be very difficult to maintain the goodness of divine providence unless free choices lay at the ultimate root of evil in the cosmos. The widely differing lot of human beings, where some live on fertile land in a kind climate while others do not, could be explained as the consequence of mistakes and sins in an existence prior to incorporation in this body of flesh (*Prin.* 2.9.3–6). Leviticus 17:14 (which says the soul or life principle is blood) ensured that Philo and Origen both knew of materialist conceptions of the soul, reinforced by Stoicism.

In the second book of his commentary on the Song of Songs, Origen gives a list of questions concerning the soul: Is it corporeal or incorporeal? composite or simple? created or uncreated? transmitted to the embryo with the physical sperm or independently from some external power? If the latter, is the soul given to the body *ad hunc* or *ad hanc* at the moment of conception? Or is it already in a divine storehouse ready to be supplied to a body when needed? Can it be reincarnated? Are all rational souls of the same *ousia* (being)? Do angels and human beings, both endowed with free will, share the same kind of soul? Or is promotion to angelic status a gift of divine grace transcending the created and natural order? Can a soul which has once acquired a state of virtue lose it?

(Parallels to this list in *C.Cels.* 4.30 and in Seneca, *Ep.* 88.34, suggest that there was a standard list of questions in philosophical schools.) In Origen's commentary on St. John there is a catalog of problems about reincarnation (6.14).

Origen's main polemical target in almost all his work was the predestinarianism of the 2nd century (and later) gnostic sects. They appealed to biblical texts, such as Paul in Romans 9:16–21 or Exodus 4:21 on God hardening Pharaoh's heart, and held that the saved and the lost are determined from the beginning, so that free human choices play no part in the path to either heaven or hell. Both Clement of Alexandria and Origen declared against these views, and this argument on behalf of freedom became a dominant theme for both writers. The third book of Origen's *De principiis* presented the case for free choice and against the view that external impressions received through the body's senses can overwhelm individual judgment. A chaste celibate confronted by a beautiful woman in undress inviting him to bed may find it impossible not to be stirred, but he still retains a rational power of decision enabling refusal both possible and responsible. Human beings are not automata, deterred from acts only by some external cause or consideration. In practice, moreover, education and discipline can change even the most uncontrolled and uncivilized people so that, after conversion, they surpass in gentleness the most courteous folk. Contrariwise, entirely respectable individuals in middle life can suddenly kick over the traces to live disordered and immoral lives. Their behavior reflects their personal decisions. Such unpredictable changes constitute for Origen strong evidence for human responsibility and undetermined choice. And this choice is not simply a physical reflex. The decision is made by the mind, not by the body.

Platonic influence is evident in the conviction, common to both Origen and the pagan opponent of Christianity, Celsus, that God, being incorporeal, can be known only by the mind. Mind is no mere epiphenomenon of matter (*Prin.* 1.1.7), a notion which is assumed by simple people who imagine God to possess physical characteristics—an old man with a long beard. The mind, being made in God's image (or, as the Platonists would say, having a kinship with God), is so constituted as to look toward the divine. Admittedly mind is hindered and rendered dull by contact with the body: "sea sickness makes the mind less vigorous" (*Prin.* 1.1.5). Nevertheless the ability of the brain to cope with arguments of extreme subtlety and to remember words and events of the past surely points to incorporeality.

Like pagan Platonists, Origen thought the soul midway between flesh and spirit, capable of ascending to be united with and even transformed into spirit (e.g., Commentary on Romans 1:5, or on John 32:18). It also has the capacity to be united with soggy materiality. Nevertheless, like Plotinus, Origen held that every soul has a guardian, a *paidagogos,* which is commonly called the conscience. This is an inner judgment, combining awareness of an action done or a word spoken with a sensation of pain at the memory, but also in certain cases vindicating the act or the word when others are critical. The martyr was called to be true to his integrity. Origen was skeptical of the notion that conscience is a separate and substantial organ (Commentary on Romans 2:9).

Everyone who goes against his conscience "kindles his own fire" (*Prin.* 2.10.4). "Outer darkness" is a condition of the soul, not a place (2.10.8). A "longing for reality" is implanted in us (11.4), and paradise will be a school in which holy people will learn the answer to many questions which baffle them in this life (11.5).

The majority of Origen's writings consisted of biblical exposition, either in the form of homilies preached to congregations in Caesarea (Palestine), whither he moved after difficulties with the bishop of Alexandria, or full-scale commentaries, all of which were too voluminous to survive intact. Scribes become exhausted. His understanding of human nature is therefore distributed over a wide area. But in the early work *On First Principles* and the late reply to the pagan Platonist Celsus a consistent picture emerges. He was passionately committed to defending the goodness of God manifest in providential care and the freedom of the rational being (angelic or human). "Take away freedom from moral virtue and you destroy its essence." Divine care is unendingly patient, and has a perspective far longer than "the fifty years or so of this life." Against the gnostic estimate of the total earthliness and irredeemability of lost humanity, Origen asserts that "a totally depraved being could not be censured, only pitied as a poor unfortunate" (*In Ev.Joh.* 20.28.254). The entire process of human existence is a gradual education, and the miseries of human life are part of that operation, to prevent our being too comfortable and forgetting about higher things. Therefore Origen regarded as gnostic the idea that any fallen being endowed with rationality and freedom is beyond redemption, even including Satan. Like a wise tiller of the land, God is not in a hurry, and what seems difficult or impossible will simply require longer time. "Love never fails," wrote the apostle, and Origen thought it a fundamental principle, even if the retention of freedom as a permanent endowment of all rational beings must carry the corollary that they may choose to fall once again.

Augustine's critical comment was that Origen's concept of human destiny was "endless real misery punctuated by short periods of illusory happiness" (*City of God* 12.20). At a time of religious crisis while residing in Milan, Augustine was given by an anti-Christian pagan "books of the Platonists" in Latin translation (almost certainly pieces of Plotinus and Porphyry). Plotinus's account of providence and evil convinced him. Neoplatonism brought to him the doctrine of the body as instrument of the soul, as taught in the Platonic *Alcibiades*. At the same time Bishop Ambrose of Milan was preaching eloquent sermons, of which he admired the oratory but went on to be impressed by the content. Ambrose found congenial matter in Plotinus and Porphyry and had a command of Greek greater than Augustine had acquired. Ambrose's discourse on the life of the patriarch Isaac was both Christian and Neoplatonic. The philosophical dialogues written by Augustine at Cassiciacum during the months between his conversion and baptism are also indebted to Porphyry and Plotinus, not least in the express conviction that the true self is the soul, to which the body is a distraction and at best secondary.

It remained Augustine's conviction that "our bodies are not what we are"

(*Vera relig.* 89). The doctrine that the body is the instrument of the soul occurs a few times, but principally with the emphasis that when we do wrong the fault lies not in the body but in the soul which uses it. Augustine liked triads, and for describing the fragility of goodness especially cited 1 John 2:16, "the lust of the flesh, the lust of the eyes, the pride of life." The primal sin of the soul is pride, which impels the soul to play at being God (*Mor.* 1.12.20). The early writings of Augustine restate the notion, found in Philo and Origen, that humanity in Adam was originally created spiritual—that is, with a tenuous body of light such as the spirits in heaven possess—but this state was lost at the Fall. More mature texts affirm the positive qualities of the body as intended by the divine Creator. Sexual differentiation is in the body, not in the soul. Augustine insists that in mind and soul male and female are equal in the human race. The biological function of women as childbearers gives them a private and domestic role which has to be socially secondary to that of their husbands. Augustine knew of strong-minded women who wholly dominated their husbands (*Gen. c. Manich.* 2.29.). On the other hand more than one text speaks of women as possessing far deeper feelings about sexual partnership than many men are capable of achieving, and the tendency to have superficial and brief affairs is described as "a common male disease" (*Adult.conjug.* 1.6). Against exegetes of 1 Cor. 11:5–7 (such as Ambrosiaster), Augustine devoted some part of his argument in *De Trinitate* (12.7.9f.) to opposing the notion that women are not in the image of God as men are. His doctrine that the image of God is entirely in the mind made that conclusion natural and inevitable.

Controversy with the Manichees (with whom he had been associated for a decade) ensured that Augustine affirmed the positive value and beauty of the human body, and was not inclined to think it a merely accidental or secondary element in the constitution of the human person. In oblique criticism of his elder contemporary Jerome he wrote a work of protest against the disparagement of marriage and its physicality. The early Augustine could echo Porphyry's advice that for the higher life "one must escape from the body." The mature Augustine could readily say that in the limitations of this present physical life there are hindrances, "ignorance and difficulty," where the latter term tends to mean the emotion of desire. But like Origen he did not believe that even a powerful sexual impulse was irresistible. That the human body was recalcitrant was evident, especially in the fact that the sexual impulse is not rational. But the fallen state of humanity is one of both body and soul together, not simply of body. And in sexuality the body manifests its fallenness by wanting sexual pleasure when the mind knows it cannot be, or in not wanting it when the rational mind knows that it would be appropriate (*Nupt. et Concup.* 1.6.7) and would have the procreative intention which was deemed essential by ancient moralists, both pagan and Christian. It was never Augustine's intention that posterity should associate sin and sex. In the *Literal Commentary on Genesis* (10.13.23) he wrote scathingly of some who talk "as if the only sins are acts performed with the genital organs."

A problem that much occupied Augustine's anxious attention, and on which he decided not to make up his mind, was how the soul and the body came to be joined together. Porphyry had written a small treatise for a friend named Gaurus on this issue; but for Christian thinkers the matter had special interest and importance because it had a bearing on human responsibility. The Platonist view was that the soul preexists the body, and from a storehouse somewhere a soul comes to animate the embryo. Among Christians Origen not only held to the preexistence of souls but even thought divine providence would be very hard to defend without this doctrine. His critics however associated preexistence with reincarnation, and cordially disliked the fatalistic treadmill which went with this view. Many texts of Augustine, especially in the *Confessions,* use language that comes close to the notion of preexistence of souls, but the associations of the idea prevented him from giving assent. That left two remaining alternatives: traducianism, or the doctrine that the soul is transmitted from the parents with the seed and egg, a view which carried the implication that the soul has material qualities; and creationism, or the doctrine that the soul is created by the omnipotent Creator in response to the conception of the physical embryo. For Stoics traducianism explained why children frequently resemble their parents not only in physical appearance but in character. In his *De Anima* Tertullian provided an eloquent statement of a Christian doctrine of heredity, which for him explained the "fault in origin" *(vitium originis)* that Augustine would name original sin. Augustine conceded that traducianism made it easier to account for the church's practice of baptizing infants, which carried the implication of a stain to be washed away by the sacrament. On the other hand, traducianism sounded very Manichee to orthodox ears, and therefore there emerged a preference for the creationist view, even though it seemed to involve the Creator, or some angel delegated to take care of the matter, in unending fuss, including the provision of newly minted souls for embryos conceived in immoral circumstances. The last point was easily answerable with the consideration that the bastardy of such children in no way added to the personal responsibility that they would come to carry.

Of the three possible hypotheses the doctrine of preexistence carried the most pessimistic implications for human nature, traducianism being less somber. Creationism obviously asserted a clean start for the infant soul, and therefore made "original sin" a more social than individual thing, the child being sinful by becoming a member of the group which manifests egocentricity on a scale far beyond that of individuals.

Augustine's determined agnosticism about the bonding of soul and body showed that he regarded it as a secondary or insoluble question. What was certain to him about the self was the "inward war" that goes on within the individual person. The observation was as old as Plato (*Laws* 626d). Poor wretches, people sin in hope that it will help them out of a difficulty, and then find the situation far worse (*City of God* 14.4). Sin or wrongdoing is ultimately rooted in treating ends as means and means as ends (*Against Faustus* 22.78; again a Platonic echo, *Republic* 443d). The perversity of the heart is visible in the delight taken in performing an act which is known to be forbidden, and if that act is being done by a group of which one is a member, it can seem irresistible. (Hence the adolescent theft of bad pears described in *Confessions* 2.)

So the soul is beset by self-made problems, not merely human transience in a life which is "a race toward death," not merely the ignorance of the right and the good, but an actual resistance to what is right and the will of God when this is known. "Human beings are ambitious for nothing so much as power" (*On St. John* 43.1). Their lust for venting anger is sometimes directed at blameless inanimate objects (*City of God* 14.15). Above all, the fetters of habit bind the soul so that what begins as a free choice becomes necessity (*Confessions* 8, 5, 10). Humanity, social by nature, becomes anti-social by corruption (*City of God* 12.28).

Yet God has mercy and gives grace. The late works of Augustine say that this is given to God's elect. Earlier Augustine can write of a universal intuition in the human heart, brought from potential to actual by God's love and presence within. The innermost self is indistinguishable from this divine presence, "deeply hidden yet most intimately there within" (*Confessions* 1.4.4). So to love God is also to love oneself. "Love is within the mind, and therefore God is nearer than my brother" (*Trin.* 8.8.12).

In his work on the Trinity Augustine expressed reservations about the terminology for the Trinity, traditional in Latin theology since Tertullian—namely three persons, one *substantia*. But the thesis in that work that the persons of the Trinity are relations suggested to him that the term "person" could convey the meaning of a human self defined by relations, and in letter 137.11 this becomes explicit. The Latin word did not previously carry this meaning for the individual constituted of body and soul together. The context was one of mysterious and incomprehensible depth. A frequent theme in Augustine's writings is the unfathomable depth of the human mind, knowing what it does not know it knows, remembering joys and griefs of the past, so that the memory can be described as "the stomach of the mind" (*Confessions* 10.13.20) but never capable of authentic self-understanding. "I do not know what kind of man I am—how much less do you know" (*Sermon* 340A 8). A fundamental mark of the human mind is restlessness, and the overriding theme of the *Confessions* is the incompleteness of humanity, which can find its true self and true rest only in God.

Although the Christians of late antiquity found themselves in much sympathy with the language of the Platonists, the generalization holds good that in the long run they were to take a more positive view of the physical realm of nature, and of the human body in particular. This is evident already in Nemesius of Emesa, *On the Nature of Man*, in which the debt to Porphyry is at least equaled by that to Aristotle. For the upholders of a dualism of soul and body, there was, perhaps is, always an issue in the background: human responsibility. An entirely materialist view of the mind or soul has acute difficulties in maintaining that a human being is actually a moral agent with capacities for deliberation and argument on grounds of reasoning, capable of changes of mind. Birds need feathers to fly. Human beings need brain cells to produce the most baffling of things in consciousness. But in consciousness there are aspirations beyond the material world.

Notes

1. In the 5th century Neoplatonist Proclus, the number nine can carry a heavy weight of symbolism, e.g. in his commentary on *Timaeus* 3.193.17ff., where "ennead" signifies the creator gods. Porphyry was well known to have detected nine distinct hypotheses in the text of Plato's *Parmenides* (Proclus, *Theol.Plato.* 1.10). In Proclus's commentary on *Timaeus* 35b (2.215.20), reporting Iamblichus's views, it is said that "the Ennead has an affinity to the Monad."

2. Augustine (*City of God* 10.30) once allows himself a sentence of gentle mockery at the Neoplatonic reverence for Plato as a sacred text.

3. Julian *Ep.* 89a Bidez-Cumont; Iamblichus on *Timaeus* 47b–d in Proclus, *In Tim.* 153.10 (= frg.16 Dillon with his commentary, p. 282).

4. See Anne Sheppard, "Proclus' Attitude to Theurgy," in *Classical Quarterly* 32 (1982): 212–224.

RELIGIOUS COMMUNITIES

Garth Fowden

In November or December of the year 408, when Alaric was besieging Rome and its inhabitants were on the brink of cannibalism, certain Etruscan diviners found their way into the city and reported how, by their rituals, they had recently repelled the Goths from the town of Narnia. Pompeianus, the prefect of the city and probably himself a polytheist, sought Bishop Innocent I's leave for the Etruscans to conjure the gods on Rome's behalf. In the words of the historian Zosimus, also a follower of the old religion, Innocent agreed to "put the salvation of the city before his own belief, and authorized them to perform their rites in secret."[1] The Etruscans answered that the traditional rituals must be performed openly and at public expense.[2] The Senate must go as a body to the Capitol, and invoke the gods there and in the marketplaces, if their prayer was to be heard. But nobody dared turn the clock that far back, and the city fathers resorted once more to bargaining with Alaric.

Not all Christians shared Innocent's flexibility—or perhaps they had not found themselves in so tight a corner. In 391 Bishop Theophilus of Alexandria, supported by the imperial authorities, had attacked and destroyed the great temple of Sarapis in the Egyptian metropolis.[3] Sarapis was responsible for the annual flooding of the Nile; and when the flood was delayed, some polytheists angrily demanded they be allowed to sacrifice to their god. The governor appealed to the emperor; and Theodosius I refused, adding that he would sooner the river stopped flowing altogether. We also read that at this time Christians went around chipping off the reliefs of Sarapis that adorned lintels and other parts of private houses throughout the city, and painting crosses in their place. On the one hand we have the worshipers of the old gods, who believed that on their cults depended Egypt's prosperity and indeed the world's, so that all stood to be penalized for the Christians' impiety. On the other hand we have the new Israelites whose dwellings, as in the days of Moses, the vengeful Lord would surely pass over, if only they marked their lintels and doorposts with the appropriate sign.

In both these sets of events we see articulated under duress an ancient sense of community which before Constantine's conversion had rarely needed to make itself explicit. We can sense its presence, though, in certain gravestones of ordinary foreigners buried at Rome that identify them simply by their village or town of origin.[4] The polytheist envisaged his native place as a unique whole defined by geography, climate, history, and the local economy, as well as by the gods who particularly frequented it, ensured its prosperity, and might even assume its name. No part of this identity, a delicate interweaving of divine, natural, and human which was often itself worshiped as a Tychē or Fortuna, could be subtracted or neglected without impairing the harmony and viability of the whole. In times of danger one addressed the gods with a single voice, often according to formulas revealed by an oracle to a representative deputation of leading citizens. Travel abroad might, admittedly, acquaint the member of such a community with exotic gods; yet honor paid them was attended by no sense of abandoning one religious and therefore social system for another. The vocabulary might change, but not the grammar; and even those who sought to explain the distinctive characteristics of particular peoples in terms of the influence of ethnarch-gods saw no religious incompatibility, since all mankind was subject to the king of the gods.[5]

Christians, by contrast, might add to their gravestones a statement of belief, such as a roughly carved cross, which attached them to a universal community of faith while separating them from compatriots who were not Christians.[6] Before the 3rd century this idea of a *religious* community, founded on self-consciously distinctive beliefs about the divine world and what those beliefs implied for conduct of individual and communal life, would have made sense only to certain philosophers, to Jews and those who sympathized with Judaism without having fully accepted it, and to Christians. The members of such a community accepted a more or less defined and internally coherent, and to some extent even written—that is, scriptural—system of belief and practice, and tended to exist in a reactive, mutually defining relationship with other such (theoretically) closed systems, that is, other religious communities. Such coexistence further implied the possibility of abandoning the community of one's birth for another—in other words, the possibility of conversion. Acceptance across broad sections of society of this previously rare type of self-consciousness was among the distinguishing characteristics of the late antique world.[7]

The unselfconsciousness of traditional religion in the Roman empire—what we call "paganism" or "polytheism"—is manifest especially in its lack of a distinctive name for itself. *Thrēskeia, eusebeia,* and *nomos; hieros, hosios,* and *hagios; religio* and *pietas; sacer* and *sanctus:* all these words lack the specific historical reference contained in such terms as "Jew" or "Christian."[8] Relations with the gods were conducted not according to the commandments of a scripture and an orthodoxy derived from it, but on the basis of traditional behavior—an orthopraxy—reinforced by the ad hoc pronouncements of oracles or sometimes of sages, men like the 1st century Pythagorean Apollonius of Tyana or Emperor Julian, or the 5th century Platonist Proclus, who had studied the writings of ancient authorities and especially the poets, such as Homer and Hesiod.[9] Even to begin to form a mental picture of this vast, complex world of traditional polytheism, one needed exceptional resources and opportunities. Emperor Caracalla (211–217), for example, probably had a better grasp of the range of religious life in his day than almost anyone else alive, since he spent most of his time traveling or campaigning, and was so troubled in both mind and body that he made a point of visiting the principal oracular and healing shrines wherever he went.[10] It was Caracalla's mother, Julia Domna, who commissioned from Philostratus a biography of Apollonius of Tyana; but although the semi-fictional account Philostratus wrote takes its protagonist to holy places from Cadiz to the Ganges, it offers nothing to hold together the many gods and rituals Apollonius encountered except the philosopher's own curiosity and piety.

In cities there was a greater variety of cultic activity concentrated in one place, and therefore a higher level of self-consciousness, than in the village. Yet distinctions between groups of worshipers, and even between associations that adopted the name of one god or another, tended to reflect personal choice and ethnic or occupational categories rather than any notion that preference for one god over another might imply a special way of life.[11] Many worshipers of Mithras were officials or soldiers; Jupiter Dolichenus, too, appealed to those with an army background. At Leptis Magna in Tripolitania, the temple of Sarapis was frequented—to judge from its totally Greek epigraphy—mainly by merchants and others from the east.[12] The cult association of the Iobacchi at Athens duly observed the festivals of Dionysus, and even on occasion assembled to hear a "theological" discourse in his honor; but the vivid inscription of ca. 175, which is our best source, exudes the clubbishness of those who need to remind themselves they have arrived.[13] Some divinities, like Isis, do seem to have been exceptionally widely esteemed, but their status was manifested more by association with other gods than by distinction from them, hence the tendency of Isis to adopt as epithets the names of numerous other goddesses (polyonymy).[14] If, in the 4th century, certain prominent polytheists liked to point out that it is natural for humans to pursue truth by many different ways, this observation was provoked not by tensions among rival groups of coreligionists but by the threat from Christianity, which denied the very existence of the traditional gods.[15] Judaism had struck polytheists as assimilable, because its austere monotheism did not, on the whole, seek to impose itself on non-Jews by proselytism.[16] It could, if necessary, be treated as one more ethnic cult.[17] But Christianity addressed itself to all mankind; and by the time of the Severans (193–235), the tendency toward dissolution of the traditional sense of local community that was likely to result from this may have been already apparent.

In either 212 or 213 Emperor Caracalla issued what has come to be known as the *Constitutio Antoniniana,* extending Roman citizenship to almost all his subjects with no distinction on grounds of faith. According to the fragmentary text preserved in a papyrus now at Giessen, Caracalla proclaimed that his motive for taking such a momentous step toward the integration of the empire was a wish to honor the gods and fill their sanctuaries with grateful worshipers.[18] The social model implicit here strongly resembles the traditional Roman civic one, with the whole community expected to come to the gods to give thanks and ensure continued favor: the Etruscan diviners were still demanding the same thing two centuries later. If Caracalla applied this traditional model to the whole empire rather than just the city, he was hardly innovating—official cults of emperors and of Rome had long sought to reinforce such broader loyalties. But Caracalla was perhaps also aware of a growing absenteeism from the temples at the local level, and he may have connected this with the spread of Christianity. Certainly the *Constitutio* sought to reinforce the dwindling Roman sense of community that acknowledged differences of race and much else among the empire's peoples and gods alike, but saw no need for an idea as implicitly divisive as that of rendering God's to God and Caesar's to Caesar, since there could be no way of telling these two spheres apart. Nonetheless, the challenge presented by Christianity had, a century and a half later, become an oppressive everyday reality. Emperor Julian's response was blunt in the extreme: if the citizens of Pessinus wished to enjoy his favor, they should supplicate the Mother of the Gods forthwith, in a single body, *pandēmei*. Otherwise, he might even take measures against them (*Ep.* 84.431d–432a).

Only in the philosophical milieu—of which Julian was a representative—did the polytheist world offer something that resembled the religious communities fostered by scriptural religions. Philosophy was often set down in texts which were carefully preserved and expounded, albeit not normally regarded as above criticism. And to adopt the philosophical life involved a choice—a conversion—which implied a rejection of alternatives and an introduction of distinctions and divisions into the prevailing model of society. Philosophers were perfectly aware of this, and divided about its possible consequences. Stoics insisted that the sage should continue to participate in the civic cults;[19] but the followers of Epicurus, who treated their founder and his literary legacy with unusual reverence, and formed closed circles defined solely in terms of belief, were regarded by outsiders with the suspicion the polytheist world reserved for private or surreptitious religion.[20] The conviction of the rabbis and philosophers, that study makes holy, was nonetheless destined for a long and influential life. In the ecumenical perspective characteristic of learned late polytheists, Porphyry of Tyre (234–ca. 301–305) drew particular attention to the habits of the Egyptian priesthood. Quoting one of its members, Chaeremon, Porphyry underlined how it had formed a caste apart (*De abstinentia* 4.6–8). Its members had lived in highly regulated communities, and had deplored the impiety of those who traveled outside Egypt and exposed themselves to alien ways. They had also been dedicated to science and the knowledge of the gods. Having discovered in their past this religious and almost scriptural community as a model, groups such as the later Platonists, and the Egyptian coteries that composed treatises under the name of Hermes Trismegistus, could adopt what they imagined to have been its conventions in their own lives and discourse. Perhaps this model even served, alongside the example offered by the church, as an impulse for the reforms to the priesthood proposed by the last polytheist emperors, Maximinus Daia and the philosopher Julian.[21]

Not surprisingly, it was under an Egyptian priestly pseudonym, Abammon, that Porphyry's pupil the Syrian Platonist Iamblichus of Apamea (d. ca. 320–325) sat down to write the only surviving account of ancient polytheism as a closed, coherent system. The title *De mysteriis Aegyptiorum*, by which Iamblichus's *Abammonis responsio ad epistolam Porphyri* is now generally known, is an inappropriate Renaissance invention, since Egyptian doctrines are touched on only summarily and toward the end, while the primary subject matter is the whole range of polytheists' experience of the divine. This experience Iamblichus sees as compounded of both thought and action, theology and theurgy. By welding together a sophisticated Platonism and the wide spectrum of traditional cult, including sacrifice, divination, and oracles, Iamblichus aroused opposition among polytheists as well as Christians. And the perfected "theurgists" who had mastered the whole of this sacred science, from healing and rainmaking to the vision of the demiurgic God, were bound to be a tiny elite, deploying skills easily misrepresented.[22] Yet unprejudiced study of the *Abammonis responsio* reveals an understanding of the divine and human worlds as a coherent, interlinked hierarchy (4.2.184; 5.22); while the need for a clear exposition of this vision is underlined by veiled yet hardly ambiguous reference to the propaganda of the "atheist" Christians (3.31.179–180; 10.2). That Iamblichus saw fit to compile this *summa* of polytheist belief and cult implies that he thought there could be a polytheist or, as he put it, theurgical community with an acquired consciousness of distinct identity as well as, of course, an appreciation of the variety of religious practice that was bound to occur within a genuine community with all its necessary range of human types. "One must make available this [material, corporeal] manner of worship to cities and peoples that have not been liberated from participation in generation and from close communion with bodies; otherwise one will fail to obtain either immaterial or material goods. For the former one will (anyway) not be able to receive, while as regards the latter one will not be offering that which is appropriate . . . That which comes to one man with great effort and after a long time, at the culmination of the hieratic art, we should not declare to be common to all men, nor make it immediately the shared possession of novices in theurgy or even of those who are already half-initiated; for these people give a somewhat corporeal character to the practice of piety" (5.15.219–220, 20.228). And along with consciousness of distinct identity, such a community would also acquire a capacity for self-explanation and self-defense. The *Abammonis responsio* is itself, as its correct title makes plain, a polemical work, written to counter certain objections to theurgy raised by none other than Porphyry.

Clearly Iamblichus believed that this theurgical community would be stronger and more likely to survive than if polytheists just went on pretending there was nothing new in their environment, and ignoring the need to articulate themselves. Iamblichus's admirer Julian pushed this idea further when he became emperor, and tried to endow his tradition with some of the features that had contributed to the church's success: a hierarchically organized and well-instructed priestly class, regular liturgy and preaching, an accessible religious literature, and philanthropic ideals and institutions.[23] And Julian too was aware of the need for a name. Iamblichus had called the approach to the gods that underlay the whole tradition "theurgy," studiously preserving polytheism's avoidance of specific historical reference in the vocabulary it used to talk about itself, and implying a refusal to fight on an equal footing with Jews and Christians. Julian abandoned this high ground. By calling worshipers of the gods "Hellenes" and Christians "Galileans," he acknowledged that both sides were at least in the same arena, even if the Christians were an upstart provincial minority.[24] But both Iamblichus's and Julian's solutions were problematic, in that they might too easily be applied to a part rather than the whole. Just as theurgists—the accomplished masters of the tradition, that is—could be seen as a tiny elite, and even encouraged the idea,[25] so too Hellenism was not necessarily what every polytheist wanted to identify with.[26] Polytheism simply did not have a founder, revelation, or scripture of sufficient stature to generate a name that could be applied to the whole tradition—proof, if one is needed, that in the end this was a more than usually "imagined" tradition.

There are modern parallels, in Indonesia for example, to this reactive type of identity imparted by monotheistic and scriptural religions to the adherents of older ways.[27] In order to survive as communities, such traditions necessarily adjust, even at the cost of imposing on themselves a spurious homogeneity and watering down that instinctive understanding of divinity that comes through dwelling together with the gods in a certain place, a precise local knowledge that no distant prophet would or could ever make into a scripture. Survive, though, these local traditions do, and did in late antiquity as well. Seen from one perspective, late antiquity is primarily of interest for its "formation of Christendom"; but it also generated another model, the empire of communities—against authority's better judgment in the Roman sphere, with the connivance of authority in the Sassanian world, and as a matter of policy in the Islamic caliphate. And alongside or in succession to these empires there were also commonwealths, built in part on political but primarily on cultural—that is, religious—foundations.

Increasingly, polytheism survived as a mere remnant, though quite widespread in certain regions, or underground as crypto-polytheism, which might allow small local groups to develop a sharply focused religion-based sense of community in the face of adversity but was not a viable basis for regional structures.[28] Only in the minds of a few intellectuals like Iamblichus or Julian did polytheism as a whole, at all social levels, come to be seen as a religious community. And even intellectuals were in practice more likely to experience the community as a diachronic succession, perhaps involving very few people at any given moment, rather than as a substantial, autonomous social organism. The *Lives of the Philosophers and Sophists* by the rhetor Eunapius of Sardis (ca. 345–ca. 414) is a good example of this approach from the end of the 4th century, and introduces the phenomenon of group biography, which not only bulks large in our evidence for religious communities at this period, but also itself helped define them. The production by both Nicaean Christians and their opponents of a number of such compilations from about the time of Theodosius I onward underlines the success of this emperor and his heirs in confirming Rome's adoption of Christianity, in particular its Nicaean version, as the official religion of the state.

Christianity had, of course, been a religious community long before it became the state religion. In the Acts of the Apostles and the Epistles, its adherents are most frequently referred to without explicit mention of their distinctive faith in Jesus Christ. They are "saints" or "brothers" or "disciples," who follow a "way"; but in Acts we also read how "for a whole year [Barnabus and Paul] met with the Church and taught great numbers of people; and the disciples were first called Christians at Antioch" (11:26). This pregnant passage implies much of what we need to know about Christianity as a religious community.

Especially at this early stage, leaders—here Barnabus and Paul—were the *sine qua non*, since only through their teaching did the congregation, "great numbers of people" consisting entirely of converts, exist at all. Just as Acts is centered on the missionary work of the apostles, so Eusebius's *Ecclesiastical History*, the next most important account of the church's early progress, is built around the "apostolic succession" of bishops who led the major sees and, by fair means or foul, constantly consolidated and widened their territory.[29] On this hierarchy were focused the church's necessary institutions. Its self-organization presupposed a place of assembly, the *ekklēsia*. Here were accommodated all the community's gatherings, especially the liturgy. And during the 4th and 5th centuries there evolved also a distinctive type of Christian art, or rather, a Christianization of late antique art, so that churches came to be adorned with images which, even when they seemed to preserve an earlier idiom, conveyed an unmistakably Christian message for those with eyes to see. In or near the church was a place for administering the sacrament of baptism, without which there was no true membership in the communion of the saints, or hope of salvation. As time went by, provision was also made for the poor and the sick. Indeed, Luke's very next verses (Acts 11:27–30) describe an act of charity, and toward fellow believers not at Antioch but in Palestine, for each *ekklēsia* was but the local manifestation of a wider and potentially universal communion.

We are reminded by the fact that Barnabus and Paul tarried at Antioch "a whole year" how time as well as space was encompassed by the Christian revelation and the community it generated. The revelation itself had of necessity been made within historical time, by God become man. The foundation documents of the faith were therefore, at one level, historical narratives. Then the succession of bishops, generation by generation, reinforced the possibility not only of perpetuating the teaching of the apostles, but also of creating a Christian chronology. On the profoundest level, sanctification of time was effected by the liturgy; by the development, especially during the 4th century, of a daily cycle of offices; and by an ever evolving calendar of festivals.[30] These commemorated the events of Christ's life, his sacrifice upon the Cross—a Pascha calculated never to coincide with its Jewish predecessor[31]—and his closest imitators the martyrs, over whose relics the Eucharist was celebrated in a powerful image of community and continuity.[32] Simultaneously the participant might see reflected the heavenly liturgy, and glimpse the angels gathered around God's throne in eternal praise.[33] The cycle of liturgy, offices, and festivals also offered a means of instruction, which Acts says was the apostles' chief concern at Antioch. In conjunction with homilies and catechisms and reading, the act of worship inculcated knowledge of the Scriptures and of the theology derived from them; and without its Scriptures, Christianity would at an early date have lost direction and been absorbed back into the synagogue. From the Scriptures, the community drew the narrative, belief, and discipline, even the very language that was at the heart of its identity.[34] All that was needed to confirm and proclaim that identity was a name.

Jesus had said he would be present even "where two or three are gathered together"; but it was on the whole felt that size and variety were positive factors in helping a community surmount the obstacles it was bound to encounter. Communities built of only one sort of person—virgins, for instance—were no more than sects, whereas the ship of Christ's church is made of many different woods.[35] Families, though they offered an effective medium for the dissemination of the gospel,[36] might easily be corrupted by heresy if the bishop did not exercise constant supervision.[37] As for numbers, Bishop Cornelius of Rome observed of the heretic Novatian that "this vindicator of the Gospel did not know that there should be one bishop in a catholic church, in which he was not ignorant—for how could he be?—that there are forty-six presbyters, seven deacons, seven subdeacons, forty-two acolytes, fifty-two exorcists, readers and doorkeepers, and above one thousand five hundred widows and persons in distress, all of whom are supported by the grace and loving kindness of the bishop. But not even did this great crowd, so necessary in the Church, and through God's providence abundant in number and multiplying, nor an immense and countless laity, turn him from such a desperate failure and recall him to the Church."[38] Nonetheless, there was an optimum number for even the most energetic bishop's flock. And who would shepherd the bishops themselves? There was no avoiding this issue once Constantine resolved to make the whole empire Christian.

In certain of Constantine's pronouncements preserved by Bishop Eusebius of Caesarea, as well as in Eusebius's own works, it is possible to discern an ideal image of a Christian Roman empire treated as a single religious community.[39] Under one God reigned one emperor, who called himself "bishop of those outside [the Church]"; while the "bishops of those within" were regarded as providing absolute Christian authority, under Christ, each in his own community of course, but a fortiori when deliberating collectively in regional councils or, at Nicaea, in a council designed to represent all Christendom, including the church in Iran.[40] The function of such gatherings was to provide guidance under the authority of Scripture and the Holy Spirit. And they excluded those who felt unable to communicate together in the same sacraments. Acceptance of scriptural and episcopal authority, and participation in the sacraments, defined the Christian community both during the proceedings of the council—a rare, paradigmatic, even, as described by Eusebius, ideal event—and also whenever or wherever else Christians gathered together. But still there was room for interpretation and therefore disagreement. Who would have the final word? Before Constantine, Christian congregations enforced their decisions by excluding those who did not comply. Under Constantine, the church succumbed to the temptation to repress its deviants, and with fatal logic made the emperor God's active representative on earth. With this move, the theoretical preconditions for the conversion of Rome into a single homogeneous religious community had been met.

If the Constantinian model had a decidedly vertical, exclusivist, and repressive aspect to it, reality organized itself, as usual, somewhat more horizontally—or better, perhaps, segmentally. Eunapius's work reveals painful awareness of the Constantinian model and simultaneously demonstrates its failure to eradicate dissent. From the 320s onward, polytheist philosophers were under constant suspicion, especially if their theurgical and in particular divinatory rituals were felt to be inspired by curiosity about the prospects of those in authority; but for Eunapius's readers these men and women were also proof of historical continuity and a living reinforcement, by example, of their doctrine. That such readers existed is guaranteed by the production of later works such as Marinus's biography of Proclus (d. 485) or Damascius's of Isidore (d. before 526), whose length and digressiveness, apparent even in its present fragmentary state, made of it, in effect, another group biography; it seems also to have been called a *Philosophical History*. In these works a polytheist intellectual community comes to life, and thanks to them this community dominates our view of late Greek philosophy and even late Greek religion. It is an urban community dominated by scholars and founded on study of philosophical texts and on the right worship of the gods wherever and whenever possible. From a strictly sociohistorical point of view, it seems apter to describe these groups as circles rather than as a community; yet Eunapius's concentration on them to the exclusion of most of the rest of society (whose fortunes he treated in a separate work, the *History)*, his skillful foregrounding of Julian, the only polytheist emperor after Constantine, and his emphasis on the groups' historical continuity as part of a "succession" *(diadochē)* create the comforting illusion of community amid a world of rapid and alienating change.

In the study of late polytheism, illusionism is far from being the prerogative only of late antique writers. A romantic and of course very political school of thought used to hold that ancient polytheism—that of the temples rather than the schools—"survived" under a decent yet not suffocating veiling of Christianity.[41] In the extreme case of crypto-polytheism one might indeed literally turn around an icon of Christ and find Apollo painted on the back.[42] But what more usually happened was that late polytheism went on evolving, often—as in the case of Iamblichus and Julian—under the direct or indirect influence of Christianity, but also itself influencing the practices of ordinary Christians, so that in the resultant local fusions there was much, on both sides, that was passed to posterity, although impure and thoroughly alloyed. In the year 348, for example, according to an Arian historiographer, "a mighty earthquake hit Beirut in Phoenicia, and the larger part of the town collapsed, with the result that a crowd of pagans came into the church and professed Christianity just like us. But some of them then introduced innovations and left, stripping off as it were the conventions of the Church. Dedicating a place of prayer, they there received the crowd, and in all things imitated the Church, resembling us just as closely as the sect of the Samaritans does the Jews, but living like pagans."[43]

And then there was Augustine of Hippo, trying hard to dissuade his flock from holding a drunken festival in honor of one of their martyrs in the very church itself. He even tried to explain to them the historical background to their situation: "When peace was made after many violent persecutions, crowds of pagans were anxious to come over to the Christian name but were hindered by the fact that they were accustomed to spend their feast days with their idols in drunkenness and excessive banqueting, and could not easily abstain from those baneful but long-established pleasures. So our predecessors thought it good to make concessions for the time being to those weaker brethren, and to let them celebrate in honor of the holy martyrs other feast days, in place of those they were giving up, unlike them, at any rate, in profanation, though like them in excess. Now that they were bound together by the name of Christ and submissive to the yoke of his great authority, they must inherit the wholesome rules of sobriety, and these they could not oppose because of their veneration and fear for him whose rules they were. It was now high time, therefore, for such as had not the courage to deny that they were Christians, to begin to live according to the will of Christ, casting behind them, now that they were Christians, the concessions made to induce them to become Christians" (*Ep.* 29, trans. J. H. Baxter).

In these situations, the church was unlikely ever to purge itself thoroughly of the old ways the converts brought; while the theological or, rather, pastoral principle of "economy" that Augustine alludes to in this passage might at times be unashamedly abused, as when Archbishop Theophilus of Alexandria consecrated Synesius bishop of Ptolemais even though, as a philosopher, he refused to entertain the idea that all matter will pass away, and had reservations about the resurrection as conventionally understood.[44] But it was no doubt sincerely believed that the old ways, of the philosophers and the illiterate alike, would not remain entirely untouched by the powerful liturgical and iconographical context in which they were now embedded, and that the new theology would seep, however slowly and anecdotally, into the subconscious of those unruly congregations.

Christians at the beginning had been forced to define themselves by reaction to a polytheist world. In the Christian world of late antiquity polytheists were in a similar position. Some even found the experience stimulating. Adjustments and accommodations were made by both sides. Even so, the influence of the different Christian communities on each other was naturally far more insidious:

at the end of the letter just quoted, Augustine remarks how, even as he spoke to his own flock, "we could hear in the basilica of the [Donatist] heretics how they were celebrating their usual feastings" (*Ep.* 29.11). Opponents and supporters of Nicaea experienced the same proximity. In the eastern empire from 337 until the accession of Theodosius I in 379 (except under Julian and Jovian), opponents of Nicaea carried at any given moment considerable and at times overwhelming weight, and from 354 to 360 in the western empire too. Under Julian, Arians acquitted themselves with distinction, gaining many martyrs. Probably under Theodosius I, when the Arian ascendancy was threatened, these martyrs' *acta* were gathered together into an Arian martyrology, another group biography designed to set a good example, this time to Arian congregations called on to resist Nicaean persecution. Eventually, the triumphant Nicaean church was to adopt these soldiers of Christ as its own, drawing a discreet veil over their Christological shortcomings.[45] Try as the church might to apply legal exclusions to heretics, their communities were interwoven with those of the Nicaean Christians, while their culture was often too closely related to that of the "orthodox" to be distinguishable.

In order to solve precisely this problem of how Christians, or at least their pastors, might tell sound from unsound doctrine, the church generated a variant form of group biography, the catalogue of heresies. Irenaeus and Hippolytus were early exponents of this genre, which was closely related to the combination of philosophical biography and doxography we find in Diogenes Laertius's *Lives and Opinions of Eminent Philosophers*. But the most impressive collection of heresies is to be found in the "medicine chest," the *Panarion*, that Bishop Epiphanius of Salamis was busy stocking up between ca. 375 and ca. 378. Among the more extensive compendia of "research" to have survived from antiquity, the *Panarion* contains historical and biographical information about the heresiarchs and their followers, and summaries and refutations of their teaching. Such works were used for reference and as sources of proof texts during the deliberations of church councils, which proceeded according to the same principle that animated the heresiologists, namely that Christian doctrine was best defined in brief, pregnant statements such as the Nicaean creed or the *De fide* appended to the *Panarion*, and elaborated only when it became necessary to exclude some specific error. As a principle on which to found a universal religious community, this avoidance of the temptation to spell out every last detail, especially in the sphere of the individual's personal knowledge of God, had much to commend it. It compensated somewhat for Christianity's insistence on adherence to credal formulations, however summary, instead of the general gratitude and reverence that Caracalla had thought sufficient for the maintenance of the polytheist empire.

The career of Epiphanius of Salamis illustrates the way that monks were among the most zealous drawers of boundaries (especially against polytheism) and upholders of what they saw as doctrinal rectitude. In the monastic sphere we find in the late 4th and 5th centuries a tremendous interest in the use of group biography in order to define and propagate a communal way of life. The anonymous *History of the Monks in Egypt* (ca. 400) and Palladius's *Lausiac*

History (ca. 419–420) are travelogues and recollections of personal encounters that did much to crystallize the image of the ascetic way of life. The various collections of sayings of the desert fathers, the *Apophthegmata patrum* that were compiled in the later 5th century, tend to a more doxographical or gnomological approach, but still abound in anecdotal biography. They are of special interest because they appear to preserve either the prevalent inside view of the anachoretic community that developed at Nitria, Kellia, and especially Scetis, or at least the views of persons who considered themselves the community's direct heirs.[46]

A wide and flexible range of relationships prevailed among the anchorites in the *Apophthegmata,* who could nevertheless be portrayed as members of a community in the loose sense. The *Lives* of Pachomius, whose writers' anecdotal style suggests an origin in materials similar to the *Apophthegmata,* depict a far more formal, structured style of living together, the cenobitic monastery under the governance of an abbot.[47] In the sense that Pachomius's life (and *Life*) was itself as good as a rule, his monasteries were founded on individual example; but the monk's personal relationship with God was worked out in a strictly corporate context which encouraged members of the community to participate in each other's practical spiritual development. Theological speculation was of little concern in these circles—it might too easily lead to schism, as in the wider church. Instead, Pachomius offered his followers a light. He once told them of a dream in which he had seen brothers wandering lost in a vast, gloomy, pillared hall—apparently one of the temples of the old Egyptian gods. From all sides they could hear voices crying: "See, the light is here!" But it was impossible to work out where the voices were coming from, and eventually they began to despair. Then they beheld a lamp advancing in the dark, and a crowd of men following it. The brothers followed, each holding onto the shoulder of the one in front. Those who let go were lost in the shadows, and all those behind them. But as many as followed steadfastly were able to ascend through a doorway toward the light (*Vita prima S. Pachomii* 102).

The charming simplicity of this vision would have bemused Athanasius. Not that Pachomius was ineffective in the environment he created: the monks became in turn the shock troops of Nicaea. But neither Nicaea's triumph under Theodosius I nor Arianism's retreat to the Germanic successor states in the west (where it was just what was needed to reinforce Gothic identity against the siren song of *romanitas*) prevented the Christological debates that rekindled in the 5th century from bringing about a situation in which the Constantinian paradigm could be imposed only on a much reduced Balkan and Anatolian empire, while the eastern provinces went their own way. The "solution" proposed at the fourth ecumenical council at Chalcedon in 451 was to split the empire into irrevocably hostile communities, and fracture even the monastic world.

From the moment Justin I (518–527) became emperor, it was evident that Constantinople would no longer compromise with Chalcedon's opponents, the

Miaphysites, who emphasized the one incarnate nature of the Word, but only in extreme cases doubted the Savior's consubstantiality with man—against the fourth ecumenical council's insistence on two natures inseparably united (an apparent Dyophysitism that could all too easily be denounced as Nestorianism).[48] Until the 520s, pro- and anti-Chalcedonian factions commonly coexisted, without open rupture, within the same see; but once Justinian was enthroned, the council's opponents took the steps needed to create their own episcopal hierarchy, in order to guarantee ordination of priests to celebrate sacraments free of Chalcedonian pollution. The wide-ranging missionary activities of figures such as Jacob Baradaeus and Simeon of Beth-Arsham simultaneously propagated the anti-Chalcedonian position and maintained contact between far-flung communities; while the frequently repressive response of the Chalcedonian hierarchy and the imperial authorities focused and strengthened allegiances at the local level, which often crystallized around anti-Chalcedonian monastic communities.[49] John of Ephesus, in his *Lives of the Eastern Saints* (ca. 566–588), provided an attractive and inspiring group biography, at least for the Syriac-speaking world. The anti-Chalcedonian churches of Egypt, Syria, and Armenia were aware, despite often bitter disputes among themselves, of a shared faith, and of the desirability of apparent unity. Constantine and Nicaea were their slogans, and they continued to pray for the emperor in Constantinople and for his illumination, because their Roman identity remained strong. Although in the immediate present they were a persecuted and outlawed community, they believed in the restoration of a single Roman Christian church, even if this hope sometimes took on an eschatological tinge.[50] It became increasingly apparent that the Roman empire had entered a phase of semi-permanent credal segmentation. It had become an empire of two main communities, both of them Christian.

But what of Christians outside the empire? Rome's self-identification with the church had created a situation in which Christians beyond the frontiers might be implicated in the empire's political aspirations. For this reason, Christians in Iran were eventually prepared to identify themselves with theological positions that Rome labeled Nestorian, so as to underline their separate identity for the benefit of their Sassanian rulers. And once Rome's own eastern provinces began to dissociate themselves from the imperial church, it was natural for anti-Chalcedonian views to take root in Iranian territory too.[51] Syria-Mesopotamia was geographically a continuum, and the political boundary that ran through it had little cultural significance. In the contested sphere between the two empires, a string of sometimes more, sometimes less independent Christian polities—Armenia, the Ghassanid Arabs, Himyar, Aksum, and Nubia—saw advantage in the emergence of a powerful anti-Chalcedonian community free from Constantinople's supervision. In the vast area between the Taurus and the Arabian Sea, the Zagros and the Mediterranean, there emerged a commonwealth of peoples held together by the distinctive form of Christianity they shared, and by their hankering after a Constantinian paradigm occluded but by no means invalidated by the Christological strife since Nicaea. The force of this Constantinian and Nicaean ideal was such that the commonwealth was clearly east Roman in its orientation, just as its theological culture was essentially Greek. Yet only beyond the Roman frontier, in the polities that perched uneasily between Rome and Iran, or in the Iranian empire itself, could Chalcedon's opponents breathe freely. The Sassanians recognized both them and the majority Nestorian church as official religious communities, with a status inferior to that of official Mazdaism, but comparable to that of the Jewish community.

Sassanian monarchs might marry Christians or Jews, and even display personal interest in the teachings of these religions, but none of them ever converted. They were too dependent on an aristocracy and a priesthood, the magi, at once hereditary and strongly Iranian. Mazdaism itself was very much a religion of Iranians, and was highly conservative, doing without a written version of its scripture, the *Avesta,* until perhaps as late as the 6th century, and preserving markedly polytheist elements even longer.[52] But the magi knew a threat to their social and political position when they saw one. Right at the beginning of the Sassanian period, the Mesopotamian prophet Mani (216–276) had challenged them on their own territory. Manichaeism was a dynamic, polyglot, scriptural dualism of thoroughly universalist aspiration, deeply indebted to both Christianity and Mazdaism.[53] Had it captured the Iranian empire—Shapur I (239/240[241/242?]–270/272) apparently showed some interest—it would surely have become as involved in the exercise of power as the Christian church under Constantine and his heirs.[54] But the magi counterattacked, Mani died in prison, and his followers concentrated their energies on the missions Mani himself had set in motion, so that small Manichaean communities were soon scattered across the Mediterranean world as far as the Atlantic, as well as eastward into Central Asia. But within the Roman and Sassanian empires, the Manichaeans were always feared and repressed. Only to the east of the Sassanian realms did they manage to take firmer root.

As an original religious teacher who wrote his own scriptures rather than leaving the job to disciples, created a structured community, launched organized missions, and thought seriously about the possibility of converting the rulers of this world, Mani was rightly feared. He reminds us more of Muhammad than of Christ. Likewise, it is the Sassanian rather than the Roman empire that presents the clearer precedent for the political arrangements adumbrated in the Qur'ān. Something should be said of Iran's Christians, and of the Jews in both empires, in their own right and in the perspective of Islam.

The Jewish communities in the Roman and Iranian empires were led—sometimes nominally, at other times very actively—by hereditary officials of allegedly Davidic lineage called respectively patriarch and exilarch.[55] But although the imperial authorities appreciated the advantage of having a single Jewish interlocutor, the line of patriarchs died out in 429, while the exilarchate went through difficult times under the later Sassanians. And anyway it was the rabbinical class that took the lead in organizing local communal institutions, encouraged the religious observances without which there could be no living sense of a community and its boundaries, and produced those two bodies of commentary on the Torah, namely the Mishnah and the Talmud, from which we derive most of our knowledge of late antique Judaism, and to which Judaism was thenceforth to look for a touchstone of communal identity. This rabbinical literature adopts a gnomological and occasionally anecdotal format that reminds one of the *Apophthegmata patrum*—though the subject matter is very different.[56] Once more we observe that characteristic phenomenon of late antiquity, the formation of a community identity by a class of people either learned or holy or both, acting in person, of course, but also making themselves known to much wider circles through gnomology and group biography.

This is not to say that these literary genres excluded the development of others more discursive in style, such as the vast mass of Christian patristic literature made up of treatises, commentaries, sermons, letters, and so forth. But the popularity of gnomological literature and anecdotal biography is especially significant, because it underlines the role of memorization and of a basic literacy, at least an oral literacy, at all social levels, acting to form a community around a written tradition, but also around individual exponents of that tradition—the sages. Judaism and Islam in particular, lacking the sacramental dimension of Christianity, were to become communities of students, religions built on texts in languages that were intrinsically sacred, all the more so for being incomprehensible even to many of those who learned by rote texts written in them, squatting long hours in childhood, maturity, and old age by the pillars of synagogue or mosque. At the heart of these communities, a pure world of signs was—and is—being performed rather than rationally reflected upon. But the performance, the recitation, reveals a different sort of rational triumph, that of the spirit-filled man of God over the brute urges which at all times threaten the community's integrity.[57]

Christianity, too, revered its sages, the apostles and the Fathers of the church. But until the 4th century, sanctity meant quite simply martyrdom, surrendering one's life for one's belief in Christ, as Christ himself had suffered for humanity's redemption. Study had no necessary part in the making of saints, while historical memory of their sacrifice was maintained as much through the liturgy as through hagiography. But as the church adapted to the world, its literature came to reflect a more complex relationship. Accordingly, Sassanian Christianity is accessible to us today mainly through two literary genres which are both eloquent about the formation of community.[58] The so-called *Acts of the Persian Martyrs* circulated widely west of the frontier as well, and were an important medium through which Roman Christians became aware of their cousins in Iran.[59] Most of the martyrs gained their crowns during the four decades of persecution that ended with Shapur II's death in 379, and their deaths were presumably caused by the Magians' wish to forestall any repercussions of the Constantinian revolution east of the Euphrates. In this they were successful, and the Christian community was ever thereafter careful to underline its loyalism, although its favoring of Antiochene (Nestorian) Christology may have been a reaction to the spread of Miaphysitism in Iranian territory, as well as an attempt to mark its distance from the empire of east Rome.

The other main literary—or at least written—legacy of Sassanian Christianity is contained in the proceedings of its ecclesiastical synods. Like the Torah and its successive layers of interpretation, the canon law formulated at these synods came to cover all civil matters—marriage, property, and inheritance—and not just church business narrowly defined. And like the Jewish exilarch, the *katholikos* or patriarch of the east at Seleucia was made responsible not only for the administration of justice to his fellow religionists (and thus also for their good behavior), but also for the collection of taxes. In effect, the church became a state agency. In this way the community both tightened its own bonds and acquired a secular, administrative identity recognizable to those who had no knowledge of Christian doctrine. That doctrine, meanwhile, as well as being spread through the liturgy, was disseminated within the community through a network of schools that reached down to the village level and taught the Antiochene theology of Theodore of Mopsuestia rendered into Syriac and made accessible to the uneducated through hymns. The monasteries were another major factor in the formation of a Nestorian identity, for the monks were vigorous teachers and proselytizers, and acutely aware of the difference between themselves and the Miaphysites, from whom they distinguished themselves even in their costume and tonsure.

Naturally enough, the community boundaries so sedulously built up and maintained by religious elites were constantly being eroded by the everyday reality of intercourse between ordinary people, especially in commercial contexts. Nonetheless, the compact nature of the Jewish and Christian communities of the Sassanian empire, compared to their counterparts under Rome, did give them a certain innate coherence, which was further sharpened by the unsympathetic Mazdean environment and by the intense competitiveness of the Christian sects. The relatively uncentralized character of the Sassanian state, especially before the reforms of Kavad I (488–496, 499–531) and Khosro I (531–579), likewise favored the development of community identity. And whereas in the Roman empire the Jews were the sole recognized community other than the approved variety of Christianity, the Sassanians recognized Jews, Nestorians, and non-Chalcedonians or Miaphysites, as well as Mazdeans. This coexistence of recognized and scriptural communities not only continued after the Muslim conquest, but also provides the clearest precedent in the pre-Islamic world for the Qur'ān's general principle that "people of the Book" should be tolerated.[60]

Initially, at least, Islam was an *Arabic* monotheism, and the army and state were run by a Muslim Arabian elite, which had no motive either to force the conversion of those whose beliefs were reasonably inoffensive—that is, not polytheistic—or to deny the universality of the Qur'ān's teaching by actively impeding those who wished to join the *'umma* (community) of Islam. Recognition of separate and subordinate communities of non-Muslims, obliged to pay a special tax *(jizya)* in return for protected status *(dhimma)*, turned out to be an ideal device for regulating the large and sophisticated populations that suddenly had fallen under Muslim rule.[61] Unlike Christian Rome, the Islamic empire was prepared to preserve the religious life of any community that had a scripture; while unlike the Sassanian state, the caliphate was committed in principle to this policy, for it had been enjoined by Allah on the Prophet Muhammad.

The approved communities, the "people of the Book" *(ahl al-Kitāb),* are named in three passages in the Qur'ān (2:63, 5:69–70, 22:18) as the Jews, the Christians, and the Sābi'a. Although the Qur'ān also contains much criticism of these peoples' beliefs, they are distinguished from the polytheists, whose traditions Muhammad knew well and rejected utterly. As a response to major religious communities of the late antique world, and to the problem of how to create a new one that could learn from its predecessors' mistakes, the Qur'ān is a unique document that deserves a more prominent place in the study of late antique religion than has so far been accorded it. To convey in a brief space the way in which the Qur'ān's statements on this subject brought about, in practice, the transition from polytheism to membership in the Islamic empire of communities, we may consider the Sābi'a and a minor but instructive incident that occurred in the year 830.

For Muhammad, it seems that the Sābi'a were a sect of baptizers, probably identical with the Elchasaites of Mesopotamia, the sect into which Mani had been born; but this group was never widely known in the lands of Islam.[62] In the year 830, the Caliph al-Ma'mūn passed through the city of Harran in northern Mesopotamia on his way to campaign against the east Romans, and was struck by the peculiar garb and hairstyle of some of those who came to greet him. In this way he discovered that the city contained a substantial remnant of star worshipers, who probably owed their survival to the sensitive position they occupied between the Roman empire on the one hand and the Iranian empire and later the caliphate on the other. Enraged by the persistence of such a substantial group of idolaters within the caliphate, al-Ma'mūn ordered them to adopt one of the approved religions before he returned from his campaign against the Christian empire.

Although some complied and became Muslims or Christians, others devised the ingenious stratagem of renaming themselves Sābi'a. After all, if nobody else knew who these people were, why not adopt their identity and claim the protection the Qur'ān afforded? In this way the "Sabians" managed to survive for at least another two centuries, and perennially to fascinate Muslim historians and geographers, who describe them as a community with a priesthood, a highly developed calendar of religious observance, and a marked sense of its own history and identity. This fascination was not just antiquarian. Muslims believed that polytheism had once been the religion of all mankind; and these earlier polytheists, too, they naturally called Sābi'a, or Sabians. The first to perceive the error of this belief, and to proclaim the unicity of God, had been Abraham, who had lived under King Nimrod's rule in Babylon before he fled via Harran to Palestine. Eventually, with his son Ishmael, he built the Ka'ba at Mecca.[63] In effect, Abraham had been the first Muslim. The continued existence of a Sabian polytheist community at Harran must have seemed a stunning confirmation of the Qur'ānic story of the origins of monotheism; while the figure of Abraham, the rejected prophet, along with a whole succession of other such "messengers" culled from the pages of the Hebrew Bible and ending with Jesus, son of Mary, provided a firm and universally familiar genealogy for the last and most evolved of all religious communities, the *'umma* that Muhammad had brought into being (see, for example, Qur'ān 21).

There was, though, some elasticity regarding "peoples of the Book." In only one of the three Qur'ānic passages in question is Mazdaism alluded to, and even then ambiguously and in direct association with polytheism. Even so, it was tolerated in practice, as a kind of third-class religion.[64] And Islam itself did not for long remain monolithic. The *'umma* soon became bitterly divided by struggles between different parties that saw themselves as Muhammad's heirs and could not decide whether inspiration should be regarded as having dried up on the Prophet's death, or as being still available within the community—the fateful divergence, in other words, between Sunnis and Shiites. Only after 'Abd al-Malik reestablished order in the 690s did it become possible to draw tighter the bonds that held the caliphate together, from the Indus to the Atlantic, and to impose a more explicitly Islamic style in place of the earlier imitation of Roman and Sassanian models. And perhaps it was at this point that the classical Islamic *'umma* first came clearly into focus, since it is likely that, in the early decades of the new faith's dissemination, amidst the heat and confusion of rapid conquest and internal strife, local loyalties and identities had tended to prevail over any wider vision.[65]

That wider vision was focused in part on the person of the caliph, who held in his hands interdependent religious and politico-military authority, just as the Prophet himself had exercised absolute authority in order to make of the Muslim community an effective brotherhood (Qur'ān 49.11) and a substitute for the traditional clans its members had abandoned. Behind the caliph lay the Qur'ān, other sayings of the Prophet (hadith), and the whole complex of dogma and practice in the context of community that went under the general heading of *sunna*. In daily life, the community's identity and coherence were most clearly expressed not in the marketplace, as in Graeco-Roman cities, but at the place of congregational worship and indeed of judgment, the *masjid;* while the pilgrimage to Mecca, the hajj, imprinted in the mind of every participant the ecumenical dimension of Islam and its sacred history right back to the time of Abraham.[66] Rooted as it was in a world rich in Jewish, Christian, and Mazdean communities and traditions, Islam naturally drew on all of these; but to the cultural continuities thus accepted, a distinctively Muslim tone was always imparted, as one can see already in the Qur'ān's constant emphasis on the fact that Muhammad is called to purge the error of the monotheist and prophetic tradition of the Jews and Christians.

The mid 8th century transition from Umayyad to Abbasid rule, and the loss of Spain, did not weaken the Islamic empire, which attained its greatest glory under the early Abbasid caliphs ruling from the new capital at Baghdad. By al-Ma'mūn's day, though, strains were showing; by the early 10th century the empire was in full dissolution. But the social and cultural foundations of the Islamic world had by then been firmly laid, and could not be shaken by any degree of political fragmentation. Conversion to Islam was by the 10th century making substantial inroads into the "peoples of the Book."[67] Nevertheless, these communities inherited from late antiquity remained vital contributors to the flexibility, entrepreneurial spirit, and international contacts that characterized the Islamic commonwealth; while the commonwealth became in turn one of the crossroads of the world economic system that began to emerge between the China Sea and the Atlantic by the 11th century and matured in the 13th.[68]

If 10th or 11th century Cairo, for example, seems to us the quintessential example of the classical Islamic city of communities, that is partly because Islam in general accorded a degree of recognition to other religions for which even the Sassanian world had offered only partial precedent, and partly because, as Shiites, the ruling Fatimids favored other minority communities that were also attempting to survive in a Sunni environment.[69] And these communities were often by now beneficiaries of secondary identities accumulated over the centuries, best exemplified by the vast and increasingly systematized commentary literatures they had been producing throughout late antiquity. As well as the Torah, the Jews now had a Mishnah and a Talmud, none of which had been written down much before the year 200; while the Christians had generated an enormous body of theological writing, a luxurious growth that had spilled out from the narrow terraces of Scripture and could now, under Islam, be trained, pruned, and shaped at leisure. Hence John of Damascus's compilation of Christian doctrine, *De fide orthodoxa,* which in precisely 100 chapters covers everything from proof of God's existence to circumcision, in a systematic, accessible fashion that had seemed unnecessary when the church was comfortably enshrined within the all-powerful empire of Christian Rome. To his heirs in the Greek-speaking world John of Damascus bequeathed narrower horizons and a refusal to think constructively about Islam, typified by his supercilious account of Muhammad's life and teaching, the last entry in a catalogue of (again) 100 Christian heresies. But increasingly Christians, especially in John's Chalcedonian or "Melkite" tradition, wrote in Arabic too; and some were clever enough to see that the unrivalled clarity of the Qur'ān's language about God might be used in the service of the gospel as well.[70] In the Islamic world as in the Roman, religious communities derived from the experience of coexistence a sharper understanding of their own identity.

On the life of the Christian communities under Islam, literary sources such as the Arabic *History of the Patriarchs of Alexandria* throw only a partial light, since their concern is with the way in which an elite—in this case, the leadership of the anti-Chalcedonian, Coptic church of Egypt—dealt with the Muslim authorities and conspired to fix succession to the community's highest offices, especially the patriarchal throne.[71] But the contents of the document depository of the synagogue of the Palestinians at Fustat, better known as the Cairo Geniza, have made possible an in-depth portrait of this not especially influential or privileged community's everyday life—a portrait that has been triumphantly drawn by S. D. Goitein in his *A Mediterranean Society: The Jewish Communities of the Arab World As Portrayed in the Documents of the Cairo Geniza.*

Through Goitein's five vast volumes we come to know the Jews of Fustat as *pars pro toto* of the international Jewish community, in a world where long-distance travel was common and law was personal, not territorial: one was free to appeal to leading judges from one's own community even if they were resident in a foreign state. And this right of self-government, exercised within relatively small groupings in which a significant degree of individual participation was feasible (2:57), gave Christians and Jews one privilege denied to the great mass of Muslims, who had little opportunity to express a point of view in the hearing of those who controlled their destiny. There were no ghettoes either: the religious communities of Fustat were at once supraterritorial and closely intermixed, much more so than one would ever guess from literary sources like the *History of the Patriarchs of Alexandria.*

The deepest foundations of personal and communal identity were of course laid at home: "Before taking food or drink of any kind one would say the appropriate benediction, and grace . . . after . . . followed by an Amen by those present, so that the children learned them by listening. For them, opening the mouth for food without opening it first for a benediction would soon become awkward and unusual" (5:352).[72] But it was in the synagogue or church that the community felt itself most truly a community. "A high claim to pride for any Geniza person was his ability to read and recite in public the Torah and the Prophets in their original language—a task to which he had dedicated most of his years in school. The emotion accompanying this performance found its expression in the benedictions said by him before and after the recital, respectively: 'Blessed be you . . . who chose us of all nations and gave us his Torah' and 'who, by giving us a true Torah, planted eternal life within us'" (5:348).

If space allowed, I would say more about the formation of scriptural canons and commentaries, the formulation of liturgies, and the organization of study. These are processes that point to eternity, yet take place within historical time; and their prominence in the formation of religious communities illustrates how those communities' self-consciousness is in significant part historical memory, focused of course on the origin and development of their own distinctive beliefs and practices. Such memory—unlike awareness of eternity, or the need to conform to the annual cycle of the seasons—may be lost. In 1890, the British traveler and archaeologist David Hogarth crossed Lake Egridir in Anatolia to visit "a remnant of fifty Christian families huddle[d] at one end of the island, where is a church served by two priests. No service is held except on the greatest festivals, and then in Turkish, for neither priest nor laity understand a word of Greek. The priests told us that the families became fewer every year; the fathers could teach their children nothing about their ancestral faith, for they knew nothing themselves; the Moslems were 'eating them up'. We had to force the church door, and brush dust and mould from a vellum service-book dated 1492. It was all like nothing so much as a visit to a deathbed."[73]

But while communities die out, their individual members may live on with new identities, and in so doing add in distinctive ways to the community of their adoption. Where there has been a long-term, intimate interpenetration, as in Ottoman Anatolia between Christians and Muslims, this is a relatively natural and easy process; but we have seen that something similar happened even in the more abrupt transition from polytheism to Christianity. In particular, the rapid rise of the cult of saints just as the temples were closing indicates that many communities never fully abandoned a diffused understanding of divinity. Once the trauma of transition had been healed, the same scriptural religions which in urban environments defined themselves in opposition to polytheism and each other turned out to be no less capable than polytheism of responding to the need of simple rural communities for a faith that expressed both their undivided, relatively unselfconscious identity and their awareness of dependence on a natural world whose external manifestations are multiple and seem, at times, contradictory. Just because in other places there were known to be fellow religionists of different hue, or even people who professed other faiths entirely, members of such Christianized or, eventually, Islamized communities did not necessarily feel constrained to relativize everything, or to deny the possibility of expressing man's intuition of the essential oneness and holiness of all creation in a specific, unique, and exclusive religious language. As the anthropologist Juliet du Boulay wrote in her account of a village in Northern Euboea in the 1960s: "Their own religion they consider to be the only correct path to God, for they find on the whole what they hear of non-Christian practices incredible and ludicrous, and what they hear of other denominations of Christianity strange and shocking. Inevitably, therefore, except when they are consciously defining ethnic and cultural differences, their concept of mankind is either an implicit extension of the Christian Orthodox world to cover all humanity of whatever actual faith, or the idea of humanity in general as Christendom, from which non-Christians are unconsciously excluded."[74]

The possible merits of unconscious exclusivism are not much considered in our time. Yet the variety of religious communities—which some see as offering grounds for comparison with modern situations[75]—was not what most struck late antique observers. Almost all the literary evidence drawn on in this essay is oriented toward a single community or tradition and, whatever that community's debt to others, shows no disinterested curiosity about them, let alone esteem for the inherent merits of variety.[76] The Qur'ān, though it takes an exceptionally considered and generous approach to the religious communities of the late antique world, does so summarily, from the perspective of a revelation at the apex of a long historical development, and addressed to Arabs, in Arabic. Eventually Muslim scholars, most famous among them al-Shahrastānī, dealt with their materials from a firmly monotheist, and ultimately Qur'ānic, perspective.[77] Even to educated city-dwellers, accustomed to pluralism, their own community's orthodoxy and coherence mattered most.

Notes

1. Zosimus 5.40–41; and compare Sozomen, *Historia ecclesiastica* 9.6.3–6. Apparently both depend on a lost account by Olympiodorus, whose angle is probably reproduced more faithfully by his coreligionist Zosimus.

2. Compare Sextus Pompeius Festus (2nd century), *De significatione verborum,* 284 (Lindsay): "Publica sacra, quae publico sumptu pro populo fiunt."

3. Sozomen, *Historia ecclesiastica* 7.15, 20; Rufinus, *Historia ecclesiastica* 9.29; G. Fowden, *The Egyptian Hermes: A Historical Approach to the Late Pagan Mind* (Cambridge, Eng., 1986; repr. with new preface, Princeton, 1993), 13.

4. *IGUR* 2:478–480. Only a minority of Roman epitaphs of Greek-speaking polytheists state the place of origin; but almost none allude to religious belief: I. Kajanto, *A Study of the Greek Epitaphs of Rome* (Helsinki, 1963), 2, 38.

5. *Myst.* 5.25.236; Julian, *Contra Galilaeos* fr. 21 (Masaracchia).

6. Eusebius, *Vit.Const.* 2.23.2, records how Constantine sent out a letter in two versions, one "to the Churches of God," the other "to the peoples outside, city by city."

7. See also J. North, "The Development of Religious Pluralism," in J. Lieu, J. North, and T. Rajak, eds., *The Jews among Pagans and Christians in the Roman Empire* (London, 1992), 174–193.

8. W. Burkert, *Greek Religion* (Oxford and Cambridge, Mass., 1985), 268–275; J. Irmscher, "Der Terminus *religio* und seine antiken Entsprechungen im philologischen und religionsgeschichtlichen Vergleich," in U. Bianchi, ed., *The Notion of "Religion" in Comparative Research* (Rome, 1994), 63–73.

9. Philostratus, *Vita Apollonii* 4.24; Julian, *Epistulae* 89.300c–302a; Marinus, *Vita Procli* 15, 32.

10. Dio Cassius 77.15.5–7.

11. F. Poland, *Geschichte des griechischen Vereinswesens* (Leipzig, 1909), 5–6, 65, 173–176.

12. M. F. Squarciapino, *Leptis Magna* (Basel, 1966), 117.

13. *IG* 2–3².1368.

14. For example, *P Oxy.* 1380.

15. For example, Symmachus, *Relatio* 3.10; Augustine, *Epistulae* 104.12 (quoting the addressee, Nectarius of Calama).

16. See, recently, E. Will and C. Orrieux, *"Prosélytisme juif"? Histoire d'une erreur* (Paris, 1992); P. van Minnen, "Drei Bemerkungen zur Geschichte des Judentums in der griechisch-römischen Welt," *Zeitschrift für Papyrologie und Epigraphik* 100 (1994): 253–258.

17. Julian, *Contra Galilaeos* frs. 19–20 (Masaracchia).

18. *P Giess.* 40 I; K. Buraselis, *Theia Dōrea* (Athens, 1989), 20–21; P. A. Kuhlmann, *Die Giessener literarischen Papyri und die Caracalla-Erlasse* (Giessen, 1994), 217–239.

19. Marcus Aurelius 5.33, 6.30.

20. Numenius, fr. 24 (des Places); Aelian, fr. 89 (Hercher).

21. Compare, for example, Chaeremon's account with Julian, *Epistulae* 89.302d–303b.

22. Iamblichus, *Myst.* 5.16–18, 10.6.

23. Julian, *Epistulae* 84, 89; Sozomen, *Historia ecclesiastica* 5.16; Sallustius, *De dis et mundo.*

24. Note especially Julian, *Epistulae* 98.400c, applying the term indiscriminately to all the polytheist inhabitants of a town in Syria. Julian's highly political use of names is decried by Gregory of Nazianzus, *Orationes* 4.76.

25. For example, Julian, *Orationes* 8.172d–173a.

26. *Corpus Hermeticum* 16.1–2; Philostratus, *Vita Apollonii* 3.32; Iamblichus, *Myst.* 7.5.259.

27. C. Geertz, *The Interpretation of Cultures* (New York, 1973), 181–189; R. S. Kipp and S. Rodgers, eds., *Indonesian Religions in Transition* (Tucson, 1987).

28. On crypto-polytheism see, for example, Libanius, *Orationes* 30.28; Zacharias Scholasticus, *Vita Severi,* 17–37 (Kugener); Procopius, *Anecdota* 11.32.

29. On the role of episcopal violence in the definition of the community see P. Brown, *Religion and Society in the Age of Saint Augustine* (London, 1972), 326–331; G. Fow-

den, "Bishops and Temples in the Eastern Roman Empire A.D. 320–435," *Journal of Theological Studies* 29 (1978): 53–78.

30. C. Jones et al., eds., *The Study of Liturgy* (2nd ed., London, 1992), esp. 403–420, 472–484; and cf. R. Taft, *The Liturgy of the Hours in East and West: The Origins of the Divine Office and Its Meaning for Today* (Collegeville, Minn., 1986), 331–334.

31. Eusebius, *Vit.Const.* 3.18.

32. Ambrose, *Epistulae* 22.13. On the role of saints and their relics in the formation of Christian community, see P. Brown, *The Cult of the Saints: Its Rise and Function in Latin Christianity* (Chicago, 1981).

33. John Chrysostom, *De sacerdotio* 6.4 (*PG* 48.681); Palladius, *Historia Lausiaca* 18.25; Cyril of Scythopolis, *Vita Euthymii 19*; Gregory the Great, *Dialogi* 4.60.3; *Liturgy of S. Basil*, in F. E. Brightman, ed., *Liturgies Eastern and Western*, vol. 1 (Oxford, 1896), 312.

34. But see *Apophthegmata patrum* (Greek alphabetical series), in *PG* 65.128c–d, on preferring the language of the (desert) Fathers to the dangerous idiom of the Scriptures.

35. Epiphanius, *Panarion* 61.3.4–8.

36. Sozomen, *Historia ecclesiastica* 5.15.14–17.

37. For example, Leo the Great, *Epistulae* 1.1; and see H. O. Maier, "The Topography of Heresy and Dissent in Late-Fourth-Century Rome," *Historia* 44 (1995): 235–244.

38. Eusebius, *Historia ecclesiastica* 6.43.11–12 (adapted from trans. by J. E. L. Oulton).

39. A. Grillmeier, *Jesus der Christus im Glauben der Kirche*, vol. 1 (3rd ed., Freiburg, 1990), 386–403; G. Fowden, *Empire to Commonwealth: Consequences of Monotheism in Late Antiquity* (Princeton, 1993), 85–97.

40. Eusebius, *Vit.Const.* 4.24; compare 2.23.2, and 1 Cor. 5:12–13 (where it is God who judges those outside).

41. M. Herzfeld, *Ours Once More: Folklore, Ideology, and the Making of Modern Greece* (Austin, 1982), 116–117.

42. John of Ephesus, *Historia ecclesiastica* 3.3.29.

43. "Arian historiographer," J. Bidez and F. Winkelmann, eds., *Philostorgius, Kirchengeschichte* (3rd ed., Berlin, 1981), 202–241.

44. Synesius, *Epistulae* 105. On "economy" as a necessary compensation for the rigidities and tensions of a Christian empire, see G. Dagron, "La règle et l'exception: Analyse de la notion d'économie," in D. Simon, ed., *Religiöse Devianz: Untersuchungen zu sozialen, rechtlichen und theologischen Reaktionen auf religiöse Abweichung im westlichen und östlichen Mittelalter* (Frankfurt am Main, 1990), 1–18.

45. H. C. Brennecke, *Studien zur Geschichte der Homöer der Osten bis zum Ende der homöischen Reichskirche* (Tübingen, 1988), 93–94, 152–157. The martyrology apparently formed part of the work of the "Arian historiographer" (see n. 43). Compare also I. Shahīd, *The Martyrs of Najrān: New Documents* (Brussels, 1971), 200–207, for a similar conversion of anti-Chalcedonian martyrs into Chalcedonians in the 6th century.

46. G. Gould, *The Desert Fathers on Monastic Community* (Oxford, 1993), 1–25.

47. I rely on P. Rousseau's sensitive account, *Pachomius: The Making of a Community in Fourth-Century Egypt* (Berkeley, 1985).

48. W. H. C. Frend, *The Rise of the Monophysite Movement: Chapters in the History of the Church in the Fifth and Sixth Centuries* (Cambridge, 1972; corrected repr. 1979), 184–254; Fowden, *Empire to Commonwealth*, 100–137 and esp. 124–137, for documentation of the points made in the next two paragraphs. "Miaphysitism" is a less misleading name than "monophysitism," which implicitly excludes the human aspect of Christ's one and undivided nature.

49. A. Palmer, *Monk and Mason on the Tigris Frontier: The Early History of Ṭur ʿAbdin* (Cambridge, 1990), 149–153.

50. As in the national epic of Ethiopia, the *Kebra Nagast*, parts of which appear to go back to the 6th century.

51. M. Morony, *Iraq after the Muslim Conquest* (Princeton, 1984), 372–380; Palmer, *Monk and Mason*, 153–154.

52. Morony, *Iraq*, 280–305.

53. Fowden, *Empire to Commonwealth*, 72–76.

54. Cologne Mani Codex, 134–135, 163–164 (A. Henrichs and L. Koenen, eds., *Der Kölner Mani-Kodex: Über das Werden seines Leibes* [Opladen, 1988], 96, 112); C. E. Römer, *Manis frühe Missionsreisen nach der Kölner Manibiographie* (Opladen, 1994), 154–159.

55. Rome: *C.Th.* 16.8; L. I. Levine, *The Rabbinic Class of Roman Palestine in Late Antiquity* (Jerusalem, 1989); M. Goodman, "Jews and Judaism in the Mediterranean Diaspora in the Late Roman Period: The Limitations of Evidence," *Journal of Mediterranean Studies* 4 (1994): 208–212, 220–221. Babylon: Morony, *Iraq*, 306–331.

56. See the interesting remarks by H. L. Strack and G. Stemberger, *Introduction to the Talmud and Midrash* (Edinburgh, 1991), 66–68.

57. J. Glicken, "Sundanese Islam and the Value of *Hormat:* Control, Obedience, and Social Location in West Java," in Kipp and Rodgers, eds., *Indonesian Religions*, 240–244; B. Anderson, *Imagined Communities: Reflections on the Origin and Spread of Nationalism* (2nd ed., London, 1991), 12–16.

58. J. P. Asmussen, "Christians in Iran," in W. B. Fisher and others, eds., *The Cambridge History of Iran* (Cambridge, 1968–1991), 3:924–948; Morony, *Iraq*, 332–383, 620–632.

59. E. K. Fowden, *The Barbarian Plain: Saint Sergius between Rome and Iran* (Berkeley, 1999), chap. 2.

60. Note Ṭabari, *Ta'rīkh* 1.991 (tr. T. Nöldeke, *Geschichte der Perser und Araber zur Zeit der Sasaniden* [Leiden, 1879], 268), for a succinct statement of this policy attributed to Hormizd IV.

61. C. E. Bosworth, "The Concept of *Dhimma* in Early Islam," in B. Braude and B. Lewis, eds., *Christians and Jews in the Ottoman Empire* (New York, 1982), 1:37–51.

62. T. Fahd, "Sābi'a," *Encyclopedia of Islam*, 2nd ed., 8:675–677. On the "Sabians" of Harran see D. Chwolsohn, *Die Ssabier und der Ssabismus* (St. Petersburg, 1856); Fowden, *Empire to Commonwealth*, 62–65.

63. H. Schützinger, *Ursprung und Entwicklung der arabischen Abraham-Nimrod-Legende* (Bonn, 1961); R. Firestone, *Journeys in Holy Lands: The Evolution of the Abraham-Ishmael Legends in Islamic Exegesis* (Albany, 1990).

64. Qur'ān 22.18; M. G. Morony, "Madjūs," *Encyclopedia of Islam*, 2nd ed., 5.1110–18; S. D. Goitein, *A Mediterranean Society: The Jewish Communities of the Arab World as Portrayed in the Documents of the Cairo Geniza* (Berkeley, 1967–1993), 5:334.

65. On the *'umma* see Morony, *Iraq*, 431–506; Fowden, *Empire to Commonwealth*, 153–159.

66. Not that one should forget the sanctity of the Roman marketplace (Maximus of Madauros, in Augustine, *Epistulae* 16.1), or the use of the courtyards of large Syrian temples as public squares (*C.Th.* 16.10.8).

67. For recent comment on this complex subject see M. G. Morony, "The Age of Conversions: A Reassessment," in M. Gervers and R. J. Bikhazi, eds., *Conversion and Continuity: Indigenous Christian Communities in Islamic Lands, Eighth to Eighteenth Centuries* (Toronto, 1990), 135–150.

68. J. L. Abu-Lughod, *Before European Hegemony: The World System A.D. 1250–1350* (New York, 1989), especially chap. 7, "Cairo's Monopoly under the Slave Sultanate." On the Islamic Commonwealth see Fowden, *Empire to Commonwealth*, 160–168.

69. But Goitein, in *Mediterranean Society*, opines that the Fatimids "excelled in laissez-faire, out of indolence . . . rather than conviction" (2:404–405).

70. S. H. Griffith, "The First Christian *Summa Theologiae* in Arabic: Christian *Kalām* in Ninth-Century Palestine," in Gervers and Bikhazi, eds., *Conversion and Continuity,* 15–31.

71. *History of the Patriarchs of Alexandria,* ed. and trans. B. Evetts, *PO* 1(2,4), 5(1), 10(5). See also H. Kennedy, "The Melkite Church from the Islamic Conquest to the Crusades: Continuity and Adaptation in the Byzantine Legacy," in *The 17th International Byzantine Congress: Major Papers* (New Rochelle, N.Y., 1986), 325–343.

72. See also J. Assmann, *Das kulturelle Gedächtnis: Schrift, Erinnerung, und politische Identität in frühen Hochkulturen* (Munich, 1992), 16: "In the Seder celebration the child learns to say 'we,' as he becomes part of a history and a memory that creates and constitutes this 'we.' This problem and process is basic to every culture, although seldom so clearly visible."

73. D. G. Hogarth, *A Wandering Scholar in the Levant* (London, 1896), 84.

74. J. du Boulay, *Portrait of a Greek Mountain Village* (Oxford, 1974; corrected repr. Limni, 1994), 42.

75. E.g. Morony, *Iraq,* 524.

76. See also Goitein, *Mediterranean Society,* 2:277.

77. See al-Shahrastānī, *al-mital wa'l-niḥal,* trans. D. Gimaret, G. Monnot, and J. Jolivet, *Livre des religions et des sectes* (Leuven, 1986–93).

Barbarians and Ethnicity

Patrick J. Geary

The concept of "barbarian" was an invention of the Graeco-Roman world, projected onto a whole spectrum of peoples living beyond the frontier of the empire. Except for the Persians, whose cultural and political equality the Roman world begrudgingly recognized, Romans perceived all other societies through generalized and stereotypical categories inherited from centuries of Greek and Roman ethnographic writings. Each people's complex of traits, along with geographical boundaries, became the determining factors in Roman ethnic classification.

If barbarians were a Roman invention, ethnogenesis, or ethnic formation and transformation, was emphatically not. Classical systems of territorialization and classification, typical of Roman concerns for precision and order, objectified and externalized the identity of peoples, relegating them to an eternal present. Geographers such as Pliny delighted in combining as many sources as possible, mixing peoples long disappeared with contemporary ethnic groups in his *Natural History*. The result was a sort of law of conservation of peoples: no people ever disappeared, no trait ever changed. At best, a group might acquire a new name and novel, even contradictory customs and characteristics. Moreover, the geographical location of peoples took on increasing importance as Roman contact with barbarians increased. The maps of the Roman world became crowded as their compilers sought to fill their land masses with as many peoples as possible. These peoples, like other natural phenomena, had no real history: they encountered history only when they entered the sphere of the civilized world. Thus the concept of ethnogenesis was alien to the Roman understanding of their neighbors. Typical of the Roman explanation of peoples is this account of the emergence of the Goths: "Now from this island of Scandza, as from a hive of races or a womb of nations, the Goths are said to have come forth long ago under their king, Berig by name. As soon as they disembarked from their ships and set foot on the land, they straightway gave their name to the place" (Jordanes, *Getica,* ed. Mommsen [Berlin, 1882], 60). Thus begins the 6th century account of Gothic origins by the Gotho-Roman Jordanes, writing in the Constantinople of Justinian. The account reflects traditional concepts of Graeco-Roman ethnography more than Gothic oral traditions. The Goths (to Jordanes, equivalent to the Getae) are but one more of the innumerable peoples who emerged from the north in a timeless "long ago" and began their long migration toward Italy and thereby entered the sphere of Roman civilization.

In contrast to this classical image of peoples as static, eternal, and without history, an inscription erected by a Turkic Khagan presents an alternative understanding of the origin of a people: "My father, the khagan, went off with seventeen men. Having heard the news that [he] was marching off, those who were in the towns went up mountains and those who were on mountains came down [from there]; thus they gathered and numbered seventy men. Due to the fact that Heaven granted strength, the soldiers of my father, the khagan, were like wolves, and his enemies were like sheep. Having gone on campaigns forward and backward, he gathered together and collected men; and they all numbered seven hundred men. After they had numbered seven hundred men, [my father, the khagan] organized and ordered the people who had lost their state and their khagan, the people who had turned slaves and servants, the people who had lost the Turkish institutions, in accordance with the rules of my ancestors" (Tariat Tekin, *A Grammar of Orkhon Turkic* [Bloomington, Ind., 1968], 265). In this model of the origin of a people, one sees a new creation brought about through military success: as a war leader is successful, he draws more and more followers to himself, and they become a band and then an army. This critical mass of warriors under a successful commander is converted into a people through the imposition of a legal system. Peoplehood is the end of a political process through which individuals with diverse backgrounds are united by law. So conceived, a people is constitutional, not biological, and yet the very imposition of law makes the opposite appeal: it is the law of the ancestors. The leader projects an antiquity and a genealogy onto this new creation.

In general, three models of barbarian ethnic formation can be discerned among the peoples who came into contact with the late Roman empire. The first and most closely studied is that which took its identity from a leading or royal family. Among the Goths, the Longobards, the Salian Franks, and other successful barbarian peoples, members of a successful family of warriors succeeded in attracting and controlling a following from disparate backgrounds that adhered to the traditions of the family. In such peoples, the legendary origins of the royal family became the legendary origins of the people that coalesced around this "kernel of tradition." These traditions traced the origin of the family or people to some distant, divine ancestor who led the people out of their original territory, won a significant victory over another people or peoples, and went on to find a place within the Roman world. The success of such peoples depended on the ability of their leading family to destroy alternative claimants to leadership and to find a way of grafting onto the fluid barbarian cultural and political tradition Roman institutions of law, polity, and organization. Thus, these barbarian peoples were dependent for their survival on the cooperation and recognition, however grudgingly accorded, of the emperors.

The second model of ethnogenesis drew on traditions of Central Asian steppe peoples for the charismatic leadership and organization necessary to create a people from a diverse following. The primary model for such an ethnic formation was the Huns of Attila, although the Alans, the Avars, and later the Magyars also were steppe empires. These polyethnic confederations were if anything even more inclusive than the first model, being able to draw together groups which maintained much of their traditional linguistic, cultural, and even political organization under the generalship of a small body of steppe commanders. The economic basis of these steppe confederations was semi-nomadic rather than sedentary. Territory and distance played little role in defining their boundaries, although elements of the confederation might practice traditional forms of agriculture and social organization quite different from those of the steppe leadership. Thus the Goths in the kingdom of Attila and the Bulgars in the kingdom of the Avars could not only maintain but even develop their own traditions while remaining firmly attached to the central organization of the empire. The survival of such confederations required constant military successes to an even greater extent than did the first model. A combination of terror and military victory held them together. The death of a leader or his defeat at the hands of another barbarian or Roman army could lead to the rapid disappearance of the mightiest of these empires. Reversals such as that of the Huns following the death of Attila, or of the Avars following Charlemagne's successful penetration of their kingdom in the late 700s, resulted in their rapid and total disappearance. At the same time, the disintegration of these vast steppe confederations generated new and transformed peoples. The Ostrogoths, Gepids, and Longobards emerged from the empire of Attila; and the Bulgars and other Slavic peoples emerged from the ruins of the Avar empire.

The last model, that of decentralized peoples such as the Alamanni, perhaps the Bavarians, and certainly the Slavs, is perhaps the most difficult to understand. In these configurations, whatever traditions may have informed the community were transmitted not by a central royal family but in a more communal form. It is impossible to know to what extent such peoples had any consciousness of communal identity at all. The Alamanni appear in Roman sources from the 3rd century, but no evidence of any collective legends, traditions, or genealogies has survived that would indicate the emergence of a common sense of identity among the Germanic peoples living on the upper Rhine. In the case of the Slavs, some have hypothesized that these peoples were the amalgamation of the Germanic-Sarmatian peasant populations left behind in those regions from which warrior bands and their leaders of the first type departed for the lure of the Roman empire. This may be so, but whenever the Slavs appear in sources, they do so not as peasants but as fierce warriors, loosely organized into short-lived bands. Centralized leadership was not the norm and often came in the form of outside elements, from nearby Germanic peoples such as the Franks, or from Iranian Croats, Turkic Bulgars, or Scandinavian Rus'.

Regardless of the form of ethnogenesis, it must be understood as a continuing process rather than a historical event. Ancient names could and did come to designate very different groups of people. Alternatively, certain groups underwent repeated, profound social, cultural, and political transformations such that they became essentially different peoples even while maintaining venerable names. The only way to understand the varieties of ethnogenesis, then, is to observe the historical transformations of the most significant of these groups across late antiquity.

By the 5th century, Romans and barbarians had learned a great deal about each other, much of it through painful contact and all of it filtered through their own modes of understanding the world. Romans viewed barbarians through the inherited categories of classical ethnography stretching back over four centuries, but also with the more pragmatic eyes of conquerors and adversaries whose faith in Roman superiority had been severely shaken in the last quarter of the 4th century. Barbarians viewed the Roman empire as the home of the great king, as a source of inexhaustible wealth, and frequently as a powerful but treacherous ally. Still, this empire was deemed as essential to the barbarians as it was alien to the Romans. The Visigothic ruler Athaulf was said to have contemplated replacing the empire with his own, but abandoned the idea as a chimera. Four hundred years later another barbarian ruler, Charlemagne, absorbed the empire into his person, having himself acclaimed emperor on Christmas Day, 800.

Romans of the 5th century contemplated the barbarians of their own day from the perspective of almost a millennium of interaction with the barbarian world. These centuries of Roman presence had profoundly influenced the peoples living along the frontiers. Roman policy dictated the creation of client buffer states that could protect the empire from contact with hostile barbarians further afield; provide trading partners for the supply of cattle, raw materials, and slaves; and, increasingly from the 4th century, fill the ranks of the military with mercenary troops. Thus the empire supported friendly chieftains, supplying them with weapons, gold, and grain in order to strengthen the pro-Roman factions within the barbarian world. The effect on not only the barbarians living along the *limes* but also those further away was considerable. Roman economic and political power destabilized the rough balance of power within the barbarian world by enabling pro-Roman chieftains to accumulate wealth and power far in excess of what had been possible previously. These chieftains also gained both military and political experience by serving in the Roman military system with their troops as federates. At the same time, fear of the Romans and their allies drove anti-Roman factions into large, unstable, but occasionally mighty confederations that could inflict considerable damage on Roman interests on both sides of the borders. This had happened in the time of Caesar among the Gauls and at the end of the 1st century among the Britons. In the late 2nd century a broad confederacy known as the Marcomanni tested and temporarily broke the Danubian frontier. In the aftermath of the Marcomannic wars, new barbarian peoples appeared along the Rhine-Danube frontiers in the course of the 3rd century. A loose confederation along the upper Rhine known as simply "the people" (Alamanni) appeared in the early 3rd century and a similar confederation on the lower Rhine, "the free" or "the fierce" (Franci), came to the attention of the Romans a generation later, as did a confederation of Germanic, Sarmatic, and even Roman warriors along the lower Danube under the generalship of the Goth Cniva. Behind these constellations on Rome's borders stood still other groups, such as Saxons beyond the Franks, Burgundians beyond the Alamanni, and Vandals beyond the Goths.

These confederations were in turn composed of small communities of farmers and herders living in villages along rivers, seacoasts, and clearings from the North and Baltic Seas to the Black Sea. Most members of the society were free men and women, organized in nuclear households governed by the husband or father. Status within the village depended on wealth, measured by the size of a family's cattle herd, and military prowess. Some wealthier individuals presided over households that included not only their wife or wives and children, but free dependents and slaves housed in outbuildings around the leader's home.

Households were in turn integrated into the larger kindred group known to scholars as the Sip (German: *Sippe*) or clan. This wider circle of kin included both agnatic and cognatic groups who shared a perception of common descent, reinforced by a special "peace" that made violent conflict within the clan a crime for which no compensation or atonement could be made, by an incest taboo, and possibly by some claims to inheritance. This wider kindred might also form the basis for mutual defense and for pursuit of feuds. However, membership in this larger circle was elastic. It provided the possibility but not the necessity of concerted action since individuals might select from a variety of possible broader kin affiliations depending on circumstances. The nuclear family, not the wider clan, was the primary unit of barbarian society.

Village life was directed by the assembly of free men under the leadership of a headman whose position may have come from a combination of factors including wealth, family influence, and connections with the leadership of the people beyond his village. Binding together this larger entity was a combination of religious, legal, and political traditions that imparted a strong if unstable sense of unity.

Members of a people shared ancestry myths, cultural traditions, a legal system, and leadership. However, all of these were flexible, multiple, and subject to negotiation and even dispute. Ancestry myths took the form of genealogies of heroic figures and their exploits. The founders of these genealogies were divine, and the chain of their descendants did not form a history in the Graeco-Roman sense of a structured narrative of events and their broader significance. Rather, these myths preserved an atemporal and apolitical account of individuals, woven together through ties of kinship and tales of revenge and blood feud, to which many individuals and families could claim ties. Other cultural traditions, too, such as dress, hairstyles, religious practices, weapons, and tactics provided strong bonds but also fluid and adaptable ways of creating unity or claiming difference. Legal traditions were an outgrowth of this religious and cultural identity. In the absence of strong central authority, disputes were regulated through family leaders, village assemblies, and war leaders. Control was exerted to preserve peace or at least to set the rules for feuds to take place in a manner least destructive of the community. Finally, these religious and cultural groups were organized under political leadership, a leadership that underwent profound transformation in the early centuries of contact with Rome.

When the Romans first came into contact with the Celtic and Germanic peoples, these populations were largely governed by hereditary, sacral kings, who embodied the identity of their people by their sacred ancestry. This traditional type of king, termed *Thiudan* (from *thiuda*, "people" in east Germanic languages such as Gothic) or in Celtic languages *rhix*, continued among peoples far from the Roman *limes* in portions of the British Isles, in Scandinavia, and in the Elbe region. In the course of the 1st and 2nd centuries, those living in proximity to the Romans had largely abandoned their archaic sacral kings in favor of warrior leaders who might be selected from old royal families or, as frequently, from successful aristocratic fighters. This change favored the empire, since Rome could more easily influence new leaders emerging from oligarchic factions than heirs of ancient religious authority. These leaders were raised up by their heterogeneous armies and formed the centers around which new traditions of political and religious identity could develop and onto which, in some cases, older notions of sacro-social identity could be grafted. The legitimacy of these leaders (termed *duces, reges, regales* by different Roman sources; *kuning,* that is, leader of the family, in west Germanic languages; or in Gothic *reiks,* borrowed from the Celtic *rhix*) derived ultimately from their ability to lead their armies to victory. A victorious campaign confirmed their right to rule and drew to them an ever growing number of people who accepted and shared in their identity. Thus a charismatic leader could found a new people. In time, the leader and his descendants might identify themselves with an older tradition and claim divine sanction, proven by their fortunes in war, to embody and continue some ancient people. The constitutional integrity of these peoples then was dependent on warfare and conquest—they were armies, although their economies remained dependent on raiding and a combination of animal husbandry and slash-and-burn agriculture. Defeat, at the hand of either the Romans or other barbarians, could mean the end not only of a ruler but of a people, who might be absorbed into another, victorious confederation.

At any given time, therefore, within these broad confederations, a variety of individuals might claim some sort of kingship over portions of the people. The Alamannic confederation that fought the emperor Julian in 357, for example, was led by an uncle and nephew termed "the most outstanding in power before the other kings," five kings of second rank, ten *regales,* and a series of magnates. Although Roman sources termed all of these leaders "Alamanni," they also observed that the Alamanni were composed of such groups as the Bucinobantes, Lentienses, and Juthungi under the leadership of their own kings. These subgroups could be termed *gentes,* implying a social and political constitution, or *pagi,* suggesting that organization was at least in part territorial; or, as in the cases of the Lentienses, both. Similarly the early Franks were composed of groups such as the Chamavi, Chattuarii, Bructeri, and Amsivari, and had numerous *regales* and *duces* who commanded portions of the collectivity and disputed among themselves for primacy. In the late 4th century, for example, the Frankish war leader Arbogast, although in Roman service, used his Roman position to pursue his feud with the Frankish *regales* Marcomer and Sunno in trans-Rhenian territory. Further to the east, the Gothic confederation with its military kingship splintered under Roman pressure. The most eastern portions of the Goths in modern Ukraine accepted the authority of the Amals, a royal family of the new type that nevertheless claimed ancient and divine legitimacy, while among the western Gothic groups numerous *reiks* shared and disputed an oligarchic control.

Warfare, whether large-scale attacks led by the *reiks* or *kuning* or small-scale cattle raids carried out by a few adventurous youths, was central to barbarian life. Warfare within the family was forbidden; within the people it was controlled by the conventions of the feud; but between peoples it was the normal state of affairs. Raiding was a normal way of acquiring wealth and prestige as well as of reestablishing the balance of honor within the community. Successful war leaders gathered around themselves elite groups of young warriors who devoted themselves to their commander in return for arms, protection, and a share of booty. These bands of retainers formed powerful military units that could be invaluable in war, but also, in tendency to fight each other and dispute over spoils, dangerous sources of instability. The following of a successful war leader could grow enormously, as young warriors from surrounding villages and even other peoples joined. In time the warrior band and its dependents could splinter off to create a new people.

For the most part, warfare was directed against neighboring barbarians, and raids and plundering maintained a relative equilibrium within the barbarian world. However, the presence of Roman merchants within this world and of the riches of the empire on its frontiers proved irresistible to barbarian leaders who needed to win glory in battle and to acquire iron, horses, slaves, and gold for their following. For as long as it existed, the empire could serve this purpose in one of two ways, either as the employer of barbarian military bands or as the victim of these same bands.

Until the last quarter of the 4th century, barbarians had found direct assaults on imperial armies less effective than service to them. Barbarian military successes against the empire tended to result from Roman disputes and weaknesses. Barbarian armies were never a match for a competent emperor at the head of his army. Sporadic raiding across the frontier, often carried out by isolated warrior bands, brought severe reprisals, at times through punitive expeditions into the barbarian world accompanied by thorough devastation in the Roman tradition. Large-scale raiding was possible only when the Roman frontier garrisons were withdrawn or weakened by urgent needs elsewhere in the empire. In the 250s, during the darkest hours of the 3rd century crisis for example, the Gothic King Cniva led his mixed confederation into the province of Dacia while Gothic pirates attacked the Black Sea coast from the mouth of the Danube. When legions from along the Rhine were shifted east to deal with internal and external problems, barbarians took the opportunity to raid across the poorly defended frontier. Alamannic bands overran the Roman trans-Rhenian Decumatian territories and Frankish armies advanced deep into Gaul and even Spain. The actual identities of the peoples involved in these raids is difficult to ascertain. Often Roman sources speak of the barbarian inhabitants along the Rhine as simply "Germani." At other times, they tend to identify those on the upper Rhine as Alamanni, those on the lower as Franci, although the extent to which the raiders would have recognized such labels themselves is impossible to determine. Moreover, Romans were aware that other groups such as Burgundians and Vandals and Saxons participated in these raids as well.

However, although neither Dacia nor Decumania was entirely retaken by the empire, Emperor Gallienus (253–268) and his successors decisively defeated the Franks and the Alamanni, and Emperor Aurelian (270–275) crushed Goths in a series of campaigns that splintered their confederation. Raiding continued sporadically, but the frontiers were essentially secure for another century.

For some barbarian armies, defeat meant the destruction of their identity as a cohesive social unit. The devastation caused by barbarian raids into the empire paled in comparison with the wasting and slaughter meted out by Roman armies engaged in expeditions across the Rhine or Danube. A panegyric of the year 310 describes the treatment to which Constantine subjected the Bructeri after a punitive expedition he led against them: the barbarians were trapped in an area of impenetrable forest and swamp, where many were killed, their cattle confiscated, their villages burned, and all of the adults thrown to the beasts in the arena. The children were presumably sold into slavery. In other cases, surviving warriors were forced into the Roman army. These *dediticii* or *laeti*, following a ritual surrender in which they gave up their weapons and threw themselves on the mercy of their Roman conquerors, were spread throughout the empire in small units or settled in depopulated areas to provide military service and restore regions devastated by barbarian attacks and taxpayer flight. One such unit of Franks sent to the shores of the Black Sea managed a heroic escape, commandeering a ship and making their way across the Mediterranean, through the Straits of Gibraltar and ultimately home, but most served out their days in the melting pot of the Roman army.

Defeat also meant major changes for barbarian peoples on the frontiers of the empire not forced into service or sold into slavery. Deprived of the possibility of supporting their political and economic systems through raiding, the defeated barbarian military kings found an alternative in service to the Roman empire. After defeating a Vandal army in 270 Emperor Aurelian concluded a treaty with them as federates of the empire. Similar treaties with Franks and Goths followed before the end of the century. *Foederati* obligated themselves to respect the empire's frontiers, to provide troops to the imperial army, and in some cases to make additional payments in cattle or goods. Barbarian leaders favorable to Rome found that they could reach previously unimaginable heights of power and influence by fighting not against the empire, but for it.

In the course of the 4th century, internal conflict and pressure on the Persian frontier as well as a desire to minimize imperial expenses led to the progressive incorporation of these barbarian leaders and their followings into the Roman military system. Constantine I led the way, not only designating Frankish military units as auxiliary units of the imperial army but also promoting barbarians such as the Frank Bonitus to high military office. Bonitus was the first of a long series of Franks in Roman service. In 355 his son, the thoroughly Romanized Silvanus who was commander of the Roman garrison at Cologne, was proclaimed emperor by his troops. Although Silvanus was quickly assassinated by envoys of Emperor Constantius, subsequent barbarian commanders such as Malarich, Teutomeres, Mallobaudes, Laniogaisus, and Arbogast avoided usurpation but exercised enormous power within the western empire. Ultimately one of these Frankish Roman commanders, Clovis, would eliminate the remnants of the Roman state in Gaul and receive imperial recognition.

For the most part, these Roman generals maintained close ties with the members of their peoples outside the empire. Shortly after Silvanus's assassination, Franks sacked Cologne, possibly in revenge for his murder. Mallobaudes, who participated in Gratian's victory over the Alamanni in 378, was simultaneously termed *comes domesticorum* and *rex Francorum* by the Roman historian Ammianus Marcellinus. Others such as Arbogast used their position within the empire to attack their enemies across the Rhine. Still, their situation was extremely precarious both within the empire and without. Frequently they were the objects of suspicion to their Roman competitors, even though they generally were no less reliable than Romans in high command. At the same time, as Roman officials and as adherents of Roman religion, whether Christian or pagan, they were always targets for anti-Roman factions at home. Assumption of high Roman command generally meant forgoing the possibility of retaining a position at the head of a barbarian people outside of the empire.

Around the Black Sea, the Gothic confederation experienced a similarly ambiguous relationship with the eastern portions of the empire. By the 4th century the more eastern Gothic peoples, the Greuthungs or steppe peoples, had absorbed characteristics of the Scyths. In the western regions, the Tervingi or forest people had come under the greatest direct influence of Rome. Both were sedentary agrarian societies, although in the former the military elite was composed primarily of infantry while in the latter horsemen in the tradition of the ancient Scyths formed the core of the army. In the 4th century, the Tervingian Goths had expanded their lordship over a wide spectrum of peoples with different linguistic, cultic, and cultural traditions.

Settled in agricultural villages and governed by local assemblies of free men, the population of this Gothic confederation was nevertheless subject to the central authority of the oligarchic authority of Gothic military leaders under the authority of a nonroyal judge. In 332 Constantine and the Tervingian judge Ariaric concluded a treaty or *foedus*. Ariaric's son Aoric was raised in Constantinople and the emperor even raised a statue in the city in honor of the judge. Under Ariaric, Aoric, and his son Athanaric, these western Goths became progressively integrated into the Roman imperial system, providing auxiliary troops to the eastern region of the empire. One effect of this closer relationship with the empire was their implication in internal imperial politics. In 365 the usurper Procopius convinced the Tervingians to support him as the representative of the Constantinian dynasty in his opposition to Emperor Valens. After Procopius's execution, Valens launched a brutal punitive attack across the Danube that ended only in 369 with a treaty between Athanaric and the emperor.

Religion was a binding force in the Gothic confederation, but the heterogeneous constitution of the confederation created difficulties in maintaining this religious unity. Christians, large numbers of whom were incorporated into the Gothic world from the Crimea during the time of Cniva, and others who were carried off in trans-Danubian raids, proved the most difficult religious minority to assimilate, both because of the strong exclusivity of their monotheistic faith and because of the importance of Christianity in the political strategies of the Roman empire. Gothic Christians represented the spectrum of Christian beliefs, from orthodox Crimean Goths to the Audian sect that confessed the corporeality of God among the Tervingi, to various Arian or semi-Arian communities in the Gothic Balkans. The most influential Gothic Christian was Ulfila (whose Gothic name means "little wolf"), a third-generation Goth of relatively high social standing whose Christian ancestors had been captured in a raid on Cappadocia sometime in the 260s. In the 330s Ulfila came to Constantinople as part of a delegation, resided in the empire for some time, and in 341 was consecrated "bishop of the Christians in the Getic land" at the council of Antioch and sent to the Balkan Goths. Ulfila's consecration and his mission to the Goths and other peoples in the Gothic confederation were part of an imperial Gothic program, which may have precipitated the first persecution of Gothic Christians in 348 under Aoric and a second beginning in 369 under Athanaric. During the first persecution Ulfila and his followers were exiled to Roman Moesia, where he preached in Gothic, Latin, and Greek to his heterogeneous flock, wrote theological treatises, and translated the Bible into Gothic. Ulfila and his followers attempted to steer a middle course between the Catholic and Arian positions on the nature of the divine persons, a position that inevitably resulted in being labeled Arian by future generations of orthodox believers. In the short run, however, Athanaric's persecution was as ineffective as had been earlier persecutions of Christians by Rome. He succeeded only in badly dividing the Gothic peoples, creating an opportunity seized by the Gothic aristocrat Fritigern, who contacted the Roman emperor Valens and agreed to become an Arian Christian in return for support against Athanaric.

These political and religious tensions between and within the Roman and Gothic worlds were rendered suddenly beside the point by the arrival of the Huns, a steppe nomadic confederation under Central Asian leadership, in the area of the Black Sea in 375. These nomadic riders were like no people seen before by Romans or barbarians: everything from their physical appearance to their pastoral lifestyle to their mode of warfare was foreign and terrible to the old world. The Huns were never, except for the short period of the reign of Attila (444–453), a united, centralized people. Rather, the Huns, commonly referred to as Scyths by Roman sources, were disparate groups of warrior bands sharing a common nomadic culture, a military tradition of mounted raiding, and an extraordinary ability to absorb the peoples they conquered into their confederations. Their startling military success was due to their superb cavalry tactics, their proficiency with short double-reflex bows that allowed them to launch a volley of arrows with deadly accuracy while riding, and their tactical knowledge of the steppes and plains of western Asia and Central Europe that allowed them to appear without warning, inflict tremendous damage, and disappear into the grasslands as quickly as they had come.

Within a generation, these nomadic warrior bands destroyed first the Alans and the Greuthung kingdom and then the Tervingian confederation. With the destruction of the authority of Gothic leadership, constituent groups of the old Gothic confederations had to decide whether to join the Hunnic bands or to petition the emperor to enter and settle in the Roman empire.

The semi-nomadic confederation known as the Huns provided a model for the enormous but fragile steppe confederations such as that of the later Avars. They easily absorbed a vast spectrum of other peoples and profited from their position between the eastern and western halves of the empire, but vanished when their leaders were no longer able to lead them to victories over their victims.

For most of the Goths defeated by the Huns, entering the confederation was an obvious choice. Although a Hunnic core of Central Asians provided central leadership to the Hunnic armies, the peoples they conquered were assimilated with ease. Good warriors, whether of Gothic, Vandal, Frankish, or even Roman origins, could rise rapidly within the Hunnic hierarchy. Even among the central leadership, this polyethnicity was obvious. The Hunnic leader Edika was simultaneously a Hun and a Scirian, and ruled the short-lived Scirian kingdom as king. The greatest of the Hunnic leaders, Attila, bore a Gothic name (or title): Attila means "little father." Gothic, Greek, and Latin were used alongside Hunnic in his court, and among his advisers were not only leaders of various barbarian peoples but even former Greek merchants. For a time the Italian aristocrat Orestes, father of the last Roman emperor in the west, Romulus Augustulus, served the Hunnic king.

To maintain the unity of this heterogeneous Hunnic confederation, its chieftains needed a constant flow of treasure, the principal source of which was the empire. Initially, raids on the Illyrian and Thracian borders of the empire provided the bulk of the booty, supplemented by annual subsidies from the emperors to prevent further incursions; thus the ability to conduct successful military operations was essential for the survival of Hunnic leaders. During the first decades of the Hunnic confederation leadership was shared by members of a royal family, but in 544 Attila eliminated his brother Bleda after Hunnic successes began to abate and unified the Huns under his command. Under Attila annual subsidies from the emperor increased from 350 pounds of gold to 700, and eventually to 2,100, an enormous amount to the barbarians but not a devastating burden on the empire. Theodosius found it easier to pay than to defend against Hunnic raids. In addition to gold, Attila demanded that the empire cease harboring Hunnic refugees and return those who had fled his authority. Those who were returned were impaled or crucified.

After the death of Theodosius in 450, his successor Marcian refused to continue preferential treatment of the Huns. With this source of funding gone, Attila apparently considered himself too weak to extract adequate booty by raiding the eastern empire and turned his attention to the western empire of Valentinian III. He led his armies west in two long raids. The first in 451 reached far into Gaul before being stopped at the battle of the Catalaunian Plains between Troyes and Châlons-sur-Marne. There Attila's army, probably composed primarily of subject Germanic peoples from the western areas of his control—Suebi, Franks, and Burgundians in addition to Gepids, Ostrogoths, and Central Asian Huns—was stopped by an equally heterogeneous army of Goths, Franks, Bretons, Sarmatians, Burgundians, Saxons, Alans, and Romans under the command of the patrician Aetius. The second raid came the following year, when Attila led another army into Italy. Again, in keeping with Hunnic priorities the expedition was primarily undertaken for pillage, not for lasting political objectives, and ended at the gates of Rome when Pope Leo I paid off the Huns, who, weakened by disease and far from their accustomed terrain, were probably all too ready to return to the steppe.

The essential fragility of an empire such as Attila's was demonstrated by its rapid disintegration following his death. Steppe empires built on victory could not endure defeat. A separatist coalition under the leadership of the Gepid Ardaric revolted against Attila's sons. The rebels were victorious and the defeat of Attila's sons led to the splintering of the old confederation and new processes of ethnogenesis. In addition to the Gepid alliance emerged the Rugii, the Sciri, and the Sarmatians along the Danube, and the Ostrogoths, who gathered the remnants of the Greuthungs and entered Roman service as *foederati*. Some of Attila's sons continued to lead splinter groups, some apparently returning to Central Asia, others entering Roman service within the Roman military aristocracy. Within a few generations, they and their followers had become Ostrogoths, Gepids, or Bulgars.

A different fate met those barbarians who fled the Hunnic onslaught in 375. While the majority of the Greuthungs and Alans were absorbed into the new Hunnic confederation, a minority, augmented by deserting Huns, fled toward the *limes*. So too did most of the Tervingi, who abandoned Athanaric's leadership and fled with Fritigern across the Danube. The flight of the Tervingi into the empire set in motion a decisive transformation in the identity of this people. From the Roman perspective, they were but one more barbarian group of *dediticii*, received into the empire and allowed to settle in Thrace, where they were expected to support themselves through agriculture while supplying troops to the military. The reality was that in quality and quantity, the Tervingian refugees' situation was very different from that of earlier *dediticii*. First, these Goths were far more numerous than earlier barbarian bands allowed into the empire, and they overwhelmed the Roman administrative abilities. Second, the Romans did not force them to surrender their arms as was the usual practice. When Roman mistreatment and Gothic hunger pushed the refugees to armed resistance, the result was a series of Gothic victories. Soon the refugee cavalry of the Greuthungs, Alans, and Huns joined the Tervingi, as did Gothic units already in the Roman army, Thracian miners, barbarian slaves, and the poor. The Gothic victories culminated in 378 with the annihilation of the imperial army and the death of Valens at Adrianople.

After Adrianople, Rome could no longer treat the Goths as *dediticii*. In a treaty concluded in 382, the Goths were recognized as a federated people but were allowed to settle between the Danube and the Balkan mountains with their own governors, creating in effect a state within a state. Tax revenues traditionally collected for the support of the military were redirected to the support of the barbarians. In return they were required to provide military support to the empire, but they did so under their own commanders, who were subordinated to Roman generals.

At the same time, the unprecedented success of the Tervingians and their allies led to a fundamental transformation of this disparate band of refugees into the Visigoths, a new people with a new cultural and political identity. The Visigoths quickly adapted the mounted tactics used so effectively by the Greuthungs, Alans, and Huns in the campaigns against Valens, in effect transforming themselves into a highly mobile cavalry on the Scythian model. For the next generation the Visigoths struggled to maintain themselves as a Gothic confederation and simultaneously as a Roman army. Their king Alaric, a member of the royal clan of the Balths, sought recognition and payments at once as ruler of a federated people and as a high-ranking general, or *magister militum*, in imperial service with de facto command of the civilian and military bureaucracies in the regions under his authority. He pursued both of these goals through alternate service to and expeditions against the eastern and western emperors and their imperial barbarian commanders.

Alaric's insistence on his dual role stood in contrast to an older model of imperial barbarian embodied by Stilicho, the supreme military commander in the west and intermittently Alaric's commander, ally, and bitter enemy. Stilicho was of Vandal birth, but he, like pagan Frankish and Alamannic Roman commanders before him, had entirely abandoned his ethnic barbarian ties. He was a Roman citizen, an orthodox Catholic, and operated entirely within the Roman tradition, alternately serving and manipulating both the imperial family (as guardian and later father-in-law of the emperor Honorius) and barbarian federates such as Alaric. Stilicho's path proved fatal when he was unable to maintain the integrity of the Rhone and Danube *limes*. On the last day of the year 406, bands of Vandals, Suebi, and Alans crossed the upper Rhine to ravage Gaul and penetrate as far as Spain unhindered. Around the same time, Gothic bands fleeing the Huns invaded Italy from Pannonia. In spite of Stilicho's ultimate success in defeating the Gothic invaders, these twin disasters played into his enemies' hands. In 408 he was deposed and executed on orders of his son-in-law. Following his death, thousands of other assimilated barbarians living in Italy were likewise slaughtered.

Surviving barbarians in Italy rallied to Alaric, whose dual role as barbarian king and Roman commander offered a more durable model. His efforts to win recognition and payments to support his followers led to his invasion of Italy in 408. Botched negotiations led, after numerous feints, to the capture and pillage of Rome on August 24–26, 410. Although his subsequent attempt to lead his people to the fertile lands of Africa failed and he died in southern Italy, Alaric had established an enduring form of barbarian-Roman polity.

Alaric's successor and brother-in-law Athaulf led the Goths out of Italy and into Gaul. At Narbonne in the year 414 he married Galla Placidia, sister of the emperor Honorius captured in Rome, in the hope of entering the imperial family of Theodosius. The chimera of political advantage through marriage into the imperial family would recur over the next century, with Attila's claims to Honoria, the sister of Valentinian III, and with the marriage between the Vandal pretender Huneric and his hostage Eudocia, Valentinian's daughter. None of these attempts accomplished either peace or parity with the Roman empire.

Athaulf fell to an assassin and after futile attempts first to reenter Italy and then to reach North Africa, his successors accepted a new *foedus* with the mandate to clear Spain of rebel Bagaudae as well as of Vandals and Alans. Following their return to Toulouse in 418, the Visigoths began the form of political and social organization that would characterize their kingdom and those of other federated barbarians, notably the Burgundians and the Ostrogoths.

The barbarians, whatever their ethnic origins, formed a small but powerful military minority within a much larger Roman population. As mounted warriors, they tended to settle in strategic border areas of their territories or in the political capitols. Support of these barbarian armies was provided by the assignment of a portion of traditional tax revenues that had gone to the imperial fisc, thus minimizing the burden of the barbarian occupation on the land-owning Roman aristocracy and keeping these professional warriors free for military service. Collection and distribution of these taxes remained in the hands of the municipal *curiales,* likewise minimizing the effects on the landowning aristocracy that monopolized these offices. At least this seems to have been the arrangement with the Visigoths in 418, the Burgundians in 443, and the Ostrogoths in Italy during the 490s. In some other cases, such as that of a group of Alans settled around Valence in 440, the barbarians were assigned tax debts no longer being collected by imperial officials. Through these tax shares, barbarian kings were able to provide for their followers and keep them from dispersing into the countryside in order to supervise their estates. In the tradition of Alaric, barbarian kings were not only commanders of their people but simultaneously high-ranking Roman officials (*magister militum, patricius,* and so forth), who exercised supreme authority over the civilian administrative system in their territory, effectively governing the two elements of the Roman state that had been separate since the time of Diocletian.

The territorialization of barbarian armies within these terms set into motion a further ethnogenesis. Barbarian kings began the attempt to transform the culturally disparate members of their armies into a unified people with a common law and sense of identity while maintaining their distance from the majority Roman population of their kingdoms. This identity was drawn from vague family traditions reinterpreted and transformed by the new situations in which they found themselves. For the Visigoths, the Balth family provided the center of this tradition. For the Vandals, it was the Hasdings; for the Ostrogoths, the Amals. These royal families projected their imagined past onto the people as a whole, providing a common sense of origin to be shared by the whole of the military elite.

To a lesser extent, barbarian kings likewise used religion to found a common identity. The Gothic royal family, like those of the Vandals, Burgundians, and other peoples, were Arian, and the Arian faith became closely identified with the king and his people. Arianism was neither a proselytizing faith nor a persecuting one. At the most, Arians demanded the use of one or more churches for their worship. Otherwise, orthodox Christianity was not proscribed or persecuted. The exception appears to have been the Vandal kingdom of North Africa, but even here the persecutions and confiscations directed against the orthodox church seemed to have had more to do with confiscation of land and repression of political opponents than doctrinal differences.

Barbarian kings also relied on legal tradition to forge a new identity for their peoples. Nothing is known about barbarian law codes before the Visigothic Code of Euric, which dates from ca. 470–480. Although in general barbarian law codes appear to stand in sharp distinction to Roman law, with their system of tariffs for offenses *(Wergeld)*, the use of oaths, and formal oral procedure, such traditions may not have been much different from local vulgar legal practice in large areas of the west by the 5th century. The laws sought to delineate rights and responsibilities of barbarians and Romans and seem to have been territorial laws, intended to be applied to barbarians and Romans alike, although not to the exclusion of other Roman legal traditions alive in the territories granted to the barbarian armies.

Royal efforts to forge new and enduring ethnic and political identities within these dual kingdoms met with indifferent success. The distinction between the barbarian military and political minority on the one hand and the Roman population on the other remained most sharp in Vandal Africa. The Vandals, unlike most of the other barbarian peoples to create kingdoms within the empire, had done so without benefit of a treaty with the empire and had proceeded to confiscation of property on a wide scale. These confiscations won for them the enduring hatred of aristocratic landowners as well as that of the African orthodox church that had learned political activism during decades of opposition to Donatists. Many of the landowning aristocracy fled or were exiled, as were the Catholic bishops, who returned only in the 520s. Vandal kings eventually won imperial recognition, but even then their rule remained tenuous. Hated and isolated from the rest of the population, the Vandals were easy prey for Justinian's army in 533. Two decisive battles broke the kingdom and the remaining Vandals were deported and dissolved into various federated barbarian armies in the eastern Mediterranean. Within less than a decade, the Vandals had entirely disappeared.

The Ostrogothic kingdom in Italy established by Theoderic the Great in the 490s began with greater prospects but likewise fell to Byzantine reconquest. The Ostrogoths emerged from the ruins of the Hunnic empire as one of the Germanic factions alternatively allying with and fighting against the eastern empire. In 484 Theoderic, who claimed descent from the pre-Hunnic royal Amal family, united a number of these groups under his command and four years later led a polyethnic army into Italy on behalf of the emperor Zeno against Odoacer, a barbarian commander in the tradition of Stilicho who had made himself master of Italy. In 493 Theoderic gained control of the peninsula, eliminated Odoacer, and took over the Roman fiscal and administrative system.

Theoderic sought to transform his heterogeneous, mobile barbarian army into a stable, settled, Gothic people capable of peaceful coexistence within Roman Italy. His goal for his Gothic following was to convince them to adopt *civilitas*, the Roman principles of the rule of law and the traditions of tolerance and consensus in civic society which they were to protect by their military valor. Nevertheless, he intended to maintain Goths and Romans as separate communities, one military, one civilian, living in mutual dependence under his supreme authority. Thus, although Theoderic received the loyal support of Roman administrators and even of the close advisers of Odoacer such as the senator Cassiodorus, like other barbarian kings he sought to strengthen the Gothic element of his rule by appointing his personal agents or *comites* to supervise and intervene throughout the Roman bureaucracy. He likewise privileged the Arian church as the *ecclesia legis Gothorum*, but he saw to it that it remained a minority church which he prohibited from proselytizing among the orthodox majority.

Theoderic's attempt to bring about a new Gothic ethnogenesis failed. The boundaries between Ostrogothic warrior and Roman civilian blurred as many barbarians became landowners sharing the same economic and regional concerns as their Roman neighbors. Their children, educated in the traditions of the Roman elite, grew even further apart from the warrior culture. At the same time, some Romans rose in the ranks of the military and adopted Gothic tradition, even to the extent of learning the Gothic language and marrying Gothic women. In reaction to this loss of Gothic distinctiveness, an anti-Roman reaction set in among a portion of the military concerned about the rapid Romanization of many in their ranks. Tensions mounted following Theoderic's death and culminated in the murder of his daughter Amalasuntha in 535. Justinian took the murder as an excuse to refuse to recognize the legitimacy of the Gothic king Theodehad, Theoderic's nephew, and to invade Italy. Unlike the reconquest of Africa, however, which was accomplished in two battles, the war lasted almost two decades and devastated Italy more profoundly than had all of the barbarian invasions of the previous two centuries. The final result was, however, just as in North Africa: the total disappearance of the Ostrogoths.

In Gaul, the Gothic kingdom of Toulouse and the Burgundian kingdom met similar fates. Both continued to serve as federates, participating for example in the defeat of the Huns in the battle of the Catalaunian Plains. They likewise profited from imperial weakness by expanding their territories. The Goths eventually extended their control north to the Loire and south through Spain, while the Burgundians expanded east until being driven back by the Gepids. Still, the Visigoths remained a small Arian minority and disappeared north of the Pyrenees after a single defeat at the hands of the Franks in 507. Their survival in Spain was due to the intervention of Theoderic, who assisted them in maintaining their independence in Spain. Thereafter they retreated into Spain, where they abandoned their Arianism and thus their separate gentile identity only in 587. The Burgundians rapidly lost any cultural, religious, or genealogical identity they may have had, and by the 6th century "Burgundian" seems to have designated little more than the holder of what had originally been the military allotments first divided among the barbarians.

The type of barbarian polity pioneered by the Visigoths and largely adopted by the Vandals and Ostrogoths—the creation and maintenance of two communities, one orthodox, Roman, and civilian, the other Arian, barbarian, and military, under the unified command of a barbarian king holding an imperial commission—ended in failure. More enduring were the unitary kingdoms created by the Frankish king Clovis as well as by the petty kings of Britain. The reasons for these successes are several. In part, their distance from the core of the Byzantine world meant that by the early 5th century these regions were already considered expendable by the empire, and in the 6th century they lay beyond the reach of Justinian. In part, too, the transformation of Roman civil administration may have been sufficiently advanced that little remained for barbarian kings to absorb: in the case of the Franks, this was only the individual *civitates;* in the case of the Saxons, not even that. Finally, the barbarians themselves were different. Although the Franks and the Saxons initially served as federates of the empire, they had no direct experience of the Mediterranean world of Constantinople or even Italy. They, like the provincial Romans they absorbed, were far removed from the cultural and administrative traditions of a Theoderic or a Cassiodorus. The result was a simpler but in the long run more thorough transformation of these peoples into new social and cultural forms.

In the early 5th century Britain and northern Gaul, long peripheral to the concerns of Ravenna and Constantinople, were forced to look to their own protection and organization. In both areas, old Celtic regional affinities began to take precedence over more recent Roman organization, and new political constellations of Roman, Celtic, and Germanic elements emerged. In Britain, the Roman centralized government ceded to a plethora of small, mutually hostile kingdoms. During the later 5th and 6th centuries, Germanic federates drawn from the Saxons, Frisians, Franks, and other coastal peoples came to dominate many of these kingdoms, particularly in the southwest. Although migration from the coastal regions of the continent was significant, particularly in the 6th century, the frequent appearance of Celtic names in the genealogies of early Anglo-Saxon kingdoms as well as the survival of Christian communities within these kingdoms indicates that the Anglo-Saxon ethnogenesis was the gradual fusion of indigenous populations and new arrivals under the political leadership of families that in time came to regard themselves as descended from mythical Germanic heroes. Indeed most Anglo-Saxon royal genealogies traced their ancestry back to the war god Woden.

Frankish society was the result of a similar fusion that took place in the northern portions of Gaul, those most removed from Mediterranean concern. In the course of the 5th century, a series of rival kingdoms emerged from the ruins of Roman provincial administration, each headed by a warlord or king. Some of these leaders were Frankish kings who commanded largely barbarian units and had ties on both sides of the Rhine. Others were members of the Gallo-Roman aristocracy and drew support from mixed Roman provincial and barbarian armies. Among the former were members of the Merovingian family, who commanded barbarian troops descended from Salian Franks probably settled within the empire in the late 4th century. Ethnic affiliation was much less significant in these constellations than political expediency: the Frankish followers of the Merovingian Childeric, who had grown wealthy and powerful in the service of the empire, temporarily transferred their allegiance to the *magister militum* Aegidius.

Beginning in 486 Childeric's son Clovis expanded his power south and east from his father's kingdom centered around Tournai. He captured Soissons, the administrative center of Belgica Secunda, temporarily dominated the Thuringians, and defeated the Alamanni between 496 and 506. In 507 he defeated and killed the Visigothic king Alaric II and began conquering the Visigothic kingdom north of the Pyrenees. None of his conquests appears to have been based on a commission or treaty with Constantinople, but following his victory over Alaric emissaries of Emperor Anastasius granted him some form of imperial recognition, probably an honorary consulship. He spent his final years, until his death around 511, eliminating other Frankish kings and rival members of his own family who ruled kingdoms in Cologne, Cambrai, and elsewhere.

Ethnogenesis proceeded differently in Clovis's Frankish kingdom from that in Ostrogothic Italy or Visigothic Aquitaine. He did not base his conquests on an imperial mandate nor did he attempt to create the sort of dual society erected by an earlier generation of barbarian kings. Salian Franks had been deeply involved in imperial and regional political struggles in Gaul for generations. Clovis's authority had been recognized by representatives of the Gallo-Roman aristocracy such as Bishop Remigius of Rheims since the death of his father in 486. His absorption of rival power centers caused much less dramatic change than had the conquests of earlier barbarian kings. He certainly took over the remnants of civil administration, but these probably were already in serious decay and in any case did not extend above the level of individual *civitates*.

Moreover, there is little evidence that the Franks had or attempted to create as strong a sense of identity distinct from the Roman population as had Theoderic or other Gothic commanders. Clovis's family apparently claimed some semi-divine descent and counted a minotaur-like beast among its ancestors, but no Frankish genealogical lore could rival the generations of heroes and gods in Gothic tradition. Already in the 6th century Franks may have claimed Trojan ancestry, thus connecting themselves genealogically to their Roman neighbors. Nor were the Franks long separated from their Gallo-Roman neighbors by religion. Prior to the 6th century some Franks had been Christian, whether Arian or orthodox, while others, including Clovis's family, had retained a pagan religious tradition. Clovis probably flirted with the Arianism of his great neighbor Theoderic, but ultimately accepted orthodox baptism, although when in his career this took place remains open to debate.

United by a common religion and a common legend of origin, Clovis's Franks and the Roman provincials of his kingdom found no obstacles to forging a common identity. This they did with considerable rapidity. Within only a few generations, the population north of the Loire had become uniformly Frankish and, although Roman legal traditions persisted in the south and Burgundian and Roman legal status endured in the old Burgundian kingdom conquered by Clovis's sons in the 530s, these differing legal traditions did not constitute the basis for a separate social or political identity. The great strength of the Frankish synthesis was the new creation, within the Roman world, of a unified society that drew without a sense of contradiction on both Roman and barbarian traditions.

As Frankish, Longobard, Anglo-Saxon, and Visigothic kingdoms assimilated surviving Roman political and cultural traditions, they became the center of post-Roman Europe, while new barbarian peoples, most notably the Saxons, Slavs, and Avars, replaced them on the periphery. Ethnic labels remained significant designations within the Romano-barbarian kingdoms, but they designated multiple and at times even contradictory aspects of social and political identity.

In Italy, the Longobards, a heterogeneous amalgam including Gepids, Herulians, Suebs, Alamans, Bulgarians, Saxons, Goths, and Romans who had arrived in Italy in 568 from Pannonia created a weak, decentralized union of rival military units of duchies. The duchies combined traditional military units or *farae* with the Gothic-Roman military and administrative tradition. Religious as well as political divisions ran deep in Longobard Italy: in the 6th century "Longobards" included pagans, Arians, schismatic Christians, and orthodox Christians. Some dukes allied themselves with the Byzantine exarch of Ravenna while others, particularly in the south, remained fiercely autonomous.

In the last decades of the 6th century, however, the constant challenges that the ambitious Longobard armies posed to the Byzantines to the east and the Franks to the west led these two powers to coordinate their attacks on the Longobards. Threatened with annihilation between these two foes, the Longobard dukes restored the monarchy that they had abandoned shortly after their arrival in Italy. This kingship owed much to Gothic precedence, especially in the use of the name Flavius, which sought to connect the new Longobard identity with the imperial Flavian name and tradition, as a claim to universal recognition on the part of all inhabitants of the kingdom. Still, Longobard identity and organization remained porous. The great duchies of Beneventum and Spoleto remained essentially independent of the king throughout the entire history of the Longobard kingdom.

In the course of the 7th century, the Longobard kings solidified their position both externally and internally. They formed marriage alliances with Franks and especially the Bavarians, whose own Agilolfing dukes were closely related to Longobard kings. They strengthened the Arian party within the Longobard kingdom while maintaining a balance between orthodox and "Three Chapter" Christians, a tripartite Christian tradition that ended only around 700. Most important, beginning with Rothari (636–652) Longobard kings published legal codes for their kingdom, codes that enunciated a theory of cooperation between king and people, the former initiating and improving tradition, the latter, through the army and the magnates, accepting the code. The Edict of Rothari (643) also presents a reshaping of a Longobard ethnic myth, centered on the line of Longobard kings. Rothari styles himself the "seventeenth king of the Longobard people," a number meant to assimilate the Longobards to the Romans and the Goths (both Romulus and Theoderic the Great were held to be seventeenth in their lines). The very creation of this claim to an ancient royal history and ethnic identity is proof of the deep assimilation of Gothic and Roman values and identity.

Like the Longobard kingdom, the Frankish world remained divided in fundamental ways through the later 6th and 7th centuries. Core areas of the kingdom—Neustria, Austrasia, and Burgundy—often had their own kings, who drew their legitimacy through descent from Clovis. The peripheral areas of the Frankish kingdom—Aquitaine, Provence, Bavaria, Thuringia, and Frisia— were governed in the name of the Frankish kings by dukes or patricians, often men with central Frankish ties who rapidly integrated themselves into the local power structures.

The Frankish name came to designate the inhabitants of the core territories ruled by the Frankish kings and acquired increasingly a geographical rather than ethnic connotation. Legal codes for the Thuringians, Bavarians, and other peoples within the Frankish realm were essentially regional law codes, modeled on Salic law even while incorporating some local traditions and imposed on peripheral areas of the Frankish realm. In general the vocabulary of ethnic terminology occurs most frequently in the context of military organization, since contingents from different areas were mustered and led by their dukes and counts, the institutional descendants of late Roman military officers.

Merovingian kings of the 7th century, once characterized as incompetent if not mentally deficient, are now recognized to have been nothing of the sort. Still, from the early 7th century, when powerful leaders such as Chlothar II

(584–629) and Dagobert I (623–638) could exercise effective control over a unified Frankish kingdom, a gradual decline in royal authority worked to the benefit of regional aristocracies. However, this growth of regionalism was seldom if ever the result of deep ethnic or cultural differences. The leading families in Austria, Neustria, and Burgundy as well as in the peripheral duchies of the Frankish realm were generally themselves descendants of representatives of the Frankish monarchs with both central and regional ties that they used to their own advantage. The struggles between aristocratic factions that eventually led to the rise of the Carolingian dynasty are remarkable for their lack of ethnic overtones, in spite of the attempt by some modern historians to read ethnic conflict into these contests.

In the Visigothic kingdom, the integration of barbarian and Roman populations began with Leovigild (569–586) and his son Reccarid (586–601). Leovigild reunited a much divided Visigothic kingdom and expelled most of the remnants of Byzantine control from the peninsula. Once the orthodox Byzantine presence was eliminated, orthodox Christianity ceased to be the political threat that it had been, and Leovigild began to move his Arian elite toward orthodox Catholicism. His son brought this to completion at the council of Toledo in 589 that followed the conversion of Reccarid himself in 587.

The conversion of the Visigoths had fundamental consequences for the identity of the Visigothic people and kingdom. The Catholic hierarchy and the political and social leadership of the communities they represented became fully integrated into the Gothic state and people. The periodic councils of Toledo that began in the 630s developed into the fundamental institution unifying Visigothic Spain. These councils treated matters of faith, morals, and ritual, as well as politics and administration. Toledo became in time the preeminent metropolitan see of Spain, able both to extend its authority throughout the Spanish church and to define royal legitimacy not in terms of family, as in the case of the Merovingian family, but rather in terms of having received royal unction in the city. The extent of episcopal and royal cooperation in the transformation of the Visigothic kingdom and state was unprecedented in western Europe.

The British isles never knew the kind of unity of people and kingship known on the continent. In Scotland, Ireland, and Wales, as in England, a sense of identity never translated into a political structure. Through the 7th century, southeastern England was closely connected to the cultural and political world of Merovingian Gaul. Political unity was never an issue. At various times petty kings of southeastern England attempted to dominate their neighbors, and in the later 7th century some rulers of Northumbria temporarily managed to enforce some sort of lordship over other kingdoms. However, such claims never amounted to an institutionalized overlordship. The office of a high king, the so-called Bretwalda, is essentially a modern myth. Nevertheless, a *gens Anglorum* was perceived to exist, although it was largely defined by opposition to the British enemies to the west, south, and north. And yet membership in the *gens Anglorum*, through participation in one of the petty Anglo-Saxon kingdoms, was open to people of British and Germanic background alike. Once more, membership in the Anglo-Saxon people was a question of constitution, not simply of inheritance.

Although Roman sources often presented barbarian peoples' ethnic identities as fixed, we have seen that new identities were constantly being established and transformed through contacts with the Romans. The barbarian *gentes* in turn came to play an integral and transformative role in the later Roman empire.

Select Bibliography

Amory, Patrick. *People and Identity in Ostrogothic Italy, 489–554.* Cambridge, Eng., 1997.

———— "Ethnographic Rhetoric, Aristocratic Attitudes and Political Allegiance in Post-Roman Gaul," *Klio* 76 (1994): 438–453.

———— "The Meaning and Purpose of Ethnic Terminology in the Burgundian Law-Codes," *Early Medieval Europe* 2 (1993): 1–28.

———— "Names, Ethnic Identity and Community in Fifth and Sixth-Century Burgundy," *Viator* 25 (1994): 1–30.

Bäuml, Franz H., and Marianna D. Birnbaum. *Attila: The Man and His Image.* Budapest, 1993.

Balsdon, J. P. V. D. *Romans and Aliens.* Chapel Hill, N.C., 1979.

Campbell, James, ed. *The Anglo-Saxons.* London, 1982.

Collins, Roger. *Early Medieval Europe 300–1000.* New York, 1991.

———— *Early Medieval Spain: Unity in Diversity, 400–1000.* London, 1983.

Drinkwater, John, and Hugh Elton, eds. *Fifth-Century Gaul: A Crisis of Identity?* Cambridge, 1992.

Geary, Patrick J. *Before France and Germany: The Creation and Transformation of the Merovingian World.* New York, 1988.

———— "Ethnicity as a Situational Construct in the Early Middle Ages," *Mitteilungen der anthropologischen Gesellschaft in Wien* 113 (1983): 15–26.

Goffart, Walter. *Barbarians and Romans A.D. 418–584: The Techniques of Accommodation.* Princeton, 1980.

———— *The Narrators of Barbarian History (A.D. 550–800): Jordanes, Gregory of Tours, Bede and Paul the Deacon.* Princeton, 1988.

———— *Rome's Fall and After.* London, 1989.

James, Edward. *The Franks.* Oxford, 1988.

Jarnut, J. *Geschichte der Langobarden.* Stuttgart, 1982.

Maenchen-Helfen, Otto. *The World of the Huns.* Berkeley, 1973.

Murray, Alexander C. *Germanic Kinship Structure: Studies in Law and Society in Antiquity and the Early Middle Ages.* Toronto, 1983.

Pohl, Walter. *Die Aawren: Ein Steppenvolk im Mitteleuropa 567–822 n. Chr.* Munich, 1988.

———— "Conceptions of Ethnicity in Early Medieval Studies," *Archaeologia Polona* 29 (1991): 39–49.

———— "Tradition, Ethnogenese und literarische Gestaltung: Eine Zwischenbilanz," in Karl Brunner and Brigitte Merta, eds., *Ethnogenese und Überlieferung: Angewandte Methoden der Frühmittelalterforschung.* Vienna, 1994, 9–26.

———— "Telling the Difference: Signs of Ethnic Identity," in Walter Pohl and Helmut Reimitz, eds., *Strategies of Distinction: The Constitution of Ethnic Communities, 300–800.* Leiden, 1998, 17–69.

Todd, Malcolm. *The Northern Barbarians*. London, 1987.

Wenskus, Reinhard. *Stammesbildung und Verfassung: Das Werden der frühmittelalter-lichen Gentes*. Cologne, 1961.

Wolfram, Herwig. *History of the Goths*. Berkeley, 1988.

———— "Gothic History and Historical Ethnography," *Journal of Medieval History* 7 (1981): 309–319.

———— *The Roman Empire and Its Germanic Peoples*. Berkeley, 1997.

Wolfram, Herwig, and Walter Pohl, eds. *Typen der Ethnogenese unter besonderer Berücksichtigung der Bayern*, vol. 1. Vienna, 1990.

Wood, Ian N. *The Merovingian Kingdoms 450–751*. London, 1994.

Zöllner, Erich. *Geschichte der Franken*. Munich, 1970.

WAR AND VIOLENCE

Brent D. Shaw

I know well that war is a great evil—indeed the worst of all evils." So opined the author of a treatise on strategy written in the reign of Emperor Justinian (*Peri strat.* 4; Dennis, 1985: 20–21). The sentiments and the judgment were those of a man of pragmatic battlefield experience, and they evoke the hard realities of a fighting soldier's life. These bitter words are embedded in the otherwise cool and technical prose of a military manual, a genre which by the time of our anonymous author had a millennium-old tradition in the Greek world. Throughout the Mediterranean and the Near East during late antiquity this "worst of all evils" was fundamental to the making and unmaking of political and cultural worlds. The social orders of the time were constituted and maintained by brute force and compulsion. Yet despite a tradition of historical writing that placed the conduct of war at the center of its narratives, the obstacles to a reasoned understanding of war are considerable.

Some of the most daunting problems are posed by the written sources themselves. For the third quarter of the 4th century that is covered by the extant books of Ammianus Marcellinus, we are reasonably well informed; the same applies to the middle quarters of the 6th century that are covered by Procopius's *History of the Wars of Justinian*. For the period after the Battle of Adrianople (378) to the early 6th century, however, we are at the mercy of fragments and summaries preserved by later historians and compilers, none of which permits a systemic understanding of the nature of war. For the Roman empire, at least these remnants have survived. For other equally important places and periods in late antiquity, we face even greater difficulties. As attempts to provide general analyses of warfare among the illiterate societies of the Eurasian plains north of the Roman and Sassanid empires have shown, archaeological evidence alone is no substitute for written sources (Todd, 1992: 162). Although an understanding of social structure and political power in these societies is critical to an evaluation of the war system of late antiquity, claims about the formation of proto-states and the development of incipient class structures or political hier-archies based on the mute remains of a few wood huts are both unconvincing and frustrating (Hedeager, 1978, 1988, 1992; Todd, 1992: 65–75). So too, apart from Roman historical sources (mainly Ammianus and Procopius, and later Agathias) little can be said of the military developments and institu-tions of the Sassanid empire. In the Persian case there are no surviving contem-porary literary sources of importance; the basic source materials for a valid reconstruction and analysis of Sassanid military force and practice are surpris-ingly deficient (Schippmann, 1990: 103–106). The much later Arabic sources, such as al-Tabarī, that are used to fill the gap are difficult to interpret, and are often fantastic in their narratives (Howard-Johnston, 1995: 169–180; 211–212). Whereas it is true that some of the first Sassanid monarchs, including Shapur I, provided epigraphical *res gestae* of their reigns that highlighted their military accomplishments, the practice quickly fell into desuetude. With no tradition in which to place them and with very little other indigenous Iranian literary evidence to provide context, evaluations of the information they pro-vide on war are fraught with difficulties.

In the surviving books of the Greek and Roman historians, the focus of their accounts on single dominant narrative characters produces basic distortions. In the historian Ammianus, for example, Julian's campaigns in Gaul in 355–357 are described in considerable detail. But when Julian moves to the eastern Mediterranean, impelled by the demands of civil war, Ammianus leaves Gaul behind. The historian's narrative dutifully follows Julian and his successors eastward. Hence we have a marvelous exposition of the disastrous Persian expedition of 363; a coherent narrative of the cycle of events leading up to the crossing of the lower Danube by groups of Tervingi in 376; and a vivid descrip-tion of the incompetence and chaos leading to the Battle of Adrianople in 378. We therefore happen to be reasonably well informed about the events con-nected with the breach of one riverine frontier of the empire. But in the case of a similar, indeed more serious, breach of the Rhine frontier on that fateful New Year's Eve of 406, all we know, basically, is that it happened. For critical events of the 5th century—the wars connected, for example, with the rise and fall of Alaric or of Attila—we know, and can know, so much less.

Moreover, even in the case of the Roman empire, for which there exists a consistent narrative historical tradition, many of the ancillary primary sources are rather disappointing. Prime among these is the list of civil and military offices of the state *(Notitia Dignitatum),* which purports to provide complete lists of the principal units of the Roman army along with its command struc-ture (Seeck, 1876; Jones, 1964: 1429–50; Goodburn and Bartholomew, 1976). Apart from the constantly debated problems connected with the document's provenance, composition, and dating (especially of its divergent eastern and western halves), it should provide a good guide to the strategic distribution and organization of the late Roman army. Alas, the Roman army in action as described in narrative prose histories of the late 4th and early 5th centuries is often difficult to connect with the bureaucrat's ideal of the imperial army (Hoff-mann, 1969: 490f.; Liebeschuetz, 1990: 40–41). A quirky 4th century pamphlet entitled "On Warfare" *(De rebus bellicis)* reveals something of the ideology of a reform-minded civilian from the large landowning classes, and reaffirms the commonplace that one of the few places where technological innovations were sought and lauded was in the realm of the devices of war—but not much more (Thompson, 1952; Liebeschuetz, 1994). Vegetius's manual "On the Military" *(De re militari)* would be of great utility were it not that it was written as a picture of how the Roman army used to be (Goffart, 1977; Barnes, 1979; Stelten, 1990; Milner, 1993). The nostalgia signals that the army of Vegetius's own day no longer resembled his model of centralized organization, training, logistics, and command. By contrast, some of the advice found in later Byzantine handbooks on "stratagems" of war (that is, on tactics—not strategy in the modern sense of the word) actually addresses current problems of field combat in the 7th century, and so is more directly useful (Dennis, 1985: 1–2).

Another serious problem is that classical historiography and allied forms of literature had developed canons of reporting violence that were stereotypical and schematic, and that depended on typecast descriptions derived from literary prototypes. These conventions compelled the writer to respect the limits of what was acceptable in the description of violence, even if he was a historian who had been an eyewitness to the events. In modest contravention of these standards, Procopius's reports on the effects of war in peninsular Italy resulting from the battles waged between Gothic and Byzantine forces do sometimes offer a glimpse of the more human sides of war. Of the populace in the regions of Aemilia and Etruria during the warfare of 539 he claims that "many of them as lived in the mountains were reduced to eating loaves made of the acorns of the oak trees, which they ground up like grain. The result of this was that most of the people fell victim to all types of disease . . . It is said that of the Roman farmers in Picenum no less than fifty thousand died from famine, as did a great many more in the region north of the Adriatic" *(Wars* 6.20.18–33). Procopius offers what purport to be eyewitness accounts of women reduced to cannibalism, and scenes of hunger in which people, overcome by starvation, chance upon a patch of grass and rush to pull it out and consume it on the spot. Indeed, it is manifest from Procopius's account that the Byzantine reconquest turned formerly civil areas of the western Mediterranean, especially North Africa and peninsular Italy, into a war zone on the western frontier of the Byzantine state. The eastern Roman military intervention was probably the principal cause of the permanent decline of the city of Rome into a miserable village (Wickham, 1981: 26–29; Cameron, 1985: 193–194) and of the disintegration of the networks of municipal towns that had been the hallmark of a flourishing Roman economy in North Africa *(Wars* 2.58.52; and *Anecdota* 18.1–9; but see Cameron, 1985: 171–172).

In wars of the period, combat was often reduced to brutish hand-to-hand fighting. In his description of the siege of Rome in the year 538, Procopius gives a vivid description of some of the wounds inflicted: "One of the barbarians shot Trajan in the face, above the right eye and not far from the nose. The whole of the iron point penetrated his head and disappeared entirely, although the barb on it was large and very long; but the shaft of the arrow broke off and fell to the ground" (*Wars* 6.5.25–27). In his account of the combat around Rome during the previous year, Procopius offers more reportage of war wounds: a man named Arzes, one of the guards of Belisarius, "was hit by a Gothic archer between the nose and the right eye. The point of the arrow was embedded as far as the back of his neck, but did not penetrate out; the rest of the shaft projected from his face and shook about as he rode his horse" (*Wars* 6.2.15–18). Procopius gives testimony to the aftermath of these brief "fire fights" outside the city walls: "When all the men had returned to the city, they attended to the wounded. In the case of Arzes, although the doctors wanted to draw the weapon out of his face, they were reluctant to do so for some time. They hesitated not because of the eye, which they supposed could not be saved, but for fear lest, by the cutting of membranes and tissues such as are very numerous in the region of the face, they would cause the death of a man who was one of the best in the household of Belisarius" (*Wars* 6.2.25–36). These are just a few of the human costs in one of the seventy or so brief and vicious encounters outside the walls of Rome during the year 537.

These are extraordinary pieces of historical narration, striking because they are not, like most of Procopius's accounts of sieges and set battles, dependent on rhetorical devices and images adopted from earlier historians. Such realism in the description of combat is unusual. When Ammianus offers such reportage, most of his descriptions tend to replay stereotypical scenes and rhetoric (19.2.7–15; 19.8.6–7; 19.9.9: the siege of Amida in 359; 27.2.8; 31.7.14; 31.13.4: Adrianople in 378).

Despite the difficulties posed by the primary evidence, to comprehend the real face of war is very important because many modern-day analyses of war in late antiquity assume that it consisted mainly of one army fighting another—battles of Roman armies against Gothic, German, or Persian forces (Luttwak, 1976; Ferrill, 1986, 1991; Wheeler, 1993). But any full understanding of the actions of armies has to confront the cruel fact that a great deal of the violence consisted of attacks that were deliberately planned to terrorize civilian populations. Time and again, Ammianus reports attacks on indigenous communities across the Rhine and Danube that were not much more than massacres of unarmed civilian populations in their villages and rural farmsteads (Amm.Marc. 17.10. 5–9; 17.13.10–11, 358; 27.5.4; 30.5.13f., 374). Procopius's accounts of the brutalities of war in the Byzantine reconquest of North Africa and Italy are strewn with more violent actions of this type, which were deliberately perpetrated by army commanders and their men (e.g., *Wars* 6.7.25–34; 6.10.1–1; 6.17.1–3; 6.21.38–40). To these planned atrocities must be added the normal pillaging and looting that followed most successful forays—actions that threatened to transform an army from a hierarchically controlled unit under the command of officers to an anarchical mob.

Along with love, its ideological opposite, there is perhaps no human activity that is more insistently dialogical than war. An analysis of war as a total phenomenon therefore entails an understanding of the parties on both sides. The problem is that we are usually well informed about only one of the two parties, the Roman state. The tendency to understand war in late antiquity from a

Roman perspective is also a historiographical tradition, which has been compounded by a pervasive, almost unconscious, desire to share the Roman point of view (Bury, 1928: 3–4). So the Battle of Adrianople of 378 is a catastrophe; and the sack of Rome by Alaric in 410 is a political disaster. Similarly, the defeat of Attila and his Huns on the Catalaunian Plains in 451 is a good thing. Historians offer endless recipes for how Roman forces could have been better organized or deployed; few are willing to expend much energy on devising more successful strategies for Alaric or Attila the Hun. Instead, we are asked to identify our problems with those of the Roman empire, and to draw from its grand strategies messages for our own late 20th century military predicaments (Luttwak, 1976: 2–3; Ferrill, 1986, 1991). A better understanding of how war functioned for the sum of all persons and societies as they engaged each other in this particular form of violent behavior is not likely to be enhanced by these vicarious identifications. To understand war, it is imperative to understand all war: not only what was done by armies and soldiers, but also what was not done by them—in fact, what could not be done.

Late antiquity was not an era of any great military revolution. There were few, if any, strictly technological advances in the practice of war—whether scythed chariots; heavily armored cavalry, either *cataphractarii* or *clibanarii* (Eadie, 1967; Bivar, 1972; Speidel, 1984); newfangled *ballistae,* heavier composite bows, or even "Greek fire"—that permanently transformed the nature of battle in the period (Van Creveld, 1991). The dominant social, economic, and geographical forces in which warfare was embedded conduced to a basic continuity in the conduct of war itself, even during momentous social and political transitions (Haldon, 1993). The Parthian and Sassanid states did develop a type of warfare that was very well adapted to the ecological constraints of their world—a state-organized type of war that emphasized large numbers of heavy cavalry, mobility over large open spaces, and the use of long-range strike archery (Patterson, 1966; Kolias, 1988), whereas classic Mediterranean warfare was based on massed heavy infantry formations. The repeated confrontation of these two war cultures naturally produced a degree of adaptation on the part of either side to the techniques of the other, a movement that is consciously reflected in their military manuals (Dagron, 1993).

But these adaptations did not constitute a revolution in war technology. Although there was a certain fascination with innovation in the implements of war (e.g., Amm.Marc. 21.21.8–9; 28.4; *Wars* 8.11.27, 550), the decisive forces were those of sheer size, combined with the intensive organization and deployment permitted by a bureaucratic infrastructure. Thus the Roman state remained throughout this period the major and determinant practitioner of war in the Mediterranean, with few competitors on any of its frontiers other than Sassanid Persia. The balance of the evidence supports Hans Delbrück's thesis that for this type of premodern warfare it was the mobilization of manpower that mattered in the long run (Delbrück, 1902/1921). From the great to the small powers, there was a constant pressure to recruit beyond the bounds of one's own ethnic group or state in order to acquire the manpower needed to meet or exceed the enemy's.

It has frequently been argued that the Roman empire faced constant recruiting crises, and that the pressures created by a need for military manpower that could not be met because of a decline in the population of the empire compelled the late Roman state to recruit more and more barbarians (Boak, 1955; *contra*: Elton, 1996: 136–151). In the simple terms in which this argument has often been made, however, it cannot be true. Even if we accept the highest estimates of military manpower under the aegis of the late Roman state (on the order of 650,000 men), the government never drafted more than 1 percent of the whole population of the empire. In terms of raw demographic resources, there were always enough men to provide recruits for Roman armies. There is no need to postulate an enforced "barbarization" of the Roman army of the 4th century for these reasons, or indeed a second barbarization of the 6th century Byzantine army after the great plague of the 540s (Whitby, 1995: 103–106). There were indeed serious difficulties with recruiting, but the principal causes were social and political, not demographic. It was an established truism that Italians were resistant to military service in a way that Gauls, for example, were not (Amm.Marc. 15.12.3, 355–357). The late Roman law codes repeatedly refer to persons who were willing to mutilate their bodies rather than serve in the military (C.Th. 7.13.4–5, 367).

The propensity of Roman citizens in Italy to avoid military service is well attested from the early principate, and was a potential problem even in the heyday of the Roman republic. The main difference was the response of the late antique Roman state. Cities and landowners tended to commute their recruiting requirements to cash or gold bullion payments to the state *(aurum tironicum)*. Wealthy landowners made certain that their rural workforces were kept from the recruiting officer's grasp. Slaves were always banned from army service (except in extreme state crises such as that faced by Rome in 406/7), and *coloni* on imperial estates were formally and legally exempted from military service. The Roman state took the most convenient way out of this reluctance to serve: it redeployed tax revenues from the center of the empire to pay for the armed service of men recruited from its peripheries, creating a dangerous circle of military dependency into which the late Roman state fell (C.Th. 7.13.7, 375). For social, economic, and political reasons, therefore, the real recruiting base of the empire was rather narrow and regionally specific. In 359 when the Limigantes asked for permission from Constantius to cross the Danube and to settle on lands within the empire, the emperor's advisers argued that the resettlement would achieve two objectives. It would provide the emperor with more child-producing, tribute-paying subjects from whom he could draft soldiers; and, since "the provincials are happy to contribute gold to save their bodies," the emperor would also be able to collect commuted recruiting payments from them which he could then use for his own purposes (Amm.Marc. 19.11.7). The advisers of Emperor Valens appealed to the same rationale in support of allowing large numbers of Goths to cross the lower Danube into the empire in 376 (Amm.Marc. 31.4.4–5).

Thus all social orders, whether those of large states like Rome and Persia or those of small segmentary lineage societies such as the Goths or Gepids north of the Danube, tended to recruit polyethnic armies. The "Goths" that crossed the lower Danube in force in 376 incorporated several subethnic groups of Goths (Tervingi, Greuthungi) along with Huns and Alans—a combination of ethnic groups that continued to cooperate after the Battle of Adrianople (Amm.Marc. 31.8.3; 31.16.3). The Sassanid state was no different (Shahbazi, 1986: 497). When Shapur II led his expedition into Mesopotamia in 359, his army included Armenians, Arabs, Albani, Chionitai, Gelani, Segestani, and others (Amm.Marc. 18.6.1; 19.2.3). Sometimes the boundaries of ethnicity and military service were well defined, as in the Roman armies of the high empire, which distinguished between the Roman citizen components of the army and the allied ethnic contingents that constituted at least half of the army's strength. The forces that Belisarius commanded in Italy in the mid-530s included Armenians, Goths, Isaurians, Gepids, Huns, Sklaveni, Antai, Mauri, Thracians, and Iberians (*Wars* 5.5.1–5; 5.27.1–3). The armies that he led in the east in 542 drew recruits from Armenians, Goths, Thracians, Illyrians, Heruls, Vandals, Mauri, and others (*Wars* 2.21.5).

Naturally, various societies of late antiquity policed the connections between social status and military service differently. To the very end, the civil state polities that were part of the Graeco-Roman tradition drew the line at the recruitment of unfree persons (*C.Th.* 7.13.8, 380). Only fearful emergencies justified the breach of this social rule, and even then the propensity was to manumit slaves before enrolling them in the army (*C.Th.* 7.13.6, 406; Whitby, 1995: 83). In contrast, the segmentary lineage societies of northern Europe and the Near East seem regularly to have accepted slave or servile elements as part of their armed forces. This was as true of the Sarmatians along the Danube in the 4th century (Amm.Marc. 17.12.18; 17.13.1; 19.11.1; 29.6.15) as it was of the Heruls who were in the service of Belisarius in the mid 6th century (*Wars* 2.25.27–28). Perhaps more to the point, given later developments in Muslim armies (Crone, 1980; Pipes, 1981), there was also a tradition of slave soldiers in the Ethiopian armies (the kingdom of Aksum) and among peoples across the Red Sea in the Arabian Peninsula (*Wars* 1.20.2).

The other great constraining forces to warfare were limits on communication. All sides, of course, had their paid spies and informants (*Wars* 1.21.11). The problem was that the knowledge obtained by even these professionals was faulty and contradictory (Austin, 1979: 22–40; Lee, 1993; Burns, 1994: 32). Much of the vaunted intelligence apparatus of Rome was provoked more by fears of civil war and potential internal challenges to the emperor's power than by any real outside threats (Austin and Rankov, 1995). Most often, commanders had to deduce what might happen from actual movements of men and supplies, rather than from intelligence reports. Decisions concerning the initiation of war were concentrated in the person of a king and his advisers, who found it difficult to gain any sure knowledge (Amm.Marc. 21.13.4, 361). To the end of late antiquity, therefore, emperors, like Anastasius in the year 503, could send their armies deep into enemy lands without firm knowledge about where the enemy was or what its intentions were (*Wars* 1.8.8–9). Those who did know were usually men on the front line. In the late Roman army this usually meant the generals or *duces* who commanded the different sectors of the imperial frontier, and the frontline soldiers who fed information back to the generals in their field reports (Amm.Marc. 21.7.6–7; 26.6.10–11). In fact, beyond the frontier even wars took place in a no-man's land of the unknown. Distance, difficult terrain, lack of records, illiteracy, and other factors combined to produce a profound ignorance (Heather, 1994). As Ammianus states, reports of major conflicts among the barbarian peoples beyond the northern frontiers of the empire tended to be discounted by the Romans "because wars in those regions are not ordinarily heard of by those living at a distance from them until after they are finished or after the violence has already faded back to quiet" (Amm.Marc. 31.4.3).

These physical restrictions on war meant that actual fighting turned on individual set battles—and the operational units of battle, over the long term, devolved into smaller rather than larger field units: "For all these reasons, battle and war tended to coincide: war properly speaking only began when battle was joined . . . there was a very real sense in which strategy as understood by Clausewitz—namely, that of employing battles in order to forward the aims of war—did not exist, which of course might explain why the term 'strategy' in anything like its modern sense, only entered the English language around 1800" (Van Creveld, 1989: 16–17). Despite their large size, the Sassanid and Roman empires of the period fielded small combat units. The classic legion of the Roman principate, about six thousand men, was reduced to about one thousand men, bringing it close to the standard size for most operational units in the late imperial army. The down-sizing was the result of the practice of permanently removing detachments *(vexillationes)* from their parent legions. The gradual move to smaller operational units of combat was accompanied by an increased premium placed on mobility and a greater importance placed on the cavalry, which became a separate operational branch of the Roman army during this period (Carrié, 1993: 99–103). The Sassanid army also operated with much the same unit scales and a concomitant emphasis on mobility (Shahbazi, 1986: 497–498). The later military development of both states was therefore characterized by forces that became larger overall and more fixed in separate regional armies, but paradoxically came to operate with smaller units that contributed to greater mobility of forces.

The move to smaller operational units and the need to deal with armed threats in geographically limited zones of confrontation meant that what passed for strategy and planning, even in the largest states, were often ad hoc decisions made either by the commander in the field or, given the political dangers of such autonomy, made by him after consultation with the king or the emperor (Millar, 1982). Decision making was therefore highly personalized, and was vested directly in the person of the general or monarch. Indeed, battle capabilities and political power were so inextricably linked with one person that, whether in Rome or Persia, long royal reigns produced, and were reproduced by, military stability. Short reigns, by contrast, were both cause and effect of weakness in war, whether internal or external. The longest reigns, whether Roman (Augustus, Constantine, Justinian) or Persian (Shapur I, Shapur II, Kavad I, Khosro I), were marked by recovery from civil war, the institution of new dynastic regimes, and military reforms that presaged stronger and more stable military states (Rubin, 1995). There is less information on the politics of the frontier ethnic groups of either state, but Theoderic I, king of the Visigoths (418–451), is at least one known case that exemplifies the common pattern.

The close connection between war and political power put constant pressure on monarchs to direct war in person on the field of battle and, indeed, to prove their worth as rulers by showing (most often at the inception of their reigns) success in war. Thus the advent of each new ruler tended to provoke a perceived need to challenge the status quo. So Byzantine emperors of the 5th century, from Anastasius I on, felt compelled to test their greatest enemy's strength, almost as a rite of passage to legitimate their own power (Shahid, 1995). The same is true of the contemporary Sassanid monarchs who, like Bahram V and Yazedgird II in 421–422 and 439, went to war near the beginning of their reigns to strengthen their credentials as kings.

The need for the emperor to be personally close to his troops was provoked more by the threat of internal than external war. One of the more extraordinary documents that exemplify this relationship is a recorded dialogue between Constantine and his soldiers about their terms of employment that is preserved in the late Roman law codes (C.Th. 7.20.2 = C.Just. 12.47.1; 326). The conversation reflects a personal camaraderie that would be rather unusual for the emperor to have had with the humble civilian subjects of his empire. The emperor's presence and active participation in battle were reestablished as part of the Roman imperial system by Marcus Aurelius and the emperors of the 3rd century crisis, and remained true of the empire down to Theodosius. Although the Byzantine state managed to achieve the restoration of a civil state, its monarchs were still under unremitting pressure actively to participate in war. The severe troubles of the early 7th century compelled Heraclius once again to take the field in person at the head of the army.

The constraints on manpower and leadership that were faced by the large states of late antiquity were connected with their transition from conquest states to civil polities. The shift was usually marked by an increasing reluctance to serve on the part of the ordinary citizens of the conquering state, and an increasing professionalization of military service and drawing of recruits from the war zones of the state. The result was a dramatic shift in the war capabilities of the state. The vast citizen and allied levies of the Roman republic formed an enormous recruiting reserve which in turn had produced one of the great and paradoxical secrets of success of the republican state in war: it could lose battles. Indeed, by the standards of almost any ancient state, it could lose on a staggering scale and still return to the field of battle, finally to win the war. The government of the later Roman state was no longer in this enviable position. It ruled an empire that was many times the geographical size and population of peninsular Italy, but commanded armed forces that were not much more than double the size of the manpower reserves of the republic. The state had been divided into civil and military moieties, such that the former funded but otherwise did not participate in the latter. It was an acceptable compromise of empire.

Even when conducted by the Roman and Sassanid states that had the greatest centralized resources at their command, war remained subject to constraints of topography and climate. Weather imposed seasonal rhythms on war, dictating periodic campaigning seasons that were followed right to the end of antiquity. In Gaul and on the Rhine frontier, for example, the war season was signaled by the beginning of summer (Amm.Marc. 14.10.1; 27.10.6f; 30.5.1; 30.5.14; 30.6.2). These temporal patterns were so well known that they were regularly presented as part of normal tactical advice. When Valentinian was contemplating attacking the Alamanni in the autumn of 374, his advisers warned that he should hold back until the beginning of spring, noting that "the roads, hardened with frost, where neither any grass grew that would serve as fodder nor anything else that would be of use to the army, could not be penetrated" (Amm.Marc. 30.3.3). The cycle of Roman war on this frontier, with its annual forays to the Rhine, the *pax* conveniently "agreed to" just in time by cringing and repentant barbarians, and the following retreat to winter quarters, can be seen as a process determined by the harsh winter conditions in these lands. The regular cycle from a winter retreat from war to a summer campaigning season was compelled no less upon Persian monarchs (Amm.Marc. 19.9.1: beginning of October; 20.7; 21.6.7; 27.12.18; 30.2.16). Sometimes these responses to natural conditions were translated into traditional cultural prohibitions, such as the time around the spring equinox when Saracens entered a two-month-long sacred period during which they refused to undertake raids against their enemies (*Wars* 2.16.18).

With the arrival of inclement autumn weather, the armed forces of the Roman state regularly retired to winter quarters where stored supplies could be guaranteed. The external peoples along the northern frontiers, however, sometimes found themselves facing midwinter subsistence crises that drove them to enter the developed regions of the empire. So in midwinter 365–66, the Alamanni crossed the Rhine in large numbers on the day after New Year's (Amm.Marc. 27.1.1); the Lentienses crossed the frozen Rhine for similar reasons in mid-February of 378 (Amm.Marc. 31.10.4). The crossing of the Rhine by German ethnic groups on New Year's Eve of 406 dramatically replayed these same patterns. So too, on the eastern frontier between Persia and Rome, in the year 536, compelled by several dry seasons that left nomadic herds without pasture, a large number of Arabs led by the phylarch al-Mundhir attacked settlements in the agricultural zone of Euphratensis (Marcell. Com. *Chron.* 2.105; see also Shahid, 1995: 194–196). At least some of the Hephthalite attacks into the northern frontier zone of Sassanid Persia in the late 4th and early 5th century were provoked by famine (Thompson, 1996: 35). Climate variations also hampered the movement of armies. When Theodosius transferred troops from Gaul to deal with the Firmus rebellion in North Africa in 372, his soldiers, accustomed to the colder climates of the north, found it very difficult to adjust to the scorching heat of the high plains of central Algeria

(Amm.Marc. 29.5.7). The Roman troops besieging Theodosiopolis in 541 fell severely ill with fevers. The explanation proffered for their sickness was that the land was very hot and dry, not the type of climate to which troops brought in from Thrace were accustomed (*Wars* 2.19.31–32). Such impediments could be partly cultural as well; the local German troops recruited by Julian in Gaul in the mid-350s made it a condition of their enlistment that they would never be transferred beyond the Alps (Amm.Marc. 20.4.4; 20.8.7; 8.15.360).

Cultural, climatic, and topographical factors combined to fix limits to warfare, frontiers that could not be altered even by the most strenuous combat. Kings and monarchs tended to adjust their war frontiers to existing ecological ones (Whittaker, 1994: 86–97). Excessive long-term costs caused Diocletian to withdraw the Roman army from regions below the first cataract on the Nile and to attempt to establish a new frontier near Elephantine and the temples of Philae (*Wars* 1.19.28–30). But the classic instance is the war frontier between the late Roman and Persian states in the Near East. Persian monarchs, including Shapur II (340s–350s) and Khosro I (540s), sometimes managed to stage military forays and raids on a massive scale into the fertile zone along the Mediterranean that was under Roman or Byzantine aegis. Similarly, Roman emperors, from Julian (363) to Heraclius (622–630), staged large-scale raids that struck deep into Persian territory along the Tigris and Euphrates. But neither side was ever able to achieve a permanent change in the frontier. Individual cities and forts, especially those in the confrontation zone of Mesopotamia, might change hands for periods of time; but the regional strategic situation remained fundamentally unaltered by the practice of war. From the mid 6th century onward, when recurrent episodes of protracted war erupted—with the concomitant tremendous cost of property and toll in human life, especially in the first decades of the 7th century—cultural and ecological frontiers still determined the limits of battle. It has been noted that "the blood spilled in the warfare between the two states brought as little real gain to the one side or the other as the few meters of land gained at terrible cost in the trench warfare of the First World War" (Frye 1983: 139).

Perhaps the greatest permanent constraint on war in late antiquity, however, is not visible in the surviving records because it is simply not recognized in this period. The fundamental breakthrough that powered the military revolution in early modern Europe was fiscal; the opening of the resources of trading companies, banks, and other institutions of credit enabled nation-states to amortize the expenses of war, both men and equipment. The financing of armies and war in late antiquity, by contrast, was brittle and inflexible, constrained by fixed ceilings of expenditure that were crudely linked to the limits of the tributary system of the state. It was more probable that the entire fiscal, currency, and tribute-collecting system of the ancient state would have to change under the pressure of war, rather than that war would provoke any revolution in modes of banking (Carrié, 1995). The relationship between state, fiscal instruments, and economy was a brutal zero-sum game. There were no private fiscal institutions with massive surplus monies to invest in the high-risk venture of war. The one institution in late antiquity that possessed hoarded wealth on the requisite scale, the church, did provide such a loan on one occasion. Emperor Heraclius, facing a desperate situation in 622, is reported to have taken the hoarded resources of "pious houses" *(euagoi oikoi)* as just such a war "loan" (Theophanes, *Chron.* a.m. 6113). It was a singular occurrence that did not bear repetition, much less developed an institutional linkage between high finance and war (Jones, 1964: 316; Haldon, 1990: 225; Treadgold, 1995: 205–206). The cold fact is that the exorbitant costs of war had to be recouped by the seizure of property, including the stored wealth of sacred institutions. The massive confiscation of pagan temple treasure enabled Constantine to coin enough gold to pay his soldiers' donatives. In presenting his seizure as a loan, Heraclius was being more polite, proper, and pious. Sometimes costs could be recouped during the political purges that followed bouts of civil war, but the usual compulsion was to find another war whose booty would pay for the one just waged.

There are various calculations that estimate the size of the armed forces of the high empire at about 400,000–450,000 men (MacMullen, 1980). The army of the later empire was larger, but certainly not quadruple that of the principate, as is sometimes claimed based on misreading a famous passage in Lactantius (*De mort.pers.* 7.2). Reasonable guesses are that the size of the later Roman army had risen to about half again the size of the army of the high empire—that is, to about 600,000–650,000 men. The army was therefore by far the largest organization of the Roman state, dwarfing its civil administration and any other corporate body before the advent of the Christian church. It was also the most costly. Rough estimates of what this cost might have been are based on what is presumed to be the single largest item: the soldiers' wages, rewards, and benefits. It is generally agreed that by the early 3rd century this amount rose to about a billion sesterces per annum in a state budget with total revenues of about a billion and a half sesterces per annum, or something on the order of three-quarters of the annual budget of the Roman state (MacMullen, 1984; Duncan-Jones, 1994: 45, and chap. 3; see also Ferrill, 1991: 37). Although wages were never paid out in full (a good part of a soldier's pay was docked for various expenses), whatever allowance is made for their reduction must have been more than compensated for by the state's expenditures for weaponry and fixed defensive fortifications. Military expenditures for the late Roman and Byzantine states remained at a similarly high level of about three-quarters of the total state budget (Treadgold, 1995: 166–167, 195–197). These modern calculations are confirmed by the anonymous 6th century author of the manual *On Strategy*, who states bluntly that soldiers' wages alone consumed most of the annual public revenues of the Byzantine state (*Peri strat.* 2.18–21; Dennis, 1985: 12–13). Since the military budget was by far the single largest item in the annual disbursement of the state's assets, it follows that the military was the state-driven force that had the greatest effect on the economy of the Mediterranean world. It is most important to remember that the largest proportion of this military expenditure was directed (or redistributed) to the periphery of the empire, indeed mainly to the war zones on the frontiers where most of the military establishment was located.

When Libanius announced that money constituted "the sinews of war," therefore, he was part of a long tradition that consistently recognized the importance of the tributary infrastructure of the state to the conduct of war (Libanius, *Or.* 46; cf. Cicero, *Phil.* 5.2.5, harking back to Thucydides 1.83.2). The observation raises a second point: that the regular annual receipts (tribute) required for the armed forces of the state were almost at the limit of what the fiscal-political system could bear. (This is not strictly measurable for late antiquity, but reasonable estimates can be provided for the principate, where better data are available.) Therefore, mobilizing the state's military forces to active war, either internal or external, quickly exhausted the liquid cash reserves stored in the imperial treasury. The great surpluses that Antoninus Pius had amassed (675 million denarii, or 2.7 billion sesterces) were soon expended on the northern wars of Marcus Aurelius, who according to legend was reduced to selling his wife's furniture, crockery, and clothing at auction in the Roman forum to meet state expenses (Historia Augusta, *Marc. Aurel.* 17.4). The same pressures also weighed on the Byzantine state. By 457 Emperor Marcian had hoarded a large peacetime surplus (7.2 million nomismata), but almost all of it was run through in paying for Leo I's disastrous expedition against the Vandals in 468 (Treadgold, 1995: 193–194). It was therefore predictable that the vicious cycle of civil conflicts that rent the empire through the mid 3rd century would bankrupt the Roman state and severely undermine its currency. Indeed, it has been argued that fiscal pressures of the military and war expenditures caused the substantial alteration of the fiscal apparatus of the late Roman state under Diocletian and his successors (Jones, 1964: 42–68; Carrié, 1986: 462–469). The anonymous late 4th century pamphleteer who urged basic reforms on the state noted that "it is because of vast expenditures on the army that . . . the whole mechanism of tax collection is collapsing" (*De rebus bellicis*, 5.1).

The development of war in the Mediterranean and Near East was also determined by political preconditions. The most immediate political factor was the presence of the two great states: the Roman empire, centered on the Mediterranean, and the Sassanid empire, centered on Mesopotamia and the Iranian plateau. The Roman empire was a relatively centralized, quasi-bureaucratic patronal imperial state. The Sassanid empire, on the other hand, was a relatively decentralized, quasi-segmentary ethnic or feudal state, but one whose ruling elite commanded complex bureaucratic capabilities (Widengren, 1976; Shahbazi, 1986: 494–495, 497–498; Schippmann, 1990; Howard-Johnston, 1995: 212–226). When it comes to the technical means by which these states supported war, however, the best narrative source materials tend to fail. The infrastructure of the conduct of war, so critical to its success or failure, is imperfectly known even for the Roman state. There is enough evidence to show that the Roman state increasingly assumed the responsibility by its own arms manufactories *(fabricae)* for the provision of armor and heavy weaponry from its arsenals (Bishop, 1985; James, 1988; Ferrill, 1991: 51–54). How and by what means the Sassanid state coped with these same problems is still largely unknown, although there seems to have been a developmental pattern similar to that of the Romans, was marked by the army reforms instituted by Khosro I

(531–579) to create a more professional standing force equipped by the resources of the central state (Rubin, 1995; Howard-Johnston, 1995: 211–220). Although state-based logistics were an important advantage in the conduct of war, we know so little about this critical infrastructure that we cannot be sure when and how it began to fragment into purely local and isolated means of supply (Haldon, 1990: 220–232; Ferrill, 1991: 27–29; Bachrach, 1993; Kaegi, 1993; Treadgold, 1995: 179–184). State systems of logistics were technically far superior at the supply of large numbers of mobile troops. Armed ethnic groups in conflict with the state, unless they could become parasitic on the existing state systems, very quickly encountered the limits imposed by the exigencies of supply. Gothic forces besieging the city of Rome in 538 were reduced from many tens of thousands of men to a few by famine and disease (*Wars* 6.6.1). The invasion of a large armed force of Franks that entered Italy in 540 ground to a halt when a third of them perished from starvation (*Wars* 6.25.16–18).

The convergence of cultural and environmental constraints with the physical settings in which wars were actually contested produced different types of combat. Take, for example, the peculiar form of static war characterized by armed assaults on heavily fortified urban centers. Siege warfare arose when there was a clearly defined frontier between relatively balanced opposing forces and when large and heavily fortified urban centers were present in the frontier zone. The classic case of late antiquity was the land frontier between the Roman and Sassanid states. Where the two empires converged the Syrian desert formed a large arch-like interstitial space. North of this arid zone, in the great plain between the upper Tigris and Euphrates rivers, where more permanent and extensive human settlement was possible, the two empires confronted each other directly along a shared land frontier. The principal objective of war in this frontier zone was the wealth stored in the treasuries of the heavily fortified cities that studded the plain. The presence of urban centers that dominated the countryside, the emergence of a line of direct permanent engagement, and the relative stability and balance of the forces on either side combined to produce a classic zone of siege warfare. But siege frontiers were just as characteristic of internal wars: a city like Aquileia that was located on the borderland between the two halves of the empire was besieged (unsuccessfully) many times (Amm.Marc. 21.12.1: 361). As ecological, political, and military conditions altered to produce new frontiers of permanent engagement, siege warfare became characteristic of regions, like the Italian peninsula during the 6th century, where it had not previously been dominant. Therefore, the determinant characteristic of this type of warfare is the manner in which geopolitical factors dictated the location of siege warfare, rather than the technical tactical details of individual sieges.

Both the narrative accounts of actual sieges and the technical advice on how to besiege a city offered in military manuals like that of Vegetius (*Mil.* 4) describe a highly routinized kind of conflict that seems to have been imposed on both the besiegers and the besieged by the limitations of this type of warfare. Heavily walled urban centers were very expensive to attack (Amm.Marc.

21.13.2). Siege technology was therefore almost entirely under the command of the large states that had the requisite resources to support it. Smaller ethnic peoples, such as those along the northern flank of the Roman empire, were known not to have siege capabilities (Amm.Marc. 19.6.12: Quadi and Sarmatians; 31.6.4; 31.8.1; 31.15.1: Goths; Procopius, *Aed.* 2.9.4–5: "Saracens"). But even when the large states could afford to subvent this costly form of war, its limitations immediately became apparent. Usually the besieging forces first made a tremendous display of power, a parade of armed might by which they hoped to frighten the besieged into submission. If this ploy failed, it was usually followed by a parlay in which the besiegers attempted to negotiate the surrender of the city on equitable terms by a mixture of threats and offers of security and safe-conduct. If these moves failed, the besiegers then moved to the next step: simultaneous attacks directed at the full circuit of the city's walls. The hope was to find a weak spot or to effect a surrender by demonstrating the seriousness of the besiegers' intentions. If this failed, the attackers finally moved to the most serious and costly step—the assemblage of heavy siege equipment and the beginning of large-scale mining operations. Through all of this, the siege had its own temporal rhythms, which tended to be both seasonal and quotidian, with the darkness of each night imposing a cessation of hostilities (Amm.Marc. 19.9.1; 20.7 at Amida; 20.11.20 and 24 at Bezabde; *Wars* 5.25.8–11: Belisarius at Rome, 536).

Because it was also subject to environmental impediments, combat on the high seas has justifiably been allotted a rather small role in histories of warfare in late antiquity. Naval warfare remained peripheral not only for the great land-centered power of Sassanid Persia, but even for the Mediterranean-centered states of Rome and Byzantium (Jones, 1964: 610; Treadgold, 1995: 72–76, 173–177). This is not to say that these powers did not have ships, or in certain periods large collections of boats, oarsmen, and marines that served as naval forces. But the basic historical truth remains that the states and powers of the time were land-based and the decisive types of war were firmly terrestrial. Ethnic groups that did not otherwise have the technical resources of the larger states, such as the Goths in the mid 3rd century, could seize ships to use for raiding or more often simply for transportation (Whittaker, 1994: 194–195). But the usual, if not exclusive, function of seaborne power transporting land-based forces, whether those of large states, as in the case of the Byzantine fleets that shipped forces to North Africa in 468 and again in 534, or of ethnic-based powers, as with the boats used by the Vandals to cross the Straits of Gibraltar to North Africa in 429. Because the great majority of the potential protagonists, whether the ethnic armed groups along the Rhine and Danube, the Hephthalite Huns and Turkic groups of the Eurasian steppe, or the large state powers of Rome and Persia, were land-based powers, almost all combat was necessarily based on infantry and cavalry forces. Control of seas, rivers, or lakes remained important, but mainly for logistical reasons: the most convenient mode of transporting large stores of supplies and large numbers of men was by water (*Wars* 6.7.17; 6.24.13–16). Similarly, denying sea and riverine transport and supply to your enemy was tactically important (Höckman, 1986). But such imperatives never generated a decisive naval warfare, and the strategists of the period reflected this fact in the modest space they allotted to the tactics of seaborne fighting. For instance, Vegetius devoted only a truly exiguous portion of his whole manual to it (*Mil.* 4.31–33); and the classic Byzantine manuals have nothing on the subject (Dennis, 1985).

The purposes of wars varied according to the different social structures that sustained them. The large states fought external wars to maintain the territorial integrity of the state, whereas internal wars were waged to acquire the total resources of the state's territories. The myriad ethnic groups these large states confronted principally fought to dominate other groups and to compel surrender of their personal resources (Pohl, 1980: 244–246; Isaac 1992: 394–401). It is perhaps easy to underestimate the significance of payments that could be described as tribute. For all social groups outside the realm of state structures, war tributes were part of what Aristotle, centuries earlier, had specified as perfectly valid means of economic subsistence. In illiterate and institutionless societies, whose leadership had constantly to be reinforced by military success and material redistribution, this parasitic economy had considerable impact. When Valamir the Scythian broke the treaty and began ravaging Roman lands and towns in 459–461, it was to ensure that Roman envoys would guarantee the payment of 300 pounds of gold each year. In his own words, Valamir claimed that he had been compelled to war out of sheer necessity—because of the hardships suffered by his people (Priscos, frg. 37 Blockley). In the protection racket that was instituted by both state and ethnic forms of violence, these payoffs could be variously portrayed as an immoral extortion, as wages for armed service, or as a tribute (taxation) justly owed to the state (Blockley, 1992: 149–150). The large-scale payments made by the Roman and Byzantine states to the Huns and Hephthalites could be seen, from the state's perspective, simply as the continuation of war by other means (Gordon, 1949; Blockley, 1985; Iluk, 1985; Thompson, 1996: 211–218, 268). The more such fiscal instruments were institutionalized, the more the cycle of dependency on them was confirmed, and the more their stoppage made a return to violence the only economic alternative. Attila blamed the outbreak of war in 441 on the nonpayment of tribute by Theodosius II (Thompson, 1996: 281); Antalas, the African chieftain, went into armed revolt in 543–44 when the Byzantine commander Solomon stopped the usual imperial payments (*Wars* 4.21.17). The linkage between this type of economic dependency and war did not apply just to ethnic groups, however: major wars with Persia were directly provoked by the refusal of Justin II to pay reverse tribute (Menander, frg. 19.1; 12.7; 9.3; Rubin, 1986a; Isaac, 1992: 129–132). Perhaps the most serious consequences of ending tribute payments of this sort were the estoppages that provoked the Arab invasions in the early 630s (Theophanes, *Chron.* a.m. 6123, de Boor, 335f.; Donner, 1981: 115–117; Kaegi, 1992: 89–91; Isaac, 1992: 131–132).

From these basic structural constraints, let us turn to the principal diachronic developments that produced patterns of warfare in late antiquity. The best analytical point of departure is to follow the paradigm of the Roman empire, which remains the most completely documented case. The first great expansion of the Roman state over the Mediterranean was marked by a long cycle of warfare that lasted from about the mid 4th to the mid 1st century B.C.E. The Roman army fought increasingly successful and violent wars, mainly in the heartlands of the Mediterranean Basin. By the end of this period, the great threat to the Roman state was not external but rather internal. Within the Roman state the linkages between political institutions and armed force were inadequate to contain the consequences of state violence. Unresolved political and structural problems threatened to unravel the great success of its violent unification of the Mediterranean. The last century of the republican state was marked by a cycle of civil wars that brought an end to its system of government. The Augustan restoration stabilized the imperial military system by reconfiguring the political institutions to make them concordant with a centralized autocracy and by refashioning and redeploying the central army (Goldsworthy, 1996). These Augustan remedies provided a means for managing the internal threats of war and its effects; with two striking exceptions, they produced a long-term peace in the core areas of the empire. But they simultaneously contributed to a new form of state-driven violence which produced many of the new problems that were to haunt the conduct of war in the Late Roman state.

The Augustan system began with a general relocation of military forces to the land borders of the empire. The legionary and auxiliary units of the army were located at naturally occurring boundaries, either along rivers (the Rhine and the Danube on the northern frontier) or along road systems that ran between the desert and cultivated lands (in Syria and Palestine in the east, and in North Africa to the south). Permanent army bases were located where they could be supplied along dependable networks of communication. Augustus also professionalized armed service. The republican ideal of the citizen who was bound by duty to fight on behalf of his community continued to be mooted, but the need to stabilize the relationship between soldier and state was recognized by making military service a paid occupation, even a well-paid one. This physical and social refashioning of the Roman army effectively demilitarized the center of the empire, and thereby permanently separated the civilian core of the empire from its militarized periphery. Causally linked to this polarization of soldier and civilian was the increasing disinclination to military service of the great majority of men in the empire who did not happen to reside in the frontier provinces. Despite rewards offered to new volunteers, the state still had to resort, rather frequently, to conscription and "press gang" tactics in order to fill the ranks of the army (Jones, 1964: 615–619; Brunt, 1974; Haldon, 1979; Whitby, 1995; Elton, 1996: 128–150, 135–136). The location of most of the army camps along the frontiers of the empire and the rejection of military service by the center made recruiting increasingly provincial. The critical fact is that army recruiting was firmly rooted not just in the frontier provinces, but specifically in the war zones along the periphery of the empire. Indeed, the main bulk of all men recruited to the army was drawn increasingly from the northern frontier zones of the empire.

By implementing measures such as these, the Augustan restoration resolved one of the persistent problems of the late republic: the threat of the army and civil war to the state. By exporting its armed problems to the periphery of the empire and keeping them there, the new order effectively stripped the center of the empire of any substantial military force that might threaten the internal stability of the state. By thus disarming the core of the empire, however, Augustus and his successors, who had to sustain this new military system, simultaneously created a new condition of violence that was to become increasingly difficult to control—a permanent armed frontier around the outer periphery of the empire. Armies and their commanders might no longer emerge from violent conflicts in Italy and the center of the Mediterranean to threaten the state, but the new secret of empire, more insidious than Tacitus imagined, was that civil and military power could not be so easily detached from each other and maintained in discrete sectors. It was not so much that Roman emperors could be created outside Rome, but rather that both the political power and indeed the center of the state itself would gravitate inexorably to its heavily armed periphery. In a long-term geopolitical trend, the newly militarized imperial periphery provoked the concentration of capital cities, military supply factories, and even state mints in regions close to the frontier (Christol, 1977; Carrié, 1986: 463–465; Hollard, 1995; James, 1988).

Along the new post-Augustan frontiers of the Roman empire, the dialectical relationship between local army garrisons and external threats produced border areas of two broad categories: war zones and civil zones. In a war zone the state deployed a significant proportion of its military force in the expectation that major external wars would be fought in the region. On the civil frontier, the armed forces were principally involved in the maintenance of local order—in various forms of policing, quelling local banditry, and controlling minor rural insurgencies and occasional spates of ethnic and urban violence (Isaac, 1992: 161–218, 269–310). The war zones of the Roman empire extended along the length of the Rhine and Danube, and along the eastern face of the empire in a line from Armenia in the north to the frontiers of Syria and Mesopotamia, where Roman forces directly confronted those of Sassanid Persia. The frontier of the whole southern face of the empire—from modern-day Morocco in the west through Egypt in the east, and farther east to regions encompassing the southern areas of Palestine that faced on the Syrian Desert—was a more pacific frontier, where the civil core of the state extended almost to its natural boundaries (Isaac, 1992: 112–118, 138–140, 198–218). Military policing by the Roman state primarily involved advanced observation and control, with "tentacles" extended, like sensitive antennae, into the desert itself—the so-called *praetenturae* found on both the North African and Arabian desert frontiers (Kennedy and MacAdam, 1985; Speidel, 1987; MacAdam, 1989). The basic determinants in the creation of the two types of frontier were ecological; geopolitical forces established their respective war zones. This was just as true for the internal wars as it was for external wars.

The Roman empire was the largest, wealthiest, and most coherent state structure that dominated the Mediterranean and Near East. Recurring internal wars would therefore become the single most important military factor in the whole *oikoumenē*. And since the military establishment was the most expensive item in the state budget, the fiscal effects of civil wars were especially traumatic because they would tend to be recouped from the internal system itself. The shoring up of loyalties among the soldiers in such circumstances, against the internal competition for their resources, cost the state considerably. The dramatic civil war that preceded the 3rd century crisis, the war waged among Septimius Severus, Clodius Albinus, and Pescennius Niger in 192–93, consumed immense resources. Septimius Severus, once he became emperor, had to recover the costs from the resources of his political opponents by conducting a purge of wealthy senatorial and equestrian landowners and by appropriating their wealth for the state (indeed, the *res privata* came to rival the *patrimonium* of the emperor in size and importance). Almost every episode of internal warfare exacted an additional toll of accusation and persecution, invariably connected to the confiscation of the wealth of the landowners who had supported the losing party. Constantine, Constantius, and Magnus Maximus all recovered the costs of civil war in this manner (Jones, 1964: 158f.). Julian staged a purge of the adherents of Constantius (Amm.Marc. 22.3.1–12, 361). Procopius had to activate the services of men skilled in raising money in the cities of Asia Minor in order to support his war efforts (Amm.Marc. 26.8.14, 365); but his conqueror Valens initiated a general slaughter of Procopius's supporters in order to acquire their wealth to pay for the war (Amm.Marc. 26.10.9, 365).

The cycle of civil wars that began to afflict the Roman state during the half-century following the late 230s signaled the breakdown of the "Akzeptanz-System" at the heart of the Augustan restoration (Flaig, 1992). These internal wars also exacted a much greater toll on its resources and its leaders— only one of the fourteen emperors who died violently during this period did so in battle against the external enemies of the empire—than did the barbarian incursions which they did so much to encourage (Carrié, 1993: 93–94). It is a reasonable estimate that at least one-third of the 4th century was consumed by internal wars of one part of the Roman state against another. For a large number of the years that remained, the politics of emperors and armies were determined in no small part by a considerable fear of potential or impending civil conflict. Because of the military resources the Roman state had at its command (much greater than those of the next largest state in the region and vastly superior to those of the various ethnic groups around its frontiers), internal wars within the Roman state had a profound effect on war in general. But the repercussive effects of wars within the empire tended to focus on specific points in the imperial landscape. Fundamental geographical forces encouraged the grouping of the lands west of the Adriatic into one region and those east of the Adriatic into another. This geopolitical fact was recognized by the reforms of Diocletian that divided the empire into eastern and western halves and formally divided the fiscal and military resources of the empire between the rulers of the east and the west. The region of Illyricum and the adjacent mountainous lands between the great Danube bend and the Adriatic coast, located on the midpoint of this division, became the most important internal war frontier of the empire. The collected forces of the eastern half of the empire were regularly pitted against those of the western half along the middle Danube.

The reforms of the Roman central state under Diocletian and Constantine were Augustan in nature. They were new, but stereotypical, answers to the social, economic, political, and military problems caused by repeated fissioning of the empire into its geopolitical components and by the relapse into repeated bouts of civil war. The modular structure of the tetrarchy, with a hierarchy of powers nested one within the other, was meant to countervail the threat of civil war while at the same time answering to the need to have several concurrent emperors in command of armed forces close to the different frontiers of the empire. But the tetrarchy solution only tended to exacerbate the problems of civil conflict, which resurfaced with ferocity among the successors of Constantine. The creation of mobile field armies *(comitatus)* during the period was provoked less by the need to do battle with external enemies of the state than it was by the overwhelming pressure for each emperor and subemperor to have his own military forces directly under his command to protect himself from internal threats (Jones, 1964, 97–100; Hoffmann, 1969–70: 131–140; Ferrill, 1986: 47; Carrié, 1993: 124–125).

As the new realities forced a breakdown of the old consensus, any legitimate power player became a potential ruler. Losers were labeled usurpers or tyrants, while winners became emperors. This ex post facto labeling makes it difficult to deduce from the surviving data valid conceptions of usurpation and legitimacy (Flaig, 1997). The new facts of political life caused decisions made by emperors and their subordinates to be overshadowed by a pervasive fear of civil war that repeatedly entered into their calculations (Amm.Marc. 14.7). Emperors such as Constantius might be renowned as warriors, but in his case it was for his good fortune in fighting civil wars rather than external ones (Amm.Marc. 14.11.8, 354). Roman soldiers decided whether to follow him and to obey his orders based on their experience of earlier battles, which convinced them that Constantius had good fortune in fighting internal wars but bad luck when it came to external ones (Amm.Marc. 14.10.16; 21.15.1). It was a reputation of which Constantius was aware and in which he himself firmly believed (Amm.Marc. 21.13.7). He constantly weighed the threats and problems connected with civil war against wars that he might be compelled (or wish) to wage with external enemies. The preparations for war were just as rigorous in either case (Amm.Marc. 20.9.3, 360; 21.6.6, 361; 21.7.1; 21.13.1–2). The same calculations also had to be made by Constantius's opponent, the future emperor Julian. He had reason to fear Constantius's known record of winning civil wars, and he made sure to acquire the services of Arbitrio, an army officer well known for his extensive prior success in civil wars (Amm.Marc. 21.13.16, 361).

Civil wars were often more threatening because they pitted well-trained and well-equipped Roman armies against each other. Almost invariably this parity of power caused a rush to acquire new manpower reserves that would make the difference in the final confrontation, and a haste to settle the matter in a set battle before one's opponent could marshal more recruits. The additional manpower was always to be found among the so-called barbarians. The civil war that pitted Constantine against Maxentius provoked Constantine to draft large numbers of Franks and Alamanni. The civil war of Licinius against Constantine impelled the former to draft large numbers of Goths into his service. The civil war of Constantius against Magnentius compelled the latter to recruit Saxons and Franks to bolster his forces (Julian, *Or.* 1.34c–d). Constantine himself drafted heavily from frontier ethnic groups to create the first mobile strike force, or *comitatus,* of the Roman army (Zosimus, *Hist.eccl.* 1.15; Hoffmann, 1969–70: 130–141, 169–173; Liebeschuetz, 1990: 7).

Civil wars were also the main cause of the systematic recruiting of barbarians along the northern frontiers into the Roman army. Constantius invited barbarians (probably more Franks and Saxons) to cross into the empire and attack his rival Magnentius from the rear. The same recruitment of barbarians characterized the civil wars between Julian and Constantius; and between Procopius and Valens, in which Procopius, relying on personal connections to Constantine's family, recruited from the Goths. And it remained true of the great civil wars that Emperor Theodosius fought, first against Magnus Maximus (387) and then against Eugenius (392–394), in which he recruited on a large scale from Alans, Arabs, Goths, Huns, Iberians, and Isaurians (Pacatus, *Pan.Lat.* 12.32.3–4; 32.3–5; 33.4–5; Liebeschuetz, 1990: 30). These wars were characterized by the same large-scale recruiting of frontier ethnic groups, including Goths (Socrates, *Hist.eccl.* 5.25; Zosimus 4.45.3, 4.57.2), Huns (John of Antioch, frg. 87), and Franks (Orosius, *Adv.Pag.* 7.35.11–12; Rufinus 11.33). Almost every leader in a civil war castigated his opponent for recruiting barbarians, but then did it himself. Julian criticized Constantine, but recruited in the same region and indeed from the same ethnic groups. Magnus Maximus paraded an avowed hostility to Germans, but nonetheless recruited them in large numbers (Ambrose, *Ep.* 24.8). Not only did each contestant in civil war recruit from his own frontier peoples, but he also followed the common practice of inducing ethnic groups on his opponent's frontier to attack his rival from the rear. So Magnus Maximus accused Bauto of inciting "barbarians" to invade his territory (Ambrose, *Ep.* 24.4.6–8).

From the 3rd century crisis onward, therefore, civil wars were the single most important determinant of war for the Roman empire and for war in the Mediterranean and Near East in general. The great internal conflicts within the Roman state compelled contestants to draw on the manpower reserves of ethnic groups along and beyond the frontiers of the empire. This embroiled ethnic groups in a war economy and in recurrent cycles of war from which they could not easily escape. The effects of external recruiting for these internal wars were geographically specific. Only along the Rhine and Danube were found the permanently structurally fragmented social and political orders and the high population levels that both enticed and impelled the leaders in Rome's internal wars to the systematic recruitment of these populations. One important long-term consequence of the interlocking and interdependence of Roman and ethnic warfare on the northern face of the empire was the destabilization of a frontier that was already fragmented along ethnic lines. Then again, the systematic involvement of ethnic groups along the Rhine and Danube in this internal war oriented them permanently toward military service in the Roman state. Like a magnetic force, the rewards of the military tended to attract ethnic groups from ever farther afield to the line of the Rhine and Danube (Pohl, 1994: 75). War service, in which most of them were well experienced, was one of the very few useful things that they could offer to an empire that had the resources to pay.

The permanent involvement of ethnic groups along the northern frontiers in the internal wars of the Roman state affected the late Roman military command structure. In the long series of civil wars that began in the late 230s, which had only a temporary respite with Constantine's victory in 324, the significance of armed ethnic groups to the total manpower of Roman armies increased dramatically. This factor, along with the concentration of operational units of the Roman army in the war zones of the empire's periphery, led to the high command positions in the Roman state of experienced military men whose careers were made by service on these frontiers. It cannot surprise that the same Rhine-Danube war zone that regularly produced Roman emperors from Maximinus Thrax (reputedly the first emperor actually to fight personally in combat) onward also produced the empire's military elite of high-ranking army officers. This was the logical result of the military reforms instituted by Augustus. The permanent location of the army along the periphery of the empire and the heavy recruiting of soldiers from the northern war zone to a professional army created a military with its own frontier war economy, culture, and ideology. The constant exchanges and confrontations in military matters alone, such as weaponry and types of combat, produced a convergence of tactics and modes of operation (Kunow, 1986; Traina, 1986–87; Dagron, 1993: 279–280).

It was only a matter of time before the soldiers who shared this military culture would enforce not only their own regional interests but also their conviction that only professional soldiers were fit to command. The increasing exclusion of senators from high commands in the Roman army, traditionally ascribed to a single act by Emperor Gallienus, was the natural preference of armed forces that favored a local and professional command over a distant and amateur civil aristocracy (Carrié, 1993: 88–90). Bauto the Frank, who served Constantine, and his son Silvanus, who later fought for Magnentius, were both examples of men advanced in status by Romans in the context of civil wars; by the end of the 4th century a considerable proportion of the highest commands in the Roman army (*magistri militum*) were consistently held by such men (Waas, 1971: 10–14; Elton, 1996: 147–151). The separation of military and civilian into distinct spheres formalized the alienation of the two parts of the state from each other, with malign consequences for both sides. When Alaric brought the culture of the frontier to the gates of Rome in 409, the civil aristocracy and the Senate arrogantly rebuffed his requests—an arrogance betraying paralyzing ignorance of what sort of men they had created on the frontiers of their own empire.

The increased dependence on ethnic recruits and the rise of frontier men to high-level army commands have been rather misleadingly characterized as the "barbarization" of the Roman army, the malign effects of which have probably been exaggerated (Elton, 1996: 128–154). Its significance lies instead in the consequences of the dynamic relationships between Roman armed forces and frontier peoples. The patterns of behavior created by this system of war must seriously modify traditional claims that the empire was invaded by northern barbarians. Instead, the original historical sources are replete with repeated solicitations of northern ethnic groups and their leaders to enter the service of a given emperor or pretender in order to serve that leader's interests. The presence of large armed polyethnic bands within the frontiers of the empire cannot be blamed in any simple fashion on barbarian invasions. There was not a single leader of such a large-scale ethnic armed force, from Alaric to Attila, who had not been invited into the empire for the purpose of armed service (Heather, 1991: 193–213; Liebeschuetz, 1990: 48–85). This peculiar dynamic prevailed only on the northern frontier of the Roman empire because this frontier alone harbored large populations whose fragmentary and small-scale social units exposed them so readily to exploitation by the superior resources of the Roman state. The pattern persisted to the bitter end in the west: when in the late 560s Narses, the Byzantine commander (exarch) in Italy, fell into conflict with the eastern emperor Justin, he invited the Longobards into the peninsula (*Hist.Lang.* 2.5; Christie, 1991; 1995: 60–62). He had centuries of precedent before him.

In the dominant explanations of the historical causes of war in late antiquity, internal wars within the great states have not generally been assigned a leading place in the hierarchy. Even though they have been the object of some criticism, hypotheses on the nature of war in late antiquity are still governed by variations on what might be called the domino theory of causation (Goffart, 1980: 3–39; 1989). The domino explanation is committed to the "fact" that there were large-scale wanderings of peoples across the Eurasian steppe and western European plains, and that these movements were impelled by forces endogenous to the economies of the barbarian peoples (Todd, 1992: 55). These developments produced overpopulation and allied economic pressures that compelled the barbarians regularly to seek new lands for settlement (Demougeot, 1969–1979; Musset, 1975; Heather, 1996, chap. 2). As one northern people moved violently into its neighbor's territory, there was a "push on" effect that eventually forced the peoples closest to the northern frontiers of the Roman empire to move against the empire itself. A simple reading of a text in Ammianus Marcellinus (31.2.1) finds in it the paradigm of such a chain of causation: the Huns attack their neighbors, the Alans and Goths, thereby causing the last-named people to "flood" across the Danube in 376 (Ferrill, 1986: 59; Burns, 1994: 23; Thompson, 1996: 33–34; Heather, 1995 and 1996, chap. 4). Ammianus's words, however, have perhaps been made to sustain a greater interpretive weight than they can reasonably bear (Pohl, 1994: 75). Detailed studies of the actual modalities of the so-called barbarian incursions into the empire, beginning with Delbrück's revisionist analysis of the numbers involved, have shown that small-scale, recurrent local infiltrations of the frontier zone were the more usual threat to Roman frontiers. The revisionists assert that set battles were not typical of the multifarious confrontations between barbarian and Roman; rather, prevalent types of frontier violence were closer to petty raids and acts of brigandage, aimed at the immediate acquisition of booty (Whittaker, 1994: 152–191).

The Sassanid state, for which we know so much less, alas, was apparently no less prone to spates of civil or internal war, and for much the same causes as those that applied to the Roman empire. The king had preeminent significance as head of state, and because his position was sustained by being perceived as a successful war leader, failure to uphold this role was likely to provoke armed insurrections by pretenders (Whitby, 1994). When the strength of Bahram II was brought into question at the beginning of his reign by the successful attacks on Sassanid lands by the Roman emperor Carus (in 283), the response was an armed revolt of one of the eastern provinces, led by Bahram's brother Hormizd (Zonaras 12.30; Historia Augusta, Carus, 8). These internal wars were renewed in 293 with the death of Bahram II. His son ruled only a few months and was then overthrown by his uncle Narseh, who was then a general in Armenia. As in the Roman case, the prevailing tendency was for military commanders on the frontier to threaten a weakened center. The crises of the Sassanid state in the 5th century followed much the same pattern. Like Roman monarchs, Yazdgerd II (440–457), in his attempts to stabilize attacks on the northeastern frontier, was compelled to move both court and army to the periphery of empire. Alas, he met with no success, and his failure to control violence on the frontiers of the Sassanid empire only provoked the internal fragmentation of the state and civil war between his two sons, Hormizd and Peroz.

When Peroz became Shāhānshāh, however, he faced the same problems. His defeat by the Hephthalites in 482 produced internal dissension and armed rebellions by local men of power in the Sassanid empire, who appointed one of their own, Balāsh Valgāsh, as King of Kings. In a manner reminiscent of Aetius in the Roman west, Kavad, the son of Peroz, who had served time as a hostage among the Hephthalites, used his personal connections to mobilize the frontier peoples to assist him in the acquisition of central power. In 496, when Kavad was deposed in one of these internal wars, he managed to escape to the Hephthalites and engaged in large-scale recruiting of them to his army so he could restore himself to the throne. As in the Roman west, military dependency on the frontier peoples only served to increase the indebtedness of the state to them. These debts provoked Kavad to a series of aggressive moves against the Roman frontier on the northwest in 502–503 to extort from the Byzantine state the monies he needed to pay off the Hephthalites. Thus, the episodes of civil war within the Sassanid state produced much the same compulsion to recruit armed manpower from its northern periphery as did the internal conflicts of the Roman empire. The northern frontier was the important recruiting zone for the Sassanid state for the same reasons as Rome's own northern frontier was for the Roman empire: it harbored a large number of segmentary, dispersed, stateless societies whose main resource was their own population. The processes of war were comparable to those of the Roman state, but the precise conduct of it was different, since the populations of the Eurasian steppes were mainly pastoral nomads, with less dense populations dispersed over much larger geographic spaces, and the Sassanid state was more loosely structured than the Roman.

Although their imperial ideologies denied it, both the Roman empire and Sassanid Persia had internal frontiers which were potentially just as dangerous as many of their external ones. Indeed, all of the autonomous societies and polities located in the Mediterranean and the Near East were prone not only to external wars with foreign enemies, but also to warfare that involved internal components of the state or social order. The Roman empire offers the best evidence for this phenomenon and for understanding its significance, but this type of internal war was just as characteristic of the Sassanid state, and of the larger ethnic polities beyond the Rhine and Danube. Even within the outer frontiers of large states like Rome and Persia, however, there existed what might be called inner frontiers—large regions where the state's monopoly of violence was contested in a fashion comparable to that on the outer frontiers themselves. The existence of such inner frontiers has been doubted for the Sassanid state (Howard-Johnston, 1995: 184–185), but the paucity of evidence on the military history of the Sassanians makes one skeptical of the claim, especially since such recalcitrant inner frontiers are well documented for the Achaemenid period (Briant, 1976; 1982: 57–112). The most important reasons for the existence of the inner frontiers were ecological—a combination of climatic, topographic, demographic, and economic factors. And of the topographical factors, by far the most important were mountains. The highland zone of the Taurus mountain range called Isauria, located in the southeastern quadrant of Asia Minor, was a classic example of just such an autonomous land within the Roman empire (Shaw, 1990). All narrative accounts of war from late antiquity, including the representation of the province in the *Notitia dignitatum*, reveal not only the great difficulties that the Roman state had in controlling Isauria, but also its development as a kind of internal *limes* of the empire, marked by local effusions of state coinage typically associated with intrusive large-scale concentrations of the armed forces of the central state (Mitchell, 1989; 1995: 208–217).

Even modest mountain highlands seem to have presented the Roman state with considerable difficulties of armed control and political domination. The mountains of North Africa, especially the Qabiliyya (Kabyle) or "tribal lands" of the coastal ranges of Algeria, were a classic instance of the highland autonomy that presented the Roman state with constant problems of political integration. A late 4th century incident from North Africa reported in detail by Ammianus exemplifies the characteristic pattern: Since mountainous regions were known to be reservoirs of freedom, the local "big men" were constantly suspected of trying to enhance their own power at the expense of the central state. In the early 370s suspicions of rebellion and usurpation fell on one Firmus, son of Nubel (Kotula, 1970). "Flavius" Nubel was a paradigm of the frontier man who lived simultaneously in two worlds: he was at once an autonomous and powerful chieftain in his own community (*regulus per nationes Mauricas potentissimus*: Amm.Marc. 29.5.2) and a high-ranking officer *(comes)* in the late Roman army (*ILCV* 1822). Firmus, his son, became involved in a complicated set of machinations, mainly provoked by the problems plaguing a disintegrating central court (Matthews, 1976; 1989: 367–376). He tried to protest his loyalty to the central government, but to no avail. The incidents of guerrilla warfare and heavy policing that ensued were concentrated around Firmus's home terrain in the mountains of north central Algeria (Amm.Marc. 29.5). The general of the cavalry forces in Gaul, Theodosius, was dispatched to the area with a large expeditionary force that set sail from the port of Arelate. It is important to note that Theodosius's campaigns in North Africa stuck to the Roman roads that ran around the periphery of the mountains. He ultimately prevailed through constant patrolling of the lowlands immediately around the mountains and through imposing trade embargoes to convince Firmus's main followers that it was too costly to support him. In the end they abandoned him, and Firmus was compelled to commit suicide (Amm.Marc. 29.5.51–54).

Although large states like Rome and Persia could conduct their surrogate battles in a mountainous region like Armenia (or Lazica, Colchis, or Iberia), neither state ever managed finally to control the local dynasts, who were always able to retreat into ever more remote highland zones (Amm.Marc. 27.12, 368–70; Braund, 1994: 287–311). To the end of antiquity one encounters descriptions of zones of permanent insurgency in mountain highlands that were characterized, from the perspective of central states, by types of violence that they labeled "banditry" *(latrocinium, lēsteia)*. Such were the Tzanic people of Armenia, who could always be defeated by the Romans or the Persians in a set military confrontation, but who were never finally dominated as a people since they were always able to retreat into the mountain heights, only to return later to reassert their autonomy (*Wars* 1.15.21–15, 530). These internal highland frontiers were no less significant than the northern Rhine-Danube frontier had been in the 4th century, and played the same role as a provider of raw recruits for the Roman army. Indeed, the highland zones of Armenia, Isauria-Cilicia, and the mountains of the Lebanon and the Anti-Lebanon had been a regular source of manpower for imperial armies (Speidel, 1980, 1983; Kennedy, 1989; Mitchell, 1994). They became inland war zones of the empire, characterized by the same types of economic development as its outer frontiers (Mitchell, 1995: 212–214). The loss of the traditional Roman recruiting sources along the war frontier of the Rhine and Danube in the 5th century, however, only served to increase the importance of the eastern highlands in Isauria and Armenia for army recruiting, which brought them still more power as the eastern highlands became primary war zones. Isauria now provided the rising military men, like Longinus, Tarasikodissa, and Flavius Zenon, who became high-ranking military officers and even monarchs of the eastern empire in the third quarter of the 5th century (Shaw, 1990: 250–256).

The long-term history of warfare involving the large states that dominated Mesopotamia and the Iranian highlands—first the Parthians and then the Sassanians—is one of extraordinary stability. As long as Rome and Persia, the large states on either side, remained internally stable and were perceived to be strong militarily, then the relationships between the two, though based on a permanent armed confrontation, tended to be characterized by long periods of peace and stability. The fragmentation of the Roman state through a long spate of civil conflicts up to the middle of the 3rd century destabilized its extreme outer frontiers, both on the far east and the far west. Where the central state was not able to fulfill its critical war function of protection against invaders, local powerful figures arose to perform this task for their own regions. Thus on the western periphery the so-called local empire of the Gauls assumed this function for a long period (Drinkwater, 1987). The weakness and fragmentation of the Roman central state encouraged repeated Persian forays through the mid 3rd century, and with these the rise of a peripheral protector kingdom centered on Palmyra. The restabilization of the Roman state under Diocletian and Galerius at the end of the 3rd century, however, returned the eastern frontier to a long-term balance between the two empires. Despite the permanent marshaling of a large proportion of all the armed resources of either empire along their shared frontier, peace prevailed along the border between the two great states for over two centuries. The great peace was broken by occasional expeditionary forces and raids by either side, some of them of considerable scale (in 338–340, 358–360, and 363; and again in 421–422 and 441–442), but these sudden forays deep into each other's border zones are remarkable for their brevity and their infrequency. Every incident was rather quickly followed by a peace agreement.

War on this frontier also had an ethnic component, but the peoples who were open to recruitment by either side were locked in an interstitial zone—the large unsettled desert arch between the agricultural lands directly protected by Roman forces and the western limits of the settled areas of the Sassanid state. The interstitial desert zone was populated by ethnic groups first labeled Arabs, but later Saracens (Isaac, 1992: 235–236). Their leaders, recognized by the Roman or Persian states as rulers of their people, were granted the title of tribal chief or phylarch. Not wishing permanently to commit any sizable forces outside the zones of agricultural settlement, both the Roman and the Sassanid states forged links with the Arabic phylarchs as a means of patrolling the desert and harassing their opposites. Connections between pastoral nomadic groups and states in the region, which had a very long history, tended to be limited to the use of armed elements as surrogate policemen of the desert periphery. The long-term opposition of two great central states on either side of the Syrian desert, however, encouraged an increasing integration of warlike forces inside the desert zone itself (Isaac, 1992: 235–249). The formalization of these relationships seems to have reached a threshold of sorts in the aftermath of the long cycle of Roman civil wars that ended with Constantine. In the latter part of Constantine's reign one Imru' al-Qays, buried at Nemara in 328, was recognized as not just an isolated Arab tribal phylarch, but rather king of all the Arabs (Shahid, 1984b: 31–53; Isaac, 1992: 239–240). As Ammianus later remarked, before his time the previously disparate Arabic groups had come to unify in war and so were now seen as Saracens, a term which seems to be derived from a word that signified a larger conglomerate of ethnic groups (Bowersock, 1975, 1983: 138–

147; Graf and O'Connor, 1977; *contra*: Shahid, 1984a). By the 6th century, the heyday of these confederations, the two principal leaders—Arethas, whose Ghassanids were allied with the Romans; and al-Mundhir, whose Lakhmids cooperated with the Sassanians—assumed increasingly independent courses of action (Shahid, 1995: 209–235; 529–540). The fundamental difference between the armed ethnic servitors on this frontier and those on the northern frontiers of the Roman and Sassanid states, however, was that the former were firmly contained by the two major states in the region. The Arab allies of both states, even in the most ambitious moments of the larger war groups of the 6th century, remained contributors to the existing war system in the Near East.

Like the ethnic groups along the northern frontier, the Arab tribes were also segmentary lineage societies, and their power arrangements were structured accordingly. Only civil wars within one of the two larger states, or prolonged outbreaks of full-scale war between them, might have threatened the balance of the recruiting of the Arab tribes. Continuous wars between Rome and Persia, however, were not common until the 6th century, and even then the wars tended to be limited to the contact zone of Mesopotamia or to the Armenian highlands to the north. Neither the Sassanians nor the Romans had any serious possibility of recruiting each other's subject populations; by social and cultural disposition, the inhabitants of the settled areas on the borderlands of both empires were tied to the political structures and interests of their respective states. The crossover from one side to the other was truly minimal, and the desertion of a local big man, such as the Antoninus reported by Ammianus (18.5; 359), was usually balanced by the odd Persian nobleman who went in the opposite direction (*Wars* 8.26.13). Beyond these individual shifts, the dangers for the major states in the recruitment of Arabic ethnic groups were never that great. Because two states were competing for their resources, collaboration would tend to balance between the employers. Then again, the absolute population levels in the desert were low—certainly by comparison with those of the two large states. Even if most men of military age were co-opted (half by one side, half by the other), the immediate consequences for battlefield conditions between Rome and Persia were never great enough to change the basic nature of war on this frontier.

The northern contact zone between the lands north of the Rhine and Danube and north of the Black Sea, and the peripheries of the Roman and Sassanid states was different from the frontier between the two states. The European stretch of this long northern frontier can be divided into an eastern and a western zone incorporating the lands lying east and west of the Hungarian plain (Elton, 1996: 19–30). To the east of the European part of this northern frontier, and to the north of the Black and Caspian seas, were the great Eurasian steppelands. These different ecological zones tended to sustain different modes of war. Whereas the indigenous peoples in the western European zone conducted wars almost solely with infantry forces, in the eastern European zone, and further east to the Eurasian steppe, warfare was increasingly dominated by cavalry forces. Despite these distinctions in warfare, the societies that inhabited these zones shared some strong continuities. Ethnic groups were subdivided into small, sometimes very small, social groups. They had basic subsistence agro-pastoral economies, were illiterate, and had no complex state or bureaucratic structures through which they could marshal resources for war (Heather, 1994). Although descriptions of their social structures are few, biased, and difficult to interpret, it is reasonably certain that almost all of these societies functioned on the basis of segmentary lineage systems (Thompson, 1966; 1996: 36, 48–50, 64–66, 80). Their technologies of war were therefore exceedingly simple: "It is remarkable that despite fairly frequent contact with Roman frontier armies, and despite endemic intertribal disputes and private feuds, no great advances were made in arms and armor, with the exception of sword blades, during the centuries of the [Roman] empire" (Todd, 1972: 99-102; at 102; Raddatz, 1985). Warfare and low-level violence (feuding, raiding) seem to have been endemic to all of these societies, which had their own species of internal wars as well as larger-scale conflicts that involved the cumulated resources of their respective peoples (e.g., Orosius, *Adv.Pag.* 7.37.3 on wars involving the Huns, Alans, and Goths). Although a knowledge of these local indigenous wars is very important to a general understanding of war in late antiquity, the plain fact is that very little evidence about them has survived.

Usually, the wars waged by these northern peoples, even external ones, aimed at achieving a form of domination over other people that was analogous to the bonds of power within their own segmentary and illiterate societies: the production of a dependent following such as the "countless retinue" of the Gepid "king" Ardaric (Jordanes, *Getica,* 99). On the one hand, this politics depended on dramatic gestures and public assertion of personality (Pohl, 1994: 71). On the other hand, as Tacitus noted, the instruments of violence were of critical importance: "It is impossible to maintain a large following of warriors except by violence and war" (*Germ.* 14). Faith and trust—and one might add fear—held these men together. They tied Ardaric to the following of Attila and thereby reveal how the Huns could rapidly mushroom into a large ethnic war band. Successes in war encouraged larger numbers of adherents and solidified their loyalties. Failures, which were just as frequent, broke them. Thus warrior bands, such as that headed by Sarus the Goth at the beginning of the 5th century, could suddenly expand or diminish in size (Zosimus 6.2.4–5, 13.2, 36.2; Liebeschuetz, 1990: 38–39).

The dynamic composition of these ethnic war groupings made loyalty and motive critical to the attachment of component units to a single leader. One might think of the Gepids and their king Ardaric. In reality, his "Gepids" were a large conglomerate composed of Rugi, Heruls, Sarmatians, Suebi, Sciri, and others (Pohl, 1980: 260–261). The Longobard army that Alboin led into Italy in 568–69 was a composite band of Longobards, Saxons, Bulgars, Sarmatians, Pannonians, Suebi, Noricans, and others (*Hist.Lang.* 2.26; Christie, 1995: 64). Far from being the occasion of ethnogenesis or the forging of a specific and stable ethnic identity by means of violent confrontation with "others," war just as often impelled the creation of large polyethnic followings. Although their members might be called by a single name, like Gepid or Hun, in reality these groups were weak multiethnic conglomerates that constantly threatened to break down into their original ethnic and segmentary parts. No sooner did the Longobards conquer Italy than they redispersed and fragmented into the numerous segments *(Farae)* from which their society had been constituted (Christie, 1995: 65, 77–82).

The long-term benefits of the northern peoples' parasitic attachments to the Roman state were not inconsiderable. For their leaders, such links were probably necessary to maintain their position of superior power within their ethnic conglomerate. From the perspective of the Roman state, however, these frontier peoples posed a number of serious problems. The northern borderlands were inhabited by a great number of diverse ethnic groups, none of which were organized along state lines. Almost all of them were involved in intermittent warfare with each other, conflicts that occasionally threatened to spill over into the empire. Moreover, quite unlike the civil frontiers along the southern half of the empire, the northern frontiers had substantial population densities. The consistent Roman and Byzantine response to the serious threats posed in this war zone was the obvious one: to manipulate the local forces of violence, most often by using one ethnic group as a check on its neighbor. This response required constant readjustments, however, since the more the central state intervened with advice and exhortation, weaponry and material support, prestigious ranks and rewards, and large amounts of money and precious metals, the more violence increased. And the greater the intensity of the violence, the less predictable and controllable it became. The escalating rewards and the escalating violent behavior became part of frontier ethnic groups' learned behavior—and expectations. There was thus created along this frontier what might be aptly labeled a "parasitic economy," in which local chieftains and men of power came to depend on the acquisition of war rewards and prestige goods from their Roman employers as the critical economic means by which they sustained their own position with their followers (Pohl, 1980: 268; Todd, 1992: 86–87).

Compared to the eastern frontier, which was made unusually stable by the existence of bureaucracy, institutions, literacy, and the capability of setting fixed agreements that would hold for large geographical spaces and for long periods of time, the northern frontiers were continually threatened by war precisely because of their extreme instability. Any peace agreement on the Rhine or Danube was necessarily made with a finite ethnic group that covered only a relatively small geographic space and functioned wholly in an oral mode. The agreement had to be a spoken one between the Roman emperor and a specific ethnic head (the *rex, regulus, subregulus,* or *reiks*) who made spoken promises and swore oaths to keep his agreements (Amm.Marc. 17.1.13; 17.10.9; 30.6.2). The Roman state therefore had to deal with these peoples in the same oral mode in which they dealt with each other (Amm.Marc. 31.3.1: Huns and Alans, about 370). Alliances that were confirmed by what was said and heard by either side (Amm.Marc. 30.3.5, 374), however, were only as good as the individual chief who made them, and were based on the same networks of personal connections that constituted hierarchy in the local society—an order that constantly threatened to unravel with the provocation of some local feud or some other minor shift in local relationships that impaired the power of the individual who had made the promise to the Roman emperor. These attachments were also viewed on the ethnic side as highly personal. Gothic chieftains who made agreements with Constantine in the mid 330s passed these down to their descendants, who regarded themselves in a personal relationship with the familial descendants of that particular Roman and no other. Such a system of peace agreements was only as dependable as the oral and ritualistic personal links that sustained them from one generation to the next. The potential for misunderstanding was very great and sometimes involved the Roman emperor in grotesque scenes of farcical confusion as well as real danger, as when Constantius tried to stage a ritual ceremonial to confirm his relations with the Limigantes in 359, and almost lost his life in the ensuing wild melee (Amm.Marc. 19.11.10–13).

Warfare along the northern face of the empire, while it did involve both the congeries of ethnic groups and the massive resources of the Roman state, never produced a simple dichotomy of barbarians against Romans. The constant intrusion of the economic and political forces of the Roman state, and its exploitation of the frontier peoples for its own purposes, transformed the frontier between the two into an intensive war zone in which whole ethnic groups were repeatedly drawn into a vortex of violence. The powerful economic and social forces set in motion by these wars did on occasion contribute to the forging of new ethnic identities, in a process labeled ethnogenesis by modern-day historians—the Salian Franks being a striking example of a long-term identity defined in part by their military service for the Roman state (Anderson, 1995; see also Barlow, 1995). The identity of the whole generation of "Goths" that Alaric led across the northern war zone, from Illyricum into Italy, had been forged by the very processes of war and military service that made and unmade the circumstances of their daily lives (Liebeschuetz, 1990: 49–83). This was one of the creative faces of the northern war zone. But there was also a genocidal aspect to this frontier warfare—not, one must be careful to caution, in the sense of the physical extinction of all persons belonging to a given social group, but rather entailing the destruction of their social formations and identities. Ethnic groups were destroyed by the very forces of war that had initially helped to sustain them. As they were drawn into the vortex of violence that ground back and forth along the line of the middle Danube, Heruls, Huns, Rugi, Gepids, and others simply went out of existence as coherent and recognized peoples. It is difficult to describe this effect of war on cultural identity—the term ethnocide might be appropriate—but it was certainly no less pervasive than ethnogenesis.

The so-called Hun empire of Attila is one of the better attested cases of this general phenomenon. The factors that created an Attila were just stronger variants of those that had created Alaric half a century earlier on the same frontier. Various Hun groups had been drawn into warfare with other peoples along this northern periphery, including the Alans and the Tervingi; they began to coalesce into large coherent groups encouraged by Roman employment and by repeated invitations to intervene in civil wars within the Roman empire. The process accelerated the pyramiding of Hun clans and allied ethnic subgroups into a much larger collection of peoples under ever more powerful leaders in the period between Uldin (ca. 408–412) and Rua (420s), and culminated in the domination of Attila (ca. 435–450). Just as with the ethnic army commanded by Alaric in the late 390s and early 400s, however, even in the midst of their expansionist phase the Huns experienced several dramatic recessions of their power (Thompson, 1996: 33–35). Given the forces that made and unmade ethnic armies along this frontier, the acme of Hun power coincided with the large-scale employment of Huns by Aëtius in the court wars of the Roman state in the mid 420s to 440s (Heather, 1995: 17–19, 26–27; Thompson, 1996: 69–86). This Hun power and its social structure, however, were wholly parasitic. When the personal power relations and economic benefits of armed service that sustained it were removed, the whole edifice vanished more quickly than it had formed. In the decades after the collapse of the Hun domination, Rugi, Heruls, and others faced this same extinction of social identity in the violent gristmill of the Danubian war zone.

Contributing to the general matrix of violence in the north, war on this frontier was made more complex by internal wars, which were just as characteristic of the smaller ethnic groups as they were of the great empires. These local episodes of violence had serious implications whenever they became intermingled with the same processes within the Roman state. The expansion of any given ethnic group, such as that of the Longobards, generated internal pressures that encouraged the fission of the group's social structure and the outbreak of internecine conflicts over the appropriation of rewards and leadership—for example, in the Longobard case, in the war of Waccho against Tato and his son Hildechis fought around 510. Internal wars within the various ethnic congeries were characteristic of the system of personal power by which leaders of tribal cantons or segments built up their domination through the forcible incorporation of neighboring groups. They were also a natural result of the fission or fragmentation of an ethnic group into its smaller components.

These internal wars were just as important to the fate of any given ethnos as civil wars were to the larger states. A single case must suffice. The historian Socrates (Hist.eccl. 4.33) gives details of a civil war (emphulios polemos) between opposed segments of the "Goths" headed by Athanaric and Fritigern that broke out in the years before 370 (Lenski, 1995). The war was both cause and consequence of the fission of the Goths into two parts. When Athanaric appeared to be getting the upper hand in the war, Fritigern responded by trying to recruit Romans to assist him. In this case, Fritigern appealed for assistance from the Romans and Emperor Valens gave him the military aid that he needed. The civil war intertwined Roman and Gothic to the extent that when Fritigern and the large number of Goths attached to him won the war, they showed their gratitude to Valens by adopting his deity and his peculiar religious beliefs.

The great economic forces that flowed from the much more highly developed Mediterranean must also have contributed greatly to wars among the ethnic groups beyond the northern frontier. We cannot trace all the cause-and-effect relationships, but they included the routine redistribution of arms, luxury goods, and status symbols, and control of access to these (Todd, 1992: 86–103; Whittaker, 1994: 122–131). A particular sector of the northern frontier was rather special in this regard: the borderland zone across the lower Danube, extending northward and eastward into the present-day Ukraine. Both literary and archaeological evidence suggest that this was the premier "slaving frontier" of the Roman empire (Thompson, 1966: 38–39; Braund-Tsetskhladze, 1989). The deeply established business and power connections here went back through the period of the late Roman republic over a millennium or more, and involved all types of collusion, official and otherwise, on both sides of the frontier (Crawford, 1977). This trade (and the concurrent slaving operations of the Huns, Goths, and others) was likely to have had a considerable effect on the ethnic societies north of the Danube. It must have contributed substantially to the escalation of interethnic violence. Likewise, the sudden reduction of this enormously valuable trade in human commodities was bound to devastate the subsistence economies of the war zone that depended heavily for wealth and power on this monocrop economy (Amm.Marc. 27.5.7; 31.4.11; 31.5.1). Practically the only truly valuable "natural resource" this frontier had to offer the economy of the Roman state was its human population, whether for soldiers or for slaves (Todd, 1992: 19).

The northern frontiers of the Sassanid state were not greatly different in the typical results of interaction between the state and ethnic groups. The dimensions of the problem were different because the peoples in the Eurasian steppe, though just as segmented and as illiterate as their western counterparts, did not have as great a population density and faced more serious geographical barriers separating them from lands to the south—the great water barriers of the Black and Caspian seas, and the mountain ranges, above all the Caucasus. Yet the structure of the Sassanid state meant that responses would be modulated differently. Although so much less is known of the northern periphery of the Sassanid empire, it seems that it too was an important barbarian frontier, dominated by pastoral nomadic groups generally characterized as Hunnish, whose cultures were based on segmentary lineage structures (*Wars* 1.3.5–7). The comparable ecological and social forces meant that in the long run the warfare of the Persian state in the east tended to replicate that of Rome to the west. The hardening of the northern frontier by the building of large walls used to impede and to monitor the mobile pastoral populations, and the movement of the monarch and the royal court from Ctesiphon to the war zone itself, are but a few of the characteristic features that were duplicated by the Sassanids (Frye, 1983: 138–139; Howard-Johnston, 1995: 191–197).

There were two basic changes in the classic war system of late antiquity. The first centered on the war zone along the northern frontiers of the Roman empire and involved a complex and extended interplay of forces that were set in motion by the Augustan military restoration. Given the demographic resources and modes of social organization along this frontier, the massive militarization of this periphery by the Roman state only contributed to its final destabilization. The prolonged internal or civil wars of the empire drew in one ethnic group after another—a process which finally led to the disintegration of the part of the Roman state that directly faced this frontier. The vortices of internal conflict within the northern war zone, as well as their relationship to conflicts within the central state, compelled the fragmentation of the basic operational units of war into smaller regional units. The end of the process was marked by the emergence of independent local warlords of the type perhaps best attested for 5th and 6th century Gaul (Drinkwater, 1992; Liebeschuetz, 1993; Whittaker, 1993; 1994: 243–278). Viewed from the perspective of the system in general, therefore, Piganiol's famous dictum (1972: 466) on the end of the western empire—that "it was murdered" *(elle a été assassinée)*—could just as usefully be rephrased as *elle s'est suicidée.*

Even as biological metaphors, however, the phrases are misleading representations of a process that involved not only both parties in the west, but other parts of the organism in the east that survived rather well in consequence of the demise of its "other half." For the other profound change transformed the relationship between the two great states on the frontier between the Mediterranean and the Near East. The fundamental change was marked by the breakdown of the long stability between the Byzantine and Sassanid states, especially in the first decades of the 7th century. The transformation of attitude was reflected in an intensification of war aims, in which the leaders of each state began to think more in terms of a "total war" aimed at the extermination of the other (Isaac, 1992: 127; Howard-Johnston, 1995: 164). Neither state in its much weakened state was prepared to meet the massive coalition of Arab forces that came out of the Hijāz and struck at the southern faces of both states. There is no evidence that they were even conscious of any special military threat emanating from this direction. In their war preparations, which presumably reflected their mental disposition, they continued to be obsessively concerned with each other, and with the millennium-old frontier that converged on the great fertile crescent that joined northern Syria and Mesopotamia.

The war system of the late antique Mediterranean and Near East was therefore determined by the resources of the large states. Rome, the power focused on the Mediterranean, was counterpoised to Sassanid Persia, centered on the great land masses of Mesopotamia and the Iranian highlands (Rubin, 1986b). The geopolitical location of these states, and the manner in which they expanded militarily, caused them to leave open frontiers, mainly on their northern flanks and along the narrow land frontier in Mesopotamia where they confronted each other. When the attacks of the Banu Quraysh erupted from the Hijāz and the southern parts of the Syrian desert in 633–640—attacks that were aimed no longer just at raiding and pillaging but at land conquest—the basic shift in the direction and meaning of war was not expected by the major contestants, who had hitherto defined the nature of war in the region. The Arabs came out of a region that had never been considered a serious war frontier of the type shared by Rome and Persia during the preceding half millennium. Whether centrally organized or not (Landau-Tasseron, 1995; *contra:* Donner, 1981; 1995), the Arab forces easily drove deep into the exposed civil undersides of both states and changed the war system of late antiquity forever. As with the successor states in the Roman west, this was another very successful case of violent parasitism. (See Heather, 1996, chaps. 7–10, for the parallel case of the Goths in the west.) But so little is known about how and why it happened that the conquest is as much a puzzle, and a surprise, to modern-day scholars as it was to the Byzantines and Sassanians when it happened. The same silence of the literary sources that bedevils our knowledge of war among the ethnic groups beyond the northern frontiers of the Roman empire also leaves us ignorant of the Arabs who achieved this great feat of violent appropriation.

For our mental image of war in late antiquity, we have therefore tended, almost by default, to adopt the classical interpretation so powerfully created by Edward Gibbon. It is a perspective that is Rome-centered, suffused with a vocabulary of decline, and marked by a dichotomy between the good internal forces of the state and the evil destructive forces of external enemies. It should perhaps be a matter of some concern that Gibbon himself, not long after the completion of his *Decline and Fall,* had serious misgivings about the division of war that he had offered his readers. He had already become convinced that problems of war internal both to Rome and Persia were as important as the classic battlefield clashes with external enemies (Bowersock, 1977). The whole problem of war, so critical to the making and the unmaking of the ancient world, must be viewed from a panoramic perspective that integrates the oecumenes of both the Mediterranean and the Near East, as well as the internal and external aspects of the social orders that were created and destroyed by violent force. Because of the peculiar interests of classical historiographies, ancient and modern, it is a subject on which considerable bodies of fact have been accumulated and analyzed. But the dominant paradigms of thinking have served to obscure a clearer view of the general dynamic of war itself. Despite the great assemblage of data for the Roman part of this story, one has the uneasy feeling that we are only beginning to understand the problematic nature of this "worst of all evils."

Works Cited

Anderson, T. A. 1995. "Roman Military Colonies in Gaul, Salian Ethnogenesis and the Forgotten Meaning of *Pactus Legis Salicae* 59.5," *Early Medieval Europe* 4: 129–144.

Austin, N. J. E. 1979. *Ammianus on Warfare: An Investigation into Ammianus' Military Knowledge.* Brussels.

Austin, N. J. E., and N. B. Rankov. 1995. *Exploratio: Military and Political Intelligence in the Roman World from the Second Punic War to the Battle of Adrianople.* New York.

Bachrach, B. S. 1993. "Logistics in Pre-Crusade Europe," chap. 4 in John A. Lynn, ed., *Feeding Mars: Logistics in Western Warfare from the Middle Ages to the Present,* 57–78. Boulder, Colo.

Barlow, J. 1995. "Kinship, Identity and Fourth-Century Franks," *Historia* 45: 223–239.

Barnes, T. D. 1979. "The Date of Vegetius," *Phoenix* 33: 254–257.

Bishop, M. C. 1985. "The Military *Fabrica* and the Production of Arms in the Early Principate," 1–42 in M. Bishop, ed., *Production and Distribution of Roman Military Equipment: 220–366*. Oxford.

Bivar, A. D. H. 1972. "Cavalry Equipment and Tactics on the Euphrates Frontier," *Dumbarton Oaks Papers* 26: 271–291.

Blockley, R. C. 1985. "Subsidies and Diplomacy: Rome and Persia in Late Antiquity," *Phoenix* 39: 62–74.

——— 1992. *East Roman Foreign Policy: Formation and Conduct from Diocletian to Anastasius*. Leeds.

Boak, A. E. R. 1955. *Manpower Shortage and the Fall of the Roman Empire*. London.

Bowersock, G. W. 1975. "The Greek-Nabataean Bilingual Inscription at Ruwwāfa, Saudi Arabia," 513–522 in *Le monde grec: Hommages à Claire Préaux*. Brussels. Repr. in Bowersock, *Studies on the Eastern Roman Empire*. Goldbach, 1994.

——— 1977. "Gibbon on Civil War and Rebellion in the Decline of the Roman Empire," *Daedalus* 105: 63–71. Repr. in G. W. Bowersock, J. Clive, and S. R. Graubard, eds., *Edward Gibbon and the Decline and Fall of the Roman Empire*. Cambridge, Mass., 1977.

——— 1983. *Roman Arabia*. Cambridge, Mass.

Braund, D. 1994. *Georgia in Antiquity: A History of Colchis and Transcaucasian Iberia, 500 BC–AD 562*. Oxford.

Braund, D., and G. R. Tsetskhladze. 1989. "The Export of Slaves from Colchis," *Classical Quarterly* 39: 114–125.

Briant, P. 1976. "'Brigandage', dissidence et conquête en Asie Achéménide et Hellénistique," *Dialogues d'Histoire Ancienne* 2: 163–258.

——— 1982. *État et pasteurs du Moyen-Orient ancien*. Cambridge, Eng.

Brunt, P. A. 1974. "Conscription and Volunteering in the Roman Imperial Army," *Scripta Classica Israelica* 1: 90–115. Repr. in Brunt, *Roman Imperial Themes*. Oxford, 1990.

Burns, T. S. 1994. *Barbarians within the Gates of Rome: A Study of Roman Military Policy and the Barbarians, ca. 375–425 A.D.* Bloomington-Indianapolis.

Bury, J. B. 1928. *The Invasion of Europe by the Barbarians*. London. Repr. New York, 1963.

Cameron, A. 1985. *Procopius and the Sixth Century*. Berkeley–Los Angeles.

———, ed. 1995. *The Byzantine and Early Islamic Near East, 3: States, Resources, and Armies*. Princeton.

Carrié, J.-M. 1986. "L'esercito, trasformazioni funzionali ed economie locali," chap. 12 in Andrea Giardina, ed., *Società romana e impero tardoantico*, vol. 1: *Istituzioni, ceti, economie*. Rome-Bari, 1986: 449–488; 760–771.

——— 1993. "Eserciti e strategie," 83–134 in A. Schiavone, ed., *Storia di Roma*, vol 3: *L'Età tardoantica, 1: Crisi e trasformazioni*. Turin.

——— 1995. "L'état à la recherche de nouveaux modes de financement des armées (Rome et Byzance, IVe–VIIIe siècles," 27–60 in Cameron, 1995.

Christie, N. 1991. "Invasion or Invitation? The Longobard Occupation of Northern Italy, A.D. 568–569," *Romanobarbarica* 11: 79–108.

——— 1995. *The Lombards: The Ancient Longobards*. Oxford.

Christol, M. 1977. "Effort de guerre et ateliers monétaires de la périphérie au IIIe s. ap. J.-C.: L'atelier de Cologne sous Valérien et Gallien," 235–277 in Christol, *Armées et fiscalité dans le monde antique*. Paris.

Crawford, M. 1977. "Republican *Denarii* in Romania: The Suppression of Piracy and the Slave-Trade," *Journal of Roman Studies* 67: 117–124.

Crone, P. 1980. *Slaves on Horses: The Evolution of the Islamic Polity*. Cambridge.

Dagron, G. 1993. "Modèles de combattants et technologie militaire dans le *Stratègikon* de Maurice," 279–284 in F. Vallet and M. Kazanski, eds., *L'armée romaine et les Barbares du IIIe siècle au VIIe siècle*. Condé-sur-Noireau.

Delbrück, H. 1902/1921. *Geschichte der Kriegskunst im Rahmen der politischen Geschichte*, 2.1: *Die Germanen: Römer und Germanen*. Berlin: 1st ed., 1902; 2nd ed., 1909; 3rd ed., 1921. English ed.: *The Barbarian Invasions,* trans. W. J. Renfroe. Westport, Conn., 1980.

Demougeot, E. 1969–1979. *La formation de l'Europe et les invasions barbares,* 2 vols. Paris.

Dennis, G. T. 1985. *Three Byzantine Military Treatises*. Washington, D.C.

D'Huys, V. 1987. "How to Describe Violence in Historical Narrative," *Ancient Society* 18: 209–250.

Donner, F. M. 1981. *The Early Islamic Conquests*. Princeton, 1981.

———— 1995. "Centralized Authority and Military Autonomy in the Early Islamic Conquests," 337–360 in Cameron, 1995.

Drinkwater, J. F. 1987. *The Gallic Empire: Separatism and Continuity in the Northwestern Provinces of the Empire, AD 260–274* (Historia Einzelschriften 52). Wiesbaden.

———— 1992. "The Bagaudae of Fifth-Century Gaul," 208–217 in J. F. Drinkwater and H. Elton, eds., *Fifth-Century Gaul: A Crisis of Identity?* Cambridge, Eng.

Duncan-Jones, R. 1994. "The Imperial Budget," 33–46 in Duncan-Jones, *Money and Government in the Roman Empire*. Cambridge, Eng.

Eadie, J. W. 1967. "The Development of Roman Mailed Cavalry," *Journal of Roman Studies* 57: 165–169.

Elton, H. 1996. *Warfare in Roman Europe, 350–425*. Oxford.

Ferrill, A. 1986. *The Fall of the Roman Empire: The Military Explanation*. London. Repr. 1991.

———— 1991. *Roman Imperial Grand Strategy*. London-Lanham.

Flaig, E. 1992. *Den Kaiser herausfordern: Die Usurpationen im Römischen Reich*. Frankfurt–New York.

———— 1997. "Für eine Konzeptionalisierung der Usurpation im spätrömischen Reich," in F. Paschoud and J. Szidat, eds., *Usurpationen in der Spätantike*. Wiesbaden.

Frye, R. N. 1983. "The Political History of Iran under the Sasanians," 116–180 in E. Yarshater, ed., *The Cambridge History of Iran*, 3.1: *The Seleucid, Parthian and Sasanian Periods*. Cambridge, Eng.

Goffart, W. 1977. "The Date and Purpose of Vegetius' *De re militari*," *Traditio* 33: 65–100. Repr. in Goffart, *Rome's Fall and After*. London, 1989.

———— 1980. "The Barbarians in Late Antiquity," 3–39 in Goffart, *Barbarians and Romans*. Princeton.

———— 1989. "The Theme of 'The Barbarian Invasions' in Late Antique and Modern Historiography," 87–107 in Evangelos K. Chrysos and Andreas Schwarcz, eds., *Das Reich und die Barbaren*. Vienna-Cologne.

Goldsworthy, A. K. 1996. *The Roman Army at War, 100 BC–AD 200*. Oxford.

Goodburn, R., and P. Bartholomew, eds. 1976. *Aspects of the Notitia Dignitatum*. Oxford.

Gordon, C. D. 1949. "Subsidies in Roman Imperial Defence," *Phoenix* 3: 60–69.

Graf, D. F., and M. O'Connor. 1977. "The Origin of the Term Saracen and the Rawwāfa Inscription," *Byzantine Studies/Etudes Byzantines* 4: 52–66.

Haldon, J. F. 1979. *Recruitment and Conscription in the Byzantine Army, c. 550–950: A Study on the Origins of the Stratiotika Ktemata* (Österreichische Akademie der Wissenschaften, Philosophisch-historische Klasse: Sitzungsberichte, vol. 357). Vienna.

———— 1990. "The State and Its Apparatus: Military Administration," 208–253 in Haldon, *Byzantium in the Seventh Century: The Transformation of a Culture*. Cambridge.

———— 1993. "Administrative Continuities and Structural Transformations in East Roman Military Organisation, ca. 580–640," 45–53 in F. Vallet and M. Kazanski, eds., *L'armée romaine et les Barbares du IIIe siècle au VIIe siècle*. Condé-sur-Noireau.

Heather, P. J. 1991. *Goths and Romans, 332–489*. Oxford.

——— 1994. "Literacy and Power in the Migration Period," 177–197 in A. K. Bowman and G. Woolf, eds., *Literacy and Power in the Ancient World*. Cambridge, Eng.

——— 1995. "The Huns and the End of the Roman Empire in Western Europe," *English Historical Review* 110: 4–41.

——— 1996. *The Goths*. Oxford.

Hedeager, L. 1978. "A Quantitative Analysis of Roman Imports to Europe North of the Limes (0–400 AD) and the Question of Roman-Germanic Exchange," 191–216 in K. Kristiansen and C. Paludin-Muller, eds., *New Directions in Scandinavian History*. Copenhagen.

——— 1988. "The Evolution of Germanic Society, 1–400 A.D.," 129–143 in R. F. Jones et al., eds., *First Millennium Papers: Western Europe in the First Millennium AD*. Oxford.

——— 1992. *Iron-Age Societies: From Tribe to State in Northern Europe, 500 B.C. to A.D. 700*. Oxford.

Höckman, O. 1986. "Römische Schiffsverbände auf dem Ober- und Mittelrhein und die Verteidigung der Rheingrenze in der Spätantike," *Jahrbuch des Römisch-Germanischen Zentralmuseums* 33: 369–416.

Hoffmann, D. 1969–70. *Das spätrömische Bewegungsheer und die Notitia Dignitatum*, 2 vols. Düsseldorf.

Hollard, D. 1995. "La crise de la monnaie dans l'Empire romain au 3e siècle après J.C. Synthèse des recherches et résultats nouveaux," *Annales* 50: 1045–78.

Howard-Johnston, J. 1995. "The Two Great Powers in Late Antiquity: A Comparison," 157–226 in Cameron, 1995.

Iluk, J. 1985. "The Export of Gold from the Roman Empire to Barbarian Countries from the 4th to the 6th Centuries," *Münstersche Beiträge zur Antiken Handelsgeschichte* 4: 79–102.

Isaac, B. 1992. *The Limits of Empire: The Roman Army in the East*, rev. ed. Oxford.

James, S. 1988. "The *Fabricae*: State Arms Factories of the Later Roman Empire," 257–331 in J. C. Coulston, ed., *Military Equipment and the Identity of Roman Soldiers*. Oxford.

Jones, A. H. M. 1964. *The Later Roman Empire, 284–602: A Social, Economic, and Administrative Survey*, 3 vols. Oxford. Repr. in 2 vols., Baltimore, 1986.

Kaegi, W. E. 1992. *Byzantium and the Early Islamic Conquests*. Cambridge, Eng. Repr. 1995.

——— 1993. "Byzantine Logistics: Problems and Perspectives," 39–55 in John A. Lynn, ed., *Feeding Mars: Logistics in Western Warfare from the Middle Ages to the Present*. Boulder, Colo.

Kennedy, D. L. 1989. "The Military Contribution of Syria to the Roman Imperial Army," 235–246 in D. H. French and C. S. Lightfoot, eds., *The Eastern Frontier of the Roman Empire*. Oxford.

Kennedy, D. L., and H. I. MacAdam. 1985. "Latin Inscriptions from the Azraq Oasis, Jordan," *Zeitschrift für Papyrologie und Epigraphik* 60: 97–108.

Kolias, T. G. 1988. *Byzantinische Waffen: Ein Beitrag zur byzantinischen Waffenkunde von den Anfängen bis zur lateinischen Eroberung*. Vienna.

Kotula, T. 1970. "Firmus, fils de Nubel, était-il usurpateur ou roi des Maures?" *Acta Antiqua Academiae Scientiarum Hungaricae* 18: 137–146.

Kunow, J. 1986. "Bemerkungen zum Export römischer Waffen in das *Barbaricum*," *Limes: Studien zu den Militärgrenzen Roms*, 3, Stuttgart (1986): 740–746.

Landau-Tasseron, E. 1995. "Features of the Pre-Conquest Muslim Army in the Time of Muhammad," 299–336 in Cameron, 1995.

Lee, A. D. 1993. *Information and Frontiers: Roman Foreign Relations in Late Antiquity*. Cambridge, Eng.

Lenski, N. 1995. "The Date of the Gothic Civil War and the Date of the Gothic Conversion," *Greek, Roman, and Byzantine Studies* 36: 51–87.

Liebeschuetz, J. H. W. G. 1990. *Barbarians and Bishops: Army, Church and State in the Age of Arcadius and Chrysostom*. Oxford.

——— 1993. "The End of the Roman Army in the Western Empire," 265–276 in J. Rich and G. Shipley, eds., *War and Society in the Roman World*. London–New York.

——— 1994. "Realism and Fantasy: The Anonymous *De Rebus Bellicis* and Its Afterlife," 119–139 in E. Dabrowa, ed., *The Roman and Byzantine Army in the East*. Cracow.

Luttwak, E. 1976. *The Grand Strategy of the Roman Empire: From the First Century A.D. to the Third*. Baltimore.

MacAdam, H. I. 1989. "Epigraphy and the *Notitia Dignitatum*," 295–309 in D. H. French and C. S. Lightfoot, eds., *The Eastern Frontier of the Roman Empire*. Oxford.

MacMullen, R. 1980. "How Big Was the Roman Army?" *Klio* 62: 451–460.

——— 1984. "The Roman Emperor's Army Costs," *Latomus* 43: 571–580.

Matthews, J. 1976. "Mauretania in Ammianus and the *Notitia*," 157–186 in R. Goodburn and P. Bartholomew, eds., *Aspects of the Notitia Dignitatum*. Oxford. Repr. as chap. 11 in Matthews, *Political Life and Culture in Late Roman Society*, London, 1985.

——— 1989. *The Roman Empire of Ammianus*. London.

Millar, F. 1982. "Emperors, Frontiers and Foreign Relations, 31 B.C. to A.D. 378," *Britannia* 13: 1–23.

Milner, N. P. 1993. *Vegetius: Epitome of Military Science*. Liverpool.

Mitchell, S. 1989. "The Siege of Cremna, AD 278," 311–327 in D. H. French and C. S. Lightfoot, eds., *The Eastern Frontier of the Roman Empire*. Oxford.

——— 1994. "Notes on Military Recruitment from the Eastern Provinces," 141–148 in E. Dabrowa, ed., *The Roman and Byzantine Army in the East*. Cracow.

——— 1995. *Cremna in Pisidia: An Ancient City in Peace and in War*. London.

Musset, L. 1975. *The Germanic Invasions: The Making of Europe, A.D. 400–600*, transl. Edward and Columba James. London.

Patterson, W. F. 1966. "The Archers of Islam," *Journal of the Economic and Social History of the Orient* 9: 69–87.

Piganiol, A. 1972. *L'empire chrétien (325–395)*. Paris.

Pipes, D. 1981. *Slave Soldiers and Islam*. New Haven–London.

Pohl, W. 1980. "Die Gepiden und die *gentes* an der mittleren Donau nach der Zerfall des Attilareiches," 239–305 in H. Wolfram and F. Daim, eds., *Die Völker an der mittleren und unteren Donau im fünften und sechsten Jahrhundert*. Österreichische Akademie der Wissenschaften, Philosophish-Historische Klasse: Denkschriften, vol. 145. Vienna.

——— 1994. "La sfida Attilana: Dinamica di un potere barbaro," 69–89 in S. Blason Scarel, ed., *Attila: Flagellum Dei?* Rome.

Raddatz, K. 1985. "Die Bewaffnung der Germanen vom letzten Jahrhundert vor Chr. Geb. biz zur Völkerwanderungszeit," *ANRW* 2.12.3: 281–361.

Rubin, Z. 1986a. "Diplomacy and War in the Relations between Byzantium and the Sassanids in the Fifth Century A.D.," 677–695 in Philip Freeman and David Kennedy, eds., *The Defence of the Roman and Byzantine East*. Oxford.

——— 1986b. "The Mediterranean and the Dilemma of the Roman Empire in Late Antiquity," *Mediterranean Historical Review* 1: 13–62.

——— 1995. "The Reforms of Khusro Anushirwan," 227–297 in Cameron, 1995.

Schippmann, K. 1990. *Grundzüge der Geschichte des Sasanidischen Reiches*. Darmstadt.

Seeck, O., ed. 1876. *Notitia Dignitatum*. Berlin. Repr. Frankfurt, 1962.

Shahbazi, A. S. 1986. "Army (i) Pre-Islamic Iran," 489–499 in E. Yarshater, ed., *Encyclopedia Iranica* 2.5.

Shahid, I. 1984a. "The Term *Saraceni* and the Image of the Arabs," 123–141 in *Rome and the Arabs: A Prolegomenon to the Study of Byzantium and the Arabs*. Washington, D.C.

———— 1984b. *Byzantium and the Arabs in the Fourth Century*. Washington, D.C.

———— 1995. *Byzantium and the Arabs in the Sixth Century,* vol. 1. pt. 1: *Political and Military History*. Washington, D.C.

Shaw, B. D. 1990. "Bandit Highlands and Lowland Peace: The Mountains of Isauria-Cilicia: Parts I and II," *Journal of the Economic and Social History of the Orient* 33: 199–233; 237–270.

Speidel, M. 1980. "Legionaries from Asia Minor," *ANRW* 2.7.2: 730–746. Repr. in Speidel, 1992, vol. 1.

———— 1983. "The Roman Army in Asia Minor: Recent Epigraphical Discoveries and Researches," 7–34 in S. Mitchell, ed., *Armies and Frontiers in Roman and Byzantine Anatolia*. Oxford. Repr. in Speidel, 1992, 1:273–300.

———— 1984. "*Catafractarii Clibanarii* and the Rise of the Later Roman Mailed Cavalry: A Gravestone from Claudiopolis in Bithynia," *Epigraphica Anatolica* 4: 151–56. Repr. in Speidel, 1992, 2:406–11.

———— 1987. "The Roman Road to Dumata (Jawf in Saudi Arabia) and the Frontier Strategy of *Praetensione Colligare*," *Historia* 36: 213–221. Repr. in Speidel, 1992, 2:369–78.

———— 1992. *Roman Army Studies*, 2 vols. Stuttgart.

Stelten, L. F. 1990. *Flavius Vegetius Renatus: Epitoma Rei Militaris*. New York.

Thompson, E. A. 1952. *A Roman Reformer and Inventor, Being a New Text of the Treatise De Rebus Bellicis*. Oxford. Repr. New York, 1979.

———— 1966. *The Visigoths in the Time of Ulfila*. Oxford.

———— 1996. *The Huns*. Oxford.

Todd, M. 1972. *The Barbarians: Goths, Franks and Vandals*. London–New York.

———— 1992. *The Early Germans*. Oxford. Repr. 1995.

Traina, G. 1986–87. "Aspettando i barbari: Le origini tardoantiche della guerriglia di frontiera," *Romano barbarica* 9: 247–280.

Treadgold, W. 1995. *Byzantium and Its Army, 284–1081*. Stanford, Cal.

Van Creveld, M. L. 1991. *Technology and War: From 2000 B.C. to the Present*, rev. ed. New York.

Waas, M. 1971. *Germanen im römischen Dienst*. Bonn.

Wheeler, E. L. 1993. "Methodological Limits and the Mirage of Roman Strategy, Part I and II," *The Journal of Military History* 57: 7–41, 215–240.

Whitby, M. 1994. "The Persian King at War," 227–263 in E. Dabrowa, ed., *The Roman and Byzantine Army in the East*. Cracow.

———— 1995. "Recruitment in Roman Armies from Justinian to Heraclius (ca. 565–615)," 61–124 in Cameron, 1995.

Whittaker, C. R. 1993. "Landlords and Warlords in the Later Roman Empire," 277–302 in J. Rich and G. Shipley, eds., *War and Society in the Roman World*. London–New York.

———— 1994. *Frontiers of the Roman Empire: A Social and Economic Study*. Baltimore–London.

Wickham, C. 1981. *Early Medieval Italy: Central Power and Local Society, 400–1000*. London.

Widengren, G. 1976. "Iran, der grosse Gegner Roms: Königsgewalt, Feodalismus, Militärwesen," *ANRW* 2.9.1: 219–306.

EMPIRE BUILDING

Christopher Kelly

On 11 May 330, Rome ceased to be the most important place in the Roman empire. Five hundred miles east of the Eternal City, on a site occupied by modern Istanbul, a new imperial capital was dedicated and (like Rome before it) named after its founder: Constantinople, the city of Emperor Constantine. The inauguration ceremonies were magnificent.[1] On the first of forty days of celebrations, parades, and largesse, the imperial court assembled at the foot of a tall porphyry column erected in the center of the city's new forum.[2] This column marked the place where six years earlier Constantine, in response to a vision from the Christian God, and with the advice of the Neoplatonic philosopher Sopater, had proclaimed the founding of the city and proceeded to mark out its territory.[3] The column also symbolized Constantine's claim that his new city's roots ran deep into the classical past. According to some, the column's seven smooth purple drums had come from Troy. Later Byzantine writers also claimed that the base of the column concealed the Palladium. This ancient Trojan statue of Pallas Athena, thought to ensure the safety of the city in which it was venerated, had been recovered from the Greeks and taken to Rome by Aeneas.[4] A thousand years later, Constantine—keen to secure a talisman which would protect his new capital and assert its antiquity—was believed to have had the Palladium secretly removed and brought to Constantinople.[5]

Constantine's column was also a Christian reliquary, whose sacred contents exotically multiplied with successive retellings of the city's foundation. In the column's base, along with the Palladium, was placed the stone Moses struck to provide water for the Israelites in the wilderness, the haft of the adze Noah used to build the ark, and the wicker panniers used by the disciples to distribute the loaves and fishes at the feeding of the five thousand.[6] The column itself was topped by a statue of Constantine in the likeness of Apollo. This golden image was raised on the day of Constantinople's inauguration, to the acclamation of the assembled crowd and the repeated chanting of the *Kyrie*.[7] The statue's head was crowned by a radiate diadem like the rising sun; each of its seven glittering rays contained a sliver from the nails used to crucify Christ.[8] Inside the statue, as a further guarantee of the city's security, was hidden a splinter from the True Cross.[9]

Following the dedication of the statue, the emperor and his entourage—senior officials, military commanders, and palace functionaries—processed in splendor to the imperial box in the Hippodrome to enjoy a day of chariot racing. Constantine himself was magnificently robed, standing out even amid such courtly brilliance. He wore, perhaps for the first time in his reign, a diadem encrusted with pearls and other jewels.[10] By all accounts, the high point of the day's events was the entry into the arena of a golden chariot bearing a gilded image of the emperor escorted by a crack company of the imperial guard in full ceremonial dress, all carrying long white tapers.[11] This stunning ritual was repeated each year on Constantine's orders to mark the anniversary of the city's dedication. For the next two hundred years, as the golden image rounded the turning-post of the Hippodrome and neared the imperial box, Roman emperors and their courtiers prostrated themselves before Constantinople's glittering founder.

The striking ceremonies and magnificent parades marking the inauguration of Constantine's new capital provide important insights into both the system of government and the political ideology of the later Roman empire. The empire's center was dominated by a godlike emperor, surrounded by high-ranking court officials, soldiers, and bureaucrats. The governance of empire largely depended on these groups. They channeled, mediated, and (on occasion) blatantly misdirected imperial power. Emperors moved to contain abuses as far as they were able. Against the ever present threat of courtiers' rival interests and inducements, they enforced, in both practical and symbolic terms, the dependence of all upon an imperial center. Loyalty was buttressed by the chance of reward; disloyalty threatened with horrific torture and public punishment.[12] In a delicate balancing of competing claims, emperors and their supporters continually emphasized, and in their ceremonies openly displayed, the advantages of upholding the prevailing regime. By and large, these tactics were effective. Later Roman emperors were remarkably successful in controlling both an elaborate court society and a sophisticated and highly complex bureaucracy. In the century after Constantine, that success permitted the central government to exercise a greater control over the human and economic resources of the Mediterranean world than at any time since the foundation of the Roman empire.[13]

But the effectiveness of later Roman government was only partially dependent on organizational rules which strengthened the position of emperors and helped to tip the balance of struggles in their favor. It was also underpinned by a political ideology which reinforced those rules. In electing to support Christianity in 312, Constantine adopted a religion whose monotheism presented a view of a heavenly kingdom ruled by one God. The theology of the incarnation of Christ offered a figure who blurred the distinctions between humanity and divinity and served in his inexpressible majesty as the sole mediator between this world and the next. Such images were not always easily accepted; but their attractiveness to a highly centralized, autocratic government is not surprising. Later Roman emperors sometimes represented themselves as Christlike, or offered subsidies and taxation immunity to the Christian church.[14] Of course, here as well, there were competing interests to be negotiated. The church, itself a highly complex organization vital to the dissemination of this new religion, could not be expected unquestioningly to be subordinate to secular authority. For many, too, deeply ingrained pre-Christian beliefs died hard. Part of Christianity's strength lay in its evident ability both to accommodate and to incorporate a wide variety of religious systems and ritual practices. That broad base of support made Christianity doubly effective: it helped promote a new system of rule without rejecting outright all that had gone before. It was crucially important to the success of Constantine's new religion as an effective political ideology that the transitions from Apollo to Christ to later Roman emperor not be too difficult.

The focus of the carefully choreographed ceremonies in Constantinople in May 330 was the emperor himself. According to the surviving, openly enthusiastic accounts, Constantine was the center of attention at the dedication of his statue in the city's principal forum, and he was loudly cheered as he processed to the Hippodrome where (before the races began) all eyes were turned toward him as he took his place amid the acclamations of the crowd. The exaltation of the emperor was the insistent theme of imperial ceremonial. The more loyal the crowd, the more worshipful the regime's historians, artists, and orators, the more magnificent the emperor. When, five years earlier, Constantine opened the Council of Nicaea (a conclave of bishops called to debate important doctrinal and credal matters), all present stood and in silence faced the entrance of the assembly chamber. The emperor—in the words of his Christian court-biographer, Eusebius of Caesarea—then appeared "like some heavenly messenger of God, clothed in a shining raiment, which flashed as if with glittering rays of light . . . and adorned with the lustrous brilliance of gold and precious stones."[15]

Court occasions demanded a similar splendor. Meetings of the *consistorium*, the most important imperial council of advisors, were conducted with all standing except the emperor.[16] Those formally introduced into the imperial presence were required, having prostrated themselves, to "adore the purple"—to kiss on bended knee the hem of the emperor's robe.[17] All approaches to the imperial person were hedged with similar protocols. A magnificent silver platter made to celebrate the tenth anniversary of the accession of Theodosius I in 388 shows the emperor enthroned between his junior colleagues Valentinian II and Arcadius. Behind stand the imperial bodyguard. In front, kneeling, a splendidly attired official receives in reverently veiled hands his letters of appointment. Beneath, a half-naked woman representing the fruitful earth reclines in a field of corn; around her playful *putti* romp joyously. The whole scene, skillfully constructed, displays to the viewer the prosperity and rewards of a world which revolves around the emperor as the personification of good order.[18]

To the regime's supporters, imperial ceremonies presented an ideal map of the political world. The emperor was at the center, and on that center the security, the position, and the magnificence of all depended. When, in 388, Theodosius I, victorious over the rebel general Magnus Maximus, entered the Slovenian town of Emona, he was greeted before the walls by its chief citizens and priests. In the version of the emperor's progress presented by the Gallic orator Pacatus before the court in Rome twelve months later, Theodosius was said to have passed through gates bedecked with garlands and, to the sound of choirs, paraded through streets hung with banners and lit with blazing torches.[19] In similar terms, the historian Ammianus Marcellinus described the entry of Constantius II to Rome thirty years before: the emperor, greeted by the senate and populace drawn up in strict order of precedence, proceeded through the city "in a golden chariot, shimmering in the glitter of various kinds of precious stones . . . on either side, there marched a double line of armed men, their shields and crests flashing with a dazzling light."[20] The appearance of an emperor imposed order on society. The status and importance of any individual or group could instantly be gauged by observing their distance from the imperial center. That subordinate position was acknowledged (most obviously) by those who participated in, or later favorably described, these ceremonies; but it was also affirmed by those who, dressed in their festival best, stood at the roadside shouting their approval or singing hymns as the emperor and the carefully graded ranks of his entourage passed by. For actors and onlookers alike, imperial ceremonies dramatically displayed the benefits and advantages of a particular system of rule. They represented perfect working models of centralized autocracy.[21]

Once seen, these magnificent events were never forgotten. Those who beheld Constantine in his golden raiment were said by Eusebius to be "stunned and amazed at the sight—like children who have seen a frightening apparition."[22] But away from court and capital, emperors rarely appeared in person. In the provinces, their presence was represented by statues and other images. Municipal squares were dominated by imperial statues; the portraits of emperors hung in official buildings, shops, theaters, and public porticoes.[23] The imperial likeness might also be used to decorate everyday items such as coins or medallions, or to add efficacy to rings or amulets.[24] An early 4th century silver ringstone shows the delicately carved profiles of Constantine and his mother Helena with the inscription FVRIVS VIVAS—"Long life to Furius!"[25] In the workplace, iron weights cast in the shape of imperial busts conveyed to the customer an impression of solidity, reliability, and accuracy.[26] Some imperial representations—like modern coronation plates, mugs, and dishtowels—were more garishly amusing. One of the most splendid pieces in the recently unearthed Hoxne treasure from Norfolk in eastern England is a silver pepper-pot, complete with its internal grinding mechanism, skillfully made to represent Helena, the mother of Constantine.[27]

In their range and variety, imperial images made emperors omnipresent. This presence was rendered all the more powerful by a continual confounding of the emperor's person and his image. That deliberate confusion was key to the ceremonies at the inauguration of Constantinople. In the forum, Constantine presided over the dedication of a statue of himself; in the Hippodrome, the crowd applauded not only the emperor but also his image as it was paraded before them, surrounded—like the emperor himself—by the imperial body-guard. Fifty years later, in an even more elaborate visual conceit, the base of an obelisk erected on the central spine of the Hippodrome facing the imperial box displayed an impressive bas-relief of Emperor Theodosius I and his court seated in the imperial box watching the chariot races in the Hippodrome.[28] These mirror images of majesty not only made permanent the transitory messages of imperial ceremonial, but were designed to blur the distinction between emperors and their representations. When Constantius's procession entered Rome in 357, the emperor (again in Ammianus Marcellinus's description) sat immobile in his golden chariot "as if his neck were firmly clamped, he kept his gaze fixed straight ahead . . . nor was he ever seen to spit, or wipe, or rub his face or nose, or to move his hands about." Onlookers saw not just an emperor, but an emperor who looked to them "as though he were a statue of a man."[29]

In the absence of a real emperor (and of such sophisticated metropolitan witticisms) a similar conflation of the emperor with his representations was achieved by a rigid insistence on the performance of the same rituals and ceremonies before imperial images as before the emperor himself. Those approaching an emperor's statue were required to prostrate themselves "not as though they were looking upon a picture, but upon the very face of the emperor."[30] A proper atmosphere of sanctity was to be maintained at all times. An imperial edict issued in 394 banned the posting of advertisements for plays or chariot racing "in public porticoes, or those places in towns where our images are accustomed to be dedicated."[31] These injunctions were not to be breached lightly. In 386, the citizens of Antioch in Syria rioted, pulling down the statues of Emperor Theodosius I, pelting them with filth, and dragging them through the streets of the city.[32] John Chrysostom, a future patriarch of Constantinople who was then a priest in the city, graphically described the fear of Antiochenes in the days which followed as they expected "the wrath of the emperor to come like fire from above." An ominous silence descended on the once busy public squares and porticoes as many fled to the desert: "For as a garden when the irrigation fails shows trees stripped of their foliage and bare of fruit, so now indeed is it with our city . . . she stands desolate, stripped of nearly all her inhabitants."[33]

The reverence accorded imperial images was in part the result of fear and coercion—as the so-called "Riot of the Statues" strikingly demonstrates. (The shattered visages of usurpers' images served as more permanent reminders of the consequences suffered by those who had unsuccessfully challenged the regime.)[34] But such deference also resulted from a keen awareness of the advantages which might accrue from supporting the prevailing system. In a beautifully illustrated calendar produced for a wealthy aristocrat in Rome, the magnificently bejeweled Constantius II is depicted seated in a rigid, statuesque pose. From his outstretched right hand cascades a ceaseless flow of gold coins.[35] The question which confronted many was how best to be placed to "dip into the stream" of imperial benefits.[36] Some thought it in their interests to adver-

tise their loyalty publicly. In 425, following the elevation of Valentinian III to
co-emperorship with Theodosius II, the town of Sitifis in Mauretania (modern
Sétif in Algeria) erected a four-line metrical inscription which aimed to celebrate
Valentinian's military prowess, to praise his mother Galla Placidia (the influential daughter of an emperor), and to compliment Theodosius's more bookish
inclinations:

> Rising as the brightest star of this earthly realm,
> Valentinian, under the guardianship of the illustrious Placidia,
> Devoted to the clash of arms, preserved the empire:
> Theodosius, benefiting from the peace, pursued his learned studies.[37]

No doubt the townspeople in turning their popular image of these emperors
into verse (although of no great pretension) hoped that they had got it right: in
425 Valentinian was, after all, only six years old. Regrettably, nothing is known
of the reaction in Sitifis ten years later when Mauretania was sacked by the
Vandals as they moved from Spain through North Africa.

All praise involves risk; public praise raised the stakes higher still. Well-
judged support, if successful, might bring considerable benefits. The advantages
of proximity to the emperor were well known. The rise of Valentinian I and
Theodosius I to power in the late 4th century also saw the elevation of many of
their provincial contacts to high-ranking military and administrative posts.[38] In
similar fashion, Ausonius—a teacher of rhetoric from Bordeaux and tutor in
the 360s to the future emperor Gratian—secured from his former pupil great
offices for himself, his son, his son-in-law, and his octogenarian father.[39] More
dramatically, the bureaucrat Flavius Eupraxius owed his rapid advance at court
to his presence of mind at a ceremony in 367 where he was the first to cheer
Valentinian's announcement of the elevation of Gratian to the rank of co-em-
peror.[40]

Lesser men could hope to emulate these tactics, if given the chance. In 340 an
Egyptian soldier, Flavius Abinnaeus, petitioned Emperor Constantius II. The
issue was a simple one: After thirty-three years' military service in Egypt, Abinnaeus had been selected to escort an embassy of Blemys (a Nubian tribe) to
Constantinople. At court on at least one ceremonial occasion, kneeling in the
imperial presence, he had "adored the purple." There followed promotion and
a posting to the command of a cavalry detachment at Dionysias in the Fayum.
But when, on his return to Alexandria three years later, Abinnaeus presented
himself for service, he was told that there were other nominees for the same
post, supported by Valacius, the commander of military forces in Egypt. Abinnaeus had only one claim for priority over these local rivals. He played it to the
full. Petitioning the emperor, he explained the situation as he saw it: "But when
your sacred letter was presented to Valacius, his office replied that other men
had presented letters of promotion. Since it is clear they were advanced by
influence, but I by your sacred decision . . . may your Clemency vouchsafe that
I be appointed."[41] Abinnaeus was successful; by March 342 he was in place at
Dionysias. His contact with the imperial court allowed him to cut through

competing networks of influence and preference. It was a striking demonstration of the tangible benefits which might flow from a seemingly distant imperial center. Even so, it is unlikely that those who had been supported by Valacius and elbowed out of the queue for promotion were keen listeners to Abinnaeus's endless tales of the court and Constantinople.

It is worthwhile pausing for a moment to reflect on the delighted satisfaction of Flavius Abinnaeus in journeying to court, in securing his command, and in telling the story for years afterward; on the awestruck reaction of the crowds who chanced to see an emperor and his entourage; on the chill fear which ran through the people of Antioch as they contemplated the broken, mud-splattered statue of Theodosius; and on the reverence more usually shown toward imperial images. Such emotions—which must be taken seriously—strongly indicate an awareness of a powerful imperial center. No doubt many subjects of the empire were unable to name the current emperor, or to distinguish one emperor from another, or even to conceive of the magnificence of the court at Constantinople, but that does not mean that they were insensible to a model of society which placed at its apex the emperor and the *potestates excelsae* ("lofty powers") who surrounded him.[42] Success stories continually retold, like ceremonies repeatedly reenacted, helped both to construct and to reinforce a model of society dependent on an imperial center. The image of the emperor dominated the later Roman world as the statue of Constantine towered above his capital. In times of trouble a crowd might gather in an all-night vigil at the foot of the porphyry column to pray and sing hymns. The candle which each suppliant left burning at the column's base was, itself, a striking affirmation of imperial power, as well as a public declaration of the hope that such an affirmation might result in a glittering stream of imperial benefits as yet untold.[43]

There were (of course) severe limitations on the exercise of imperial power.[44] In an empire of sixty million people—stretching from Hadrian's Wall in the north to the river Euphrates in the east—in which, even at the best of times, it might take up to a month for an imperial edict issued in Constantinople to reach Antioch in Syria, emperors inevitably faced restrictions on their ability to rule.[45] Their difficulty was neatly summed up by Synesius, a late 4th century bishop of Ptolemais in Cyrene (modern Tulmaythah on the coast of Libya): "Now to seek to know each place, each man, and each dispute would require a very thorough survey, and not even Dionysius of Syracuse, who established his rule over a single island—and not even over the whole of that—would have been capable of performing this task."[46] Emperors were trapped. Faced with a Mediterranean-wide dominion, they had little option but to depend on secondhand advice or information; no choice but to rely on distant subordinates to carry out their commands. Delegation was an inescapable corollary of autocracy. To be sure, emperors ever since Augustus had relied on a staff of palace functionaries to collate incoming information, draft documents, and oversee the implementation of various imperial policies and projects.[47] But the continued growth of the state bureaucracy beginning with the reigns of Diocletian and Constantine significantly separated the nature of imperial rule in the early Roman empire from that of the later. The absolute number of bureaucrats was still tiny. The best estimates place the total of salaried officials in the whole of the later empire at somewhere around thirty-five thousand—roughly equivalent to the staff of the modern State Department in Washington.[48] But their impact should not be underestimated. Without a well-developed bureaucracy, imperial rule in the later Roman empire would have been considerably less pervasive, intrusive, and effective.

The formal structure of later Roman bureaucracy was concisely summarized in a document known as the *Notitia Dignitatum.* The *Notitia omnium dignitatum et administrationum tam civilium quam militarium* was, as its full title implies, a "list of all ranks and administrative positions both civil and military." The copy which survives provides a fairly comprehensive picture of the organization of imperial administration in the eastern half of the empire at the end of the 4th century.[49] The detail is complex, and—like most bureaucratic lists—the document does not make for interesting reading; but it does convey a strong impression of the meticulous classification of administrative tasks and the careful grading of imperial officials.[50] The basic unit of government throughout the empire remained the province: 114 are listed in the *Notitia,* each administered by a governor responsible for local judicial, financial, and administrative affairs.[51] The provinces were grouped into fourteen dioceses, each under the control of a *vicarius,* who had a general supervisory role and in some cases heard appeals from provincial courts. Dioceses, in turn, were grouped into four prefectures—Gaul (which included Britain and Spain), Italy (which included Africa), Illyricum, and the East—each in the charge of a praetorian prefect.

Praetorian prefects were the most powerful civil officials in later Roman government. They had overall responsibility for the administration of the empire, and in judicial matters, along with the emperor, were the final court of appeal. They also headed important financial departments, overseeing the levying of taxation to finance imperial public works, the administration, and the army (both wages and *matériel*), and to ensure the supply and transport of grain to the empire's capital cities.[52] Prefects, *vicarii,* and provincial governors each headed a permanent administrative department. The *officium* of the eastern praetorian prefect was divided into two branches: the administrative and judicial, and the financial. The former was headed by a *princeps officii* (with overall supervision of the branch's activities as well as of the department as a whole) and his deputy the *cornicularius;* beneath these officials, in descending order, were the *primiscrinius* or *adiutor* (responsible for the enforcement of judgments and court orders), the *commentarius* (mainly concerned with criminal trials), the *ab actis* (dealing with civil cases and judicial records), the *curae epistolarum* (in charge of the paperwork associated with official reports and of correspondence with *vicarii* and provincial governors), and the *regendarius* (responsible for issuing warrants for the use of the imperial postal system). Each of these officials—excepting the *princeps*—had three assistants *(adiutores)* who, in turn, were assisted by *chartularii*. These latter were drawn from the *exceptores*, a *corps* of junior officials, divided into fifteen groups *(scholae)*, which formed the basic administrative staff of the prefecture. Below these were a set of subclerical grades—ushers, messengers, doorkeepers, and attendants—each, at least on paper, carefully organized with a similar precision and regimentation.[53]

Of course, late Roman officialdom, like any bureaucracy, was infinitely more subtle in its workings than any formal listing of administrative tasks and grades could reveal. One of the most important aspects of the system in operation was a continual tension between emperors and their officials. On the one hand, emperors were strong supporters of bureaucracy—the *Notitia Dignitatum* was, after all, drawn up by the *primicerius notariorum,* the head of the imperial secretariat (staffed by *notarii*) responsible directly to the emperor himself.[54] More broadly, imperial officials retained on retirement their high rank and status, had privileged access to the courts, and were granted taxation immunity for themselves and their families.[55] On the other hand, the increase in officialdom, with the inevitable growth of rules, regulations, and standard procedures, continually threatened to limit an emperor's right to intervene in any matter, at any time, for any reason, and without necessarily any justification. Imperial power depended in great part on an emperor's ability to reward or punish spectacularly and to do so on occasion without warning. Against the pressing strictures of administrative procedure, later Roman emperors felt an insistent need—as policy, desire, or whimsy took them—to assert their own authority, to break rules, or to subvert organizational hierarchies which on other occasions they might strongly uphold.[56]

This continual balancing of the institutional needs of autocracy and bureaucracy can be seen in the selection, appointment, and promotion of imperial officials.[57] As in any administrative organization, seniority was a significant factor. In 331 Constantine affirmed this principle for the advancement of *exceptores* in the eastern praetorian prefecture: "each shall succeed to a position according to his rank-order in the department and his merit, insofar as he would have deserved to obtain that position by length of service."[58] But on other occasions emperors issued laws upholding the right of retiring officials to appoint their sons to junior posts, or affirming that promotions were to be made on grounds of proficiency or competence.[59] These criteria were always difficult to define. Indeed, in a bureaucracy without entrance examinations or formal qualifications, assessment of a candidate's ability was unavoidably dependent on personal recommendation. *Suffragium*—the influence exercised by family or friends (and their well-placed connections)—was frequently key to ensuring a successful career. In the mid 4th century, Libanius, a famous teacher of rhetoric in Antioch who had an extensive network of contacts among high-ranking officials, frequently wrote recommendations on behalf of his pupils. In an elegantly phrased letter to Domitius Modestus, *comes orientis* (the title given to the senior *vicarius* in the eastern praetorian prefecture), Libanius was full of praise for the gracious support which some of his wealthier proteges had received, but also pointedly suggested that Modestus in his generosity might consider advancing others as well: "Of my young stock—led from the fields of the Muses—which I have given up to you, you see that there are those who have been favored by you, and those not as yet so favored. I am happy indeed for those who have received preferment at your hands, but I wish to bring the others to your notice . . . For you should turn your attention to all; to the wealthy so that they may gain honor, and to the poor, so that riches may come to them."[60]

Access to grand patrons and their connections, recommendations for office, and often even the position itself could sometimes also be secured through payment of money.[61] (Many wise aspirants no doubt relied on a judicious combination of all the tactics available to them.) In 362 Emperor Julian legislated to prevent litigation for the recovery of moneys paid out in exchange for recommendations by those who had benefited from such transactions.[62] In similar terms, in 394, Theodosius I affirmed that contracts to exchange gold, silver, movables, or urban or rural property in return for a recommendation were enforceable in the courts.[63] As these legal provisions indicate, such transactions might be concluded openly and officially sanctioned. That should come as no surprise. What mattered from an emperor's point of view was maintenance of a flexible system of criteria for promotion. A potentially threatening coalition of interests within the bureaucracy might be weakened by an emperor's insisting on promotion by seniority or merit, rather than by the recommendation of senior officers or other influential persons; candidates not part of existing networks might be brought into a department through the purchase of office. Conversely, a favored individual might be allowed to strengthen his position by recommending the appointment of friends, family, or associates. In such a system, emperors were able both to underline the degree to which a successful career depended upon imperial favor and, more significantly, to emphasize to all the importance of their own position at the center of government.

Yet inevitably not all matters were resolved to an emperor's best advantage. Some officials did not always enjoy—or could not always secure—imperial favor; some, understandably, attempted to reduce the risk of disfavor, while at the same time trying to protect their current position or advance their careers. When in the 340s Flavius Abinnaeus, back from Constantinople, presented his letters of appointment to the office of the military commander in Egypt, he was met with a cool response. Other, comparable documents had also been presented, documents obtained—as Abinnaeus claimed in his petition to the emperor—not as the result of imperial favor to one who had adored the purple, but *ex suffragio*, "as the result of influence."[64] Abinnaeus's success in using his courtly contacts to overcome his rivals must be seen in the light of others' expectations of promotion on the basis of documents issued (through connections or purchase) without imperial sanction and, in this case, against explicit imperial preference. For these officials, and those whom they helped, it was better for the emperor not to know what went on. After all, there was no particular reason to suppose that imperial intervention might result in the appointment of a better or more highly qualified candidate. For those at court, close to the center of government, "leakages" in imperial power could be even more deftly exploited. In 354, the decision to send to Antioch to recall Gallus

Caesar (Constantius II's heir apparent) and his subsequent execution in transit were rumored to be the result of a whispering campaign conducted by eunuchs in the royal household, who "while performing duties of an intimate nature" convinced Constantius that his son was plotting against him.[65] But such stories could also be turned. It was sometimes better too for emperors not to know. Constantius, subsequently accused of murder, forcibly retorted—with what truth it is impossible to say—that he had rescinded his order for Gallus's execution, but that regrettably his instructions had not been carried out.[66]

The continual see-sawing of advantage between emperors and the officials on whom they inescapably relied, and the tactics used by both sides to strengthen their positions, undoubtedly impaired the efficiency of later Roman bureaucracy. The resulting uncertainties and insecurities would not be considered good management practice in a modern organization. But they were the high cost emperors were prepared to pay to maintain a careful and delicately engineered balance between the establishment of a bureaucracy and the preservation of some measure of imperial autonomy. These "inefficiencies" did not necessarily render later Roman bureaucracy ineffective. Indeed, there is good evidence to suggest that officials were able to collect and present detailed information, to plan and execute complicated administrative tasks, and to record and monitor the results. On a grand scale, the *Notitia Dignitatum* provided a conspectus of the ranks and seniority of all senior officials in the empire. Likewise, the *Theodosian Code,* promulgated by Emperor Theodosius II in 438, was the first official consolidated collection of imperial edicts.[67]

Away from court, a telling picture of bureaucracy in action is provided by the instructions issued in advance of Emperor Diocletian's visit to Egypt in September 298. A papyrus roll, which preserves copies of some of the outgoing correspondence of the *strategos* of the Panopolite *nome* (the chief official in an administrative district roughly one hundred miles downstream from modern Luxor, near Sohag), contains a series of requisition orders issued to ensure that troops escorting the emperor were supplied with sufficient lentils, meat, chaff, bread, barley, wine, and vegetables.[68] A bakery, a smithy, and an armory were ordered to be made ready. Nile boats and their crews were to be kept on continual standby for the imperial post.[69] A similar, almost obsessive attention to detail marks the near contemporary work of Diocletian's land commissioners. In an edict promulgated in 297, the emperor sought to establish a single unit of assessment for all taxable land, based on its use and fertility. Officials were appointed to survey the empire accordingly and, as a necessary preliminary, to resolve ownership and boundary disputes. The evidence of their work in the form of a series of inscribed boundary stones, some in the most far-flung places, "shows that the demands and decisions of the state in this precise period penetrated into the most remote of country districts."[70] The state's new concern with the detailed assessment of tax liability was matched by an interest in accurate documentation and the surveillance of arrears. In July 372 Julius Eubulius Julianus, the governor of the Thebaid (the Egyptian province centered on modern Luxor), mounted an investigation, perhaps following the discovery of a shortfall in the province's revenue account. He sent a circular order to various cities instructing local magistrates that all officials in the villages who had been responsible for collecting taxes in the previous year, and in the three years prior to that, should be dispatched forthwith to the governor's headquarters for questioning.[71]

These are striking vignettes. The surviving documentation points toward a strong expectation on the part of central government that it would be able to exercise control both over its own personnel and over the resources of the Mediterranean world. It indicates too a significantly higher level of administrative activity than at any previous period under the empire. Of course, the overall impact of central government and its bureaucracy is difficult to gauge precisely; no doubt it varied markedly from time to time, and from place to place. Yet in broad terms it is worth bearing in mind that, in the 4th century, the Roman state raised enough revenue to enable it to pay for a professional standing army larger than that under the Principate, to fund a greatly increased bureaucracy, to support a new religion, to subsidize heavily barbarian tribes on its frontiers, and to found a second imperial capital at Constantinople. For a preindustrial empire, these achievements should not be underrated. Without some increase in the effectiveness of its officials, the later Roman government could not have operated in so many new areas or have hoped to pay for so many new obligations. Undeniably, the tense relationship between emperors and officialdom impaired administrative efficiency. Even so, from the reigns of Diocletian and Constantine, the growth in the number and responsibilities of imperial officials was an important element in the successful formation and financing of a highly centralized state. On balance, bureaucracy helped rather than hindered imperial rule. Despite its undoubted failings it was one of the most significant factors enabling later Roman emperors to establish a degree of control over empire not reached again in Europe until the 18th century absolutisms of France and Prussia.

In the late 4th century, the Christian mystic Dorotheus had a vision. He dreamed that he was transported to a heavenly palace. In the audience hall, guided by heaven's palace attendants, he saw God the Father and God the Son surrounded by their angelic courtiers. The archangel Gabriel stood next to a figure described by Dorotheus, in strict bureaucratic terminology, as "the Lord's *primicerius*"—head of the corps of secretaries *(notarii)* who staffed the imperial palace.[72] After a series of tests, Dorotheus found himself promoted through the ranks of God's palace guard and invested with a uniform familiar to anyone who had seen the troops flanking an emperor (or his image) on ceremonial occasions: "I did not have simple clothing . . . but I was wearing a cloak made for me from two different sorts of linen. I stood with a kerchief around my neck and around my legs I wore long breeches and a multicolored belt."[73]

Visions of the divine which commingled the outward and visible forms of sacred and secular power were not uncommon in the later Roman world. Atop its tall porphyry column in Constantinople, the shining golden statue with its radiate crown might be seen as Emperor Constantine, or Apollo, or Christ, or as some combination of all three. These carefully contrived confusions were deftly exploited by those keen to legitimate the position of the emperor as the undisputed center of a highly centralized state. In 336, in a speech celebrating the thirtieth anniversary of Constantine's accession, the emperor's biographer Eusebius of Caesarea described the emperor as "the friend of the all-ruling God; arrayed as he is in the image of the kingdom of heaven, he pilots affairs here below following with an upward gaze a course modeled on that ideal form."[74] Imperial ceremonies were given heavenly archetypes. Both emperors and divinities were cloaked in a distancing, awe-inspiring splendor. Eusebius congratulated his audience on appearing like a celestial court in its angelic array: "So let those who have entered within the sanctuary of this holy place—that innermost, most inaccessible of places—having barred the gate to profane hearing, narrate the sovereign's most secret mysteries to those alone who are initiated in these things."[75] For John Chrysostom, patriarch of Constantinople at the turn of the 4th century, the city of God was like an imperial palace adorned with innumerable courts and buildings: "Here angels stand not before a mortal king, but before him who is immortal, the king of kings and lord of lords."[76] Christ in the splendor of his second coming could be compared to an emperor surrounded by his retinue processing in full ceremonial panoply before an awestruck crowd: "the men in golden apparel, and the pairs of white mules caparisoned with gold, and the chariots inlaid with precious stones, and the snow-white cushions . . . But when we see the emperor we lose sight of these. For he alone draws our gaze: the purple robe, and the diadem, and the throne, and the clasp, and the shoes—all that brilliance of his appearance."[77] Colorful language was matched by magnificent art. From the mid 6th century, visitors to Ravenna in northern Italy could see in the church of S. Apollinare Nuovo a series of mosaics on gospel themes, each with Christ dressed in imperial purple.[78] In S. Vitale they saw images of Christ, Emperor Justinian, and his wife Theodora, all surrounded by similarly attired attendants, all staring with equal wide-eyed confidence past the viewer and into an eternity beyond.[79]

Images drawn from the new state religion helped sanctify a new system of rule. An empire is held together not only by military force and an efficient administration; it also requires an effective ideology to proclaim to all involved the rightness and legitimacy of its government. Christianity's monotheism and its vision of a hierarchical heaven ruled by an omnipotent divinity offered to the Roman state a means of comprehending and justifying an imperially dominated, centralized pattern of power. The ceremonial monarch, surrounded by the glitter of an immobile court, was presented as a potent icon of majesty whether in heaven or on earth. Whatever Constantine's personal motivations for conferring state patronage on Christianity, the theology and imagery of this new religion were undoubtedly useful for creating a political ideology which could complement changes in the nature, extent, and effectiveness of imperial government.[80] In addition, part of Christianity's success lay in its ability to accommodate itself to long-standing classical traditions. Arguably, one of the most significant factors in its growth throughout the 4th century was a recognition—in both liturgical practice and theology—of the value of pagan learning, philosophy, and ritual. This recognition was particularly attractive to members of the well-educated urban elite. The expensive classical education that marked their superior status was also an indispensable prerequisite for understanding and manipulating the highly rhetorical language of power which since Augustus had "provided a permanent background music to the consensus in favor of Roman rule skillfully fostered among the civic notables of the Greek world."[81] A Christianity in tune with classical culture provided an ideological framework which both shored up traditional urban hierarchies and gave the empire's municipal elite (on whose loyalty the stability of imperial rule ultimately depended) an appropriate language with which they could continue to exercise influence over central government and its representatives. In political and religious terms, the rise of Christianity in the later Roman world was dependent not only on its ability to attract adherents in the present, but also on its success in converting the empire's classical past.

But the advantages which this new religion offered the Roman state and its supporters did not go unchallenged. For the first three centuries after Christ, Christianity had survived as a close-knit sect firmly opposed to the religion and culture of the society which surrounded it. A classical education was regarded by many with suspicion. In a famous passage the 2nd century African writer Tertullian trenchantly asked: "What has Athens to do with Jerusalem? What has the Academy to do with the Church? . . . Away with all attempts to produce a Stoic, Platonic, and dialectic Christianity."[82] In the later empire, a dramatic rejection of the classical world and its learning—that "great dust cloud of considerations"[83]—remained important for those who sought holiness in the silence and solitude of the desert. Antony, one of the most famous of Egyptian monks, was said always to have worsted wily philosophers who sought to ridicule him for his professed illiteracy. Once a debate turned to a discussion of thought and writing. Antony asked which came first. The philosophers replied that, of course, thought was primary and through it writing and literature were generated. Antony pressed home the advantage: "Now you understand that in a person whose thought is pure there is no need for writing."[84] For those in the wilderness, that was a common theme. On turning forty, Arsenius, the highly educated son of a senatorial family and once tutor to the imperial princes Arcadius and Honorius in Constantinople, renounced the delights of high civilization for a monk's cell in the Egyptian desert. To those who would marvel at his rejection of such an influential position at court (perhaps thinking of the successes Ausonius enjoyed under his former pupil Gratian), Arsenius, pointing to his new teacher, would reply: "I once knew Greek and Latin learning; but with this peasant, I have not yet mastered my ABC."[85]

Aphorisms such as these were important in the presentation of a church militant, strongly resisting contamination in a world deeply wedded to its classical past. But against the rejection of classical learning advocated by holy men and monks must be set the conviction of those Christians who saw reverence for the classical past as a firm foundation for their own faith. For these deeply committed believers, Christ's teaching of his disciples could be envisioned as a philosopher's education of his pupils. In a beautiful early 5th century mosaic in the apse of S. Pudenziana in Rome, a seated Christ, holding a scroll in one hand, gestures didactically with the other; his disciples, decorously arranged in a semicircle on either side of their instructor, pay polite attention like well-bred students in some divine academy.[86]

The fusion of Christianity with classical learning illustrated by such images was perhaps best represented by the theological works of the Cappadocian Fathers. This group of highly educated bishops from Asia Minor drew freely on both classical literature and Neoplatonic concepts and vocabulary in their elucidation of Christian doctrinal problems. The justification for such an approach, they claimed, was firmly located in scripture. Writing in the late 390s, Gregory of Nyssa in his *Life of Moses* sought to demonstrate how the patriarch's great knowledge of "the wisdom of the Egyptians" had made him suitable to receive the divine law on Mount Sinai.[87] In the hands of the learned, argued Gregory, classical philosophy—"the wealth of Egypt"—might become "at certain times a comrade, a friend, and a lifetime companion for the higher way."[88] In that sense, Moses was a model for all educated men. Set afloat among the bulrushes in his papyrus coracle, he prefigured the true Christian, swaddled in classical learning, successfully navigating the hazards of "this stream of life."[89] The intellectual agility shown by the Cappadocian Fathers in sanctifying classical culture had a wide appeal, far beyond the abstruse subtleties of their weighty theological tracts. Once legitimated, a sophisticated synthesis of Christianity with traditional wisdom provided limitless opportunities for the display of knowledge and the erudite wittiness so prized by the *beau monde* of the Roman world. In the late 4th century, the well-educated elite of Kourion on entering the eastern portico of the house of Eustolius—no doubt to admire the splendid views along the Cypriot coast—might pause to admire an inscription neatly worked into the mosaic floor:

> This house in place of massy stones and solid iron,
> Burnished bronze and even adamant,
> Is now girt with the much hallowed signs of Christ.

The more learned would have been pleased to note that this forthright assertion of Christianity was couched in deliberately archaizing Greek. Perhaps too they paused to puzzle over some of the Homeric vocabulary, or to scan the elegant old-fashioned hexameter verses.[90]

The importance of this cultural fusion between paganism and Christianity was clearly evident in Constantine's carefully contrived ceremonies for the consecration of Constantinople in May 330. The emperor's statue (with its multiple possible meanings) looked out across a capital whose churches and cathedrals allowed it to lay claim to being a truly Christian city.[91] Yet the famous sculptures, bronzes, and monuments removed from towns and cult centers throughout the empire that crammed its public spaces must also have made it seem the ultimate classical city.[92] The principal forum, itself dominated by the porphyry column taken from Troy, contained statues of Athena, Juno, the Judgment of Paris, Daniel in the lions' den, and the Good Shepherd.[93] Above all, the collection of relics believed to be hidden beneath the column's base—the Palladium taken from Rome, the holy nails, Noah's adze, Moses's stone, and the wicker panniers—symbolized the self-conscious incorporation of a classical and Hebrew past into a Christian present. This was a deliberate and elegantly constructed ambiguity, best epitomized in Constantine's own name for his imperial capital built on seven hills by the Bosphorus: "New Rome."[94]

In one sense, the open display of Christianity in Constantinople was a striking indication of the effect of this new religion on the empire's government and its importance in the representation of imperial power. Equally, as the stress on "Roman" tradition indicated, the success of the Constantinian revolution depended on the continued loyalty and support of the empire's elites, understandably made nervous by an increasing concentration of authority in the hands of emperors and bureaucrats. The striking of a difficult balance between these two pressing concerns inevitably meant the survival of many traditional pagan institutions well into the new Christian empire: Constantine himself permitted the building of a temple to the imperial cult at Hispellum in Umbria; until well into the 5th century, emperors on their death were granted the title of *divus* ("deified"); the excited crowd which was said to have streamed out of Emona in 388 to greet the victorious Theodosius I included at its head municipal pagan priests *(flamines)* resplendent in their robes of office and distinctive tall conical hats.[95] But in the longer term, the assimilation of many traditional beliefs and practices hastened the acceptance of Christianity and the imperial regime which sponsored it.

Even in Rome itself—often seen as the last stronghold of a committed pagan aristocracy—by the mid 4th century there were clear signs of rapprochement. The Codex-Calendar of 354 produced for the wealthy Christian Valentinus included a meticulous record of pagan holidays and observances proper to the imperial cult.[96] The sarcophagus of Valentinus's contemporary, Junius Bassus, who died in office as urban prefect of Rome in 359, was decorated with scenes from the life of Christ juxtaposed with Bacchic cupids enjoying a plentiful grape harvest.[97] Like the ambiguities of Constantine's capital, this sophisticated melding of the old and the new had a strong political significance. An inscription on the upper edge of the sarcophagus clearly proclaimed Bassus's Christian belief and recorded his deathbed baptism.[98] It was complemented by flamboyant verses on the lid (neatly framed by representations of the sun and moon) which listed his offices and stressed his high social rank. As Bassus's cortege passed by, they proclaim,

> Even the roofs of Rome seemed to weep,
> And then the houses themselves along the way seemed to sigh.
> Grant him the highest honors of the living, grant these honors,
> Lofty is the height which death had assigned to him.[99]

The public advertisement of Christian belief coupled with traditional iconography and the celebration of high office indicates that adherence to the new religion was compatible both with long-standing cultural expectations and with the maintenance of a superior social status. The success of Christianity among the empire's elite was linked closely with its ability to make sense of the present—in stark political as well as cultural terms—without rejecting the hard-won advantages of the past. Indeed, for confident Christian aristocrats like Junius Bassus, the surety of promotion under an emperor could be matched by an equally firm expectation of elevation to a lofty place in Christ's celestial hierarchy.

For members of the ruling elite throughout the empire the possibility that Christianity might help preserve their social and political clout (if only in this world) was unquestionably attractive. In the cities of the later Roman world, in growing numbers throughout the 4th century, the well-educated sons of the urban elite sought ordination and were in time raised to the episcopate.[100] As bishops, in time-honored upper-class fashion, they were in a position to support their family, to seek favors for their friends, and to secure preferment for their proteges. (In many of their concerns there is little to separate the letters of Basil of Caesarea from those of his pagan contemporary Libanius, the well-connected professor of rhetoric at Antioch.)[101] As bishops, these men continued also to fulfill the long-standing obligation of leading citizens to beautify their home towns. As their forebears had built splendid baths, temples, and porticoes, so their Christian descendants erected magnificent basilicas, churches, and hospices. An inscription set into the floor of the ambulatory in the early 5th century cathedral at Salona makes the point simply and clearly: "New things follow old; begun by Bishop Synferis, finished by his grandson Bishop Hesychius, with the help of the clergy and people, this gift of a church, O Christ, is freely given."[102] Finally, as bishops these municipal worthies remained well placed to cultivate a special relationship with the imperial government and its official representatives. Their advantageous position was publicly displayed in their rank, privileges, and immunities; in the grants of jurisdiction which allowed them to hear a range of civil and criminal matters; and in their role as spokesmen and advocates for the interests of their cities.[103] Imperial government continued to listen—as it had always done—to these civic grandees. It is no surprise to find that it was Basil, worried about the status and prosperity of Caesarea, who led a campaign against the division of the province of Cappadocia, or that, following the Riot of the Statues in Antioch, it was the intercession of the city's patriarch at court which secured the emperor's pardon.[104]

For the urban elite of the empire adherence to Christianity offered a way of confirming their traditional place at the head of municipal society; more widely, it gave them a recognizable place in the empire-wide hierarchy at whose distant apex stood both God and emperor. That security in both positions is reflected in a magnificent mosaic in the late 4th century cathedral at Aquileia in northern Italy. The central panels display portraits of the principal civic benefactors who had contributed to its construction. Their comfortable expressions—confident in the church as a guarantor of their identity and importance in local society—

are matched by the smug frankness of the inscriptions recording their generosity: "Januarius vowed this gift for God: 880 square feet of mosaic."[105] A similar certainty that the church could be invoked to uphold the existing social and moral order was neatly captured on a bronze tag from Rome once attached to the collar of a slave. Should the slave run away, the finder is asked to return the fugitive to his owner: "Seize me and return me to Maximianus the copyist in the Forum of Mars." For added efficacy (and Christian moral support) the inscription is neatly punctuated with the Chi-Rho monogram of Christ.[106]

The union of slavery and Christianity, churches decorated with portraits of wealthy benefactors, or the eclectic collection of relics under Constantine's porphyry column would have been unlikely to secure the approval of St. Antony or Arsenius. But away from the stark simplicities of the desert and its holy men who had turned their back on the cities of the Roman world, the accommodation between Christianity and the habits, customs, and social expectations of many in the empire was a vital factor in securing the widespread acceptance of the new imperial religion. On that acceptance the later Roman empire was substantially built. Christianity permitted the development of a sophisticated ideology of power; it was a key element in the establishment of a transcendent justification for the highly centralized rule imposed by the later Roman state. Earthly monarchy reflected heavenly archetypes: in churches, emperors appeared like Christ; in visions, angels appeared like bureaucrats; and in the expectations of many, the carefully graded hierarchies of this world prefigured the divinely ordained ranks of the next. Equally important, a Christianity which permitted the participation of leading members of the empire's elite (and, in many cases, helped secure their status within their own cities) provided both an ideological framework and an institutional structure for the exercise of influence on the actions of imperial government and its representatives. A shared language of power based on a coalition between Christianity and classical culture allowed emperors to emphasize their distant, godlike status while at the same time making possible the effective voicing of praise or disagreement by those whose cooperation and participation remained essential for the collection of taxes and the maintenance of good order in the provinces.

Despite the gloss of political and cultural unity which Christianity gave to the later empire, though, the shift toward a strong, centralized government should not be downplayed. One of the best indicators of that movement remains the expansion in the size and competence of the later Roman bureaucracy, particularly at the imperial court, and the change in the nature and scope of much of the surviving administrative paperwork. Of course, there were limits on both effectiveness and efficiency. Above all, emperors were wary of any restriction on their (sometimes capricious) freedom of action that might be imposed by a bureaucracy's inevitable reliance on rules, regulations, and standard procedures. While actively encouraging the growth of a more centralized system of rule, emperors insisted that the success and security of all was dependent on them alone. The importance of continued imperial favor was reflected in the vast ceremoniousness of later Roman government. Memorable rituals enacted before emperors or their images were designed to present an exemplary model of society which emphasized the dependence of all upon the imperial center and stressed the benefits which might flow from the recognition of an emperor's sovereignty. To be sure, ceremony had always played an important part in the representation of Roman imperial power, but in the later empire it acquired a heightened and more complex meaning.[107] Nowhere was this more clearly on show than in Constantine's new capital, a city consciously designed as a brilliant backdrop for the staged display of imperial power. Seven years after the city's inaugural celebration, another ceremony was played out before an awe-struck crowd in Constantinople. Under military escort, Constantine's body was carried through the grief-stricken city. Encircled by candles, the emperor lay in state in the main audience hall of the imperial palace, attended day and night by officials: "presenting a marvelous spectacle, and one such as no one under the sun had ever seen on this earth since the world began." Mourners were admitted in strict rank-order of precedence; the same court ceremony was observed before the dead emperor's golden coffin as before a living emperor's throne.[108] Constantius II, on his succession, commemorated his father's death by issuing a series of coins whose design explicitly drew on the classical imagery of Roman imperial apotheosis: Constantine was shown guiding a four-horse chariot across the sky as a veiled hand reached out to welcome him into heaven.[109] Yet the emperor was buried by his son in the Church of the Apostles, newly built on one of the most prominent hills in Constantinople: "this building he carried to a great height" and roofed with bronze, "and this too was splendidly and sumptuously adorned with gold, reflecting the sun's rays with a brilliance which dazzled the distant onlooker." At its center twelve splendid shrines "like sacred pillars" had been consecrated to Christ's apostles. In their midst, in a glittering catafalque, lay the magnificent sarcophagus of Constantine, the self-proclaimed thirteenth apostle of Christianity—a new official religion capable, when linked to proper reverence for the classical past, of both justifying and sanctifying a striking shift toward a more autocratic and highly centralized pattern of Roman rule.[110]

Notes

I should like to thank both Keith Hopkins and Richard Miles for their thoughtful, perceptive, and sympathetic comments on this essay.

1. There is no straightforward ancient account of these ceremonies: most versions were written later; many represent an almost baroque accretion of various stories; all contradict each other at some point. What follows draws substantially on the *Chronicon Paschale* (Easter Chronicle) for the years 328 and 330, and John Malalas 13.7–8; with the reconstruction of events by Gilbert Dagron, *Naissance d'une capitale: Constantinople et ses institutions de 330 à 451* (Paris, 1974), 32–47; Raymond Janin, *Constantinople Byzantine: Développement urbain et répertoire topographique* (Paris, 2nd ed., 1964), 18–19, 23–26; David Lathoud, "La consécration et de dédicace de Constantinople," *Échos d'Orient* 23 (1924): 289–314 and 24 (1925): 180–201; Richard Kraut-

heimer, *Three Christian Capitals: Topography and Politics* (Berkeley, 1983), chap. 2, esp. 55–56, 60–67, plates 51–53.

2. Cyril Mango, "Constantinopolitana," *Jahrbuch des Deutschen Archäologischen Instituts* 80 (1965): 305–336, at 306–313, repr. in Mango, *Studies on Constantinople* (London, 1993), chap. 2; id., "Constantine's Column," ibid., chap. 3; Janin, *Constantinople Byzantine,* 77–80. The column—known as the Çemberlitaş—or Colonne Brûlée—still stands; see Wolfgang Müller-Wiener, *Bildlexicon zur Topographie Istanbuls* (Tübingen, 1977), 255–257.

3. Sozomen, *Hist.eccl.* 2.3.3, ed. Joseph Bidez and Günther Hansen (Berlin: GCS, 1960); Nicephorus Callistus, *Ecclesiastical History* 7.48 (*PG* 145; 1324C); Philostorgius 2.9, ed. Joseph Bidez (Berlin, GCS, 3rd ed., 1981); John Lydus, *On Months* 4.2.

4. Procopius, *Gothic War* 1.15.9–14; Virgil, *Aeneid* 2.162–170.

5. Charles Diehl, "De quelques croyances byzantines sur la fin de Constantinople," *Byzantinische Zeitschrift* 30 (1929–30): 192–196, at 193–194; Andreas Alföldi, "On the Foundation of Constantinople: A Few Notes," *Journal of Roman Studies* 37 (1947): 10–16, at 11.

6. Nicephorus Callistus, *Ecclesiastical History* 7.49 (*PG* 145: 1325D); Hesychius 41 note, ed. Theodor Preger, *Scriptores originum Constantinopolitanarum,* 2 vols. (Leipzig, 1901–1907), 1: 17; A. Frolow, "La dédicace de Constantinople dans la tradition byzantine," *Revue de l'histoire des religions* 127 (1944): 61–127, at 76–78; Lathoud, *Echos d'Orient,* 23, 299–305.

7. *Breves Chronographicae* 56, ed. Preger, *Scriptores,* 1: 56–57; *Patria* 2.49, ed. Preger, *Scriptores,* 2: 177–178; Theodor Preger, "Konstantinos-Helios," *Hermes* 36 (1901): 457–469.

8. Zonaras 13.3.

9. Socrates, *Hist.eccl.* 1.17 (*PG* 67: 120B).

10. John Malalas 13.8; Richard Delbrueck, *Spätantike Kaiserporträts von Constantinus Magnus bis zum Ende des Westreichs* (Berlin, 1933), 59–61; Jules Maurice, *Numismatique Constantinienne,* 3 vols. (Paris, 1908–1912), 2: 486–487.

11. *Breves Chronographicae* 38, ed. Preger, *Scriptores,* 1: 42; *Patria* 2.42, ed. Preger, *Scriptores,* 2: 172–173.

12. Ramsey MacMullen, "Judicial Savagery in the Roman Empire," *Chiron* 16 (1986): 147–166, repr. in MacMullen, *Changes in the Roman Empire: Essays in the Ordinary* (Princeton, 1990), chap. 20.

13. A. H. M. Jones, *The Later Roman Empire 284–602: A Social, Economic, and Administrative Survey,* 3 vols. (Oxford, 1964; repr. in 2 vols, 1973), 1: 406–410; John Matthews, *The Roman Empire of Ammianus* (London, 1988), 253–262. For a contrasting view, see Ramsey MacMullen, *Corruption and the Decline of Rome* (New Haven, 1988), parts 3–4, esp. 167–170.

14. *C.Th.* 16.2.1–16; see Jean Gaudemet, *L'Eglise dans l'Empire romain (IVe–Ve siècles),* Histoire du droit et des institutions de l'église en occident, rev. ed. (Paris, 1989), 172–179, 240–245, 311–320; T. G. Elliott, "The Tax Exemptions Granted to Clerics by Constantine and Constantius II," *Phoenix* 32 (1978): 326–336.

15. Eusebius, *Life of Constantine* 3.10.3, ed. Friedhelm Winkelmann (Berlin: GCS, 1975).

16. Wolfgang Kunkel, "Consilium, Consistorium," *Jahrbuch für Antike und Christentum,* 11/12 (1968/1969): 230–248, at 242–246; repr. in Kunkel, *Kleine Schriften: Zum römischen Strafverfahren und zur römischen Verfassungsgeschichte,* ed. Hubert Niederländer (Weimar, 1974), 405–440, at 428–437.

17. William Avery, "The *Adoratio Purpurae* and the Importance of the Imperial Purple in the Fourth Century of the Christian Era," *Memoirs of the American Academy in Rome* 17 (1940): 66–80.

18. Missorium of Theodosius I (now in the Real Academia de la Historia, Madrid): see Sabine MacCormack, *Art and Ceremony in Late Antiquity* (Berkeley, 1981), 214–

221; Richard Delbrueck, *Die Consulardiptychen und verwandte Denkmäler* (Berlin, 1929), 235–242.

19. *Latin Panegyrics* 11.37, ed. Édouard Galletier, 3 vols. (Paris, 1949–1955); for the background, see C. E. V. Nixon and Barbara Saylor Rodgers, *In Praise of Later Roman Emperors: The Panegyrici Latini, Introduction, Translation, and Historical Commentary* (Berkeley, 1994), esp. 441–447.

20. Amm.Marc. 16.10.4–10, with the useful remarks in MacCormack, *Art and Ceremony*, 39–45, and Matthews, *The Roman Empire of Ammianus*, 231–235.

21. MacCormack, *Art and Ceremony*, 1–14; Keith Hopkins, *Conquerors and Slaves* (Cambridge, Eng., 1978), 197–200; Michael McCormick, "Analyzing Imperial Ceremonies," *Jahrbuch der Österreichischen Byzantinistik* 35 (1985): 1–20.

22. Eusebius, *In Praise of Constantine* 5.6, ed. Ivar Heikel (Leipzig, 1902).

23. For a description of the Embolos, the principal commercial area of Ephesus in Asia Minor, see Clive Foss, *Ephesus after Antiquity: A Late Antique Byzantine and Turkish City* (Cambridge, Eng., 1979), 65–74; more generally on imperial statues, see Kenneth Setton, *Christian Attitude towards the Emperor in the Fourth Century Especially As Shown in Addresses to the Emperor* (New York, 1941; repr., New York, 1967), chap. 8; Helmut Kruse, *Studien zur offiziellen Geltung des Kaiserbildes im römischen Reiche* (Paderborn, 1934), chap. 2; Hopkins, *Conquerors and Slaves*, 221–231.

24. Coins: Delbrueck, *Spätantike Kaiserporträts*, 71–104; Medallions: Andreas Alföldi and Elizabeth Alföldi, *Die Kontorniat-Medaillons* (Berlin, 1976–1990), vol. 1, nos. 440–482, 148–156.

25. Gisela Richter, *Catalogue of Engraved Gems: Greek, Etruscan, and Roman, in the Metropolitan Museum of Art, New York* (Rome, 1956), no. 500, 109. The inscription is restored.

26. David Buckton, ed., *Byzantium: Treasures of Byzantine Art and Culture from British Collections* (London, 1994), nos. 31–32, 49; Kurt Weitzmann, ed., *Age of Spirituality: Late Antique and Early Christian Art, Third to Seventh Century* (New York, 1979), nos. 324–328, 343–345.

27. Roger Bland and Catherine Johns, *The Hoxne Treasure: An Illustrated Introduction* (London, 1993), 1, 25–26.

28. The Obelisk of Theodosius I: see Dagron, *Naissance d'une capitale*, 311–312, 323–324; Janin, *Constantinople Byzantine*, 189–191; the most comprehensive publication remains Gerda Bruns, *Der Obelisk und seine Basis auf dem Hippodrom zu Konstantinopel* (Istanbul, 1935), esp. 33–68. For the position of the imperial box, see Rodolphe Guilland, "Études sur l'Hippodrome de Byzance: Le palais du Kathisma," *Byzantinoslavica* 18 (1957): 39–76, repr. in Guilland, *Études de topographie de Constantinople byzantine*, 2 vols. (Berlin, 1969), 1: 462–498); Janin, *Constantinople Byzantine*, 188–189. The obelisk still stands on the site of the Hippodrome in Istanbul: see Müller-Wiener, *Bildlexicon*, 64–71.

29. Amm.Marc. 16.10.10.

30. Severianus of Gabala, *On the Holy Cross*, in John of Damascus, *On Images, Oration* 3.385 (*PG* 94: 1409A).

31. *C.Th.* 15.7.12 = *C.Just.* 11.41.4.

32. Glanville Downey, *A History of Antioch in Syria from Seleucus to the Arab Conquest* (Princeton, 1961), 426–433.

33. John Chrysostom, *Homilies on the Statues* 2.1 (*PG* 49.35); see Frans van de Paverd, *St. John Chrysostom, The Homilies on the Statues: An Introduction* (Rome, 1991), 15–159.

34. Gregory of Nazianzus, *Oration* 4.96 (*Sources chrétiennes* 309: 240).

35. Michele Renée Salzman, *On Roman Time: The Codex-Calendar of 354 and the Rhythms of Urban Life in Late Antiquity* (Berkeley, 1990), 34–35, fig. 13.

36. John Chrysostom, *On Vainglory* 4 (*Sources chrétiennes* 188: 78) with Peter

Brown, *Power and Persuasion in Late Antiquity: Towards a Christian Empire* (Madison, 1992), 83–84. The image was an old one; see Pliny the Younger, *Letters* 3.20.12.

37. *CIL* 8.8481 = *ILS* 802; on Sitifis, see Claude Lepelley, *Les cités de l'Afrique romaine au Bas-Empire*, 2 vols. (Paris, 1979–1981), 2: 497–503.

38. John Matthews, *The Roman Empire of Ammianus*, 271–274; id., "Gallic Supporters of Theodosius," *Latomus* 30 (1971): 1073–99, repr. in Matthews, *Political Life and Culture in Late Roman Society* (London, 1985), chap. 9.

39. Keith Hopkins, "Social Mobility in the Later Roman Empire: The Evidence of Ausonius," *Classical Quarterly*, n.s. 11 (1961): 239–249; Hagith Sivan, *Ausonius of Bordeaux: Genesis of a Gallic Aristocracy* (London, 1993), 131–141.

40. Amm.Marc. 27.6.14.

41. *P. Abinn.* 1.11–14. For Abinnaeus's career see E. G. Turner in H. I. Bell, V. Martin, E. G. Turner, and D. van Berchem, *The Abinnaeus Archive: Papers of a Roman Officer in the Reign of Constantius II* (Oxford, 1962), chap. 2; and the suggestions of Timothy Barnes, "The Career of Abinnaeus," *Phoenix* 39 (1985): 368–374, repr. in Barnes, *From Eusebius to Augustine: Selected Papers 1982–1993* (London, 1994).

42. Amm.Marc. 28.6.9.

43. Philostorgius 2.17; Theodoret 1.34.3, ed. Léon Parmentier and Felix Scheidweiler (Berlin, 1954).

44. Some of the arguments in the opening parts of this section are more fully worked out in Christopher Kelly, "Emperors, Government, and Bureaucracy," in Averil Cameron and Peter Garnsey, eds., *The Cambridge Ancient History, vol. 13: The Late Empire, A.D. 337–425* (Cambridge, Eng., 1998), chap. 5.

45. Richard Duncan-Jones, *Structure and Scale in the Roman Economy* (Cambridge, Eng., 1990), chap. 1.

46. Synesius of Cyrene, *On Kingship* 27, ed. Antonio Garzya (Turin, 1989).

47. For useful surveys, see P. R. C. Weaver, *Familia Caesaris: A Social Study of the Emperor's Freedmen and Slaves* (Cambridge, Eng., 1972), part 3; Nicholas Purcell, "The *Apparitores*: A Study in Social Mobility," *Papers of the British School at Rome* 51 (1983): 125–173, esp. 128–131.

48. Jones, *The Later Roman Empire*, vol. 3, n. 44, 341–342; Roger Bagnall, *Egypt in Late Antiquity* (Princeton, 1993), 66. See also MacMullen, *Corruption*, 144, roughly estimating a hundredfold increase in salaried officials from the early empire.

49. John Mann, "The *Notitia Dignitatum*—Dating and Survival," *Britannia* 22 (1991): 215–219; Werner Seibt, "Wurde die notitia dignitatum 408 von Stilicho in Auftrag gegeben?" *Mitteilungen des Instituts für Österreichische Geschichtsforschung* 90 (1982): 339–346. There are good introductions to the *Notitia* in Jones, *The Later Roman Empire*, 3: 347–380; Roger Goodburn and Philip Bartholomew, eds., *Aspects of the Notitia Dignitatum* (Oxford, 1976).

50. The most compact introduction to the formal structure of later Roman bureaucracy is Alexander Demandt, *Die Spätantike: Römische Geschichte von Diocletian bis Justinian, 284–565 n. Chr.* (Munich, 1989), 231–255; see also Jones, *The Later Roman Empire*, chaps. 11, 12, 16, 18. The functions of palatine departments—not described here—are well set out in Karl Noethlichs, "Hofbeamter," *Reallexikon für Antike und Christentum* 15 (1991): 1111–58.

51. *Not.Dig.(oc.)* i 57–128, *(or.)* i 50–121.

52. *Not.Dig.(oc.)* ii–iii, *(or.)* ii–iii; see Wilhelm Ensslin, "Praefectus praetorio," *Pauly-Wissowa: Realencyclopädie der classischen Altertumswissenschaft*, 22.2 (1954): 2391–2502, at cols. 2426–2478.

53. The details are disputed; see Ernst Stein, *Untersuchungen über das Officium der Prätorianerpräfektur seit Diokletian* (Vienna, 1922), esp. 31–77, repr. ed. Jean-Rémy Palanque (Amsterdam, 1962); Jones, *The Later Roman Empire*, 1: 586–590; Ensslin, *Pauly-Wissowa*, 22.2, cols. 2478–2495.

54. *Not.Dig.(oc.)* xviii 3–4, *(or.)* xvi 4–6; see Guido Clemente, *La "Notitia Dignitatum," Saggi di storia e letteratura 4 (Cagliari, 1968)*, 360–367; H. C. Teitler, *Notarii and Exceptores: An Inquiry into Role and Significance of Shorthand Writers in the Imperial and Ecclesiastical Bureaucracy of the Roman Empire* (Amsterdam, 1985), esp. chap. 6.

55. *C.Th.* 6.35.1 = *C.Just.* 12.28.1; *C.Th.* 8.4.1; Jones, *The Later Roman Empire*, 1: 525–530, 535–537, 543–545. The most useful survey of the evidence remains Emil Kuhn, *Die städtische und bürgerliche Verfassung des römischen Reichs bis auf die Zeiten Justinians*, 2 vols. (Leipzig, 1864–1865), 1: 149–226.

56. Christopher Kelly, "Later Roman Bureaucracy: Going through the Files," in Alan Bowman and Greg Woolf, eds., *Literacy and Power in the Ancient World* (Cambridge, 1994), chap. 11, at 166–168; Jones, *The Later Roman Empire*, vol. 1, 377. Karl Noethlichs, *Beamtentum und Dienstvergehen: Zur Staatsverwaltung in der Spätantike* (Wiesbaden, 1981), 3–18, 34–37, makes an instructive comparison between later Roman and modern western bureaucracies.

57. The evidence is discussed in Jones, *The Later Roman Empire*, 1: 383–396, 602–604; and in Fritz Pedersen, "On Professional Qualifications for Public Posts in Late Antiquity," *Classica et Mediaevalia* 31 (1970): 161–213, at 175–205, repr. as Pedersen, *Late Roman Public Professionalism* (Odense, 1976), at 23–46.

58. *C.Th.* 8.1.2.

59. *C.Th.* 6.27.8.2; 7.3.1.

60. Libanius, *Letters* 154; see Paul Petit, *Les étudiants de Libanius* (Paris, 1957), 158–166, 183–188; J. H W. G. Liebeschuetz, *Antioch: City and Imperial Administration in the Later Roman Empire* (Oxford, 1972), 192–198. More generally, see Geoffrey de Ste. Croix, *"Suffragium:* From Vote to Patronage," *British Journal of Sociology* 5 (1954): 33–48.

61. For perceptive surveys of the evidence (and contrasting conclusions to those presented here) see Claude Collot, "La pratique et l'institution du *suffragium* au Bas-Empire," *Revue historique de droit français et étranger*, 4th ser., 43 (1965): 185–221, at 190–211; Detlef Liebs, "Ämterkauf und Ämterpatronage in der Spätantike: Propaganda und Sachzwang bei Julian dem Abtrünnigen," *Zeitschrift der Savigny-Stiftung für Rechtsgeschichte* 95 (1978): 158–186, at 170–183; Noethlichs, *Beamtentum und Dienstvergehen*, 69–72; MacMullen, *Corruption*, 150–151.

62. *C.Th.* 2.29.1, with Walter Goffart, "Did Julian Combat Venal *suffragium*? A Note on *C.Th.* 2.29.1," *Classical Philology* 65 (1970): 145–151; Timothy Barnes, "A Law of Julian," *Classical Philology* 69 (1974): 288–291.

63. *C.Th.* 2.29.2 = *C.Just.* 4.3.1.

64. *P. Abinn.* 1, line 12.

65. Amm.Marc. 14.11.3. Imperial eunuchs were frequently at the center of such stories; see, generally, Keith Hopkins, "Eunuchs in Politics in the Later Roman Empire," *Proceedings of the Cambridge Philological Society* 189 (1963): 62–80, repr. in Hopkins, *Conquerors and Slaves*, chap. 4; Peter Guyot, *Eunuchen als Sklaven und Freigelassene in der griechisch-römischen Antike* (Stuttgart, 1980), chap. 7.

66. Philostorgius 4.1.

67. See, generally, Tony Honoré, "The Making of the *Theodosian Code*," *Zeitschrift der Savigny-Stiftung für Rechtsgeschichte* 103 (1986): 133–222; Jill Harries and Ian Wood, eds., *The Theodosian Code: Studies in the Imperial Law of Late Antiquity* (London, 1993).

68. *P Panop. Beatty* 1, lines 241–248, 277–333; T. C. Skeat, *Papyri from Panopolis in the Chester Beatty Library, Dublin* (Dublin, 1964), xxii–xxiii.

69. *P Panop. Beatty* 1, lines 213–216, 252–255, 332–337, 342–346.

70. Fergus Millar, *The Roman Near East: 31 BC–AD 337* (Cambridge, Mass., 1993), 193–196 and appendix A, quoting 193.

71. *P Lips.* inv. no. 366; Bärbel Kramer, "Zwei Leipziger Papyri," *Archiv für Papyrusforschung* 32 (1986): 33–46, at 33–39.

72. *P Bodm.* 29, line 49. On this text see A. H. M. Kessels and P. W. van der Horst, "The Vision of Dorotheus (*P Bodm.* 29) edited with Introduction, Translation, and Notes," *Vigiliae Christianae,* 41 (1987): 313–359; Jan Bremmer, "An Imperial Palace Guard in Heaven: The Date of the Vision of Dorotheus," *Zeitschrift für Papyrologie und Epigraphik* 75 (1988): 82–88.

73. *P Bodm.* 29, lines 329–334. Generally on late antique uniforms see Ramsey MacMullen, "Some Pictures in Ammianus Marcellinus," *Art Bulletin* 46 (1964): 435–455, esp. 445–451, repr. in MacMullen, *Changes in the Roman Empire,* chap. 9, esp. 95–102.

74. Eusebius, *In Praise of Constantine* 5.4 and 3.5.

75. Ibid., *Prologue* 4. On Eusebius's political theology see Timothy Barnes, *Constantine and Eusebius* (Cambridge, Mass., 1981), esp. chap. 14; Raffaele Farina, *L'Impero e l'imperatore cristiano in Eusebio di Cesarea: La prima teologia politica del Cristianesimo* (Zurich, 1966), esp. 166–183, 195–203; Johannes Straub, *Vom Herrscherideal in der Spätantike* (Stuttgart, 1939; repr. 1964), 113–129; Setton, *Christian Attitude,* chap. 2.

76. John Chrysostom, *Homilies on the First Epistle to the Thessalonians* 6.4 (PG 62: 434).

77. Ibid. 14.10 (PG 60: 537); Setton, *Christian Attitude,* 187–195.

78. Friedrich Deichmann, *Frühchristliche Bauten und Mosaiken von Ravenna* (Wiesbaden, 1969), nos. 113 (Christ with Angels—with detail at 116–117), 156 (The Miracle of the Loaves and Fishes), 161 (Healing the Blind), 174 (Parable of the Sheep and Goats), 180 (The Last Supper), 184 (Gethsemane), 187 (Betrayal); for detailed description, see id., *Ravenna: Geschichte und Monumente* (Wiesbaden, 1969), 176–197.

79. Deichmann, *Frühchristliche Bauten und Mosaiken,* nos. 311, 351–353 (Christ), 358 (Theodora), 359 (Justinian); see also id., *Ravenna: Geschichte und Monumente,* 234–256; MacCormack, *Art and Ceremony,* 259–266; Marion Lawrence, "The Iconography of the Mosaics of San Vitale," *Atti del VI congresso internazionale di archeologia cristiana, Ravenna, 1962* (Vatican City, 1965), 123–140. Generally, on imperial imagery in Christian art, see Ernst Kitzinger, *Byzantine Art in the Making: Main Lines of Stylistic Development in Mediterranean Art, 3rd to 7th Century* (London and Cambridge, Mass., 1977), esp. chap. 2; André Grabar, *The Beginnings of Christian Art: 200–395,* trans. Stuart Gilbert and James Emmons (London, 1967), esp. chap. 1 and 193–207; and, challenging some of their approaches, Thomas Mathews, *The Clash of Gods: A Reinterpretation of Early Christian Art* (Princeton, 1993), esp. chap. 6; J. Elsner, *Art and the Roman Viewer: The Transformation of Art from the Pagan World to Christianity* (Cambridge, 1995), esp. 177–189.

80. There is a daunting literature on these themes. Recent discussions of some of their important aspects include Barnes, *Constantine and Eusebius,* part 3, reviewed by Averil Cameron, "Constantinus Christianus," *Journal of Roman Studies* 73 (1983): 184–190; G. W. Bowersock, "From Emperor to Bishop: The Self Conscious Transformation of Political Power in the Fourth Century A.D.," *Classical Philology* 81 (1986): 298–307; Robin Lane Fox, *Pagans and Christians* (London, 1986), part 3; J. H. W. G. Liebeschuetz, *Continuity and Change in Roman Religion* (Oxford, 1979), 277–308; Garth Fowden, *Empire to Commonwealth: Consequences of Monotheism in Late Antiquity* (Princeton, 1993), chap. 4.

81. Brown, *Power and Persuasion,* 40, and chaps. 1–2.

82. Tertullian, *Prescription against Heresies* 7.9 and 11 (CCSL 1: 193).

83. *Life of Antony* 5 (PG 26.848A)

84. Ibid. 73 (PG 26.945A); see also 72 (PG 26.944B–C), 74–80 (PG 26.945B–956A).

85. *The Sayings of the Fathers: Arsenius* 6 (PG 65: 89A); on the holy effects of the Egyptian desert, see Peter Brown, "The Rise and Function of the Holy Man in Late Antiquity," *Journal of Roman Studies* 61 (1971): 80–101, at 82–84, repr. in Brown, *Society and the Holy in Late Antiquity* (London, 1982), 103–152, at 109–112.

86. Mathews, *The Clash of Gods*, 98–114, fig. 71. The best reproduction remains Joseph Wilpert, *Die römischen Mosaiken und Malereien der kirchlichen Bauten vom IV. bis XII. Jahrhundert*, 2nd ed., 3 vols. (Freiberg im Breisgau, 1917), 2: 1066–69, 3: plates 42–44.

87. *Acts* 7:22; Gregory of Nyssa, *Life of Moses* 1.18, ed. Jean Daniélou, 3rd ed. (Paris, 1968).

88. *Life of Moses* 2.112 and 37.

89. Ibid. 2.7–8. For Moses as a model of virtue to be emulated see 1.14–15 and 77; 2.48–50 and 319. For good introductions to the intellectual project of the Cappadocian Fathers, see Werner Jaeger, *Early Christianity and Greek Paideia* (Cambridge, Mass., 1962), esp. 68–102; Jean Daniélou, *Platonisme et théologie mystique: Essai sur la doctrine spirituelle de Saint Grégoire de Nysse* (Paris, 1944).

90. T. B. Mitford, *The Inscriptions of Kourion* (Philadelphia, 1971), 353–354 (with photograph); John Daniel, "Excavations at Kourion: The Palace," *University of Pennsylvania Museum Bulletin* 7:2 (1938): 4–10.

91. Eusebius, *Life of Constantine* 3.48.1; Dagron, *Naissance d'une capitale*, 388–401.

92. Jerome, *Chronicle* Olympiad 277, ed. John Fotheringham (Oxford, 1923); Eusebius, *Life of Constantine* 3.54.1–3.

93. *Life of Constantine* 3.49; Nicetas Chroniata, *On Statues* 3 (PG 139: 1044B); Janin, *Constantinople Byzantine*, 63; R. J. H. Jenkins, "The Bronze Athena at Byzantium," *Journal of Hellenic Studies* 57 (1947): 31–33.

94. Sozomen 7.9.2; Dagron, *Naissance d'une capitale*, 45–47; Janin, *Constantinople Byzantine*, 4–6, 22–23; Louis Bréhier, "Constantin et la fondation de Constantinople," *Revue historique* 119 (1915): 241–272, esp. 247–255; Lathoud, *Echos d'Orient*, 23, 296–297.

95. Hispellum: *CIL* 11.5265 = *ILS* 705 = *ILCV* 5; Mario de Dominicis, "Un intervento legislativo di Costantino in materia religiosa (Nota a C.I.L., XI, 5265)," *Revue internationale des droits de l'antiquité*, 3rd ser., 10 (1963): 199–211. Divus: *C.Just.* 5.17.9. Emona: *Latin Panegyrics* 11.37.4. Good discussions on the survival of the imperial cult into the later empire include Louis Bréhier and Pierre Batiffol, *Les survivances du culte impérial romain: A propos des rites shintoïstes* (Paris, 1920); G. W. Bowersock, "The Imperial Cult: Perceptions and Persistence," in Ben Meyer and E. P. Sanders, eds., *Jewish and Christian Self-Definition: vol. 3, Self-Definition in the Graeco-Roman World* (London, 1982), chap. 10, esp. 176–182; Lepelley, *Les cités de l'Afrique romaine*, 1: 362–369; Salzman, *On Roman Time*, 131–146.

96. Salzman, *On Roman Time*, 199–205 and chap. 4, esp. 118–131.

97. Elizabeth Struthers Malbon, *The Iconography of the Sarcophagus of Junius Bassus* (Princeton, 1990), gives a detailed description and analysis; diagram 1-1 on p. 6 presents, at one view, the complete iconographical scheme.

98. Ibid., 1.

99. Ibid., 114–115, quoting lines 7a–8b. For good discussions of the Christianization of the Roman aristocracy, see ibid., 136–153; Salzman, *On Roman Time*, chaps. 5–6; Peter Brown, "Aspects of the Christianisation of the Roman Aristocracy," *Journal of Roman Studies* 51 (1961): 1–11, repr. in Brown, *Religion and Society in the Age of St Augustine* (London, 1972), 161–182. A range of views is conveniently canvassed in Alan Cameron, "Forschungen zum Thema der 'heidnischen Reaktion' in der Literatur seit 1943," in Alföldi and Alföldi, *Die Kontorniat-Medaillons*, 2: 63–74.

100. Useful discussions include Werner Eck, "Die Episkopat im spätantiken Africa: Organisatorische Entwicklung, soziale Herkunft, und öffentliche Funktionen," *Historische Zeitschrift* 236 (1983), 265–295, esp. 284–293; Aline Rouselle, "Aspects sociaux du recrutement ecclésiastique au IVe siècle," *Mélanges d'archéologie et d'histoire de l'Ecole français de Rome* 89 (1977): 333–370, esp. 362–370; Frank Gilliard, "Senatorial Bishops in the Fourth Century," *Harvard Theological Review* 77 (1984): 153–175.

101. Barnim Treucker, "A Note on Basil's Letters of Recommendation," in Paul Fedwick, ed., *Basil of Caesarea: Christian, Humanist, Ascetic, A Sixteen-Hundredth Anniversary Symposium*, 2 vols. (Toronto, 1981), 1: 405–410.

102. *ILCV* no. 1843; Giuseppe Cuscito, "Vescovo e cattedrale nella documentazione epigrafica in Occidente: Italia e Dalmazia," *Actes du XIe Congrès international d'archéologie chrétienne*, 3 vols. (Rome, 1989), 1: 735–778, at 771–775, fig. 21.

103. Gaudemet, *L'Eglise dans l'Empire romain*, 230–240. Among recent discussions of the civic role of bishops, see Brown, *Power and Persuasion*, esp. chap. 3; Rita Lizzi, *Il potere episcopale nell'Oriente romano: Rappresentazione ideologica e realtà politica (IV–V sec. d.C.)* (Rome, 1987), chap. 3; Henry Chadwick, "The Role of the Christian Bishop in Ancient Society," in Edward Hobbs and Wilhelm Wuellner, eds., *Protocol of the Thirty-Fifth Colloquy (25 February 1979)* (Berkeley, 1979), 1–14, repr. in Chadwick, *Heresy and Orthodoxy in the Early Church* (London, 1991), chap. 3. There are also perceptive reflections on this wider context in some recent hagiographies: see Philip Rousseau, *Basil of Caesarea* (Berkeley, 1994), chap. 5, esp. 169–175; Neil McLynn, *Ambrose of Milan: Church and Court in a Christian Capital* (Berkeley, 1994), chap. 5; Timothy Barnes, *Athanasius and Constantius: Theology and Politics in the Constantinian Empire* (Cambridge, Mass., 1993), chap. 19.

104. Basil, *Letters* 74–77; Sozomen, *Hist.eccl.* 7.23.3–5; see also Thomas Kopecek, "The Cappadocian Fathers and Civic Patriotism," *Church History* 43 (1974): 293–303; Raymond Van Dam, "Emperor, Bishops, and Friends in Late Antique Cappadocia," *Journal of Theological Studies*, n.s. 37 (1986): 53–76.

105. Rita Lizzi, *Vescovi e strutture ecclesiastiche nella città tardoantica (L'"Italia Annonaria" nel IV–V secolo d.C.)* (Como, 1989), 139–145; Giovanni Brusin and Paolo Zovatto, *Monumenti Paleocristiani di Aquileia e di Grado* (Udine, 1957), 49–58, esp. fig. 21, and 79–89, esp. figs. 34–36; Heinz Kähler, *Die Stiftermosaiken in der konstantinischen Südkirche von Aquileia* (Cologne, 1962), esp. plates 1–14.

106. *CIL* 15.7190 = *ILS* 8730 = *ILCV* 712a; Giovanni Battista di Rossi, "Dei collari dei servi fuggitivi," *Bullettino di archeologia cristiana*, 2nd ser., 5 (1874): 41–67, 41, 51–55, 58–61. I thank Richard Duncan-Jones for his help in locating this reference.

107. MacCormack, *Art and Ceremony*, 116; see also Andreas Alföldi, "Die Ausgestaltung des monarchischen Zeremoniells am römischen Kaiserhofe," *Mitteilungen des Deutschen Archäologischen Instituts (Römische Abteilung)* 49 (1934): 3–118, at 3–6, repr. in MacCormack, *Die monarchische Repräsentation im römischen Kaiserreiche* (Darmstadt, 1970).

108. Eusebius, *Life of Constantine* 4.65–67, quoting 66.1; MacCormack, *Art and Ceremony*, 115–121.

109. Maurice, *Numismatique Constantinienne*, 2: 548, plate 16, no. 16; Leo Koep, "Die Konsekrationsmünzen Kaiser Konstantins und ihre religionspolitische Bedeutung," *Jahrbuch für Antike und Christentum* 1 (1958): 94–105, esp. 96–97, plate 6b; MacCormack, *Art and Ceremony*, 121–127; Bowersock, "The Imperial Cult," 178–179.

110. Eusebius, *Life of Constantine* 4.58–60, quoting 58 and 60.3; Sozomen 2.34.5–6; Socrates, *Hist.eccl.* 1.40 (*PG* 67: 180B). The details of Constantine's funeral are exhaustively discussed in Agathe Kaniuth, *Die Beisetzung Konstantins des Grossen: Untersuchungen zur religiösen Haltung des Kaisers* (Breslau, 1941, repr. Aalen, 1974); P. Franchi de' Cavalieri, "I funerali ed il sepolcro di Costantino Magno," *Mélanges d'archéologie et d'histoire de l'Ecole français de Rome*, 36 (1916–17): 205–261. For discussion of the Church of the Apostles, see Dagron, *Naissance d'une capitale*, 401–408; André Grabar, *Martyrium: Recherches sur le culte de reliques et l'art chrétien antique* (Paris, 1946), 1: 227–234; Suzanne Alexander, "Studies in Constantinian Church Architecture," *Rivista di archeologia cristiana* 47 (1971): 281–330, at 325–329, fig. 23; Müller-Wiener, *Bildlexicon*, 405–411.

CHRISTIAN TRIUMPH AND CONTROVERSY

Richard Lim

Under this sign conquer" *(en toutōi nikā)*—by this message, Emperor Constantine had understood the Christian God, his new patron, to be a bringer of victory in battles. Triumph in the context of traditional religions largely meant the military conquest of a people and therefore of its gods; polytheists rarely envisioned the victory of one set of beliefs over another. The rise of a universalistic monotheism altered this formula.[1] Persecuted Christians sometimes looked toward an eschatological settling of scores, while Lactantius's angry God struck down persecuting emperors. But Constantine's conversion in 312 lent impetus to more ambitious hopes than the mere redress of wrongs: Eusebius's ideal prince held out a thoroughgoing form of victory, for he was to promote the one faith throughout the empire and beyond. First promised by the house of Constantine and later realized by that of Theodosius I (379–395), the alliance of Christianity with the Roman state incorporated imperial victory ideology into ecclesiastical thinking and expectations. Following the end of the 4th century, Christ triumphant over death in resurrection scenes became a favorite iconographic subject.[2]

Yet even before Eusebius could fully articulate his theory of Constantinian triumph and proclaim the peace of the church, Christian communities had become polarized by proliferating disputes over discipline and belief. Conflicts between Donatists and Catholics in Roman North Africa nominally began in 311 over the status of *traditores,* priests who had surrendered sacred books during times of trouble. Around 319, Arius, presbyter of Alexandria, set into motion and defined the terms of an enduring theological dispute when he challenged his bishop's public doctrinal statements. These two developments, together with the Melitian schism in Egypt, posed a painful paradox: Why was it that the unlooked-for conversion of Constantine, a turn of events that portended such good, should coincide with the outburst of ever more fissiparous and inveterate controversies? And how could a church divided triumph in the world?

Rather than treat in detail and in historical order the ruptures that checked Christian triumphalism, I will paint in broad strokes certain aspects of Christian religious unity and diversity, techniques of controversy, and their consequences.[3] Theological disputes engendered fierce strife and bitter enmities, but more importantly, they sharpened doctrinal formulations—notions of orthodoxy and heresy—and eventually gave rise to stronger and more coherent religious communities. These conflicts also created a more elaborate set of rules for defining religious legitimacy. But creeds and anathemas, conciliar and episcopal authority, a bolstered ecclesiastical hierarchy, denunciation in heresiography and imperial edicts, together with outright religious coercion, finally served only to reinforce rather than reconcile divergent worldviews and group identities.

The religious landscape that emerged following the imperial imposition of orthodoxy under Theodosius I was neither tranquil nor monolithic, but oddly diverse and still pluralistic. Within a shrinking empire, establishment churches coexisted and competed with a variety of nonconforming communities. Sassanian Iran, with its resurgent militant Zoroastrianism, nevertheless tolerated autonomous Nestorian and Monophysite churches in its midst. The fragmentation of Rome's political universalism in the 5th century and the rise of successor Germanic kingdoms that retained Arian Christianity as an emblem of ethnic difference linked religious affiliation with regional or national identity.[4] Within these states, "dissident" groups continued to survive, aided not by openminded tolerance but by a religious taxonomy that marginalized minority communities, insulating them from each other. But even the reconquests and religious persecutions of Justinian failed to impose unity. Throughout a world on the brink of the Muslim conquest, many came to despair of complete victory or even of compromise; instead, Christians, although very much engaged in theological controversy, focused more on their own communities, tending to the business of survival.

Roman victory guaranteed cultural and religious pluralism in the Mediterranean world so long as the emperors chose to practice salutary neglect and shunned militant universalism. Polytheists' assimilative mythology, and their idiosyncratically diverse practices and multivalent religious claims, allowed them to coexist with even the oddest bedfellows so long as none challenged the *pax deorum* with provocative atheistic claims or sacrilegious acts.[5] Philosophers could likewise debate metaphysical issues or scorn traditional religion in the secluded privacy of the Academy and deliver diatribes against followers of other *hairēseis* in the agora without fear of consequences.[6] Neither Graeco-Roman polytheism nor its philosophical tradition boasted the categories of orthodoxy and heresy in the later Christian sense—only differences, sometimes polemic, and always rivalry.[7]

Except in times of political insurrection, Romans freely allowed Jews, who flatly denied the gods' existence, to worship according to their ancestral custom.[8] Even though its adherents proselytized and attracted converts and sympathizers in places, Judaism was regarded by the Romans as a *Volksreligion* that had its own recognized hierarchy, distinctive laws, rituals, and institutions.[9] Thus for a nonconforming minority religion the secret to survival rested on being set apart and hedged by clear group boundaries. Whenever purveyors of religious ideas aggressively sought converts across established social and ethnic lines, their success met with stiffer opposition. Though universalistic in aspiration, the so-called mystery religions did not seek to monopolize religious devotion but offered added options under the rubric of polytheism. But the missionary efforts of Christians and later of Manichaeans, neither of whom could boast unambiguous ethnic identities, posed a more threatening challenge to the existing order; their brand of transgressive proselytism alarmed local opponents and caused them to be intermittently persecuted by the state.

Imbued with an imperative to prevail over others by spreading the gospel, early Christians had deliberately and repeatedly engaged in controversy. First they had to differentiate themselves from the matrix of Graeco-Roman Judaism and to claim the legitimacy and heritage of *verus Israel*.[10] Conflicts between Christians and Jews often assumed the form of competing exegesis of biblical prophecies because both sides readily accepted the authority of the Hebrew Bible.[11] Such contests, ranging from face-to-face verbal jousts to literary skirmishes, provided the *mise en scène* for Tertullian's *Adversus Judaeos* and Justin Martyr's *Dialogue with Trypho,* gentle precursors to a long-lived war of pamphlets and innuendo that soon turned ugly.[12] This *Adversus Judaeos* literature, compiled by Christians from a growing collection of arguments and *catenae,* chains of biblical proof-texts, supported their claims to scriptural prophecies and to the social respectability that Romans begrudgingly granted Judaism, a *religio licita*.[13]

Christians sought to subordinate Jews, but they had to win over pagans. Since Christianity moved, within the Roman empire at least, within predominantly gentile circles, Jewish-Christian controversy ultimately aimed not to convert Jews, whose "hard-heartedness" had been accepted by the gospel writers and allowed for in Christian soteriology, but to impress polytheists, especially those who harbored sympathies for Judaism.[14] Unable to engage in formal controversy because they lacked a shared biblical culture, Christians and pagans competed with each other over claims to power. The mystery religions attracted adherents by *son et lumière*—through processions, ceremonies, and aretalogies. According to Ramsay MacMullen, "signs, marvels and miracles" were the primary vehicle for converting pagans.[15] Easily graspable signs of power, divine miracles demonstrated the Christian God's superiority to a plethora of pagan deities. In the *Acts of Peter,* Peter confronts Simon Magus before a pagan audience by working a miracle that wins the people's acclamation: "There is but one God, the God of Peter!"[16] In a more true-to-life scenario in the Pseudo-Clementine literature, Peter debates Simon Magus but fails to win decisively; likewise, Barnabas, who only tells stories of miracles and does not perform them, receives a mixed reception from his audience. In literary accounts, public miracles ensured instant triumphs, but such narrated victories leave a loose thread: How might Christians show that their god was the one and only true deity when such a cognitive claim could not be proved by power alone? Surely, the *kerygma* still had to be based on the *logos* and the persuasion of words.

Public preaching and set disputations appear in the early literature as favored missionary tactics, whereas it was mostly in smaller and humbler settings and through tightly knit networks of households that Christians disseminated their beliefs and persuaded others.[17] Thus Celsus accused Christians of being able to impress only women, children, and old men, individuals who according to contemporary elite opinion were ill equipped to judge.[18] At times, Christian reliance on miracles and paradoxes turned the contest for converts into an intellectual debate over rational demonstration.[19] Some Christians sought to answer pagan critiques by condemning the irrationality of ancient myths and cultic observance, using chiefly "off-the-rack" philosophical *topoi;* the multivalence of set arguments, textually transmitted, remained a persistent feature of ancient religious controversy. Christian apologists made ample use of the contrast between their own alleged universalism and *homonoia,* and the manifest lack of unity among pagan philosophers, who contradicted and refuted each other: since the truth is one, the consensus of Christians proves beyond doubt that they alone possess it.[20] Confident of their triumph over the entire polytheist tradition, some Christians even asked whether the whole purpose of the *pax romana* was not to prepare for Christ's coming.[21]

Late antique Christians looking back from a vantage point after the late 4th century might see their victory over polytheism as ideologically clear-cut and unproblematic. Events such as the violent destruction of the Serapeum in 391 merely confirmed Christ's triumph over the powers of the lower world. Likewise, they thought that Jews, with their laws superseded by a new dispensation and their fortunes in steady decline since the Temple was destroyed, would ultimately be converted when Christ returned.[22] But these same Christians could find no such comforting assurance when examining their own history, marked by factionalism and divisions. Indeed, later explanations for why Eusebian hopes of Christian triumph soon turned to ashes point to the success of the devil's ruse of sowing seeds of internal discord, a last-ditch attempt to delay Christianity's final victory.[23] What determined Christian unity and disunity, and how did Christian communities resolve disputes before and after the reign of Constantine?

Frequently sectarian in a sociological sense, early Christian communities endured institutional fragmentation, schisms, and mutual accusations of heresy. Recurring admonitions to beware of "false teachers" and their *heterodidaskalia* in early Christian texts bespeak a dynamic climate of claims and counterclaims. In this environment, the church universal and apostolic succession were ideals favored and promoted by certain Christians in their struggle for advantage or survival. Recent scholarship, following the influential work of Walter Bauer on orthodoxy and heresy, shuns the anachronistic and partisan bias that the wholesale acceptance of these ideals necessitates, and accepts instead a plurality of Christianities and the conclusion that those later deemed heretical often once represented a local "catholic" majority.[24]

Clustered in isolated small groups, sometimes in semi-autonomous house-churches, early urban Christians easily accommodated a variety of different beliefs and practices. Gnostic Christians questioned the authority of ecclesiastical hierarchy and apostolic tradition, preferring a living wisdom rooted in revealed scriptures, and for this reason did not concern themselves much with the integrity of the *ekklēsia* as a social body.[25] While Ignatius of Antioch had theorized on the monarchical episcopacy, and Cyprian of Carthage, another champion of episcopal authority, had rejected the notion of the plurality of churches on the basis of a strictly defined *disciplina*, only a few pre-Constantinian bishops were able to impose conformity.[26] Instead, emerging factionalism in a Christian community normally required careful treatment by a combination of moral persuasion and authority. A regional synod might be convened so that those in disagreement could discuss their differences in the open.[27] Origen of Alexandria (ca. 185–254) employed his charisma and exegetical acumen to help reconcile various divided Christian communities after he debated and refuted a number of other Christians without shaming them.[28] Dionysius (bishop 247–ca. 264), his pupil, traveled from Alexandria to confront a millenarian movement in the Fayum that justified itself by a literal interpretation of the Apocalypse of John.[29] He finally succeeded in persuading his interlocutors to accept his views because he spent three trust-building days arguing with them: his reminiscences of the event dwell on the deference and eagerness for truth that both sides displayed.[30]

Dionysius's employment of patience and mutual deference was rarely repeated by his successors, who more and more relied on the direct exercise of authority. At the same time, the willingness of church members to defer to authority diminished as the right and ability to expound on scriptures ceased to be a monopoly exercised by a privileged few; rather, the commitment to a *via universalis*—in Momigliano's words, "the Christian abolition of the internal frontiers between the learned and the vulgar"—made virtually every Christian a potential exegete and theologian.[31] The early Arian controversy began when the presbyter Arius (ca. 250–336) dared to challenge the ecclesiastical authority of his bishop because he thought the latter had incorrectly explained Christian doctrine.[32] Perhaps all would have been well if only Arius had deferred to Alexander of Alexandria (313–328) instead of publicizing and popularizing their disagreements; indeed, later traditions would blame this rift on Arius's prideful ambition, even—anachronistically—on his dialectical cunning.

The Christian *oikoumenē* adopted by Constantine thus contained a church monolithic and universal in name only. Diversity had been a fact of life for Christians, partly resulting from their widespread diffusion and the lack of central organization. Even within each city, the indeterminacy of Christian authority, distributed among charismatic ascetics and confessors, scriptures, synods and communal consensus, and holders of ecclesiastical offices, gave ample room for differences to arise while also making them difficult to resolve. The success of local attempts to settle intra-Christian disputes depended on the initiatives and strengths of particular individuals and communities.

Constantine, to whom Christian divisions appeared bewildering and unnecessary, repeatedly urged the parties to reasonable compromise, especially during the first few years of the Donatist and early Arian controversies.[33] Drawing on their own experience with provincial synods, *koina* and *concilia,* emperors chose to invest the collective decisions of assemblies of bishops, which were already becoming important in the 3rd century, with imperial dignity.[34] Constantine's personal presence and his exhortations to *homonoia* at Nicaea in 325 prevailed upon most disputants to sign on to a compromise solution. By promoting the products of the conciliar process as reflecting a *consensus omnium gentium,* and by exiling opponents who refused to sign on, Constantine and his successors mistakenly believed they could forestall future ruptures.

Yet the emperor's selective patronage did strengthen episcopal authority, counterbalancing the centrifugal forces exerted by charismatic ascetics and confessors and the aristocratic patronage of household communities. Adapting the imperial tradition of relying on the leading men of local cities to rule, emperors dealt primarily with bishops as ranking heads of a hierarchy and as Christian spokesmen.[35] The emperors' support and their expectation that such men, now in principle given judicial authority over internal Christian disputes, would keep their own houses in order caused local bishops to aspire to more effective control over their communities.[36]

While many modern studies have been concerned with the theoretical underpinnings of imperial religious interventions, the notion of Caesaropapism, and the constitutional relationship between church and state, recent works examine the practical aspects of imperial religious policies and the precise historical interactions between emperors and bishops.[37] Thanks to the efforts of T. D. Barnes and others, understanding of imperial involvement in Christian controversy has gained greater definition.[38] The imperial presence after Constantine altered the course and aims of Christian religious controversies. Formerly, disputants who lacked formal powers of coercion and thus also the prospect of outright triumph had two main options: to follow the pattern of traditional dispute settlement in which persuasion, compromise, and consensus building represented a normative ideal, or to boycott and rhetorically condemn their opponents. Now protagonists on either side could hope for an enforceable decision in their favor when they appealed to the emperor's arbitration. Such dreams of victory too frequently chased away the willingness to compromise.

Beyond perpetuating Christian controversies, imperial patronage actually inflamed them by giving protagonists more booty to fight over. Grants of liturgical exemptions and endowed basilicas to qualified priests turned the possession of the *nomen christianum* from a badge of belonging for any who dared claim it to a title even more worth having. Disputed successions to the episcopacy were a common cause of violence and disorder, as rival parties sought to install their candidates. On occasion a number of communities within the same city would lay claim to the same real estate. A Christian quarrel over the ownership of a church was first heard by Aurelian (270–275), a pagan. Christian disputes turned into competitions over concrete possessions and imperial recognition during the 4th century as control over large urban churches became a coveted prize that could not be shared, as Ambrose of Milan's involvement in the basilica conflict of 386 shows.[39]

But by this I do not mean to suggest that theological controversies were only about politics, wealth, and vested interests, or that the disputed ideas served merely as excuses for Christians to engage along established lines of civic factional rivalry. Edward Gibbon had early on credited Christianity with making "the abstruse questions of metaphysical science" that elite philosophers once meditated in quiet leisure a preoccupation of the masses: "These speculations, instead of being treated as the amusement of a vacant hour, became the most serious business of the present, and the most useful preparation for the future, life. A theology which it was incumbent to believe, which it was impious to doubt, and which it might be dangerous, and even fatal, to mistake, became the familiar topic of private meditation and popular discourse. The cold indifference of philosophy was inflamed by the fervent spirit of devotion."[40] In its crudest and most reductive form, an approach to these disputes through the history of ideas might see them as struggles between monotheism and dualism, rationalism and mysticism, Platonism and Aristotelianism, or Greek philosophy and Christian *paideia*.[41] But, as Gibbon knew equally well, not every theological controversy was a clash of rarefied ideas. Even though Christian controversies were not uncommonly fed by the tensions between divergent strands of the classical tradition and the need to reconcile scriptural expressions, which often undergirded communal beliefs and practice, with Greek philosophical precepts, the motivations of the individuals involved were rarely pure and never simple. Positions on such issues were seldom taken in the abstract, particularly by those who played a public role.[42] The individual preferences of the protagonists tended to reflect specific concerns; the need to argue against immediate rivals frequently determined the manner in which individual Christians eclectically appropriated past traditions.

Even so, the theoretical element of Christian controversies remains crucial and should not be brushed aside as mere window dressing for age-old rivalries. At a minimum, the importance of biblical warrants to Christian actions allowed individuals and groups who disagreed for any number of reasons to conduct their mutual contest by means of a scriptural debate.[43] Scriptures could serve established authority or challenge it, justify a social movement or delegitimize it. Many Christians in practice insisted on applying rules of faith or creeds to circumscribe the scope of exegesis; biblical interpretation unrooted in tradition might easily give impetus to radical changes.

A particular kind of argument based on scriptures became a source of widespread disorder for Christians. Aristotelian dialectic emerged as an important element in the later Arian controversies of the late 4th century and remained prevalent until much later, as Christians who engaged in Trinitarian and Christological controversies needed to find a precise logic for defining the relationship among nouns, adjectives, and predicates.[44] The doctrinal controversies surrounding the figures of Aetius the Syrian (ca. 313–370) and Eunomius of Cappadocia (ca. 335–394), variously called Neo-Arians or Anomoeans today, encapsulate the competitive environment that the unregulated social use of dialectic might entail.[45] Aetius had learned to pose philosophical and theological *aporiai* publicly in the form of syllogisms, and made available his method through his *Syntagmation,* a collection of alternating questions and answers that enabled readers to reproduce or adapt deductive syllogisms that were irrefutable in controversy.[46] His disciple and associate Eunomius so developed and propagated the use of dialectic and syllogisms that he gained from adversaries the label of *technologos,* in grudging recognition of his turning theological discourse into a precise yet popular *technē.*[47] The agonistic flavor of dialectic and the necessity of syllogistic reasoning, together with the logical principle of the excluded middle, allowed the identification of winners and losers in arguments; but by rendering outright victory possible they also decreased the likelihood of patient compromise.[48]

Exacting dialectical questions stripped Christian leaders of the security of their office and social standing. The anxious requests for help from Amphilochius of Iconium (ca. 340–395) to Basil of Caesarea, and Gregory of Nyssa's famous observation regarding the widespread culture of questioning in late 4th century Constantinople, are but two examples of the challenges this verbal culture presented.[49] Called to account by those of lower or no rank who no longer deferred to authority, elites found themselves susceptible to challenge from those who claimed *isēgoria* based on a competitive form of knowledge; moreover, the solidarity of the communities they led was disrupted as individuals bandied urgent and challenging questions at each other, undermining accepted certainties, established friendships, and loyalties.[50] For a brief moment, it was feared that even Theodosius might be swayed by the arguments of Eunomius if Empress Flacilla were to succeed in securing an audience for him.[51]

A number of ad hoc textual weapons were sent into the fray, often for defense. Ready-made responses or retorts, often in the form of catechetical or question-and-answer dialogues, were provided to arm common as well as elite Christians against anticipated questions;[52] creeds were also sometimes put to use in this context to quell further discussion.[53] Later, Anastasius of Sinai (d. ca. 700) combined text and icon in his *Hodēgos,* a multimedia prophylactery designed to put a stop to provocative Monophysite questions.[54] In short, no effort was spared to prevent Christians from engaging in frank and unmediated exchanges over particular theological issues. A growing selection of theological writings, ranging from catechetical pamphlets such as Theodoret of Cyrrhus's *Eranistes* to more ponderous system-building treatises, provided individuals with ready-made arguments against challenges from familiar quarters. The authority of this literature delineated and patrolled the boundaries of theological communities; it also helped harness dialectic to the task of defending a group's position against outside attacks.

The ideological strategies for managing conflict in such situations were fundamental to the development of the later orthodox identity and culture. Such tactics included appeals to the authority of simple but steadfastly faithful ascetics, who abhorred sophistry and dialectical disputation; reliance on the traditional authority of patristic consensus expressed in *florilegia* and in councils; and the elaboration of a mystical theology—all of them a part of the ideological fence, erected to contain freewheeling theological debates, that finally helped solidify Christian communities formed around set theological ideas.

Sometimes treated as marginal to theological controversy, the phenomenon of asceticism first entered the fray as certain Christians began to validate their own claims by invoking the charisma and *virtutes* of ascetics, who were represented as paragons of orthodoxy; rival groups, who portrayed them as itinerants and Manichaeans, regarded them as purveyors of dangerous teachings. The positive emphasis on the *habitus* of these ascetics served as a counterpoint to the ad hominem ethical invective against adversaries castigated as sophistic dialecticians, whose allegedly dissolute way of life only confirmed their scant regard for truth.[55] Christians who asserted that simple and God-loving ascetics professed the same true faith which they also embraced thus exploited the cultural capital of ascetics in "antiheretical" polemics.[56] A story connected with the Council of Nicaea has an unlearned confessor put an end to ongoing dialectical disputations by challenging those present to confess together to a short and simple creed.[57]

In this story, the bishops at Nicaea found themselves in such disarray that they had to be rescued from their war of words by a charismatic confessor.[58] But the ability of individuals to challenge authority with dialectical questions at councils would be checked by patristic consensus as the authority of *florilegia patrum* came to be more widely accepted. These collections of sayings from eminent "Fathers of the church" were often used with *catenae* of proof-texts culled to establish particular interpretations of scriptures; together they became a fixture of conciliar proceedings, whereby a particular *florilegium* would be affirmed by the acclamations of attending bishops.[59] This combination of diachronic and synchronic consensus circumscribed the ability of individuals, even trained dialecticians, to pose fresh questions and arguments in council. When those engaged in controversy expected their own arguments to be measured against authoritative precedents, they would be less likely to argue dialectically from first principles or from a few scriptural premises. By thus removing theological formulations from close questioning and constant reexamination, a precious element of stability could be introduced into these controversies— even as protagonists soon learned to compile their own partisan *florilegia* and *catenae*. Now transposed to the level of written authorities, Christian disputes became less sharply agonistic: victory would go to those who championed views that accorded with established consensus, allowing for the operation of analogical reasoning.

As growing weight was placed on the examination of written evidence in conciliar proceedings, similar to senatorial and legal methods, the principle of agreement with established norms became a criterion for judging orthodoxy. Later traditions would represent the scriptures enshrined as the ultimate authority at the Council of Constantinople in 381. Theodosius I, who allegedly asked for written statements of faith from disputing Christian groups so that he could render judgment based on them, decided after prayer to accept only those that agreed with the Nicene creed.[60] At the Council of Ephesus in 431, Nestorius received the collective anathemas of the assembled bishops after his views were found by Cyril's partisans to conform not to the Nicene creed but rather to the condemned views of Paul of Samosata, who had been branded a heretic at the Council of Antioch in 268.[61]

Authoritative creeds were both a tool and a product of controversy. What later came to be known as the Nicene creed had been subsequently modified or even set aside in numerous councils until it was reestablished by imperial fiat as the canon of orthodoxy at Constantinople 381.[62] As the language of theological controversy became ever more complex and convoluted, short credal statements could rarely serve, on their own and without specifically attached interpretations, as an adequate guarantee of orthodoxy.[63] But a creed whose language was extremely precise would also likely be exposed to criticism, leading to an unending cycle of controversy.

Concerned that every championed idea provoked a response, particularly if the precise terms used lent themselves to dialectical and syllogistic reasoning, some Christians turned to a strategy of mystification. The Cappadocians, in their argument against Eunomius, had insisted that human language and thought were inadequate for grasping the divine essence.[64] John Chrysostom (ca. 347–407) and Gregory of Nazianzus (329–389), who as priest and bishop came into intimate contact with the culture of dialectical questioning, opposed what they termed *polupragmosunē*, meddlesome curiosity, with a robust assertion of divine mystery that put the knowledge of God's attributes beyond the reach of ordinary believers.[65] Their homilies on the incomprehensibility of the divine essence, occasioned by immediate controversies, later developed into the mystical theology of Pseudo-Dionysius the Areopagite (ca. 500), according to whom the hierarchical chain of beings could know God only anagogically and in part through intermediary signs. That this view came to the fore when Aristotelian dialectic was being employed by both sides during the ongoing Monophysite controversy may not be sheer coincidence.[66]

Borrowing ideas from a venerable philosophical tradition of apophaticism, the Christian *via negativa,* instead of being seen as a form of irrationalism that blocked advances in theology and science, may be considered the price that a society had to pay for greater social harmony. By asserting that unaided human reason could not grasp the divine essence, mystics established the need for Christians to adhere steadfastly to creeds and to participate in liturgical prayer and worship. Such strategies enhanced rather than undercut Christian solidarity. Competitive forms of knowledge such as Aristotelian dialectic were subordinated to an apophatic, mystical *theōria* that stressed the importance of a hierarchical status quo and the mediation of priests in the spiritual anagogy.[67] Christian communities, thus rallied around local priests and bishops, became more unified bodies with distinct group identities and boundaries. Competition and conflict between Christians did not cease; but they increasingly took place at the edges of communities: as the battle-lines were drawn, contests tended to take place between rival congregations rather than within groups. In fact, with the heightened sense of belligerence that controversy bred, differences between encapsulated communities tended to become even more intractable.

H. I. Marrou speaks of the 4th century as "a century of strong personalities, men of steel who knew how to withstand the powerful forces of the day and oppose violence with the firmness of their faith."[68] This statement betrays a prevalent bias of patristic scholarship. To examine religious controversies as a historical phenomenon, it is not enough to focus just on select patristic figures, or even on the more colorful "heresiarchs." The nature of Christian leadership must be placed under careful scrutiny. Beginning with the 4th century, bishops increasingly hailed from the upper strata of society, entering ecclesiastical office with firmer notions about the exercise of power. As part of a macrosocial elite, these bishops knew that they had to seek allies abroad and build on their own power bases at home to secure their own future in an uncertain, fractious world.

Somewhat sweepingly, W. H. C. Frend has portrayed the religious controversies of the 4th century as sustained by bishops, while those of the 5th were pursued by the populace as a whole.[69] Though the importance of individual Christian leaders and later ecclesiastical parties (frequently connected with the imperial court) in religious disputes in the 4th century has been overstated, it did pale in significance in the course of the 5th century as popular participation expanded, a result of deliberate efforts by the leaders to widen the controversies. The process had in fact already begun in the 4th century, if not even earlier: Arius was said to have popularized his views through metrical songs contained in his *Thalia,* while Athanasius of Alexandria, a consummate political fighter and an ideologue equally capable of mobilizing a community, appealed with simple words to monks in the Egyptian desert.[70] More concrete involvements of communal organizations in religious rivalry included popular acclamations and the singing of antiphonal songs during processions through cities such as Antioch and Milan.[71] Chanting provocative words served as a clarifying ritual that rallied the catholic congregations, giving them a visible and solid identity and openly challenging Arian Christians. As Christian leaders embroiled in controversy sought to increase their bases of support by securing regional constituencies, bishops of Alexandria such as Cyril and his successor Dioscoros (bishop 444–454) mobilized the desert monks outside the city, whose biblical fundamentalism and unquestioning adherence to the Nicene creed made them stalwart allies against Nestorius once the latter's views had been recast by the Alexandrians in simple terms and encapsulated in slogans.[72] Without taking into account how leaders shaped the controversies as well as both the intended and unintended consequences of popularization, historians will continue to pose moot questions such as whether the majority of Christians understood the intellectual issues in dispute.[73] As certain leaders deployed demagogic rhetoric and tailor-made appeals to create or galvanize communities, it is impossible to examine doctrinal disputes as having a single underlying cause. These leaders' actions have greatly vexed the longstanding scholarly discussion concerning whether the Christian heresies were also national or regional movements.[74]

The consequences were reaped in the 5th century, when monastic participation and activism in controversy became much more noticeable: monks accused their own bishops of heresy and even violently disrupted the Council of Ephesus in 431.[75] Monks did not always have a predetermined inclination to particular theological views (many in Syria were Chalcedonian while those in Egypt were mostly Monophysite), yet their tendency to starkly dualistic worldviews added uncertainty and volatility to already difficult situations. The involvement of unlettered monks, who attacked heretics as they would a polluted pagan temple—with hatred and determination—exacerbated intra-Christian contests by giving protagonists without imperial support the option of prevailing through physical violence. A patriarch of Alexandria might even turn to the strong right arms of the 500 *parabalani* (hospital attendants) under his charge to impose his will.[76] The Christians' incitement of popular violence against each other soon made imperial repression of disputes more palatable, which in turn led to further resistance. Emperors might prevail upon individuals and crush ecclesiastical parties by cajoling, threatening, or exiling leaders, but a *dēmos* or *populus* in arms was a tougher nut to crack.[77] The operation of imperial pressure and consensual politics behind closed doors became well-nigh impossible.

But the inability of conciliar proceedings to resolve disputes and prevent further controversies cannot be blamed entirely on those who disrupted the proceedings of particular councils. The councils' transformation from occasions for consensual compromise and moral exhortation into a forum for the exercise of authority weakened their ability to settle differences. Because many councils were openly partisan, interested groups that failed to prevail at them quickly sought to undercut their authority. The lack of a disinterested and neutral broker was another problem: as emperors became more embroiled in religious controversies, rival parties turned the imperial court into an arena for ecclesiastical political maneuvers, through persuasion or even bribery.[78] But although protagonists in controversy increasingly learned to play the game and gained sophistication in shaping such proceedings, select councils were still regarded by later Christians as inspired. Those who opposed their decisions, as Arius and Nestorius were said to have done, came to be called *theomachoi,* those who resisted God, in the later orthodox tradition. Councils such as Nicaea and Constantinople became sanctified icons for most Christians, while Monophysites anathematized Chalcedon.[79] As Cyril's victory at that council was won by questionable means, its decisions served only to entrench divisions among Christians and eventually split the empire. In vain, emperors tried to close the book after such a general council. Marcian (450–457) forbade future discussion of the subject three years after Chalcedon to protect its decisions.[80] Zeno (474–491) issued his *Henoticon* in 482 containing the twelve anathemas of Cyril of Alexandria, the creeds of Nicaea and Constantinople, and a ban on further debate. Two subsequent imperial attempts at compromise, including Heraclius's *Ecthesis* in 638 and Constans II's *Typus* in 647/48, came too late because the rival communities had by then become far too well established and entrenched in their differences. Instead a separate and increasingly important discourse of Christian consensus grew up in the form of hagiography, especially of the *saloi*, "fools for the sake of Christ": the holy men of the late empire embodied a positive, broad-based religiosity that overrode the effects of theological controversy on many Christian communities.[81]

While Christians had long entertained a notion of orthodoxy, the state's support gave it definition and weight. How was one to identify orthodox Christians, who alone could claim considerable privileges and imperial gifts? For a half-century after Nicaea, a fixed and precise definition of orthodoxy did not yet obtain, as emperors and bishops continued to revisit the decisions of 325, but closure began to be achieved under the reign of Theodosius I: orthodox Christians held communion with named bishops; they adhered to specific short creeds; and they accepted the conclusions of designated councils.[82]

Theodosius I tried and failed to create a thoroughly Christian society.[83] He prohibited polytheists' sacrifices, both private and public, and demanded the closing of temples.[84] Groups that had existed at the margins of catholic communities, such as the Manichaeans and those who had sympathies with the theological views and methods associated with the Anomoeans Aetius and Eunomius, were pushed out and doors shut behind them.[85] The emperor's sanction of the use of physical force to address religious nonconformity enshrined a practice that had been selectively applied by Constantine, Constantius, and Valens. Now entitled to apply coercion against rivals, some Christian bishops such as Augustine quickly rationalized its use.[86] Pagans and their temples were the most immediate target, but the momentum of growing zeal caused Donatist Christians, who had earlier been treated as schismatics, to be indiscriminately lumped with heretics.[87] Deprived of churches, their priests exiled and suffering other indignities, nonconforming Christians nevertheless found ways to survive. As polytheists had once learned, religious persecution rarely succeeded in extirpating its target; instead, well-organized dissident groups merely hardened under pressure, as they developed their own internal hierarchies, textual authorities, communal rituals, and group memory.

Imperial edicts against named heresies, which relied on the religious taxonomy and labels generated by disputing Christians, turned mud-slinging among them into a far more consequential enterprise.[88] Heresiologues such as Epiphanius of Salamis (ca. 315–403), Filaster of Brescia (d. ca. 397), and Augustine drew on earlier precedents to present a taxonomy of Judeo-Christian sects that splintered from the one original truth by coupling descriptions of sectarian fragmentation with explanations of each group's peculiar beliefs and customs.[89] By naming sects after supposed eponymous founders or by caricaturing an aspect of their beliefs, these compendia of religious ethnography reflect a clear bias toward orthodox views; any sect that bore a particularistic name could not be catholic or true. But ultimately they generate a cognitive map that contains carefully delineated spaces even for dissenting "heretics."

Demonizing opponents appealed to "God-bearing" desert monks accustomed to contending with the devil in the wilderness, yet it also appeared in cities, where a different set of conditions encouraged the stigmatization of rivals. Urban Christianity, with its plurality of study groups and networks of patronage and friendship, furnished fertile ground for peripheral diversity in domestic spaces even as centers were being formed by bishops around basilica churches.[90] As bishops encouraged the homogenization of Christian beliefs and practices through preaching *ex cathedra,* direct supervision over liturgical life, and administration of communion, their practical hold over the large urban community long remained incomplete. The unsupervised networks of people and information that continued to exist became the targets of polemic: slanders against Manichaeans, for instance, focused on their performance of unspeakable crimes in closeted spaces, just as libelous claims against Christians at an earlier period had done. By mobilizing public opinion, by allowing rumors to spread and pamphlets that cast aspersions on the private activities of such marginal groups to circulate, those in authority hoped to undercut their legitimacy and appeal, and perhaps even to force them to justify themselves in a public forum that Christian bishops could control.[91] The tactic that Augustine used against the Manichaeans while he was bishop of Hippo combined the pressure of rumors, the threat of coercion, an imposing episcopal presence, and the use of stenography to record the victorious proceedings for later use and for posterity; the shift in the locale of the disputations from public baths to the bishop's palace is equally suggestive of the constriction of civic dialogue.[92]

The heresiological discourse increasingly cast the orthodox community as a body that was assailed by the disease of heresy, for which it prescribed dismemberment—shunning and excommunication—to protect the whole when the infected part was thought beyond cure. Once the social lines between the orthodox community and named heresies had been drawn, intra-Christian controversy continued between rival communities. Creeds, anathemas, and abjuration formulas, common weapons in the arsenal of war, implied above all inclusion and exclusion from social bodies.

Yet symbolic forms could enable sanctioned and outlawed groups to coexist ideologically, particularly if the leaders of nonconforming groups, even polytheists, belonged to the social elites and accepted their own subordinate status.[93] Such a *modus vivendi* with local Arians was important to Roman emperors before the reign of Justinian because, with Arian Germanic peoples ruling over large catholic populations of *Romani* in the west and as *foederati* at home, persecutions against Arians on imperial soil might occasion reprisals against one's own people, as indeed happened in Vandal Africa. Justinian's reconquest had reclaimed Italy and North Africa for the *imperium,* making possible the assertion of Roman political and religious universalism.[94] After the Burgundians and the Suebi converted to catholic Christianity, the Visigoths, who under Euric (466–484) had persecuted Catholics, turned to orthodoxy. Reccared convened a council at Toledo in 589 to mark the change, at which the king and his nobles swore to uphold the creeds established at Nicaea, Constantinople, and Chalcedon, burned Arian books, and anathematized Arian beliefs. By establishing Chalcedonian Christianity as its *Reichskirche,* Visigothic Spain aimed to become a fully Christian society, a rival to Byzantium.[95] The time for pluralism was past: efforts were made to forcibly convert Jews within the kingdom to Christianity.[96]

But even with these changes, and with the widespread forced conversion of pagans under Justinian, the Christian *oikoumenē* did not suddenly become unified in one confession. As religion and society became harder to separate, religious controversies and endemic civic and intercity rivalry also tended to come together. The dispersal of religious authority into often rival centers further perpetuated and accentuated theological differences among the Christian population.[97] The growing confidence expressed by bishops of metropolitan sees such as Alexandria, Antioch, Constantinople, Jerusalem, and Rome added fuel to the flames of controversy. Rome intervened more actively and was repeatedly appealed to by eastern prelates about to lose an ongoing struggle at home. While often seen as naives by modern scholars, Roman bishops such as Leo asserted their own voices in the definition of orthodox doctrine, sometimes derailing imperial efforts to achieve compromise and unity. Heraclius (610–641), anxious to rally Monophysite communities in the face of the Persian threat, promoted his *Ecthesis* as a compromise document.[98] It was immediately derided in Monophysite Egypt and rejected the following year in Rome at a synod convened by Pope Martin (649–655), attended by a large number of eastern bishops who approved instead a mainly Greek *florilegium* compiled by Maximus the Confessor (ca. 580–662).[99] This assertion of Roman primacy was premature, as Martin was soon exiled from the city by imperial order.

The theological controversies that continued from the 5th century onward tended to have heavier regional accents. But as long as marginal groups retained hopes of being one day accepted by the emperor, they continued to remain loyal to the empire. After Nestorian Christians were deprived of the Christian name in 435, they began to move eastward and eventually crossed into the Persian empire in 457, from which they were to expand into Central Asia and China.[100] Monophysites became alienated from the Chalcedonians championed by Constantinople after numerous attempts at reconciliation failed; but only more determined persecutions under Justinian caused them to create their own churches. When pressured further, these dissident communities retreated into the remoter regions of the empire and even into Persian territory with their own full-fledged ecclesiastical hierarchy, organized monasteries, and schools.[101]

Originally, categories of heresy and orthodoxy operated differently in the Sassanian empire than in the Christianized Roman empire. Zoroastrians prized orthopraxy above all and condemned as heretics only those who refused to acknowledge Ahura Mazda with appropriate rites. While the magi, whose worship at the fire temples safeguarded the prosperity of the state, remained alert to challenges from others—especially Manichaeans—the *zindīq*s, kings of kings from Yazdegird (399–420) onward, normally acknowledged the Christians' right to exist, supporting their synods and confirming the bishop of Seleucia-Ctesiphon as their *katholikos* and spokesman.[102] The later success of Nestorians in converting Iranians away from Zoroastrianism and their ill-advised destruction of fire temples provoked repressive measures. Periodically persecuted, Nestorian and Monophysite communities, as sizable subject minorities like the established Jewish population in Mesopotamia, nonetheless found in the Sassanians reasonably tolerant masters, even while the Chalcedonians were singled out for intense persecution as imperial allies in conquered Byzantine lands.

It is salutary to remind ourselves that religious controversies of the sort described here were not unique to Christians in the Mediterranean world.[103] A religion of the book, Islam accepted Jews and Christians as subject peoples but insisted on the conversion of pagans; for this reason the polytheists of Harran famously attempted, ultimately without success, to pass themselves off as Sabians.[104] Membership in the 'umma, the Islamic community, could be gained by anyone who professed the belief that God was one and that Muhammad was his last and most eminent prophet; in practice, it was largely limited to Arabs in the first century or so after the *hijra*. The Umayyad caliphs, who combined religious and political authority, had no reason to desire mass conversion because it could result in a loss of revenue; taxes raised from the conquered population served as the financial basis of the state. While Muslim heresiographers, perhaps following Christian predecessors, noted in retrospect the continuous fragmentation of the true faith, no reliable source portrays an Umayyad caliph as having sought to impose religious uniformity. Beliefs regarding doctrine remained open to question, though there were already hints that the scriptural authority of the Qur'ān was becoming a source of contention.[105] Interestingly, the intellectual roots of important sectarian political movements that the state attempted to suppress were downplayed: the Azāriqa (a splinter group of the Khārijites) and Shī'i Muslims were viewed by what became the Sunnī majority community as schismatics and religious extremists respectively, not heretics.[106] *Bid'a,* arbitrary theological innovation, was frowned upon rather than condemned. Persecution against *zindīq*s, such as the Manichaeans, intensified under al-Mahdī (775–785) and came closest to the categorical rejection of heretics in contemporary Byzantium; but this exception rather proves the rule.[107]

The loose association between the Umayyad caliphate and Muslim theologians safeguarded the freedom of doctrinal discussions. The Abbasids, particularly during the reign of al-Ma'mūn (813–833), the first caliph also to claim the imamate, began to form a tighter bond between the state and an established religion.[108] Al-Ma'mūn's adviser was a chief advocate for Mu'tazilism and through him an alliance was forged between the caliphate and those individuals who championed the view that the Qur'ān was created rather than coeternal with God, who alone was transcendent. Sometimes characterized as rationalists, Mu'tazilites believed that God, and hence correct belief about him, could be discovered by applying reason to the exegesis of Qur'ānic revelation. The caliph, using inquisitorial procedures, sought to compel the major religious scholars in Baghdad and elsewhere to accept this doctrine and transformed the matter into a litmus test for political loyalty as well as religious orthodoxy. The resulting controversy spread far beyond the intellectual circles of theologians as communities coalesced in support of or in opposition to the imposed dogma. Such a precedent soon resulted in a backlash beginning in 848, as a succeeding caliph, al-Mutawakkil (847–861), the Islamic Theodosius, gave the Mu'tazilites a taste of their own medicine; his zeal went beyond this controversy to the persecution of Jews and Christians, who had previously been left alone if they would pay a poll tax. This setback encouraged the Mu'tazilites to settle into more coherent schools based in Basra and Baghdad, which in the 10th century developed their own distinctive traditions; they also found safe havens in rival centers on the Iranian plateau where local rulers lent them support. The history of Mu'tazilism shares the same ingredients with the earlier history of Christian religious triumph, controversy, and survival: state formation, revealed scriptures, Greek philosophical rationalism, regional diversities, and an initial dichotomy between theologians and ordinary believers that was later overcome through popularization.

Notes

My warmest thanks go to Peter Brown, Keith Lewinstein, and Jennifer M. Miller for their generous help in the preparation of this essay.

1. On the connection between monotheism and intolerance, see E. Peterson, *Der Monotheismus als politisches Problem: Ein Beitrag zur Geschichte der politischen Theologie im Imperium Romanum* (Leipzig, 1935); A. Momigliano, "The Disadvantages of Monotheism for a Universal State," in id., *On Pagans, Jews, and Christians* (Middletown, Conn., 1987), 142–158; and G. Fowden, *Empire to Commonwealth: Consequences of Monotheism in Late Antiquity* (Princeton, 1993).

2. A. Grabar, *Christian Iconography: A Study of Its Origins* (Princeton, 1968), 123–127; on Roman triumphalist ideology, see M. McCormick, *Eternal Victory: Triumphal Rulership in Late Antiquity, Byzantium and the Early Medieval West* (Cambridge, Eng., and Paris, 1986), esp. 100–111.

3. For general accounts, see S. L. Greenslade, *Schism in the Early Church* (London, 1953); id., "Heresy and Schism in the Later Roman Empire," in D. Baker, ed., *Schism, Heresy and Religious Protest* (Cambridge, Eng., 1972), 1–20; and J. Meyendorff, *Imperial Unity and Christian Divisions: The Church from 450–680 A.D.* (Crestwood, N.Y., 1989). J. Stevenson, *Creeds, Councils and Controversies: Documents Illustrative of the History of the Church to AD 337* (2nd ed., London, 1987), provides a selection of pertinent texts in translation,

4. M. Meslin, "Nationalisme, état et religions à la fin du IVe siècle," *Archives de sociologie des religions* 18 (1964), 3–20, and *Les ariens dans l'occident, 335–430* (Paris, 1967).

5. A. Momigliano, "La libertà di parola nel mondo antico," *Rivista storica italiana* 4:83 (1971): 499–524; and P. Garnsey, "Religious Toleration in Classical Antiquity," in W. J. Shiels, ed., *Persecution and Toleration* (Oxford, 1984), 1–27.

6. See J. Hahn, *Der Philosoph und die Gesellschaft: Selbstverständnis, öffentliches Auftreten und populäre Erwartungen in der hohen Kaiserzeit* (Stuttgart, 1989); on philosophical polemics, see G. E. L. Owen, "Philosophical Invective," *Oxford Studies in Ancient Philosophy* 1 (1983), 1–25; on philosophical sectarianism and schools, see J. P.

Lynch, *Aristotle's School: A Study of a Greek Educational Institution* (Berkeley, 1972); and D. Runia, "Philosophical Heresiography: Evidence in Two Ephesian Inscriptions," *Zeitschrift für Papyrologie und Epigraphik* 72 (1988), 241–243.

7. See M. Simon, "From Greek *hairesis* to Christian Heresy," in W. R. Schodel and R. L. Wilkens, eds., *Early Christian Literature and the Classical Intellectual Tradition in honorem Robert M. Grant* (Paris, 1979), 101–116. On the management of conflict in Late Platonist circles, see Richard Lim, *Public Disputation, Power, and Social Order in Late Antiquity* (Berkeley, 1995), 31–69.

8. See J. G. Gager, *The Origins of Anti-Semitism: Attitudes towards Judaism in Pagan and Christian Antiquity* (Oxford, 1985), 39–66; and A. M. Rabello, "The Legal Condition of the Jews in the Roman Empire," in H. Temporini and W. Haase, eds., *ANRW* II.19.662–762; for the later period, see the fine overview in N. de Lange, "Jews and Christians in the Byzantine Empire: Problems and Prospects," in D. Wood, ed., *Christianity and Judaism* (Oxford, 1992), 15–32.

9. For diaspora Judaism, see P. R. Trebilco, *Jewish Communities in Asia Minor* (Cambridge, Eng., 1991); for Palestinian Judaism, see M. Avi-Yonah, *The Jews under Roman and Byzantine Rule: A Political History of Palestine from the Bar Kokhba War to the Arab Conquest* (New York, 1984). On conversion to Judaism, see M. Goodman, "Proselytizing in Rabbinic Judaism," *Journal of Jewish Studies* 40 (1989): 175–185; on god-fearers, see J. Reynolds and R. Tannenbaum, *Jews and God-Fearers at Aphrodisias: Greek Inscriptions with Commentary* (Cambridge, Eng., 1987).

10. See M. Simon, *Verus Israel: Etude sur les relations entre chrétiens et juifs dans l'empire romain (135–425)*, rev. ed. (Paris, 1964). M. S. Taylor, in *Anti-Judaism and Early Christian Identity: A Critique of the Scholarly Consensus* (Leiden, 1995), now argues that there was no actual direct competition between Jews and Christians in the first two centuries and that Christian anti-Judaism was wholly an ideological construct.

11. See O. Skarsaune, *The Proof from Prophecy: A Study of Justin Martyr's Proof-Text Tradition* (Leiden, 1987).

12. W. Bousset, *Jüdisch-christlicher Schulbetrieb in Alexandria und Rom* (Göttingen, 1915); on Jewish-Christian dialogues, see M. Hoffmann, *Der Dialog bei den christlichen Schriftstellern der ersten vier Jahrhunderte* (Tübingen and Leipzig, 1966); and B. R. Voss, *Der Dialog in der frühchristlichen Literatur* (Munich, 1970).

13. A. L. Williams, *Adversus Judaeos: A Bird's Eye View of Christian Apologetic until the Renaissance* (Cambridge, Eng., 1955); and H. Schreckenberg, *Die christlichen Adversus Judaeos Texte und ihr literarisches und historisches Umfeld (1.–11. Jahrhunderte)*, 2nd ed. (Frankfurt am Main, 1990).

14. H. Remus, "Justin Martyr's Argument with Judaism," in S. G. Wilson, ed., *Anti-Judaism in Early Christianity II: Separation and Polemic* (Waterloo, Ont., 1986).

15. R. MacMullen, *Christianizing the Roman Empire (A.D. 100–400)* (New Haven, 1984), 25.

16. *Acta Petri* 8.26. See J. Colin, *Les villes libres de l'orient gréco-romain et l'envoi au supplice par acclamations populaires* (Brussels, 1965), 109–152.

17. R. MacMullen, "Two Types of Conversion to Early Christianity," *Vigiliae Christianae* 37 (1983): 174–192.

18. Origen, *Contra Celsum* 2.55.

19. See, e.g., R. Walzer, *Galen on Jews and Christians* (London, 1949), 15–16; and S. Benko, "Pagan Criticism of Christianity during the First Two Centuries," *ANRW* II.23.2.1055–1118. On Christian paradoxical discourse, see Averil Cameron, *Christianity and the Rhetoric of Empire: The Development of Christian Discourse* (Berkeley, 1991).

20. K. Ochler, "Der Consensus Omnium als Kriterium der Wahrheit in der antike Philosophie und der Patristik: Eine Studie zur Geschichte des Begriffs der allgemeinen Meinung," *Antike und Abendland* 10 (1961): 103–130. The pagan Celsus used this argument against Christians: Origen, *Contra Celsum* 3.11–12.

21. See Eusebius, *Praeparatio evangelica* (compiled ca. 318).

22. Eusebius, *Hist.eccl.* 2.26, 3.5–6.

23. Evagrius Scholasticus, *Hist.eccl.* 1.1; Nicetas, *Encomium of Gregory of Nazianzus* 16.

24. W. Bauer, *Orthodoxy and Heresy in Earliest Christianity,* trans. R. A. Kraft and G. Krodel (Philadelphia, 1971).

25. G. Levesque, "Consonance chrétienne et dissonance gnostique dans Irénée 'Adversus haereses' IV, 18, 4 à 19,3," *Studia Patristica* 16 (Berlin, 1985): 193–196.

26. Ignatius, *Ep. ad Eph.* 3–5 and Cyprian, *Ep.* 66; *De ecclesiae catholicae unitate* 3–24.

27. C. J. Hefele, *Histoires des conciles* (Paris, 1907–1908), vols. 1–2. For the ideology of early councils, see H. J. Sieben, *Die Konzilsidee der Alten Kirche* (Paderborn, 1979), 384–447; and C. Vogel, "Primalialité et synodalité dans l'église locale durant la periode anténicéenne," in M. Simon, ed., *Aspects de l'orthodoxie: Structure et spiritualité* (Paris, 1982), 53–66.

28. Eusebius, *Hist.eccl.* 6.18 and 6.33; Origen, *Dialogue with Heraclides,* J. Scherer, ed., *Entretien d'Origène avec Héraclide,* Sources Chrétiennes 67 (Paris, 1960). See Lim, *Public Disputation,* 16–20, and "Religious Disputation and Social Disorder in Late Antiquity," *Historia* 44 (1995): 204–231, at 209–210.

29. Eusebius, *Hist.eccl.* 7.24. See Lim, *Public Disputation,* 20–22, and "Religious Disputation," 211–215.

30. R. MacMullen, "Personal Power in the Roman Empire," *American Journal of Philology* 107 (1986): 513–524. See also E. P. Thompson, "Patrician and Plebeian Society," *Journal of Social History* 7 (1974): 382–405, and *Customs in Common* (London, 1991); and J. G. A. Pocock, "The Classical Theory of Deference," *American Historical Review* 81 (1976): 516–523.

31. A. Momigliano, "Popular Religious Beliefs and the Later Roman Historians," in G. J. Cuming and D. Baker, eds., *Popular Belief and Practice* (Cambridge, Eng., 1972), 1–18, at 17.

32. Arius has recently been rehabilitated by scholars as a rigorous ascetic with deep theological convictions. On Arius and early Arianism, see R. C. Gregg and D. E. Groh, *Early Arianism: A View of Salvation* (Philadelphia and London, 1981); R. Williams, "The Logic of Arianism," *Journal of Theological Studies* n.s. 34 (1983): 56–81, and *Arius: Heresy and Tradition* (London, 1987); R. C. Hanson, *The Search for the Christian Doctrine of God: The Arian Controversy 318–381* (Edinburgh, 1988). For later developments, see essays in M. R. Barnes and D. H. Williams, eds., *Arianism after Arius: Essays on the Development of the Fourth Century Trinitarian Conflicts* (Edinburgh, 1993).

33. Lim, "Religious Disputation," 217–219.

34. F. Millar, *The Emperor in the Roman World (31 B.C.–A.D. 337)* (London, 1977), 385–394.

35. P. R. L. Brown, *Power and Persuasion in Late Antiquity: Towards a Christian Empire* (Madison, Wis., 1992), 3–34.

36. H. von Campenhausen, *Ecclesiastical Office and Spiritual Power in the Church in the First Three Centuries* (Stanford, 1969; orig. German ed. Tübingen, 1953); E. W. Kemp, "Bishops and Presbyters at Alexandria," *Journal of Ecclesiastical History* 3 (1952): 125–142; H. Chadwick, "The Role of the Christian Bishop in Ancient Society," in *Protocol of the 35th Colloquy,* Center for Hermeneutical Studies (Berkeley, 1980) = *Heresy and Orthodoxy in the Early Church* (London, 1991), III; G. W. Bowersock, "From Emperor to Bishop: The Self-Conscious Transformation of Political Power in the Fourth Century, A.D.," *Classical Philology* 81 (1986): 298–307; R. Lizzi, *Il potere episcopale nell'oriente romano* (Rome, 1987); and Brown, *Power and Persuasion,* 71–117.

37. E.g., E. Schwartz, *Kaiser Constantin und die christliche Kirche*, 2nd ed. (Leipzig, 1936); F. Dvornik, "Emperors, Popes and General Councils," *Dumbarton Oaks Papers* 6 (1951): 1–27; C. Pietri, "La politique de Constance II: Un premier 'césaropapisme' ou l'*imitatio Constantini*?" *L'église et l'empire au IVe siècle*, Entretiens sur l'antiquité classique 34 (Vandoeuvres, 1989), 113–172; and G. Dagron, *Empereur et prêtre: Étude sur le 'césaropapisme' byzantin* (Paris, 1996), esp. 141–168.

38. T. D. Barnes, *Constantine and Eusebius* (Cambridge, Mass., 1981), and *Athanasius and Constantius: Theology and Politics in the Constantinian Empire* (Cambridge, Mass., 1993).

39. See A. Lenox-Conyngham, "Juristic and Religious Aspects of the Basilica Conflict of A.D. 386," *Studia Patristica* 18 (Kalamazoo, Mich., 1985), I, 55–58; D. H. Williams, "Ambrose, Emperors and Homoians in Milan: The First Conflict over a Basilica," in Barnes and Williams, *Arianism after Arius*, 127–146; and N. McLynn, *Ambrose of Milan: Church and Court in a Christian Capital* (Berkeley, 1994), 187–196.

40. E. Gibbon, *Decline and Fall of the Roman Empire* (New York, 1932) 1:682.

41. See, e.g., A. Meredith, "Orthodoxy, Heresy and Philosophy in the Latter Half of the Fourth Century," *Heythrop Journal* 16 (1975): 5–21; essays in G. Vesey, ed., *The Philosophy in Christianity* (Cambridge, Eng., 1989); and the fine survey in C. Stead, *Philosophy in Christian Antiquity* (Cambridge, Eng., 1994).

42. In Basil's *Hexaemeron* and Augustine's *De Genesi contra Manichaeos*. See Lim, "The Politics of Interpretation in Basil of Caesarea's *Hexaemeron*," *Vigiliae Christianae* 44 (1990): 351–370. Arian Christians, sternly opposed by Basil and Augustine (both of whom had once rejected allegory), also opposed allegories in favor of literal readings that legitimated their subordination of the Son to the Father (their attachment to literalism was such that they even accused their Nicene opponents of introducing nonscriptural terms such as *ousia* and *hypostasis*). See T. E. Pollard, "The Exegesis of Scripture and the Arian Controversy," *The Bulletin of the John Rylands Library* 41 (1989): 289–291.

43. A. H. Armstrong, "Pagan and Christian Traditionalism in the First Three Centuries, A.D.," *Studia Patristica* 15 (Berlin, 1957), 414–431.

44. J. de Ghellinck, "Quelques appréciations de la dialectique d'Aristote durant les conflits trinitaires du IVe siècle," *Revue d'Histoire Ecclesiastique* 26 (1930): 5–42; on scriptural traditionalism, see A. H. Armstrong, "Pagan and Christian Traditionalism in the First Three Centuries, A.D.," *Studia Patristica* 15 (Berlin, 1957), 414–431.

45. See R. P. C. Hanson, *The Search for the Christian Doctrine of God: The Arian Controversy 318–381* (Edinburgh, 1988), 594–636; Lim, *Public Disputation*, 109–148.

46. See L. R. Wickham, "The *Syntagmation* of Aetius the Anomean," *Journal of Theological Studies* n.s. 19 (1968): 532–569.

47. M. Wiles, "Eunomius: Hair-Splitting Dialectician or Defender of the Accessibility of Salvation?" in R. Williams, ed., *The Making of Orthodoxy: Essays in Honour of Henry Chadwick* (Cambridge, Eng., 1989), 157–172.

48. See Lim, "Religious Disputation," 204–231, esp. 222–228.

49. Basil of Caesarea, *Ep.* 234–235; and Gregory of Nyssa, *De deitate filii et spiritus sancti* (PG 46.557).

50. E.g., Gregory of Nazianzus, *Or.* 27.2.

51. Sozomen, *Hist.eccl.* 4.18.

52. On this issue, see Averil Cameron, "Texts as Weapons: Polemic in the Byzantine Dark Ages," in A. Bowman and G. Woolf, eds., *Literacy and Power in the Ancient World* (Cambridge, Eng., 1994), 198–215; and Lim, *Public Disputation*, 165–166. See also J. A. Munitz, "Catechetical Teaching-Aids in Byzantium," in J. Chrysostomides, ed., *Kathegetria: Essays Presented to Joan Hussey on Her 80th Birthday* (Camberley, 1988), 78ff.

53. Gregory of Nazianzus, *Or.* 29.21.

54. A. D. Kartsonis, *Anastasis: The Making of an Icon* (Princeton, 1986), 40–67.

55. R. P. Vaggione, "Of Monks and Lounge Lizards: 'Arians', Polemics, and Asceticism in the Roman East," in Barnes and Williams, *Arianism after Arius,* 181–214; and Lim, *Public Disputation,* 144–149, 182–216.

56. See *Vita Danielis* 90.

57. See E. Jugie, "La dispute des philosophes païens avec les pères de Nicée," *Échos d'Orient* 24 (1925): 403–410; and Lim, *Public Disputation,* 182–216.

58. Skill in debate was not a monopoly of Arians; see *Altercatio Heracliani,* in C. P. Caspari, ed., *Kirchenhistorische anecdota nebst neuen Ausgaben patristischer und kirchlichmittelalterlicher Schriften* (Christiania, 1883), 1:133–147.

59. M. Richard, "Notes sur les florilèges dogmatiques du Ve et du VIe siècle," in *Actes du VIe Congrès Internationale d'Études Byzantines* (Brussels, 1950), 1:307–318.

60. See J. Taylor, "The First Council of Constantinople (381)," *Prudentia* 13 (1981): 47–54, 91–97.

61. *Acta Oecumenicorum Conciliorum* I.1.1, 18 (Schwartz, ed., 101).

62. See A. de Halleux, "La réception du symbole oecuménique, de Nicée à Chalcédoine," *Ephemerides Theologicae Lovanienses* 61 (1985): 5–47.

63. On increasingly exact definitions of orthodoxy, see *C.Th.* 16.5.14 (388) on the targeting of Nicene Apollinarians who opposed Cappadocian Christology.

64. Gregory of Nyssa, *Contra Eunomium* 1.683 (Jaeger, ed., 1:222).

65. See Lim, *Public Disputation,* 149–181.

66. Corpus of Pseudo-Dionysius: *PG* 3, 119–1064; see also R. Roques, *L'univers dionysien: Structure hiérarchique du monde selon le pseudo-Denys* (Paris, 1954).

67. Lim, *Public Disputation,* 175–177.

68. H.-I. Marrou and J. Daniélou, *The Christian Century I: The First Six Hundred Years,* trans. V. Cronin (London, 1964), 234.

69. W. H. C. Frend, *The Rise of the Monophysite Movement: Chapters in the History of the Church in the Fifth and Sixth Centuries* (Cambridge, Eng., 1972), 141: "The Chalcedonian crisis was not only a crisis of the intellectuals. It was a crisis involving the totality of Christians in the eastern Mediterranean. This marks it off from the Arian controversy a century before for the latter was primarily a crisis of bishops. Throughout the Monophysite dispute, the key role was always to belong to the monks." Frend's characterization of the elite nature of the Arian controversy is now increasingly under challenge.

70. W. H. C. Frend, "Athanasius as an Egyptian Christian Leader in the Fourth Century," *New College Bulletin* 8 (1974): 30–27; reprinted in Frend, *Religion Popular and Unpopular in the Early Christian Centuries* (London, 1976).

71. Socrates, *Hist.eccl.* 6.8.

72. Frend, *Rise of the Monophysite Movement,* 137.

73. H. J. Carpenter, "Popular Christianity and the Theologians in the Early Centuries," *Journal of Theological Studies* n.s. 14 (1963): 294–310.

74. E. L. Woodward, *Christianity and Nationalism in the Later Roman Empire* (London, 1916); W. H. C. Frend, *The Donatist Church* (Oxford, 1952); J. P. Brisson, *Autonomisme et christianisme dans l'Afrique romaine* (Paris, 1958); A. H. M. Jones, "Were the Ancient Heresies National or Social Movements in Disguise?" *Journal of Theological Studies* n.s. 10 (1959): 280–295; W. H. C. Frend, "Heresy and Schism as Social and National Movements," in D. Baker, ed., *Schism, Heresy and Religious Protest* (Cambridge, Eng., 1972), 37–56. See survey of these approaches by R. A. Markus, "Christianity and Dissent in Roman North Africa: Changing Perspectives in Recent Work," in Baker, ed., *Schism, Heresy and Religious Protest,* 21–36.

75. S. H. Bacht, "Die Rolle des orientalischen Mönchtums in den Kirchenpolitischen Auseinandersetzungen um Chalkedon (432–519)," in A. Grillmeier and H. Bacht, eds., *Das Konzil von Chalkedon* (Würzburg, 1953), 2:193–314. On the effects of having

monks living near cities, see G. Dagron, "Les moines et la ville: Le monachisme urbain à Constantinople," *Travaux et Mémoires* 4 (1970): 229–276.

76. *C.Th.* 16.2.42–43.

77. T. Gregory, *Vox Populi: Popular Opinion and Violence in the Religious Controversies of the Fifth Century* (Columbus, Oh., 1979); R. MacMullen, "The Historical Role of the Masses in Late Antiquity," in MacMullen, *Changes in the Roman Empire: Essays in the Ordinary* (Princeton, 1990), 25–76, 384–393; and N. McLynn, "Christian Controversy and Violence in the Fourth Century," *Kodai* 3 (Tokyo, 1992), 15–44.

78. P. Batiffol, "Les présents de saint Cyrille à la cour de Constantinople," in *Etudes de liturgue et d'archéologie chrétienne* (Paris, 1919), 159–173; and Brown, *Power and Persuasion,* 15–17.

79. On the Monophysite rejection of Chalcedon, see Michael the Syrian, *Chron.* 9.26. On the liturgical celebration of select councils, see S. Salaville, "La fête du concile de Nicée et les fêtes de conciles dans le rite byzantin," *Echos d'Orient* 24 (1925): 445–470, and "La fête du concile de Chalcédoine dans le rite byzantin," in Grillmeier and Bacht, *Das Konzil von Chalkedon,* 2:677–695.

80. *C.Just.* 1.1.4 (Krueger, ed., *Corpus Iuris Civilis,* II, 6).

81. See, e.g., V. Déroche, *Etudes sur Léontios de Néapolis* (Uppsala, 1995), 270–296; see also 226–269 on the miracle as a consensual symbol of holiness.

82. *C.Th.* 16.1.2 (= *Cunctos populos,* 380); 16.1.3 (= *Episcopis tradi,* 381).

83. N. Q. King, *The Emperor Theodosius and the Establishment of Christianity* (London, 1961); T. D. Barnes, "Religion and Society in the Age of Theodosius," in H. A. Meynell, ed., *Grace, Politics and Desire: Essays on Augustine* (Calgary, 1990), 157–160.

84. *C.Th.* 16.10.11–12 (391–392). G. Fowden, "Bishops and Temples in the Eastern Roman Empire, A.D. 320–425," *Journal of Theological Studies* n.s. 29 (1978): 62–69.

85. Lim, *Public Disputation,* 103–108.

86. Brown, "St Augustine's Attitude to Religious Coercion," *Journal of Roman Studies* 65 (1964): 107–116; J. Vanderspoel, "The Background to Augustine's Denial of Religious Plurality," in Meynell, *Grace, Politics and Desire,* 179–193. On pagan reactions, see F. Paschoud, "L'intolérance chrétienne vue et jugée par les païens," *Cristianesimo nella storia* 11 (1990): 545–577.

87. Brown, "Religious Coercion in the Later Roman Empire: The Case of North Africa," *History* 48 (1963): 283–305; and B. Shaw, "African Christianity: Disputes, Definitions and 'Donatists,'" in M. R. Greenshields and T. A. Robinson, eds., *Orthodoxy and Heresy in Religious Movements: Discipline and Dissent* (Lewinston, Queenston, Lampeter, 1992), 5–34. See Augustine's new sermons, in F. Dolbeau, "Nouveaux sermons de S. Augustin sur la conversion des païens et des Donatistes," *Revue des études Augustiniennes* 37 (1991): 37–78 and *Recherches Augustiniennes* 26 (1992): 69–141.

88. On moral categorization, see L. Jayussi, *Categorization and the Moral Order* (Boston and London, 1984).

89. A. Le Boulluec, *La notion d'hérésie dans la littérature grecque (IIe–IIIe siècles* (Paris, 1985); and R. Lyman, "A Topography of Heresy: Mapping the Rhetorical Creation of Arianism," in Barnes and Williams, *Arianism after Arius,* 45–62.

90. Peter Brown, "The Patrons of Pelagius: The Roman Aristocracy between East and West," *Journal of Theological Studies* n.s. 21 (1970): 56–72; E. Clark, *The Origenist Controversy: The Cultural Construction of an Early Christian Debate* (Princeton, 1992); H. O. Maier, "Private Space as the Social Context of Arianism in Ambrose's Milan," *Journal of Theological Studies* n.s. 45 (1994): 72–93, and "The Topography of Heresy and Dissent in Late Fourth-Century Rome," *Historia* 44 (1995): 232–249.

91. Mark the Deacon, *Life of Porphyry of Gaza,* 85–91, in H. Grégoire and M.-A. Kugener, *Marc le diacre: Vie de Porphyre évêque de Gaza* (Paris, 1930), 66–71; and Augustine, *Contra Felicem* (in CSEL 25).

92. Lim, *Public Disputation,* 93–102.

93. Brown, *Authority and the Sacred: Aspects of the Christianization of the Roman World* (Cambridge, Eng., 1995), 29–54.

94. See Cyril of Scythopolis, *Vita Sabae* 72 on the religious aspects of the reconquest.

95. J. Herrin, *The Formation of Christendom* (Princeton, 1987; rev. ed., 1989), 228–229.

96. Isidore of Seville, *Historia de regibus Gothorum, Vandalorum et Suevorum* 52–53 (on the Council of Toledo), 60 (on the conversion of Jews).

97. See Herrin, *Formation of Christendom,* 90–127, 250–290.

98. See Meyendorff, *Imperial Unity,* 336–380.

99. *Acta Oecumenicorum Conciliorum* II.1 (= R. Riedinger, ed., *Concilium Lateranense a. 649 celebratum,* Berlin and New York, 1974), 2–29 (the proceedings according to the *primus secretarius*), 425–436 (the *florilegium* = *Codex Vaticanus Graecus* 1455, fol. 165r–176r).

100. *C.Th.* 16.5.66 (435).

101. On the school of Nisibis, see J.-B. Chabot, "L'école de Nisibis, son histoire, ses statuts," *Journal Asiatique* 9 (1896): 43–93; A. Vööbus, *Statutes of the School of Nisibis* (Stockholm, 1961/62), and *History of the School of Nisibis,* CSCO 266 (Louvain, 1965).

102. On Christian synods in Persia, see J.-B. Chabot, ed., *Synodicon orientale ou recueil de synodes nestoriens* (Paris, 1902).

103. Fundamental studies include J. Wellhausen, *Die religiös-politischen Oppositionsparteien im alten Islam* (Berlin, 1901); T. Nagel, "Das Problem der Orthodoxie im frühen Islam," *Studien zum Minderheitenproblem im Islam* (Bonn, 1973), 1:7–44; M. Cook, *Early Muslim Dogma* (Cambridge, Eng., 1981); and J. van Ess, *Theologie und Gesellschaft im 2. und 3. Jahrhundert Hidschra: Eine Geschichte des religiösen Denkens im frühen Islam* (Berlin, 1991–1992), vols. 1–2. W. M. Watt, *The Formative Period of Islamic Thought* (Edinburgh, 1973), provides an accessible introduction to the subject.

104. See M. Tardieu, "Sābiens coraniques et 'Sābiens' de Harrān," *Journal Asiatique* 274 (1986): 1–44.

105. W. Madelung, "The Origins of the Controversy concerning the Creation of the Koran," in J. M. Barral, ed., *Orientalia Hispanica sive Studia F.M. Pareja octogenario dicata* (Leiden, 1974), 1:504–525 = *Religious Schools and Sects in Medieval Islam* (London, 1985), V.

106. K. Lewinstein, "The Azâriqa in Islamic Heresiography," *Bulletin of the School of Oriental and African Studies* 44 (1991): 251–268.

107. See G. Vajda, "Les *zindiq*s en pays d'Islam au début de la période abbaside," *Rivista degli studi orientali* 17 (1937–38): 173–229; Van Ess, *Theologie und Gesellschaft,* 1:136–137, 416–458, 2:4–41; and S. Shaked, *Dualism in Transformation: Varieties of Religions in Sasanian Iran* (London, 1994), 58–59: Manichaeans were called *zindiq*s *(zanadaqa)* because of their "twisted" exegesis of the Avesta *(Zand).*

108. Madelung, "Imāmism and Muʿtazilite Theology," in T. Fahd, ed., *Le Shīʿism imāmite* (Paris, 1979), 13–29 = *Religious Schools,* VII.

Islam

Hugh Kennedy

Of all the dividing lines set up between academic disciplines in the western intellectual tradition, the frontier between classical and Islamic studies has proved among the most durable and impenetrable. Great monuments of scholarship like A. H. M. Jones's *Later Roman Empire* and the *New Cambridge Ancient History* take it as axiomatic that the coming of Islam in the early 7th century marked a change so complete that there was no advantage in pursuing the topics that had been discussed into the new era. To a certain extent this is simply a result of linguistic difficulties—the coming of a new language of high culture and historiography (Arabic) meant that the source material was simply incomprehensible—but it is also cultural in a broader sense: whereas late antiquity can be seen as part of the broader history of western civilization, the history of the Islamic world cannot. Yet reflection will soon suggest that the changes cannot have been so sudden and dramatic, especially at the level of the structures of everyday life, and that the Islamic was as much, and as little, a continuation of late antiquity as was western Christendom.

It would be easy to see late antiquity as a unit in the history of the Near East and to see broad continuities from the 4th century to the beginning of the 7th century. The development of a Greek-Christian high government and culture would support this. Yet more than three centuries elapsed between the adoption of Christianity as the official religion and the coming of Islam, and in this period the structures of everyday life continued to evolve and develop. Insofar as the Muslims were the heirs of late antiquity, they inherited the world of Heraclius, not of Constantine; the cities and villages they came to rule were those of the early 7th, not the 4th century; and comparisons which look back from the formation of the early Islamic world to a homogenous late antiquity can be either unhelpful or actually misleading.

To examine these issues, I have chosen to concentrate on greater Syria, the lands the Arabs call Bilad al-Sham—that is to say, the lands of the eastern

Mediterranean from Antioch in the north to Gaza in the south and their hinterlands. There are good reasons for choosing this area. The literary and archaeological evidence allows us to form a fuller impression of what the end of antiquity and the coming of Islam entailed than in any other area of the empire and this wealth of evidence provides a much more nuanced picture than we can find in Egypt or North Africa.[1] The changes which took place in this area between the 6th and the 8th centuries affected all aspects of society. In this essay I will discuss ethnic change, political and administrative change, religious change, and change in the patterns of settlement and the built environment.

The Muslim conquest of the Near Eastern lands of the Byzantine empire was neither particularly violent nor particularly destructive. That does not mean, of course, that there was not bloodshed and disruption: the Byzantine armies were defeated, cities like Damascus and Caesarea were taken by siege and storm, refugees were driven from their homes, and some clerics were forced to flee to Constantinople or even Rome. However, compared with later invasions, like those of the Crusaders or the Mongols, or even of the Persian invasions which immediately preceded the coming of Islam, neither the literary sources (such as they are) nor the archaeological records show evidence of extensive destruction. The Muslims came not as a *Volkswanderung*, nor as tribes migrating with their families and their beasts, but rather as organized armies with commanders and strategic objectives. The Muslim conquest was a stage in the long-term penetration of Arabic-speaking peoples into the Near East which seems to have begun in about 200 C.E. and continued to the 10th and 11th centuries. Certainly the Muslim conquest, bringing as it did a new religion and a new language of high culture, marks an important stage in this process—but a stage nonetheless.

The early Islamic state in Syria may have been the heir of late antiquity but it also inherited from the *jāhilīya,* the world of pre-Islamic tribal Arabia with its cult of poetry and warrior heroes and fierce loyalty to tribe and kin. This heritage was temporarily eclipsed by the coming of Islam, which rejected its values, but was rediscovered and to an extent reinvented in the first century after the Prophet's death. In the 8th century the collection of poems and stories relating to the *ayyam,* the "days" or battles of the pre-Islamic tribes, were studied with almost as much love and veneration as the traditions of the Prophet himself, and the world of the pagan Arabian nomad became as integral to the history of Islam as the works of classical pagan authors did to the Christian intellectual tradition.

Many of the early Muslim conquerors of the Near East were not nomads at all but came from the settled fertile areas of highland Yemen, from a world of stone-built towns and carefully terraced mountainsides. The Muslims who first settled in Egypt and Spain largely came from tribes like the Khawlan, Madhhij, Ma'afir, and Hadramawt, long settled in south Arabia. The people of this area were used to irrigation culture and had produced, in the Marib dam, one of the most impressive hydraulic works of the ancient world. They also had a political tradition of powerful monarchy, and memories of the lords of Himyar and Dhu Raydan who had ruled as kings when the ancestors of the Umayyad caliphs were no more than shepherds and peddlers.

Closer to Syria itself had been the pre-Islamic kings on the desert margin of the crescent: the Lakhmids of Hira in southern Iraq, who had guarded the lands of the Sassanian kings, and the Ghassanids, who had performed the same service for the Byzantines. Around both these courts, a Christian Arabic culture had developed, a world of palaces, hunting, and poetry. Though the political independence of both groups had ended in the late 6th century, the memory of their rule and their style persisted in literature and tales and was probably a potent source of inspiration for Umayyad court life.

It was the monarchy of Sassanian Persia, however, which provided the most pervasive of the legacies to the Islamic world.[2] Here again there was an ancient cultural tradition, a memory of kings like Khosro and heroes like Rustam whose more or less mythical stories were to provide material for poets and painters for centuries. There was also a more practical legacy of political and administrative structures and theories of statecraft from the well-remembered Sassanian monarchy of the 6th and early 7th centuries, not to speak of the presence of administrators who had actually worked for the old kings. These competing influences diluted the culture of late antiquity, but it still remained important, especially in Syria and Egypt, which had been so thoroughly Hellenized.

Although the Muslim conquests swept away the superstructure of Byzantine power, the emperor and the governors he had appointed, the early Muslims took on much of the lower-level Byzantine administrative practice. The provincial boundaries of the Byzantine empire largely disappeared, to be replaced by a system of *jund*s (military provinces) based on the need to supply troops. Attempts to discover the origins of these *jund*s in the nascent *theme* system of the Byzantine empire have not met with favor but the logic behind the new Muslim divisions remains obscure.[3] Each of the new divisions stretched from the seacoast on the west to the desert in the east, and the Arab population had different tribal and regional origins. From the beginning, the Muslims recognized two major administrative areas, Syria (al-Sham) and Palestine (Falastin), which were in turn subdivided. Instead of two Syria provinces based on Antioch and Apamea, two Phoenicias based on Tyre and Damascus, three Palestines based on Caesarea, Scythopolis and Petra, and the Provincia Arabia with its metropolis at Bostra there were now *jund*s of Palestine, Jordan (Urdunn), Damascus, Homs (Emesa), and Qinnasrin (Chalcis). While the *jund* of Qinnasrin covered some of the same territory as Syria I and Homs the same as Syria II, the frontiers were significantly different. Farther south, Damascus, Tiberias, and from the early 8th century Ramla were the new provincial capitals.[4] Most of this area had been conquered by the Persians in the first decade of the 7th century and restored to Byzantine rule only in 628, less than ten years before the Muslim conquest. It is likely that the old Byzantine administrative divisions had not been fully reestablished and that the Muslims were working with a *tabula rasa* when it came to local boundaries.

If the boundaries had been eroded or had disappeared, there were still people who had operated the late antique administrative systems who were in a position to help the newly arrived Muslim rulers make the best use of the resources of their new-won lands. Until the reign of 'Abd al-Malik (685–705) Greek remained the language of administration. We know this not just from references in the Arabic chronicles but also from the evidence of papyri from Egypt and Nessana in the Negev, where we can see this early Islamic, Greek-using administration in action.[5] It seems as if even the *diwan,* which recorded the names of the Muslim soldiers and their entitlement to stipends, was sometimes compiled in Greek.[6]

The use of Greek in the administration meant that knowledge of the language continued to be a valuable skill; throughout the 7th century and into the 8th a Greek culture continued to thrive in Palestine and Syria, perhaps more vigorously than in Constantinople itself. The most important figure in this culture was of course St. John of Damascus (d. ca. 754), who came from an Arab family with a tradition of working in the Byzantine administration and whose name before he entered the church was Mansur. He had worked for the Byzantine administration before taking service with the Umayyads. Despite working for a Muslim court he retained the faith of his ancestors and his defense of the use of icons in Christian worship was perhaps the most important contribution to Greek theology in the 7th and 8th centuries. When Greek ceased to be an official language, Greek education withered, as it was no longer a qualification for a lucrative career, and became confined to a few monasteries. By the 9th century, Christian intellectuals like Theodore Abu Qurra (ca. 740–ca. 820) and the historian Agapius of Manbij (d. ca. 950) were writing in Arabic even when discussing questions of theology and Christian doctrine.[7]

Early Islamic administration may have inherited the language and some of the forms of late antique government but it put them to rather different use. The Muslims came with their own ideas about administration and taxation and they felt no need to look to late Roman models. These ideas were certainly only half-formed in the early days, but it must not be forgotten that the Prophet was the ruler of a small state as well as the Messenger of Allah and that even this small state had developed a rudimentary fiscal structure. The Muslims may have not had a fully worked-out taxation system but they did have an ideology of taxation; reference to late antique practice carried no weight to devotees of the new religion.

In reality, the Muslims probably borrowed more from late antiquity in this area than they normally admitted. The fiscal system developed in Medina in the time of the Prophet was based on booty from war, the taxes paid by the protected non-Muslims *(dhimmī)* and the tithe *('ushr)* that richer Muslims were enjoined to pay for the support of widows, orphans, and Muslims in need. In both the Byzantine and Sassanian empires, the main source of revenue was the land-tax paid on all cultivated property. At first the Muslims took this over for their own purposes and obliged non-Muslims to pay it to them. As the pace of conversion increased, however, an ever higher proportion of the population claimed immunity. By the end of the 8th century Muslim rulers demanded the land-tax, now generally known as the *kharaj,* of almost all landowners, very much as it had been in the great empires of antiquity.[8]

In most preindustrial states, the proceeds of taxation were largely used to support the ruler and the military and elite elements who sustained his power. The Byzantine empire in late antiquity and the early caliphate both shared this common characteristic, but there were significant differences. In late antiquity, Syria was a provincial area, a rich and culturally significant area certainly, but it did not support an independent court and bureaucracy. Although we have no figures, it must be assumed that a considerable proportion of the taxes raised in Syria were exported to Constantinople. While emperors and the imperial government could and did spend money on ecclesiastical and military buildings in the province, we would probably be correct to assume that Syria was a net exporter of wealth.

In the earliest phases of Islamic rule Syria remained a province of a larger empire, but in the chaotic conditions of the years immediately after the conquests it is unlikely that much revenue was exported from Syria to the Muslim government in Medina. After the Umayyad Muʿāwiyya ibn Abi-Sufyān became governor in 639 it is probable that the revenues of Syria were spent in the province itself. The seizure of the caliphate by Muʿāwiyya in 661 changed the province's position yet again and Syria now become the capital of an empire which stretched from the Atlantic to Central Asia and the Indus valley. In its early phases, the administration of this empire was very decentralized and most of the revenue raised in the various provinces was distributed to the Muslim conquerors and their descendants in the province without ever having been sent to the capital.

Successive Umayyad caliphs attempted to break down this fiscal autonomy and secure at least a proportion of the tax revenues for the caliph. The leading figures in this policy of centralization were ʿAbd al-Malik and Hishām (721–743). They encountered stiff and sometimes violent opposition, but the evidence suggests that they did secure a share of the revenues of the rest of the caliphate. For the first and only time in its millennial history, Syria became the center of a widespread empire; the wealth which flowed into the country is reflected in great prestige building projects like the Umayyad mosque in Damascus and the development of the Dome of the Rock and the Aqsa mosque in Jerusalem. Nothing on this scale was ever attempted in the later Islamic history of Syria, and it is striking testimony to the importance of its imperial role that the two major Muslim monuments of Syria and Palestine were built within twenty years at the end of the 7th century and the beginning of the 8th.

The Muslim conquerors brought with them the outlines of a new system of rewards for the military which owed nothing to Byzantine models. The Byzantine army had been paid out of tax revenue by the imperial treasury. Until the middle of the 6th century, the frontiers had been defended by *limitanei,* who were assigned lands in exchange of their military services. This system seems to have been abolished, or simply fallen into disuse under Justinian (527–561). Maintaining the security of the desert frontier was now the responsibility of the

Ghassanid phylarchs, Arab leaders who acted as intermediaries between the Bedouin tribes and the Byzantine authorities. The Persian and Muslim invasions marked the end of the late antique military system in the Byzantine empire as well as in the Muslim world. It is true that the Byzantines did still have paid soldiers based in Constantinople, but the reduced resources of the battered empire could no longer sustain a regular salaried army in the provinces. Instead the land was divided into *themes* and peasant soldiers were enrolled to defend their native soil against outside attack. In many rural areas, the slide to a nonmonetary economy meant that there was no longer any paid army in the area.

The Muslim military finance system owed nothing to late antique models and was a direct product of the settlement which followed the initial Muslim conquests.[9] The early stages of this development are difficult to recreate but its beneficiaries ascribed it to the decisions of the caliph 'Umar ibn al-Khaṭṭāb (634–644), thus elevating it above criticism and change. According to this traditional story, 'Umar had decreed that the victorious Muslims should not disperse through the conquered lands, settling as proprietors or farmers, but should establish Muslim cities known as *amṣār* (singular *miṣr)*. The revenues from the subject people would be collected and distributed to the Muslims as ata' (salaries) and *rizq* (supplies). In this way the Muslims would remain a small elite "tax-eating" caste and so retain their religion and culture.

In Iraq, Kufa and Basra became the main centers of Muslim habitation; in Egypt it was Fustat or Old Cairo; and in Ifriqiya (Tunisia), Qayrawan was founded as the local *miṣr*. In Syria too a *miṣr* was founded at Jabiya in the Golan Heights, but the Muslim conquerors never settled in it in large numbers and were instead dispersed through the ancient cities, notably Damascus, Homs, and Qinnasrin. Why this should have happened in Syria is not clear but it may have been a result of the Arabization of the population before the coming of Islam. Many of the Muslim conquerors came, in fact, from tribes already resident in Syria or its frontier districts, like the Kalb of the Palmyrena or the Lakhm and Judham of southern Palestine. It was inconceivable that they should reside as outsiders, isolated from the local population of which they were in a sense part and with which they had well-established links.

Nonetheless in Syria, as elsewhere in the Muslim world, the pattern of a caste of conquerors paid from local revenues was the ideal if not the practice. Soon, however, this system came under increasing strain and pressure, even in those areas where it was well established. The problems stemmed ultimately from the fact that membership of the *diwan*, the register of the names of the tax-eaters, was hereditary. Furthermore, salaries varied greatly according to the *sabiqa* or precedence in Islam of the family concerned; early converts and their descendants were highly paid whereas late arrivals to the Muslim fold were at the bottom of the scale. This may have been acceptable in the first generation when men were rewarded for their own faith and commitment, but as the conquerors died off and their privileges were inherited by their sons and grandsons, it caused increasing resentment.

The system could function only as long as the Muslims were a small minority and there was no provision for new, post-conquest converts to enter the *diwan*. As conversion gathered pace, the pressure from those outside the system increased until it became irresistible. At the same time, the hereditary militia whose names did appear on the *diwan* became increasingly militarily ineffective. Like 18th century janissaries in the Ottoman empire, they rarely took up arms except in defense of their own privileges and even then they were not especially successful. As a military force for policing and defending the empire, they were virtually useless.

Unable to rely on this cumbersome and inflexible system, the Umayyad and early Abbasid rulers tried to step outside it. The later Umayyads recruited troops from the Bedouin tribes of the Syria desert, whether or not their ancestors had fought in the original conquests, and set about finding resources to pay them. The Abbasids, unable to draw on the Syrian tribes who had supported their rivals, looked outside the Muslim world entirely and began to employ Turkish mercenaries and slaves, recruited in Central Asia.

By the reign of the caliph al-Mu'tasim (833–842), the old *diwan* system had broken down almost entirely. The hereditary Muslim militia had been replaced by a professional army paid from the land-tax *kharaj* imposed on Muslim and non-Muslim alike (though, of course, non-Muslims were still obliged to pay the *jizya* or poll tax). In a curious way the raising of taxes and armies had come full circle; the Muslim rulers of the 9th century operated a system broadly similar to that of their Byzantine and Sassanian predecessors in late antiquity.

Nor was this similarity entirely unconscious. Muslim rulers and, even more, their bureaucrats knew that they were following pre-Islamic models of statecraft and they became proud of it. However, the legacy they looked to was not Byzantine but Sassanian.[10] This was partly because many of the bureaucrats were themselves of Persian origin, although in Umayyad and even in Abbasid times considerable numbers of Syrians were still employed in the bureaucracy. The Byzantine empire still existed, of course, and it was perhaps controversial for any Muslim ruler to admit that he was following the practices of the ancient enemy. The Sassanians, however, posed no such threat and their memories could be called on to sanction present practice. "Anushirvan the Just" (largely based on Khosro I Anushirvan, 531–579) was the figure to whom Muslim rulers felt able to appeal to legitimize their practice. Indeed it would be possible to argue that Khosro I and Muhammad shared the honor of being the two great begetters of Muslim statecraft. But we may perhaps see, lurking in the shadows, the image of the Roman empire of late antiquity from which, it can be suggested, Khosro himself received his political education.

The end of late antiquity meant the coming of a new religion of government and power. The Byzantine empire was fiercely Christian, so loyalty to religion could have consolidated resistance to the invaders even if ties of blood and language drew many Syrians to the new Muslim arrivals. In the event things were not as simple as this: the Christians were not as homogenous nor the new religion as clear-cut and aggressive as might have been imagined. By the end of antiquity, it is likely that the vast majority of the population of Syria were either Christians or Jews. Paganism had continued to flourish well into the 5th century and classical mythology was familiar to the designers of mosaic floors even in quite remote rural areas like the Hawran; a few pockets, notably the Sabaeans of Harran (Carrhae), maintained their ancient beliefs into the Islamic period.[11] The triumph of Christianity did not, however, mean that religious conflict had disappeared.

Relations between Jewish communities and the Byzantine authorities were marked by periods of persecution by the government and unrest among the Jews. In 556 an uprising of Jews and Samaritans resulted in the death of the governor of Caesarea, but the accusations that the Jews supported the Persian attack on Jerusalem in 614 probably owe more to the imagination of later Christian apologists, seeking to explain away the successes of Persian and Muslim conquerors, than to contemporary historical fact. There were also violent Samaritan revolts in 484 and in 529, when Scythopolis, the capital of Palestine II, was sacked. There is no doubt that Jews and Samaritans were second-class citizens in late antiquity and that, from time to time, decrees were issued that they should be converted to Christianity. Archaeological evidence, however, suggests that the fearsome legislation was not enforced with any vigor and that many Jewish populations, especially in Galilee, shared in the general prosperity of late antiquity.[12]

The Jews remained second-class citizens after the Muslim conquest, being classed as *dhimmīs* or protected people.[13] The great difference, however, was that they were no longer alone: the Christians too were now *dhimmīs*; indeed, *dhimmīs* formed the overwhelming mass of the population. The Muslim conquest certainly did not bring the two communities together in adversity, and Christian-Jewish controversy and polemic continued to be as shrill as ever, but the Jews were no longer the targets of legislation directed solely at them. We cannot be certain whether the poll tax demanded by the Muslims was more or less than the taxes required by the Byzantines, but we do not hear of large-scale Jewish unrest. In some ways the situation of the Jews did improve: though Tiberias still remained the most important Jewish city, Jews were allowed once more to settle in Jerusalem itself, though the bulk of the population of the Holy City remained Christian.

The Christian church was far from united in late antiquity. Syria was the scene of a fierce and prolonged struggle between the Monophysites and the Dyophysites.[14] The dispute centered on the nature of the incarnation, the Dyophysites maintaining that Christ had two distinct and complete natures, one human and one divine. The Monophysites regarded this as blasphemy and claimed that Christ had a single, divine nature and only took on the appearance of humanity. This apparently technical dispute went to the heart of Christian belief and aroused violent passions, each sect regarding its opponents as the vilest of heretics. These theological differences were compounded by cultural conflicts. Though there were important exceptions, the Dyophysites were mostly to be found among the Greek-speaking inhabitants of the towns and coastal areas, the Monophysites among the Syriac-speaking populations of the inland rural areas: the Monophysites were strongest in the north of Syria, while Palestine was almost entirely Dyophysite.

The broad outlines of the dispute had developed during and after the church council at Chalcedon in 541, which had adopted a Dyophysite position (hence the Dyophysites were often known as Chalcedonians), but the dispute did not become a real schism until the 6th century. Emperor Justinian tried to enforce Chalcedonian uniformity and this led militant Monophysites like Jacob Bar 'Adai (Baradaeus) to break away and after 536 to set up an alternative church with a parallel hierarchy. This church is often referred to as Jacobite. Despite attempts to reach a compromise in the second half of the 6th and early 7th centuries, the church in Syria was painfully divided and many Syrian Christians were alienated from the official church. There is no evidence that the Monophysites were disloyal to the empire in the face of Persian and Muslim attacks. They wanted an empire which was Christian and, as they saw it, orthodox, but their disaffection with the empire may account for the lack of popular resistance to the Muslim conquest in many areas.

The coming of Islam radically affected the status of the Christian churches.[15] The Chalcedonian church, from being the religion of the elite, became simply another sect among several and the links with the emperor, which had ensured its success in earlier days, now became an embarrassment rather than a help.[16] The conquests shattered the hierarchy; we do not even know if the patriarchates at Antioch and Jerusalem were filled during the later part of the 7th century. However, as long as Greek remained the language of administration, the Chalcedonian church still had wealthy patrons; there is archaeological evidence that new churches continued to be built in the Umayyad period. From the mid 8th century, the Christians' position became more precarious and the general insecurity and impoverishment of Syria from 750 onward caused increasing problems.

In these circumstances, the Chalcedonian church reinvented itself. Whether intentionally or not, it was cut off from Constantinople and the Greek heritage. The liturgical language changed to Syriac and then to Arabic, which also became the language of Christian religious writing and polemic. Priests and bishops were recruited from the members of the local churches. This church, commonly referred to as the Melkite or Royal church (in memory of its ancient links with the Byzantine emperors), has survived to the present day, and, despite the constant attrition of converts to Islam, remains the most numerous of the Christian denominations of Syria.

The Muslim conquests significantly improved the status of the Jacobite church in the short term. For the first time in a century, the Jacobite patriarch of Antioch was able to reside in the city from which he took his title, and the Muslim authorities granted the Jacobites the same status as the Melkites, with the added advantage that their church was not tainted by association with the Byzantine enemy. The Jacobites were now free to preach and make converts, which had been forbidden under Byzantine rule. However, Syriac was never a language of government and the Jacobites seem to have been slower to adopt Arabic than their Melkite rivals. The church remained firmly entrenched in the villages of northern Syria and the areas of the Byzantine frontier but failed to achieve any ascendancy over its hated competitors.[17]

The most obvious feature of the Muslim conquest was that it brought a new elite religion; yet despite the military ascendancy of the Muslims the spread of the new religion was slower and more hesitant than might be imagined. Not only were many of the bureaucrats Christian but so were some of the Syrian Bedouin, like the leaders of the Kalb, who supported the Umayyads against their Muslim rivals. It is very difficult to assess the progress of conversion. Bulliet's model, which is based on statistics from Iranian biographical dictionaries of Muslim scholars, suggests that conversion in the first century and a half of Islam was very slow, and that it was not until the 10th century that the Muslim element in the population began to increase rapidly.[18] There is little if any evidence of forced conversion except among the Christian Bedouin, though churches and monasteries certainly did suffer in periods of general lawlessness, like the disorders and rebellions which followed the death of the caliph Hārūn al-Rashīd in 809.

The new religion needed high-status architecture to assert its identity against the surviving monumental architecture of Christianity. Almost miraculously, the two most important of these buildings have survived, with some alterations, down to the present day: the Dome of the Rock in Jerusalem and the Umayyad Mosque in Damascus.[19] The Dome of the Rock, constructed during the reign of the caliph 'Abd al-Malik (685–705), is a centrally planned, domed structure; it stands over the rock that projects in the middle of the great paved terrace which had once supported Herod's Temple and which the Muslims know as the Haram al-Sharif. The purpose of the building remains a subject of controversy. It was probably both a pilgrimage center and a conspicuous rival to the Christian Church of the Holy Sepulcher, whose dome could easily be seen across the narrow streets of the city. In both construction and decoration, it owed much to the late antique building traditions of Syria. The overall design has a number of precursors in the centrally planned churches of Christian architecture. The construction, with its thin walls, classical columns, and wooden roofing and dome, derives directly from the ecclesiastical architecture of the 5th and 6th centuries. The decoration, too, is heavily Byzantine in style, as is shown by the veined and patterned marble panels which decorate the lower parts of the walls and the glass mosaics on the drum of the dome. Only the absence of representations of the human figure and the Arabic dedicatory inscription reveal this building as a mosque.

The Umayyad mosque in Damascus, built by the caliph al-Walīd (705–715), stands on the site of the cathedral of St. John, which in turn stood within the *temenos* of the ancient temple of Haddad/Jupiter, whose origins go back to remotest antiquity. It is striking evidence of the continuity of cult centers that the Muslims decided to take over this ancient holy place. Unlike the Dome of the Rock, this is a congregational mosque, where the Muslims could gather in large numbers to worship together on Fridays. As well as being a religious center, it had a political function, for it was here that caliphs and governors could address the Muslims, and it soon acquired judicial functions, as the setting for the court of the Muslim judge *(qāḍī)* and as a center of Muslim education. In one direction, the design of the mosque looked back to the origins of Islam, for the first such mosque and community center had been the house of the Prophet himself in Medina, built, as it was, around a large courtyard where the Muslims could gather. Yet the mosque, with its open court and three-aisled prayer hall, also derived from the forum and the basilica of antiquity. Nowhere is this clearer than in Damascus, where the great rectangular court of the mosque still constitutes the only formal open space with the old city walls and whose architecture, despite the vicissitudes it has suffered, still reflects its origins in the antique townscape.

Mosques were of course built in most towns, but the great structures of the Dome of the Rock and the Umayyad mosque in Damascus give a somewhat misleading impression of the relative importance of these structures. The mosque at Jerash (Gerasa), a town of some prosperity in the Muslim Umayyad period, was little more than a large room with a *miḥrāb* in the shadow of the giant remains of antiquity and large numbers of Christian churches. In Subeita in the Negev, the mosque was a very modest hall fitted into a corner of the narthex of the splendid south church, more tentative than triumphant. In other cities, like Hims, the Muslims continued to share the main church with the Christians, as indeed they had done at Damascus until the time of al-Walīd.

Muslim government arrived in Syria with dramatic suddenness in the decade after 632, but the new religion was much slower to establish itself among the people. The decline of Christianity can be attributed to many causes. Among these were certainly the grinding burden of the poll tax, the fierce rivalries between Christian sects, often eager to appeal to the Muslim authorities for support against their hated opponents, and the tendency of ambitious figures in the Christian community to convert for career reasons. The Christian populations, being largely unarmed and unmilitarized, also suffered disproportionately from the impoverishment and Bedouinization of the country in the 9th and 10th centuries. Despite these problems, there were still important Christian populations, especially in northern Syria, at the coming of the crusaders in 1099, and the Christian society of late antiquity only gradually gave way to the Muslim society of the later Middle Ages.

The Islamic city conjures up visions of winding, narrow streets; crowded, bustling *sūq*s; calm and spacious mosques; and secluded houses, presenting only blank walls to the outside world but enclosing private courtyards where domesticity and even luxury flourish, unseen by the outside world.[20] How different such a city appears from the monumental city of antiquity. There we find broad, straight, colonnaded streets; open fora; magnificent temples, theaters, and baths; and, in general, an atmosphere of spacious, ordered elegance. Of course this is a simplistic view but it has achieved a certain scholarly respectability, and the Islamic city has been the object of considerable academic discussion. As in so many investigations into late antiquity and Islam, the true picture is much more complex and the differences much less clear-cut.[21] The Muslims did not inherit the classical city. No new theater had been constructed in Syria for four hundred years before the Muslims invaded, and the temples had been closed three centuries before al-Walīd ibn ʿAbd al-Malik began the construction of the Umayyad mosque in Damascus. Instead the Muslims inherited the cities of late antiquity, which had evolved significantly.

Two factors lay behind this evolution. The first was the prolonged period of civil war and disturbance in the mid 3rd century. This had brought to an end the great building boom of the 1st and 2nd centuries. When the emperors recovered their authority under Aurelian, Diocletian, and Constantine, the civic autonomy which had characterized and made possible the construction of the classical city had largely disappeared: city treasuries were confiscated, and the cities of Syria no longer minted the bronze coins which had advertised their individuality and status. The second major change was the coming of Christianity, which became the official religion in 313 with the Edict of Milan: by the end of the 4th century most of the temples in the cities had been closed. The main buildings in many cities thus had become derelict, and the courts which surrounded them and the ceremonial ways which led up to them were now redundant. In Gerasa, for example, the ceremonial way which led from the river up to the temple of Artemis was blocked off, and part of what had been a colonnaded street was roofed over and converted into a church.

Other public buildings in the city were allowed to decay. It is difficult to tell from the archaeological evidence when the great baths of antiquity or the aqueducts and nymphaea which supplied running water to the city fell into disuse. The construction of new, much smaller baths in Gerasa in the mid 5th century suggests that the two huge ancient structures in the city were no longer in use. Theaters survived rather longer, as the setting for the performances the early Christians so strongly condemned but also as a site of political occasions, where a governor could hear the acclamations (and complaints) of the people. But even so, it is likely that most theaters were in an advanced state of decay before the coming of the Muslims.

The loss of civic self-government and the end of paganism changed not just the physical structures of the city but the ideological environment which supported it. The classical city was dependent on the generosity of its citizens, who demonstrated their status by paying for and maintaining public buildings and were, in return, commemorated by inscriptions and statues. The cult of the city was the essential underpinning of this beautiful but fragile urban environment.

The Christians of late antiquity had other priorities.[22] The building of churches was the most obvious, and cities of any size were endowed with a fair number of them. In Gerasa for example some fifteen have been discovered, and there were no doubt others now lost, varying in size from the great city center churches of the cathedral and St. Theodore to much smaller structures which may have been little more than local chapels. It is arguable that Christianity put more emphasis on the family and hence on the family house. It almost seems that the people of late antiquity turned their backs on the public open spaces which their ancestors had seen as the setting for their lives and retreated inside, locking the doors and windows on the street scene.

The character of the streets themselves began to change. The wide straight streets with colonnaded sides and covered pavements were gradually encroached on as shops and houses invaded the previously public open spaces. The streets narrowed as pack animals came to replace wheeled vehicles as the main means of transporting goods. There were attempts to turn the clock back: when Justinian built his great Nea Church in Jerusalem, he extended the ancient colonnaded *cardo* to the south and constructed a broad straight city street which any Hellenistic builder would have been proud of. But without the intervention of a revivalist emperor, such projects were doomed; commercial pressures and social indifference gradually eroded the fabric of Hippodamian (rectilinear) planning.

The Muslim conquerors inherited this late antique city, with its narrow streets and blank-walled houses, a city whose only public buildings were the churches. The first century of Muslim rule saw the continuation and completion of many of the developments of the previous three centuries. The Muslims kept up the ancient tradition of bathing, but the Muslim *hammam* looked much more like the Byzantine bath of the mid 5th century than the great structures of antiquity. Hypocausts were still used and the procession of rooms from cold to hot was maintained but the palaestra and social areas were gone and the scale was more intimate, the business more commercial: baths became a source of revenue for mosques and other religious endowments (*awqāf,* singular *waqf*) rather than a subsidized relaxation for the citizens.

The theater was now entirely useless. The public life of early Muslim cities contained no dramatic performances of any sort. The political function of the theater was transferred to the mosque; it was there that the governor would lead the people (at least the political classes, that is, the Muslims) in prayer and address them from the pulpit. If theaters were still used at all, it was as the setting for pottery kilns.

The most noticeable changes occurred in the street pattern. The houses and shops continued to intrude on the pavement as the streets became narrow, winding, and in some cases blocked entirely. But there was nothing specifically Islamic about these changes; they were the continuation of trends which had begun in late antiquity. Clear evidence of the process has emerged in a number of recent excavations: at Jerash, where extensive and well-built Umayyad houses have been discovered that spill out from the hillside onto the sidewalk and use the pillars of the colonnade as the cornerstones of the front wall. This privatization of previously public spaces can be seen again at Beisan/Scythopolis, where the Umayyad buildings occupy the sidewalk and parts of the main carriageway.

Market areas underwent the same sort of transformation. In 1934 Sauvaget published a famous model, demonstrating how the broad, colonnaded street of antiquity slowly evolved into the narrow, crowded *sūqs* of the premodern Near Eastern city.[23] It was a classic piece of theoretical archaeology but until recently there was no site where the crucial stages of this transformation could be directly observed. Excavations at Palmyra have, in a sense, provided the missing link.[24] Palmyra boasted one of the grandest of all classical street layouts.

The vast porticoed way which forms the spine of the plan was unsurpassed in its scale and the richness of its decoration. In the Umayyad period a *sūq* was built on the paving of the main street, consisting of narrow but substantially built stone booths which used the pillars of the classical design to frame their entrances. The main surface of the street was now completely blocked and passage was allowed only on the old sidewalk or along a narrow alley behind the shops.

More than thirty years after his death, Sauvaget's theory was triumphantly vindicated, except in its chronology. He argued that the "degradation" (as the value-laden language of the day put it) of the classical street had taken place in the Fatimid period in the 10th century, when, he argued, civic government disappeared, allowing traders to usurp the public spaces. Archaeological evidence has since proved beyond all reasonable doubt that this process began in late antiquity and gathered pace in the first Islamic century. But the legacy of antiquity was not entirely obliterated: in the three greatest cities of Syria—Jerusalem, Damascus, and Aleppo—the Roman street plan underlay and determined the street plan, not just in early Muslim times, but right down to the present day.

The Muslims did not simply occupy and develop ancient cities; they founded new ones as well. The most important of these were the major *amṣār* at Kufa and Basra in Iraq, Fustat in Egypt, and Qayrawān in North Africa, as well as the failed *miṣr* at Jabiya in Syria. The archaeological record for these *amṣār* is not very helpful. Fustat has produced a good deal of evidence, mostly from later periods but, as in the Iraqi examples, the early phases of urban development can be discerned only in very general outline from the written sources. Qayrawān is a stone-built town whose origins go back to the first century of Islam, but the urban history and topography of the site have not been investigated in depth.

The Islamic new towns in Syria are on a much smaller scale.[25] Two sites can be singled out for discussion: Anjar, near Baalbek in the Biqaa Valley; and Ayla (Aqaba), on the gulf of that name in the Red Sea. Both sites are comparatively small and very obviously planned, more or less square in shape and surrounded by walls with round interval towers and four gates, one in the center of each side. The plan within the walls at Anjar is well preserved, showing straight streets crossing in the center in a very classical manner. Another example of such planning is the small madina at Qaṣr al-Hayr al-Sharqi: again the city is surrounded by walls with towers.[26] Inside there is a regular pattern of dwellings and a mosque. At the center there is a large, square courtyard which originally had an arcade around it. The striking feature of all these foundations is the concern with formal urban planning.

How far such planning was a reflection of antique practice is doubtful: settlements of comparable size in late antiquity—Umm al-Jimal in the Hawran, or Subeita in the Negev, for example—show no such concern for order. As we have seen, the formal regularities of the classical city may not have been very apparent to the incoming Muslims. The distinction is probably not between late antique order and Muslim chaos but between planned and informal, organic growth in both cultures. The square enclosures with their regularly spaced towers are certainly reminiscent of Roman structures like the legionary fortresses of Lajjun, but before we assume that this form was entirely derived from ancient practice we should consider the evidence from Arabia.

At a site known today as Qaryat Faw, on the road from Najd and Yamama to Yemen, excavations have uncovered a *sūq* probably dating from the 3rd to the 5th century.[27] It consists of a square, walled enclosure about 30 × 25 m, with small square towers at the corners and on the middle of each side. There is one entrance. In the interior, shops, which in their present form postdate the enclosure wall, are arranged around a sub-rectangular court which contains a deep cistern. Outside the enclosure a secondary market has been found, less strongly defended but still within a rectangular wall. Qaryat Faw demonstrates that planned fortified settlements could be found in Arabia well before the coming of Islam or the Muslim conquests. Like the architecture of early mosques, the development of these fortified settlements seems to represent a fusion, or at least an interaction, of Arabian and antique forms.

One of the features which makes the archaeology of late antique Syria so interesting and important is the wealth of rural settlement. Remains of numerous villages have survived in areas such as the limestone massif of northern Syria and the Hawran. As far as we can tell from dated structures, most of these villages were constructed approximately between 350 and 550. These villages seem to reflect a thriving rural economy; much of the domestic architecture seems to demonstrate considerable affluence, with simple and massive but curiously elegant houses being found in large numbers, even in the most out-of-the-way communities. Most of the surviving examples of these villages are found in marginal areas, where there was little or no settlement in antiquity and none since the 8th or 9th centuries. The best known and most fully researched of these areas of rural settlement are to be found in the rolling limestone hills of northern Syria, between Antioch and Aleppo.[28] This distribution may be due to accidents of survival; settlements in more obviously inviting areas, like the plains around Tripoli or the vale of Jezreel, have been overbuilt. However, it is clear that late antiquity was an era of expanding settlement and it seems likely that the Syrian countryside was more densely populated in the 5th and early 6th century than at any period before the present century.

The importance of villages in this pattern of rural settlement should be noted. There are many affluent-looking houses in villages like Serjilla or Refada, but little evidence of large estates or latifundia. It is possible that estates and villages were owned by the numerous monasteries in the area. The only aristocratic rural residence which can be clearly identified is the mid 6th century complex of palace and church at Qaṣr Ibn Wardan, on the edge of the desert northeast of Hama. This was obviously the residence of a large landowner or military commander but, unfortunately, we have absolutely no indication who the builder might have been. The thriving village economy may have faltered in the late 6th century. These is very little evidence for the construction of new houses after this date (possibly simply reflecting that people no longer inscribed dates on their dwellings), and the series of plagues which ravaged the area from 540 onward must have taken their toll. Archaeological evidence from Dehes in northern Syria, the only site which has been subjected to systematic excavation, suggests that the houses continued in use during the first two centuries of Muslim rule, even if new houses were not being built.[29]

The early Islamic period also saw an expansion of rural settlement in marginal areas, but one very different in character. Whereas the settlements of late antiquity were largely villages inhabited by free peasants—a social structure reflected in the high quality of individual houses combined with a lack of overall planning—the settlements of the Umayyad period took the form of large estates with high-status buildings. These developments were undertaken and financed in the early 8th century by important members of the Umayyad family.

There were good fiscal reasons why they should do this. Because the early Islamic fiscal system assigned revenues from conquered lands to those people whose names were entered in the *diwan* for the area, there was a strong feeling—vigorously, sometimes violently defended—that money raised in a given province should be disbursed among the Muslims of that province. This feeling made it difficult for the Umayyad caliphs in Damascus to tap into provincial resources, and though they did secure a share of the revenues, it was never as much as they hoped for or needed. Even in Syria itself, much of the revenue was already hypothecated in this way and the opportunities for expanding the caliphs' resource bases were very limited. It was a principle of both Roman and Islamic law that "dead lands" which were brought into cultivation belonged to the cultivator. For the Umayyad ruling elite, bringing new land on the desert margins into cultivation was the most effective, sometimes the only, way of providing much-needed resources. Hence the need for large-scale agricultural development projects.

Such activities gave rise to what can fairly be described as the cult of the gentleman farmer in Umayyad times. The anecdotes which reflect this are mostly centered on the caliph Hishām, a figure renowned for his shrewdness in administrative and financial matters. He is often portrayed as a farmer or gardener, inspecting crops himself and giving instructions to his subordinates about the harvesting and marketing of produce. The literary evidence for the expansion of agriculture is fullest from Iraq, where we have descriptions of the building of new canals and the irrigation of large, previously uncultivated areas. As often, however, the best archaeological evidence comes from Syria. Two sites illustrate this phenomenon, Qaṣr al-Hayr West and Qaṣr al-Hayr East.

Qaṣr al-Hayr West lies on the course of the old highway between Damascus and Palmyra, in an area where dry farming on a large scale is impossible.[30] The Romans had built a dam at Habarqa in the nearby mountains to retain water for the use of troops in frontier garrisons but this fell into disuse in late antiquity. In Byzantine times a monastery was founded in the plains by the road where the later palace was to be. In the 720s the area was extensively developed. The reservoir behind the dam, which had become silted up, was brought back into use and a canal dug to bring water to the plains, where it was distributed to gardens, a watermill, a khan, a bathhouse, and a luxuriously decorated palace.

Qaṣr al-Hayr East lies deep in the Syrian desert, halfway between Palmyra and the Euphrates in an almost completely arid landscape. The site consists of two square buildings, both surrounded by walls with interval towers and a central courtyard. There is also a freestanding bathhouse. The larger complex was described in a (now lost) inscription as a madina or city and consists of a series of dwellings, a mosque, and an olive press, arranged in strict symmetry around a central court. The smaller enclosure has a series of chambers arranged around a court and has been interpreted as a khan or possibly as a palace. As with Qaṣr al-Hayr West, the water-harvesting arrangements are impressive. In this case rainwater was gathered in the shallow wadis around the site and canalized into a walled enclosure. The olive press and the possibility that the site was called Zaytuna, or olive grove, point to an agricultural function.

In both these estates, we can see the careful management of water allowing agriculture in areas which were not cultivated either before or since. The village civilization of late antiquity was replaced by a demesne farming regime in the early Islamic period but agricultural development continued. It was not until after the fall of the Umayyads and the creation of a centralized, land-tax-based government by the Abbasids in the 9th century that investment in these large-scale projects became unprofitable and was abandoned.

The transition from the world of late antiquity to that of early Islam was gradual and multifaceted. Society and culture in the area changed slowly but markedly between the 4th century coming of Christianity and the fall of the Umayyads in 747–750. Despite the change in official language and elite religion, early Islamic society built on and developed the late antique legacy. In many ways the great earthquake of 747 and the coming of the Abbasids in 750 mark a bigger break than the coming of Islam; they spelled the real end of late antiquity and with it the end of the prosperity of Syria's golden age. Perhaps the archaeological record shows it most clearly: between the death of Hārūn al-Rashīd in 809 and the coming of the Fatimids in 969 there is not a single extant dated monument in the entire area of greater Syria. The contrast with the vast building activity of late antiquity and the Umayyad period could not be more striking.

Notes

1. There is a large and growing literature on Syria in late antiquity. For a helpful introduction, see Clive Foss, "The Near Eastern Countryside in Late Antiquity: A Review Article" in J. Humphrey, ed., *The Roman and Byzantine Near East* (Journal of Roman Archaeology, Supplementary Series 14, 1995), 213–234. See also the three volumes of *The Byzantine and Early Islamic Near East*, ed. A. Cameron, L. Conrad, and

G. R. D. King (Princeton, 1992, 1994, 1995). For the Islamic conquest of Syria, see Fred Donner, *The Early Islamic Conquests* (Princeton, 1981), 91–155, and Walter Kaegi, *Byzantium and the Early Islamic Conquests* (Cambridge, Eng., 1992).

2. The Sassanian legacy to the early Islamic state is fully discussed in Michael Morony, *Iraq after the Muslim Conquest* (Princeton, 1984).

3. Irfan Shahid, "Heraclius and the Theme System: New Light from the Arabic," *Byzantion* 57 (1987): 391–403, and "Heraclius and the Theme System: Further Observations," *Byzantion* 59 (1989): 208–243.

4. The best English-language guide to the geography of Muslim Syria is still Guy Le Strange, *Palestine under the Moslems* (Cambridge, Eng., 1890).

5. C. J. Kraemer, ed., *Excavations at Nessana*, vol. 3: *Non-Literary Papyri* (Princeton, 1958).

6. For this suggestion see H. Kennedy, "The Financing of the Military in the Early Islamic State" in Cameron, *Byzantine and Early Islamic Near East III* (Princeton, 1995), 361–378.

7. On this Christian Arab tradition see Sidney H. Griffith, *Arabic Christianity in the Monasteries of 9th-Century Palestine* (Aldershot, 1992).

8. On taxation in early Islam, see D. C. Dennett, *Conversion and Poll-Tax in Early Islam* (Cambridge, Mass., 1950).

9. On this system see H. Kennedy, "The Financing of the Military in the Early Islamic State," in Cameron, *Byzantine and Early Islamic Near East,* 361–378.

10. See H. Kennedy, "The Barmakid Revolution in Early Islamic Government," in *Pembroke Papers,* ed. C. Melville (Cambridge, Eng., 1990), 89–98.

11. For a good recent discussion, see G. W. Bowersock, *Hellenism in Late Antiquity* (Cambridge, Eng., 1990).

12. There is a considerable literature on the Jews in late antique Palestine: see M. Avi-Yonah, *The Jews of Palestine: A Political History from the Bar Kokhba War to the Arab Conquest* (Oxford, 1976); G. Alon, *The Jews in Their Land in the Talmudic Age (70–640 C.E.),* 2 vols. (Jerusalem, 1980; repr. Cambridge, Mass., 1988); and Averil Cameron, "The Jews in Seventh Century Palestine," *Scripta Classica Israelica* 13 (1994): 75–93.

13. For the Jews in early Islamic Palestine, see Moshe Gil, *A History of Palestine, 634–1099* (Cambridge, Eng., 1992), 490–776.

14. See William H. C. Frend, *The Rise of the Monophysite Movement* (Cambridge, Eng., 1972) and J. Meyendorff, *Imperial Unity and Christian Divisions* (New York, 1989).

15. For a general survey, see Gil, *History of Palestine, 430–489.*

16. For the Chalcedonian (Melkite) church in this period, see H. Kennedy, "The Melkite Church from the Islamic Conquest to the Crusades," in *17th International Byzantine Congress: The Major Papers* (New Rochelle, N.Y., 1986), 325–343.

17. There is no good survey of the Jacobite church in Syria in the early Islamic period, but see Morony, *Iraq after the Muslim Conquest, 372–380,* and the discussion of the Tur Abdin area (southern Turkey) in Andrew Palmer, *Monk and Mason on the Tigris Frontier* (Cambridge, Eng., 1990), 149–181.

18. Richard Bulliet, *Conversion to Islam in the Medieval Period* (Cambridge, Mass., 1979), 104–113.

19. The literature on these two buildings is vast. For a concise discussion of the early development of the mosque, see Robert Hillenbrand, *Islamic Architecture* (Edinburgh, 1994), 31–74. See also Oleg Grabar, *The Formation of Islamic Art* (New Haven, 1973).

20. For an overview of this subject, see H. Kennedy, "From Polis to Madina: Urban Change in Late Antique and Early Islamic Syria," *Past and Present* (1985): 3–27.

21. The fullest archaeological survey of an indivdual city in this period remains C. H. Kraeling, ed., *Gerasa: City of the Decapolis* (New Haven, 1938). For other important urban sites see Y. Tsafrir, "Beisan/Scythopolis" in King and Cameron, *Byzantine and*

Early Islamic Near East II (Princeton, 1994); Maurice Sartre, *Bostra: Des origines à l'Islam* (Paris, 1985); G. Downey, *Antioch in Syria* (Princeton, 1961). For the smaller towns of the Negev, see J. Shcreshevski, *Byzantine Urban Settlements in the Negev Desert* (Jerusalem, 1991).

22. See the recent discussion of changing values in the late antique city in Annabel Wharton, *Refiguring the Post Classical City* (Cambridge, Eng., 1995).

23. Jean Sauvaget, "Le plan de Laodicée-sur-Mer," *Bulletin d'études orientales* 4 (1934): 81–116.

24. K. al-As'ad and F. M. Stepniowski, "The Umayyad Suq in Palmyra," *Damaszener Mitteilungen* 4 (1989): 205–223.

25. For these smaller towns, see A. Northedge, "Archaeology and New Urban Settlement in Early Islamic Syria and Iraq," in King and Cameron, *Byzantium and Early Islam,* II.

26. See the classic account: Oleg Grabar, *City in the Desert,* 2 vols. (Cambridge, Mass., 1978).

27. Described in A. R. Al-Ansary, *Qaryat al-Fau: A Portrait of Pre-Islamic Civilisation in Saudi Arabia* (London, 1981).

28. See the classic account: G. Tchalenko, *Villages Antiques de la Syrie du Nord,* 3 vols. (Paris, 1953–1958), and the more recent discussion in G. Tate, *Les campagnes de la Syrie du Nord du IIe au VIIe siècle* (Paris, 1992).

29. See J.-P. Sodini et al., "Dehes (Syrie du Nord) Campagnes I–III (1976–78): Recherches sur l'habitat rural," *Syria* 57 (1980): 1–304.

30. For this site, see D. Schlumberger, *Qasr El-Heir El Gharbi* (Paris, 1986).

THE GOOD LIFE

Henry Maguire

In his tenth homily on Paul's Epistle to the Philippians, John Chrysostom, at that time patriarch of Constantinople, gave a vivid description of the good life as it was flaunted by the wealthy and powerful of his day. The preacher criticized the extravagance of the rich man's house, with its display of porticoes, columns, and precious marbles, its gilded ceilings, and its pagan statues. He spoke of the elaborate confections served in the dining room, made to satisfy the pleasure and vanity of the host. He complained of the clothes of the well-to-do, costing a hundred pieces of gold and worn in many layers, so that the wealthy appeared sweating beneath their finery. Finally, he ridiculed the rich men's wives, weighed down with jewelry and decked out like their mules and horses with gold.[1] This characterization of the prosperous lifestyle during late antiquity was not mere rhetorical exaggeration, for archaeology has shown that the picture painted by John Chrysostom was true. This essay reviews a selection from the abundant material evidence of domestic prosperity in late antiquity, including the interior furnishings of houses, the silver vessels used for eating, drinking, and bathing, silk clothing, and jewelry. I also look at imitations of these objects made in cheaper materials, through which the less fortunate emulated the success of the rich. The second part of the essay turns from the objects themselves to the images used to decorate them, which evoked the idea of prosperity in various ways, primarily through personifications, motifs drawn from nature, and mythology. Finally, I consider the attitudes toward those images that were adopted by Christianity, Judaism, and Islam, and the degree to which each religion opposed, assimilated, or rejected the visual expressions of domestic prosperity in late antiquity.

In the Roman and Byzantine worlds, marble was always an important emblem of wealth and consumption. The effect of this material upon the clientele of the wealthy aristocrats of Rome was described in scathing terms by the 4th century historian Ammianus Marcellinus: "Idle gossips frequent their houses, people who applaud with various flattering fictions every word uttered by those whose fortune is greater than their own . . . In the same way they admire the setting of columns in a high facade and the walls brilliant with carefully selected colors of marble, and extol their noble owners as more than mortal" (Amm.Marc. 23.4.12). Such late antique houses, featuring arcades with marble columns and walls expensively clad with marble revetments, have survived in nearby Ostia; a well-preserved example is the House of Cupid and Psyche, which featured a marble-lined dining room and a columnar arcade, as well as statuary of the type criticized by John Chrysostom, including the group of Cupid and Psyche that gave the house its modern name (fig. 1).[2] Many wealthy homes had floors covered with colorful tessellated mosaics. Among the best preserved are the 6th century pavements discovered in the Villa of the Falconer at Argos in Greece, which had a dining room looking out onto a courtyard that was surrounded on two sides by columnar porticoes. The floor of the *triclinium* (dining room) was decorated with a mosaic of Dionysus with satyrs and maenads, which was placed so that it could be admired by diners reclining on the couch set at the back of the room (fig. 2). The position of the semicircular couch is marked on the mosaic floor, together with that of the sigma-shaped table in front of it. Even the meal of two fish on a platter was indicated in the center of the table. The porticoes of the courtyard also were paved with mosaics. In front of the dining room were scenes of hunting with dogs and falcons, activities which provided food (ducks and hares) for the table (fig. 3). The other portico was decorated with personifications of the months holding their seasonal attributes (figs. 4 and 5).[3]

Textiles were very important in the decoration of late antique houses, although their effect is more difficult to visualize today than that of the splendid mosaic floors that have survived in their original locations. A luxurious copy of the poems of Virgil, possibly produced in Ravenna during the 6th century, contains a painting of Dido entertaining Aeneas in her palace which gives some idea of the contribution made by textiles to the late antique dining room: blue, green, and red hangings and swags cover the walls, white and purple cloths decorate the couch (fig. 6).[4] A number of domestic wall-hangings executed in tapestry weave, some of considerable size, have been excavated from graves in Egypt, where they had been used to wrap corpses for burial when they were no longer needed in the house. The rich imagery of these tapestries includes beneficent personifications (fig. 7); bearers of gifts (fig. 8); servants (fig. 9); trees, fruits, and flowers (fig. 10); animals and hunting scenes; and figures from mythology. Houses were also decorated with curtains, which were hung in doorways and between the columns of arcades. As may be seen from the example illustrated in figure 11, curtains were made of a lighter weight material than the wall-hangings, being typically woven of linen with intermittent repeat patterns executed with dyed woolen threads.[5] Such a curtain, decorated with a repeating pattern of flowers on a neutral ground, may be seen hung across a doorway in the 6th century mosaic of Empress Theodora and her retinue from the church of S. Vitale in Ravenna.[6]

Diners in late antiquity well appreciated the aura of luxury that finely woven textiles brought to a dining room. In one of his poems, the 5th century Gallic aristocrat Sidonius Apollinaris wrote how his experience of a feast was enriched by the red- and purple-dyed cloths of wool and linen that adorned the couch. He describes a textile woven with hunting scenes, showing hills and "beasts rushing over the roomy cloth, their rage whetted by a wound well counterfeited in scarlet," so that "at the seeming thrust of a javelin, blood that is no blood issues." On the same textile he admired the motif of the Parthian shot, in which "the Parthian, wild eyed and cunningly leaning over with face turned backwards, makes his horse go [forward] and his arrow return, flying from or putting to flight the pictured beasts" (*Epistulae* 9.13.5; trans. W. B. Anderson). Such couch-covers, woven with scenes of horseback riders hunting in landscapes, are depicted on the lids of some 3rd century Attic sarcophagi.[7] As for the Parthian shot, it is depicted in surviving textiles, such as a fragment of draw-loom silk now preserved in the treasury of St. Servatius at Maastricht, which dates to the 8th century (fig. 12).[8] Besides hunting scenes, textiles used to cover household furnishings were woven with many other figural subjects, as may be seen in the fragment of wool and linen tapestry weave in figure 13, which may have come from the border of a couch cover showing a series of beneficent personifications.[9] The rich 4th century silk shown in figure 14, depicting the Nile in his chariot accompanied by *putti,* aquatic creatures, and waterfowl, could also have been part of a spread or a cover, although its original function is uncertain.[10]

One further element of the furnishing of the late antique houses should be mentioned here, even if it is preserved only in the imagery of poets and weavers: in the aristocratic dining room a profusion of greenery and flowers provided color and fragrance, as is described in the poem by Sidonius: "Let the round table show linen fairer than snow, and be covered with laurel and ivy and vine-shoots, fresh and verdant. Let cytisus, crocus, starwort, cassia, privet, and marigolds be brought in ample baskets and color the sideboard and couches with fragrant garlands" (*Epistulae* 9.13.5).

Another feature of entertaining in late antiquity was the display and employment of a large variety of silver vessels for serving drink and food. The discovery of several hordes of late antique silver has shown the astonishing richness and variety of this ware; the 4th century treasure discovered at Kaiseraugst, on the river Rhine in Switzerland, for example, included a big rectangular salver, large circular and polygonal platters (fig. 15), dishes specially shaped for serving fish, bowls of various sizes, long- and short-handled spoons, wine strainers, beakers, an elaborate candlestick, a handbasin, and even toiletry implements such as toothpicks and ear cleaners.[11] Other treasures have contained silver jugs of various shapes and sizes, as well as sauce bowls equipped with lids and handles. The painting of Queen Dido's banquet in figure 6 shows some of this ware in use. The servant on the left offers a silver beaker of wine to the guests, which he has filled from the silver jug in his right hand (the artist has indicated the purple liquid at its brim). The servant on the right, who holds another silver jug and a long-handled silver bowl, is probably preparing to pour water over the hands of the guests to clean them. A good host was expected to keep his silver well polished, as we learn again from Sidonius Apollinaris, in a letter praising the Gothic king Theoderic II: "When one joins him at dinner . . . there is no unpolished conglomeration of discolored old silver set by panting attendants on sagging tables . . . The viands attract by their skillful cookery, not by their costliness, the platters by their brightness, not by their weight" (*Epistulae* 1.2.6). Much of this silver tableware was decorated, either with chasing or with motifs executed in relief; often the designs were enriched with niello or gilding. Fine examples of such pieces are the great platters from the Kaiseraugst and the Mildenhall treasures, which portray, respectively, scenes from the early life of Achilles (fig. 15) and a Bacchic revel surrounding a central mask of Ocean (fig. 16).[12] This kind of decoration, also, was described by Sidonius: "Let the attendants bend their heads under the metal carved in low relief, let them bring in lordly dishes on their laden shoulders" (*Epistulae* 9.13.5). Nor should one forget the repeated pleasures of the food that was served with such splendor: "I have overextended myself by eating everything," wrote the poet and bon vivant Venantius Fortunatus in the 6th century, "and my belly is swollen with various delicacies: milk, vegetables, eggs, butter. Now I am given dishes arranged with new feasts, and the mixture of foods pleases me more sweetly than before" (*Carmina* 11.22).

Silver vessels also played a prominent role in bathing, another luxury enjoyed in the houses of the rich. Late antique villas were frequently equipped with their own private bathhouses, some of which contained floor mosaics illustrating the rituals of cleanliness and beautification. One such mosaic has been preserved in the baths of a large villa discovered at Sidi Ghrib, in Tunisia (fig. 17). The mosaic, which dates to the late 4th or early 5th century, shows the lady of the house at her toilette. On the left, a maid proffers jewelry in a silver tray, while her mistress tries on an earring. Another maid holds up a mirror, so that the resulting effect can be admired. On either side of the mosaic appears the silver that has been used in bathing: to the left is a scalloped washbasin, similar to one that survives in the Kaiseraugst treasure, and a silver-gilt chest containing a towel or a garment.[13] A similarly shaped gilded chest was preserved in the mid 4th century treasure found on a slope of the Esquiline hill in Rome (fig. 18).[14] Such silver vessels, made expressly for bathing, were described about one hundred and fifty years earlier by the early Christian writer Clement of Alexandria, who wrote scornfully that women went to the public baths with "a great paraphernalia of vessels made of gold or silver, some for drinking the health of others, some for eating, and some for the bath itself . . . Parading with this silverware, they make a vulgar display of it in the baths" (*Paedagogus* 3.31).

Another way of publicly displaying one's wealth was through clothing, and especially through the wearing of patterned silks. Both pagan and Christian writers criticized the extravagance of such garments. Ammianus Marcellinus described the extreme fineness of the mantles worn by the Roman senators, which "were figured with the shapes of many different animals" and which shone when their wearers moved (14.6.9). A contemporary of Ammianus, Asterius, bishop of Amaseia, condemned the luxury of silks and the vanity of those who wore garments decorated with "lions and leopards, bears, bulls and dogs, forests and rocks, hunters and [in short] the whole repertory of painting that imitates nature." He also castigated those who wore garments decorated with scenes from the gospels. Such people, he declared, "devise for themselves, their wives and children gay-colored dresses decorated with thousands of figures . . . When they come out in public dressed in this fashion, they appear like painted walls to those they meet."[15]

The fashions evoked by these texts are borne out by images and by survivals of the textiles themselves. The mosaic of Theodora with her retinue in S. Vitale shows the ladies of her court wearing draw-loom silks with repeating patterns, including flowers and ducks. The empress herself has a gospel scene, the Adoration of the Magi, embroidered into the hem of her cloak. As for the male garments, a late 4th century silk tunic has been preserved in relatively good condition in the church of S. Ambrogio in Milan (fig. 19). Even if it may not have been the garment of the saint himself, as tradition would have it, the textile is almost certainly of his date. The tunic had a linen lining, over which was an outer layer of white silk damask woven all over with repeating designs of lions being hunted by men and dogs in a landscape evoked by trees and bushes.[16] Less expensive tunics had applied bands and roundels of silk rather than a continuous surface of the costly material, but the effect of these garments could still be rich (figs. 20 and 21).

As in the villa at Sidi Ghrib, late antique floor mosaics demonstrate the importance of jewelry in the self-image of the rich (fig. 17). A similar scene appears in the famous late 4th century mosaic of Dominus Iulius, which was found in a house at Carthage. Here scenes of the life of an estate revolve around the main house, depicted with its columned porticoes and its domed baths (fig. 22). At the lower left appears the mistress of the domain, leaning on a column and gazing at herself in a mirror, while she stretches out her hand languidly to receive a necklace proffered by a maid who holds the box containing her jewelry.[17] Magnificent examples of jewelry from late antiquity still survive. Two necklaces from the 7th century are illustrated in figures 23 and 24, one composed of eleven openwork plaques of gold set and hung with pearls and precious stones, and another adorned with a pendant portraying a golden Aphrodite in a lapis lazuli shell.[18]

The accouterments of the good life—the marbles, the silver, the silks, the gold, and the gems—were well enough appreciated to inspire imitation in cheaper materials. In North Africa, for example, panels of floor mosaic frequently imitated the veining of marble, which was a more expensive material; figure 25 illustrates a mosaic of the second half of the 4th century found at Thuburbo Majus which reproduces green "cipollino," a marble imported from Greece.[19] Such false marble panels were frequently installed at important places in the floor, such as at thresholds. On occasion, mosaic itself might be imitated in the medium of fresco. This occurred in the early Islamic period at the Umayyad palace of Qaṣr al-Hayr West, where there are floors paved with frescoes whose designs, characterized by hard-edged contrasts of color, imitate the effect of tessellated pavements (fig. 26).[20] Even the great tapestry wall-hangings, luxurious in themselves, imitated the greater luxury of spacious marble arcades and porticoes. This emulation explains the popularity of textile compositions that framed their subjects beneath arches or between columns, as seen in figures 8–10.

The imitation of silverware in ceramic is a phenomenon well attested for many periods and cultures, but it was especially pronounced in North Africa during late antiquity. Here potters decorated their earthenware vessels with raised motifs in imitation of the repoussé decoration of silver, and even went so far as to reproduce the shapes of rectangular silver vessels in clay, a form that could not be manufactured on the potter's wheel. They also copied the iconography associated with silverware, as can be seen in figure 27, which reconstructs part of a rectangular earthenware tray decorated in relief with scenes from the life of Achilles, similar to those appearing on the 4th century polygonal dish from Kaiseraugst (fig. 15). Even though these pottery dishes were cheaper imitations of more precious models in silver, they were prized by the poorer folk who owned them; in several cases there is evidence that the ceramics were repaired in antiquity.[21]

Silk-weaving was often imitated in less precious materials, as is shown by a medallion of the 7th century showing two mounted lion hunters which originally adorned a domestic textile such as a tunic (fig. 28). This piece, a tapestry weave of dyed woolen threads on linen, carefully reproduces the bilateral symmetry characteristic of silks produced on the draw loom.[22] The red ground and the border containing floral motifs are also copied from silks; compare the fragmentary silk medallion at Maastricht (fig. 12). The manufacturers of tapestry weaves even went so far as to imitate gold and jewelry in their humble materials. A particularly striking example is a fragment of a tunic woven in linen and wool with gold threads (fig. 29). This garment was decorated with two imitation necklaces at the neckline, one of which has pendants like the real piece of jewelry in figure 23.[23]

The houses and objects possessed by the rich and the would-be rich were adorned with images that expressed the prosperity projected and desired by their owners. It would be inaccurate to call these motifs decoration, which implies they had no function other than to provide visual delight to the beholder. Often these designs were invested with a stronger significance, which approached a numinous power; that is, the images were both an expression and an assurance of abundance.

In many cases the prosperity of the late antique house was illustrated literally, in compositions such as the Dominus Iulius mosaic from Carthage (fig. 22). In this mosaic the activities of the estate are focused on the ease and comfort of the owners, in a cyclical composition that evokes the gifts of the seasons. Immediately above the representation of the villa sits the lady, fanning herself as she receives offerings from her servants: ducks and a basket of olives on the left, and a lamb on the right. At the lower left she is presented with jewelry, as we have seen, and also with a fish and a basket full of roses, while on the right sits the master of the estate, who receives birds, a basket of grapes, and a hare. Similar imagery of servants or personifications bringing gifts can be found on tapestry hangings. In one example we find two attendants under jeweled arches, one carrying a fish and three pomegranates, and the other holding a bowl and a small elongated flask of a kind that could have contained scent for sprinkling over the hands of guests (fig. 8). (This recalls the line "iuvat ire per corollas / alabastra ventilantes" ["It is pleasant to pass through garlands while swinging perfume boxes"] in Sidonius's description of a feast, *Epistulae* 9.13.5.) A fragment of another hanging shows a servant pulling back a curtain hanging between two columns (fig. 9); it evokes a privileged setting, where, at the appointed time, curtains are drawn aside by the hands of half-hidden minions.[24]

Beneficent female personifications were a popular presence in the household. While many of these personifications alluded to moral qualities, and may have had Christian overtones, they also evoked material wealth, prosperity, and security. They include Ktisis (Foundation or Creation), Kosmēsis (Ordering or Adornment), Ananeōsis (Renewal), and Sotēria (Security or Salvation). To these may be added personifications more directly associated with physical prosperity, such as Tychē Kalē (Good Fortune), Apolausis (Enjoyment), and Hestia Polyolbos (the Blessed Hearth). The last-named is depicted in a splendid 6th century wool tapestry that was woven to be fitted into an arched niche (fig. 7). As often with these personifications, Hestia Polyolbos is richly dressed. She wears a heavy jeweled necklace and pendant earrings, and is enthroned like the mistress of an estate flanked by her attendants. The six boys who approach her on either side hold disks inscribed with her blessings, namely "wealth," "joy," "praise," "abundance," "virtue," and "progress."[25] Hestia Polyolbos is clearly identified by an inscription above her head, but frequently the richly attired female personifications were left unnamed, as unspecific beneficent presences. Such a figure, wearing a pearl headband, a pearl necklace, and pearl pendants on her earrings, can be seen in the fragment of tapestry band illustrated in figure 13.

Another group of propitious personifications evoked nature and its cycles: the earth, the ocean, the seasons, and the months. The seasons and months were often depicted in floor mosaics, as in the 6th century villa at Argos, where each of the personified months holds the attributes appropriate to it (fig. 4). Since many of these attributes are in the form of seasonal produce enjoyed by the owner of the villa—such as ducks from February, a lamb from April, a basket of flowers from May, and grain from June—the months in effect take the place of the servants who catered to the owners' pleasure on the Dominus Iulius mosaic from Carthage (fig. 22). A similar promise was embodied in the personifications of the earth and the ocean, which occurred not only in floor mosaics but also on a smaller scale in textiles worn as clothing. The fragment of silk illustrated in figure 20 originally formed half of one of the two sleeve bands of a tunic. The complete band depicted the earth surrounded by the ocean;

Earth was personified by four repeated busts of a crowned woman wearing a heavily jeweled collar and holding up a fruit-laden cloth in front of her chest, and the ocean was signified by means of fishes and water plants in the border. A similar personification of Earth was portrayed elsewhere on the garment, in medallions at the ends of the four bands that descended from the shoulders, and in four small circles that were affixed to the lower part of the tunic at the level of the knees.[26] These motifs, which miniaturized the abundance of the whole earth into a small charm repeated sixteen times on the same garment, illustrate the magical potential of these personifications of the power of nature. The silk tunic band in figure 21 shows at the bottom a similar female personification, wearing a crown and a jeweled collar; here she accompanies birds, plants, and hunting scenes, which signify the terrestrial domain.[27] Ocean, also, appeared on household objects, such as the magnificent platter from the 4th century Mildenhall treasure, where he appears as a mask with dolphins leaping from his hair and beard at the center of a marine *thiasos* of nereids riding upon sea beasts (fig. 16). Like the personification of Earth, Ocean had both a metaphorical and a magical value. According to John Chrysostom, in 4th century Antioch a public benefactor could be compared by grateful citizens to the ocean on account of his generosity: "he in his lavish gifts is what the Ocean is among waters."[28] But it was also possible for the personification to have protective value, as is demonstrated by a mosaic discovered at Ain-Témouchent, near Sétif, in Algeria. Here a head of Ocean with enlarged eyes is accompanied by an inscription invoking the gaze of the mask as protection from the misfortunes caused by envy (fig. 30).[29]

Another subject that conveyed good fortune was the river Nile with its flora and fauna, for the flooding of the Nile was seen as emblematic of prosperity not only in Egypt itself but in much of the Mediterranean world. The imagery of Nilotic abundance was evoked in a pagan hymn, written around the year 300:

> Fishes and not oxen dwell in the plain,
> for the Nile inundated the land formerly accessible by foot . . .
> Dark earth, you flourish in your water which produces corn.
> Be gracious king of the rivers, Nile nourisher of children . . .
> You are present bringing to mortals full baskets.[30]

The motifs of this hymn—the fishes, the children, the baskets, the abundance of produce—were reproduced on textiles, on tableware, and on floors. In the 4th century silk illustrated in figure 14, the personified river is accompanied by *putti* holding wreaths and garlands and by a variety of aquatic creatures. Sometimes the Nilotic subject matter is accompanied by an inscription specifying its propitious value. This can be seen in the case of a large 5th or 6th century mosaic, recently excavated in a secular building at Sepphoris, in Galilee. It displays a variety of conventional motifs, including the personified Nile accompanied by the usual aquatic plants and birds; a personification of Egypt reclining on a basket full of fruit and holding a cornucopia; and boys engaged in engraving the high-water mark on a nilometer. All of this is accompanied by an inscription in the border enjoining the viewer to "Have good fortune."[31]

The wealth of earth and sea was invoked not only by personifications, but also by the numerous portrayals of animals and plants throughout the home. The rich acanthus borders of the floor mosaics in the Villa of the Falconer at Argos are inhabited by a variety of creatures, including birds such as ducks and waders, reptiles such as snakes and lizards, and mammals such as rabbits and deer, together with fruits and vegetables (fig. 5). While these motifs undoubtedly provided visual pleasure to the beholder, they also gave an assurance of continuing life and prosperity. Birds were especially favored as a decoration on textiles, whether curtains (fig. 11) or the silks worn by the ladies at court. Plants and their products appeared in numerous guises. Large tapestry hangings portrayed lines of trees (fig. 10)—in one case at least eight in a row.[32] The significance of such representations is indicated by a fragment of a curtain which depicts a tree in full leaf with the invocation *Euphori* ("Flourish!") written upon its trunk (fig. 31).[33] Sometimes the imagery of plants was enhanced by the richness of gems, as can be seen in the case of the 6th or 7th century tunic band in figure 21, where the central motif, a stylized plant crowned by a pomegranate, rises from a jeweled vase.

In this evocation of plenty and abundance through images drawn from nature, there was a supporting role for the old pagan deities, even if the patrons were Christian. The domestication of pagan gods in Christian households can be seen both in art and in literature. The epithalamia of Dioscorus of Aphrodito, a 6th century Egyptian lawyer whose father had founded a monastery, strikingly combine references to Zeus, Ares, Apollo, Heracles, Dionysus, Ariadne, Demeter, and other deities with invocations to the Christian God. In the poem for the wedding of Count Callinicus and Theophile, for example, which he wrote sometime before 570, he declared: "You [the bridegroom] raise up the honey-sweet grape-cluster, in its bloom of youth; Dionysos attends the summer of your wedding, bearing wine, love's adornment, with plenty for all, and blond Demeter brings the flower of the field . . . They have woven holy wreaths round your rose-filled bedroom." In another epithalamium, for the wedding of Isakios, Dioscorus invokes "garlanded Dionysos" and "the Nile with his many children," before exclaiming "Go away, evil eye; this marriage is graced by God."[34] This easy combination of nature imagery with the evocation of pagan deities in the context of a Christian wedding finds a parallel two centuries earlier in the reliefs on the casket of Projecta, where the toilette of the bride is mirrored by a marine Venus portrayed on the lid (fig. 18). Here, in spite of the explicit evocation of the pagan goddess, the Christian orientation of bride and groom is not in doubt, for on the rim of the casket's lid appears the inscription *Secunde et Projecta vivatis in Chri[sto]* ("Secundus and Projecta, may you live in Christ").

The appearance of pagan deities on domestic furnishings from late antiquity should not, therefore, necessarily be taken as evidence of outright paganism on the part of their owners; rather, the pagan motifs should be read as embodying ideas of plenty and good fortune. The 4th century treasure from Mildenhall in

Suffolk contained both spoons engraved with the Christian Chi-Rho monogram and dishes decorated with figures from pagan mythology. The latter included the great platter with its central mask of Ocean surrounded by a Bacchic revel portraying the drinking contest of Dionysus and Hercules in the company of dancing satyrs and maenads (fig. 16). These subjects, in the eyes of many Christians as well as pagans, evidently signified the respective gifts of the waters and the earth, the seafood and the wine that should accompany a feast.[35] Likewise, the woman of the 7th century who wore the gold and lapis lazuli pendant portraying Aphrodite was probably a Christian (fig. 24); but she may, nevertheless, have hoped that her charm might bring her some good things. Such a wish is expressed by a 5th century mosaic discovered in a bath building at Alassa on the island of Cyprus, which depicts the goddess beautifying herself under the inscription EP AGATHOIS ("for a good cause").[36]

The late antique repertoire of images drawn from nature was not confined to the homes of pagans and Christians; some of it survived into the decoration of early Islamic palaces. It formed a common cultural frame of reference, evocative of well-being and prosperity, which was not the exclusive preserve of one faith. For example, the offering of the products of the land, a theme depicted in floor mosaics and textiles (see figs. 4, 8, and 22), also appears in the 8th century stucco reliefs set into the courtyard facades of Qaṣr al-Hayr West, where there are attendants holding, among other things, pomegranates, birds, lambs, and vases filled with flowers.[37] One of the frescoed floors in the palace at Qaṣr al-Hayr West even portrays a personification of the Earth (fig. 26). As in the silk tunic ornaments discussed above (fig. 20), she is portrayed in a medallion as a bust-length figure holding a scarf in front of her, while the surrounding ocean is evoked by aquatic creatures, in this case marine centaurs. The fresco is bordered by vine scrolls containing bunches of grapes, a motif also frequently encountered in pre-Islamic art (compare the borders of the casket of Projecta, shown in fig. 18). Although it would certainly be possible to read into this fresco a political meaning of conquest and hegemony, given its presence in a palace of the Umayyad rulers, its motifs also belonged to a common vocabulary of abundance inherited from late antiquity.[38]

Even though the evidence of material culture demonstrates that many Christians were perfectly happy to accept pagan imagery into their houses, there was also an undercurrent of opposition and unease. Sidonius Apollinaris, in a description of a villa at Avitacum, praised its bath building because its walls were unadorned concrete: "Here no disgraceful tale is exposed by the nude beauty of painted figures, for though such a tale may be a glory to art it dishonors the artist . . . there will not be found traced on those spaces anything which it would be more proper not to look at; only a few lines of verse will cause the new-comer to stop and read" (*Epistulae* 2.2.5–7). This somewhat puritanical viewpoint, with its disapproval of nudity and pagan myth, finds some confirmation in the archaeological record, for there are a few instances in which figural images were removed from the floor mosaics of houses. A case in point is the so-called House of the Sea Goddess at Seleucia, near Antioch. In one of the rooms of this villa, the late 5th or early 6th century floor mosaic exhibited the heads of four female personifications set in medallions, which were excised at a later period and replaced with slabs of marble.[39] A similar intervention occurred in a pavement of the baths of a Roman house at El Haouria, in Tunisia, where there was a frontal mask of Ocean accompanied by an apotropaic inscription against envy, similar to the mosaic of the same subject at Ain-Témouchent (fig. 30). Some time after the setting of the mosaic at El Haouria, the face of the mask was carefully picked out, leaving behind only Ocean's curved beard and the claws that had projected from his hair. The images that had framed the mask in the four corners of the composition, erotes and hippocamps, were allowed to remain, presumably because they were deemed to be more innocuous.[40]

Such archaeologically attested instances of the destruction of mosaics with pagan connotations in private houses give credence to certain stories in the saints' lives that might otherwise be dismissed as pure fantasy. One is found in the biography of St. Eutychius, a 6th century patriarch of Constantinople, which was written by his pupil Eustratius. It relates the story of a young artist residing at Amaseia in the Pontos, who was made to remove an old mosaic representing the story of Aphrodite from the walls of a private house. The mosaic was inhabited by a demon, who got his revenge upon the young man by causing his hand to become so severely infected that it had to be amputated. Eventually, the hand was restored through the agency of St. Eutychius, after which the grateful artist set up the saint's image in the house, in the place of the pagan goddess.[41] The story demonstrates that some Christians of the 6th century opposed and feared the pagan imagery that was still current in domestic contexts, even while other Christians were prepared to accept it.

In addition to these instances of domestic iconoclasm, there are other cases in which it may be possible to speak of private patrons manipulating traditional iconographic schemes so as to avoid the representation of pagan deities. For example, a curious mosaic survives on the floor of one of the three apses of a luxurious dining room attached to a large house north of the Antonine baths in Carthage (fig. 33). According to the latest investigations, the mosaic probably dates to some time after the beginning of the 5th century. The central subject of the floor was an open domed tholos, beneath which four boys danced with a garland held in their outspread hands against a background scattered with flowers. On either side of the tholos were projecting wings, above which grew fruiting vines.[42] This scene, which appears to make the domed building the central focus of the design, has no direct parallels in North African art. It is, however, reminiscent of later mosaics from Christian Monophysite and Islamic contexts, which eschewed portrayals of sacred figures in favor of buildings and plants (see fig. 42).[43] The mosaic at Carthage can be related to a composition that was relatively frequent in North African mosaics of the 4th century, namely a central shrine containing the image of a pagan deity, flanked by motifs such as creatures, plants, and dancers that were suggestive of abundance. Such a mosaic was excavated in another house at Carthage (fig. 33). Dating to the first half of the 4th century, it shows Venus sitting on an island beneath an open domed structure supported on columns, with flowers and garlands spread at her feet, and with a chorus of dwarfs and musicians dancing in boats on either side.[44] We know that pagan art was an especially sensitive subject in Carthage at the turn of the 4th and the 5th centuries; archaeology shows that at this time it was even necessary for some householders to hide their pagan statuary in the basement.[45] It is possible, therefore, that the mosaic of the *tholos* represents one patron's solution to the problem. He has preserved the ebullient motifs of the frame—the elaborate domed building, the flowers, and the dancers—but the offending deity has been removed.

If Christians were occasionally unsure about the suitability of personifications and pagan deities as decoration for their houses, it might be assumed that they would be even more reluctant to admit such images to their places of worship. However, after a brief phase at the end of the 4th century during which aniconic floors were in favor, the repertoire of images from nature that had expressed domestic well-being began to make itself increasingly at home in churches.[46] By the 6th century, in spite of earlier condemnations of domestic luxury, ecclesiastical buildings were displaying much of the visual splendor that was characteristic of a magnate's villa or palace.[47] They avoided explicit portrayals of pagan myths, but minor pagan deities such as Pan might occasionally slip into the decoration of church pavements.[48] The naves and aisles of church buildings, which Christian cosmographic interpretations identified with the earth, exhibited nature personifications as well as a rich repertoire of creatures and plants, motifs that could be subject to Christian allegorization on the part of the patron or the viewer.[49] A good example of such decor is provided by the newly excavated church at Petra, in Jordan. Here the nave, the sanctuary, and the central apse were covered with an expensive *opus sectile* pavement of purple sandstone and imported marble, but the two side aisles were carpeted in the 6th century with the cheaper medium of tessellated mosaic. The mosaic in the north aisle displayed a vine scroll filled with a rich assortment of motifs evocative of the earth and its produce, including birds and beasts of various kinds, trees, baskets and fruits, and vases, goblets, and bowls. The south aisle portrayed more creatures of land, air, and sea, together with personifications of the earth, the ocean, the four seasons, and wisdom. The season of summer appeared as a bare-breasted woman wearing earrings and brandishing a sickle (fig. 34), while Ocean was portrayed as a half-nude man distinguished, as in the domestic mosaics, by claws growing from his hair.[50] These bold personifications have parallels in other 6th century churches, for example in the nave mosaic of the East Church at Qaṣr-el-Lebia in Libya, dated to 539–540, where the four rivers of Paradise (Gihon, Pishon, Tigris, and Euphrates) are portrayed as reclining nude figures, in the same manner as pagan river gods; they are joined in this composition by the pagan oracular spring Castalia, now converted by the power of Christ (fig. 35).[51] Several churches preserve Nilotic scenes, among the finest examples being the 5th century floor mosaics in the transepts of the

Church of the Multiplication of the Loaves and the Fishes at Tabgha in Galilee,[52] and the carvings on the westernmost of the wooden beams over the nave
of the church at Mount Sinai, which date from between 548 and 565 (fig. 36).[53]

Such evocations of the powers of nature in the context of Christian churches
became possible because of a new way of thinking which saw them as subjects,
rather than as rivals, of Christ. In one of his epithalamia, the 6th century poet
Dioscorus of Aphrodito bound the power of the Nile to Christ in order to
convey a blessing on the bride and groom: "Easily protecting . . . the Nile with
his many children, may God grant a superlative marriage free from the accursed
envy of others."[54] A 6th century papyrus from Antinoe in Egypt contains a
hymn addressed to the Nile which begins in a manner reminiscent of pagan
invocations, but closes with an appeal to the Christian deity:

> O most fortunate Nile, smilingly have you watered the land;
> rightly do we present to you a hymn . . .
> you are full of wonders in all Egypt, a remedy for men and for beasts;
> [you have brought] the awaited season . . .
> the fruit of your virtue is very great . . .
> you have displayed to us a strange miracle;
> you have brought the benefits of the heavens . . .
> True illumination, Christ, benefactor, [save] the souls of men, now and
>   [forever].[55]

There is nothing explicitly Christian about most of this poem. Only at its end is
there a prayer to Christ, the true source of the river's power. It is as if the
supplicant is appealing to the river as Christ's agent, almost in the same way
one might appeal to a saint.

By the 5th century a nave pavement decorated with creatures and plants was
considered to be a typical part of a church, as is demonstrated by a tomb
mosaic from a church at Tabarka, in Tunisia (fig. 37). The mosaic depicts a
basilica labeled Ecclesia Mater, symbolizing the reception of the deceased into
the eternal repose of the church. In an "exploded" view, we are shown the apse,
the altar, the interior colonnades, the clerestory windows, and the tiles of the
roof. Only the further line of columns, on the south side of the building, is
depicted at full height, from the bases to the capitals. The nearer line of columns, on the north side of the church, is cut off at half height, so as not to
obscure the south side of the church from the spectator's view. Between the
truncated columns appear glimpses of the floor mosaic, which is composed of
different types of birds and plants.[56] While one might assume that the creator of
this panel, being himself a mosaicist, would have a particular interest in floors,
it is striking that the pavement, with its motifs drawn from nature, is the only
part of the building's decoration to have been shown. But such motifs, as we
have seen, were not confined to floors. They flourished also on the fittings of the
church, whether they were carved in wood, such as doors and ceiling beams
(fig. 36), or in stone, such as chancel screens, pulpits, and capitals. Walls and

vaults also received decoration evoking the profusion of terrestrial creation, as is shown by the mid 6th century mosaic that arches over the chancel of S. Vitale in Ravenna (fig. 38).[57] This composition in green and gold, with its scrolling plant rinceaux bearing fruit and flowers and framing several species of beasts, birds, and reptiles, is a richer version of the borders of the mosaics in the provincial villa at Argos (fig. 5).

A similar imagery of abundance was incorporated into the decoration of Jewish synagogues during the late antique period, although with a somewhat more restricted repertoire than in Christian churches. A popular composition for the floors of synagogues, which has been found at several locations, is represented by a 4th century pavement discovered at Hammath Tiberias. Here the widest of the four aisles of the hall, leading to the raised alcove that contained the Torah chest, displays a handsome mosaic divided into three sections (fig. 39). The southern section, closest to the Torah niche, contains signs of the Jewish faith, such as the Ark of the Law, menorahs, and other ritual objects. The northern section contains inscriptions naming founders or donors, flanked and watched over by two lions which also serve as guardians of the entrance. The largest of the sections represents at its center Helios, shown as a young man with a halo, riding in his chariot within a circular frame containing the signs of the zodiac. The circular border is itself framed by a square, in the four corners of which appear personifications of the seasons holding their attributes.[58] Thus the biggest section of the floor evokes the cycle of the year and the good things brought by the seasons. Even though it is set beside a panel containing cultic images and another invoking blessings upon members of the congregation, it has few specifically Jewish elements; most of its subjects can be found depicted in the houses of the pagans.[59] A similar composition—Helios surrounded by the signs of the zodiac and the four seasons, the Ark of the Law, and the menorahs—is found in the 6th century floor mosaic of a synagogue at Na'aran, but here with the addition of a geometric carpet of octagons and circles filled with fruits, baskets, and creatures of earth, sea, and air. In addition, this pavement contains a biblical subject: the Prophet Daniel is depicted standing in prayer in front of the Ark, flanked by two large lions.[60]

Another composition that is found on several synagogue floors is the inhabited vine scroll, which occurs at Gaza, Ma'on, and Beth Shean. The medallions framed by these vines contain a wide variety of creatures, both the more common species such as snakes and hares, and relatively exotic ones such as zebra and giraffe. In addition, the vines at Ma'on and Beth Shean contain specifically Jewish symbols, such as the menorah. Other motifs displayed on these floors include bowls, vases, baskets, and fruit. Inscriptions set into the medallions of the mosaics or adjacent to them commemorate the donors of the pavements and, at Beth Shean, the artist ("Remembered be for good the artisan who made this work").[61] These floors, which all date to the 6th century, closely resemble depictions of inhabited vines appearing in Christian churches, such as the basilica discovered at Shellal, which is dated by an inscription to the year 561–62.[62]

Such figured floors were not confined to synagogues in Palestine. A pavement presenting a large repertoire of creatures was found in a synagogue at Hamman Lif (Naro), eleven miles from Tunis (fig. 40). Here the main hall was carpeted with mosaics depicting, among other motifs, fishes hooked on lines; ducks, quails, and peacocks; a lion, a hare, and a bull; as well as palm trees and baskets of fruit and possibly bread. All of these images surrounded the inscription of the donor, Juliana, which stated that she had at her own expense provided the mosaic for her salvation.[63]

As in the case of the Christian churches, these motifs from nature were capable of specific symbolic interpretation on the part of the faithful. Lions, for example, could represent Judah, or, as at Na'aran, they could refer to the salvation of Daniel. The continuing underlying message, however, was always of well-being and prosperity. And among the Jews, as among the Christians, there was a current of opposition to these motifs. In a recently discovered synagogue at Sepphoris there is a pavement depicting the chariot of the sun surrounded, as at Hammath Tiberias, by the signs of the zodiac and the seasons. In this case, however, the chariot is not driven by the personified Helios, but instead carries the sun itself, represented by a circle surrounded by rays.[64] It may be surmised that those who commissioned the mosaic were uncomfortable with the portrayal of the sun as a human figure. In this case an image redolent of paganism was avoided at the initial creation of the mosaic, but there were also several cases of floors whose images were removed after they had been laid, as can be seen in the mosaics at Na'aran, where not only the human figures but even the beasts and the birds were carefully picked out of their frames. The date at which these interventions took place has not yet been determined, but since the iconoclasts were often at pains to preserve the Hebrew letters, it seems to have been the Jews themselves who undertook the destruction.[65]

Islamic attitudes to figural representations excluded much of the late antique imagery of abundance from their religious architecture, where the portrayal of living creatures was scrupulously avoided. This absence of figural motifs left only plants and vegetation to evoke the fecundity of organic nature within the confines of cult buildings. Such a decoration may be seen in the late 7th century wall mosaics of the Dome of the Rock in Jerusalem, where plant forms of various kinds spring from jeweled vases and cornucopias (fig. 41).[66] In their design, some of these plants and gems recall the ornaments of tunics, such as the one illustrated in figure 21. The most extensive employment of plant forms in the decoration of an early Islamic religious building is to be found in the courtyard mosaics of the Great Mosque at Damascus, which date to the early 8th century (fig. 42). These mosaics, which present lines of trees, some with fruit and some without, interspersed with buildings, are devoid of any portrayal of living creatures, but show a striking variety of arboreal species.[67] Their overall effect recalls not only the earlier floor mosaics of villas set in bucolic surroundings (fig. 22), but also the tapestry hangings, displaying different varieties of trees together with architectural features such as columns, that were displayed on the walls of wealthy houses (fig. 10).[68] Whatever the symbolic meanings that could be projected upon the Jerusalem and Damascus mosaics by Muslim viewers, their ancestry lay in the imagery of well-being that had characterized the domestic environment of late antiquity.

At Damascus portrayals of living creatures were avoided, but in mosques there were also instances in which figural elements were deliberately destroyed. This happened at the Great Mosque of Kairouan, constructed in the 9th century, which contained sculptures appropriated from earlier Byzantine buildings, most of which must have been churches.[69] Many of the reused Byzantine capitals were of the two-zone type with projecting animal protomes at the corners. The Islamic builders of the mosque carefully cut off the features of the birds and beasts of the protomes, ingeniously converting them into nonfigural elements of the capital, such as volutes (fig. 43). The other decorative elements of the capital, however, such as leaves and cornucopia filled with fruits, they allowed to remain; in some cases the wings of the birds were recut and redrilled to become leaves. As in the mosaics of the Great Mosque of Damascus, some elements of the late antique imagery were preserved—the foliage and the horns of plenty— while the objectionable figural motifs were excised.

The material trappings of the good life in late antiquity, especially as it was enjoyed in the domestic sphere, displayed a rich imagery of personifications and motifs drawn from nature that evoked prosperity in the homes of the well-to-do. This imagery was a common frame of reference for pagans, Christians, Jews, and Muslims alike, but it was not completely neutral; it was sufficiently powerful to provoke opposition, demonstrated both by texts and by iconoclastic interventions in the monuments themselves. Nevertheless, many of the motifs that expressed abundance and well-being were eventually incorporated into the decoration of cult buildings after the removal of elements that were deemed unacceptable—such as the major pagan deities in the case of the Christians, or living creatures in the case of the Muslims. The Christians went the furthest in introducing the imagery of abundance into their places of worship; their permissiveness in this respect may even have contributed, by way of reaction, to the later adoption of stricter stances on the part of Jews and Muslims.[70] Borrowing much of the iconography of secular abundance and pleasure, the Christian authorities converted the good life dominated by the late Roman aristocrats into a good life that was controlled by the church. Thus, while the deities changed, the rich frames within which they had been presented survived.

Even among the Christians, however, there was an undercurrent of unease at this assimilation, and in the end the frames themselves came under increasing suspicion. The iconoclastic controversy of the 8th and 9th centuries, although primarily concerned with sacred portraiture, sensitized Christians anew to the issue of the suitability of motifs drawn from nature as a decoration for churches. John of Damascus wrote in the 8th century: "Is it not far more worthy to adorn all the walls of the Lord's house with the forms and images of saints rather than with beasts and trees?"[71] A famous passage in the iconodule Life of St. Stephen the Younger accuses the iconoclast Emperor Constantine V of scraping the pictures of Christ's miracles off the walls of the church at the Blachernae, and replacing them with mosaics representing "trees and all kinds of birds and beasts, and certain swirls of ivy leaves [enclosing] cranes, crows, and peacocks," thus turning the building into a "store-house of fruit and an aviary."[72] After iconoclasm, there was little place in medieval Byzantine churches for elaborate tessellated floors with animals and personifications from nature; these motifs were, in many churches, replaced by aniconic compositions in intarsia, which did not compete with the sacred company depicted upon the walls.[73] Hereafter, the good life was to be lived with the saints, not with the wealth imaged by the material world.[74]

Notes

I thank Stephen Zwirn for his critical reading of this essay.

1. *PG* 62.259–264.

2. G. Becatti, "Case Ostiensi del Tardo Impero," *Bollettino d'Arte* 33 (1948): 105–107.

3. Gunilla Åkerström-Hougen, *The Calendar and Hunting Mosaics of the Villa of the Falconer in Argos* (Stockholm, 1974).

4. Vatican Library, ms. lat. 3867, fol. 100v. Facsimile and commentary: Carlo Bertelli et al., *Vergilius Romanus, Codex Vaticanus Latinus 3867*, 3 vols. (Zurich, 1985–1986).

5. Eunice Dauterman Maguire et al., *Art and Holy Powers in the Early Christian House* (Urbana, 1989), 48.

6. Friedrich Wilhelm Deichmann, *Ravenna: Hauptstadt des spätantiken Abendlandes,* vol. II, 2, *Kommentar* (Wiesbaden, 1976), 180–187.

7. Friedrich Matz, *Die dionysischen Sarkophage* (Berlin, 1968), vol. 1, nos. 11–11A, pls. 18, 22.

8. Annemarie Stauffer, *Die mittelalterlichen Textilien von St. Servatius in Maastricht* (Riggisberg, 1991), 102–103.

9. Maguire, *Art and Holy Powers,* 51.

10. Mechthild Flury-Lemberg, *Textile Conservation* (Bern, 1988), 412–420.

11. Herbert A. Cahn and Annemarie Kaufmann-Heinimann, *Der spätrömische Silberschatz von Kaiseraugst* (Derendingen, 1984).

12. Ibid., 1: 225–315; K. S. Painter, *The Mildenhall Treasure* (London, 1977), 26.

13. Abdelmagid Ennabli, "Les thermes du thiase marin de Sidi Ghrib," *Monuments et Mémoires,* Fondation Eugène Piot, 68 (1986): 42–44.

14. Kathleen J. Shelton, *The Esquiline Treasure* (London, 1981), 72–75.

15. *Homilia I; PG* 40.165–168; trans. Cyril Mango, *The Art of the Byzantine Empire, 312–1453* (Englewood Cliffs, N.J., 1972), 50–51.

16. Alberto de Capitani d'Arzago, *Antichi tessuti della Basilica Ambrosiana* (Milan, 1941), 15–67; Hero Granger Taylor, "The Two Dalmatics of St. Ambrose?" *Bulletin de Liaison du CIETA* 57/8 (1983): 127–173.

17. Wulf Raeck, "Publica non despiciens," *Mitteilungen des Deutschen Archäologischen Instituts, Römische Abteilung,* 94 (1987): 295–308.

18. Kurt Weitzmann, *Age of Spirituality* (New York, 1979), 310, 313–314.

19. Margaret A. Alexander et al., *Corpus des Mosaiques de Tunisie,* vol. 2.4, *Thuburbo Majus* (Tunis, 1994), 100.

20. Richard Ettinghausen, *Arab Painting* (Geneva, 1962), 33–35.

21. J. W. Salomonson, "Late Roman Earthenware," *Oudheidkundige Mededelingen* 43 (1962): 56, 74–81, 89.

22. W. Fritz Volbach, *Il tessuto nell'arte antica* (Milan, 1966), 74–76.

23. Jutta-Annette Bruhn, *Coins and Costume in Late Antiquity* (Washington, D.C., 1993), 33–34.

24. Larry Salmon, "An Eastern Mediterranean Puzzle," *Boston Museum of Fine Arts Bulletin* 67 (1969): 136–150.

25. Paul Friedländer, *Documents of Dying Paganism* (Berkeley, 1945), 1–26.

26. Margaret T. J. Rowe, "Group of Bands Adorning a Tunic: Dossier," *Bulletin de Liaison du CIETA* 17 (1963): 9–13.

27. Annemarie Stauffer et al., Textiles of Late Antiquity (New York, 1996), 45, no. 24.

28. *De inani gloria,* 4; cited by Peter Brown, *Power and Persuasion in Late Antiquity* (Madison, 1992), 83.

29. Katherine M. D. Dunbabin, *The Mosaics of Roman North Africa* (Oxford, 1978), 151–152.

30. Raffaella Cribiore, "A Hymn to the Nile," *Zeitschrift für Papyrologie und Epigraphik* 106 (1995): 97–106; translation on 100.

31. Ehud Netzer and Zeev Weiss, *Zippori* (Jerusalem, 1994), 46–51.

32. On this class of tapestries, see Annemarie Stauffer, *Textiles d'Egypte de la collection Bouvier* (Fribourg, 1991), 35–53.

33. Henry Maguire, "Garments Pleasing to God: The Significance of Domestic Textile Designs in the Early Byzantine Period," *Dumbarton Oaks Papers* 44 (1990): 217.

34. Leslie S. B. MacCoull, *Dioscorus of Aphrodito: His Work and His World* (Berkeley, 1988), 88–89, 111–112; translations by MacCoull.

35. Lambert Schneider, *Die Domäne als Weltbild: Wirkungsstrukturen der spätantiken Bildersprache* (Wiesbaden, 1983), 150.

36. D. Michaelides, *Cypriot Mosaics,* 2nd ed. (Nicosia, 1992), 93, no. 51.

37. Daniel Schlumberger, "Les fouilles de Qasr el-Heir el-Gharbi (1936–1938)," *Syria* 20 (1939): 330, fig. 25, pl. 47.3.

38. Ettinghausen, *Arab Painting,* 36.

39. The personifications, whose inscriptions survived, were Ktisis, Ananeōsis, Euandria, and Dynamis; Doro Levi, *Antioch Mosaic Pavements* (Princeton, 1947), 349–350, pl. 132.

40. Louis Poinssot, "Mosaïques d'El-Haouria," *Revue Africaine* 76 (1935): 183–206.

41. *Vita S. Eutychii,* 53; PG 86.2333–36.

42. Dunbabin, *Mosaics of North Africa,* 142–144; Margaret A. Alexander, Aïcha Ben Abed, and Guy P. R. Metraux, "Corpus of the Mosaics of Tunisia, Carthage Project, 1992–1994," *Dumbarton Oaks Papers* 50 (1996).

43. On aniconic mosaics of the early 6th century preserved in a Monophysite church, see Ernest J. W. Hawkins and Marlia C. Mundell, "The Mosaics of the Monastery of Mar Samuel, Mar Simeon, and Mar Gabriel near Kartmin," *Dumbarton Oaks Papers* 27 (1973): 279–296.

44. From the Maison d'Ariane; Dunbabin, *Mosaics of North Africa,* 156.

45. Katherine M. D. Dunbabin, "A Mosaic Workshop in Carthage around A.D. 400," in John Griffiths Pedley, ed., *New Light on Ancient Carthage* (Ann Arbor, 1980), 77–78; Henry Maguire, "Christians, Pagans, and the Representation of Nature," *Riggisberger Berichte* 1 (1993): 151–152.

46. Maguire, "Christians, Pagans," 132–136.

47. See André Grabar, "Recherches sur les sources juives de l'art paléochrétien, II: Les mosaïques de pavement," *Cahiers archéologiques* 12 (1962): 115–152, esp. 132–134.

48. Elisabeth Alföldi Rosenbaum and John Ward-Perkins, *Justinianic Mosaic Pavements in Cyrenaican Churches* (Rome, 1980), 41–42, pl. 11.3.

49. Henry Maguire, *Earth and Ocean: The Terrestrial World in Early Byzantine Art* (University Park, Pa., 1987); Marek-Titien Olszewski, "L'image et sa fonction dans la mosaïque byzantine des premières basiliques en Orient: L'iconographie chrétienne expliquée par Cyrille de Jérusalem (314–387)," *Cahiers archéologiques* 43 (1995): 9–34.

50. Zbigniew T. Fiema, Robert Schick, and Khairieh 'Amr, "The Petra Church Project: Interim Report, 1992–94," in J. H. Humphrey, ed., *The Roman and Byzantine Near East: Some Recent Archaeological Research* (Ann Arbor, 1995), 294–295.

51. Maguire, *Earth and Ocean*, 45–51.

52. Alfons M. Schneider, *The Church of the Multiplying of the Loaves and Fishes* (London, 1937), 58–63, figs. 2–17.

53. Maguire, *Earth and Ocean*, 29, figs. 32–33.

54. MacCoull, *Dioscorus of Aphrodito*, 111–112.

55. M. Manfredi, "Inno cristiano al Nilo," in P. J. Parsons and J. R. Rea, eds., *Papyri Greek and Egyptian Edited by Various Hands in Honour of Eric Gardner Turner* (London, 1981), 56.

56. Noël Duval, "La représentation du palais d'après le Psautier d'Utrecht," *Cahiers archéologiques* 15 (1965): 244–247.

57. Deichmann, *Ravenna*, vol. II, 2, *Kommentar*, 177–178.

58. Moshe Dothan, *Hammath Tiberias* (Jerusalem, 1983), 33–60.

59. See, for example, a floor from the Maison de Silène at El Djem depicting busts of the sun and the moon accompanied by the four seasons (Dunbabin, *Mosaics of North Africa*, 160, pl. 159), and another from the *oikos* of a villa at Bir-Chana showing the planetary deities surrounded by the signs of the zodiac (ibid., 161, pl. 162).

60. Michael Avi-Yonah, "Na'aran," in Ephraim Stern, ed., *The New Encyclopedia of Archaeological Excavations in the Holy Land* (Jerusalem, 1993), 3: 1075–1076.

61. A. Ovadiah, "The Synagogue at Gaza," in Lee I. Levine, ed., *Ancient Synagogues Revealed* (Jerusalem, 1981), 129–132; Dan Barag, "Ma'on," in *The New Encyclopedia of Archaeological Excavations in the Holy Land*, 3: 944–946; D. Bahat, "A Synagogue at Beth-Shean," *Ancient Synagogues Revealed*, 82–85.

62. A. D. Trendall, *The Shellal Mosaic* (Canberra, 1957).

63. Jean-Pierre Darmon, "Les mosaïques de la synagogue de Hammam Lif," in Roger Ling, ed., *Fifth International Colloquium on Ancient Mosaics* (Ann Arbor, 1996), 7–29.

64. Netzer and Weiss, *Zippori*, 56–58.

65. Avi-Yonah, "Na'aran," 1076.

66. K. A. C. Creswell, *Early Muslim Architecture* (Oxford, 1969), vol. I, 1, 213–322, pls. 7–37; Oleg Grabar, *The Formation of Islamic Art* (New Haven, 1987), 55–62.

67. Creswell, *Early Muslim Achitecture*, vol. I, 1, 323–372, pls. 50–58; Grabar, *Formation of Islamic Art*, 88–89; Gisela Hellenkemper Salies, "Die Mosaiken der Grossen Moschee von Damaskus," *Corsi di cultura sull'arte ravennate e bizantina* 35 (1988): 295–313.

68. Tadeusz Sarnowski, *Les représentations de villas sur les mosaïques africaines tardives* (Wroclaw, 1978); Stauffer, *Textiles d'Egypte*, 45–46.

69. K. A. C. Creswell, *Early Muslim Architecture* (Oxford, 1940), 2: 220.

70. See Ernst Kitzinger, "The Cult of Images in the Age before Iconoclasm," *Dumbarton Oaks Papers* 8 (1954): 130, n. 204; Grabar, *Formation of Islamic Art*, esp. 94.

71. *De imaginibus oratio I*, PG 94.1252.

72. *Vita S. Stephani iunioris*, PG 100.1120; trans. Mango, *Art of the Byzantine Empire*, 152–153.

73. On the archaeological evidence for the destruction of such motifs in the pavements of churches in Jordan, which seems to have occurred not earlier than the 8th century, see Michele Piccirillo, *The Mosaics of Jordan* (Amman, 1993), 41–42, and

Michele Piccirillo and Eugenio Alliata, *Umm al-Rasas Mayfa'ah*, vol. 1, *Gli scavi del complesso di Santo Stefano* (Jerusalem, 1994), 121–164. See also Urs Peschlow, "Zum byzantinischen opus sectile-Boden," in R. M. Boehmer and H. Hauptmann, eds., *Beiträge zur Altertumskunde Kleinasiens: Festschrift für Kurt Bittel* (Mainz, 1983), 435–447, pls. 89–93.

74. See Peter Brown, *The Rise of Western Christendom* (Oxford, 1996), esp. 250–253.

1 Ostia, House of Cupid and Psyche
(photo: Henry Maguire)

2 Floor mosaic from the dining room of the Villa
of the Falconer, Argos Museum (from G.
Åkerström-Hougen, *The Calendar and Hunting
Mosaics of the Villa of the Falconer in Argos*
[Stockholm, 1974])

3 Hunting with falcons, detail of a floor mosaic from the Villa of the Falconer (Åkerström-Hougen, *Calendar and Hunting Mosaics*)

4 May (holding a basket of flowers) and June (holding a sheaf of grain), detail of a floor mosaic from the Villa of the Falconer (Åkerström-Hougen, *Calendar and Hunting Mosaics*)

6 Dido's feast (Biblioteca Apostolica Vaticana, MS. lat. 3867, fol. 100v., Roman Virgil)

5 Acanthus border, detail of a floor mosaic of the months from the Villa of the Falconer, Argos Museum (photo: Henry Maguire)

7 Hestia Polyolbos, tapestry weave hanging (Dumbarton Oaks, Washington, D.C.)

8 Bearers of gifts, fragment of a tapestry weave hanging (Dumbarton Oaks, Washington, D.C.)

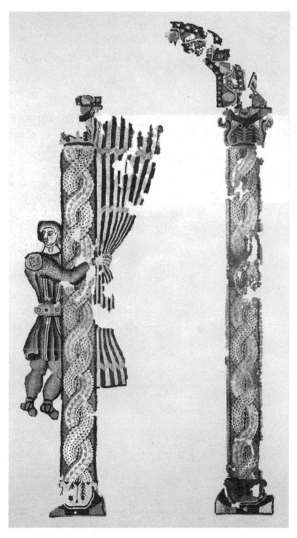

9 Servant behind a column, fragment of a tapestry weave hanging (Museum of Fine Arts, Boston)

10 Fruiting trees, fragment of a tapestry weave hanging (State Hermitage Museum, St. Petersburg)

11 Curtain fragment (Walter Massey Collection, Royal Ontario Museum, Toronto)

12 Rider making the "Parthian" shot, fragment of a silk roundel (Treasury of St. Servatius, Maastricht)

13 Female personification, fragment of tapestry weave (University of Toronto Malcove Collection)

14 Nilotic themes, silk fragment (Abegg-Stiftung, Riggisberg)

15 Scenes from the life of
Achilles, silver dish from
the Kaiseraugst treasure
(Römermuseum Augst,
Basel)

16 Ocean and Bacchic scenes,
silver dish from the
Mildenhall Treasure
(© The British Museum,
London)

17 The lady's toilette, floor mosaic (from Abdelmagid Ennabli, "Les thermes du thiase marin de Sidi Ghrib," *Monuments et Mémoires* 68 [1986], pl. 14)

18 "Projecta Casket," silver casket from the Esquiline treasure (© The British Museum, London)

19 Lion hunt, detail of silk tunic (from Alberto de
Capitani d'Arzago, *Antichi Tessuti della Basilica
Ambrosiana* [Milan, 1941], fig. 20)

20 Personifications of Earth, surrounded by the ocean, fragment of
silk sleeve band (Yale University Art Gallery, New Haven)

21 Lion hunters, plants, and personification, silk band (Metropolitan
Museum of Art, New York)

22 Estate of Dominus Iulius, floor mosaic from Carthage (Bardo Museum, Tunis)

23 Gold
necklace
with gems
and pearls
(Staatliche
Museen,
Berlin)

24 Shell-shaped pendant with Aphrodite,
necklace (Dumbarton Oaks, Washington,
D.C.)

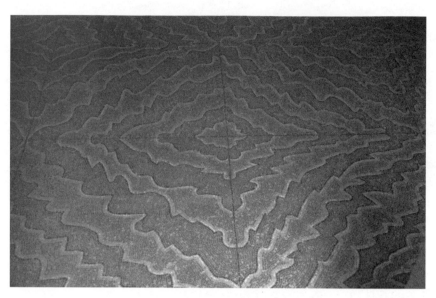

25 Imitation marble, floor mosaic from Thuburbo Majus (Bardo Museum, Tunis)

26 Personification of Earth, floor fresco, Qaṣr al-Hayr West (© 1962 and 1977 by Editions d'Art, Albert Skira SA, Geneva)

27 Scenes from the life of
Achilles, reconstruction of
North African pottery *lanx*
(National Museum of
Antiquities, Leiden)

28 Lion hunters, tapestry
woven medallion (Cooper-
Hewitt National Design
Museum/Art Resource,
New York)

29 Imitation necklaces, neckline
of a tunic (Museum of Fine
Arts, Boston)

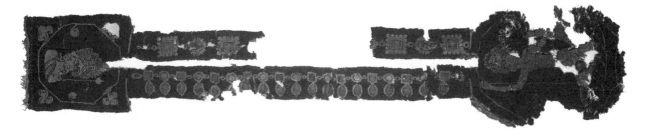

30 Mask of Ocean, floor mosaic from Ain-Témouchent (photo: Katherine Dunbabin)

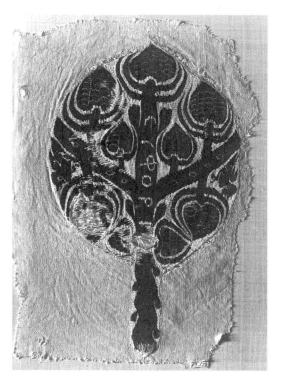

31 Flourishing tree, curtain fragment (Museum of Fine Arts, Boston)

32 *Tholos* with dancers, floor mosaic, house north of the Antonine baths, Carthage

33 Venus and dancers, mosaic from the Maison d'Ariane in Carthage (Bardo Museum, Tunis; photo: Margaret Alexander)

34 Summer, detail of floor mosaic in the south aisle, church east of the Temple of the Winged Lions, Petra (photo: Henry Maguire)

35 Detail of floor mosaic in the nave, East
Church, Qaṣr el-Lebia (from Elisabeth Alföldi-
Rosenbaum, *Justinianic Mosaic Pavements in
Cyrenaican Churches* [Rome, 1980])

36 Nilotic motifs (crocodile, boat, and ostrich), detail of carved ceiling beam over the nave, St. Catherine,
Mount Sinai (Michigan-Princeton-Alexandria Expedition to Mount Sinai)

37 View of a church with its floor mosaic, tomb mosaic from Tabarka (Bardo Museum, Tunis)

38 Mosaics in the vault over the chancel, S. Vitale, Ravenna (Hirmer Fotoarchiv, Munich)

39 Floor mosaic in principal aisle, synagogue, Hammath Tiberias (from Moshe Dotha, *Hammath Tiberias* [Jerusalem, 1983])

40 Floor mosaic in main hall, synagogue, Hamman Lif (Naro) (from Erwin Goodenough, *Jewish Symbols in the Greco-Roman Period,* © 1988 by Princeton University Press)

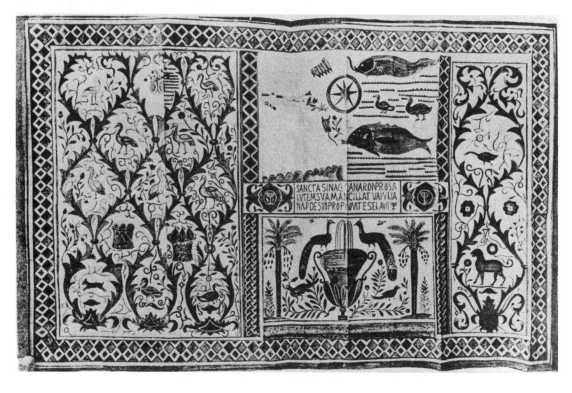

41 Plant and jewels, wall mosaic in the drum, Dome of the Rock, Jerusalem (photo: B. Brenk)

43 Bird converted into leaves and volutes, reused Byzantine capital, Great Mosque, Kairouan (photo: Henry Maguire)

42 Trees and buildings, wall mosaic in the western portico, Great Mosque, Damascus (photo: B. Brenk)

Habitat

Yizhar Hirschfeld

The dwellings of the inhabitants of the empire in late antiquity express various and at times contradictory trends. During this time the gap between the aristocratic class and the simple folk widened. Yet there was also a significant increase in the economic power of the middle class, which comprised landowning free farmers as well as city dwellers dealing in small industry, commerce, and services. The high point of private construction came in the 4th century, which saw the building of magnificent urban complexes and of fortified villas in rural areas. The prevailing economic prosperity also found expression in the houses of simpler people. The decline that followed was not uniform: in the west, prosperity ended in the 5th century, in contrast to the east, where it continued until the mid 8th century.

The Roman villa of late antiquity, both urban *(villa urbana)* and rural *(villa rustica)*, underwent a renaissance. The end of the 3rd century and beginning of the 4th witnessed a dynamic process of consolidating properties into private hands. This process, which was initiated in part by the emperors, created an affluent social stratum across the empire. The wealth of the elite found expression in the villas they built—which functioned not only as dwellings, but also as centers of social and economic activity. The existence of substantial villas, both in the city and village, attest to a high standard of living. Their regular plan and high-quality construction (including architectural decoration) reflect the economic resources of members of the middle class. Many of the houses of this period contained facilities for the processing of agricultural produce; this private enterprise also helped raise the standard of living.

The abundance that earlier, in the Roman period, was at the disposal of the few became widespread among the residents of settled lands and also extended to outlying areas. Farmhouses of varying sizes have been discovered in regions that were previously sparsely settled or not settled at all. These well-constructed buildings often served as the production centers of local landowners.

In the east the construction of farmhouses in peripheral areas continued into the 8th century. There the economic prosperity of this period influenced the nomadic desert population to make the transition to seminomadic or permanent settlements.

On the outskirts of settled areas we also find the dwellings of monastic communities—an innovation on the landscape of late antiquity. The communal monasteries (coenobia) were for the most part very similar to the villa rustica, but they always preserved their special function as institutions of prayer as well as hospitality. The monasteries of the recluses (lavrae) and individual monks' places of seclusion, or hermitages, were unlike any secular buildings. The use of the natural landscape—cliffs, caves, and rock shelters—as dwellings emphasized the importance of monks as spiritual patrons. These people, many of whom gained admiration as holy men, were immeasurably more accessible than the landowning patrons living in the city, who offered financial sponsorship. The contrast between these two forms of patronage is among the signs of late antiquity.

Our information about dwellings and domestic life in late antiquity comes from an array of sources. Hagiographic literature contains various references to houses, primarily in the rural settlements, as well as detailed descriptions of monastic dwellings transmitted to us in the written lives of the saints. Other literary works from the 4th and 5th centuries, such as the descriptions of banquets in the writings of Ausonius or Paulinus of Nola, inform us of daily life in the villa. Relevant information regarding private building is occasionally found in imperial laws as well. For example, in the writings of Julianus of Ascalon, a 6th century architect who composed a book about the laws of construction, we learn about the urban bylaws regulating the height of construction, distances between houses, the location of windows, and so on.

Rabbinic literature is a rich historical source for the lifestyle of dwellings in the east. The corpora of halakha (Jewish law), such as the Mishnah, Tosefta, and Talmuds, and of midrash written by the Jewish religious leadership in Palestine and Babylonia, reflect daily life in the Roman-Byzantine period. In them we find references to almost every aspect of existence, including the most intimate ones concerning the home. Although this literature was written in the cities of Palestine, such as Sepphoris, Tiberias, and Caesarea, it expresses the way of life of the Jewish population as a whole, the majority of whom lived in rural areas.

In addition to literary sources, a trove of information about rural life in Egypt can be derived from papyrological evidence. These documents usually deal with landed property and estates; the descriptions of houses are incidental. This valuable material is found in the papyri of Oxyrhynchus, the capital of the desert located about 180 km south of Cairo. Detailed references to estates—dwellings and landed property—are found in the papyri of Petra in Jordan from the 6th century and in the papyri of Nessana in the Negev, which date a bit later (6th and 7th centuries). These documents complement what we know from the papyri discovered in Nahal Hever in the Judaean desert, which date to the 2nd century C.E. These papyri inform us of various details about the dwellings of the inhabitants of the desert oases around the Dead Sea, such as Ein Gedi and Zoar.

Epigraphical evidence is particularly important because it includes dedicatory inscriptions that provide names of homeowners and construction terms. So, for example, we learn about the various elements of the house, such as the *triclinium* (dining hall), *stablon* (stable), or *aulē* (courtyard), from inscriptions found on the walls or ceilings of houses.

The archaeological evidence of dwellings from late antiquity is very rich. Although the study of archaeological sites in the west is quite developed and has a relatively long tradition, it naturally has focused on villas and manor houses, the better preserved remains of the period; details of the homes of simple farmers in the west, which were often constructed of brick, are not so readily studied. In contrast, remains of all types of dwellings in the east have been preserved, both in cities and rural regions, since their construction was largely of stone. Moreover, in the peripheral areas of the east, human activity after antiquity waned; therefore many of the dwellings from the Roman-Byzantine period were left in the relatively good state of their last occupation. In the desert areas of North Africa and the Negev, for instance, many houses were preserved intact to a height of over one story, while Hauran houses from the Roman-Byzantine period were inhabited by the local population until recently. Archaeological finds enable us to trace the dynamics of expansion and renovation, as well as those of reduction, abandonment, and destruction.

Another important source of information is the depiction of houses and manors in mosaics of the 5th century, primarily from North Africa. In the urban villas of North Africa's upper classes, very precise, almost photographic depictions of their rural manors have been found. These mosaics, and mosaics from sites throughout the empire, also contain scenes of banquets and social events that were held in halls intended for these purposes *(convivia)*. These scenes appear alongside the images from Greek mythology favored by upper classes in the 3rd–4th centuries.

The wealth accrued by the urban aristocracy supported the building of dwelling complexes of outstanding splendor and size. Much simpler dwellings, and occasionally even houses bearing a rural character, stood side-by-side with these urban complexes.

Remains of houses of the well-to-do have been found throughout the empire, in both the east and west. These houses were usually located in the center of the city, following the local Roman tradition, or on the city's periphery, where there was ample building space. Although the houses of the urban aristocracy varied in their layout and details, they all had some combination of two elements: an apsidal reception hall *(oikos)*, and a central courtyard surrounded by columns (peristyle). The peristyle courtyard was the heart of the house. The entrance hall leads from the street to the courtyard, from which one gains access to the reception hall and dining rooms (triclinia), where the homeowners received their guests. This is a departure from the design of the Pompeiian house of the Roman period, in which the peristyle courtyard was situated at the back. In the center of the courtyard, or in one of its corners, a fountain or pond containing exotic fish was almost a standard fixture. In the west, the peristyle courtyard disappears in the 5th and 6th centuries, but in the east we know of examples of houses with peristyle courtyards that were in use until the 8th century, such as those at Pella and Gerasa, cities of the Decapolis in Jordan.

The reception hall and dining hall opened directly onto the courtyard (through one wide entry or three narrower ones), so guests could enjoy the air and light as well as the pond or fountains in the courtyard. Opposite the entrance facing the courtyard, on the other side of the hall, there was almost always an apse or an arrangement of three apses (in this case, the hall is termed *triconchos*). The apse occasionally framed the official seat of the homeowner. It was in the reception hall that the homeowner would receive his guests. Since according to the system of patronage that characterized late antiquity many people were dependent upon a wealthy person's sponsorship, the reception hall served in the daytime as a place to receive people seeking help. The ceilings in such rooms were often supported in the center by two rows of columns; inscriptions found on mosaics called these halls *basilica*.

Next to the reception hall was the triclinium, where business or social dinners were held. It also served as the place of reception in houses that lacked a separate oikos. The social function of rooms of this type was depicted in the magnificent mosaic floors decorating them. These floors were characteristically divided into four colored panels arranged in a T shape: three panels forming a horizontal row with a fourth, larger panel perpendicular to them. The diners would sit around the mosaic panels and look out at the view through the courtyard entrance.

The banquets held in these rooms are depicted on many mosaic floors. In the triclinium of the Orpheus House—a large dwelling recently discovered in Sepphoris in the Lower Galilee—a festive banquet is depicted. The central panel depicts four members of the dining party sitting on a semicircular sofa *(stibadium)*, of the type that was fashionable in the 5th–6th centuries. This semicircular sofa surrounds a three-legged dining table, next to which stands a three-legged urn *(milliarium)* for heating wine. The triclinium in which this mosaic is found is a large hall measuring 6 × 8 m. The house is named after the figure of Orpheus appearing in the center of the mosaic.

Another element often found in the villa urbana is the private bathhouse, sometimes added on to an existing structure. At Ostia, large houses with halls heated by a hypocaust were found, as were private bathhouses with toilets. It appears that aristocratic homeowners saw a need to separate themselves from the masses that frequented the public bathhouses. Such private bathhouses were also found in the large manors in the rural areas.

The rooms of the villa urbana were arranged in various configurations, although the villas of the west continued to uphold the strict Roman tradition of symmetry. The homeowner's living quarters were usually on the ground floor, while the second floor held the rooms of servants and others in the homeowner's employ, and those considered part of the household's *familia*. The villa also accommodated its owners' commercial occupations: the facade of the villa urbana often contained shops that sold agricultural produce from the rural manors of the homeowners, who were also large landowners. Some of these shops were rented to the highest bidder. Often at the entrance to the house there was a stone-paved courtyard for the loading and unloading of merchandise. Sometimes a room for a guard who watched those entering and leaving the premises was positioned next to the entrance.

Houses of the urban aristocracy have been found at a large number of sites. Near the Athenian agora, spacious houses of the well-to-do from the 4th–5th centuries have been uncovered. These houses range between 1000 and 1300 sq m (unlike houses in Roman Athens, whose area is 350–420 sq m). Magnificent villas have been uncovered at Antioch and its nearby port of Seleucia. The focus of these houses was their triclinia, which were decorated with colored mosaics. It appears that the importance of the triclinium was expressed by its size; whereas the average width of the 2nd century triclinium was 4–5 m, in the 5th century it was 7–8 m. Other impressive houses of the urban aristocracy were discovered at Sepphoris in the Galilee (Dionysius House) and at Nea Paphos in Cyprus, among other places.

The most beautiful examples of the houses of the wealthy come from the cities of Africa Proconsularis. The villas of the local aristocracy, who had accrued much wealth, were exceptionally large and magnificent. Their triclinia usually contained three or more apses; in the Bacchus House in Djemila we find a triclinium with seven apses. This complex, which stretches over an area of 7000 sq m, is one of the largest dwellings found in North Africa. Another complex is the 4th century House of the Hunt uncovered at Bulla Regia. The area of this complex is 2800 sq m and includes a front courtyard for carriages at the entrance to the house and a peristyle courtyard in its center. Signs of renovations and additions are evident in these houses.

From the late 2nd century until the end of the 4th, various cities in the west saw the building of villas with peristyle courtyards. An impressive aristocratic house from the 4th century was uncovered near the Cologne cathedral. In its center was a huge courtyard with a fountain lying on the same axis as the triclinium, which was adorned with scenes from the life of Dionysius. At the front of the house were a large portico and a row of shops. Aristocratic houses from the 4th century have been found in other cities as well, such as Bordeaux, Ravenna, Ostia, and Rome. Late Roman Ostia, the port town of Rome, marks a breaking away from the Roman *insula* (apartment block) and a preference for the *domus* (freestanding house). When the city's decline beginning in the 2nd century caused the prices of rented apartments in the insulae to plummet, these buildings were abandoned and destroyed. In contrast, this period witnessed a flourishing of the peristyle dwelling, the domus. This house is characterized by marble floors, gardens, and fountains in a peristyle courtyard, as well as a frequently used warm-air heating system beneath the floors. One such domus is the House of Cupid and Psyche, built around 300. A magnificent garden with a nymphaeum and a privy occupied one-third of the ground floor. The rear of the garden opened onto a large hall paved with floors worked in beautiful colored marble *(opus sectile)*, next to which were three bedrooms. In the course of the 5th and 6th centuries these houses were abandoned, some converted into monasteries.

Near the urban peristyle aristocratic houses were various types of simpler dwellings. A densely built residential quarter from the 6th century has been uncovered in Jerusalem, south of the Temple Mount. In this quarter, twenty-two houses were found built one next to the other. Most of them were two stories high; the rooms on the ground floor were used for storage and services, while those on the upper floor served as living quarters. Bordering these were single-story houses with one or two rooms, and bordering them, agricultural tracts that were worked by their owners. Another example of an urban dwelling with a rural character was found at Pella in Jordan. In the eastern quarter of the city, archaeologists uncovered a house that was built in the 4th century and destroyed in the great earthquake of 749. The rooms on the ground floor of this two-story house served as stables and storerooms. The remains of a horse, two cows, and a goat were found beneath the rubble of the earthquake.

The central courtyard was a prominent feature in the dwellings of late antiquity. The extended family, which was the primary social unit in this period, lived in apartment buildings arranged around a common courtyard. An apartment building typical of the 7th–8th centuries has been discovered at Gerasa. In the front of the building, which faced the *decumanus,* were three shops and an entranceway leading into an irregularly shaped inner courtyard. Around it, five or six separate dwelling units were built for members of one family. Each unit had two rooms: a front room for daily living and a back room for sleeping. The area of the complex was about 600 sq m.

Workplace elements were found in many urban houses. A good example of this are the houses from the 4th–7th centuries uncovered in Alexandria. The houses' facades were integrated with shops that served simultaneously as workshops *(ergasteria),* equipped with kilns, dye vats, a glass factory, and so on. Various workshop facilities were found inside the houses as well, which required the homeowners to enlarge their dwelling complexes. The expansion at times came at the expense of the street area; this process marked the appearance of the Oriental *sūq* (bazaar) in the cities of the east as early as the 6th century. Dwellings with shops and workshops are known from the 7th–8th centuries (Umayyad period) at Apollonia on the coast of Palestine, north of Tel Aviv.

In many cities, especially in the east, monasteries had become a new type of dwelling. These were communal institutions (coenobia), complexes containing enclosed inner courtyards and surrounded by a wall, housing for the most part modestly sized monastic communities. An example is the 6th century Monastery of the Lady Mary discovered in Beth Shean/Scythopolis, which was named after one of the donors mentioned in the mosaic floor. It was situated not in the city's center, but rather next to the northern wall. The plan of the monastery is reminiscent of the aristocratic houses of the period: a central courtyard (though not peristyle) and a church paralleling the apsidal reception hall (oikos) of the secular villa. The remaining rooms of the monastery—the monks' cells, dining room, and kitchen—are arranged around the courtyard. As in the villas, here too the floor is composed of colored mosaic depicting animals and agricultural scenes. These subjects were close to the hearts of the monks, many of whom worked in agriculture (producing wine and oil) while living in the monastery.

Thousands of sites with manor houses and farmhouses have been found throughout rural areas of the empire, both in the east and west. In the east some of these survived after the urban centers had waned. For example, farmhouses in the Negev continued to be used in the 8th and 9th centuries, although the main settlements of Avdat, Nessana, and Shivta ceased to exist at some point in the 7th century. A similar phenomenon occurred in the west. At the end of the 4th century and during the 5th, some cities lost their function as commercial centers, and the economic center of gravity shifted to the rural areas. The simple dwelling that characterized the rural areas of the west in late antiquity continued to be used in the early Middle Ages as well. This "aisled house" contains a main hall divided by two rows of wooden posts into a central nave flanked by two side aisles. The internal division of these spaces depended upon the needs of the residents of the house.

The countryside of late antiquity was characterized by large rural manors which usually served as the hub of vast estates. We know of examples of urban villas that were built according to Roman tradition—on beautiful landscapes, on the coast (in North Africa), or along large rivers (in Germany and Belgium)—but they are in the minority. The dominant type of manor house in late antiquity was the fortified villa which, influenced by military architecture, continues the eastern Hellenistic tradition of fortified courtyard houses, equipped with up to four towers. The tower, rising to a height of three or four stories, was a status symbol; it was also functional, as it enabled the homeowner or estate manager (*villicus*) to oversee and supervise the manor.

The large rural manor houses are familiar to us first and foremost from depictions on mosaics from North Africa. These mosaic floors, dating to the 4th and 5th centuries, were usually found in the dining rooms of large aristocratic urban houses such as the ones in Carthage, Cherchel, Tabarka, and elsewhere. The wealth of these homeowners was derived from their rural manors, which were clearly a source of pride. We can imagine these aristocrats dining with their guests and, during the banquet, proudly pointing to the depictions of their manors in the mosaic. The manor houses are depicted standing in an open landscape surrounded by orchards and fields. Occasionally, as in the famous mosaic of Dominus Iulius in Carthage, the lord of the manor and his wife are depicted. The manor building in this mosaic is typical: a fortified structure with two towers. The arched entrance gate leads into the central courtyard, where the reception hall and adjacent private bathhouse are depicted. The reception hall was used by the lord of the manor for receiving his guests and subjects, as was the custom in the city. The bathhouse is depicted as a structure with domes venting smoke from the heating system.

The typical villa rustica, which had three components, is depicted in detail in a 4th–5th century mosaic discovered at Tabarka. The mosaic adorned a trifoli-ate triclinium, so that each of the room's three apses depicted one part of the villa. The central apse shows the main structure, the *pars urbana,* where the owner lived when he was in residence. This was an enclosed structure with a main gate leading into an inner courtyard. One can see the domes of the bathhouse inside the courtyard, and opposite them the two-story residential wing with its portico and two towers. The side apses depict portions of the *pars rustica,* that is, the parts of the manor that served as living quarters for the workers and animals and for food storage and the processing of agricultural produce; the right-hand apse pictures the main structure, with a horse tethered to it; the left-hand apse, a simple farmhouse with storerooms, animal pens, and barns.

The manor house symbolized the wealth of the homeowner. In the Dominus Iulius mosaic, the lord of the manor is seen on the left coming to visit his manor and, on the right, leaving for a hunt—a popular occupation of the elite. Above and beneath the manor house are detailed depictions of agricultural activity according to the seasons of the year. The entire image illustrates the patron-age system, as the lord and his wife receive presents from the tenant farmers *(coloni)* who live on the manor. The coloni dwellings were much more modest, as attested by the mosaic floor at Oudna, which depicts a tent that apparently served as their seasonal home. Next to the tent a shepherd stands at the en-trance to a simple farmhouse.

The villas in the mosaics from North Africa are the fortified villas that were widespread from the 4th century on. They are characterized by high walls on the ground floor, windows and porticoes on the upper floors, and towers in the corners. The fortified villa of late antiquity may be viewed as the prototype of the medieval château.

Archaeological finds confirm the mosaic depictions of villas. At Nador, which lies in the rural area of Mauretania, stood a large (2000 sq m) 4th century complex surrounded by walls. The front wall, facing north, boasted an arched gate with round towers in each corner, similar to the facades of fortified farms depicted in mosaics. Inside the complex is a large courtyard surrounded by various installations associated with the processing of agricultural produce: wine presses, olive presses, and storerooms for food. The residential section of the farm (pars urbana) occupies less than one third of the structure's area, indicating that the lord of the manor was an absentee owner, an urban dweller who was away from the manor most of the year. Fortified farms like the one at Nador became an integral part of the rural landscape of North Africa. In various inscriptions, such a farm was called *turis* or *centenarium,* terms bor-rowed from the realm of military architecture. It was apparently designed to defend its inhabitants and property from invasions by barbarians or local theft.

The remains of dozens of much simpler farmhouses have been found next to the fortified farms. In an archaeological survey conducted in Tunisia, 67 farm-houses were discovered within an area of 47 sq km, which is 0.7 sq km per structure. These farmhouses were built and used from the 2nd to 7th centuries. The preferred structure was long and narrow, with the length varying according to the number of rooms (usually 1 or 2); in contrast, the house's width was more or less fixed at 3.5–4 m, according to the length of the wooden beams that were available to the builders. The entrance facade to the houses generally face east or south, to ensure maximal exposure to sunlight and minimal penetration of cold winds in the winter. Next to the house there was always a large courtyard with various agricultural installations. One surprising find in this Tunisian survey was the discovery of 15 to 20 rural bathhouses, most of which were built in the 4th–5th centuries. This phenomenon is a clear sign of Roman urban cultural influence on the rural populations.

A unique type of tower-like farmhouse was developed in the semiarid peripheral areas of the empire. Dozens of structures of this type were discovered in the semidesert strip of Libya, about 200 km south of the coastline. These dwellings, called *gusr* in Arabic, were built in the 3rd and 4th centuries by local landowners. They are fortified tower-like structures rising to a height of two to three stories and ranging in area between 70 and 240 sq m. In their center is a compact courtyard surrounded by rooms. The quality of the construction and the stone ornamentation attest to the employment of professional builders. Next to the main tower-like structure are the remains of courtyards, annexes, agricultural installations, and terraces. The gusr were thus dwelling complexes for the extended family, numbering up to fifty people. Dedicatory inscriptions found above the entrance lintels to the gusr mention the centenarium, originally a military term, but in this context referring to a fortified dwelling place for landowners. The Negev of southern Palestine was also dotted with similar dwellings.

Various versions of fortified villas have been discovered throughout the empire. At Ramat Hanadiv, northeast of Caesarea in Palestine, a fortified villa built sometime between the 5th and 7th centuries has been discovered. This complex, measuring 520 sq m, was built around a central courtyard flanked by wings on three sides: two two-story wings and one single-story wing. The rooms on the ground floor were used for various functions, including food storage and sleeping quarters for animals, while the rooms on the upper floor were living quarters. This layout characterizes private rural construction. A fortified farm similar to the one at Ramat Hanadiv was discovered at Monte Birro in southern Italy; it also dates from the 5th and 6th centuries.

The manor houses of the west prospered in the 4th century. A 2nd century villa in Chedworth, England, for instance, added a portico, triclinium, and two private bathhouses in the 4th century. Another example is the villa rustica excavated at Gadebridge Park in England. This house was also initially built in the 2nd century, but its principal period of construction was in the 4th. The main structure consisted of a number of rooms joined by a portico in the front. Like the farmhouses of North Africa, it was flanked by two towers. The notable additions of a private bathhouse and large swimming pool were among the house's 4th century modifications, attesting to the high standard of living enjoyed by the villa's residents.

The Gadebridge house is a typical example of the corridor villa that characterized the northwestern provinces of the empire (Britain, Germany, and Belgium). In Gaul (southern France) and Spain, villa design was influenced by the Mediterranean concept of the central courtyard. The enormous villa excavated in Lalonquette, France, has at its center a wide peristyle courtyard, surrounded by living quarters, halls, and other amenities.

The most impressive manors perhaps in the entire empire have been found in Sicily; famous among them is Piazza Armerina, a striking complex covering an area of over 5000 sq m. This manor house, which belonged to a wealthy landowner, was built in the early 4th century in central Sicily. The house displays the repertoire of components characteristic of the villa urbana, such as an enormous peristyle courtyard, apsidal reception halls, and magnificent triclinia. The entire complex is covered with a colored mosaic floor containing depictions of daily life inside and outside the manor.

The intricate layout of the Piazza Armerina complex and the exceptional opulence of its mosaics have led to various theories regarding its owners. Among other suggestions, it has been proposed that this site was the palatial dwelling of the emperors of the west in the early 4th century, although not a single piece of evidence has been found to justify this claim. Parallels from other sites in Sicily support the more reasonable assumption that the owner of the Piazza Armerina complex was a local wealthy senatorial nobleman.

For an example of imperial dwellings in late antiquity we can look at Diocletian's palace in Split. This huge complex (160×200 m), erected around the year 300 on the Adriatic coast, is surrounded by a wall with four corner towers. The interior is distinguished by its symmetrical division into intersecting streets around large courtyards. Adjoining the courtyards were the dwelling quarters of the emperor's coterie and personal military guards, as well as large reception halls and the emperor's residential wing overlooking the sea. This wing contained a private bathhouse. The construction of the palace was influenced by the military architecture of the era, but it also continued the eastern Hellenistic tradition of building fortified palaces with four corner towers—*tetrapyrgia*, as they are called in the sources.

Both Piazza Armerina in Sicily and the palace in Split were surrounded by the hundreds of modestly built farmhouses that typically stood nearby to magnificent complexes. Thus in the countryside one would find settlements containing: (1) The *small farm*, a simple rectangular structure containing 7–15 rooms, without amenities, 300–400 sq m in area, the dwelling of a small farmer or tenant; (2) the *medium farm*, 500–2500 sq m, including a courtyard house or a house with a double hall and 20–50 rooms (and often a separate wing with a bathhouse), the property of landowners of medium estates; (3) the *large farm*, extending over an area of over 2500 sq m, an enormous complex containing dozens of built structures surrounding two or three courtyards. The opulence of these structures is evident in the mosaic floors, decorative fountains, and other installations. The owners of these palatial centers lived in the city.

In a study conducted of about two hundred sites of this type, it became clear that most of the complexes were built in the 2nd century, underwent a period of decline in the 3rd, and prospered again in the 4th. In the early 5th century, the scope of the settlements began to contract, and toward the end of that century most of the sites were abandoned. It therefore appears that there was a high rate of settlement in the 3rd and 4th centuries, mostly an increase in the number of medium farms. There are no signs of the creation of huge estates, *latifundia*, at the expense of the small farmers; indeed, the number of large manors diminished in relative terms. There was also a decrease in the number of small farms, in contrast to the rise in the number of medium farms belonging to independent landowning farmers. This pattern is repeated in all the provinces of the west (England, France, and Spain) and also characterizes rural settlement in the northern provinces of the Danube region (Moesia, Pannonia, Noricum, and Dalmatia).

This phenomenon also characterized the provinces of the east (Syria, Jordan, Palestine); the prosperity of the 4th, 5th, and 6th centuries found expression in the construction of well-built and adorned dwellings, similar to the medium farm in the west. This construction attests to an increase in the broad class of independent farmers who had established themselves financially. However, unlike in the west, where settlement was primarily in the farm setting, the dominant settlement in the east was (and still is) the village.

The rural dwellings of the east suggest a homogeneous rural society without distinctive class differences. The houses are built one next to the other, without preconceived plan. The difference in the sizes of the houses expresses the difference in the farmers' economic standing. The large dwellings of more prosperous families are usually located in the center of the village next to the house of prayer (synagogue or church). At Chorazin, north of the Sea of Galilee, five or six large courtyard houses (900 sq m each) were discovered next to the synagogue. These houses contained many rooms, as well as storerooms and stables. Simpler rural houses, with an adjacent courtyard, were found next to them. Another example is the village of Behyo in northern Syria, which blossomed in the 5th–6th centuries. In this period, spacious courtyard houses, with portico facades facing the courtyards, were built in the center of the village. These houses were the dwellings of wealthy landowners, while the simple rural houses were occupied by the rest of the farmers, who worked as tenants or hired day-laborers.

The modest rural house was a square or rectangular structure facing a courtyard. The 4th–5th century house excavated at Horvat Shema' in the Upper Galilee is composed of two rooms built one on top of the other; the room on the ground floor (2.3 × 3.6 m, or 8.3 sq m) served as a storeroom and workshop, while the room above it functioned as a dwelling. A stone staircase outside the house connected the two rooms. The main activity of the house's inhabitants took place in the courtyard: a raised surface in the corner of the courtyard served as a place for sitting, working, and sleeping; the center of the courtyard contained a cistern. Rabbinic sources inform us that most domestic activities, such as cooking and laundry, were performed in the courtyard, which also housed farm animals.

The dominant trend in the design of rural houses in late antiquity was the transition toward a more closed plan, an inclination toward separating parts of the house by function, and the establishment of the family living unit around a courtyard. Thus we witness development of large courtyard houses that served as dwellings for extended families. A good example of this are the dwellings preserved at Umm el-Jimāl, which in the 6th century numbered 128 complexes built to a height of two or three floors. Each house had a clear separation between the ground floor, which was reserved for work and agricultural purposes, and the floors above it, which served as living quarters. The large rooms of the ground floor were roofed with a single arch and used as a silo and animal pens or stable. Five to ten stone troughs attest to the presence of animals. In the corner of the room there was often a toilet. It is possible that these stables also accommodated the hired day-laborers. A typical example is house no. 119, a relatively modest complex measuring 40 × 40 m built around a large central courtyard. There are seven rooms on the ground floor, including a large stable (7 × 8 m) containing troughs for horses and cows. The complex was built in the 4th century and remained in use until its destruction in the great earthquake in the mid 8th century.

A rise in the rural standard of living is evident from the interior plan of the house. The functional separation between different parts of the house, usually achieved by building a second story, characterizes private construction in the east after the Hellenistic period. The ground floor, opening onto the courtyard, was used as a service area and for storing food and stabling animals, while the floor above it served as living quarters. The rooms on this floor were well illuminated, open to the landscape, allowing cool breezes to stream through them. The area of the second story was often smaller than that of the ground floor. In this case, the rest of the roof may have been used as a veranda for sitting or as an area for drying food (for example, raisins and figs). The two floors were connected by an exterior stone, or sometimes wooden, staircase. A characteristic feature of the two-story houses is the portico—a row or two of columns standing parallel to each other at the front of the house. The columns supported the veranda that gave access to the rooms on the upper floor of the house. The shaded area created beneath this porch gave shelter to the workers on the ground floor.

Another separation instituted in rural private construction was the partition between the sleeping quarters and the dining area (triclinium). The larger triclinia were gracefully built spaces that usually had a separate entrance. A rural dwelling discovered at Horvat Susiya in southern Judaea, built in the 6th century and used continuously until the 8th century, is a single-story house with a regular plan (160 sq m). The front of the house facing the courtyard had two entrances: a northern one leading into three residential rooms and a southern one leading into a spacious room that served as a dining room. In the rear of the house, two shops were built facing the street. We may therefore conclude that the homeowners dealt not only in agriculture, but also in commerce. The incorporation of shops into dwellings was a widespread phenomenon in the villages. In Shivta in the Negev, a courtyard house adjoining three shops facing the street was discovered. Two of them were connected by entrances into the house, while the third shop was isolated and possibly intended for rental.

The rural dwellings of northern Syria exhibit the prosperity of the 4th, 5th, and 6th centuries. These were stone houses with simple plans, but well built and decorated with great opulence. Most of the houses are rectangular two-story buildings with two or three rooms on each floor. Galleries as well as cellars and olive presses were constructed in many houses. No triclinia were found, not even in the large houses. The high point of private construction in Syria was in the 5th century, although these structures remained in use until the 8th century. The architectural uniformity of these houses expresses a homogeneous society with limited class distinctions.

A similar situation characterizes private building in the large settlements of the Negev—Shivta, Nessana, and Rehovot. These are large, densely built villages without preconceived plan. The superior construction exploited the local limestone. The dominant type of structure is a spacious courtyard house, ranging in area between 200 and 400 sq m. The courtyard of each house had a cistern. The living quarters surrounding the courtyard included one larger room that served as a dining room. The larger houses had towers similar to those of the rural manor houses. Division of the villagers by family is reflected in the Nessana papyri, which deal almost entirely with familial property of modestly sized tracts of land.

The rural settlement of the Negev in the 4th through 7th centuries is characterized, among other things, by a wide distribution of hamlets, or clusters of modest farmhouses. These are small settlements of five to ten dwelling units at an average distance of 20–25 m. The houses are simple rectangular structures consisting of two or three rooms facing a courtyard. Occasionally, another wing was built perpendicular to the existing structure. Hundreds of structures of this type that have been surveyed in the Negev and elsewhere in the east attest to the safe conditions prevailing in the remote peripheral areas of the empire. These conditions apparently did not change after the Muslim conquest, since these hamlets and farmhouses continued to exist until the end of the Umayyad period.

In addition to the villages, hamlets, and farmhouses in the peripheral areas, a new settlement phenomenon involved the desert nomads. During the 6th, 7th, and 8th centuries, nomads working in agriculture established seasonal settlements. The dwellings characterizing these settlements are round stone huts with a diameter of 4–8 m. The walls were built to a height of 1.5–2 m without bonding materials. The huts were roofed with foliage. The inhabitants of these huts worked in agriculture in the winter and spring months, while in the summer and fall they herded their flocks. The Negev surveys have yielded hundreds of sites of this type, occasionally including 20–30 dwelling units. Next to some of them were open mosques that are considered among the earliest in Islam. The nomadic settlements continued until the 9th century and then ceased completely.

Another new settlement phenomenon characterizing the rural areas in late antiquity is the various monasteries and hermitages. Among monasteries we can distinguish two types: the communal monastery (coenobium) and the monastery of recluses (lavra). The coenobium, built in an open rural area, is in many respects reminiscent of the fortified villa. It was surrounded by a wall with one or two entrances leading into a large inner courtyard. Around the courtyard were living quarters, as well as a dining room, kitchen, and church hall. The construction was often two stories high, in the plan characterizing the large farms.

A marvelous example of a coenobium may be found at the Martyrius monastery in the Judaean Desert, 5 km east of Jerusalem. It was erected at the end of the 5th century and assumed its final form in the 6th. Like the fortified villas of North Africa, it is a large complex surrounded by a wall. An entrance gate leads into a large courtyard occupying about 40 percent of the monastery's area. A large church was built east of the courtyard, and a large dining hall (refectory) at the north. The monks' dwellings were located in various rooms on the building's upper floor, above the service quarters (including stables) on the ground floor. A private bathhouse was found at the west side of the courtyard (according to monastic regulations, only sickly monks or monastic leaders were allowed to use the bathhouses). Well-tended vegetable gardens and orchards adorned the interior and exterior of the monastery; from afar it would have appeared like one of the fortified villas depicted in the mosaics of North Africa.

The lavra, in contrast, is reminiscent of a desert hamlet. It consisted of a cluster of cells surrounding communal structures, including a small church and a storehouse for food and supplies. The monks' cells, small structures with one or two rooms, were separated from one another. Often next to the cells were garden plots worked by the monks. The distance between the cells was about 30–35 m and a path (Greek: *lavra*) connected the cells with the church and the communal structures. The lavra could have looked like an idyllic, well-cared-for village with fruit and vegetable gardens.

In addition to the lavrae, monastic places of seclusion can be found in the remote desert areas, or between cliffs or in caves or rock shelters in the hills. An example is the secluded site of Sousakim (el Quseir) in the Judaean Desert, where the holy man Cyriac lived; it consisted of a cave and a fenced garden plot with a cistern in front of it. At a later stage, a dwelling cell with a prayer niche was built for the holy man. Such a dwelling was part of its natural surroundings and open to visitors. Here Cyriac received his many admirers among the monks and the local rural population. The phenomenon of patronage, which became institutionalized in this period, took on a completely new dimension. Unlike the urban patron, who was difficult to approach, and to whom entrance was blocked by officers and bodyguards, the holy man in his remote dwelling place was easily and immediately accessible. Here his admirers could receive spiritual healing as well as relief from pain. The monastic simplicity of early Christianity was a new phenomenon in late antiquity.

The dwellings throughout the Roman empire reflect several of the main characteristics of late antiquity. The economic prosperity that followed the resolution of the 3rd century crisis affected the quality of housing construction in all social strata and in all forms of settlement. From the 4th century onward, existing dwellings were expanded and renovated, while new houses were built at sites hitherto unsettled. Although this prosperity in the western empire lasted only until the 5th century, in the east it continued until the end of the Umayyad period in the 8th century.

The discovery of dwellings in remote, previously unsettled areas—where we find the diverse dwellings of farmers, nomads, and monks—is an impressive aspect of private building in this period. This development expresses a shift of the cultural center of gravity from the city to the rural areas. In this respect, the dwellings of late antiquity express the character of the period as moving from the classical world into the culture of the early Middle Ages.

Bibliography

Dunbabin, K. M. D. "Triclinum and Stibadium," in W. J. Slater, ed., *Dining in a Classical Context* (Ann Arbor, 1991), 121–148.

Ellis, S. P. "The End of the Roman House," *American Journal of Archaeology* 92 (1988): 565–576.

Frantz, A. "The Athenian Agora," in *Late Antiquity* A.D. 267–700 (Princeton, 1988), 30–45.

Hirschfeld, Y. *The Palestinian Dwelling in the Roman-Byzantine Period* (Jerusalem, 1995).

Possiter, J. "Convivium and Villa in Late Antiquity," in W. J. Slater, ed., *Dining in a Classical Context* (Ann Arbor, 1991), 199–214.

Sodini, J.-P. "Habitat de l'antiquité tardive," *Topoi* 5 (1995): 151–218; 7 (1997): 435–577.

Stillwell, R. "Houses of Antioch," *Dumbarton Oaks Papers* 15 (1961): 47–57.

Tate, G. *Les campagnes de la Syrie du nord du IIe au VIIe siècle,* I (Paris, 1992).

Thébert, Y. "Private Life and Domestic Architecture in Roman Africa," in P. Veyne, ed., *A History of Private Life,* I: *From Pagan Rome to Byzantium* (Cambridge, Mass., 1987), 313–409.

Villeneuve, F. "L'économie rurale et la vie des campagnes dans le Hauran antique (Ier siècle av. J.-C.–VIIe siècle ap. J.-C.): une approche," in J.-M. Dentzer, ed., *Hauran—recherches archéologiques sur la Syrie du sud à l'époque hellénistique et romaine* (Paris, 1985), 63–136.

1 Dome of the Rock, Jerusalem: mosaic spandrel inside octagonal arcade, from the late 7th century.

2 Manuscript illumination: Rabbula Gospel Miniature. Manuscript completed on February 6, 586, by the calligrapher Rabbula working in a monastery north of Syrian Apamea.

3 Christ Pantocrator holding a jeweled Gospel book. A 6th century icon, 84 x 45.5
cm, in the Monastery of St. Catherine at Mount Sinai.

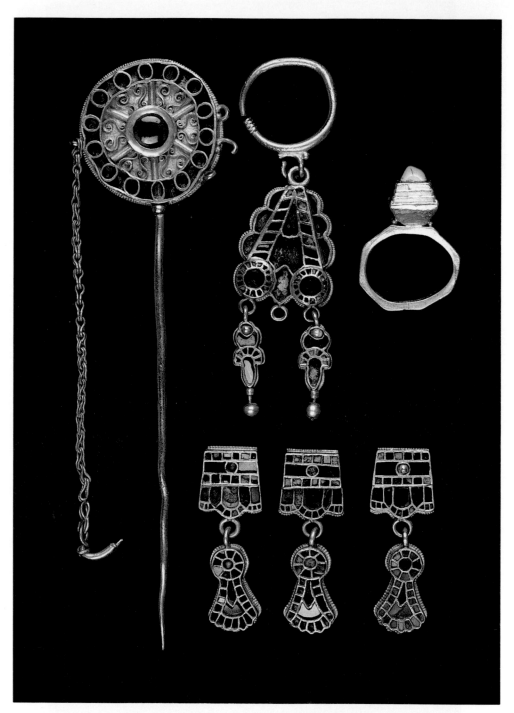

4 Women's jewelry from the Treasure of Domagnano (Republic of San Marino) dating to the late
5th or early 6th century. Hairpin with chain, earring, ring, and pendants from a necklace.

5 Large plate in silver from the Treasure of Sevso, whose name appears in the Latin verses inscribed around a central medallion that depicts hunting scenes with an al fresco banquet alongside a stream or lake. Of unknown provenance and dating probably to the second half of the 4th century.

6 Mosaics from the Church of St. Stephen, Umm ar-rasas (ancient Mefaa) in Jordan. *Top:* "The Holy City" (Jerusalem). *Bottom:* Iconoclastic removal of human figures. The inscription is dated to the 8th century by a reference in the last line to the era of the defunct Roman province of Arabia.

7 Germanic gold bracteate pendant from the late 5th to early 6th century.
The design imitates an "Urbs Roma" coin, with the head of Roma above
a wolf suckling Romulus and Remus.

8 Mosaic with a wolf suckling Romulus and Remus at Maʿarrat al-Nuʿman, Syria, with inscription showing that
the mosaic came from a hospital built in 511.

9 Panel of an ivory diptych: "The Emperor Triumphant." Late 5th to early 6th century, Constantinople.

10   The court of the Empress Theodora. wall mosaic in S. Vitale, Ravenna.

11 Sassanian "Cup of Khosro" in the Treasury of St. Denis.

12 Mosaics at Maʿarrat al-Nuʿman, Syria. *Top:* Heracles standing before Zeus; 3rd or 4th century. *Bottom:* Section of a floor mosaic dating to the early 6th century.

13 Mausoleum of Galla Placidia, Ravenna: mosaic depicting the martyrdom of St. Lawrence. Early 5th century.

14 The Wadi Ramm in southern Jordan (late antique Third Palestine), looking south.

15 Landscape in Turkey to the east of Lake Van, near Harrâka.

Abbasids

The Abbasids, the second ecumenical Islamic dynasty (750–1258), based their claim to rule on their descent from al-'Abbas, uncle of Muhammad the Prophet. They led a ruthless revolution against the Umayyads that manipulated the resentment of the supporters *(shī'a)* of the house of 'Ali and the large class of Islamized Persians. The Abbasids soon eliminated their dangerous allies and established themselves as the definitive successors to the Prophet Muhammad and the protectors of the growing consensus around his tradition *(sunna),* which was to develop into the doctrine of the orthodox majority.

Al-Manṣūr, the second caliph (754–775), was the real architect of the Abbasid empire and the founder of its capital, Baghdad, near Ctesiphon, the seat of Sassanian kings on the Tigris River. His perfectly round and concentrically planned city symbolized the eastward orientation of the regime and the hierarchical order it sought to impose. The new image of an absolute, secluded sovereign was more influenced by Persian traditions and court ceremony than by Arabic tribal customs. The Arabs soon lost their supremacy in the state and were replaced, first by Khurasanian supporters and later, starting with the caliphate of al-Mu'tasim (833–842), by Turkish mamluks, who dominated the political scene until 945. A new and grandiose capital, Samarra, was built in 836 but was abandoned in 883, and Baghdad regained its old eminence.

Islamic civilization began to acquire its contours in 9th and 10th century Baghdad, at that time the largest, richest, and most cultured city in the world west of China. Theologians, literati, scientists, philosophers, and ascetics (later known as Sufis) all sought patronage there. Hellenistic culture, as preserved in scholarly communities in Syria and Iraq, played an important role in shaping Islamic philosophy and science. Caliph al-Ma'mūn (813–833) sponsored the translation of Greek (mostly through Syriac renditions), Persian, and Sanskrit texts into Arabic and tried, but failed, to impose a single official interpretation of Islam based on the teaching of a group of rationalist theologians called the Mu'tazilites. Though scripturalism ultimately dominated Islamic theology, Mu'tazili—and hence Greek-influenced—reasoning was never totally abandoned.

Under the Abbasids territorial conquests ceased, and the caliphate began to settle within its frontiers and adjust to its role as one empire among others. Predictably, its integrity under a central political authority did not last. It lost Spain at the outset to a surviving Umayyad, and after the empire's zenith under Hārūn al-Rashīd (786–809), it started to lose its hold on outlying regions in North Africa and Central Asia. Slowly a new modus operandi was established by which powerful amirs could maintain their independence while recognizing the caliph in Baghdad as the leader of the faithful. This development accounts for the longevity of the dynasty and the semireligious aura it achieved, so that even after the Mongols destroyed Baghdad and killed its last caliph in 1258, an Abbasid figurehead was installed in Cairo to lend legitimacy to the upstart Mamluk sultanate.

BIBL.: M. M. Ahsan, *Social Life under the Abbasids* (London and New York, 1979). W. F. Buckler, *Harunu'l-Rashid and Charles the Great* (Cambridge, Mass., 1931). Hugh Kennedy, *The Early Abbasid Caliphate: A Political History* (London and Totowa, N.J., 1981). Jacob Lassner, *Islamic Revolution and Historical Memory: Abbasid Apologetics and the Art of Historical Writing* (New Haven, 1986). Muhammad Abd al-Hayy Muhammad Shaban, *The Abbasid Revolution* (Cambridge, Eng., 1979).   N.R.

'Abd al-Malik

'Abd al-Malik Ibn Marwan, the fifth Umayyad caliph (685–705), came to power in a time of civil strife and when a Byzantine army was threatening the northern borders. At first his dominions were limited to Syria and Egypt. The revolt of Ibn al-Zubayr and his establishment of a rival caliphate in Mecca constituted the greatest menace that 'Abd al-Malik faced. The Syrians, who constituted his loyal army, succeeded in due course in crushing rebel forces and recapturing Iraq and Arabia (in 691 and 692, respectively). Iraq and the rapidly expanding eastern provinces were to be held for the rest of his reign by the famous al-Hajjāj, a skillful and exceedingly cruel strategist.

'Abd al-Malik was an energetic and determined caliph whose knowledge of Islamic tenets was undisputed and whose sense of sovereignty *(mulk)* uncompromising. He belonged to the first Medinese generation brought up from birth in the Islamic faith and was considered among the most trustworthy *fuqaha* (jurists) before he moved to Damascus. His alleged rejection of pious manners after becoming caliph is inconsistent with the multitude of references to his adherence to Islamic precepts throughout his rule.

In the second part of his rule, 'Abd al-Malik resumed the conquest efforts and initiated the process of Arabizing the administration and Islamizing the coinage to create an imperial Islamic image of the state. Under his son al-Walīd I, the process was carried further, and the imperial image was expressed in monumental mosques built in major cities of the empire, including Mecca, Medina, Damascus, and Jerusalem. But the most impressive if enigmatic monument was the Dome of the Rock, built by 'Abd al-Malik in Jerusalem when he was still struggling to assert his authority.

BIBL.: Al-Baladhuri, *Ansab al-Ashraf,* vol. 5, ed. S. D. Goitein (Jerusalem, 1938), 158–180. W. Ahlwardt, *Anonyme arabische chronik,* vol. 2 (Greifswald, Ger., 1883), 1–78, 266–356. S. A. Natur, *Tajdid al-dawlah al-Umawiyah fi ahd al-khalifah Abd al-Malik ibn Marwan,* 69 H/685 M–86 H/705 M (Irbid, Jordan, 1996). G. R. Hawting, *The First Dynasty of Islam: The Umayyad Caliphate A.D. 661–750* (Carbondale, Ill., 1987).   N.R.

Acclamations

Acclamations—public expressions of opinion or faith by an assembled group—were important in all preliterate societies as the simplest method of communicating opinion. The kings of Israel were acclaimed by the people; in the Graeco-Roman world the existence of large, resonant auditoriums in all the major cities made this form of expression particularly practical. It was in the theater at Ephesus in the 1st century C.E. that the people expressed disapproval of the activities of the apostle Paul, through the traditional acclamation of adoration for their own goddess, "Great is the Artemis of the Ephesians," which they shouted for two hours (Acts 19:23–41). Religious acclamation passed quickly into Christian practice. In hagiography, miracles commonly brought shouts of "Praise God!" or "God is One!" from onlookers. Certain acclamations ("Alleluia," "Kyrie eleison") became regularized and passed into the liturgy. To this day, the cry "God is Great" ("Allāhu Akbar") begins Islamic worship.

Acclamations served to present an appearance of unanimity, and in religious contexts such as miracle stories and episcopal elections, a supposedly spontaneous outcry could be taken as evidence of divine inspiration. It was commonly held that the Holy Spirit spoke through the unanimous acclamations of the bishops assembled at church councils. Acclamations could also serve a polemical purpose (e.g., the accusations shouted between the Egyptian and eastern factions of bishops at the council of Chalcedon) or incite confrontation by putting forward a controversial doctrinal statement, such as the Monophysite addition of the phrase, "who was crucified for us" to the Trisagion, which led to riots in Constantinople.

In late antiquity, acclamations became much more important as a means of establishing public political opinion than they had been during the Hellenistic and early imperial periods. In 331, Emperor Constantine ruled that popular acclamations for or against provincial governors should be reported directly to the emperor (*C.Th.* 1.16.6, = *C.Just.* 1.40.3). From the beginning of the 4th century acclamations are recorded with increasing frequency, inscribed on stone (e.g., at Aphrodisias) or reproduced in official documents. The *Theodosian Code* includes a list of the acclamations pronounced by Rome's Senate when it was promulgated in 438. The acts of the church councils of the 5th and 6th centuries include numerous acclamations, as do the accounts of the proclamations of new emperors in this period (Constantine Porphyrogenitus, *De caeremoniis* 410–412, 418–425, 426–430). To turn the voices of many into one unanimous expression, acclamations used set formulas and repetition and were chanted in regular meter. In larger cities such as Alexandria or Antioch, claques of professional "cheerleaders" usually associated with the theater sometimes organized and directed the shouts of the crowd.

The content of acclamations was usually either highly laudatory or harshly polemical: "Many years to the pious and orthodox emperors! O emperors, you are victorious!" or (at church councils) "You speak the faith of the Fathers! The Holy Spirit speaks through you!" alternated with "Throw out" or "Dig up the bones of" a supposedly corrupt or heretical public official or bishop. Often, a demonstration would include both lavish praise of the emperor and denunciations of lower officials or unpopular taxes. This tactic allowed the people to express dissatisfaction with government policy without directly challenging the authority of the emperor, who in turn could blame and punish the underling named by the crowd and thus back off from an unpopular policy without losing face.

The development of acclamations had complex implications. The more authority attributed to acclamations, the more this empowered those acclaiming. Libanius describes a governor filled with fear when the crowd remained silent, withholding the support they would normally give by acclamation (*Orat.* 41.1–2). The most common occasion for acclamation was when the people were assembled in an auditorium—a theater or, in larger cities, a hippodrome. By the 5th century audiences had come to be divided into supporters of the so-called Blue or Green circus factions. This gave the leaders of those factions the power to influence an activity of political significance. The extraordinary situations this could produce are exemplified in the Acts of Kalopodios, in an exchange in Constantinople in the 530s between a crowd in the hippodrome, using acclamatory formulas, and the emperor's representative (Theophanes, *Chronographia* 181.30–184.1). Only gradually were the factions, and their acclamations, regularized and absorbed into the imperial ritual that is recorded in the *De caeremoniis* of Constantine Porphyrogenitus.

BIBL.: Charlotte Roueché, "Acclamations in the Later Roman Empire: New Evidence from Aphrodisias," *Journal of Roman Studies* 74 (1984): 181–199. On acclamations in miracle stories, see E. Peterson, *Eis theos* (Göttingen, 1926). On acclamations in liturgy, see Ernst Kantorowitz, *Laudes Regiae* (Berkeley, 1946).   C.R.

Acta

The government authorities of late antiquity enjoyed broader rights in compiling acts *(ius actorum conficiendorum)* than authorities of earlier times. Organized bodies at all levels of the hierarchy compiled protocols, giving a step-by-step account of their sessions. Administrative authorities (civil and military judges, financial agents, and so on) used the same means to record how formal procedures within their province were being carried out. Unlike the brief *commentarii* of the high empire, these *acta* or *gesta* (*hypomnēmata* in Greek) related the acts of assemblies, tribunals, and bureaus word for word. As the practice spread,

a specialized secretarial staff of stenographers and clerks *(exceptores, notarii, chartularii)* had to be set in place.

The *acta* were composed in Latin or Greek, depending on the language used by the intervening parties. In the east, they were normally in both languages (the preliminaries were still in Latin), except within the church, where conciliar acts were entirely in Greek. The *acta* were rendered in direct speech *(oratio recta)*. In terms of palaeography, they are noteworthy for their use of an archaic cursive Latin for the initial date.

Extant documentation is vast and diverse. Originals on papyrus exist in Italy (Ravenna) and in Egypt. Examples of epigraphy are very rare; the literature consists primarily of the acts of councils. The best-represented genres are the minutes of judicial hearings and the proceedings of assemblies. Records of actions taken against Christians were a source for several accounts of martyrs; the authenticity of these *acta sincera* can be inferred, since they are consistent with the original protocols (on papyrus) of sessions with provincial governors. The protocols of assemblies consisted of individual statements and collective acclamations. We possess those of the Senate of Rome at the time the *Theodosian Code* was published (438). The events and slogans of popular demonstrations were also recorded (for example, the *acta* of the Constantinople hippodrome during the Nika rebellion of 532). Beginning with Constantine I, acclamations of provincials were the object of protocols, transmitted to the central government for its consideration. Municipal councils kept their own *acta* on papyrus. The largest body of *acta* by far concern bishops' assemblies, or councils, whether local (especially Gallic and African) or ecumenical (these are virtually complete beginning with the Council of Ephesus in 431). The conciliar acts are, for antiquity, exceptionally complete and accurate. They explicitly illustrate the complex procedures for taking down, editing, and authenticating the *acta* (see the *Collatio* of Carthage of 411).

Beginning in the 5th century, a growing number of formal procedures of private law (wills, adoption documents, and so on) were recorded *apud acta*. These acts, authenticated by the authorities, had the legal value of *instrumenta publica*.

The original *acta* were kept by the appropriate agencies in their archives. Copies circulated widely within the administrative system. Citizens, either individually or collectively, could obtain an abstract of the acts *(editio actorum)*. The declaratory form of the charters of early medieval Wales preserve the late Roman practice of transactions recorded *apud acta*.

BIBL.: R. A. Coles, *Reports of Proceedings in Papyri* (Brussels, 1966). W. Davies, "The Latin Charter Tradition in West Britain, Brittany and Ireland," in *Ireland in Early Medieval Europe*, ed. D. Whitelock (Cambridge, Eng., 1982), 258–280. H. C. Teitler, *Notarii and Exceptores* (Amsterdam, 1985).   D.F.

Actors and Acting

There is no indication that either comedies or tragedies, as represented by whole plays, survived as performance pieces much after the early 3rd century in the Greek east, and both forms had probably disappeared at an earlier date in the Latin west. In terms of actual performance, tragedies seem to have metamorphosed into successions of excerpts recited or sung by a *tragicus cantor* or *tragoidos,* perhaps accompanied on the kithara. The *tragoidos* wore a distinctive costume—a gaping mask and a long-sleeved garment—and he performed in high-heeled boots, sometimes on stilts.

The most popular forms of theater in late antiquity appear to have been mime and pantomime. The former was, with the exception of a written prologue, usually improvised from a comic scenario. Mime performances were short, often just one act, with a fairly rambling plot in which the dramaturgical rules of consistency in time and place were completely ignored and prose, verse, song, and dance were intermixed. With the exception of mythological mimes, the actors performed without masks and, unlike in pantomime, professional actresses were employed. Pantomime first appears on the stages of Latin-speaking areas of the Roman empire from the end of the 1st century B.C.E., but it was not accepted into Greek sacred festivals until the late 2nd century C.E. Pantomime drew its themes and stories from tragedy; all the scenes were dance solos performed by a virtuoso masked actor, backed by musicians, while another actor or a chorus might be used to provide narrative continuity.

Epigraphic evidence would seem to indicate that pantomimes were included in "sacred contests" from the 2nd century onward. Mimes clearly were considered to be of lower status, but by the 3rd century they were also being admitted to some competitions. For example, a 3rd century inscription from Tralles honors a mime whose victories included one at the Asian games. It is recorded that the subject had received the typical honors given to victors from other disciplines, such as being made a member of the council or *gerousia,* of various cities (*I.Tralles* 110). In later antiquity such honorific inscriptions for victors disappear and the bulk of the evidence for their activities comes from literary sources, the most important being the antitheater diatribes in the homilies of John Chrysostom and the orations of the later sophists Libanius and Choricius in defense of pantomimes and mimes, respectively (Libanius, *Orat.* 64; Choricius, *Orat.* 8). Pantomimes are also the subject of several epigrams by the 6th century poets of the *Cycle of Agathias* and feature in the *Dionysiaca* of Nonnus.

By late antiquity there is no unambiguous evidence that the trade guilds in which theatrical performers had traditionally been organized were still in existence; instead it seems that mimes and pantomimes had become associated with the circus factions. For instance, the theater at Aphrodisias contains many examples of graffiti associating performers with a particular faction (see Rouechè, *Performers and Partisans,* 31–43). Each color-named faction at Constantinople had its leading pantomime, who seems to have had an important role in the administration of the faction. John Malalas in his history records several incidences of pantomimes' being exiled because of continued fighting between the factions (*Chronographia* 393–394, 417–418). Even in Ostrogothic Rome the performances of pantomimes had to be closely controlled by city authorities (Cassiodorus, *Variae* 1.31).

Art gives some indication of theatrical style and costume in late antiquity. For instance, an ivory statuette of a drunken young man and a slave from late 3rd century Milan provides a good example of the formality of comic costume in this period: The man wears a mask complete with long curling hair falling back over his shoulders and a tall, crowning headpiece of a kind that must have been developed as a counterpart to the *onkoi* of tragedy. An early 6th century ivory diptych commemorating the consul Anastasius indicates that the formality and elaboration seen in the Milan statuette have been taken a step further, as there the actor's mask has gained a far more decorative crowning element. A number of masks from later periods have large, deep openings for the eyes and mouth through which the features of the actor could be clearly seen. It has been suggested that this might indicate that masks had become little more than a concession to tradition and were far less important as definers of character. Another example of the change of styles is seen in the costume worn by the actor Marcus Varenius Areskon on his funerary relief in Thessalonica (*I.Thessalonike* 9815). He is shown wearing an elaborately decorated costume on which color traces remain. The costume is heavy with broad embroidered bands, and the *onkos* reminds us that such tall headpieces imply a style of performance in which the head was not readily turned sideways.

Stage performers served as important *exempla* in both Christian and non-Christian texts in late antiquity. The 4th century sophist Eunapius of Sardis uses the catastrophic effects of the performance of an unnamed *tragoidos* on an untrained barbarian audience as a cultural marker emphasizing and reaffirming his own and his readership's *paideia* (*Historici graeci minores* frg. 54; for other examples see Libanius, *Orat.* 64.75; Choricius, *Orat.* 8.118 and 141–142). Christian writers condemn stage players for their licentiousness and deceit (see, for instance, John Chrysostom, *Homilia contra ludos et theatra*). The antipathy between the church and the stage was marked, with the church becoming the butt of many jokes in the theater (see Gregory of Nazianzus, *Orat.* 2, and *Nov.Just.* 123). Stage performers, in turn, were favorite subjects for Christian texts about ascetics and martyrs, charting the redemption of the fallen. (See, for instance, Bollandus, *Acta sanctorum march vii* 751–754, for the martyrdom of the mime Philemnon, and *Pélagie la pénitente: Métamorphoses d'une légende* [Paris, 1984] for a collection of tales concerning Pelagia, the leading mime actress and the leader of the chorus girls of Antioch, who became the celebrated "monk" Pelagius.)

The imperial authorities' attitude toward theatrical performers reflects the conflicting pressures of Christian disapproval and the need to supply public entertainment. There are thirteen entries in the *Theodosian Code* under *De scaenicis*. Acting had always been a profession that carried the stigma of *infamia*. The edicts reflect strong disapproval of actors' activities while at the same time legally binding such performers to their profession (see *C.Th.* 15.5).

Mime seems to have survived into the Byzantine period in the form of small-scale, private entertainments for the rich (see, for instance, the household accounts of the Apions in 6th century Oxyrhynchus indicating payments to mimes [*P Oxy.* 2482, line 43]), whereas pantomime, with its need for space, scenery, and musical support, seems to have died out after the end of the 6th century.

BIBL.: W. Weissmann, "Gelasius von Heliopolis, ein Schauspieler-Märtyrer," *Analecta bollandiana* 93 (1975): 39–66. C. Lepelley, *Antiquités africaines* 25 (1989): 258–260. C. Roueché, *Performers and Partisans at Aphrodisias in the Roman and Late Roman Periods* (London, 1993).   R.M.

Adulis

Adulis was the principal port of the kingdom of Axum (Ethiopia). Its name is attested only in Greek and Latin; its designation in the indigenous language, Ge'ez, is unknown. The only precise data on the location of Adulis are found in *Periplus of the Erythraean Sea* (middle to late 1st century C.E.). They suggest that, at the time, Adulis—the port as well as the residential neighborhoods—stood on the site of modern Mesewa in Eritrea, across from the Dahlak Archipelago. Significant ancient relics have been found 35 km southsoutheast of Mesewa and 6 km from the bank of the Haddas River, near modern Zula (whose name may be derived from "Adulis"). They are in all likelihood the remains of the residential section of the Byzantine city (4th to 6th centuries). The city may have moved away from the port to obtain better water resources. Axumite coins and the remains of a church with a semicircular apse have been found.

Adulis exported ivory, rhinoceros horn, and tortoiseshell *(Periplus)*. A bishop from Adulis may have attended the Council of Chalcedon in 451. Cosmas Indicopleustes came through Adulis early in the reign of Justin I (518–527), when Elesboas (Kaleb Ella Asbeha), *negus* (king) of the Axumites, was preparing to invade Yemen in response to the persecution of the Himyarite Christians of Najran (November 523). Ka-

leb assembled a fleet of seventy ships at Gabaza, port of Adulis. The last mention of Adulis is made by Nonnosos, an ambassador sent to the *negus* by Justinian (Photius, *Bibliotheca*). With the rise of Islam in the 7th century, the center of Ethiopian power shifted southward and inland, away from the Red Sea. Adulis seems to have been destroyed by the Arabs in the 8th century.

BIBL.: F. Anfray, "Deux villes axoumites: Adoulis et Matara." *IV congresso internazionale di studi etiopici* (Rome, 1974), 745–772. Lionel Casson, "The Location of Adulis," in *Coins, Culture and History in the Ancient World,* ed. L. Casson and M. Price (Detroit, 1981), 113–122. Lionel Casson, ed., *The Periplus Maris Erythraei* (Princeton, 1989), 102–106. Cosmas Indicopleustes, "Topographie chrétienne," ed. and trans. W. Wolska-Conus, *Sources chrétiennes* 141, 159, 197 (1968–1973). *The Christian Topography of Cosmas, an Egyptian Monk,* ed. and trans. J. W. McCrindle (New York, 1898).   C.J.R.

Advocates

During the late Roman empire the terms *advocatus* and *causidicus* became synonymous; each was applied to persons who exercised the profession of *advocatio* as defined by the 3rd century jurist Ulpian: "We must regard as advocates all those who work on pleading cases with a certain degree of application; but those who regularly receive remuneration for drafting a case without being present at the hearings will not be regarded as advocates" (*Digest* 50.13,1,11). The advocate thus assisted his clients with legal advice before and during a trial and pleaded their case in court. The legal sources for the late empire confirm these duties (*C.Th.* 2.11–12, *C.Just.* 2.6–10, *Nov.Theodosius* 10, *Nov.Valentiniar* 2.2).

The skill of the advocate lay in his rhetoric, both in his preparation of written material for submission to the court and in his expertise in pleading the case before the magistrate. The rhetorical schools were thus the training ground for the advocate, and the surviving late Latin treatises on rhetoric testify to the teaching of technical points of Roman procedural law (*Rhetores latini minores,* ed. Carolus Halm [Leipzig, 1858]), as do the letters of Libanius. In legal material from the 3rd to the 7th centuries the terms *orator, rhetor,* and *scholasticus* are often used in place of *advocatus*.

Evidence from ecclesiastical writers and early Byzantine papyri testify that the role of advocate remained distinct from that of *iurisconsultus* (in the Greek papyri denoted by *nomikos*), whose duty continued to be that of giving juristic advice and legal opinions on points of substantive Roman law relating to the case in hand. "The *advocatus* is paid for legal protection and the *iurisconsultus* for truthful advice" (Augustine, *Ep.* 153.25). The separateness of the professions was maintained despite the increasingly exacting legal qualifications imposed on advocates by imperial constitutions in the 5th and 6th centuries.

The most important development in the profession of advocacy was not in function but in professional organization. From at least the time of Diocletian, advocates were organized into corporations with both statutory and supernumerary members, attached to the tribunals of particular magistrates. In a constitution from 368 the bar is classed as a *militia* (*C.Th.* 1.29.1), and in the 5th century advocates are described as *officiales cohortales* (*C.Just.* 2.7.11 [460] and 2.7.17 [474]). Their rights *(privilegia et immunitates)* and duties were regulated by imperial orders, offering opportunities for promotion by merit to other bureaucratic posts. These posts included appointment as the prestigious *advocatus fisci* (*C.Th.* 10.15.2), *defensor civitatis*, and *defensor ecclesiae*. A constitution of Theodosius II dated 442 states that it was a frequent practice for the praetorian prefect to entrust the government of a province to an advocate who had distinguished himself in the *patrocinium causarum* (*C.Just.* 2.7.9). Many advocates made a sideways career move and exercised their skills in the service of the late imperial and early Byzantine church. C.HUM.

Agens in Rebus

The corps of *agentes in rebus* (a euphemism meaning "those active in affairs"), attested beginning in 319, may have been created during the tetrarchy. The corps was conceived to replace the *frumentarii,* special agents of the emperor who were despised by the general public, which succeeded in obtaining their suppression under Diocletian. The *agentes in rebus* appear to have followed the same evolution as their predecessors, even acquiring the same nickname, *curiosi,* among provincials. The chancellory itself adopted this term; thus, the *Theodosian Code* devotes a chapter to them entitled *De curiosis* (6.29), in addition to the chapter *De agentibus in rebus* (6.27). The latter term, which has intrigued commentators, was already the group's official name in 326, and it should not be considered a slang expression. Like the *frumentarii,* who were under the orders of the praetorian prefects (military personnel at that time), the *agentes in rebus* may have come into being as a military structure. They retained several formal traits of the military even after Constantine placed them under the authority of the newly created *magister officiorum* (hence the corps' Greek nickname, *magistrianoi*). They continued to constitute a *schola,* and their ranking and career profile were modeled on those of the cavalry *(eques, circitor, biarchus, centenarius, ducenarius, princeps)*. There is no doubt, however, that the *agentes* were now civilians, assimilated into the palace staff.

At the start of his career, an *agens in rebus* served as a simple courier on horseback, carrying imperial messages. In the higher ranks, they were primarily responsible for administering and managing the public postal system *(curas gerere et cursus publicum gubernare),*

with one or two *agentes* assigned to each province, depending on the era. Their authority also extended to seaports and shores. They quickly began to abuse their power, however, which made it necessary for the emperors to restrict their mission. Constantius II prohibited them from imprisoning people without reporting it to the judicial authority. This was a venial crime, all in all, when one realizes that the same Constantius recruited *agentes* (and some of the notaries) to carry out his base political schemes (the assassination of Gallus, for example). Such combining of duties triggered a chorus of protests from contemporaries, who were also disturbed to see the corps growing. The privileges of the *schola* were attracting "unworthy" candidates, who used corrupt means to break down the doors of recruitment. Even Constantius could not control their growing numbers. Although Julian reacted forcefully to such excesses, decimating the corps, which was briefly held in disrepute, his measures did not survive him. As Libanius lamented, after Julian the *agentes in rebus* began once more to proliferate, to such a degree that in 430 Theodosius II claimed he was satisfied to be able to limit their number *(matricula)* to 1,174. Under Leo (475–470), a new line was drawn at 1,248, for the east alone. Many of these posts were pure sinecures, passed on from one generation to the next.

A law of Valentinian I indicates that an *agens in rebus,* at the end of his career, could serve for one year as secretary general *(princeps officii)* of a large administrative agency such as a praetorian prefecture or, later, an urban prefecture, a vicariate, a proconsulate of Africa or Achaea, or an eastern duchy. But this system, which placed "senior members of his trusted corps . . . as watchdogs in the office of every important civilian officer in the empire" (Jones, 128), can be traced back at least to Constantius II. A. Giardina has shown that, contrary to earlier analyses, the term *princeps* designated a single category of personnel who continued to belong to the *schola* even when detached into an *officium*. Giardina also redefines the duties of the *magister officiorum,* overseer of all administrative agencies of the empire, as a "bureaucrat par excellence endowed with policing powers" and a supervisor of all the sensitive areas of state security, from roads to weapons factories, from the transmission of messages to the management of the *officia* (Giardina, 71). Under direct orders of the *magister,* the *principes officii* engaged in political surveillance and intelligence and oversaw the provincial administration's operations and the application of laws.

Giardina's redefinition lends new support to the classic interpretation of the *agentes in rebus* as political police that has been called into question by Jones. According to Jones, the execrable reputation they acquired under Constantius II (the reign to which the sources invoked invariably refer) led historians to overestimate their policing powers and to attribute to them a political influence and a social position they never had, unlike the *notarii,* to whom they were excessively compared. In fact, the *agentes in rebus* gradually took over duties that had come to be beneath the notaries; in the 5th century, they succeeded notaries as "secretaries of the divine consistory." They followed the notaries in their climb up the ladder of power and respectability, but the gap that separated them at the beginning never diminished. Sixth century regulations often linked them to the *memoriales,* mere service employees of the archives. An Egyptian example from the same period confirms the stages of ascension in the palace hierarchy: two sons of an *agens in rebus* became *tribuni* and *notarii.* One need not be impressed by their access to the rank of senator (in 386 for the *principes*) or by the progression of the *ducenarii* from the rank of proconsul (in 410) to that of *spectabilis* (in 426), since such honors must be situated within the general inflation of titles. At best, the *principes* could become provincial governors.

After their well-known excesses, were not the *agentes in rebus* brought back into line? Clearly, if one accepts the hypothesis of an all-powerful corps of political police, it is difficult to understand why the emperors would have constantly worked to rein in *agentes in rebus,* limiting them to their specific responsibilities and, in particular, combating their usurpation of policing powers and their interference in the provincial administration. This is an untenable hypothesis, unless we posit that all the authorities (and not just Constantius) were consistently hypocritical. In the same vein, how can we explain the fact that Libanius depicted some of them as perfectly pleasant persons? The *principes,* sharing the exemption from curial duties with other *palatini,* could accede on retirement to a municipal career in their city-state. Such was the case for a certain Comitas in the 6th century, an *agens in rebus* and "father of the city" in Mopsuestia in 550. Contrary to Jones's claim, we cannot be sure that he was "not even a citizen of the town" (*Later Roman Empire,* 760). A similar situation can be seen in the continuing institution of *defensor civitatis,* or judicial magistrate. Candidates were recruited by preference from among various categories of former administrators, including ex–*agentes in rebus.* There were also many curials who sought admission to their *schola* to escape curial obligations.

The later accounts thus give a more bureaucratic and civilized image of the *agentes in rebus.* Perhaps their strength lay more in their exceptional esprit de corps than in some unknown terror they might have inspired.

BIBL.: Andrea Giardina, *Aspetti della burocrazia nel basso impero* (Rome, 1977). A. H. M. Jones, *The Later Roman Empire, 284–602,* 3 vols. (Oxford, 1967); repr., 2 vols., 1973. William G. Sinnigen, "The Roman Secret Service," *Classical Journal* 57 (1961): 65–72.   J.C.

Agriculture

In the late antique world, from 300 to 800, agriculture evolved as part and parcel of the world in which it was practiced. In particular, it was conditioned by changes in populations, degrees of urbanization, the scope of the money economy, the supply of labor, taxation, and security of life and property. Quite possibly it was also affected by changes in climate that are not yet well understood. Although advances in the science of agriculture played little or no part in agricultural evolution, the westward diffusion of crops, irrigation techniques, and other technologies had, over the centuries, a significant impact.

In the western European provinces of the later Roman empire, scholars have commonly held—at least until recently—that from roughly the middle of the 2nd century onward agriculture was affected by falling population levels, decreasing supplies of slaves, the shrinkage of cities, a progressive demonetization of the economy and a decline of trade, growing insecurity both internally and along the borders, and heavy taxation. The result of these changing circumstances could be seen in a widespread abandonment of land, the decline of smaller "yeoman" farms, and the transformation of large, slave-operated *latifundia* into late-Roman colonates. The latter operations relied increasingly on the labor of tenants of two kinds: *servi casati,* or former slaves to whom dwellings and tenancies had been given, and *coloni,* who came from outside—ex-soldiers, former city dwellers, and yeoman farmers who, willingly or unwillingly, commended their persons and perhaps their land to the great landowners. In keeping with the decline in urban markets and long-distance trade, and perhaps also with the desire of tenants to produce a larger proportion of their own food, colonates became more self-sufficient, producing nearly all the food and more of the industrial products consumed by their inhabitants. And as the powers of the central government waned, the resident owners, or *domini,* as they had come to be known, began to assume some functions of the state—notably defense, and the administration of justice and taxation—while the formerly free *coloni* became bound to the soil and to their masters. In short, there occurred a protofeudalization of the countryside.

In the past two decades, however, revisionist scholars have questioned the documentation on which this model was based, and they have adduced new archaeological evidence that does not sit easily with some of its tenets. They have cast doubt on the extent and permanence of land abandonment. They point to the continuing presence of many farms that, to judge from their buildings, appear to have been small or of moderate size; particularly striking is the great number of apparently affluent estates that are smaller than the very great colonates but far more substantial than small farms. And they have also argued that the first half of the 3rd century was a time of prosperity everywhere except in Italy, and that after the disorders of the second half of the 3rd century, prosperity reappeared in all parts of the western empire except northern Gaul, Belgica, and Italy. Yet this same body of evidence shows that the maximum occupation of the land was reached by the end of the 1st century in Italy and in the 2nd century in Britain, Belgica, northern Gaul, and northern Spain. In the second half of the 3rd century, declines in occupation seem to have been great in northern Gaul, Belgica, and Italy, and all regions of the western empire show considerable abandonment of sites through the 5th century. Archaeological evidence from western Europe also suggests a continuing decline in the relative importance of small farms through the later centuries of the empire, a substantial shrinkage of cities, a falloff in long-distance trade, and a probable contraction of the money economy. Inevitably, all these changes affected agriculture, encouraging the development of largely self-sufficient estates.

While the impact of the Germanic invasions of the 5th and 6th centuries varied according to region—the more exposed parts of the empire, such as Britain, Belgica, northern Gaul, and Bavaria, experienced great destruction while elsewhere there was more continuity—the period following the invasions saw similar developments in most areas. Peasants congregated in nucleated settlements, sometimes on hilltops or other easily fortified sites. Where these settlements did not already have a lord, there was a tendency for them to fall under the control of one as the system of lordship spread and small farmers found it hard to survive on their own. Lords were granted—or they assumed—increasing powers over the villagers under their control, and there seems to have been a significant shift of surplus agricultural production away from the state and toward the lordly class. Particularly noticeable was the growth of royal and ecclesiastical properties in which the king, other members of the royal family, and ecclesiastics served as lords; in many regions these accounted for as much as half of the farmland. In the near absence of slaves and wage labor, these estates were worked almost entirely by tenants, who farmed their tenancies with the help of family members and other villagers; the land reserved for the use of the lord, his demesne, was cultivated by tenants performing obligatory services. In most places, contacts with the outside world were few and production was almost entirely for the consumption of the lord, his dependents, and the villagers. In short, this period saw the rise of the manor. Though it varied greatly over time and place, according to economic and political contexts, this was to remain the dominant mode of agricultural exploitation through the European Middle Ages.

At the same time, there seems to have occurred a fusion between Germanic farming traditions, in which livestock production was prominent, and Roman traditions, which concentrated almost exclusively on crops. In the more Romanized parts of western Europe this is evidenced by a marked increase in the production of animals, and in the more northerly parts of the Continent by the spread of cereal cultivation. The "cerealization" of the north, which is almost certainly linked to rising population densities, was greatly facilitated by two innovations: the heavy plow, which made it much easier to plow the heavy clay soils of the European plain, and an essentially new cereal crop, rye, which was more tolerant than wheat of cold, drought, and poor soil. A sign that growing crops and raising animals were becoming more tightly integrated may be seen in the appearance, from the 7th century onward, of "open" or "common" fields, which were used alternately for the cultivation of crops and the pasturing of livestock. As such arrangements were consolidated and became villagewide activities, the cultivated lands of the manor came to be divided into just a few large fields in which both lords and peasants held plots; after harvesting and during fallow periods, an entire field was grazed by the animals of the lord and his villagers. With new, villagewide controls governing the use of these lands, private property rights were extinguished in favor of rights that were shared among lords, tenants, and the community at large.

The eastern part of the Roman empire (or, after 330, Byzantium) was subject to many of the same pressures as the western empire, especially internal and external threats to regional security. But agriculture was more resilient than in the west on account of the east's higher population densities, its large and prosperous cities, the greater availability of slave labor, its more monetized economy, the strength of both local and long-distance trade, the strong presence of the state in the countryside, and, ultimately, the ability of the state to fend off invaders—at least until the middle of the 7th century. Nevertheless, the eastern empire, like the western, saw heavier and at times oppressive taxation in the countryside, the binding of the *coloni* to the soil (in the 4th century), and the growth of large estates at the expense of small farms. From the 3rd century onward, abandonment of land is frequently mentioned in texts, and it probably accelerated with the "plague of Justinian," which struck in 542 and persisted until late in the century; though this plague also hit western Europe, it appears to have been particularly devastating in the Byzantine east. Inter alia, its effects may be seen in the abandonment of cultivation and settlement in such places as the *villes mortes* around Aleppo. The plague probably also accounts for the appearance of huge deposits of silt along the lower reaches and at the mouths of many rivers: this phenomenon is best explained by the abandonment of cultivation in marginal hilly lands, from which, as terraces collapsed and eroded, soil was washed into streams and rivers.

A new period in Byzantine agriculture begins, however, in the 7th century, with the reforms of Heraclius (610–641) and the loss of Egypt and the Near East to the Arabs. The burden of taxation on the countryside was reduced; most peasants were freed from military service; and the peasantry, no longer bound to the soil, became free to move from place to place. Some moved onto previously abandoned lands. Almost everywhere peasant-owned farms became conspicuous and important. These could be tiny properties (sometimes the result of the division of lands through inheritance) that were barely viable without supplementary earnings; or they could be much larger, market-oriented farms with consolidated lands or, more commonly, plots scattered among the lands of a nucleated village. Larger estates by no means disappeared, but—except for the notable growth of ecclesiastical properties—their expansion seems to have been contained. Labor on the larger peasant farms and the great estates came from four sources: the peasant-owner and family, slaves, tenants, and wage laborers; these last might be villagers with little or no land of their own, itinerant rural workers, or city dwellers who came to help at harvest time. This period lasted until the 9th century, when peasants were once more burdened with heavier taxes and military service, and large estates again grew at their expense.

The practice of agriculture varied from place to place according to climate, soil, water resources, political and economic context, and familiarity with technologies and crops. Yet up until the 7th century there were many features common to agriculture throughout the Mediterranean basin and western Europe. In general, the raising of livestock and the growing of crops were separate activities that shared a sometimes hostile relationship; they usually made use of different lands and labor forces, but at the margins they often competed for land. Livestock production was usually confined to lands that were too arid, hilly, rocky, or infertile for cropping. As year-round pastures were seldom available, many animals were slaughtered in their first year, often while still suckling; the remaining animals might have to be driven long distances in search of grazing grounds.

Crops were grown on irrigated and rain-fed land. Although irrigation works had been extended through the early centuries of the Roman empire, irrigated land was still very limited, consisting usually of river valleys and places where water from flash floods could be captured; water was generally available only while rivers were in flood or during the season of rains. Furthermore, during the later centuries of the western empire, and in the 6th and early 7th centuries in Byzantium and the Sassanian empire, many irrigation works seem to have fallen into disrepair. But where available, irrigation made land much more productive, and irrigated lands tended to produce more cash crops and fewer crops for subsistence. On rain-fed lands crops were of two types: "permanent" crops that remained in the soil for many years, typically grape vines, olive trees, fruit trees, and date palms; and crops that were sown annually on plowed fields. The latter were principally grains, which were the staple foods almost everywhere; some grains were also fed to animals or used for fermented drinks. The commonly grown grains included einkorn, emmer, spelt, brome, rivet wheat, common wheat *(Triticum aestivum),* common millet, foxtail millet, barley, oats, and, eventually, rye. Whether hard wheat was also grown is not certain: it does not seem to be mentioned in the classical agricultural texts, and the carbonized grains of various naked wheats found by archaeologists cannot be distinguished with currently available technology. Other rain-fed crops included legumes—mainly lentils, chickpeas, fava beans, and peas—as well as some vegetables that might be grown as field crops. In general, fields were sown shortly after the autumn rains and harvested in the spring. Lands were then fallowed for a year and a half—or longer—to restore moisture and fertility. By the 8th century there are signs in France of the appearance of a three-phase rotation in which land was cropped two years out of three, with summer and winter crops alternating; in later centuries this practice would spread through much of temperate Europe.

Following the Arab conquests of the 7th to 9th centuries, many innovations were introduced into the agriculture of the Near East, Egypt, the Maghreb, Spain, and Sicily. These changes diversified production and intensified land use. At the core of what might be called an agricultural revolution were many new crops that were for the most part found by the Arabs in the lands of the former Sassanian empire and in the province of Sind (in northwestern India). These crops diffused westward on a large scale. They included rice, cotton, sugarcane, sorghum, various citrus fruits, bananas, watermelons, spinach, eggplants, indigo, henna, and possibly hard wheat. A second component of this revolution was the extension and improvement of irrigation, in part through the westward diffusion of eastern technologies such as the *noria,* or waterwheel, for the lifting of water, and the *qanaat,* or underground canal, which tapped an aquifer and channeled its water, often over long distances. As a result, more water was brought to more land over a longer period of the year—often through the entire year. These improvements were linked to the new crops, many of which needed heavy watering and were grown in summer, when irrigation water had previously been scarce or unavailable. In turn the new crops and the improvements in irrigation allowed new rotations that used land much more intensively and raised its productivity. In many places land was cropped two or more times every year and fallowing was done away with; where such heavy cropping was not possible, other rotations were introduced that reduced the time that the land lay idle. All these changes in the agriculture of the early Islamic world should be understood in the context of a society in which the population was growing and becoming more urbanized; the scope of the money economy was expanding as local and long-distance trade grew; laws enshrined private property and favored the extension of irrigation; taxes were generally low; security of life and property was generally good; and there was a widespread movement of soldiers, merchants, scholars, pilgrims, and migrants who carried westward new technologies, skills, plants, and tastes.

The agricultural literature of the ancient world was preserved and transmitted through late antiquity in a number of works, for the most part compilations, which were translated into Greek, Syriac, Persian, and Arabic. In the 4th century Vindanius Anatolius of Beirut compiled a treatise in Greek that drew, directly or indirectly, on the works of earlier Greek, Latin, and Phoenician authors. Anatolius and the classical Latin agronomes were the main sources for Palladius's late 4th century compendium in Latin, while Isidore of Seville (d. 636) in his *Etymologiae* drew directly on classical Greek and Latin sources; these two works transmitted agricultural writings of antiquity into the medieval west. Anatolius was also one of the principal sources for the compilation in Greek by Cassianus Bassus, completed around 600. Around the middle of the 10th century Anatolius's compilation was reworked to form the Byzantine *Geoponica*. During the 9th and early 10th centuries the treatises of both Anatolius and Cassianus were translated from Greek into Syriac and thence into Arabic, as well as directly from Greek into Arabic. The work of Anatolius was also translated into Armenian and that of Cassianus into Persian. The Arabic translations of Cassianus, known to the Arabs as Qustūs al-Rūmī, or Kasīnūs, were one of two main sources of ancient traditions cited by later Arabic agronomes, particularly those of Muslim Spain in the 11th and 12th centuries. The other principal source was the so-called *Nabataean Book of Agriculture*, an enormous work that appeared in Arabic in the early 10th century and purported to be a translation by one Ibn Waḥshīya of the agricultural traditions of the Nabataean (or Syriac-speaking) peoples of Iraq. In fact this work appears to draw on a number of different sources: several otherwise unknown eastern works, containing much superstition, which perhaps go back as far as the 1st century C.E.; various ancient Greek and Latin authors, whose works were used to an extent that is difficult to determine without extensive textual analysis; and fresh observations made either by Ibn Waḥshīya himself or by a near contemporary.

Apart from the new material added to Ibn Waḥshīya's compilation, and a very few references to new crops in the Arabic translation of Cassianus, this literature appears to add nothing to the agricultural knowledge of the ancients. It was left to later scholars—in Islamic Spain from the 10th century onward and, much later, in Christian Europe—to make new observations and to propose explanatory theories.

BIBL.: Tamara Lewit, *Agricultural Production in the Roman Economy*, A.D. 200–400 (Oxford, 1991). Michel Kaplan, *Les hommes et la terre à Byzance* (Paris, 1992). Andrew M. Watson, *Agricultural Innovation in the Early Islamic World: The Diffusion of Crops and Farming Techniques, 700–1100* (Cambridge, Eng., 1983). Chris Wickham, "The Other Transition: From the Ancient World to Feudalism," *Past and Present* 103 (1984): 3–36.   A.W.

Agri Deserti

Agri deserti (deserted lands) are prominent in the later Roman empire for three reasons: Roman historiography, fiscal law, and barbarian invasions. Roman tradition, which regarded the fall of all empires as "biologically" inevitable, was modified by Christian apologists, who seized on rural disasters as providential forerunners of the second coming, and by secular contemporaries, who exaggerated agrarian misfortunes to praise or damn individual emperors. Cyprian's description of sterility was written from Africa, and Lactantius's attack on the rural misery caused by Diocletian's reforms came from Syria, where archaeology has in fact revealed extensive prosperity. Many laws in the codes dealt with *agri deserti,* but they were more concerned with rent taxes than productivity. It is uncertain whether the land was always abandoned. Tax remissions to wealthy landowners in Campania in 395 (*C.Th.* 11.28.2) and a similar concession in Africa in 422 (*C.Th.* 11.28.13) were probably motivated politically rather than economically. The most favored fiscal instruments were long-lease *emphuteusis* and restrictions on movements of *coloni.* But both were less relevant to deserted lands than the unwieldiness of imperial estates, especially in Africa, where agriculture was booming. Although no one would deny that some land was abandoned in the disturbed conditions and invasions of the later empire, it was often deserted by rich proprietors but still cultivated by poor tenants, squatters, or foreign settlers, as certainly happened in northern Gaul. In Italy a new tax regime imposed by Diocletian drove marginal land out of use. But empirewide assessments of the archaeological evidence are less pessimistic than those derived from the literary sources.

BIBL.: Clive Foss, "The Near Eastern Countryside in Late Antiquity: A Review Article," *Journal of Roman Archaeology,* supplementary series 14 (1995): 213–234. T. Lewit, *Agricultural Production in the Roman Economy,* A.D. 200–400 (Oxford, 1991). C. R. Whittaker, "Agri deserti," in *Land, City and Trade in the Roman Empire* (Brookfield, Vt., 1993). C.W.

Ahura Mazda

Ahura Mazda (Lord Wisdom, or Wise Lord) was originally one of several Indo-Iranian *ahuras* or *asuras*— "spiritual lords"—that included Mithra and Varuna. Adopted by the prophet Zoroaster as the source of righteousness, he became the creator deity of Zoroastrianism.

Ahura Mazda was extolled by Zoroaster in the *Gathas,* and invocations to him permeate the rest of the *Avesta.* He came to be worshiped by the Achaemenians as Ahuramazda, the greatest of deities and the giver of kingship. Under the names Aramazd, Ohrmazd, and Hormizd, he was venerated during the Parthian, Sassanian, Umayyad, and Abbasid eras as a perfect, good, rational, and omniscient spirit. Zoroastrianism of late antiquity, as codified in a Pahlavi catechism called the *Shkand Gumanig Wizar* (Doubt-Dispelling Exposition), proposed that imperfection could not arise from a perfect being. As a result, Zoroastrians of that time claimed that Ahura Mazda had created the spiritual and material worlds completely pure, and that all sin, disease, decay, and death were created by the opposing evil spirit Angra Mainyu, or Ahriman, to corrupt humans. The struggle between Ahura Mazda and Angra Mainyu came to be seen as a cosmic battle between light and darkness, good and evil, humans and demons for the destiny of the world and all creation. A detailed description of the beneficence of Ahura Mazda, the hostility of Angra Mainyu, and the universal dualism between opposing forces, starting with cosmogony and ending with eschatology, is provided by the Pahlavi *Bundahisn,* or *(Book of) Primal Creation.* A monist version of Zoroastrianism was also present during late antiquity, in which Ahura Mazda and Angra Mainyu were viewed as offspring of Zurvan, "time."

During Sassanian times Ahura Mazda was depicted in anthropomorphic form on investiture rock reliefs at sites such as Naqsh-i Rostam (in Fars). As Zoroastrians encountered other faiths, Ahura Mazda came to be equated to Zeus, Yahweh, and Bel.

BIBL.: F. B. J. Kuiper, "Ahura Mazda 'Lord Wisdom'?" *Indo-Iranian Journal* 18 (1976): 25–42. J.K.C.

Aila/Ayla

Located at the head of the Gulf of Aqaba, Aila emerged as a Nabataean city by the 1st century B.C.E. It served as a transshipment point for trade between the Roman empire and its eastern neighbors. Following the Roman annexation of Nabataea in 106 C.E., Aila was the southern terminus of the Via Nova Traiana, which ran north through Transjordan to Syria. By ca. 300 it was garrisoned by Legio X Fretensis, and it remained a military post until at least the early 5th century. Records attest to bishops in Aila beginning in 325. Excavations have revealed a possible 4th century Christian basilica and that the city was fortified in the late 4th or early 5th century. The city flourished through the Byzantine period and peacefully submitted to Muslim rule in 630.

The Muslims founded the new city of Ayla next to the older settlement, possibly under 'Uthmān ibn 'Affān, ca. 650. Excavations have revealed a city modeled on the older legionary camps: a *miṣr,* or very early Islamic city. This transformation of artifacts parallels the emergence of Islamic political and cultural identity. The city prospered in the Abbasid period (9th and 10th centuries), participating in the commercial world of the Indian Ocean and in pilgrim traffic to Mecca and Medina from Egypt and Palestine. In the last Fatimid period, bedouins sacked the town in 1024 and a hoard of gold dinars minted in Sijilmasa, Morocco, was lost. The town was damaged in the earthquake of 1068 and abandoned with the arrival of the crusaders in 1116.

BIBL.: Paul M. Cobb, "Scholars and Society at Early Islamic Ayla," *Journal of the Economic and Social History of the Orient* 38 (1995): 417–428. S. Thomas Parker, "The Roman Aqaba Project: The 1994 Campaign," *Annual of the Department of Antiquities of Jordan* 40 (1998): 231–257. Donald Whitcomb, *Ayla: Art and Industry in the Islamic Port of Aqaba* (Chicago, 1994). T.P., D.W.

Alaric

Alaric first appears in the early 390s as a Visigothic military leader. In 394 he served in Theodosius's campaign against the usurper Eugenius, but then, unhappy about not receiving a sufficient reward, he revolted. Between 395 and 397 he and his Goths devastated Thrace and Greece, sacking a number of famous cities and escaping destruction by the western *magister militum* Stilicho on several occasions. In 398 or 399 he was granted the office of *magister militum* (Master of Soldiers) of Illyricum. In spite of this honor, he invaded Italy in 401 and besieged Emperor Honorius in Milan. In 402, he was defeated at Pollentia and again at Verona by Stilicho, who then allowed him to withdraw from Italy. In 407, Alaric was engaged by Stilicho in a plan to seize Illyricum, then administered by the east, for the western empire, but this scheme was frustrated by the revolt of Constantine III in Britain and Gaul (407–411).

After Stilicho's murder in 408, many of his partisans joined Alaric, who had moved into the province of Noricum on the northern Italian border. Then, when Honorius refused to pay Alaric for past services, the Visigoths invaded Italy once again in 408 and besieged Rome, having been promised assistance from a group of Visigoths and Huns led by Alaric's relative Athaulf. A long series of negotiations then ensued that involved Alaric, the Senate at Rome, and Honorius, who by then was safely installed in Ravenna. The siege of Rome was lifted and renewed several times as Honorius continued to delay, the main sticking point being his refusal to make Alaric a western *magister militum.* In 409, Alaric allowed the Senate to name a new emperor, Priscus Attalus, who granted Alaric his desired rank.

Finally in 410, after being joined by Athaulf and attacked by imperial forces, Alaric returned to Rome, which he captured and sacked beginning on 24 August. The sacking lasted only three days, and churches, at least, generally were left untouched. The damage was more psychological than material. For the first time in 800 years Rome had fallen. No longer could the city be called Roma Invicta (Unconquered Rome).

After leaving Rome, Alaric and his band, which had been augmented by many stray barbarians and even Romans, traveled south, hoping to cross to Sicily. Foiled in this endeavor when the Gothic fleet was wrecked, Alaric turned back north, and on this journey he became ill and died in Bruttium. He reportedly was buried in the bed of the Busento River after the stream had been diverted. His position then was taken by Athaulf, who two years later led the Goths into Gaul.

Alaric and his Goths had a devastating effect on the Roman national consciousness. The Goths' ability to roam the empire freely, under their own commander, put an end to the belief in Roman military superiority. Other barbarian groups quickly followed the Gothic example. The sack of Rome, in particular, was a devastating blow. Shortly thereafter, pagan arguments that Roman failures were the result of the abandonment of the pagan gods were countered by Augustine in the *City of God*. The Visigoths, meanwhile, went on to found kingdoms based first at Toulouse and then in Spain.

BIBL.: Thomas S. Burns, *Barbarians within the Gates of Rome: A Study of Roman Military Policy and the Barbarians, ca. 375–425 A.D.* (Bloomington, Ind., 1994). E. Demougeot, *De l'unité à la division de l'empire romain* (Paris, 1951). Theodor Mommsen, "Stilicho und Alarich," *Hermes* 38 (1903): 1–15.   R.W.M.

Alchemy

Alchemy—or more correctly for late antiquity, the "sacred" or "divine" art—refers to the harnessing of metalworking techniques for religious goals. It is uncertain when and where a theory of the salvific value of the transmutation of metals arose. Egypt is usually held to be the country of origin, though this may merely repeat a late antique topos. Papyrological evidence and the first major compiler of alchemical traditions, Zosimus of Panopolis, both point to the second half of the 3rd century C.E. Diocletian's order at the end of that century to burn "the ancient books of Chemia dealing with gold and silver" (John of Damascus, the *Suda*) evinces the prestige and power of these techniques.

The earliest extant texts associated with alchemy, the Leiden X and Stockholm papyri (mid-3rd century), were part of a rich collection of esoterica found in a tomb at Thebes. These texts include metalworking techniques unlikely to yield any practical results, indicating a shift from considerations of jewelry making to new social concerns. Similar recipes appear in the earliest texts in Berthelot's idiosyncratic reconstruction of the alchemical "corpus" (1888), including Pseudo-De-

mocritus's *Physical Things and Mysteries*. In this text recipes are combined with a narrative recounting the author's search for true illumination, culminating in the optimistic revelation that the process for "conquering" the natural world is obtainable from the natural world.

Zosimus's theology of alchemy (before 400 C.E.) reflects spiritual desires to make the corporeal incorporeal, to undo through ascent the fall of the first man into the body and his consequent subjection to fate, and to transform nature. Zosimus also preserved excerpts both from "legendary" authors of the previous several centuries and from Maria the Jewess, a historical figure probably of the 1st century C.E. Maria refined the standard alchemical operations on volatile substances by distillation and sublimation and elucidated the vocabulary of transmutation. Her simple goal was to impart a series of color changes to metals: to make them black, white, yellow, and violet. These external changes represented inner changes undergone by the metals. Metals were believed to represent the natural world, and changes in them were evidence of natural processes. Every metal was seen as on its way to being gold; the alchemist merely sped up the process by adding a catalyst.

Alchemists grounded their work in ancient traditions based on divine revelation and related to sacrificial practices. In the context of late antique cosmological beliefs, alchemical practices were understood to transform the lower order (earthly) matter into higher order (heavenly) matter. In contrast to the "Gnostic" vision, which sees an unbridgeable gulf between matter and divinity, alchemical metallurgy implies a positive attitude toward the natural world and a belief in its redeemability even at the lowest level of nature. In addition to these theoretical concerns, late Roman alchemy continued to be concerned with the technology of imparting worth to worthless objects through dyeing, gilding, and silver plating. An interest in the techniques of applied chemistry survived throughout late antiquity.

For several centuries after Zosimus, alchemical texts and pseudoepigraphical works were collected and commented on by Byzantine authors. Some attempted to explain the meaning of alchemical processes in the context of Neoplatonic ideas, others in terms of Christian spirituality. When the Muslims began to study the Greco-Egyptian tradition of alchemy in the 7th century, they found a wide array of texts in several languages, including Syriac and Coptic. A work of Aristotle, for example, was translated into Syriac in 618 C.E. at the bidding of Heraclius; the Bishop of Sinjar (in Mesopotamia) wrote a commentary on it that still exists in an Arabic translation. Some of the important early Greek texts were preserved most fully (or solely) in Arabic translations of the 8th and 9th centuries. Although alchemical recipes were known in western Europe in late antiquity, alchemy did not become a scientific discipline there until the 12th century, when a large number of Arabic texts (translations of earlier texts and original works) were translated into Latin. The idea of the alchemical process as an allegory for the spiritual transformation of the alchemist became popular in early modern Europe but was not common in late antiquity.

After the Muslim conquest of Egypt in the 7th century, the Arabs became acquainted with ancient Egyptian, Hellenistic, and Byzantine traditions. Other transmissions of texts may have taken place through contacts with Christians in the east. In addition, there are Chinese and Iranian influences on alchemy in the Islamic world. The earliest historical figure associated with the science is Khālid ibn Yazīd, an Umayyad prince who died around 704. He reputedly learned alchemy in Alexandria from the monk Marianos (Morienus) and ordered that Greek and Coptic scientific works be translated into Arabic. Jābir ibn Ḥayyān (d. ca. 812) is considered the first major figure in Islamic alchemy.

From the corpus of early Egyptian and Greek teachings on alchemy, Muslim alchemists derived both terminology and techniques. The Islamic tradition is significant not only for its preservation of texts but also for its emphasis on scientific experiments and observation. Plant, human, and animal substances were added to the array of materials used in alchemical processes, leading to advances in the related fields of pharmacology and medicine. Early Muslim alchemists were concerned with cosmological theory and natural philosophy, but the religious and allegorical interpretations associated with Zosimus did not become prevalent in the Islamic world until the 11th century.

BIBL.: George C. Anawati, "Arabic Alchemy," in *Encyclopedia of the History of Islamic Science*, vol. 3, ed. Roshdi Rashed with Régis Morelon (London and New York, 1996). Marcellin Berthelot, *Collection des anciens alchimistes grecs* (Paris, 1888; repr. London, 1963). Joseph Bidez et al., *Catalogue des manuscrits alchimiques grecs* (Brussels, 1924). Robert Halleux, *Les alchimistes grecs* (Paris, 1981). Robert Halleux, "Alchemy," and Michael W. Dols, "Alchemy, Islamic," in *Dictionary of the Middle Ages*, ed. J. Strayer (New York, 1982–1989), 134–142.   N.J.

Alexandria

Despite the 3rd century ravages of plague, civil war, and foreign occupation, Alexandria in late antiquity retained its place as one of the preeminent cities of the Mediterranean. With a population of several hundred thousand, it vied with Antioch and later Constantinople as the Byzantine empire's second largest city. Alexandria owed its continued prosperity to its unique geographical setting. Linked to the Canopic branch of the Nile via canals and Lake Mareotis, Alexandria served as the Mediterranean entrepôt for the produce of Egypt and for luxury goods carried overland from

the Red Sea port of Berenike. During the 5th and 6th centuries, the Alexandrian grain fleet provisioned Constantinople with nearly 36 million *modii*, or approximately 220,000 tons, of Egyptian grain per annum. Other widely exported goods included papyrus, wine, olive oil, fine glassware, linen, ivory and bone carvings, embroidered fabrics, medicines, and precious stones. Alexandria's economic prosperity and status as a major trading center continued with only minor setbacks until the Tulunid period in the 9th century.

Although the late antique city preserved the basic gridlike configuration that dated from its Hellenistic foundation, the centuries had taken their toll on several famed topographical features. The palace district of Bruchion was destroyed during the 270s, and with it possibly the tomb of Alexander the Great and the celebrated museum. In addition, the Alexandrian gymnasium, the focal point of Hellenism in the city, is not attested past the early 3rd century. With the decline of these sites, other urban locales, like the Agora (or Mesopedion) and the hippodrome, increasingly became the foci of the city's ceremonial life—a development common to other late antique cities. Other prominent urban sites survived into late antiquity, owing to their Christianization during the 4th century. The Caesarion, which dominated the waterfront of the Great Harbor, was transformed into the patriarchal cathedral (or Great Church) during the mid-4th century. Likewise, near the Great Harbor, the Ptolemaic Temple of Kronos became the Church of St. Michael during the 320s. The Serapeum, the massive temple of the city's patron deity, was forcibly turned into the Church of St. John by the patriarch Theophilus in 391. Despite these alterations in the city's landscape, they took place within a relatively unchanging circuit of the city's walls, at least until the Sassanian and Arab occupations in the 7th century. Moreover, they all occurred within a topographical framework dominated by the city's principal east-west artery, the Via Canopica, and by the city's bustling twin harbors. The Pharos, the city's immense multistoried lighthouse, loomed over these harbors and acted as a beacon to sailors some dozens of miles out to sea. The Pharos is well attested in late antique pilgrim itineraries, and it stood substantially intact until the earthquake of 955.

Throughout late antiquity, Alexandria continued as the chief administrative center for the post-tetrarchic Egyptian provinces. At the apex of this administrative structure was the *praefectus Augustalis*, successor after ca. 380 to the *praefectus Aegypti*. Prefectural courts heard petitions submitted from all over Egypt concerning tax liability, estate division, and civic obligations. The prefect entrusted the assessment and collection of taxes (both monetary and in kind) to subordinate financial officers such as *logistēs*, *katholikos*, and the *procurator rei privatae*. Other prefectural officials included the *procurator Phari* who collected harbor dues at the ports of Alexandria and protected shipping lanes

Map of Alexandria in late antiquity.

near the city; the *praepositus monetae,* who supervised the imperial mint located in the Caesarion; and the *praefectus annonae Alexandrinae,* who oversaw the vast bureaucracy that facilitated the collection and transport of grain to Alexandria—and eventually to the rest of the empire. The prefect and his administration worked in concert with the *dux Aegypti* (sometimes known as the *comes Aegypti*), the senior military officer in lower Egypt. The *dux* commanded the legionary troops garrisoned at the suburban camp of Nicopolis, and he frequently deployed troops to restore order in the city or to enforce imperial directives. Alexandria's political life was also directed by its civic aristocracy, the *bouleutai,* a hereditary class of notables eligible for local offices, positions usually denoted by a seat on the Alexandrian council, or *boulē.* The *boulē* had been restored by Septimius Severus and was presided over by the city's chief magistrate, the *prutanis.* Although many traditionally aristocratic offices disappeared after the tetrarchy and the *boulē* seems to have lost much of its power across late antiquity, the bouleutic class still exerted considerable influence through its wealth and patronage in the city. As a consequence, it remained a pivotal group and was courted or bullied by the emperor's representatives during the conflicts that troubled the city.

The 3rd century trend of factional conflict fed by rebellions against imperial authority culminated in the usurpation of power by Domitius Domitianus and later by his lieutenant, Aurelius Achilleus, in 297–98. After a protracted siege, Diocletian crushed this rebellion, and thenceforth Alexandria was free from similar blatant challenges to imperial rule. However, the growing power of the Christian community served to destablize the city's political life during the 4th and early 5th centuries. Led by able patriarchs like Peter I (300–311), Athanasius (328–373), Theophilus (385–412), and Cyril (412–444), the Christian community challenged the cultural hegemony long enjoyed by the city's pagan community and also threatened the status of the city's prominent Jewish community. Added to this volatile mix was the heavy hand of imperial authority, as the emperor's representatives sought to tip the scales of intercommunal competition, as well as to favor various factions arising from conflicts within the Christian community—notably the Arians during the mid-4th century and the Chalcedonians in the period after 451. As a consequence, riots attended the episcopates of the Arian bishops Gregory (339–345), George (357–361), and Lucius (367–378); pagan-Christian violence racked the city in 356, 374, 391 (the destruction of the pagan cult at the Serapeum), 415 (the murder of the philosopher Hypatia), and finally during the antipagan pogroms of the 480s; Jewish-Christian violence escalated until 414–415, when rioting led to the expulsion of a large portion of the Jewish community. Chalcedonian-Monophysite violence erupted in 451 with the deposition of the patriarch Dioscorus. This violence resulted in the murder of the Chalcedonian bishop Proterius in 457 and continued sporadically until the Arab conquest in 642.

Throughout these centuries Alexandrian cultural life thrived, confirming the city's status as one of the empire's greatest intellectual and religious centers. The reputation of Alexandrian medical education was unsurpassed, producing several imperial court physicians. The city's schools of philosophy and mathematics drew many students to the lectures of Olympius, Theon, Hypatia, Ammonius, Asclepiodotus, and Horapollon. Christian rhetoricians and philosophers, such as Aphthonius, Theodore, and John Philoponus, demonstrate that Alexandria's intellectual achievement also spread across communal boundaries. In addition, the successive heads of the Christian catechetical school—Origen, Pierius, and Didymus the Blind, for example—contributed to the city's rich legacy of patristic exegesis and theology, exemplified by the works of Athanasius and Cyril.

The contours of urban life in late antique Alexandria have become much better known through recent archaeological work carried out in an area of the city's center known as Kōm el-Dikka. A portion of the excavated site consists of an inhabited quarter dated to the 4th through 7th centuries. This quarter grew up on either side of a broad colonnaded street that ran in front of an elegant theaterlike structure that seated up to six hundred spectators. Just to the north, excavators uncovered a large imperial bath complex and three conjoining lecture halls—the latter providing unprecedented archaeological testimony of the city's intellectual life. Along a nearby parallel street were found cisterns, taverns, glass workshops, and well-preserved private dwellings. Significant discoveries from this quarter include a large mural of an enthroned Madonna and other wall decorations that serve as clear evidence for the development of Coptic artistic forms in a cosmopolitan urban setting—not just in the Egyptian countryside. Graffiti from the theater supply data concerning the factions of the hippodrome, particularly during the rebellion of Nicetas and Heraclius. It appears that the quarter's public buildings were all erected at approximately the same time during the 4th century. These late Roman building projects reflect the renewed vigor of urban conditions in Alexandria immediately following Diocletian's capture of the city in 298.

BIBL.: A. J. Butler, *The Arab Conquest of Egypt* (Oxford, 1902; 2nd ed., ed. P. M. Fraser, Oxford, 1978), chap. 24, "Alexandria at the Conquest," with Fraser's additional bibliography, lxxiii–lxxvi. C. Haas, *Alexandria in Late Antiquity: Topography and Social Conflict* (Baltimore, 1996). Annick Martin, *Athanase et l'église d'Égypte au IVe siècle* (Rome,

1996). M. Rodziewicz, *Les habitations romaines tardives d'Alexandrie à la lumière des fouilles polonaises à Kōm el-Dikka, Alexandrie*, vol. 3 (Warsaw, 1984).   C.H.

ʿAlī ibn Abī Tālib

ʿAlī ibn Abī Tālib, whose date of birth was probably around 598, was a relative of the Prophet Muhammad and one of the first Meccans to believe in the Prophet's mission. He became one of Islam's earliest heroic and legendary warriors. He married Muhammad's daughter Fatimah and fathered two sons, Hasan and Husain.

Soon after the death of the Prophet in 632, he appeared as a possible successor and caliph because of his family ties to the Prophet. But his claims were rejected, and it is only in 656 that he managed to become the fourth caliph, having in the meantime incurred the enmity of large segments of the Muslim population. He was not a successful caliph and, in spite of his strong base in Kufa in Iraq, he failed to win over Muʿāwiyyah, became involved in all sorts of sectarian conflicts, and was eventually assassinated in 661. His primary importance lies in the fact that he was the original leader of the movement known as Shīʿism, which held that the rule of the Muslim community must remain in the hands of the Prophet's descendants. This movement was destined to play a major role in the history and culture of Islam, and a complex hagiography eventually developed around ʿAlī ibn Abī Tālib, a person whose historical role was quite weak, if not pitiful.

BIBL.: "Ali b. Abi Talib," Ehsan Yarshater, ed., *Encyclopedia Iranica* (London and Boston, 1982–).   O.G.

Almsgiving

Almsgiving is the act of providing for the needy. Judaism viewed almsgiving as a religious obligation for which God rendered reward. The Torah contains numerous regulations enjoining the care of the poor. Deuteronomy 14:28–29 attests to the antiquity in Jewish tradition of an organized system of relief; in the common era, Jewish religious leaders oversaw distribution from their community food chests, as at Aphrodisias in the 3rd and 4th centuries. Rabbinic writers presented almsgiving as an essential foundation of religious life (for example, Mishnah, *Avot* 1.2).

The "doing of good works" in Graeco-Roman tradition—*euergetism* for the Greeks and *beneficences* for the Latins—formed part of the patronage activity that made up civic duty. The recipients of such giving, however, were not the poor but rather the patron's clients, friends, or fellow citizens. The patron gave as a demonstration of power and wealth, devotion to the civic community, and worthiness as a public figure; loyalty and public acclaim were the expected rewards. The poor were not included in this system. The Roman bread dole was a limited practice, available only to certain citizens in certain cities, and not inclusive of the destitute poor. On the other hand, the Stoics viewed justice as a necessary component of piety. Seneca (*Clem.* 2.6.3.) advocated fair treatment of the unfortunate, toward whom the good judge "like a god" should show mercy. The Cynics begged for their sustenance, and preached that material poverty enabled the highest virtues of the soul. Voluntary poverty and the sharing of goods were ideals of utopian communities both Graeco-Roman and Jewish.

Christianity followed Judaism in its presentation of almsgiving as obligatory. Throughout the New Testament the faithful are urged to provide for the voluntary and the involuntary poor and to look after all in need, defined as the poor, widows, orphans, prisoners, strangers, the sick, and the afflicted. By the 2nd century, almsgiving, fasting, and prayer were advocated as the three religious acts effecting forgiveness of sin (2 *Clem.* 16.4). Clement of Alexandria and Cyprian of Carthage cast wealth in religiously positive terms, for it enabled almsgiving. After its legalization, the Christian church was able to establish an array of organized responses to poverty—food distribution, hospitals, hospices, orphanages, and leper colonies—operating under the direction of the episcopacy, monastic communities, or even local churches. Bishops took over the traditional role of the civic patron, now recast with the explicit responsibility of care for the poor. Basil of Caesarea, John Chrysostom, Ambrose of Milan, Rabbula of Edessa, and John the Almsgiver were renowned figures in this development. Augustine proclaimed that all excess wealth belonged to the poor (*Enarr. in Ps.* 147.12).

Following Matthew 25:40, Christian writers added a Christological foundation to the understanding of almsgiving as redemptive: "Christ lies bleeding in the marketplace, fainting from hunger" was a homiletic commonplace. The distinction between voluntary and involuntary poverty was keenly understood. A frequent theme in hagiography was the poor saint who, receiving alms, gave them to the destitute.

Following Sirach 3:30, it was believed that the regular giving of alms was an effective "daily remedy" for the small sins of everyday life, and that such alms would also benefit the souls of the departed: in other words, like cured like—small sums of money, the almost unconscious "surplus" of daily life, redeemed the category of sins that were, themselves, the almost unconscious result of "surplus" energy and excessive involvement in "the world" (Augustine, *Enchiridion* 18.69).

The giving of alms (*zakāt* in Arabic, from a root meaning "to be pure in heart, to be righteous") is mentioned thirty-two times in the Qur'ān as an obligation for the faithful. It is almost always connected with the obligation to pray and is seen in part as an act of charity and in part as a form of purification. The gathering and distribution of alms were functions of the central mosque of each city, at least during the first century and a half of Islam.

BIBL.: Peter Brown, "Poverty and Power," in *Power and Persuasion in Late Antiquity: Towards a Christian Empire* (Madison, 1992), 71–117. Gildas Hamel, *Poverty and Charity in Roman Palestine, First Three Centuries C.E.* (Berkeley, 1990). R. Hermes, "Die stadtrömischen Diakonien," *Römische Quartalschrift* 91 (1996): 1–120. Evelyne Patlagean, *Pauvreté économique et pauvreté sociale à Byzance 4e–7e siècles* (Mouton, 1977). B. Ramsey, "Almsgiving in the Latin Church: The Late Fourth and Early Fifth Centuries," *Theological Studies* 43 (1982): 226–259. T. Sternberg, *Orientalium more secutus* (Münster, 1991). S.A.H.

Alphabets

The development of new alphabetic scripts in late antiquity was a phenomenon primarily of the eastern lands of the Roman empire and the contiguous Sassanian territory. It reflects the enormous economic and strategic importance of Egypt, Syria, and Anatolia, and the presence of settled, indigenous civilizations there. Writing systems were already in use in most of these places, but proficiency in them had been limited to priestly and scribal classes. Alphabets are easier to learn than Egyptian hieroglyphics and Mesopotamian cuneiform, for example, and they developed in this period thanks to the unprecedented proliferation of evangelistic religions with universalist claims, by far the most important of which was Christianity. The replacement of the unwieldy scroll with the more durable and compact codex happened at the same time. It seems to be an advance in technology that caught on because it served the same needs as the alphabet: popularization and diffusion of the written word.

Origen (*C.Cels.* 2.30) suggests it was by divine providence that Jesus was born at the same time that Augustus had consolidated a single vast empire, for had there been many kingdoms, it would have hindered the spread of his word. But there remained many languages, and the Gospel had to be translated if it was to reach all peoples. Egypt was the granary of the empire, and an alphabet was developed there for Coptic, a late form of the Egyptian language written with Greek letters, to which seven symbols from cursive Demotic were added for sounds not represented in Greek; the earliest datable documents in Coptic come from the 5th century C.E. Greek had been used extensively in Egypt since Alexander's conquest in the 4th century B.C.E., and Greek documents reproduce Egyptian personal and month names. It is not surprising that Coptic should possess many Greek loanwords; but the vocabulary is also heavily Christian, so dissemination of the Gospel to the native population in a medium easily learned was the main impetus for the development of Coptic literature. Egyptian hieroglyphics, knowledge of which had always been restricted to pagan priests and scribes, fell out of use as Christianity permeated

Egypt in a way Hellenism had never sought to. The Neoplatonists' mistaken belief that the hieroglyphics represented wholly abstract concepts is an indication of the great distance separating Egyptians from Greeks before Christianity.

Antioch in Syria was the de facto capital of the Roman empire through much of the 4th century: the region was of critical military importance and heavily urbanized, a center of both pagan learning and Christian piety, and it was the western terminus of the Silk Road. Greek settlement there, too, goes back to the first Seleucids, but no systematic effort was ever made to Hellenize the indigenous population. Stone inscriptions in the local dialect of Aramaic-Syriac in Estrangela script are datable to 73 C.E.; the earliest inscriptions not on stone, to 243 (a parchment found at Dura-Europus). Again, it was Christianity that brought Syriac, with its beginnings at Edessa, to prominence and wide diffusion as the principal written form used by the Persian church across the border. The Christians of Soghd, in Central Asia, translated Christian literature into their eastern Iranian language, employing Syriac script; in the Islamic period, Syrians who had lost their native command of Syriac but retained their Christian faith wrote Arabic in Syriac letters (Karshuni): the alphabet had become a marker of religious identity. In Ottoman Turkey, Armenians were permitted to print books in Armeno-Turkish (Turkish in Armenian letters); the printing of books in Turkish in Arabic script was forbidden because Arabic letters were sacred and had to be written only reverently, by hand. Armenian writing and the status of the Armenian *millet* (nationality, or religious group) were coterminous. Similarly, the square-character Aramaic in which Hebrew was written in the late antique period came to be a marker of all Jewish writing, whether Judeo-Persian as far east as Khotan, or Judeo-Spanish on the shores of the Atlantic.

Pre-Christian Armenia had employed both Aramaic and Greek for limited inscriptional purposes, but it seems that Armenia itself possessed only an oral literature. After the conversion of the Armenian royal family early in the 4th century to Christianity, Syriac and Greek books were used for nearly a century, until St. Mesrob Maštocʻ created an alphabetic script, based primarily on Aramaic and Greek, for the translation of the Bible and a range of classical and Syriac texts into Armenian. He seems also to have borrowed one character, *č*, from Coptic, and the final letter, representing aspirate *k*, is the Chi-Rho, the Chrismon: Christ's assertion that he is the omega as well as the alpha becomes the literal truth of Armenian script. The letters of Armenian are separated, too, unlike Syriac (or later Arabic); the vowels are represented by seven distinct characters; and the verticals are thick, as with Latin and Greek uncials. Thus the alphabet has a western, Christian orientation, just as the vast translation project undertaken by the school of Maštocʻ anchored

Armenian culture forever after in Christendom and the Mediterranean world, not the Iranian. Maštocʻ was a charismatic visionary who accomplished his task at a time when Armenia stood in danger of losing both its national identity, through partition, and its newly acquired Christian faith, through Sassanian pressure and reversion to paganism. By preaching in Armenian, he was able to undermine and co-opt the discourse founded in native tradition, and to create a counterweight against both Byzantine and Syriac cultural hegemony in the church. Maštocʻ also created the Georgian and Caucasian-Albanian alphabets, based on the Armenian model. Elsewhere in Anatolia, Greek simply replaced the local languages—only a few words from Zoroastrian Cappadocian survive, transcribed into Greek in Greek texts. In the north Caucasus, Alan Christians have left a grave memorial in Ossetic in Greek characters. The character and activities of Maštocʻ are typical of grammatogenists and may be compared with the career of the Hmong visionary of the early 1970s, Shong Lue Yang, who created during the Vietnam War a complex, ingenious script some Khmer also adopted, that helped his people to cohere in difficult times and was connected to millenarian religious teaching.

In Ethiopia, the South Arabian alphabet was adapted to a script employed for royal inscriptions and Christian evangelization in the late 4th century: like Armenian, it survives, little changed, to this day, and Ethiopian Christian literature bears many striking similarities to Armenian, perhaps because both countries possessed strong indigenous cultures that have asserted their distinct identity as Christian in their Muslim surroundings.

In the Sassanian empire, the 3rd century prophet Mani and his followers adapted a form of the Aramaic alphabet to Middle Persian and other Iranian languages in which Mani's dualist, Gnostic gospel was preached: Sogdian Manichaeans employed this script for their literature, while their Christian compatriots used Estrangela. The Zoroastrians themselves, probably in response to Manichaean and Christian evangelism through literature, created in the 5th century a clear, precise alphabet for the written edition of the *Avesta,* instead of using the awkward, rebarbative Pahlavi script. The latter had evolved naturally as a kind of shorthand from the cursive Aramaic of the scribes of the Achaemenid court: as many as five different letters might be represented by the same stroke, and Pahlavi was rich, besides, in heterograms. For example, the word *šāh*, "king," was written as *MLKʾ*—Aramaic *malkā*. A scribe would write in Aramaic what his master dictated in Persian, and the scribe who received and read out the document in another satrapy to his own master—a Bactrian or Sogdian speaker—would pronounce *MLKʾ* as *khwatāw* or the like. Other Iranian lands preserved local developments of this *Reichsaramäisch* (imperial Aramaic): Sogdian Buddhists and Zoroastrians continued to employ a cursive form of it. (Sogdian script, without the heterograms, was borrowed and modified by Uighur, then Mongolian—where it survives to this day.) After the conquest of Iran by the Muslims in the 7th century, Zoroastrians used Pahlavi script for books in Middle Persian, and the Avestan alphabet for the *Avesta* and for the transcription of Persian (Pāzand). But however much sense the allographic character of Pahlavi or Sogdian might have made at one time, by the 10th century it was impossibly difficult and senselessly archaic, and it stood no chance against Arabic.

Writing is not needed to preserve literature, but it can introduce a new discourse that drowns an older one; it can transmit large amounts of information rapidly over great distances; and the written word itself becomes a concrete relic, a facet of a religion's iconography. Arabic, the alphabet whose perfection and diffusion mark the end of late antiquity as surely as does the rise of Islam itself, exemplifies these characteristics. Based on Nabataean, it became both the means to teach a new religion to the Arabs and to define them as a people, and the vehicle of a universalist, aggressively evangelist faith that absorbed and transformed the entire earlier culture of the Middle East. As Coptic had been written in Greek, with the addition of a few letters and many Christian terms, so Persian, Turkish, and Hindustani were to be written in modified Arabic script, their vocabulary irrevocably Islamized; and so the Qur'ān itself would become the primary icon of Islam.

BIBL.: Peter T. Daniels and William Bright, eds., *The World's Writing Systems* (New York, 1996). B. Gruendler, *The Development of the Arabic Scripts,* Harvard Semitic Studies 43 (Atlanta, 1993). A. Harvey, "Early Literacy in Ireland: The Evidence from Ogam," *Cambridge Medieval Celtic Studies* 14 (1987): 1–15. James R. Russell, "On the Origins and Invention of the Armenian Script," *Le muséon* 107.3–4 (1994): 317–333. E. Motke, *Runes and Their Origin: Denmark and Elsewhere* (Copenhagen, 1985). R. I. Page, *Runes* (London, 1987).　　　　　　　　J.R.R.

Altars

In pagan cults, altars were used as the place to perform sacrifices. They took a wide variety of forms. For the public sacrifice of animals, monumental altars, often richly adorned, were built in front of temples; for first-fruit offerings in the fields, rustic altars were set up, sometimes simply made of turf; for domestic sacrifices, small, often portable altars were used in private houses. Improvised altars and permanent ones dotted the landscape and allowed all kinds of sacrifices to be performed. Some altars had special designs to let the blood of animals flow, while others could contain hot coals for burning incense or wine in offering. Under Christianity, because of their association with sacrifices, pagan altars were desacralized and sometimes destroyed, in conformity with the imperial legislation against pagan cults. In 357 under Constantius, and again in 384 under Gratian, the altar of Victory, where senators used to offer incense and libations, was removed from the Curia in Rome. In 407–408, a new law ordered the destruction of pagan altars in all places. Landowners were compelled to destroy all pagan altars standing on their property. The stones from some of these altars were eventually reused in new buildings.

In Judaism, altars were used for sacrifices in the Temple of Jerusalem, until its destruction by the Romans in 70 C.E., but they were not part of the synagogue furnishing. The altars of the Jerusalem Temple remained an object of commentary and an inspiration for iconography in late antique Judaism, along with the rest of the religious objects that once stood in the Temple.

In the New Testament, Jesus shared an important meal with his disciples before his crucifixion, asking them to continue the custom in remembrance of him. This common meal of the disciples evolved into the celebration of the Eucharist, in which bread and wine were consecrated on an altar by members of the clergy. The history of the emergence of early Christian altars is extremely difficult to follow, because they were not essentially different from other tables placed in churches. At first made of wood and portable, Christian altars evolved into fixed marble or stone tables during late antiquity. Wooden altars nevertheless remained in some churches until the Middle Ages, and missionary priests used portable altars to offer the Eucharist wherever they went. Late antique Christian altars were of different sizes and forms, and they sometimes bore inscriptions or Christian designs.

The location of the main altar in Christian churches differed according to regional traditions. Always highly visible, the altar formed the center of the sanctuary to which only the clergy had full access, and it was approached with gestures of respect. Its importance was underscored by its central position and by such architectural ornaments as ciboria and chancel barriers. The use of light and incense also enhanced the solemnity of the altar area. In Rome and Constantinople, churches benefiting from imperial funding had altars covered with silver, gold, and precious stones.

Christian altars were sacralized by the Eucharist and by the deposition of relics. In 386 Ambrose, the bishop of Milan, had the relics of the martyrs Gervasius and Protasius placed at the right of the altar in his newly dedicated cathedral. Thereafter it became customary to consecrate a new church by placing relics under or close to the altar. They were sometimes incorporated in the table or in the foot of the altar, sometimes placed in cavities or crypts built under the altar. Specific rituals of consecration were created for new altars. These might include aspersion of the table with blessed or exorcistic water, unction of the four corners of the table with fragrant oil, and the burning of a cross of incense on the altar, as well as the deposition of relics and various prayers of blessing. Altars were veiled with a cloth, often made of linen. In the Hagia Sophia church in Constantinople, the precious altar donated by the emperor Justinian was covered with a cloth embroidered with purple and gold threads. In the west, the evolution of eucharistic practices, along with the celebration of masses for the soul of the departed and the multiplication of relics, led to an increase in the number of consecrated altars inside churches. In 596, Pope Gregory the Great sent relics of Roman saints to Leuparicus, the Gallic bishop of Saintes, builder of a church containing thirteen altars, of which four awaited relics for their consecration. The 9th century plan of the church of St. Gall envisioned seventeen altars to allow the simultaneous celebration of masses offered for its numerous donors and the deceased.

East and west evolved differently in this matter. In Byzantine Christian churches, tables were set up beside the main altar for the receiving or preparing of offerings, but they were not consecrated as altars. One altar per church remained the rule. In some Byzantine churches, chancel barriers evolved into screens that hid from the faithful the sacred mysteries. These screens were later covered with icons and became iconostases. Christian commentaries on the liturgy often equated the altar with Christ's tomb or with Golgotha, others with the table of the last supper. Some compared it to the throne of God. In all Christian traditions, with the exception of a few sects, the altar was the center of liturgical life and the most sacred area in the church.

BIBL.: J. Braun, *Der christliche Altar in seiner geschichtlichen Entwicklung* (Munich, 1924). R. Etienne and M. T. Le Dinahet, eds., *L'espace sacrificiel dans les civilisations méditerranéennes de l'antiquité* (Paris, 1991). B.C.

Amber

The word *amber* denotes two distinct materials, gray amber, or ambergris, and yellow amber. The term, originally used for the former item, was gradually extended to the latter.

Ambergris is a waxy substance produced in the intestines of sperm whales. When directly obtained from a dead whale it is soft, black, and foul smelling. But when it has weathered—as when it has floated ashore—ambergris becomes a grayish-white solid with a musky fragrance. Ambergris was renowned in late antiquity as a fixative for perfumes, as an incense that burned brightly, and as a spice. Therapeutic qualities were also attributed to it. Its European name combined the Arabic *'anbar*, Pahlavi *ambar* (which entered Latin as *ambra*) and *gris* (from Indo-European *gher-* "gray"). An Arab tribe, the Banu 'l-'Anbar, is believed to have been named after this substance. Muslim tradition associated ambergris with the Meccan traders of pre-Islamic and early Islamic Arabia. It was also said

to have been sent as tribute by Iranian governors in Yemen to the Sassanian royal court in Iran during the late 6th and early 7th centuries C.E. Later Muslim scholars, such as al-Qazwini, grouped ambergris with naphtha, tar, and sulfur. They commented about its marine origin, particularly in the Indian Ocean, and speculated on its medicinal properties, which supposedly included invigoration of the heart, brain, and senses.

Yellow amber is a hard, translucent, yellow, orange, or brown fossil resin from evergreen trees. Known to the Iranians by the Pahlavi compound word *kah-ruba* (from *kah* "straw" plus *rubay* "attract, snatch," referring to its electrical properties), which entered Arabic as *kahraba'* or *kahraba*, it too was called amber in Europe (Old French and Middle English *ambre*). Found along the southern shore of the Baltic Sea, yellow amber reached the Middle East and western Europe via trade. Its coastal acquisition may have been one reason yellow amber came to be designated by the same term as ambergris. Moreover, like ambergris, the resin could be burned as an incense. The resin's most popular use was, however, for ornamentation—easily cut and polished, it could be transformed into beautiful jewelry.

BIBL.: J. Kolendo, "Napływ bursztynu z Polnocy na tereny imperium rzymskiego w I–VI w n.e.," *Prace Muzeum Ziemi* 41 (1990): 91–100. Z. Krumphanzlova, "Amber: Its Significance in the Early Middle Ages," *Pamatky Archeologicke* 83 (1992): 350–371. P. Petrequin et al., "L'importation d'ambre balte: Un échantillonnage chronologique de l'est de la France," *Revue archéologique de l'est et du centre-est* 38 (1987): 273–284. J.K.C.

Ambrose

As a provincial governor and the son of a praetorian prefect, Ambrose unexpectedly became bishop of Milan when he intervened in a riotous episcopal election and was promptly acclaimed bishop by the crowd. Still a catechumen at the time of his election, Ambrose quickly passed through the various ranks of the clergy, being consecrated bishop only a week after his baptism. The circumstances surrounding Ambrose's acclamation as bishop are deeply puzzling, and the significance of this episode is disputed, but the new bishop's initiatives during the next few years—which included the sponsorship of female asceticism, the initiation of a lavish building program, and a well-publicized commitment to scholarship (all familiar expressions of 4th century aristocratic piety)—suggest attempts by a controversial figure to mobilize a consensus.

The conflict that propelled Ambrose to office pitted Nicenes against the Arian supporters of the previous bishop, Auxentius, and during the subsequent decade Ambrose emerged as the leading western spokesman for the Nicene position. At the council of Aquileia (381) he engineered the deposition of two senior Arian bishops, one of whom produced a blistering protest that has fortuitously been preserved in the margins of a manuscript. Opinions on the quality of Ambrose's arguments, as opposed to the undeniable efficiency of his management of the proceedings, vary widely; nor is it clear how closely fought was Ambrose's eventual victory. An important aspect of the controversy was that Ambrose won the favorable attention of the emperor Gratian, who made Milan his base (381–383): the first of six resident *Augusti* with whom Ambrose had important and often tense dealings.

Popular support served Ambrose well in the confrontations with imperial authority that mark the most dramatic highlights of his career: his refusal to yield a basilica to Valentinian II for an Arian service (385–386), his insistence that Theodosius I leave unpunished the Christian zealots who had attacked the synagogue at Callinicum (388), and his demand that Theodosius do penance after a massacre of civilians at Thessalonica (390). Ambrose prevailed by his skillful exploitation of the uncertainties of rulers temporarily resident in a part-time capital; his success consisted essentially in negotiating favorable terms for a partnership between court and church. Another aspect of the same process is represented by his memorial speeches for Valentinian (392) and Theodosius (395). Ambrose used this alliance to obstruct the reinstatement of the altar of Victory after it had been removed by Gratian (382).

One of Ambrose's most important constituencies comprised imperial officials and courtiers, who appreciated his allusive sermons and shared a similar social background and outlook. The most notable example of this type is Augustine, who abandoned his political ambitions to receive baptism from Ambrose (387). Another key element in Ambrose's power base was the solid support of his clergy, in whom he instilled a firm discipline and whose loyalty was rewarded, in several cases, by promotions to Italian bishoprics.

Ambrose continued the work of Hilary of Poitiers, promoting the Nicene formulation in the west. His Christology is dependent on the Greek Fathers. Unlike many Latin churchmen, Ambrose read Greek well. His familiarity with Philo, Origen, Athanasius, and Basil helped to further integrate these eastern theologians into western Christianity. But his attention was primarily devoted to practical pastoral issues rather than theology. In addition to a large number of exegetical works, Ambrose composed treatises on the duties of the clergy, on baptism and the Eucharist, and on living a life of virginity.

Ambrose had grown up in the home of his widowed mother and his sister Marcellina, a dedicated virgin. As bishop he became an advocate for the movement of aristocratic Roman women that was dedicated to celibacy. In support of their cause he preached the perpetual virginity of Mary, a relatively new teaching, not undisputed in Italy at the end of the 4th century. He divided Christians into groups of varying merit based on their degree of sexual purity: the chastely married, continent widows, and dedicated virgins. Ambrose urged male clergy to adopt the virtue of celibacy practiced by the women in their congregations.

Ambrose harnessed other sources of sanctity. In the midst of tensions between the bishop and the emperor Valentinian II, Ambrose presided over the discovery *(inventio)* of the martyrs Gervasius and Protasius. Their relics offered the court an invitation to reconciliation and also consecrated the basilica that was reserved for Ambrose's own burial. The *inventio* of another martyr, Nazarius, almost a decade later reaffirmed the alliance between the church and the court of Stilicho. Ambrose appropriated relics from a more distant provenance when he delivered his memorial oration for Theodosius. He is the first western source to connect the *inventio* of the True Cross with Constantine's mother, Helena. Ambrose gives political significance to the legend that Helena sent the nails from the True Cross to Constantine to be put in his helmet and bridle. The nails given to the emperor announced a new hereditary Christian rule. Ambrose claimed that their promise applied not only to Constantine's family, but also to Theodosius's young sons Honorius and Arcadius.

The two most enduring images of Ambrose were created in Africa, after his death (397), by representatives of his palatine and clerical constituencies. Having eulogized him in the *Confessions*, Augustine subsequently used Ambrose's works as the foundation of the imposing "catholic faith" that he deployed against Pelagius; he also commissioned a biography from Ambrose's former secretary, the Milanese deacon Paulinus. The continuing influence of Paulinus's presentation of Ambrose as an indomitably resolute "tower of David" puts it among the most successful hagiographical projects of late antiquity.

Ambrose is remembered as one of the four doctors of the western church (with Augustine, Jerome, and Gregory the Great). The antiphonal singing of psalms by the congregation, which Ambrose used to secure basilicas against imperial troops, became a lasting part of western liturgy, as did the singing of metrical hymns, which he developed. Ambrose's legacy was not limited to the west. Paulinus's *Vita* was translated into Greek, an anonymous Greek life was compiled, and Greek hymns were dedicated to his feast day (7 December).

BIBL.: G. Madec, *Saint Ambroise et la philosophie* (Paris, 1974). Neil B. McLynn, *Ambrose of Milan: Church and Court in a Christian Capital* (Berkeley, 1994). Christoff Markschies, *Ambrosius von Mailand und die Trinitätstheologie: Kirchen- und theologiegeschichtliche Studien zu Antiarianismus und Neunizänismus bei Ambrosius und im lateinischen Westen (364–381 n. Chr.)* (Tübingen, 1995). Daniel H. Williams, *Ambrose of Milan and the End of the Arian-Nicene Conflicts* (Oxford, 1995). H. Savon, *Ambroise de Milan* (Paris, 1997). N.M.

Ammianus Marcellinus

The historian Ammianus Marcellinus (ca. 330–395) wrote the first major history in Latin after Tacitus. His *Res gestae* recorded events from Nerva to Valens (96–378) in thirty-one books, of which books fourteen to thirty-one survive (covering the years 354–378). Because of his reliability, powers of observation, vividness of expression, and range of interests, Ammianus remains the central source for the political, diplomatic, and administrative history of his age. He includes much material about the social life of the period, and his comments on religious issues, though few, are incisive. Had he written in classical Latin, he might well be judged the greatest of Roman historians.

He is a complex and elusive figure, known only from his *History* and (perhaps) Libanius's letter 1063. His major motivations appear to have been the desires to write a personal memoir and to record, and in some sense to justify, the career of Emperor Julian. He wrote as a "former soldier and a Greek" ("*ut miles quondam et Graecus,*" 31.16.9), yet he chose to compose his *History* in Latin. Apparently from Antiochene origins, he served as an officer in Gaul and on the Persian frontier in the 350s, was in the Persian campaign of 363, and traveled widely in the Mediterranean after leaving the army. In the mid-380s, he appears to have settled in Rome, where he completed the research for and composition of his work around 390.

BIBL.: John Matthews, *The Roman Empire of Ammianus* (Baltimore, 1989). T. D. Barnes, *Ammianus Marcellinus and the Representation of Historical Reality* (Ithaca, 1998). S.B.

Amphitheater

An elliptical building designed for public entertainments, to showcase gladiators and exotic wild animals, the Roman amphitheater appeared all throughout the empire, especially in the Latin west, where most cities boasted at least one. In the Greek east, where some theaters and stadia were temporarily converted for such shows, inscriptions indicate that gladiatorial games had also become widespread by the 2nd century C.E. Amphitheatrical shows consisted of gladiatorial and animal combats (*munera* and *venationes*) as well as public executions of criminals or captured enemies; the latter were at times staged as mythological scenes. *Munera,* which were originally duels to the death between armed slaves, staged by private individuals to placate the shades of the familial dead, became a form of mass entertainment through which aristocratic and imperial games givers (*munerarii, editores*) displayed their munificence and gained popular support. Gladiators were commonly slaves or criminals who had sworn an oath, or *sacramentum,* to fight in the arena, although at times free men, including members of the elite, also fought in this fashion. The drilling of gladiators took place under trainers, or *lanistae,* in special schools, or *ludi.* Ranging from the rank beginner, or *gregarius,* to the seasoned professional who could command a price ten times that of a novice, the gladiator was a popular symbol of Roman martial *virtus.* While mortality was certainly high, valiant and successful gladiators could hope to receive their freedom; some even commemorated this fact on their funerary stelae. Despite their professional standing and popularity, gladiators suffered from the social stigma and lifelong *infamia* that attached also to charioteers, animal fighters, and stage performers. Elite pagan moralists such as Seneca criticized the games for their capacity to excite the emotions of the audience, which was seated in the amphitheater according to the gradations of Roman social hierarchy. Christian writers such as Clement of Alexandria, Tertullian, Minucius Felix, and Lactantius, adapting Stoic arguments, also condemned the *crudelitas amphitheatri,* the games' ability to turn spectators into savage, bloodthirsty individuals. Indeed, Augustine famously narrated such a transformation in relation to Alypius's reaction to gladiatorial fighting in Rome. Such games, which for fiscal reasons had been previously banned (temporarily) and regulated in some places—as a Gallic inscription of 177 C.E. shows, they were categorically outlawed for the first time by Constantine in 325 (*C.Th.* 15.12.1), though in fact they continued. The uncle of Libanius put on *munera* in Antioch a few years later, and various imperial laws attest to the survival of the games through the 4th century. *Munera* (and *venationes*) remained an important part of the mandatory games put on by incoming Roman magistrates and the celebrations of imperial victories, anniversaries, and *adventūs.* Along with imperial and civic fiscal crises, shortages of personnel threatened the games after the emperors ruled in 365 that no Christian criminal could be condemned *ad arenam* and ecclesiastical leaders began to refuse baptism to those gladiators who continued in their trade. Since the emperors had already issued a law in 357 forbidding soldiers and palatine officials from hiring themselves out to *munerarii,* it appears that a shrinking supply of gladiators (and the concomitant rise in the price of a *munus*) might have been a factor in the games' slow decline. There were also strong ideologically driven pressures coming from certain Christians to end the blood sport. Prudentius urged that *venationes* be retained while *munera,* which he regarded as pagan human sacrifice, be ended. Theodoret of Cyrrhus attributed the end of the games to the intervention of the monk Telemachus at the Flavian Amphitheater when *munera* were being staged: his death at the hands of an angry crowd subsequently caused Honorius to forbid gladiatorial shows—a vivid but surely apocryphal tale. While evidence for gladiatorial games disappears after the first quarter of the 5th century, animal hunts continued for much longer as a popular offering in the amphitheater and as an integral part of consular inaugurations and other state

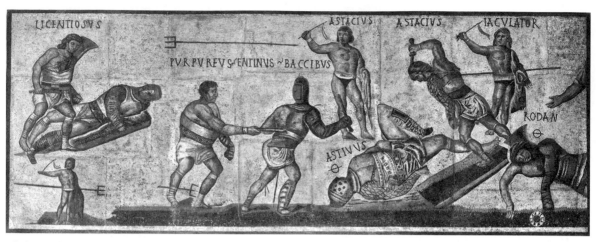

Gladiatorial combat depicted on a 4th century mosaic from Torra Nuova. Villa Borghese, Rome.

celebrations. Animal fighters also became heroic figures, the embodiment of martial valor and success that gladiators used to represent.

BIBL.: K. Coleman, "Fatal Charades: Roman Executions Staged as Mythological Enactments," *Journal of Roman Studies* 80 (1990): 44–73. J. P. Kirsch, "Das Ende der Gladiatorenspiele in Rom," *Römische Ouartalschrift für christliche Altertumskunde und für Kirchengeschichte* 26 (1912): 207–211. P. Leveau and J. C. Golvin, "L'amphithéâtre et le théâtre de Cherchel," *Mélanges de l'école française de Rome: Antiquité* 91 (1979): 817–843. G. Villes, "Les jeux de gladiateurs dans l'empire chrétien," *Mélanges de l'école française de Rome: Antiquité* 72 (1960): 273–335.   R.L.

Amphorae (East)

The east, a region that saw intensive agricultural cultivation, seems to have made use of a more limited spectrum of imported amphorae than other regions of the Roman empire. Most of the excavations in the region of the eastern empire have yielded many more or less local amphorae and only single foreign pieces.

The most common eastern types are the cylindrical, dull-brown "Gaza amphorae" (Peacock-Williams Class 49), transport vessels for the famous Gaza wine (ca. 425 C.E. to the [late?] 7th century); the long vessels with ribbed bodies (Peacock-Williams Class 44/British B ii), also used for transporting wine as well as dried fruits, that originated probably in Cilicia near Adana; and the bag-shaped amphorae with shallow grooving on the body (Carthage Late Roman 6) from northern Palestine (Beisan?), dating from the 5th to the 7th century and continuing well into early Islamic times. There is also a very similar Palestinian type (Peacock-Williams Class 46/Carthage Late Roman 5) made from sandy, buff to mostly reddish clay, often with black slip and white painting on the close-ribbed body. From the early 8th century, these appear with white clay and red painting, and with simplified rims. It seems that they were used as water jars.

Typical for northern Syria are cylindrical amphorae with curved walls and brown painting on the shoulders. They started appearing in the 4th century and were still common in the Umayyad period. Additionally, there are many other local types of amphorae that were used for oil or water storage.

BIBL.: John W. Hayes, "The Pottery," *Excavations at Saraçhane in Istanbul II* (Princeton, 1992), 61–79. D. P. S. Peacock and D. F. Williams, *Amphorae and the Roman Economy: An Introductory Guide* (London and New York, 1986). John A. Riley, "The Coarse Pottery from Berenice," in John A. Lloyd, ed., *Excavations at Sidi Khrebish, Benghazi (Berenice II): Supplements to Libya Antiqua V 2* (Tripoli, 1979).
M.K.

Amphorae (West)

Amphorae, primarily used to transport wine, oil, and preserved fish, were one of the major commercial products of late antiquity in the Mediterranean basin. Other ceramics, especially fine ceramics, such as those known as African red slip, then became secondary accessories in that commerce. Western centers of amphora production were located in Africa Proconsularis/Byzacena, in Mauretania Caesariensis, in Tripolitania and in Hispania, particularly in the Levant of Tarraconensis, the south of Lusitania, and Baetica.

Oriental amphorae from the second half of the 4th century are distributed in relative abundance, from the eastern Mediterranean coast and the Aegean to the north of Africa and the western Mediterranean. But amphorae produced in northern Africa at the end of the fourth and beginning of the fifth centuries are also widely distributed. Archaeological contexts in the western Mediterranean show very high quantities of these African amphorae. In Italian sites, in Ostia and

Rome, for example, they represent as many as 50 percent of the containers found; in the case of Tarraconensis, they account for 70 to 80 percent. The distribution of African amphorae toward the eastern zone of the empire was also important, although they are detected to a much lesser degree there than are African fine ceramics.

Amphoric products of the 5th century are characterized by a change in form, becoming larger. The distribution of African amphorae is still confirmed in the stratigraphy of some sites on the Italian peninsula, such as Rome and Naples, as well as on islands of the western Mediterranean—for example, Sardinia—although they appear much less frequently than those from previous periods, representing nearly 40 percent of documented containers. This reduction in the distribution of African amphorae is probably due to the arrival in western ports of wine-carrying amphorae produced in Asia Minor, the islands of the Aegean, and the southeastern Mediterranean. At the same time, amphorae filled with wine from Calabria and Sicily, notably those made in Naxos (identified as amphorae of type Keay LII), were reaching many points in the coastal zones of the western Mediterranean, especially Italy, Sicily, Sardinia, Gallia, and Hispania. Amphorae characteristic of late antiquity, originating in the Aegean and the mid-eastern zone also reached these coastal zones. Even if there were some variants in terms of wine transport, it can be observed that significant exportation of grain, oil, and *garum* (fish sauce) from Africa to Italy and Constantinople continued throughout the 5th century, although other products were obtained from the Orient in exchange.

Starting at the end of the 5th century and throughout the first half of the 6th, in some Italic sites, such as Naples and Rome, the number of imported African amphorae appears to have been cut in half; even cylindrical amphorae appear in smaller quantities, and they

are not replaced by the spindle-shaped amphorae, called *spatia*, that were renowned as oil containers and were produced up to the 7th century in Tunis. However, African amphorae do continue to be exported throughout the 6th century, as the findings on the islands of Corsica and Sardinia attest. In the coastal zone of Tarraconensis, it seems that numbers of imported African amphorae were reduced in the first half of the 6th century. It is quite possible that this reduction in the distribution of African amphorae was brought about by an increased presence of Oriental containers.

BIBL.: S. J. Keay, *Late Roman Amphorae in the Western Mediterranean: A Typology and Economic Study: The Catalan Evidence* (Oxford, 1984). Clementina Panella, "Merci e scambi nel Mediterranneo tardoantico," in *Storia di Roma*, vol. 3, *L'età tardoantica, 2: I luoghi e le culture* (Turin, 1993), 613–697. D. P. S. Peacock and D. F. Williams, *Amphorae and the Roman Economy: An Introductory Guide* (London and New York, 1986). Paul Reynolds, *Trade in the Western Mediterranean, A.D. 400–700: The Ceramic Evidence* (Oxford, 1995). G.R.

Amrah

Quṣayr 'Amrah, a small bathhouse located 50 miles east of Amman, well-preserved and restored, is datable to the first half of the 8th century. There are traces nearby of a hydraulic system and of what may have been a residence, although the absence of significant quantities of shards casts some doubt about the building as connected with a permanent residence.

The design of the building (a tripartite hall with an apse, which is often called a throne room, and three small rooms, two of which are equipped with heating equipment) is typical of late antique city and village baths found all over the Levant.

The most remarkable feature of Quṣayr 'Amrah is

Wall painting of a dancer in the main hall of Quṣayr ʿAmra.

Amulets

Amulets—small, inscribed objects or containers meant to be worn close to the body with the expectation of their supernatural effect—are found throughout the Mediterranean world in excavated grave sites, houses, temples, and even the very workshops that produced them. By far the more common type of amulet historically, those made of organic material—wood, plant, or animal parts—survives mostly in the witness of ancient writers: Abbot Shenoute (5th century Egypt) reports the wearing of fox claws, snake heads, and crocodile teeth. As Shenoute here refers to the practices of Christians, it is certain that the practice of wearing amulets did not by any means diminish when cultures gave their allegiance to Christianity or Islam. Yet amulets did evolve under Christianization and Islamization to incorporate, on the one hand, the distinctive contagious charisma of living saints and, on the other hand, the supernatural potential of the written word (as had long been exploited in Egyptian and Jewish traditions).

A representative sample of late antique amulets from various provenances in Europe and the Mediterranean world (Kotansky, 1994) shows a wide variety of applications: medical and apotropaic (not strictly distinguished in amuletic spells), mortuary, judicial, and domestic (preserving the home from threats meteorological, human, and supernatural). The media out of which such powers were expected to work likewise extend from aniconic forms made from wood, bone, clay, or stone, to simple containers filled with particular substances deemed powerful because of their connection with sacred places or people, to elaborately decorated gems and the most meticulously inscribed papyri or metal leaves. Semi-iconic amuletic figures in Coptic culture, for example, often emphasize the eyes or female fecundity (breasts, vulva). Inscribed gems (large corpora of which have been published by Campbell Bonner, and Armand Delatte and Philippe Derchain) show a particular eclecticism of religious themes and symbols from around the Mediterranean world, mixing Egyptian tableaux, Hebrew invocations, Greek writing, and Babylonian names.

The relationship of the amulet to the contagious power of special places or people was crystallized in early Christianity in the phenomenon of the relic. The appeal of the relic as a link with the mediating powers of a saint certainly antedates Christianity, but the peculiar attention to sacred body parts and contiguous substances became characteristic of the Christian movement at an early stage. Saints' lives record the efficacy of "blessings": water, dust, oil, or, as in Syria, *hnana*, a mixture of oil and dust, taken from the environs of the living saint or his or her tomb. These were widely believed to protect homes from rats, travelers from danger, and infants from illness. The containers for these substances, produced in workshops near the shrines, subsequently acquired talismanic properties them-

that its walls are entirely covered with frescoes; these were copied in 1901 and restored between 1971 and 1974, but only partially published. Greek and Arabic inscriptions are found in this painted decoration, which is a unique example of late antique secular painting in situ, and its interpretation has inspired many arguments. Some have seen in it a coherent program representing the life and aspirations of an aristocratic court and including a prince enthroned, surrounded by musicians, dancers, clad and unclad women, hunting scenes, and narrative or symbolic events (the Six Kings, including Roderic of Spain, thus dating the work after 717, greeting their Umayyad successor; nude men and children walking toward a bathhouse; the construction of a building; possibly a representation and glorification of Sarah; signs of the zodiac and constellations taken from a hemisphere). Others, noting the many stylistic and qualitative variations in these paintings, have seen them as a more haphazard collection painted for an unknown Umayyad aristocrat.

BIBL.: K. A. C. Creswell, *Early Muslim Architecture* (Oxford, 1969). M. Gorbea et al., *Qusayr Amra* (Madrid, 1975). O. Grabar, "Umayyad Palaces Reconsidered," *Ars orientalis* 23 (1993).   O.G.

selves, as artisans began to include representations of the saints' lives on the vessels. Such representations linked an amulet's owner visually with the saint or a particular legend of the saint, much like Byzantine icons did. Ancient writers describe how saints actively used these portable representations (or simply the "blessing" substances alone) as supernatural pathways by which they could intervene for the amulets' owners.

The written word had its own supernatural aura in a world of sparse literacy, and the large number of amuletic texts from Egypt and early Judaism suggests that the ancient scribal institutions of these cultures had long included amulet preparation as one of their functions. A simple list of demons, illnesses, and dangers, prepared by a monk or priest, might protect a Coptic Christian in the same way that similar "misfortune lists" from native temples had protected Egyptians of an earlier time. Extending a tradition as archaic as the mezuzah and tefillin (specific biblical passages placed on home or body for sacred purposes, as per Deut. 6:8–9), Jewish rabbis drew on common supernatural associations with certain Psalms and other Scripture when composing amuletic texts. Muslim clerics worked from similar associations with Qur'ānic suras (and these traditions operate quite widely today). Christian literati likewise composed amulets from Christian Scripture (canonical and extracanonical), often imputing power to the merest Gospel incipit. John Chrysostom describes how, in 4th century Antioch, "Women and children suspend Gospels from their necks as a powerful amulet, and carry them about in all places wherever they go" (*Hom.* 19.14). Doubtless inspired by these traditions of "Scripture magic," other cultures of the Mediterranean world came to endow their own book traditions with supernatural efficacy: a fragmentary manual from 4th century Egypt instructs how to wear Homeric verses to gain favors (*PGM* 4.467–474, 820–824, 2145–2240). Out of these conceptions arose also the widespread practice of inscribing amulets with "divine"—incomprehensible—words or characters.

Manuals for the preparation of amulets give a fuller picture of the practices surrounding the use of amulets than would be apparent from the objects themselves. In addition to the precise words and figures to be inscribed, instructions often include the utterance of a spell and the consecration of a place or the amuletic substance, altogether rendering the mundane medium sacred and efficacious. In some cases the inscribed amulet is meant to function as a kind of perpetual recitation of the initial oral incantation or, alternately, as a seal or guarantee of some one-time ritual performance (as in the case of exorcisms). In the manuals, a spell usually includes "DD" where the client's name should be inserted on the actual amulet, and some amulet makers perfunctorily copied this generic "blank." Some amulets, especially gems and images already endowed with power, have an original client's name erased and a new name added. Inscribed metal sheets *(lamellae)* were the easiest to customize, but after a sheet had been inserted into its carrying tube, an amulet's original function and owner might be forgotten, the whole apparatus thus becoming an all-purpose charm.

That an amulet originally commissioned for a specific illness might be worn for an owner's entire life, and then even into the grave, shows both the devotion people felt toward these protective objects and also the increasingly generic sense in which any consecrated object could be viewed and deployed. The strongly local, even personal, context in which amulets were produced, chartered, and worn in the late antique world, a context in which expediency and immediate circumstances dominated ritual expression far more than orthodoxy, allowed their spells and their iconography to retain a degree of religious or symbolic synthesis (syncretism) that would be unusual for texts and images with more public or institutional contexts. The simple and miniature format of the amulet also allowed people to collect them and to construct, out of these condensed links to various geographical and historical points of supernatural power, their own domestic memorials or shrines.

BIBL.: Roy Kotansky, *Greek Magical Amulets,* vol. 1, Papyrologica Coloniensia 22 (Opladen, Ger., 1994). J. Naveh and S. Shaked, *Amulets and Magic Bowls* (Leiden, 1985). J. Russell, "The Archaeological Context of Magic in the Early Byzantine Period," in Byzantine Magic, ed. H. Maguire (Washington, D.C., 1995). G. Vikan, "Art, Medicine, and Magic in Early Byzantium," *Dumbarton Oaks Papers* 38 (1984): 65–86. K. Hauck, *Die Goldbrakteaten* (Munich, 1985).   D.T.F.

Anastasius I

Born in Dyrrachium, the silentiary Anastasius (ca. 430–518), noted for his character and culture, was made emperor in 491. Successor to the Isaurian Zeno, he married Zeno's widow, Ariadne. His twenty-eight-year reign, through its prudent foreign policy and its domestic reforms, prepared the way for the prosperity of the century of Justinian. He restored order to the army, essentially as part of a defensive strategy: domestically, the emperor put an end to the Isaurian uprising (491–498) and the revolts of Vitalianus in Thrace (513–515); externally, he secured a truce ending four years of war against Persia (502–506). Innovative legislation in the areas of civil and military administration, urban institutions, and the status of peasants helped put public finances on a more solid footing. Major reforms targeted taxes and currency: the creation of the *comes patrimonii;* the abolition of the *chrysargyron* (498), the tax on trades; new methods for collecting the *annona (coemptio);* and the reform of copper currency (498), which was thereafter based on a *follis* of forty *noummia.* The state, enjoying a rich treasury, financed an active public works policy (construction of the Long Wall of Thrace; the foundation of Dara). At the same time, the empire was weakened by the religious policy of Anastasius, who opposed the Council of Chalcedon. Because he was a devoted Monophysite, the emperor supported the patriarchate of Alexandria; in the east, he favored the advent of Severus to the patriarchate of Antioch (512). Exacerbating the break with the church of Rome, he entered into conflict with the church of Constantinople and forced two of its patriarchs into exile, Euphemius in 496, and Macedonius in 511.

BIBL.: C. Cappizzi, *L'imperatore Anastasio I (491–518)* (Rome, 1969). D.F.

Anchorites

Anchorites (from the Greek *anachorēsis*, withdrawal) were those who fled the world to seek a life of solitary prayer. The term gained a near mythic power in late antique spirituality, exemplified by Egypt's legendary desert saints alone in their caves, far from human habitation and utterly cut off from social interchange. The ideal linked absolute inaccessibility with absolute devotion to God: the more remote the saint, the greater his or her sanctity. In legend, for example, Mary of Egypt lived forty-eight years in the desert without encountering any living thing before the priest-monk Zosimus found her; Onuphrios lived so deep into the desert that he could only be found if divine aid sustained the traveler. The Syrian orient was renowned for the extreme methods of its anchorites, who sometimes lived in cages or other contraptions, on pillars, or naked in the wilderness. Holy fools were anchorites who sought withdrawal in the midst of city life, as a living admonishment (frequently echoed in homilies and letters) that withdrawal was an interior condition rather than an exterior situation. Basil of Caesarea argued that the cenobitic life was superior to that of the anchorites, for the latter could not fulfill the commandment to love one's neighbor, nor practice the necessary virtues of humility and obedience (*Long Rules*, 7). Dadisho (d. 690) identified six classes of "solitaries" (Syrian *ihidaye*) distinguished by the degree and duration of their withdrawal; the highest in perfection were those in utter seclusion, the true "anchorites" (Syrian *noucarite*; Greek *anachorētēs*).

BIBL.: Derwas J. Chitty, *The Desert a City: An Introduction to the Study of Egyptian and Palestinian Monasticism under the Christian Empire* (Oxford, 1966). James E. Goehring, "The Encroaching Desert: Literary Production and Ascetic Space in Early Christian Egypt," *Journal of Early Christian Studies* 1 (1993): 281–296. A. Monachi-Castagno, "Il vescovo, l'abbate e l'eremita: Tipologia della santità nella *Vita Patrum* di Gregorio di Tours," *Augustinianum* 24 (1984): 235–264. Ignace Peña, Pascal Castellana, and Romuald Fernandez, *Les reclus syriens: Recherches sur les anciennes formes de vie solitaire en Syrie* (Milan, 1980). S.A.H.

Angels

The notion that supernatural beings mediate between the divine and human realms in the capacity of "messengers" (*mlk*; Greek *angelos*) appears throughout the ancient Mediterranean world, but it is the biblical formulation of angels that underlies their complex development and definition in late antiquity.

The Dead Sea Scrolls, which offer a microcosm of sectarian Jewish angelology in the Graeco-Roman period, posit angels both as representatives of the divine presence and as models of participation in that presence. The imitation of the angels' liturgies is a theme that continues throughout late antiquity. The idealization of the Jerusalem Temple in the Graeco-Roman period also led to the concept of a heavenly temple and a cult staffed with angelic priests. In the Byzantine period, images of the heavenly throne room mirrored the emperor's court, with angels depicted as eunuchs in court apparel.

Another idea articulated in Jewish and Christian texts of the early Roman period that influenced late antique belief was the division of heaven into zones. These divisions, based on proximity to the divine throne, protected the heavenly realm from the impure (*Ascension of Isaiah, Apocalypse of Elijah*). Numerous texts and amulets show a popular idea in late antique angelology in which particular angelic names and "personalities" were invoked against particular demons and misfortunes (Tobit, *Testament of Solomon, 1 Enoch*). Such traditions continued with great resilience throughout Judaism and Christianity and are maintained even today in Ethiopian Christianity.

This complex series of angelological traditions, when coupled with the various indigenous Mediterranean and Near Eastern beliefs about divine mediators in the world (often designated *angeloi* in descriptions), led to the definition of a Christian angelic "pantheon" so well represented in Byzantine icons and texts. From the 4th century through the course of western and Byzantine Christianization, local sacred places often came to be redefined as sites of angelic visitation and service (when they were not rendered as saints' shrines or else castigated as demonic). Local legend and iconography of these angels' activities often preserve the traditions of earlier divinities.

Fourth century theologians, in reaction to Arian Christology, were concerned to distinguish between angels, Christ, and the Holy Spirit. Christ was the head of the angels, but angel Christology was rejected. Basil of Caesarea insisted that the Holy Spirit was not one of the "ministering spirits" created by God. Angels were created by God either before or concurrently with the creation of the material world. The bodies of angels were often thought to be made of a spiritual substance, less corporeal than those of humans. The primary function of angels was to praise God, but they possessed free will. Satan was the leader of fallen angels.

In the 6th century Pseudo-Dionysius the Areopagite developed Christian angelology in his *Celestial Hierarchy*. He organized angels into a hierarchy between humans and God, consisting of three triads. Those closest to God were the seraphim, cherubim, and thrones. The middle group included virtues, dominations, and powers. Principalities, archangels, and angels were the orders of angels most active in the human sphere. Gregory the Great and Maximus the Confessor developed these ideas, which proved influential in later medieval angelology.

In late antiquity asceticism came to be identified with the "angelic life." Ascetic commentary on the Gospel, (and Tatian's Diatessaron) interpreted Matthew 22:32 to mean that those who neither married nor were given in marriage in this life were like the angels.

Byzantine liturgy and liturgical art preserved the older Jewish apocalyptic understanding of angels as signs of divine presence and human-divine commingling. Even before the 3rd century development of the Sanctus or Trisagion portion of the liturgy (based on the mysterious vision in Isa. 6:1–5), Christian ritual had emphasized communion with angels as its apex. Byzantine liturgy put ever more emphasis on the belief in angelic participation, not only expanding the Trisagion but also including angelic iconography in processions and ecclesiastical decoration. Processional fans bear the esoteric figures of seraphim, while the later Byzantine development of the iconostasis was meant to represent the immediate proximity of heaven and its angelic liturgy within the liturgical space.

Of the three archangels recognized by the church, Michael, Gabriel, and Raphael, the first two are more frequently depicted. The cult of Michael, located primarily in Asia Minor, was more developed than that of any other archangel. He was also revered in Constantinople, with many churches dedicated to him dating from the 6th century.

In Islam, angels are the guardians of humans, cognizant of and recording the deeds of every person (Qur'ān 82:11). In the Qur'ān, God commands them to bow down before Adam (for example, 2:34), the significance of this being the primacy of humankind in God's creation. Angels are present in heaven near God and were created to praise him, but other tasks are mentioned as well. In several verses they figure prominently in the deaths of mortals, when they punish unbelievers (7:50) or cause them to die (47:27). The most visual description of them says that they are "messengers with wings two, three, and four" (35:1). There is no separate conception of archangels in Islam; however, Mīkāl (Michael) and Jibrīl (Gabriel) are two of the very few angels mentioned by name. The latter is the figure who appears to Muhammad and conveys to him the revelation from God. Iblīs (Satan) is an angel who refused to make obeisance to Adam and was subsequently cast out of heaven, but since he is also described as one of the jinn (18:50), a third category of intelligent beings, Muslim commentators have taken his mixed nature to be the cause of his imperfection and disobedience. The two remaining named angels present a unique case. These are the "Babylonian" angels Hārūt and Mārūt, who teach humans sorcery that could "cause a man and wife to separate" but do so with God's permission and warn their victims of their intentions beforehand (2:102). Georges Vajda has argued that their names may be linked to two Zoroastrian "archangels," Haurvatāt and Ameretāt.

The activities and characters of the Qur'ānic angels were considerably fleshed out by early Muslim commentators and collectors of legends. Other angelic figures, including Isrāfīl, the trumpet blower, and 'Izrā'īl, the angel of death, were added to the core of Muslim beliefs. Many of the stories are based on the traditions of Christianity, Judaism, Zoroastrianism, and local Arabian lore. In general, Islamic angels are most often depicted as figures who perform a variety of services in connection with the period of death and resurrection. An elaborate eschatology of the "punishment in the tomb" alluded to in several Qur'ānic verses developed around two non-Qur'ānic angels, Munkar and Nakīr, who are said to question the dead about their belief on the night after burial. In Shī'ism, angels also attend the imams in a variety of ways, joining them in prayer and shaking their wings over the imams' children.

BIBL.: Richard Bell and W. M. Watt, *Bell's Introduction to the Qur'an*, rev. and enlarged by W. M. Watt (Edinburgh, 1970). B. Caseau, "Crossing the Impenetrable Frontier between Earth and Heaven," *Shifting Frontiers in Late Antiquity*, ed. R. Mathisen and H. Sivan (Aldershot, Eng., 1996), 333–342. C. Mango, "Saint Michael and Attis," *Deltion Christ. Arch. Etaireias*, series 4, 11 (1986): 39–62. G. F. Hill, "Apollo and St. Michael: Some Analogies," *Journal of Hellenic Studies* 36 (1916): 134–162. Glenn Peers, "Apprehending the Archangel Michael," *Byzantine and Modern Greek Studies* 20 (1996): 100–121. Christopher Rowland, *The Open Heaven: A Study of Apocalyptic in Judaism and Early Christianity* (New York, 1982). Individual angels in Islam can be found in the *Encyclopedia of Islam*, new ed. (Leiden, 1954–). D.T.F., EDS.

Angels in Iconography

The Bible established the ethereal nature of angelic beings (Ps. 104:4, Heb. 1:7) and this quality posed difficulties for Christian artists. Early representations reveal different approaches to depicting immaterial beings. The Via Latina Catacomb (Rome, 4th century) shows the angelic manifestation as smoke and fire, from Exodus. The appearance of Gabriel to the Virgin Mary (Luke 1:28–38) is represented in the Catacomb of Priscilla (Rome, late 2nd century) by a wingless man. This literalism evidently was not sufficiently descriptive of the bodiless nature of angelic beings, and attributes such as color (St. Apollinare Nuovo, Ravenna, ca. 557–570), cloud (St. Demetrius, Thessalonica, 6th century), and wings were used to indicate the allusive nature of these representations. Stylistic differences between human and angelic figures also underlined the essential differences between the two (as in the icon of the Virgin and Child flanked by SS. George and Theodore at the Monastery of St. Catherine's, Sinai, from the 6th/7th century). Wings were, of course, the preeminent distinction for angels. They appear first on two figures on the Sarigüzel sarcophagus (Archaeological Museum, Istanbul, ca. 400) in a manner clearly derived from pagan funerary art. The Christian angels are distinct, however, in dress and gender as well, and angels and Nike figures can coexist on the same monument, as for instance, in the Barberini diptych (Louvre, Paris, ca. 500). Despite the clear indebtedness of Christian artists to pagan models, Scripture had already established a connection between wings and angelic beings (for example, Isa. 6) and early exegetes (such as Tertullian, *Apologeticum* 22.8) viewed wings as symbols of angels' transcendental nature. The winged youth can be an inclusive symbol for any angel (for instance, on the entrance gate of the Alahan complex, 5th century; in the *Vienna Genesis,* fol. 2v, 6th century; and in the Church of the Dormition, Nicaea [Iznik], ca. 700).

Pagan models of court ritual determined the triumphant iconography of apse mosaics; compare, for instance, the apse mosaic at S. Vitale (Ravenna, 548) with the silver *missorium* of Theodosius I (Römisch-Germanisches Zentralmuseum, Mainz, 388). If in official art, however, the transition is largely self-evident, in cult practice the progression toward Christianizing elements of pagan art is not nearly so clear. For example, the foundation legend of the shrine of the archangel Michael outside Constantinople, the Sosthenion, reveals the shadowy history of artistic transfer from gods to angels. This absorption of pagan practice and iconography excited opposition in conservative quarters (from Severus of Antioch, for instance).

The most exalted members of the hierarchy, the cherubim and seraphim (in the hierarchy of Pseudo-Dionysius the Areopagite, who had a negligible impact on iconography of this period), were most often depicted in liturgical contexts. The Trisagion, the "Holy, holy, holy" chanted by the seraphim (Isa. 6:3, Rev. 4:8), influenced representations of cherubim and seraphim. The earliest depiction of the seraphim and the tetramorph cherubim, in the 5th to 6th century apse mosaic in the Church of St.

David in Thessalonica, conflates the visions of Ezekiel's cherubim (1:4–28, 10:12), Isaiah's seraphim (6:1–3), and the six-winged creatures of Revelation (4:2–10). The iconography in the St. David mosaic is the first example of the liturgical *maiestas.*

BIBL.: Kurt Weitzmann, ed., *Age of Spirituality: Late Antique and Early Christian Art, Third to Seventh Century* (Princeton, 1979). Marco Bussagli, *Storia degli angeli: Racconto di immagini e di idee* (Milan, 1991). Glenn Peers, "The Sosthenion near Constantinople: John Malalas and Ancient Art," in *Byzantion* 68 (1998).　　　　　　G.P.

Anicia Juliana

Within the (long ago destroyed) Church of St. Polyeuktos in Constantinople, one of several churches Anicia Juliana was credited with building or embellishing, there was inscribed a dedicatory poem—preserved for us entire in the *Greek Anthology* (1.10)—in which she did not blush to be ranked alongside the emperors Constantine and Theodosius as a benefactor of the imperial city, nor to declare that the temple she had erected had surpassed that of Solomon himself.

Anicia Juliana could well associate herself with such distinguished company. Born at Constantinople about 461, possessed of both an enormous fortune and ster-

Portrait of Anicia Juliana from the frontispiece of a treatise by Dioscorides.

ling prestige, she established herself there as a prominent patron and a leading citizen, holding the title of *patricia*. In her the bluest blood of the western Roman aristocracy joined with that of the Theodosian imperial dynasty. The Anicii, on her father's side, were one of the wealthiest and most influential noble lineages in late antiquity. Her mother, Placidia, was the daughter of the emperor Valentinian III and a descendant of emperors through both her parents.

Juliana's own father, Anicius Olybrius, ruled as emperor over the west for a few months prior to his death in 472. But any aspirations Juliana might have had to become an empress herself went unsatisfied. Her husband, Areobindus, declined an invitation to usurp the crown during a riot in the capital in 512. Much of his appeal to the rioters lay not only in his wife's connections but also in her staunch Chalcedonianism, which contrasted favorably with the Monophysite sympathies of the reigning emperor Anastasius and made Juliana a figure of some significance in the ecclesiastical controversies of the day. She nonetheless allied her family with the royal house through the marriage of her son Olybrius to the emperor's niece. After Anastasius, however, the succession would fall into other hands.

Her portrait survives as the frontispiece to a manuscript she commissioned of the medical treatise of Dioscorides, now preserved in Vienna. She died about 528.

BIBL.: C. Capizzi, "Anicia Giuliana (462 ca.–530 ca.): Ricerche sulla sua famiglia e la sua vita," *Rivista di studi bizantini e neoellenici*, new series 5 (1968): 191–226. C. Mango and I. Ševčenko, "Remains of the Church of St. Polyeuktos at Constantinople," *Dumbarton Oaks Papers* 15 (1961): 243–247. J. R. Martindale, ed., *The Prosopography of the Later Roman Empire*, vol. 2, s.v. Anicia Iuliana 3 (Cambridge, Eng., 1980): 635–636. C.P.

Annona

Although it once meant "annual harvest," the word *annona* came to designate the provisioning of large communities (the city of Rome, the imperial army), and then, in the later Roman empire, the tax in kind that supplied for such needs *(res annonaria)*.

The civil *annona* was a key preoccupation of government authorities, and in the west it was the major responsibility of the urban prefect. In 375, L. Aurelius Avianius Symmachus (father of the writer), a former prefect, was held partly responsible for the inadequacy of the supply and the rise in prices (the "wine scandal") and was expelled from Rome, his house burned by rioters. He was more fortunate than Gabinius Barbarus Pompeianus, who was murdered by a mob in 409 for similar reasons. Thenceforth, grain from Africa supplied Rome, and Egyptian grain was reserved for Constantinople, to which the privileges of the Roman plebs had been extended. Durliat argues that the Byzantine state took charge of food distribution in many provincial cities, but provides no real proof. The *annona civica* was always limited to a portion of the population of capital cities and was even paid for in part by the beneficiaries (not only meat and oil but even bread—*panis gradilis*—cost them something). The institution kept its civic and limited character to the end, and whatever the demographic estimate adopted, the proportion of beneficiaries within the overall population did not increase. A tax was the major but not sole source of provisions. Wine distributions (in Rome, under the porticoes of the Temple of the Sun on the Campus Martius) were soon being financed by a tax in kind imposed on the southern provinces of Italy. A system of public purchases also operated on behalf of a few megalopolises such as Alexandria.

When bread replaced grain, the methods and structures of the distributions changed. Where there had once been a single distribution location (the Porticus Minucia), now there were various *gradus* dispersed throughout the districts of the city. The *annona* distributed bread for free *(panis popularis)* or for a price *(panis fiscalis)*. The financial operation of the institution was supported by special funds *(arca olearia, arca vinaria;* the role of the *arca frumentaria* is less clear).

The imperial state did not ensure the transport of goods for the *annona*. It preferred long-term contracts with individuals who belonged to "associations of public law" *(corpora)* with fixed obligations *(munus)*. The financial stability of these organizations was guaranteed by real property, or by *praedia navicularariorum* in the case of overseas transport. A number of trade associations (bakers, loaders, measurers) were organized on the same principles. The imperial legislation concerned only those *corpora* in the state's service doing work related to public distributions, for free or for a political price. It is thus quite wrongly that commentators have extended its application to the professional Roman world as a whole and asserted that the state completely took over urban provisioning. This complex organization, then, can no longer be seen as a demonstration of some "totalitarianism" of the later empire. Rather, it was the late empire that put an end to it in the 5th century. This occurred for various reasons: in the west, the loss of the *frumentarii* provinces necessitated a new supply map; in the east, the choice was voluntary, probably the result of disadvantages in the *corpora* system. In any case, no trace of that system remained under Justinian. From then on, the government relied on contracts with private transporters and requisitioned transports *(angariae)*. But at no time did private and totally free activities cease to play an important role in the transport of the *annona* and the provisioning of large city-states. This is especially true given that public distributions reached only a portion of the population and always left a significant share of the market to free trade, particularly that of great landowners. These circumstances, maintained by the purchasing power of the salaried urban plebs, remained in place in Rome throughout the 5th century and stimulated the Italian economy. This explains the prosperity of pork farmers in southern Italy, which the excavations of St. Giovanni di Ruoti and St. Vincenzo al Volturno have revealed for that period.

Food problems were no less keen in the other large urban centers of the empire that did not benefit from any state aid. A benefactor's generosity or municipal funds, possibly supplemented by a bequest, sometimes allowed certain of them to undertake short-term civic distributions more or less inspired by those of the capital cities. These populations also held their ruling classes responsible for supplying the market and maintaining prices at an acceptable level, and mobs in a city-state such as Antioch were no less volatile than those in Rome or Constantinople.

From the fiscal point of view, the innovation of the late period did not lie in the universalization of the tax in kind *(annona)* but rather in the integration of the *annona militaris* into the land tax, which was then supplied directly to the troops. As much as possible, local resources provided for provincial garrisons. Nonetheless, the new military structures increased the need to convey supplies over long distances *(expeditio, prosecutio annonae, parapompē)*. Organizing these transports became increasingly complex and bureaucratized; still imposed on the municipalities in the 3rd century, the responsibility for this *pastus primipili* fell to provincial chiefs of *officia* when they left office. Concurrently, the provision of goods *(species)* became concentrated in certain zones, where the fiscal system may have taken the dominant or exclusive form of a tax in kind. Thus, several provinces in the eastern prefecture were given the long-term assignment of supplying the armies of the prefecture of Illyricum. The same was true for the vicariate of northern Italy with respect to the western *comitatus*—hence its name, Italia Annonaria. The tax in kind did not become universal, however, contrary to repeated assertions by 20th century historians. In the new terminology, the expression *res annonaria* covered all land taxes (those that filled the chests of praetorian prefectures); this does not authorize us to maintain that land taxes were collected in kind in all places. Furthermore, we cannot ignore the large number of personal taxes in currency (destined for the *largitionalia*), levied on a still largely money-based economy. At the same time, the army continued to collect a significant part of its remuneration in currency.

Just as Rome's loss of its African supply source may have precipitated the decline of the city beginning in 439, Byzantium's loss of Egypt in 642 ended the free civic distributions. In their newly conquered possession, the Arabs continued to levy the *annona* in kind, for their army and later for the population of Baghdad.

BIBL.: Jean-Michel Carrié, "Les distributions alimentaires dans les cités de l'empire romain tardif," *Mélanges de l'école française à Rome* 87 (1972): 995–1101. Jean Durliat, *De la ville antique à la ville byzantine: Le problème des subsistances* (Rome, 1900). P. Mayerson, "The Port of Clysma (Suez) in Transition from Roman to Arab Rule," *Journal of Near Eastern Studies* 55 (1996): 119–126. Boudewijn Sirks, *Food for Rome: The Legal Structure of the Transportation and Processing of Supplies for the Imperial Distributions in Rome and Constantinople* (Amsterdam, 1991). J.C.

Anthology

Anthologies (collections) in late antiquity took several forms, both secular (collections of verses, mainly epigrams and collections of moral or improving excerpts from secular authors) and religious (typically collections of scriptural or patristic citations [*florilegia*] for use in theological argument, or of ascetic texts or decisions taken by church councils).

The *Greek Anthology* is the most important example of the first category. In its surviving form it is a composite from the Byzantine period amounting to fifteen books that incorporate all or parts of several earlier collections beginning from the Hellenistic period, and it includes verses by poets of late antiquity, including Palladas and Christodorus of Coptus, and the Christian epigrams of Gregory of Nazianzus. It also includes the *Cycle* of epigrams collected by Agathias Scholasticus in Constantinople in the 6th century. Some of the epigrams in the *Anthology* were originally verses inscribed on monuments rather than literary compositions. In contrast, the *Latin Anthology* is a collection of epigrams put together in Vandal Carthage immediately before the Byzantine reconquest (533–534 C.E.); while their technical quality varies, the poems by Luxorius and others show that secular Latin education was still available in the 6th century, and they reveal a degree of patronage for letters by the Vandal aristocracy and court.

Another type of anthology was the *gnomologion,* or collection of *gnomai,* improving sayings or extracts, collected and recommended by rhetoricians. Stobaeus (4th to 5th century) produced a collection of extracts taken from Greek literature in four books, supposedly for the instruction of his son; it became popular in Byzantium, and Protius recommended it for its utility.

In the 4th century Basil and Gregory of Nazianzus produced a *Philokalia* of extracts from the works of the 3rd century writer Origen, and from the 5th century onward *florilegia* of extracts from Scripture or from the Fathers were produced for use in dogmatic disputes. *Catenae,* which also begin during this period, are *florilegia* of extracts from biblical exegesis, attached to a biblical text. Dogmatic *florilegia* became particularly important during the 7th and 8th centuries, during the controversies over Monothelitism and Iconoclasm, when rival *florilegia* circulated or were produced to justify particular theological positions; as the level of theological debate intensified, so *florilegia* proliferated. *Florilegia* were also attached to polemical or controversial treatises, and examples of the *Adversus Iudaeos* literature, which flourished during this period, often incorporated *florilegia* of scriptural citations chosen to support a Christian and anti-Jewish reading of the Hebrew Bible.

Collections of a hundred extracts or quotations were known as centuries, such as the *Centuries on Charity* of Maximus Confessor (7th century). The *Sacra Parallela,* a Byzantine collection of extracts divided into three books on God, man, and virtue and vice, perhaps meant to balance the secular collection of Stobaeus, seems to derive from an 8th century original, attributed to John of Damascus. Sets of questions and answers and problems *(ambigua, dubia)* on religious matters also circulated, and there were ascetic *florilegia* for use in monastic environments, the early prototypes of the orthodox anthology known as the *Philokalia,* which in its present version was put together in the 18th century.

BIBL.: Alan Cameron, *The Greek Anthology* (Oxford, 1993). Averil Cameron, "Texts as Weapons: Polemic in the Byzantine Dark Ages," in A. K. Bowman and G. Woolf, eds., *Literacy and Power in the Ancient World* (Cambridge, Eng., 1994). A.M.C.

Antinomianism

The term *antinomianism* was coined in the 16th century to describe the behavior of some Protestant sectarians whose radical Paulinism entailed total rejection of biblical law and libertarian behavior. The term is useful, however, for describing various Gnostic or dualist movements of the first Christian centuries, for whom the message of the New Testament meant a complete refusal of the God of Israel and the Hebrew Bible. The creator God was conceived as a lower deity, sometimes even stupid, ignorant, revolted, or evil, and in any case directly or indirectly responsible for the existence of evil in the world. In opposition to this demiurge, the antinomian dualists postulated the supreme God, father of a Christ who had not suffered on the Cross, often conceived as a purely spiritual mythical figure.

Among the main antinomian thinkers of the 2nd century, one must mention the Alexandrian Basilides—perhaps the first Christian philosopher—and Marcion of Sinope, who argued most consistently that Christians ought to reject the Hebrew Bible and expurgate the New Testament of various texts written under the inspiration of the lower god, the demiurge. For Marcion, the demiurge was only just *(justus),* while Christ's father, the supreme God, was also good *(bonus).* Arguing against such heretics, the Christian writer Clement of Alexandria (late 2nd century) offers a taxonomy of antinomian attitudes on the margins of Christianity. From their recognition of the evil nature of the material world, two different attitudes can be observed.

Some antinomians reject any ethical behavior, proclaiming that good and evil are indifferent *(adiaphora),* while others develop a radical asceticism, or encratism, reflecting their hatred for this world and their refusal to have any contact with it *(Stromateis* 3.5.40).

Most Gnostic sects disappeared before the end of the 3rd century. A major exception is that of the Marcionite church. We can follow traces of Marcionite communities in the Near East as late as the 8th century. Hiwwi al-Balkhi, a Jewish heresiarch whose views seem to have been close to those of Marcion, dates from the same period. His figure excepted, we possess very few sources about the existence of Jewish antinomians in late antiquity. Another exception is that of the Mandaeans, a late antique Gnostic Baptist sect living in the marshes of Khuzistan, whose writings strongly reject Christianity as ultimately stemming from Satan.

As proponents of a radical dualism both cosmological and anthropological, the Manichaeans strongly objected to the Hebrew Bible and conceived this world as remaining under the sway of Satan, the Prince of Darkness, while the Church of the Elect, the Manichaeans, belonged to the camp of the Father of Light. The two camps were to remain in constant conflict until the final apocalyptical salvation, when the sons of light would leave forever the material earth. Such principles entailed some radical ethics, which included, for the core members of the sect—the elect—a total rejection of sexual relations. In that sense, Manichaean encratism fits the second category of antinomianism as described by Clement of Alexandria. The Manichaeans were perceived as a radical threat to public life by the proponents of all theologies (Greek philosophers, Christians, Zoroastrians, and Muslim theologians alike), and were persecuted by all political powers, the Romans (before and after Constantine), the Sassanians, and the Umayyads. Despite persecution, Manichaeism seems to have exerted a powerful attraction and to have been remarkably resilient: the religion of light, whose believers could be found from North Africa to Central Asia, survived for about one thousand years. It appears to have offered a serious challenge to both Christian and Muslim theologians, mainly in questions of ethics.

BIBL.: K. Rudolph, *Gnosis* (Edinburgh, 1983). S. Stroumsa and G. G. Stroumsa, "Anti-Manichaean Polemics in Late Antiquity and under Early Islam," *Harvard Theological Review* 81 (1988): 37–58. G.STR.

Antioch

Antioch on the Orontes, modern Antakya, is located 25 km from the Mediterranean Sea. It was formerly the Seleucid capital and became the capital of Roman Syria. For the most part, its vast *chōra* extends east and southeast of the region known as the limestone massif.

On several occasions during the 4th century, Antioch served as a capital city, particularly during the prolonged stays of Constantius II (337–350) and Valens (371–378), which were necessary for operations against the Sassanids. The *comes Orientis*, the *magister militum* of the east, and the civil governor of the province of Syria Coele, then of Syria Prima, all resided there. The patriarch of the east also had his seat there. These different civic functions faded away, however, and after the 4th century, emperors stayed in Antioch only rarely. The Muslims, after their arrival in 638, made it a city secondary to a military district; Palestine and then Cyprus were detached from the patriarchate in the 5th century; and theological quarrels further weakened the Chalcedonian patriarchs.

Antioch's apogee occurred in the late 4th century—the era of the rhetor Libanius and of John Chrysostom—and in the 5th century. The population is estimated to have been between 150,000 and 300,000. The city, built on the east bank of the Orontes, on the slopes of Mount Silpius, and on an island occupied by its palatine district, was surrounded by walls that were built or rebuilt under Theodosius II and Justinian. The suburban areas, including Daphne, were vast. A long street, 36 m wide, lined with colonnades and shops, crossed Antioch north to south over a distance of 3 km. This street was the essential element of urban development, and it was rebuilt for the last time under Justinian. The octagonal Great Church, built on the island by Constantine, was Antioch's most famous religious building. It was destroyed by an earthquake in 588.

In the 6th century, the sacking of the city by the Persians (540), the deportation of residents, numerous earthquakes, and a plague led to the city's decline. During the same period, economic expansion on the limestone massif ended. Internal and external factors joined to make 7th and 8th century Antioch a modest city that occupied only the southern part of its former area, surrounded by Justinian's ramparts, with a very small number of new constructions.

BIBL.: G. Downey, *A History of Antioch in Syria* (Princeton, 1961). H. Kennedy, "Antioch: From Byzantine to Islam and Back Again," in *The City in Late Antiquity*, ed. J. Rich (London and New York, 1992), 181–198. J. H. W. G. Liebeschuetz, *Antioch: City and Imperial Administration in the Later Roman Empire* (Oxford, 1972).   P.-L.G.

Antony

Antony of Egypt (ca. 250–356) is the primary exemplar of the desert monk. As a young man, Antony sold his extensive property, entrusted his sister to a community of Christian virgins, and abandoned village society to practice solitary asceticism in the Egyptian desert. Although it is unlikely that Antony was the first to take such a step, he became the most famous monk to do so. Even in his own lifetime Antony attracted numerous admirers and disciples, but his worldwide fame was achieved posthumously thanks to an idealized biography, the *Life of Antony*, written by Bishop Athanasius of Alexandria (ca. 295–373). According to this work, Antony took up residence in the remote "inner desert" after living near other ascetics outside a village and then spending twenty years shut up in an abandoned military fort. This latter feat gained Antony immediate notoriety within Egypt.

The only literary remains of Antony himself are seven letters, which he wrote in Coptic but which now survive in several ancient translations. These letters reveal that Antony was a literate man with philosophical interests who saw the ascetic life as a means of transforming the body into a more spiritual version of itself and of gaining knowledge of God and self. Athanasius's *Life*, however, presents Antony as illiterate, empowered by Christ to perform exorcisms or healing miracles, and obedient to bishops and priests; his ascetic life is described as a means of warfare with demons. This literary depiction of Antony so captivated ancient Christians that many of them, including Augustine of Hippo, adopted the ascetic life.

BIBL.: David Brakke, *Athanasius and the Politics of Asceticism* (Oxford and New York, 1995), 201–265. James E. Goehring, "The Origins of Monasticism," in *Eusebius, Christianity, and Judaism*, ed. Harold W. Attridge and Gohei Hata (Detroit, 1992), 235–255. Samuel Rubenson, *The Letters of St. Antony: Monasticism and the Making of a Saint* (Minneapolis, 1995).   D.B.

Aphrahat

Aphrahat, the Syriac form of the Persian name Farhad ("perspicacious"; Aphraates in Greek), was the name given by medieval sources to the self-effacing author of twenty-three acrostically ordered Syriac demonstrations in rhetorical prose. The dates of their composition can be determined by references to different political events: the first half of the demonstrations date to 337 C.E., the second half to 344, and the last demonstration to 345. Aphrahat refers to himself as one of a number of *hakkime*, or wise men, and, like them, as a "disciple of Holy Scripture," although he sometimes speaks on behalf of the whole Christian church.

Aphrahat is called Jacob in one 5th century manuscript but cannot be identified with Jacob of Nisibis, with whom he is confused in Armenian and Ethiopian tradition and in Gennadius, since Aphrahat is a subject of the Sassanian empire, possibly living near Nineveh. He expected the Roman empire—which he referred to as "the sons of Shem/Esau" and identified with the "fourth animal" in Daniel's prophecy—to triumph over the Persians and rule until the return of Christ. Aphrahat is an example of a Persian Christian whose sympathies lay with Constantine, who claimed to be the protector of the Christians living under Persian rule. After Constantine's death cut short the campaign against Persia, Shapur II, suspicious of the loyalty of his Christian subjects, began the "destruction of the churches" in 339–340. Aphrahat survived this attack, as well as the same shah's "great annihilation of blood-witnesses in the land of the East" in 343–344, and is not himself said to have died a martyr.

Aphrahat's argument with one of his Jewish counterparts, even if invented, shows that the synagogue was not persecuted at that time, so his demonstrations against Judaism may be evidence that some Christians avoided official harassment by embracing, or reverting to, Judaism. He reports that Jews taunted Christians, saying that their God could not protect them from persecution. Although there is no specific evidence that he was trained in a rabbinical school, as has been suggested, Aphrahat does assume that his audience accepts the Hebrew Scriptures as authoritative. He does not allegorize the stories in the Hebrew Bible but recognizes biblical law as legitimate for the Jews of that time. He does, however, try to downplay the salvific significance of the ritual law, emphasizing, instead, its practical purposes. Unlike some of his western contemporaries, Aphrahat shows no need to make the biblical God compatible with the ideals of Greek philosophy.

Aphrahat reveals other Jewish criticism of Christianity: the Jews mocked the Christians for their idealization of celibacy (which offended Zoroastrians as well). Aphrahat, who evidently belonged to the *qyama,* the "elite corps" of men and women who made a vow of celibacy at baptism, defends the high value attached to *ihidayuta,* "singleness." He did not consider celibacy a condition for baptism, or even its preservation after baptism a condition for salvation, as has been claimed; but, in writing for ascetics, Aphrahat (like the encratite Tatian who edited Aphrahat's gospel) did associate baptism and the presence of the Holy Spirit closely with asceticism. Perhaps responding to criticism, he recognized marriage as a good created by God but insisted that celibacy remained superior.

Aphrahat deplores the hypocrisy and power mania of certain unnamed leaders in his community. His belief in the "sleep of the soul"—that the soul falls asleep with the body and will be resurrected at the end with the body—has puzzled theologians, while the many titles with which he names Christ have delighted them. His creed and paschal computation show no knowledge of the Council of Nicaea, which was approved by the Persian church only in 410; he lacks interest in Christological speculation. Aphrahat cites copiously a Syriac Bible apparently consisting only of the Peshitta with 1–2 Maccabees, Tatian's harmony of the gospels—the *Diatesseron,* Acts, and the Pauline epistles. He may have been unknown to his younger contemporary in Roman Mesopotamia, Ephrem, with whom, nevertheless, he has much in common, especially in his use of images and names.

Although his demonstrations are referred to by some learned writers in the 8th and 9th centuries, they are not widely known. Aphrahat is almost lost to later Syriac tradition: his identity is confused, and his demonstrations survive in only a few manuscripts.

BIBL.: For Aphrahat's demonstrations, see Syriac with Latin trans. by J. Parisot, in *Patrologia syriaca* 1 and 2 (1894, 1907); French trans. and extensive intro. by M.-J. Pierre, in *Sources chrétiennes* 349 (1988) and 359 (1989); German by P. Burns, in *Fontes christiani* 5, nos. 1, 2 (1991). For English translations of some demonstrations, see *Select Library of Nicene and Post-Nicene Fathers* 2.13 (1898); J. Neusner, *Aphrahat and Judaism* (Leiden, 1971), and *Journal of the Society for Oriental Research* 14 (1930) and 16 (1932). See also T. D. Barnes, "Constantine and the Christians of Persia," *Journal of Roman Studies* (1985) 75: 126–136. Sidney H. Griffith, "Asceticism in the Church of Syria: The Hermeneutics of Early Syrian Monasticism," in *Asceticism,* ed. Vincent Wimbush (Oxford, 1995), 220–245. Robert Murray, *Symbols of Church and Kingdom: A Study in Early Syriac Tradition* (London, 1975). T.D.B., EDS.

Aphrodisias

Capital of the province of Caria, Aphrodisias was the seat of a governor and a metropolitan archbishop. Its school of pagan philosophy flourished through the 5th century, and its ancient tradition of sculpture remained productive in late antiquity. Three of the most famous local sculptors flourished in the 4th century, and remarkable portraits were still being made in the 6th. It also had an important Monophysite church.

The city is best known for its extensively excavated remains. They reveal a high level of sophistication and prosperity that was partially interrupted by earthquake and flooding in the 5th century but recovered substantially in the 6th. Most public works of antiquity were maintained, restored, or transformed. The cathedral, remodeled from the Temple of Aphrodite in the mid-5th century and flanked by the palaces of the bishop and governor, dominated the city center, while the theater, stadium, odeum, baths, basilicas, marketplaces, and broad streets occupied most of the monumental area within the 4th-century walls. The lavish 1st century Sebasteion, built for the imperial cult, apparently became a market. Most buildings were made of marble and were decorated with sculpture and frescoes. Numerous inscriptions reveal much about the political, religious, and intellectual life of the city and illustrate the revival under Justinian. They show the overwhelming importance of the governor and the extravagant praise some incumbents attracted. Aphrodisias was destroyed in the early 7th century, apparently by earthquake, and never recovered. Known in the Dark Ages as Stauropolis, it was confined within new walls built around its ancient theater.

BIBL.: R. Cormack, "The Temple in the Cathedral," *Aphrodisias Papers,* ed. C. Roueché and K. Erim, *Journal of Ro-*

man Archaeology, suppl. (1990): 75–84. Kenan T. Erim, *Aphrodisias* (London, 1986). Charlotte Roueché, *Aphrodisias in Late Antiquity* (London, 1989).   C.F.

Aphroditopolis

Called Aphroditō in Arabic documents and Aphroditēs komē in texts of the Byzantine era, Aphroditopolis (modern Kom Ishgaw) lies on the west bank of the Nile, 400 miles south of Alexandria, halfway between Lycopolis/Asyūt and Akhmīm/Panopolis and not far from Pachomian strongholds. Archaeologically unexplored, the site is nonetheless the best-documented locality of 6th century Egypt, if not of the Byzantine east as a whole, thanks to the archives of one of its most illustrious citizens and *prōtocomētēs,* the poet Dioscorus.

The ancient capital of a nome, later downgraded to the administrative rank of a village dependent on Antaeopolis, Aphroditopolis preserved characteristics of its urban past, both in its sociocultural structure and in the size of its population (estimated at fifteen thousand). Its residents had a direct relationship with the emperor that was sustained by petitions, sometimes taken to Constantinople by a delegation, to defend the privilege of independent tax collection or to denounce the machinations of corrupt public employees (in particular, the pagarchs).

Long the object of harsh judgments, Dioscorus (born about 520) is now being rehabilitated. He "exemplified the kind of local *propriétaire* who supported and made possible the high creativity of Coptic culture" (MacCoull, 8). He combined Coptic spirituality, the classical literary tradition, and the legal competence of the age of Justinian. His archives show that this remote Egyptian province of the 6th century remained well integrated in the economic, political, cultural, and religious circuits of the Byzantine world.

Aphroditō's life under the Arab administration in the 8th century can be followed through tax records recovered on the site and published primarily in *P London* 4 and *P Schott-Reinhardt.*

BIBL.: Jean Gascou and Leslie S. B. MacCoull, "Le cadastre d'Aphroditō," *Travaux et mémoires* 10 (1987): 104–158. James G. Keenan, "The Aphrodite Papyri and Village Life in Byzantine Egypt," *Bulletin de la société d'archéologie copte* 26 (1984): 51–63. Leslie S. B. MacCoull, *Dioscorus of Aphrodito: His Work and His World* (Berkeley, 1988).   J.C.

Apocrypha

The word *apocrypha* (literally, "things hidden away") is used to designate a group of fifteen religious writings from antiquity that are included in the Greek Septuagint and Latin Vulgate but are not in the Hebrew Scriptures. With minor exceptions, the traditional apocryphal works are 1 Esdras, 2 Esdras (Vulgate: 4 Ezra),

Tobit, Judith, Additions to the Book of Esther, the Wisdom of Solomon (also called Wisdom), Ecclesiasticus (also called Sirach, or the Wisdom of Jesus ben Sirach), Baruch, the Epistle of Jeremiah, the Additions to the Book of Daniel (or, individually, the Prayer of Azariah and the Song of the Three Young Men; Susanna; and Bel and the Dragon), the Prayer of Manasseh, and 1 and 2 Maccabees. The Septuagint lacks 2 Esdras but includes 3 and 4 Maccabees, which are absent from the Vulgate. Among Roman Catholics and Eastern Orthodox Christians, most of the texts listed above are regarded as deuterocanonical, meaning books belonging to a second layer of the canon but with no implication that they are of less worth than the others. The authorized (or King James) version of the Bible of 1611 included the Apocrypha between the Old and the New Testaments.

The importance of these books arises from their having been composed later than the canonical writings of the Hebrew Scriptures and (apart from 2 Esdras) before the books of the New Testament. They are valuable not only for their insight into the national consciousness of Jews in the Diaspora but also for the light they shed on political, religious, and cultural developments in the later Hellenistic and early Roman periods—and thus on the background of rabbinic and early Christian thought.

Furthermore, when considered as to their own individual importance, several of the apocryphal books represent typical examples of literary genres. Tobit is a romantic eastern tale depicting very human characters and illustrating high ethical teachings. Judith is a fictitious story of a heroic Jewish woman who accomplishes the deliverance of her people by using feminine wiles. The Wisdom of Solomon, a patently pseudonymous work, is an early attempt to fuse two different intellectual traditions, the Jewish and the Greek. The Prayer of Manasseh, which was not part of the original Septuagint and is deuterocanonical for only some eastern churches, purports to be the penitential prayer uttered by the infamous King Manasseh of Judah while exiled in Babylon (referred to in 2 Chron. 33:12–13 and 18). Although only fifteen verses long, it is recognized as one of the finest examples of ancient Jewish devotional writing. First Maccabees is a sober and reliable, albeit partisan, historical source for the struggle of the patriotic Jews against Hellenism during the intertestamental period. The book depicts the Hasmonaeans as God's chosen agents of salvation, rewarded for their faithfulness to the Mosaic law. Susanna and Bel and the Dragon are among the earliest detective stories ever written.

In addition to the set of books traditionally designated as the Apocrypha, there are a large number of Jewish and Christian works (3rd century B.C.E. to 6th century C.E.) that rewrite portions of the Hebrew Bible or are attributed to figures in the Hebrew Bible. Designated Pseudepigrapha ("writings falsely ascribed"), they have been important in both Jewish and Christian traditions.

BIBL.: R. H. Charles, ed., *The Apocrypha and Pseudepigrapha of the Old Testament*, 2 vols. (Oxford, 1913). J. H. Charlesworth, ed., *The Old Testament Pseudepigrapha*, 2 vols. (Garden City, N.Y., 1983, 1985). C. Carozzi, *Eschatologie et au-delà: Recherches sur l'apocalypse de Paul* (Aix-en-Provence, 1994). A. Dufourcq, *Étude sur les gesta martyrum romains* (Paris, 1988). B. M. Metzger, *An Introduction to the Apocrypha* (New York, 1957). B.M.

Aquileia

In the region known as the "Gauls' land" *(ager Gallorum),* where 12,000 Transalpine Gauls forced out by overpopulation and famine had hoped in 186 B.C.E. to found their fortified center (Livy 39.22.6–7 and 55), 3,000 soldiers and coloni from Rome, victorious against them with Consul Marcellus (183), laid the foundations of Aquileia, a Latin *colonia.* The amount of land given to the soldiers determined the structure and economic future of the town. Fifty *iugera* were given to *pedites,* 100 to *centuriones,* 140 to *equites,* and this was enough to enable the new farmers to invest money not only in the land, but also in commercial enterprises as small landowners. This happened very quickly, thanks to the Romanization of the area. In 187 the Via Aemilia had been extended to Aquileia. In 148 and 147 B.C.E. the town would become the terminal point of Via Postumia, which connected the Tyrrhenian Sea to the Adriatic. In 132–131 the Via Annia would link Adria with Aquileia, continuing the route of Via Popillia between Rimini and Adria.

In 169 B.C.E. another 1,500 coloni arrived in Aquileia, called by the *colonia* itself to help defend it against Histri and Illyri (Livy 43.1–5). Thus from the very beginning, the town grew because it was the strongest point of defense against threats by way of the many easy passages through the Alps. The progressive juridical integration of the Cisalpine region into Italy during the Augustan period produced its economic strength. In Aquileia arrived, in particular, many Istrian products—olives, olive oil, wine, wheat—some of which were consumed by the local people, and some transported to other regions by families involved in such commerce, such as the Barbii and Statii. Aquileia's port system testifies to its lively and large-scale trade in the early imperial period. Its role as commercial emporium promoted local crafts production by immigrating workers. Wool, imported from Istria, was woven by Aquileia's *vestiarii,* so that the garment factory for *militia* enlisted in the *Notitia Dignitatum* probably continued as a local tradition of craftsmanship. During the first two centuries of the empire, the production of amber and engraved gems increased.

Later, while these products diminished, the manufacture of glass was well established.

Aquileia's twofold nature as a center of trade, increasingly dominated by oriental goods, and a strategic and logistical base for military and civilian transport between Rome and transalpine provinces enabled it to prosper during the empire. It seems that Aquileia was one of the few destinations (along with Ravenna and Milan) of Augustus's short trips away from Rome (Suetonius, *Augustus* 20.3). By then, it was already one of the preferred observation posts from which the emperor could keep track of events in the provinces. In the 2nd century Marcus Aurelius transformed Aquileia into the operational base for his Illyric campaigns against the Marcomanni: the imperial *praetorium* resided there in 168–169. And the emperor Maximinus, who was killed by his own soldiers under Aquileia's walls, had planned to turn the town into his strategic base (Herodian 8.6.3).

Aquileia was actually used in just this way from the 4th century onward. While Milan became the frequent residence of the western emperor, Aquileia was the main terminal for many eastern ports (Alexandria, Antioch, Constantinople) and the town through which roads from Noricum, Pannonia, and Illyricum led. Emperors reached many of their eastern seats by passing through Aquileia, as the high percentage of laws issued there can show. The frequent presence of the imperial court, with its military and bureaucratic entourage, was a significant stimulus for the economic, political, and cultural life of the town. Before the end of the 3rd century Aquileia had a local mint, and in the 4th century the *consularis Venetiae et Histriae,* the *praefectus Venetorum classis,* the *comes thesaurorum,* and the *comes Italiae* (the last one was delegated to defend the fortifications of the eastern Alps) all had administrative offices in Aquileia.

Aquileia was probably the first center of Christian expansion in the Padane region. The older examples of Christian architecture are to be found there. During Theodorus's episcopate (308–319) the first cult *aulae* were built, characteristic double basilicas that are similar to the 3rd century Christian *domus* in Dura-Europus. The *aulae*'s marvelous mosaics, still partly preserved, had been offered by the faithful who contributed to the building of the church. Chromatius, bishop of Aquileia in 388–408, started to erect at least three churches, stimulating nearby towns (such as Concordia, which had then its first bishop, and Gradus) to do the same. Even if only the early phases of these churches can be attributed to Chromatius, his building plans were extensive. The situation is comparable to that in Milan, where Ambrose in two decades completed at least four churches.

When Alaric moved down into Italy (402), Honorius decided to move his court from Milan to Ravenna, which was not a salubrious town but was well defended by its marshes. As the new imperial seat grew in importance, Milan and Aquileia were weakened. Aquileia's mint closed in 425. Attila with his Huns arrived in 452 from Pannonia. They conquered Aquileia, Padua, Verona, Milan, Pavia. They plundered and left ruins everywhere in Venetia, Lombardy, Emilia. While the other towns recovered quickly, Aquileia could not. Ravenna had already replaced it as a port of connection with the eastern court.

BIBL.: A. Calderini, *Aquileia romana: Ricerche di storia e di epigrafia* (Milan, 1930). S. Panciera, *Vita economica di Aquileia in età romana* (Venice, 1957). R. Lizzi, *Vescovi e strutture ecclesiastiche nella città tardoantica* (Como, 1989), 139–169. L. Cracco Ruggini, "Aquileia e Concordia: Il duplica volto di una società urbana nel IV secolo d.c.," in *Antichità altoadriatiche* 24, (Udine, 1987), 57–95. *Da Aquileia a Venezia* (Milan, 1980). R. LIZ.

Arab

The Semitic word *'Arab* has two meanings. It was used as a geographical term meaning desert or steppe, and it also designated the collectivity of the nomadic or seminomadic desert dwellers in the Middle East. For much of the late antique period the term did not connotate ethnicity or a special language. Geographically *'Arab* can denote the Egyptian desert east of the Nile toward the Red Sea, the desert east of the Dead Sea in Jordan, the Syrian desert west of the Euphrates, or the northern Mesopotamian steppe between the Euphrates and Tigris east of Nisibis. In the desert area there was a demographic and economic interdependency between desert dwellers and the sedentary population in villages and towns. By the beginning of our period many Arab tribesmen *(arabiyē)* were already settled in Palmyra in the middle of the Syrian desert; in Edessa in northern Mesopotamia; in Petra, capital of the kingdom of the Nabataeans; and in Hatra situated in the Mesopotamian desert near ancient Assur. Classical authors usually call the roaming population Saracens or *skēnitai* (tent dwellers).

Almost the entire desert area of the Middle East became part of the Roman empire with the exception of the Mesopotamian steppe, which belonged to Parthia and after 224 to the Sassanian kingdom. The desert area was important in the wars between Rome and the Parthians and later between Byzantium and the Sassanians. At the end of the 3rd century, during the reign of the emperor Diocletian, the Romans started to build the desert frontier, a row of forts and military installations along the edge of the desert from the Euphrates to the Red Sea and the Negev, many of which are still visible today. Some sectors in northern Mesopotamia and northern Syria guarded against the Parthians and the Persian Sassanians, but the main function of the desert frontier was to control the desert population and to safeguard the trade routes. The bulk of the Roman army was garrisoned in the towns and cities, not in the desert.

Rome, Byzantium, and the Sassanians all made alliances with desert tribes. Arab tribesmen carried out raids into enemy territory and also served as auxiliaries in the regular armies. The Tanūkh and Salīh tribes were confederates of the Romans at the end of the 4th century in the Syrian and Mesopotamian desert; from the late 5th century the Romans were allied with the Ghassanids. The Lakhmid dynasty based at Hira on the Tigris was a long-time ally of the Sassanians. The Lakhmid-Ghassanid rivalry continued into the 6th century wars between Byzantium and the Sassanians.

Throughout late antiquity the Arab population of the desert could travel freely, and there is evidence of large-scale movement between the Roman and the Sassanian empires. Political alliances shifted as well. A famous example is Aspebetos, chief of an Arab clan, who was first a Persian ally but went over to the Romans in 420 C.E. and was made "phylarch of the Roman confederates in Arabia." His clan converted to Christianity, settled in Palestine, and Aspebetos became bishop under the name Petrus.

Most of the desert dwellers remained pagan for a long time, and Christianity gained converts from among them only during the 5th and 6th centuries. Little is known about Arab pagan religion; inscriptions contain names of deities but yield scant information about religious practice. The Arab allies of Byzantium were usually adherents of Monophysitism, whereas the tribes on the Sassanian side were mainly Nestorians. The Islamic conquests of the 7th century put an end to the independent Arab reigns, and the desert population gradually became Muslim. There is some 6th century evidence of a common cultural identity among the Arabs. By the early 7th century Arabic dialects were spoken throughout the Arabian Peninsula, except in Yemen, where pre-Arabic languages endured. In Muhammad's time, the term *'Arab* continued to refer to nomads and seminomads, but as the Islamic empire expanded it also came to refer more precisely to the bedouin.

BIBL.: G. W. Bowersock, *Roman Arabia* (Cambridge, Mass., 1983). Toufic Fahd, *Le panthéon de l'Arabie central à la veille de l'Hégire* (Paris, 1968). Benjamin Isaac, *The Limits of Empire: The Roman Army in the East*, rev. ed. (Oxford, 1992). David Kennedy and Derrick Riley, *Rome's Desert Frontier from the Air* (London, 1990). A. H. Saleh, "Les bédouins d'Égypte aux premier siècles de l'Hégire," *Revista degli studi orientali* 55 (1981): 137–161. Irfan Shahīd, *Rome and the Arabs: A Prolegomenon to the Study of Byzantium and the Arabs* (Washington, D.C., 1984); *Byzantium and the Arabs in the Fourth Century* (Washington, D.C., 1985); *Byzantium and the Arabs in the Fifth Century* (Washington, D.C., 1989); *Byzantium and the Arabs in the Sixth Century* 2 vols. (Washington, D.C., 1995). J. Spencer Trimingham, *Christianity among the Arabs in Pre-Islamic Times* (London, 1979). H.J.D.

Arabia, Roman

Changes in the boundaries of Roman Arabia, beginning in the Severan age, then under Diocletian, and finally between 451 and 535, shifted the province northward, where it touched Damascus. To the south, it ended at Wadi Mujib, in the middle of the Dead Sea. The Arabia of late antiquity, centered around Bostra (but minus Petra), measured about 250 km from north to south. It was composed of fertile agricultural regions bordered on the east by steppes.

In Roman Arabia the duties of civil governor and military *dux* were separate but were often performed by the same person. The reforms of Justinian, who in 536 named a *moderator* in Arabia, were aimed at restoring the splendor of civil governors vis-à-vis Ghassanid dukes and phylarchs. Two legions were stationed in Arabia, the Fourth Martia in Betthoro (Lejjun) and the Third Cyreniaca in Bostra. We do not know what became of them after the 4th century. Numerous fortresses housed other troops along the Via Nova, which crosses the province from north to south, about 20 km farther to the east. Three great periods of military construction are to be distinguished: the tetrarchy, the mid-2nd century (360–379), and the second decade of the third century (410–419). Beginning with Justinian, imperial policy promoted the military use of nomad tribes under the direction of phylarchs, at the expense of fortresses. A great number of fortresses seem to have been abandoned by the army.

Geographical surveys, primarily in Jordan, and excavations show that late antiquity was a period of demographic and economic expansion. Lands in the steppes and mountainous regions were densely populated. Cities and villages grew in number and size. Before the 20th century, the region was never so completely occupied as during that time. The expansion even seems to have lasted longer in Arabia than in Syria proper. The first half of the 7th century may have been as prosperous as the 6th. The role played by outside influences—trade with Hejaz or pilgrimages—is in dispute but must have been limited. The region's real prosperity was based on agricultural development. Studies of the cities of Bostra and Gerasa, however, show that they underwent a transformation in the 7th century, perhaps begun before then. They lost their public spaces and some of their monuments. The functions of the cities of Arabia, no longer centers of power, changed.

Christianity reached Arabia fairly early, shown by the presence of sectarian or heretical groups as early as the 3rd and 4th centuries. Monophysitism, supported by Ghassanid phylarchs, later divided the clergy of the provinces. Nonetheless, Arabia, totally Christianized, was largely Chalcedonian on the eve of the Islamic conquest. One characteristic of the region, an exception for the Near East, was the number of religious constructions, much greater in Arabia than in equivalent villages of northern Syria. Mefaa had fourteen churches, for example, and Rihab nine. A second characteristic was the pursuit of urban development projects and the application of mosaics in churches in the 7th and 8th centuries. These are attested by Greek inscriptions. A third characteristic was the use in the southern part of the province of a particular written Aramaic dialect, distinct from Syriac, in the 6th and 7th centuries.

BIBL.: G. W. Bowersock, *Roman Arabia* (Cambridge, Mass., 1983). Fergus Millar, *The Roman Near East: 31 BC–AD 337* (Cambridge, Mass., 1993). M. Sartre, *Trois études sur l'Arabie romaine et byzantine* (Brussels, 1982). P.-L.G.

Arabic

Arabic is the designation for the Semitic language originally in wide use as a high language in central and northern Arabia, as attested in pre-Islamic poetry and, above all, in the Qur'ān in the 7th century. It has served as the principal language of Islam ever since, and an immense corpus of literature of all kinds has been produced in it. It continued in use in Muslim religious and scientific writing even when, beginning with about the 10th century, Muslims speaking other, very different languages (such as Persian) developed flourishing literatures of their own. They adopted the Arabic script as well as many Arabic words, often those for the most meaningful religious and cultural concepts. Minority groups in arabophone countries, such as Christians and Jews, largely accepted Arabic as their written and spoken language.

With the spread of Islam, spoken dialects of Arabic took root throughout the Near East and extended westward to northwest Africa and Spain. In proportion to their geographical distance from the Arabian center, they developed differences often to the degree of mutual incomprehensibility, while the written language remained seemingly unchanged and was widely understood. The precise linguistic relationship of the spoken dialects to this "classical Arabic" and to the Arabic dialects spoken in the Arabian Peninsula before the rise of Islam has been the subject of much inconclusive scholarly debate. In its phonetic and many of its grammatical features, classical Arabic represents a highly archaic type of Semitic speech. Case endings in nouns and modal endings in verbs, for instance, have been preserved. Their actual use in the language is confirmed by the quantitative meters of poetry; however, the consonantal spelling of the Qur'ān suggests that they were largely lost in ordinary speech.

The pre-Islamic history of related forms of Arabic is known, if imperfectly, for about fifteen hundred years for the northern regions of Arabia. The Semitic language called South Arabian is to be sharply distinguished from this Arabic, although the geographical and ethnic-tribal dividing lines between Arabic and South Arabian cannot now be precisely determined.

More than ethnic designations such as *Aribi* from Assyrian times or Greek *Arabes* and *Sarakēnoi*, it is linguistic characteristics that are decisive for safely establishing Arab ethnicity. Phonetic features in personal names and the names of deities provide reliable criteria. For example, Arabic phonetics are found in proper names from early Christian Palmyra such as Ouballathos, or Wahb-Allāt ("Gift of Allāt") and Odenathos, or Udhayna(t) ("Little Ear"). The Nabataeans centered in Petra were ethnic Arabs writing in an Aramaic dialect with occasional Arabisms. The poetry of the prominent tribes of the Lakhmids and the Ghassanids that is preserved in Islamic literature suggests that it was linguistically identical with Arabic poetry in general, though practically nothing is known directly of their Arabic language.

Many inscriptions, all of them brief and written in ancient variants of the South Arabian alphabet, have been found in northwest Arabia and Jordan. Known as Lihyanite (Dedanite), Thamudic, and Safaitic, the former two can be dated into pre-Christian times whereas Safaitic belongs mainly to the first three centuries of the Christian era. So far, direct precursors of later Arabic are known only from a few inscriptions of some size dating from the 4th and 5th centuries, among them the oldest Arabic inscription named after the location where it originated, the Namāra inscription. It is dated 328 C.E. and describes the "King of all Arabs" Imru'al-Qays, son of ʿAmr, who was buried there and his victorious dealings with various Arab tribal groups. The script was Nabataean, and the word for *son* was still the Aramaic *b-r,* instead of Arabic *b-n.*

As to how much Arabic in any form was used before Islam for written literary texts, it remains a matter for speculation—such as, for instance, how much of the orally transmitted poetry was also at times fixed in writing, or whether there existed a written translation of the Bible or parts of it for use by Christian Arabs. Be this as it may, Arabic in some form served as a medium for much of late Hellenistic civilization. Cultural influences from the surrounding Hellenistic world as well as from Persia had naturally extended south into central Arabia, where Islam was to originate, and beyond it to southern Arabia, leaving a good many traces in the language. The expansion of Islam then assured the continuity and survival of earlier intellectual and artistic achievements. Arabic translations have made contributions to our knowledge of classical Greek works, and they have also preserved much information on the intellectual life of late antiquity. Many subjects are more accessible in Arabic translation than in preserved or postulated Greek originals. Thus, much late scientific writing (especially in the fields of medicine, alchemy, astrology, and musical theory) as well as late Hellenistic popular philosophy, is reflected in Arabic translation.

The spread of Arabic as a lingua franca in the early Islamic empire has been discussed primarily in historical studies on conquest and conversion. Although a formalized Arabic was used in religious contexts and came to be used in imperial administration, different regions of the Islamic empire adopted Arabic as a spoken language at different times. In some places, the original language of the region endured alongside Arabic for several centuries or even up to the present, as with Berber dialects and Persian.

BIBL.: J. A. Bellamy, "A New Reading of the Namarah Inscription," *Journal of the American Oriental Society* 105 (1985): 31–48. François Déroche, *The Abbasid Tradition: Qurʾans of the Eighth to the Tenth Centuries,* vol. 1 of the Khalili Collection of Islamic Art (Oxford, 1992). Fred Donner, *The Early Islamic Conquests* (Princeton, 1981). "Kitābāt," *Encyclopedia Islam,* 2nd ed. Johann Fück, *Arabiya: Untersuchungen zur arabischen Sprach- und Stilgeschichte* (Berlin, 1950). Irfan Shahīd, *Rome and the Arabs* (Washington, D.C., 1984); *Byzantium and the Arabs in the Fourth Century* (Washington, D.C., 1984). Kees Versteegh, *Pidginization and Creolization: The Case of Arabic* (Amsterdam and Philadelphia, 1984). F.R.

Aramaic

A Semitic language closely related to Hebrew and Arabic, Aramaic is attested uninterruptedly as a living language from about the 9th century B.C.E. to the present. For much of the time, its historical and cultural importance has far surpassed the ethnic and political power of its speakers. Spoken in ancient times in northern Arabia and Syria, Aramaic also soon conquered, linguistically and ethnically, all of Mesopotamia. It achieved the status of an official language for communication within the far-flung Achaemenid empire and replaced other languages in the Fertile Crescent. By virtue of its official status, it infiltrated the Iranian languages in their written forms and survived there in remnants often called ideograms (logograms, heterograms), that is, Aramaic words written but replaced in reading by their Persian equivalents. Official Aramaic is most amply documented by numerous Aramaic papyri and ostraca and some writings on leather found in Egypt. The early literary production in Aramaic has left a few remnants, the most accessible being the fragments of the Aramaic version of the Ahiqar story. The use of Aramaic—in the past often wrongly called Chaldaean/Kasdean—in some portions of the Hebrew Bible in the books of Ezra and Daniel has given it a special place in western civilization. Original Aramaic texts of biblical Apocrypha as well as secular documents have been discovered among the Dead Sea material. Much of this Aramaic literature is, however, preserved only in translation. In the case of the New Testament, this situation has given rise to much speculation about possible Aramaic originals.

In later antiquity, the flourishing of Aramaic in the pre-Christian Near East was succeeded by its complete linguistic dominance throughout the region, resulting in a vast literature in a number of dialects. As the hold of Official Aramaic had been diminishing slowly but steadily in the preceding centuries, local dialects were able to establish themselves and become written languages in their own right, thus initiating another glorious period of Aramaic history that arguably surpassed that of Official Aramaic times in intellectual productivity as well as lasting influence on world civilization. When in the 7th century the religious and political victory of Islam ensured the superiority of Arabic, Aramaic struggled valiantly, and in many ways successfully, to remain alive.

The Christianization of the Near East gave pride of place among Arabic dialects to that of Edessa (Orhāy [related to Osrhoëne], Arabic ar-Ruhā, Turkish Urfa), known as Syriac. It spread widely and came to dominate the region. Its origin in northern Mesopotamia allies Syriac with the Eastern Aramaic dialects. Among other dialects of this Eastern group, Mandaic, the language of the Mandaeans, the only bona fide present survivors of ancient Gnosticism, produced a highly poetic and aesthetically haunting religious literature. The original language of the Manichaeans also was no doubt an Eastern Aramaic dialect. Inscriptions found in recent years in Hatra, the ancient Ashshur, offer some glimpses of an earlier stage of pagan Eastern Aramaic. The dialect originally used by the Sabian Gnostics of Harran, whose literature is now lost, possibly was of a similar character. The Jews of Mesopotamia employed an Aramaic dialect quite close to Mandaic in their religious discussions, which most notably resulted in the creation of the Babylonian Talmud.

Jews throughout the Near East had experienced a long process of restricting the use of their Hebrew language in favor of Aramaic. This made it necessary for them to explain Holy Scripture in Aramaic for the common people and also to employ the language for scholarly discussions and for the homiletic and didactic exposition of biblical text in the midrash literature. Among the Bible translations known as Targums, the so-called Targum Onkelos became most prominent; its conservative Aramaic hints at some kind of original or secondary Eastern Aramaic affiliation. Other more interpretative translations, such as the Targum Yerushalmi/Neofitti, are true representatives of Western Aramaic, as is the Jerusalem Talmud. In later centuries, the Jews made artificial use of Aramaic as their second holy language in important literary products such as the Zohar of the Kabbala.

The Samaritans employed their Western Aramaic dialect for the translation of the Pentateuch as well as works of their own composition, outstanding among them the poetic midrash *Memar Marqa*. They also developed their own quite peculiar tradition of Aramaic pronunciation. Christians in the western region used Syriac basically unchanged in their literary language, with slight differences in pronunciation. However, some of them also used their Western Aramaic dialect for biblical and religious literature; it is conveniently designated in scholarly works as Christian Palestinian Aramaic. Modern spoken dialects representing Western Christian Aramaic are known from Maʿlūla and neighboring villages in the Anti-Lebanon. Christian and Jewish communities originally from Kurdistan, now mainly displaced and widely scattered all over the world, as well as Christians in the Ṭūr ʿĀbdīn region, have continued Eastern Aramaic speech forms, as have, to a minor degree, some surviving Mandaeans.

The Aramaic script deserves to be singled out for having made a strong impact on civilization throughout much of the world. The earliest documents in Aramaic show an adaptation of the linear alphabet that was developed by the Phoenicians, speakers of a closely related group of Semitic dialects, and passed on to Asia Minor and, ultimately, Europe. That Aramaic script took on many different forms among speakers of the various dialects. A form very close to that used in Official Aramaic became what is now known as the Hebrew alphabet, which in fact is distinct from the genuinely Hebrew script of earlier times that continued in full use among the Samaritans. Aramaic writing also spread eastward to speakers of non-Semitic languages native to Iran. Different forms were developed in Mesopotamia, such as those known from the Hatran inscriptions and the writings of the Mandaeans. In Palmyra, a conservative form of the alphabet was reserved mainly for monumental inscriptions, while its more cursive development was employed throughout the region in places such as Dura-Europus on the Euphrates and Edessa. The neighboring Nabataeans centered in Petra transformed earlier Aramaic writing into a script known mainly from monumental inscriptions but now also shown to have been developed in a cursive form for use on soft writing materials. The Nabataean script is widely acknowledged to have been the starting point for the development of Arabic writing, which gives it wide and lasting importance.

BIBL.: S. A. Kaufman, ed., *A Comprehensive Aramaic Lexicon*, forthcoming.   F.R.

Architecture

Originally shaped by the monuments of the earlier Roman empire, the profile of late antique architecture throughout the Mediterranean world gradually evolved in the direction of a strident eclecticism as it reflected changes in the fabric of town and country life. With its roots reaching back to Hellenistic and especially Roman early and high imperial sources of inspiration, the architecture of late antiquity became dominated by religious and domestic buildings, as governmental edifices, public baths, and theaters slowly fell into disuse. After the plagues of the 6th and 7th centuries, which reduced the population of Constantinople and Asia Minor, and the subsequent Persian invasions and Arab conquests, new monuments ap-

Interior view of Hagia Sophia, Constantinople.

capital's major boulevard, the Mese. Both oval and rectangular in shape, they were bordered by porticoes and displayed traditional propagandistic triumphal arches, commemorative columns, and honorific statues of members of the imperial household; the Forum Tauri commissioned by the emperor Theodosius I at Constantinople was consciously modeled on Trajan's Forum at Rome. But late antique forums were not enclosed within the high walls that were characteristic of the imperial forums of the old Rome. In time commerce shifted from the forums to colonnaded streets where shops and temporary booths were set up, and the forums were put to different uses. At Philippi in Thrace the 2nd century forum was originally surrounded by low-profile religious, governmental, and commercial edifices. In the 5th and 6th centuries these structures were replaced by tall church buildings that dominated the entire cityscape. This new pattern was followed elsewhere as well.

A major focus of architecture and social and political life in early late antiquity was the hippodrome, or circus, which was used for horse and chariot racing and other events such as the proclamations of emperors, the celebration of triumphs, and the reception of foreign embassies. The hippodrome's attenuated hairpin form, its grandstands, *spina,* gates, and other amenities, had all long before achieved their definitive form. In the new tetrarchic capitals of Antioch, Nicomedia, Thessalonica, Sirmium, Milan, and Trier, an imperial residence rose in proximity to the hippodrome, a juxtaposition followed by the imperial residence that Constantine the Great began at Constantinople. While the hippodrome of Constantinople continued in use until the late Byzantine period, hippodromes elsewhere were abandoned in the 6th and 7th centuries as chariot racing declined as an urban sport.

The bathing establishment continued the earlier imperial custom of providing a major center for leisure and social intercourse. Many older baths were still in use, and new ones arose, though on a reduced scale. Early in the 5th century, Constantinople possessed as many as 9 public and 153 private baths. The monumentality and rigidly symmetrical design of high empire baths were continued in the imperial baths of Trier, the two baths erected by Diocletian and Constantine in Rome, and the bath in Antioch, but the more common neighborhood bath (the *balneum*) was significantly smaller and far more informally arranged.

peared on a reduced scale and with less frequency. Cities and towns diminished in size or were abandoned for strongly fortified hilltops. The big monuments of days past became towering ruins for all to behold and were subject to quarrying for building materials.

At first the earlier urban pattern was maintained. Urban centers were usually laid out irregularly, following the local terrain, but some followed orthogonal plans. Provisions for the water supply and for burial adhered to earlier practice. Archaeological excavations have revealed that nearly the entire repertory of building types of the early empire deemed necessary for civilized life appeared in early late antiquity: colonnaded streets; the agora, or forum; governmental buildings; the hippodrome, or circus; theaters, or odeons; baths with gymnasiums; cisterns; warehouses; and the residences and apartment buildings of the rich and poor. Slums must have existed, but they await the spade.

The forum of older cities continued to function as a major center of public life at the start of late antiquity. At Constantinople, new forums, ultimately seven in number, were strung out at intervals along the new

At the end of the 4th century a Christian woman named Scholastikia financed the remodeling of a bath at Ephesus that included (it is believed) a brothel on its upper floor. It is no surprise, then, that the church, regarding public baths as dens of immorality, condemned frequent visits to them by clergy and issued regulations prohibiting mixed bathing. Nevertheless bishops rebuilt baths in Gerasa and Gaza in the 5th and 6th centuries, respectively. After the 6th century large public baths fell into disuse because of population declines and the expense involved in their maintenance. Some were converted to different functions.

In late antiquity the most ubiquitous buildings were dwellings, and they took two forms: the substantial private residence *(domus)* and the apartment house *(insula)*. In large urban centers the vast majority of the population lived in *insulae*. At Rome in the mid-4th century there were 46,602 *insulae* and 1,797 *domus;* seventy-five years later Constantinople possessed 4,388 *domus*. In a metropolis, apartment buildings might attain a height of five stories, and they consisted of modest rectangular rooms. Along the colonnaded streets of late antique cities and towns (e.g., at Sardis) small merchants or their representatives might live in their shops or in the rooms overhead, while affluent citizens sometimes dwelt in one- or two-story town mansions that occupied an entire *insula*. At Ephesus the precipitous slope of the northern side of the Street of the Kuretes required the construction of artificial terraces upon which rose town houses covering up to 10,000 square feet; these were remodeled several times between the 1st century and the seventh, when a devastating earthquake struck. Impoverished freedmen and slaves occupied the hovels in the vaulted basements of these town houses. Deriving ultimately from the Hellenistic peristyle house, the *domus* was centered on a peristyle court around which were grouped rooms forming the outer walls of the house. It might feature a reception room for clients and visitors, a *triclinium* for dining, bedrooms, a bath, kitchen, latrines, plumbing and heating systems, and storage rooms, as well as mosaic pavements and painted walls. Near the end of late antiquity it also would sometimes include a private family chapel. Grand mansions and even palaces of the aristocracy and high-ranking government officials are recorded at Constantinople, Antioch, Stobi, and elsewhere, and they were even more imaginatively laid out and lavishly appointed.

The wall emerged as a hallmark of architecture in late antiquity, and it did so in two different ways. The economic and political crisis of the 3rd century led to the enclosing of cities, towns, military outposts and forts, farmhouses, villas, and country monasteries with massive walls for defense against attack by barbarians. Under the threat of invasion, the emperor Aurelian provided the city of Rome with new walls in 271. The Aurelian ramparts were not only tall and massive but also marked by numerous towers and daunting gateways. Their design was to be repeated elsewhere, including in the early Islamic world. The Constantinian land-wall of Constantinople was displaced by Theodosius II in 413 with new land-walls on virgin soil—a triple rampart with a moat some four miles long. Today the ruins of the Theodosian land-walls remain one of the truly memorable sights from the late antique world. By contrast, at Philippi in Thrace and other sites, circuit walls were rebuilt on earlier foundations. Towered ramparts lent a new and sharper profile to the urban periphery than had existed in the earlier empire, and they were accompanied by new political and social systems of urban control.

Within cities and towns individual buildings, secular and ecclesiastical alike, attained greater height than was common in the architecture of the earlier empire. Unlike fortifications, these structures give witness to a process of skeletalization through the inclusion of generous numbers of large, round-arched windows, sometimes arranged in superposed rows (e.g., the audience hall of Constantine the Great at Trier, Hagia Sophia at Constantinople). As a consequence, the interiors of buildings were brilliantly illuminated for the first time since Minoan architecture. This light fused with the color of the interior decoration—marble columns and ornately carved capitals, marble revetments, painted stucco moldings, mosaics, frescoes—and thereby dematerialized the mass of these edifices.

Reused building materials, *spolia,* from abandoned pagan temples and empty public buildings appeared with frequency in late antique edifices and imparted an aesthetic new in the history of ancient architecture. Sometimes the *spolia* were adopted unconsciously, and sometimes they were chosen deliberately as status symbols of a venerable architectural heritage. In either case these monuments lacked the classical quality of concinnity. Likewise the arcade: arches supported on freestanding columns. Although the arcade appeared as early as the 1st century B.C.E., it was rare compared with trabeation, which predominated in classical buildings. In late antiquity the interior arcade triumphs.

What especially distinguishes the late antique from earlier Roman architecture are the buildings constructed for the newly enfranchised Christian church. Public church buildings began to appear with the reign of Constantine the Great and proliferated in the 5th and 6th centuries; the number of the new foundations began to fall off dramatically in the 7th century. In cities and towns these churches were sometimes accompanied by clerical residences, baptisteries, and structures for the care of virgins, children, and the poor, creating conspicuous ecclesiastical centers reflecting the ever increasing wealth and power of the church. In isolated localities pilgrimage sites sprang up that featured churches, monasteries, baptisteries, vast hostels, and other amenities catering to heavy pilgrim traffic (e.g., Qal'at Sem'an in northern Syria). The most innovative aspects of architectural planning in late antiquity are found in church buildings, especially central-plan buildings (cruciform, polygonal, quatrefoil, and the like). By far the most prevalent type was the aisled basilica, which, like all the public buildings of the period, took as its model the civil basilica introduced in the Roman Republic. Likewise the late antique synagogue adopted the basilica form. The most celebrated of all late antique buildings, Justinian's Hagia Sophia in Constantinople, is an aisled basilica, and it was constructed with techniques rooted in earlier Roman practice in Asia Minor. Yet the Hagia Sophia, the cathedral of the capital and the patriarchal church, exhibits the most innovative and daring planning and execution in all of late antiquity, proving that architects of the period were capable of achieving originality and greatness within the framework of a well-established building type.

BIBL.: Richard Krautheimer, *Early Christian and Byzantine Architecture*, 4th ed. rev. (New Haven, 1986), 39–330. Cyril Mango, *Byzantine Architecture* (New York, 1985), 9–107. John Bryan Ward-Perkins, *Roman Imperial Architecture* (New Haven, 1981), 415–466.   W.E.K.

Aristocracy

Before ca. 250 C.E., elite status in the Roman empire had three distinct, if not entirely separate, manifestations: the senators of Rome, high bureaucratic functionaries who achieved equestrian status and local landowners, who were organized into largely self-governing town councils. This third category was by far the largest. The Senate of Rome consisted of a few hundred families, and there were only 182 equestrian bureaucrats in office in 249 C.E.

In the 4th century, the aristocratic boundaries were redrawn. By 367, senatorial status had become the ultimate reward for a host of imperial servants, both civilian and military. At the same time, the bureaucracy increased dramatically in size. By ca. 400, it included at least three thousand very good jobs in each half of the empire (defined as those positions that brought the holder senatorial status, at least upon retirement). There was a total of at least twenty-three thousand jobs overall.

This revolution profoundly affected the lives of local elites. At the same time that new opportunities opened up in the bureaucracy, the cities were becoming subject to increasingly centralized financial regulation. Service in the bureaucracy thus became more attractive to urban elites, because money and status were increasingly controlled from the imperial center. A few well-known cases aside, bureaucratic recruitment took place among those previously constituting the local elites. Even some of the nonsenatorial jobs were attractive to such individuals.

Throughout the 4th century the length of bureaucratic service tended to decline and a new, cyclical career pattern evolved. Landowners would spend part of their life in the central bureaucracy and then return home, forming a new provincial elite of retired former bureaucrats (the *honorati*) who were given key rights and functions, such as setting their neighbors' tax rates. An intense literary education conducted by a grammarian (in Latin or Greek, as appropriate), lasting up to ten years and paid for privately, remained the key marker of elite status, but there was some change in higher education. Instead of further Greek studies with rhetors such as Libanius—suited to an old-style career in the cities—elite offspring gravitated to Latin, law, and other studies they thought would better secure their bureaucratic advancement.

Patterns of political dissent suggest, however, that some parts of the empire, such as Britain, were dominated by local elites excluded from the vast patronage system of the late Roman bureaucracy. Likewise, across the frontier, another type of aristocracy dominated non-Roman, largely Germanic Europe. Fourth-century Germanic groups near the frontiers were dominated by kings and great men, some of the rulers being subsidized by Roman diplomatic payments. The extent to which a defined nobility had evolved among these groups is questionable, and perhaps it varied. Social stratification among Germanic groups clearly increased in the first four centuries C.E. Some of the groups invading the Roman empire after ca. 375 were dominated by an elite of freemen that was still too large and undifferentiated to be called a nobility. Among the Goths, the freeman elite amounted to between one-fifth and one-half of all adult males. Among the Burgundians, by contrast, a high-status group within the freeman class is already identified in laws of ca. 500 C.E. Germanic elites shared with Roman aristocrats the characteristic of landholding, but otherwise lifestyles were completely different. Germanic (and other non-Roman) elites formed warrior aristocracies among whom reading and writing played little, if any, role.

The later 4th and the 5th century brought these two aristocracies together. By ca. 600, groups of intruders had established new kingdoms on former Roman soil all the way from Italy to Britain. At one end of the spectrum of possible patterns of interaction lay Britain. There, considerable conflict between indigenous and invading elites (in a variety of combinations) destroyed much of the fabric of Roman life. In Ostrogothic Italy, although not Lombardy, by contrast, Roman landowners took a largely neutral stance as the kingdom was created, and then accommodated themselves to the new regime. Somewhere in between lay the Frankish and Visigothic kingdoms in Gaul and Spain, where Roman landowners chose a variety of options between armed resistance and passive accommodation as the new political order evolved.

By ca. 700, a unified Catholic aristocracy had emerged within all these kingdoms. Vestigial memories of the different traditions of the two contributing parties (Roman and non-Roman) may have remained, but a new set of norms now shaped the behavior of all western European aristocrats. The Christianity and literacy of this new elite must be given due weight. Its offspring did not spend a decade with the grammarian, and did not, by and large, actively compose literature, but royal authors are known, and post-Roman kings and aristocrats had a healthy respect for Roman learning and also needed to read Latin to be good Christians.

The descendants of Frankish, Gothic, and other non-Roman aristocrats thus acquired Christianity and some Latin culture. Likewise, established processes of social transformation continued, and a more defined nobility evolved among those newly established on Roman soil. At the same time, bureaucratic careers declined drastically in number and importance, and military service was required of all landowners in the new kingdoms. Surviving Roman families are often held to have retreated into episcopal office, but this is mistaken. Everywhere from Britain to Byzantine Italy, landowners swapped bureaucracy for the battlefield. Indeed, a wealthy bishopric (of which there were not a large number) became a final prize sought by many, whether Roman or non-Roman in origin, after an otherwise secular career, and bishops were essentially appointed by kings. In this way the royal courts of post-Roman Europe generated a new elite. Militarized, and landowning, it was also Christian and, to some extent, literate. Active, compositional literacy in classical Latin no longer led directly to a bureaucratic career, however, so the classical grammarians quickly went out of business. Classical Latin would be restored as the standard language of the educated class with the Carolingian Renaissance, but active lay literacy would not again become a norm until after the year 1200.

BIBL.: P. J. Heather, "New Men for New Constantines: Creating an Imperial Elite in the Eastern Mediterranean," in P. Magdalino, ed., *New Constantines* (London, 1994). A. K. Bowman and G. Woolf, eds., *Literacy and Power in the Ancient World* (Cambridge, Eng., 1994). J. F. Matthews, *Western Aristocracies and Imperial Court AD 364–425* (Oxford, 1975). B. Näf, *Senatorisches Standesbewusstsein in spätrömischer Zeit* (Fribourg-en-Suisse, 1995). P.H.

Arles

Roman Arles was a *colonia* founded by Tiberius. In the ensuing years it became a city of some significance, with numerous monumental buildings. Under the tetrarchy, it was still no more than a *civitas,* capital of the province of Viennensis, but it had a significant position within the empire, housing a monetary atelier from 313 and providing a residence for the emperor on a number of occasions in the 4th and 5th centuries. Further, perhaps as early as 407 and certainly by 418, the seat of the pretorian prefect of the Gauls was moved from Trier to Arles, reflecting the disasters that had hit the former city.

The distinction between the relatively low position of Arles in provincial organization and its significance within the empire led to tensions, especially between Arles and the metropolitan city of Vienne. These tensions were not purely secular, since the diocese of Arles, echoing provincial organization, was subordinate to that of Vienne. There was a long-running conflict between the bishops of Arles and Vienne over their respective status; this was originally legislated by the Council of Turin (398) and only concluded in 499–500, when Pope Symmachus decreed that Arles should be the metropolitan see for all of Viennensis except for Vienne and four other dioceses.

Arles was represented in this conflict by a series of notable bishops: in particular, Hilary, Leontius, and, finally, Caesarius. The last episcopate, however, was more notable for the bishop's monastic interests than for his preaching: his sermons give a fine picture of the religious life of the city in the opening decades of the 6th century. Caesarius's *Vita* also provides crucial evidence for the city under Visigothic, Ostrogothic, and Frankish rule.

BIBL.: W. E. Klingshirn, *Caesarius of Arles: The Making of a Christian Community in Late Antique Gaul* (Cambridge, 1994). *Topographie chrétienne des cités de la Gaule des origines au milieu du VIII siècle*, ed. N. Gauthier and J.-Ch. Picard, vol. 3: *Provinces ecclésiastiques de Vienne et d'Arles* (Paris, 1986). I.W.

Armaments

However much they differ from earlier Roman forces, late antique armaments are best understood as slowly evolving Roman armies. The old legions and *auxilia* (*alae* and cohorts), while much reduced in strength, still defended the imperial frontiers in late antiquity. But they shared this duty with new-style units forged in the great crisis of 230 to 280 and in the civil wars that ensued until Constantine's victory over Licinius in 324. One contender after another raised strong forces that afterward had to be strung out along the frontiers. (For well-trained troops, even if they posed a loyalty risk, were too precious to disband.) From such repeated upheavals came the many units of Equites Dalmatae, Mauri, Stablesiani, Promoti, Sagittarii, and Scutarii that throng the *Notitia Dignitatum* lists of the frontier armies. Whether on the frontier or in the administrative entourage, they are part of the provincial forces commanded by dukes.

New in late antiquity were standing field armies. Earlier Roman emperors had only the praetorian guard and the horse guard of the Equites Singulares Augusti for a standing field army, but from Gallienus onward emperors kept large cavalry strike forces at the ready in strategic provinces. These were the *vexillationes comitatenses*. Their elite members, largely recruited from among foreign forces, were the *vexillationes palatinae,* first known in the mid-4th century.

The new field army also included infantry in two classes of units, palatine and comitatensian. Rome's most reliable troops had been the praetorians; hence the best palatine legions, such as the Lanciarii, Ioviani, and Herculiani, derived from praetorian field detachments. Further palatine legions derived from frontier legions that since the mid-3rd century had maintained permanent detachments in the emperors' expeditionary armies, like the Pannoniciani and Moesiaci stationed, for example, at Aquileia. Other legionary detachments, called up for a campaign but afterward not sent back, became the lower-ranking comitatensian legions.

For the first time, infantry *auxilia* belonged to the elite troops. Maximianus (285–310) recruited the earliest palatine *auxilia* from tribes across the Rhine. During the 4th century they grew to become the largest class of units, amounting to half the field army.

In the *Notitia dignitatum,* written around 400 C.E., the five classes of troops are ranked thus: *vexillationes palatinae, vexillationes comitatenses, legiones palatinae, auxilia palatina, legiones comitatenses.* Tellingly, the two highest ranking categories are cavalry. While in the early empire, infantry units (legions) always outranked cavalry units, in late antiquity cavalry units *(vexillationes)* outranked infantry. Just as striking is the fact that *auxilia* took precedence over (comitatensian) legions.

In the 4th century, field army units stood, on average, 500 strong. The 900 units of the *Notitia Dignitatum* could thus amount to 450,000 troops, as against 300,000 men of the 1st century C.E. In the 6th century Agathias (5.7) gives the strength of the army on paper as 645,000, yet he adds in the same breath that Justinian kept barely 150,000 men under arms, a figure so small it is hard to believe.

Constantine and his co-emperors also raised a new type of guard, the *scholae palatinae,* all horsemen. Under Theodosius, the eastern *magister officiorum* commanded seven such *scholae,* the western *magister* five, for a grand total of 6,000 horse guards. By contrast, in the 3rd century the guard had consisted of 15,000 praetorians, mostly foot, and 2,000 *Equites Singulares* horse guards. Thus the horse guard had tripled while the foot soldiers disappeared from the guard altogether: the cavalry became the "queen of the battlefields." The *scholae palatinae* served as shock troops for the 4th-century army. They won the Battle at the Milvian Bridge in 311, but in 378 their untimely attack turned Adrianople into a reckless rout. During the 5th century the guard lost its role as a strike force. Since the emperors no longer took the field, the *scholae* became mere palace guards within the garrison of Byzantium.

The rise of the cavalry was not yet complete in the 4th century. Emperor Julian (*Orat.* 2.63c–d) said of the Sassanian armament besetting Nisibis in 350, "First of all came horsemen who wore cuirasses, then archers, another overwhelming throng of horsemen. Finding infantry useless in war, [the Persians] think little of it. Nor do they need it, for their whole land is flat and bare. Our state, on the other hand, facing all kinds of foes, yet winning through by wisdom and good luck, has rightly been fitted to every kind of weapon and to other equipment." There is some truth in Julian's statement: Nisibis, under Constantius II, was saved by infantry, and Julian himself fought the battle of Strasburg where the vaunted cataphracts gave ground to the Alamanni.

On a wider view, though, the shape of the land mattered not so much. The driving forces for the change from foot to horse were the irresistible fighting techniques invented on the Eurasian steppe. They reached Rome mainly via Germans and Persians: already in the 2nd century Quadi were training Roman cavalrymen (Arrian, *Tact.* 44) in handling the long spear during intricate wheelings, a skill they had learned from their Sarmatian neighbors. Persia, close to the steppe horsemen, had excellent archers and mailed horsemen (cataphracts; *clibanarii*). Rome adopted cataphracts but found them not overly useful: strong infantry could stop them; swift cavalry could undo them. Archery gained the upper hand. In the 6th century Procopius proudly praised the versatile horse archer, who overcame the Goths in Italy. While Vegetius's handbook on warfare in the early 5th century deals mainly with infantry and sword or spear fighting, Maurice's treatise in the late 6th century stresses cavalry and archery.

Army units, by the end of the 6th century called by the Gothic term *banda,* tended to become smaller, some 200 strong. Even so, they sought to be self-contained by using several different kinds of weapons.

With the empire on the defense, fortifications mattered now much more than before. Forts, watchtowers, and fortified farms studded the frontier lands; all cities were walled. Even today the walls of Rome, Byzantium, and Amida awe the viewer. Fortifications offered not only refuge to retreating armies but also allowed them to store food and equipment, which often gave imperial troops the edge over their foes.

In the civil war that lasted from Gallienus to Constantine, powerful generals (Aureolus, Probus, Aurelian) led the new cavalry strike forces. They stood next in power to the emperor and often turned usurper, but there were always several generals active at any one time, which helped maintain the status quo. Constantine later appointed single commanders-in-chief but stymied would-be usurpers by splitting the command in two: one over cavalry *(magister equitum),* the other over infantry *(magister militum).* Mostly foreigners, the *magistri militum* dared not reach for supreme power but stayed loyal (or appointed emperors that suited them). In the east, Theodosius divided the command into two court armies and three regional armies.

In a change from the late republic and early empire, in late antiquity Romans, high or low, no longer wanted to enroll in the army. Recruits, forcibly collected like so much tax, often deserted. Foreigners, if well paid, willingly took their place, but the good of the *res publica* meant little to them; they widely oppressed civilians and quickly switched sides. Field army recruits, in the 4th century largely German, from the 5th century onward also came from Isauria or Armenia. In the 7th century, when the field armies had their own lands *(themes),* recruitment became local and was stabilized, in that mainly soldiers' sons joined the elite troops.

In late antiquity, military training grew more formalized. Emperor Maurice, in his *Strategicon,* describes impressive training and planning efforts. Typical for Byzantium, training in this period benefited from handbooks.

Thanks to the empire's rich tax base, mercenaries from warlike nations formed a vital part of the armament. When this tax base shrank, Heraclius settled the army on the land through the allotment of *themes.* In this way the army renewed itself and thus could weather the Avar and Arab invasions.

BIBL.: J.B. Campbell, *The Emperor and the Roman Army, 31 B.C.–A.D. 235* (Oxford, 1984). Alexander Demandt, *Die Spätantike* (Munich, 1989), 255–272. John Haldon, *Byzantine Praetorians* (Bonn, 1984). Ramsay MacMullen, *Soldier and Civilian in the Later Roman Empire* (Cambridge, Mass., 1963). D. Nicole, "Arms of the Umayyad Era," in Y. Lev, ed., *War and Society in the Eastern Mediterranean* (Leiden, 1997), 9–100. M. Speidel, *Riding for Caesar: The Roman Emperors' Horse Guards* (Cambridge, Mass., 1994). M.P.S.

Asceticism

A term deriving from the Greek word *askēsis* (training), asceticism is the practice of a disciplined life in pursuit of a spiritual condition. In late antiquity this discipline was exercised through a physical and mental process of ordering the self in relation to the divine. Physical practices commonly employed involved abstinence from sexual relations, food, and physical comforts; voluntary poverty; control of the passions; and renunciation of worldly power.

As a practice and as a cultural ideal, asceticism was present to greater or lesser degrees in every religious tradition of the Roman empire, pagan, Jewish, Christian, and Manichaean. It was practiced throughout the spectrum of social organization—from households to philosophy schools to utopian and monastic communities to desert caves—by men, women, and children of every social class. Motivations for and types of asceticism varied dramatically across the social and religious spectrum, as did its meanings. Celibacy might indicate a rejection of the body as intrinsically evil, a belief that marriage is a sinful state, a return to the pre-Fall condition, or the virtue of sexual continence. There could

also be contrasting results: ascetic men often renounced worldly power and influence, while women could gain precisely these advantages through a sustained ascetic life. The voluntary poverty of the monastic community brought humility to former aristocrats but security and stability to those who entered from the lower classes.

The Graeco-Roman schools of philosophy had cultivated a physically disciplined way of life that would inculcate certain habits, leading to a life of virtue. In middle Platonism and Neoplatonism, asceticism was specifically identified with divine contemplation. Benign neglect of the body and detachment from the world were exemplified by Plotinus, Porphyry, and Iamblichus as necessary for the soul's ascent to the divine.

Rabbinic sources advocated disciplined practices to sustain a distinct religious identity. Self-denial that exceeded the requirements of biblical law could be lauded under certain conditions (although almost never for women), especially in association with the sages or to uphold an ideal of religious perfection, as in discussions about the Nazirite (a rhetorical rather than historical presence after the destruction of the Temple in 70 C.E.). But rabbinic writers were hostile to the Christian ideal of lifelong ascetic renunciation and saw it as the violation of, rather than supererogatory devotion to, divine will.

For Marcionites, Manichaeans, certain Gnostic and Encratite groups, the issue was the actual evil at work in and through the physical realm. "Mainstream" Christians, like the philosophers and rabbinic sages, rejected this motivation, consistently upholding the intrinsic worth of the created order—even in its fallen condition. Pre-Nicene Christian texts had advocated moderate asceticism for all believers as the highest Christian ideal, with justifications blending philosophical dispositions (most notably in Clement of Alexandria) with eschatological hope. Such advocacy was heightened by Origen in the 3rd century with the achievement of an ascetic exegetical tradition through which to interpret biblical texts.

The rise of monasticism over the course of the 4th century provided tremendous impetus for the ascetic movement. St. Antony of Egypt was immortalized as one who made "the desert a city" (*Vita* 14). Yet one need only read the homilies of John Chrysostom or Ambrose of Milan to hear the ecclesiastical exhortation that the city should become a monastery. Prayer, fasting, celibacy (or chastity in marriage after the birth of one's heir), vigils, almsgiving, and avoidance of bodily comforts were preached no less from the pulpit than from the monastery gate or the hermit's cave. Gregory of Nazianzus praised the ascetic devotion of his sister Gorgonia—faithful wife, mother of five, mistress of a sizable household—in the same terms his friend Gregory of Nyssa used for his sister Macrina, who had declared her ascetic vows at age twelve, converted her family to the ascetic life, and founded a monastic community for men and women. The rhetoric of late antique Christian literature advocated the Christian life, wherever located and in whatever circumstances, as necessarily ascetic.

Because the surviving literature is heavily dominated by the ecclesiastical and monastic elite, it is difficult to measure the social reality behind the rhetoric. However, between the 4th and 7th centuries there was a marked drop in birth rates as well as a gradual shift in economic structuring, away from the civic household as the basic unit through which money circulated to the monastery as the major location for tax collection, land management, and welfare distribution. Inherent in the ascetic impulse, the rejection of the old social order was also a move to create a new order, a new human family, a new city.

Christian asceticism became distinctive also for the severity of its practices. The words of the Egyptian monk Dorotheus represent a not uncommon view: "My body kills me; I will kill it" (Palladius, *Hist.Laus.* 2). Pagan and Jewish critics found this aggravation of asceticism alarming. Yet Christians understood asceticism (moderate or severe) through a theological perspective that rendered even the most negative practices positive. The life of faith required participation in the cosmological battle between God and Satan. Christians fought demons in their bodies just as Christ had fought Satan in the wilderness. Prayer was described as spiritual combat as well as contemplation. Eschatological expectations were sustained by the view that asceticism also enacted a realized eschatology. The life of ceaseless prayer was the attainment of the angelic life: a life without bodily needs, without marriage, a life of continual liturgy.

Only occasionally was Christian asceticism simply a rejection of the body. More commonly it meant the forging of a new body, the body of the new Adam. Abba Alonius said, "If I had not destroyed myself completely, I should not have been able to rebuild and shape myself again" (*Apoph.patr.*, alph. coll., Alonius, 2). Asceticism was the remaking of the human person in the image of its maker. The curse of the Fall was undone: in death, Macrina's mortal body glowed with the radiance of incorruptibility (Gregory of Nyssa, *Vita S. Macr.*, 32.8–12).

BIBL.: Peter Brown, *The Body and Society: Men, Women, and Sexual Renunciation in Early Christianity* (New York, 1988). Susanna Elm, *"Virgins of God": The Making of Asceticism in Late Antiquity* (Oxford, 1994). Vincent L. Wimbush and Richard Valantasis, eds., *Asceticism* (New York, 1995).

S.A.H.

Astrology

Astrology in late antiquity was the product of an earlier confluence of three intellectual traditions: Chaldaean or Babylonian belief in the dominion of planets and stars (probably resulting in the zodiac) combined with Egyptian speculation on the nature and influence of time and Greek astronomy and mathematics. Indeed, astrology and astronomy were often regarded as a single discipline. Well-known Greek astronomers whose ideas decisively influenced astrology include Hipparchus (2nd century B.C.E.) and Claudius Ptolemaeus, or Ptolemy (2nd century C.E.). Later western astrologers included Firmicus Maternus (4th century), author of *Mathēseōs libri VIII*.

From Mesopotamia and Egypt, astrology entered Iran and reached India by the 2nd century B.C.E. The *Syntaxis mathematikē* or *Almagest* of Ptolemy and astrological treatises by Dorotheus of Sidon were copied into Pahlavi during the 3rd and 4th centuries. Hellenistic scholars who relocated to Sassanian Iran in the 6th century also translated astrological and astronomical texts from Greek into Pahlavi. Around the same time, an Indian named Varahamihira compiled a Sanskrit corpus—the *Panchasiddhantika*—of available astrological knowledge from Graeco-Roman, Egyptian, Indian, and possibly Iranian sources. Indian refinements were, in turn, picked up by Iranians and recombined with Hellenistic and Mesopotamian material—for example, the Sassanians attempted to reconcile their own astronomical table, or *zij*, with those of the Indians and Greeks. The resulting astrological tradition affected Zoroastrian beliefs—passages in the *Bundahisn* and the *Wizidagiha* of Zadspram (9th century) demonstrate that foreign celestial concepts were assimilated into Magian exegesis. Iranian astrological lore survived the Arab Muslim invasion, was preserved in Umayyad and Abbasid libraries, was used by scholars like Abu Maʿshar al-Balkhi, or Albumasar (ca. late 8th to late 9th century) in his Arabic *Zij al-ḥazarāt*. Ptolemy's calculations were revised after the introduction of trigonometry, but his methods would be accepted as standard. These Arabic manuals eventually formed the basis of medieval European astrological suppositions and astronomical calculations.

Astrological practices fell into broad categories: one being particular to individuals, for predicting the course of their life based on the position of astral bodies at the time of birth; a second providing auspicious times for important activities; a third yielding responses to specific queries; a fourth employing celestial guidelines for the practice of medicine; and a fifth relating to events supposedly destined to reshape the course of regions or cultures. Briefly, the astrological system consists of a zodiac with twelve constellations: Aries (Ram), Taurus (Bull), Gemini (Twins), Cancer (Crab), Leo (Lion), Virgo (Virgin), Libra (Scales), Scorpio (Scorpion), Sagittarius (Archer), Capricorn (Goat), Aquarius (Water-carrier), and Pisces (Fish), in order of their ascent. These constellations are classified according to gender, attribute, and appearance: Taurus,

Virgo, and Capricorn are earth signs; Gemini, Libra, and Aquarius are air ones; Aries, Leo, and Sagittarius are fire ones; and Cancer, Scorpio, and Pisces are water signs. Each constellation took up 30 degrees along the ecliptic, with further subdivision into three decans. The zodiac was believed to revolve through a series of eight or, more commonly, twelve houses or mansions, representing life, fortune, siblings, parents, offspring, health, marriage, death, travel, fame, friends, and foes (Indians, followed by Iranians, used twenty-seven mansions). Seven "planets," the Moon, Mercury, Venus, the Sun, Mars, Jupiter, and Saturn, were viewed as rotating through these constellations and mansions in geocentric orbits. Specific horoscopes showing the relative positions of planets and signs of the zodiac were produced, in which the combinations of constellations, mansions, and planets, and the qualities attributed to them, provided many possible astrological predictions. Until the advent of modern science, astrology and astral lore exerted a powerful influence on people, individually and collectively. Rulers and other nobles usually hired court astrologers to chart the sky and prescribe propitious times for action or suggest favorable courses to take. Commoners frequently consulted astrologers before making life-altering decisions.

BIBL.: Hans G. Gundel, *Astrologumena: Die astrologische Literatur in der Antike und ihre Geschichte,* Sudhoffs Archive 6 (Wiesbaden, 1966). W. Hübner, "Das Horoskop der Christen," *Vigiliae christianae* 29 (1984): 120–157. David A. King, "Astronomy," and David Pingree, "Astrology," in *The Cambridge History of Arabic Literature: Religion, Learning, and Science in the 'Abbasid Period,* ed. M. J. L. Young, J. D. Latham, and R. B. Serjeant (Cambridge, Eng., 1990), 274–289, 290–300. David N. MacKenzie, "Zoroastrian Astrology in the Bundahishn," *Bulletin of the School of Oriental and African Studies* (London) 27 (1964): 511–529. U. Riedinger, *Der Heilige Schrift im Kampf der griechische Kirche gegen die Astrologie* (Innsbruck, 1956). J.K.C.

Astronomy

Astronomy in late antiquity was concerned mainly with the apparent motions of the sun, the moon, and the five planets visible to the naked eye. Its ancestry can be traced to the Babylonians of the 1st millennium B.C.E., who discovered the periodic nature of the phenomena of the heavenly bodies and learned how to predict them using sophisticated mathematical models based on simple arithmetic. Hellenistic astronomers took over many elements of the Babylonian science and adapted them to a different kind of modeling that decomposed the celestial motions into circular revolutions. This Greek tradition reached its acme in the mid-2nd century with Claudius Ptolemy. Three of Ptolemy's writings became the nuclei around which subsequent astronomy crystallized: the *Mathematical Syntaxis* (later diffused under the Arabic-Greek title *Almagest,*

or "Greatest") demonstrated how to accommodate geometrical models of planetary motion to specific observations, and how to translate these models into tables for predicting the phenomena; the *Handy Tables* made these predictive methods accessible in a convenient format, especially for the astrologer; and the *Planetary Hypotheses* refined the models into a coherent geocentric cosmological system of nested rotating spheres. These writings were so successful that by the end of the 3rd century, reading the *Almagest* had become the culmination of a mathematical education in Alexandria, and Ptolemy's tables were the preferred tool of astrologers, not only in the intellectual centers of the Roman empire but also in provincial Egyptian towns. Of the ancient societies that learned part of their astronomy directly from the Greeks, only India felt none of Ptolemy's influence.

The astronomical literature in Greek that survives from this time until its twilight in the early 7th century consists mostly of commentaries and scholia on the *Almagest* and *Handy Tables.* The Alexandrian pedagogues Pappus (c. 320) and Theon (c. 360) composed huge works aimed mostly at helping the student through the mathematical arguments; the lost commentary on the *Handy Tables* by Theon's fabled daughter Hypatia was probably similar. The 5th century Neoplatonist Proclus, on the other hand, wrote a lucid nontechnical summary of the *Almagest.* Several of Proclus's associates and pupils showed a lively interest in astronomy; for example, the brothers Heliodorus and Ammonius made a series of observations of the planets about 500 C.E. This line of scholarship, centered in Alexandria and Athens, comes to an end with a voluminous introduction to the *Handy Tables* attributed in the manuscripts to the emperor Heraclius (but likely ghostwritten by Stephanus of Alexandria). Between that time and the end of the 8th century there are few glimmers of astronomical activity in Byzantium. A genuine revival would not come until the 11th century, under the stimulus of contacts with Islamic science.

The Latin west had inherited only a nontechnical, and rather unreliable, body of astronomical lore from Roman times. The surveys of Macrobius, Martianus Capella, and Isidore of Seville are of historical interest for the tidbits of information that they transmit from otherwise poorly attested theories, but the Plinian habit of retailing disjointed facts was not conducive to teaching a coherent astronomical system. A Latin translation of the *Handy Tables* dating from the 530s failed to establish a foothold for computational astronomy and survived to the later Middle Ages only in fragmentary form. The needs of the calendar, including of course the Easter computus, involved only the most elementary knowledge of solar and lunar periods. Computus also accounts for a large component of pre-Islamic Ethiopic astronomy, which is wholly of a basic and practical character. In the works of the 7th century Armenian scholar Ananias of Shirak, one finds a slightly more advanced level of astronomical knowledge influenced by translations of Greek writings.

Syria and Sassanian Persia, however, possessed astronomical traditions that were comparable to that of Byzantium, and indeed were of much historical importance because they remained vigorous during the centuries of the ebb of Greek science. Not coincidentally, astrology was prominent in these societies, and the Greek influence was balanced to varying degrees by teachings filtered through from Sanskrit texts in India. By way of a translation of the *Handy Tables,* and probably also of the *Almagest,* Ptolemy's system was well represented in Syriac in the 7th and 8th centuries. Original astronomical works by Severus Sebokht survive from the middle of the 7th century, of which the best known is a treatise on the astrolabe modeled on a lost text by Theon of Alexandria. The *Almagest* had been accessible in Persia as early as the reign of Shapur I in the mid-3rd century, which is barely a hundred years after it was composed. But the important set of tables entitled the *Zīk-i Shahriyārān,* which was composed in Pahlavi about 450 and revised in the 6th century and again in the 7th, was primarily founded, so far as we can tell from later Arabic references, on Indian texts.

It was of course the Islamic world that assumed the central role of integrating and rediffusing the various streams of astronomy that existed in late antiquity, ultimately awarding primacy to the legacy of Ptolemy, and then introducing the first significant empirical corrections to Ptolemy's parameters and the first serious criticisms of his models since his own time. Most of these developments came after the late antique period. The first Arabic astronomical tables, however, were compiled in the first half of the 8th century in Sind, based chiefly on Sanskrit models. Astrological computations and tables were in use under the early Abbasids, based at first on Persian and subsequently on Indian originals. Between 771 and 790 Muḥammad ibn Ibrāhīm al-Fazārī and Yaʾqub ibn Ṭāriq produced an influential oeuvre merging Indian, Persian, and a few Ptolemaic elements. The confrontation of these methods with the authentic texts of Ptolemy, first translated into Arabic a few years later under Hārūn al-Rashīd, was a stimulus to the revival of observational astronomy in Baghdad and Damascus.

BIBL.: O. Neugebauer, *A History of Ancient Mathematical Astronomy* (New York, 1975). S. C. McCluske, "Gregory of Tours, Monastic Timekeeping, and Early Christian Attitudes to Astronomy," *Isis* 81 (1990): 9–22. D. Pingree, "The Greek Influence on Early Islamic Mathematical Astronomy," *Journal of the American Oriental Society* 93 (1973): 32–43. J. P. Mahé, "Quadrivium et cursus d'études au VIIe siècle en Arménie," *Travaux et Mémoires* 10 (1987): 159–206.   A.J.

Athanasius

Born ca. 298 into an Alexandrian family of modest means, Athanasius was noticed as a boy by Alexander, who became bishop of Alexandria ca. 313 and groomed him as his successor. Athanasius attended the Council of Nicaea in 325 as a deacon and was consecrated bishop of Alexandria after a disputed election on 8 June 328. He was deposed by councils of eastern bishops meeting outside Egypt on at least five occasions (in 335, 338, 339, 349, and 351) for tyrannical behavior as bishop, and he spent many years in exile in the west (335–337 and 339–346) or in flight in rural Egypt (most of the years 356–363).

The details of Athanasius's stormy episcopal career can be reconstructed only with difficulty, since his successive defenses of his conduct, which have usually been taken at face value by ecclesiastical historians ancient and modern, conceal or misrepresent many salient facts. The vicissitudes of his career, however, reflect the important fact that Athanasius's political power within Egypt was such that the emperors Constantius and Valens were compelled to conciliate him when their own position was challenged by usurpers in 350–351 and 365–366. Athanasius consistently identified his cause with that of imperiled orthodoxy, a claim that received validation only when the status of the creed of the Council of Nicaea as the sole touchstone of orthodoxy came under increasing challenge in the east in the 340s. It may have been Athanasius himself who brought the creed of 325 to the center of theological debate in the 350s by encouraging Liberius, the bishop of Rome, and other western bishops to claim it as justification for their refusal to accept later eastern attempts to define the relationship between God the Father and God the Son.

From a historical point of view, Athanasius's most important writings are, first, the pair of apologies *Contra gentes* and *De incarnatione,* which he probably wrote ca. 326 to establish his theological credentials; second, three *Orations against the Arians* composed later, probably in Rome ca. 340; third, a series of works composed for use in his political and theological struggles that were collected into a corpus perhaps even during his lifetime; and fourth, the pastoral letters he wrote for each Easter from 329 to 373: a Syriac translation preserves the first half of what appears to be a conflation of two scholarly collected editions made in Alexandria and Thmuis, shortly after his death.

Athanasius's precise theological significance is hard to evaluate for two principal reasons. His letters and pastoral and homiletic works survive only haphazardly, often in fragments or in Coptic and Syriac translations; thus it must be suspected that later generations did not wish to preserve original and speculative ideas that they considered improper for a sober champion of orthodoxy. And most modern expositions of the theology of Athanasius are based in large part on the *Life of Antony,* whose attribution to Athanasius is highly doubtful. Although Athanasius was universally accepted as its author from 380 to 1877, the vocabulary and some basic ideas and assumptions in the *Life* differ greatly from his undoubtedly genuine works.

BIBL.: M. Geerard, *Clavis patrum graecorum,* vol. 2 (Turnhout, Belg., 1974), 12–36, nos. 2090–2170. T. D. Barnes, *Athanasius and Constantius: Theology and Politics in the Constantinian Empire* (Cambridge, Mass., 1993). A. Martin, *Athanase d'Alexandrie et l'église d'Égypte au IVe siècle (328–373),* Bibliothèque des écoles françaises d'Athènes et de Rome 216 (Rome, 1996).   T.D.B.

Athens

In 267 C.E., a year that has often been considered a decisive moment in the history of the decline and fall of Athens, a Germanic tribe from the Black Sea area, the Heruli, sacked the city. Soon after, a wall was constructed, using material from old ruined buildings, to protect only the central parts of the city and the Acropolis. A special commissioner, the *corrector provinciae Achaeae,* was charged by Diocletian with the task of restoring the Library of Hadrian, perhaps because it housed the cadastral archives that were indispensable for effective taxation.

Despite the raid, various cultural activities flourished in late antique Athens after only a brief lapse, and although Neoplatonic philosophy was not very much in fashion there before the beginning of the 5th century, there were active circles of philosophers, or sophists, in Athens in the 4th century. Athenian pottery was soon again well established in the market.

There are very few signs of Christian influence in Athens in the 4th century, if one excepts Bishop Pistus, who represented the Athenian congregation at the Council of Nicaea in 325, and the presence of the Cappadocian church fathers Basil the Great and Gregory of Nazianzus, who were there later in the same century.

Some late literary sources seem to indicate that Alaric and his Visigoths did not sack Athens at all in 395–396 when they invaded Greece. However, recent archaeological discoveries in the Agora excavations, on the Acropolis's south slope, and east of the Acropolis attest Alaric's destruction of the city. The consequences of this raid are reflected in the keen building activity that immediately followed. Athens was rebuilt predominantly as a "pagan" city. Several of her traditional secular buildings, such as the Theater of Dionysus and the Library of Hadrian, were restored once again, the former to serve also as the site for popular assemblies and philosophical lectures, and the latter to continue as the complex where the cadastral archives

were kept. Recent finds south of the Theater of Dionysus precinct would seem to indicate that the last home of the School of Plato may have been situated somewhere in that area. Panathenaic processions were again organized, and new buildings were constructed to supply traditional needs.

Despite the devastations the Athenian way of life continued quite undisturbed until as late as the second half of the 5th century, although some signs of Christian influence became common. A tetraconch, a church of unusual design resembling a quatrefoil, was constructed in the central area of the Library of Hadrian. It probably replaced a shrine for the imperial cult that originally existed somewhere in the library complex. It has been suggested that this tetraconch church was the first cathedral of Athens; according to the most recent studies concerning the Acropolis, the Parthenon did not become a church before the second half of the 6th century.

Another attack was made on Athens by the Vandals toward the end of the 5th century. As a consequence of this sparsely documented raid, the character of the Agora area changed definitively: water mills appeared there and its "industrialization" began.

Apart from some isolated incidents, Christian intolerance seems to have reached Athens as late as toward the end of the 5th century. While the life of an ordinary citizen was not much changed, as no sharp distinctions between pagan and Christian lifestyles were observed, the new attitude seems to have affected the official forms of cult and religious life. The archon, *patricius,* and senator Theagenes, a prominent member of the imperial elite in the 5th century, was a native of Athens and—characteristically enough—claimed to be a descendant of Miltiades and Plato. He was married to Asclepigeneia, the great-granddaughter of the famous Neoplatonist philosopher Plutarchus, who belonged to another prominent Athenian family of theurgists and intellectuals. Perhaps after the raid by the Vandals, Theagenes and his father in law Archiadas commented on the losses they had suffered and claimed that they would willingly have spent that amount of money on organizing Panathenaic processions. However, by that time the processions were no longer acceptable.

Even Proclus, *scholarch* (principal) of the School of Plato, who was widely respected and on very good terms with the leading personalities of the town, had to leave Athens for a year, which he spent in his native Asia Minor. After his death in 485 the Christians "occupied" the Temple of Asclepius and sent his successor Marinus into temporary exile in Epidaurus. At about the same time, Christian tombs appeared in the area of the Odeum of Pericles in the immediate vicinity of the Theater of Dionysus. Later, perhaps in the 6th century, a one-aisled basilica was built in the eastern parodos of the theater, perhaps to "Christianize" this venerable construction. Also in the 6th century (roughly contemporary with the transformation of the Parthenon into a church), a villa on the northern slope of the Areopagus may have become the house of the bishop of Athens. The closure of the Platonic school by Justinian followed, in 529 (the same year that St. Benedict founded the Abbey of Montecassino), though the emperor closed the school more for educational than religious reasons. Its few but highly esteemed philosophers and students were thenceforth directed to the biggest cities of the empire.

The disintegration of Athens was soon completed by an invasion by a band of Slavs and Avars, perhaps in 582. The tetraconch church was destroyed, and by that time the Parthenon may have become the Cathedral of Athens. There are in the Parthenon some Christian graffito epitaphs, the earliest of which mentions a certain Bishop John who died probably in 595. Some other similar epitaphs date from the 7th century.

Apart from the tetraconch church and the basilica in the Parthenon, about twenty other churches are known to have existed in central Athens and her immediate outskirts ca. 600 C.E. Their names; the names of a few distinguished citizens; short lists of other, undistinctive names; and a record of the visit to Athens by the Emperor Constans II in 662–663 are almost the only pieces of information we have on life in Athens in the 7th and 8th centuries.

BIBL.: Alison Frantz, *The Athenian Agora: Results of Excavations Conducted by the American School of Classical Studies at Athens*, vol. 24: *Late Antiquity: A.D. 267–700* (Princeton, 1988). Alison Frantz, "From Paganism to Christianity in the Temple of Athens," *Dumbarton Oaks Papers* 19 (1965): 187–205. Alison Frantz, "Did Julian the Apostate Rebuild the Parthenon?" *American Journal of Archaeology* 83 (1979): 395–401. G. Fowden, "Late Roman Achaea: Identity and Defence," *Journal of Roman Archaeology* 8 (1995): 549–567.

P.C., M.G.

Atlantic Ocean

Traditionally the Atlantic marked the edge of the world: promontories that jutted into it were truly *fines terrae*. Yet for those peoples who lived on the western fringes of Europe, the Atlantic had long provided a major network of communications. Communication along the coasts of Spain and Gaul, across to Britain, and thence to Ireland was well established even in the pre-Roman period. In the last century of the western empire these routes were occasionally and partially appropriated by barbarian groups who sailed across the Channel and from thence down to Gaul and Spain. Franks, for instance, are said to have attacked Spain by way of the Atlantic Ocean prior to 313, and Heruls are recorded as doing the same in 455 to 457. At the same time some British communities, following well-worn lines of communication, left Britain for Brittany to avoid the incoming Anglo-Saxons.

After the period of the barbarian invasions, the western seaways apparently continued to have some economic and cultural significance. African red-slip pottery was reaching Britain, notably Tintagel, in the 5th and 6th centuries, and some fragments of the ware have even been found in Ireland. The pots themselves presumably contained wine, indicating a taste for one element of Mediterranean culture in the courts of western rulers and perhaps reflecting the demand for wine in the Christian liturgy.

Religious contacts along the old Atlantic seaways in the 5th century and beyond can be traced from other information. A number of British clerics left Britain for Brittany: notably Samson, Paul Aurelian, and perhaps Gildas. Members of a British ecclesiastical community seem even to have reached Spain in this period, as the group was represented at the synod of Braga in 572.

In this context it is reasonable to ask whether intellectual exchange took place along the same routes. It has been argued that the works of Isidore of Seville, for instance, were transmitted directly from Spain to Ireland, although it is perhaps more likely that Gaul acted as a staging post.

More intrepid were Irish ascetics, some of whom treated the coast and islands of the Atlantic as their equivalent of the Egyptian desert, notably on the rocky island of Skellig Michael off the coast of Kerry, where there are extensive remains of a medieval monastic settlement. Other more adventurous holy men even attempted to explore the ocean itself. Most famous of the Irish navigators was St. Brendan of Clonfert (d. ca. 575), whose explorations were subsequently recorded in the somewhat legendary *Navigatio sancti Brendani*. Brendan's attempt to find the "Island of the Blessed" in the Atlantic points to the continuity of Celtic pagan traditions about the existence of a supernatural world beyond the western horizon. Some of the explorations of Celtic monks did, however, bear fruit. It is clear that when the Vikings discovered Iceland they came across an island that had already been settled by Irish ascetics.

BIBL.: S. McGrail, ed., *Maritime Celts, Frisians and Saxons* (London, 1990).

I.W.

Attila

King of the Huns from ca. 439 to 453, Attila succeeded his uncle Rua (or Ruga) as ruler of the Huns of the great Hungarian plain. He at first ruled jointly with his brother Bleda, but in 443 Attila murdered Bleda so he could rule alone. Attila died a decade later, suffocating from a nosebleed in a drunken stupor on the last of his wedding nights.

Under Attila's rule, the Hunnic empire reached its apogee, the result of centralization among the Huns and progressive conquests of non-Hunnic groups. The Huns' formidable military power showed itself in a series of wide-ranging campaigns. In 441–443 and 447, Attila mounted two (possibly three) major Balkan campaigns against the eastern Roman empire, sacking cities, destroying armies, and extorting large monetary tributes. In 451 he crossed the Rhine into Gaul and advanced as far as Paris before being defeated in the Champagne. In 452 he attacked Italy, sacking Aquileia and other towns prior to a retreat that owed more to disease than to the apocryphal intervention of Pope Leo I.

On his death, Attila's several sons squabbled over the empire, dividing its Hunnic core. This allowed the previously defeated subject groups to reassert their independence. By 469, the Hunnic empire had ceased to exist. Older views saw this collapse as the direct result of the loss of Attila; more modern ones have concentrated on structural explanations for the Huns' dramatic rise and fall, and have even gone so far as to blame the latter on the incompetence of Attila's leadership.

BIBL.: I. Bona, *Das Hunnenreich* (Bonn, 1991). M. Kazanski, "L'archéologie de l'empire hunnique," *Francia* 21, no. 1 (1993): 127–145. O. J. Maenchen-Helfen, *The World of the Huns* (Berkeley, 1973). W. Pohl, "La sfida Attilana," *Attila: Flagellum Dei?* (Rome, 1993), 69–89. E. A. Thompson, *The Huns* (Oxford, 1996).   P.H.

Augustine

Bishop of the North African city of Hippo from 396, Augustine (354–430) was an intellectual and doctrinal giant of the late Latin church. Almost all of his prodigious literary output survives, securely dated thanks to the catalogue to his own works that he assembled late in life, the *Retractationes* (428). Besides his formal works—commentaries, treatises, polemical tracts, speculative theology—there remains a large (and recently expanded) dossier of sermons and letters, as well as his singular, brilliantly original theological treatise that combines exegesis, epistemology, and polemic with haunting autobiographical meditation: the thirteen books of his *Confessions* (397).

Augustine did some of his best thinking when arguing. The conventional periodization of his life in terms of the controversies that engaged him can, accordingly, lend some insight into his development as a theologian and ecclesiastical campaigner. His first and formative battle was against the Manichees. From the age of sixteen as a student in Carthage, until his reintroduction to Catholicism some twelve years later in Milan, Augustine himself had been involved in this ascetic, dualist sect. As radical Paulinists, the Manichees repudiated material creation together with the Hebrew Bible and its god, seeing their warrant for such a rejection in Paul's opposition of law and Gospel, light and darkness, spirit and the flesh. They resolved the problem of evil, cosmic and moral, by postulating two independent and opposed realms, Light and Darkness, which battled with each other: man was a miniature instance of this cosmic conflict, his moral failings a reflection of the triumph of Darkness. Augustine's so-

journ in Milan in the mid-380s, at the height of a renascence of Platonic studies, provided him with both a new metaphysics that enabled him to answer Manichaean dualism (namely, that evil did not have its own existence but was rather the absence of good) and, particularly through the preaching of Ambrose, an allegorizing biblical hermeneutic through which he could see the Hebrew Bible as a genuine vehicle of Christian revelation. His longest and most definitive repudiation of Manichaeism, the *Contra Faustum* (398), he produced once back in Africa; but virtually all his writings in this first period, from his conversion (386) to the *Confessions*, are to some degree motivated by anti-Manichaean concerns.

Augustine's middle period was particularly taken up with combating the Donatists. In Catholic eyes a schismatic community, the Donatist church embodied the rigorist position taken by African Catholics during Diocletian's persecutions in 303–305. In their view, clergy who had complied with imperial demands to turn over the Scriptures were *traditores* whose sacraments were illegitimate and who themselves had to be reintegrated into the church through rebaptism. Neither transmarine episcopal authority nor the prestige of the newly Christian government under Constantine could shake the Donatist position; in Augustine's time they were still the significant North African church.

Augustine waged a war on two fronts against them. First, adopting the arguments of one of their own alienated theologians, Tyconius, he argued against any possibility of a visible church of the saints in the period before the End: the church was a *corpus permixtum*, and therefore Donatist perfectionism was both impossible and wrong. Second, and momentously, he threw his prestige behind a new legal and political opportunity in 405 to prosecute Donatists through the power of the state. His writings from this period ultimately serve to support the state coercion of Christian minorities.

The Donatist controversy had sunk Augustine into specifically North African issues; against the Pelagians, he again moved onto an international stage. With the Vandal invasion of Italy in 410, cosmopolitan Italian Catholics were driven as refugees into the narrower world of North Africa, where a young colleague of Pelagius, Caelestius, inadvertently detonated the controversy by refusing to assent to some peculiarly North African theological positions when he sought ordination in Carthage. From 411 until the very end of his life in 430, Augustine contributed to the escalation of what was originally a clash of theological styles. In the course of this controversy, he went back to many of the issues that had defined his debate with the Manichees: the status of the body, and of sexuality; the effect of Adam's sin on humanity; the role of the soul in sin; the correct way to read Paul (Pelagius, like Augustine, had commented on the epistles). The Pelagian controversy ultimately defined Augustine's positions on heritable original sin, on sexuality as a premier (but by no means sole) expression of the ineffectiveness of man's will, and on the individual's absolute dependence, to act rightly and even to believe, on God's grace.

Two other original theological positions, on Jews and on Christian millenarianism, developed in the course of these controversies, and are related to them and to each other. Against the Manichees, drawing on Tyconius as he reread Paul, Augustine came to emphasize Paul's own positive statements on the law. Against anti-Judaism, Augustine argued that biblical law was a medium of revelation and salvation continuous from the period of the Old Testament to the New; that Jesus, Paul, and other apostles of the first generation had been Torah-observant Jews; and that contemporary Jewish communities, in their insistence on observing the law's ordinances, performed a valuable service as witnesses to the church. In contrast to the coercion he was prepared to exercise against "deviant" Christian groups, Augustine made a principled exception of the Jews, arguing that any prince or person who coerced them to give up their practices stood under the seven-fold curse by which God protected Cain. Further, he argued that voluntary conversion of Jews to Christianity had always happened and would always happen, and that such conversions signaled nothing in terms of the approach of the End.

This rereading of Judaism fed into Augustine's opposition to apocalyptic millenarianism, which was endemic in most forms of Christianity both popular and clerical in the 4th and 5th centuries. Several centuries of erudite calculations had named the zone of time between 400 and 500 as the due date for the second coming, to occur when the world was 6,000 years old; persecutions (especially for the Donatists), natural disasters, the appearance of heresies, the fall of Rome, and, on the positive side, the fact that the government was now Christian, all stimulated this foundational Christian expectation.

Against this, and again drawing on Tyconius, Augustine argued that the period outside of biblical history was eschatologically opaque, that one could not know from current events anything of the divine plan: disasters always occur, government, whether pagan or Christian, is simply a secular imposition of order on disorder; and the church (here his anti-Donatist ecclesiology figures) will remain an imperfect, mixed body until God closes the age.

All these themes come together to shape Augustine's last masterwork, the *City of God*. Opening with a comprehensive indictment of Roman and classical culture as a moral failure, Augustine proceeds to trace history since creation, organized according to the object of love, *amor sui* or *amor dei*. Those who love God are citizens of the heavenly city; those who love themselves, of the earthly city. The two cities of apocalyptic tradition, Jerusalem and Babylon, thus transmute to two opposed moral communities existing, indefinitely

mixed, in time. Only biblical history in its two movements, Old and New Testament, clearly reveals God's will: in the present, all is indefinite and opaque, though the eruption of miracles in daily life displays the manifest power of the saints. Life in history is life in exile, an exile that will end only when time itself ends. Against his millenarian coreligionists, Augustine adds to the traditional admonition that none can know the hour of the End his own radical innovation, that though the kingdom will include the saints raised in the flesh, it will come not on a transformed earth but in heaven. His huge work closes with a meditation on the heavenly Jerusalem as the *visio pacis,* the vision of eternal peace.

Augustine himself knew no such peace. His last years were marred by his increasingly bitter conflict with Julian of Eclanum, spokesman for the Pelagian position. At the end of his life Catholic Africa was shattered by the invasion of Arian Vandals, who besieged Hippo as he lay dying. The city burned, but his library, and his tremendous legacy, endured.

BIBL.: Peter Brown, *Augustine of Hippo* (Berkeley, 1967). R. A. Markus, *Saeculum: History and Society in the Theology of St. Augustine* (Cambridge, Eng., 1970). P. M. Hombert, *Gloria Gratiae* (Paris, 1996). S. Lancel, *Saint Augustin* (Paris, 1999). G. Wills, *Augustine* (New York, 1999). James J. O'Donnell, *Augustine: Confessions,* 3 vols. (Oxford, 1992). *Bibliothèque augustinienne: Oeuvres de Saint Augustin* 46B: *Lettres 1–29* (Paris, 1987). R. Eno, trans., *Letters VI* (Washington, D.C., 1989). *Vingt-six sermons au peuple d'Afrique,* ed. F. Dolbeau (Paris, 1996). E. Hill, trans., *Complete Works of Saint Augustine. Sermons III/i: Newly Discovered Sermons* (New York, 1997). P.F.

Augustinianism

The term *Augustinianism* denotes various aspects of western culture that, in one way or the other, show the mark of Augustine, whether in questions of doctrine (original sin, predestination), philosophy (psychology of perception and of the soul), worldview (the secularization of history, church, and government), or personal style (traditions of literary confession, e.g., Petrarch). Along with Paul, whose letters he interpreted—in many ways decisively—for the west, Augustine had more of an impact on the European learned religious tradition than any other single figure.

This impact has an ironic quality. In 1933, Arquillère used the term *augustinisme politique* to designate a systematic misunderstanding and distortion of Augustine's position on the noneschatological quality of the earthly political realm. Gregory VII and the papal monarchy to the one side, Alcuin and Charlemagne to the other, sought to invest their respective spheres with an absolute value that Augustine himself would have denied. In addition to political Augustinianism, one might further distinguish historiographical Augustinianism, which linked earthly institutions to salvation history (e.g., the works of Orosius, and Otto of Freising), and chronological Augustinianism, which sought to fix a terminal date to the "invisible millennium" since the establishment of the church, a period whose duration Augustine himself had argued was unknowable in principle.

Augustine died as his city was beseiged by invading Vandals. If Poitiers and Tours fought over St. Martin's body, those escaping Hippo had no question about the matter: they rescued Augustine's *corpus scriptorum*. In those days, where the prestige and importance of relics stood firmly at the heart of Catholic culture, this was a significant choice. Augustine was above all the saint of the literate, the clerical, the learned. His most lasting influence on subsequent western Christian culture, then, might be measured by the formation of a certain personality type. For centuries after his death, his writings continued to form and inspire men of the highest energy and acumen—mystics (Bernard of Clairvaux, Hugh of St. Victor), chronographers (Bede, Otto of Freising), political thinkers and inquisitors (Giles of Rome, Bernard Gui), great reformers (Hildebrand, Luther, Calvin)—who, like Augustine himself, combined theological brilliance with equally profound ecclesiastical commitment, and who identified their own, sometimes idiosyncratic opinions, with the fundamental traditions of the church.

BIBL.: Henri Xavier Arquillère, *L'augustinisme politique: Essai sur la formation des théories politiques du moyen-age* (Paris, 1934). Henri Marrou, *St. Augustine and His Influence through the Ages* (New York, 1958). J. J. O'Donnell, "The Authority of Augustine," *Augustinian Studies* 22 (1991): 7–35.   P.F., R.A.L.

Ausonius

"I love Bordeaux, Rome I venerate. I am a citizen [*civis*] of the former and a consul in both. Bordeaux is my cradle, Rome holds my consular chair" (*Ordo urbium nobilium* 167–168, Green). With these words Ausonius summed up the outlook that typified provincial climbers in late antiquity whose loyalties remained firmly within the circumference of their province but who held sentimental attachment to the memory of the city they had never bothered to visit.

Born in Bordeaux ca. 310 to a family noted for its medical and pedagogical professionalism, Ausonius embarked on a teaching career there and contracted a useful marriage with a local woman. His literary fame, his contacts, and the presence of the imperial court in Gallic Trier led to an invitation from the emperor Valentinian I (364–375) to tutor his son and heir, Gratian. Upon the accession of his imperial charge in 375, Ausonius enjoyed rapid promotions up the imperial administrative ladder and helped to place his relatives and friends in prominent positions as well. His own career included a praetorian prefecture (of the Gauls)

and the consulship (in 379), for which his *gratiarum actio* to Gratian is extant.

Ausonius's success as an imperial administrator was short-lived. When the imperial court moved to Italy in 381–382 new influences, primarily emanating from Ambrose of Milan, shaped Gratian's preferences. Ausonius retired to his rural estates and died in Aquitania ca. 395. His grandson Paulinus (of Pella) is the last self-recording member of the family. His poem *Eucharisticon* sums up the vicissitudes of the Ausonii in the 5th century. Paulinus retired to a monastic life in Marseilles ca. 440 (or ca. 420?) while his sons attempted, in vain it seems, to regain the family's wealth and influence by serving the barbarian monarchs established in Gaul in the 5th century.

Ausonius's claim to lasting fame is based on his literary output as well as his influence on noted poets, such as the Spaniard Prudentius. Among Ausonius's more original poems are two series of brief biographies commemorating his family (*Parentalia*) and his teaching colleagues (*Professores*). His most famous poem describes the river Moselle, which runs across Trier. Ausonius also corresponded with a gallery of contemporary notables, ranging from the emperor Theodosius I (379–395) to the Italian aristocrat Symmachus.

Through Ausonius's correspondence with his pupil Paulinus (of Nola) important light is shed on the Christianization of the Gallic aristocracy in the late 4th century. The letters reflect two kinds of aristocratic Christianity, a respectable (Ausonian) mixture of visibility through attendance at public celebrations in the city and of scholarly curiosity in scriptures, and an extreme form of ascetic piety (Paulinian) that seemed out of place in Gallic aristocratic circles. Among Ausonius's most intriguing compositions (now lost) is a comparative compilation on the Hebrew and Athenian names of the months and on Hebrew (biblical?) names (*Libellum de nominibus mensium et hebreorum et atheniensium; Item de eruditionibus hebreorum et interpretationibus hebraicorum nominum librum unum*).

BIBL.: R. Green, *Works of Ausonius* (Oxford, 1991). H. Sivan, *Ausonius of Bordeaux: Genesis of a Gallic Aristocracy* (London, 1993).   H.S.

Avars

A nomadic people of inner Asia, the Avars formed a state in Pannonia in the latter part of the 6th century C.E. While the origins of the European Avars remain a matter of some dispute, their name is connected with the Apar/Abar/Awar (Chinese *Jou-jan* or, more derogatorily, *Juan-juan,* "wriggling worms"), a Proto-Mongolian tribal confederation that formed a khaghanate in Mongolia in the 4th century C.E. and was later destroyed by their subjects, the Turks, in 552. Theophylactus Simocattes, in a muddled account (7.7), states that the European Avars were not the true Avars but rather a tribal grouping of the "Ouar and Chounni" who assumed the name of the fearsome Avars to frighten their neighbors. However, recent scholarship (Czeglédy) has shown that the inner-Asian Avars consisted of "War" (Chinese Huol Hua) and Hun (Hsiung-nu) elements, as did the Hephthalite tribal union, whose relationship with the inner-Asian Avars is equally problematic. The Hephthalites were crushed by the Turks and Sassanids in 557. An inner-Asian connection for the European Avars is confirmed by archaeological data from Hungary, the ultimate area of settlement.

Priscus (frg. 40–41) first mentions them as an inner-Asian link in the chain of migrations, ca. 463, that brought the Oghur Turkic peoples into the Pontic steppes. The Syriac *Ecclesiastical History* of Pseudo-Zacharias Rhetor places the "Abar," ca. 555, in the northern Caucasian steppes. By 558 the "European Avars," now in the Pontic steppe zone, were negotiating, with Alanic assistance, an alliance with Byzantium, offering the latter their "efficient protection" in exchange for land and annual payments. Their hegemony over the Pontic steppe peoples was short-lived, however, for by 567–568, the Turks were threatening. The Avars, now allied with the Lombards, displaced the Gepids from Pannonia; after having dispensed with the Lombards as well, Pannonia came into their full possession. There they were joined by, or they brought with them, some Oghuric Turkic peoples and the Zabender, who were also of War-Hun origin. Their establishment in Danubian Europe coincided with increased Slavic raiding expeditions into the Balkans, an activity in which the Avars became actively engaged. The nature of the Avaro-Slavic relationship (symbiotic, hegemonic) in this early stage has been variously interpreted. Subsequently, Avar oppression of the Slavs became legendary in Rus' sources.

The settlement of a powerful nomadic people in their immediate environs was undoubtedly a factor in Slavic movements south of the Danube where, increasingly, they established permanent settlements. The Byzantines were as fearful of their "allies" the Avars, under their Khaghan Bayan, as of the Slavs whose raids were ostensibly to be stopped by their presence on imperial lands. A Byzantine counteroffensive mounted by the emperor Maurice (582–602) drove back both Avars and Slavs for a time, but a massive Avar attack on Constantinople (599) was halted only by the plague. Avar assaults on the capital continued, reaching a crescendo in 626, when an attack was coordinated (or perhaps only coincided) with a Persian expedition. Although it was unsuccessful, the emperor Heraclius (610–641) who had allied himself with the Turk-Khazars to halt the Persians in the east, now sought to foment trouble in the Avar rear. In 623, some western Slavic subjects of the Avars had revolted under the leadership of Samo, a Frankish merchant. These "White" Croats (who successfully warred with the Avars) and the Serbs were brought into the Balkans to

form a new bulwark against them. In addition, the Turkic Bulgar tribal union, under Qubrat, was encouraged to revolt (successfully) against Avar overlordship ca. 631–632. The establishment of the Balkan Bulgar state after 679 constituted another obstacle to Avar attacks.

We are much less well informed about subsequent Avar history. Some Bulgar groupings, their state having been broken up by the Khazars, came under Avar overlordship in Pannonia. Avar pressure on the Balkans, however, appears to have eased considerably. There are fleeting references to Avar conflicts with the Bavarians, the Lombards, and other neighbors. In the late 8th century these drew the attention of Charlemagne. In a series of campaigns (791–799), the now fragmenting Avar state was defeated, and ca. 820–830 it was subjected to Carolingian administration; Avar remnants in the east were subsumed by the Bulgar state of Krum.

BIBL.: R. C. Blockley, *The Fragmentary Classicising Historians of the Later Roman Empire: Eunapius, Olympiodorus, Priscus and Malchus,* 2 vols. (Liverpool, 1981, 1983). *Theophylacti simocattae historiae,* ed. C. de Boor, rev. P. Wirth (1887; repr., Stuttgart, 1972); English: *The History of Theophylact Simocatta,* trans. M. and M. Whitby (Oxford, 1986). K. Czeglédy, "From East to West: The Age of Nomadic Migrations in Eurasia," trans. P. B. Golden, *Archivum eurasiae medii aevi* 3 (1983): 25–125. A. Kollautz and H. Miyakawa, *Geschichte und Kultur eines völkerwanderungszeitlichen Nomadenvolkes,* 2 vols. (Klagenfurt, 1970). W. Pohl, *Die Awaren: Ein Steppenvolk in Mitteleuropa* (Munich, 1988), 567–822. S. Szádecky-Kardoss, "The Avars," in *The Cambridge History of Early Inner Asia,* ed. D. Sinor (Cambridge, 1990), 206–228.   P.B.G.

Avesta

Probably meaning "pure instruction," *Avesta* is the title of the Zoroastrian Scripture. Two dialects in which it was composed can be identified: Old Avestan and Young or Younger Avestan. The Old Avestan corpus includes *Gathas* ("songs"; *Yasna* 28–34, 43–46, 47–51, 53), *Yasna Haptanhaiti* ("sacrifice or worship of seven chapters"; *Yasna* 35–41), *Yenhe Hatam* ("all those beings"), *Ashem Vohu* ("righteousness is good"), *Yatha Ahu Vairyo* or *Ahuna Vairya* ("as is the lord") and *Airyema Ishyo* ("may the desirable tribe") prayers (*Yasna* 27, 54), *Srosh Yasht* ("hymn to Sraosha"; *Yasna* 57), praise of *Nemah* ("prayer"; *Yasna* 58), and the *Fravarane* ("declaration of faith"; *Yasna* 12–13). The five *Gathas* can be attributed to Zoroaster himself. The *yasna,* meaning sacrifice, or worship service, is the main liturgical part of this canon. The other Old Avestan texts were composed by members of the early Zoroastrian community prior to approximately the 9th century B.C.E. Young Avestan materials comprise *Yashts* (hymns) to *yazatas* (divinities) such as Anahita, Mithra, and Haoma (*Yashts* 1–21, *Yasna* 9–11), who were incorporated into Zoroastrianism from earlier

Iranian belief; *Visprad*, "(a prayer to) all the patrons"; *Niyayishns*, "praises"; *Gahs*, "divisions of the day"; *Siroza*, "thirty days"; *Afrinagans*, "blessings (for the dead)"; the remainder of the *Yasna*; and ritual prescriptions in the *Videvdad*, "code for abjuring demons." The Young Avestan corpus also includes fragmentary texts such as the Herbedestan, "priestly code"; *Nerangestan*, "ritual code"; *Aogemadaecha*, "we accept," a prayer for the dead; *Pursishniha*, "questions"; and the *Hadokht Nask*, "book of scriptures." These Young Avestan materials date from the 6th century B.C.E. to the 2nd century B.C.E. But several of the *Yashts* represent, in fact, revisions of hymns older than Zoroaster's *Gathas*. The *Avesta* as a whole was memorized by Zoroastrian priests and transmitted orally from generation to generation for hundreds of years.

The word *Avesta* (Pahlavi *Abestag*) actually originated in late antiquity and refers to the received tradition, as distinct from the *Zand* (commentary), or priestly exegesis. It is possible that the terms *Abestag* and *Zand* were calques on Greek *epistēmē* and *gnōsis*, respectively. Since the *Avesta* and its *Zand* were written together, interlinearly, the composite text has often been incorrectly called the *Zend-Avesta*. The *Avesta* apparently received its extant written form between the 4th and 7th centuries C.E., under the oversight of chief magi such as Adurbad i Maraspandan and Wehshapur and Sassanian kings such as Shapur II and Khosro I. At that time, a canon of twenty-one Avestan *nasks* (divisions, books) covering not only liturgy but also sacred history, hagiography, myth, and law was assembled and its *Zand* composed in the Pahlavi language. The cursive Avestan script, specially derived from Aramaic via Book and Psalter Pahlavi, had thirty-five consonants and sixteen vowels. Magi in late antiquity continued to memorize and orally transmit the *Avesta* and *Zand* much as their ancestors had done, even though they no longer spoke Avestan. Thus, very few written versions of the *Avesta* probably existed. Attenuation of memory over time, coupled with dispersion and degeneration of textual copies, led to the loss of several *nasks*. As a result, the extant *Avesta* contains only a small portion of the Sassanian one.

Indeed, the oldest surviving but greatly incomplete manuscript dates to 1278 C.E.

BIBL.: Harold W. Bailey, "Apastak," in *Papers in Honour of Professor Mary Boyce* (Leiden, 1985), 9–14. James Darmesteter and Lawrence H. Mills, trans., *The Zend-Avesta*, 3 parts, Sacred Books of the East 4, 23, 31 (Oxford, 1887–1895; repr., Delhi, 1981). Karl F. Geldner, ed., *Avesta: The Sacred Books of the Parsis*, 3 vols. (Stuttgart, 1886–1895; repr., Delhi, 1982).   J.K.C.

Azraq

Azraq is a large oasis in the eastern desert of Jordan. Its location at the northwest end of the Wadi Sirḥān, a main travel route between the northern Arabian Peninsula and southern Syria, has made Azraq a natural halting point for caravans throughout the ages. A number of Roman forts and watchtowers were built in the area, starting in the Severan period (2nd century), including a large early *castellum* (detectable in aerial photographs) that awaits further investigation. An altar dedicated to Diocletian and Maximian (292–306) and another inscription recording repairs in the time of Constantine (326–333) date the extant, as yet unexcavated, *castellum* to the 4th century. That castellum, constructed of the local black basalt, is not quite square (79 m by 72 m) and has projecting corner towers, rows of rooms along the enclosure walls, and an open central courtyard area. Inscriptions show that the name of Azraq in the 4th century was Basie (or Basia), its ethnic either Basieneis (or Bwianis). No clear trace has been detected of any early Islamic occupation predating the Ayyubid (13th century) rebuilding of the castellum, but it is scarcely likely that it was unoccupied at least in the Umayyad period.

BIBL.: David Kennedy, *Archaeological Explorations on the Roman Frontier in North-East Jordan*, British Archaeological Reports, International Series 134 (Oxford, 1982), 69–136. S. Thomas Parker, *Romans and Saracens: A History of the Arabian Frontier* (Winona Lake, Md., 1986), 16–21. M. Speidel, "The Roman Road to Dumata (Jawf in Saudia Arabia) and the Frontier Strategy of *Praetensions colligare*," *Historia* 36 (1987): 213–221.   R.S.

B

Bactria

Bactria was the name given to the region between the Oxus River (Amu Darya in Uzbekistan) and the Hindu Kush mountain range (in northern Afghanistan). Probably named after the Bakhtri River, its major city was Bahl (called Bactra by the Greeks), later known as Balkh. Like Soghd to the north, it definitely came to be inhabited by Iranian people from 1000 B.C.E. onward. Prior to that time, settlements (perhaps by Indo-Iranian peoples) existed since approximately 1900 B.C.E. The region has at times been associated (incorrectly) with the prophet Zoroaster's ministry.

Called Bakhtrish, it was the twelfth satrapy or province of the Achaemenian empire. The region became famous for its gold objects—now amply attested in archaeological excavations and in the so-called Oxus treasure. Following Alexander the Great's conquest, Greek-style cities, such as Ay Khanum, were established. Previously existing metropolitan areas were Hellenized under the Seleucids. An independent Graeco-Bactrian kingdom followed (ca. 247–130 B.C.E.), and next came nomadic rulers. In late antiquity, Indian influences entered the region via trade and conquest. Under the Kushans, Bactria emerged as a major center of Buddhist praxis and art. A famous temple, the Nawbahar (new vihara), functioned at Balkh. The Bactrian language, written in a modified Greek script, came into use and survived until about the 8th century. Sassanian governors, who bore the title *kushanshah,* or king of the Kushans, controlled the area during the 3rd and 4th centuries. They were ousted by Hephthalite tribesfolk who were expanding southward. Around the year 558, the Sassanians regained control over Bactria. Muslims captured Bactria in the late 7th and early 8th centuries. After the region was colonized by Arabs and the local inhabitants had been slowly converted to Islam, Bactrian cities like Balkh and Termez emerged as important Muslim scholarly centers of late antiquity.

BIBL.: Wilhelm Barthold, *An Historical Geography of Iran,* trans. Svat Soucek (Princeton, 1984), 6–34.   J.K.C.

Bagaudae

In the mid-280s the new emperor Diocletian sent his colleague Maximian to Gaul to subdue the "country folk and bandits whom the inhabitants called Bagaudae." Although a panegyrist and later historians may have belittled Maximian's opponents as "rustics" and "agrarian bandits," these epithets must not be taken to imply that the Bagaudae were participants in a class war, peasants in revolt, or even mere brigands. More likely they were Gauls who were simply resisting barbarian incursions by rallying around local leaders, one of whom may even have assumed the imperial title of Augustus.

The appearance of Bagaudae highlighted the increasing ineffectiveness of Roman administration in outlying or mountainous regions of Gaul and Spain. Throughout most of the 4th century an imperial court was resident at Trier; upon its departure Bagaudae reappeared. During the 5th century, Bagaudae in the western Alps blocked a Roman army that was retreating to Italy; in central Gaul, Bishop Germanus of Auxerre represented them at the prefect's court; and Bagaudae skirmished in northern Spain, where local aristocrats were resisting Suebis and Visigoths. The use of the label Bagaudae thus represented the retreat of Roman imperialism and the rollback of its cultural hegemony. The Gallic priest Salvian sympathetically conceded that the Bagaudae were people who were being abandoned by the Roman empire and denied "the dignity of the Roman name." Their own name probably derived from the Celtic word for war; however much the central administration denigrated them, locals honored them as warriors defending against the barbarians. Eventually Christian traditions even reinterpreted the Bagaudae as heroic martyrs.

BIBL.: J. Drinkwater, "Patronage in Roman Gaul and the Problem of the Bagaudae," in *Patronage in Ancient Society*, ed. A. Wallace-Hadrill (London, 1989), 189–203. A. Giardina, "Banditi e santi: Un aspetto del folklore gallico tra tarda antichità e medioevo," *Athenaeum* 71 (1983): 374–389. L. Cracco Ruggini, "Établissements militaires, martyrs bagaudes et traditions romains dans la *Vita Baboleni*," *Historia* 44 (1995): 100–119. R. Van Dam, *Leadership and Community in Late Antique Gaul* (Berkeley, 1985), chaps. 2–3.

R.V.

Baghdad

Baghdad was founded by the second Abbasid caliph, al-Manṣūr, in 762 C.E. It is located in what was the heart of Mesopotamia (Iraq), on the west bank of the Tigris River at the closest juncture between that waterway and the Euphrates River. The city eventually spread along both banks of the Tigris. The imperial capital of the former Parthian and Sassanian empires had been nearby—a metropolis called Seleucia (on the west bank of the river) and later Ctesiphon (Pahlavi Tesfon, on the east bank of the river). Despite attacks by Romans and Byzantines, flooding, plague, and occasional civic strife, Ctesiphon and its suburbs developed into the largest Near Eastern city of late antiquity—gaining the title al-Mada'in, "the Cities," from Arab Muslim invaders who captured it in 637 C.E. Officially named Madinat al-salām, City of Peace, by the Abbasids, Baghdad served as the caliphate's capital until the Mongol army entered it in 1258. Only briefly, during the 9th century, did Baghdad cease for a time to be the Abbasid capital. Baghdad's preeminence as the cultural center of the Islamic and Arabic-speaking world declined, however, by the 11th century. Its popular name, Baghdad (god given) was of Iranian origin.

Baghdad had been planned as a round city, perhaps following the oval rampart layout of Ctesiphon. Like such Sassanian round cities as Firuzabad, Baghdad had four main gates. Within the new city's walls were located the caliph's palace and main congregational mosque. Medieval Muslim historians, including

al-Ṭabarī, recorded that al-Manṣūr instructed his prime minister (vizier) Khalid ibn Barmak to utilize materials stripped from buildings at Ctesiphon in construction of the new city. Outside the walled citadel lay the rest of the town, which was divided into quarters. The population consisted of Arab and Iranian settlers and local Aramaeans. In addition to the Muslim population, the city, like its Parthian and Sassanian predecessors, had sizable Jewish, Christian, and Zoroastrian communities. Baghdad reached its zenith as a cosmopolitan center during the reign of Hārūn al-Rashīd.

BIBL.: Robert Adams, *Heartland of Cities: Surveys of Ancient Settlement and Land Use on the Central Floodplain of the Euphrates* (Chicago, 1981). Jacob Lassner, *The Shaping of Abbāsid Rule* (Princeton, 1980). Jacob Lassner, *The Topography of Baghdad in the Early Middle Ages: Text and Studies* (Detroit, 1970).

J.K.C.

Baladhuri

Ahmad Ibn Yahya Ibn Jabir al-Baladhuri (d. ca. 892) is one of the most important historians of the formation of the Arabic Islamic empire. He was probably born in Baghdad and lived most of his life there, but he traveled in Iraq, Jezira, and Syria to collect his historical material. Among his teachers he counted al-Mada'ini and Ibn Sa'd, two paragons of the Medina school of history. He had strong contacts at the Abbasid court, especially with the caliphs al-Mutawakkil (who ruled from 846 to 861) and al-Musta'in (862–865). His *nisba* (designation), al-Baladhuri, is said to be derived from his fondness for *baladhur*, an anacardiaceous plant whose juice was believed to be a memory stimulant. Excessive use may have caused his mental derangement before his death, but the account is puzzling because the same *nisba* was attached to his grandfather.

Two of his books have survived. *Futuḥ al-Buldān* (1863–1866; English trans. 1916 and 1924), the most complete account of early Islamic conquests in Arabia, Syria, Jezira, Egypt, Maghreb, Iraq, Persia, and Sind, is reported to be a condensation of a longer and missing history. *Ansab al-Ashrāf* (Lineage of the Nobles) is a large, and apparently never completed, work of genealogy (less than half the extant work has been published to date). It begins with Muhammad, then his kin, the rest of Quraysh, and finally other important Mudari tribes. The reigns of Umayyad and Abbasid caliphs are discussed at length in the sections devoted to their respective clans. Al-Baladhuri is probably the most reliable source on the Umayyads, despite his connections with the Abbasids. Moreover, he was among the first historians to methodically organize the material culled from oral reports and the few earlier biographies and campaign accounts, always giving their chains of transmission.

BIBL.: Abdel 'Aziz al-Duri, *The Rise of Historical Writing* among the Arabs, ed. and trans. L. I. Conrad (Princeton, 1983). Amanullah Khan, *A Critical Study of al-Baladhuri as a Historian* (Lahore, 1987). Muhammad Jasim Hammadi Mashhadani, *Mawarid al-Baladhuri an al-Usrah al-Umawiyah fi Ansab al-Ashraf,* 2 vols. (Mecca, 1986).   N.R.

Banditry

From the perspective of the Roman imperial administration, bandits were men who used violence to threaten the political, social, and moral order of the Roman state. Some of these bandits were simply continuing a traditional lifestyle that had always included thievery, rustling, and extortion, while others deliberately resorted to force to challenge the power of imperial magistrates or local notables. The label *latrocinium,* or banditry (Greek *lēsteia*), thus reflected not necessarily rampant lawlessness but rather the indignation of administrators and notables at their inability to impose their authority in outlying regions. Since the Roman imperial administration was most effective in cities, in lowlands, and in frontier zones dominated by Roman troops, bandits seemed to be especially prevalent in regions isolated by difficult topography. The swamps around the Nile Delta, for instance, were acknowledged to be infested with *boukoloi* ("cowboys") who had founded villages and raised families. The most common hideouts for bandits were mountains. Isauria in particular had a notorious reputation for its autonomous highland lords, whom Roman troops tried eventually to isolate by enforcing a blockade.

To survive, bandits relied on the resources of local communities and sometimes even entire regions; in Syria one village was filled with opulent homes because its men had plundered neighboring villages by disguising themselves as soldiers and merchants. Great landowners offered refuge to bandits in exchange for their service as armed protectors. Thus, controlling bandits was difficult. Cities maintained only small police forces and relied on local notables to serve as peace officers and to organize posses. Governors were expected to maintain order in their provinces, and some even hired bounty hunters and professional killers. Emperors occasionally ordered army troops to track down bandits, or appointed special "prefects for repressing bandits," but in what was perhaps the most successful strategy, they also simply co-opted bandit chieftains by offering them formal friendship and recruiting their supporters into the Roman army.

Because bandits existed on the economic, cultural, and geographical margins of Roman society, they came to represent a symbolic paradigm whose alleged attributes of lawlessness and cruelty (and even cannibalism) were advertised as the reverse of normal society. Ancient novelists, historians, and even rabbis in Judaea played with these ideological categories in order to comment on the nature of power and justice, sometimes implying that bandits were more just than current rulers. Emperors also manipulated the stereotypes of banditry to define political legitimacy: during periods of uncertain succession, civil war, and pressure on the frontiers, they were quick to stigmatize their rivals as mere bandits. By representing a livelihood based on the use of force and defiance, bandits clearly defined the practical limits of state control; by being included in an ideology of state legitimacy, they also hinted at the potential for the emergence of new rulers or even the formation of an alternative state. The best understanding of the ongoing dialectic between banditry and state power came, typically, from Bishop Augustine of Hippo (*City of God* 4.4): "If justice is removed, what are kingdoms but gangs of bandits on a large scale?"

BIBL.: C. E. Bosworth, "Liss," *Encyclopaedia of Islam, New Edition* (Leiden, 1954–). B. Isaac, "Bandits in Judaea and Arabia," *Harvard Studies in Classical Philology* 88 (1984): 171–203. J. L. Kraemer, "Apostates, Rebels and Brigands," *Israel Oriental Studies* 10 (1980): 34–73. B. D. Shaw, "Brigands in the Roman Empire," *Past and Present* 105 (1984): 3–52. J. Winkler, "Lollianus and the Desperadoes," *Journal of Hellenic Studies* 100 (1980): 155–181. V. Neri, *I marginali nell'Occidente tardoantico* (Bari, 1998).   R.V.

Baptism

Through baptism, one entered the Christian community: indeed, through baptism the community was formed. Its ceremony reveals much about the self-image of the community, and about the advantages expected from initiation.

By the time of Constantine, the chief elements of the baptismal ceremony were established and soon had growing public impact. At the beginning of Lent, those wishing to be baptized were formally enrolled, supported by a Christian guarantor. During Lent, the catechumens were regularly exorcized: they stood barefoot and simply clothed, hands uplifted, while priests commanded demons to depart from them. The bishop instructed them in the meaning of baptism and in the tenets of Christianity generally. We possess many such addresses by almost every major churchman of the patristic period—John Chrysostom, Cyril of Jerusalem, and Theodore of Mopsuestia being the most notable. On Good Friday, the catechumens knelt to renounce Satan and identify themselves with Christ. They were then anointed on the crown or forehead. The following morning, they professed their faith by reciting the creed. During the vigil of Easter, stripped naked, they were anointed again from head to foot—a standard practice at the baths, here sacralized for Christian purposes and linked symbolically with athletic contest. The sexes were segregated, and the catechumens went down into the baptismal pool in small groups, standing knee or waist deep, while water was poured on their head and shoulders or clerics, invoking the names of the Trinity, plunged them three times into the pool itself. Then, clothed in simple white garments and carrying lights, they reentered the assembly of believers, where they were anointed with chrism, embraced with the kiss of peace, and admitted for the first time to communion.

This impressive ceremony reinforced the Christian presence in the cities of the empire. Substantial baptisteries were erected within or beside basilicas. Their *piscinae* were symbolic in form—circular, hexagonal, octagonal, cross-shaped, or flower-shaped, sometimes combining several such elements. They were a meter or more deep, often with steps, and they lay at the center of lofty, columned rooms of a similar shape. Baptisteries added an awesome component to the burgeoning building program inseparable from Christian expansion. The earliest examples known to us in the period after Constantine were erected at Aquileia, Milan, and Rome.

The central role in baptism claimed by the bishop was another element in his hold over the community, reaching in this case beyond the fully committed. Some catechumens, it seems, enrolled for several years without completing initiation. Others postponed baptism until old age or death. Churchmen urged their wider audience to avoid such delay and to seal their identification with the community of believers. Around the ritual, therefore, a debate was conducted between church leaders and the wavering or doubtful. Final submission marked a deliberate and openly declared choice, and placed the initiate safely within a clear boundary between the demonic and the redeemed.

During the 5th century, changes took place; in particular, the catechumenate waned. In the east, the *Ecclesiastical Hierarchy* of Dionysius the Areopagite and the sermons of Severus of Antioch suggest that fewer adults came forward for baptism, that those who did might be baptized at times other than Easter, and that correspondingly more infants were being presented for initiation. Infant baptism was not new: it had long been permitted in times of danger and even recommended. The eastern church allowed baptized infants to proceed at once to anointing with chrism and reception of the Eucharist; in the west, infant baptism was regarded more as a promise to be fulfilled, demanding a subsequent and formal education and a postponed anointing. The differences were more than superficial. While in theory each boy or girl needed the salvation that only baptism could guarantee, the practice of the church created the impression of a self-generating community. The forming of Christians was now regarded as a continuous process, conducted during the weekly liturgy: fewer sermons were dedicated specifically to the Lenten preparation, and baptism could

now occur during ordinary eucharistic celebrations. Assuring the Christian loyalty of baptized infants was seen as a community responsibility, undertaken especially by godparents, who gained greater prominence at this time. The differences marked the shift from a "Christianizing" church to a Christian society.

Developments in the west have an interest of their own, because of the presence of new "barbarian" settlers. For ritual information, we depend chiefly on the *Gelasian Sacramentary* and the *Ordo romanus*. Their late 6th and 7th century dates make it difficult to identify earlier phases, but they bear witness to the increasing influence of Roman custom. A new factor was that of "mission," the outreach of Mediterranean Christians to peoples beyond the region's traditional boundaries. The commitment of the devotee was now less important than the enthusiasm of the wandering preacher. Acquisitive aggression displaced cautious surrender. Baptism became an instrument in the conversion of whole communities and nations. Clovis provides a famous example (although not the first), and the pattern continued in early Anglo-Saxon England and in Frankish missions to peoples further east. More was involved than a Germanic emphasis on family, kin, or tribe—the notion that, where father or leader went, others were expected to follow. Cyril and Methodius journeyed similarly beyond the imperial sphere. In the west, many early barbarians were already Christian, and missionary expansion helped them to mark out their new kingdoms as Christian "peoples" or "nations" vis-à-vis remoter groups that were to be resisted or absorbed. In the east, the trauma of loss in the face of Islam made self-confidence dependent on a comparable push northward. The intimate demons exorcized in the basilicas of the 4th century were now seen as mastering territories and their inhabitants.

Infant baptism and mass conversion accentuated the problem of subsequent lapse, and a complex penitential system emerged, especially in the west. Again notions of formation and personal development were involved, and a new relationship was established between penitent and priest. In addition, the prayers and anointings that had immediately followed baptism in earlier times were now divided into a longer series of commitments and blessings, including postponed confirmation by the bishop—another example of the gradual formation that now defined and nurtured the Christian people. The impressive mystery of solemn commitment gave way to years of arduous reflection and effort.

BIBL.: Sebastian Brock, "Some Important Baptismal Themes in the Syriac Tradition," *The Harp* 4 (1991): 189–214. A. Khatchatrian, *Les baptistères paléochrétiens: Plans, notices, et bibliographie* (Paris, 1962). Thomas M. Finn, *Early Christian Baptism and the Catechumenate: West and East Syria* (Collegeville, Minn., 1992). Victor Saxer, *Les rites de l'initiation chrétienne du IIe au VIe siècle: Esquisse histori-*

que et signification d'après leurs principaux témoins (Spoleto, 1988).   P.R.

Baptisteries

The mystery of baptism marked the believer's full admission into the Christian community; only after baptism was the initiate allowed to share in the Eucharist, the other central mystery of the cult. According to Matthew (28:19) and John (3.5), the ritual was prescribed by Jesus and modeled after his own baptism by John the Baptist (Matt. 3:13–17, John 1:32–34; also see Mark 1:9–11, Luke 3:21–22). Paul provided the basis for a common understanding of the rite: by participating in Jesus's death and resurrection through baptism, believers were cleansed of their sins and admitted into the body of the church (Rom. 6:2–4, Col. 2:12, 1 Corinthians 12:13).

During the 1st to early 4th centuries, baptism was commonly, though not necessarily, performed outdoors, after the example of Jesus's baptism in the Jordan and other baptisms described in the Book of Acts (8:36–38, 16:13–15). Justin Martyr described initiates as simply being led "to a place where there is water" (1 *Apol.* 61). The *Didache* recommended running water, although if it were not available, any water would do (7.1–2). Tertullian insisted that "it makes no matter whether one is washed in the sea or in a pond, a river or a fountain, a cistern or a tub" (*De baptismo* 4).

The earliest structure identified with some assurance as having functioned as a baptistery was excavated at Dura-Europus in Syria. In converting a private dwelling into a Christian building in the 240s, the northwest room was modified to serve as a baptistery. Although smaller than the congregational hall of this *domus ecclesiae*, the baptistery was the only space in the building to be decorated with figural frescoes, including a representation of the Good Shepherd over the baptis-

mal font. Episodes from the New Testament and the Hebrew Bible (the healing of the paralytic, Peter saved from drowning, the woman at the well, David and Goliath) as well as a processional image (commonly identified as the women at the tomb or the wise and foolish virgins) appear on the walls. The room between the baptistery and the meeting hall has been speculatively identified as the *katēchoumenon*, where prospective initiates gathered for exorcism and catechism, or as the *consignatorium*, where they were confirmed. Rooms attached to baptisteries are often so labeled, though collaborative evidence is rarely available.

With Constantine's legitimation of Christianity, baptisteries increased in scale and elaboration. The character of these baptisteries depended on such factors as local building tradition, the size and wealth of the congregation, the ambition of the church patron, and regional liturgical practice. Scholars have documented variations in baptismal services, although the basic features of the rite had become remarkably consistent throughout the Roman empire by the 4th and 5th centuries. Easter eve was universally recognized as the most appropriate moment for baptism; it might also occur legitimately at Pentecost or at any time a candidate was in extremis. Baptizing on the feasts of the Nativity and Epiphany was repeatedly denounced in the west (Leo the Great, *Letter* 16, *PL,* 54.695–704), although it was sanctioned in the east. In the urbanized areas of the Roman empire, the bishop enrolled initiates at the beginning of Lent, then catechized and exorcised them regularly before their initiation. The ceremony itself involved a contractual renunciation of Satan and acceptance of Jesus, a triple immersion or affusion linked with the recitation of a trinitarian formula, anointment and confirmation, and the participation with the congregation in the Eucharist.

At least in the west, baptism was controlled by the bishop, and large baptisteries were associated with episcopal complexes. Intercity diocesan competition may well have promoted the building of large baptismal halls, as well as great cathedral churches. The earliest surviving baptistery with urban prominence, S. Giovanni in Fonte in Rome, was a large, central-plan structure built by Constantine as part of the Lateran episcopal complex. According to the *Liber pontificalis,* among Constantine's appropriations for the baptistery were a porphyry font overlaid with silver, a five-foot-high gold lamb, silver statues of Christ and John the Baptist, and seven silver stags that spouted water. Pope Sixtus III (432–440) reconstructed the baptistery with a high, light dome supported on eight porphyry columns (collected but not used by Constantine), embraced by an octagonal ambulatory.

Reconstruction of the baptistery at Dura-Europus.

Centralized baptisteries, perhaps responding to Constantine's Lateran baptistery as well as to contemporary centralized tombs and martyria, proliferated in Italy in the later 4th and the 5th centuries. Excavations of the late 4th century baptistery of the Cathedral of St. Thecla in Milan revealed a large, octagonal font enclosed in an octagonal structure elaborated internally with alternating square and semicircular niches. A much discussed verse supposedly transcribed from the baptistery and attributed to Ambrose suggests that the octagonal form of the structure carried considerable meaning for at least some members of its late antique audience: "Eight-niched soars this church destined for sacred rites, eight corners has its font, the which befits its gift. Meet it was thus to build this fair baptismal hall about this sacred eight: here is our race reborn" (trans. F. van der Meer, *Atlas of the Early Christian World* [London, 1958], 129).

Two examples of freestanding octagonal baptisteries survive in Ravenna, which in 404 succeeded Milan as the imperial residence of the west Roman emperor. The Orthodox Baptistery was built ca. 400 as a wooden-roofed octagon with alternately niched and flat walls. A light domical vault constructed of ceramic vessels decorated with an elaborate mosaic program was added by Bishop Neon (ca. 451–ca. 473). There a medallion with the scene of Jesus's baptism is encircled by a procession of crown-bearing apostles, and, in a lower register, by a series of alternating thrones and altars in perspectively rendered architectural settings. The late 5th century Arian Baptistery in Ravenna modified the architecture and decorative program of its orthodox rival to fit the liturgical and ideological needs of the Ostrogoths.

Other early Christian polygonal baptisteries of northern Italy and the Adriatic include those in Aquileia (late 5th century; rebuilt in the early 11th); Grado, at St. Euphemia, and another associated with the church on Piazza Vittoria (5th or 6th century); and Poreč (mid-6th century). The polygonal of Albenga (late 5th or early 6th century) retains part of its original mosaic decoration in the southeast niche: a problematically restored inscription naming several saints on the face of the arch, a Chi-Rho in the vault surrounded by twelve doves in a star-filled, blue field, and lambs flanking a cross in the lunette of the back wall. This imagery, by no means exclusively baptismal, appears in a number of different 5th-century contexts, including the "Tomb" of Galla Placidia in Ravenna and S. Maria della Croce in Casaranello, as well as the baptistery at Naples and the lost baptistery in Nola (Paulinus of Nola, *Carmen* 28). Outside central and northern Italy, freestanding octagonal baptisteries are less common, although the Small Baptistery of Hagia Sophia in Constantinople indicates that the form was known in the east.

Distinct traditions of baptistery construction have been associated with other regions of the empire.

For example, Megaw identified a group of tripartite baptisteries in which the font is set in a small, screened space flanked by subsidiary chambers, and associated this type with the diocese of Antioch (St. Theodore, late 5th century, and St. John the Baptist, 6th century, in Jerash; late 4th- or early 5th-century baptisteries at Kourion, Agia Trias, St. Philon, Carpasia, and Salamis; and perhaps the baptistery at the Holy Sepulcher in Jerusalem). The intimate spaces of these baptisteries, as well as the elaborate explanations of nakedness in the catechetical lectures of Cyril of Jerusalem and John Chrysostom in Antioch, suggest that at least in the east initiates continued to be baptized in the nude.

Most early Christian baptisteries do not, however, conform to a regional type. The most common form of baptistery throughout the late empire was an apsed or simple rectangular chamber directly attached to a church. For example, the 6th century tetraconch church in Resafa has an apsed rectangular space with an octagonal font to the north of the sanctuary; Basilicas 2 and 3 in Leptis Magna both have square baptisteries of the 6th century with cruciform fonts to the north of the apse; the font excavated at S. Stephano on Via Latina in Rome is placed in a square room to the northwest of the west-oriented sanctuary; at Sabratha, Basilica Three has two rectangular baptisteries, one of the late 4th century on the south and another of the 6th century to the north of the west-oriented church. One of the more elaborate and well preserved examples of a rectangular baptistery is that attached to the cathedral of S. Restituta in Naples built by Bishop Soter between 465 and 481. The dome and squinches that vault the square plan retain much of their original mosaic decoration. At the apex a Chi-Rho is depicted on a starry field; lush festoons and curtains entrame eight impressionistically rendered narrative episodes, among which the *Traditio Legis*, the Samaritan woman at the well, the marriage at Cana, and the draught of fishes can still be identified. Shepherds flanked by either sheep or drinking stags appear above the evangelist symbols, which occupy the squinches. On either side of the windows are crown-bearing apostles.

Although the particular form of a baptistery cannot serve as an indication of its provenance, eastern and western baptisteries may perhaps be distinguished by their distribution. In contrast to the west, where large baptisteries are, with important exceptions, associated with cathedrals, in the east and in parts of North Africa impressively scaled baptisteries commonly appear in rural as well as urban sites, suggesting that initiation was controlled by holy ascetics as well as bishops. Elaborate baptisteries are, for example, associated with the great pilgrimage shrines of St. John in Ephesus (5th or 6th century), St. Symeon at Kal'at Sim'an, Syria (late 5th century), and Abu Mena in Egypt (late 5th and beginning of the 6th century). Smaller monaster-

333

ies, like Alahan Monastir in Asia Minor (late 5th century), also might have elaborate baptisteries.

With the shift from adult to infant baptism that marked the progressive dominance of Christianity in the empire, the rite of initiation lost its spectacular civic character. Typically newborns were baptized by parish priests. Although some old baptisteries continued to function, new, large baptismal halls were rarely built except in those areas on the periphery in which there was still significant adult conversion to Christianity. The revival of large baptismal halls in Italy in the high Middle Ages is apparently related to citizenship and polity in the emerging communes rather than to significant liturgical changes in the rite of baptism.

BIBL.: Enrico Cattaneo, "Il battistero in Italia dopo il mille," *Miscellanea Gilles Gerard Meersseman*, Italia sacra, Studi e documenti di storia ecclesiastica 15 (Padua, 1970), 171–195. Charles Delvoye, "Baptisterium," *Reallexikon zur byzantinischen Kunst*, 1 (Stuttgart, 1966), cols. 460–496. Thomas M. Finn, *Early Christian Baptism and the Catechumenate: West and East Syria* and *Early Christian Baptism and the Catechumenate: Italy, North Africa, and Egypt*, Message of the Fathers of the Church, vols. 5 and 6 (Collegeville, Minn., 1992). Armen Khatchatrian, *Les baptistères paléochrétiens* (Paris, 1962). Spiro K. Kostof, *The Orthodox Baptistery of Ravenna* (New Haven, 1965). A. H. S. Megaw, "Excavations at the Episcopal Basilica of Kourion in Cyprus in 1974–1975: A Preliminary Report," *Dumbarton Oaks Papers* 30 (1976): 345–372.   A.J.W.

Barbaria

Barbaria is the name given in the anonymous *Periplus Maris Erythraei* (*Periplus of the Erythraean Sea*, mid-1st century C.E.) to two stretches of the coast of East Africa: Barbaria proper, from below ancient Berenice on the Red Sea to above Ptolemais Theron, and "farside" Barbaria, from the Straits of Bab el Mandeb to Ras Hafun. In Ptolemy's *Geography* (mid-2nd century C.E.) the name is given to the next stretch of coast, from Ras Hafun to, roughly, Zanzibar. The native population throughout was primitive, made up of tribes the Greeks called *ichthuophagoi* (fish eaters), *rhizophagoi* (root eaters), and the like. Greeks entered the area in the 3rd century B.C.E., when the Ptolemies planted settlements up to Cape Guardafui to serve as bases for hunting elephants to train for war; those settlements along the shore of the Gulf of Aden, a prime source of myrrh and frankincense, continued in use throughout antiquity for the export of those valued substances to the Mediterranean world. Besides myrrh and frankincense, Barbaria—as understood by both the *Periplus* and Ptolemy—was also a source of ivory and tortoiseshell, and there were numerous small ports along its length to handle that trade.

The coast between the two Barbarias in *Periplus* was more or less dominated by the kingdom of Axum. On it, near modern Massawa, was the port of Adulis, the kingdom's sole access to the sea. Adulis was in its heyday from the 4th to the 7th century C.E., when it served as the port par excellence for ships in the trade between the west and India.

BIBL.: L. Casson, *The Periplus Maris Erythraei* (Princeton, 1989). Ptolemy, *Geography* 4.7.28.   L.C.

Barbarian

The term *barbarian*, derived from Greek ideals of cultural "otherness," sat uncomfortably with Roman traditions of inclusion. Goths and Franks were called Scythians, Getae, Sicambri, as though they were the barbarians of Herodotus and Tacitus, yet Frank and Goth generals commanded armies of Rome without rancour. Inevitably there were tensions between an ideology that asserted that Rome possessed a unique capacity to rule and the reality that the empire had been won with the aid of non-Romans. But there was no objective view of "barbarity," no precise distinction between barbarian and savage.

The image of *barbaricum* began at the frontiers. But the idea of a wall around the empire, separating Rome from the outer *gentes*, was an image never reconciled with Rome's civilizing mission. Julian voyaged down the Danube with "all barbary kneeling on the left bank making abject prayers" (*Pan.Lat.* 11[3] 7.2), and imperial iconography regularly portrayed emperors trampling barbarian enemies underfoot or leading them to captivity by the hair. Every "good" emperor set up inscriptions of himself as *domitor gentium barbararum*, corresponding to the actual image he paraded in the circus with prostrate prisoners (Symmachus, *Relatio* 47). But there was also a theme of conquest by other means, with the emperor as universal savior, the dispenser of *philanthropia*, as Themistius famously advocated to Theodosius (*Orat.* 15), probably reflecting the accord with the Goths in 382. Since all emperors were more worried about usurpers from within than enemies without, they readily admitted barbarian settlers as Roman soldiers, and the regular *receptio* (receiving) of outsiders was more significant than the ideology of barbarian *deditio* (surrender). The conflicting images are captured on the obelisk of Theodosius at Constantinople, depicting both the submission of kneeling barbarians and long-haired barbarian soldiers standing at the emperor's side.

The term *barbarian* focused generalizations—giving an appearance of unity to disjointed and fractious groups—that again were contradictory. Barbarians were contemptible, unworthy enemies, "a people not much to be feared," as Ammianus Marcellinus said of the Quadi (Amm.Marc. 29.6.1), or fit only for slave dealers, as he described the Goths (Amm.Marc. 22.7.8). Or they overwhelmed everything like waves, floods, and volcanic lava. Barbarians were portrayed as destroyers when in reality most wanted land. Alaric's aims were distorted into, "So many Getic jaws open for the spoils of Latium" (Claudian, *Bell.Goth.* 29–30). Many stereotypes were simply ethnocentric, characteristic of societies under pressures of social change. Barbarians were natural slaves, animals, faithless, dishonest, treasonable, arrogant, drunken sots. Race riots occurred when Goths became a dominant presence, and Stilicho's politics were undermined by his barbarian origins. Both Constantius II and Theodosius were attacked for their concessions to barbarians, regardless of political necessity. Eunapius (frg. 59) pointedly recounted how Theodosius dined with Goths while they plotted treachery "beyond the normal savagery of barbarian custom."

Christians were not detached from the construction of these images. The fall of the Goth general Gainas and the massacre of his followers in 400 was represented by paintings in the circus with the caption, "The hand of God driving off the barbarian" (Eunapius, frg. 68), although another Goth, Fravitta, was appointed in his place. Some, like Ambrose, projected barbarians as drunks and faithless savages, although open to conversion; others detected God's hand using barbarians to punish Roman sins. By the 5th century, Salvian, Augustine, and Orosius were reconciled to the barbarian presence as a new order that compared well with the pagan past.

BIBL.: Y. A. Dauge, *Le barbare: Recherches sur la conception romaine de la barbarie et de la civilization* (Brussels, 1981). W. Goffart, "Rome, Constantinople and the Barbarians," in *Rome's Fall and After* (Ronceverte, W.V., 1989), 1–32. G. B. Ladner, "On Roman Attitudes towards Barbarians in Late Antiquity," *Viator* 7 (1976): 1–26.   C.W.

Barbarian Settlements

The Roman empire had a long history of "receiving" barbarians from beyond the frontiers to settle within the adjacent provinces, but references in the sources to such *receptio* increase significantly between the late 3rd and early 5th centuries, and most concern the frontier provinces of the Rhine and Danube. Typical is an idealized scene on a medallion of Constantine from Lyons illustrating barbarians being led across the Rhine at Mainz. But not all immigrants were settled on the frontiers. Ammianus (Amm.Marc. 28.5.15, 31.9.4), for instance, tells of Alaman and Tailfal prisoners who received lands in northern Italy; toponyms in Gaul suggest settlements as far south as Burgundy and the Auvergne; some Goths were settled in Asia Minor.

The majority of settlers probably entered under conditions of surrender *(deditio)* and semisubjection, since *dediticii* were denied Roman citizenship by the Edict of Caracalla (212 C.E.). But other names, such as *laeti* (confined to Gaul) and *tributarii,* were also used, sometimes without distinction, which makes it difficult to differentiate their precise status. Almost all immigrants appear to have been compelled to work the

land, assist in public corporations, or serve in military units, not unlike some *coloni,* with whom they are sometimes associated. A Gallic panegyricist (*Pan.Lat.* 6[7] 6.20) says, "They assist the Roman peace by cultivation and army conscription"; while an edict of 319 linked *tributarii* with *coloni* as those for whose debts a landlord was responsible (*C.Th.* 11.7.2). Some prisoners, like the Hunnish Sciri, were distributed as labor to private landowners under conditions of *ius colonatus* (*C.Th.* 5.6.3 [409]); others, like the Franks settled by Julian in Toxandria, appear to have formed virtually self-governing local enclaves. The status of *dediticius,* however, probably disappeared, like that of freedmen, in the succeeding generation; the usurper Magnentius rose through military service despite what some sources claimed were his laetic origins. A further term, *gentiles,* was probably confined to ethnic military units, such as the Sarmatians, who subsequently settled in the empire, or to border tribes, some of whom spanned the frontiers, as on the *limes Tripolitanus.*

It is impossible to be precise about total numbers, often cited in tens of thousands, as when Constantine supposedly settled 300,000 Sarmatians in the Danube provinces (Anonymus Valesianus 6.32). Although ancient sources are unreliable, we know barbarian settlers were regarded (by the Gallic panegyricists, for example; *Pan.Lat.* 8[5] 21) as a significant source of labor replacement after barbarian attacks, while sixteen laetic or gentile units are recorded on the *Notitia Galliarum* in northern Gaul and Germany. Even a conservative guess of 20,000 settlers in northeastern Gaul would represent about 2 percent of the population, but the reality could be ten times greater. The "countless multitude" (Amm.Marc. 31.4.8) of Goths who migrated across the Danube under pressure from the Huns and Alans in the late 4th and the 5th centuries was perceived as a major demographic event, even if the figure of 200,000 (Eunapius, frg. 42) before Adrianople was a fantasy.

In the later 4th century and the 5th century a new source of settlers appeared in the form of federate groups who were granted access to land under treaty *(foedus).* Although doubts have recently been expressed about the difference between such agreements and earlier terms of *receptio,* there is no doubt about the increasing employment of federate soldiers. Since many remained as settlers, their status was probably superior to that of previous subject immigrants, and we read, for example, of Goths who were given citizenship. The policy change is usually associated with treaties struck by Theodosius I and Gratian with the Goths in 382, but it accelerated when large numbers of federates were employed in the west to bolster the frontiers in the 5th century and were subsequently rewarded with land. Typical was the installation of Alans near Orléans, where rich *domini* were ordered by the Roman general Aetius to give up their lands to the soldiers (*Chronica Gallica of 451,* a. 442). It was a short step from this sort of settlement to the first barbarian kingdom of the Visigoths in Aquitaine in 412 C.E. Although the origins of Alaric and his Goths remain obscure, there is a fair possibility that he came from a community of Goths settled within the empire under treaty.

The archaeology of barbarian settlements has proved elusive. The appearance of belt fittings and buckles, weapons and ornamental fibulae was once thought to provide evidence of German settlers. Many such items were found in cemeteries composed of "row graves" whose dates extended into periods long after the breakdown of Roman administration, such as in the famous cemetery of 5,000 graves on the site of the Roman Rhine fort of Gelduba (modern Krefeld-Gellep). More recently doubts about the German origin of the weapons and artifacts have been expressed, since they have been found only within the Roman empire and are now attributed to a new frontier military culture that included Germans, Goths, and Romans. Hence it is impossible to be categorical about the ethnic character of the settlement archaeology. Recent study of the northern Gallic and German provinces make it clear that, despite considerable damage in the late 3rd century and even more radical changes in the mid-4th century, the land itself was not abandoned by the native rural inhabitants, many of whom remained as squatters on the Roman villa sites. In some cases wooden longhouses and dugout huts (Grubenhäuser), which look like German dwellings, were added to the farm buildings, and the cemetery evidence suggests new social groupings of warrior leaders and their followers, some of them Gallo-Romans.

This symbiotic process is consistent with the literary evidence, which attributes large numbers of German immigrants to the period of the usurpations of Magnentius in the rule of Constantius II, followed by the restoration of order under Julian, when the Roman authorities gave extensive permission to settle. Most of the Roman settlements and villas are thought to have been abandoned in the 5th century, but there are serious contradictions in the dating of late Roman pottery finds and the identity of early Merovingian sites, almost all of which are graveyards. New evidence, however, is beginning to come to light. The cemetery at Vron (Somme) shows continuity from the 4th to the 7th century, and Condé-sur-Aisne has revealed hundreds of building structures between the same dates. In general, therefore, historians are less inclined to describe the barbarian settlements in terms of rupture and to see them instead as a process of continuous assimilation.

BIBL.: P. J. Heather, *Goths and Romans 332–489* (Oxford, 1991). E. James, *The Franks* (Oxford, 1988). A debate centers around the work of Walter Goffart, *Barbarians and Romans, A.D. 418–584* (Princeton, 1980); see C. Wickham, *Land and Power: Studies in Italian and European Social History, 400–1200* (London, 1994), 41 and n. 21.   C.W.

Basil of Caesarea

Known as Basil the Great and one of the three Cappadocian Fathers, Basil of Caesarea was born ca. 330 into a wealthy Christian family in Pontus. He sat briefly at the feet of Libanius in Constantinople and completed his education in Athens, where he was taught by Himerius and Prohaeresius among others. That combination of religious and cultural instruction enabled him to write his later influential *Address to Young Men,* which discussed what a Christian might gain from the traditional curriculum. He might have embarked on a teaching career himself, but the influence of Eustathius of Sebaste, reinforced by his own travel to the great cities and monastic sites of the eastern provinces, inclined Basil to asceticism. He withdrew to family property in Pontus, where his mother and sister Macrina had already established a household ascetic community. He was accompanied for a time by Gregory of Nazianzus, his fellow student and lifelong friend. During this period the two compiled the *Philocalia,* an anthology of long extracts from the works of Origen. Others were also attracted by Basil's rigor and shrewd reflection.

Basil's ascetic experience was distilled chiefly in his *Asceticon,* more commonly known as the *Long Rules* and *Short Rules.* They were neither wholly "monastic," since he believed his ascetic principles were applicable to all Christians, nor were they "rules" in the strict sense but rather responses to the inquiries of the devout. They exalted the cenobitic or communal ideal over the anchoritic life and emphasized moderation in the practice of ascetic disciplines. Basil presented asceticism as a life of service to God through liturgical and private prayer, obedience, voluntary poverty, charity, and manual labor. His *Rules* became foundational for monastic organization in the east, influenced St. Benedict's establishment of a Rule for the west, and have remained the guiding light for Greek and Slavonic monasticism.

Engaging in church affairs from 360, Basil was active in theological controversies and ecclesiastical politics. He allied himself with Basil of Ancyra and developed a lifelong loyalty to Melitius of Antioch. He consistently advocated a straightforward attachment to Nicaea, adding only (in both the *Contra Eunomium* and the *De spiritu sancto*) a fuller reflection on the divinity of the Spirit. With the other Cappadocians, he worked out an understanding of the Trinity that emphasized the individuality of persons *(hypostaseis)* while also insisting on the divine unity—a formulation of the doctrine that was incorporated in the wording of the Niceno-Constantinopolitan Creed. Owing to his cautious language regarding the divinity of the Spirit, Basil was viewed with some suspicion by more forceful opponents of Arianism in both Alexandria and Rome, but he was admired for his courage in his dealings with Valens, and he refuted with some success the Arian theologian Eunomius. His family relations were less successful: he distanced himself from his sister Macrina and despaired of the practical abilities of his brother Gregory of Nyssa; but his subsequent reputation probably owed much to Gregory and to his youngest brother, Peter.

He became bishop of Caesarea in 370 after some hesitant years as a priest, and at first faced challenge and unpopularity, caused chiefly by the circumstances of his election and by his characteristic combination of ascetic fervor and social concern. On the outskirts of the city he established a complex of buildings to serve the needs of the sick, the indigent, poor travelers, and strangers. The social service program he instituted became a model for Byzantine philanthropy in subsequent centuries. His care for the sick and the poor was supported financially by Valens himself—a credit to both men—and the emperor showed further admiration and trust by sending Basil in 373 to restore order to church affairs in Armenia.

His letters tell us much about life in Cappadocia and elsewhere. They are both intimate and condescending, revealing both friend and patron, and rich in allusion to church practice and secular government. His homilies are polished, humorous, and vivid. Their image of the church is sympathetic and inventive, the work of a conscientious pastor, a fearless social critic, and an optimistic visionary. Among his greatest achievements was his *Hexaemeron,* comparable to Augustine's major works and imitated by Ambrose. An attempt to present a complete Christian cosmology, these homilies draw extensively on the classical tradition, show sensitivity to contemporary philosophy and science, display a deep and humane affection, and present an exalted image of the future.

Basil died in 379. In addition to his monastic, theological, and social contributions, he was revered in Byzantium for his liturgical activity. Reflecting his inspiration if not his direct authorship, the liturgy of St. Basil predominated in the Byzantine church until ca. 1000. Eastern Orthodox Christians consider Basil, along with Gregory of Nazianzus and John Chrysostom, one of the three hierarchs of the faith.

BIBL.: *Lettres,* ed. Y. Courtonne, 3 vols. (Paris, 1957–1966). *Contre Eunome,* ed. B. Sesboüé et al., Sources Chrétiennes 299, 305 (Paris, 1982, 1983). *Sur le saint-esprit,* ed. B. Pruche, 2nd ed., Sc 17 bis (Paris, 1968). *Homélies sur l'hexaéméron,* ed. S. Giet, 2nd ed., Sc 26 bis (Paris, 1968). *Regulae fusius tractatae, PG* 31.889–1050. *Regulae brevius tractatae, PG* 31.1080A–1305B. N. G. Wilson, ed., *Saint Basil on the Value of Greek Literature* (London, 1975). *The Philocalia of Origen,* ed. J. A. Robinson (Cambridge, Eng., 1893). Gregory of Nazianzus, *Orat. 43, PG* 36.493–605, ed. Jean Bernardi, SC 384 (Paris, 1992). Stanislas Giet, *Les idées et l'action sociales de S. Basile* (Paris, 1941). Jean Bernardi, *La prédication des pères cappadociens: Le prédicateur et son auditoire* (Paris, 1968). Paul Jonathan Fedwick, ed., *Basil of Caesarea: Christian, Humanist, Ascetic* (Toronto, 1981). Jean Gribomont, *Saint Basile: Évangile et église: Mélanges,* 2 vols. (Abbaye de Bellefontaine, 1984). Philip Rousseau, *Basil of Caesarea* (Berkeley, 1994). Anthony Meredith, *The Cappadocians* (London, 1995).   P.R.

Basilica

Descended from the Hellenistic "royal portico" *(basilikē stoa),* the late antique basilica was a monumental public building, situated in most Roman cities next to the forum and used as a market, for public gatherings, and as a law court. A related type of basilica served as reception or audience hall in a private or official palatial residence. There were regional variations—in the east, for example, the normal plan was longer and narrower than in the west—but basilicas everywhere were longitudinal (longer than wide) and frequently either had internal colonnades enclosing a hypaethral (open-air) court or a truss roof supported on colonnades that divided the interior into a nave and two aisles. The nave of a roofed basilica might be brightly lit through large windows that pierced clerestorey walls above the colonnades. On one of the short sides, or alternatively looking over one of the aisles, there would be a tribunal for the presiding magistrate and his attendants, often separated from public space by a chancel screen and contained in an attached apse.

The Roman basilica was essentially secular, and there is little evidence from the 1st through 3rd centuries that basilical architecture influenced buildings designed from the outset for religious use. The 3rd century synagogue at Sardis in Asia, for example, occupied a wing of a bath and gymnasium that had already been converted into a basilical hall with an apse and aisles before the Jewish community took possession. Yet public basilicas enclosed a space replete with holiness and power. Among other divine images, they housed the emperor's statue, essential in law courts, and the typical adornment of sculptured colonnades and entablatures—stone masonry or its imitation in stucco—and coffered ceilings with painted or gilt decoration likewise evoked religious and imperial majesty.

By the early 4th century, a typical plan featured a narthex, a single nave without aisles, an apse on the long axis, and grand scale. The best preserved example of all is the basilica that Constantine built in Trier in 305 to 312 as the audience hall of the imperial palace. This had a truss roof and coffered ceiling, but the traditional colonnades and decorative sculpture were suppressed in favor of flatter wall decoration, suggestive of the future style, that consisted of mosaics, painted stucco, and multicolored marble revetments.

Constantine then selected this building type, with its desirable implications of imperial patronage and ready adaptability to the liturgical needs of Christian congregations, for the first truly monumental Christian churches. The earliest was St. John Lateran, built 312/13–ca. 320 to be the see of the bishop of Rome, which had four aisles, two on each side, separated by colonnades. Most characteristic, though, was Constantine's church in Jerusalem at the site of the Holy Sepulcher. Also a four-aisled basilica, this church, built in the years 325–336, had a coffered ceiling and was preceded on the east by a colonnaded atrium. In a letter to the local bishop, Constantine ordered construction of "a basilica finer than any other" (Eusebius, *Vit.Const.* 3.31), explicitly placing this church in the mainstream of the basilica tradition.

Thereafter, roofed basilicas were usually built as churches, but curiously the term *basilica* was infrequently used for them. In late antiquity the word usually meant a covered colonnade or a hypaethral court surrounded by colonnades, as in the *basilikē* that Emperor Valens built in Antioch ca. 375 (John Malalas, *Chronographia,* 338–339).

BIBL.: Richard Krautheimer, "The Constantinian Basilica," *Dumbarton Oaks Papers* 21 (1967): 117–140. Idem, *Early Christian and Byzantine Architecture,* 3rd ed. rev. (Harmondsworth, 1981). Glanville Downey, "The Words *Stoa* and *Basilike* in Classical Literature," *American Journal of Archaeology* 41 (1937): 184–211.   K.G.H.

Bathing

So deeply rooted was the custom of public bathing in Roman culture that sheer momentum carried it well into the world of late antiquity. Rome received two of its largest baths, the *thermae* of Diocletian and the *thermae* of Constantine, at the very end of its tenure as the center of imperial power. Early in the 5th century Rome had 856 small baths; Constantinople had 153, and Antioch must have had several dozen. In the enumeration of municipal expenses under Justinian, the costs of heating and maintaining the baths were listed next to those of the army. Even small cities and villages in distant provinces matched the unflagging interest of metropolitan populations in keeping their baths in good order. A petition sent by the Lydian peasants to a Byzantine emperor complained that their village "had been forced to give up even its public baths" in order to meet the excessive burden of taxes imposed by a multitude of greedy imperial tax collectors.

Although St. Jerome's forceful injunction, "He who has bathed in Christ once has no need of a second bath," echoed through centuries and shaped conservative Christian attitudes to our own time, the early church never formulated a universal and dogmatic ban against bathing. Perceiving them as lucrative business enterprises, some practical-minded church concerns even owned and operated baths. Often a part of ecclesiastical palaces and monasteries, baths were sometimes opened for the ritual cleansing of the laity and the poor. Perhaps the populist Christian distaste for bathing was largely a residue of ascetic feelings against the perceived luxury of bathing in Roman culture, as

well as a contemptuous association of baths with the rising world of Islam.

On a more practical level, however, the growing influence of Christianity left its impact on the customs of bathing. Concerns for modesty, as well as shrinking municipal budgets, must have been responsible for the gradual abandonment of communal bathing in large pools in favor of the smaller, personal tubs and hip baths typical of Byzantine and early Islamic baths. Foremost among the pagan institutions rejected by the church was the gymnasium, the quintessential cultural foundation of the classical world and one that had become closely related to Roman baths in the form of palaestras intended for athletic exercise. None of the baths established after the 4th century combined a bath and a palaestra; some already existing palaestras were either built over by neighboring structures or paved in stone, changing them from exercise grounds to civic plazas.

In the east, the transition of classical bathing culture to its early Christian and Islamic forms was remarkably smooth. The small, compactly designed baths of Syrian market towns such as Serdjilla, Brad, and Babiska offered not only the welcome amenities of water and hygiene at the edge of the desert but also the pleasures of a friendly gathering in their comfortable lounges and courtyards. After the habit of following hot bathing with a cold plunge was abandoned, the *frigidarium* proper gradually was replaced by the social hall. Lavishly decorated bathing suites that form an important component at Qasr al-Amrah and Khirbat al-Mafjar, hunting lodges and fortified desert palaces of the Umayyad period (8th century) in Jordan, provide glowing testimony to the acceptance of the classical tradition of bathing as a social and cultural institution by the upper echelon of Islamic society. The baths and bathing habits of the late antique world, Christian or Islamic, symbolized something more than amenities. They symbolized the continuity of urban civilization in a world that perpetually threatened it.

BIBL.: H. Groztfeld, *Das Bad im arabisch-islamischen Mittelalter* (Wiesbaden, 1970). G. Schöllgen, "Balnea mixta: Entwicklung der spätantiken Bademoral," in *Festschrift K. Thraede* (Münster, 1995), 182–194. Fikret Yegül, *Baths and Bathing in Classical Antiquity* (New York, 1992; repr. 1995). Y. Hirschfeld, *The Roman Baths at Hammat Gader* (Jerusalem, 1997).   F.Y.

Bedchambers

Bedchambers (Greek *koitōn* and Latin *cubiculum*), especially those of the Byzantine emperor or empress, are mentioned in texts on court ceremonial and the rankings of officials in the imperial palace in Constantinople. Courtiers and servants attached to the bedchamber were traditionally eunuchs. The office of *praepositus sacri cubiculi,* or grand chamberlain, was instituted by Constantine the Great and included managing the bedchamber, imperial wardrobe, and receptions; the *cubicularii* assigned to the bedchamber were the most important class of palace servants by the 5th century. Of these, the office of *parakoimōmenos*, the one "sleeping next to" the emperor, attested from the late 6th century, became self-sustaining by the 10th century. This high ranking and powerful official served as an imperial bodyguard and presided over the *koitōnitai* serving in the bedchamber.

Corippus's poem *In Laudem Iustini* (ca. 565) (1.97–114) allows us to visualize an imperial bedchamber, shining with light and ornaments and situated so as to provide views of the sea and the harbor. In the *Klētorologion* of Philotheos (ca. 900), court dignitaries are described by rank, including those managing the bedchamber of the emperor and empress. The *Book of Ceremonies* of Constantine Porphyrogenitus (ca. 957) frequently refers to the emergence of the emperor from or retirement to the *koitōn* of the Daphne and the Octagon Palaces within the imperial palace, usually in relation to a change of ceremonial garb. The *Vita Basilii* (ca. 950, v. 89) gives us a long description of a bedchamber in the Kainourgion Palace, with its floor mosaics depicting peacocks and eagles and wall mosaics of the imperial family, accompanied by an inscription giving thanks to God. Anna Comnena's *Alexiad* (ca. 1148) (8.2, n. 4) notes the ancient tradition of Byzantine empresses giving birth in a splendid hall of the palace known as the porphyra.

While archaeological evidence for Byzantine imperial bedchambers is lacking, there is some reason to think they followed Roman precedent. Excavation has yielded a clear idea of the typical late Roman or late antique villa, in which the bedroom is easily identified. The bed was often installed on a raised dais or in a part of the room with less ornate floor mosaics. Reception rooms were often juxtaposed near bedrooms, showing the interspersal of public and private spaces; bedrooms were sometimes grouped around a secondary peristyle, and they were numerous in large villas. The preserved *cubiculum* from a villa of 40–30 B.C.E. at Boscoreale, near Pompeii, now reconstructed at the Metropolitan Museum in New York, provides an example of a Roman bedroom with frescoes and floor mosaics. An early Islamic villa or small palace of 711–715 excavated at Qaṣr 'Amrah (Jordan) shows a layout similar to that of Roman villas, with symmetrically arranged bedchambers adjacent to a reception hall joined to a bath; these bedchambers also have preserved frescoes and mosaic floors.

BIBL.: J. B. Bury, *The Imperial Administrative System in the Ninth Century with a Revised Text of the Kletorologion of Philotheos* (New York, n.d.). Constantine Porphyrogenitus, *Le livre des cérémonies,* ed. Albert Vogt (Paris, 1967). K. A. C. Cresswell, *Early Muslim Architecture* (Oxford, 1932 and 1940; repr. 1969). Rodolphe Guilland, *Recherches sur les institutions byzantines* (Berlin and Amsterdam, 1967). H. Schlinkert, "Vom Haus zum Hof: Aspekte höfischer Herrschaft in der Spätantike," *Klio* 78 (1996): 452–482. Yvon Thébert, "Private Life and Domestic Architecture in Roman Africa," in *A History of Private Life,* vol. 1: *From Pagan Rome to Byzantium,* ed. Paul Veyne (Cambridge, Mass., 1987), 313–405.
C.C.

Belts

Attested since prehistoric times by archaeological evidence, belts served practical, decorative, and amuletic purposes. In the late Roman west, inhabitants wore belts *(cinguli, zonae)* of cloth, rope, leather, or metal to gather in their long tunics. Distinctive belts served as insignia of high civil or military status (*C.Th.* 14.10.1.1), perhaps due to ancient symbolism of binding and loosing. From a leather girdle *(cingulum)* or shoulder belt *(balteus)* with metal plaques, late Roman and early medieval soldiers hung their weapons (Isidore of Seville, *Etymologies* 19.33). Beginning in the 4th century in Gaul and Germany, belts were buried in graves with their owners, since they expressed ideal status and protected their bearers. Such belts were usually composed of sturdy leather or metal, since they were made to carry armament or, when worn by women and children, everyday and symbolic objects including keys, knives, amulet bags, and utensils. Gregory of Tours observed that gem-bedecked gold belts were offered along with swords as precious gifts and tribute (*History of the Franks* 7.38; 10.21). Among Christians, while liturgical belts are not well attested in the east or west before the 9th century, girding one's loins had long constituted an outward sign of ascetic behavior (Luke 12:35–37). Hence, the 6th century Rule of St. Benedict included belts among the possessions of a monk (c.55), and instructed that they be worn day and night (c.22). Venantius Fortunatus praised Queen Radegund's donation of her gold girdle to the poor (*Life* of St. Radegund 1.13). Burgundian belt buckles were often noted for bearing biblical images such as Daniel in the lions' den. In Ireland and on the early medieval continent, buckles sometimes had hollowed spaces for holding relics or amulets.

A belt or girdle was part of the distinguishing clothing that Christians and Jews in Islamic lands were required to wear according to the laws of differentiation *(ghiyār)* decreed by Muslim rulers. These laws were intended to maintain recognizable differences between Muslims and non-Muslims. The belt was usually called a *zunnār* (from *zōnarion* in Greek; *zonara* in Syriac), the name for a belt worn by Christians in pre-Islamic times in some of the areas that came under Islamic rule in the 7th century.

BIBL.: Mark R. Cohen, *Under Crescent and Cross: The Jews in the Middle Ages* (Princeton, 1994). Birgit Dübner-Manthey, "Kleingeräte am Gürtelgehänge als Bestandteil eines charakteristischen Elementes der weiblichen Tracht," in Werner Affeldt and Annette Kuhn, eds., *Frauen in der Geschichte,* vol. 7 (Düsseldorf, 1986), 88–124. H. Leclercq, "Ceinture," *Dictionnaire d'archéologie chrétienne et de liturgie,* vol. 8 (Paris, 1909), 2779–2794. M. Sommer, *Die Gürtel und Gürtelbeschläge des 4. und 5. Jahrhunderts im römischen Reich* (Bonn, 1994).   B.E.

Benedict

Benedict of Nursia, St. Benedict (ca. 480–547), is considered the father of western monasticism. Benedict's career illustrates the disorder of monastic life in the early 6th century and the difficulty of formulating a successful rule of common life.

Benedict was born in Nursia, about 70 miles northeast of Rome, around the year 480. His parents were wealthy enough to send him to Rome for his education. Finding his peers too worldly, Benedict gave up his studies and renounced his home and inheritance. He took up religious life (ca. 500), retiring to a cave at Subiaco, about 35 miles from Rome. A monk named Romanus from a neighboring monastery supplied Benedict's daily needs. Gradually Benedict the hermit became known and gained disciples. He was chosen to serve as abbot of a neighboring monastery on the death of the monks' leader, but Benedict's severity led the monks to poison his wine. Escaping their plot, Benedict returned to the wilderness.

Again Benedict's life as a hermit attracted followers. Gregory's account credits him with establishing twelve monasteries in the area of Subiaco, three of them on barely accessible rocky heights. Once more Benedict became the target of hostility and homicide, this time from a priest, Florentius, in a neighboring church. Having escaped a second poisoning, Benedict left the area with several of his followers (ca. 529), after first reorganizing his monasteries and appointing priors to help govern them.

Benedict and his followers settled in Monte Cassino, a citadel about 75 miles south of Rome. The monastery endured attacks from the Ostrogoths in the 540s. After Benedict's death, it was destroyed by the Lombard duke Zotto in 589 and was not rebuilt until 720. Benedict remained at Monte Cassino until his death ca. 547, when he was buried in the same grave as his sister, St. Scholastica.

The principal document of Benedict's life is the *Dialogues* of Gregory the Great, written about 594. Gregory reports what is told to him by four witnesses who knew Benedict: Constantine and Simplicius, who succeeded Benedict as abbot; Honoratus, who was abbot at the first monastery where Benedict lived; and Valentinian, who was abbot of the Lateran monastery. Gregory credits Benedict with writing a Rule "noteworthy for its discretion." The Benedictine Rule relies principally on the *Regula magistri,* and is also related

to the Rule of Basil, and to Augustine, Cassian, Caesarius of Arles, and the Desert Fathers. Benedict's feast day is July 11 in the western church and March 14 in the eastern church.

BIBL.: J. Chapman, *Saint Benedict and the Sixth Century* (London, 1929). A. de Vogüé, *Saint Benoît: Sa vie et sa règle: Études choisies,* Vie Monastique 12 (Bellefontaine, 1981). O. L. Kapsner, *A Benedictine Bibliography,* 2nd ed. (Collegeville, Minn., 1962), 2 vols.   C.S.

Berber

Although the term *Berber* has many layers of meaning for cultural identity in North Africa today, it was originally used by the Muslim Arabs who conquered North Africa in the 7th century to refer to the non-Roman natives of the region, who belonged to a wide variety of tribal groups and confederations. The term was borrowed from the Latin *barbari,* which referred to peoples who did not speak Greek or Latin. In the modern historiography of Roman and early Islamic North Africa, it continues to refer to tribal groups who were linked linguistically and sometimes culturally, but not necessarily ethnically. The script of a single language group has been found in widely different parts of the region; it was much influenced by Punic, which is believed to be the ancestor of Tifinagh, spoken by the Touareg Berbers today. In late antiquity, Berber was a collective term for tribes whose distinctiveness in fact countervailed the implied homogeneity.

The Romans were more geographically specific when they referred to the natives of Africa as Libyci, Gaetuli (inhabitants of the areas outside the provinces of Numidia and Mauritania), Mauri, and so on. Libyan and southern *gentes* on the frontier fringes are recorded in the 5th century as manning forts of the frontier ditch called the *fossatum.* Many, like the Arzuges noted by Augustine in southern Tripolitania or those described in southern Algeria as *Barbari transtagnentes,* migrated seasonally across borders. Others in the mountainous fastnesses of the Aures and Kabylie lived on fortified estates, constructing *centenaria* and *castella,* but recent archaeology shows how deeply Romanization had penetrated. One Berber chief, Nubel, whose sons Firmus and Gildo led rebellions against Rome in the late 4th century, was a Roman officer and a founder of Christian churches. Successor kings, such as Masties in the Aures (ca. 455) or Masuna in western Algeria (ca. 508), carried on aspects of Roman culture well into the Islamic period.

The term *Berber* is relevant in the modern historiography of the later Roman empire, first in the cultural debate concerning Romanization and the resistance of a so-called *permanence berbère,* and second in the debate about a "forgotten Africa" (a term coined by Christian Courtois), supposedly untouched by Rome, which gave rise to later "Berber kingdoms." The survival of artistic and social characteristics, such as geometric designs, religious practices, and folklore, into modern times is also debatable, since many are shared by rural Arabs. Attempts to discover traces of such features in Donatism have been challenged.

BIBL.: M. Brett and E. Fentress, *The Berbers* (Oxford, 1996). G. Camps, *Berbères: Aux marges de l'histoire* (Paris, 1980). C. Courtois, *Les Vandales et l'Afrique* (Paris, 1955; repr. 1964). *Encyclopédie Berbère* (Aix-en-Provence, 1984–). M. Shatzmiller, "Le mythe d'origine berbère: Aspects historiographiques et sociaux," *Revue de l'occident musulman et de la Méditerranée*, 35 (1983): 145–156. C.W.

Bible Translations

During the late antique period the Bible (or parts of it) was translated into Latin and Gothic in the west, and in the east into Syriac, Coptic, Armenian, Georgian, Ethiopic, and Arabic.

The earliest Latin translations of various books of the Bible probably date from the second half of the 2nd century. Old Testament books were not translated from the Hebrew but were based on the Greek version known as the Septuagint. During the 3rd and 4th centuries independent translations of New Testament books, made in North Africa and in Italy, resulted in a welter of diverse renderings. The ever-increasing divergencies, the defective textual tradition, and the lack of literary elegance in the Old Latin versions prompted Pope Damasus (366–384) to urge Jerome to prepare a revision that might, it was hoped, become the common biblical text of the western church.

Despite Jerome's initial reluctance to undertake a task that, he suspected, would expose him to charges of tampering with Holy Writ, he nevertheless acceded to the pontiff's request. For the New Testament he made comparisons with ancient Greek manuscripts and altered the Old Latin rendering only when it seemed absolutely necessary. This procedure accounts for the diverse renderings of identical expressions in Greek; for example, "high priest" is usually translated in Matthew and Luke as *princeps sacerdotum,* in Mark as *summus sacerdos,* and in John as *pontifex.*

Jerome's growing interest in Hebrew led him to take up residence in Bethlehem. There during the years 390–405 he translated the Old Testament directly from the Hebrew text. In subsequent years his rendering gradually supplanted the various Old Latin translations and eventually became for the western church its standard version, called since about the 9th century the Vulgate *(versio vulgata).* Of the thousands of extant Vulgate manuscripts, the *Codex Amiatinus* of the 8th century, now in the Laurentian Library at Florence, is one of the most important.

The Gothic alphabet and the Gothic version of the Bible, notable as being by several centuries the earliest surviving monument in a Teutonic language, were made about 350 C.E. by Ulfilas, bishop of the West Goths. His translation is severely literal, the order of the Greek being almost always retained, often against the native Gothic idiom. Except for a deluxe copy of the four Gospels, written in the 6th century with silver ink on purple-dyed parchment and now in Uppsala, Sweden, only half a dozen other Gothic manuscripts have survived, and most of them are exceedingly fragmentary.

Among important eastern translations of the Bible, the Peshitta ("simple") Syriac version of the Old Testament was produced probably in the 2nd or 3rd century from the Hebrew. The Peshitta New Testament (which does not include 2 Peter, 2 and 3 John, Jude, and Revelation) took final form about 400. It is preserved in several hundred manuscripts, some from the 5th century. In the 6th and 7th centuries two other Syriac translations, the Philoxenian and the Harclean, were produced, the latter being an exceedingly literal rendering of the Greek.

Translations into several Egyptian Coptic dialects began to appear in the 3rd and 4th centuries. The most important of these were the Sahidic and the Bohairic; the latter became the accepted version of the Coptic Orthodox church.

The creation of the Armenian alphabet and the translation of the Bible are traditionally associated with the patriarchs Mesrob and Sahak (early 5th century). Based originally on an Old Syriac version, the translation was later made to conform with copies of the Greek Bible brought from Constantinople. The oldest dated manuscripts are from the 9th century.

The Georgian Bible, often called the twin sister of the Armenian, was completed by the end of the 6th century. The original version, made by several hands, rests on an Armenian-Syriac foundation but discloses some Greek influence.

The Ethiopic version was translated, it appears, from the Greek by the 5th century, but the earliest surviving manuscripts date from about the 14th century.

Several Arabic versions of the New Testament are known, but none seems to antedate the age of Muhammad; some were made from Syriac or Coptic (Bohairic), rather than Greek. The oldest surviving manuscript (8th century) is a translation of the Syriac Peshitta.

BIBL.: Bruce M. Metzger, *The Early Versions of the New Testament: Their Origin, Transmission, and Limitations* (Oxford, 1977). Ernst Würthwein, *The Text of the Old Testament,* 2nd ed., trans. Erroll F. Rhodes (Grand Rapids, Mich., 1995). B.M.

Bishops

In theory, bishops were chosen as religious leaders by the whole Christian community, and in fact the voice of the plebs did have its place, even if at times it was the voice of frustrated powerlessness or dissent. In the appointment of new bishops, it was quickly recognized that the support of neighboring bishops was essential to religious unity. The need for due order is defended in *1 Clement,* and such matters of practicality were reinforced by theological reflection—appealing to an episcopal succession that reached back to the apostles, tying a bishop to the sacramental economy of baptism and the Eucharist, and linking earthly authority with heavenly according to the slogan, "One God, one Christ, one bishop."

Between the Councils of Nicaea in 325 and Chalcedon in 451, the tolerant but intrusive interest of the state made church structures more rigid and complex. A minimum of three bishops assisted at each new consecration, with the approval of local colleagues. The bishop of the capital city in each civil province (the "metropolitan") acquired a veto over ecclesiastical elections, and the "patriarchs" of major sees—Antioch and Alexandria, Rome, Jerusalem, and, finally, Constantinople—had even wider powers. Twice a year bishops within each province held a council, or a bishop might invite colleagues to a local synod; only the emperor could convene an ecumenical or universal council. From the time of Theodosius I, the bishop of Constantinople was virtually an imperial nominee.

There were never as many aristocratic bishops as some literary evidence may suggest: most were *curiales* or less prominent officials. Nevertheless, while biblical exegesis, cultic purity, and moral leadership demanded both learning and virtue, congregations and colleagues soon recognized the additional advantages of good birth and public experience. Even emperors valued a bishop's usefulness as advocate, diplomat, and ambassador. And whether electors favored qualities of holiness or learning, there was also an increasing demand that candidates be drawn from the ranks of experienced priests.

Episcopal authority did not go unchallenged. It represented a choice among valued charisms, enhancing cult at the expense of insight and abnegation. Bishops might strive to imitate in their official lives the virtues of learning and asceticism, or they incorporated the learned and ascetic into their pastoral programs. Hence their admiration for virginity and their inclusion of women, widows as well as virgins, particularly in charitable enterprises. Bishops themselves were often married at the time of their election, but subsequent sexual relations were frowned upon, and there were always those who preferred a continent or virginal candidate. Bishops were nevertheless well able to institute a family monopoly of leadership in their diocese, even if their own children were not favored.

From early times, each city had its own bishop, and the small scale of most urban communities would have made him well known to the majority of his flock. To a lesser and sometimes disputed extent, a bishop's authority also reached out into the surrounding *territorium.* Once elected, a bishop was virtually irremovable, and he was forbidden by canonical custom to move from diocese to diocese. Apart from the emperor, no other figure in the empire enjoyed such powerful longevity. The restriction on movement, however, locked competent men into lower levels of the system and exposed prominent sees to lengthy government by the inexperienced.

Christians expected their bishops to interpret Scripture and to identify obligations. This they did through reflection, writing, and oratory. Bishops had much in common, therefore, with the philosophers and rhetors of the classical tradition. Yet they were not merely interpreters of a culture, even of a new biblical culture: they summed up in themselves the communities they led and were in effect suspended as intercessors and guides between human inadequacy and heavenly fulfillment. A bishop's status and influence, therefore, while based on personal qualities and the theological understanding of his office, could extend well beyond the religious sphere. Constantine inaugurated the *audientia episcopalis,* a court to which, by mutual agreement, litigants could refer their case (*C.Th.* 1.27.1; see *Sirmondian Constitutions* 1). The bishop's judgment was final, and the popularity of the court lay in its reduced exposure to bribery and its emphasis on reconciliation rather than strict justice. Bishops were able to imitate other persons of status by supporting clients before officials and judges; and within their own jurisdiction they quickly found the need to set up legal structures, such as for the payment of fees and the employment of the officials known as the *defensores ecclesiae.*

Bishops also wielded economic power. Hospitality toward strangers and the care of the poor were essential duties, supported by Constantine's decision to allow bequests to the church and by the growing expectation that persons of substance would leave as much as one-third of their property to the church. A special relationship with the poor had as its obverse a critical but close alliance with the rich: collaboration with lay patrons remained crucial to episcopal success. Bishops wished to encourage fresh ways of circulating wealth, appealing to ancient habits of public service and a new sense of social cohesion and moral responsibility.

In both the legal and the financial spheres, tolerance and privilege offered undeniable temptation, especially to personal luxury and material grandeur in ceremony and public buildings—as, for example, in the "lithomania" charged against Theophilus of Alexandria. The temptations arising from the vast concentration of wealth and power controlled by bishops often led to abuse, a fact that is nowhere better demonstrated than in the colorful accounts of charges brought at church councils against miscreant bishops. Although undoubtedly exaggerated or invented in some specific cases, these charges nevertheless give us some idea of the ways in which people reasonably expected episcopal misbehavior to manifest itself. At the Synod of the Oak in 403, John Chrysostom was charged with a long list of offenses ranging from battery and unlawful imprisonment to too-frequent bathing (a sign of luxury and vanity). Occupants of the more powerful sees were not above using violence or the threat thereof to intimidate opponents. Primian, Donatist bishop of Carthage, reportedly destroyed the houses of his critics and had one hapless presbyter thrown down a drain. Libellants presented at the Council of Chalcedon described how Dioscorus of Alexandria harassed and persecuted relatives of his predecessor, Cyril, to extort from them the wealth they had inherited from Cyril. Dioscorus had also engineered the condemnation of several prominent Syrian bishops by cooperating with local clergy and monks who had been making various complaints of misconduct against their bishops for several years; in Dioscorus they had finally found someone powerful enough and ready to listen to charges that served his own political and theological agenda. Ibas of Edessa allegedly pocketed gold given to the church for the support of the needy and the ransom of captives; provided poor-quality, spoiled wine for communion while keeping better vintages for himself; lent money at interest and then extorted repayment by threats of violence; sold ordinations; and took bribes from pagans to overlook their sacrifices.

The sins of clergy and lesser bishops were held against their superiors: between a third and half of all charges brought against bishops actually refer to crimes committed by others whom the bishop had ordained. In addition to his own misdeeds, Ibas, as metropolitan of Osrhoëne, had installed some very unqualified relatives in his suffragan sees, such as his nephew Daniel of Harran, a young, drunken playboy who lavished church wealth on his mistress, and Sophronius of Tella, who practiced astrology and was caught engaging in a complicated divination ritual involving a brass cauldron, a donkey, and a naked boy.

Later in the west, especially in Gaul, episcopal rank was seen as a way of preserving influence and family property, and a developing cult of local saints reinforced bishops' hold over the cities. Western churchmen, Pope Gelasius in particular, did much to develop the notion of "two powers": the emperor (or king) and his associates deferred to bishops in matters of religion, while bishops deferred to them in secular affairs. Ambrose of Milan was in part the architect of this view, and Gregory the Great was a prominent beneficiary. In practice, bishops exercised considerable influence outside the religious sphere (for example in fostering legislation), while emperors like Constantius, Zeno, and Justinian were never hesitant in taking the lead where doctrine was concerned. Changing circum-

stances in the west also encouraged a missionary impulse, obvious in the despatch of Augustine to Kent but earlier apparent in attempts to evangelize the countryside (often furthered by collusion with landowners against peasants), as by Gregory the Wonderworker in the 3rd century, by Martin of Tours and Maximus of Turin in the 4th, and by Jacob Baradaeus in the 6th. Conjoined with a decline of the *civitas*, these developments did as much as doctrinal disagreement to distinguish religious government in the Byzantine heartland of the imperial church from other provinces both east and west.

BIBL.: Peter Brown, *Power and Persuasion in Late Antiquity: Towards a Christian Empire* (Madison, 1992). Henry Chadwick, "The Role of the Christian Bishop in Ancient Society," in *Thirty-fifth Colloquy of the Center for Hermeneutical Studies* (Berkeley, 1980), 1–14. V. Déroche, *Études sur Léontios de Néapolis* (Uppsala, 1995), 136–153. M. Heinzelmann, "Bischof und Herrschaft von spätantiken Gallien bis zu den karolingischen Hausmeiern," in *Herrschaft und Kirche*, ed. F. Prinz (Stuttgart, 1988), 23–82. B. Jussen, "Über 'Bischofsherrschaften' in Gallien, *Historische Zeitschrift* 206 (1995): 673–718. J. Lamoreaux, "Episcopal Courts in Late Antiquity," *Journal of Early Christian Studies* 3 (1995), 143–167. *Vescovi e pastori in epoca teodosiana*, Studia Ephemeridis Augustinianum 58 (Rome, 1997).   P.R.

Black Sea

The ancients first called the Black Sea "inhospitable" *(axeinos),* but as it became familiar to them through the colonization of its coasts, it became "hospitable" *(euxeinos).* Probably the original name meant "dark," as does the present one in a variety of modern languages (Persian, Turkish, Slavic, Georgian, and others). Its Latin name was Pontus Euxinus. The Roman author most familiar with the sea was Arrian, whose surviving *Periplus of the Black Sea* presents much information.

Many ancient authors writing about the Black Sea (Herodotus, Ps.-Scylax, Strabo, Varro, Arrian, and others) tried to estimate its extent but they came to different conclusions in a variety of measurements. Modern calculation gives it a maximum length of 1,130 km and a breadth of 610 km. The climate varied from region to region but was generally colder in ancient times than now. The sea level has changed six times in the past 6,000 years. It last rose in the 1st to 2nd centuries, by 3 to 5 m (different scholars have made different calculations), leaving many Roman sites underwater.

The Black Sea was of considerable importance to the Romans for its location and resources (including slaves, honey, wax, fish, and grain: Polybius 4.38.4–6). Several provinces were situated around it. It was famous for its piracy—against which the Roman empire devoted much effort—and the hostility of the local population to Roman rule. Although the Romans' first knowledge of the Black Sea dated to the 2nd century B.C.E. (the kingdom of Pontus), their real interest developed only after 65 B.C.E. (Pompey's expedition to the Caucasus). Not until the time of the emperors Claudius and Nero, and later, did Roman garrisons arrive in the Black Sea. As a result of their presence, the Pontic *limes,* or frontier, was established.

The eastern shore of the Black Sea (Colchis) was the principal part of the province of Cappadocia, which included the kingdom of Pontus. The Bosporan kingdom was the most important buffer state, standing between Cappadocia and the threat of invasion by the Scythians and Sarmatians, who inhabited the whole of the Crimea and much of the steppes. The arrival of the Goths in the 3rd century severely impaired Roman domination. After destruction of the Bosporan kingdom by the Huns in the 4th and 5th centuries, life thereabouts was effectively extinguished for several centuries. Chersonesus, the main Roman outpost in the Crimea, flourished under Roman rule (the Goths and Huns did not pass through it); it became the main base for the Byzantine expansion and influence in the northern Black Sea.

The Danube was the northern frontier of imperial territory for many centuries. Every Roman province from the Alps to the Black Sea bordered it. The Danube's local population always caused the Romans problems, and the Goths threatened these provinces also. The problems along the Danube contributed to the decision to create a new Roman capital, Constantinople, but this could not halt the Goths who, in 378, settled across the Danube and defeated the emperor Valens at Adrianople, ending forever Roman hopes of ruling the Danube region.

Dacia became the subject of Roman interest around 106 and continued as an imperial province to 271. It supplied gold, silver, and other metals to the emperors. The Romans faced problems with Dacians, Roxolani, and other local populations who never accepted Roman rule. Another barbarian province always troublesome to the Romans was Moesia (Superior and Inferior), which was far less Romanized than any other Danubian province. There Greek traditions were quite strong.

Thrace was one of Rome's most important Danubian provinces, protecting the lines of communication from Macedonia via Byzantium to Bithynia and Asia Minor (particularly important after the 4th century, with the creation of Constantinople). Until the Romans arrived urbanization was absent but subsequently many cities were established (Plotinopolis, Traianopolis, Philippopolis, and others). Thracians made excellent soldiers. The Goths passed through this province, destroying everything in their way. Barbarian ravaging of Thrace continued in the 4th and 5th centuries. From the 6th century Thrace was under Byzantine influence.

BIBL.: M. V. Agbunov, *Antichnaya Geographia* (Moscow, 1992). Benjamin Isaac, *The Limits of Empire: The Roman Army in the East,* rev. ed. (Oxford, 1992). Fergus Millar, *The Roman Empire and Its Neighbours,* 2nd ed. (London, 1981).

G.T.

Bnay and Bnat Qyama

Syriac Christianity was distinctive for the emergence by the 3rd century of a consecrated lay office known as the Bnay and Bnat Qyama, the "Sons and Daughters of the Covenant," or "Covenanters." These men and women took vows of celibacy and simplicity (by the 5th century explicitly a vow of poverty); lived in segregated households within the Christian community, alone or with their families; and worked in the service of the parish priest or bishop. With the development of a separate monastic movement, the duties of the Covenanters became increasingly specified in canonical legislation of the 5th through 9th centuries. All Covenanters had the task of keeping the prayer offices and services in the local churches, and particularly chanting the Psalms; Daughters of the Covenant had special choir duties. Covenanters served in hospitals and among the poor, assisting the priests. Forbidden to hold certain types of secular employment, Covenanters were supported by the church or by their families. It became common for families to dedicate a child to the order of the Covenanters. These children were educated in monastery schools until they could take their place in the larger community. Sons of the Covenant were sometimes ordained as clergy. Daughters of the Covenant were often exploited: the 5th century Rabbula canons ruled that they must not be "compelled by force" to weave garments for the clergy. In the 7th century, Dadisho described the four kinds of Christian life in ascending rank: the laity, the Covenanters, the monastics, and the solitaries.

BIBL.: Sidney H. Griffith, "Monks, 'Singles,' and the 'Sons of the Covenant': Reflections on Syriac Ascetic Terminology," in Ephrem Carr, et al., eds., *Eulogema: Studies in Honor of Robert Taft, S. J.* (Rome, 1993), 141–160. George Nedungatt, "The Covenanters of the Early Syriac-Speaking Church," *Orientalia christiana periodica* 39 (1973): 191–215, 419–444. Arthur Vööbus, *Syriac and Arabic Documents regarding Legislation Relative to Syrian Asceticism* (Stockholm, 1960).

S.A.H.

Boethius

Anicius Manlius Severinus Boethius was born ca. 480 and died ca. 525. He presents himself as the scion of an ancient family, and it is clear that he had ancestors whose deeds can be traced a century and more before his birth. He is hard to localize: his principal seat of activity seems to have been Rome, but the prodigiousness and idiosyncrasy of his learning lead to serious speculation about time spent in studies abroad (Athens? Alexandria?), and his public career, brief though it was, took him as well to the Ostrogothic court and thence to a criminal's death, apparently outside Pavia.

Boethius's reputation rests chiefly on his philosophical oeuvre, and above all on *The Consolation of Philosophy*, a favored book of world-weary readers from Alfred the Great to Elizabeth I. But his real achievement lay in acquiring a remarkably accurate knowledge of Platonic philosophy as it was practiced in late antiquity down to his own day and in beginning a huge and never-finished project to represent that knowledge to a Latin audience. At the same time, he found application for his philosophical skills in writing short theological treatises (four or five of them survive) related to ecclesiastical controversies of the day.

The poignancy and vividness of his literary work is heightened by his personal story. He held the consulship himself when young, under the patronage of near relatives, and had in turn the extraordinary distinction of introducing his two sons as joint consuls for the year 522. At about that time, he entered government service for the Gothic regime of Theoderic as *magister officiorum*. The coincidence of events and later outcomes suggests that the distinction of having two consular sons in the same year reflected high favor shown to Boethius from the imperial government in Constantinople. That favor may have reflected a quid pro quo for services rendered, either past or prospective. (Modern scholarship reveals that the theological treatises written ten years earlier had all had as their subtext a pro-Constantinopolitan attempt to reconcile eastern and western theology at a time when it was in the interest of the Gothic regime to encourage separatism.) At any rate, Boethius's term and office ended badly, with accusations of disloyalty that his most strenuous professions of indignation do not quite suffice to refute completely. Versions of his death vary, but it seems to have been gruesome. His family found refuge at the court of Constantinople and were still there, wealthy and influential, a generation later.

No record from the 6th century tells us of *The Consolation of Philosophy*, but Boethius had to have written it during a period of confinement shortly before his death. (Whether he anticipated death as the outcome of his disgrace at the time of the writing is unlikely, but possible.) The work is a Menippean satire—that is, a prose narrative mixed with verse, in which the first person narrator, Boethius, recounts his life's fortunes and misfortunes to a mysterious and powerful woman who personifies Philosophy itself. She treats him as an errant disciple whom she praises highly but needs to enlighten, and the narrative of the book has Boethius moving from self-pity to consoled enlightenment by contemplation of the providence and justice of God. The text is explicitly Platonic (its most famous passage is a poem digesting Plato's *Timaeus*) and bears either no trace or (depending on scholarly argument) the slightest and faintest of traces of any influence of the

Christian doctrines that Boethius had written of in earlier years. It is conventional among moderns to puzzle at this lack of influence, but it certainly did not bother generations of devout Christian medieval readers, who happily accepted its praise of divine providence and human freedom while borrowing the image of the "wheel of fortune" as a metaphor for life's ups and downs.

If none of his works had survived, Boethius would be a historical figure of enigmatic interest. If only the works preceding his arrest had survived, he would be a philosopher worthy of respect even in the century of Philoponus. What we know of his end and the success of his *Consolation* are what make him a figure of more than ordinary reputation.

BIBL.: H. Chadwick, *Boethius: The Consolations of Music, Logic, Theology, and Philosophy* (Oxford, 1981). Margaret Gibson, ed., *Boethius: His Life, Thought, and Influence* (Oxford, 1981). L. Obertello, *Severino Boezio*, 2 vols. (Genoa, 1974). J.J.O.

Books

Throughout the era from the 3rd to the 8th century, Greek and Latin books, constructed in different formats and exhibiting a wide variety of styles, were primary vehicles for the transmission of learning and information, played leading roles in public and private worship, entertained and edified, and were in themselves important objects of material culture. The prominence of the book in the thinking world of those times is attested both in literature and in images presented by various artistic media, where roll and codex appear regularly as symbols of learning, social and educational status, and authority. In many respects the late antique book was similar to its ancient predecessor. However, in the 2nd century C.E. certain developments were already under way that, though gradual in their progress, were destined by their cumulative effect over the course of a few hundred years to bring about some profound changes in the nature of the artifact, most notably in structure, material, and content.

Until the 2nd century the normal type of book in use for general literary purposes was the papyrus roll, but the same century saw the slow rise in the popularity of a different format, the codex. The Latin term *codex* (like the English word *book*, which is connected with beech) preserves the memory of its remote origins in the wooden tablets that were widely employed in the ancient world for simple everyday needs like letter writing, school exercises, and business records. An arrangement consisting of multiple tablets strapped to one another eventually led to the idea of sewing together sheets of papyrus or folded parchment leaves to produce the kind of object that is more familiar to us. For reasons still not entirely clear, the Christians of the 2nd century favored this kind of manuscript over the roll for biblical texts, with the result that by the end of

Scene with books: Frontispiece of the Codex Amiatino I.

copies. Eusebius (ca. 260–340) has left us the interesting report that, when the industrious Origen began his extensive commentaries on the Scriptures, a wealthy friend provided him with the services of more than seven shorthand writers and at least that number of scribes, as well as girls who had been trained in calligraphy (*Hist.eccl.* 6.23). We must also allow for the real likelihood that important bishoprics organized the apparatus necessary to supply basic liturgical works for their churches. The main repository for manuscripts, at least for pagan authors, will have been the private collections of well-placed citizens and devoted literati, including Christians. Direct evidence for the involvement of such individuals in the transmission of classical authors between the 4th and 6th centuries can be reconstructed from the subscriptions of Latin codices containing works by Cicero, Caesar, Virgil, Horace, and Livy.

In monastic communities, which began to spring up in the 4th century, writing was pursued as one of the forms of manual work that were central to the ascetic life of men and women. Palladius (ca. 365–425) lists a series of nine crafts he saw being practiced in a Pachomian monastery where, among rooms set aside for weavers, fullers, smiths, and so on, there was also a scriptorium (*Lausiac History* 32). Obviously religious establishments first entered the business of bookmaking as part of the effort to be self-sufficient and were primarily interested in supplying their own needs in the areas of education, the liturgy, and devotional reading. By extension, the call for school materials, the interests of more intellectually inclined monks, and commissions from influential churchmen and others in the outside world will have led to the development of major scriptoria in many of the larger monasteries, production centers that perhaps as early as the 6th century were responsible for a good number of the new codices coming into circulation. The vast majority of these books contained ecclesiastical works in a broad sense, but secular literature would have been on occasion catered for as well, especially when connected with schooling. It is an undeniable fact that there were in all periods of Christianity pockets of genuine hostility and resistance to pagan writings, but it is equally true that theologians, learned members of the clergy, and even monastic leaders were often at the forefront of book-related activities that must have helped to save many an ancient author from extinction. Learned men and friends of the book in the east include Origen (ca. 185–254), Basil of Caesarea (ca. 329–379), and Gregory of Nazianzus (ca. 330–390), while in the west the prominent figures include Boethius (ca. 480–524), Cassiodorus (ca. 485–580), and Isidore of Seville (ca. 570–636). Had it not been for the cultural and studious activity of individuals like these, the effects of ignorance and neglect, combined with the ravages of war and ruined economies,

the 4th century the ultimate triumph of the new religion over paganism was matched by an equally final ouster of the roll by the codex as the standard book form. And while papyrus continued to be used, for limited purposes, even into the Middle Ages, it too had been fully overtaken by parchment as the codex writing material of choice before the beginning of the 5th century. And as for content, the successful rise of the Christian religion gave birth to a completely new body of writings that absorbed more and more of the energies spent on book production and by its sheer mass alone became one of numerous factors militating against the preservation of earlier, non-Christian literature.

Other changes took place in the late antique period. We read next to nothing about the public libraries in the larger cities that were common in previous times, and the type of flourishing book trade that is evident from the frequent comments of 2nd century writers like Aulus Gellius, Galen, and Lucian appears to have gradually died out. The manufacture and circulation of Greek and Latin books, until the coming of monastic scriptoria, must have been largely in the hands of private persons with means sufficient either to assemble their own manpower or to commission the making of would have seen to the loss of many of the secular works that did manage to make their way into the Middle Ages.

Needless to say, the secular and religious book of late antiquity must have come in a great variety of sizes and styles, with marked differences in levels of quality. The relatively few extant examples, the more abundant evidence from the early medieval period, and common sense indicate as much. Among manuscripts that have managed to survive in whole or in part (thanks largely to their own beauty and to good fortune) are a small number of outstanding cases that deserve special mention. They are books in which the elements of script, decoration, and illustration have been executed to such a high degree of craftsmanship and artistry that they can still be regarded as masterpieces of western bookmaking. It is no surprise that many of these early deluxe editions carry the texts of the Bible, Virgil, and Homer. Leading examples are: the remains of an *Iliad* with miniature paintings, perhaps dating from the 4th century, now in Milan (Ambros. F 205 inf.); a richly illustrated text of Virgil's works, made around 40 C.E., housed in the Vatican library (Vat. lat. 3225); the Rossano Greek Gospels of the 6th century, on purple parchment with the main script in silver and the incipits in gold lettering (Rossano, Museo Arcivescovile); and a majestic 6th century copy of Dioscorides's *De materia medica* in Vienna (Nat. Lib., med. gr. 1) that has almost five hundred miniatures and six full-page illustrations.

The political and social conditions of the 7th and 8th centuries in much of the east and west were not good for cultural life in general and certainly not for the creation of well-made manuscripts, even those of religious content. Latin books of very high quality, however, were produced in scriptoria on the islands of Britain and Ireland, as well as in some continental centers where Celtic missionaries were active. From these came a steady stream of elaborately ornamented copies of texts of the Bible, including some superb examples: the Book of Durrow (ca. 650), the Lindisfarne Gospels (ca. 700), and the monumental *Codex Amiatinus* with writing in two columns on 1,030 folia (ca. 700). Insular manuscript making reached its artistic climax in the Book of Kells (ca. 800) at a time when the Carolingian Age was already introducing the next momentous changes in the history of the European book.

BIBL.: Bernhard Bischoff, *Latin Palaeography: Antiquity and the Middle Ages*, trans. Dáibhí Ó Cróinín and David Ganz (Cambridge, Eng., 1990). G. Cavallo, "Il libro come oggetto d'uso nel mondo bizantino," *Jahrbuch für österreichische Byzantinistik* 31 (1981): 395–423. R. Lane Fox, "Literacy and Power in Early Christianity," *Literacy and Power in the Ancient World*, ed. A. K. Bowman and G. Woolf (Cambridge, Eng., 1994), 128–148. L. D. Reynolds and N. G. Wilson, *Scribes and Scholars: A Guide to the Transmission of Greek and Latin Literature*, 3rd ed. (Oxford, 1991).

C. H. Roberts and T. C. Skeat, *The Birth of the Codex* (London, 1983). J.M.D.

Bordeaux

Situated on the banks of the Garonne River, the city of Bordeaux (ancient Burdigala) is conveniently linked to the Atlantic and the Mediterranean. This strategic location led to its initial Roman foundation under Augustus and to the city's considerable affluence during the early empire (1st to the 3rd centuries). The tokens of this wealth, in the shape of inscriptions and funerary stelae, were incorporated in the city walls, which were erected at the beginning of the 4th century. Encircling 32 hectares of the inhabited area, only a portion of the city and its population, the walls nonetheless included the inner harbor, thus ensuring Bordeaux's continuing economic vitality. From the 4th to the 6th century the city acted as a shipping center for merchandise from Aquitania, Britain, and Spain. Recent excavations *intra muros,* at various locations, have revealed a large commercial and industrial center (St. Christoly) and a 4th century mithraeum (Parunis). The prosperity of both the city and its countryside in late antiquity is attested by contemporary poetic descriptions (Ausonius in the 4th century; Venantius Fortunatus in the 6th) and by a series of excavations that have revealed the existence of numerous villas (like St. Emilion and Plassac).

Capital of the province of Aquitanica II in the 4th century, and briefly of the entire southern Gallic diocese, Bordeaux passed into the hands of the Visigoths in 418 to become one of the capitals of the Gothic Aquitanian kingdom. The attraction of the Gothic court at Bordeaux to both Romans and barbarians is described by Sidonius Apollinaris (ca. 410–485) in a poem honoring Euric, the Gothic monarch (466–484; *Ep.* 8.9, *Carm.*). Bordeaux's strategic importance also invited Frankish raids as early as the 480s, and after 507 the city passed into Frankish hands. In the 6th and 7th centuries Bordeaux remained under Merovingian sovereignty as a succession of semi-independent rulers claimed revenues and even minted coins there. At the beginning of the 8th century Bordeaux became a battleground in the conflict between Saracens and Carolingians and a key to the military success of Charles Martel.

Among Bordeaux's famous sons in late antiquity is Ausonius (ca. 310–390), poet and politician, who rose to eminence under the emperors Valentinian I (364–375) and Gratian (375–383). He was one of a class of educated provincials, many of whom taught at the famed schools of Bordeaux and elsewhere in the empire in the 4th century (Ausonius's *Professores* commemorates thirty of these educators). Paulinus (c. 354–430), Ausonius's pupil, acquired fame after his migration from Bordeaux to Italian Nola, where he became the patron of a local saint. In the 6th century, distant relatives of Paulinus, the Pontii Leontii, founded an episcopal dynasty and were instrumental in transforming Bordeaux into a Christian city (Venantius Fortunatus, *Carm.*, esp. 15).

Christianity reached Bordeaux in the late 3rd century, as far as reliable records attest. In 333 an unknown Bordelais embarked on a pilgrimage to the Holy Land and produced a diary of the journey (the *Itinerarium Burdigalense*). In the 380s Priscillian of Avila reached the outskirts of Bordeaux and in 385 was condemned of heresy by a synod assembled under the auspices of Delphinus, the city's bishop. Priscillian's Bordelais host, Euchrotia, was executed with him at Trier, while another female supporter, Urbica, was stoned to death just outside Bordeaux.

The first Christian edifices were built outside the walls, in the cemetery where the Church of St. Seurin was constructed in the 4th or 5th century. Sometime during this period the affluent members of the community also interred their dead in carved marble sarcophagi, which still decorate the crypt of St. Seurin. The Cathedral of St. André was constructed in the 6th century, marking the Christianization of the urban landscape inside the walls.

BIBL.: M. de Maille, *Recherches sur les origines chrétiennes de Bordeaux* (Paris, 1959). P. Garmy and L. Maurin, *Enceintes romaines d'Aquitaine* (Paris, 1996). C. Balmelle, *Recueil général des mosaïques de la Gaule IV: Province d'Aquitaine; 2 of 3 vols. have been published (Paris, 1980 and 1987). J. P. Bost, et al., *Les racines de l'Aquitaine* (Bordeaux, 1992).

H.S.

Bostra

Bostra (modern Buṣrā-eski-Shām in Syria), lying southwest of the Hauran, is on the edge of the Nuqra, a rich cereal plain. The Nabataean city became the capital of the province of Arabia, which was created in 106. It remained the capital city throughout late antiquity, even though the boundaries of the province changed. Bostra had Roman institutions, which earned it its rank as a colony in the 3rd century, a designation still in place in late antiquity. The territory of Bostra covered a vast zone, especially in the steppe south of the city, including the Jordanian sites of Samra, Rihab, and Qaṣr el-Hallabāt.

Bostra is known to have had bishops, metropolitans of Arabia, beginning in the 3rd century, and some of them, such as Beryllos and Titus, were theologians and scholars. That tradition continued with Antipater in the 5th century. Theological controversies were marked early on, with Origen's two visits to Bostra. Accounts indicate outbursts of violence between pagans and Christians at the time of Emperor Julian. In the 6th century, the confrontation between Chalcedonians and Monophysites led to the creation of a dual ecclesiastical hierarchy: the leader of the Mono-

physites in the southern zone of Syria received the title of bishop of Bostra, while the Chalcedonian bishops of Bostra continued to reside there, at the head of an Arabia that was in large part subject to them.

The remains of six churches are known. It is unclear which buildings are to be attributed to St. Job and which to the Virgin Mary. A large four-sided building, recently discovered, may have been the cathedral. Its colossal dimensions are much greater than those of the Church of Ss. Sergius, Leontius, and Bacchus, also four-sided, the only Christian building identified. That church, transformed into a basilica of smaller dimensions, continued to function until the 12th century. The reparation of fortifications and the construction of a "tetraconch sigma," an aqueduct, and a new praetorium are indicated in the epigraphy of late antiquity. The episcopal palace might have been the building now called the Palace of Trajan, rather than the large dwelling located near SS. Sergius, Leontius, and Bacchus.

Islamic traditions are attached to the Church of Baḥīra and to the Mosque of al-Mabrak, located outside the walls. It is said that during one of his journeys Muhammad met the monk Baḥīra at the church, and Baḥīra announced Muhammad's mission to him. The camel that brought the first Qur'ān to Damascus is said to have knelt in the mosque, beneath 'Uthmān ibn 'Affān. The mosque of al-Umari dates from before 745. Despite its role as a station of the pilgrimage, Bostra, no longer a regional capital, lost its importance in the Umayyad era. Its monumental appearance changed. The porticoes were converted into a *sūq* and the thermae in the south of the city became a bakery.

BIBL.: M. Sartre, *Bostra, des origines à l'Islam* (Paris, 1985). R. Al-Muqdad and J.-M. Dentzer, "Bosra," *Syrian-European Archaeology Exhibition* (Damascus, 1996), 123–129. R. Al-Muqdad and R. Farioli-Campanati, "Bosra," ibid., 167–170.

P.-L.G.

Bread

In the Christianized empire, bread took on new value as a religious symbol. As a result, it was introduced as a motif in the catacombs and became part of the repertoire of anti-Christian mockery in the *Historia Augusta*. It nonetheless conserved its traditional connotation, as well, as a first level of nutritional comfort: in the free civic distributions, it replaced rations of grain relatively late (under Septimius Severus), obliging the *annona* organization to hire *pistores* (bakers), increase the frequency of distributions, and build water mills to augment flour production (the Janiculum mills date from the 3rd century, the same era as that now accepted for Barbegal, near Nîmes). Whenever possible, efforts were made to procure fresh bread for soldiers by ordering city authorities to organize temporary *pistrina*. Desert saints abstained from eating bread; like the poor, they confined themselves to eating porridge or "roots," that is, various plants.

There were all kinds of bread, from coarse loaves generously mixed with bran (*panis sordidus,* or *plebeius*) to white bread combining clear and top-quality flour (*panis mundus, candidus,* or *siligineus*), not to mention *buccellatum* (a type of biscuit made for the army in the countryside), which gave its humble name to a category of troops, the *buccellarii.* At an equal cost to the public, the *annona* organization could distribute a smaller ration of better quality bread or sacrifice quality for quantity. The quality of the bread also depended on the conditions for preserving grain. When supplies were corrupted, there was a great temptation to set aside the unspoiled grain for bread to be sold—*panis fiscalis*—at the expense of free bread—*panis popularis.*

BIBL.: Malcolm Bell, "An Imperial Flour Mill on the Janiculum," in *Le ravitaillement en blé de Rome* (Naples and Rome, 1994), 73–89. M. Dembinska, "Diet: A Comparison of Food Consumption in Eastern and Western Monasteries," *Byzantion* 55 (1985): 431–462. Y. Hirschfeld, "The Importance of Bread in the Diet of Monks in the Judaean Desert," *Byzantion* 66 (1996): 143–155. Emil Tengström, "Bread for the People: Studies of the Corn Supply of Rome during the Late Empire," *Acta Instituti Romani regni Sueciae Ser.* in 8, XII (1974). Kenneth D. White, "Cereals, Bread and Milling in the Roman World," in *Food in Antiquity,* ed. John Wilkins, David Harvey, and Mike Dobson (Exeter, Eng., 1995), 38–43. J.C.

Brooches

Brooches in antiquity were not simply ornamental items but frequently were employed to join pieces of clothing. However, most examples show some form of decorative elaboration, either through being made of showy metals or by being engraved or decoratively enlarged and used as a setting for gems, pendants, or cameos. Some of the most spectacular examples of purely ornamental brooches for women can be seen to have been a feature of demotic eastern fashions, as illustrated on the funerary busts from Palmyra. Although these date from the 2nd and 3rd centuries C.E., the style of brooch then in use appears to be closely related to the more elaborate styles of the late Roman and early Byzantine periods.

Brooches were a prominent element of state dress in that they provided the shoulder fastening of the soldier's cloak, the *paludamentum* or *chlamys.* Pliny wrote that Brutus had complained of the gold clasps worn by military tribunes (*Nat.Hist.* 33.12). This fashion came to be adopted, along with the military uniform, by civilian administrators of the later empire. Prior to late antiquity, men's brooches in Roman figural depictions are generally shown as round, but a second form was subsequently in official use, having spread from the northern provinces. This brooch type consisted of a curved, bow-shaped section, the ends of which formed the mounting for the fastener so that the brooch functioned rather like a modern safety pin. This is the brooch form usually depicted in late Roman art.

In images from late antiquity emperors are shown wearing a specific form of shoulder clasp. It is a huge object with pendant chains *(pendula),* considerable jeweling, and elaborate detail. A hint concerning its development may be provided by brooches worn by a barbarian hoard from Simluel Silvaniei in Romania. This type included a composite clasp with a plate affixed to bow elements supporting a huge sardonyx. It is quite possible that the late Roman emperors' brooch was a similar hybrid, its form perhaps dictated by the desire to display the largest possible gem in the context of the fashionable bow brooch. The first appearance of the emperors' special brooch occurs on the coins of Constantine at the same time that a jeweled diadem also appears on the imperial bust on coins, that is, ca. 325 C.E. The emperor Leo declared that the brooches of officials worn on the *chlamys* were to be free of any sort of gems. They were to be "precious only for their gold and for their craftsmanship" (*C.Just.* 11.11.1). The official relationship between the emperor, with his jeweled brooch, and the subordinate noble servant wearing the gold bow-brooch is prominently displayed in the Justinian mosaic panel of S. Vitale in Ravenna. Leo's legislation did not concern itself with women's jewelry, indicating that this was not so much sumptuary legislation as it was aimed at preserving important symbolic distinctions in official uniform.

BIBL.: R. Delbrueck, "Der spätantike Kaiserornat," *Die Antike* 8 (1932): 1–21. D. Janes, "The Golden Clasp of the Late Roman State," *Early Medieval Europe* 5 (1996): 127–153. D.J.

Bucellarii

The term *bucellarii* originated as a scornful nickname for soldiers, derived from the dry biscuits (*bucellatum*) they ate, according to Olympiodorus (frg. 12), who wrote about 420, but the name was by then evidently official, since *bucellarii* were already listed in the *Notitia Dignitatum* (Or. 7.25). The ancestry of this class of soldier lies in the growing numbers of official bodyguards and irregular retainers used by both public officials and private grandees in the 4th century under names such as *armigeri, amici, clientes, satellites, comites, domestici,* and (in the east) *paramenontes.* Rufinus, the praetorian prefect of the east in 392–395, was accompanied always by "an armed band of clients serving his private standards" (Claudian, *In Ruf.* 2.76–77). Although often seen as a German innovation, as in the warrior bands attached to barbarian leaders (see Sidonius Apollinaris, *Ep.* 4.20), the *bucellarii* were always Romans until Honorius's reign (Olympiodorus, frg. 74). They require, therefore, sociopolitical explanations, such as patronage, warlordism, and weakening of central state powers. The *bucellarius* in Euric's

Code was regarded as *in patrocinio constitutus,* while the use of irregulars increased in the 5th century so much that Leo banned "everyone throughout the cities and countryside from keeping *bucellarii* or Isaurians or armed slaves" (*C.Just.* 9.2.10, 468). In the 6th century they served regularly as crack mobile units of the official army. But since they were often maintained as a fiscal obligation on the estates of the great *oikoi,* such as that of the Apiones in Egypt, the line between public and private was inevitably blurred.

BIBL.: H. J. Diesner, "Das Bucellariertum von Stilicho und Sarus bis auf Aetius (454/55)," *Klio* 54 (1972): 321–350. J. Gascou, "L'institution des bucellaires," *Bulletin de l'Institute française de l'archéologie orientale* 76 (1976): 143–156. J. H. W. Liebeschuetz, "Generals, Federates and *Bucellarii* in Roman Armies around A.D. 400," in P. Freeman and D. L. Kennedy (eds.), *The Defence of the Roman and Byzantine East,* British Archaeological Reports S 297 (Oxford, 1986), 463–474. O. Schmitt, "Die *Bucellarii:* Eine Studie zum militärischen Gefolgschaftswesen in der Spätantike," *Tyche* 9 (1994): 147–174.   C.W.

Buddha

Buddha, meaning "awakened one," is a Sanskrit (later Pali) epithet for individuals who are believed to have attained enlightenment. The founder of Buddhism was Gautama Šākyamuni (Siddhartha Gautama). After his demise Gautama was accorded the title of Buddha by the Buddhist clergy *(bhikkus, bhikkṣus)* and laity, who saw him as the enlightened being of this cosmic era. Gautama was believed to have honed his mental and physical perfection over several lifetimes, in endeavors recounted in the *Jātaka* stories. The dates of his life are unclear: 624–544 (alternatively 563–483) or 448–368 B.C.E., according to ancient Sinhalese chronicles like the *Mahāvaṃsa* and old Indian documents, respectively. Hagiography, dating from the 1st to 5th centuries C.E. (based on oral traditions several hundred years older), claims he came from the Hindu *kṣatriya,* or princely class, married, had a child, and then renounced the world. His ascetic quest came to fruition under a bo tree *(Ficus religiosa)* at Uruvilva in northeast India, a town later called Buddh Gaya. After years of ministry, Gautama died, probably of dysentery, at Kushinagara. Buddhists regarded this demise not as death but as the achievement of *parinirvāṇa,* or freedom from an endless cycle of rebirth. After cremation, his bones were deposited in a *stūpa* (burial mound). These remains were later divided; new *stūpas* containing his relics were built in India, Sri Lanka, and central Asia. By the 3rd century C.E., Buddhists began making pilgrimages to the sites of his birth, enlightenment, first sermon, and death. Devotional statuary also developed during late antiquity, first at Mathura (in north-central India), using indigenous styles, and later at Gandharan sites such as Taxila (in the upper Indus Valley), in styles following Hellenistic conventions.

Gautama Buddha preached that life involves suffering that stems from desire, which can be overcome, and that an Eightfold Path of correct beliefs, goals, words, behavior, vocation, striving, thinking, and meditation would lead to freedom from rebirth. The "triple gem" *(triratna),* or three focuses, of Buddhist veneration are: the Buddha himself; his life, teachings, and experiences *(dharma)*; and the community *(saṅgha).* Distinct schools of Buddhist philosophy developed by the 5th century C.E.: the Theravada (Way of the Elders), Sarvastivada (All Things Are Real), Madhyamika (Middle Path), and Vijnanavada (Consciousness Alone) schools. Different understandings of the means for attaining salvation led to three groupings or "vehicles" *(yāna)* of thought—the Hinayana or lesser vehicle, including the Theravada and Sarvastivada schools; the Mahayana or greater vehicle, in which it was believed that people's struggle to achieve enlightenment could be assisted by supernatural beings; and the Vajrayana or diamond vehicle, in which tantric methods were employed.

Ashoka (around 270–232 B.C.E.), third ruler of the Maurya dynasty, adopted Buddhism, and missionaries journeyed to Sri Lanka and to central Asia under his patronage. By the 2nd century B.C.E., Buddhism had come under attack from a Hindu resurgence sponsored by the Shunga kings. Despite eventually fading from India, Buddhism gained converts among the Sinhalese people, who followed the Hinayana Theravada school, and the Indo-Greeks, who accepted Mahayana notions. From the Kushan state (ca. 50–320 C.E.) the faith moved into eastern Iran before being stopped by Zoroastrianism under the Sassanians. A series of *naubahars,* "new viharas," may have flourished in eastern Iran and Afghanistan into early Islamic times—their western limit was at the cities of Balkh and Qandahar. In its spread northward, Buddhism endured at Tarim Basin sites such as Khotan, Tumshuq, Dunhuang, and Kocho into the 9th and 10th centuries before Islam won over the inhabitants. Clerics from India and Sri Lanka and Sogdian merchants from the Silk Road cities transmitted Buddhism to China. By the 6th century it reached Japan. During the 7th century, Buddhists from central Asia, northern India, and China penetrated Tibet. This extensive spread resulted in the translation of Buddhist Scriptures into Sinhalese, Gandharan Prakrit, Sogdian, Saka, Chinese, Tibetan, and Japanese, among other languages.

As devotees speculated about the possibility of additional teachings, the concept of past and future Buddhas arose. The Pali *Buddhavaṃsa* (Chronicle of Buddhas) records lives of twenty-four previous enlightened ones. Future Buddhas *(bodhisattvas)* could also arise—the next would be named Maitreya, "friendly one." His veneration became important in the Kushan kingdom, in central Asian mercantile cities, and in China between the 4th and 7th centuries. Mahayana literature discussed the possibility of enlightened beings on other worlds—for instance, the Buddha Amitābha, "boundless light." His cult appears to have originated in central Asia, then spread to China and Japan as the Sukhavati (Pure Land) tradition between the 6th and 10th centuries.

BIBL.: Alfred Foucher, *The Life of the Buddha according to the Ancient Texts and Monuments of India,* abridged trans. Simone B. Boas (Middletown, Conn., 1963). Peter Harvey, *An Introduction to Buddhism: Teachings, History, and Practices* (Cambridge, Eng., 1990). Frank E. Reynolds, "The Many Lives of Buddha: A Study of Sacred Biography and Theravada Tradition," in *The Biographical Process: Studies in the History and Psychology of Religion,* ed. Frank E. Reynolds and Donald Capps (The Hague, 1976), 37–61.

J.K.C.

Buddhism

First preached by Gautama Šākyamuni (Siddhartha Gautama) on the Himalayan foothills of modern Nepal during the 6th to the 5th century B.C.E., Buddhism offers a message of universal salvation based on personal moral and spiritual behavior, irrespective of a follower's gender and caste. The Buddha's teaching of the Four Noble Truths and the Eightfold Path, aimed at securing release from the endless cycle of rebirths in which all beings are trapped, stresses a middle way of cultivating enlightenment that avoids more extreme forms of bodily asceticism. Many of his followers became itinerant monks who traveled, with help from a pious laity that hoped to gain merit from their patronage, to disseminate his message; later, monasteries, *sanghas,* were established.

The religion flourished in northern India in the mid-3rd century B.C.E. upon receiving the support of King Ashoka—grandson of Chandragupta, to whom Seleucus Nicator had ceded the Punjab in exchange for elephants—who boasted of having sent Buddhist missions to the western lands ruled by the Hellenistic successor kings. Under this Mauryan patronage, Buddhism reached Transoxiana, where it established deep roots. Later, as Mauryan political power declined, many Graeco-Bactrians and Indo-Greeks (i.e., those who invaded India from Bactria) were supposedly influenced by Buddhist teachings, such as King Menander, the eponymous protagonist of the *Questions of Milinda* (extant in Pali), in which he debated the Buddhist sage Nagasena. After the Yüeh-chih, or Scythian, tribes that ended Greek rule in northwest India established the Kushan dynasty, King Kanishka (ca. 100 C.E.) emerged as a champion of the *dharma,* the Buddhist law. He convoked a universal Buddhist council and undertook the collection and codification of Buddhist Scriptures. Under the Kushans, artisans of Gandhara drew on Hellenistic and Roman aesthetic canons to create statues and other artworks celebrating the Buddhist cult. Buddhism spread to Parthia, Sogdia, and the oasis towns of central Asia, where it encoun-

tered worthy religious competitors in Nestorian Christians, Manichaeans and, later, Arab Muslims. The Amitābha (Buddha of Infinite Light) sect, originating in Kushan territories, may have been influenced by Iranian Zoroastrianism. Even the conquest of Kushan itself by the Sassanians toward the end of the 3rd century C.E., and later severe repressions at the hands of the Hephthalites, failed to destroy Buddhist influence in this region of central Eurasia, from which it spread to China, Korea, and Japan through Parthians and other intermediaries. One such notable figure was An Shih-kao, a Buddhist monk of the royal Arsacid line who became the first translator of Buddhist texts in China after he arrived in Lo-yang, the Han capital, ca. 148 C.E. In turn, converts from China, among them Fa-hsien (399–414), Sung Yün (516–523), Hsüan-tsang (596–664), and I-tsing (671–695), would later undertake laborious pilgrimages back to the "Buddhist countries."

While East Asia would eventually prove to be a safe haven for Buddhism, the religion's westward movement is much less well documented. The Roman discovery of the Indian Ocean monsoons, which they named for Harpalus, intensified seaborne trade between the Mediterranean and southern India and Sri Lanka. Graeco-Roman travelers who sailed to India could have returned with some knowledge of Buddhism. Also, among the enterprising Indians who traveled by sea to Alexandria, the entrepôt par excellence of this east-west trade, some might have professed the Buddhist faith. But little about this is known.

More notably, Buddhist influences entered the Roman empire through the agency of Manichaeans. Mani appended himself to a prophetic lineage that included Moses, Buddha, Zoroaster, Jesus, and Paul; he also traveled to India in search of superior alien wisdom, just as Apollonius of Tyana is said to have done in the *Vita Apollonii* by Philostratus. There, according to a tradition surviving in Parthian texts, Mani converted Tūrān Shāh, a Buddhist ruler in Baluchistan, as well as learned Buddhist doctrines, which he then adapted and combined with Iranian, Gnostic, and Judaeo-Christian elements to produce his own distinctive syncretistic cosmogony and salvific myth. Mani, called the Buddha of Light in some Manichaean texts, might indeed also have borrowed from Buddhist missionary techniques, texts, and monastic organization. Even so, whether he adapted the organization and practices of the Buddhist monastery and then transmitted them, indirectly, to the Christians of the late Roman east remains a tantalizing and virtually unanswerable question. Mani's assertion that Manichaeism was uniquely successful in establishing a presence in both east and west—therefore unlike either Christianity or Buddhism—suggests that he personally knew of few traces of Buddhists and Buddhism west of the Indus and the Oxus. Such an observation reinforces the impression given by Graeco-Roman authors from Megasthenes on, whose descriptions focus almost entirely on the Punjabi gymnosophists famously encountered by Alexander during his Indian campaign.

Clement of Alexandria appears to be the first Graeco-Roman author even to mention the name of the Buddha, whom he described as a deity venerated by some Indians. In the west, even among the learned, knowledge of the religion and its founder remained vague and imperfect at best. Jerome's comment that Buddha was the founder of a sect of the gymnosophists confuses Buddhist ascetics with those better known Brahmin priest-philosophers. Later, Cosmas Indicopleustes wrote about the wise gymnosophists but failed to mention Buddhist monks. The Islamic conquest ruptured direct east-west communications, though some knowledge and texts, perhaps even people, continued to travel along the established trade routes. The Christian Greek romance *Barlaam and Ioasaph* was based on a Buddhist prototype that told the story of the Buddha and Bodhisattva. While the authorship, transmission, and even date of its *Ur*-text are all poorly known, the work shows how repackaged Buddhist material could still be introduced into the Mediterranean world during the middle Byzantine period. Its textual and redactional history, however, suggests a key reason that Buddhist influences there were not perceived as such: few transmitted beliefs, texts, or organizational principles still wore the label of this world religion upon their arrival in the west. Rather, Buddhist ideas typically first underwent a process of cultural conversion and assimilation that effectively obscured their origin.

Buddhism as an institutionalized religion gradually died out in central Asia after the arrival of Islam and the Arab victory over the T'ang Chinese army at the Battle of Talas in 751; even so, some modern scholars theorize that its spirit had passed on to the practitioners of Sufism, a tradition said to have been developed under the residual influence of Buddhism in Tocharistan, ancient Bactria.

BIBL.: C. Colpe, "Heidnischer und christlicher Hellenismus in ihren Beziehungen zum Buddhismus," *Vivarium: Festschrift T. Klauser* (Münster in Westfalen, 1984), 57–81. David Scott, "Christian Responses to Buddhism in Pre-medieval Times," *Numen* 32 (1985): 88–100. Michel Tardieu, "La diffusion du Bouddhisme dans l'empire kouchan, l'Iran et la Chine, d'après un Kephalaion manichéen inédit," *Studia Iranica* 17 (1988): 153–182.   R.L.

Budget

The Roman imperial state was no more inclined toward improvisation in finances than it was in other areas. Although the empire has left us almost no trace of its budget accounts, everything leads us to believe that it inherited from its predecessors several simple but proven methods for adapting its resources to its expenses. In the late period, it further improved its knowledge of citizens' ability to pay, strengthened its control over the system for collecting funds, and standardized its procedures. In appearance, its demands increased in proportion to its needs; in fact, tax collection was more broadly and—theoretically at least—more equitably shared. However anachronistic the word *budget* may be, once stripped of the concepts of modern national bookkeeping, it is not as inappropriate as it might appear. Every year, financial bureaus fixed the government's total costs and set tax rates *(indictio)*, which were similar to our "finance laws." Lacking the means for deficit spending, which borrowing and the administration of public debt made possible in later times, the state could spend more than it had in its coffers only if it manipulated currency or deferred payment of its obligations (for example, military salaries). These were politically delicate methods, as was the temptation to make revenue demands above an acceptable level. The state had to cover expenses incurred on a yearly basis as well as unforeseen needs; make contingency plans in case of an unexpected drop in revenues during a bad year; and allow for misappropriation due to administrative dishonesty at every level. It also had to redistribute money across provinces to correct for local budget shortfalls or surpluses.

It is customary to limit the Roman Byzantine budget to three essential areas of outlay—the army, the civil administration, and special expenses (such as the *annona* in capital cities, public construction, various spectacles)—and to one principal source of revenue—the land tax. This leaves out numerous elements, however. Among the outlays, one would have to add reimbursements for requisitions and public purchases, and the price paid to buy external peace; among revenues, customs duties and traffic fees, legal fines, the resale of confiscated property, revenues from the imperial patrimony, and—as is always forgotten—the issuance of currency, which was in itself a considerable source of profit. Nevertheless there is no doubt that military expenses represented the most important budget item for the empire, however hard emperors sought to reduce them. Military taxes specific to the tetrarchy, theoretically earmarked for precise areas, were progressively replaced by an undifferentiated tax in gold.

The state's primary budget obligation recurred every five years, in the form of the *donativum* to soldiers, but the theoretical regularity of this basic calendar was disrupted by anniversaries of reigns or emperors, which occurred from time to time and also gave rise to *donativa*. Taxes too were collected on a five-year cycle: beginning with Constantine, three five-year periods constituted one revenue indiction. In fact, taxes were collected annually but tallied only in the fifth year (hence the apparently contradictory data concerning the commercial *chrysargyron* or senatorial *oblatio*). The high degree of monetization of public finances in the 6th century can no longer be considered the antithesis of a budget in kind imposed by "demonetization," which supposedly marked the period 250–360 and culminated in the tetrarchic period. In every era, in fact, the budget was sustained partly by taxes in kind *(canonica),* and partly by currency *(largitonialia).*

Every effort to calculate the revenue and expenses of the Roman-Byzantine treasury is necessarily approximate and disheartening. For the period between the tetrarchy and the early 6th century, proposed estimates range from 7–8 million *solidi* to 10–13 million per annum (that is, between 97,000 and 180,500 pounds of gold).

BIBL.: Richard Duncan-Jones, *Money and Government in the Roman Empire* (Cambridge, Eng., 1994). Michael H. Hendy, *Studies in the Byzantine Monetary Economy c. 300–1450* (Cambridge, Eng., 1985). Keith Hopkins, "Taxes and Trade in the Roman Empire (200 B.C.E.–C.E. 400)," *Journal of Roman Studies* 70 (1980): 101–125.   J.C.

Building

Late antiquity was a period of profound change in public building. The classical tradition of constructing pagan temples and secular amenities gradually disappeared and was replaced predominantly by the provision of places of worship for the new religions (Christianity in Byzantium and the west; Islam in the east). After about 600, in much of the former Roman empire the advent of hard times is reflected in an overall decline in the scale and splendor of the buildings that could be erected.

We know very much more about religious buildings (churches and mosques) in late antiquity than we do about other types of structures, but this is partly an accident of survival. Churches and mosques remained in use for centuries—indeed are often still in use today—which ensured their preservation, whereas other buildings have tended to go out of use and be destroyed, and so are known only when excavated. However, public buildings other than churches and mosques were definitely still being erected in late antiquity, and being built on a scale designed to impress. Constantinople saw a vast panoply of traditional secular buildings (baths, forums, porticoed streets, ceremonial arches, and others) erected in the 4th to 6th centuries, including, for instance, two historiated marble spiral columns, imitating Trajan's column in Rome. It also had a number of spectacular new buildings that were highly functional, including the great land-walls (which are perhaps the most famous and successful fortifications ever built) and an array of immense water cisterns (some subterranean, some open).

Outside Constantinople, traditional building continued on a lesser scale, but in the east at least, it could be impressive, including, for instance, the massive porticoed monumental street, the Arcadiane, in Ephesus. In the west, traditional secular building of this type was definitely in decline by the beginning of the 4th century, but late antique emperors and some of the bar-

barian successor kings still felt it incumbent on themselves to erect or maintain traditional buildings in their capitals. Theoderic, the Ostrogothic king of Italy (493–526), was an enthusiastic builder in the traditional mode (because he was particularly eager to be seen in the guise of a good Roman ruler). As late as 577, the Frankish king Chilperic ordered circuses to be built in Paris and Soissons, certainly in order to imitate Byzantine ceremonial use of the hippodrome.

All rulers—western barbarian kings, Byzantine emperors, and Arab caliphs—expended effort and money on their palaces, designed to impress subjects and foreign ambassadors alike. Unfortunately, very little is known of these buildings, though we do have Constantine's magnificent audience hall (the Basilica) in Trier and some wonderful, heavily classicized 6th century mosaics from the Great Palace at Constantinople, as well as many contemporary and later written accounts of this same building.

Although secular buildings should not be ignored, there is no doubt that much of the most spectacular building efforts in late antiquity went into religious buildings—often, as with traditional classical buildings, as much designed to impress viewers with the splendor and munificence of the patron as to glorify God and ease the builder's path to heaven. Some of these buildings are very large, such as the great pilgrimage churches in Tebessa in North Africa and in Qalat Siman in Syria (the latter was a four-armed basilica centered on a domed crossing that covered the column on which Symeon the Stylite had spent his life). The biggest projects of all were those commissioned by rulers: in early 4th century Rome, Constantine's five-aisled Basilica of St. Peter, 100 m long and preceded by a vast open atrium; in 6th century Constantinople, Justinian's huge, domed, central-plan Church of Hagia Sophia; and in Jerusalem and Damascus, between 691 and 715, the caliphal Dome of the Rock and the Great Mosque, both buildings of an imperial scale and sumptuousness, designed to mark the advent (and triumph) of a new religion in the Holy Land and to celebrate the glories of the new Arab empire.

But it is not just the scale and richness of the most spectacular new buildings that should impress. The quantity of smaller new religious buildings erected in late antiquity is also striking. In the provincial city of Gerasa (Jerash, in modern Jordan), at least fourteen churches were built in the period up to 611. In village settlements, too, large numbers of new churches were constructed, as is clear, for instance, in the limestone villages of northern Syria.

Toward the end of the late antique period, in the 7th and 8th centuries, the difficult times through which the west and Byzantium were passing are marked by a dramatic falling off in the scale and quantity of new churches being built. Byzantine and western church architecture entered a dark age whose achievements are characterized by maintenance (of many of the spectacular buildings of the past) and by the addition of minor decorative schemes and small chapels. Larger buildings were achieved only when abandoned classical buildings were adapted to ecclesiastical use, as when Pope Boniface IV (608–615) took over the Pantheon in Rome and dedicated it as the Church of St. Maria ad Martyres. Only in the Islamic Near East were new public buildings on a spectacular scale still being erected at the end of the 7th and in the early 8th century, as is seen not only in the large and richly decorated mosques of Jerusalem and Damascus, but also in the so-called desert palaces of the new Arab rulers. At Anjar a caliph in the early 8th century even erected a new centrally planned town, complete with mosque, palace, baths, porticoed monumental streets, and central ceremonial arch.

BIBL.: K. A. C. Creswell, *A Short History of Early Muslim Architecture*, rev. and supplemented by James W. Allan (Aldershot, Eng., 1989). Cyril Mango, *Byzantine Architecture* (London, 1979). Bryan Ward-Perkins, *From Classical Antiquity to the Middle Ages: Urban Public Building in Northern and Central Italy* A.D. *300–850* (Oxford, 1984).   B.W.

Bulgars

The Bulgars were a Turkic tribal confederation that gave rise to the Balkan Bulgar and Volga Bulgar states. The ethnonym derives from the Turkish *bulgha-*, "to stir, mix, disturb, confuse." The confederation appears to have taken shape among Oghur tribes in the Kazakh steppes following the migrations that were touched off by movements of the Hsiung-nu. Later Byzantine sources (Agathon, Nicephorus Patriarchus, Theophanes) closely associate or identify the Bulgars with the Onoghurs, who were enemies of Sassanid Iran in the late 4th century. When or how this connection developed is unclear. If we discount several (most probably) anachronistic notices on the Bulgars in Moses Khorenats'i (Moses of Chorene), the earliest references to them are perhaps to be found in an anonymous Latin chronograph of 354: "Vulgares." They are absent from Priscus's account of the migration, ca. 463, of the Oghuric Turks into the Pontic steppes, but by 480 they are noted under their own name as allies of Constantinople against the Ostrogoths.

Amity with Byzantium was short-lived. By 489 the Bulgars had initiated a series of raids on Byzantine Balkan possessions. Their habitat, at this stage, appears to have been in the eastern Pontic steppes stretching into the Azov region and North Caucasus. It is here that Jordanes and Pseudo-Zacharius Rhetor place them in the mid-6th century. Shortly afterward, they were overrun and subjugated by the Avars and then the Turks. When Turk rule weakened, sometime after 600, the Avars appear to have reestablished some control over the region. It was against Avar rule that the Bulgars—under their leader Qubrat, whom Heraclius had been cultivating for some time (he and his uncle were

baptized in Constantinople in 619)—revolted ca. 631–32 and founded the Onoghundur-Bulgar state. Sometime after Qubrat's death (660s?), this Pontic-Maeotian Bulgaria, whose Balkan descendents would also claim Attilid origins, came into conflict with the Khazar khaganate, successor to the Turk empire in western Eurasia. The Khazars emerged victorious from the contest, and parts of the Bulgar union broke up and migrated. One grouping under Asperukh in 679 crossed the Danube into Moesia and, having subjugated a local Slavic confederation, there laid the foundation for the Balkan Bulgarian state. Yet other groups joined the Avar state in Pannonia (where some would prove to be rebellious subjects) or took up residence in Italy around the five Ravennate cities, to live as Byzantine subjects. The other Bulgars either remained in the Pontic steppe zone (the "Black Bulgars" of Byzantine and Rus' sources) or later migrated (perhaps as early as the mid-7th century or as late as the mid-8th to early 9th century) to the middle Volga region, giving rise there to the Volga Bulgarian state, which remained, however, a vassal of the Khazars.

Balkan Bulgaria soon became an important element in Byzantine politics, on occasion supporting contestants to the throne and also helping to defeat the Arab attack on Constantinople of 717–18. The iconoclastic Emperor Constantine V (741–775) began a series of wars against them that remained a constant theme of Byzantine-Bulgarian relations until the destruction of the first Bulgarian empire by Basil II (976–1025). In 864 the Bulgarian king Boris, outmaneuvered by Constantinople, converted to Christianity. Thereafter, the Turkic Bulgars underwent Slavicization, and Balkan Bulgaria became one of the centers of medieval Slavic civilization.

The Volga Bulgars, however, converted to Islam in the early 10th century and created a highly sophisticated, urbane, mercantile Muslim society that, after stout resistance, was conquered by the Mongols in the early 13th century.

BIBL.: V. Beševliev, *Die protobulgarische Periode der bulgarischen Geschichte* (Amsterdam, 1980). J. V. A. Fine, Jr., *The Early Medieval Balkans* (Ann Arbor, 1983). A. V. Gadlo, *Etnicheskaia istoriia Severnogo Kavkaza IV–Xvv.* (Leningrad, 1979). P. B. Golden, *An Introduction to the History of the Turkic Peoples* (Wiesbaden, 1992). J. Werner, "Der Grabfund von Malaia Pereščepina und Kuvrat, Kagan der Bulgaren," *Bayerische Akademie der Wissenschaften: Abhandlungen*, NF 91 (Munich, 1984). I. Zimonyi, *The Origins of the Volga Bulgars*, Studia uralo-altaica 32 (Szeged, Hung., 1990).

P.B.G.

Burial

Zoroastrianism was the state religion of Iran during the Sassanian dynasty (223–642) and the dominant religion in the independent Iranian-speaking principalities of central Asia in the same period. Funerary practices were governed by the precepts of the *Avesta,* the Zoroastrian holy book, especially those set out in the *Vendidād,* the section on purity laws believed to have reached its final version in Iran during the Parthian period. Preliminary exposure to flesh-eating animals in an open space is described as the only acceptable way to dispose of a body, as there is no other one that avoids desecration of the deified elements of fire, earth, and water. Subsequent collection of the bones was recommended but not compulsory. Funerary places had to be kept apart from dwelling areas, as they tended to attract daemons. Cremation and immersion were punishable by death, whereas the attitude toward inhumation appears less rigid: only corporal punishments are prescribed (in practice, these were convertible into fines). Although the sin of burial was theoretically irremissible if the corpse was not exhumed within two years, it could still be cleared if it was committed on bad advice and the sinner repented. The land on which a grave had been dug became pure again after fifty years. Such distinctions suggest an effort to come to terms with persisting practices that arose either from different traditions or from the practical difficulties sometimes encountered with the ritual of exposure in areas of intense cultivation.

In central Asia, archaeology tends to suggest that exposure had been fairly generalized at an early period, possibly even predating the spread of Zoroastrianism (as no cemetery is known between the early Iron Age and the Greek conquest). A Chinese report from the 7th century indicates that at Samarkand corpses were thrown to dogs that were kept in an enclosure near the city, while the remains of a "Silent Tower" more probably frequented by vultures still stand on the hill of Chilpyk in Choresmia (south of the Aral Sea). But in some places corpses were laid to decompose naturally on the benches of freestanding mausoleums until the bones were eventually heaped together, a compromise that at least preserved the purity of the earth.

From the 5th and 6th centuries onward, bones were often gathered in ossuaries, which were either reused jars or specially manufactured caskets of baked clay, plaster, or, more rarely, stone. Some have small perforations, no doubt made to comply with a prescription contained in a contemporary ritual treatise: the bone containers had to give access to the sun (the final resurrection will take place in daylight). Central Asian ossuaries have recently attracted much attention, as they are sometimes adorned with inscriptions of blessings or with very informative images, especially in the Samarkand region. These show, in particular, funerary ceremonies (fire tending, or violent lamentations including self-mutilation, a practice theoretically condemned by Zoroastrian texts and probably inherited from the Scythians); the advent of the soul in paradise; and Zoroastrian deities celebrating an office at the time of the final resurrection.

In contrast, Sassanian Iran is entirely devoid of funerary iconography. Not a single specimen of a portable ossuary has been confirmed (except in the frontier province of Merv). It seems that excarnated bones were usually left scattered on the ground; a practice that, according to Agathias, shocked the Athenian philosophers traveling to the court of the Sassanian king, as it ran counter to the Greek concept of piety. Installations for Zoroastrian funerary rituals are preserved only on the mountain slopes of Fars. They are hewn in the rock and comprise open coffins, niches, and cavities, which are sometimes combined and were presumably intended, respectively, for the exposition of bodies, the preservation of bones, and the tending of a purifying fire. A few inscriptions describe these complexes as *dakhmas,* a word originally reserved for the excarnation place only. Some archaeologists have proposed that isolated columns, too, were used to carry bone-caskets. The fact that inhumation was sometimes tolerated is indicated by some graves found at Susa and near Persepolis (in the latter case, the deceased had the Charon's obol in his mouth, a possible Greek legacy also found in some central Asian ossuaries). However, in the Sassanian court circle, one case is known in which the accusation of burying a relative resulted in a death sentence (see Procopius, *Wars,* 1.11.37).

The custom of embalming Sassanian kings, attested by the medieval poet Ferdowsi, came from the Achaemenian tradition and was perhaps justified by the concept that kings' bodies were not of the same nature as those of other men. But no Sassanian royal grave has been discovered other than that of Shapur I (240–272), which was found in a mountain cave in Fars, where his gigantic statue carried the vault.

In Zoroastrian society, purity laws were supposed to be enforced on followers of other religions as well. Jews, who had had their own tradition of ossuaries in Palestine, had no difficulty complying with this regulation. In fact the only pre-Islamic Jewish cemetery known to archaeologists, in Merv (6th century), has provided ossuaries identical to those used by local Zoroastrians but bearing Hebrew inscriptions. For Christians, excarnation and dismembering of bones ran counter to the hope of the resurrection of the flesh. In periods of tolerance they obtained the right to bury their dead, but when this policy was reversed under Vahrām V (420–438), mass exhumations were committed by the authorities. In fact, archaeology shows that official pressure, and possibly also habits kept by new converts, often led Christians to follow local customs: bone niches cut in the rock and topped with a Nestorian cross are known on the island of Kharg, and ossuaries similarly marked have been excavated in the Choresmian cemetery of Mizdakhkan. But in Bactria, Buddhists kept to the Indian ritual of cremation.

In the end, the Arab conquerors of central Asia occasionally chose mausoleums as places for crucifying rebellious local rulers, an initiative no doubt meant to provoke the horror of the Zoroastrian spectators, who were convinced that people perishing in this manner had no chance of escaping the daemons.

In Islam, preparation for burial included washing and dressing the body, except in the case of martyrs, who were to be buried unwashed, wearing the clothes in which they had died. Graves could be either level with the ground or raised in a mound. Muslim burial customs reflect the common belief that the dead were present and even mentally aware in their graves. Bodies were thus susceptible to heat, to thirst, and perhaps even to the weight of buildings over the grave. According to several hadith, Muhammad outlawed some pre-Islamic Arabian practices, notably sacrificing animals at the graveside. Libations left at the tomb or palm fronds attached to the grave to cool it were considered permissible.

Early Muslim scholars debated the legitimacy of erecting funerary structures. In the hadith we find the injunction to level existing graves (taswiyat al-qubūr). Many interpreted this to mean that funerary architecture was a vain or idolatrous custom; partly for this reason, large-scale monuments such as mausoleums were not erected until the mid-9th century. It may be that the Prophet encouraged his followers to remove signs of pre-Islamic practices—that is, those of unbelievers—and also intended to prevent future worldly extravagance at grave sites. At the same time, specific instructions for the construction of tombs are also found in the hadith, indicating that building over graves was a common practice in early Islam.

BIBL.: Frantz Grenet, *Les pratiques funéraires dans l'Asie centrale sédentaire de la conquête grecque à l'islamisation* (Paris, 1984). Dietrich Huff, "Zum Problem Zoroastrischer Grabanlagen in Fars. I: Gräber. II: Das Säulenmonument von Pengan," *Archäologische Mitteilungen aus Iran* 21 (1988): 145–176, pl. 44–56, and 25 (1992): 207–217. A. S. Tritton, "Muslim Funeral Customs," *Bulletin of the School of Oriental and African Studies* 9, no. 3 (1938): 653–661. Judith Lerner, "Central Asians in Sixth-Century China: A Zoroastrian Funerary Rite," *Iranica antiqua* (1995): 179–195.

F.G.

Cadastres

One must be wary of the habit adopted by modern commentators when speaking of "cadastres": the term cannot apply to the type of documentation kept by the Roman administration or by the municipal archives. The Roman cadastre, notes André Déléage, "is not a real estate record and does not allow us to establish a real estate record based on it." Conversely, the only illustrated cadastral maps that have come down to us were produced not to estimate revenues but to allot territories newly acquired by the conquest (such as the colony of Arausio, or Orange, in France). The "life-size cadastres" known as centuriations also date from earlier eras. The term *cadastre* will thus be understood in the sense of "tax base."

The epigraphic inventories found in Asia Minor and in the Aegean Islands, known under the name of "revenue cadastres" (Mylasa, Thera, Lesbos, Chios, Cos, Tralles) existed so that a "bivalent" system of *jugatio-capitatio* could be set in place. This single tax with a dual schedule was created by combining the land *capita* and the personal *capita*. Such inventories categorized surface area by type of agriculture, resident labor force *(coloni, adscripti)*, and livestock. Illustrating the procedures described both in *Panegyricus* 8 (for Gaul) and in Lactantius's *De mortibus persecutorum*, these documents thus date from the tetrarchic era.

The ungainliness of these operations (particularly the cadastral review, which in Egypt took no fewer than fifteen years) excludes the possibility that the imperial administration could have proceeded at regular and closely spaced intervals and explains the immuta-bility of the cadastral base, which then served to establish tax registries. Even partial reviews were undertaken only as a last resort. Papyri describe precisely the procedure for surveying parcels; this was undertaken by itinerant commissions headed by a *censitor*. A text called *De iugeribus metiundis*, ascribable to the 6th century, which reappears in the compilation *Gromatici veteres*, provided the *mensores* with approximate formulas for calculating surface area. It thus offered a tool comparable to those that Byzantine treatises on geometry later provided the tax bureau. One may assume that these "recipes" for pragmatic calculation, these simple techniques for surveying, were already at the disposal of tetrarchic *mensores*. They were then transmitted from one generation to the next through a specific education inculcated in the Byzantine *notarii*, tax agents, or private lawyers. The census of persons, which rested on the individual declarations of heads of families, might seem to have been easier to keep current. Yet, here again, the list of taxpayers was reestablished every year, and the state was helpless before the frequent underreporting of income.

Diocletian's census and cadastre were probably the first since Augustus. There may have been another under Honorius. A "state" reorganization of the Egyptian cadastre seems unthinkable for the first centuries of Muslim domination. The *rawk*, or cadastral survey, mentioned in the sources is the continuation of the Byzantine *katagraphon* (registry by locality, name of farmer, surface area, and crop grown). It gradually became more complete over the course of five centuries, as the Arab administration increased its direct control. In the west the Roman cadastral tradition, made null and void by the regression in the tax system, still operated in the internal management of the great Merovingian domains, as seen in their polyptychs.

Another cadastral preoccupation resulted not from taxing practices but from private interests. If property rights were to be guaranteed, inheritances divided up, or other changes made, the property had to be precisely delimited. In authenticated archival contracts, parcels were identified by measuring the distance between landmarks and indicating the neighboring owners. No drawings of the lands were made (at least none that have come down to us).

BIBL.: A. R. Congès, "Modalités pratiques d'implantation de cadastres romains," *Mélanges de l'école française de Rome: Antiquité* 108 (1996): 299–422. André Déléage, *La capitation du Bas-Empire* (Mâcon, 1945). Jacques Lefort, R. Bondoux, J.-C. Cheynet, J.-P. Grélois, and V. Kravari, eds. and trans., *Géométries du fisc byzantin*, with the collaboration of J. M. Martin (Paris, 1991). Arnold H. M. Jones, "Census Records of the Later Roman Empire," *Journal of Roman Studies* 43 (1953): 49–64; repr. in *The Roman Economy: Studies in Ancient Economic and Administrative History*, ed. P. A. Brunt (Oxford, 1974), 228–256.   J.C.

Caesar

In antiquity, Julius Caesar remained a two-faced figure; his assassination difficult to interpret. On the one hand, that famous murder might hint at a last attempt by republicans to save their state from tyranny; on the other, it might be seen as a bloody regicide by those determined to destabilize a regime that had clearly demonstrated the benefits of imperial rule.

Such ambiguities were still keenly exploited nearly five hundred years after Julius Caesar's death. In the late 4th century, the wealthy and well-born Roman aristocrat Julius Toxotius traced his family back through the Julian family to Aeneas; Toxotius's wife Paula claimed descent from the Gracchi and the Scipios (Jerome, *Letters* 108.1 and 4). Early in the century, on the inscribed base of a commemorative statue erected by the Senate, C. Ceionius Rufius Volusianus, urban prefect of Rome and consul in 314, had his consulship dated not by reference to the emperor Constantine's offices or titles, but *"post caesariana tempora."*

Such references to Caesar were two-edged. In part they admitted that he might be regarded as the first Roman emperor; but in part they also sought to link him to a specifically Roman preimperial history, a history that allowed Roman aristocrats—with their carefully constructed fictive genealogies—to assert their preeminence as the direct heirs of a glorious republican past.

In late antiquity, much less ambiguous versions of Caesar were also available. Caesar (like Augustus) was a title borne by all emperors. It had been used by Diocletian specifically to mark out his two junior colleagues in the tetrarchy, and it continued to be used as the conventional title designating imperial princes as heirs apparent. Caesar was an imperial name. Julius Caesar was presented as the first ruler of the Julio-Claudian dynasty. In a set of short poems on Roman emperors written by the late 4th century court poet Ausonius, Julius Caesar heads the series; his brutal murder is presented as a pitiless gang-style killing (*Caesares* 1.49).

This was a version of Julius Caesar that could be taken further. Against aristocratic accounts of the Roman republic, the imperial court and its supporters sought to impose a more exclusively imperial history in which kingship was presented as a natural and deep-rooted institution. In the preface to a law issued in 537, the emperor Justinian offered a framework for viewing Rome before the Julio-Claudians, dividing it into three significant periods of kingly rule—first Aeneas, then Romulus and Numa, and finally Julius Caesar and Augustus.

Such versions of republican history were important both in establishing emperors' legitimacy and in edging out competing claims to the prestige conferred by the distant past. On Justinian's model, all Roman history was regal history. There was no break between republic and empire; no Roman revolution; no room for nostalgic republican sympathy. The past was uninterruptedly joined with the present. Julius Caesar bridged the gap between the mythical rulers of early Rome and the undoubtedly imperial Augustus and so, by implication, on up to Justinian himself. In this smooth, kingly version of history, Julius Caesar—as his name retrospectively suggested—was clearly (and surprisingly) a Roman emperor.

The Greek equivalent of Caesar, *kaisar,* became *qesar* in Aramaic and *qaysar* in Arabic. Although not in the Qur'ān, it appears frequently in hadith literature and in early historical texts with two meanings: the Byzantine emperor, whomever he might be, and the emperor in general. In the latter sense, it is often used pejoratively to imply an un-Islamic way of life.

BIBL.: M. Maass, "Roman History and Christian Ideology in Justinianic Reform Legislation," *Dumbarton Oaks Papers* 40 (1986): 17–31.   C.K.

Caesarea

Commonly called Caesarea Palaestinae (to distinguish it from other cities of the same name), this Caesarea was a Roman city on the Mediterranean coast approximately 40 km north of modern Tel Aviv. The Jewish king Herod the Great built Caesarea and its harbor, Sebastos, in 20–10 B.C.E., naming both after the first emperor. From 6 C.E. to the end of antiquity Caesarea was the headquarters for the Roman governor. In 306 Caesar Maximinus presided over spectacles in the city's amphitheater, witnessing executions of Christian martyrs. In about 500, Emperor Anastasius restored the harbor. After a Persian occupation from 614 to 628, the city withstood a Muslim siege before it fell in 640 or 641.

At Caesarea, shortly after the crucifixion, St. Peter founded the earliest Gentile church anywhere, in the household of the centurion Cornelius (Acts 10). This church may have continued without interruption. Bishop Theophilus headed a thriving community there ca. 190 and was metropolitan of Palestine. In 231 Origen, escaping from Alexandria, settled in Caesarea, where he attracted pupils, disputed with the city's eminent rabbis, and compiled the parallel biblical texts known as the Hexapla, which attracted St. Jerome and other scholars to Caesarea. The priest Pamphilus enriched Origen's library and taught the historian Eusebius, Caesarea's bishop ca. 314–338, who included a vivid image of Caesarea, still pagan and dominated by the governors, in *Martyrs of Palestine*. After the Council of Chalcedon (451), Jerusalem replaced Caesarea as metropolitan see.

Greek in culture by the 4th century, Caesarea was known for its excellent rhetoricians and historiographers. Like Eusebius, Gelasius, bishop ca. 380–394, wrote ecclesiastical history. On the secular side, Procopius, historian of Justinian's wars, descended from the local landholding aristocracy. In his *Secret History* he lamented damage to his class interests when Samaritan peasants rebelled in Caesarea's countryside in 529–530.

Large-scale excavations since 1989 have revealed a prosperous city in late antiquity. The harbor's Herodian breakwaters had already succumbed to tectonic slippage and coastal surge by the 2nd century, but shipping and pilgrim traffic still contributed much to the local economy. Warehouse complexes suggest a large export-import trade in grain, wine, oil, and other commodities. Inscriptions show the local aristocracy still prominent in communal affairs, including public building. The city's expanding population required new fortifications in the 5th century that enclosed twice the urban space of the earlier circuit. In the 6th century the authorities restored the aqueducts and renewed ancient streets, along with the water pipelines and sewer channels that ran beneath them. Four public or commercial bathing establishments from the period have now come to light. The city's theater, of Herodian age, still functioned in late antiquity, as did a Roman-style hippodrome. The Roman amphitheater, scene of martyrdoms, was despoiled during the period.

Caesarea was Christianized during the 4th century, but the city's main temple, Herod's Augusteum, presumably deconsecrated and dilapidated, still dominated the city from its platform above the harbor. An octagonal church, built from the same stones, replaced this temple ca. 500. It was perhaps the attested church of St. Procopius, the city's first martyr and the namesake of numerous inhabitants. The *Life of St. Anastasius the Persian* mentions churches of the Theotokos, of Pamphilus, and others, amid accounts of the saint's miracles at Caesarea during and after the Persian occupation, on the eve of the Muslim conquest.

BIBL.: Walter Emil Kaegi, Jr., "Some Seventh Century Sources on Caesarea," *Israel Exploration Journal* 28 (1978): 177–181. Avner Raban and Kenneth G. Holum, eds., *Caesarea Maritima: A Retrospective after Two Millennia* (Leiden and New York, 1996). R. Lindley Vann, ed., "Caesarea Papers," *Journal of Roman Archaeology*, Supplementary Series 5 (1992). K.G.H.

Caesarius of Arles

As a monk, monastery founder, and bishop of Arles, Caesarius (469/70–542) devoted his life to propagating a demanding set of biblical and ascetic values and practices for the Christians of post-Roman Gaul, many of whom preferred traditional customs or alternative expressions of piety, such as consulting diviners and dancing at saints' feasts. As a political figure, Caesarius resembles the other powerful bishops with whom he corresponded—Avitus of Vienne, Ennodius of Pavia, and Symmachus and Hormisdas of Rome—all of whom found that success as local church and civic leaders required close diplomatic relations with the barbarian kings who were contending for their territories. Though largely anonymous, Caesarius's influence on the medieval church, as disseminated by an ambitious and well-informed *Life*, the canons of the church councils over which he presided, his *Rule for Nuns*, and the hundreds of sermons that he had written down and sent out over Gaul, shows up clearly in later Merovingian monastic rules, Carolingian programs of church reform, and sermon collections in Latin and the vernacular languages.

Caesarius was born in Chalon-sur-Saône, where he served for two years in the lower clergy, and he arrived in Arles early in the 490s after a stay of some years at the island monastery of Lérins. Under the patronage of his kinsman Aeonius, bishop of Arles ca. 485–502, he advanced rapidly in the local church. His aristocratic patrons in the city included the pious matron Gregoria and her relative (probably husband) Firminus, dedicatee of Book 9 of Sidonius's *Letters*. Their attempt to polish his "monastic simplicity" through the teaching of Iulianus Pomerius, a noted *grammaticus* and rhetor (Kaster, *Guardians of Language*, no. 124), suggests, as do his sermons and other writings, that his education was more Christian than classical.

Caesarius was consecrated bishop of Arles in December 502 by the choice of the late Aeonius and the permission of the Visigothic king. Faced with attempts by disaffected clerics to depose him, under both the Visigoths and the Ostrogoths who succeeded them in 508, Caesarius remained in office through skillful court diplomacy and a network of outside supporters. These included his newly elected suffragan bishops (whose consecration he alone, as metropolitan, could approve), the bishops of Rome, and high-ranking local officials such as Liberius, praetorian prefect of Gaul from ca. 510/11–534, whose relationship with Caesarius was particularly close. (Both Liberius and his wife, Agretia, were reportedly healed by the bishop's prayers, and one of the bequests in Caesarius's *Testament* was of a slave woman named Agritia, probably a gift from Agretia.) Indeed, it was during Liberius's administration that Caesarius's most important accomplishments occurred: the founding, with his sister Caesaria, of the first nunnery in Arles (512); the reform councils of Arles (524), Carpentras (527), and Vaison (529); and the doctrinal council of Orange (529), whose canons against semi-Pelagianism were signed not only by the bishops who attended but also (unusually) by seven aristocrats, including Liberius, whose construction of a basilica the council celebrated.

When Provence was ceded to the Franks in 536, Caesarius's political position rapidly declined. Drawn into the larger orbit of Merovingian church politics, where he was simply one metropolitan bishop among many with no privileged royal access, he found it impossible to maintain his former prominence. He died on 27 August 542 and was buried in the basilica of his nunnery, which until its dissolution during the French Revolution also preserved several of his possessions—most famously a splendid ivory buckle depicting two soldiers leaning on their spears, sleeping at the Holy Sepulcher—now held by the museums of Arles.

BIBL.: D. Bertrand et al., *Césaire d'Arles et la christianisation de la Provence* (Paris, 1994); R. A. Kaster, *Guardians of Language: The Grammarian and Society in Late Antiquity* (Berkeley, 1988); W. E. Klingshirn, *Caesarius of Arles: The Making of a Christian Community in Late Antique Gaul* (Cambridge, Eng., 1994); and R. Markus, *The End of Ancient Christianity* (Cambridge, Eng., 1990).   W.KLI.

Caliphate

When the Prophet Muhammad died in 632, he had neither designated a successor nor established a system for the political leadership of his community. Abū Bakr was chosen by the Prophet's companions as the *khalīfat rasūl Allāh,* the successor to the Messenger of God, to lead the emerging polity in Medina. The term *caliph (khalīfa),* which can mean both successor and deputy in secular and Qur'ānic usage, thus came to refer to the ruler of early Islamic society. The English word *caliphate* refers to the ruling institution of the caliph.

The first four caliphs were occupied with military expansion and the formation of an administrative system, as well as with leading the new religious community. Although these caliphs made no claims of continuing Muhammad's prophetic mission, the extent to which the early Muslims expected to be led by a religious authority remains a question. Part of the community felt that leadership should be based on the ability to maintain the religious legacy of Muhammad, and

some saw this in the person of 'Alī ibn Abī Ṭālib, the Prophet's son-in-law and cousin who became the fourth caliph, and in his progeny.

'Alī was assassinated in 661 during a civil war that brought to power the Umayyads, who began to choose successors from among their own family. To many Muslims, the bitter conflict had clearly established the Umayyad caliphate, now based at Damascus, as a temporal rather than a religious regime. In an attempt to assert their religious legitimacy, the Umayyad caliphs adopted the controversial title of *khalīfat Allāh,* or "deputy of God." Thereafter caliphs often emphasized the divine foundations of the caliphate. This was particularly true of the Abbasids, who succeeded the Umayyads in 750 and moved the caliphate to Baghdad.

BIBL.: Patricia Crone and Martin Hinds, *God's Caliph: Religious Authority in the First Centuries of Islam* (Cambridge, Eng., 1986). A. K. S. Lambton et al., "Khalīfa," *Encyclopaedia of Islam,* new ed. (Leiden, 1954–). Wilferd Madelung, *The Succession to Muhammad: A Study of the Early Caliphate* (New York, 1996). W. Montgomery Watt, "God's Caliph," in *Early Islam: Collected Articles* (Edinburgh, 1990), 57–63.   M.R.

Camels

The three centuries following the death of Alexander the Great witnessed profound changes in the pastoral and transportation economies of the Middle East and North Africa. At the same time, one-humped camels, previously known only in the Arabian Peninsula and its northward desert extensions, transformed the herding economies of the southern highlands of the Sahara and became a factor in the development of the Silk Road. The simultaneity of these developments indicates changes in the role and status of the primary herders of one-humped camels, the Arabs.

Comparing depictions of Arabs on Assyrian bas-reliefs of the 7th century B.C.E. and descriptions of them several centuries later reveals significant changes. Judging from costume and accoutrements, the earlier Arabs had few imported goods and lived, in material terms, very simple lives. The later Arabs had horses, spears, and swords, all indicating material improvement, and their caravan cities traded in imported luxuries. The apparent reason for these changes was a new North Arabian camel saddle design, which was more efficient militarily than the South Arabian saddle. The earlier design seated the rider on the animal's rump and made it so difficult to wield a bow and arrow that, in fighting the Assyrians, the Arabs resorted to a two-man saddle—placing one rider on the camel to drive and one to fight. The new northern saddle seated the rider over the hump with a high, firm pommel and cantle that allowed him to strike downward against attacking horsemen.

The prosperity of the caravan city of Petra in the 1st

century B.C.E. attests to the fact that the Arabs had by then gained control of the lucrative incense trade that had for centuries traversed the Arabian Peninsula bringing only minimal benefit to the pastoralists who supplied the camels. The social elite of Petra and other caravan cities consisted of traders. It is presumably they who expanded Arab trading enterprise across the Red Sea into the routes linking the seaports to the Nile. Once local peoples established a herding economy in Egypt's eastern desert, camel use spread westward from one desert ethnic group to another. Because there was little trade in the southern Sahara at that time, the technologies of the early Saharan camel herders reflect military applications more than commercial ones. In later centuries, however, peoples like the Tuareg became key factors in trans-Saharan trade.

Arab traders were probably responsible, as well, for the crossbreeding in southern Mesopotamia of one and two-humped camels to produce particularly strong animals for traveling the Silk Road. Though forgotten today, this breeding industry endured for many centuries and played a role in the dominance of one-humped camels, who gradually supplanted native two-humped camels from western Iran to northern India.

Once Arab prosperity and enterprise had brought the desert nomads into closer relations with the settled peoples of the surrounding lands, opportunities arose to capitalize on the camel's strength and cheapness. Diocletian's edict on prices of 301 C.E. indicates a 20 percent savings for hauling a load on a camel instead of an oxcart, and there are other indications that camel breeders took over much of the transportation economy. As a consequence of this, and perhaps other factors, wheeled transport virtually disappeared from the Middle East by the time of the Islamic conquests, except in Anatolia, which was probably too cold for the Arabs' camels. Carts proved slightly more enduring in Egypt and North Africa, but they mostly succumbed to camel competition there too.

The disappearance of wheeled transport had a pronounced effect on urban topography. Since camels needed much less room to maneuver, narrow and winding streets tended to replace broad, straight avenues in many late antique cities.

The camel was used as a pack animal throughout the Mediterranean as far as Gaul (Gregory of Tours, *History* 7.35; *Vita Eligii* 2.12). Its predominance in the transport systems of the Middle East surprised only northerners (Adomnán, *de locis sanctis* 2.28), but it was viewed as a vaguely uncanny beast. Its erratic stride reminded churchmen of the twisted ways of the pagans and of the fluidity of earthly goods (Gregory the Great, *Moralia in Job* 1.15). It made appearances in the circus in comic roles (*Lamentations Rabbah, Petihta* 17: where the camel, dressed in mourning robes, laments that the Jews are so poor that they have eaten up his favorite food, the camel thorn) and for displays of acrobatic camel riding (*Life of Theodore of Sykeon*

3.13). Boiled camel, reputed to be the favorite dish of the nomads, was in fact a sign of their famished condition and was regarded with abhorrence (Michael the Syrian, *Chronicle* 9.29, trans. Chabot, p. 247; al-Ṭabarī, *ad annum Hegirae* 20, de Goeje, pp. 2590–2591: trans. Juynboll, *History of al-Tabari,* vol. 13 [Albany, 1989], 173–174). To be paraded on camelback through the city was a common punishment, the height of the animal providing visibility and its awkward stride inflicting exquisite humiliation on those accustomed (in the west) to showing their status by riding on horseback (Procopius, *Wars* 7.32.3 and *Secret History* 11.37; John Malalas, *Chronicle* 18.47, ed. Dindorf, p. 529; Fredegar, *Chronicle* 4.42 [Queen Brunhilda]; Julian of Toledo, *Historia Wambae* 20 [Visigothic noble rebels]).

BIBL.: Roger S. Bagnall, "The Camel, the Wagon, and the Donkey in Later Roman Egypt," *Bulletin of the American Society of Papyrologists* 22 (1985): 1–6. Richard W. Bulliet, *The Camel and the Wheel* (Cambridge, Mass.), 1975. Richard W. Bulliet, "Botr et Baranès: Hypotheses sur l'histoire des Berbères," *Annales: Économies, Sociétés, Civilisations* (Jan.–Feb. 1981): 104–116.   R.B.

Camps

The Roman defenses, after the breakdown of the late 3rd century, were restored and strengthened under the tetrarchy and the house of Constantine. Most earlier legionary fortresses and lesser forts remained in use, especially along the Rhine and the Danube. In addition some new networks appeared, such as the forts of the Saxon shore in Britain and the fortified strata Diocletiana in Syria. There are, however, very few excavated late Roman camps, and the dating of many fortifications remains conjectural, especially in the east. A striking variety of ground plans cannot be translated into chronology, as widely divergent features were apparently contemporary. It seems that parts of some works usually attributed to the tetrarchy could be in fact of a 4th or even 5th century date.

The late Roman camps are better protected but usually smaller than the well-known *limes* installations of the principate. This agrees with the commonly admitted reduction of the late legions to units of roughly one thousand strong, although many fortresses could have been manned by detachments of the large legions as well. Similarly, the typical *quadriburgia (tetrapyrgia)* are obviously too small and too many to accommodate complete auxiliary units.

The only excavated legionary fortresses founded in late antiquity are in the east: Lejjun in Jordan, Palmyra in Syria, and Luxor in Egypt. Many legions were stationed in cities, where their quarters are not necessarily distinguishable today, especially without excavations. The often-quoted passage of Zosimus (2.34) attributing the practice of stationing legions in cities to Constantine is incorrect and biased, as the camps of

Legio III Cyrenaica in Bostra and of Cohors XX Palmyrenorum in Dura-Europus are much earlier, and the explanation could be simple practicality in the urbanized east: the 4th century Persian wars consisted largely of sieges of strongly fortified Mesopotamian cities.

The camp of Lejjun (probably Betthorus, of Legio IV Martia) in the provincia Arabia, built about 300 C.E., covers barely 4.6 hectares, about one quarter of a stationary camp of the principate. Its layout was conservative, with the *principia* in the middle, at the meeting of the *via praetoria* and the *via principalis,* and a regular pattern of barracks.

The camp of Legio I Illyricorum at Palmyra was founded before 303 on the outskirts of the city, but it is included within the same ramparts as the city itself. Only a continuous line of shops divided it from the town, while the water supply and baths were common for both. The two camp streets cross at right angles in the middle, and the *principia* are sited on a slope of the hill at the far end. The serviceable surface of the camp hardly exceeded 4 hectares, about as much as at Lejjun, and also as in a square unexcavated fort found inside the walled frontier city of Sura, on the Euphrates, which probably accommodated the Legio XVI Flavia Firma. In spite of the massive use of older architectural members, the military buildings at Palmyra surely belong to the tetrarchic period. The central crossing can be also found in some other 4th century fortresses (Diocletian's palace at Split, for example, and Portchester and Drobeta, although the plans of the latter two are subject to doubt). It is repeated twice in the tetrarchic camp at Luxor, on either side of the pharaonic temple in which the chapel of the imperial cult found its place.

The traditional plan of *principia* is still followed in Lejjun and Palmyra. In later camps the absidal chapel survives alone at the end of a colonnaded approach along the sole axis of the camp, as in Iatrus (Bulgaria) and Dionysias (Egypt, Fayum). The regular layout of the Roman camp seems to have disintegrated completely after the 4th century, although some camps survived down to the Islamic conquest.

It has been argued that the Roman camp plan was behind the composition of several Umayyad settlements, such as Anjarr in Lebanon and Qaṣr al-Hayr East in Syria. In addition, the Near Eastern nomadic tradition had a pattern of camps about which little is known, but which may well have influenced the new Islamic cities of Kufa and Basra in Iraq and Fustat (the word means "tents"), the forerunner of Cairo in Egypt. In a sense, the plan of Baghdad, with its four entrances facing cardinal points, can be related to the octagonal pattern of a Roman camp.

BIBL.: David Kennedy and Derrick Riley, *Rome's Desert Frontier from the Air* (London, 1990). H. Kennedy, "From *Polis* to *Madina:* Urban Change in Late Antique and Early Islamic Syria," *Past and Present* 106 (1995). Harald von Petrikovits, "Fortifications in the North-Western Roman Empire from the Third to the Fifth Centuries AD," *Journal of Roman Studies* (1971): 178–218. Michel Reddé, "Dioclétien et les fortifications militaires de l'antiquité tardive," *Antiquité tardive* 3 (1995): 91–124.

M.G.

Cappadocia

In the early Roman empire, the province of Cappadocia came to include most of eastern Asia Minor between the Black Sea, the upper Euphrates River, and the Taurus Mountains. Because this high plateau was isolated from the Mediterranean, it had had limited contact with Greek civilization, and it long remained one of the most backward regions in the Roman empire. Its harsh climate contributed to its seclusion as well, since every year winter buried the inhabitants in a "night that lasted six months." Before the reign of Constantine, very few Cappadocians served in the imperial administration, acquired senatorial rank, or even received Roman citizenship. Because the region contained only a few cities, the opportunities for studying classical culture were limited; one sophist from Caesarea who did become a distinguished teacher in Rome and Athens during the later 2nd century was nevertheless criticized for the thickness of his accent, "as is common among Cappadocians."

By the 370s emperors had divided the earlier large province into several smaller provinces, among them Cappadocia Prima and its capital of Caesarea, and Cappadocia Secunda and its capital of Tyana. By then, too, the region had become central to imperial plans. Since the main roads between Constantinople and Antioch passed through Cappadocia, emperors often visited the region. The emperor Constantius, for instance, stopped there to hunt at a game park and to check on his young cousin, the future emperor Julian, whom he had had confined to an imperial estate near Mt. Argaeus; the emperor Valens passed through Caesarea several times as he prepared for his eastern campaigns. Imperial factories and weaving mills produced armor and clothing for the magistrates and troops on the eastern frontiers, and the numerous imperial ranches contributed horses for campaigns against the Persians. Local aristocrats from Cappadocia took advantage of their access to the imperial court in order to hold offices in the imperial administration or acquire membership in the new Senate at Constantinople. Others became bishops or clerics. The most influential and by far the most prominent were the three Cappadocian Fathers: Bishop Basil of Caesarea, his brother, Bishop Gregory of Nyssa, and their friend Gregory of Nazianzus, who served briefly as bishop of Constantinople. Other notable Cappadocian churchmen included Bishop Amphilochius of Iconium, a cousin of Gregory of Nazianzus, and Bishop Eunomius of Cyzicus, whose theological treatises were nevertheless quickly dismissed as heretical in a cavalcade of opposition led by Basil, Gregory of Nyssa, and others.

After the 4th century emperors again neglected Cappadocia, and one emperor simply used it as a prison for the confinement of two usurpers. Large landowners in Cappadocia became so powerful that they intimidated even the court at Constantinople; because of his "embarrassment" over these "ruthless bandits" and their seizure of imperial estates, the emperor Justinian proposed changes in the administration of the region. While waging his wars against the Persians, Heraclius finally became the first emperor to visit Cappadocia in more than two centuries. Soon thereafter the Arab conquest of Syria transformed Cappadocia into what it would remain for centuries in the Byzantine empire, a frontier zone.

BIBL.: F. Hild and M. Restle, *Kappadokien (Kappadokia, Charsianon, Sebasteia und Lykandos) = Tabula Imperii Byzantini*, ed. H. Hunger, vol. 2., Österreichische Akademie der Wissenschaften, philosophisch-historische Klasse, Denkschriften, Bd. 149 (Vienna, 1981). S. Mitchell, *Anatolia: Land, Men, and Gods in Asia Minor*, 2 vols. (Oxford, 1993). R. Van Dam, "Emperor, Bishops, and Friends in Late Antique Cappadocia," *Journal of Theological Studies* n.s. 37 (1986): 53–76. R.V.

Carthage

Situated on the protected side of an arrowhead-shaped peninsula jutting into what is today the Bay of Tunis, centrally located in the Mediterranean between east and west, Carthage originated as a Phoenician trading town and rose to later prominence as one of the three great ports of the Roman Mediterranean. With a population estimated in the early 3rd century at perhaps 300,000, Roman Carthage became the second city of the western empire. A magnet for trade, overseas visitors, and refugees in late antiquity, the city was known for its deep attachment to Roman culture and civic life.

Carthage was a lightning rod for the tensions within the African church in the 4th through 7th centuries. The Donatist schism was born in the city in 312 and ended officially in the Baths of Gargilius, in the summer of 411. Carthage was also the site, in 645, of the climactic debate between the Monothelite Pyrrhus and Abbot Maximus.

The environs of Roman Carthage were stable enough that a defensive wall was first erected around the city ca. 425, long after it became the capital of the diocese of Africa under Diocletian and just before it was captured by Gaiseric and made the center of the Vandal kingdom in 439. Carthago Justiniana was the capital city of the prefecture of Africa after 533 and later became the seat of the Byzantine exarch. The emperor Heraclius considered moving his administration to Carthage in 620, although a generation later the exarch Gregory, after declaring himself emperor in the city in 646, moved his capital to Sufetula to meet the Arab threat.

Because Africa's agricultural heartland had come through the depredations of the 3rd century comparatively well, Carthage remained the major supplier of grain and oil to Italy in the 4th and 5th centuries and to Constantinople in the 6th and 7th. Control of these commodities was an effective political tool in the hands of Count Gildo in 397, the Vandal kings in the 5th century, and the exarch Heraclius in the early 7th, as a means of resisting imperial authority. The city was the site of a Vandal mint, which continued a tradition begun in the late Roman period and renewed by the Byzantines. Archaeological evidence suggests that parts of the city continued to be rich and cosmopolitan in the 6th century, especially in the later Vandal period. While some city streets and public buildings suffered from periodic neglect or were even destroyed, church buildings, private houses, and some baths were built or rebuilt and adorned with the mosaics and sculpture of local ateliers as well as the latest in imported architectural decorations. Ceramic assemblages from the last quarter of the 5th century through the mid-6th century show a great diversity and quantity of imports. Carthage in this period was the setting for the civic and literary patronage of King Thrasamund and his successors, commemorated by the African poets of the *Latin Anthology*. The city's traditional economy must have collapsed around 650 when its harbors went out of use and African red slip ware was no longer produced.

BIBL.: C. Lepelley, *Les cités de l'Afrique romaine au Bas-Empire* (Paris, 1981), vol. 2, 11–53. F. M. Clover, "Felix Karthago," *Dumbarton Oaks Papers* 40 (1986): 1–16. S.T.S.

Cassiodorus

Flavius Magnus Aurelius Cassiodorus Senator (known as Senator by his contemporaries, and as Cassiodorus for posterity) came from an arriviste family in the far south of Italy. The family home was near Squillace, in modern Calabria. Cassiodorus was born ca. 490, apparently while his father was governor of the local province. His grandfather and great-grandfather had also been dignitaries in the regimes of imperial and subimperial Italy of the 5th century, but the family cannot be traced back beyond the early 5th century in Italy and seems to have come west from an eastern origin around that time.

Cassiodorus's own father was praetorian prefect for Italy under the Gothic king Theoderic ca. 500–507. Under his father's patronage, Cassiodorus made his debut as a panegyrist, and at about the time of his father's retirement he became quaestor, a post in which he wrote elaborately formal letters and edicts in the king's name. He served in that role from approximately 507 to 511. Not long after, he held the office of consul for the year 514 and enjoyed the dignity of having no colleague share the office. Cassiodorus remained active in the service of the Gothic regime as long as he could, both as author of flattering works of history and as sedulous administrator. He served from 523 to 527 as *magister officiorum* (master of offices) and thought himself instrumental in assuring the smooth succession of the child-king Athalaric after the death of Theoderic. Another interlude out of office was followed by his crowning service, from 533 to approximately 540, as praetorian prefect for Italy under first Athalaric and then a succession of Gothic kings and generalissimos. During Cassiodorus's time as prefect, the Justinianic war of reconquest began its inexorable demolition of the regime Cassiodorus had labored to serve. His public life seems to have ended with his going to Constantinople as something like a hostage or a refugee; he remained there until 554, when the Justinianic war was settled.

While in Constantinople, Cassiodorus maintained an interest in the affairs of Italy but began to devote himself to theological writing as well. On returning to Italy, he settled at his family estate near Squillace, which he called Vivarium, after the fishponds that decorated its grounds (and that may have been rediscovered in modern times). There he attracted a small community of Christian monks and devoted himself to the establishment of a library of Christian literature. The ambitions he had for such a library were connected in some way with his failed attempt to found a Christian school of higher studies in Rome in the 530s, but the mix of retirement and Christian learning he chose was one already exemplified elsewhere (e.g., in Cassiodorus's lifetime, by Eugippius, who lived near Naples), and it would have a long life after him; it is unclear how directly influential Cassiodorus may have been in propagating the model.

Cassiodorus's known works include his *Variae* (*Miscellanies,* an anthology of public letters written for the Gothic regime), *Chronicon* (an outline of world history written to flatter a Gothic prince), fragments of panegyrics for the Gothic regime, and a *Gothic History* (not surviving, but reflected in the *Getica* of Jordanes, written in Constantinople ca. 551 and purporting to be a digest of Cassiodorus's work). At the end of his public career, Cassiodorus wrote a short philosophical treatise, *De anima* (On the Soul), then (apparently in Constantinople) a complete commentary on the Latin Psalter. Back at Vivarium, his *Institutiones* set out a plan of sacred and secular studies, and the books supporting them, for his monks. The work is a distinctive mix of church Fathers and the seven liberal arts, and the two halves of *Institutiones* led sometimes separate lives in the Middle Ages. Other works written or patronized by Cassiodorus at Vivarium have chiefly to do with scriptural studies, but in his ninety-third year he wrote

a digest of grammarians' rules on spelling for the benefit of his monks' scribal activity. His death occurred sometime in the 580s. By the reign of Pope Gregory the Great (590–604), the monastic community Cassiodorus left behind seems shrunken and paltry. His books were widely read in the Middle Ages, exercising a utilitarian influence with little of either inspiration or controversy about them.

BIBL.: S. J. B. Barnish, *The Variae of Magnus Aurelius Cassiodorus Senator* (Liverpool, 1992). J. J. O'Donnell, *Cassiodorus* (Berkeley, 1979). A. Momigliano, "Cassiodorus and Italian Culture of His Time," *Proceedings of the British Academy* 41 (1955): 207–245; repr. in his *Studies in Historiography* (London, 1966), 181–210.   J.J.O.

Catechesis

Catechesis, or oral instruction, was the teaching given in preparation for Christian baptism (see Acts 8:26–39). Some matter used in Jewish synagogues for instructing Gentile proselytes could be adapted, e.g., a document used in the Didache and the epistle of Barnabus on "the Two Ways." The *Qumran Manual of Discipline* also has analogies. Candidates for admission to Christian society needed to be told what moral conduct would be expected of them (Acts 15:29) and how to understand the Bible, baptism, and the Eucharist. They needed to be given some grasp of the pattern of Christian doctrine—i.e., the creation of this world as good but dependent on the will of God; the mixed nature of humanity, made in the divine image with freedom and responsibility but fallen and flawed by selfishness; the need for divine redemption, the story of which is traced through the choice of Israel's patriarchs and prophets, culminating in the Messiah or Christ of prophetic hope; the salvific function of his community of disciples, the church, his "body," deriving from the universal significance of God's anointed and inspired Messiah; the redemption mediated through faith and adherence to this society that leads to salvation or bliss in the world to come, in which individuality is not lost and each bears responsibility and faces judgment.

Within this story of God's providence in history, crucial importance attached to the discernment that the coming of Jesus the Messiah fulfilled the prophets, and in the surviving documents of early catechesis the argument about (or from) prophecy looms strikingly large.

The epistle to the Ephesians declared for "one Lord, one faith, one baptism." This presupposed a common pattern of normative instruction given by a teacher bearing authority derived from the first, or apostolic, generation. This teacher might be a well-educated layman (e.g., Justin Martyr or Clement of Alexandria). At Alexandria, in the interests of maintaining the church there in the truth, safe from Gnostic vagaries, the bishops set up a catechetical school. Since the bishop was the normal minister of baptism, in which the symbolic descent into the water represented the redemptive death of Christ's crucifixion and resurrection, he usually administered the sacrament at the annual commemoration of Easter and preceded that by a course of catechetical lectures. In time an originally interrogatory form of three baptismal questions concerning faith in Father, Son, and Holy Spirit became an affirmation: "I believe in . . ." The text of this creed, together with the "Our Father," or Lord's Prayer, was disclosed to the candidates as part of their initiation.

Prior to this, perhaps some years earlier, there was a ceremony of admission as a catechumen (a person under instruction). In this rite, the entrant received the sign of the Cross on the forehead, the imposition of hands, an exorcism to expel evil powers together with an insufflation with similar purpose, and special prayers. In some places the confession of sins played a part, and if the sins were of any notoriety, they would be confessed before the congregation. In the Latin west the emphasis in catechism lay on moral correction, with questions of theology being secondary, whereas in the east it tended to be the other way around. Because of the seriousness attached to baptismal vows, catechumens were often reluctant to give their names for baptism, and at Sunday worship would be told to leave before the Eucharist was offered.

The attitude of educated pagan Platonists toward Christian catechesis may be summed up in the words of the Egyptian Alexander of Lycopolis in about 300: he said that he found Christian doctrine obscure, but it was clear that it all had something to do with being good.

BIBL.: M. Arranz, "Evolution des rites d'incorporation et de réadmission dans l'église selon l'euchologe byzantin," *Gestes et paroles dans les diverses familles liturgiques* (Rome, 1978), 36–53. M. Dujarier, *A History of the Catechumenate: The First Six Centuries* (New York, 1979). William Harmless, *Augustine and the Catechumenate* (Collegeville, Minn., 1995). E. Rebillard, "La figure du catéchumène et le problème du delai du baptîme," *Augustin prédicateur*, ed. G. Madec (Paris, 1998). H.C.

Caucasus

The Caucasian Mountains, situated between the Black Sea and the Caspian, are divided into two ranges: the Greater and the Lesser Caucasus. The highest peaks are Mount Elbrus and Mount Kazbegi. The Caucasus region contains many rivers and lakes. To the south is Transcaucasia, home to the ancient civilizations of Colchis, Iberia, Armenia, and Albania. In the high mountains, especially in the North Caucasus, many local tribes lived a barbarian life. Crossing the Caucasian Mountains, linking North Caucasia with Transcaucasia, the best-known passes are the Dariel and Derbend; there are thirty-six other passes between Mounts Elbrus and Kazbegi alone. The protection of these passes against hostile North Caucasian tribes, who were prone to attack Cappadocia to the south,

was the main preoccupation of the Romans in this region.

Little was known about the Caucasus until Pompey's campaign there. Previously only the name and the great size of this range of mountains were known. Some ancient authors described it as a single vast, high mountain populated by primitive people. Here Prometheus was chained, on Mount Elbrus. The Caucasus was the land of arimasps and griffins, who guarded its gold treasures. The best-known ancient myth set in the Caucasus is that of Jason and the Argonauts, who sailed there to steal the golden fleece. For many centuries this myth retained its great popularity (particularly the image of Medea) in ancient art and literature.

The Romans first became familiar with the Caucasus, especially Colchis, Iberia, and Albania, when Pompey vanquished Iberia in 65 B.C.E. Colchis and Albania then became a Roman vassal state, enjoying internal independence. Roman garrisons were established in Colchis in the reign of Nero. The Caucasian frontier, with its fortresses on the eastern shore of the Black Sea (Apsarus, Tsikhisdziri, Phasis, Sebastopolis, and Pityus), became a main part of the Pontic *limes* and the province of Cappadocia. It was the task of the Caucasian frontier to protect shipping and trade along the shores of the Black Sea by preventing the local tribes (Achaei, Zygi, Heniochi, and others) from engaging in piracy. It also served the strategic functions of projecting Roman power to the client kingdoms of Iberia and Albania and controlling the Caucasian passes (again, to prevent attacks from local tribes, the most dangerous being the Alani).

Under the principate, close relations were established between Rome and Iberia in consequence of Rome's eastward penetration, especially into Armenia. Iberia played an important role as a buffer kingdom in relations between Rome and Parthia. In the 3rd and 4th centuries, after the creation of the Sassanid empire, Roman influence declined, despite the Christianization of Iberia (and Colchis). By the end of the 4th century Iberia was under Persian control. In western Transcaucasia, Lazica (Colchis) remained under the Romans; in the 5th century it was lost, but in 522 a new Lazic king returned to the Roman fold. In the middle of the 6th century Lazic territory was the arena for wars between the Byzantine and Persian empires, leading to a Byzantine alliance with Lazica that lasted for two centuries more.

Armenia, another important Caucasian kingdom, was proclaimed a Roman province during Trajan's eastern campaign (113–117). From the 3rd century on, the Sassanids coveted it. In 296 Diocletian and Narses signed a treaty giving all of Armenia to Rome, but only as a protectorate. Armenia's Christianization was of benefit to the Romans because of its location, straddling the trade routes to the east. Armenia remained under Roman control until 287, when the Sassanids took half of it. Starting in the 6th century Armenia established close links with the Byzantine empire.

BIBL.: David Braund, *Georgia in Antiquity: A History of Colchis and Transcaucasian Iberia, 550 BC–AD 562* (Oxford, 1994). D. C. Braund and G. R. Tsetskhladze, "The Export of Slaves from Colchis," *Classical Quarterly* 39 (i) (1989): 114–125. *Il Caucaso: cerniera fra culture del Mediterraneo alla Persia (secoli IV–XI)*, Settimane di Studi sull'Alto Medio Evo 43, 2 vols. (Spoleto, 1996). F. Thélamon, *Paiens et chrétiens au IVe siècle* (Paris, 1981), 85–122. G. A. Tiratsyan, *Kul'tura drevnei Armenii* (Erevan, 1988). G.T.

Celibacy

The English term *celibacy* preserves the Latin meaning of *caelebs, caelibatus* to indicate persons who, though physically and socially able, are not, never have been, and publicly announce they never will be married, often for religious reasons. They abstain from that which society and the law define as marriage.

Celibacy is thus distinct from *virginity,* the nonconsummation of the sexual act; *continence,* abstinence from all sexual acts; and *chastity,* which involves the control and use of sexuality according to specific religious and ethic precepts. As such, celibacy can exist without the other three, but in Christianity celibacy includes sexual continence.

In late antiquity, celibacy increasingly signified a way of life, a conscious, religiously motivated choice. It involved men and women who remained "single" *(monachos, monachē)* and lived as such within their family, alone, in loose association with others (as *anchōritai*), or in regulated communities, either of men and women together or separated according to the sexes. In the writings of ancient authors this lifestyle reflected, in conscious contrast to non-Christian forms of celibacy, a stringent application of biblical precepts, such as Matt. 22:30 and Mark 12:25 regarding the temporal nature of marriage; Matt. 19:12 on eunuchs for the sake of heaven; and Gal. 3:28 proclaiming the irrelevance of gender differentiation in Christ.

The diffusion of the celibate lifestyle during the 4th and 5th centuries was paralleled by an increase in celibate members of the clergy. According to the 5th century church historians Sozomen (*Hist.eccl.* 1.23), Socrates (*Hist.eccl.* 1.11), and Gelasius (*Hist.conc.Nic.* 2.32), the question of a canon requiring clerical celibacy was a hotly debated issue at the Council of Nicaea in 325. Since the Council of Elvira in Spain (ca. 300) had already stipulated that those who entered the clergy as celibates had to remain so (can. 33), it is possible that the Spanish participants at Nicaea (Osius) introduced the suggestion. However, despite general opinion in favor, the strenuous opposition of the Egyptian ascetic, confessor, and bishop Paphnutius carried the day. The story, which does not appear in sources contemporary to the council, may in any case be more representative of the attitudes of the late 4th and early 5th century. Clerical celibacy remained a personal option rather than a legally binding prescription, though it was increasingly demanded by moral pressure.

Councils in Toledo (400), Carthage (401), and Turin (401) prohibited the "use of marriage" for married priests and deacons; Leo I made celibacy obligatory for subdeacons as well. Most prominent church Fathers, such as Innocent I, Ambrose, Jerome, John Chrysostom, and Epiphanius, promoted the incompatibility of marriage and clerical office, against others, such as Helvidius, Jovinian, and Vigilantius, who were later declared heretics. While a law promulgated by Honorius and Theodosius in 420 stipulated that no member of the clergy was allowed to dissolve his marriage on the pretext of chastity (*C.Th.* 16.2.44), Justinian excluded those who were married, and those who had children and grandchildren, from clerical office, because of the inevitable distractions of everyday life (*C.Just.* 1.3.41).

A prosopographic study of bishops in Italy from 350 to 450 reveals that out of fifty-seven known bishops, ten were married and two had one or more children. Indeed, only the Third Lateran Council of 1139 (decretal of Innocent II) declared marriages contracted by clerics invalid, while the council in Trullo in 692, against Roman usage, permitted all clerics except bishops to continue marital relations contracted prior to ordination; subdeacons, deacons, and priests who married after their ordination were to be deposed.

Though increasingly prominent in the Christian church, celibacy was fiercely attacked as an impious practice by Zoroastrians (Elishe Vardapet, *History of Vardan* 2). It was treated by Muhammad as an illegitimate accretion to the original teachings of Jesus (*Qur'ān* 57:27). Some Muslim mystics and ascetics chose not to marry as a sign of personal religious devotion, but celibacy never became prevalent in the Islamic world.

BIBL.: E. Beck, "Das christliche Mönchtum im Koran," *Studia orientalia* 13 (1946): 3–29. Susanna Elm, *"Virgins of God": The Making of Asceticism in Late Antiquity* (Oxford, 1994). R. Gryson, *Les origines du célibat ecclésiatique du premier au septième siècle* (Gembloux, Belg., 1970). S.E.

Celtic

Ancient authors are not always clear about the distinction between Celts and Germans, and neither are we. By late antiquity, a number of distinct peoples are known to have spoken related languages today called Germanic (e.g., Gothic, Frankish), while a number of others spoke "Celtic" languages, including the Galatians and the Gauls. Gaulish is probably the oldest Celtic language to leave any trace in the written record. Julius Caesar noted that although the Gauls were literate, they preserved their culture orally and used writing only for quotidian purposes such as making lists. Gaulish survives in a few inscriptions (including graffiti, evidence for literacy among skilled workmen), most notably in the Calendar of Coligny (2nd century C.E.), a bronze tablet found near Lyons containing a five-year calendar; it stops being written in the 4th century. Irish is the next oldest.

Taxonomically, the Celtic languages subdivide into Continental Celtic and Insular Celtic. There is not enough evidence for more than speculative divisions within Continental Celtic, but Insular Celtic again subdivides into two main groups, known as *p*-Celtic and *q*-Celtic. This "shorthand" for a major morphological difference in the treatment of consonants is easily illustrated: in Welsh, a *p*-Celtic language, we find forms such as *map* (son) and *pen* (head); in Irish, a *q*-Celtic language, the equivalents are *mac* (Archaic Irish *maqqos*) and *cenn*. By far the best preserved Celtic literatures are those of the British Isles: Irish, with its offshoot Scottish Gaelic; Welsh, with its relatives Cornish, Manx, and Breton (debate continues to rage as to whether any dialects of Breton are influenced by Gaulish). Of all Celtic languages, only Irish has a literary history stretching back to late antiquity: some Welsh poems (notably the *Gododdin*) reflect events of the 6th century, but they survive only in medieval versions that have been updated to an unguessable extent.

Attempts to identify a common Celtic culture are mostly tendentious beyond a few simple statements. It is clear from much recent work that there was a great deal of cultural common ground between the speakers of Celtic and Germanic languages. But some differences are also apparent, such as a distinctive group of gods worshiped by many Celtic-speaking peoples, notably Lug, who has given his name to a number of European cities (e.g., Lyons and Laon in France, Leiden in the Netherlands, Carlisle in England, and Louth in Ireland). In art, spiral decorative motifs are strongly associable with speakers of Celtic languages. Like the Germans, the Celtic peoples we know about had a warrior aristocracy. Gaulish, British, and Irish Celts also had a professional learned class, the druids, which the Romans were at great pains to suppress as a natural focus of resistance to their rule.

BIBL.: Karl Horst Schmidt, "The Celtic Languages in Their European Context," in *Proceedings of the Seventh International Congress of Celtic Studies*, ed. D. Ellis Evans et al. (Oxford, 1986): 199–221. Joshua Whatmough, *The Dialects of Ancient Gaul* (Cambridge, Mass., 1970). P. Sims-William, "Celtomania and Celtoscepticism," *Cambrian Medieval Celtic Studies* 36 (1998): 1–35. J.S.

Ceramics (East)

Research into Roman pottery has proceeded very differently in the various landscapes of the eastern Mediterranean. Whereas in Palestine archaeological exploration has covered the cities as well as rural settlements, military installations, and ecclesiastical sites, in Syria and Turkey investigations outside the metropolis are scarce, and only a few places now provide evidence for the development of pottery in late antiquity and early Islamic times. Moreover, studies there have concentrated on fine wares and lamps.

In spite of a decline in local fabrication of fine wares in the eastern Mediterranean about 150 C.E., greater numbers of North African Samian imports do not appear in the region until the second quarter of the 3rd century (Sigillata chiara A and C), when the North African kilns increased their production. Whereas earlier African imports are mostly to be found in such urban centers as Jerusalem, Antioch, Dura-Europus, and Athens, they spread farther from the late 3rd and early 4th century on, when a coarser product, the so-called D-fabric, was invented, that from about 350 allowed mass production. Imports of North African Samian ware reached their peak in the eastern Mediterranean in about 550, with regular imports continuing well into the early 7th century and beyond. Among the three "Egyptian" types of fine ware, only quality "C" emerges with single pieces in the 7th century.

In the late 4th century there were several production centers for Samian ware on the west coast of Turkey, delivering an extremely limited variety of forms in a very typical and simple fabric (Late Roman C ware). They supplied only the eastern Mediterranean, where their products dominated the market from about 450 (Hayes form 3 and 10). It is amazing that Cypriot kilns, situated much closer to the Levantine coast, at the same time marketed only a fraction of their products in the eastern provinces, especially in northern Syria. Only some later forms seem to appear more frequently.

In addition, Macedonian "Terra Sigillata Grise" (late 4th to early 5th century), "Athenian ware" (ca. 250 C.E. to the late 5th century), "Palestinian ware" (second half of 4th century?), and various forms from Asia Minor (ca. 450 C.E. to the early 7th century) should be mentioned as eastern products, imitating mainly African red slip and Late Roman C wares for the local market, often with stamped decoration as their prototypes. An oriental equivalent are the "Jerash bowls" mostly with painted instead of stamped decoration, found in a limited area around Gerasa and dating from ca. 525 to ca. 675.

As to coarse wares, it is possible to distinguish three different "ceramic provinces" in the Near East, each covering a certain repertoire of vessel types and probably reflecting different ceramic traditions as well as the radius within which kilns distributed their products. These are roughly southern Palestine and the Dead Sea region; northern Palestine and southern Syria, including the upper Orontes Valley; and northern Syria from the Belus to the Euphrates. These production areas remained active into the early Umayyad period. Thanks to a long and intense tradition of studies of Roman pottery in northern Palestine and southern Syria, and recently increasing research in the

Euphrates region, we are able to trace, besides the occurrence of typical early Islamic ceramics, the continuity of the Romano-Byzantine pottery tradition. This means that there was no break in the economic structures at the beginning of Umayyad rule but rather a slow development of handicrafts responding to various demands.

BIBL.: Pierre Canivet and Jean-Paul Rey-Coquais, ed., *La Syrie de byzance à l'Islam: VIIe–VIIIe siècles* (Damascus, 1992), 195–261. John W. Hayes, *Late Roman Pottery* (London, 1972; supplement, 1980). Jodi Magness, *Jerusalem Ceramic Chronology circa 200–800 CE* (Sheffield, 1993). Estelle Villeneuve and Pamela Watson, ed., *La céramique byzantine et protoislamique en Syrie-Jordanie (IVe–VIIIe siècles),* forthcoming in *Bibliothèque archéologique et historique Beyrouth.*

M.K.

Ceramics (West)

Fine ceramics for cooking and table use must be considered as items produced in a series but understood at the same time as a craft. Their classification as mass produced is due to their being wholly for mass consumption. In the west, the centers of production and distribution for these ceramics in late antiquity extended throughout the western provinces of the Roman empire, and were found particularly in Africa Proconsularis. This zone would become the purveyor to markets, above all Italic ones. The production and distribution centers of Carthage and Hadrumetum stand out as the most important in the production of fine ceramics commonly called African red slip. This is confirmed starting from the end of the 3rd century and the beginning of the 4th, a time when principal fabrication centered on the red-slip pottery known as African terra sigillata C, from the shops of central Byzacena, and African terra sigillata D, from the region of Carthage. In addition, one of the major commercial ceramic products coming from Africa was cookware. African producers of cookware supplied the Italic markets, as is demonstrated by the stratigraphies of various Mediterranean sites, outstanding among them, Ostia on the Italian coast and, on the Hispanic coast, Tarraco.

Dating from the first half of the 4th century, from its creation in the year 330, Constantinople became a new pole of attraction for commerce with the *pars orientis;* hence the observed trade in African fine ceramics in some cities of the Aegean and on the coast of Asia Minor. But in the western part of the Mediterranean, the arrival of ceramics originating in Asia Minor is also observed at this time, as is the case with Phocean red-slip ware and late Roman cookware (Late Roman C). This great commercial opening from east to west and vice versa does not preclude the appearance at the time of new productions of sigillata, which were locally restricted. We find examples of this in the red-slip ware designated African terra sigillata E, produced in central, eastern, and southern Tunis. Imitations of African and non-African ware were also being produced in Tripolitania and Argelia (such as Phocean Red Slip, Cypriot Red Slip, and Late Roman E and D). In Egypt, new products arose, such as Egyptian terra sigillata A, or Coptic ceramic (Egyptian Red Slip A), whose fabrication was centered mostly in Aswan with some variants in Luxor, and the ceramics of the delta and Fayum (Egyptian Red Slip B and C). From all this it can be inferred that despite the arrival of oriental materials and despite local productions, Africa became, from the 4th century on, one among many production centers of extraordinary vitality in the Mediterranean. Commercialized African products, in the east as in the west, were not only imitated but copied.

This vitality in African products continued throughout the 5th century, even if traditional historiography has always assumed that with the arrival of the Vandals there came decadence and a rupture in relation to the previous economy. What is certainly evidence of the Vandal presence is that African products, above all those of eastern Africa Proconsularis, tended to penetrate into the interior, while coastal points were abandoned. This finding confirms that food production and ceramic centers coincided in their locations (rural nuclei) and that the two processes were carried on conjunctively.

Starting in the early 5th century there appear in certain production sites in Tunis the well-known classical African lamps whose production and distribution would endure until the 7th century, although they were imitated by common local ceramics producers in some cases (e.g., in the form Carandini, *Atlante* VIII). In a reverse trend, the renowned cookware from the area of Carthage ceased to be exported, and common ceramics from southern Italy and the islands of Sardinia and Sicily reached the African coast. On western coastlines—for example, in Italy (Naples and Rome), in Sardinia, and in Gallia (Marseilles)—the only fine ceramics in use throughout the 5th century were of the African red-slip type (terra sigillata C, C3, C5, and D), as compared with a very scarce arrival (some 10 percent) of ceramics such as *derivée de sigillée paléochrétienne,* Late Roman C, and painted local ceramics. An example of restricted commercialization is found in the ceramic termed *lucente,* a very fine ceramic similar to clear terra sigillata B, produced throughout the 4th and first half of the 5th centuries. The distribution of *lucente* was limited to the southeast of Gallia.

The wide diffusion of Late Roman C ware (Phocean red slip), whose exportation was particularly dense toward the end of the 4th century and the beginning of the 5th, provoked a certain decline in imports in the east. Western centers of reception for this ceramic were distributed throughout the provinces, even in Britain, but as these markets were saturated with African ceramics, Phocean did not have such great success. Nevertheless, African tableware was preferred, and African lamps as well. In their turn they were imitated, and their distribution varied in the Mediterranean, due to the concurrence of products from the eastern Mediterranean and the Aegean. There was, however, a clear route to Italy, with the export of fine tableware and lamps, and another to Constantinople, exporting or exchanging fine ware and lamps for wine, fabrics, glass, or marble.

The period from the end of the 5th century to the first half of the 6th was characterized by a certain restriction in the export of African ceramics, above all that of sigillata C from Byzacena and sigillata E from the southern part of Tunis. Sigillata D was also less abundant. So far as lamps are concerned, the form Carandini, *Atlante* VIII ceased to be produced, and the classical African *Atlante* X took its place. The survival of the commercial axis from Carthage to the east is also notable, since the African city continued to receive ceramics from the Aegean and the southeastern Mediterranean, even as ports in the Aegean and the Asian coast up to Antioch, continued to receive African ceramics.

Starting from the second half of the 6th century and throughout the 7th, it seems that the various production centers tended to consume their own product, as was observed in some places in Tunis. However, following a profound revision of the historical material, as is being carried on at the present time, this view could change drastically. For example, throughout the 7th century one can detect the production and distribution of African terra sigillata D, created in the region of Carthage, which continues to supply both eastern and western centers. Likewise, there is confirmation that eastern products reached the most westerly ports, such as Hispanic Carthago Spartaria, up to the first half of the 7th century. This favorable commercial situation in the Mediterranean, with the exchange of ceramics and other products, is no longer perceptible toward the end of the 7th century.

BIBL.: D. Bayard, "L'ensemble du grand amphithéâtre de Metz et la sigillée d'Argonne au Ve siècle," *Gallia* 47 (1990): 271–319. A. Carandini et al., *Atlante delle forme ceramiche* (Rome, 1981). J. W. Hayes, *Late Roman Pottery: A Catalogue of Roman Fine Wares* (London, 1972; supplement, 1980). Richard Hodges and David Whitehouse, *Mahomet, Charlemagne, et les origines de l'Europe* (1983; enl. ed., Paris, 1996). Clementina Panella, "Merci e scambi nel Mediterraneo tardoantico," in *Storia di Roma, III, L'età tardoantica, 2, I luoghi e le culture* (Turin, 1993). Paul Reynolds, *Trade in the Western Mediterranean, AD 400–700: The Ceramic Evidence* (Oxford, British Archaeological Reports, i.s., 604, 1995).   G.R.

Chalcedon, Council of

The Fourth Ecumenical Council was held in October 451 at the martyrium of St. Euphemia in Chalcedon. About 520 bishops were present. The council produced the Chalcedonian Creed in response to the Christological controversies of the 5th century.

The convocation of Chalcedon was essentially a reaction against the excesses that many felt had occurred at the Council of Ephesus in 449, where Dioscorus of Alexandria had secured the condemnation of Flavian of Constantinople, Ibas of Edessa, Theodoret of Cyrrhus, Comnus of Antioch, and other bishops. The proceedings at Ephesus were tainted by accusations of illegality and violence. Opposition to Dioscorus and his "Robber Council" centered on Pope Leo of Rome (whom Dioscorus had arrogantly excommunicated) and the empress Pulcheria, who after the death of Theodosius II in July 450 was able to consolidate power and (with her new imperial consort Marcian) begin preparation for a new council. The council had originally been called to meet in Nicaea, but Marcian, busy fighting the Huns in Thrace, relocated it at the last minute to the suburb opposite Constantinople so that he could attend its sessions more easily. The imperial couple was determined to exercise the tightest possible supervision over the proceedings to prevent any repetition of the excesses of Ephesus. Pulcheria ordered the governor of Bithynia to expel "riotous" monks and clergy, who had no legitimate reason to be present at a council reserved for bishops. At both previous councils of Ephesus, the emperor had given the presidency to the bishop of Alexandria. Now a secular committee that included many of the most powerful figures in the imperial administration (praetorian prefect, urban prefect, *magister militum, comes domesticorum,* and a number of influential senators and ex-prefects) set the agenda and maintained order. Marcian and Pulcheria themselves attended the 6th session, where the bishops acclaimed them as "New Constantine" and "New Helena." The council's emphasis on law and order was reinforced by its canons, which stressed obedience to the official, legitimate episcopal hierarchy by placing monasteries under the close supervision of the local bishop; restricted the movements of lower clergy and monks; and expressly prohibited priests and monks from forming "conspiracies" against their bishops—a clear reaction to the events of 448–49. Although the pope's representatives enjoyed great influence at the council, they were unable to prevent the adoption of the controversial canon 28, which claimed for the church of Constantinople (New Rome) equal authority and honor with the papal see, a provision that would create endless friction between Rome and Constantinople for centuries to come.

The first session of the council featured a careful examination of the records of Ephesus II and also of Flavian's synod against Eutyches in 448. The record preserves angry exchanges between the eastern bishops, shouting for justice against Dioscorus, "the murderer of Flavian," and the Egyptians, who protested the admission of "Nestorians" such as Theodoret of Cyrrhus, whom they felt had been lawfully condemned by the previous council. As the session dragged on, many of Dioscorus's initial supporters (including, most prominently, Juvenal of Jerusalem) publicly repudiated or denied their statements and actions at the previous council. At the third session, Dioscorus (no longer present) was deposed for his failure to appear and answer charges regarding his violent persecution of opponents in Alexandria. Later Monophysite tradition made much of the fact that even though Dioscorus went into exile still proclaiming a one-nature Christology, he was never actually condemned as a heretic.

After much acrimonious debate, the council finally produced a definition of faith based largely on the *Tome* of Pope Leo, a document that Dioscorus had attempted to suppress at Ephesus. The *Tome* included the formula "two natures after the incarnation" and specified that Christ is consubstantial *(homoousios)* with the Father in the godhead and consubstantial with us in humanity. Chalcedon presented itself as a correct middle way between the opposite extremes of Nestorius and Eutyches, both of whom were condemned anew. The "two natures" definition was a victory for Leo and for Antiochene Christology, but the council also accepted Alexandrian teachings from the first council of Ephesus and the writings of Cyril as a basis of orthodoxy. Cyril's inconsistent use of Christological terms such as *ousia, physis,* and *hypostasis* through his vast corpus of writings allowed both Chalcedonian and Monophysite camps to claim him as their own. The Chalcedonians felt that "two natures" made a necessary distinction between the human and divine in Christ, and prevented the human nature from being completely subsumed. They accused the Monophysites of teaching that Christ was somehow less than fully human, and of attributing suffering and death to the immortal and omnipotent divinity. The Monophysites, in turn, felt that any language distinguishing separate natures in Christ came unacceptably close to dividing Christ into two separate persons, and thus ran the risk of calling the one who died on the Cross a "mere man," a heresy that had been (unfairly) attached to the name of Nestorius. For the Monophysites, Chalcedon represented a thinly disguised revival of Nestorianism, a betrayal, and an apostasy. Attempts by the imperial government to impose its Chalcedonian "solution" led to violent resistance in many areas, particularly Palestine, where in 451–453 followers of the monk Theodosius seized control of the Jerusalem area and expelled Bishop Juvenal, and Alexandria where in 457 the pro-Chalcedonian bishop Proterius was lynched by an angry crowd. The church history for the next two centuries is largely the story of failed attempts to end the schism created at Chalcedon.

At the Second Council of Constantinople in 553, the emperor Justinian attempted to disarm Monophysite opposition by retrospectively condemning three bishops who had been accepted as orthodox at the Council of Chalcedon—Theodore of Mopsuestia, Theodoret of Cyrrhus, and Ibas of Edessa. This was done on the basis of a dossier of their works called *The Three Chapters.* The condemnation of the *Three Chapters* implied the right to excommunicate the dead on the strength of their *literary* output—a departure that betrayed the increased "textualization" of dogma. The undermining of the authority of Chalcedon implied in the decision on the *Three Chapters* raised a storm of opposition in Africa and caused a schism in the church in northern Italy that lasted well into the 7th century.

BIBL.: E. Schwartz, *Acta Conciliorum Oecumenicorum,* vol. 2 (Berlin-Leipzig, 1933). A. J. Festugiere, *Ephèse et Chalcédoine: Actes des conciles* (Paris, 1982), and *Actes du Concile de Chalcédoine* (Geneva, 1983). Francis X. Murphy, *Peter Speaks through Leo: The Council of Chalcedon* A.D. 451 (Washington, D.C., 1952). A. Grillmeier and H. Bacht, eds., *Das Konzil von Chalkedon,* 3 vols. (Würzburg, 1953). P. T. R. Gray and M. W. Herren, "Columbanus and the Three Chapters Controversy," *Journal of Theological Studies* n.s. 45 (1994): 160–170. P. T. R. Gray, "Covering the Nakedness of Noah," *Byzantinische Forschungen* 24 (1997): 193–205. Ernest Honigmann, "The Original Lists of the Members of the Council of Nicaea, the Robber-Synod and the Council of Chalcedon." *Byzantion* 16 (1942): 20–80. R. V. Sellers, *The Council of Chalcedon: A Historical and Doctrinal Survey* (London, 1953).   J.M.G.

Chant

Vocal music played an important role in the religious cults of the ancient world. Hymns were sung in many civic religious ceremonies, often by choirs of children. The texts of many Greek hymns survive, and there are also some in Latin, such as Horace's *Carmen saeculare* to Apollo and Diana, composed for the Secular Games of 17 B.C.E. Hymns connected with most of the known mystery religions are also extant, including the Eleusinian and Dionysiac mysteries and the cults of Isis and Osiris, Cybele and Attis, and Mithras. Gnostic hymns are known from a more recent period, beginning about the 4th century C.E. Though the word *hymn* as used today refers to a poetic text, there are many ancient prose texts in praise of the gods that are hymnlike in content but more comparable to the modern sermon because of their prose form. Very few ancient hymns survive with music notation indicating the melody. The most important of these are Greek hymns to the Muse Calliope, Apollo, Helios, and Nemesis by Mesomedes, musician to the emperor Hadrian (who reigned from 117 to 138 C.E.). Older and better known are two paeans to Apollo from the 2nd century B.C.E., preserved in stone inscriptions from the Temple of Athena at Delphi.

Greek Christian hymns that are similar in language and style to Hellenistic pagan hymns are preserved in the writings of Hippolytus and Clement of Alexandria (early 3rd century) and Synesius of Cyrene (late 4th century). The only such hymn that survives with music notation, however, is the fragment in Oxyrhynchus papyrus 1786. Christians also made use of prose hymns modeled on the parallelistic structure of the biblical Psalms. Many texts in the New Testament are thought to be quotations of such hymns (e.g., Luke 1:46–55, Phil. 2:5–11, Rev. 19), and a collection of psalmlike hymns survives as the *Odes of Solomon*, from about the 2nd century C.E. The Acts of the Apostles contains an example of a prayer (4:24–31) that incorporates part of a psalm but also is not unlike a sermon. Some such text may have been the "song [*carmen*] to Christ, as to a God" that provincial governor Pliny the Younger (61–114) reported hearing about from Christians he had interrogated.

Jewish hymns in Hebrew, clearly written in imitation of the biblical Psalms, survive in abundance among the Dead Sea Scrolls. Jewish psalmodic hymns in Greek survive among the apocryphal and deuterocanonical books of the Bible, such as the songs of the three Hebrew children added to chapter three of the Book of Daniel. An important account of Jewish ritual singing is preserved in *De vita contemplativa* by Philo Judaeus (d. ca. 50 C.E.). It describes the Therapeutae sect's ritual banquets, which were preceded by Bible reading, preaching, and the singing of psalms and hymns by soloists, with and without congregational refrains or responses. After the meal there was singing and dancing, with the men and women separated into two different groups. The description and terminology closely resemble those of the early Christians, testifying to their close relationship with Hellenistic Judaism. Evidence that Greek-speaking Jews chanted the text of the Bible, as later Jews and Christians certainly did, has been seen in a papyrus fragment of the Septuagint in which the syntactic units of the text are clearly marked off, as if for singing, in a way that foreshadows the punctuation accents and musical signs that both Jews and Christians developed during the Middle Ages.

BIBL.: James McKinnon, *Music in Early Christian Literature* (Cambridge, Eng., 1987). Egert Pöhlmann, *Denkmäler altgriechischer Musik: Sammlung, Übertragung und Erläuterung aller Fragmente und Fälschungen,* Erlanger Beiträge zur Sprach- und Kunstwissenschaft 31 (Nuremberg, 1970). E. J. Revell, "The Oldest Evidence for the Hebrew Accent System," *Bulletin of the John Rylands Library* 54 (1971–72): 214–222.   P.J.

Characene

Characene was an independent kingdom ruled by the Hyspaosinid dynasty from ca. 141 B.C.E. and centered around Spasinou Charax (the "palisaded" city of Hyspaosines, former Alexandria-on-the-Tigris, now identified at Jabal Khayābir, 17 miles south of al-Qurna in southern Iraq). The word *Characene* disappears from

historical sources in 222–224 C.E. when the last king, Abinergaos (Tabarī = Bandu), was killed by Ardashir. Most of the classical and oriental sources refer to the region as Mesene from its Aramaic name, Maysān.

Limited to the west by the desert, the area is characterized by large lakes and marshes resulting from the confluence of the Euphrates, Tigris, and Karkheh Rivers. Strongly affected by tidal movements, the landscape of the semiflooded region has changed many times, especially in the 5th and 7th centuries C.E., owing to rising sea level, diversion of rivers, irrigation canals, and so on. The country was famous for its date gardens.

From the beginning Mesene was inhabited by Aramaic-speaking people; Arabs were occasionally mentioned (the *skēnitai* from the west, the Palmyraneans from the north), and Persians (military and civilian) were numerous in the province at the time of the Muslim conquest (Khālid ibn al-Walīd in 633). During the Sassanid and early Islamic periods, thousands of Indians were settled in the region, among them the *Zuṭṭ*; Arab sources name the country ardh el-Hindh. Slaves from eastern Africa known as the Zānj were strong enough to hold a major rebellion in the 9th century.

As part of the province Assyria of the Sassanid empire, Mesene (in Sassanian, Mēshān) was ruled by a king, and later by a governor. Manichaean sources attest that the princes of Mesene were members of the royal court. It is not clear whether the Persian Gulf was a dependent of Mesene (a tradition since the Seleucids) or of Persis, as the bishoprics of the gulf are subordinated to the metropolis of Rev Ardashīr/Bushir.

The city Charax survived as Astārābādh Ardashīr(?), Syriac Khark Mayšān, but lost its preeminence to its fluvial emporium Forāt, situated on the left bank of the Tigris halfway between Charax and al-Uballa. The Aramaic name Forat probably derives from the Euphrates, which at some time joined the Tigris there. The city mentioned by Pliny probably became Bahman Ardashīr, and is mentioned in the Syriac sources as Pᵉrath Mayšān; it disappeared after the foundation of Basra. When al-Ubulla was founded is not known; some authors would identify it with Teredon, cited by the classical sources. The literary evidence from Hellenistic texts to early Arab authors (no archaeological research was carried out in the area) confirm that the basic function and wealth of Charax, Forāt, and al-Ubulla was the eastern trade with the Persian Gulf, India, and the Indian Ocean: several texts refer to the area as the market of oriental merchants.

The religious milieu of Mesene was rich. Jews are mentioned from the 1st century C.E., sometimes as merchants. Magianism is attested also, and Manichaeism spread in the region after Mani's voyage to India (mid-2nd century). Manichaeans were later powerful in Khark Mayšān and in northeastern Arabia. Legendarily evangelized by Mari in the 1st century, Mesene became a metropolis in 310 (first at Pᶜrath Mayšān, later at Basra), heading seven bishoprics; the (late) *Chronicle of Seert* provides a lively description of the Christian communities in the region. The Islamization of the country was rapid and deeprooted, although Christianity survived for several centuries after the destruction of the churches of Basra in the reign of Hārūn al-Rashīd.

Basra was founded ca. 638–639 after the Muslim conquest of Iraq. Originally a military and administrative center built on desert land about 14 miles east of al-Ubulla, it rapidly grew as a major city linked to the Persian Gulf through the (present) nahr az-Zubayr and Khor Abdullah, or to the Tigris. In the 7th century, Basra was able to provide 43,000 armed men to the Khurāsān wars (Tabarī). In the 9th century, it became the point of concentration of all the eastern trade. The city started declining from the 10th century (today it is known as az-Zubayr); modern Basra was built on the supposed site of ancient al-Uballa.

BIBL.: Jean-Maurice Fiey, *Assyrie chrétienne*, Dar el-Machreq Éditeurs (Beirut, 1968), esp. vol. 3. John Hansman, "Charax and the Karkheh," *Iranica antiqua* 7 (1967): 21–58. Michael G. Morony, "Maysān," *Encyclopaedia of Islam*, vol. 6, col. 919–923. Paul Sanlaville, "Considérations sur l'évolution de la basse Mésopotamie au cours des derniers millénaires," *Paléorient* 15 (1989): 5–27.   J.-F.S.

Children

Late antiquity inherited competing schemes of the stages of life. Traditionally Roman society understood a life span as having three parts. From the Greeks came other ideas: Plato used four ages, a tradition from Solon to Philo employs seven, and the Stoic model was of seven-year blocks. The seventh year usually separated older *pueri, puellae,* and *paides,* terms that were also used for slaves, from prerational children, *parvi parvuli, infantes, pisinni, pullali, paidia, brephoi,* and *nēpioi,* terms that stressed smallness and immaturity. Popular images of life divisions have been preserved on late Roman sarcophagi.

Children were generally nursed to the age of two or three. Although experts advocated the ideal of mothers nursing their own infants, the use of wet nurses was prevalent among members of the Roman aristocracy. Rabbinic law urged maternal breastfeeding for twenty-four months. Christian art depicted the Virgin Mary nursing her son; an early version of the *virgo lactans* appears in a fresco of ca. 500 at Saqqara in Egypt. Jews and Christians appear to have commemorated deceased children more than pagans, although commemorations of children under two months are infrequent. Christian children were buried at martyrs' shrines, and epitaphs testified to parents' hopes for the afterlife. We also have examples of children's sarcophagi. Poetry of bereavement for children is found in the

Islamic world. The fragility of children contributed to Christianity's development as a healing religion. Augustine, for example, described miracles at St. Stephen's shrine where a crushed boy was revived whole, another was resurrected with its oil, and a garment that had touched the shrine resurrected a girl (*De civ.Dei* 22.8). Therapeutic bathing of the child was sacralized, appearing in Byzantine representations of the Christ child and in an Infancy Gospel from Arabia. Anointing and swaddling of babies were understood by the church as symbols of mortality.

Childbirth rituals dealt with protection and parental acknowledgment. Seclusion and purification were especially important in Judaism, which prescribed a thirty-three or sixty-six day separation of the new mother from the community, ending in a sacrifice of atonement (Lev. 12); this period was interrupted by the eighth-day circumcision of male infants. Christians rejected the practice of circumcision, though its place in Scripture was conceded, as was the significance of its endurance by Christ (Ambrose, *Epistula* 78.2ff.; Augustine, *Epistula* 23.4ff.). Islamic books of *Ethica* describe how prayers were uttered into the newborn's ears and dates were placed in the mouth; on the seventh day came naming and the sacrificial ransom in which the father offers himself in place of the child, life for life, blood for blood, bone for bone, hair for hair, skin for skin. A Muslim youth was usually circumcised in his seventh year.

Christian infant baptism was disputed but widely practiced by the 4th century and sanctioned by the Council of Elvira. Infants were even believed to be miraculously resurrected for the purpose of baptism (Fortunatus, *Vita Hilarii* 12). Augustine preferred immediate to eighth-day baptism and argued its necessity against Pelagius and others, citing the common practice of rushing dying children to the church (*Enarr. in Ps.* 50.10). Baptism may have served as a naming ceremony as well. John Chrysostom spoke scathingly about the persistence of giving pagan names to babies (*Serm. de Anna* 1.6).

Sexuality was a bridge into adulthood. One who was not yet legally responsible was an *impubes,* unable to reproduce. Asceticism, as Origen had suggested, offered a prolonged childhood (*Commentarius in Matthaeum* 13.16). Christianity had expressed a hostility toward pedophilia (*Ep. Barnabae* 19.5), and early monastic sources warned against living with boys. The spread of Christianity may have increased the age of marriage for girls. However, girl martyrs and virgins were sexualized in literary and visual representations.

The spiritual status of children was paradoxical. On the one hand, they were born unclean, tainted with original sin and in need of ransoming. On the other hand they were innocent, as in a Rabbinic image likening them to new paper that absorbed what was written on it. Christians "became children" through baptism in order to enter the kingdom of heaven. Muslims held that God had created children in a state of innocence and that it was the duty of parents and educators to ensure that they were rightly guided in morals and religion.

Children, as figures of purity, participated in religious life as bearers of sacred objects in pagan rituals, as cultic initiates, and in choirs. Judaism introduced children gradually to ritual, educating them for a year before the Day of Atonement fast (*Yoma* 8.4A–B). Baptized Christian children took communion. Children served in the church as *lectores,* reciting lessons for the priest's homily, and they were choristers, like Prudentius's "chorus of little ones" at Christmas (*Cathemerinon* 9.109) and Egeria's "chicks" in Jerusalem; children also reenacted Palm Sunday crowds in those services (*Peregrinatio* 36.1–5).

BIBL.: Susanne Dixon, *The Roman Family* (Baltimore, 1992), and *The Roman Mother* (Norman, Okla., 1985). Peter Garnsey, "Child-Rearing in Ancient Italy," in D. I. Kertzer and R. P. Saller, eds., *The Family in Italy from Antiquity to the Present* (New Haven, 1991). Avner Gil'adi, *Children of Islam: Concepts of Childhood in Medieval Muslim Society* (London, 1992), and "Saghir," in *Encyclopaedia of Islam,* new ed. (Leiden, 1954–), 821–827. Blake Leyerle, "Appealing to Children," *Journal of Early Christian Studies* 5, no. 2 (1997): 243–270. L. S. B. MacCoull, "Child Donations and Child Saints in Coptic Egypt," *East European Quarterly* 13 (1979): 409–415. A. de Vogüé, *La règle de Saint Bénoît: VI* (Paris, 1971), 1355–1368.   S.C.

Children, Exposure of

The late antique attitude toward exposure was formed by a variety of earlier influences. The Greeks regarded the exposure of infants—particularly female infants—as normal, if undesirable. A principal reason for the act was probably a family's need to maintain a size and a sex ratio that would enable it to survive severe shortages. In the Roman imperial period, pagan moralists begin to question child exposure, while concomitantly Jews such as Philo, for whom the Sixth Commandment forbade the taking of human life, denounced it vociferously. The opposition of official Christianity was absolute, though this was not expressed until postapostolic writings (*Didache XII Apost.* 2.2, *Sources chrétiennes* 248, p. 148). From the beginning of their new religion, Christians established extensive social networks that may have saved children from possible or actual exposure by assigning them to families in need of, or able to provide for, extra members.

From Augustus on, Roman emperors struggled with the many legal problems raised by exposure (Pliny, *Ep.* 10.65–66). With Constantine's conversion to Christianity, there began a process of restricting and finally outlawing the practice. In 313 the emperor legalized the sale of children, thus offering parents who might otherwise have resorted to exposure a less inhumane alternative. In later years he provided subsidies to indigent parents, and (reversing the precedent of pagan emperors) ruled that the rearers of an abandoned, exposed child had absolute discretion to decide whether that child would be slave or free. It was not until 374, however, that Valentinian laid down the principle that parents should raise their own children and criminalized exposure. In 529 Justinian completed the process begun by Constantine, ruling that all exposed children were to be free, whatever their previous status.

The campaign against exposure was aided by the rise of cenobitic monasticism. St. Macrina is said by her brother, Gregory of Nyssa, to have "collected infant girls when they were abandoned in the streets at the time of the famine, to have nourished and raised them, and educated them in the pure and incorruptible life" (*Vita Macrinae* 26, *Sources chrétiennes* 178, p. 233). In the same period began the practice of families' offering their young to be brought up in monasteries. Basil of Caesarea in his *Long Rules* states that orphans must be welcomed without question, but children with parents were to be accepted only in the presence of witnesses, "so that we may not give an excuse to those . . . who spread slander against us" (*Regulae fusius tractatae* 15, PG 31.952B).

Even if the adoption of Christianity did not end child exposure, the practice had ceased to be morally neutral. What had been a matter of choice was now illegal, and social structures existed that were intended to help indigent families and to receive unwanted children. There is no evidence to show how effective these measures were, or whether infants previously considered hopeless, such as those born blind or deformed, had a better chance of survival than before.

In Islam, the Qur'ānic prohibitions against infanticide dramatically challenged a widely accepted social practice in Arabia in which newborns were killed by being buried alive. Parents who killed their children are condemned to hellfire, according to Islam, and the verses specifically state that fear of poverty is no justification (sura 17:31). As elsewhere, female infanticide was more common than male infanticide in pre-Islamic Arabia; the Qur'ān mentions the polytheists' dislike of their daughters as a motive for killing them (16:58–59). It affirms the infant's innocence when, on the Day of Judgment, "the infant girl buried alive is asked for what sin she was slain" (81:8–9). Additionally, the Qur'ān frequently enjoins charity and fairness toward orphans, as do many hadith. Muhammad himself was orphaned at a young age and raised by an uncle.

BIBL.: Amira al-Azhary Sonbol, "Adoption in Islamic Society: A Historical Survey," in E. W. Fernea, ed., *Children in the Muslim Middle East* (Austin, 1995), 45–67. Maria Bianchi Fossati Vanzetti, "Vendita ed esposizione degli infanti da Costantino a Giustiniano," *Studia et documenta historiae et iuris* 49 (1983): 179–224. John E. Boswell, *The Kindness of*

Strangers (New York, 1988), ch. 3. William V. Harris, "Child-Exposure in the Roman Empire," *Journal of Roman Studies* 84 (1994): 1–22.   C.J.

China

The first historical links between the European antique world and China occurred ca. 130 B.C.E., when Chang Ch'ien visited Ferghana, the Tocharians, Bactria, and Sogdiana, and wrote short descriptions of the Parthian (An-hsi) and Seleucid (Li-kan/T'iao-chih) empires, with whom China exchanged embassies soon afterward. In 97 C.E., Kan Ying was sent on a mission to Ta-Ch'in (the Roman empire) but reached only Mesopotamia. Pliny (1st century C.E.) mentions silk and iron from the Seres, a term thought to refer to the Chinese. Ptolemy (mid-2nd century) records that the Macedonian Maes Titanios sent merchants who reached the Stone Gate, and Chinese sources record the arrival of an embassy from Meng-ch'i Tou-le (Macedonia?) in 100 C.E., almost certainly the same merchants. In 166, merchants claiming to be envoys from An-tun (Antoninus Pius or Marcus Aurelius Antoninus) reached China. This trip was the first by sea. Thereafter, in 226 and 285, merchants traveled from the Roman empire to China by sea, via Ceylon and Southeast Asia, though it is not recorded that any Chinese traveled the other way. Chinese sources mention a long list of Roman products, including asbestos, glass, and pearls.

The initial name of Li-kan for the west (probably referring to "Rekem," the Semitic name of Petra, the capital of the Nabataean kingdom, rather than to Alexandria) was replaced by Ta-Ch'in ("Greater Ch'in") after the expedition of 97 C.E. By the 5th century, the terms P'u-lan and later Fu-Lin were used (transcriptions into Chinese of the word *Rome*). According to the Chinese annals, embassies from Rome (P'u-lan) were sent to the northern Wei court during the reigns of Marcian (450–457) and Leo I (457–474). During the reign of Justinian, according to Procopius, silk-worm eggs were smuggled out of China for the first time. In 643, an embassy from Fu-Lin was sent to China with gifts for the T'ang dynast T'ai-tsung and received silk garments in exchange.

Sassanid Persia was in much closer contact with China, with regular embassies traveling in both directions from 455. Khosro I (531–579) treated China as a great power. Peroz, the last king of Persia, was granted asylum in Ch'ang-an in 671, along with thousands of his followers who had fled the Arabs. Various commodities, as well as animals and plants, were transmitted both ways during this period. Religions, such as Zoroastrianism, Nestorian Christianity, and Manichaeism (and possibly Islam and Judaism) spread from Persia into China. Chinese descriptions of the Persian and later Arab rulers are accurate, though less is said about religion and culture. Chinese Buddhists are known to have visited Persia in the 7th and 8th centuries. Arab embassies came regularly, the first under 'Uthmān in 651. In 715 the Arab general Qutaiba reached the border of China. In 751 the Arabs defeated the Chinese at Talas in central Asia. Tu Huan was captured and taken to Baghdad, where he wrote a lengthy description of Arab Islamic culture. Around this time, Chinese inventions such as paper are thought to have been transmitted to western Asia, and thence later to Europe.

Roman and Greek writers from the reign of Augustus mention the Seres as producers of silk. Virgil has the Seres obtaining silk from trees; Strabo reports that they live for two hundred years; and Pliny describes them as "blue-eyed, with fair hair," presumably referring to intermediaries in the silk trade rather than to the Chinese themselves. Ptolemy (2nd century) places the Seres in the north and the Thin (Sinae) in the south. Several sources (e.g., Ammianus in the 4th century and Moses of Chorene in the 5th) write of their peaceful nature, or their long life and great height. Others give snippets of true information about the far-off land, the farthest to the east according to Martianus Capella (5th century) and Cosmas Indicopleustes (6th century). Bardaisan and Eusebius both mention the large population. Theophylact Simocatta (early 7th century), among other sources, portrays the Roman and Chinese empires as equals. Pausanias (mid-2nd century) recognizes an animal origin for silk. Origen (early 3rd century) describes the Seres as atheists, a hint of Confucian attitudes; Caesarius notes their emphasis on ancestral customs rather than law.

However, it is only from the Arabic writers that we get a real picture of China. "Sulaiman" in 851 gave a remarkable description of Chinese customs as well as the life of Arabs settled in Kuangzhou (Canton). This account, the best description of Chinese customs by a westerner before the 17th century, is preserved in the *Silsilat* (ca. 915) of Abu Zaid, who also adds information from Ibn Wahab (ca. 878).

BIBL.: P. A. Boodberg, "Theophylact Simocatta on China," *Harvard Journal of Asia Studies* 3 (1938): 223–242. H. Miyakawa and A. Kollautz, "Ein Dokument zur Fernhandel zwischen Byzanz und China zur Zeit Theophylaktus," *Byzantinische Zeitschrift* 77 (1984): 6–19. D. D. Leslie, *Islam in Traditional China* (Canberra, 1986). D. D. Leslie and K. H. J. Gardiner, *The Roman Empire in Chinese Sources* (Rome, 1996). S. N. C. Lieu, *Manichaeism in the Later Roman Empire and Medieval China*, 2nd ed. (Tubingen, 1992). P. Saeki, *The Nestorian Documents and Relics in China* (Tokyo, 1951). P. Schreiner, "Eine chinesische Beschreibung Konstantinopels," *Istanbuler Mitteilungen* 39 (1989): 493–505.

D.D.L.

Chronicles

The chronicle was a creation of late antiquity: Christian historiography par excellence. The genre had the overall aim of presenting the history of salvation—

God's intervention in the shaping of the world—from Adam and creation down to the author's time. It was generated by fusing a number of separate lines of inquiry. Annalistic record keeping began in the Graeco-Roman world as early as the 5th century B.C.E.. This quickly stimulated an interest in organizing all knowledge of the past along such lines, so that synchronisms could be worked out: as, for instance, in the *On Time* of Dionysius of Halicarnassus. The rise of Christianity saw the natural extension of this activity to the Hebrew Bible, while scholars such as Tatian and Clement of Alexandria attempted to demonstrate the chronological priority of Moses over Homer so that, where teachings overlapped, the former could be considered the teacher. Others produced chronological schemes that also embraced the future as portrayed in Christian prophecy. In his work, Sextus Julius Africanus in the 3rd century argued that the world would last 6,000 years, and that Christ had been born in the year 5500.

These strands were brought together in the *Chronicle* of Eusebius of Caesarea. Eusebius laid out the history of known peoples in parallel columns, briefly noting significant individuals and events; his emphasis throughout was firmly on salvation history. Eusebius's *Chronicle* stopped early in the 4th century, but it soon found continuators. Jerome translated it into Latin and continued the story of salvation down to the 370s, and the 5th and 6th centuries saw many continuators in both Latin and Greek. The work's success caused a problem. Later contributors consciously continued chosen predecessor(s), editing and remodeling as they worked. Manuscript traditions are thus highly complicated, and it is often impossible to reconstruct any particular author's "original" text.

In format, chronicles were simple and homogeneous. The author first needed a list of years—usually starting with a list of consuls, sometimes taken from city records (examples using those of Constantinople and Antioch have been identified)—to which extra information was then added. The added information was usually brief, sometimes even terse, but not always so. The *Chronicon Paschale* incorporates very substantial documents within its text, while Hydatius and Malalas devoted parts of their works to reasonably circumstantial historical narratives. Chroniclers also tended to be obsessive about chronology, but again this was not always so. In much of his text, Malalas was content to date events by decade, within imperial reigns. Authors' purposes also varied. Apart from the shared interest in salvation history, some, such as Cassiodorus, also wrote for particular patrons. His *Chronicle* celebrated the consulship of the heir to the Ostrogothic throne, Flavius Eutharic Cilliga. Thus, in late antiquity Christian authors created the chronicle genre by incorporating biblical events and Christian soteriological prophecy into an established Graeco-Roman tradition of annalistic record keeping. The extra infor-

mation authors chose to add, however, gave them ample opportunity to make these texts express their own interests and concerns.

BIBL.: S. Muhlberger, *Fifth-century Chronicles* (Leeds, 1990). R. W. Burgess, *The Chronicle of Hydatius* (Oxford, 1993). E. Jeffreys et al., eds., *Studies in John Malalas* (Sydney, 1990). A. A. Mosshammer, *The Chronicle of Eusebius and Greek Chronographic Tradition* (Lewisburg, Pa., 1979).

P.H.

Church Architecture

The earliest Christians, lacking special cult places, met in private homes spacious enough to receive guests, usually the homes of well-to-do patrons of the community. In such homes the community heard the Christian message, shared the common meal *(agapē)*, and prayed together (Acts 2:42, 46; 5:42; 10:22–33; 22:7–9; 1 Cor. 11:17–34). When a patron delivered such a private home over more or less exclusively to community use, it became a *domus ecclesiae*, "house of the church" or (better) "house of the congregation." By ca. 200, however, the Eucharist had developed into an act of worship separate from the common meal and required an assembly hall rather than a dining room. Hence the Christians at Dura-Europus in Syria adapted a private house in 240–241 for congregational use. From the exterior it still resembled a dwelling, but inside a wall was removed to transform the dining room into a rectangular hall that accommodated sixty persons, with a raised dais for the bishop on the narrow eastern wall. Nearby, across the courtyard, another room became a baptistery, identified by a canopied tub and mural paintings on the theme of salvation and resurrection. Between the baptistery and the assembly hall was a room for catechumens, where the unbaptized could attend and hear without actually witnessing the liturgy of the faithful.

Similar adaptation of private houses for Christian worship occurred across the Roman empire. Excavation beneath the 5th century Church of St. Peter at Capernaum above the Sea of Galilee revealed an earlier *domus ecclesiae* and beneath it a typical village dwelling (the "House of St. Peter"). The *tituli*, or parish churches, of Christian Rome descended similarly from private dwellings identified by a plaque *(titulus)* giving the owner's name and making the house over into "houses of the congregation." By ca. 300, however, some of these early churches had already begun to impose themselves on the neighborhood. When Emperor Diocletian began persecuting Christians in his imperial capital at Nicomedia in 303, he ordered the destruction of a "conspicuous church" *(fanum editissimum),* prominently sited and visible from the imperial palace (Lactantius, *De mort.pers.* 12.4–5). Beneath S. Crisogono in Rome are remains of its predecessor, dated likewise shortly after 300, which was a large (15.5 m by 27 m) rectangular hall flanked by an external portico and entered through three arches in the facade.

Although Christians were already asserting themselves architecturally in Roman society, it was Constantine's embracing of Christianity in 312–313 that first gave rise to a monumental church architecture. Ordering the construction of two churches, St. John Lateran in Rome and the Holy Sepulcher in Jerusalem, the first Christian emperor established the basilica as the normative design for buildings of Christian assembly. The basilica brought to church architecture the requisite atmosphere of holiness and imperial or magisterial power, and it responded to the need for a more spacious interior that suited the maturing Christian liturgy. The basilica's atrium accommodated catechumens and the nave processions of the faithful and the clergy, and, where segregation by sex was practiced, either the aisles or galleries above provided space for the congregation's women. In the apse, the semicircular synthronon provided magisterial seating for the bishop and clergy, where once the Roman governor had presided. The raised bema, or chancel, projected from the apse into the nave and was separated from it at the edges by a parapet that enclosed the space reserved for priests and the altar table. From the bema the bishop or other speaker could reach the ambo, or pulpit, located farther forward in the nave, by a raised bridge. The baptistery, frequently an immersion pool with steps, occupied an attached building or room off the atrium or one of the aisles.

From the reign of Constantine through the end of antiquity, basilical churches remained typical in both east and west. Variants reflected local or regional custom and differing liturgical practice, and included double basilicas, basilical halls sheltering graves in cemeteries surrounding martyrs' tombs, and basilicas with transepts like Old St. Peter's in Rome, built ca. 319–325. From the later 4th and the 5th century, elaborate programs of figural mosaics and wall paintings enriched the elegant but relatively simple interior decoration of Constantine's basilicas. In the 6th century, Syrian triple-apsed basilicas became fashionable in the Latin west.

A *martyrium* was simply a "martyr" or "witness" church, testifying to an event in the life of Christ, like the nativity or the resurrection, or to a martyr's ultimate act of faith. Hence Constantine's basilica at the Holy Sepulcher was known, in Greek, as the Martyrion, and any church might be called a *martyrium* once relics had been translated and deposited in it, a normal practice from the later 4th century. Even so, the term *martyrium* is often used specifically for a church built on a central plan, usually circular, octagonal, or cruciform, in contrast to the longitudinal plan of the basilica. Such churches derived from ancient *herōa*, tomb temples, and monuments of Roman funerary architecture like the Mausoleum of Diocletian at Split,

or perhaps from centrally planned dining or reception rooms in imperial palaces.

It was again Constantine and his successors who first built Christian monuments on a central plan. These included the octagonal *martyrium* that Constantine built over the Grotto of the Nativity in Bethlehem and the Apostles' Church in Constantinople, which was cross-shaped with a drum above the crossing that rose over the tomb of Constantine himself, surrounded by cenotaphs dedicated to the twelve apostles. S. Constanza in Rome, the tomb of Constantine's daughter, had a dome above a circular colonnade and barrel-vaulted ambulatory. By ca. 380 the circular Anastasis (Resurrection) Church enclosed the Holy Sepulcher itself, now disengaged from the rocky slope just west of Constantine's basilica.

Thus the central plan, like the basilica, established itself in the Holy Land, the imperial capitals, and the rest of the empire. Provided with a bema and apse, it took on the same liturgical functions as the longitudinal plan. The Golden Octagon in Antioch, also begun under Constantine, sheltered no major relics but served as the city's cathedral, and so perhaps did the octagonal church, dated ca. 500, uncovered recently at Caesarea in Israel. In the 6th century, the architects of Justinian made the brick-vaulted, domed, central-plan church the standard major church form across the empire. This tradition culminated, in the west, with S. Vitale in Ravenna, completed ca. 548, and ultimately with Charlemagne's Palatine Chapel at Aachen. In the eastern empire it yielded Hagia Sophia in Constantinople, dedicated in 537, the last great architectural monument of the ancient world.

Architects of the Justinianic age likewise created the cross-domed church, drawing on both the basilica and the central plan. The Church of St. John at Ephesus, for example, has crossed basilical halls, a dome at the crossing resting on pendentives—the curved masonry structures that form the transition between the square plan of the crossing and the circular base of the dome—and five further domes on pendentives above the four wings of the cross. Like the basilica and the central church, this was a plan rooted firmly in Roman traditions of design and construction that would have a long life in medieval Byzantium.

BIBL.: N. Duval, "Études d'architecture chrétienne nord-africaine, *Mélanges de l'école française de Rome: Antiquité* 84 (1972): 1071–1125, and "L'évĝue et la cathédrale en Afrique du Nord," *Acts du XIe congrés international d'archéologie chrétienne,* Collection de l'école française de Rome 123 (Rome, 1989), vol. 1, 345–403. André Grabar, *Martyrium: Recherches sur le culte des reliques et l'art chrétien antique* (Paris, 1946; repr. London, 1972). B. Gui, *Basiliques chrétiennes de l'Afrique du Nord* (Paris, 1992). Richard Krautheimer, *Early Christian and Byzantine Architecture,* 3rd ed. rev. (Harmondsworth, 1981); L. Michael White, *Building God's House in the Roman World* (Baltimore, 1990). K.G.H.

Cilicia

Cilicia is a semicircular region in south-central Turkey that is defined geographically by the Mediterranean to the south, the Amanus Mountains to the east, and the broad curving spine of the Taurus Mountains (approximately 300 km by 50 km) to the north and west. The Lamas River divides the fertile Cilicia Pedias (or Cilicia Campestris) in the east from the semi-arid Cilicia Tracheia (or Cilicia Aspera) in the west. The political boundaries of the Roman province were altered by Diocletian (286–305), who attached most of Cilicia Tracheia to the new province of Isauria. The Metropolis of Tarsus, which had served as the provincial capital of Cilicia from 72 C.E. was further diminished in 409 when the eastern half of the Pedias became the new province of Cilicia Secunda, which was administered by the Metropolis of Anazarbus. However, Tarsus remained the capital of Cilicia Prima, which included a portion of the Tracheia east of the Calycadnus River, and continued as the region's most important city. It controlled access along the coast to the Adana-Antioch highway and served as the southern terminus for the strategic route from Cappadocia (via the Cilician Gates). Despite its long coastline, Cilicia provided few good ports; many of those in the Tracheia were well defended by cliffs but small and shallow. Heavy siltation from the rivers in the plain required constant dredging of the eastern harbors. Progressive deforestation in late antiquity exacerbated the problem to such an extent that Tarsus could be rescued from frequent floods only by the construction (ca. 550) of an elaborate canal system (Procopius, *Aed.* 5.5.17–20).

The majority of Cilicia's inhabitants lived in relatively self-sufficient agricultural and fishing communities: their chief exports were wheat, fruit, olive oil, timber, rope, linen, hides, salted fish, and a Madeira-type wine. Settlements in the Pedias were widely scattered and ranged from villages to small cities. The latter, such as Anazarbus, Castabala, Flaviopolis, and Mopsuestia, were built in the 3rd through the 5th centuries on the Roman provincial pattern, with at least one central colonnaded street, flanking temples, a triumphal arch, baths, fountains, aqueducts, a stadium, a theater, and several necropoleis. The Christian population carefully maintained the pagan civic buildings and frequently incorporated the spolia of demolished temples into their three-aisled hall churches, the standard type of ecclesiastical construction. To the west of Tarsus the settlements of the Tracheia, such as Akkale, Canbazli, Canytella, and Yanikhan, were confined to the coast and the adjoining highlands. Unique in the area between the Lamas and Calycadnus Rivers are the numerous examples of Christian basilicas built into pagan temples; the best documented cases are at the Cave Church near Corycus, and at Diocaesarea, Se-

baste, and Seleucia. The vast majority of Cilicia's monastic communities occupied the same area. The two most famous monasteries, Sancta Thecle, or Meriamlik, and Alahan, were both founded in the 4th century and received the patronage of Emperor Zeno in the last quarter of the 5th century.

Despite widespread persecutions, Christianity had extended across Cilicia in the late 3rd century and was firmly established by the mid-4th century. In 325 the Cilician bishops appeared on council lists for Nicaea. The Orthodox church was under the authority of the patriarch of Antioch. A large minority of Syrian Jacobites appointed their own bishops from the late 6th through the 13th centuries. The geographical isolation of Cilicia fostered a degree of religious nonconformity. The bishop-theologian of Tarsus, Diodore (378–390), led an active campaign against Arianism. In 518 the emperor Justin I expelled Monophysite bishops from a number of cities, including Anazarbus.

There is no fully convincing archaeological or textual evidence to explain the gradual decline of the population across Cilicia in the early 7th century. Certainly pestilence, earthquakes, climatic change (with the resulting crop failures), and the brief Persian invasion provide reasons for the abandonment of specific communities. It is certain that the emperor Heraclius's order to evacuate all garrisons east of Tarsus in the wake of the Arab victories in Syria left the civilians of Cilicia Pedias vulnerable to attack in the late 640s. By 672 the Arabs had captured Tarsus, and by the 8th century they had established permanent agricultural communities of Muslim emigrants and a defensive zone (the *thughūr*) that reached to the Lamas River.

BIBL.: Paul C. Finney, ed., *Encyclopedia of Early Christian Art and Archaeology* (forthcoming). Friedrich Hild and Hansgerd Hellenkemper, *Kilikien und Isaurien* (Vienna, 1990). R.E.

Circumcellions

A militant group in the North African countryside, the Circumcellions were closely associated with the Donatist movement. Our evidence for the Circumcellions depends almost entirely on hostile Catholic sources such as Optatus and Augustine, who characterize their activities as fanaticism or "banditry" (a catchall term for any form of organized violence not controlled by the state and therefore "illegitimate"). Although modern scholarship has attempted to explain the Circumcellions in terms of social or economic conflict, they themselves, as well as their opponents, saw their activities as fundamentally religious. The word *circumcellion* is most plausibly derived from the cellae in which they often gathered. Their leaders were called "captains of the saints" *(duces sanctorum);* Augustine accused them of "falsely" claiming to practice asceticism.

The Donatist church saw itself as the true church

of the martyrs and the Catholic church, with its imperial sponsors, as little more than paganism in a new disguise. Donatist martyr stories, in which Catholics and imperial officials take the part of persecutors, seem to have inspired some Circumcellions into wild quests for martyrdom that bordered on the suicidal. They allegedly sought out soldiers and magistrates and demanded to be put to the sword, or hurled themselves off of cliffs, presumably in imitation of the martyrdom of Marculus. They recklessly smashed pagan altars and idols, thus inviting violent retaliation—a practice condemned by the Council of Elvira (ca. 305) and by Augustine. The sixty Christians massacred at Sufes in 399 for smashing a pagan statue (Augustine, *Ep.* 50) may well have been Circumcellions.

The Circumcellions are most notorious for their attacks on the Catholic church and its clergy. In the time of Optatus (the 360s) the Circumcellions, led by Donatist clergy, fought with Catholics for possession of church buildings, causing much bloodshed and at least a few deaths in the process. Upon taking over a Catholic place of worship, the Donatists performed a variety of cleansing rituals (whitewashing walls, scraping altars, sprinkling holy water, melting down vessels) that demonstrated that they regarded Catholic churches as polluted, little different from the daemon-haunted pagan temples that Christian monks in the eastern empire were demolishing at the same time. Treating all Catholic sacraments as irretrievably tainted by the "original sin" of the *traditores* Felix and Caecilian, they forcibly rebaptized Catholics and threw Catholic host—the eucharistic bread—to the dogs.

In the forty years between Optatus and Augustine, Circumcellion activities seem to have taken a decidedly nasty turn, emphasizing savage physical attacks on Catholic clergy. Priests and bishops were abducted from the roads and subjected to public humiliation, brutal beatings, and often fatal injury. Augustine himself narrowly escaped such an ambush; his disciple and biographer Possidius was not so lucky. Maximian of Bagai helped obtain anti-Donatist legislation by displaying his scars to a shocked imperial court in Ravenna. Most bizarre was the Circumcellion practice of blinding victims by forcing a caustic mixture of powdered lime and vinegar into their eyes—an act they justified by recalling how Christ had converted the persecutor Saul into the disciple Paul by striking him blind on the road to Damascus (Acts 9). For all their ingenious varieties of brutality, however, the Circumcellions seem to have made a point of not "shedding blood" (in place of swords or knives they used cudgels, which they called "Israels") and therefore claimed to be using only moderate or "nonlethal" force. The Donatist Passions of Donatus and Advocatus, and of Maximian and Isaac, show imperial soldiers committing the same hypocrisy.

Though they often worked in concert, the Circumcellions were not completely controlled by the Donatist episcopal hierarchy, and there is evidence that at least some prominent Donatists, such as Tyconius, condemned the Circumcellions and their methods. In this respect their position in relation to the church establishment could be compared to that of the gangs of monks who roamed the eastern empire destroying pagan temples and intervening violently in church controversies. The imperial government's severe crackdown on Donatism that began after the Conference of Carthage in 411 seems to have gradually suppressed Circumcellion activities, and we hear no more of them after the coming of the Vandals in 429.

BIBL.: Salvatore Calderone, "Circumcelliones," *Parola del passato* 22 (1967): 94–109. W. H. C. Frend, "Circumcellions and Monks," *Journal of Theological Studies* n.s. 20 (1969): 542–549. Claude Lepelley, "Circumcellions," in Cornelius Mayer, ed., *Augustinus-Lexikon*, vol. 1 (Basel, 1992), 930–936, and "Iuvenes et Circoncellions: Les derniers sacrifices humains de l'Afrique antique," *Antiquités africaines* 15 (1980): 261–271. Zeev Rubin, "Mass Movements in Late Antiquity—Appearances and Realities," in *Leaders and Masses in the Roman World: Studies in Honor of Zvi Yavetz*, ed. I. Rubinsohn and Z. W. Malkin (Leiden, 1995), 129–187. E. Tengström, *Donatisten und Katholiken* (Göteborg, 1964). Maureen A. Tilley, ed. and trans., *Donatist Martyr Stories: The Church in Conflict in Roman North Africa* (Liverpool, 1996).   J.M.G.

Civitates

Like the polis of the Greek-speaking East, the *civitas* was the essential building block of administration and power in the Roman west. The empire was divided into *civitates,* territories of greater or lesser size, each administered by an aristocratic *curia* based in the *civitas*'s principal town. Furthermore, the *civitas* was not just a political and administrative unit. Its capital was also a cultural center—local aristocrats, whether in Italy or out-of-the-way Britain, were expected to serve in the *curia* and to spend much of the year living in opulent townhouses within the civitas capital, financing public spectacles and public buildings.

Not surprisingly, the widespread changes and frequent turbulence of late antiquity in the west brought considerable change to the *civitates.* An early victim was probably traditional aristocratic public munificence (euergetism). The evidence from Italy, Gaul, and Britain suggests that before 300 C.E. this had already more or less disappeared from the *civitas* capitals of the northwestern provinces, surviving only in Rome itself and in the south Italian provinces dominated by the estates of the senatorial aristocracy. However, in Africa, which was very prosperous in the 4th century, and which had suffered little in the troubles of the 3rd century, euergetism survived as a much more continuous tradition, right up to the time of the Vandal conquest in the early 5th century.

In the very period that euergetism disappeared and

the traditional secular public buildings (like baths, amphitheaters, and forums) slowly crumbled away, the *civitates* gained a new function, and an entirely new type of building. The organization of the Christian church, officially recognized in the west after Constantine's triumph in 312, was closely modeled on the organization of the empire, with a bishop for each *civitas*, based in the local *civitas* capital. Indeed only very gradually—and usually after the late antique period—did the bishop loosen his direct control of the entire territory of a *civitas*, through the establishment of rural churches and (eventually) a pastoral organization through rural parishes. In late antiquity, the episcopal church was *the* church of the *civitas*, and the local aristocracy was expected to come into town to mark the great festivals of the Christian year.

As the church grew in wealth and number of souls, so, gradually, did the number and size of church buildings increase within the episcopal towns (the *civitas* capitals). By the 5th and 6th centuries each episcopal town had one major church (the *ecclesia* of the bishop himself), often flanked by secondary oratories and an episcopal palace, and also a crop of other churches, such as those built outside the walls, over the graves of the martyrs. By 600 C.E. the church was perhaps the most solidly established institution of each *civitas* capital, and increasingly the church also provided a new heavenly patron to defend the city, such as Martin for Tours or Hilary for Poitiers.

The *civitas* also remained the basic unit of secular administration within the late empire, though under ever tighter imperial control, and often without the trappings of a classical monumental past. The tax and requisition system, on which the very survival of the empire depended, remained the responsibility of the *civitas* and its *curia*. So too did the enforcement of imperial commands and the maintenance of law and order, at least in those *civitates* away from the frontiers and the direct influence of the imperial army.

In much of the west, this secular administrative role persisted in the Germanic successor states. *Curiae* are documented into the 8th century, but it is clear that increasingly the *civitates* were no longer under the control of these local aristocratic councils but under the direct command of royally appointed officials, all with a military bent and most of Germanic origin, such as the counts of Ostrogothic Italy, Visigothic Spain, and Frankish Gaul, and the dukes of Lombard Italy. The testimony of Gregory of Tours shows that, under their counts and bishops, the *civitates* of 6th-century Gaul remained the basic units of administration for the raising of both taxes and military units, and for the provision of justice and public order.

The central administrative role of the *civitas* persisted in much of the west throughout the early Middle Ages, but in some regions it did decline and even disappear. In Britain it went very early, in the 5th century—but Britain was an extreme case, and there even the

church ceased to be based around the old Roman *civitates*. In Gaul, after the 6th century the secular role of the *civitas* was gradually eroded, to be replaced in part by that of a different unit, the *pagus*, which was often centered on a rural estate. However, at least in the form of the bishop and his diocese, the *civitas* proved one of the most durable and influential legacies of antiquity in the west.

BIBL.: N. Christie and S. T. Loseby, eds., *Towns in Transition: Urban Evolution in Late Antiquity and the Early Middle Ages* (Aldershot, Eng., 1996). *La fin de la cité antique et le début de la cité médiévale*, ed. C. Lepelley (Bari, 1996). John Rich, ed., *The City in Late Antiquity* (London and New York, 1992). *Villes et peuplement dans l'Illyricum proto-byzantin*, Collection de l'école française de Rome 77 (Rome, 1984).

B.W.

Claudian

Claudius Claudianus, born in Alexandria (ca. 370), came to Rome in 394. His first Latin poem celebrated the consuls of 395, Probinus and Olybrius, but thereafter most of his poems served the interests of his patron and the emperor Honorius's chief minister, the Vandal general Stilicho. Claudian wrote panegyrics for the third (396), fourth (398), and sixth (404) consulates of Honorius, for the consulate of Mallius Theodorus (399), and for the consulate of Stilicho (in three books, 400); invectives against the eastern ministers Rufinus (in two books, probably 396 and 397) and Eutropius (two books, 399); and historical epics on the campaigns against the African warlord Gildo (*De bello Gildonico*, 398) and against Alaric in 401–402 (*De bello Getico*, 402). An epithalamium, or nuptial hymn, accompanied by four *Fescennini*, celebrates the marriage of Stilicho's daughter Maria to Honorius (398). Separately transmitted are a collection of *Carmina minora*, including epigrams, ecphrases, verse epistles, an incomplete verse panegyric of Stilicho's wife, Serena, and the beginning of a *Gigantomachia* (the subject also of a fragmentary Greek poem of Claudian's youth); and three books of an unfinished mythological epic, *De raptu Proserpinae* (of uncertain date; book one, perhaps 396–397, books two and three, 400–402). Nothing is heard of Claudian after 404—a number of his poems are incomplete—and it is likely he died in that year or soon thereafter.

For his poetic achievements and service to Stilicho, Claudian was appointed tribune and notary and received the honor of a statue in the Roman forum (*CIL* 6.1710). He owed his marriage, to the daughter of an African landowner, to the good offices of Stilicho's wife, Serena. Claudian's religious affiliation is uncertain. Both Augustine (*De civ.Dei* 5.26) and Orosius (7.35) identify him as a pagan, but he wrote for a Christian court, and one of his poems (*De salvatore*, *Carm.min.* 32) has explicitly Christian content. He may have been at least nominally Christian. His deepest devotion, however, was to the poetic and ideological traditions of Rome. His poetry is full of allusions to classical poets, with a special affinity for writers of the 1st century C.E.; his invocation of the city and the imperial mission of Rome reflects the ideals of the western ruling class, which was his audience. Claudian initiated a tradition of Latin verse consular panegyrics; his *De bello Gildonico* and *De bello Getico* are the earliest surviving Latin historical epics on contemporary subjects. The distinction between panegyric and epic in Claudian's poetry is blurred. The panegyrics (and still more, invectives) contain a large narrative element, while the poems arranged according to a chronological sequence of events often have substantial sections of panegyric. In the narrative, whether mythological or historical-panegyrical, descriptions and set-piece speeches predominate, often attributed to personifications (especially to the goddess Roma). The recounting of actions is kept to a minimum. In this Claudian conforms to broader tendencies in late Latin poetry, but he is unusual in his restrained use of catalogues and figures of lexical accumulation.

BIBL.: Alan Cameron, *Claudian: Poetry and Propaganda at the Court of Honorius* (Oxford, 1970). S. Döpp, *Zeitgeschichte in den Dichtungen Claudians* (Wiesbaden, 1980). M. Roberts, *The Jeweled Style: Poetry and Poetics in Late Antiquity* (Ithaca, N.Y., 1989). —M.J.R.

Clients

In the principate the institution of clientage lost part of its political role but preserved its social importance. For aristocrats, clients were a sign of stature and prestige. There are lines of essential continuity between late antique clientage and that of the principate. The former is well attested, since it is mentioned in the most disparate sources: by historians such as Ammianus Marcellinus and Zosimus, by epistolographists (Symmachus, Sidonius Apollinaris), by poets (Ausonius, Paulinus of Pella, Dracontius), and by Christian writers (Ambrose, Jerome, Augustine). These authors reflect the social reality in the most important regions of the western empire (Italy, Gaul, North Africa). Clientage is also mentioned in the legal sources (*C.Th.*, *C.Just.*, *Nov.* 5). The majority of patrons were presumably wealthy people, mostly senators and *honorati* (in his sermons Augustine refers to *divites* and *potentes*). However, the status of clients is not so certain: in spite of the pejorative sense of the word, one should not assume all clients came from a lower social position.

Clients were basically bound to *obsequium* toward the person who engaged them, the patron. *Obsequium* assumed various forms, the most typical of which were offering the morning *salutatio* to the patron and being present next to him in special circumstances. Relations between patron and client are often presented in the sources in terms of their intrinsic instability and some-

times as analogous to those between master and slave: the patron is the *dominus* to whom the *cliens* owes service (*servitia*; for the principate, cf. Martial 2.18.7f., 2.32.9, 9.92). Patrons were often criticized for their lack of generosity. Since the most important advantages, such as assistance in court, were granted in return for material compensation, patronage relations could be corrupt. The venal *suffragium* is supposed to originate from clientage. Nevertheless, in late antiquity there is no clear distinction between the client-patron relation and *suffragium*. *Suffragatores* were often suspected of deceiving their clients by taking compensation for a *suffragium* that in the end never took place (*fumum vendere*: Historia Augusta, *Ant.Pius* 11.1; Heliogab. 10.3; Alex.Sev. 35f.). Often patrons' orders turned out to be onerous to clients. Clients who balked could be charged with *laesa fides* (disloyalty)—the crime of abandoning a patron as soon as he fell into trouble.

Like slavery, the institution of clientage was not strongly criticized by Christian thinkers. The formulas, law codes, and especially the conciliar legislation of Visigothic Spain are informative on this subject. In the 6th century, the church in particular was concerned to preserve the dependency of those whom it released from slavery. Freedmen and women were therefore required to render *obsequium* to their patron, the church. Since the patron-church was undying, a freedman, and his descendants for generations after him, could remain in a client position to successive bishops. Later, royal legislation in Spain became equally restrictive. The Visigothic evidence is insufficient for understanding exactly what constituted proper *obsequium*, although there are indications that in addition to personal services, monetary payments and even military service were possible. However, what appears in the 7th century to have been an emerging "feudal" order was disrupted by the Islamic conquest in 711.

Islamic society also had a system of clientage. While various forms of clientage were known in pre-Islamic Arabia, it developed in early Islam largely as a way of integrating non-Arab converts into a society still dominated by Arab tribes. Both patron and client were known as *mawlā* (pl. *mawālī*). Theirs was a bond of loyalty and financial obligation between two socially unequal individuals: generally between a protégé and a benefactor, but more precisely between a freed slave and his manumitter or a convert and his Muslim sponsor. Clients were often stigmatized in Umayyad society, yet the system endured into the Abbasid period, during which the caliphs relied heavily on their *mawālī* for political administration.

BIBL.: D. Claude, "Freedmen in the Visigothic Kingdom," in *Visigothic Spain: New Approaches*, E. James, ed. (Oxford, 1980), 159–180. Patricia Crone, "Mawlā," *Encyclopaedia of Islam* (Leiden, 1954–). J.-U. Krause, *Spätantike Patronatsformen im Westen des Römischen Reiches* (Munich, 1987). Jacob Lassner, *The Shaping of Abbasid Rule* (Princeton,

1980). N. Rouland, *Pouvoir politique et dépendance personelle dans l'antiquité romaine* (Brussels, 1979). P. Veyne, "Clientéle et corruption au service de l'état: La vénalité des offices au bas-empire romain," *Annales* 36 (1981): 339–360.

A.MAR.

Clothing

There are very few original garments preserved from antiquity. Those that are conserved are mostly from dry regions such as Egypt and the Syrian desert. Very little is known about late antique clothing in Spain, France, and Germany, and there are almost no examples of Roman garments. Hints about clothing in late antiquity have to be taken from depictions in art and written sources.

As in textile production in general, different traditions can be recognized within the Roman empire in late antiquity: clothes in the north (France, Germany, England) were different from those in Spain, Italy, and the Balkans and from those in the Near East and North Africa. In general, clothing rules become less strict from the 3rd century onward. Shapes became simpler, the garments themselves became less bulky. The toga, a symbol of Roman citizenship, was worn almost only at official events.

The main pieces of men's clothing were the light undertunic *(tunica)* with narrow long or half-long sleeves; the dalmatic, or overtunic *(dalmatica/collobium)*, with large, long sleeves that touched the hands; and the cloak. The *lacerna* was a large semicircular cloak, closed by a fibula on the right shoulder. The *pallium,* a large rectangular, and in later times also semicircular, garment was wrapped around the body. In early Byzantine times it was closed by a fibula on the right shoulder. The purple-dyed *pallium* became one of the emperors' insignia. The *paenula,* another type of cloak, was less bulky. It was triangular, closed in front, and had a V-shaped opening for the head. The *paenula,* being a garment designed for travelers, was shorter than the *lacerna* and the *pallium.*

Working people and slaves wore a short tunic *(tunica exomis)* that reached only to the knees. If necessary, it could be tucked up with a girdle. On some occasions this short tunic with narrow sleeves was also worn by aristocrats, together with a short shoulder mantle *(paenula/sagum),* for example for hunting. The military costume basically consisted of the same two pieces: a short tunic and short cloak, decorated according to the rank of its owner.

The main pieces of women's clothing were an undertunic with narrow long sleeves, an overtunic or stola with large sleeves, and a large cloak *(paenula/palla).* Married women wore their stola with a girdle. Women's dresses were long-sleeved and covered the ankles, except those worn by servants. Married women in eastern and western provinces covered their heads on official occasions, either by pulling a mantle over the head or by wearing different kinds of headdresses or veils—in the east called *maphorion.*

Heavier garments were required in northern provinces for protection against cold weather. Thus heavy woolen cloaks *(birrus)* and hooded cloaks *(cucullus),* kerchiefs, and long woolen socks were of main importance. The most typical garments in the northwestern parts of the empire were trousers *(braccae)* and breeches *(uddones),* worn with a type of long-sleeved shirt and high boots. Instead of the *palla* women wore a bulky cloak *(paenula),* closed in front over the breast by a fibula. Wool was the main material for garments in these regions, because it is warm and water repellent. Occasionally cloaks and tunics were lined with fur. Lighter clothing used as underwear was made of flax, hemp, or sometimes even nettle fiber. Elaborate clothing from the northern provinces was often patterned and decorated with small trimmings.

Special pieces of clothing were known in eastern parts of the empire. The coexistence of Roman and local customs—a typical feature of late antique times in general—was most evident in clothing worn by people in Pannonia or the inhabitants of Syrian towns situated on the Parthian frontier. In Palmyra, for example, aristocrats wore both the Parthian costume (consisting of trousers, shirt, and caftan) and the Roman tunic and toga. In the east garments were made of fine wool or flax, according to local custom. Egypt, for example, used a lot of flax, while finds from Palestine, Syria, and the Black Sea coast generally consist of fine wool or silk. Finds from Palmyra show that silk was mainly imported from China, both as woven fabric with typical Chinese patterns and in the form of raw silk. A considerable amount of cotton fabric and cotton clothing from India reached the Near East and Egypt by sea trade. Probably as a result of intensified economic and cultural contact between the Parthian empire and the Far East, clothing in the Near East became more colorful and decorated. This new fashion spread from Syria and Palestine in the 1st century C.E. and reached Egypt and Italy in the early 4th century.

The classic decoration for tunics consisted of two vertical stripes running from the shoulders downward, and one or two stripes at the end of the sleeves. If these stripes did not reach the seam of the tunic, they were called *clavi.* Additional decoration consisted of symmetrically arranged medallions *(orbiculi)* and squares *(tabulae).* Cloaks were decorated with angel-shaped forms *(gammadion)* or H-shaped stripes. Such garments were made by specialists and distributed by traveling merchants. This clothing was made in more or less one size for adults and one size for children. Individual fit was achieved by cinching and tucking the garments with belts. Fabric for most late antique clothing was woven in the necessary shape, tunics as well as semicircular mantles.

Garments made of silk were most precious. They were rare until the 7th century. Diocletian's Edict (301

C.E.) lists dalmatics made entirely of silk and those made with only a silk warp or weft. In the course of the 7th century silk became more popular in the whole Mediterranean area. The most precious garments of late antiquity were those made of purple-dyed silk. An edict of Emperor Theodosius I from 395 C.E. reserved the wearing of purple silk as a privilege for the emperor and his family and prohibited its use by others. The large cloak *(paludamentum)*, the trousers, the handkerchief *(mappa)*, and the shoes, all dyed purple with murex shells, became insignia of the Byzantine emperor.

Both men and women in early Islamic Arabia wore clothing consisting of a loin cloth *(izār)* or drawers *(sirwāl)*; a shirt *(qamīṣ)*; a tunic or robe; and, when in public, a mantle over all. The same basic items were common in other parts of the early Islamic empire as well, but were wrapped and draped differently according to the sex of the wearer and different regional styles. While the central Islamic lands saw ankle-length garments, the basic outer garment in North Africa was a shorter tunic.

A great variety of garments existed in the Islamic world, made from wool, linen, leather, silk, and other fabrics. Beginning with the caliph Hishām (who ruled 724–743), the Umayyads began to produce luxurious embroidered textiles in palace factories, a practice that continued in Abbasid times. Called *ṭirāz*, these fabrics became widely popular and were an immense source of revenue.

Continuing an ancient Near East custom, Muslim men and women covered their heads, with the exception of some Berbers who did not wear headgear until well into the Islamic period. Men wore a variety of caps and turbans, most known from pre-Islamic times. Arab women covered part or all of their face with a veil and in addition wore a mantle from head to toe, as had been the custom earlier. Men occasionally veiled themselves as well, often using their mantle or turban cloth.

BIBL.: R. P. A. Dozy, *Dictionnaire détaillé des noms de vêtements chez les arabes* (Amsterdam, 1845). Hero Granger-Taylor, "Weaving Clothes to Shape in the Ancient World," in *Textile History* 13 (1982): 3ff. Francisco Garcia Jurado, "La revolución indumentaria de la antiquedad tardía: Su reflejo en la lengua latina," *Revue des études augustiniennes* 42 (1996): 97–109. J. L. Sebaste and L. Bonfante, *The World of Roman Costume* (Madison and London, 1994). Yedida Stillman, "Libās," *Encyclopaedia of Islam*, new ed. (Leiden, 1954–). R. Warland, "Status und Formular in der Repräsentation der spätantiken Führungsschicht," *Deutsche archäologische Institut: Römische Mitteilungen* 101 (1994): 175–202. John Peter Wild, "Clothing in the North Provinces of the Roman Empire," *Bonner Jahrbücher* 168 (1968): 166ff.   A.S.

Clovis

Clovis was largely responsible for the establishment of the Frankish kingdom as the dominant force in what had been Roman Gaul. His father, Childeric, had clearly established himself in the region around Tournai, where he was buried with a magnificent quantity of grave goods in ca. 481. Clovis extended his father's power, initially in the direction of Soissons, where he destroyed the power bloc of the Roman Syagrius ca. 486. He expanded Frankish power westward, toward Brittany, and made a number of forays south of the Loire before 500. In that year he took advantage of divisions within the Burgundian kingdom to make the Burgundians tributary. Six years later he attacked the Alamans, largely destroying their kingdom, and in 507 he turned against the Visigoths in Aquitaine. His success in defeating them at Vogliacum (probably Voulon, rather than the traditional Vouillé), and his seizure of much of Aquitaine the following year, led the Ostrogothic king Theoderic to take reprisals against the Franks and their Burgundian allies. For the remainder of his reign Clovis seems to have consolidated his power among the Franks, destroying rival kingdoms. He died apparently in 511.

Although Clovis's reign can be reconstructed with reasonable certainty, there are difficulties in interpretation, notably because the majority of the evidence comes from the *Histories* of Gregory of Tours, in which Clovis is presented as a model for future generations. Most significant in this regard is the question of the king's conversion to Catholic Christianity. Gregory dates this event in the year 496 and sees the king as converting directly from paganism. Earlier sources, notably the writings of Clovis's contemporary Avitus, bishop of Vienne, suggest that Clovis did not convert suddenly from paganism to Catholicism but weighed the options over a long period, finally choosing the Catholic faith of his wife perhaps as late as 508. The last years of Clovis's reign saw a flurry of religious activity, starting with legal support for Catholic clergy in the course of the Vogliacum campaign and concluding with a church council at Orléans in 511, largely for the benefit of the clergy of newly conquered Aquitaine.

Clovis's reign was also significant for its secular legislation. The earliest Frankish law code, the so-called *Pactus Legis Salicae*, was apparently issued under Clovis before the king's conversion—although the text makes no claim to be royal law.

When Clovis died he left his kingdom to his four sons. One of the sons, Theuderic I, the son of a concubine, was already a proven warrior; the other three, all of them minors, were the sons of Queen Chlothild. Thereafter the Merovingians seem to have regarded the practice of dividing the Frankish kingdom among all the sons of a dead king as the norm. More significant for the immediate future, the fact that three out of four heirs were minors at the time of Clovis's death meant that Frankish power was in retreat for a decade or more, and that Merovingian domination of Gaul did not come to fruition until the destruction of the Burgundian kingdom in 534 and the takeover of Gothic Provence in 537.

BIBL.: W. M. Daly, "Clovis: How Barbarian, How Pagan?" *Speculum* 69 (1994): 619–664. M. McCormick, "Clovis at Tours: Byzantine Public Ritual and the Origins of Medieval Ruler Symbolism," *Das Reich und die Barbaren,* ed. E. Chrysos and A. Schwarcz (Vienna, 1989), 155–180. I. N. Wood, *The Merovingian Kingdoms 450–751* (London, 1994). I.W.

Codex

A codex is the form of book, familiar for the last fifteen hundred years, with writing on both sides of sheets that are gathered together and bound along one edge, usually within a cover. In later Latin, *codex* already had this usage, derived from the term for a tree's trunk, *caudex,* because it originally referred to wooden tablets with wax panels for writing. These were used for taking notes, and almost by definition for ephemeral purposes. By the 1st century of the Christian era, there are references to bound gatherings not of wooden tablets but of parchment—that is, prepared animal skins—still used for notes rather than for books. In contrast, books were written on one side of a long roll, usually of papyrus, called a *volumen,* or in Greek, *biblos.* Martial refers to the use of portable parchment codices of his poems in the late 1st century, but this was clearly rare. Abundant evidence concerning the shift from the roll form to the codex form for longer books survives only from Egypt, and the sample may be unrepresentative, but it does support the now widely held view that the shift was especially associated with Christian literature. By the later 2nd and early 3rd century, the preponderance of Christian literature is in codex form, written on parchment or papyrus, whereas non-Christian literature retained a preference for the roll form. Only gradually and sporadically did the codex become the dominant form for all books, a process largely completed by the end of the 4th century.

The shift from roll to codex had a profound impact in many spheres, clearly affecting the development of the Christian scriptural canon and the notion of the Bible as a single corpus of writings. The enhanced compactness and portability of the codex may have been associated with and supported missionary activity, while encouraging a style of referring to authority in a written canon. The shift also seems to have created a book form both more expensive and more durable, which had important effects on literacy. The codex made elaborate pictorial decoration of books a reasonable activity for the first time, and from the late 4th century a few luxurious codices, both Christian and non-Christian in content, were provided with elaborately painted pictures that begin the story of book illumination, which by the end of late antiquity became a major artistic genre.

BIBL.: Alain Blanchard, ed., *Les débuts du codex: Actes de la journée d'étude organisée à Paris les 3 et 4 juillet 1985* (Turnhout, 1989). Harry Y. Gamble, *Books and Readers in the Early Church: A History of Early Christian Texts* (New Haven, 1995), 49–66. M. McCormick, "The Birth of the Codex and the Apostolic Life Style," *Scriptorium* 39 (1985): 150–158. Colin Roberts and T. C. Skeat, *The Birth of the Codex* (London, 1983). L.N.

Coinage

In late antiquity coinage was highly homogeneous as long as the Roman and Persian empires, each with its characteristic system, remained intact. Successor states in the east and west imitated imperial coins before developing independent coinages of their own, a process completed by the 8th century.

In the Roman empire, Diocletian subsumed the independent production of provincial mints under imperial control and thus increased the number of public mints *(monetae publicae)* to fourteen. His system gave most (though not all) dioceses at least one mint. This number and the mint locations remained fairly constant throughout the 4th century. Under Constantine I, gold and silver began to be coined by a staff that followed the imperial comitatus *(moneta comitatensis).* From 368 the *moneta comitatensis* controlled precious metal coinage altogether and distinguished its production with the mint mark "COM." In the 5th century most western mints, except those in Rome, Ravenna, and Milan, drastically cut production and eventually closed. Lyons reopened under the Burgundians, and Rome remained the center of Ostrogothic production, but most barbarian production reflected the disintegration of centralized factories in the west. Justinian later reopened mints in Rome, Ravenna, and Carthage. In the east, all of the 4th century mints except that in Heraclea operated down to the 7th century, when Heraclius closed all but the mints at Constantinople and Alexandria. The *monetae publicae* were staffed by *monetarii,* who were organized into divisions *(officinae)* under a *praepositus.* The *Comes sacrarum largitionum* controlled the *moneta comitatensis,* which was broken into ten production divisions and further compartmentalized by task (*C.Just.* 12.23.7). From 395, when emperors ceased extensive travel outside the capital, the *moneta comitatensis* acquired a permanent place in Constantinople, though it occasionally transferred some staff to other mints for temporary production.

Coinage was primarily in gold, issued where the emperors resided, and in bronze, struck everywhere. Both were produced for the convenience of the state, not the public, with the gold playing a major role in the salaries and donatives of the troops. Excavations show that all coins had a wide circulation and that the bronze coins facilitated exchange in local markets.

The main gold coin was the *solidus,* struck at seventy-two to the pound; because of its consistent purity, it remained the standard well into the Middle Ages. The *tremissis*, worth one-third of the *solidus*, was also generally issued. Silver formed little part of the imperial coinage except in the second half of the 4th century, when issues were plentiful. Bronze coins were produced in vast quantities, in a series of denominations now difficult to understand because inflation constantly reduced the size and weight of the coins and generated frequent reforms in which new, larger coins were struck. By the mid-5th century, the bronze had deteriorated to one tiny denomination of about 8 mm in size. In 498 Anastasius introduced a new bronze coinage; these coins bore on the reverse not pictorial types but numbers to mark their value. The largest and most common was a piece of 40 *nummi*; 20, 10, 5 *nummi* coins were also issued, as well as 12 and 6 for Egypt. This system remained stable, though the 40 *nummus* inevitably tended to shrink and the smaller denominations to disappear. By the mid-7th century the minor coinage of the eastern empire consisted of vast quantities of small, crudely struck 40 *nummus* pieces.

At first, the reverse side of the coins displayed a variety of images reflecting contemporary events and imperial policies (the obverse always had the head of the emperor); the issues of Constantine, on which the pagan gods vanish though Christianity barely makes an appearance, are especially rich. Later types are limited to abstractions and celebrations of imperial anniversaries (the occasions for donatives). By the 5th century, even these disappear, with the bronze bearing numbers and the gold restricted to four main types: the emperor or an angel with a long cross on the solidus and a seated Victory or a cross on the tremissis.

In the west, the Germans, who had no indigenous coinage of their own and whose rulers called themselves king, not emperor, issued gold in the name of the emperor of Constantinople through the 6th century and rarely struck silver or bronze coins. After a period of variety, a standard silver coinage appears in the 8th century.

The Vandals and Ostrogoths conformed most closely to the Roman pattern, striking coins in all three metals. The emperor's head normally appeared on the gold, the king's on the silver, and the bronze featured municipal images. The Burgundians and Suebi issued imitative imperial gold, as did the Visigoths and Franks (with some exceptions) until the late 6th century.

From Leovigild (568–586) until the Arab conquest of 711, the Visigothic kings struck broad thin *tremisses* in their own names. The Lombards issued imitative *tremisses* until Cunicpert (688–700) inaugurated a royal coinage of distinctive type. The Franks produced *solidi* with their king's image throughout the 7th century. Far more abundant, though, were the *tremisses* issued locally; the obverse bears a head and the name of the mint, with a cross and moneyer's name on the

reverse. Their metal was constantly debased until it was virtually indistinguishable from silver. Finally, Pepin III (751–781) issued a broad thin silver piece, probably imitated from the Arab *dirhem* of Spain, which became the characteristic coin of medieval Europe. The Anglo-Saxons, who had no coinage at all until about 600, generally followed the lead of the Franks.

The Sassanian coinage was even more conservative than the Roman. From the beginning of their kingdom, they struck primarily in silver (gold was extremely rare and bronze coins were issued only sporadically, in small denominations). The coins of all metals bore unvarying types: the head of the king, differentiated by his elaborate crown, on the obverse, and a fire altar flanked by attendants on the reverse. These were dated and were issued at a large number of mints. The style and purity of metal gradually deteriorated, and the coins, which were struck in enormous quantities, became broader and thinner, but they did not change their types for 400 years.

When the Arabs occupied the Near East, they found two totally different systems of coinage, the Roman in Egypt and Syria, the Persian in Mesopotamia and Iran. During the 7th century they copied what they found, most faithfully in the east. The first Islamic coins are of pure Sassanian type, only with the addition of "in the name of God" in the margin. Similar coins were struck bearing the names of Umayyad governors. In Syria, for some time, the bronze coinage of Constans II (642–668) was used or imitated in great quantity with varying degrees of accuracy. Later, more standardized types were issued from mints named in Greek or Arabic, but still bearing the image of the emperor carrying a cross. In Egypt, the dumpy bronzes of the mid-7th century were generally imitated until replaced by a new though still Christian-looking type. 'Abd al-Malik (685–705) eventually issued coins bearing his own image holding a sword with a stylized design derived from a cross on the reverse. They were inscribed in Arabic.

Finally, in 696–697, 'Abd al-Malik created a distinctive and original Islamic coinage consisting of broad thin gold *dinars* and silver *dirhems* with no image, but only Qur'ānic quotations, the date, and the mint. Issued throughout the empire to a fixed standard in great quantity, they remained unchanged during the Umayyad and Abbasid periods. Bronze coins also adopted aniconic types, bearing the name of the Prophet; these underwent some variation until they generally ceased being issued in the early 9th century.

BIBL.: Claude Bénoît, "Du monnayage impérial au monnayage mérovingien: L'exemple d'Arles et de Marseille," *La fin de la cité antique et le début de la cité médiévale*, ed. C. Lepelley (Bari, 1996), 147–160. A. Bursche, *Later Roman-Barbarian Contacts in Central Europe: Numismatic Evidence*, Studien zur Fundmünzen der Antike 11 (Berlin, 1996). *Coin Finds and Coin Use in the Roman World*, ed. C. E. King and D. Wigg (Berlin, 1996). P. Grierson, *Byzantine Coins*

(Berkeley, 1982). M. F. Hendy, *Studies in the Byzantine Monetary Economy c. 300–1450* (Cambridge, Eng., 1985). D. Sellwood et al., *Sassanian Coins* (London, 1985).　C.F.

Colonate

The difficulty about the institution we call the colonate in the later empire is that most of the evidence comes from scattered laws that were not united until the *Code* of Justinian. Consequently, it is not possible to trace a systematic history of its evolution or to define its scope and application. The alternative literary evidence is, though less theoretical, essentially anecdotal.

We can begin with three negative assertions. There is no proof that *coloni* were everywhere the dominant form of labor on the land; there was no single law of the colonate; and there was no single aim to the legislation. The haphazard character of the legal evidence warns us that, although there are occasional references to "the colonate" *(ius colonatūs),* there was no comprehensive law that applied to all *coloni.* Although they were the successors of the colonus farmers of earlier periods who usually held legally enforceable contracts of tenancy *(locatio-conductio),* tenants in the codes appear under a variety of names—*inquilini, originarii, originales, adscripticii*—and form a spectrum from relatively rich to servile poor. The most prosperous tenants, the *coloni idonei* of the earlier empire, were now never called *coloni* but *conductores,* and they held long lease contracts that often made them de facto owners of estates. The poorest probably never had held legal contracts even in the earlier empire, to judge by the appeals they made to the emperors. Beyond these there are numerous references in the sources to other types of labor—journeymen, reapers, and slaves—quite apart from extensive evidence of independent farmers. If in the end many smallholders became tenants of the rich in order to survive, there was an opposite tendency for some rich landowners to abandon their farms to former workers and barbarian settlers.

The aim of legislation regarding the colonate was primarily fiscal, to sustain the level of taxes and rents by ensuring that the land was farmed. The first reference to workers tied to the land, in an edict of 332 (*C.Th.* 5.17.1), concerned their payment of the capitation tax, which had probably been initiated by Diocletian's reforms. Much of the legislation, including the first reference to *ius colonatūs* in 342 (*C.Th.* 12.1.23), occurred in the context of imperial estates, granting privileges to the tenants but restricting their movement. Like the laws on emphyteutic leases, the objective was to induce tenants and *conductores* to keep up the level of rents by offering attractive terms. No doubt laws that restricted movement of *coloni* on imperial lands were also popular and ensured tax collection when extended to private landowners.

But rent-tax does not explain all the *coloni* laws,

since after the abolition of the capitation tax in provinces such as Thrace, movement of *coloni* was still restricted, and in 371 *coloni* in Illyricum were declared to be tied not by the tax but because of their status (*C.Just.* 11.53.1). A progression of laws from the mid-4th century deprived *coloni* of further rights, such as the freedom to dispose of property and to marry as they wanted. By 393 *coloni* were called "slaves of the land" (*C.Just.* 11.52.1), but in the east Anastasius distinguished between "free *coloni*" who paid their own taxes, and *adscripticii* whose property belonged to their master (*C.Just.* 11.48.19). By 530 a rescript of Justinian rhetorically demanded what difference existed between slaves and *adscripticii* (*C.Just.* 11.50.2). Shortage of manpower and general attempts to stimulate the economy are unsatisfactory explanations of such laws, since they make assumptions about demographic changes that cannot be proved. The tenor of the legislation fits into other utopian attempts by the state, that were doomed to failure, to freeze society into castes.

The precise categories within the range of *coloni* are hard to interpret. The terms *originales* and *originarii* probably covered those registered as citizens within the city or estate where they were born. *Inquilini* defined those who, as outsiders or foreigners, were probably registered purely by residence, while *adscripticii* probably derived their name from registration on the tax lists. But we also have references to *coloni* who made private contracts "as though they were their own masters and free" (*C.Just.* 11.1.14; 371 C.E.) and to *coloni* who paid their own taxes or who were free plebs. No doubt over several hundred years definitions changed, categories overlapped, and rights were eroded (or even improved). Under certain conditions, a law of 400 conceded that *coloni* and *inquilini* could become *curiales* (*C.Th.* 12.19.2). Even the imperial chancellery in that same year found *inquilini* and *originales* "almost" the same (*C.Just.* 11.48.13), although only for tax purposes. Augustine in the 5th century was fully aware of the differences between *originarii* and *inquilini,* the latter surprisingly being able to make contracts on property (*Enarr. in Ps.* 148.11).

There are striking links in legislation between *coloni* and *laeti, tributarii,* and *dediticii,* and in one law of 409 landlords were permitted to employ Sciri prisoners of war as *iure colonatūs* (*C.Th.* 5.6.3), probably indicating how the barbarian settlements influenced general thinking about *coloni.* By the 5th century the distinction between free and servile *coloni* seems to have hardened. In the east, legislation established that free *coloni* effectively became peasant-owners, a characteristic of Byzantine civilization, although a similar evolution may be shown by Sidonius Apollinaris in Gaul, who stressed the difference between an *inquilinus-tributarius* on the one hand and *cliens* with a plebeian *persona* on the other (*Ep.* 5.19).

There are equal ambiguities and differences in the

rights of movement by *coloni*. Augustine in 5th century Africa provided insight into the reality of tenant mobility, whatever the legal ideal. Despite a restatement in 419 of the legislation that required a *colonus originalis* to be returned to his home estate (*C.Th.* 5.18.1), this did not restrain the movement of *coloni* on one of the estates in Augustine's diocese of Hippo, quite apart from other examples of landowners who reduced their tenants or their tenants' children to slavery or indentured service. As elsewhere in the later empire, there was constant tension between the fiscal demands of the state and the growing powers of patronage enjoyed by landowners. It was taxation that drove so many poorer citizens to "flee into the laps of the most powerful houses" (*C.Th.* 12.1.6; 318 C.E.), and not surprisingly many small farmers preferred what Salvian in 5th century Gaul called "the yoke of abject *inquilini*" to the freedom of oblivion through taxation.

BIBL.: J. M. Carrié, "Le 'colonat du bas-empire': Un mythe historiographique," *Opus* 1 (1982): 351–370. W. E. Heitland, *Agricola: A Study of Agriculture and Rustic Life in the Greco Roman World* (Cambridge, Eng.; repr. Westport, Conn., 1970). Miroslava Mirković, *The Later Roman Colonate and Freedom* (Philadelphia, 1997). D. Vera, "Dalla 'villa perfecta' alla villa di Palladio: Sulle trasformazioni del sistema agrario in Italia fra principato e dominato," *Athenaeum* 83 (1995): 189–211, 331–356.   C.W.

Comitatus

The term c*omitatus* (retinue) had been used to refer to the immediate associates of the emperor since the 1st century C.E. By the late 3rd century, when the emperor traveled widely, it was applied to the entire entourage of civilian staff and military personnel that accompanied him. Civilian officers of the comitatus included the emperor's personal household (the *cubiculum,* with its staff and guards) and his administrative council (the consistory, with its secretaries, guards, the quaestor, the master of offices, the count of the domestic guards, the counts of the imperial largesse and imperial estates, and one of the praetorian prefects). When multiple emperors ruled, each had his own comitatus, which together amounted to a mobile capital of about 6,000 officers and guards. Constantine drew a firm distinction between these civilian personnel and the mobile army that also accompanied the emperor. Even so, the migratory nature of the civilian comitatus made its staff "no strangers to the dust and toil of the camps" (*C.Th.* 6.36.1) until the emperors ceased extensive travel after 395.

Comitatus also designated the large, mobile corps of troops (*comitatenses*) who accompanied the emperor on military expeditions, as distinct from the stationary troops (*ripenses* or *limitanei*) who remained in fixed garrisons near the frontiers. Since Gallienus, troops detached from regular legions had been used to form standing mobile divisions; such field troops were al-

ready being designated *comites* or *comitatenses* under Diocletian and Maximian (*ILS* 664, 2781; *AE* (1981) 777; *P Oxy.* 43.A.II). However, Zosimus (2.34; cf. 15) indicates that Constantine first employed mobile troops in large numbers and firmly established their units as a central element in the military organization. The enlarged field army he created (110,000 to 120,000 men) consisted of Roman infantrymen and cavalry units (*legiones* and *vexillationes*) and a large number of auxiliaries (*auxilia*) drafted from barbarian troops; all were commanded by newly created officers, the master of the infantry (*magister peditum*) and master of the cavalry (*magister equitum*). When multiple emperors ruled, each had his own field army in attendance; from the mid-4th century, large field armies were also detached from the imperial retinue to serve under separate masters of the cavalry in Gaul and the east, and smaller mobile groups were dispatched under lesser commanders (*comites*) into other territories. This separation of mobile troops led to a distinction between *palatini*, who served in the emperor's presence (*in praesenti*) and *comitatenses*, who did not. The distinction is first attested in a law of 365, which also first attests the mobilization of border troops (*limitanei*) into the field army under the title *pseudocomitatenses* (*C.Th.* 8.1.10). Theodosius I fixed the eastern comitatus in the five groups that appear in the *Notitia Dignitatum*: two around the capital (*praesentales*) and three in outlying regions (the eastern frontier, Thrace, and Illyricum). The *Notitia* shows the western command as it was fixed under Stilicho: central administration under a single master of the soldiers *in praesenti*, who retained a subordinate master of the infantry *in praesenti* and a number of regional commanders, mostly *comites*. The western comitatus disappeared with the collapse of Roman rule in the west in the late 5th century; in the east, the old comitatensian units continued to exist into the 6th century, although they tended to become stationary in the provinces where they were garrisoned and often ceased to be referred to as *comitatenses*.

BIBL.: D. Hoffmann, *Das Spätrömische Bewegungsheer und die Notitia Dignitatum,* 2 vols. (Düsseldorf, 1969–1970). P. Southern and K. R. Dixon, *The Late Roman Army* (New Haven, 1996). D. Van Berchem, *L'armée de Dioclétien et la réforme Constantinienne* (Paris, 1952).   N.L.

Commerce

Modern historians have long maintained that commercial trade in the Mediterranean region declined beginning in the 3rd century as a direct consequence of a decline in economic prosperity and urban civilization in the empire. Depending on the school of thought, the later empire experienced either a "crisis" in an early precapitalist system, or the immobility of nondevelopment. Following Pirenne, however, there has been a tendency to reassess the vitality of the late economy in various domains—agriculture, crafts, commercial exchanges, monetary economy, imperial largesse *(euergetism)*, and public construction. The theory of decline has been expressed in another form by Keith Hopkins. He establishes a link between the tax system and commercial trade and assumes that, beginning with Diocletian, the relation between the two was reversed, because of the development of a tax system in kind at the expense of exactions of currency. However, two contradictions in the traditional theories to which Hopkins remains indebted—namely, the partial maintenance of a currency-based tax system and evidence of sustained commercial activity—allow us to extend this model's application into the late period. All the same, monetary circulation spurred by state finances remained available for commercial needs. According to other historians analyzing the late Roman economy as "state-administered trade," later commerce was monopolized by the state, the church, and large property owners. These three dominant economic actors, placing social exchange above the profit economy, are believed to have developed "nonmarket activities" that withdrew a growing portion of commerce from commercial free enterprise. Using their own organizations and their own personnel, they are said to have irremediably made private commercial enterprise noncompetitive, and to have afflicted the Mediterranean economy with "decommercialization." This model makes the postulate of a decline in specifically commercial trade compatible with the evidence of strong economic production; unfortunately, the sources offer no support for such a theory.

Just because production was primarily agricultural does not mean that commercial trade remained low. Large-scale transfers of agricultural products were necessary to maintain the urban populations (especially in the east) and a sizable army, a responsibility the *annona* organization was far from assuming. The foundations of the often-cited estimate that 6th century agriculture produced something like twenty times the revenue of commerce and industry are simply too fragile. There are now historians who reject Moses Finley's belief in an insignificant level of artisanal production and his dogma of peasant autarky. In the most recent analyses, the low level of trade in antiquity, compared with the level reached in developed economies, tends to be attributed primarily to an inadequate interregional division of labor and the low level of commodity capital.

Historians long believed that the deterioration of currency led users to bypass money as much as possible, returning to barter, royalties, or salaries in kind. But we need only glance at the Egyptian documentation for the years 250–350 to see that this was not at all the case. Monetary disorder (mid 3rd century to mid 4th century) may have complicated commercial life, momentarily paralyzing the banks, but it was not a serious obstacle; nor was the government's attempt, in conjunction with its monetary policy, to fix the price of various articles in an authoritarian manner (edict on prices, in the year 301). The result was a two-level price scale (official and free).

Certainly trade movements (increased flow of eastern products to the west beginning in the 5th century), products, and routes played a large part in commercial life, but very often artisanal objects were marketed at the factories themselves, like those that have been studied in Sardis, Jerusalem, Gerasa, and Caricingrad. The most important products (clear sigillated ceramic from Africa) were traded locally, within provinces, and between different regions. As for luxury items, marble objects from Proconnesus conquered vast markets, even in the west. Without taking literally the idyllic picture painted in the *Descriptio totius mundi et gentium,* a work whose pretensions are more cultural than economic, we must admit the vitality of Mediterranean trade in the 4th century. Trade "from the Indies" was more active than ever. It did not place the metallic reserves of the empire in greater peril than before through some mythic "gold flight," but it did determine a good portion of eastern policy. In the only area where legislative and administrative obstacles to private commercial activity were erected, the state required all trade with the outside to pass through particular control points, the *commercia*. This allowed the state to monitor contacts between individuals and an external world it judged dangerous, and it facilitated the collection of duties.

Until recently, information relating to the *annona* organization was unduly extended to trade in late antiquity. That organization, preponderant in the sources, has distorted our vision. The *corpora* hired by the state to provide public services insured by individuals were in no way professional guilds in the strict sense of the term. Their goal was to provide the permanent organizational and financial structure necessary for the proper operation of maritime transport of goods over the long term. Similarly, the *navicularii* were chosen from among large landowners rather than professional navigators, for reasons that were the result of wealth, not economic pressure. That did not rule out a preponderant role for large *possessores* in the free market of food products. In general, historians have looked to the legal sources for a reflection of a socioeconomic reality they were not designed to describe. Because the sources very rarely allude to private commercial activity, scholars have inferred a decline in such activity, even though lawmakers had no reason to speak of commerce except when it intersected tax questions.

When commercial activities became subject to taxation (Constantine's notorious *chrysargyron*, which raised protests disproportionate to its real weight), lawmakers had to state precisely what was meant by commerce as a profession *(negotiatio)*. They had to distinguish commerce strictly speaking (which has to do with products made by others) from the marketing of one's own products. Even though the imperial state recognized the public usefulness of traders, these legal criteria were somewhat parallel to the traditional representation of commerce, conceived as nonwork because it was nonproductive and nontransformative. The state continued to use the term *sordidus,* that is, unworthy of a person of quality (Libanius, Basil of Caesarea, and so on). Christian authors at first adopted this ideological bias against commerce, which was considered the archetype of all dishonest activity by the homilist of the *Opus imperf. in Matthaeum,* 41, a text that was constantly reread throughout the early Middle Ages. At most, a few passages from Augustine and Ambrose suggest a move beyond these deeply rooted prejudices, which continued to afflict commerce and traders.

BIBL.: Jean-Michel Carrié, "Les échanges commerciaux et l'état antique tardif," in Jean Andreau et al., *Les échanges dans l'antiquité: Le rôle de l'état* (Saint-Bertrand-de-Comminges, 1994), 175–211. Keith Hopkins, "Taxes and Trade in the Roman Empire 200 B.C.–A.D. 400)," *Journal of Roman Studies* 70 (1980): 101–125. *Mercati e mercanti nell'alto medioevo: L'area euroasiatica e l'area mediterranea* (Spoleto, 1993). Charles R. Whittaker, "Late Roman Trade and Traders," in *Trade in the Ancient Economy,* ed. Peter Garnsey, Keith Hopkins, and Charles R. Whittaker (London, 1983), 163–180.   J.C.

Concubinage

In Roman legal terms, *concubinatus* was a monogamous, semipermanent relationship, an alternative rather than a supplement to legal marriage. Generally the male partner had a substantially higher social and legal status than the female and so *concubinatus* was considered more socially appropriate than marriage, as with a man and his freedwoman. Sometimes marriage was legally impossible, as with a senator and a freedwoman, who could not marry under the Augustan marriage legislation. Status, as the jurist Ulpian said, was what distinguished a wife from a concubine (*Digest* 32.49.4).

Since *concubinatus* was not legal marriage, any offspring were illegitimate and would not inherit from their father upon intestacy. Pre-Constantinian law allowed a man to leave legacies to his illegitimate children, but he would be unlikely to make a concubine's child his heir if he also had children from a legal marriage. Gifts to a concubine were valid, unlike gifts to a wife, who could not own property separate from her husband. In late Roman law, concubines and their offspring receive considerable attention. A law of Constantine declares, "No one is permitted to have a concubine in his home while he is married" (*C.Just.* 5.26.1, 326). This simply codifies the Roman view of *concubinatus,* but perhaps was directed to regions where married men did have concubines. Constantine

also forbade senators and provincial and municipal officeholders to give anything, in their lifetime or in their will, to lowborn concubines and their offspring (*C.Th.* 4.6.2–3, 336). However, he encouraged men whose concubines were freeborn to marry them and legitimate their children retroactively (cf. *C.Just.* 5.27.5, 477). Post-Constantinian policy toward concubines and their offspring fluctuated but was somewhat more liberal in the eastern empire, where by the mid-5th century illegitimate children could receive by will up to one-fourth of their father's estate if he had no legitimate heirs, and could inherit fully if he enrolled them in his local *curia* (*C.Th.* 4.6.4–8; Theodosius II, *Nov.* 22.1 and 22.2.11; *C.Just.* 5.27.2–7). Justinian continued this relatively favorable policy and also abolished the classical prohibitions on marriage between high-ranking men and lowborn women that had sometimes made concubinage necessary (*C.Just.* 5.27.8–12; 5.4.28–29). Children born in a *concubinatus* relationship that was later converted to legal marriage were to have the same legal rights as their legitimate brothers, and a slave concubine and her children could be freed after her master's death and could inherit his estate, assuming he had no legal wife (*C.Just.* 5.27.10; 7.15.3; *Nov.* 117.4).

Augustine, who lived in a monogamous union with a concubine for almost fifteen years, provides evidence of *concubinatus* in late antiquity from a personal perspective. The relationship, which early produced a son, ended only when Augustine became betrothed to a girl whose social standing would aid his career ambitions. His concubine returned to Africa, leaving the child with his father and vowing that she would never know another man. During the two years before his fiancée reached marriageable age, Augustine took another concubine. His spiritual awakening ended both marriage and career plans (*Confessions* 6.15).

Augustine's personal experience clearly influenced his views on concubinage. He saw his former relationship as based solely on sex and condemned men who had acted as he had. In *De bono coniugali,* he stressed that a union that was not intended to be permanent or to produce offspring was not marriage and could even be equated with adultery. A man who dismissed a concubine to take a wife was an adulterer. And he said that a woman should not enter such a relationship when she knows the man will eventually dismiss her. But what if she remains faithful even after the relationship ends and never takes another man? "I probably would not easily presume to call her an adulteress," Augustine wrote. And a monogamous and permanent relationship, in which procreation was not prevented even though it was not the union's purpose, could "perhaps not absurdly be called *conubium*" (*De bono coniugali* 5).

Emphasis on intent and permanence as distinguishing a relationship rather than validity under secular law appears in other early Christian sources; around

400, the Council of Toledo barred from communion men who had both wife and concubine but accepted those who had a concubine instead of a wife (canon 17). Others, however, followed imperial law in condemning such unions and, unlike Augustine, did not condemn a man who dismissed his concubine to make a legal marriage. "Not every woman joined to a man is the man's wife, because not every son is the heir of his father . . . Thus a wife is one thing, a concubine another," declared Pope Leo in regard to one such case (*Ep.* 167, *inquisitio* 4, dated ca. 458). The church's ambivalence to concubinage continued into the Middle Ages, as did concubinage itself; ironically, ecclesiastical prohibitions on the marriage of clerics opened the way for a new type of concubinage.

BIBL.: Joelle Beaucamp, *Le statut de la femme à Byzance (4e–7e siècle), I: Le droit impérial* (Paris, 1990). Thomas A. J. McGinn, "Concubinage and the Lex Iulia on Adultery," *Transactions of the American Philological Association* 121 (1991): 335–375. Susan Treggiari, "Concubinae," *Papers of the British School at Rome* 49 (1981), 59–81.   J.E.G.

Conscription

Conscription provided the majority of military recruits in the 4th century, though volunteers were also welcomed. Three forms of conscription were common for Roman citizens: the sons of veterans were required to enlist as soldiers or be forced into curial service (*C.Th.* 7.22); occasional levies were raised in the 5th century from holders of honorary ranks or codicils (*honorati*), though this was often commuted to gold; regular annual levies compelled all landowners to provide recruits (*C.Th.* 7.13). The third, compulsory levy was probably instituted under Diocletian and more fully articulated over time thus: only large landowners were expected to provide a single recruit each year; others formed themselves into consortia (*temones* or *capitula*) in which responsibility for providing a recruit rotated; the members of each consortium paid a prorated sum to the one whose turn it was to offer a recruit (an obligation called *prōtostasia*, first attested in 324 [*P Oxy.* 45.3261]); the annual levy could also be commuted to a gold tax (*aurum tironicum*), which seems to have varied according to military necessity between ten and forty *solidi* per man (*P Lips.* 34, 35), though thirty seems to have been most common after 370 (*C.Th.* 7.13.7; 13; 20; Valentinian, *Nov.* 6.3). In the 5th century the compulsory levy was generally commuted to the gold tax, which may have continued to be levied through the 6th century. By then imperial authorities relied entirely on voluntary recruitment for Roman citizens. Heraclius's Persian counteroffensive saw the reintroduction of hereditary military service, and subsequent countermeasures against the Arabs led to the permanent settlement of soldiers in threatened communities. Out of these circumstances derived the Byzantine system of manning provincial armies (*themata*) with hereditary soldiers who equipped themselves and were paid and provisioned only when they were mobilized for campaigns.

Recruits were also levied from barbarians, many of whom volunteered for service in comitatensian units. Some (*dediticii*) were also forcibly conscripted, particularly when their tribe had surrendered unconditionally to Roman authority. *Dediticii* were either split from their tribal groups and distributed into regular units or subsumed en masse to form new auxiliary units. In the west, some barbarian groups were settled in Roman territory and apparently drafted as if they were regular citizens (*laeti* and *gentiles*, *Not.Dig.[oc.]* 42). Theodosius's treaty with the Visigoths in 382 initiated the process of enlisting barbarians who were settled under their own leadership inside Roman boundaries. Such barbarians, later referred to as *foederati*, became crucial for expeditionary forces in the 5th and 6th centuries.

Age limits, varying over time between 18–25 and 35–40, were enforced, and conscripts were required to be of a certain height, and of free, noncurial status. Law codes and military manuals call for further discretion but they also indicate laxity in enforcing regulations in the face of recruitment shortages. Unwilling conscripts went so far as to amputate their thumbs to avoid service, although exemption for mutilation was forbidden, at times on pain of death. Recruits and the sons of veterans often tried to avoid service or to desert but were faced with penalties ranging from obligatory curial service to execution. Upon induction recruits were branded (or tattooed) to ensure identification in case of desertion. To encourage enlistment, incentives were offered including bounties for volunteers and exemption from the poll tax (*capitatio*) for all soldiers and for the wives and parents of comitatensian troops. Veterans were rewarded with special exemptions, privileges, cash, and land grants (*C.Th.* 7.20).

BIBL.: H. Elton, *Warfare in Roman Europe, AD 350–425* (Oxford, 1996). J. F. Haldon, *Recruitment and Conscription in the Byzantine Army c. 550–950* (Vienna, 1979). W. Treadgold, *Byzantium and Its Army, 284–1081* (Stanford, 1995).   N.L.

Constantine

It is universally agreed that the reign of the emperor Constantine I (306–337) constituted a watershed in the transformation of the ancient world and the development of the Christian church. Born sometime in the 270s at Naissus (modern Nish) in the Danubian province of Moesia, Constantine grew up in a privileged world as son of Constantius I, one of the four coemperors who ruled in the college of emperors set up by Diocletian. That world came crashing down in 305 when, on his retirement, Diocletian passed over Constantine in the selection of new emperors. Constantine rejoined his father in Gaul, and was at his side when he died on July 25 in the year 306 while on campaign in Britain. Elevated to the purple by his father's troops, Constantine began to play a skillful game of alliance and maneuver that, by 324, left him sole emperor of the Roman world.

Although he helped destroy the tetrarchic system set up by Diocletian, replacing it with an overtly dynastic model, in other ways Constantine continued to rebuild the empire along the lines laid out by his great predecessor. He completed the separation of the army into frontier and field forces, and of provincial government into separate military and civil duties. Exhibiting the same concern for order and predictability that characterized Diocletian's thinking, he took steps to keep all classes bound to their positions. Later, hostile sources blamed him for opening high military commands to the Germanic peoples who would eventually replace Roman government, as Christianity would replace the traditional Roman religion.

Christian policy is, indeed, the area where Constantine broke most dramatically with his predecessor. Where Diocletian persecuted its followers, Constantine favored the new religion. After seizing control of Rome following the Battle of the Milvian Bridge on October 28, 312, Constantine met his ally, the eastern emperor Licinius, at Milan in February 313. The agreement that emerged from that meeting is traditionally known as the "Edict of Milan," although the document we possess actually was issued by Licinius in Nicomedia after he returned to the east. Recognizing Christianity as a legal religion, the emperors removed disabilities imposed by Diocletian and ordered restitution of property seized in the Great Persecution. About the same time, Constantine convened the Council of Arles to hear charges leveled against Catholic bishops by dissident Christians in North Africa, the Donatists. Lessons learned in that encounter served Constantine a decade later when, after seizing the eastern empire from Licinius, he attempted to settle the Arian controversy by convening the epochal Council of Nicaea in 325. The final decade of his reign was marked by the founding of Constantinople, the confiscation of pagan treasures, his continued involvement in disputes between the bishops, and an elaborate church building program that included St. Peter's in Rome and the Holy Sepulcher in Jerusalem. After his death on 22 May 337, Constantine was laid to rest amid memorials to the twelve Apostles in a church he had built for that purpose in Constantinople, deliberately fostering the association that would make him *isapostolos*, or "equal to the Apostles," in the eastern Church.

Traditionally it was said that Constantine's conversion to Christianity was due to the "Vision of the Cross," a miraculous event witnessed by his entire army as he marched to Rome in 312. In a biography published shortly after Constantine's death, Bishop Eusebius of Caesarea gives the account as told to him years afterward by the emperor himself. "He said that about noon, when the day was already beginning to decline, he saw with his eyes the trophy of a cross of light in the heavens, above the sun, and bearing the inscription, 'Conquer by This'" (*Vit.Const.* 1.28). The story became the foundation legend of the Christian empire, leading eventually to forgery of the "Donation of Constantine," by which the emperor supposedly assigned jurisdiction over the western empire to the bishop of Rome. With his mother, Helena, Constantine also became a central figure in the popular Legend of the Cross, in which Helena recovers the wood and nails of the Cross, thereby sanctifying the reigns of both the eastern emperor and, eventually, the new Germanic kings in the west.

As guarantor of the medieval church, Constantine inevitably suffered from the scholarship and skepticism produced by the Reformation, which culminated in Jacob Burckhardt's *Die Zeit Constantins des Grossen* (1859), a powerful though flawed portrait of an emperor whose only "vision" was to see how the church might be used to achieve his own secular goals. Norman Baynes put Constantine scholarship on a sounder footing with his 1930 lecture, "Constantine the Great and the Christian Church," in which he argued that "the true starting-point for any comprehension of the reign must be Constantine's own letters and edicts."

Today there is less debate over the sincerity of Constantine's conversion, but also more attention given to the type of Christian he became. Older studies assumed that all Christians were intolerant by nature, and that Christians of the late empire were engaged in a life-and-death struggle with their pagan neighbors. From this premise it followed that Constantine, if he were indeed sincerely converted, must have instituted the coercive practices that characterized Christian behavior by the end of the 4th century. Instead of this black-and-white terrain, scholars now see a much more nuanced landscape in the Constantinian period, filled with pagans who abhorred the excesses of the persecution and Christians who argued that true belief could not be coerced. At the same time, late antique paganism had less need for the practices, such as blood sacrifice, that had offended Christians, and had evolved its own monotheistic beliefs.

Seen against this backdrop, steps Constantine took that seemed controversial under the old conception take on more coherence. He avoided specific religious terminology in his public utterances, for instance, preferring neutrally worded phrases like "Supreme Sovereign" or "Highest God," and he kept pagan philosophers, such as the Neoplatonist Sopater, at his court. Apart from a few instances of temple destruction that can be described as police actions, Constantine took no steps against pagan cults, and he warned zealous Christians in an edict published shortly after he won control of the eastern empire that their initiatives in this direction, however laudatory, would not be tolerated. The consistent message of Constantine's policy appears to have been that acknowledgment of a "Highest God" whose personal emissary was the emperor and whose cult did not require "superstitious" practices was sufficient for citizens to participate in public life. More specific definitions, as he wrote to the principals in the Arian controversy, could be left to the privacy "of your own minds and thoughts" (Eusebius, *Vit.Const.* 2.64–72).

Despite disagreements that may remain about Constantine's Christian policy, it undeniably included a massive redistribution of patronage resources to the bishops and unprecedented recognition of their importance to the successful functioning of imperial government. As with his use of Germans in the military, Constantine's use of Christians in his government may show that his genius lay in an ability to reach out to new sources of strength. Whatever his motives, his use of these two forces will alone ensure that his reign remains a turning point in western history. Like many spectacular emperors, he was not remembered only for his historic deeds: a perfumed soap that Constantine had used to hold his hair in place beneath his diadem was still known by his name in 5th century Gaul (Polemius Silvius, *Laterculus* 5).

BIBL.: T. D. Barnes, *Constantine and Eusebius* (Cambridge, Mass., 1981) and *The New Empire of Diocletian and Constantine* (Cambridge, Mass., 1982). H. Dörries, *Das Selbstzeugnis Kaiser Konstantins* (Göttingen, 1954). H. A. Drake, "Lambs into Lions: Explaining Early Christian Intolerance," *Past and Present* 153 (1996): 3–36. Robin Lane Fox, *Pagans and Christians: Religion and the Religious Life from the Second to the Fourth Century A.D.* (New York, 1987).

H.D.

Constantinople

Constantine began searching for a new capital in 324, soon after defeating his rival Licinius at Chrysopolis. Plans for a new imperial center removed from Rome and identified with a particular emperor were not new for the late antique world, accustomed as it was to such initiatives in the tetrarchic period. Byzantium (modern Istanbul), an ancient urban site surrounded on three sides by water—Keras, or the Golden Horn (modern Haliç), Bosporion (the Bosphorus), and Propontis (the Sea of Marmara)—was not Constantine's first choice. The emperor had already laid foundations near Troy, in the Hellespont, before he turned to Byzantium. Why he changed his mind remains open to question. The move from the mythological Troad to Byzantium may, however, indicate a desire to put distance between foundation of the new capital and the mythological foundations of Homeric inspiration.

When Constantinople was officially inaugurated on May 11, 330, large urban areas within its land-walls still lay empty. Initially population growth was modest and the urban space remained relatively undeveloped. Yet the city could boast of an infrastructure consistent with Roman tradition. The Via Egnatia linked Constantinople with the west, while at least two roads led east into Asia Minor via the cities of Chalcedon and Nicomedia. Maritime commerce on the Black Sea and the Mediterranean took advantage of two harbors established in the Golden Horn. These harbors received the *annona civica*, wheat from Egypt for free consumption, which originally was sent to Rome but was now reserved for Constantinople.

Although its earliest physical remains are scarce, both the urban plan and many of Constantinople's monuments can still be identified. No traces survive of Constantine's original circuit of land-walls, but written evidence makes it possible to locate their position and establish that the Via Egnatia entered the city through a ceremonial gate in the southwest wall and led to the Capitolium. At that point it met another avenue that originated in the northeast and passed by Constantine's dynastic mausoleum. From the Capitolium the two roads joined to form a large colonnaded avenue, the Mese, which descended first toward the circular Forum of Constantine, with the emperor's porphyry honorific column (modern Cemberlitas) erected at its center, then to the domed four-columned Milion, and finally to the large porticoed square of the Augusteum. The Mese gained in splendor as it drew nearer to the city center, sporting a two-storied arrangement of marble columns on each side with shops lining the porticoes. The *omphalos,* or heartbeat of the city, was the area of the Augusteum, bordered on the east by the Senate and west by the imperial or Great Palace. The palace, a self-contained, multifunctional series of buildings arranged along a terraced hill on the southwest, commanded a spectacular view of the Bosphorus. Attached to the palace on its west via the *kathisma,* or imperial lodge, was the hippodrome, scene of some of the most furious athletic and political dramas of the age. Constantine built the church of Hagia Irene nearby, on the edges of the ancient acropolis, in an area nonetheless curiously unaffected by the new urban layout and that would indeed remain untouched for several centuries to come. Both the central area of the city and other neighborhoods further out underwent significant symbolic transformation under Constantine's successor, Constantius II, builder of the Megalē Ekklēsia, or Hagia Sophia. Constantius II's religious patronage also included the Church of the Holy Apostles, adjoining his father's mausoleum.

In the 5th century, building activity accelerated to such a degree that Constantinople became a metropolis. The *Notitia urbis Constantinopolitanae* provides an impressive list of the civic, private, and religious establishments that had emerged. The urban landscape comprised 14 churches, 52 colonnaded roads, 153 private bath complexes, and several open air and underground cisterns. For its water needs, which now included many public fountains and nymphaea, the Theodosian emperors looked to the city's hinterland, creating an elaborate water supply system there. Three more forums, the largest of which was the Forum of Theodosius, or Forum Taurii (modern Beyazit), had been added along the Mese leading to the ceremonial gate. Furthermore, the addition of a tripartite defensive system, built during the reign of Theodosius II (ca. 413) and located some 1.5 km west of the Constantinian walls, both provided stronger defenses and enlarged the enclosed area of the city. Set within the new wall was the Golden Gate, which was linked to the Via Egnatia and served as the city's main ceremonial entrance.

The 5th century also brought new emphases. The number of church foundations increased hand in hand with the intensification of urban monasticism. The monastery of St. John of Stoudios constituted one of the most impressive, active, and durable of these foundations. Another shift is evidenced in one of the most emblematic images of the 5th century, a distinctly anti-classicizing relief picturing Emperor Theodosius I in the imperial *kathisma* surrounded by a court of mixed ethnic origins. This image, which stands on the base of the Egyptian obelisk in the *spina* of the hippodrome, speaks vividly of the accruing cultural changes. Constantinople had greatly distanced itself from its *romanitas*.

With the 6th century the process of Christianization found new outlets of expression. Lavish religious complexes such as the St. Polyeuktos, built by the aristocrat Anicia Juliana, show that the enlightened classes, as religious patrons, were now as creative and uninhibited by imperial influence as they were active. At the same time, the emperor Justinian pursued his markedly religious building program in Constantinople as vigorously as in other parts of the empire. Two of the most notable examples are the Church of SS. Sergius and Bacchus, erected within the mushrooming Great Palace complex, and the newly reconstructed Hagia Sophia, which replaced an earlier structure destroyed during the Nika riot of 532. Inaugurated in 562, Hagia Sophia was as daring as it was innovative in its articulation of the domed basilica plan on such a grand scale. It soon became a defining symbol of Constantinople as a Christianizing capital.

Constantinople arguably reached its peak in the opening decades of the 6th century. The city's impressive infrastructure was now complete, the population had been growing steadily, the monumental layout and urban decor reflected an elegant if eccentric mixture of tastes and materials brought in from all corners of the *oikoumenē*, and religious establishments of various sorts had filled out the city's landscape. The religious stamp of the capital was further marked by sanctuaries hosting holy relics, the most notable being the sanctuary of the Virgin of the Blachernae, which housed the Honorable Robe of the Virgin.

All of this and much more was available to Constan-

tinoplitans until 542, when a plague decimated the city and dramatically upset its social life, economic productivity, and defense capabilities. The loss of Egypt and most of Asia Minor in the subsequent century further weakened Constantinople's position. The Persian and Arab sieges of 626 and 717–718, respectively, both of which brought the city to the brink of disaster, demonstrated the point further. Modern historians generally point to a complete break in urban continuity during this era. Archaeologists may be inclined to reserve judgment on the degree of urban decline, however, until further material evidence comes forth.

BIBL.: Gilbert Dagron, *Naissance d'une capitale: Constantinople et ses institutions de 330 à 441* (Paris, 1974). Cyril Mango, *Le développement urbain de Constantinople (IVe–VIIe siècles)* (Paris, 1990). Wolfgang Müller-Wiener, *Bildlexikon zur Topographie Istanbuls* (Tübingen, 1977).

A.RIC.

Contraception and Abortion

The Romans employed a variety of birth control methods: sexual abstinence, coitus interruptus, contraceptives, abortion, and infanticide. Of these means, drug contraceptives and abortifacients appear most frequently in medical, religious, and legal texts as well as in anecdotal evidence in literary sources.

Because the marriage age was young, fourteen and fifteen years of age for women, delayed marriage was a strategy not employed on a sufficiently large scale to alter the population. In the late 3rd and the 4th centuries, Christians advocated stricter codes for sexual activity, notably approving sex only between married couples, but it is questionable how extensive the results were. Barrier methods, such as condoms, were seldom employed; it is unlikely that condoms existed. Rhythm, or timing intercourse for the least fertile period, was either not used or was ineffective because the period of maximum fertility enhancement was poorly understood. Male withdrawal before climax *(coitus interruptus; amplexus reservatus)* was not extensively used. By the 4th century Christians cited Genesis 38, in which the "sin of Onan," for which God took his life, was "spilling his seed on the ground," a statement they interpreted as prohibiting male withdrawal in general. (Now the Genesis passage is understood to mean that God was angry because Onan refused to sire a child by his brother's wife.) Infanticide, practiced by early Romans, was increasingly condemned, although never criminalized, during the empire.

Ancient society and, with it, Roman law, did not recognize or protect fetal life. A single exception to this was the rule to protect the unborn child of a husband. In this case, a woman was not free to abort; if she did so, she could be charged with committing a felonious act. With this exception, however, women were free to regulate their reproduction, and judging by contemporary accounts as well as modern estimates of population size, Roman women had fewer children than if there had been no purposeful intervention.

Juvenal said that "we have surefire contraceptive and abortion drugs" (*Satire* 6.595–596). Ancient vocabulary distinguished between contraception (*atokios, sterilus*) and abortion (*phthorion, abortum*). Soranus, who lived during the time of Trajan and Hadrian and wrote about gynecology and birth control, said that contraceptives were preferable to abortifacients, and that oral drug contraceptives were better than those administered as vaginal suppositories. A number of herbs were taken to stimulate or block reproductive hormonal actions in women. Women, in particular, seem generally to have possessed the knowledge that medical writers record. Important plants, contraceptives, and abortifacients were rue, chaste tree, pomegranate, juniper, pennyroyal, Queen Anne's lace, and the squirting cucumber.

Stoic philosophy raised the question of when life begins and concluded that it began when the neonatal infant took its first breath of air, but that the potential for life began with fetal development. A few Romans, such as Pliny the Elder, opposed contraception and abortion, but there was no systematic attack on such practices by most ancient peoples. Christian writers condemned abortion after the formation of the fetus (when it was thought capable of independent life), but they were divided on the subject of contraception and, for the most part, did not reject early-term abortifacients. In elucidating Exodus 21:22, Augustine wrote: "If what is brought forth is unformed [*informe*], but at this stage some sort of living, shapeless thing [*informiter*], then the law of homicide would not apply, for it could not be said that there was a living soul in that body, for it lacks all sense, if it be such as is not yet formed [*nondum formata*] and therefore not yet endowed with its senses" (*Quaestiones Exodi*, 80.1439–1445). Basil (ca. 330–379) spoke harshly against women who "destroyed a fetus," irrespective of "whether the fetus was formed or unformed." Even though opposition to birth control developed from the 3rd and 4th centuries, Roman women were largely free to exercise a number of effective birth control means.

BIBL.: Angus McLaren, *A History of Contraception from Antiquity to the Present Day* (Oxford, 1990). B. F. Musallam, *Sex and Society in Islam* (Cambridge, Eng., 1983). John M. Riddle, *Contraception and Abortion from the Ancient World to the Renaissance* (Cambridge, Mass., 1992). J.R.

Conversion

The history of conversion in late antiquity may be said to have begun with that of the emperor Constantine. Although interpretations differ as to the chronology of his conversion, it is clear that the emperor's religious affiliations developed over a long period of time. And while it can be said that he experienced some religious transformation at the time of the Battle of the Milvian Bridge in 312, he was not actually baptized until he was on his deathbed in 337, thus highlighting an important distinction between the psychological process of conversion and the *rite de passage* of baptism.

Constantine's conversion is only one of a number of high-profile changes of religion in the 4th century, each of which is distinctive. Julian, for instance, abandoned Christianity for paganism; Synesius of Cyrene clearly had difficulty rejecting his pagan Neoplatonism, despite being elected bishop of Ptolemais; Jerome and Augustine of Hippo, by contrast, both experienced deep psychological and spiritual crises, and in each case the conversion was not from paganism to Christianity, but from nominal Christianity to a far greater spiritual commitment.

The famous conversions of the later Roman empire, therefore, are individual experiences. It is also possible to identify the working of imperial influence, chains of patronage, and the developing influence of the church—exerted through preaching, the liturgy, and patronage, as well as pressures exerted by pious governors and zealous ascetics, notably in Egypt. This process may usefully be described as Christianization, to distinguish it from the personal conversion of individuals. The Christianization of the empire as a whole was thus an extremely complex set of developments, religious, cultural, social, and political. It was also an extended process: as late as the controversy over the Altar of Victory in 382, pagans and Christians could both claim to be in the majority in the Senate.

The conversion of barbarians is represented in a very different way in the sources: there is rarely much detailed evidence for the conversion of an individual, and there is nothing to compare with the psychological detail available in the *Confessions* for the spiritual development of Augustine of Hippo. Nor is the Christianization of whole barbarian peoples represented as being the same complex process it was for the peoples of the Roman empire: rather, the conversion of a ruler or leader went hand in hand with or was followed shortly after by the Christianization of his people.

Despite the presence of Christians among the Visigoths prior to their entry into the empire in 376, the Christianization of the people seems to have been a condition of their settlement on Roman soil. What spiritual developments took place must have followed official conversion, and were apparently carried out largely by Ulfilas and his disciples. In many ways the Visigoths provide a model for the representation of the subsequent conversion of many other tribes. Christianization often followed entry into the Roman empire (although one should note that some tribes, like the Thuringians, who never entered the empire, seem to have converted relatively early), and the whole tribe was supposedly converted at once. Further, because Ulfilas accepted the established doctrines of the 360s and 370s that were subsequently to be condemned as Arian, the Christianity accepted by the Visigoths came to be regarded as Arianism; and since the Visigoths played a role in the Christianization of other Germanic peoples, Arianism was initially the dominant form of Christianity among those peoples.

Traditionally the first Germanic king to convert directly from paganism to Catholicism was Clovis, and by extension, the first Germanic people to become Catholic were the Franks. In fact this statement needs some modification: the Suebi were certainly Catholics and were ruled by Catholic kings long before Clovis's conversion, and the Burgundians may also have been, although Gundobad, who ruled between ca. 476 and 516, was unquestionably Arian. Further, it is clear that Clovis spent some time considering the rival merits of the Catholic and Arian variants of Christianity.

The Burgundians finally abandoned Arianism in 516, while the Visigoths made a clear break with the heresy at the Third Council of Toledo in 589, following the accession of King Reccared. The Lombards, late entrants into the empire and thus latecomers to Christianity, continued to hesitate between Arianism and Catholicism until the mid-7th century.

The conversion of Ethelbert of Kent and the Christianization of the Anglo-Saxons marks the end of the expansion of Christianity among the direct successors to the Roman empire. In certain respects, however, the Christianization of England presented particular problems. Unlike the kingdoms established within what had been the Continental lands of the western Roman empire, the English had not accepted Latin as an official language. The conversion of Ethelbert and subsequently of Edwin of Northumbria thus posed linguistic problems, which certainly troubled Gregory the Great's chosen missionary to England, Augustine of Canterbury. Nevertheless Augustine achieved great success, supposedly baptizing ten thousand people at Christmas 597, within one year of his arrival in Kent. One factor underlying this success was supposedly Augustine's success as a wonder-worker. The conversion of Ethelbert himself also had an impact on other kings in southern England who acknowledged his overlordship.

In contrast to the history of the Christianization of Germanic kingdoms on the Continent, a recurrent feature of the Christianization of the English kingdoms was a subsequent lapse into paganism. In the case of Kent, this was led by Ethelbert's son, Eadbald, who seems not to have been converted with his father, thus suggesting either that the Christianization of England differed from that of the Continental successor states, or that the representation of Christianization on the Continent is oversimple. Like Kent, other Anglo-Saxon kingdoms experienced a period of apostasy after initial Christianization. In the south of England the second phase of Christianization was carried out, like the first phase, by Continental missionaries: in Northumbria, however, the second and lasting attempt at Christianization was carried out by Irish monks, led by Aidan from the monastery of Iona. The final Anglo-Saxon kingdom to be Christianized was Sussex, ca. 680. With that the initial phase of the Christianization of the barbarian peoples was concluded.

Effectively the territories once held by Rome were all Christian at this point, although the Danube region was to present problems until the Christianization of the Hungarians in the 10th century. Further, although the focus of Christianization before the 8th century was largely on what was or what had been part of the Roman empire, some had rather wider visions: notably, in the 5th century, Pope Celestine, who wished to spread Christianity in Ireland; Patrick, who worked in Ireland of his own accord; and Amandus, who attempted to evangelize the Slavs in the 7th century.

Conversion to Islam required only an oral statement of faith in the presence of another person. There was no baptism or formal ceremony. During Muhammad's mission in Mecca, in early Islamic Medina, and in Muslim communities in the early Islamic empire, conversion would have involved participation in communal worship and the fulfillment of other ritual obligations. Mass conversion was rare and was usually a consequence of capitulation. It occurred primarily among the pagan tribes of Arabia at the time of Muhammad and among the Berbers in North Africa during the Muslim conquests of the second half of the 7th century. In most parts of the early Islamic empire, however, conversion was not encouraged, and the Muslims remained a small elite who ruled over a predominantly non-Muslim population. Those from the subject populations who did convert typically entered into a client relationship with an Arab Muslim. This was the main way in which non-Arab converts were assimilated into Muslim communal life. Non-Arab converts often took Arab names. Circumcision of male children was condoned in Islam, and it was an important sign of being a Muslim. The issue of circumcision arises occasionally in discussions of suspected apostasy, particularly among the sons or grandsons of converts in areas such as Iran.

BIBL.: Richard W. Bulliet, *Conversion to Islam in the Medieval Period* (Cambridge, Mass., 1979). Ramsay MacMullen, *Christianizing the Roman Empire (A.D. 100–400)* (New Haven, 1984). Michael Morony, "The Age of Conversions: A Reassessment," in *Conversion and Continuity: Indigenous Christian Communities in Islamic Lands,* ed. Michael Gervers and Ramzi Jibran Bikhazi (Toronto, 1990). F. Thélamon, *Païens et chrétiens au IVe siècle* (Paris, 1981). Frank R. Trombley, *Hellenic Religion and Christianization c. 370–529,* 2 vols. (Leiden, 1993–1994). I. N. Wood, "Pagans and Holy Men," *Ireland and Europe: The Bible and the Missions,* ed. P. Ní Chatháin and M. Richter (Stuttgart, 1987), 347–361. I.W.

Copts

The term *Copt* refers nowadays to a Christian people
of Egypt who are in many ways culturally distinct from
the Arab-Islamic majority. It should be noted that contemporary Copts' venerable linguistic and religious
heritages have influenced our use of the term for the
period of late antiquity, although there was no such
designation then. *Copt* is an anglicized version of the
Arabic *Qibt*, which was itself a variant of the Greek
Aigyptios, meaning, simply, Egyptian. Throughout late
antiquity, "Egyptian" had a generic sense, but there
were specific cultural connotations as well. Egyptian
could also be used negatively to emphasize non-Greek
(or non-Roman) cultural identity. Egyptian identity,
then, was viewed along a spectrum paralleling that of
"Hellene," an indicator of incorporation into the cultural hegemony of the late Roman empire that continued to evolve along with the spread of Christianity.
Later Arab usage of *Qibt* referred similarly to the Arab
context, meaning non-Muslim and, until the 9th century, non-Arabic-speaking. Consequently, diachronic
cultural developments during and after late antiquity
are critical to our understanding of who and what is
meant by the term *Copt*.

In late antique Egypt, the population was mixed, not
as a homogenized Greco-Egyptian culture but, as one
New York City mayor once said, as "a glorious human
mosaic." The chief part of the population was surely
Egyptian in a modern racial sense of the term; however, specifics of actual ethnic identities are difficult to
discern in the terse prose of tax rolls and census records, where proper names, for example, drew from
Greek, Egyptian, and biblical traditions. The Ptolemaic dynasty had introduced a small but privileged
class of Greeks, and indeed, until after the Arab conquest, the Greek-speaking east provided the cultural
matrix for Egypt's administrators and social elite. Language is essential to any discussion of late antique
Egyptian culture: Roman and Byzantine Egypt were
multilingual, and Greek, not Coptic, was the official
language for legal transactions. Moreover, it is from
the long-Hellenized stratum of society—who conducted business in Greek, read Greek literature, and
composed in Greek—that we have a great deal of our
documentary evidence. Thus, it should be noted that
our historical narratives may be skewed in favor of the
arrangements made in their wills, the running of their
estates, and the administration of their cities. Archaeological projects have also focused on urban sites,
finding, predominantly, Greek city planning and architecture as well as the production and consumption of
Greek-style goods. In contrast, the next largest category of archaeological efforts, which explored monasteries as the rural, antisecular, and mainly Egyptian
counterparts (indeed, opponents) of cities, instead
found material remains attesting to the same broad
cultural repertory.

This complexly multicultural population has been
much discussed in recent years, and there is presently
an insistence on reevaluating the previously alleged antagonism between city and hinterland, especially the
nationalism of rural and monastic Egyptians, who
were seen in opposition to the Hellenized populations
of the cities, populations that had been thought to be
strongholds of a dying paganism. Some Greek texts,
it is clear, do adopt a pejorative tone toward rustic
Egyptians, and this may well reflect the urban social
contexts of these texts rather than a religious divide
between city and countryside or ethnic animosity between Greek and Copt. It should be remembered, for
example, that apostolic tradition looks to St. Mark's
mission in Alexandria, Egypt's premier city, as the root
of all Christianity in Egypt. Current scholarship recognizes Christian activity in cities where, in the 5th century, for example, bishops became increasingly important urban administrators, as did priests and deacons
in town and village administration. At the same time,
churches and monasteries began to appear as significant landowners in both city and countryside.

Religion is key to any description of the emergence
of Copts as a distinct group. In Egypt, as elsewhere,
late antiquity was a time of religious coexistence, transition, and turmoil. Throughout the period, Jews were
a significant, legally recognized minority, who maintained considerable social and economic interaction
with the rest of the population. Polytheists, in the
majority at the beginning of the 3rd century, participated in official government-sponsored persecutions of
Christians until the end of the 3rd century. Imperial
toleration of Christianity encouraged conversion, and
during the late 4th or early 5th century, the balance
tipped in favor of a Christian majority. Outbreaks of
persecutions of pagans by Christians ensued. There
was, however, no single united Christian community in
late antique Egypt. Most significant for the continued
multiplicity of Christian sects in Egypt was the Monophysite controversy of the mid-5th century. This debate over the nature of Christ split the eastern church
in half. Against the Dyophysite Greek church based in
Constantinople, there were Monophysite churches in
Egypt, Syria, and Armenia, as well as in Nubia and
Ethiopia, which lay outside the empire's administration but well within its sphere of influence. In the 7th
century, Heraclius attempted unsuccessfully to defuse
the situation by introducing the compromise theology
of Monothelitism, and for the last decade of Byzantine
rule, Egyptian Monophysites endured persecutions by
the Melkites. Silence in both Coptic and Greek documents on the subject of the Arab conquest is especially
suggestive. Was there greater freedom for religious
practice in the early years of Arab domination? Certainly Egypt entered a different cultural orbit after the
Arab conquest, as Egyptians—overwhelmingly Christians by this time—were subject to the poll tax required of all non-Muslims and gradually, as a conse-

quence of assimilation and emigration, declined to a minority population. As a result of this change in status and relative cultural identification, what we mean by "Copt" is a product of both the Arab conquest and the triumph of Monophysitism in Egyptian Christianity.

BIBL.: G. W. Bowersock, *Hellenism in Late Antiquity* (Ann Arbor, 1990). A. K. Bowman, *Egypt after the Pharaohs, 332 BC–AD 642: From Alexander to the Arab Conquest* (Berkeley, 1986). F. D. Friedman, *Beyond the Pharaohs: Egypt and the Copts in the 2nd to 7th Centuries AD* (Providence, 1989). Gawdat Gabra, *Cairo: The Coptic Museum and Old Churches* (Cairo, 1993). *Graeco-Coptica: Griechen und Kopten in byzantinischen Ägypten,* ed. P. Nagel (Halle, 1984).

T.T.

Corruption

Much in vogue in recent decades for obvious topical reasons that have made it an object of general interest, the theme of corruption has not advanced the study of late antiquity, at least when scholars have been content to paraphrase without critical distance the discourse of witnesses and actors of the time, who spoke endlessly on the subject. Ambrose was distressed that *"omnia pretio distrahebantur"* ("everything was sold for a price"): an eternal theme. From Libanius to the anonymous *De rebus bellicis,* from Basil of Caesarea to Synesius, accusations of corruption rained down on provincial governors. The criticism extended to their subordinates as well, from Basil of Caesarea's homily against the rich (adapted by Ambrose in *De Nabuthae historia*) to the *Institutio Traiani* (under Honorius). It is customary to cite Valens's letter (370) on the abuses of provincial justice: "While a grasping advocate is briefed, the *princeps* who guards the door of the court is softened by large bribes, the record of the trial is sold by shorthand clerks, those who administer justice demand more in fees [*commodi nomine*] from the successful litigant than his opponent is going to pay him" (*C.Th.* 1.29.5; trans. A. H. M. Jones). That observation appears even darker in that it was supposed to justify the creation of the *defensor civitatis,* an economic justice system accessible to the *rustici* (peasants). It has been easy to characterize the emperors' attitude as impotence (MacMullen) or, more subtly, as hypocrisy (Veyne, who accuses the emperors of being quick to encourage what they pretended to repress).

Above all, corruption in late antiquity consisted of influence peddling in two forms, *suffragium* and *patrocinium. Suffragium,* which spread in the 4th century, was a debased form of *commendatio,* which had been practiced in earlier periods. We know that in Roman practice, the nominator of a man for office was responsible for his nominee and named himself in writing as his guarantor. The recommendation, though committing its author less stringently, could also appear as a moral guarantee. That explains, for example, the sys-

tem of naming *agentes in rebus* through *petitio,* or the recognized right of a certain number of administrative staff members to nominate a candidate, with a limit of one per year (*C.Th.* 6.27.8, year 396). The degeneration of the system arose when the support given by high-placed or influential figures was remunerated. This was encouraged by the candidates themselves, who began to multiply when an honorary office no longer procured merely honorific advantages (for example, when Fronto recommended Appian to Antoninus Pius) but rather offered the same considerable privileges (tax exemptions, fixed services) that imperial authorities attached to the real exercise of public duties. Hence we have the contract of 345 between an Egyptian curial and Abinnaeus, an Egyptian officer leaving for the comitatus in the east: it required the *curialis* to obtain an *epistula exactoriae* for the officer and committed him to reimburse all expenses incurred by the action *(P Abinnaeus 58).* The *suffragium* also functioned as a request for undue or accelerated promotion, and to oppose that practice, the emperors first sought to impose the rule of advancement based on seniority. Later they tolerated the *suffragium* (beginning with the Valentinians), and finally they recognized it by codifying it (394).

The concept of *patrocinium* (protection) provides a good illustration of the ambivalence of this entire semantic field. A single term, initially neutral and descriptive, could, depending on the context, acquire either a positive or a negative value: it could refer to a legitimate defense of the weak (*C.Th.* 1.29.1, the *patrocinium* granted to the peasants by the *defensor*), or to reprehensible influence peddling (*C.Th.* 12.1.34, concerning the *honorariae dignitates*), or even to the protection of colonists against taxation in exchange for their work or their land (Libanius). Hence it is easy to understand why corruption, which twisted certain fundamental principles of the Roman administration, was so difficult to eradicate.

Current interest in the corruption of the later empire appears to be largely a by-product of the theme of "decadence," though it has managed to escape the latter's disrepute. Before lamenting what is believed to be the degradation of Roman public morality, we would need to know more about what was going on previously. Hence, venality of offices already existed under the republic, as a means for obtaining a place within the *ordo scribarum* (Cicero, *Verr.* 3.184), and continued under the empire. In addition, numerous texts invoked to demonstrate corruption have been misinterpreted, although this does not call into question the spread of the phenomenon. Thus, the expression *stationes vendere* (*C.Th.* 8.4.10) must be dissociated from the problem of venality of offices and attributed, rather, to the sale of tax *stationes,* that is, collection duties. The practice of being replaced by a *vicarius,* or of supplementing one's official salary with fees and perquisites from the public, also goes back to the republican era. Fourth century emperors who reaffirmed the privilege of scribes *(decuriales),* now provincialized, to be paid for publishing legal documents (*C.Th.* 8.9.1) and extended it to all provincial *officiales* were thus following a long tradition. The savings thus realized on public salaries had to be made up by users, who were forced to pay the cost of a venal and corrupt justice system.

BIBL.: C. Kelly, "Later Roman Bureaucracy: Going through the Files: Literacy and Power in the Ancient World," ed. A. K. Bowman and G. Wolf (Cambridge, Eng., 1994), 161–176. Wolfgang Schuller, ed., *Korruption im Altertum: Kostanzer Symposium . . . 1979* (Munich, 1982). Richard Talbert, review of Ramsay MacMullen's *Corruption and the Decline of Rome* (New Haven, 1988) in *Phoenix* 45 (1991): 85–87. Paul Veyne, "Clientèle et corruption au service de l'état: La vénalité des offices dans le bas-empire romain," *Annales* 36 (1981): 339–360.   J.C.

Councils

The council was the ruling municipal body in every town of the empire. Council members numbered in the hundreds in the big cities and a few dozen in the small centers. The members of the councils, the *curiales,* were landowners willing to assume the honors and burdens of local government. From what evidence we have, in late antiquity there was no great competition to obtain the magistratures that were held in turn by the *curiales*—or at least by those who were the most powerful and wealthy. In the first centuries of the empire, the council would either present the people with a list of candidates among whom they might choose or, alternatively, submit single names to be approved. In late antiquity the elections did not provide for any form of popular participation and the whole procedure of nomination began and ended in the council. Only Africa seems to have been an exception: we can infer from a law of Constantine that there, electoral procedure included some form of popular approval.

The recruitment of new members for the councils was by co-optation, and sons and descendants of *curiales* normally represented the first choice. Membership presupposed property of land, and normally entry was barred to the *liberti,* but not to their sons. The emperors of late antiquity never tied people to the work and status of their father, and consequently membership in the councils was not hereditary by law. Sons of *curiales* might decline the position; new landowners might seek it. The chief preoccupation of the emperors and municipalities was practical: the lands of the *curiales* were subject to the obligations of providing wood, stones, oil, and other material for the maintenance of civic life. They feared only that lands belonging to the *curiales* might be transferred to another, non-*curialis* owner and be lost to local needs.

The *curiae* or *bouleutēria* were the meeting places of the councils, and the councils kept the acta of their meetings and deliberations. From the 4th century, imperial laws required that private documents be kept in the municipal archives after being certified by a local magistrate. This procedure, the *insinuatio,* gave a surer legal value to the documents because it prevented falsification.

The lack of a solid central government, and barbarian incursions into the provinces of the empire in the hard days of the 3rd century, affected the mentality and the behavior of the members of the local leading class. They became much more individualistic, seeking personal power in a more ruthless way, and they lost in great part the desire to assume burdens for their town and fellow citizens. The powerful *curiales* of late antiquity enhanced their personal power with grand private houses and sought popular fame by organizing magnificent games, but, with some good exceptions, they were less interested in the upkeep of public buildings and in enhancing local cultural life. This process of disaffection was accelerated by the grand project of restoring and renovating the structures of government initiated by Diocletian. The *curiales* saw their duties increase sharply; at the same time, they astutely perceived that by entering the imperial bureaucracy they could push the authorities for exemption from their curial obligations. The poorest among the *curiales* often tended to escape from the councils by entering the army or leaving their town for the service of some powerful landowner. The flight of *curiales* from the councils constituted a major trend in late antiquity, and as a result the councils and the towns were to a certain extent impoverished. But the process was not uniform, and we know of rich *curiales* and their munificence in Africa until the Vandalic invasion, and in the eastern provinces until the last part of the 5th century.

Another blow to city life was given by a law issued by Constantine or Constantius II according to which the central government confiscated municipal money derived from the renting of public lands and various other kinds of local taxes. Subsequently, after a total restitution of these funds to the towns was ordered by Julian, many laws were issued on the subject, but generally the towns were permitted to retain only a part of their revenues.

The process of disaffection of the *curiales* toward their towns can be seen clearly in the deterioration of urban plans, a trend that emerged from Theodosius's reign and is attested by imperial laws and the archaeological evidence. The lessening of attention paid to a city's appearance and monuments testifies to a change in local elites' tastes and interests. For example, spaces in the archways were filled with shops, and new buildings, mostly for commercial use, invaded the forums and pushed out into the streets. Against such development, laws failed to curb the greed of the local ruling classes, who very often were in collusion with provincial governors.

In big provincial capitals powerful local elites still struggled for preeminence, and the governors were involved in these political struggles. Alliances between a governor and some dominating group of *curiales* were perhaps more common than confrontations between the council as a body and the imperial administrator.

In the second half of the 4th century the legal privileges held by the *curiales* were undermined because they lost their immunity from corporal punishment. Immunity was thenceforth reserved by law for the so-called *principales*, a select group of rich and influential members of the councils who had held all the *munera* and the magistratures and to whom the emperors gave honorary rank in the imperial administration.

It is hard to assess the process of change in the councils during the 5th century. It is certain that in the east some cities were rich and were led by powerful *curiales*. On the other hand, it is hard to believe that in the Balkan area, struck by barbarian invasions, many towns were able to maintain their traditional civic life; and there are great doubts about the survival of the councils in Vandalic Africa. In Italy the invasions caused civic life to come almost to a stop, but according to the emperor Majorian, the *curiales* were still considered the backbone of the empire.

Justinian tried to revitalize the councils, but in his time the process of decline of the *curiae* was almost complete: according to the complaint in *Novella* 38 (536), at that time there were only a few councillors in the towns, and they were not rich people. Among *curiales* the practice of selling their property to be freed from their duty toward the city became more and more widespread. John Lydus, who wrote after 550, remembered the meetings of the councils as a thing of the past. In his time, the cities were ruled according to a totally new system, by the bishops who kept the archives and by the rich landowners. In the west, the council remained an institution capable of certifying and preserving legal documents at Rieti (557) and at Ravenna until 625.

BIBL.: F. Jacques, *Le privilège de liberté* (Rome, 1984). Claude Lepelley, *Les cités de l'Afrique au bas-empire*, vol. 1 (Paris, 1979). Ariel Lewin, *Assemblee popolari e lotta politica nelle città dell'impero romano* (Florence, 1995), 89–112. J. H. W. G. Liebeschuetz, *Antioch: City and Imperial Administration in the Later Roman Empire* (Oxford, 1972).

A.L.

Countryside

The importance of the countryside in antiquity is obvious: the economy was primarily agricultural, peasants made up the bulk of the population, and the main tax was assessed on land. This was even more true for late antiquity. Because of urban decline, ornate mausoleums and sumptuous villa estates attest a stronger elite presence in the countryside. Yet the countryside has long been neglected by historians.

It is indeed difficult to give an accurate picture of the countryside in late antiquity, given the heterogeneity and the bias—or worse, the silence—of our sources. Literary texts, written by and for an urban elite, usually do not pay much attention to the countryside and its inhabitants, and often reproduce classical topoi. The only agricultural treatise for the period (Palladius, mid-5th century) lays down more or less the same rules as Columella (1st century). The legal documents are mostly interested in taxation. Inscriptions and papyri come from the viewpoint of the properted classes and are largely the voice of urban populations and interests. The mosaic pavements of rural villas, far from reflecting the surrounding countryside, usually offer to the landowner a reassuring image of his own wealth or an ideal setting for his favorite leisure.

But the recent proliferation of archaeological surface surveys has made possible a major breakthrough in rural history. It is too early even to attempt a synthesis encompassing the whole late antique world, but there are enough results to demolish the view once prevalent that most independant farmers came under the domination of rich landlords, and to seriously challenge the bleak picture of a general decay of rural life in late antiquity owing to a shortage of manpower and an increasing tax burden. North Africa, at least before the Vandal raids, was famous for its wealth. Even in Italy, which undoubtedly suffered badly from barbarian incursions, the pattern varies from place to place: the reduction of farm sites in Etruria from the 2nd to the 6th century can be opposed to the massive increase in rural activity in Lombardy during the 4th century and a major upturn in rural productivity with the Ostrogoth king Theoderic. The late Roman period was also marked by a dramatic recovery in Greece. In the east, we are particularly well informed about Syria, where the rural vitality and dense population are attested, up to the mid-6th century, with large and well-built villages. The Mediterranean coast of Asia Minor shows a strikingly parallel development. In Egypt, tax documents suggest the permanence of small independent farming next to large estates. In short, it has become obvious that different regions must be treated on their own terms.

To complement these fragmentary data, one can also point out some major continuities and changes in the perceptions, positive and negative, of the countryside. Most of the members of the urban upper class, pagan and Christian alike, still relished a civilized countryside adorned by beautiful houses and pleasant vineyards and fields, and populated by benevolent landowners and tenants full of respect and gratitude. But because of the growing insecurity, the country villa surrounded by a garden was replaced by the castle. Poets of late antiquity, such as Claudian and Venantius Fortunatus

(6th century), praise a countryside protected "by so many rivers and fortresses" and "the mighty towers contrasting with the peace of field and vineyard." They still celebrate the country as a place for relief and leisure, far removed from the troubles of the city. But with the rise of asceticism, the "desert" and the dread vastness of solitude successfully compete with the graciousness of the gardens and the charms of a cultivated countryside, as demonstrated by a famous letter of Basil.

The countryside also remained a foil for the values of urban and Christian life. Beside its pleasing prospects, there is the dismal picture of "fields ruined by the war and land becoming wild again" (Claudius Namantianus), with greedy landowners eager to enlarge their estate, poor farmers oppressed by tax collectors and helped by holy monks, boorish peasants sometimes turned into ruthless bandits. As opposed to the Christian cities, the countryside, with its *pagi* (dispersed settlements), is often perceived as the last stronghold of paganism and a safe retreat for outlawed sects and heretics. When it is praised, it is for negative reasons: in contrast to the city, which is filled with impiety, the peasants are "purer than gold on account of their innocence and simplicity" *(Life of Simeon the Fool)*. This is enough to suggest that the countryside, for better and for worse, was still perceived from the viewpoint of the town, as an opposite.

During the first two centuries of Muslim rule, two contradictory attitudes prevailed. One emphasized the superiority of urban living and tended to denigrate the country as lacking in cultured amenities. The other saw in the country, primarily the desert, a place where traditional, especially linguistic, values were preserved.

BIBL.: N. Christie, "Barren Fields? Landscapes and Settlements in Late Roman and Post-Roman Italy," in *Human Landscapes in Classical Antiquity,* ed. G. Shipley and J. Salmon (London, 1996). P. van Ossel, *Établissements ruraux de l'antiquité tardive dans le Nord de la Gaule, Gallia* Supp. 51 (Paris, 1992). P. Périn, "La part du Haut Moyen Age dans la génèse des terroirs de la France médiévale," *Le roi en France et son royaume autour de l'an mil* (Paris, 1992), 225–234. M. Roberts, "The Description of Landscape in the Poetry of Venantius Fortunatus: The Moselle Poems," *Traditio* 49 (1994): 1–22. L. Schneider, *Die Domäne als Weltbild* (Wiesbaden, 1983). S.S.

Crime and Punishment

The empires and states that ruled over Europe, the Mediterranean, the Fertile Crescent, and Iran from the 4th to the 9th century classified human acts as crimes and inflicted punishment on their authors in the light of political, religious, and social traditions they both upheld and redefined. The *Codex Theodosianus* (438 C.E.), Justinian's *Corpus Iuris Civilis* (534 C.E.), and the Germanic codes of the 5th to 7th centuries consti-

tute attempts to codify the legal dimension of the political traditions and to assign it a normative function. Religious traditions also partook in this effort: the Talmud, which took its written form between the 2nd and the beginning of the 6th century; the priests of Mazdaism, who shaped Sassanian religious policy; the burgeoning canon law and the popes; the bishops in the Byzantine commonwealth and the Germanic kingdoms; and the *qaḍīs'* jurisprudence in the Muslim caliphate all defined crimes against religion or the state. The importance of ethnical legal traditions is underlined by the codes of the Germanic kingdoms, which often refer to the personality of the law.

Late antiquity was a period of normative pluralism. Though corporal and capital punishment were mainly administered by secular institutions, religious courts and norms played a major role. Even though the Roman authorities, after 212, considered Jewish jurisdiction as mere arbitration, they tolerated capital punishment imposed by Jewish courts. In the Sassanian empire, religious courts existed side by side with secular ones and the decisions of the high priest were without appeal. The Christian church exerted jurisdiction over crimes of clerics in the Byzantine empire and the Frankish kingdom. In the Muslim empire, Islamic law was applied by the *qaḍīs*, who were nominated by the caliphs. Other forms of justice of a more political character existed side by side with the *qaḍī* courts, and non-Muslims were allowed to exert their own jurisdiction over their religious communities.

None of the legal systems of late antiquity defined its structure in terms of a clear division between civil and penal law. Many of them (the Germanic codes, the custom of the Slavs, Jewish and Muslim law) defined the infliction of bodily harm on another person as a private offense: action against the perpetrator had to be brought by the victim or by his next of kin. The culprit had to pay a monetary compensation, and tariff systems for the various limbs and wounds regulated the amount of the compensation to be paid. But if the victim did not sue the perpetrator, the private offense of bodily harm entailed no legal consequences.

All legal systems of late antiquity defined crimes that had to be punished by the ruler or his judiciary (*crimina* in Roman law, *ḥudūd* in Islamic law). These were acts directed against the public order, religion, and the dominating sexual morality. Murder was a case on the borderline: it was defined as a crime in Jewish and Roman law, a mixed offense in Islamic law, and it could be either a public or a private offense in the Germanic codes.

In trials concerning crimes, most legal systems of late antiquity legalized the application of torture. The postclassical Roman judiciary utilized torture when investigating the *crimina laesae maiestatis*, crimes against the sovereign's sacrosanct dignity and power.

Their number was constantly increased by the emperor's *mandata* and *rescripta*. Even the persecution of the Christians under Roman law was justified not as a defense of religion but as the punishment of a *crimen laesae maiestatis*. In the Byzantine empire, crimes against the emperor were submitted to him and decided according to his instruction. Trials concerning corporal and capital punishments were mostly administered by military dignitaries. Witnesses in these trials were tortured routinely. The Sassanians applied torture in their trials against Manichaeans, Christians, and Mazdakites. The Germanic kingdoms applied torture whenever people were suspected of crimes against the state and religion. In addition to testimony of witnesses and avowals of the accused, they also recognized ordeals as means of proof. Only Jewish and Muslim law (in most of its law schools) took a strong doctrinal stance against judicial torture (which was not always heeded by the political authorities).

The monotheistic religions of late antiquity stressed the importance of the soul, but the political and legal systems concentrated their quest for punishment on the body (only Christian penitentials and Muslim *kaffarat* indicate a discipline based on the expiation of public offenses). The penalties fixed by the various doctrines of law included crucifixion (Roman and Muslim law), amputation (Jewish, Sassanian, and Muslim law), strangling or hanging (Jewish, Roman), and decapitation, imprisonment, and flogging. The praxis of all political systems of the era added an amazing array of mutilations, castrations *(lex salica),* blindings, and other torments. Only the Jewish legal doctrine, following theological (the concept of bodily resurrection) and political considerations, replaced older forms of execution, such as stoning and burning, with strangling, a less public form of execution that leaves fewer traces on the body. During late antiquity the tendency of not applying capital punishment at all became predominant in Jewish justice.

The political implications of the ruler's right to impose the death penalty on his subjects did not escape the peoples of late antiquity. The Muslim jurists, the Germanic codes, and the Slavic peoples were reluctant to grant the ruler power over the life and death of his subjects in matters of homicide. For the same reason, Muslim law had no equivalent to the *crimen laesae maiestatis,* which in postclassical Roman law among the Byzantines and, later, among the emperors of western Europe was the paradigmatic crime against the state. In Islamic law, the political leader of the community, according to the Hanafite jurists, was subject to the *ius talionis* for private offenses; he was not sacrosanct. But he could not be castigated for the abuse of his penal jurisdiction, because nobody else was entitled to punish in order to defend God's claims. The justification for the Muslim ruler's power over life and death was thus religious in character: he acted as God's representative in the defense of the divine law. According to the Hanafites, he was entitled to do so only where he ruled de facto: the limits of his political power defined the realm in which corporal and capital punishment according to sacred law could be legally applied. This limitation remained a matter of debate among Muslim jurists throughout late antiquity and beyond. But they all justified the ruler's power over life and death through his function as the protector of God's law and the representative of God's claims *(huquq allah)*.

Over and above the pluralism of judicial institutions and legal norms, a basic difference thus prevails in the sphere of crime, between the legal traditions of Judaism and Islam, on the one hand, and Rome, Byzantium, and Europe on the other: whereas for the first, the protection of true prophecy and divine law constituted the basic norm from which the ruler's power over the life and death of his subjects was derived, in the second group it was the protection of the sovereign's sacrosanct dignity and power. In late antiquity the second group turned out to be politically much less tolerant of religious pluralism than Muslim law, which became the most powerful representative of the sacred law tradition and adopted coexistence with other religions on the basis of their legal and political subordination to the Muslims and their rulers.

BIBL.: D. Bracken, "Immortality and Capital Punishment: Patristic Concepts in Irish Law," *Peritia* 9 (1995): 167–186. Centro Italiano di Studi sull'Alto Medioevo, *La giustizia nell'alto medioevo (secoli V–VIII),* 2 vols. (Spoleto, 1995). David Daube, *Collected Works, I: Talmudic Law,* ed. Calum M. Carmichael (Berkeley, 1992).   B.J.

Crowns

Among many purposes, crowns in late antiquity served as symbols of rulership, as accoutrements of office, as rewards, and as offerings in public and private ceremonies. The crown's symbolic message, usually referring to power, depended on its ritual function, design, and material, and was often based on Greek and Roman usages. These included dynastic, religious, military, honorific, dedicatory, and funerary functions, though no meaning remained absolutely discrete. The blending of coronal typologies, denotations, and nuanced connotations, for example to identify divinities, to differentiate the status of rulers, or to distinguish among victories (over enemies or death), was a major factor in their widespread use (see Pliny, *Natural History,* 21.1–9, 22.4–6).

Crowns ranged from ephemeral circlets of grass, leaves, and flowers to permanent insignia made of gold and gems. Their shapes also varied, from wide bands to diadems, tiaras, and *tainia* (ribbons). The type used depended on the ritual context as well as the status of the wearer. Although much was written about crowns from the 4th century B.C.E. to at least the 4th century C.E., relatively little of this literature remains.

Throughout the reigns of the Roman and early Byzantine emperors, contemporary Christian apologists developed significant interpretations of pagan crowns and what Christian attitudes toward them should be. One especially critical assessment was made by Tertullian *(De corona militis)*, reacting to military awards and their strictly pagan meanings. After the recognition of Christianity (Edict of Milan, 313) and the institution of imperial support of the church by Constantine I, who introduced the gem-studded diadem as an imperial insignia, the protocols of wearing and offering crowns *(aurum coronarium)* merged metaphorically as their symbolic interpretations became inextricably bound. This is vividly demonstrated in the late 4th century collection of poems, *Peristephanon,* by the Christian poet Prudentius.

The most important visual sources for imperial crowns are found on coins. Additionally, abundant contemporary works of Roman, Byzantine, and Sassanian art represent men and women wearing crowns at a wide variety of events.

There has been much debate as to whether and when crowns (Arabic, *taj*) came into use by Umayyad and early Abbasid rulers. Most of the texts arguing for an Umayyad usage are tendentious. However, representations of presumed Muslim rulers at Khirbat al-Mafjar and Qasr al-Hayr show them wearing imitations of Sassanian crowns, which could reflect the origins of the representations rather than actual practice. Early Arabic coins (before the reform of 692 that stopped images on coins) do not show crowns, but possibly a cylindrical cap known as the *qalansuwah.*

BIBL.: Pierre Bastien, *Le buste monétaire des empereurs romains,* 3 vols. (Wetteren, 1992–1994); Karl Baus, *Der Kranz in Antike und Christentum* (Theophaneia 2) (Bonn, 1940). Prudence O. Harper, *Silver Vessels of the Sasanian Period, vol.* 1: *Royal Imagery* (New York, 1981). G. C. Miles, "Mihrab and Anaza," *Archaeologica Orientalia in Memoriam Ernst Herzfeld* (Locust Valley, N.Y., 1952). S.Z.

Curiales

In late antiquity the members of the councils of the towns of the empire were called *curiales.* They had the honor of ruling the town and holding the traditional magistratures and enjoyed as well some legal privileges above other citizens. They were also charged with complex duties *(munera)* toward their town.

From the middle of the 3rd century, many provinces suffered from disruptions caused by barbarian raids; the lack of a strong central authority and widespread economic difficulties throughout the empire created a general feeling of uncertainty and growing individualism. At the same time, many towns required exceptional efforts and great expense for the restoration of their public buildings and the reorganization of civic services. And another, and in great part new, burden derived from the emperors themselves, for they needed a constant supply of food and clothing for their armies and their bureaucracy, which also entailed the erection of buildings and structures to house the growing central administration; consequently, further time-consuming duties and expenses fell on the *curiales.*

Two main trends appeared in late antiquity: first, *curiales* increasingly judged *munera* as excessive, and second, Diocletian and his successors actively sought educated men to serve in the imperial bureaucracy. Many *curiales* entered into imperial service and immediately requested to be freed of their duties toward their town. In a short time, service in the bureaucracy, in the army, and, with the rising of the Christian empire, in the clergy automatically conferred an exemption from curial duties. Buying fictitious codicils of rank, which gave exemption from curial duties, became widespread. *Curiales* who were not wealthy often tried to escape from their duties by fleeing their town and entering the service of powerful landowners. Until the end of antiquity the emperors struggled to block illegal channels of escape from the councils. Not all *curiales* of late antiquity were in difficulty, however. There is evidence for the existence of rich and powerful *curiales* in some areas of the empire well into the 5th century. It is easy to imagine that, when they strove to enter the highest levels of the imperial administration, the wealthy did so for personal ambition. In the biggest towns, the councils were bodies with hundreds of members, but in the minor centers they might number not more than a few dozen; everywhere powerful magnates sat near small landowners. A great part of the misfortune of smallholding *curiales* was caused by the domination of the more powerful councillors.

From the second half of the 4th century, the most powerful group in the councils, the *principales,* obtained by law particular power and privileges above those of the other *curiales* who, in the same period, were losing their traditional immunity from the harshest punishments the law reserved for the *humiliores.* Nonetheless, in the first half of the 5th century the bishop of Marseilles, Salvianus, denounced the *curiales* as a class of powerful oppressors of the people.

What of municipal vitality survived was finally destroyed by the reforms of Anastasius. In Justinian's time the councils were agonizing, and he complained that the *curiales* were mostly people of few means. Some vestiges of the *curiales* seem to have persisted until the end of the 6th century or the beginning of the 7th, but it is difficult to assess the degree to which they could still be considered a ruling class.

BIBL.: Peter Brown, *The Making of Late Antiquity* (Cambridge, Mass., 1978), 47–53. Fergus Millar, "Empire and City, Augustus to Julian: Obligations, Excuses and Status," *Journal of Roman Studies* 73 (1983): 76–96. A.L.

Cursus Publicus

The *cursus publicus,* or public postal service, created during the reign of Augustus, was placed under the authority of praetorian prefects and governors during the late period. At the time of its greatest extension, the network stretched along 75,000 km. Major and minor stations (*mutationes* and *mansiones*), furnished with personnel and providing fresh mounts at closely spaced intervals, had to be secured. Of the two branches of the *cursus publicus,* the *cursus velox* seems to have been the more important; it allowed messengers and agents of the government to move rapidly from one end of the empire to the other, all the while taking only official routes. As for the heavy transport service *(cursus clabularis),* which is less well known and was not available throughout the entire network, it transported certain tax goods, in particular, clothing produced by state manufacturers. Historians have also linked it to the *annona militaris,* but the latter had its own circuits (the *res privata* also used organized transports, the *bastaga privata*). Wherever and whenever the "heavy" service did not exist, it was replaced by requisitioned transports *(angariae).*

The heavy transport service used oxen (Holmberg, Jones). Although John Lydus (*Mag.* 3.61) differentiated between the two branches on the basis of whether vehicles were used—a criterion that may have held true for his era—it seems we need to add to the usual list a service of somewhat heavy transport carried out by the *cursus velox:* light vehicles drawn by four or five pairs of mules (*C.Th.* 8.5.8) were used to transport loads of 1,000 to 1,500 pounds (less than 500 kg). Following Lefebvre-Desnouettes, that weight limit has been universally attributed to a supposed technological weakness of yokes in antiquity (*contra* Burford). A law of 386 (*C.Th.* 8.5.48) shows that, in reality, monetary freight was limited by security considerations rather than technology, since the maximum weight authorized for silver was double that for gold, and the weight authorized for the *largitionalia* double that for the *res privata.* Strong horses *(veredi)* in the rapid postal service could themselves serve to transfer public funds (*C.Th.* 8.5.47) in their saddle or in sealed official sacks. The permanent endowment for the *cursus* grew, and additional mounts, yokes, and vehicles (*paraveredi, parangariae*) were requisitioned temporarily, by means of a supplementary tax classified as *munera sordida.* The *cursus publicus* was also responsible for organizing these exceptional modes of transportation.

Under the Severi, the postal service was not operated by the military or by the state. The example of Pizos (Thrace) in the 3rd century shows that the need to free the army from managing a road *statio* led to the creation of an entirely new civic structure capable of providing the curials with the necessary support. For the tetrarchic era, the papyri of Panopolis confirm that stationmasters were civilians, designated by the *boulē* from among the low-ranking decurions or even from among noncurials. In this same text, the order to supply the *mansiones* temporarily in preparation for an imperial visit proves that the Severi had not given the stations the primary and permanent mission of centralizing the *annona militaris* in kind, to distribute it to the garrisons. The postal stations are not to be confused with the *thesauri* (granaries or warehouses of the public treasury).

Called indiscriminately *praepositus* or *manceps* (in the east, *conductor*), the head of a *mansio* was a *liturgus* named by his curia, except during a brief interlude under the Valentinians, when the curials were ousted. The stationmaster was assigned for five years. He was paid for his service but was required to be present at all times, an intolerable condition for the designates who, for that reason, seem to have frequently hired replacements. The staff of a *mansio,* which included an accountant *(tabularius),* a veterinarian, grooms, and rider-messengers, was designated by the word *familia.* This has led to the incorrect conclusion that they were public slaves; for a long time, *familia* had designated all sorts of civilian and military communities, not only servile groups.

The emperors continued to require restricted use of the postal service, limiting the manpower, the space for waiting mounts and vehicles, the number of daily movements, and the number of warrants *(evectiones)* issued. For the east, the *Notitia Dignitatum* indicates the annual allowance of warrants for each duke or vicar. In theory, there was a concern to contain the maintenance costs falling to the provincials. But by means of the allowances, the emperor could control and limit all movements of political and military staff: think of Ursicinus summoned from Nisibis to Milan by Constantius, *"acceptis litteris et copia rei vehiculariae data"* (Amm.Marc. 14.11.5). The ease with which the *agentes in rebus* moved from their official duties as controllers of the *cursus* to that of informers also becomes clear. The file on movements was carefully kept, as the extant registries of station leaders attest (*P Oxy.* 40.4087–4088). Despite such strict regulation, abuses multiplied, and emperors were the first to lavish warrants on their favorites (for example, on bishops traveling to synods).

In the eastern prefecture and in certain other provinces, the *cursus clabularis* was abandoned in 467–468 and replaced by requisitions or even contracts with private transporters. In Egypt in 610, however, the *cursus publicus* continued to exist in its two overland forms (*P Oxy.* 1.138) and in a river-based form (already mentioned in 318). It continued under Arab domination. The long-held theory of the decline of the Roman state organization has led commentators to assume that Egyptian great landowners developed a private postal system as the decay of the imperial postal service, reduced to using donkeys in place of horses, became more pronounced. These are but cruel shadows cast on the portrait of Justinianian greatness. In fact, that was not at all the case, since commentators mistook for privatization what was the assumption by the magnates' *oikoi* of previously municipal liturgies. This type of obligation might just as easily have fallen on professional guilds, as was the case in Oxyrhynchos during the same period (*P Gothenberg* 9).

The Roman-Byzantine *cursus publicus* had its counterpart in the Persian empire. An indispensable instrument for a state that extended its power over such a vast space, the *cursus publicus* was also a symbol of international standing, a particularly visible sign of a state with worldwide pretensions.

BIBL.: Alison M. Burford, "Heavy Transport in Classical Antiquity," *Economic History Review,* 2nd series, 13 (1960): 1–18. Erik J. Holmberg, *Zur Geschichte des Cursus Publicus* (Uppsala, 1933). Arnold H. M. Jones, *The Later Roman Empire* (Oxford, 1964), vol. 2, 830–834, with notes, and vol. 3, 274–279.   J.C.

Customs and Tolls

The concept of *portorium* was not limited to customs duties but encompassed a multitude of taxes (tolls, fees), often local, on sea or land, that affected traffic within the empire. As for the state *portorium,* which sustained the *sacrae largitiones,* it was the primary tax in certain fiscally uncontrollable regions (Illyricum, for example). In the 3rd and 4th centuries, a tax of one-fortieth on the value of transported goods was still attested in Gaul (Massilia tablet) and in Ostia ("relief of the Tabularii," protests by Symmachus against the *mancipes'* tax on animals for quaestorial games). The state also returned to a system of auctioning off leases to *conductores.* Duties were assessed on merchandise entering and leaving the empire, barring exemptions. The rate attested (between 2 and 5 percent *ad valorem*) remained stable throughout the late period. In addition there were some new inventions, such as the strait toll (under Justinian).

Numerous *portoria* were municipal, but the tax bureau appropriated their receipts, and praetorian prefects returned only a portion of them to the city-states. The anticipated expenses became less and less municipal (hence the Alexandrine *exagogium*).

The purpose of border stations was not merely financial; they were also a matter of security. Both factors, finances and security, worked to limit the number of points—less than ten in all—called *commercia,* through which merchandise had to pass. Customs duties, called *octavae,* may have been reduced to 12.5 percent, or they may have been collected twice, from the buyer and the seller, reaching the rate of 25 percent that has been previously attested. In support of the second hypothesis, one might invoke the *quadruplatores* (collectors of a 25 percent *portorium*) mentioned by Sidonius Apollinaris. Since these duties were levied

exclusively on luxury goods, even a high tax would not have affected consumption. Therefore there was no protectionist intention on the part of the imperial powers, nor any idea of favoring exports. It is perfectly anachronistic to speak of a "customs policy." Finally, with the consolidation of the monopoly on eastern commerce (especially silk), custom duties on foreign goods tended to become confused with the state organization of international trade.

BIBL.: R. Andreotti, "Su alcuni problemi del rapporto fra politica di sicurezza e controllo del commercio nell'impero romano," *Revue internationale des droits de l'antiquité,* 3rd series, 16 (1969): 215–257. Roland Delmaire, *Largesses sacrées et res privata: L'aerarium impérial et son administration du IVe au VIe siècle* (Rome, 1989).   J.C.

Cyril of Alexandria

Patriarch of Alexandria (412–444) and famed exponent of the Alexandrian School of Christology, Cyril (ca. 378–444) was the nephew of the previous bishop, Theophilus (385–412), who was known for his destruction of the Serapeum and his vendetta against John Chrysostom. The young Cyril spent several years living among the monks at Nitria. Although Theophilus was clearly grooming him to be his successor, in 412 Cyril was still just a reader, and only after three days of struggle with Timothy the archdeacon was Cyril able to take the patriarchal throne.

Like his predecessor, Theophilus, and his successor, Dioscorus, as head of the Alexandrian church Cyril controlled a vast power structure covering all of Egypt and Cyrene. When journeying to Ephesus to confront Nestorius in 431, Cyril brought numerous monks from Nitria and Upper Egypt, the notorious *parabalani* (a group of more than 500 strong men employed by the Alexandrian church as "hospital attendants"), and many supporters from among the sailors who manned the Alexandrian grain fleet. These groups filled the streets and occupied the churches, terrifying many bishops into joining Cyril's assembly and even intimidating the imperial officials and soldiers who had come in support of Nestorius. The immense wealth commanded by the Alexandrian church is graphically illustrated by a detailed and itemized inventory of numerous expensive "gifts" sent to prominent people in the imperial court to gain their support against Nestorius (Cyril, *Ep.* 96).

Cyril did not rule unchallenged in his home city. In the first few years of his episcopate, Alexandria was shaken by several violent episodes. In 415 a gang of Cyril's followers brutally lynched the pagan philosopher and mathematician Hypatia, who was apparently a casualty of the hostility between Cyril and the prefect Orestes. Orestes, who was attempting to resist the patriarch's encroachments on secular authority, was himself attacked and wounded by a group of monks. On that occasion, however, the Alexandrian populace rushed to the defense of the prefect. At about the same time, conflict with the Jews escalated into a nocturnal bloodbath that led to the expulsion of the city's Jewish community and Cyril's seizure of their synagogues.

Over the course of his career Cyril generated a massive body of writing, much of which is still extant and includes scriptural exegesis as well as polemic against Arians and pagans. His written response to the anti-Christian treatise of Julian shows that Cyril still considered paganism to be very much a threat even sixty years after Julian's death. Cyril's reputation as a church father and a teacher of orthodoxy, however, rests largely on the Christological teachings he produced in the course of his conflict with Nestorius and his later campaign against Diodore of Tarsus, Theodore of Mopsuestia, and Antiochene Christology in general. Following Alexandrian tradition, Cyril's Christology emphasized the incarnation as "the divine word made flesh," sometimes appearing to downplay the human element to such an extent that opponents accused him of Apollinarianism. Cyril disliked the Antiochene emphasis on strict distinction between the human and divine elements in Christ. Through the vast corpus of his writings he was sometimes vague or inconsistent, using words such as *hypostasis* and *physis* interchangeably, so that in the decade after his death both the Chalcedonian exponents of "two natures" and the Monophysite supporters of "one nature" could plausibly claim to find support for their views in Cyril. The veneration accorded him in the tradition of Monophysite and Chalcedonian churches contrasts sharply with the controversy he provoked in his own time, expressed in Theodoret's caustic remark that a heavy stone should be placed on top of his grave, lest he so irritate the spirits of the dead that they expel him from hell (Theodoret, *Ep.* 180).

BIBL.: Johannes Quasten, *Patrology, Volume III: The Golden Age of Greek Patristic Literature from the Council of Nicaea to the Council of Chalcedon* (Westminster, Md., 1959), 116–142. John I. McEnerney, ed. and trans., *Cyril of Alexandria: Letters,* 2 vols. (Washington, 1987). Maria Dzielska, *Hypatia of Alexandria,* trans. F. Lyra (Cambridge, Mass., 1995). E. Gebremedhin, *Life-Giving Blessing: An Inquiry into the Eucharistic Doctrine of Cyril of Alexandria* (Uppsala, 1977). Christopher Haas, *Alexandria in Late Antiquity: Topography and Social Conflict* (Baltimore, 1997). Joseph M. Hallman, "The Seed of Fire: Divine Suffering in the Christology of Cyril of Alexandria and Nestorius of Constantinople," *Journal of Early Christian Studies* 5 (1997): 369–391. John A. McGuckin, *Cyril of Alexandria: The Christological Controversy: Its History, Theology, and Texts* (Leiden, 1994). Tito Orlandi, *Storia della chiesa di Alessandria: Testo Copto, traduzione e commentario* (Milan, 1970). J. Rougé, "La politique de Cyrille d'Alexandrie et le meurtre d'Hypatie." *Cristianesimo nella storia* 11 (1990): 487–492. Eduard Schwartz, "Cyril und der Mönch Viktor," *Sitzungsberichte: Akademie der Wissenschaften in Wien, philosophische-historische Klasse* 208, no. 4 (1928): 1–51.   J.M.G.

Daphne

On the old road between Antioch on the Orontes (Antakya) and Laodicea ad Mare, Daphne was located 8 km south of Antioch on a plateau that has several permanent springs. Beginning in the Hellenistic era, it was the setting for the legend of Daphne, who was transformed into a laurel tree. Temples of Apollo and Artemis were built there, side by side near a famous cypress wood. The renown of Daphne was such that the capital of Syria was called "Antioch near Daphne."

Diocletian was responsible for major construction projects in Daphne: the chapels of Nemesis and Zeus in the Olympic stadium (where some of the Olympic Games took place, the others being held in Antioch); a subterranean Temple of Hecate, reached via a staircase with 365 steps; and the imperial palace; in addition to renovations in the Temple of Apollo. Theodosius later had the palace refurbished. Two important monuments, the Bath of Ardaburius and the Antiforum of Mammianus, were provided by rich private donors in the second half of the 5th century. There are several known Christian sanctuaries in Daphne: St. Babylas, St. Euphemia, St. Michael the Archangel, and St. Leontius, built on the remains of a synagogue burned in 507 by a riot of the Green circus faction.

The destruction of the large oracular sanctuary of Apollo occurred in several stages. In about 351–354 Caesar Gallus had a martyry of St. Babylas built in the sanctuary, which led to the oracle's silence. But under Constantine and Constantius columns had already been removed to be placed in public buildings and churches in Antioch. Even before his arrival in the capital, Julian endeavored to have the sanctuary repaired; then, moved by the modesty of the feasts of Apollo in August 362 and by the cessation of the oracle, he ordered the remains of Babylas sent to Antioch. The temple fire on 22 October 362 destroyed the chryselephantine statue of Apollo. Julian blamed this on the Christians, who were persecuted as a result.

Daphne was surrounded by wealthy residences, such as the villa of Yakto, where a mosaic from the late 6th century has been found. The mosaic depicts a series of monuments stretching from Antioch to Daphne. But this chic suburb lost its importance, a victim of the demolitions carried out by the Persians, the suppression of the Olympic Games after 520, and the crisis in Antioch during the 6th century. Despite various bans, the cypress trees in the wood were cut down; in 526, some were used to rebuild the Great Church of Antioch. The silence of the sources illustrates the profound decadence that rapidly set in.

BIBL.: B. Cabouret, "L'oracle de la source Castalie à Daphné près d'Antioche," *Mélanges Vatin* (Aix-en-Provence, 1994), 95–104. G. Downey, *A History of Antioch in Syria, from Seleucus to the Arab Conquest* (Princeton, 1961).

P.-L.G.

Defensor Ecclesiae

Under late Roman law, the church was classified as a corporation. It thus had the right to request the institution of a permanent body of legal *defensores*, recruited from practicing advocates, to promote and defend its interests in all legal processes. This right was not automatic but was conceded as a privilege by the imperial court. (The analogous *defensores civitatis* and *defensores senatus* had similar origins.) In the context of fierce legal battles against schismatics and heretics, the African church petitioned for and obtained the faculty of *defensores ecclesiae* in 407 (*Registri Ecclesiae Carthaginensis Excerpta* Canon 97 and *C.Th.* 16.2.38).

Pope Innocent I (402–417) established a permanent corpus of *defensores* for the Roman church, and this practice became standard throughout the eastern and western churches during the course of the 5th century. Both laymen and clerics acted as *defensores* in civil and ecclesiastical forums. There is evidence that in some cases they ranked as a distinct *ordo* within the church hierarchy.

By the beginning of the 6th century the *defensores* were an established institution with special honors and privileges. Their duties included acting as advocates and legal representatives for their bishop and church, the care and administration of episcopal goods, and the defense of church dependents.

In the 7th and 8th centuries their responsibilities and social prestige were enhanced as the bishops took on an ever increasing role in the civil administration of the cities. The corporation of papal *defensores* evolved into an elite body of legal experts, admitted by examination; this had important implications for the development of medieval canon law.

BIBL.: S. Lancel, "L'affaire d'Antoninus de Fussala," in *Les lettres de Saint Augustin découvertes par Johannes Divjak* (Paris, 1983), 277–278. F. Martroye, "Les 'defensores ecclesiae' aux Ve et VIe siècles," *Revue historique de droit français et étranger* 2 (1923): 597–622.   C.HUM.

Demons

Demons were powerful spiritual beings who changed from being neutral or beneficent to being clearly malevolent entities in late antique religions. In Graeco-Roman antiquity, *daimones* (daemons) were conceived as spirits who watched over people and places. They formed legions of intermediary spiritual beings ranked between men and gods. They could be protective deities or simply neutral spirits who inhabited the cosmos. In late antiquity, these *daimones* became demons, spiritual beings of a malevolent nature who were to be feared. In Judaism and in Christianity, they were equated with the fallen angels and were held responsible for nature's disorder and for personal accidents. Adam's fall had enslaved humans in the power of demons. They could harm people, and they controlled nature; in particular, they were held responsible for illnesses. In the Bible, the Book of Job illustrates what the demon, called the Accuser, could do to a person: it deprived Job of his family, his health, and his wealth. The death of his children was the result of demonic power, as was his stinking illness. The demon's power, however, was limited by God's final control of the whole situation. Christianity inherited the Judaic vision of the demonic. Demons were invisible beings fluttering in the air. They were in control of this earth, and each person had to receive exorcism at baptism to be freed from their power. Christ had redeemed creation and freed humanity from demonic power by his death, his sojourn in hell, and his subsequent resurrection. Yet until the end of time, it was believed, the struggle would continue on a personal level. The life of Christians was seen as a struggle with demons whose hostility increased with the sanctity of the person. St. Antony went out into the Egyptian desert—a favorite dwelling place for demons—where he was fiercely attacked by demons resolved to separate him from God. After Antony, monastic life, in particular anachoretic life in the desert, was perceived as a life devoted to fighting with demons.

Demons wanted to receive the same cult that was due to God, and they misled people to make them fall into idolatry. Neoplatonists such as Porphyry already thought that demons were evil creatures that fed on libations and that bloody sacrifices attracted them to earth. In Christianity, this theme is reinforced by the rejection of idols. The heathen gods were equated with demons, their statues with the demons' dwelling places. The cult they received was analyzed by Christian apologists as the ultimate attempt of demons to usurp the worship due to the one true God. Led by their chief, Satan, the origin of all evil, demons were also believed interested in tempting humans into wrongdoing to make them despair of their salvation.

Demons could not be eliminated, but they could be displaced or relocated. In the New Testament, Jesus allowed the legion of demons tormenting a man of the Gerasenes country to enter a herd of swine once they had been expelled from the man. The power of demons could be curbed under superior powers, those that Christ had delegated to his disciples. The sign of the Cross and the name of Christ were deemed to be so unbearable to demons that they had to leave immediately, usually shouting their name and their defeat in the process. Members of the clergy called exorcists were in charge of exorcisms, yet holy persons could also perform them, as saints' lives attest. Exorcists tried to learn the name of the demon in question. It was believed that by calling his or her name—demons could be male or female—the exorcists gained power over a demon and could order it to free the person it possessed. Elaborate rituals with long lists of names were therefore written to help the clergy deal with demons. Exorcism was practiced only in serious cases of possession and with some illnesses specifically attributed to demons. Yet demons also had to be dealt with in ordinary life. Protective phylacteries, amulets, or talismans were worn bearing names of saints, angels, or Christ to protect those who feared the evil eye and the power of demons. Christians sought the protection of crosses, as making the sign of the Cross was seen as the most efficient way to protect oneself against demonic powers. Apotropaic crosses were carved on walls, on simple objects for everyday life, and even on clothes. Cleansing the earth of demons seemed to be the task of zealous Christians. Pagan statues and representations of the gods began to worry some Christians, for they were potential abodes for demons. As a result, a number of these were destroyed. This concern still existed in 8th century Constantinople, where some of the statues brought to adorn the city in earlier centuries were considered potentially dangerous and avoided.

For many persons in late antiquity, the universally recognized power of the demons created a wish to exploit them. Magic practices, in particular curse tablets, were frequently used to manipulate demons and direct their negative actions against somebody in particular. Sudden illnesses, falling in love with the wrong person, and delinquent behavior were attributed to demons, and often to black magic and the ill-intentioned intervention of some person. Saints' lives demonstrate the superior power of God's friends over demons in these cases. They acknowledge the binding power of the spells but allow the faithful who come to them for help to discover the hidden binding tablet or figure.

Demons were extremely numerous. As in exorcism, to manipulate them, for good or bad, it was necessary to know their name. Lists of names linked to specific powers are recorded in magical papyri. Demons could be borrowed from one tradition by another. In the Babylonian Talmud, demons seem to surround the living. They live in trees, in water, in closets. It is possible that this wealth in demons comes from the influence of ancient Persian religions. In Zoroastrianism, demons were very numerous and powerful. As servants of Ahriman, the Hostile Spirit, the source of all evil and suffering, they meant to harm people. Along with them worked other harmful creatures, such as insects, that should be killed by any pious Zoroastrian.

In Islam, demons (jinns) had a preference for ruins, cemeteries, and bathhouses, not unlike demons in Christianity. They could also take any form they wanted. However, jinns in Islam were different from demons in Christianity in the sense that they were not necessarily harmful. They could inflict illnesses, wreck marriages, and ruin family life, yet when left alone or treated politely, as irritable creatures should be, they could also be controlled.

Demons played an important role in all the late antique religions that shared a common recognition that invisible spiritual beings lived in the air and resided on the earth. The different traditions did not agree on the nature of their power over the living, although in most, demons appear as evil, harmful, and dangerous beings.

BIBL.: P. Brown, "Sorcery, Demons, and the Rise of Christianity from Late Antiquity into the Middle Ages," in M. Douglas, ed., *Witchcraft, Confessions and Accusations* (London, 1970). J. Gager, *Curse Tablets and Binding Spells from the Ancient World* (Oxford, 1992). P. Perdrizet, *Negotium perambulans in tenebris: Etudes de démonologie gréco-orientale* (Strasbourg, 1922). B.C.

Dendrites

Dendrites were ascetics who lived in trees (from the Greek *dendron*). Similar to the stylites, who lived on top of pillars (Greek *stylos*), dendrites used their unusual ascetic situation to combine withdrawal, vigil, and penance. The primary contrast to the stylite was in their level of public engagement. The stylite practiced a discipline of physical withdrawal—atop a pillar, up in the air—that commonly resulted in active public ministry. People flocked to the stylites for counsel, healing, and adjudication. The tree-dwelling ascetic seems to have maintained the life of a recluse without the demands for spiritual and political patronage that generally plagued the late antique holy man.

The practice of living in trees seems to have been a temporary discipline in ascetic careers marked by changing locations and practices. David of Thessalonica (ca. 450–540) began his long ascetic career by living for three years in an almond tree. The 14th century frescoes in the *parekklesion* of Kariye Camii in Istanbul depict him in his tree. In Mesopotamia in the late 5th and early 6th century, the ascetic Maro lived for many years in a hollowed-out tree segment in a corner of a monastery enclosure, next to the pillar on which his brother Abraham dwelt as stylite. When Abraham died, Maro took his place on the pillar and was deeply grieved by the burden of public responsibility he thereby inherited. Another Mesopotamian ascetic named Adolas (or Addas) confined himself in a hollow plane tree in Thessalonica soon after the renowned David.

BIBL.: David of Thessalonica: *Bibliotheca hagiographica Graeca*, 3rd ed., ed. François Halkin (Brussels, 1957), 492y-493m. John of Ephesus, *Lives of the Eastern Saints*, ch. 4, ed. and trans. E. W. Brooks in Patrologia orientalis, vol. 17 (Paris, 1923), 56–84. John Moschus, *Pratum spirituale*, ch. 69–70; trans. with commentary in John Wortley, *The Spiritual Meadow (Pratum Spirituale) by John Moschos (also known as John Eviratus)* (Kalamazoo, Mich., 1992), 51–53. S.A.H.

Denis

Later medieval legends listed Dionysius (St. Denis) as the first bishop of Paris; they also conflated several traditions by identifying him with the Dionysius converted by the apostle Paul at Athens, and by locating his martyrdom in either the late 1st or the mid-3rd century. His cult emerged only during the late 5th century when the ascetic Genovefa (St. Geneviève) encouraged the construction of a church at the site of the saint's tomb a few miles north of Paris; at some later time a monastic community was also established. The saint and his abbey gradually became associated with the Merovingian dynasty of Frankish kings. During the late 6th century King Chilperic had one of his sons buried in the saint's church, and the discovery of her signet ring helped to identify a tomb uncovered in 1959 as that of Aregund, Chilperic's mother. King Dagobert I marked the reemergence of Paris as an important capital city in the early 7th century by enlarging and richly decorating the saint's church. He and subsequent Merovingian kings also acknowledged St. Denis to be their "special patron," emancipated the abbey from the administration of the bishops of Paris, and endowed it with numerous estates, rents, concessions, and even an annual fair. The Church of St. Denis thus became a primary pantheon for Merovingian kings and their family members. During the 8th century the Carolingian family began to patronize the abbey and eventually promoted the construction of a new church. An explicit sign of the demise of the Merovingian dynasty was the burial in the Church of St. Denis of both Charles Martel, the powerful mayor of the place, and Pippin, the first Carolingian king.

BIBL.: S. M. Crosby, *The Royal Abbey of Saint-Denis from Its Beginnings to the Death of Suger, 475–1151,* ed. P. Z. Blum (New Haven, 1987). J. Semmler, "Saint-Denis: Von der bischöflichen Coemeterialbasilika zur königlichen Benediktinerabtei," in *La Neustrie: Les pays au nord de la Loire de 650 à 850: Colloque historique international,* vol. 2, ed. H. Atsma (Sigmaringen, 1989), 75–123.   R.V.

Dhimmī

A *dhimmī* is a non-Muslim living in Islamic lands who has been granted special status as a member of a religious community. Beginning in early Islam the *dhimmī's* rights and obligations in Islamic society were secured by a contract *(dhimma)* of indefinite duration established between the religious community and the Muslim rulers. In essence, the contract guaranteed *dhimmīs* protection of property and person and freedom of religion in exchange for loyalty to the Muslim state and the payment of tribute *(jizya).* The *jizya,* which evolved into a poll tax, was the most permanent feature of their submissive status (Qur'ān 9:29).

The requirements of such contracts with non-Muslims varied according to the terms of capitulation. Muhammad's treaties of mutual protection with various Jewish, Christian, and pagan tribes in Arabia established a precedent, yet it was during the period of Islamic expansion and subsequently in Islamic law that *dhimmī* status gained its contours. Christians and Jews, as members of scriptural religions recognized by the Qur'ān (e.g., 5:68–69), were the first groups given *dhimmī* status in the Islamic empire. Consequently much *dhimmī* law relates specifically to them. Other religions were also accorded *dhimmī* status, the general requirement being the possession of a revealed Scripture; but, as in the case of Hindus and Buddhists, other criteria often sufficed.

The Umayyad and early Abbasid periods saw the elaboration of laws that governed the social boundaries of a plural society. *Dhimmī* law prohibited certain public expressions of religion, and its laws of differentiation *(ghiyār)* required *dhimmī* to dress differently from Muslims. Though such restrictions may have first aimed at perpetuating visual distinctions between Muslims and non-Muslims, later sumptuary laws were a response to growing cultural assimilation. While debate continues about the extent to which *dhimmī* regulations were from the outset intended to be demeaning, the enforcement of discriminatory laws often corresponded to periods of strained relations and the programs of particular rulers.

BIBL.: C. E. Bosworth, "The Concept of Dhimma in Early Islam," in B. Braude and B. Lewis, eds., *Christians and Jews in the Ottoman Empire: The Functioning of a Plural Society* (London and New York, 1982), vol. 1, 37–51. Mark R. Cohen, *Under Crescent and Cross: The Jews in the Middle Ages* (Princeton, 1994). Antoine Fattal, *Le statut légal des non-Musulmans en pays d'Islam* (Beirut, 1958). Albrecht Noth, "Abgrenzungsprobleme zwischen Muslimen und Nicht-Muslimen: Die Bedingungen 'Umars *(aš-šur ūṭ al-'umariyya')* unter einem anderen Aspekt gelesen," *Jerusalem Studies in Arabic and Islam* 9 (1987): 290–315. A. S. Tritton, *The Caliphs and Their Non-Muslim Subjects* (London, 1930).

M.R.

Dietary Restrictions

In the Greek and the Roman religious systems, dietary restrictions were characterized mostly by their absence. A few distinct groups (such as Pythagoreans and Orphics) regulated their members' consumption of various foods and beverages; in some shrines and villages, local custom (as reported, e.g., by Pausanias) enjoined the observance of certain dietary taboos; such examples, however, were clearly the exception. In other areas of the ancient world, dietary taboos and regulations were common among several ethnic groups, some of which preserved their ancestral customs throughout the Hellenistic and Roman periods. Thus, the ongoing emigration of numerous individuals within the Hellenistic world and the Roman empire, and especially the spread of several Far Eastern cults, gave greater prominence to the issue of dietary restrictions in Graeco-Roman literature and society. In the shrines of foreign gods, visitors might be enjoined not to offer certain animals in sacrifice, or even not to enter if they had eaten any forbidden foods within a given number of days (e.g., *I. Delos* 2305, 2308, etc.); at banquets, Greek and Roman intellectuals discussed the causes and meaning of various ethnic food taboos (Plutarch, *Quaest.conv.* 4.5) and conversed with foreigners about their dietary customs (e.g., Heliodorus, *Aethiopica* 3.11). Reactions to such taboos ranged from contempt to admiration, the latter attitude often related to the numerous attempts to demonstrate the rational, ethical, or symbolic value of various food taboos, perhaps by way of a philosophical or allegorical interpretation of their meaning (as reflected, e.g., in the writings of Philo, in Plutarch's *De Iside et Osiride,* or in Porphyry's *De abstinentia*).

Because of the importance of dietary restrictions among the Jews, establishing a policy toward such taboos was among the first issues confronted by Jesus's early followers. The subject therefore figured prominently in the New Testament, in the letters of Paul (1 Cor. 10:25), in the Gospels (e.g., Mark 7:15), and in the Book of Acts, where a clear policy was formulated (Acts 15:29, 21:25) to allow Gentile converts to Christianity to eat every kind of food except meat offered to idols, blood, and animals that had been strangled. However, adopting this lenient position did not solve the problem entirely, and the issue of deviant dietary regulations among individuals or groups persistently recurs in later Christian literature. Moreover, the development within the Christian world of strong Encratite tendencies, and the subsequent emphasis on the personal asceticism of select individuals, turned dietary abstinence (from meat, wine, or other foodstuffs) into one hallmark of the late antique holy man. With the rise and spread of Islam, in the 7th century new dietary standards swept all of the Near East and much of the Mediterranean basin. In the Qur'ān, the general attitude is that all good things may be eaten (Qur'ān 5:4), but specific prohibitions regulate the slaughter and consumption of meat (2:173 and elsewhere: no pork, carrion, blood, or animals sacrificed to idols), and forbid the drinking of wine (5:90). In practice, however, avoidance of various kinds of foods differed greatly from one Qur'ānic legal school to another and from one region to the next.

BIBL.: J. André, *L'alimentation et la cuisine à Rome* (Paris, 1961). K. Böckenhoff, *Speisesatzungen mosäischer Art in mittelalterischen Kirchenrechtsquellen des Morgen- und Abendlandes* (Münster, 1907). M. Cook, "Early Islamic Dietary Law," *Jerusalem Studies in Arabic and Islam* 7 (1986): 217–277. Rob Meens, "Pollution in the Early Middle Ages: The Case of Food Regulations in the Penitentials," *Early Medieval Europe* 4 (1995): 3–19.   G.B.

Dining

In the later Roman empire the main meal was the *cena,* taken in the late afternoon; the midday *prandium* could also be a significant meal (Ausonius, *Ep.* 5.2; Sidonius Apollinaris, *Ep.* 2.9.6). For the wealthy and aristocratic, as for their precursors in the earlier empire, the entertainment of friends or clients at dinner

Dining scene from Tomb of the Banquet, Constanța, Romania.

formed the principal focus of social life. The *convivium,* or banquet, offered an opportunity to display one's luxury and wealth through the furnishings of the dining room itself, the provision of exotic and lavish food and drink, the quality of the vessels in which they were served, the throngs of well-dressed and well-trained slaves who attended the guests, and the extensive entertainment offered, which might include music, dancing, and theatrical performances.

The ceremonial that governed these events goes back in its essentials to earlier Roman custom. It was a mark of a civilized man to recline while dining; one supported oneself on one's left arm and used the right hand alone to eat. In upper-class society women also normally reclined at dinner, although in some circles or contexts they may have been seated. The layout of the traditional Roman dining room consisted of three rectilinear couches set around three sides of a square: the term *triclinium* applies both to this arrangement and to the room itself. This layout is still found in late antiquity, but whereas in the late republic and early empire the three couches had traditionally held nine guests, whose positions were hierarchically determined according to a strict system, in the later empire rooms designed for such furnishing were much larger and could evidently accommodate a greater number of guests. However, from at least the 3rd century onward another dining arrangement became much more common, the semicircular or lunate couch known as the *stibadium* or *sigma,* used with a single small round or D-shaped table. This practice is alluded to by many authors of the 4th, 5th, and 6th centuries, and is represented figuratively in paintings, mosaics, and on silver plates. Between five and eight guests could be accommodated on a single *sigma* couch, which could fit into the curved space of an apse; sometimes the design and layout of the mosaic pavements indicates the intended location of the couch in a room, as in the Villa of the Falconer at Argos. Many apsidal rooms in wealthy private houses and villas seem to have been designed as *stibadium* dining rooms, with the open space in front used for service and entertainment; rooms of this type are found in buildings of the 4th and 5th centuries in the western empire and as late as the 6th in the Greek east, for instance at Argos and Apamea.

In the grander villas of the 4th century, rooms with triple apses, or triconches, are found fairly frequently; well-known examples are at Piazza Armerina in Sicily and Desenzano in northern Italy, and there are a number of examples in Spain. Most of these were almost certainly to be used as elaborate rooms for dining with three *stibadia,* one in each apse. The very rare multiconch rooms would allow even more; there is one with seven apses at Cuicul (Djemila) in Numidia, but otherwise they are attested only in the Imperial Palace in Constantinople.

Open-air dining was also fashionable in wealthy circles. It might be associated with hunting, as in scenes of the hunters' picnic on mosaics such as those of Piazza Armerina and Tellaro and on silverware like the Sevso Plate: the hunters are seen reclining at a *stibadium* set on the ground, surrounded by attendants, and often shaded by a hanging canopy. Villas might also have permanent locations for open-air dining, continuing an earlier custom.

Another custom that survived from the earlier Roman period was that of the funerary banquet, celebrated by family or funerary colleges. Tombs might be provided with couches of masonry, where the banquet could be held on feast days or anniversaries; the earlier pagan examples, for instance at Ostia and the Isola Sacra, are succeeded by similar provisions in Christian necropolises of North Africa (notably at Tipasa) and Spain. Paintings in both pagan and Christian tombs show guests assembled at the *stibadium;* while these may sometimes be meant to show the banquet in the next world, in many renderings the mass of incidental details leave little doubt that reference is intended to contemporary life. Good examples may be seen in the Catacomb of SS. Petrus and Marcellinus in Rome, probably dating from the end of the 3rd to early 4th century, and in a recently discovered tomb of the fourth century at Constanza in Romania. Christians celebrated these banquets not only at the tombs of their own dead but also at those of the martyrs, with an enthusiasm that provoked the disapproval of church fathers such as Ambrose, who banned them (cf. Augustine, *Confessiones* 6.2); perhaps in consequence, such scenes disappear from Christian art by the end of the 4th century.

Classical dining rituals were alive among the upper levels of Roman society up to the end of the Roman empire of the west. Some barbarian rulers adopted the habit of reclining at table as a mark of Roman manners; one example was the Vandal usurper Guntharis, who was murdered at a banquet where the guests reclined on three *stibadia* (Procopius, *Bell.Van.* 4.28.1). But there are also signs that the custom of reclining to dine was dying out in the west in the 5th and 6th centuries, preserved only under exceptional circumstances or by determined upholders of traditional ways. In the eastern empire, however, the traditional customs were maintained among the upper classes at least during the 6th century. They lingered even longer in the ceremonial that surrounded the Byzantine emperors, who continued to lie down to dine on feast days as a sign of adherence to tradition, even as late as the time of Constantine Porphyrogenitos in the 10th century.

Islamic culture celebrated several social events, such as weddings and circumcisions, with feasts. Historians took note of the exorbitant amounts spent by caliphs on such occasions, when the public might also share in the feast and receive gifts. In Umayyad and Abbasid times the banqueting of the caliphs was renowned. Funeral feasts, known in pre-Islamic Arabia, also endured in Islam. Much information regarding the religious precepts of Islamic dining etiquette may be found in the hadith literature.

BIBL.: M. M. Ahsan, *Social Life under the Abbasids 170–289 A.H.* (London, 1979). K. Dunbabin, "Convivial Spaces: Dining and Entertainment in the Roman Villa," *Journal of Roman Archaeology* 9 (1996): 66–79. M. J. Enright, *Lady with a Mead Cup* (Dublin, 1996). E. Jastrzebowska, "Les scènes de banquet dans les peintures et sculptures chrétiennes des IIIe et IVe siècles," *Recherches augustiniennes* 14 (1979): 3–90. Adam Mez, *The Renaissance of Islam*, trans. S. Khuda-Bukhsh and D. Margoliouth (London, 1937). J. Rossiter, "Convivium and Villa in Late Antiquity," in W. J. Slater, ed., *Dining in a Classical Context* (Ann Arbor, 1991), 199–214. M. Roberts, "Martin Meets Maximus: The Meaning of a Late Roman Banquet," *Revue des études augustiniennes* 41 (1995): 91–111. K.D.

Dionysius the Areopagite

The enigmatic Greek writings traditionally attributed to Dionysius the Areopagite (Acts 17:34) were actually written about 500 C.E.: *The Celestial Hierarchy, The Ecclesiastical Hierarchy, The Divine Names, The Mystical Theology,* and the ten *Letters.* The author, who still eludes precise identification, was familiar with liturgical practices of western Syria and the Athenian Neoplatonism of Proclus. With an intentionally archaic style studded with neologisms like "hierarchy" and "supernatural," Dionysius used Proclus's version of procession and return as a way of understanding the Christian liturgy and the biblical names and descriptions for God and the angels; the entire method of affirmation and negation leads to silence and to union with the unknowable God. The Areopagite is especially known for this apophatic approach to the ineffable divine.

The Dionysian writings illustrate late antiquity's transition from pagan to Christian philosophy, in that this corpus began to circulate just when the emperor Justinian forced the Platonic Academy out of Athens (529 C.E.). Christian Neoplatonism thus thrived under apostolic authority in the early Byzantine era (John of Scythopolis and Maximus the Confessor) and especially in western medieval philosophy.

BIBL.: *Pseudo-Dionysius: The Complete Works,* trans. Colm Luibheid (New York, 1987). Andrew Louth, *Denys the Areopagite* (London, 1989). Paul Rorem, *Pseudo-Dionysius: A Commentary on the Texts and an Introduction to Their Influence* (New York, 1993).   P.E.R.

Dioscorus

Dioscorus (d. after 585), poet and *scholasticus,* was a native of Aphrodito (Kom Ishqāw) in the Antaeopolite Nome, one of the best documented towns of late antique Egypt. His father, Apollos, had been *prōtokomētēs* of Aphrodito. As the son of a prominent landowner, Dioscorus received a broad education in rhetoric and philosophy, possibly in Alexandria. He studied law and is attested as a *scholasticus* in 543, by which time he received the rank-indicating name of Flavius. After 547, he held his father's former position of *prōtokomētēs,* and as such defended the interests of Aphrodito in 551 at the imperial court in a dispute over the town's right of *autopragia,* or self-collection of taxes. He dwelt in Antinoopolis between 566 and 573, practicing law and writing encomiastic poetry. By 573 he returned to Aphrodito, where he spent his remaining years administering his family's property and acting as agent for a local monastery founded by his father. He is last attested in 585, from an entry in his personal account book.

At the beginning of the 20th century, a large cache of papyrus documents was discovered, many written in Dioscorus's own hand, providing an unusually rich source of information regarding his career and cultural outlook. The archive includes business contracts, poems praising local officials, legal petitions, and a Greek-Coptic glossary. The documents show Dioscorus to have been thoroughly bilingual, combining in an unaffected way Christian and pagan literary motifs and ornamentation. He exemplifies the fusion of Coptic and Hellenic cultures that culminated in Egypt during the century prior to the Arab conquest.

BIBL.: *P. Cairo Masp.* 1 (1911), 2 (1913), 3 (1916). *P. Lond.* 5 (1917). J. G. Keenan, "The Aphrodite Papyri and Village Life in Byzantine Egypt," *Bulletin de la société d'archéologie copte* 26 (1984): 51–63. L. S. B. MacCoull, *Dioscorus of Aphrodito: His Work and His World* (Berkeley, 1988).   C.H.

Diplomacy

The Roman empire of late antiquity faced significantly more difficult strategic circumstances than its classical predecessor, particularly due to the rise of Sassanian Persia to the east and the emergence of stronger new tribal groupings to the north, initially Goths, Alamanni, and Franks, then Huns, and finally Avars and Slavs. One consequence of the resulting strain on the empire's military resources was that diplomacy came to play an increasingly prominent part in efforts to maintain the empire's position vis-à-vis its neighbors, a development reflected in the gradual evolution of an institutional infrastructure for the conduct of diplomacy, albeit a relatively simple one by modern standards.

Ambassadors of this period did not reside permanently at foreign courts and, perhaps as a result, there was no specialist diplomatic corps as such. Envoys were selected for individual missions, and high-ranking government officials or military officers were the typical choice, though clergy or physicians were sometimes deemed appropriate. Ability in public speaking is mentioned as a particular recommendation, but more significant for the issue of specialization is the way in which, by the 6th century, previous diplomatic experience either on the part of the individual or a relative (especially to the same destination) increasingly features as a criterion in selection. Envoys often had to travel long distances and might be absent for many months, rendering the whole process of negotiation slow and cumbersome, though such delays could be turned to advantage both by the empire and its neighbors.

The empire never had a foreign minister as such, with policy normally being determined by the emperor in consultation with such advisers as he chose to consult. However, one of the highest court officials, the *magister officiorum* (master of the offices), came to include within his remit responsibility for many aspects of imperial diplomacy. Indicative of this is the addition of a corps of interpreters to his staff by the late 4th century, if not earlier—a highly significant institutional development in its own right—while during the 5th century, the *magister officorum* became responsible for coordinating the reception of foreign envoys in the capital and sometimes undertook important diplomatic missions in person. Best-known holder of this office was Peter the Patrician (539–565), who during his unusually long tenure led major embassies to Persia and also wrote a history of the office; surviving extracts provide invaluable information on the reception of envoys in Constantinople.

It is tempting to link these diplomatic developments with the emperors' abandonment of campaigning in person from the end of the 4th century. While they remained personally active on the frontiers, emperors retained much more direct involvement in negotiations with foreign peoples; by relinquishing this role and rarely traveling far from the capital, emperors of the 5th and 6th centuries made room for officials like the *magister* to play a greater mediating role in diplomacy. There was also more scope for the accumulation of relevant written records. Texts of treaties were being stored in archives in Constantinople by the 6th century, and probably also aide-mémoires concerning negotiations, though there is no definite evidence that the government maintained a repository of other information relevant to relations with neighboring states and peoples. There can, however, be no doubt that intelligence gathering was one of the unofficial functions of Roman envoys, and the imperial authorities increasingly took care to limit the scope that visiting envoys had for such activities while in Roman territory. At the same time, the opportunity was seized to impress foreign delegations with the empire's wealth and power through the magnificence of the imperial palace and its attendant ceremonial, presumably in the expectation that over-awed envoys would be less assertive and more amenable to Roman demands, and on returning home would be more likely to advise their ruler against infringing the empire's interests.

Late antique diplomatic protocol reached its most developed expression in the context of relations with Sassanian Persia, the empire's only neighbor of comparable sophistication. From the 4th century, emperor and shah referred to one another as "brothers" in diplomatic correspondence, while by the 6th century they formally notified each other of new accessions to the throne, had established a distinction between "major" and "minor" embassies, engaged in competitive gift giving, and normally spared no expense in ensuring the comfort of each other's envoys.

In addition to formal negotiations, the empire employed a variety of other means of a broadly diplomatic character to try to achieve its ends. Money and goods, euphemistically referred to as gifts or subsidies, were dispensed to neighbors both regularly and on a one-time basis, whether to buy peace on a particular frontier or to induce one enemy to attack another. These payments often attracted criticism from the educated elite because of their connotations of dominance and subservience and their perceived expense, but they were probably a cost-effective if unglamorous alternative to military action. When the empire was able to dictate terms, hostages from the other state, usually the sons of leading families, were often demanded as guarantees. These young men, who were typically detained for periods of years, were educated in Roman fashion, doubtless in the hope of inculcating a sympathy for imperial interests. At the same time, they must also have been valuable sources of information about their homeland. Interestingly, there is no evidence for this practice in Roman relations with Sassanian Persia, in which context hostages appear only as short-term

guarantees prior to the conclusion of agreements. There are also occasional glimpses of low-level cross-frontier contacts maintained by local commanders or officials, likewise useful for intelligence purposes and as avenues for exploratory initiatives that could then conveniently be disowned by the central authorities if developments took an unpromising turn.

The empire showed some awareness of the diplomatic potential of religion. The presence of substantial Christian communities in Persia and Armenia, and the adherence of many of the new Germanic kingdoms in the western Mediterranean to Arian Christianity made religion a vital issue in relations with those regions, and one that some emperors were prepared to exploit. Finally, the empire was not averse to kidnapping or assassinating problematic foreign leaders when other methods failed (though again, significantly, such actions were never taken against Persia).

The relationship between Arab Muslim conquerors and the places they took over, as well as between Umayyad or early Abbasid caliphs and their neighbors, often consisted in ad hoc negotiations about conditions of surrender, truces, and, later, exchanges of prisoners. Many of the texts in historical sources have been altered over the centuries to meet specific needs, and they should be used with caution.

BIBL.: R. C. Blockley, *East Roman Foreign Policy: Formation and Conduct from Diocletian to Anastasius* (Leeds, 1992), 129–163. D. Hill, *The Termination of Hostilities in Early Arab Conquests* (London, 1971). A. A. Vasiliev and M. Canard, *Byzance et les Arabes* (repr. London, 1974). A. D. Lee, *Information and Frontiers: Roman Foreign Relations in Late Antiquity* (Cambridge, Eng., 1993), 32–48, 166–170. J. Shepard and S. Franklin, eds., *Byzantine Diplomacy* (Aldershot, Eng., 1992), 1–39, 159–165, 295–303. S. Diebler, "Les Hommes du Roi," *Studia Iranica* 24 (1995): 187–218. N. Garsoian, "Le rôle de l'hiérarchie chrétienne dans les rapports entre Byzance et les sasanides," *Revue des études arméniennes* 10 (1973/4): 119–138.   D.L.

Divination

In late antiquity, divination—the prediction of future events or the gaining of information about things unseen—encompassed a range of techniques inherited from classical antiquity, Babylonia, and Sassanian Iran. Isidore of Seville (d. 636 C.E.) wrote in his *Etymologiae* that divination was divided into four categories corresponding to the four classical elements (water, earth, air, and fire). Only hydromancy was described in any detail by Isidore, while other terms (*geomantia, aeromantia,* and *pyromantia*) were coined to complete the parallel and did not reflect actual practice at the time.

While foretelling the future by consulting oracles had been important in classical antiquity, it played a greatly diminished role in late antiquity. The common Graeco-Roman practice of dream interpretation, on the other hand, passed into late antiquity through a number of treatises, especially that by Artemidorus. The practice of inducing a dream, or causing someone else to dream, can be seen in Egyptian magical papyri of late antiquity, which display a merging of Greek and Egyptian practices with some Christian influences, such as names of angels.

Augury by observing the behavior of animals (especially the flight of birds) was an early practice throughout Mesopotamia and continued in late antiquity, along with techniques for reading the future by examining the conformation of animal parts (usually shoulder blades or the liver). Hydromancy—interpreting patterns appearing on the surface of water (or on oil, ink, or any reflective surface)—was another ancient practice. Few details remain, however, of the specific methods used in these intuitive techniques.

A number of Byzantine treatises concerned divination from winds or the phases of the moon. The prediction of seasonal changes and cultivation patterns on the basis of natural phenomena such as thunder, clouds, and rainbows was the subject of Byzantine treatises called *Geoponica,* transmitted into Islam as "Nabataean agriculture."

Other forms of divination in late antiquity were less intuitive: lot casting (sortilege or cleromancy), letter-number manipulation (onomancy), and astrology. The Roman practice of lot casting (the interpretation of results produced by chance) was especially popular throughout late antiquity. Dice could be used, as well as rods or grains. A variant form (bibliomancy) involved opening a book and selecting a passage at random.

In onomancy, the numerical values of letters forming a word (often the name of a person) would be interpreted. This method could flourish only in a culture that used alphabetical numerals (Greek, Syriac, Arabic), and its legendary origins were traced back to Pythagoras. An onomantic table often present in Byzantine treatises was used to determine the victor and the vanquished by calculating the numerical value of the names of the contenders, dividing each by nine, and finding the remainders on the chart. There were similar procedures for predicting the outcome of an illness, the success of a journey, the truth or falsity of a matter, or whether or not an event would occur.

The Alexandrian astronomer Ptolemy's defense of astrology in his *Tetrabiblos,* written in the 2nd century C.E., was crucial in establishing it as the most important learned form of divination. Horoscopic astrology was practiced throughout late antiquity, as were simpler forms of zodiacal associations. The Sabian inhabitants of Harran in northern Iraq were particularly famous for the practice of astrology, and their influence extended well into the early Islamic period. A form of astrological divination especially popular in late antiquity, one combined with onomancy and omens drawn from natural phenomena, is represented by a divinatory text, *The Book of the Zodiac,* preserved in the Mandaic language of lower central Iraq, in which one can see the blending of Babylonian, Sassanian, and Hellenistic traditions.

BIBL.: *The Book of the Zodiac,* trans. Royal Asiatic Society (London, 1949). P. Athanassiadi, "Philosophers and Oracles: Shifts in Authority in Late Paganism," *Byzantion* 62 (1992): 45–62. Tamsyn Barton, *Ancient Astrology* (London, 1994). B. E. Daley, "Apollo as a Chalcedonian," *Traditio* 50 (1995): 31–54. J. Elukin, "The Ordeal of Scripture: Functionalism and the Sortes Biblicae in the Middle Ages," *Exemplaria* 5 (1993): 135–160. Georg Luck, *Arcana Mundi: Magic and the Occult in the Greek and Roman Worlds* (Baltimore, 1985). Henry Maguire, ed., *Byzantine Magic* (Washington, D.C., and Cambridge, Mass., 1995).   E.S.-S.

Divorce

Divorce under pre-Constantinian Roman law was subject to few restrictions and (in theory if not always in reality) available to both men and women. Roman marriage rested on the consent of both spouses; a partner who no longer felt marital intent (*affectio maritalis*) could seek a divorce. Women had an action for return of their dowry, though the husband might retain part of the dowry if the divorce was due to the wife's fault or if there were children (whose maintenance was the father's responsibility). Few provisions of classical divorce law survive in the *Digest,* because they were no longer valid in the time of Justinian.

Little evidence survives for divorce in practice. Almost all the divorce cases known in Rome date to the late republic and early principate and arose from the political and dynastic maneuverings of the Roman elite. Funerary epitaphs, our main source for information on family life outside the elite, rarely mention divorce but do indicate that remarriage was not uncommon (whether after divorce or widowhood is unclear). Marriage contracts from Egypt often make provision for divorce, and divorce documents survive from Egypt and Dura-Europus; evidently divorce was widespread and socially acceptable throughout the Mediterranean. Probably most divorces were by mutual consent and left few traces in the written record, especially if there were no children or no property involved. Even less is known of attitudes toward divorce. Doubtless there was considerable diversity in attitudes and practice throughout the empire.

One small but eloquent group consistently opposed divorce: Christians, who regularly included denunciations of non-Christian marital and sexual practices in their apologetical and prescriptive writings. Jesus himself had explicitly criticized contemporary Jewish law, which permitted husbands to initiate divorce and both parties to remarry. Mark (10:2–12), Luke (16:18), and Paul (1 Cor. 7:10–11) present Jesus as condemning divorce without exception, but divorce of an adulterous wife is permitted in Matthew (5:31–32, 19:3–9). This discrepancy in the New Testament accounts of Jesus's teachings caused great concern to later Christian interpreters. Opponents of the double standard declared that neither party should divorce, even for adultery, and that all remarriage after divorce was invalid, whereas the more traditionalist (or more realistic) accepted the possibility of a man's remarrying after repudiating an adulterous wife.

Late imperial law diverged sharply from classical law regarding unilateral divorce. Constantine imposed criminal penalties (exile and confiscation of property) on women who repudiated their husbands for any but the most serious reasons, and allowed an unjustly repudiated woman to seize the dowry of her ex-husband's second wife (*C.Th.* 3.16.1, 331). Julian annulled Constantine's law, but 5th century emperors reintroduced restrictions on unilateral divorce, with a less severe policy prevailing in the eastern half of the empire (*C.Th.* 3.16.2; Theodosius II, *Nov.* 12; Valentinian III, *Nov.* 35.11; *C.Just.* 5.17.8, 5.17.9). Apparently no attempt was made to restrict divorce by mutual consent until Justinian in the mid-6th century (*Nov.* 117.10), a policy overturned by his successor, Justin II (*Nov.* 140). It is reasonable to attribute these new restrictions to Christian influence, although imperial policy did not accord perfectly with the position of Christian writers like Jerome and Augustine. Christian bishops and church councils also imposed ecclesiastical penalties on those who remarried after divorcing; as with imperial law, women were treated more severely than men.

The effect of imperial legislation on actual practice is unclear. Little documentary evidence for divorce survives for the later 4th and the 5th century, but this may reflect the overall decline in papyri rather than social change. Public opinion, perhaps orchestrated by local church authorities, would have been a more potent deterrent than legal penalties. The combined force of secular and ecclesiastical sanctions that emerges in late antiquity effectively inhibited divorce and remarriage after divorce in the western world for the next fifteen hundred years.

BIBL.: Susanne Dixon, *The Roman Family* (Baltimore, 1997). Gertrude Stern, *Marriage in Early Islam* (London, 1939). Susan Treggiari, "Divorce Roman Style," *Marriage, Divorce and Children in Ancient Rome,* ed. B. Rawson (Oxford, 1991), 31–46. R. Bagnall, "Church, State and Divorce in Late Roman Egypt," in *Florilegium Columbianum: Essays in Honor of Paul Oskar Kristeller* (New York, 1987), 41–61.

J.E.G.

Documents (East)

In the late eastern Roman empire, legal acts, whether public or private, were normally carried out by means of written documents. Specialists in diplomatics for the period can consult original documents (usually on papyrus), contemporary copies (on papyrus, but also inscriptions), and medieval copies to gain an understanding of the external and internal traits of the documents. Given these conditions, the study of proto-Byzantine diplomatics largely intersects the field of papyrology, addressing the history not only of Egypt but also, by methodical extrapolation, that of the empire as a whole.

Papyrus was manufactured in Egypt in rolls (*chartai,* hence the word *charter* in modern usage). Beginning in the 5th century, the state, which controlled the production of papyrus, inscribed the *prōtokollon*—a sort of official stamp with the date of fabrication—at the top of certain rolls. Material and page makeup varied, depending on the kind of document and the agency issuing it. For the most simple documents, one sheet was sufficient (several sheets could be gathered into a roll after the fact); a more solemn document had longer lines and more space between them, running to several columns if necessary. In place of the traditional roll, the documentary codex, which was easier to leaf through, tended to take precedence beginning in the 4th century as the format for fiscal registries (cadastres, account books).

Documentary paleography excludes on principle the use of majuscule (capital, uncial) letters, which was reserved for literary texts. Documents were written in a cursive script with linked letters, and the style varied noticeably with the era and issuing agency. Influences can be observed between late Latin cursive and Greek cursive. Documents copied on stone were normally transliterated into epigraphic capital letters.

In the east, the language of documents was primarily Greek. Diocletian's attempt to impose the use of Latin for public documents in every region had an effect in certain sectors (imperial constitutions, military documents), but practically speaking, this worked only with the help of Greek translations of Latin documents. The use of Latin in eastern documents declined after the 4th century, but the proportion of Latin words borrowed from the Greek remained high in the later documents. The style of the documents reveals the growing dominance of rhetorical models (especially in the preambles), and of the literary and poetic lexicon. These developments, which occurred early in high-level public documents, later extended to lower administrations and to private documents. The Semitic languages had no known documentary use in the later empire; in Egypt, documentation in Coptic developed only after the Arab conquest.

Materially, the late antique period was hardly an exception in the general disappearance of archives from the Graeco-Roman world. Nonetheless, certain Egyptian provinces saved a few thousand documents, and they have made it possible to reconstitute sets of documents issued or conserved by a single author or authority: the (always fragmentary) "archives" of persons, often amassed in the course of exercising public duties, such as the officer Abinnaeus under Constantius II or the notary Dioscorus under Justinian. Another eastern province, Arabia, has begun to yield a deposit of archives in the form of carbonized rolls from the cathedral of Petra (6th century). A few originals written in other regions have been found in Egypt—in particular, rare documents sent from Constantinople. The chronological profile of documentation is not linear: the 4th and 6th centuries left behind more documents in Egypt than the 5th. The same is true in other eastern provinces, where epigraphic copies of official 5th century documents are rare.

The quantity and quality of the data vary depending on the place, the age, and also the category of document. Within the state's sphere, several thousands of imperial constitutions (complete or fragmentary) were compiled, especially in the Theodosian (438) and Justinianic (534) Codes; a scarce hundred others are known to epigraphy. Of the originals on papyrus, there are now only mutilated rescripts. The acts of provincial agencies (civil or military governors, bureaus, municipalities) are known both through Egyptian papyri and, to a lesser degree, through inscriptions (especially in Asia Minor). Large sets of documents from the judicial system (minutes of hearings, petitions from citizens) and the tax system have come down to us. In the sphere of private law, documentation is lacking in certain respects. Even though legislation broadened the role of lawyers *(nomikoi)* to cover a growing number of notarized acts, only a handful of documents indicate the later form of marriage licenses and wills, for example.

The disparities in extant documentation prevent us from giving a perfect assessment of the variety of documentary forms and their development over time, even at the highest level. Our knowledge, for example, of emperors' documents suffers greatly from the disappearance of the originals. In this area, the difference between the east and west seems minor (with the exception of the barbarian kingdoms). Linguistically, Greek did not become predominant in eastern legislation before the 6th century. Formally, the genres of Roman antiquity persisted: the *edictum* (in particular in Constantinople), the *mandata principis* addressed to governors, and the *oratio ad senatum* (also in the east). However, the constitutions of late antiquity established the dominance of the epistolary style, nuanced with distinctive formulas depending on the status of the addressee. In addition to legislation in the strict sense, the imperial chancellery produced masses of responses to requests from individuals or city-states; only a portion of these responses *(rescripta)* were initialed by the emperor personally *(adnotationes)*. Beginning in the 5th century, a solemn form of rescript developed, the *pragmatica sanctio*.

BIBL.: Roger S. Bagnall, "Papyrus Documentation in Egypt from Constantine to Justinian," *Miscellanea Papyrologica,*

ed. R. Pintaudi (Florence, 1980), 13–23. Franz Dölger and Johannes Karayannopulos, *Byzantinische Urkundenlehre I: Die Kaiserurkunden* (Munich, 1968). Jean Gascou, "Les codices documentaires égyptiens," in *Les débuts du codex,* ed. A. Blanchard (Turnhout, Belg., 1989).   D.F.

Documents, Islamic

Islamic documents reveal the transition from Graeco-Roman to Islamic rule and society, as well as the intervening Coptic influence. There are more than fifty thousand documents dating from 643 to 1378 C.E. housed in collections on four continents, the largest collections being in Vienna and Berlin. Several thousand Arabic documents dating primarily from the 7th to the 10th century have been catalogued and a smaller part of those published. The documents are written overwhelming on papyrus but also on ostraca, bone, wood, and linen, while post-10th century documents are on paper. Documents have been found in archaeological excavations beginning in 1824 near the pyramids, and also by grave robbers. The overwhelming majority originate from Egypt. There are more than six hundred 7th century documents from Palestine and a few early ones from Jordan, Damascus, and central Asia. Documents from Egypt from 643 until about 720 are in Greek, Arabic, or Coptic, or they are trilingual. Thereafter they are overwhelmingly in Arabic, with perhaps several thousand in Coptic. Documents from elsewhere are in Arabic; those from central Asia are in Sogdian, Arabic, and Chinese.

Among the catalogued documents, the overwhelming majority are personal letters, many incidental to business affairs. The next largest portion are administrative documents dealing with agricultural administration, including contracts, tax receipts, survey logs, and orders. Next are legal documents—regarding marriage, inheritance, property, legal disputes and settlements. A few are literary and religious.

Documentary sources are invaluable in providing us with unbiased, contemporary testimony written by and for the local population, reflecting actual day-to-day practices and circumstances. In some instances documents confirm and elucidate later Arabic narrative evidence. Documents confirm narrative sources' accounts of the Arab administration's attempt to replace Coptic officials with Muslim (because of their limited numbers, Arabs were able to replace only the highest level of native Egyptian administrators during the 1st century). On the other hand, later Arabic narrative sources can also be shown to have occasionally systematically rewritten history, suppressing earlier realities to serve then-current political, economic, religious, and social purposes. Papyri from the Umayyad period contradict later Abbasid narrative sources, which uniformly misrepresented the earlier dynasty in a systematic effort to discredit it.

Documents provide our only reliable evidence of the

pace and mechanisms of Arabization and conversion in ordinary society. In the early 8th century, parties to contracts had a choice of language in which to have their documents recorded, and they opted for Coptic. In the 11th century legal documents written in Arabic continued to be "read to the parties in Arabic and explained in Coptic," and the parties to the Arabic contracts were overwhelmingly Coptic.

On the basis of the documents, Arabization appears to have been glacially slow. And without Arabization, what of conversion to Islam? Muslim witnesses who signed contracts in the 10th century were sometimes recent converts or from families of recent converts, by the evidence of their names. In a 9th century marriage contract, a woman with a Coptic first name and patronymic marries a man with an Arabic first name and patronymic. In a 10th century document the mother of a Muslim official has a Coptic first name and patronymic. Intermarriage between Christian women from prominent families and Muslim officials represented upward social mobility and protection of family position.

Greek (and also ancient Egyptian) technical terminology was transliterated into Arabic and continued sometimes into modern times. In agriculture-related documents in particular, officials in Egypt transliterated terminology from the Coptic and the Greek. The precise meaning and usage of the terms, however, correspond more closely to later Arabic definitions than to Greek and Coptic antecedents.

Documents indicate that, early on, the Muslims reinstituted a reliable judicial system in Egypt, of which Christians chose to avail themselves. The legal documents give evidence of the change but, more important, also reveal a continuity that predates the Hellenistic period. Specifically Islamic jurisprudence is evidenced in a subtle change in Coptic legal formulary to alter a seller's testimony from a declaration of agreement to a statement that, when asked, he will testify that he had agreed. This reflects the preference of Islamic practice for oral over written testimony.

Many of the constitutive elements of formulary in Arabic contracts for the sale of legacies between Copts—formulary that is "according to the sale of Islam" and that conforms to later Islamic jurisprudence from Iraq—are the same as those elements in Coptic and Greek formulary. At first glance, this seems to indicate that the Arabs borrowed from their immediate predecessors in Egypt and disseminated those elements eastward. However, the appearance of these same formulaic elements in much earlier documents from Egypt and elsewhere in the Middle East indicates instead that the Arabs and Greeks shared a legal tradition drawn from ancient Middle Eastern forms. Further evidence that Arabic was part of the Asian world from which that legal formulary originated is the reappearance in Arabic documents and Islamic jurisprudence of legal and administrative terminology common to the ancient Semitic-speaking world.

Certain elements of the millennium-long Hellenistic presence in Egypt were reversed under the Arabs, with those elements reverting back to pre-Hellenistic Egyptian practices. Regional differences in Islamic jurisprudence sometimes correspond to pre-Hellenistic Egyptian practice in those regions. Additionally, contrary to all Islamic laws of succession but following pre-Hellenistic Egyptian customary law, a sister's share in an endowment is equal to her brother's. The unique historical equality of women in Egypt apparently survived or was revived after one thousand years of Hellenism. Finally, the Arabs reverted to using the ancient Egyptian names of major towns after a thousand-year hiatus.

In summary, the documents give evidence of a slower pace of transition, a deeper entrenchment of ancient customs, and greater degrees of continuity and commonality between the Graeco-Roman and Islamic periods than narrative sources would have us believe.

BIBL.: N. Abbott, *The Kurrah Papyri from Aphrodito in the Oriental Institute* (Chicago, 1938). G. Frantz-Murphy, "A Comparison of the Arabic to Earlier Egyptian Contract Formularies," *Journal of Near Eastern Studies* 40 (1981): 203–225, 355–356; 44 (1985): 99–124; 47 (1988): 105–112; 47 (1988): 269–280; 48 (1989): 97–107. A. Grohmann, "Arabische Papyruskunde," *Handbuch der Orientalistik, Erste Abteilung, Der nahe und der mittlere Osten, II. 1* (Leiden and Köline, 1966), 48–118. R.G. Khoury, "Du vocabulaire politico-religieux dans la plus vieille correspondance officielle en Islam," *Ktêma* 14 (1989): 79–85. Y. Ragib, "L'écriture des papyrus arabes aux premiers siècles de l'Islam," *Revue du monde musulman* 58 (1990): 14–29. G.F.-M.

Documents (West)

Legislation apart, few examples of official documents have survived from the late antique west. Fortunately, however, it is clear that various types of official documents of the classical and late Roman periods provided models that underlay those of the early Middle Ages. Not that there are many surviving official documents from the 6th and 7th century west. Where a document has been preserved, it is often because it was useful to later generations: indeed the majority of pre-7th century documents that have come down to us were transcribed onto parchment, having originally been written on the much more perishable medium of papyrus. In the event, most documents surviving from the early Middle Ages were preserved in monasteries which were concerned with their possessions and rights. Because those monasteries whose archives have survived to any extent were founded, at the earliest, in the 6th century, it is usually necessary to make inferences about documents in the late Roman west from what survives from the sixth and seventh centuries: this is also true for Italy, although it boasts a collection of papyri surviving from Byzantine Ravenna. For the east, the preservation of papyrus documents in Egypt has ensured a larger survival of classical material, which sometimes provides useful analogues for the west.

According to the traditional study of diplomatic, documents can be classified either as public or private. Public *acta,* or diplomas, emanating from the sovereign included legislation, or royal *edicta,* as well as grants of privilege and records of final settlement of cases, or *placita.* The forms of the majority of early medieval public (or royal) documents were almost certainly derived from types of documents issued in the late Roman period by provincial governors. Some Merovingian *acta* survive as originals, the most significant group of those, which date to before 750, being the 38 royal charters that were preserved at St. Denis. Private *acta* include documents recording gifts, exchanges, sales, concessions, etc. Again early medieval traditions appear to be a development of those of antiquity.

Documents were drawn up by official scribes. Those at the royal court were highly trained and could use the shorthand system of Tironian notes—named after Cicero's secretary, Tiro—to authenticate documents. Authentication also required signatures, or marks *(signa)* in the case of the illiterate, and could include the use of the seal in the case of the Merovingians. That methods of verifying the authenticity of documents were sophisticated can be seen from an episode in *Histories* by Gregory of Tours (10.19) in which documents purportedly sent by Bishop Egidius of Rheims were checked against copies in the bishop's own archive. While documents were not always required to prove possession or a right, an authentic charter carried considerable weight in a court of law.

Although the majority of documents that have come down to us were transmitted through monastic archives, it is clear that the most important archives of private documents in late antiquity were the *gesta municipalia,* registers held in the *civitates* in which every major transaction had to be registered. References in earlier administrative texts show that the *gesta municipalia* had been in existence in the late antique period, but the fullest evidence for them is found in the Merovingian formularies, which on occasion refer to the opening of the *gesta* and the registration of a new document.

The Merovingian (and Visigothic) formularies are collections of *formulae,* providing models of the most important types of documents. The formularies that survive all date from the 6th century or later: some of them can be linked to particular towns, like Clermont, Tours, or Bourges, but the most extensive of them was compiled by Marculf, apparently for Bishop Landeric of Paris ca. 700, whose formulary includes models for

public and private documents. Formularies seem to have been compiled at a time when expertise in drawing up documents was in decline, and in some cases it is clear that the compiler had in front of him a genuine archive of texts from which he was constructing models. They thus provide our fullest evidence for the use of documents at the end of antiquity in the west, as well as being evidence of the need for handbooks to maintain the tradition of written documentation.

Although the majority of late antique and early medieval documents belong to the traditional area of diplomatic, chance discoveries have shown the use of documentation to have been extensive even outside the legal context. The discoveries of fragments of a Merovingian financial document from Tours and, more remarkably, slate documents from Visigothic Spain offer indications of the extensive reliance on written documentation in the period.

BIBL.: Olivier Guyotjeannin, Jacques Pycke, and Benoît-Michel Tock, *Diplomatique médiévale* (Turnhout, Belg., 1993). I.W.

Donatism

A long-lasting schism in the North African church, Donatism was one of several rigorist movements that opposed reconciliation with those Christians who had "lapsed" under pressure of persecution. Other such groups included the Melitians of Egypt and the Novatianists in Rome, Constantinople, and Asia Minor.

During the persecution of 303–305 a number of the clergy submitted to the authorities' demand that they surrender their copies of the Scriptures. In the sight of the resisters, they became known as *traditores* (betrayers). In February 304 one group of resisters, arrested in the small town of Abitina in central Tunisia, held an impromptu council while in prison in Carthage and declared solemnly that *traditores* would not share with the martyrs (namely, themselves) in the joys of paradise. Donatism got its start at this point. Probably in 311, Mensurius, bishop of Carthage, died and was succeeded by his archdeacon, Caecilian. Immediately the schism occurred, for it was believed that Felix of Aptunga, one of Caecilian's consecrators, was a *traditor,* while Caecilian himself was rumored to have behaved oppressively toward the Abitinian confessors. The dissidents were reinforced by the arrival of seventy Numidian bishops claiming the right to consecrate the new bishop of Carthage. They held a council, declared Caecilian deposed, and consecrated in his stead Majorinus, a lector and servant of Lucilla, a rich Spanish lady whom Caecilian had offended.

This was the situation that confronted Constantine when he entered Rome in triumph on 29 October 312. Believing that there could be only one authentic ministry in the church, the emperor backed Caecilian from the outset, and subsidized him. The opposition was now led by Donatus of Casae Nigrae in southern Numidia, a charismatic figure who gave his name to the movement and governed it until his death in 355. They protested to Constantine as chief magistrate of the empire. Constantine remitted the case first to an ecclesiastical tribunal under Miltiades, bishop of Rome (2–5 October 313) and then to a council of the western churches convened at Arles (1 August 314). Both found in Caecilian's favor. In February 315 Felix of Aptunga was cleared of the charge of *traditio*. After further hesitation Constantine declared Caecilian to be rightful bishop of Carthage and proscribed his opponents. In December 320 a judicial inquiry before Zenophilus, *consularis* of Numidia, proved that some of the Numidian bishops who had condemned Caecilian were themselves *traditores*.

Despite these setbacks, the Donatist cause prospered. In 336 Donatus was able to convoke a council of 270 bishops to consider whether or not converts to his church should be rebaptized. Ten years later, he felt strong enough to petition the emperor Constans (340–350) to recognize him as sole bishop of Carthage. The two commissioners, Paul and Macarius, who were sent to North Africa to report on the situation favored Donatus's Catholic rival. There were disturbances in Carthage and Numidia. Donatus and his chief followers were exiled to Gaul, where Donatus died in 355.

The Catholic ascendancy ended with the advent of the emperor Julian (361–363). The Donatist leaders returned from exile in triumph, and under a new, non-African bishop of Carthage, Parmenian (355–391), the church entered a period of prosperity that lasted until the end of the century. As Jerome wrote in *De viris illustribus* in 393 regarding Donatus, he had "deceived nearly the whole of Africa" *("paene totam African decepit")*. A schism led by the Donatists in proconsular Africa (the Maximianists) was crushed by the Numidians at the Council of Bagai in 394. The situation was ultimately changed by the failure of Count Gildo's revolt (supported by some leading Numidian Donatists) in July 398, and the emergence of Augustine of Hippo as Catholic champion. Augustine's unceasing barrage of anti-Donatist writings was followed by a renewed proscription of the Donatist church by the emperors in 405 and their enforced attendance at a confrontation with the Catholics at Carthage in 411, presided over by the imperial commissioner Marcellinus. Donatism was condemned and finally banned by edict on 30 January 412. Though much weakened, the church survived renewed Catholic ascendancy, the Vandal conquest (429–534), and the Byzantine occupation (534–ca. 660) to reemerge as a force in southern Numidia during the pontificate of Pope Gregory I (590–604). It died out only with the onset of Islam at the end of the 7th century.

Southern Numidia (central Algeria) was the heartland of the Donatist church—"Numidia, where you predominate," as Augustine admitted, addressing the Donatists. From 1890 to 1940 archaeological evidence accumulated to support this statement. In the 1930s research by André Berthier and colleagues covering seventy-five sites revealed a uniform religious scene. Each village possessed more than one chapel (sometimes as many as seven). These were rustic buildings, each housing relics of a martyr beneath the altar enclosure in front of the apse. Some inscriptions carried the Donatist watchword *Deo laudes* (Praise God) or the names of martyrs and dates of their death. Other inscriptions indicated a liturgy, based on the Eucharist, that included triumphant singing in praise of martyrs and biblical readings emphasizing separation from and defiance against the world. The villages that housed these chapels seem to have had no other public buildings, but were dominated by granaries and olive presses. Though ostensibly prosperous, it was from among these communities that the movement of the Circumcellions arose. Eventually allied with the Donatist church, between 340 and the arrival of the Vandals in 429, the Circumcellion bands wrought terror among Catholic clergy and landowners.

The martyr ideal vividly expressed in 400 by Petilian, bishop of Constantine, linked the popular Donatism of the Numidian high plains to the Donatism of educated Christians in the towns—the "eloquent many" in the movement, as Augustine called them. The Donatists could claim parentage for their beliefs in the mainstream of North African theology in the 3rd century, as represented by Tertullian and Cyprian. Their church also was an exclusive body of the elect that denied any ecclesiastical authority to the emperor and his representatives. Sacraments had to be administered by clergy who were themselves in a state of purity. Hence apostates, such as *traditores*, were automatically outside the church, their sacraments were invalid, and if they wished to join the "true church" of Donatus they had to be rebaptized. Whereas the Catholics, represented by Optatus of Milevis (fl. 365–385) and Augustine, emphasized that the true church had to be universal, the Donatists stressed the necessity for its integrity and holiness, though they maintained a link with the See of Peter as the source of episcopacy. Suffering persecution was the touchstone of righteousness. Holiness also involved renunciation of the classics. The Bible alone defined their way of life, and their understanding of the Bible drew its inspiration from Cyprian. Not only did they call on the same biblical texts as Cyprian and his contemporaries—such as Ephesians 4:5 (one Lord, one faith, one baptism)—to justify their exclusion of "the sons of *traditores*" (i.e., the Catholics) from Communion, but also like Cyprian they understood the whole Bible in terms of typology relating in some way to Christ and his church. In Tyconius (ca. 380), Parmenian (d. 391), and Macrobius, Donatist bishop of Rome (ca. 350), they produced theologians regarded as eminent by western Catholics. Tyconius's Seven Rules for the interpretation of Scripture influenced Augustine's thought, especially in the *De doctrina christiana,* and that of early medieval theologians such as Bede and Beatus of Liebana.

The emergence of the Donatist church was the most important event in the history of 4th century North Africa until the advent of Augustine. Donatism influenced plastic art and sculpture, attitudes to the classics, and the social as well as the religious outlook of the majority of North African Christians. As a result North African Christianity became increasingly isolated. Carthage was no longer the powerhouse of western Christian thought and a potential rival to Rome, as it had been in the 3rd century. The violent suppression of Donatism may have contributed to the alienation of North Africans from Christianity itself, and prepared the way for the relatively swift and permanent transfer of allegiance to Islam.

BIBL.: W. H. C. Frend, *The Donatist Church: A Movement of Protest in Roman North Africa* (Oxford, 1952; 3rd ed. 1985). F. Leroy, "L'homélie donatiste ignorée du Corpus Escorial," *Revue bénédictine* 107 (1997): 250–262. J. L. Maier, *Le dossier du Donatisme,* Texte und Untersuchungen 134–135 (Berlin, 1987). M. Tilley, *Donatist Martyr Stories* (Liverpool, 1996). M. Edwards, *Optatus: Against the Donatists* (Liverpool, 1997). S. Lancel, *Actes de la Conférence de Carthage, SC* 194, 195, 224, 373.   W.F.

Dowry

Marriage was normally accompanied by a direct dowry, given by the wife's family to the husband. Sources from late antiquity frequently allude to the practice, mentioning, for example, that with the birth of a daughter came concern for the dowry, or that looking for a wife meant looking for a dowry. Such remarks are reinforced by biographical notes. Besides the dowry, from the 4th century on, one finds a gift was given from husband to wife. Imperial law gradually treated the dowry and the husband's donation (called an antenuptial) as two symmetrical patrimonial contributions, subject to the same rules in cases of divorce, widowhood, or remarriage, and went as far as requiring equality. In practice, however, there was a major difference: while the dowry was usually paid upon marriage, the donation often remained virtual and served as a dower for the widow. In western kingdoms the direct dowry declined in comparison with the husband's donation, which was called the *dos* (marriage portion).

Information as to dowry amounts is rare. Literary sources cite dowries from 10 to 100 gold pounds, and one of Justinian's *Novellae* confirms that 100 pounds (7,200 *solidi*) was a limit rarely exceeded. Papyri mention, among various social classes, much lower amounts (50 or 100 *solidi,* with no value for other dowry property), and, once, 50 gold and 500 silver pounds.

Since the dowry was a portion of the patrimony reserved for daughters and then, usually, for their descendants, we are inevitably dealing with property transmission within the family. Roman law, applicable throughout the empire, gave daughters on intestacy the same rights as their brothers. But to receive their inheritance, dowered daughters were required to put their dowry back into the pool. Legislation from late antiquity refined the relevant regulations, seeking equality among the children. It is generally believed that the Greek world excluded dowered girls from family inheritance and that such a custom continued into the Byzantine era. But careful study of inheritance practices shows that from the end of the 3rd to the 7th century married daughters were not excluded and participated equally with the other children.

The dowry, paid in the wife's name or by her, represented a discrete entity within the property controlled by the husband, and it was subject, from the time of Roman classical law, to complex rules establishing each person's rights. Later legislation gave new prerogatives to the wife, the "true owner" of the dowry according to Justinian: its administration, under serious circumstances, could be entrusted to her during the marriage, and a general and preferential security on her husband's property was granted to her if the dowry had already been spent. Literary sources and documents confirm that the management of the dowry estate was the husband's affair, and that the risk that the property would be mortgaged or spent during the marriage was real. It is more difficult to know whether the dowry usually represented the whole estate of a married woman. Justinian claimed that it did. But legal texts and papyri refer to more complex situations, and it is assumed that the richer the woman's family, the more likely she was to possess property besides her dowry.

In Islam, the bride receives a dowry *(mahr)* from the groom as a legal requirement for marriage. The dowry might consist of money, other objects of value, or, less often, merely a symbolic gift; it was given to the bride at or shortly after the marriage or in installments. Although the marriage contract itself was concluded between the groom and the bride's guardian, the dowry was the sole property of the bride, even after divorce or the death of her husband. This right substantially altered the Arab custom in which a dowry was given as a "purchase price." Originally the dowry in pre-Islamic times was given to the bride's guardian, though by the early 7th century the bride may have received part or all of it. In the Qur'ān, see sura 2:236–237, and many places in sura 4.

BIBL.: Antti Arjava, *Women and Law in Late Antiquity* (Oxford, 1996). Mona Siddiqui, "Mahr: Legal Obligation or Rightful Demand," *Journal of Islamic Studies* 6 (1995).   J.B.

Easter

Easter, the annual Christian feast of the "paschal mystery" of Jesus, including his passion, death, and resurrection (not just the resurrection, as later thought), was celebrated between 22 March and 25 April, on the Sunday on or after the first full moon following the spring equinox. Astronomy was therefore a crucial component of the ecclesiastical calendar. A literary method known as the computus helped to reckon consistently the date of the paschal celebration. It was then announced by the local bishop to his congregation at Christmas, as is preserved in sermons especially from North Africa.

Jewish converts to Christianity continued to observe Jewish feasts (Matt. 26:17ff.; Mark 14:12ff.; Luke 22:7ff., John 5:1; Acts 2:1, 20:16), and it is impossible to determine when Easter became a Christian feast distinct from the Jewish Passover. The New Testament employed Jewish paschal typology to explain Jesus's self-offering (Matt. 26:17–29; Mark 14:1–25; Luke 22:7–20; John 1:36, 19:31–37; 1 Cor. 5:6–8), and the Parable of the Virgins is considered a Christian Passover Haggadah (Matt. 25:1–13; Luke 12:35–40; cf. Matt. 9:14ff.; Mark 2:20, Luke 5:33–35; Rev. 19:9).

The "paschal controversy" recorded by Eusebius (*Hist.eccl.* 5.23–25) proves that Christians celebrated Easter by around 125. The dispute concerned the date of Easter, which Johannine Christian communities in Asia Minor celebrated at the Jewish Passover on 14 Nisan (21 March). That is why they were called Quartodecimans ("Fourteeners"). Other churches celebrated, as today, on the Sunday following 14 Nisan.

The earliest description of a Christian Easter service, the apocryphal *Epistle of the Apostles* 15 (ca. 150), probably from Asia Minor, describes a Quartodeciman paschal vigil celebrated on the night of 14 Nisan in memory of Jesus's death, and concluding with the Eucharist, the sign of Jesus's ongoing presence and the pledge of his second coming (1 Cor. 11:26). Early Christians fought over the date of Easter precisely because they expected the return of Jesus during the Easter vigil, at which they were "watching and waiting" for that coming (cf. Matt. 24:43; 1 Thess. 5:2; 2 Thess. 2:1ff.; Rev. 3:3, 16:15), an eschatological expectation still seen as late as the 4th century.

In the 3rd century the addition of baptism to the ritual of the vigil enriches Easter symbolism. Earlier, Jesus was the sole protagonist of Easter: only his crossing over from death to life in expectation of his coming again was commemorated. With the addition of baptism to the vigil, contemporary with a renewed emphasis on the Pauline theology of baptism (Rom. 6:3–12; Col. 2:11–14, 3:1–4), the Christian, too, becomes protagonist of the celebration: just as Jesus died and rose for our salvation, Paul teaches, so too the Christian, in baptism, dies to sin and rises to new life in Jesus.

The earliest signs of the tendency to historicize Easter into an annual commemoration of Jesus's resurrection, a narrowing of focus not justified by earlier Christian tradition, appear in the 5th century, consequent to the development of the Holy Week passion cycle in Jerusalem at the end of the 4th century. Egeria, a traveler in the east probably from Spain, recorded in her travel accounts the Easter liturgy she observed being performed in Jerusalem in 383.

In its final form the traditional Easter celebration comprised a vigil beginning Saturday evening with vespers extended by a series of readings from the Hebrew Bible illustrating the Jewish paschal typology and messianic or new covenant prophecies (for instance, the Paschal Lamb of Ex. 12; crossing the Red Sea in Ex. 14–15) believed fulfilled in Jesus and in the sacraments of baptism and the Eucharist, which celebrate the mystery of salvation and the new covenant in him. While the congregation listened to the vigil readings, the bishop baptized the neophytes in the baptistery, then led them into the church to join the waiting community for the Easter Eucharist, the first in which the newly baptized took communion.

BIBL.: Raniero Cantalamessa, *Easter in the Early Church: An Anthology of Jewish and Early Christian Texts* (Collegeville, Minn., 1993). *Egeria's Travels,* J. Wilkinson, trans. and commentary (London, 1971), 54–88, 132–140. Hans-Joachim Schulz, "Sieht, der Bräutigam kommt!" in E. Carr, S. Parenti, A.-A. Thiermeyer, and E. Velkovska, eds., *Eulogema: Studies in Honor of Robert Taft, S.J.* (Rome, 1993), 453–472. August Strobel, *Ursprung und Geschichte des frühchristlichen Osterkalendars* (Berlin, 1997). Thomas J. Talley, *The Origins of the Liturgical Year,* 2nd ed. (Collegeville, Minn., 1991).

R.F.T.

Edessa

Called Orhay in Syriac (whence Arabic ar-Ruha and Turkish Urfa), Edessa was the capital of Orrhoene, or Osrhoëne, a small kingdom on the east bank of the Euphrates. Situated between the Taurus Mountains and the Desert of Syria, it was a satellite of Iran, then of Rome, and was annexed by the latter as a *colonia* in 216 C.E. Taken by Iran in 609, by Rome in 628, by the Arabs in 639, the power of its legend was never forgotten in Byzantium; there it was exploited in favor of icons, and the legend was appropriated in 944, together with the associated relics (the letter of Christ and his miraculous image on cloth, the *mandylion*) by the Christian emperor as heir to Abgar of Edessa, the first Christian king. The supposed divine grant of immunity to Edessa, and thus to Constantinople, made the legend of King Abgar a focus of the empire's hopes in the 4th, 6th, and 10th centuries. The relationship between the king and the apostle (Thomas, Addai, or Thaddaeus) in the legend mirrored that between the emperor and the patriarch in Byzantium, and retellings of the legend (at least one of them by an emperor, Constantine Porphyrogenitus) comment indirectly on contemporary relations between church and state.

The Christians of Edessa were probably always of at least two factions, that associated with the missionary Addai being Pauline and becoming Nicene and Orthodox, and any others, who came to be generally considered as heretical. This disunity stimulated a remarkable literary creativity, which made Syriac, the Aramaic dialect of Edessa, the chief vehicle for Christian ideas east of Byzantium as far as India and China. Thanks first to the philosopher Bardesanes (d. 222) but above all to Ephraim (d. 373), much of theology developed at Edessa along poetical lines and was brought home to the people by the chanting of ballads and lyrics called *memrē* and *madrashē*. The exegetes of Edessa composed their commentaries on the Jewish Scriptures in markedly Semitic ways, though they also assimilated the teachings of the Antiochene and the Alexandrian schools. The School of the Persians at Edessa was "a communicating door between East and West" until its closure by Zeno in 489. Greek literature was avidly translated at Edessa; the exegete Theodore of Mopsuestia and the theologian Severus of Antioch were later suppressed in Byzantium and their work survived only in Syriac. Histories were written, too, at Edessa. The so-called *Chronicle of Joshua the Stylite* is a jewel of the annalistic genre composed anonymously by a steward of the cathedral of Edessa in 506; the *Chronicle of Edessa,* composed in 540, arranges selected extracts from the ancient royal annals and the more recent episcopal ones for rhetorical effect, but leaves an impression of incompleteness.

The topography of Edessa in late antiquity is hard to establish without archaeology. There is an acropolis with a steep drop to the west, where the original walled city must have stood. At some date the walls were extended to include the springs to the south, on which the kings built their palace, but to build it they had to straddle the River Daysan (Skirtos in Greek). This led to catastrophic floods in 201, 303, 413, and 525, in spite of the diversion of the river through a man-made channel to the north of the city (presumably Diocletian's work, since the traveler Egeria saw it in 384 but it was not one of the works of Abgar VIII after the flood of 201). Justinian, besides clearing the channel of silt and building the dike higher, extended the walls even further to include the citadel to the south of the springs. At the same time a new domed basilica was built to replace the one destroyed in 525. It is described in a contemporary Syriac *sūgīthā* rich in keys to Byzantine architectural symbolism. This building was counted one of the wonders of the Arab world.

BIBL.: F. Miller, "Materials for the History of Roman Edessa and Orrhoene, AD 163–337," in *The Roman Near East* (Cambridge, Mass., 1993), 553–560. A. N. Palmer, "King Abgar of Edessa, Eusebius and Constantine," in H. Bakker, ed., *The Sacred Centre as the Focus of Political Interest* (Groningen, 1992); and "Who Wrote the Chronicle of Joshua the Stylite?" *Ägypten und altes Orient* 20 (Festschrift J. Assfalg) (1990): 272–284. J. B. Segal, *Edessa* (Oxford, 1970).

A.P.

Education

The kinds of education available in late antiquity were as varied as the faces of late antique culture itself. In the home and the school, the forum and the church, the weaver's shop and the army, people learned the skills and behaviors needed to survive and (with luck) prosper in the world that birth's chances or human designs had given them. Educational possibilities ranged from the piety of a bishop's exegesis to the secularity of a goldsmith's apprenticeship; from the utilitarian shorthand in which a notary recorded the proceedings of a governor's tribunal to the fine rhetoric of the advocate whose words the notary recorded; from the formal institution of "chairs" in rhetoric or philosophy supported by civic or imperial funds in the empire's great cities to the informal intimacy of the study group that brought Augustine to Christianity at Milan. To survey all these avenues would be to survey the world of late antiquity itself. Here we can examine only the one variant most commonly meant when people speak of ancient education, the "classical" education of the male elite.

The education of young men was founded on a long tradition of learning and verbal skills that, as one teacher put it, "the brilliance of human talent ha[d] brought to a state of high polish" (Diomedes, *Gramm.Lat.* 1.299.3 Keil). The tradition's main institutions—the schools of "grammar" and rhetoric—were the main institutions, outside the family, through which the empire's governing classes created and confirmed their identity. Acquiring the modes of speech traditionally defined as correct was the first, critical step in assuming this identity. From about the age of seven or eight, a boy's experience was governed by three goals, pursued first in the school of the grammarian, then in that of the rhetorician: mastery of correct language, command of a fairly small number of classical texts, and an ability to turn the knowledge of language and literature to a facility in composition and speech.

The grammarian's main contribution to these aims consisted of the "knowledge of speaking correctly" and the "explication of the poets" (Quintilian, *Inst.* 1.4.2). Knowledge of correct speech was conveyed as a set of rules governing phonology, morphology, and the behavior of the individual parts of speech as codified in the technical handbook (Latin *ars;* Greek *technē*). Explication of the poets combined study of the language, as its larger part, with historical and ethical instruction. In line-by-line and word-by-word progress through a text—above all, Homer and Menander in Greek, Virgil and Terence in Latin—the poet's language was explained and used as a tool to confirm the grammarian's rules. Persons, events, and other realia were glossed as they occurred; the actions of men and gods were explained and judged in terms of accepted mores and so were used to confirm them.

Having secured the basic forms and rules in his memory, the student then went on to deploy them in a school of rhetoric. Again instruction combined the reading of classical texts—now predominantly prose,

especially the orators—with the professor's lectures on the main devices of persuasive speech: *inventio,* the discovery of the appropriate facts and arguments; *dispositio,* the arrangement of the latter in an effective order; *elocutio,* their expression in a becoming style; *memoria,* memorization of the speech, the better to deliver it in the most natural-seeming manner; and *pronuntiatio,* the delivery itself, with attention to voice and gesture. The climax of this schooling, and the most direct preparation for turning textbook skills to practical use as an advocate, was declamation. Here the student delivered speeches on imaginary themes, pretending to advise a noted historical figure on a course of action or, more often, arguing one side or the other (or both in turn) of fictitious forensic cases—the ancient version of the moot court competitions in North American law schools. And like winning a case in moot court, the successful delivery of a declamation was something of a rite of passage: it signaled that the student was nearly ready to enter the company of adults, and that through "tenacious memory" and "toil" he had achieved "the square-set soundness of speech and its polished brilliance produced by skill." He was then as superior to the uneducated as the uneducated were to cattle (*Gramm.Lat.* 1.299.18ff.).

This "gymnastic of the soul" (Galen, *Peri ēthōn* 4) was available to very few. The population at large, massively illiterate, was served (if at all) by "schools of letters" *(ludi litterarii),* institutions of low prestige that generally provided only basic, utilitarian literacy; those who had access to the "liberal schools" of grammar and rhetoric were effectively insulated from the lower orders. That access depended primarily on wealth of a kind that few strata of the population possessed, and was made still more difficult by the schools' sparse geographical distribution: in late antiquity all known schools of grammar and rhetoric were located in urban areas that later emerged as episcopal sees—that is, places that tended to be centers of gravity in the secular as well as the spiritual lives of their regions.

The social and geographic exclusiveness of the traditional culture had two evident and related consequences. First, "letters" (that is, liberal letters) or the like figured as one of the three or four most important marks of status—what Paulinus of Nola meant, for example, when he referred to "office, letters, and family background" *(honos, litterae, domus)* as the "tokens of prestige in the world" (*Carm.* 24.418–419). At one extreme, these "letters" provided eminence at the tomb, if nowhere else; scores of funeral inscriptions boast of the education of deceased children or youths, pathetic reminders of dignity achieved and promise cut short. At the other extreme, one's culture followed one through life: education was included regularly, for example, on inscriptions honoring men who had gone on to hold the highest offices of state. On such occasions "letters" (or "eloquence") are regularly joined with other virtues such men might claim, such as justice and integrity (e.g., *CIL* 6.1751, 1772, cf. 1698, 1735).

The phrase "other virtues" is used advisedly here. A literary education, no less than justice and integrity, was regarded as a guarantee of moral worth; acquisition of eloquence was a sign that one possessed the discipline, the diligence, the appetite for toil that marked a man fit to share in the burden of empire. *Doctrina* presumed *mores;* to be a scholar presumed that one was the right sort of person, a gentleman. Letters validated claims to status, both moral status and social, although the two were hardly separate in the eyes of the traditionally cultured man. The learned were, simply, *boni,* the good; the uneducated were *inertes,* the "crude and slothful" (Aurelius Victor, *De Caesaribus* 9.12).

This notional fusion of moral and social status helps to explain a second consequence of the traditional culture's exclusiveness, its importance in maintaining the social stability of the empire. If in theory a man of traditional education could be presumed to be the "right sort," in practice the presumption provided entry into the networks of personal relationships and patronage by which local and imperial governments were managed and through which their rewards were distributed. The man thus prized and rewarded for his culture was a figure of continuity in the empire from its beginning until its end, whatever changes the life and structure of the empire experienced. In the wake of such changes it was a function of the traditional education to continue its old job of sorting out and identifying the elite, of providing reassurance that nothing basic had shifted, that the right, honorable men were still conspicuously present and in control. Tenacious in its maintenance of a familiar order, this culture of language and texts continued to perform its job as long as the structures of the imperial government remained standing in the Latin west, and still longer in the Greek east.

BIBL.: Stanley F. Bonner, *Education in Ancient Rome* (Berkeley, 1997). R. Cribriore, *Writing, Teachers and Students in Graeco-Roman Egypt* (Atlanta, 1996). M. R. M. Hasitzka, *Neue Texte und Dokumentation zum Koptisch-Unterricht* (Vienna, 1990). P. Heather, "Literacy and Power in the Migration Period," *Literacy and Power in the Ancient World,* ed. A. K. Bowman and G. Woolf (Cambridge, Eng., 1994), 177–197. Robert A. Kaster, *Guardians of Language: The Grammarian and Society in Late Antiquity* (Berkeley, 1988). P. Riché, *Education and Culture in the Barbarian West: Sixth through Eighth Centuries,* trans. J. J. Contreni (Columbia, S.C., 1976). A. L. Tibawi, "Education in the Golden Age of the Caliphates," *Islamic Culture* 28 (1954): 418–438.

R.K.

Elections

The epigraphic silence about curiae after the tetrarchic era is not sufficient to prove the disappearance during late antiquity of all participation by the people in local political life and in the election of municipal magistrates. A relic at least of that participation appeared in Africa, a particularity *(consuetudo)* recognized by the law. Although the people were still playing a role in 412 in appointing *exactores* in Carthage, they had lost the right to nominate candidates (*nominatio* took on the sense of designation when the function shifted to the curiae). Popular *suffragia* took the form of acclamation or dissent rather than elections in the strict sense. Preferences *(vota)* were expressed in venues for public entertainment (in Lepcis Magna, Aphrodisias, and so on), and the text of the acclamations was frequently inscribed in public places.

An idea of what municipal contests had become can be inferred from ecclesiastic elections, which are described in more detail. We have the proceedings of the election of Silvanus in Cirta in 305, and of Augustine's successor in Hippo in 426. Because of the growing role of bishops in the city-states, local political issues were raised during their elections. Both desired and feared, the participation of the plebs was never questioned by ecclesiastical authorities, who defined it as the *suffragium* of the local community, subordinated to the *iudicium* of the bishops. The unanimous consent of clerics and laymen was championed by the conciliar canons and became a topos in episcopal biographies, but was implemented unevenly in reality. Certain elections of popes were particularly eventful, with the community at first divided between two pope-elects: in 366–367, between Damasus I and Ursinus; and in 418–419, between Boniface I and Eulalius. In the former election, political factors (opposition to the emperor) played a role, as did popular pressure and support (from circus people and gravediggers, the proponents of Damasus said).

BIBL.: G. W. Bowersock, "From Emperor to Bishop: The Self-Conscious Transformation of Political Power in the Fourth Century A.D.," *Classical Philology* 81 (1986): 298–307. D. Claude, "Die Bestellung der Bischöfe im merowingischen Reich," *Zeitschr. Savigny Stiftung für Rechtsgeschichte: Kanonist. Abt.* 49 (1963): 1–77. Frédéric Ganshof, "Note sur l'élection des évêques dans l'empire romain au IVe siècle et pendant la première moitié du Ve siècle," *Revue internationale des droits de l'antiquité* 4 (1950): 467–498. Claude Lepelley, *Les cités de l'Afrique romaine au bas-empire* (Paris, 1979), vol. 1, 140–149. L. Pietri, Y. Duval, and C. Pietri, "Peuple chrétien et 'plebs': Le rôle des laïcs dans les élections ecclésiastiques en Occident," *Institutions, société et vie politique dans l'empire romain du IVe siècle* (Rome, 1992), 373–395.

J.C.

Emesa

Emesa or Homs, modern Hims, is located at the point where the the road joining Palmyra to the sea crosses the road leading from northern Syria to Damascus. Close to an ancient dam on the Orontes, it lies on a rich agricultural plain. Emesa seems to have suffered from the fall of Palmyra and the collapse of trade in the late 3rd century. However, it would be wrong to believe that this large pagan sanctuary and ancient capital of a client kingdom of Rome was a fallen city during late antiquity. Joined to the province of Second Phoenicia after Phoenicia's partition in the late 4th century, Emesa became the rival of the metropolis of Damascus. It finally obtained the title of autocephalous metropolis thanks to the 452 discovery of the head of John the Baptist by monks in the monastery of Spelaion. In the 7th century, it became a *jund* capital, which augmented its role as a large regional center.

Paganism, manifested under Emperor Julian by the violent destruction of churches and the conversion of one of them into the Temple of Dionysus, does not seem to have survived much longer in Emesa than elsewhere in Syria. The rarity of Christian inscriptions—which are not more numerous in many other cities—is offset by the abundance of hagiographic and literary documents. The relic of John the Baptist, kept in the monastery of Spelaion, was transported to the cathedral in the 8th century, and the cult of Saint Julian of Emesa took its place at the monastery. A church dedicated to the Apostles and to St. Barbara was located near the *tell*; the Church of St. Thomas and the Church of the Theotokos are known to us; there were also probably sanctuaries of SS. Silvanius, Luke, and Mokimos, and Hemorroisse of the Gospel.

In the late 6th century, Emesa appears in the *Life of Simeon the Mad* as a large city with ramparts, an agora, baths, *stoa,* and theaters; various trades, from mule driver to glassmaker, are noted. The city played a large role in the early 7th century as a center for regrouping troops and a pillar of Byzantine defense in operations against the Persians and Arabs. The taking of Emesa (Homs) by the Arabs, after the population had demanded the *aman,* cost a ransom. One church became the mosque, and five hundred Companions of the Prophet moved into the city.

Archaeology has uncovered few relics of the Emesa of late antiquity, apart from a basilica—decorated with mosaics—outside the walls, and Christian tombs with paintings and mosaics.

BIBL.: P. Peeters, "La passion de saint Julien d'Emèse," *Analecta bollandiana* 47 (1929): 44–76. N. Saliby, "Die Katakomben von Emesa/Homs (Hims)," in *Syrien: Von den Aposteln bis zu den Kalifen,* ed. E. M. Ruprechtsberger (Linz, 1993), 265–273. P.-L. Gatier, "Palmyre et Emèse ou Emèse sans Palmyre," *Annales archéologiques arabes syriennes* 42 (1996): 431–436.   P.-L.G.

Emperor

Emperor is the standard modern designation for a ruler of the Roman empire. The titles commonly used in late antiquity were *Basileus* in the Greek east and *Augustus* in the Latin west. Emperors were appointed for life unless deposed; the tetrarchy instituted by Diocletian (ca. 300 C.E.) represents only a brief and failed attempt to institutionalize cycles of retirement and replacement. Modes of appointment varied. Dynastic succession tended to prevail; otherwise emperors were often chosen by the army. The usurpation of Julian and the appointment of Jovian in the mid-4th century both suggest that nondynastic appointments were negotiated in cabals of senior officers, who also took account of at least some higher-ranking civilian officials. From Diocletian to the fall of the western empire (476), there was usually more than one reigning emperor; from the reigns of Arcadius and Honorius (395), a pattern of one eastern and one western emperor became normal. By the mid-4th century, the most important seats of imperial power were Trier and Milan in the west, Constantinople and Antioch in the east. From Theodosius I onward (379–395), Constantinople predominated as the eastern imperial residence, matched in the west from ca. 408 by Ravenna.

In ideological terms, the emperor was the all-powerful, divinely appointed ruler of the Roman state. The first few centuries C.E. had seen Hellenistic concepts of kingship overtake the position of first citizen as defined by Augustus, and the adoption of Christianity merely advanced the process. As a result, the office of emperor came to be defined by the interplay of a number of related ideas. First, the Roman empire upheld (above all, by its written laws) a social order that allowed individuals to achieve their teleological maximum: the triumph of the rational mind over irrational physicality that lay at the heart of the divine plan for humankind. Second, the divinity (after Constantine, the Christian God) directly upheld the Roman state, since its triumph was thus so central to the divine plan for the cosmos. Third, the divinity directly appointed and inspired the ruler of the Roman state. Fourth, as a result, the emperor came to be seen as *nomos empsuchos,* law—i.e., divine law—personified.

This ideology dictated much of the lifestyle of a late antique emperor; ordered ceremony reflecting the emperor's supra-human status was what the public demanded. Thus Ammianus Marcellinus praises Constantius II (in other ways his villain) for his superhuman demeanor during a visit to Rome in 357, and criticizes Julian (otherwise his hero) for his unbecoming informality at court. The waking hours of emperors were increasingly consumed by a daily ceremonial routine, supplemented by a regular sequence of special events. Architecturally, the audience halls of imperial palaces were constructed as theaters for ceremonial display. Behavior within these halls was regulated by dress codes and complex laws on precedence, and by elaborately submissive norms of behavior such as prostration before the imperial person. In addition, horse and chariot racing, journeys, victories, and religious festivals were opportunities for yet more ceremonies before a wider audience. This highly developed ceremonial life communicated certainty to the people. Its rhythms reiterated that they were part of an unceasing and profoundly correct social order, maintained by the direct support of the divinity and designed to bring them to full humanity.

Some aspects of the imperial office, not least its legal responsibilities, straddled boundaries between ceremony and the more straightforwardly practical. The emperor was the fundamental source of law, and with every imperial letter having the status of law, dispute settlement became a matter of keeping up with or even identifying the latest relevant imperial ruling. At the same time, written law was seen as the great symbol of what made Roman civilization uniquely good. For two different reasons, therefore, a series of emperors attempted to codify late imperial laws: to provide lawyers (and their clients) with up-to-date handbooks and to posture as the upholders of Roman civilization.

In addition, of course, an emperor had very practical roles. Perhaps above all, he was supreme commander of the army, but this function was exercised in practice only by some. Where the emperor did not in fact take this command, it was still vital for him to secure military loyalty. Related to this, the imperial council, or Consistory, was the formal body where issues were debated and foreign and other policies formulated. It was, however, a public and formal gathering rather than a debating forum, and much of the real give and take of politics probably took place elsewhere, behind closed doors. Also in the hands of the emperor was religious policy. After Constantine, emperors increasingly controlled higher church appointments and both called major church councils and set their agendas. These rights gave emperors considerable power to set official religious policies, but they had to use it carefully. Too much interference generated opposition, and the church never in practice formed a united body. Indeed, some churchmen did not even accept the basic premise of imperial ideologies, that the emperor was God's particular agent on earth. On a more individual level, the emperor was the focus of innumerable petitions. The emperor's overall right to grant offices, exemptions from office, tax reductions, and other special favors represented formidable powers of patronage, making the imperial court and its officials, if not the actual emperor, central to the aspirations of the empire's landowning elites.

The degree to which individual emperors actually exercised personal control in these areas, and the balance between the ceremonial and directive functions in their lives, varied considerably. There was, however, a marked tendency for the ceremonial to increase over time, reflecting the rise of an articulated imperial bureaucracy, and a consequent development of a court society. Mode of appointment was also an important variable. Where the individual was the latest member of an established dynasty, especially if he inherited as a minor, then there was a greater tendency for his reign to focus on ceremonial functions. These were tendencies, however, not absolute patterns. Constantine I, son of Constantius I Chlorus, could hardly have been more actively involved in policy and patronage, and the later 6th and early 7th centuries were dominated by emperors with active military pedigrees.

BIBL.: R. Collins, "Theodebert, 'Rex Magnus Francorum,'" *Ideal and Reality in Frankish and Anglo-Saxon Society*, ed. P. Wormald (Oxford, 1983), 7–33. G. Dagron, *Empéreur et prêtre: Étude sur le "césaropapisme" byzantin* (Paris, 1996). J. F. Matthews, *The Roman Empire of Ammianus* (London and Baltimore, 1989). F. Millar, *The Emperor in the Roman World* (Ithaca, N.Y., 1977). S. MacCormack, *Art and Ceremony in Late Antiquity* (Berkeley, 1981). C. E. V. Nixon and B. S. Rodgers, *In Praise of Later Roman Emperors: The Panegyrici Latini* (Berkeley, 1994). P.H.

Encratites

Encratite (from Greek *enkrateia*, continence) was a label attached to heretical Christians and also to anyone who practiced rigorous asceticism. The name referred to the rejection of marriage, meat, and wine in opposition to the goodness of creation (1 Tim. 4:1–5). Irenaeus claimed the Encratites originated with Saturninus and Marcion, but that Tatian defined their doctrinal stance with the belief that Adam was denied salvation (*Adv.Haer.* 1.28.1). Tatian's influence on Encratite thought was extensive. Certain readings in his *Diatessaron* supported an Encratite understanding of the Gospels, ensuring his influence would be long-lasting in regions such as Syria and Mesopotamia, where the *Diatessaron* long remained the standard Gospel version. Clement of Alexandria (*Stromateis* 3.9.63; 3.12.81–82, 85; 7.17), Eusebius (*Hist.eccl.* 4.28–29), and Epiphanius (*Panarion* 47) all condemn Tatian and the Encratites for their irregular exegesis.

The Encratite understanding of the virtuous life had its roots in pre-Christian Graeco-Roman philosophical practice. Some scholars have also seen a connection with certain Jewish movements such as the Essenes or Therapeutae, although the descriptions in Josephus and Philo owe more to philosophical models than to Jewish tradition. The valuing of abstinence characterized all religious orientations of late antiquity. The Encratites differed only by degree: their complete insistence on abstinence as a requirement for all believers. Basil of Caesarea viewed Encratites as heretical because they practiced their own rite of baptism (*Ep.* 188.1, 199.47). Eventually the Encratites were absorbed into the monastic movement.

BIBL.: Ugo Bianchi, ed., *La tradizione dell'Enkrateia: Motivazioni ontologiche e protologiche* (Rome, 1985). Giulia Sfameni Gasparro, "Asceticism and Anthropology: *Enkrateia* and 'Double Creation' in Early Christianity," in *Asceticism,* ed. Vincent Wimbush and Richard Valantasis (New York, 1995), 127–146. William L. Petersen, *Tatian's* Diatessaron: *Its Creation, Dissemination, Significance, and History in Scholarship* (Leiden, 1994). S.A.H.

Ephesus

The greatest city of Asia Minor, a center of commerce, banking, administration, and education, Ephesus played a significant role in church history and legend. It was strategically located on the west coast of Asia Minor at the western end of a major road that led east into the interior. Its governor, the proconsul of Asia, held a high rank in the imperial hierarchy; he exercised considerable local and regional power and was the major patron of public works. The council, which functioned throughout the period, and the provincial assembly, attested in the 4th century, had little real power. The people expressed their will in formal acclamations and often violent riots; they supported the Blue and Green circus factions. A school of pagan philosophy—its most famous representative, the theurgist Maximus of Ephesus (who converted the emperor Julian to paganism)—was active until the late 4th century.

The Ephesian church was supposedly founded by St. Timothy and sanctified by the visit of St. Paul; legends, all narrated in late antique texts, associated it with St. John and the Virgin Mary, and with the 5th century miracle of the Seven Sleepers. Its bishop, who aspired to dominance in Asia Minor, hosted the ecumenical Council of 431 and the "Robber Council" of 449. The minutes of these meetings give considerable insight into local conditions. St. John's tomb, which exuded a miraculous curative "manna," and the shrine of the Seven Sleepers attracted numerous pilgrims.

Our knowledge of the city comes primarily from a century of excavation that shows that the antique fabric of the city was maintained through the 6th century, with characteristic modifications. Pagan buildings were destroyed or put to new uses, while churches and associated structures grew; colonnaded streets assumed greater prominence as markets and social centers. Massive public works still dominated, financed in this period primarily by the proconsul or the church, though with important imperial contributions. A theater, an agora, baths, colonnaded streets, and luxurious houses filled the center, representing continuity with the Roman past. The elaborate decoration of the houses reveals the continuing prosperity of the urban rich. Almost all existing public works were maintained or rebuilt in this period, with much activity in the 4th and 6th centuries. The great basilical churches of St. Mary (seat of the Council of 431), built in a wing of the temple of Hadrian, and of St. John, a work of Justinian on a hill outside the city, the supposed site of the evangelist's tomb, were the greatest new monuments.

Ephesus never recovered from a massive destruction around 614. Thereafter, it came to consist of two discrete centers, one by the harbor and another around the Church of St. John. Both were surrounded by new fortifications, faced largely with marble reused from ancient buildings. The ancient site was greatly reduced, its largest structures used as bastions in the new walls, and the most active part of the late antique city left outside. The Church of St. Mary was eventually replaced with a smaller though still substantial structure, while St. John remained to dominate the hilltop site that became the center of medieval Theologos, as the city came to be called, after the evangelist.

BIBL.: C. Foss, *Ephesus after Antiquity* (Cambridge, Eng., 1979). C.F.

Ephesus, Councils of

Two church councils were held in Ephesus (431 and 449) that together displayed the power of the patriarchate of Alexandria against its main rivals, Constantinople and Antioch, and established Alexandrian Christology as the basis for official Christian orthodoxy. In 431, Cyril exploited the controversy over the term *Theotokos* to bring about the downfall of his rival Nestorius. A schism between the 200 bishops who followed Cyril and the 43 who sided with John of Antioch was resolved with the Formula of Reunion in 433, after heavy pressure from the imperial government, when the Antiochenes acquiesced in the condemnation of Nestorius and Cyril withdrew his Twelve Anathemas, a particularly extreme and controversial statement of his doctrinal position. In 449 Dioscorus used the case of Eutyches as a pretext for deposing Flavian, bishop of Constantinople; established a "one nature" Christology as orthodoxy; and proceeded to condemn all the major leaders of the Antiochene movement, including Bishop Domnus of Antioch, Theodoret of Cyrrhus, and Ibas of Edessa.

On both occasions, the legitimacy of the proceedings was called into question by accusations of intimidation and violence. In 431 Cyril brought to the Council of Ephesus large numbers of Egyptian monks, Alexandrian sailors, and perhaps the notorious *parabalani,* or hospital attendants, attached to the Alexandrian church. In concert with the followers of Memnon of Ephesus, also an opponent of Nestorius, Cyril's people occupied the streets and major churches, preventing their rivals from holding services and apparently forcing the vast majority of the bishops present to join with Cyril and begin the council before John of Antioch and his Syrian bishops had arrived. Nestorius, meanwhile, stayed away from the Cyrillian assembly and surrounded his lodging with soldiers; his friends at the imperial court blockaded major roads and ports to prevent (unsuccessfully) the pronouncements of Cyril's council from reaching Constantinople. In 449 Dioscorus drew on the strength of the same Egyptian groups and also allied himself with powerful monastic leaders such as Eutyches of Constantinople and the Syrian Barsauma (an archimandrite already notorious for his savage attacks on Jews in Palestine), leading a large group of monks and lower clergy who were in open rebellion against bishops such as Flavian, Ibas, Theodoret, and Domnus, charging them with "Nestorian" teachings as well as misconduct. Charges of peculation, usury, sorcery, sodomy, blasphemy, nepotism, and other crimes brought by local clergy and monks against their bishops, though undoubtedly exaggerated or invented in many cases, offer a fascinating glimpse of church government and misgovernment at the local level. The admission of an archimandrite such as Barsauma, who was not a bishop, to an official seat at the council, symbolized the revolutionary nature of this assault on the very legitimacy of the episcopal hierarchy of the east. Dioscorus, unlike Cyril, began the council with the full support of the emperor and thus had soldiers at his command as well. At the Council of Chalcedon two years later, many bishops charged that the soldiers and the monks had beaten them, forced them to sign their names to blank sheets of paper, and even threatened their lives. Flavian apparently died of injuries sustained either at the council or on his way to exile a few weeks or months later (the exact chronology is uncertain).

The Councils of Ephesus are the first for which complete documentary *acta* are preserved (those of 449 survive only in a Syriac translation). Both councils were characterized by tight control over the production of the written record, so as to create an appearance of unanimity in the transcript. At Ephesus II, the notaries of Dioscorus attacked some other notaries who were caught trying to make an independent transcript, beat them, and destroyed their writing materials. In the Acta of Chalcedon, by contrast, complaints and protests and shouting matches between different factions are carefully recorded. Ephesus II's treatment of the records of Flavian's synod against Eutyches, and Chalcedon's of the record of Ephesus II, featured scrupulous examination and challenge to the accuracy and authenticity of the record as a means of undermining the legitimacy of the previous proceeding.

Despite the similar procedure and course of events at both councils, the long-term results of each were quite different. The Council of Ephesus in 431 has gone down in history as the Third Ecumenical Council, at which Cyril's writings and then Cyril himself came to be canonized as a touchstone of orthodoxy. Less than a decade after Cyril's death, both Monophysites and Chalcedonians claimed to be following the true teaching of Cyril as expressed at Ephesus I. In his attempt to imitate Cyril's success, Dioscorus in 449 overreached himself. Where Cyril had had the support of both the pope and the empress Pulcheria, Dioscorus had managed to turn both against him. Although he conducted the council with the full support of Theodosius II, the

death of that emperor in July 450 cleared the way for a backlash against his arrogant conduct and violent tactics. Pulcheria and her new imperial consort, Marcian, organized the Council of Chalcedon with the specific purpose of reversing everything that Dioscorus had done. Pope Leo (whom Dioscorus had unwisely excommunicated) had, historically speaking, the last word when he gave the council of 449 its infamous nickname of *Latrocinium*, or "Robber Council."

BIBL.: Eduard Schwartz, *Acta Conciliorum Oecumenicorum*, vol. 1 (Berlin and Leipzig, 1933); French trans. in A. J. Festugiere, *Ephèse et Chalcédoine: Actes des conciles* (Paris, 1982). U. Bouriant, ed., *Actes du concile d'Ephèse: Texte copte publié et traduit* (Paris, 1892). Wilhelm Kraatz, "Koptische Akten zur ephesinischen Konzil vom Jahre 431: Übersetzung und Untersuchungen," in *Texte und Untersuchungen zur Geschichte der altchristlichen Literatur*, ed. Oscar von Gebhardt and Adolf Harnack (Leipzig, 1904). J. Flemming and G. Hoffman, eds. and trans., *Akten der ephesinischen Synode vom Jahre 449* (Göttingen, 1917). S. G. F. Perry, *The Second Synod of Ephesus together with Certain Extracts Relating to It* (Dartford, Eng., 1881).

J.M.G.

Ephrem

Ephrem the Syrian (ca. 306–373 C.E.) was a deacon, hymnographer, exegete, and controversialist in the Syriac tradition of the Christian church. A few details of his biography may be gleaned from his extant writings; all other sources, Syriac, Greek, and Latin, are tendentious and present complex problems of interpretation. Born into an orthodox Christian family, Ephrem lived under an ascetic discipline unique to early Syriac Christianity. In that context the "sons and daughters of the covenant" *(bnay wbnath gyama)* lived in the towns and villages as consecrated celibates, "single ones" *(ihidaye)*—as symbols of single-minded devotion to the "only-begotten" Son. Bishop Jacob of Nisibis, upon returning from the Council of Nicaea, to which he was a signatory, selected Ephrem as his official "interpreter" *(mpashqana;* apparently of Scripture). Although the precise meaning of this appointment is unclear to modern scholars, Barhadbeshabba, the 6th-century historian of the School of Nisibis, understood it to signal the birth of that famous theological school. In any case, Ephrem began his prolific career as the bishop's interpreter and continued in this capacity to serve a succession of orthodox bishops: Babu, Vologeses, and Abraham.

Religious and political friction characterized life in Syro-Mesopotamia, especially after the death of Constantine in 337. On the one hand, establishment of Nicene orthodoxy was especially challenging, since heterodox or Jewish-Christian missionaries had evangelized Syriac-speaking Christians. On the other hand, the Sassanid Persian and Roman empires were engaged in a prolonged and brutal conflict in Mesopotamia. The political and military strife fueled both intra-Christian rivalry and broader conflict among Jews, Christians, and adherents of the traditional Graeco-Roman and Syro-Mesopotamian religions. Ephrem's writings manifest his profound involvement in these issues.

After the death of Julian, when the newly chosen Emperor Jovian ceded Nisibis to the Persians in 363, the Christian population left to resettle within the new Roman borders. Ephrem was among those who went to Edessa (Urfa), where he remained for the rest of his life. Ordained a deacon, he continued his writing and teaching and is said to have overseen the distribution of wealth for care of the hungry and the sick during a famine shortly before his death 9 June 373.

Ephrem wrote hymns *(madrashe)*, metrical homilies *(memre)*, and prose; in these compositions he presented classic 4th century orthodoxy in a richly symbolic matrix. By the early 5th century the hymns had been classified according to melody and content and gathered into collections for liturgical use—a process that ensured their preservation and centrality in Syriac worship but obscured in some degree their original sequence and context. Jacob of Sarug (d. 521) portrays Ephrem as conducting a choir of women and accompanying them on the kithara as they sang his hymns. The friendly interest his writings show toward women make this a plausible, if unproven, scenario.

With respect to their primary subject matter, the hymns may be classified variously as liturgical, historical, controversial, exegetical, ecclesiological, or hagiographical. The seasons of Christmas-Epiphany and Lent-Easter inspired his *Hymns—On the Nativity, On the Epiphany, On Fasting, On Unleavened Bread, On the Crucifixion,* and *On the Resurrection.* Ephrem's theological reflections on the major religious and political events of his time are to be found especially in the *Carmina Nisibena* and *Hymns against Julian (the Apostate).* Polemics against the Arians, Bardaisanites, Marcionites, and Manichaeans predominate in the *Hymns on Faith* and *Hymns against Heresies.* The *Hymns on Paradise* and *Hymns on Virginity* focus on symbolic and spiritual interpretations of Scripture. The *Hymns on the Church* present a wealth of ecclesiological symbolism. Finally, the *Hymns on Abraham Kidunaya* and *Hymns on Julian Saba* present these men as models of asceticism and holiness.

Although he is known primarily for his hymns, a substantial number of Ephrem's metrical homilies and prose writings also survive. In these he expounds such fundamental theological doctrines as the incarnation and the Nicene formulation of the Trinity, while he refutes the same heretical alternatives as in his hymns. In his *Prose Refutations* he displays a rudimentary awareness of Greek philosophical concepts that belies the notion that he was utterly innocent of "Greek learning"—a view espoused at least since Sozomen (*Hist.eccl.* 3.16). His *Commentaries on Genesis and Exodus* differ radically in style and occasionally in content from parallel materials in the hymns, notably

in the *Hymns on Paradise.* Several other scriptural commentaries (notably *On the Diatessaron* and *On the Acts of the Apostles*) survive in full or in part, principally in Armenian translations.

Ephrem's hymns became central to both eastern and western Syrian liturgical traditions, and his works have exerted a formative influence on all aspects of their ecclesiastical life. His reputation as hymnodist and model of the monastic life spread to all branches of the church. A vast body of writings attributed to him survive in Greek, Latin, Armenian, Georgian, Slavonic, Coptic, Arabic, and Syro-Palestinian—most of them spurious and designed to promote post-Evagrian developments in monastic spirituality.

BIBL.: Sebastian Brock, trans. and ed., *The Harp of the Spirit* (San Bernardino, Calif., 1984). S. H. Griffith, "Ephraem the Syrian's Hymns 'Against Julian': Meditations on History and Imperial Power," *Vigiliae christianae* 41 (1987): 238–266. S. H. Griffith, "Images of Ephraem: The Syrian Holy Man and His Church," *Traditio* 45 (1989–90): 7–34. Samuel N. C. Lieu, ed., *The Emperor Julian: Panegyric and Polemic: Claudius Mamertinus, John Chrysostom, Ephrem the Syrian,* 2nd ed. (Liverpool, 1989). Kathleen E. McVey, trans. and ed., *Ephrem the Syrian: Hymns* (New York, 1989).   K.M.

Epistolography

Letter writing was considered to be one of the great literary arts in late antiquity. Renowned epistolographers such as Libanius, the 4th century Antiochene rhetorician, spent much time defining what a good letter was (Libanius, *Letters* 228, 606, 716; Eunapius, *Lives of the Sophists* 496). Handbooks were also produced to teach the art of epistolography (Pseudo-Libanius, *Epistolimaioi*; Bologna Papyrus). These works are essentially collections of letters suitable for every occasion: praise and blame, advice, admonition, rebuke, consolation, mediation, accusation, accounting, and apology, which the less skilled could adapt to their particular situation.

A considerable number of letters, written by both pagans and Christians, have survived from late antiquity in published collections. It would be wrong, however, to view these letters as mere literary works. Epistolography was an essential mode of communication. Even the most seemingly banal communication fulfilled an important function, proclaiming the author's *paideia* and maintaining or establishing bonds of *amicitia* and patronage (e.g., Symmachus, *Letters* 2.68, 8.39; Theodoret of Cyrrhus, *Letters* 4, 5, 6). In their epistolographic output, men like Libanius and his contemporary Basil, bishop of Caesarea, represented themselves as important and recognized figures within the wider community of the Roman empire. This authority was demonstrated by the number of letters they sent out and the number of replies they received. However, it must be said that it was the Christian letter writers, concerned with forging a clear orthodoxy and hierarchy within their church, who maintained their vision of a united dominion long after their secular counterparts had resigned themselves to the realities of a divided empire and readjusted their sights accordingly. While Basil of Caesarea did not hesitate in petitioning the western bishops for aid in his struggle against Arianism (Basil, *Letters* 90, 92, 242, 243), the vast correspondence of Libanius contains little that is not solely concerned with his native city of Antioch and the imperial court at Constantinople.

The confidentiality of missives was difficult to enforce. Letters were often dictated and then, when received, read out aloud to an audience (e.g., Jerome, *Letter* 66.12; Libanius, *Letters* 476, 477). It was also not unusual for both the writer and the recipient to send copies of the missive to others (e.g., Jerome, *Letter* 51; Augustine, *Letter* 186.40). In addition, those who delivered letters could not always be trusted. Forgeries were not unknown (e.g., Symmachus, *Letter* 2.12.48; Basil, *Letter* 198.1–2). These shortcomings meant that sensitive information was often passed on by a trusted messenger *(tabellarius)*, with a written missive serving only as an introduction (e.g., Symmachus, *Letter* 1.46.90; Augustine, *Letter* 186.1). In some cases the letter itself seems to have been just a covering note attached to a *breviarium* or *indiculum* that contained more detailed news and information (e.g., Symmachus, *Letter* 2.25).

Often letters were collected together and published during or after their author's lifetime. Libanius, for instance, kept a file of duplicates of all his correspondence (*Letters* 88.5, 1218.2, 1307.1–3). Although formally published after his death, the corpus of Libanius's letters is generally thought to have been selected and rearranged by the author himself. The same can be said for Christian writers such as Basil and Augustine. Thus, it is clear that late antique letters often present the reader with a sanitized account of events.

BIBL.: C. W. Keyes, "Greek Letters of Introduction," *American Journal of Philology* 66 (1935): 28–44. G. Karlsson, *Idéologie et cérémonial dans l'épistolographie byzantic* (Uppsala, 1962). K. Thraede, *Grundzüge griechisch-römischer Brieftopik* (Munich, 1970). R.M.

Eras

None of the great taxonomic enterprises of late antiquity drew from a wider range of sources or engaged a wider range of collaborators than chronology. As a field of study, it took shape as early as the 5th and 4th centuries B.C.E. Antiquaries in Athens and elsewhere tried to date such great historical events as the Trojan War by collating the literary evidence with that of astronomy, on the one hand, and genealogical and other lists, on the other. Their techniques—which often rested on assumptions about the length of generations—proved both immensely durable and capable of being modified. In the Hellenistic world, scholars drew

up a standard set of dates for Greek history. Eratosthenes divided past time into three periods: chaotic, mythical, and historical. The Olympic era of 776 B.C.E. came to be accepted as the beginning of true Greek history, and lists of rulers, writers, and inventions gave more recent centuries a firm chronological spine, though debate persisted on the details.

At the same time, non-Greek scholars such as Manetho and Berossus made available records of Egyptian and Mesopotamian history—records that stretched back long before the beginnings of the Olympic era. Eschatological prophecies called forth by the extension of Seleucid and Roman rule stimulated the production of chronological schemes that covered the past as well as the future—usually in search of a hidden providential order that would bring about the end of oppression in foreseeable time. Within the Roman world as well, the crises of the late republic and early empire produced a new interest in historical dates and cycles: Varro, the greatest of the Roman antiquaries, clearly took as much interest in the future duration of Roman history as in its past, and saw chronology as a key to both.

Late antique chronologers, accordingly, inherited a rich and diverse body of materials and methods, which they assembled and used in creative ways. From the 2nd century onward, Christian intellectuals such as Tatian drew on both Jewish and pagan scholarship to argue for the priority of Moses over Homer. Eschatology continued to provide a powerful stimulus for chronological scholarship, sometimes of radically different kinds. Julius Africanus (3rd century) saw the past as falling into a neat, coherent pattern, and believed that the end of time was only two and a half centuries away. His successor, Eusebius, rejected such precise predictions and used the chronology of the Septuagint to postpone the end of the sixth millennium to long after his own time. In both cases, however, eschatology motivated chronology.

In the 4th century chronology received its definitive shape. Eusebius, perhaps imitating the *Hexapla* of Origen, laid out the histories of Egyptians and Jews, Greeks and Romans in parallel tables that included much cultural detail as well as the names and dates of rulers. This device required highly trained scribes and resulted in expensive manuscripts. Nonetheless, Jerome retained it in his Latin adaptation of the work. Numerous continuations and revisions preserved Eusebius's innovation for well over a millennium: Luther and Ussher still drew up chronologies in the same tabular and comparative format.

Tabular, comparative world chronology was intellectually expansive. It required wide coverage and allowed for constant digression. Its practitioners found room for the most up-to-date technical astronomy, that of Ptolemy, as well as for information about a very wide range of past civilizations. Chronologies became valued reference works about a vast range of subjects, from the names of the three Magi who came to adore

Christ to the date of the first Loireme. Some compendia—like the luxurious *Codex-Calendar of 354*—juxtaposed pagan and Christian materials without much apparent sense of strain. But beneath the calm, fact-studded surface of many world chronicles, debates raged. Even the date of the creation depended on one's choice of biblical text. Accordingly, some chronologers, such as Eusebius and Jerome, chose to fix a later date, like that of Abraham, as a base from which to reckon. The vast range of Near Eastern, Greek, and Roman material assembled by chronologers in Hellenistic and Alexandrian times could not always be reconciled with the Bible or with Christian practice. In 5th century Alexandria, scholars resorted to radical surgery to make Ptolemy's dates for Persian history match Daniel's. The Egyptian dynasties of Manetho seemed to start before the biblical flood. Chronology therefore remained as unstable as it was ambitious. Late antiquity bequeathed not only great compendia but a list of difficult technical questions to the Byzantine and western scholars who continued, down to the 18th century, to grapple with the problem of producing a single coherent chronology of the world from the materials known in the 4th century C.E.

BIBL.: W. Adler, *Time Immemorial* (Washington, D.C., 1989). M. Maas, *John Lydus and the Roman Past* (London, 1992). A. A. Mosshammer, *The Chronicle of Eusebius and Greek Chronographic Tradition* (Lewisburg, 1979). M. Salzman, *On Roman Time* (Berkeley, 1990).   A.T.G.

Eroticism

Eroticism can be viewed as the set of expressions of desire with which every civilization produces a particular style, and as a set of practices in love relationships. Past practices are accessible to us only through their expressions—in literary, verbal (through graffiti, for example), and iconographic documents. As a result, the disappearance of the expressions could lead us wrongly to infer the disappearance of the practices.

In effect, classical Hellenistic and Roman eroticism had its apogee in the 1st century B.C.E. It dealt frankly with both desire and practices. A romantic literature, which encouraged the dream of love, was popular between the 3rd century B.C.E. and the 3rd century C.E. The dreams analyzed in Artemidorus's *Oneirocriticon* (Interpretation of Dreams) in the 2nd century offer the most direct expression of the practices. The Greek myths, introduced throughout the Mediterranean and recounted and illustrated in painting, sculpture, and especially mosaic, provided a limitless fount of references through which to speak of desire, acts, and pleasure. The custom of holding long banquets that included debates and performances of singing and dancing continued in late antiquity, in modified and enlarged halls; mosaics with mythological themes still decorated private homes in the 5th century, in both the west and the east. But openly erotic writings and in-

scriptions were disappearing, and depictions of nude bodies lost their seductiveness and then disappeared altogether from art.

It is difficult to believe that the many Christian criticisms that, in the early centuries, accused pagans of debauchery, give a credible picture of pagan practices. We can, however, get at least an idea of these practices by making social distinctions. Monogamy was obligatory under Roman law, as Diocletian reminded polygamous peoples such as the Phoenicians and Jews in the late 3rd century, threatening them with the loss of their civil rights. We know that eroticism within marriage was discouraged. All the literature on marriage advised husbands not to initiate their wives into love practices, which were reserved for extramarital relations. Those pleasures, provided by slaves, concubines, and prostitutes of both sexes, were accepted by society.

The men of the Roman world had a marked preference for relations with very young boys and girls. The Greeks continued their tradition of loving free-born young boys, citizens, a tradition particularly well known for classical Athens. Libanius reports that during winter banquets in Antioch, guests made advances under blankets on boys younger than ten years old. He advised fathers not to take their sons to the banquets. The practice of marrying off prepubescent female citizens, rooted in Roman tradition, continued in the Byzantine world.

In addition to engaging in love relationships with free children, men habitually used slave children for sex, both boys and girls. Boys were still sometimes castrated so they would maintain their youthful smoothness (absence of body hair). The sale of free children by their fathers was forbidden, and the law attempted to shield slaves from the panders and go-betweens who prostituted them. The castration of slaves, already banned during the late empire, was better held in check. Christian sermons confirmed the need for conjugal chastity and fought against freer expressions of desire. Hagiography and the accounts of ascetics show how the body resisted when refused pleasure and what temptations arose when ascetics failed in their calling. We might even wonder whether the descriptions of temptations, and the visions and dreams of punishment, were not new modes of erotic excitation.

BIBL.: H. G. Beck, *Byzantinisches Erotikon* (Munich, 1984). Peter Brown, *The Body and Society: Men, Women and Sexual Renunciation in Early Christianity* (New York, 1988). Patricia Cox Miller, *Dreams in Late Antiquity: Studies in the Imagination of a Culture* (Princeton, 1994). Jean-Noël Robert, *Eros romain: Sexe et morale dans l'ancienne Rome* (Paris, 1997). Aline Rousselle, *Porneia: On Desire and the Body* (Oxford, 1988).   A.R.

Espionage

Espionage is a broad term encompassing a range of covert activities, but central to its meaning is the acquisition of politically or militarily valuable information. For late Roman emperors this meant information, first, about unrest and possible challenges from within the empire, and second, about external threats. They had at their disposal various institutional mechanisms through which it was sometimes possible to gain useful information in these two areas, although the clandestine nature of such activities inevitably means that the evidence is patchy.

There was no body specifically dedicated to internal surveillance, but the group of officials known as the *agentes in rebus* played an important role in this area, at least during the 4th century. Indeed the contemporary historian Ammianus Marcellinus portrayed some members of this group in such a sinister light that some modern scholars have incautiously described the *agentes* as a sort of "secret police." The formal function of the *agentes in rebus* was to carry government dispatches and to monitor the imperial courier service *(cursus publicus)*, ensuring that it was used only by those with official permits, but these responsibilities meant that they were also well placed to pick up portents of discontent and rebellion. One law instructs them to report all they see to their superior, elsewhere they are referred to as "the eyes of the emperor," and there are various incidents in which they can be seen acting as informers and agents provocateurs. All this derives from the 4th century; that they do not feature in this guise in subsequent centuries is probably due either to deficiencies in the evidence or to the necessarily furtive nature of such activities, since the formal responsibilities from which this aspect of their work evolved remained unchanged.

In the sphere of foreign relations, embassies to neighboring rulers were an obvious means of gathering intelligence about the capabilities and intentions of a people or state. This is well illustrated by the fact that one 4th century Roman envoy communicated details of Persian troop movements (and did so, moreover, by the ingenious subterfuge of a coded message concealed inside a sword scabbard). The restrictions placed by both the Roman and Persian governments on the movements of each others' embassies provide a further telling indication of their potential, which such controls would by no means have been able to curtail entirely.

Spies were also employed by both empires. According to the 6th century historian Procopius, spies in Roman pay would "enter enemy territory and gain access to the palace of the Persians, either under the guise of trading or by some other ploy; after investigating everything thoroughly, they would return to Roman territory and be able to report all the secrets of the enemy to the authorities" (*Secret History* 30.12). This is intriguing, but it also leaves many questions unanswered: how long such arrangements had been in place, the degree of formal organization, from where these spies were recruited. Accounts of particular individuals who undertook spying missions undoubtedly

survive from late antiquity, but they are of limited help in elucidating Procopius's statement, since in every case the individual is manifestly not a specialist spy—a "professional"—such as Procopius seems to describe. Procopius's optimistic assessment of the spies' effectiveness also remains difficult to verify, although the two empires' agreement early in the 5th century to restrict merchants' cross-frontier movements explicitly to combat the use of trade as a cover for espionage suggests that a serious problem existed, while the fact that, on Procopius's testimony, trade nevertheless remained a satisfactory pretext into the 6th century implies that the ability and perhaps the will to enforce the restrictions was limited. Certainly Persia offered a more favorable environment for intelligence gathering than any of the empire's other neighbors insofar as the higher degree of administrative and military organization there made it easier, paradoxically, to divine Persian intentions and to do so at an earlier stage. Moreover, although the Christian church within Persia increasingly sought to distance itself from the Roman empire to counter charges that it constituted a fifth column, ecclesiastical links across the frontier continued throughout late antiquity and could sometimes be exploited as a supplementary, informal intelligence channel not usually available elsewhere.

Although the frontier with Persia seems to have provided the greatest opportunities for intelligence gathering, espionage did also occur across other frontiers, even if less intensively. Particularly interesting is the existence in 4th century Britain of a body known, significantly, as *arcani* (literally, secret[ive] men), whose job was to move about among neighboring peoples to the north and report any signs of trouble. Frustratingly, however, nothing more definite is known about how they operated, when they were first established, or whether there were similar groups elsewhere in the empire. What is known is that the *arcani* were disbanded in 368–369 after it was alleged that they had succumbed to an unsurprising occupational hazard: accepting bribes in return for passing information to the enemy.

Besides information gathering, espionage can involve covert activities aimed at destabilizing enemy regimes, and examples of this can also be found during late antiquity. Two instances are known of plans to kidnap troublesome Alamannic leaders during the 4th century, while from the 4th and 5th centuries there are a number of cases involving the (attempted) assassination of problematic rulers, whether through the agency of an envoy or suborned retainer, or by a knife in the back while enjoying Roman hospitality. The target was almost invariably a key figure from one of the empire's northern neighbors; most notorious was the abortive plot to murder Attila. Apparently such methods were considered inappropriate vis-à-vis civilized Persia. Although extreme measures of this sort were not totally unprecedented in earlier periods of Roman history, there does appear to have been a greater willingness to resort to them during late antiquity—a development that perhaps reflects the increasingly desperate straits in which the empire found itself.

BIBL.: N. J. E. Austin and N. B. Rankov, *"Exploratio": Military and Political Intelligence in the Roman World from the Second Punic War to the Battle of Adrianople* (London, 1995), 214–243; A. D. Lee, *Information and Frontiers: Roman Foreign Relations in Late Antiquity* (Cambridge, Eng., 1993).   D.L.

Estates

Landholding—from medium-size properties to great estates—in the 4th to 7th centuries was dominated by the most powerful groups and institutions of the late antique world: the *domus divina* (imperial household), the church, the monasteries, and, to a great degree, the aristocracy. Below these groups was a mass of smaller landowners drawn from the middle bureaucracy of the provincial towns and from rich peasants and rural entrepreneurs. The "peasantry" included both the wealthier peasant proprietors and the mass of landless laborers who worked as lessees and rural laborers. Major social changes occurred in the course of the 4th and 5th centuries. Large estates in particular reflected the power of new landed groups nurtured by the transformations of the late empire. The nucleus of this aristocracy was made up of high-ranking government officials who had amassed considerable properties and in general ran their estates with mechanical efficiency. As the Apion archive shows, these nascent large landowners of the 5th century expanded their holdings through moneylending, which implies that the more powerful layers of the bureaucracy had accumulated cash reserves for investment in mortgages. The other feature worth noting is the role played by bureaucratic management of the larger estates in sustaining the permanence of the new enterprises.

Aristocratic estates generated huge revenues, of which the greater part accrued in cash. Such estates were said by a 5th century writer to have annual incomes of several hundred pounds of gold, excluding the value of the produce that was directly consumed. The characterization of the aristocracy as a "stratum of rentiers" (Vera, *Opus* II [1983] 493) is based on the unlikely assumption that the monetary component of estate revenue (three-quarters of the total) represented rent payments or the extraction of rent, whereas the underlying contrast is surely one between cash income or income accruing in monetary form and income retained in kind. These estates, then, were bound to the larger context of a restructured monetary economy which expanded slowly over the centuries. Their consistently high levels of extraction of gold also presuppose higher levels of efficiency in the organization and running of enterprises than minimalist stereotypes suggest.

In particular, the organization and use of labor were characterized by much more fluidity than historians have allowed for. Free labor was used extensively, and the dividing line between wage-labor and tenancy was far less rigid than scholars usually suppose. Landowners strove for both flexibility and control. (*P. Oxy.* 19.2239 [598] shows how carefully aristocratic estates could be supervised.) While smaller landowners depended on leasing, the aristocracy employed permanent laborers housed in special settlements called *vici* or *epoikia*. By the 6th century, the workforces resident in these settlements were largely hereditary, as a *Novella* of Justin II clearly implies. In estates based on resident labor, it is possible that some form of service tenancy was the usual method of exploitation, as it was on the Egyptian *'izbahs* of the late 19th century. The system maximized supervision of labor by its physical concentration of workers in specific localities within the estate. By contrast, in areas (mostly in the west) where seasonal migrant workers provided the bulk of labor (cf. Poncet for the French olive estates of a more recent period), landowners would have had less control over workers. This was probably true of large parts of North Africa in the 4th century, when rural laborers organized into labor gangs (*turbae*) and struggled to retain their mobility in the face of a powerful onslaught from both employers and the state. In short, rural wage earners included full-time rural laborers (*coloni*), casual employees, seasonal workers, sharecroppers, and so on, with some mobility, one presumes, between these sectors of the labor market. But slavery persisted, and rural laborers were frequently treated *like* slaves. This was most evident in the evolution of the colonate, which is best seen as a set of legal ordinances designed specifically for estates with resident workforces. A letter of Gregory the Great (*Ep.* 9.129) provides a fascinating illustration of how these might be applied in practice, and, indeed, of how they were still operative in the late 6th century on ecclesiastical estates in Sicily.

These Sicilian estates were called *massae*. Estates were described by various terms, such as *villa, vicus, fundus, massa,* and so on. *Villa* could mean either the estate as a whole or the central group of buildings from which the estate was administered. *Fundus* was a standard term frequently used for small or middle-size estates. *Massae* were agglomerations of *fundi*. In the *Liber pontificalis* the *massae* are described as yielding roughly thirteen times as much revenue as the average *fundus*. But the *Liber* also shows that *massae* varied greatly in size and productivity. In the vicinity of the towns and major urban centers, the aristocracy held "suburban estates," called *proasteia* in Greek. The ownership of villages was also a possible form of landholding. Libanius contraposed villages (*kōmai*) comprising numerous landowners to villages controlled by a single landowner (*despotēs*). The *Life of Theodore of Sykeon* refers to "villages belonging to the local church."

Again, there is the curious story in Procopius about a certain rhetor of Caesarea who purchased a "coastal village" for 21,600 *solidi,* which Justinian confiscated.

Finally, archaeological evidence has begun to reveal the late antique countryside in a more positive light. Catani's careful reconstruction of the Byzantine *fattoria* at El-Beida, in Cyrenaica, implies continuing investments in the third quarter of the 6th century and no apparent reason to suppose that production declined in the first half of the 7th century. In Egypt the huge wine factory excavated in the center of Marea on the southern coast of Lake Mareotis was surely active in the 6th century. The intense boom that stimulated investments in viticulture throughout the Byzantine period lasted well into the 7th century and could account for the dense network of estates that spread across areas like the Fayum in this period. What these individual establishments illustrate is the substantial continuity of many of these sites into the 7th century and later.

In all likelihood, both in the former Byzantine empire and in the Iranian world, estates abandoned by their owners were taken over by the Muslim state, which usually distributed the lands among members of the ruling family (as was the case in Syria and Jordan/Palestine) or among the military leadership (in central Asia).

BIBL.: Jairus Banaji, "Agrarian History and the Labour Organization of Byzantine Large Estates," in Alan Bowman and Eugene Rogan, eds., *Land, Settlement and Agriculture in Egypt from Pharaonic to Modern Times* (London, 1997). H. Finberg, "Roman and Saxon Withinton," *Lucerna* (London, 1964), 21–65. Jean Poncet, *La colonisation et l'agriculture européennes en Tunisie depuis 1881: Étude de géographie historique et économique* (Paris and The Hague, 1962), esp. 459–473. Dominic Rathbone, *Economic Rationalism and Rural Society in Third-Century A.D. Egypt: The Heroninos Archive and the Appianus Estate* (Cambridge, Eng., 1991).

J.BAN.

Ethiopia

A Greek noun derived from *aithiops,* meaning face burned (by the sun), *Ethiopia* refers to several regions of Africa. Among classical authors, it designates Nubia, south of Egypt, and, more generally, all the regions populated by blacks. That is the case in Herodotus and the New Testament. In early Christian literature, "Ethiopians" often appeared as generic figures of evil, stained black by sin—a blackness that could be "washed away" by baptism. In early monastic literature, monks were frequently tempted and tormented by demons who appeared in the form of Ethiopians.

In the 4th century C.E., the name *Ethiopia* was adopted by King Ezana to designate his kingdom, Abyssinia, in its Greek inscriptions (it was called Habashat in the indigenous language, Ge'ez). Among the late Greek and Roman authors, Abyssinia was called not Ethiopia but India, like the other countries

Stela, 67 feet high; 3rd to 4th century. One of a group of stelae at Axum carved to represent multistory buildings.

bordering the Indian Ocean (more precisely, *India ulterior* in Rufinus). The late antique Ethiopian state was also commonly called Axum (or Aksum), after its capital, which was located on the Tigrean plateau about a week's journey south and inland from the Red Sea port of Adulis.

The kingdom of Axum is mentioned for the first time in the *Periplus of the Erythraean Sea* (mid- to late 1st century C.E.). The territory of Axum included the northern part of modern Ethiopia and Eritrea, and at times may have stretched farther west into modern Sudan. In the early 3rd century, under Gadara, and again in the 6th century, under Kaleb Ella Asbeha (Elesboas in Greek), Axum brought large parts of South Arabia under its control. The chronology of the period must be established from a few royal inscriptions, coinage, and legendary royal lists found in later medieval literature.

Christianity took root in Ethiopia in the time of Constantine, through the agency of two shipwrecked Romans, Frumentius and Aedesius. Frumentius was made bishop of Ethiopia by Athanasius in 328, and was apparently still there in 357, when Constantius II wrote to King "Aizanas" (Ezana) in an unsuccessful attempt to recall Frumentius and replace him with an Arian bishop. These events, known from Athanasius's *Apologia to the Emperor Constantius* and Rufinus's *Ecclesiastical History,* are confirmed by numismatic and epigraphical evidence for the adoption of Christian ideology, at least by the rulers. In the early 4th century, the coinage of Ezana began to display the cross, long before that symbol ever appeared on Roman imperial coins.

After a very poorly documented 5th century, the next Axumite monarch known in any detail is Kaleb Ella Asbeha (Elesboas), who ruled from ca. 520 to ca. 540 and was most famous for his invasion of South Arabia in retaliation for the massacre of Christians at Najran. Kaleb was on good diplomatic terms with Constantinople. The Byzantine historian Malalas gives a colorful description of Kaleb's court. Later tradition remembers his reign as a golden age of Axumite power and portrays him as a great Christian king on the model of Constantine.

Axumite civilization is known through its architectural ruins. The greatest monuments were in the capital. They were primarily palaces of several stories, tombs, and especially the famous steles, whose ornamentation depicts very tall houses. The tallest of these steles, now broken, was 33.5 m high; another, still standing, measures 23 m. The vast 6th century cathedral Maryam Seyon (Mary of Zion) was destroyed in the 16th century: all that remain are the base, a few column fragments, and capitals very similar to those of the contemporary cathedral of San'a, built by the Axumite Abraha. Many churches and monasteries seem to have been constructed on top of pre-Christian religious sites.

The wealth of ruins in Axum is the result of the extraordinary prosperity of the kingdom in the 4th to 6th centuries, also evident in the abundant gold coinage. That prosperity was grounded in the massive exportation of African products: gold, ivory, rhinoceros horn, tortoiseshell, and live animals. The fauna were richer in antiquity than in our own time: the Byzantine ambassador Nonnosos, sent by Justinian to the king of Axum, saw a herd of five thousand elephants (Photius, *Bibl.*)

After Kaleb, Axumite power began a long decline. Axum was expelled from South Arabia by the Persians at the end of the 6th century and then cut off entirely from the Red Sea by Arab expansion in the 7th and 8th centuries. As the Ethiopian state shifted inland, Axum was abandoned as a royal capital, though it remained an important religious center.

Knowledge of Axumite Christianity depends largely on extrapolation from the customs and traditions of the Ethiopian church, as recorded in much later periods: little contemporary evidence survives. Nothing is known of the immediate successors of Frumentius, but by the end of the 4th century Christianity was sufficiently well established that Ethiopians were frequently seen in Egypt, Palestine, and Syria as pilgrims or monks (Jerome, Palladius, Synesius). Later Ethiopian tradition speaks of an influx of Syrian holy men in the late 5th or early 6th century, most famous among whom were the Nine Saints, revered as the founders of Ethiopian monasticism. They may have fled the Roman empire to escape Chalcedonian persecution, and indeed, at this time, Ethiopia followed the prevailing opinion in Egypt and Syria in rejecting the Council of Chalcedon and opting for a Monophysite definition of faith. Up to this time, Ethiopian Christianity had remained formally dependent on the church of Alexandria, with the Ethiopian primate *(abuna)* receiving consecration from the Coptic patriarch. The liturgy of the Ethiopian church seems to have been derived originally from that of 4th century Alexandria, and it also shows substantial Syrian influence. The Deggwa or antiphonary, along with other music and hymns, is traditionally attributed to the 6th century saint Yared, who was inspired by chanting he heard while on a pilgrimage to Jerusalem. Ethiopian Christianity of later times is characterized by a strong emphasis on the Hebrew Bible and a number of "Judaizing" practices such as Sabbath observance, circumcision, and dietary restrictions. From at least the 13th century, the Ethiopian royal family claimed descent from Solomon, and the Church of Maryam Seyon in Axum claims to possess the Ark of the Covenant. However, there is no direct evidence for the existence of these traditions in the late antique period.

Ethiopian monasticism, later famous for its severe ascetic practices, seems to have featured both individual hermits and large, organized communal foundations; the *Life of Antony* and the Pachomian Rule were both translated into Ge'ez during this time. Although all extant works on lives of native Ethiopian saints date from a much later period (usually the 13th century or later), they follow very much in the tradition of late antique hagiography. Evangelization by monks seems to have been mainly responsible for spreading Christianity farther south and inland from its original base around Axum and Adulis.

The Axumite empire and its civilization exercised a strong influence on the imagination of its neighbors. Mani called Axum one of four great world empires, along with Rome, Persia, and China. The early 8th century Umayyad frescoes at Qusayr Amrah depict the Axumite *negus* as one of six great kings whose rule had been superseded by Islam. Islamic tradition remembered the Ethiopians favorably for having given refuge to Muhammad's followers who had fled from persecution in Mecca. For this reason, it was later held, Ethiopia was to be spared from jihad, although this theoretical prohibition does not seem to have prevented frequent Arab-Ethiopian clashes in the following centuries. Even as the Islamic conquests of the 7th century cut off Byzantium from direct contact with Axum, Ethiopia acquired a new role in Christian apocalyptic writing as the great Christian kingdom in the south that would one day overthrow the Muslims (for example, the late 7th century *Apocalypse* of Pseudo-Methodius of Patara), anticipating the later medieval legends of Prester John.

BIBL.: U. P. Arora, "India vis-à-vis Egypt: Ethiopia in Classical Accounts," *Graeco-Arabic* 1 (1982): 131–140. F. Anfray, *Recueil des inscriptions de l'Ethiopie* (Paris, 1991). Jon Bonk, *An Annotated and Classified Bibliography of English Literature Pertaining to the Ethiopian Orthodox Church* (Metuchen, N.J., and London, 1984). Heinzgerd Brakmann, *Die Einwürzelung der Kirche im spätantiken Reich von Aksum* (Bonn, 1994). Roderick Grierson, ed., *African Zion: The Sacred Art of Ethiopia* (New Haven, 1993). Yuri M. Kobishchanov, *Axum,* trans. Lorraine T. Kapitanoff (University Park, Pa., 1979). Stuart H. C. Munro-Hay, *Aksum: An African Civilization of Late Antiquity* (Edinburgh, 1991).

C.J.R.

Ethnography

In late antiquity the terms of inclusion within the Roman imperial community changed. As Christianity came to dominate social and political expression and as the emperor took an ever more central position in the theocratic state, the sources of authority on alien peoples altered. The independent traditions of evaluating cultural difference found in Christianity, Roman law, and the classical genre of literary ethnography came together to form an "imperial" ethnography closely linked to the Roman state. This ethnography reached full development in the Byzantine east but took a different course in the west after the end of imperial control in the 5th century, when ethnographic attitudes coalesced around new power structures. In the development of Germanic successor states, Roman ethnographic traditions were widely influential.

To entertain and instruct their readers, Roman ethnographic writers translated the exotic habits of foreign peoples into familiar, comprehensible terms, thus imposing order and definition on the complex jumble of communities inside and outside the empire's borders. By fitting perceived traits into established patterns of community, these ethnographers in effect imposed identities in relation to the workings of imperial power. Thus the strategies of distinction formalized in ethnography had ideological significance, reflecting collective myths of order at the highest level. Ethnography played an active role in interpreting historical events because it supplied a repertoire of analytical and explanatory ideas with which to confront new circumstances and new peoples.

From the deceptively conservative tradition of ethnographic description begun by Greek scientists in the 5th century B.C.E., Romans inherited a well-developed contrast between civilized and barbarian society. They tailored this literary construct in two ways to fit their particular experience of conquest, governing, and assimilation. First, the governing elite accepted that Roman law and institutions could transform barbarians into Romans, though creating new Romans was only a possible consequence and not a goal of conquest. Second, they maintained a deep-seated antagonism to barbarians as a type, making aliens the foil for Roman vice or virtue. Reconciling these contradictory needs to incorporate and exclude created a lasting tension in Roman imperial ethnographic thought. Some writers attempted to describe cultural change and the assumption of new names and characteristics (e.g., Agathias 2.27.8; 2.1.6–7), presenting civilization as a political condition of cultural interchange.

Roman writers categorized alien communities by their descent *(origo gentis),* language, religion, and habits of life, and especially by the geography and climate of their homeland, as these were understood to determine character traits. Ethnographic descriptions in works of history (e.g., Ammianus Marcellinus), geography (e.g., Strabo), or chorography (e.g., Pomponius Mela), or other genres of classical Greek origin, always remained ancillary to the text's greater political or literary goals. After Procopius, historians who wrote ethnography in the classical style no longer affected ignorance of Christianity. This Christianized ethnography lost its analytical force by the mid-7th century because Christianity altered the criteria of *romanitas* and community and because classicizing genres fell out of style.

Roman law institutionalized a different set of ethnographic categories. It defined inclusion in the state primarily in terms of citizenship and status. The Constitutio Antoniniana in 212 granted citizenship to nearly all the inhabitants of the empire, thus eliminating the gradations of citizenship that had accumulated since the republic. Cities began to lose their status as significant granters of identity, though local "customary" law (as opposed to imperial law) continued to be tolerated in the provinces until the time of Justinian. After 212, foreigners who came into the empire as settlers, slaves, or soldiers took on a particular legal status in place of the generic condition of barbarian. Identity based on legal status was more negotiable than the binary identifications required by Christianity. Roman law found a place within a Christian firmament by the mid-6th century and became an instrument to pursue conformist religious goals.

On the foundation laid by Paul (e.g., Gal. 3:27–28) Christian clerics cast the relation of the Gentiles to the church in ways that challenged the absolute opposition of Roman and barbarian and undermined the utility of secular ethnography. Christianity did not require the state to be the arbiter of civilized values, nor did one need be Roman to be Christian. With Christianity as the rationale for judging foreign peoples, identifying with them, and even gaining knowledge about them, the perception and representation of cultural difference altered. The crucial development was Eusebius's introduction of providential history into the narrative of Roman history (e.g., *Proof of the Gospel* 4.9, 4.10d). Conversion to the Gospel was not only desirable for the nations but also necessary to complete a divine plan in which the Roman peace enabled the diffusion of Christianity. This fostered a teleological ethnography of empire. Outsiders in a history of salvation are people not yet saved, and when civilization is redemptive, ethnography can become heresiology. In the 4th century, orthodoxy and heresy arose as important diagnostic categories of community. Pagans emerged as an important group on the landscape mapped by the faith, and it became the emperor's obligation to facilitate their redemption. Missions of conversion became a goal of state by the 6th century. An elaborate theory of the emperor's role in God's providential plan for human salvation developed. In the Justinianic age, the emperor (and not the state in a general sense) entered ethnographic description as a Christian *artifex* of cultural transformation. Medieval ethnographies in Byzantium and the west developed on these late antique foundations.

BIBL.: *After Empire: Towards an Ethnography of Europe's Barbarians,* ed. G. Ausenda (Woodbridge, Eng., 1995). Patrick Amory, *People and Identity in Ostrogothic Italy, 489–554* (Cambridge, Eng., 1997). J. Barlow, "Gregory of Tours and the Myth of the Trojan Origins of the Franks," *Frühmittelalterliche Studien* 29 (1995): 86–95. Klaus E. Müller, *Geschichte der antiken Ethnographie und Ethnologischen Theoriebildung* (Wiesbaden, 1972). Walter Pohl and Helmut Reimitz, eds., *Strategies of Distinction: The Construction of Ethnic Communities, 300–800* (Leiden, 1997).   M.M.

Eudocia

Named Athenais at birth (ca. 400), the daughter of the Athenian sophist Leontius was baptized in Constantinople as (Aelia) Eudocia before her marriage to Theodosius II in 421. She had two brothers, Valerius and Gessius. Her daughter Licinia Eudoxia was born in 422, and in 423 Eudocia gained the title Augusta. Another daughter, Flaccilla, died young in 431. A son named Arcadius is attributed by some scholars to Eudocia, but the evidence seems unconvincing.

In 431 Eudocia was involved in the Nestorian conflict. Later on, in 438, she made friends with Melania the Younger and made her first pilgrimage to the Holy Land, giving donations en route. In Constantinople she had already founded a church of St. Polyeuctus, and she probably adorned her native Athens too.

Back in Constantinople in 439, Eudocia was at the peak of her influence, eclipsing even her sister-in-law Pulcheria. But after a series of events known to us mainly through later legends, Paulinus and Cyrus of Panopolis, both close to Eudocia, fell from grace (Paulinus was executed, Cyrus exiled). In 441 Eudocia

was more or less obliged to make her second pilgrimage to Jerusalem, this one for life. In the Holy Land Eudocia promoted monasticism and acted as a benefactress. A supporter of Monophysitism, she died an Orthodox Christian in Jerusalem in 460, after an alleged conversion.

Eudocia's poetry was acclaimed by the Byzantines, but the only substantial remains (a paraphrase of the life of St. Cyprian) shows a mediocre talent.

In modern scholarship her role has been controversial. New inscriptions (*Supplementum epigraphicum Graecum* 32, 1502 and 40, 184) have modified the legendary image of Eudocia.

BIBL.: Jane C. Biers, "A Gold Finger Ring and the Empress Eudocia," *Muse* 23–24 (1989–1990): 82–99. Julia Burman, "The Athenian Empress Eudocia," in *Post-Herulian Athens,* ed. Paavo Castrén (Helsinki, 1994), 63–87. Alan Cameron, "The Empress and the Poet: Paganism and Politics at the Court of Theodosius II," *Yale Classical Studies* 27 (1982): 217–289.   E.S.

Eunapius

Born in Sardis probably in 347, Eunapius went to Athens to study rhetoric under the sophist Prohaeresius, probably from 362 to 366. He returned to his native city, where he himself became a sophist, or teacher of rhetoric. Eunapius died sometime after 414. A serious student of Neoplatonism and medicine as well as a sophist, he is important to us as the author of a *History* and of the fully extant *Lives of Philosophers and Sophists.*

Eunapius's *History* survives only in fragments, though in Zosimus's *New History* we have an account of which much derives (or which mainly derives) from Eunapius's work. A continuator of the 3rd century historian Dexippus, Eunapius covered the period from 270 to 404. He interrupted work on his *History* to write the *Lives,* probably in 399. It is not certain what year Eunapius's historical narrative had reached by 399 or for how long the portion completed by 399 had been published (perhaps it was published in installments?); if we had this information, we would be in a much better position to assess the source-critical relationship between Eunapius's *History* and other late 4th century works, the most important being Ammianus Marcellinus's *History.* Eunapius's *History* was highly anti-Christian. The pagan emperor Julian was its hero; the Christian emperors Constantine and Theodosius were its bêtes noires. Its strident anti-Christian tone was softened somewhat in a revised edition. The work of a provincial academic as well as an impassioned religious propagandist, the *History* is hardly a model example of its genre. Its author was fond of moralizing and of rhetorical effect; he belittles chronological precision and in other ways, too, is weak in factual detail.

Eunapius's *Lives* offers sketches of thirteen philosophers, ten sophists, and five rhetorically trained physicians—almost all 4th century pagans. Among his subjects are the well-known Neoplatonic philosophers Plotinus, Porphyry, and Iamblichus and the sophists Himerius and Libanius. One of his philosophers is a woman, Sosipatra. Eunapius is especially interested in the "progeny" of Iamblichus—his pupils and the pupils of his pupil Aedesius. Julian the Apostate was taught by and had dealings with several of Aedesius's pupils, hence he appears in the *Lives* as well as in the *History*. The length of Eunapius's sketches and his judgments on his subjects vary, but three amply treated individuals whom he highly praises clearly occupy a special place in his heart: these are the philosopher Chrysanthius, the sophist Prohaeresius (despite his Christianity), and the physician Oribasius. Eunapius studied under Prohaeresius and Chrysanthius. Oribasius wrote a medical handbook for Eunapius and a memoir on Julian that he used as a source for his *History*. Through Chrysanthius, Prohaeresius, and Oribasius, Eunapius felt connected to his hero, Julian. Oribasius had been Julian's close friend. Chrysanthius had briefly taught Julian and was later summoned, unsuccessfully, to his court. Julian's relationship with Prohaeresius was characterized by a mix of admiration and annoyance.

One might say that the "real" hero of the *Lives* is no single person but traditional Hellenic learning. And for Eunapius, that learning was inseparably linked to traditional Hellenic religion.

BIBL.: R. C. Blockley, *The Fragmentary Classicising Historians of the Later Roman Empire*, 2 vols. (Liverpool, 1981–1983). G. Fowden, "The Last Days of Constantine: Oppositional Views and Their Influence," *Journal of Roman Studies* 84 (1994): 146–170. R. J. Penella, *Greek Philosophers and Sophists in the Fourth Century A.D.: Studies in Eunapius of Sardis* (Leeds, 1990). K. S. Sacks, "The Meaning of Eunapius' 'History,'" *History and Theory* 25 (1986): 52–67.

R.P.

Europe

One may assume that the term *Europe* was coined in the area of Thrace—on his way to Greece, Xerxes the Great had his army travel from Asia Minor through "Europe" (Herodotus 7.8)—and from there it was extended to denote central Greece and finally the entire Greek mainland. Through seafarers, people learned about the western Mediterranean Sea and the existence of countries surrounded by the ocean, and about lands adjacent to Greece. The name of Europe was extended to these areas and was used to denote the third part of the then-known world, distinguishing it from Asia and Africa. In principle this division into three can be found throughout ancient geography.

More detailed geographical information was given by the Romans, who since Julius Caesar had been exploring parts of the Continent, though many ideas about the conditions and the situation of the European hinterland remained rather fabulous; much of this can be found in the works of Pliny the Elder (*Nat.Hist.* 3.5). Only Strabo in his *Geographica* gives a more realistic description. The literature and science of late antiquity had to bring these ideas into accord with the Christian worldview.

Europe was seen as a part of the *orbis terrarum*, which was surrounded by the ocean. We may assume that the contrast to Asia was clearly felt and moreover that the terms *orient* and *occident* did not facilitate an *aequalis divisio* since there were three continents. The political affiliation of the province of Africa to the Roman empire may have been important, too (see Sallust, *Bell.Iug.* 17.3; Paulinus of Nola, *Carm.* 3.1.3). This became even more obvious when in 394, after the division of the empire, Africa went to the Latin world of the west (Claudian, *De bello Gildonico* 5.4 and *Panegyricus de sexto consulatu Honorii* 5.103–106).

The borders of Europe as they were assumed by Herodotus remained unchanged. It was bordered in the west by the ocean, in the south by the Mediterranean Sea from the Pillars of Hercules (Strait of Gibraltar) to the Hellespont (Dardanelles) and from there on through Pontus (the Black Sea) to the Maeotis (the Sea of Azov). There the eastern border began, running along the River Phasis (Rion) to the north. The Phasis was replaced soon by the River Tanais (Don), which rises in the so-called *riphaei montes*. Orosius (*Adversum Paganos* 1.2.52–53) drew a line from the northern coast to the mouth of the Rhine in Gallia Belgica.

The conception of Europe in late antiquity is summarized by Procopius; he reports two contemporary opinions that differ mainly in their view of the eastern border, Phasis or Tanais (Procopius, *Aed.* 4.1, 4, 8–9). Procopius saw Constantinople as the most important city and the center of the European continent, which was to be clearly distinguished from Asia within the empire (*Anecdota* 23). The famous historian's conception of Europe contains three different ideas. First, Europe included those masses of mainland that stretch from the Hellespont to the ocean in the west. Second, he refers to the European part of Justinian's empire, which was seen as an island between the Adriatic Sea and the Danube. Third, Europe also denoted a province in Thrace (cf. Cassiodorus, *Hist.eccl.* 9.2.1). From the beginning of the 5th century the term *res publica Hesperiae plagae*, or simply *Hesperia*, had been used to denote the western part of the Roman empire, competing with the name Europe. But Hesperia's real meaning became more and more blurred. In the course of time it meant merely Italy or—for pseudo-etymological reasons—Spain (Hispania) (Cassiodorus, *Hist. eccl.* 7.7.6; Isidorus, *Etymologiae* 14.14.19).

The historians of late antiquity differed somewhat on the regions they included in Europe. While Orosius (*Adversum Paganos* 1.2.52–53) includes in the empire the area from the River Tanais through Alania, Dacia, Gothia, and Germania, Jordanes (*Getica* 5.32–34) mentions the Gepidae as the easternmost people. Procopius (*Bell.Goth.* 1.12, 4.2–3) starts in the west with Spain and only mentions provinces of the empire, whereas he tells fabulous stories about peoples who live in the Caucasus. None of the authors, however, tells us whether the lands of barbaric peoples are considered parts of Europe in the original meaning. Jordanes regarded the Orcades (Orkneys) and *ultima Thule,* which had been known from Virgil's works, as parts of Europe. But apparently he regarded Germania and, what is more, Scandza (Scandinavia), which had been mentioned by Pliny the Elder, to be outside of Europe (*Getica* 1.8–9; Paul the Deacon, *Hist.Lang.* 1.1). Isidorus, however (*Etymologiae* 14.4.2–8), differentiates between the heartland of the empire that stretches to Greece; Barbaricum, between Scythia inferior and Germania, which he calls *prima Europa;* and a buffer zone to the Mediterranean Sea (Moesia, Pannonia, Noricum, Raetia). Bede (*Hist.eccl.* 1) calls Germania, Gallia, and Hispania (but not Italia) the *maximae Europae partes.* Basically all those ideas go back to the opinion of Augustine (*City of God* 3.31), who considers the Roman empire to be representative of the world. Therefore—the cultureless and little known parts excluded—it may justly be called Europe. Assuming a new settlement of the world after the Flood, Europe is generally attributed to Japhet, Noah's third son (Isidore, *Hist.Goth.,* dedicatio; *Etymologiae* 9.37). Japhet's descendants are the peoples who inhabit Europe. A genealogy of peoples based on these ideas is given by the so-called Nennius (*Hist.Britanniae,* prologue).

Increasing Christianization and the inclusion of new peoples and areas made it necessary to formulate a new concept of Europe. In the letters of Columbanus the Younger to Popes Gregory the Great and Boniface IV (*Ep.* 1 and 5), Europe appears as the continent, which is oriented toward Rome, the head of Christianity (cf. Aldhelm, *De virginitate* 25). A new Christian self-consciousness that concentrated on Europe began to replace the old imperial viewpoint, St. Martin being its symbol (Sulpicius Severus, *Dialogi* 2.17.7), and was fencing itself off not only from Asia and Africa but also from Greece.

In the 7th century *Europe* as a political term began to be interpreted in connection with the Frankish kingdom. According to a sophisticated construction, the Franks began to consider themselves of Trojan origin and therefore as equal to the Romans (Fredegar, *Chronicae* 2.5, 3.2; *Liber Historiae Francorum* cc.1–2), but at the same time they dissociated themselves from the Mediterranean area as the premise for political power. Their kingdom gained supremacy in a new Christian Europe, which was ready to expand. The characterization of Charlemagne as *Europae venerandus apex* testifies to this development.

BIBL.: Jürgen Fischer, *Oriens-Occidens-Europa: Begriff und Gedanke 'Europa' in der späten Antike und im frühen Mittelalter* (Mainz, 1957). Karl Leyser, "Concepts of Europe in the Early and High Middle Ages," in Leyser, *Communication and Power in Medieval Europe: The Carolingian and Ottonian Centuries* (London, 1994), 1–18.　　G.S.

Eusebius

Born shortly after 260, Eusebius was metropolitan bishop of Caesarea in Palestine from ca. 313 until his death 30 May 339. Formed intellectually in the tradition of Origen, whose library and voluminous writings he was able to use throughout his life, he was trained as a scholar and biblical exegete, and the style of his historical works reflects these interests. Eusebius wrote four works of a historical nature, each of which presents serious problems of chronology and interpretation.

Eusebius composed two editions of his *Chronicle.* The second went down to the twentieth year of Constantine (325–326); its layout and contents can be deduced with confidence from the early manuscripts of Jerome's Latin version with a continuation to 378. The terminal point of the first edition has been set as early as the year 277–78 and as late as 303.

There were also two editions of the *Martyrs of Palestine* (the longer composed in 311, the shorter in 313–14 as an integral part of the *History*). Of the *Ecclesiastical History,* there appear to have been four main editions. The date and scope of the first edition is in serious dispute: although the majority of modern scholars put it as late as 311, strong arguments have been advanced in favor of dating it no later than ca. 300, among them the fact that the later editions, which are attested by manuscript variants, all comprise a history of the Christian church down to ca. 280 followed by an account of the "Great Persecution," which began in February 303.

Eusebius started to assemble material for what eventually became his *Life of Constantine* ca. 325. What survives, however, is a posthumous conflation of this intended sequel to, or even continuation of, the *Ecclesiastical History* with a generically very dissimilar panegyric of Constantine that Eusebius drafted after the emperor's death in 337. Modern interpretation of this problematic work has until recently been bedeviled both by a refusal to admit that it is a conflation of two unfinished drafts and by the assumption, which Eusebius himself fostered, that the provincial bishop stood close to the first Christian emperor.

BIBL.: T. D. Barnes, *Constantine and Eusebius* (Cambridge, Mass., 1981). A. Cameron, "Eusebius' *Vita Constantini* and the Construction of Constantine," in *Portraits,* ed. M. J. Edwards and J. Strain (Oxford, 1997).　　T.D.B.

Eutyches

As an elderly presbyter and archimandrite who directed a monastery of some 300 monks in Constantinople, Eutyches (ca. 378–ca. 454) was a virulent enemy of Nestorius, a staunch supporter of Cyril, and an ally of Dioscorus. By the late 440s he enjoyed tremendous influence at the imperial court, being the godfather to the powerful eunuch Chrysaphius and spiritual adviser to the emperor himself. With the emperor's support, said Nestorius, Eutyches "set himself up to be bishop of bishops."

Eutyches seems to have preached an extreme form of Monophysitism, going so far as to deny that Christ was "consubstantial" *(homoousios)* with humans. This feature of his belief was condemned by most later Monophysites as well as Chalcedonians. He acknowledged two natures before the incarnation, but only one after. He was accused (although he denied it) of saying that the flesh of God the Word had descended from heaven and was therefore not "real" human flesh. In November 448, he was accused of heresy by Eusebius of Dorylaeum, a zealous bishop who years earlier had been among the first to denounce Nestorius. Eusebius called him to stand trial before the *synodos endēmousa* ("home synod"), a floating committee of bishops visiting the capital, under the presidency of Flavian, bishop of Constantinople. Eutyches was reluctant to appear, first claiming that he had sworn an oath never to leave his monastery but to live in it "as if in a tomb," and then pleading illness. After repeated summonses, however, he arrived with a military escort led by the silentiary Magnus, pointedly underlining his powerful connections. Eusebius claimed that Eutyches's protectors had threatened him with exile.

During his interrogation, Eutyches strove to present himself as a pious man of simple faith ("I follow Nicaea, Cyril and Ephesus") and simple mind, with no patience for the clever theological sophistries he felt the bishops were trying to force on him. In fact he was laying a trap for his interrogators. By claiming to defer to the superior authority and intellect of the bishops and accept their teachings "even though I do not find these things in scripture or in the Fathers," he effectively accused them of innovation—thus producing the pretext that Dioscorus would use to condemn Flavian and Eusebius at the Second Council of Ephesus the following year.

Condemned by Flavian's synod, Eutyches and his supporters fought back by challenging the legitimacy of the proceedings. At an official inquiry in April 449, they alleged that Eutyches's statements had been altered in the transcript, and that Flavian had written up the formal condemnation before the trial had begun. Eutyches's appeal to the emperor led to the convocation of the Second Council of Ephesus, which vindicated him and condemned his accusers. After the fall of the eunuch Chrysaphius and the death of Theodosius II in 450, however, Eutyches lost his most powerful protectors. He was condemned again at Chalcedon and exiled.

BIBL.: Eduard Schwartz, *Acta Conciliorum Oecumenicorum* 2.1.1 (Berlin and Leipzig, 1933); French trans. in A. J. Festugière, *Ephèse et Chalcédoine: Actes des conciles* (Paris, 1982). Heinrich Bacht, "Die Rolle des orientalischen Mönchtums in den Kirchenpolitischen Auseinandersetzungen um Chalkedon (431–519)," in A. Grillmeier and H. Bacht, eds., *Das Konzil von Chalkedon* (Würzburg, 1953), vol. 2, 193–314. Gilbert Dagron, "Les moines et la ville: Le monachisme à Constantinople jusqu'au concile de Chalcédoine (451)," *Travaux et mémoires* 4 (1970): 229–276. R. Draguet, "La christologie d'Eutyches d'après les actes du synode de Flavien," *Byzantion* 6 (1931): 441–457. Eduard Schwartz, *Der Prozess des Eutyches* (Munich, 1929).   J.M.G.

Exorcism

Ritual procedures for the elimination of maleficent supernatural powers, to end their control and often habitation in the home, farm, landscape, or body, were a typical facet of popular and personal religion from well before the Roman era. Consequently, the ability to purge demonic spirits and thus bring about healing or the renewal of good fortune was a sine qua non of local shrines and healers throughout the Mediterranean world. Temples, villages, and homes often set up guardian figures—usually in the form of horrific theriomorphs—that would repel demons from sacred or domestic space by their appearance: stelae from Roman Egypt reflect a widespread popular practice of appealing to the divine chiefs of aggressive ambiguous spirits, so that these chiefs would rein in their minions. Indeed, literary and iconographic sources, as well as a profusion of apotropaic amulets, make clear that much of local religious life in antiquity involved the alternate appeal to such "chief demons," ritual expulsion of demonic invasion, and simple avoidance of places associated with demonic presence and invasion (such as pools, mountains, deserts, and abandoned dwellings).

In this sense, exorcism in late antiquity was not the singular cure-all of a demon-plagued environment but rather a genus of ritual, one of a number of approaches to misfortune and illness and one that could be performed by authorities as diverse as saints (living or dead), local specialists, or amulets alone. As portrayed in literary sources and exorcistic manuals and spells, exorcistic ritual generally involved: (1) a person holding some recognized authority in the effective performance of the rite; (2) words of command directed at the demon, believed to be efficacious owing to the authority of the speaker, the series of divine names or legends invoked, or both; (3) occasionally some dramatic action at the demon's departure (a motif of the literary accounts and certainly a technique in effective performance); and (4) the sealing of the exorcism through the ingestion or application of some substance or the donning of a protective amulet, which would act as a guarantee of the exorcism's effect in everyday life. (The large number of amulets whose inscriptions begin with "I exorcize you" or "I adjure you" and appeal to Christian powers shows the importance of sealing ex orcisms and of extending the rite's power beyond the ceremony.) In the competitive religious marketplace of the Roman period, an exorcist might distinguish himself and his authority through the particularly extravagant performance of any of these components.

Jews held a particular reputation for exorcistic technique in the Graeco-Roman period. Jewish lore about the powers of King Solomon (believed to have built the Jerusalem Temple with the help of an army of demons) and an ancient battery of sacred names from Scripture and liturgical tradition provided a continual source for the composition of exorcistic spells and their pedigrees.

The importance attributed to Jesus's exorcistic technique in the Christian Gospels (Mark 5:1–20) and to that of his successors (Luke 10:17–19; Acts 19:11–17) provided one basis for Christianity's special claims to exorcistic power in its early self-presentation. Apocryphal acts and saints' legends continued this theme, invariably including the expulsion of demons as the saint's typical miracle. Exorcism also provided a vivid ritual model for performing, and then retelling, the Christianization of local shrines. It is this ideological focus on the ritual expulsion of demons that seems to have made Christianity attractive to many peoples as its missionaries moved into new regions.

Baptism itself served as the most central of the various exorcistic rites established in early Christian liturgy and preserved in handbooks, for it combined exorcistic themes with a major ritual of transition and included the application of sacred water or oil, believed to purify and insulate the initiate from demonic presence or attack.

BIBL.: Campbell Bonner, "The Technique of Exorcism," *Harvard Theological Review* 36 (1943): 39–49. P. Horden, "Responses to Possession and Insanity in the Early Byzantine World," *Social History of Medicine* 6 (1993): 177–194. Henry Ansgar Kelly, *The Devil at Baptism* (Ithaca, N.Y., 1985). Roy Kotansky, "Greek Exorcistic Amulets," in *Ancient Magic and Ritual Power,* ed. M. Meyer and P. Mirecki (Leiden, 1995), 243–277. A. Rousselle, *Croire et guérir: La foi en Gaule dans l'antiquité tardive* (Paris, 1990), 171–256.

D.T.F.

Ex-voto

Ex-voto means "in accordance with a vow" and identifies an object given or an event dedicated to a divinity or spirit as the fulfillment of a promise. This offering usually takes place after the propitious outcome of an uncertain situation or condition, for example a safe return from a voyage, or an improved state of health. Such vows reflect the dependence felt by a society—and its members—on the unpredictable intercession of supernatural power(s) in the events and experiences of life. By creating a contract, stipulating that something will be given or done in return for a successful, improved, or safer condition, faith in personalized divine beneficence is expressed by the gratified donor. Vows

may also be made against anticipated benefits, and thus the faith of the giver is extended into the future, and even into the afterlife. Such vows and their tangible fulfillments should be understood not only as proofs of slightly skeptical religious faith, but also as specie within a spiritualized culture of exchange.

The ex-voto system was widespread in Greek, Roman, and late antique culture. However, the identification of an object or event as ex-voto depends on evidence that a vow was made. Documentation can be literary, such as reports in historical writing, or inscriptional, stating an object's status as ex-voto. Despite numerous ex-voto inscriptions on extant objects, the occasion for their production most often remains unknown. Fulfilling vows was so widespread a custom that formulaic statements evolved—for example, *votum solvit,* or *votum solvit libens merito*—that became common enough to be abbreviated *v.s.* or *v.s.l.m.* Two inscriptions to Mercury on silver serving dishes from the Berthouville treasure (in the Bibliothèque National, Paris), dated to the late 2nd or early 3rd century, end with *v.s.l.m.* Like other customs in late antiquity, ex-voto dedications were adopted for Christian use. The Greek counterpart to ex-voto, *huper euchēs,* is found on many Christian objects in eastern Mediterranean regions. It was frequently linked with the expression *kai sōtērias* (and for the salvation [of]) on donations to churches. It appears on a lamp, a censer, three polycandela, and a cross-shaped suspension bracket donated to a Church of Holy Sion by an otherwise unknown Bishop Eutychianos, whose name was included in the inscriptions. These church furnishings are a part of an extensive mid-6th century ecclesiastical treasure found near Kumluca in southern Turkey (now divided between the Antalya Museum and Dumbarton Oaks in Washington, D.C.).

Other types of Christian dedications were plaques representing either the intercessory saint being or having been invoked, or a body part cured or in need of a cure, each type deriving from Graeco-Roman precedents. Examples of both types are part of the 6th to 7th century Ma'aret en-Noman (northern Syria) silver treasure: a plaque with St. Symeon Stylites on top of his column with an inscription of thanksgiving to God and St. Symeon (in the Louvre, Paris) and the far simpler plaquettes with pairs of eyes simply inscribed HELP! (in the Walters Art Gallery, Baltimore).

Such donations, whether costly or not, are testimonials of the enduring gratitude of sometimes anonymous, sometimes named donors. Whatever the type—celebratory, intercessory, curative, or functional—the practice descended from older traditions, and ex-votos would continue to be offered throughout the Middle Ages and into modern times.

Animals were frequently offered as ex-votos at shrines, so that the precincts both of temples and, in this period, of the sanctuaries of martyrs and holy men had the aspect of a zoo, filled with live or stuffed animals (*Miracles of Saint Thecla* 24; Antonius, *Life of Symeon Stylites* 15 and appendix 21).

BIBL.: M. M. Mango, *Silver from Early Byzantium: The Kaper Koraon and Related Treasures* (Baltimore, 1986). Ihor Ševčenko, "The Sion Treasure: The Evidence of the Inscriptions," in S. A. Boyd and M. M. Mango, eds., *Ecclesiastical Silver Plate in Sixth-Century Byzantium* (Washington, D.C., 1992), 39–56. D. Trout, "Christianity in the Nolan Countryside: Animal Sacrifice at the Tomb of Saint Felix," *Journal of Early Christian Studies* 3 (1995): 281–298.　　　S.Z.

Eznik of Koghb

The Armenian Christian theologian Eznik of Koghb (in Armenian, Eznik Kolbacʻi) was born ca. 390 in Kolb, Ayrarat province, and died in 455. A pupil of St. Mesrop Maštocʻ, inventor of the Armenian alphabet, Eznik (literally, little ox) was sent with Bishop Yovsēpʻ to Edessa to translate works from Syriac, then to Greek-speaking regions of Anatolia and Constantinople, where he was received by Maximianus (431–434); he returned after the Council of Ephesus to Armenia and was appointed bishop of Bagrewand. He attended the Council of Aštišat in 450.

His most important work, written in the 440s, is traditionally known as *The Refutation of Sects* (in Armenian, *Elalandocʻ*), because of its polemics against Manichaeism, pagan Hellenism, Marcion, Valentinian Gnosticism, "Chaldaean" astrology, diverse Armenian pagan beliefs, and, most of all, the Zurvanite philosophy in Sassanian Zoroastrianism. Eznik's concern in refuting this doctrine has to do with the Iranians' dualistic solution to the larger problem of evil, which the Armenian author addresses in its various aspects. But the Mazdean religion he describes is the contemporary form he actually encountered, so his work has the value of a primary source for the latter: even though Eznik's remarks parallel those of other writers, such as Theodore bar Konai and Theodore of Mopsuestia, he adds details, such as that of the demon Mahmī, who taught the god Ohrmazd how to create light, which have only recently been corroborated by the finds of Middle Iranian Manichaica at Turfan. Eznik's purpose was not primarily to expound the true nature of divinity, as C. Mercier and Louis Mariès assumed in entitling their edition and French translation *De Deo* (Paris, 1959), but to counteract actual religious movements and tenacious pagan beliefs very much alive in newly Christianized Armenia. His testimony on Armenian beliefs—in Vahagn, the god who slays submarine dragons called *višaps;* in the king Artawazd, who will rise from his long imprisonment in Mount Ararat and bring on the apocalypse; and in various demons and evil spirits—is drawn from firsthand experience, and his career was not that of a secluded monastic scholar. Eznik's purpose backfired badly in the case of the English romantic poet Byron, a determined enemy of Christianity, who found the dualism described by "Esnacius" so appealing that he presented a translation of the exposition of Zurvanite cosmology without the refutation, in a section entitled "Some Pieces of the Best Armenian Authors" appended to *A Grammar, Armenian and English* (Venice, 1819), published by his Armenian tutor, Fr. P. Awgērean (Anglicized as Aucher).

BIBL.: *Refutation of the Sects,* trans. L. Mariès and C. Mercier, *Patrologia Orientalis* 28 (1959): 549–776. J. R. Russell, "Mahmi Reconsidered," *Journal of the K. R. Cama Oriental Institute* (Bombay), 1987. J. R. Russell, *Zoroastrianism in Armenia* (Cambridge, Mass., 1987).　　　J.R.R.

Factions

The Latin term *factio* comes from the world of Roman chariot racing; this expensive activity in the Roman world did not involve individual competitors (as it did in the Greek world). It was a professional sport presented as part of public festivals and celebrations, and the chariots, horses, and charioteers were owned by groups of businessmen, *factiones,* and hired to compete on such occasions by rich magistrates or, later, by the emperor. Four factions evolved, racing under the four colors green, blue, red, and white; popular enthusiasm was for a particular color, or faction, rather than for an individual. Chariot racing was therefore a form of entertainment that the emperors could sponsor, glorifying victory, without adding luster to significant individuals (as racing had done in the Greek world).

By the 4th century C.E. this system of organization had spread to the eastern half of the empire, where an increasing number of hippodromes were built, particularly at imperial residences and most notably in Constantinople. Over the imperial period the cost of presenting chariot races had come increasingly to fall on the central government, which continued to find it convenient to deal with the factions. During the 5th century a new system evolved: the factions took on responsibility for maintaining and providing other kinds of performers, including dancers, wild-beast fighters, and actors. This development almost certainly took place in response to a general reduction in the number of festivals and spectacles, which made it more difficult for such entertainers to function independently. At the same time, two factions, the Blue and the Green, came to predominate. Only at a very rich center, such as Constantinople, would all four factions compete; the Red and White appear to have been maintained as adjuncts of the two main colors. In other cities, only the Blues and the Greens provided performers, the minimum required to retain the structure of a contest. This arrangement made organization easier, but it had unexpected consequences. The enthusiasm of the spectators was now entirely focused on one or other of two colors. Audiences were now made up of two blocks of supporters, with assigned seating. Their other concerns were subsumed in their support for the Greens or Blues. Moreover, the factions had inherited from earlier groupings of performers the responsibility for ensuring that the rulers were properly honored at public assemblies—most particularly by the chanting of acclamations, when the audience would follow the lead given by the performers. During the later empire, acclamations assumed greater importance; this inevitably empowered the crowds who raised the acclamations. From the later 5th century until well into the 7th this new focus of political power had a destabilizing effect, leading to riots and revolts; it was only in the 7th century that the factions lost the last traces of their independent origins and became completely absorbed into the structure of state control and ritual.

BIBL.: Alan Cameron, *Circus Factions: Blues and Greens at Rome and Byzantium* (Oxford, 1976). Charlotte Roueché, *Performers and Partisans at Aphrodisias in the Roman and Late Roman Periods* (London, 1993). G. Vespignani, "Il Circo e le fazioni del circo nella storiografia bizantinistica recente," *Rivista di studi bizantini e slavi* 5 (1985): 61–101.

C.R.

Factories

Fabrica, Latin for factory, came to refer specifically to state-operated arms manufactories. The *Notitia Dignitatum* lists fifteen of these in the east ([or.] 11.18–39) and twenty in the west ([oc.] 9.16–39). Though the list registers no *fabricae* for Britain, Egypt, or the southwestern empire, it appears to be complete. Each of the dioceses abutting the northern and eastern frontiers was furnished with one general arms factory or shield factory. Additional factories specializing in certain types of weaponry (bows, arrows, heavy armor, lances, swords, artillery) were distributed across the empire. All *fabricae* were controlled by the *magister officiorum.* Workers *(fabricenses)* were organized into quasi-military units under a *primicerius* and were sometimes even used for military service. Their factories, none of which has been firmly identified from archaeology, were located in secure areas, generally in walled cities, near sources of raw materials and on major highways. The *fabrica* system was probably organized under Diocletian, perhaps to supply the soldiery with arms in kind, rather than cash for their purchase. In the east the system was still operating in 539 when Justinian reformed it *(Nov.Just.* 85), but it had fallen into desuetude by the late 6th century when Maurice faced resistance to his reintroduction of state arms distributions in lieu of cash *(Theophylact Simocatta* 7.1). In the west, the state *fabricae* did not survive the barbarian invasions, though the Ostrogoths revived them in some form (Cassiodorus, *Variae* 7.18–19). The *barbaricarii (Not.Dig.* [oc.] 11.74–77; [or.] 11.45–49), who embossed arms with silver or gold, constituted a separate and much smaller corps of imperial weapons manufacturers.

State factories also existed for textile production and dying. The *Notitia Dignitatum* lists these by location in the west ([oc.] 11.46–73; 12.26–27): fourteen for wool cloth *(gynaecea);* two for linen cloth *(linyfia);* nine for purple dying *(baphia).* The eastern *Notitia* mentions neither numbers nor locations ([or.] 13.16–17; 20), but many eastern textile factories and their locations are known from other sources. These factories were also first organized under Diocletian. Each was headed by a *procurator* under the charge of the *comes sacrarum largitionum.* The *gynaecea* apparently wove cloth and produced garments for the military as a supplement to the levy of military clothing in kind *(vestis militaris),* which was entirely commuted to money by 400 C.E. No textile factory has been identified from archaeology, but they appear to have been physical entities rather than cottage industries. From the 6th century, imperial silk factories came into operation. The state also ran factories *(monetae)* for the production of coinage.

Factories were generally organized by the state to produce goods that were restricted from the general public (money, weapons, purple cloth) or in short supply for the army (wool cloth). All workers in imperial factories were hereditarily bound to their profession. Textile labor was especially burdensome, since it entailed servile status *(C.Th.* 10.20; Eusebius, *Vit.Const.* 2.34.1) and was even used to punish convicts (Sozomen, *Hist.eccl.* 1.8.3). Mint workers *(Monetarii)* were also of servile status but some enjoyed influence through their contact with money. *Fabricenses* had higher status: they received the privileges of government service *(militia),* including state rations *(annonae),* exemption from compulsory duties, and retirement after a fixed term. All factories represented a significant demographic feature in their home city; they constituted a concentrated group with mutual interests and immunities that could be formidable even to emperors (Athanasius, *Hist.Ar.* 18; Sozomen, *Hist.eccl.* 5.15.6–7; Gregory of Nazianzus, *Orat.* 43.57).

BIBL.: S. James, "The *Fabricae:* State Arms Factories of the Later Roman Empire," in *Military Equipment and the Identity of Roman Soldiers,* ed. J. C. Coulston (Oxford, 1988). J. P. Wild, "The *Gynaecea,*" in *Aspects of the Notitia Dignitatum,* ed. R. Goodburn and P. Bartholomew (Oxford, 1976).

N.L.

Fairs

In the world of late antiquity, as in virtually all premodern societies, a very large proportion of the commercial exchange of goods was carried out at periodic markets. To understand the role of these markets in the Roman economy, it is essential to establish some basic distinctions.

To begin with, it is important to differentiate between high-frequency (weekly or monthly) markets, on the one hand, and equally periodic but less frequent commercial gatherings, on the other. Although both types of markets existed in late antiquity, their economic functions were fundamentally different. For this reason alone, the term *fair* ought to be reserved for the second category. Another distinction should be made between festival-connected trade in ephemeral items, such as food and sacrificial animals, and the commercial exchange of more durable goods not destined for consumption on the spot. We can be sure that all major periodic gatherings (whether religious, political, or judicial) generated a certain amount of commercial activity, but it would not be very illuminating to designate such secondary forms of periodic trade as fairs. Instead, the label *fair* should ideally be used to refer to low-frequency periodic markets involving the distribution of less ephemeral goods over wide geographical areas. Finally, it should be realized that those commercial gatherings that meet the second criterion may perform widely varying functions. As a general rule, most fairs were strictly local occasions at which traveling traders sold their merchandise directly to final consumers. There is, however, no doubt that during the 4th and 5th centuries of the Christian era a restricted number of fairs retained or assumed regional or even interregional importance. A defining characteristic of such fairs was that they were the scene of entrepôt trade between merchants.

Needless to say, the literary sources display no interest in any such niceties. Instead, the Greek and Latin terminology is frustratingly imprecise, with general words for market (such as *mercatus, nundinae,* and *agora*) being used to denote daily, weekly, monthly, and annual markets alike. The same problem affects most references to the suspension of indirect taxes *(ateleia)* during certain periodic festivals. Although *ateleia* usually indicates that the fair was a genuine one, this cannot be confirmed without the help of additional clues. Another source of confusion is the Greek word *panēgyris;* this can refer to a genuine fair, but its usual meaning is simply "festival." To make things worse, *panēgyris* is also used to denote high-frequency periodic markets. Thus the *panēgyreis* at which the Romans and Huns engaged in commercial exchange during the age of Attila (Priscus, frg. 2, 6, and 46) seem to have been "weekly" rather than annual occasions.

Although the lack of precision characterizing much of the surviving evidence may seem to pose an insuperable obstacle to any serious study of periodic trade in the late empire, it would be wrong to take an overly pessimistic stance. This is especially true of the eastern part of the late Roman world, concerning which the patristic sources supply much valuable information. One conclusion that emerges from this material is that the entire spectrum of genuine fairs, ranging from one-day local fairs to forty-day interregional ones, is represented in the documentary sources. At one end of the spectrum we find relatively modest gatherings that were dominated by trade in agricultural produce, farm animals, and cloth. Interestingly, there is evidence that these fairs (some of which were held in out-of-the-way locations) were visited by itinerant hawkers, just as were similar fairs in later preindustrial societies. A good example is the rural fair of Imma (near Antioch), which is said to have attracted "traders from everywhere and a numberless crowd." Doubtless it was on such occasions that the empire's rural subjects bought the few town-produced luxuries they were able to afford. It does not seem far-fetched to assume that this sort of opportunity was also provided by some urban fairs, such as that of Gaza, where the booths were "copiously laden with merchandise both for the rich and for those of moderate means."

For obvious reasons, it is not always easy to draw the line between local and regional fairs. Despite this, the existence of fully fledged regional fairs during the late Roman and early Byzantine periods is an established fact. One of our few western sources relates to the rural fair of Marcelliana (Lucania), which attracted people from Calabria, Bruttium, and Campania. The trade goods included textiles, livestock, and slaves. In the east, another important fair was held near Hebron; it was visited by people from Palestine, Phoenicia, and Arabia. It would, however, be wrong to assume that regional fairs were typically rural occasions, as is shown by the existence of an eight-day fair in 4th century Tyre and another in 7th century Jerusalem. In the early Byzantine period we find the annual *panēgyris* of Ephesus, which allegedly yielded customs duties to the equivalent of 100 pounds of gold. Where fairs were held in coastal cities, it may be conjectured that they were periodic bulking points for regional exports. In other words, even in large harbor cities where trade was carried on continuously, fairs may have provided a vital link with the interior districts.

It can safely be assumed that interregional fairs were much less numerous than were their local and regional counterparts. On the other hand, the scale and importance of such gatherings is likely to have enhanced their chance of being recorded by the literary sources. In any case, the late Roman (and Merovingian) sources refer to at least three fairs that can be assigned to this category. One of these was the September fair of Batnae, where a huge crowd gathered "to traffic in the wares sent from India and China, and in the articles regularly brought there in great abundance by land and sea." Another example is the tax-free fair of Edessa, which lasted no less than thirty days. Finally, the Cilician fair of Aegae is known to have lasted for forty days and to have attracted merchants from the western half of the empire. It may not be a coincidence that this type of fair is recorded only in what is now the Middle East. The geographical pattern, at least, would be in line with the comparative evidence, which suggests that interregional fairs were typically associated with the overland trade in luxury goods. The reason for this is the uncertain duration of long sea voyages in preindustrial societies, which resulted in a tense relationship between fleets and fairs. The apparent exception of Cilician Aegae does not really contradict this assertion, since its existence can be attributed to the peculiar pattern of winds prevailing in the Mediterranean during the sailing season. Apart from that, the exceptional length of this fair seems to illustrate the tendency of major maritime fairs to dissipate into longish "business seasons."

A final set of questions concerns the nature and importance of low-frequency periodic markets in the late Roman economy. A useful starting point is provided by two patristic treatises from the late 4th century. The first of these is the *Constitutiones apostolicae,* which admonishes Christians not to attend any pagan or Jewish *panēgyreis* "except in order to purchase a slave . . . or to buy something else which is suited to bodily sustenance." The other is Basil's contemporary appeal not to turn the shrines of the martyrs "into a market, a *panēgyris,* and a common center for trade." The interest of such warnings lies in the fact that they bear witness to the unease felt by many church Fathers about the traditional bond between festivals and fairs while at the same time suggesting that they were fighting a losing battle. The ultimate reason for their failure was surely that the economic advantages of multipurpose gatherings (bearing in mind how slow and how expensive travel and transportation were) were too great to be gainsaid.

A related, but different, question is whether these annual periodic gatherings were institutions of growing importance during the last centuries of the empire. According to Rostovtzeff, fairs "*regained* importance in every part of the empire when economic life became everywhere simplified." A study of the early imperial evidence shows this statement to be misleading in the sense that local and regional fairs are likely to have *remained* important throughout the history of the empire. Another qualification that should be made is that it seems unwarranted to speak of an absolute increase in the turnover of goods at low-frequency periodic markets. Nonetheless, Rostovtzeff's observation remains a valuable reminder that the preexisting fairs of late antiquity may have become more conspicuous when institutions for continuous trade went into decline. Viewed in this light, the fact that the early Byzantine fair of Ephesus attracted the attention of the chronographer Theophanes may be interpreted as a sign that the overall volume of commerce had decreased. It seems worth noting, however, that the downturn in urban economic activity did not take place simultaneously in every part of the empire, and that it certainly occurred at a much later date than Rostovtzeff supposed. It follows that throughout the 4th and 5th centuries fairs must have been an integral part of the economy of a thoroughly urbanized society, meaning that their relationship with the permanent trading institutions of the town should be described as complementary rather than as competitive.

BIBL.: J. M. Frayn, *Markets and Fairs in Roman Italy* (Oxford, 1993). J. Gaudemet, "L'empire romain, a-t-il connu les foires?" in *La Foire*, Recueils de la Société Jean Bodin 5 (Brussels, 1953), 25–42. L. de Ligt, *Fairs and Markets in the Roman Empire: Economic and Social Aspects of Periodic Trade in a Pre-Industrial Society* (Amsterdam, 1993). B. Shaw, "Rural Markets in North Africa," *Antiquités africaines* 17 (1981): 37–83.　　　　　　　　　　　　　　　L.D.

Family

Late antique Greek and Latin had no specific term for the family as we understand it (a domestic group of related persons): *oikogeneia* did not yet designate the residential family; *sungeneia, domus,* and *familia* might relate to the family, but they also had other meanings (kinship, residence, a group of slaves).

The nuclear family (parents and children), sometimes vertically extended, dominated. The census returns prove it for Egypt in the early empire, and later papyri give the same impression. As for the west, thousands of Latin funerary inscriptions provide more wide-ranging information than literary sources do. Mentions of family ties bear witness to the growing importance of the nuclear family among the urban and suburban rural populations, even among the aristocracy. The imagery of those inscriptions does not necessarily correspond to real social units, yet the preeminence of the conjugal family, reaching even the slave's world, seems undeniable. Historians now consider that such a family type was maintained after the arrival of Germanic populations, who in the past were credited with the growth of more complex family households. The conjugal family appears to have been the fundamental structure in Visigothic Spain, Latium, and Puglia of the 8th century. Even in the Frankish world, the funerary inscriptions of Trier and hagiographic evidence question the importance of extended- or multiple-family households.

Demographic data are rare. Prosopographic researches seem to show that, in the 4th century senatorial class, families with one or two children were predominant and that, among the curials of Antioch, those with three to six children were not rare. But literary sources rarely cite complete families. Funerary inscriptions of Asia Minor lead to the conclusion—taking into account the probable completeness of the descent and the underreporting of girls and of children who died very young—that the average family size was six children with four having survived at least until the age of five or six (less in Roman Egypt). Thus, the birth rate appears high in at least one segment of the population. Infanticide and the exposure of children seem, at that time, linked to poverty. But the marriage rate is the major unknown factor.

Late antiquity was marked by a move toward rejection of the family and married life. Certain pagan traditions converged with the legacy of early Christianity, which was indifferent, even hostile, to the family. The preachings of Christ taught the rupture of family ties, and eschatological expectations canceled the very necessity of the institution; paleo-Christian iconography eliminated conjugal representation (Adam and Eve, who seem the exception, represented sin). If that rejection was expressed most radically in heretical movements of Asia Minor or Syria, there was a gap within the church, too, between those who, by insisting on the superiority of virginity and abstinence, saw marriage as a lesser evil (Gregory of Nyssa, John Chrysostom, Jerome) and those who defended the family as a fundamental social structure, willed by God, with children representing its highest achievement (Ambrose and, especially, Augustine). In any case, the ascetic and monastic ideal criticized married life and involved a rupture with the family. Its impact is difficult to judge. Imperial and senatorial families after 320 had a significant percentage of single persons, with sources referring to religious motivations. It is easy to imagine the way things went: refusal of marriage itself or later rejection of family life (especially after the birth of heirs), an open break (fleeing from parents or husband), or a consensual agreement.

However, this rejection does not mean any weakening of the family. Historians have identified an economic and social consolidation of the family from the 4th to the 8th century (perhaps even a certain tightening with the growth of intermarriage), accompanying the decline of the city and its system of social relations. In the west, with the decaying of the centralized state, the family offered the only source of protection for individuals. In the east, as in the west, it represented the main economic unit. Many urban trades existed within this framework. In rural areas, farms able to sustain couples with children were omnipresent and formed the basis of village communities. The family was the determining factor of social status, for monogamy was practiced everywhere and the weight of heredity very strong, even when legal constraints touching certain trades or stations did not exist.

Imperial law gradually confirmed the preeminence of the nuclear family. While classical family law was dominated by paternal power and by the resulting dissymmetry of family relationships (children were outsiders to their mother and her family), this lifelong *potestas* thereafter declined as children reached majority, and legislation gave more significance to the ties between husband and wife or mother and child: the role of the husband in his wife's affairs was increased, and the widow received guardianship over underage children. At the same time legal protection of the conjugal family was growing, limiting divorce and imposing heavier restrictions on remarriage, especially in favor of the first spouse's children. These changes are often imputed to the influence of Christianity, whose role is sometimes undeniable (the interdiction of marriage to kin) or perhaps only probable (measures against infanticide and the exposure of children). But the rising importance of the conjugal family regarding property transmission was not a lesser factor in this evolution. In classical law, there prevailed a strict separation of property between spouses, and the transmission was relatively independent of the marriage vicissitudes. As soon as property began to be considered as belonging to the couple, with symmetrical patrimonial contributions (dowry and antenuptial donation) destined for the children, it became more urgent to regulate and stabilize marriages.

The attitudes concerning family varied little. Family order was characterized by a hierarchical division of functions (men represented the family outside and women took care of the home), and by three forms of authority (husbands over wives, fathers over children, and masters over slaves). John Chrysostom, comparing the household to the city, with its "commandments" *(archai)*, was indeed in line with Aristotle. The strength of those attitudes is seen in the reprobation shown at any act of rebellion against the family: when religious motivations made such an action inevitable, then sources disguised it as running away or resorting to cunning.

Christian teachings reinforced the reciprocity of rights and obligations: children owed obedience and parents owed an education; spouses had a mutual obligation of fidelity and help. The effect of the most radical innovation on family structure (the assertion of marriage indissolubility) was to come later, given that the church's control over the family was still very weak.

BIBL.: Susan Ashbrook Harvey, "Sacred Bonding: Mothers and Daughters in Early Syriac Hagiography," *American Journal of Philology* 116, no. 4 (1995): 27–56. Noel J. Coulson, *Succession in the Muslim Family* (Cambridge, Eng., 1971). Susanne Dixon, *The Roman Family* (Baltimore, 1997). D. B. Martin, "The Construction of the Ancient Family: Methodological Considerations," *Journal of Roman Studies* 86 (1996): 40–60.   J.B.

Famine

Famine is a modern concept that translates badly into Greek and Latin. *Fames* and *limos* denote hunger, but they may also embrace the subsistence crises in which people go hungry. Famine is not hunger, whether episodic hunger—that is, the *event* of going hungry in consequence of a food shortage—or endemic hunger, the *state* of chronic malnutrition, which is a condition of long-term food deprivation. Nor is famine shortage. Both are subsistence crises, but of different degrees of seriousness. Historians tend to collapse famine into shortage, or variants such as dearth, scarcity, or hunger. This stands in the way of a qualitative account of famine and impedes historical comparison across time and space. The same writers, not coincidentally, talk of famine as if it were a frequent occurrence—as indeed shortage was. But famine was a rarity; it is properly defined as a particularly acute subsistence crisis, leading through hunger to a substantially increased mortality rate in a community or region, and involving a collapse of the social, political, and moral order. Shortage was common because of the nature of the physical environment and the conditions of agricultural production, the backwardness of transport facilities, and the limited range and aims of government and administration in antiquity. All these factors, in particular the first two, climate and agriculture (which between them ensured that grain, the basic staple food, was a relatively scarce commodity in the Mediterranean world), guaranteed that there would be frequent breakdowns in the food supply, but also that such breakdowns would be temporary. Typically, authorities, local or central, secular or ecclesiastical, intervened before a crisis could evolve into a catastrophe, because it was in their interest to do so and the necessary resources were not lacking.

The capacity of communities to cope with food crises varied. Inland towns were less well placed than coastal towns for receiving emergency supplies, as Gregory of Nazianzus observed, prompted by a crisis that hit the town of Caesarea in Cappadocia, about 350 miles inland. We should not exaggerate, however. The marginal cost of transport becomes less crucial to the price of wheat in periods of rising prices, and authorities in inland towns were no less alive to the need for paternalistic intervention than their counterparts were on the coast. Where local resources proved insufficient, there was still the possibility of central government intervention. The emperor Anastasius had cash and grain sent to the hapless citizens of Edessa in northern Mesopotamia, lying about 350 miles from the nearest port, but too late and in quantities insufficient to cope with the terrible three-year famine of 499–502. The case of Antioch is complicated: this was a prosperous community in its own right but also much frequented by emperors as a regional capital and a base for wars against the Persians. The imperial presence itself, together with army and entourage, provoked food crises, as in the case of Julian in 361–362, and the tensions between emperor and local leaders sometimes got in the way of quick solutions. Julian's inadequate economic understanding proved a further hindrance when he tried to end the food crisis by bringing in imperial grain and putting it up for sale at a fixed, below-market price. Because his cheap grain was not rationed, it was quickly bought up by speculators and resold at a high price in the countryside or abroad. There was, however, never any likelihood that a solution would not be found, in this case or in others, before the sufferings of the populace reached Edessan proportions.

The most imposing system for supplying an urban center with foodstuffs was that developed in Rome and adapted to Constantinople from 330. Rome retained a privileged position as the main recipient of the tax-grain of Africa and Sicily (Egyptian grain now fed Constantinople). And it could sometimes secure help from the emperor in a shortage. But Rome was no longer the imperial capital and seat of emperors, and this threw the burden of responsibility onto the local elite, that is, the Senate. There were times when rich and reluctant Roman aristocrats were constrained to feed the people. Romans, like any other provincials, now turned on their municipal government and its key officials when prices rose and starvation seemed to threaten. The chance arrival of a grain ship from Brindisi saved the urban prefect of 468, Sidonius, from condemnation and humiliation. In 397 Symmachus, having heard, or learned of, the people's "entreaties for food," judged it prudent to withdraw from the city. It was he who proposed that Gildo, who was holding up the African grain ships, should be declared a public enemy. The nature of the danger Symmachus was escaping is illustrated by the experience of the Africa-based grain officials after the fall of Gildo: paraded in Rome, they were executed or freed according to their reception by the populace. A generation earlier, in 359, Tertullus, urban prefect of Rome, had been embarrassed when the grain fleet was held up by bad weather. He was saved from death by the dramatic gesture of offering the rioters his small sons, and by a timely sacrifice to Castor and Pollux, who calmed the winds and let the ships enter the harbor.

Food riots at Rome might have been more dangerous in late antiquity than under the principate, and Roman senators more exposed, but there was little chance that Romans would starve. Acute distress in times of severe and prolonged shortage is more likely to have occurred among the poor of the countryside, who lacked access to the civic privileges and private and institutional patronage available to city dwellers. From the 2nd century we have Galen's sharp observations on the routine but increasingly desperate attempts of peasants to cope with the inexorable depletion of their food resources in times of shortage, exacerbated by the necessity of surrendering vital supplies to city residents. At Edessa, the peasants were reduced to beggary in a year, and the famine had two more years to run.

BIBL.: P. Garnsey, *Famine and Food Supply in the Greco-Roman World* (Cambridge, Eng., 1988). T. Sternberg, *Orientalium more secutus* (Münster, 1991).   P.D.G.

Fars

The large and mountainous province of Fars occupies some 200,000 square kilometers and is located in the southwest of Iran. It borders the Persian Gulf, and to the west is the province of Khuzistan, to the north Isfahan, and to the east Kirman. Fars, the Arabicized form of Pars (Old Persian Parsa, Greek Persis), was the homeland of two great Iranian dynasties, the Achaemenian Persians (ca. 559–330 B.C.E.) and the Sassanians (224–651 C.E.). The remains of many important cities and monuments are located within the province, with a concentration in the fertile Marv-Dasht plain, north of Shiraz, the site of both the Achaemenian dynastic center of Persepolis and the principal city of Fars from the Seleucid to the early Islamic periods, Istakhr. From Parthian times Istakhr had a fire temple dedicated to Anahita, of which the Sassanian family were priests.

Both the founder of the Sassanian empire, Ardashir I (224–241), and his son, Shapur I (240–272), built new cities: Ardashir Khurra (the Glory of Ardashir), or Gur, and Bishapur. Ardashir I located Gur in a fertile area some 3 km from the modern town of Firuzabad, half-way between Shiraz and the Gulf; maritime trade was important to the Sassanian kings. Its double walls were pierced by four gates and formed a circle with a diameter of more than 2 km (the city of Darabgird was also circular). Shapur I built his new city, Bishapur, on a rectangular grid. It was near Kazerun, again en route to the Gulf.

Sassanian buildings are often preserved to a considerable height. Their massive walls were constructed of stones set in gypsum mortar, their surfaces subsequently plastered. Both Ardashir's fortress, Qalch-i Dukhtar, constructed on a dramatic spur commanding the road from Shiraz to Firuzabad, and his palace set in gardens in the plain illustrate the typical design of a Sassanian structure, with an arched iwan leading into a domed room, the dome carried on squinches. Another well-preserved "palace" is located at Sarvistan, although there is some doubt as to whether it is late Sassanian or early Islamic in date. In addition to monumental structures, there are many fire temples, or *chahar taq*, in Fars, of which a well-preserved example was found near the village of Kunar Siah. It originally consisted of a pair of domed buildings, a sanctuary and a fire temple.

The early Sassanian kings followed a late Parthian fashion of carving pictures on cliffs or boulders, and they raised this art form to new heights. The majority of their reliefs were carved in Fars, mostly near Sassanian cities. Because of the paucity of internal written records and provenanced artifacts, the reliefs are important for the light they shed on the state art of the time and the preoccupations of the kings. Ardashir I and Shapur I, for instance, were concerned with legitimizing their seizure of power, and they recorded their investiture by the god Ahuramazda several times. Other images recorded their victories, showing either the crucial point of a battle, as in the vivid jousting scene at Firuzabad, or the defeated rulers dead at their feet or pleading for mercy, as in Shapur's series commemorating his remarkable victories over Rome.

BIBL.: J. E. Curtis, *Ancient Persia* (London, 1989). R. W. Ferrier, ed., *The Arts of Persia* (New Haven, 1989). G. Herrmann, *The Iranian Revival* (Oxford, 1977).   G.H.

Fayum

Fayum is the Arabic name (derived from the Coptic Phiom, meaning "lake") for the fertile, low-lying area to the west of the Nile Valley about 80 km southwest of Cairo. Although often referred to as an oasis, it is (unlike the other Egyptian oases) watered by a branch canal from the Nile, the Bahr Yussuf. Part of it, including the modern lake (Birket Qarun) lies below sea level. The lake (Lake Moeris in ancient sources) was in pharaonic times much larger than at present; the Ptolemies reduced its level considerably by controlling the inflow of water from the Bahr Yussuf, which flows through an extensive canal and drainage system into the lake. Much of the land reclaimed by this process was assigned to Ptolemaic military settlers (Ptolemy II renamed the area the Arsinoite nome after his sister-wife Arsinoe), but the new villages were also populated by Egyptians brought in from other parts of the country.

Because the Fayum was irrigated by a canal network, unlike the flood basins of the Nile Valley, the maintenance of these canals (which flow at very gentle gradients for much of their course) was central to the usability of most of the land. Perennial irrigation also made it a logical zone for extensive planting of vineyards, orchards, and gardens. Failure to maintain the canals led to the desertification of arable land, however, and some villages went through periods of abandonment when their water supply failed. These periods are in considerable measure the reason for the survival of large numbers of papyri from the Fayum.

The capital of the Fayum was variously called Crocodilopolis, Arsinoe, and Ptolemais Euergetis; most of its once-extensive remains have disappeared in the spread of the modern capital, Medinet el-Fayum. Many of the ancient villages located around the periphery of the canal system have been excavated or surveyed, the best known being Karanis, Philadelphia, Soknopaiou Nesos, Tebtunis, and Theadelphia, all of which have yielded abundant papyri. Karanis (with the archive of Aurelius Isidoros) and Theadelphia (with the archive of Aurelius Sakaon) have contributed greatly to knowledge of village administration, taxation, and economy in the 4th century. For later centuries the villages have yielded little, but 19th century plundering of the mounds of Arsinoe produced a considerable number of documents and literary papyri.

The nome was apparently subdivided in the 6th century to create a new Theodosiopolite nome; it has been argued that its capital was at Tebtunis.

Fayum (or al-Fayyum) became an important and agriculturally wealthy district of early Islamic times; its decline had taken place by the 13th century. It was populated mostly by Christians and was associated in Muslim legend with the presence of Joseph, who would have drained the marshes around the oasis.

BIBL.: Dominic Rathbone, *Economic Rationalism and Rural Society in Third-Century* A.D. *Egypt* (Cambridge, Eng., 1991). Peter van Minnen, "Deserted Villages," *Bulletin of the American Society of Papyrologists* 32 (1995): 41–56.

R.S.B.

Festivals

The modern understanding of *festival,* as an occasion for celebration, especially on a day or at a time of religious significance that recurs at regular intervals, comes close to the Latin term *dies festi.* However, the Romans, as the Greeks, stipulated that all festival days were proclaimed for the gods. Thus an ancient festival is defined as essentially sacral in character. The great public games *(ludi)* and banquets *(epulae)* were occasions for festivals, as were certain holidays *(dies feriae).* But to the Romans there was a significant difference between festivals and holidays, for another essential feature of *dies festi,* or festivals, was the element of pleasure, whereas *dies feriae* were essentially days of rest when, as legally defined, certain rites had to be performed to honor the gods and the law courts were officially closed. This distinction is apparent in Macrobius's *Saturnalia* (1.16.2–4), where he lists *ludi* separately from *feriae; Varro, too, made a careful distinction between holidays (feriae) and public games (ludi)* that fell on the same day *(Ling.* 6.20). In the Greek world, this distinction does not appear relevant; the term *hēortē* appears to cover the Roman concepts of festival and holiday. Here, festivals will be defined as including both the Latin *dies festi* and *dies feriae.*

The public holidays celebrated in late antiquity honored the traditional deities of the Graeco-Roman pantheon: Jupiter, Juno, Minerva, and so on. But as the *Codex-Calendar of 354* indicates, those deities associated with certain mystery cults—Isis, Attis, and Cybele, or the Magna Mater, as the Romans called her—had also won public recognition. Each city had its own listing of holidays; in mid-4th century Rome, there were some 56 holidays celebrated without public games, scattered throughout the year. Although this may seem like a large number, it is significantly less than the 104 weekend holidays in the modern calendar year.

The public holidays recorded in the official calendar were considered to be of benefit for the people, either as a whole or for some subgroup. Consequently they were funded by the state and magistrates were involved, either overseeing or participating in the celebration. Priests were required to carry out prescribed rites, but the public at large was not obliged to perform specific rituals of worship. It is clear, however, that many of the rites connected with the holidays were widely practiced; so, for example, at the Saturnalia (which honored Saturn), the exchange of gifts and the reversal of slave-master roles is generally attested. The popularity of such rites led some scholars to dismiss these holidays as mere popular entertainments, not religious observances. The merriment accompanying the Lupercalia, for example, when naked young men would race through Rome striking women with strips of goatskin to ensure their fertility, does not coincide with modern ideas of solemnity. Nevertheless, this should not obscure the religious nature of such ritual activity.

Most often, the holiday veneration of a deity took the form of a blood sacrifice that was performed in front of a temple by the priests of the cult. A large public banquet frequently followed, as it did to honor Jupiter in November during the Plebeian Games. At times a *supplicatio,* or day of public prayer, took the place of a blood sacrifice; the 3rd century military calendar from Dura-Europus records a *supplicatio* to Vesta on 9 June while the records of the Arval Brethren indicate a blood sacrifice on this day in Rome. Certain holidays required specific rites, such as the ritual opening and cleansing of the Temple of Vesta by women and vestals on the seventh and fifteenth of June in mid-4th century Rome. The commemoration of the

dedication of a new temple often coincided with a public holiday to honor that god, as it did in 4th century Rome on 28 August to honor Sol and Luna; a large public banquet would have followed the ritual sacrifice and commemoration.

Macrobius (*Sat.* 1.16.4–6) divides the Roman public holidays into four categories: the fixed, annual public celebrations *(feriae stativae)* that were noted in the calendar and that had specific observances, like the Lupercalia; the annual but movable celebrations *(feriae conceptivae),* such as the Compitalia, whose dates were set yearly by magistrates or priests, like our modern holiday of Easter; the holidays proclaimed for special reasons *(feriae imperativae)* by consuls or praetors, such as those to commemorate a triumph or a ritual of purification; and, finally, the *feriae nundinae,* or the nundinals, the market days recurring every eight days that were "days off" for the rural, farm populations to come together for business or private affairs. (This last group is not included in the 56 holidays cited above, for these "rest days" are not named holidays.) All but the *feriae conceptivae* were also observed in the Greek world, and it seems that this category was disappearing from late Roman calendars too.

In addition to the public holidays, Romans recognized certain private ones. These were also categorized by Macrobius (*Sat.* 1.17.7–10). First were those holidays that belonged to certain families, such as for the Julian or Cornelian families, and those that were associated with a particular family and its domestic life; here Macrobius is probably thinking of the family cult, with its worship of its particular ancestors. In addition, there are those that were for individual private concerns, such as to commemorate a birthday, the striking of (and survival from) a lightning bolt, a funeral—accompanied by a ten-day period of ritual purification of the family of the deceased—or, interestingly, those for making an atonement or expiation. This last reveals a type of personal connection to the divine that arguably comes close to the modern concept of guilt.

Public games were celebrated as festivals, but they were not, strictly speaking, holidays *(feriae).* The law courts were open and people could go about their business if they chose to do so, much like in the limited celebration of Roman Catholic saints' days in modern Italy. However, the public games were a great attraction to Romans and Greeks, so much so that Augustine's Christian friend Alypius, for example, could not resist attending them in Rome despite his religious scruples *(Confessions* 6.8).

The entertainments at the games varied: theatrical games or spectacles *(ludi scaenici)* where mimes or pantomimes performed or wild animals were hunted, chariot races *(ludi circenses),* or gladiatorial combats were offered, depending on the festival. Since all games were held on behalf of the people, they were funded with public monies and administered by state magistrates, who also often contributed funds. For example, it was one of the duties of the urban prefect to fund the games to Apollo held in Rome in July.

The public games *(ludi)* and circuses *(circenses)* were the most popular ways of celebrating festivals in late antiquity, and, arguably, they were the most significant socially. Their appeal is apparent from the text of the *Codex-Calendar of 354,* which records 177 holiday or festival days devoted to *ludi* and *circenses* (including 10 days of gladiatorial shows); this contrasts markedly with the approximately 77 days recorded in calendars of the Augustan age devoted to this type of activity. The emperor and the imperial family were honored most often by these games, followed by the pagan gods and goddesses. Games commemorated the reigning emperor's birthday, day of accession, and triumphs, and often those of his father. These changes have given some scholars the impression that the political significance of the festival games obliterated their religious importance, for it was at these festival intervals that the populace and emperor were in direct contact. Festivals also offered local and senatorial aristocrats an arena in which to display their civic prominence; one competed against others of one's class for civic honor by providing the monies for the games. In the larger cities of the empire the dominance of circus factions, which were originally aligned with the sporting teams of the circus, provides further evidence of the social and political importance of the festival games in late antiquity.

However, the essentially sacred nature of the festival games persisted into late antiquity, and this explains the ongoing opposition of Christians to their celebration. These festivals were essentially pagan: the theatrical performances reenacted myths associated with the pagan gods; the circus races were dedicated to the gods; the bloody human and animal combats offended Christian morality. Recognizing this opposition, certain Christian emperors tried to secularize the traditional festivals. For example, legislation of Arcadius and Honorius in 399 concerning Africa allowed for festival games and banquets to continue because they were traditional amusements *(voluptates; C.Th. 16.10.17).* But the difficulty of reinforcing this sanitized view of the festivals is apparent. It is evidenced most forcefully by the 5th century controversy over the celebration of the Lupercalia in Rome. Pope Gelasius opposed this holiday as "the devil's work" *(diabolica figmenta).* A Christian senator argued that this was merely an image of a once-pagan ritual that now had efficacy as a means of purification from sin (Gelasius, *Lettre contre les Lupercales et dix-huit messes du sacramentaire léonien,* no. 8, ed. G. Pomarès, *Sources chrétiennes* 65.)

Following the definition of a festival as a periodic celebration of religious significance, whether joyous or sad, it is apparent that the introduction of Christian festivals represents a significant development in late antiquity. In addition to the celebration of the Nativity of Christ and the holidays around Easter, the commemorations of the depositions of martyrs and bishops were festivals of increasing social and political import. The dates of the Nativity and of Easter, and the veneration of the martyrs varied locally. Interestingly, festivals for some martyrs did spread; Ss. Cyprian, Perpetua, and Felicitas were popular African martyrs who were also honored in areas in Rome.

One of the most intriguing phenomena of late antiquity is the assimilation of pagan festival elements into Christian ones. For example, the carrying of pictures of Isis on board her sacred ship was originally part of the popular pagan festival to Isis known as *Isidis navigium,* celebrated in the Latin west in March. This rite was retained in the Christian *carnevale,* held in conjunction with Easter, when a ship or a representation of one was carried by the assembled participants.

The Persian festival of Nawrūz, or New Year's Day, was widely celebrated from pre-Sassanian through Islamic times in Iran and Iraq. People marked the occasion by exchanging presents, lighting fires, and sprinkling each other with water. The Sassanian king would customarily offer a feast and receive gifts, and rituals were performed at the fire temples. In late antiquity Nawrūz generally coincided with the vernal equinox and was the start of the Sassanian fiscal year. Although it signaled the beginning of the Persian solar year, the Muslims adopted the day for the collection of the land tax, and later several Abbasid caliphs attempted to fix the date in the Muslim lunar calendar. Nawrūz was also celebrated with similar customs in Syria and Egypt.

BIBL.: E. Bolognesi and R. Franceschini, "The Iron Masks: The Persistance of Pagan Festivals in Christian Byzantium," *Bosphorus: Essays in Honour of Cyril Mango: Byzantinische Forschungen* 21 (1995): 117–132. A. Dihle, "La fête chrétienne," *Revue des études augustiniennes* 38 (1992): 323–335. M. Harl, "La dénonciation des festivités profanes," ed. M. Harl, *Le déchiffrement des sens* (Paris, 1993), 433–453. Adam Mez, *The Renaissance of Islam,* trans. S. Khuda-Bukhsh and D. Margoliouth (London, 1937). G. Prinzing and D. Simon, *Fest und Alltag in Byzanz* (Munich, 1990). Jörg Rüpke, *Kalender und Öffentlichkeit* (Berlin and New York, 1995). Michele Renee Salzman, *On Roman Time: The Codex-Calendar of 354 and the Rhythms of Urban Life in Late Antiquity* (Berkeley, 1990). —M.R.S.

Fish

Fish and fishing were of great importance in the antique Mediterranean world. Greek naturalists studied fish, for which the Greek language had more than four hundred names. Classical art provides large numbers of fish images in various contexts (fishing scenes, *xenia* on mosaics, mythological scenes). Various cults gave fish particular significance. For example, sacred fish were raised in the sanctuaries of Atargatis in Syria and in Hatra, where it was forbidden to try to catch them. Before the feasts of Cybele, believers abstained from eating fish. Fish were also significant in the zodiac, and the zodiac sign Pisces was the object of countless iconographic representations. Between the two poles of reality (catching and eating fish) and aesthetics (their symbolic representation) too many textual and iconographic occurrences of fish exist in the pagan and Judeo-Christian world for all of them to have the same meaning. One is unable to choose a single meaning for all iconographic instances.

Christians of the Roman empire made symbolic use of fish and the Greek word for it, *ichthus*, whose acrostic form was articulated very early (*Iēsous Christos Theou Huios Sōtēr,* Jesus Christ Son of God Our Savior). It is impossible to say whether the use of the fish as a Christian sign occurred before the initials were assigned a meaning. In the early 3rd century, Tertullian *(De baptismo)* already knew what they signified. The use of the Greek word, or of the fish as an isolated symbol, continued until the 6th century. We do not know if it was a symbol of Christ or a symbol of faith in Christ.

In the Christian context, fish, depicted more or less realistically, decorated gravestones, sarcophagi, paintings, and objects. Clement of Alexandria *(Paed. 3.11)* officially authorized the use of carved fish seals among the few images he recommended.

Other occurrences in the Scriptures gave further significance to the literary and plastic images of fish in Christianity. Such fish always appeared within the context of miracles: the fish that leaps toward Tobias; the fish that swallows Jonah (the sources tell us that Jonah's stay in the fish's belly symbolizes Christ's time in the tomb); the miraculous draft of fishes; the miracle of the loaves and fishes (the feeding of the multitude). The Christian mission is to be "fishers of men."

Paintings in catacombs and on sarcophagi from the second half of the 3rd century show fishermen (angling is associated with baptism) or one or two fish on a platter, held by Christ or placed on a banquet table next to bread. Fish, isolated or in complex scenes depicting the feeding of the multitude (with Christ and onlookers standing, or seated at a banquet), have a number of different narrative referents: the miracle of real food; spiritual food; the Eucharist; Christians themselves; Christ as Savior and as the food of communion. They may even have real-life referents, such as funeral meals of fish.

BIBL.: F. J. Dölger, *Ichthys: Das Fisch-symbol in frühchristlicher Zeit* (Munster, 1922–1943). R. I. Curtis, *Garum and Salsamenta* (Oxford, 1991). G. Dagron, "Poissons, pêcheurs et poissonniers de Constantinople," in *Constantinople and Its Hinterland,* ed. C. Mango and G. Dagron (Aldershot, 1995).

A.R.

Foederati

The term *foederati* derives from the *foedus,* or treaty, concluded by Romans with neighboring peoples, most often those on the frontiers, and thus it refers to soldiers and civilians within the Roman empire under the terms of such treaties. The discussion of "federates" in the later empire focuses on two major issues: the extent to which the Roman army came to rely on such troops, and the status of the groups who settled in the frontier regions. References to *foedera* occur throughout Roman history, but most were not treaties between equals so much as formulas for submission. Rome recognized friendly rulers, usually with diplomatic gifts or "subsidies" given in return for recruits who served as auxiliaries, often in specialized ethnic units. In the later empire, although many ethnic groups, such as Saracens, Iberians, or Juthungi, are recorded in the army lists, it is usually impossible to tell whether they were *gentiles* recruited within the frontiers or federates from beyond. This recruitment process never ceased during the later empire, when foreign troops served Rome, frequently with their chiefs. Constantine received support from Crocus and his Alamans and from Bonitus and his Franks in 306; a treaty of "slavery" (Eusebius, *Vit.Const.* 4.5) was concluded by Constantine with the Goths in 332; and in Julian's time Hortarius, the Alaman living beyond the frontier, was called *rex foederatus* (Amm.Marc. 18.2.13). The Arab tribes led by sheikhs called phylarchs have been claimed as *foederati* as well, although our sources do not normally use this term for them. In theory most federates were irregulars, not part of the army establishment, and many units did not appear on the *Notitia Dignitatum* drawn up between the late 4th and early 5th century. For example, only two units of Goths are listed there, although Theodosius recruited them extensively, while the northwestern frontier list gives the impression of a phantom army, after Stilicho had replaced many regular units with federate Franks. Federates were still considered limited-contract troops who served on ad hoc campaigns in return for rations *(annonae foederaticae)* and gold. As such, they were valuable to emperors, who were preoccupied with the costs of maintaining an army and anxious not to remove tax-producing farmers from the land.

Cost was doubtless one of the pressures that led to the increasing use of federates from the later 4th century on. But the event that marked a major change in both the numbers and the status of federates was the Battle of Adrianople and the subsequent treaties concluded with the Goths. That there was a massive influx of foreign troops into the army cannot be disputed, given the unanimity of the sources. The Gallic orator Pacatus enthused about the Goths, Huns, and Alans who filled the cities of Pannonia with soldiers (*Pan. Lat.* II(XII) 32.4), while Theodosius's rival, Magnus

Maximus, spoke of "thousands" of federates also in his service in the 380s (Ambrose, *Ep.* 24.4). No doubt many were the same Goths, Alamans, and Franks who slaughtered each other at the River Frigidus in 395 to promote a Roman emperor. The real debate, however, is about the treaty of 382, which is obscure, under which Gratian and Theodosius negotiated the entry of the Goths into the empire. Did the Goths enter Roman service as "allies and citizens" (Synesius, *De regno.* 14–15), or were they "received into servitude" (*Pan.Lat.* II(X) 22)? The sources are divided between those that suggest the Goths preserved a semi-independent political status while being permitted to settle on land inside the empire, and those that claim they were reduced to the noncitizen status of *dediticii*. In support of the former is the fact that some Goths undoubtedly did gain status, and in the 6th century Procopius (*Bell.Van.* 3.11.3) refers back to an earlier time when barbarian federates "arrived in the state, not on condition of being slaves, since they were undefeated by Rome, but on terms of total equality." Against this is not only the traditional Roman practice of *receptio* but also the fact that the literary and archaeological sources contain no clear evidence of independent enclaves of barbarian communities within the frontiers (though an ambiguous inscription, *CIL* 5.1623, in the Drave Valley is sometimes cited). Nor is it easy to see how such communities would have worked within the Roman system, unless by a program of *hospitalitas*, to which there may be some vague allusion in Themistius (*homorhophios,* "living under the same roof"; *Orat.* 34.24).

The later 4th century and early 5th century saw a rapid acceleration in the use of federates, but by this time the term covered many different categories of soldiers. Some, as earlier, were foreigners who came with their leaders from beyond the frontiers at the invitation of the Romans, as, for example, in 409 when the emperor Honorius "summoned as allies" several thousand Huns under their king, Uldin, to fight against Alaric (Zosimus 5.50). Others were recruited by Roman agents without an alliance. Aetius was sent by John in 423 "with a great sum of gold" (Gregory of Tours, *Hist.* 2.8) to recruit Huns through his personal contacts, much as Gainas used his influence to invite Goths into the empire individually. Still others came from groups already installed inside the empire under the terms of their treaties. Almost certainly this was the origin of Alaric, one of the several Goth leaders who was cultivated by Theodosius after 382 in his struggle against usurpers. And finally there were federate groups, apparently homeless *condottieri,* who lived within the empire, serving whoever paid them. They became common during the confused wars against usurpers in the 5th century and were sometimes enrolled as units into the Roman army. There was little difference between groups like this and the *bucellarii,* if we consider the band of two or three hundred men who followed the Goth leader Sarus, at least some of whom were given the title of "domestics" or bodyguards (Olympiodorus, frg. 18). The rewards of gold and land given to such groups explains the origin of the first barbarian kingdom in Aquitania, given to Wallia and his Visigoths in 418.

During the 5th and 6th centuries federates and *bucellarii* more or less replaced *comitatenses* as mobile fighting units. The wars of Aetius in Gaul were fought almost entirely with federates. By the reign of Honorius the units had ceased to be ethnically distinctive, now including Romans, which explains why some became regular army units. The Honoriaci, for example, stationed in the Pyrenees in 409, "had at one time been received into a treaty" (Orosius 7.40.7). By Justinian's rule *foederati* were regular regiments in the official army, although always separate from Roman units, since they probably still contained recruits from beyond the frontiers—almost like "foreign legions."

BIBL.: T. S. Burns, *Barbarians within the Gates of Rome: A Study of Roman Military Policy and the Barbarians, ca. 375–425 A.D.* (Bloomington, 1994). P. Heather, *Goths and Romans, 332–489* (Oxford, 1991). J.H.W.G. Liebeschuetz, *Barbarians and Bishops: Army, Church and State in the Age of Arcadius and Chysostom* (Oxford, 1990). J. Maspero, "Foederati et Stratiotoi dans l'armée byzantine au vie siècle," *Byzantinische Zeitschrift* 21 (1912): 97–109. I. Shahīd, *Byzantium and the Arabs in the Fourth Century* (Washington, D.C., 1984). C.W.

Food

Throughout the antique Mediterranean world, children were suckled for several years, a practice that made it easier to space out births if the mother did not entrust the child to a wet nurse. The basic foods of the time were grains, oil, wine, meats—generally from animals slaughtered during sacrifices—and dairy products. Farm vegetables supplemented this diet. The consumption of products that were gathered (wild fruit, thistles, wild legumes, and mushrooms) and of game, fish, and mollusks continued uninterrupted. The basic products (grains, wine, oil, and pork) were collected as taxes (the *annona*) and distributed in the largest urban centers (Rome, Alexandria, Constantinople). The rations of the Roman army in the late period included bread (replaced in the countryside by biscuits), meat (veal, fresh or salted pork), wine (or vinegar), and oil.

In the classical world, food was the object of medical, philosophical, and religious reflection. The collection of the physician Oribasius, compiled after 360, essentially transmitted excerpts from Galen on food, but the latter's writings had already borrowed from a tradition that can be traced back to Hippocrates. Oribasius first divided the texts into those dealing with plants and those dealing with animal products. He further organized the texts by diet, based on the humor to be acquired or eliminated, and then by the desired effect. Finally, he classified them according to the four fundamental diets: chilling, heating, drying, and moistening. The chapters on food preparation are also arranged by diet.

The first goal of a diet was to favor well-being through good digestion. Readers were advised to avoid heavy food. Ever since the Hippocratic treatise on diet, food had been a part of therapeutic methods. In addition to physical exercise and a proper lifestyle, the essential means for preventing illness had to do with food. Diet, determined as a function of age, sex, and the individual's disposition and circumstances, was a constant concern throughout antiquity.

Diets were also designed to improve intelligence (Hippocratic treatise on diet). Philosophy required a mastery of the appetites; in addition, ideas relating to the communication between body and spirit, especially via life-carrying blood, led to alimentary asceticism, or at the very least to self-control.

General knowledge of the sexual effects of malnutrition and anemia (it was known that male sexual impotence was brought on by famine or other deficiencies), and knowledge of the aphrodisiac or anaphrodisiac effects of certain foods, led to the use of diet to facilitate or avoid conception. Such knowledge also lent support to religious practices involving sexual asceticism during at least a part of the year.

Even though Pythagoras is believed to have been the first to give a meat diet to an Olympic athlete, tradition attributes to him the idea of the transmigration of souls, which is associated with a ban on consuming animals. That tradition, adopted for a time by Seneca and disputed by Plutarch, was commented on at length by Porphyry in the 3rd century in his treatise on abstinence. Despite the existence of butcher shops in Rome, the consumption of meat was primarily associated with the sacrificial slaughter of cattle and sheep. Poultry and game were also consumed. Both Oribasius, on the side of medicine, and Porphyry, on the side of philosophy, mention the consumption of big cats (for example, panthers). In the early 4th century, Iamblichus's defense of sacrifices gave its approval to the Neoplatonist decision to abandon vegetarianism.

In addition to the Jewish prohibition on eating pork, shared by other Semites (the Phoenicians, for example), other religions advised abstaining from certain foods. Manichaeism respected the counsel given to Manes to abstain from meat, wine, and commerce with women. Also associated with religion, the prohibition on consuming fish in the cult of Atargatis was combined with other dietary prohibitions, either permanent or on days preceding feast days. Fasting was practiced in Graeco-Roman and Near Eastern cults before certain ceremonies: the cults of Demeter, for example, and especially those of Isis and Cybele. The form this fasting took probably varied depending on the holiday, the individual, and the cult.

In Christianity, the real and metaphoric uses of diet attest to the importance of food and the rules relating to it in the practices and psychology of the time. The apostle Paul (1 Cor. 8–10) wrote that the meat of sacrificed animals was not tainted, but nonetheless warned against the consumption of such meat of idolatry. Christians, fearing they would mistakenly consume the meat of animals sacrificed to pagan gods, sometimes became vegetarians (in Bithynia in about 112 and in Lyons in 177, for example). Christian dietary asceticism had the same purpose as its pagan counterpart: to train the individual to master bodily appetites, to facilitate sexual mastery, and to give freedom and lightness to the soul in order to direct one's entire being toward God. The Jewish fast of penitence was also adopted. For every Christian, periods of fasting were a key part of asceticism. Mastery over food, as well as mastery over sexuality, was a topos of hagiography. Diets were established for solitary or cenobite ascetics after Egyptian anchorites experimented with excessive restrictions. Preparing for the stages of Christian life or for the church hierarchy implied adopting a particular diet. The Christian week and year were marked by periods of fasting, which varied depending on place and era and were regulated by popes or councils.

Suckling became the privileged metaphor for God's function as a teacher of Christians, both individuals and communities. Augustine saw the church as the "nurse" of every Christian. Prayers before meals (Prudentius, *Cathemerinon* 4) emphasized spiritual food, a gift from God.

BIBL.: Jean-Louis Flandrin and Massimo Montanari, eds., *Histoire de l'alimentation* (Paris, 1996). Herbert Musurillo, "The Problem of Ascetical Fasting in the Greek Patristic Writers," *Traditio* 12 (1956): 1–64. Aline Rousselle, *Porneia: On Desire and the Body* (Oxford, 1988). T. Shaw, *The Burden of the Flesh: Fasting and Sexuality in Early Christianity* (Minneapolis, 1998). A.R.

Foodstuffs

The inhabitants of late antique Europe, North Africa, and the Middle East fell heir to the food traditions of the ancient world. These were richly varied, showing considerable differences between regions and social classes. There were also some changes through time. Yet underlying all this variety was much similarity in eating habits, which makes it possible to treat the subject in a general way.

Cereals were the staple food almost everywhere, the exception being in marginal hunting and grazing communities that had less developed agriculture. Indeed the early Middle Ages saw an extension and intensification of cereal production and consumption throughout Germanic Europe. Prominent among the grains consumed were various *Tritica*, including emmer, rivet wheat, einkorn, spelt, and common wheat *(Triticum aestivum)*, the last of which had spread widely through the ancient world; barley and oats were also commonly eaten, and in some regions rye, brome, foxtail millet, and common millet were consumed. During the early Middle Ages rye gradually became an important grain in much of central and northern Europe, while the Arab conquests led to the diffusion of sorghum and rice into the Middle East, North Africa, Spain, and Sicily. Whether hard wheat was also used in the ancient world, and how and when it spread through the Mediterranean and into northern Europe, are questions that cannot yet be answered: the texts throw almost no light on the matter, and with present techniques, the archaeological finds of various naked wheats cannot be distinguished one from another. Primarily grains were ground into flour, either by hand-operated querns or, increasingly from late Roman times onward, by animal-drawn or water-powered mills; flour was used for the making of leavened and unleavened bread. Grains could also be made into cakes, polentas, and porridges, the last of which might also contain some legumes, vegetables, or meat; grains were added to soups and meat dishes as well. In the Islamic world there appeared a wide variety of sweet and savoury dishes made with rice.

Consumption of animal products was probably generally low. It appears to have been highest in the very wealthy classes and among fishing, hunting, and grazing communities with relatively underdeveloped agriculture. It was also probably greater through the Germanic north; as the German peoples spread into the western Roman empire, diets in the successor kingdoms probably showed some shift toward meat and other animal products. Cattle, sheep, goats, and pigs were commonly raised for meat, milk, wool, and hides, but various constraints limited production and hence consumption, most notably the lack of year-round fodder and forage in most places, the limited appeal of salted or sun-dried meat, and the need for densely settled communities to maximize calorie output by concentrating on grain production. Some meat was also available from farmyard animals such as chickens and pigeons, and villagers—and no doubt the rich—consumed some game. Fish were eaten mainly by coastal and riverine communities and by people who lived near fish ponds, though preserving fish by salting or sun drying allowed some consumption elsewhere.

Late antique peoples could also eat a wide variety of fruits and vegetables, though the importance of these in diets seems uncertain. Among the most common vegetables were legumes, such as peas, fava beans, kidney beans, chickpeas, and lentils, all of which were high in protein and often rich in minerals; leaf vegetables such as lettuce, cabbage, various cresses, and greens gathered from the wild; root vegetables such as turnips, parsnips, radishes, beets, and carrots; and various others, such as onions, garlic, leeks, celery, asparagus, cardoon, and kohlrabi. In the Middle East and Egypt, dates, figs, melons *(Cucumis melo)*, and

pomegranates were important fruits, while people in Europe and Anatolia ate apples, pears, cherries, apricots, plums, medlars, peaches, quinces, melons, and grapes. Only one citrus fruit was known in the late Roman period, the citron, which was perhaps used mainly for seasoning and as a medicine. In the wake of the Arab conquests of the 7th to 9th centuries, the range of available fruits and vegetables expanded considerably in the Near East, Egypt, North Africa, Spain, and Sicily. Among the fruits and vegetables introduced into those regions in early Islamic times were sour oranges, lemons, limes, bananas, plantains, watermelons, spinach, eggplants, colocasia (taro), and possibly shaddocks. To judge from later cookery books and the accounts of travelers, people in the early Islamic world became big eaters of fruits and vegetables.

Dishes were flavored and seasoned in a number of ways. The use of onions and garlic was almost universal, and most regions made extensive use of locally grown herbs: in his *Etymolgiae,* Isidore of Seville (d. 636) mentions parsley, fennel, lovage, anise, dill, cumin, coriander, chervil, sage, and six varieties of mint, while in the Capitulare de Villis of 815, Charlemagne ordered that gardens on imperial estates should include fenugreek, costmary, sage, rue, cumin, caraway, tarragon, anise, chicory, herb william, fennel, dill, mustard, summer savory, and mint. On the tables of the rich, spices from India and the Far East were also widely used. Diocletian's Price Edict of 301 fixed maximum prices not only for many herbs produced within the empire but also for cinnamon, cassia, and ginger of eastern origin; and in the 6th century Justinian's *Digest* sets customs duties at Alexandria on a wide variety of imports from the east, including white pepper, cinnamon, cassia, amomum, ginger, and cardamom. Though in Byzantium and the Islamic world such spices continued to be used extensively through the late antique period, it seems likely that, as long-distance trade declined, their use fell off in the western European provinces of the later empire and in the successor kingdoms; they by no means disappeared, however, as attested by a royal diploma granted to the Abbey of Corbie in 716 that mentions quantities of pepper, cinnamon, cloves, and nard.

Honey was the almost universal sweetener, supplemented in places by concentrated grape juice, date syrup, and the like. The growing of sugar cane and the refining of sugar were probably known in the Sassanian empire by the 6th century and then diffused through the Islamic world from the 8th century onward. Salt, used for preserving as well as seasoning foods, was obtained almost exclusively by evaporating or boiling water from salt springs, saltwater lakes, or the sea; it is not clear that the mining of rock salt, which was important in prehistoric times at some eastern Alpine sites, continued in the late antique period. As many regions could not produce salt, it was traded extensively. In the Germanic kingdoms of western Europe, trade in salt continued after most other long-distance trade had nearly vanished.

Fatty substances for cooking and eating were obtained from vegetable and animal sources. Vegetable oils were extracted by crushing the vegetables in bag presses, beam presses, screw presses, and roller mills; the *trapetum,* a Roman invention, was also used for making olive oil. All over the Mediterranean basin olive oil was the most common source of fat, supplemented in some places by oils from colocynths, sesame seeds, and various nuts, as well as by animal fats. In the Germanic parts of Europe, animal fats seem to have predominated, most notably pork fat, lard, butter or butterfat, and, in some places, fish oil.

Of the various beverages known in the late antique world, milk was the most ancient, but it was drunk mainly by herding communities and in the Germanic world; in the Mediterranean basin and the Middle East it was more commonly consumed in the form of cheese, which could be kept longer and was more easily digested by Mediterranean people. Wine made from grapes was the most common drink for all classes in the Mediterranean basin, and during the Roman empire there was a considerable expansion of wine production into the northern and western provinces. Though the Germanic conquests dealt a serious blow to wine drinking in the areas overrun, it seems nowhere to have disappeared; and, perhaps in part because of its use in Christian communion, its production seems to have expanded in the Germanic world from about the 8th century onward. Similarly, in the areas conquered by the Arabs in the 7th and 8th centuries, wine production suffered but still flourished among Christian and Jewish communities. The usual alternative to wine was beer, made mainly from the malt of barley: beer was a common drink in the Middle East before the rise of Islam, and in northwestern Europe, where the Germans had learned beer making from the Celts, it was the drink of choice. Other fermented drinks could be made from honey and from such fruits as dates, apples, and pears; indeed, cider and perry came to enjoy some popularity in northwestern Europe as, from the fifth century onward, the growing of apple and pear trees spread through the region.

Little is known about aristocratic cookery in the late antique period. While the recipe book of Apicius (born ca. 25 B.C.E.) appears to have been reworked a number of times up until the 5th century and perhaps beyond, and copies of later versions are known to have existed in the libraries of the monasteries of Tours and Fulda at the end of the Middle Ages, we cannot know how closely the work reflected later Roman cookery in the west nor whether it had any influence on post-Roman cuisine. What seems likely is that in the western European provinces of the later empire, the food of the rich became simpler as they retreated from the cities to their country estates and as these estates became increasingly self-sufficient; this trend probably continued in the successor kingdoms, encouraged by the church's views on gluttony and by an austerity that prevailed on many monastic estates and beyond. From Byzantium, too, there is little evidence on cookery before the 10th century, but later sources suggest that in the eastern empire Roman and Greek traditions were preserved and added to by a lavish imperial court and a large city-dwelling aristocracy. In the Islamic world, first in Damascus and from the mid-8th century in Baghdad, a new cuisine of great refinement was taking shape, which, as the caliphate broke up, was diffused westward to the courts of the newly emerging states. This cuisine incorporated elements of both Byzantine and Sassanian cooking, and made use of novelties such as sugar, rice, sour oranges, lemons, bananas, eggplants, watermelons, and spinach.

While it seems impossible to say anything about the adequacy of late antique diets, it is certain that most people endured—or succumbed to—periods of severe food shortage, for two quite different reasons. By the early centuries of the Roman empire there had developed a considerable local and long-distance trade in foodstuffs, especially wine, grain, oil, and some luxury foods. This had a number of advantages: it allowed some regional specialization and hence more efficient production; it brought exotic luxuries to the tables of the rich; and it gave a measure of protection against potential local famines. In time, however, cities came to depend on this trade for much of their food supply and became vulnerable to interruptions in it. To protect the population of the city of Rome, for example, the imperial government, through the 3rd and 4th centuries, bound to their jobs many food producers, processors, transporters, and distributors. Similar measures were taken by the councils, or *curiae,* of many other western cities. While such regulations may have had some effect, they were not altogether successful; and indeed, by destroying markets, they may often have been counterproductive. In any event, cities, particularly those in the western European part of the empire, experienced frequent food crises as long-distance trade declined and became more erratic. These shortages may have been one of the reasons for the marked decline of western cities during the centuries leading up to and following the collapse of the empire in the west.

In addition, as western society reorganized itself into largely self-sufficient rural estates, their inhabitants, like those living in the shrunken cities, increasingly relied on a restricted range of locally produced foodstuffs. Both rural and urban dwellers thus found themselves more and more at the mercy of local weather, plant diseases, and pests. When they wanted to turn to markets, they found these inadequate. Food crises punctuated their lives, as many laws and chronicles attest. When peasants were pressed to sell their worldly goods, eat the seed needed for the following season, or slaughter their draft animals to tide themselves through the crisis, the recovery could be delayed for years after the initial causes had been resolved. Although there seems to have been some revival of trade in foodstuffs by the 9th century, this at best reduced, but did not remove, the specter of famine.

BIBL.: *L'alimentazione nell'antichità* (Parma, 1985). Andrew Dalby, *Siren Feasts: A History of Food and Gastronomy in Greece* (London and New York, 1996). J. Wilkins, D. Harvey, and M. Dobson, eds., *Food in Antiquity* (Exeter, 1995). R. J. Forbes, *Studies in Ancient Technology* (Leiden, 1955–1964). vols. 3 and 5. V. E. Grimm, *From Feasting to Fasting: The Evolution of a Sin: Attitudes to Food in Late Antiquity* (London, 1996). J. Koder, *Gemüse in Byzanz* (Vienna, 1993). K. L. Pearson, "Nutrition and the Early Medieval Diet," *Speculum* 72 (1997): 1–32. F. Thélamon, "Ascèse et sociabilité: Les conduites alimentaires des moines d'Égypte," *Revue des études augustiniennes* 38 (1992): 295–321.   A.W.

Fortification

Few events can have affected the lives of the 3rd century citizens of Rome as much as the emperor Aurelian's construction of the 18 km circuit of walls started in 271 C.E. From an open city defined by the boundary stones of its *pomerium,* the imperial capital went to being fortified like a military camp. The events and military crises of the 3rd century had demonstrated that cities like Rome could no longer rely for their protection on the garrisons and defenses of the imperial frontiers. The fortification of cities and military camps was to become a major activity over the succeeding centuries, so that by the time of Justinian the principal civic enterprises recorded by Procopius were the construction of churches and fortifications.

The Aurelianic walls of Rome have few precise parallels. They were constructed of brick-faced concrete, 4 m wide and up to 7 m in height, normally with a gallery to provide a second fire platform. Rectangular towers were located at frequent intervals of about 30 m; in all, there were 381 towers. Elsewhere in the empire cities and fortresses followed a somewhat different pattern, although a distinction can be drawn between military and urban forms of fortification. Military fortifications from the later 3rd century onward display similar characteristics, from the Saxon Shore forts of Pevensy and Portchester overlooking the English Channel to the new tetrarchic legionnary fortresses of Odruh and Lejjun in Jordan. Broad curtain walls of more than 3 m in width were flanked by bold projecting towers, frequently U-shaped in form, and special provision was made for the protection of gates. Some of these late forts continued the rectilinear outline used during the principate, but many took advantage of the local terrain and were irregular in plan, such as the lower Danube forts of Dinogetia and Iatrus. Some of these 4th century forts were smaller than their predecessors, like Eining on the upper Danube, but size varied considerably across the empire. Overall the new fortifications indicate a greater concern for defense against more aggressive enemies.

Many cities also received new defenses at this time, and the pattern for urban fortification is even less consistent. In some cases, especially in Gaul and at Sparta and Athens, the new circuit defended only part of the urban area, often making extensive use of *spolia* from cemeteries and abandoned public buildings. In other cases, as in cities like Nicaea or Hisar in Bulgaria, the new circuits were made of alternate brick bands and rubble masonry with U-shaped or rectangular towers similar to many late Roman forts. The construction of both military and urban fortifications followed the established practice of the region: ashlar predominated in Syria and Roman Mesopotamia, and brick and coursed rubble are normally found throughout Europe and the Aegean provinces.

The most monumental and successful fortifications of late antiquity were the Theodosian land-walls of Constantinople, built in 412–422 when the boundary of the Constantinian city was extended 3 km to the west. This huge system of triple defenses comprised an outer ditch, an outer wall *(proteichisma),* and an inner wall 12 m high and 3.5 m broad; both inner and outer walls included ninety-six towers. The origins of this system are not clear; often claimed to represent the triple scheme described by the 3rd century B.C.E. Hellenistic writer Philo, the Theodosian walls present a more complex system than he wrote of. An attacker was confronted by a tripartite system of fortified terraces more than 60 m wide and rising from the outer ground surface by 25 m. The system of outer walls probably originated on the eastern frontier with Sassanian Persia, where Singara and Amida were fortified in the 4th century. Development of the fortress-cities of the Roman east continued until the 6th century, with the Anastasian foundations of Dara and Resafa and Justinian's fortress at Zenobia. In general these followed the tradition of fortifications established since the 4th century. Greater originality of design was found in the Balkan provinces, stemming from the new ideas in the capital. Thessalonica was refortified with a brick-built circuit including triangular towers and an outer wall, probably built in the mid-5th century. For the next hundred years, pointed towers, either triangular or pentagonal, became characteristic of urban and frontier fortifications in the Balkans and were also employed in some of the major fortifications in the east, and even at Tocra in Cyrenaica. This last site was exceptional, since the new works of Justinian's reconquest in Africa continued the tradition of rectilinear forts and towers. The Anastasian wall in Thrace was equipped with massive pentagonal towers projecting 12 m from the curtain wall. This was the last of a group of "long walls" in the Balkans built or rebuilt in the 5th and 6th centuries, including the Isthmian wall at Corinth and the fortifications at Thermopylae. The Anastasian wall was 56 km in length, and it was built only 65 km west of Constantinople. In a sense it was the last frontier, restating the vulnerability of the Danube frontier. In late antiquity the region from the Adriatic to the Black Sea became a landscape of fortified towns and villages; some were military in function, but the majority were defended settlements. A new form that developed was the fortress constructed at a strategic location in the interior, for example Veliko Turnovo and Kjustendil in Bulgaria and Markovi Kuli near Skopje. The form of their defenses indicates that they were imperial foundations, and they provided a model for the 7th century fortresses built in Asia Minor at Ephesus, Ankara, and Sardis after the invasions of the Persians and Arabs. At that time of crisis, Constantinople was forced to rely on the Theodosian walls for its protection, and successive emperors maintained the walls according to the original plan and construction methods. Like Justinian's Church of Hagia Sophia, the land-walls were a unique legacy from early Byzantine Constantinople at the apogee of its development.

BIBL.: J. Cotterill, "Saxon Raiding and the Role of the Late Roman Coastal Forts in Britain," *Britannia* 24 (1993): 227–240. K. R. Dark, "A Sub-Roman Re-defence of Hadrian's Wall?" *Britannia* 23 (1992): 111–120. J. Durliat, *Les dédicaces d'ouvrages de défense en Afrique* (Paris, 1981). C. Foss and D. Winfield, *Byzantine Fortifications* (Pretoria, 1986). G. Fowden, "Late Roman Achaea: Identity and Defence," *Journal of Roman Archaeology* 8 (1995): 549–567. D. Pringle, *The Defence of Byzantine Africa* (Oxford, 1981).   J.G.C.

Fortunatus

A native of northern Italy, Venantius Fortunatus was educated at Ravenna, which had been recently reclaimed for the Roman empire after Emperor Justinian's armies had liberated the city from Ostrogothic control. In 566 he arrived at Metz, in the heart of Frankish Gaul. There he celebrated the marriage of the Merovingian king Sigibert to the Visigothic princess Brunhild in a wedding poem that, with its learned allusions to classical mythology and use of traditional meter, may well have baffled many of the guests. He eventually moved south, visiting King Charibert's court at Paris and the Church of St. Martin at Tours. At Poitiers Fortunatus ingratiated himself with Radegund, formerly a wife of King Chlothar but now a prominent nun, honored the city's patron saint by writing a *Life* of St. Hilary and a collection of his miracle stories, and was soon ordained a priest.

Fortunatus's many poems, composed in various genres, demonstrate his deep familiarity with both pagan and Christian Latin poetry, and throughout Frankish Gaul he became an arbiter of classical rhetoric and

Latin poetry. He delivered verse panegyrics at the courts of various Merovingian kings in which he interpreted their exploits in terms of classical mythology, biblical events, and Roman history, compared them to past Roman emperors, and shrewdly reminded them of the virtues characteristic of a Christian ruler. During his travels around Gaul he was the guest of various bishops, magistrates, and aristocrats, whose accomplishments and pedigrees he commemorated in numerous poems and epitaphs and whose occasional attempts at writing verse he generously complimented. In other poems he furthermore praised their villas, the churches they had funded, and the shrines they had founded. Using stories supplied by some of his hosts, Fortunatus wrote *Lives* of various saints in a prose that was ornately, and sometimes almost incomprehensibly, baroque; he also composed a long *Life* of one of his hosts, Bishop Germanus of Paris.

Three friendships were especially important. In 573 Fortunatus celebrated Gregory's accession as bishop of Tours. One link between the two men was their mutual veneration for St. Martin, who had once healed Fortunatus's eyes at a shrine in Italy. Gregory now encouraged Fortunatus's new versification of Sulpicius Severus's writings about St. Martin, hinted that his own collection of miracle stories might also provide suitable material for a poem, and presented his friend with an estate; in return Fortunatus dedicated to Gregory his first collection of poems and helped in his defense against the suspicions of King Chilperic. At Poitiers Fortunatus composed two hymns that celebrated the arrival of relics of the True Cross, sent to Radegund by the Byzantine emperor Justin II. He also wrote many poems as gifts for Radegund, as well as for Agnes, the abbess of the convent; his poems for Agnes were so affectionate that in one he had to protest that he loved her only like a sister. After Radegund's death in 587 he wrote a laudatory *Life* of the former queen. Although Fortunatus eventually became bishop of Poitiers, his subsequent reputation was due primarily to the literary influence of his hagiography and, especially, his magnificent poems.

BIBL.: B. Brennan, "The Career of Venantius Fortunatus," *Traditio* 41 (1985): 49–78. R. Collins, "Observations on the Form, Language and Public of the Prose Biographies of Venantius Fortunatus in the Hagiography of Merovingian Gaul," in *Columbanus and Merovingian Monasticism*, ed. H. B. Clarke and M. Brennan (Oxford, 1981), 105–131. J. W. George, *Venantius Fortunatus: A Latin Poet in Merovingian Gaul* (Oxford, 1992).   R.V.

Fossatum

The term *fossatum* appears in only one source during the later empire. An imperial edict of 409 to the vicar of Africa, under the title *de terris limitaneis* (*C.Th.* 7.15.1), demands that land granted "by an ancient humane concession" to barbarians "for the fortification of the *limes* and the *fossatum*" must not be held by illegal occupants but immediately returned to "tribesmen" *(gentiles)* or to veterans. The identification of the *fossatum Africae* began in the 19th century, when French officers of the Brigade Topographique found stretches of walls and ditches in the predesert of central Algeria and western Tunisia, and it was fully accepted in 1949 when Colonel Baradez published aerial photographs of the Algerian (Numidian) sectors. Since then numerous other short walls, arbitrarily referred to as *clausurae,* have been discovered across valley entrances between the predesert and the fertile north in Tunisia and Libya (the *limes Tripolitanus*). The function of the *fossatum,* which is not continuous, is disputed, although most agree it served not as linear barrier but as a control for transhumant pastoralists. Construction dates are virtually nonexistent and not necessarily identical everywhere. The camp of Gemellae, intimately linked to an uncertain Numidian section (the Seguia bent el-Krass), was occupied in 125–126, but scarce pottery finds in other sectors yield 1st, 2nd, or 3rd century dates. Late Roman forts, many in distinctive *quadriburgi* form, appear associated and show the *fossatum* was still active in the 4th century, while the use of *gentiles* units is a well-documented feature of the late African *limes.*

BIBL.: J. Baradez, *Vue aérienne de l'organisation romaine dans le sud algérienne: Fossatum Africae* (Paris, 1949). D. J. Mattingley, *Tripolitania* (London, 1995). P. Trousset, *Recherches sur le limes Tripolitanus* (Paris, 1974).   C.W.

Frumentius

Frumentius, the first bishop of Axum, ordained by Athanasius of Alexandria, is first attested in a letter to the local rulers Aizanas (Ezana) and Sazanas by Roman Emperor Constantius II in 356 C.E. (Athanasius, *Apologia* 31). Constantius tried, unsuccessfully, to recall Frumentius and force him to submit to George, Arian bishop of Alexandria. The reports of Rufinus (*Hist.eccl.* 10.9) and other historians about the shipwreck of young Frumentius together with the philosopher Meropius and his companion Aedesius, Frumentius's arrival at Axum, and his career at the court as the educator of the royal princes, have a rather legendary quality to them, but Rufinus claims to have spoken to Aedesius himself. Frumentius was probably a native of Tyre, and the letter of Constantius makes his connection to the Axumite court certain. King Ezana became a Christian around the middle of the 4th century, as can be seen from his coins and his later inscriptions. Frumentius may have gathered Graeco-Roman merchants who lived in Adulis, the kingdom's Red Sea port, to form a Christian congregation that eventually led to the conversion of the king and his people. Today, Frumentius is revered as the founder of the Ethiopian church, according to liturgical and hagiographical tradition, under the name of Abba Salama (Father Peace).

BIBL.: H. Brakmann, *Die Einwürzelung der Kirche im spätantiken Reich von Aksum* (Bonn, 1994). W. H. C. Frend, "The Church in the Reign of Constantius II: Mission, Monasticism, and Worship," in A. Dihle, ed., *L'église et l'empire au IVe siècle* (Geneva, 1989). Françoise Thélamon, *Païens et Chrétiens au IVe siècle: L'apport de l'"Histoire ecclésiastique" de Rufin d'Aquilée* (Paris, 1981), 37–83.   A.D.

Games

Late antique games are known from archaeology and from texts that neither explain rules nor match surviving artifacts. Playing pieces and dice cannot always be differentiated from counting stones, theater or meal tokens, votive or decorative figures, and the tools for divination. Specific games may derive from limited sources (e.g., oracular lots, or another game) or from repeated inventions.

Social attitudes toward games were similar throughout the late antique world, though levels of acceptance varied regionally and chronologically. Condemnations of gambling and obsessive play appear in rabbinic commentaries and in Roman, Byzantine, Islamic, and canon law, but these had little practical effect.

Children's toys included nuts, ropes, and hoops or wheels. Ball games were widespread. Knucklebones, either real bones (usually from sheep) or artificial, were thrown by both children and adults. In play, the four largest faces of the bone had both names and numeric values.

Dice were made from bone, clay, wood, bronze, glass, and luxury materials. Most were cubes like their modern equivalents. Parallelepiped dice were common in northern Europe and were used in Britain throughout this period and in Scandinavia through the Viking era. Other variants included crouching human figures and polyhedra with seven to twenty-four sides. However, dice with more than six sides were probably used more for divination. Games normally required two or three cubic dice, dropped through a hollow tower or shaken from a cup to ensure fair throws.

Elaborate board games were mainly adult pastimes. Portable boards of wood or tile were balanced on the knees of two facing players. Other boards were cut into stone panels, buildings, and public plazas. Playing pieces were most commonly flat disks of potsherd, bone, glass, or metal (often smoothed coins), many inscribed with numbers from one to eighteen. They might be decorated with concentric circles or with images, including portraits, buildings, fruit, and religious symbols. The figural disks, some found in sets of fifteen pieces, were used for an unknown game invented in the first century B.C.E. to C.E.

Other game pieces of bone, stone, or glass (including millefiori), in different colors for opposing players, had flat bases and rounded tops. Many sets and isolated pieces have been found in Merovingian and Scandinavian graves. Anglo-Saxon burial sites, including Sutton Hoo, contain pieces made from horses' teeth. Rarer animal-shaped pieces are flattened and marked with numbers.

Partial rules are known for three board games. Merels resembled its modern version: opponents competed to arrange pieces in complete rows. In *ludus latrunculorum*, opponents captured or blocked each other's pieces on a grid. This strategy game with military terminology was considered more honorable than games of pure chance. *Duodecim scripta* resembled modern backgammon. Players threw dice to move pieces around a board with three lines of twelve places. On many boards the lines formed words cheering winners, insulting losers, or commenting on current events. Dice throws were counted either singly or together, using both chance and skill.

Little is known about these games' chronological development. The latest textual mention of *ludus latrunculorum* is from the 5th century. Isidore of Seville may refer to *duodecim scripta*. Fewer game boards are found at later sites than at imperial ones, but this may simply indicate a shift of materials to perishable wood. The northern European strategy game of *tafl* (later *hnefatafl*), with unevenly divided playing pieces and a distinctive king, may have developed from *ludus latrunculorum*.

Chess was an important late invention, a strategy game in which opponents have equal numbers of varied pieces (originally foot soldiers, horses, chariots, and elephants). The game probably originated in 6th century north India, with either two or four players and perhaps a *ludus latrunculorum* board and dice. In the late Sassanian Persian empire, chess, together with backgammon, numbered among the cultural attainments expected of educated men. Islamic culture adopted the game from the Sassanians and expanded its theoretical development. The game quickly spread among the Byzantines, but it did not reach the western empire until later. Such games were notable occasions of gambling: see Ammianus Marcellinus 14.6.14. One senator even staked, and lost, his wife to the emperor Valentinian III (John of Antioch, frg. 200).

BIBL.: Elisabeth Alföldi-Rosenbaum, "Spielmarken und Amulette: Ergänzungen zu zwei Aufsätzen von Andreas Alföldi," *Jahrbuch für Antike und Christentum* 34 (1991): 152–155. Richard Eales, *Chess, The History of a Game* (New York and Oxford, 1985). Anita Rieche, *Römische Kinder- und Gesellschaftsspiele* (Württemberg, 1984).   G.K.

Games As Contests

The "games" (from the Latin *ludi*) of the ancient world are better understood as "contests" (from the Greek *agones*); they were an integral element of the festivals with which communities honored the gods. At the festivals—normally composed of a procession, a sacrifice, and a contest—musicians, poets, wrestlers, or runners would compete in order to offer the gods the best possible achievement. Associated with this was the glorification of victory, which in the Roman period came to fit very well into the celebrations of the cult of the emperors. This concept of victory meant that one of the characteristically western forms of *ludi*—gladiatorial combat—came to be adopted in the eastern empire as part of the celebrations in honor of the emperors. The sponsoring of such activities was one of the prime forms of benefaction that rich citizens could offer to their community, and, over the centuries of the Roman empire, the civic calendars of cities were marked with more and more of such festivals.

This background explains the complex attitudes toward "games" in late antiquity. The entertainment that they offered was an integral part of civic life, and the victories they celebrated were as important as ever to

the rulers; at the same time, they had evolved as part of pagan religious practice, and they roused passions and offered distractions of which Christian preachers disapproved. As a consequence, there was a particularly substantial discrepancy between what was said and what was done.

This discrepancy is well illustrated by the banning of gladiatorial combats by Constantine (*C.Th.* 15.12.1 of 325), who nevertheless gave permission, during the 330s, for a regular festival with both theatrical performances and gladiatorial combats to be held at Hispellum in honor of the imperial house (*ILS* 705). Imperial legislation from the 4th to the 6th century reflects the wish to guarantee the pleasures of the spectators: "We do not disapprove, rather we urge that the enthusiasms of a happy populace be embraced, so that the spectacles of an athletic contest should be reestablished," says a law of 376 retained in the *Justinianic Code* (*C.Th.* 15.5.3, *C.Just.* 11.41.1); Justinian appreciated the need for *spectacula* to be provided "for the pleasure of the people" (*Nov.Just.* 105.1). The emperors limited themselves to banning "every pleasure of the theaters and the circuses" on Sundays—not because the entertainments were intrinsically wrong but because they were a distraction (*C.Th.* 15.5.5 = *C.Just.* 3.2.6 of 425).

Yet gradually the celebration of festivals did diminish. It is hard to measure exactly what was happening, since the bulk of the evidence for contests in the Roman period comes from inscriptions, and inscriptions themselves become far less frequent after the middle of the 3rd century. Some festivals were officially brought to an end: the original Olympic Games at Elis were in 392 (Cedrenus, *Chronographia*, 323D); the Olympia at Antioch in 521 (John Malalas, *Chronicle*, 417). Others seem to have withered away: the gladiatorial shows at Rome survived Constantine's ban by a century but stopped in the 5th century. Almost certainly the principal reason was not so much ideology as finance. The sacred funds that had financed many festivals had been eliminated, and the curial class no longer had the wealth or the will to undertake such lavish expenditure. The festivals dwindled, leaving their strongest traces in the metaphors of struggle, combat, and victory in Christian literature.

BIBL.: Louis Robert, "Discours d'ouverture," *Actes du VIIIe Congrès international d'épigraphie grecque et latine à Athènes, 1982* (Athens, 1984), 35–45 (= L. Robert, *Opera minora selecta*, vol. 6 [Amsterdam, 1989], 709–719). G. Ville, "Les jeux de gladiateurs dans l'empire chrétien," *Mélanges de l'École française de Rome: Antiquité* 72 (1960): 273–335.
                                                      C.R.

Gandhāra

The term *Gandhāra* is found in both Greek and Achaemenid sources and continued to be in use at least until the 7th century. The region lies to the northeast of

Peshawar between the Indus and Kabul Rivers. Art historians have tended to use the term somewhat loosely, expanding the geographic area north and west. The school of Gandhāran Buddhist art extends from Taxila and Manikyala in the south northward along the Indus to Swat and Bajaur and along the Kabul River to Afghanistan.

Usually associated with the Buddhist art of the Kuṣāṇa period, Gandhāran art is characterized by a mixture of Graeco-Roman, Iranian, and Indian themes and stylistic conventions. This heterogeneous style is the product of the long history of the region: the province was conquered by the Achaemenids, by the Macedonian armies, and then by the Mauryans. The earliest Buddhist monuments, for instance the *stūpa*s at Butkara and the *dharmarājika stūpa* at Taxila, date to this time. In the 1st century B.C.E. the Śakas ruled, then the Indo-Parthians; the great Kuṣāṇa were followed by the lesser Kuṣāṇa (Kidarite), the Hephthalites, and the Turki, and then Hindu Shahi. Then the entire region was converted to Islam.

Pre-Kuṣāṇa art has not yet been systematically explored. Terracotta images indicate the existence of separate Hellenistic and Indian traditions. Stone toilet trays are mostly dated to the pre-Kuṣāṇa period and until now have been found only in Pakistan. They are mostly decorated with Hellenistic motifs but one group has Indianizing themes, for instance the *makara* and lotus. There is also a small group of schist sculptures and stucco figures with archaic and Hellenistic features, respectively.

Recent excavations have demonstrated that Greek civilization flourished under the Graeco-Bactrian and Indo-Greek kings who established cities at Taxila (Sirkap) and Charsada (Shaikhan Dheri). Indian cultural influence can be identified already at this time. Thus, the cultural amalgam that resulted in the flowering of Gandhāran art with its "Graeco-Buddhist" character can be traced to this easternmost branch of Hellenism. Over the centuries Mediterranean influences were renewed through direct contact with Roman art. This Graeco-Roman influence can be seen in stylistic features—a more plastic and sometimes expressive treatment of the figures—as well as in the choice of iconographic themes.

Parallel with changes within Buddhism toward a more developed form of Mahāyāna, there was a great expansion in the pantheon. Different Buddhas, such as Amitābha, as well as the Bodhisattvas Avalokiteśvara and Maitreya, also became cult figures. These large-scale, deeply carved figures were often placed in niches. Narrative art, mostly related to the life and the previous lives of Buddha Śākyamuni, with a preference for linear chronological representation, was very much favored in the architectural decoration of *stūpa*s and also in monasteries.

An outline of the relative chronology for the Buddha image can be obtained from archaeology, dated inscriptions, and comparative stylistic analysis. The earliest dated image of a Buddha bears the date "5" and may be compared to the image of the standing Buddha on a rare gold coin of Kaniṣka; the schist Buddha image is clearly earlier than the schist sculpture representing the Visit to the Indrashala Cave in the Peshawar Museum, inscribed with a dated year 89; this in turn is earlier than the triad in a private collection in Brussels, also with the date 5—which should be read as 105 using the "dropped hundred" method (that is, year 5 of the second 100 years of the Kaniṣka era).

Buddhist art was produced at least until the 6th century at all the major sites in Gandhāra, such as Taxila and Haḍḍa, and some sites, such as Butkara, continued to be active into the 8th and perhaps even the 9th century, although they were functioning at a very reduced level. From the 7th century, under the Turki Shahi, Hindu cult images, often of marble, become more numerous. Important for an understanding of the history of the period is the inscribed Umā-Maheśvara from Tepe Sikandar and the recently discovered monumental Sūrya from Khair Khana, both north of Kabul, the capital of the Turki Shahi.

BIBL.: Elizabeth Errington and Joe Cribb, eds., *The Crossroads of Asia: Transformation in Image and Symbol in the Art of Ancient Afghanistan and Pakistan* (Cambridge, Eng., 1992). Maurizio Taddei, "Was bedeutete der Buddhismus für die frühe indische Kunst," in Deborah E. Klimburg-Salter, ed., *Buddha in Indien* (Milan and Vienna, 1995), 41–49. Francine Tissot, *Gandhāra* (Paris, 1985).   D.K.-S.

Gaul

Gaul was defined by the Romans, whose conquests and narratives of conquest had successively created it, above all in campaigns led by Julius Caesar. Gaul's administrative boundaries were set at the Alps, the Mediterranean, the Pyrenees, the Atlantic, and the Rhine by Augustus, who superimposed on existing divisions a pattern of provinces that persisted in its basic form into late antiquity: Narbonensis (Provence); Aquitania, Belgica, and Lugdunensis (the "three Gauls"); Alpes Maritimae; and the Rhine provinces of Germania Superior and Inferior, formally created in 90.

Though dominated in many areas by Celts, Gaul was heterogeneous in ethnic composition, language, social organization, and material culture, especially in its broad frontier zones; its component regions, moreover, were positioned to face outward (Provence toward the Mediterranean, for instance), rather than toward any political or cultural center (Caesar, *De bello gallico* 1.1.5–7). Despite this, Gaul did acquire a degree of political cohesion and cultural unity under Roman rule. This is evident, as elsewhere in the west, in the imposition of a fiscal and administrative system based on the collaboration of native elites, the gradual adoption of Latin, the construction of urban infrastructures and a military road network, and archae-ologically measurable changes in settlement, land use, and trade. That Gaul could afford this level of Romanization is an indication of the size of the (mainly) agricultural surplus that the imperial government and local aristocrats could extract from Gallic landholdings and workers in the form of taxes and rents. Of course Romanization was far from uniform or total, especially in central and northwestern Gaul, and the most deeply embedded features of native culture and society (religion, settlement patterns, forms of local authority and dependency) changed either very slowly or only temporarily under Roman control.

The incursions of Franks, Alamanni, and other Germanic groups in the 260s and 270s threatened—and in Belgica and Germania Superior substantially altered—Roman patterns of settlement and control, but did not permanently affect the rest of Gaul. With its seventeen newly reorganized provinces grouped into a northern and a southern diocese, as optimistically recorded by the *Notitia Galliarum* in the 380s, Gaul remained a relatively prosperous, lucrative, and integral part of the empire into the 5th century, especially in the south and along the Rhône-Saône-Mosel corridor to the Rhine frontier. Indeed, the cities of Trier and Arles, at opposite ends of this axis, were splendidly built up in the 4th century to serve as imperial capitals and centers of trade. Aquitaine also prospered during the 4th century, its high-Latin culture lovingly described by Ausonius, its well-appointed villas documented by archaeology. Ammianus confirms this picture by eyewitness observations made between 355 and 357: the elegant dinner parties of Aquitaine (16.8.8), the massive rivercraft that plied the lower Rhône (15.11.18), and the large number of eminent cities, especially in the south (15.11.7–15). Of course the Gaul he portrays was also heavily taxed (16.5.14; 17.3) and constantly threatened by invaders, but a high level of involvement by the emperors Julian, Valentinian I, Gratian, and the usurper Magnus Maximus managed to keep these problems in check until nearly the end of the 4th century.

Large-scale movements of non-Roman peoples into Gaul from the late 4th century initiated the end of direct imperial control. Although some groups, like the Vandals and Suebi who crossed the Rhine with the Alans in 406–407, never settled in Gaul; others, including Franks, Goths, Alans, and Burgundians, took up permanent residence by negotiation with imperial and local officials, receiving land in return for military service. Over the 5th century, as the administrative control of barbarian kings expanded, local aristocrats—deeply alert to their native political and economic interests—increasingly put aside their imperial loyalties, reverted to pre-Roman patterns of self-help, and collaborated with their new rulers. Even Sidonius Apollinaris, prefect of Rome in 468–469, whose writings depict a he-roic resistance to barbarian advances, eventually had to cooperate with the Goths, who in 475 had been given control of the Auvergne. That he did so as bishop of Clermont is a striking indication of the increasing attractiveness of episcopal office to aristocrats with strong local connections and declining opportunities for imperial service. Imperial control thus gradually receded, weakened not so much by direct military conquest as by the consequent loss of tax revenues and the end of collaboration by local aristocrats. By the 480s, Clovis's Franks were dominant in Belgica, emigrant Britons in Brittany, Goths in Aquitaine and Provence, Alamanni along the upper Rhine, and Burgundians east of the Rhône, a division of territory that reflected military and political circumstances but also the "natural" regionalism of Roman Gaul. Political fragmentation continued under the Merovingian kings, descendants of Clovis, whose control over Gaul frequently took the form of separate subkingdoms that were often hostile to one another and powerless to control outlying territories.

Culturally, much of Gaul remained recognizably Roman until the 7th or 8th century. Latin continued to be widely spoken, arguably until well past 800. Roman law profoundly influenced the written barbarian codes and long prevailed in the south. Roman civic organization and bureaucratic and fiscal practices were continued, and together with imperial landholdings they allowed rulers to maintain smaller-scale states on Roman models. The Christian church, organized according to Roman cities and provinces, governed and enriched by local aristocrats, and embraced by barbarian newcomers, preserved a high degree of continuity with Mediterranean culture in language, patterns of urban building and living, habits of reading and writing, the luxury arts, and expressions of religiosity. Contact between northern Gaul and the Mediterranean world—including the Byzantine empire—continued as well, although at a reduced level after 600, taking the form of letter writing, diplomatic missions, and the exchange of relics, textiles, ivories, and other prestigious objects.

Of course fundamental changes also occurred in Merovingian Gaul, but these were gradual—indeed, many had long been under way. Frankish customs of law, burial, kinship, and social hierarchy came to prevail, especially north of the Seine, where most Franks settled. A new nobility arose, defined by landholding, military prowess, allegiance to the king, and aristocratic forms of Christian piety, such as the founding of family monasteries. Landowners exerted progressively greater control over non-slave-dependent labor. Patterns of long-distance trade and cultural exchange were gradually reconfigured toward the North Sea and the British Isles. Finally, by the 8th century, it is possible to speak of a thoroughly post-Roman Gaul, whose *romanitas* its new Carolingian rulers could claim to have revived.

BIBL.: John Drinkwater and Hugh Elton, eds., *Fifth-Century Gaul: A Crisis of Identity?* (Cambridge, Eng., 1992). *Shifting Frontiers in Late Antiquity*, ed. R. Mathisen and H. Sivan (Aldershot, 1996). I. N. Wood, *The Merovingian Kingdoms* (London, 1994). S. Lebecq, *Les origines franques* (Paris, 1990). W.KLI.

Gaza

Situated near the coast of southern Palestine, Gaza was a cosmopolitan city poised between the Near East and the Greek civilization of the eastern Roman empire. As an outlet for the caravan routes leading from Arabia, it acquired a reputation as the "mouth of the desert." Its most prominent cult was dedicated to the local deity Marnas. In the aftermath of Alexander the Great's conquests, Gaza acquired the institutions of a Greek city, as well as a theater, a stadium, and a series of monumental wall paintings depicting scenes from Greek mythology and the *Iliad*. Greek became one of the common spoken languages, and even Marnas was identified with Zeus. In the early 2nd century the Hellenophile emperor Hadrian instituted a festival in honor of Marnas, whose shrine, the Marneion, was thought to be the most prestigious of all temples in the world.

The early Christian community in Gaza was so insignificant that its church was outside the city's walls, and pagan cults remained so dominant that the emperor Constantine responded to an appeal from the large Christian community at the port of Maiuma by removing the town from Gaza's control and giving it its own bishop. Some local notables likewise used their promotion of Christianity as a way of distinguishing themselves from their peers. The ancestors of the historian Sozomen financed new churches and monasteries. Even though Hilarion retreated to the nearby sand dunes and established himself as one of the first monks in the region, he was influential enough that imperial administrators and municipal magistrates consulted him, and his blessing once determined the outcome of a chariot race during the festival of Marnas. At the end of the 4th century Porphyry became bishop of Gaza. In response to his direct appeal, the imperial court at Constantinople ordered the destruction of pagan shrines, including the Marneion, and provided funding for the construction of a new church. In his account of Porphyry's career, Mark the Deacon noted that this new church, named after the empress Eudocia, was the largest church of its time. Other new churches followed; in the 6th century a local orator described a new church dedicated to St. Stephen as the most magnificent then known.

The well-known teacher Libanius had once praised the quality of rhetorical studies at Gaza, and these schools survived into the 5th and 6th centuries. Notable teachers and students included Aeneas, Procopius of Gaza, Choricius, and perhaps the great historian Procopius of Caesarea. The numerous monks living nearby enhanced the city's cultural milieu. Isaias of Gaza offered advice about interpreting Plato and Aristotle even as he opposed the orthodoxy of the Council of Chalcedon; Peter the Iberian was a Georgian prince who had fled the court at Constantinople; and the Coptic "old man" Barsanuphius, the "other old man" John of Gaza, and Dorotheus all composed meditations on the monastic life. Arab merchants also traveled to Gaza, among them, according to later legends, the great-grandfather of Muhammad. After Muhammad's death the Arabs soon conquered all of Palestine. Gaza (or al-Ghazzah) was the site of one of the relatively rare unsavory episodes of the Muslim conquest of Palestine, when the soldiers of the Byzantine garrison were massacred and became martyrs. The city is hardly ever mentioned in early Islamic sources.

BIBL.: G. Downey, "The Christian Schools of Palestine: A Chapter in Literary History," *Harvard Library Bulletin* 12 (1958): 297–319. C. A. M. Glucker, *The City of Gaza in the Roman and Byzantine Periods* (Oxford, 1987). D. Sourdel, "al-Ghazzah," *Encyclopedia of Islam*, 2nd. ed. R. Van Dam, "From Paganism to Christianity at Late Antique Gaza," *Viator* (1985): 1–20. R.V.

Ge'ez

A now-extinct language of northern Ethiopia, Ge'ez belongs to the Semitic family. Ge'ez is also the name of the alphabet and syllabary that notate that language. Ge'ez engendered the Tigrinya language, spoken today in Tigre (northern Ethiopia) and in Eritrea. It is closely related to Amharic and to the languages of South Arabia, both epigraphic and modern. The Ge'ez syllabary, which was formed in the second half of the 4th century C.E., developed a consonantal writing system used until the 6th century and derived from the South Arabic writing system of Yemen. It has twenty-six consonants, which take seven different forms to notate the seven vowels; in addition, four consonants can receive a diphthongized vowel. This syllabary, which has 202 signs in all, is still used today in Ethiopia and Eritrea to notate Amharic and Tigrinya. Writing moves from left to right; words are separated by a colon or a space.

Axum's conversion to Christianity in the 4th century conferred on Ge'ez the status of liturgical language of the Abyssinian church, a status that remains in place in our own time. Ge'ez is also the liturgical language of the Falasha, the black Jews of Ethiopia. Translations played a major role in Ge'ez literature, which is primarily religious in nature. The Ge'ez translation of the Bible dates from the period of Axum; it contains several books elsewhere considered apocryphal (Enoch, Jubilees). Translations of various texts in vogue in the Christian east, such as *Qerillos* (a collection of excerpts and homilies by Cyril of Alexandria and other church Fathers), the Pachomian Rule, and the *Physiologus* (a popular early Christian bestiary), were also undertaken. All these translations were made from the Greek.

A second period, which began with the restoration of the Solomonic dynasty (1270), also included a large number of translations (from Coptic or Arabic), and a few original writings as well. These include historical chronicles and the *Kebra Nagast*, or "Glory of Kings" (14th century), which established the legitimacy of the dynasty by linking its origin to Solomon. Prose works predominate: favorite themes include the lives of the saints, the celebration of the virtues of Mary, eschatology, theology, the liturgy, monastic discipline, and the edification of believers. There is also a body of poetry of religious inspiration.

BIBL.: E. Cerulli, *La letteratura etiopica,* 3rd ed. (Florence and Milan, 1968). *Kebra Nagast,* ed. and trans. C. Bezold (Munich, 1909); English trans.: E. A. Wallis Budge, *The Queen of Sheba and Her Only Son Menyelek (I)* (Oxford, 1932). Thomas O. Lambdin, *Introduction to Classical Ethiopic (Ge'ez),* Harvard Semitic Studies (Cambridge, Mass., 1978). Wolf Leslau, *Comparative Dictionary of Ge'ez (Classical Ethiopic)* (Wiesbaden, 1987). C.J.R.

Gems

The Hellenistic gem cutter's art had its origin in the Black Sea area but had spread all around the Mediterranean in Roman times. In connection with the development of the polychrome mosaic art, natural colored stones had great importance. The cutting of precious stones was, however, a more exclusive art that in the Roman empire was found in larger towns and in some cases in military garrisons. The cutting of larger stones, either as cameos or as intaglios, specially from sardonyx and onyx, or harder gemstones such as carnelian, amethyst, rock crystal, and garnet, was an art that was closely connected to die cutting for coins and therefore belonged to power elite serving the Roman emperor.

Necessary for gem cutting was a manually driven rotating wheel or drill with a hard abrasive surface of emery. In late Roman times gem cutting became more mechanized and cutting was done with a continuously rotating wheel, sometimes powered by water, and by drills with diamond points. In the Byzantine empire, conditions for practicing the art were the same, but the importance of precious gems was enhanced, as they were used to express the Christian faith as well as the power of the emperor. The red garnet, or carbuncle, began to gain in importance, especially for cloisonné inlaying, a technique that has certain affinities to the mosaic art. Garnet gems were so highly appreciated not only for their red color but also because the stones were used in the Jewish high priest's jeweled breast-

plate, where it symbolized the tribe of Juda; among Christians, the garnet was then taken over as a symbol for Jesus Christ.

The art of cutting gems—e.g., cameos and intaglios—rapidly declined after the fall of the Roman empire, and in the fifth century the only continuous practice within the empire was the cutting of garnets for cloisonné work. The gold cloisonné with garnets has its widest distribution in finds from the barbarian peoples—the Huns, the Alans, the Avars, and the Germanic peoples—and migration-period garnet jewelry was long thought to be a barbarian product. A closer analysis, however, shows that the most brilliant examples of early garnet work are found on Christian cult objects such as reliquaries, patens, and chalices, as well as on book covers. These products most probably originate from Constantinople. In that city a more profane cloisonné industry seems also to have existed for the adornment of weapons, buckles, mounts, and harnesses. The emperor used the profane jewelry as gifts for his allies, and this explains its spread among the barbarians. The most splendid examples of this profane cloisonné art are among the grave finds from Apahida in Hungary and the grave of the Frankish king Childeric, found in Tournai. In both these sites were found, among other items, heavy gold buckles inlaid with garnet cloisonné of the same type as in the collection of the Saray in Istanbul. In the Germanic area there was also an import market for cut but unmounted garnets, as well as cloisonné panels, which were mounted on Germanic items. In time locally produced garnet jewelry industries started up, especially among the Franks, and probably directly inspired by Constantinople, since one of the key centers seems to have been Trier. However, the quality of this jewelry at its best (e.g., the Sutton Hoo jewelry) never compares with what was produced in Byzantium. Typical of Byzantine garnet jewelry are large (more than a square centimeter) flat or slightly domed garnets cut in stepped patterns or in flower shapes. The settings are commonly furnished with green malachite and blue lapis lazuli and in some cases even black and white banded onyx. In the 7th century the Byzantine production of garnet jewelry seems to fade out, and by then there are also very few examples of cut gems from the area. Small Gnostic gems made of steatite or hematite were produced, but their artistic quality is low. In addition there might have been pieces of cut rock crystal. The gem cutter's art, which since Hellenistic time also existed in Persia and was taken over by the Sassanians, seems to have found its last home in Islam. In the Byzantine empire cameos of glass or glass paste were used, and a frequent practice was the remounting of Roman gems, which were highly appreciated on both profane and ecclesiastical items.

BIBL.: B. Arrhenius, *Merovingian Garnet Jewellery: Emergence and Social Implications* (Stockholm, 1985). B.A.

Genovefa

Aside from brief entries in liturgical texts, St. Genovefa is known only from a laconic mention by Gregory of Tours and a *Vita* that was written by a devoted hagiographer in the early 6th century. She was born ca. 420 at Nanterre outside Paris, the daughter of Severus and Gerontia. In 429 she met bishops Germanus of Auxerre and Lupus of Troyes when they were on their way to Britain. With the encouragement of Germanus, she subsequently devoted herself to the religious life. At the age of fifteen, she was consecrated as a religious by Bishop Vilicius of Bourges. Then, after the death of her parents, she went to live with her godmother in Paris, where she again met Germanus during his second trip to Britain in 445.

After overcoming some initial opposition to her activities, she went on to take a leading role in city life. When Gaul was invaded by the Huns in 451, "She persuaded the men that they should not remove their goods from Paris, because the cities they deemed safer would be devastated by the raging Huns while Paris, guarded by Christ, would remain untouched by her enemies." Later, she interceded on behalf of captives with the Frankish kings Childeric and Clovis, and she provided relief during the Gallic famine of 471. She also built a church in honor of St. Dionysius.

Most of her *Vita* details St. Genovefa's miracles. Along with curing the sick, she also was able to create wine and oil ex nihilo, to light candles, and to cause doors to open of their own accord. Some of her miracles were somewhat sinister in nature and could have been associated with sorcery. She caused those who provoked her to become ill or disabled: on three occasions she blinded them, and one was her own mother. She also could predict the future, read minds, summon and subdue sea monsters, and control the weather.

Genovefa died shortly after 500 C.E. at more than eighty years of age and was buried on 3 January. She was interred in a church begun in her honor by Clovis and completed by his wife Chlotilde, both of whom also were buried there. During the French Revolution the church was secularized as the Pantheon, and her remains were scattered. Her *Vita* is significant not only for the light it throws on this troubled and poorly known period but also for providing insight into the role of women at the very end of Roman Gaul.

BIBL.: B. Krusch, ed., *Vita Genovefae,* Monumenta Germaniae historica, Scriptores rerum Merovingicarum 3 (Berlin, 1896), 215–238; Eng. trans.: Jo Ann McNamara and John E. Halborg, *Sainted Women of the Dark Ages* (Durham, N.C., 1992), 17–37. E. Coltra, "Per una nuova edizione della Vita Genovefae virginis parisiensis," *Scripta philologa* 3 (1982): 71–118. P. Croidys, *Sainte Geneviève et les barbares: La splendeur du christianisme au Ve siècle* (Paris, 1946). M. Heinzelmann and J.-C. Poulin, *Les vies anciennes de Sainte Geneviève de Paris* (Paris, 1986).   R.W.M.

Georgia

The area of modern Georgia was divided into two separate kingdoms in late antiquity: Lazica in the east and Iberia in the west. Late antique sources use the name Lazica to denote the area east of the Black Sea that earlier writers (and later classicizers) had named Colchis and that the Georgian historical tradition referred to as Egrisi. It is a large triangle of land with its base formed by the coast and its sides bounded by the Main Caucasus to the north and the Lesser Caucasus to the south. It was separated from Iberia to the east by the Likhi Range (the Surami Ridge), which was fortified in late antiquity, notably at Sarapanis (modern Shoraponi) and Skanda (modern Skande). While much of the interior was hilly (as at Cotais, modern Kutaisi, or Archaeopolis, modern Nokalakevi), Lazica became a low wetland as it came down to the sea at Phasis. Its main crop seems to have been millet, though other grains were grown in the drier uplands. By late antiquity the various peoples of the region (notably the Abasigi, Sanigae, Apsilae, Misimiani, Scymni, and Suani) had been brought under the control of the Lazi, whose origins lay on the central lowland and in the regions to the south.

To the east of Lazica was the kingdom of Iberia, bounded by Albania to the east and Armenia to the south. The local tradition of Armenia tended to see both Lazica and Iberia as northern provinces. The Main Caucasus separated Iberia from the Asian steppes. From Hellenistic times, Iberia seems to have been divided between the urbanized population of the plain and the peoples of the mountains, who maintained close links with the steppes beyond. Iberia was important throughout antiquity particularly because its kings controlled passage across the Caucasus, albeit uncertainly. The capital of Iberia until ca. 500 C.E. was Mtskheta, located at the junction of the rivers Cyrus (Georgian Mtkvari) and Aragvi, which flowed down from the Daryal Pass in the north (known in antiquity under names akin to Biraparakh; Priscus, frgs. 41:47). Thereafter, the capital seems to have moved to Tiflis (modern Tbilisi), according to Georgian tradition, under King Vakhtang Gorgasali, whose connection (if any) with Procopius's Gourgenes remains unclear. In 626–627 the emperor Heraclius took the newer capital by siege.

For centuries after Pompey's campaign in the Caucasus in 65 B.C.E., both Lazica and Iberia exploited their positions on the marchlands of Rome and Parthia/Persia. The rise of the Lazi in Colchis from the 2nd century C.E. onward (and especially from the 4th century) seems to have been at least encouraged by Roman support, while Persian diplomacy seems to have favored dismemberment of the Lazian "empire." For Persia and Rome, Lazica had major strategic significance: located on the Black Sea, the region also controlled passes across the mountains, whether north to the Huns, northeast through Suania, east into Iberia, south into Armenia, or southwest into the difficult mountains of Tzanica. In the 4th century, in particular, substantial cities were established in Lazica, at Archaeopolis, Rhodopolis (modern Vardtsikhe), and Cotais. Yet the Lazi were not passive objects of Persian and Roman ambitions. They seem to have used their significant position to pursue their own ends by playing the two great empires against each other.

Rome and Parthia/Persia also sought Iberia as an ally. While during the principate Rome developed a close relationship with Iberia, in the 3rd and 4th centuries, with the rise of the Sassanian empire, Persia exercised increasing influence in the region. Roman engineers built up Iberia's defenses in 75 C.E., while under Antoninus Pius the Iberian king Pharasmanes II was received in great style at Rome itself. Both Marcus Aurelius and the court of Ardashir I sent diplomatic gifts, which were deposited as grave goods at Armaziskhevi, close to Mtskheta. In the 3rd century, both Shapur I and Narseh claimed Iberia for Persia. Under the Treaty of Nisibis (298), it was from Rome that the Iberian kings were to receive their symbols of office. However, Persian links were still maintained: Ammianus complains that Shapur II bestowed a diadem on the Iberian Asparuces "in order to show his contempt of our authority" (27.12.4). In approximately 370 Rome sent twelve legions to restore to the Iberian throne Asparuces's cousin Sauromaces, who had been ousted. Briefly Iberia was divided along the line of the Cyrus River: southern and eastern Iberia were to belong to Asparuces, while Sauromaces held the lands of Iberia that bordered Lazica. Although details remain obscure, by 380 Iberia was Persia's. The Persians also claimed Suania (modern Svaneti) to the north and west of Iberia.

After the 4th century, Lazica, rather than Iberia, occupied the primary position in Roman foreign policy in Transcaucasia. The Lazis' manipulation of diplomatic ties with the Persian and Roman empires resulted in a series of wars in the region in the 5th and 6th centuries. The beginning of this conflict is not well documented. While in 422 Persia had acknowledged Roman suzerainty in Lazica, Rome waged war on the Lazi ca. 456. The meeting of the Lazian king Gobazes I with the emperor Leo in 466/7 seems to have been a turning point: Gobazes flaunted his Christianity and was taken to meet Daniel the Stylite. Yet Gobazes was also open to Persia, and by 470 Persia had established dominance in Lazica. This dominance lasted until 522, when King Tzathius received both Christianity and royal regalia from the emperor Justinian. He also received a Roman wife: marriage and religion were the principal bonds between Lazica and Byzantium.

In 541, encouraged by renewed difficulties in Iberia, the Persian king Khosro I invaded Lazica, beginning twenty years of warfare. Persia supplied its armies in Lazica from Iberia. Rome now treated the strongholds of Pityus and Sebastopolis as part of Pontus Polemoniacus, but built up Petra (modern Tiskhisdziri) from which to administer Lazica. Petra became a focal point of Lazian discontent with Byzantium and of the warfare that ensued from 541 until the formal conclusion of peace in 561–562, when the Persians agreed to cede Lazica to Byzantium.

Archaeological evidence suggests a gradual spread of Christianity in Lazica and Iberia in the 4th century. However, local tradition, supported by Rufinus, emphasizes the dramatic conversion of the Iberian king Mirian in 337 by the slave woman St. Nino. As the political history indicates, religion was a recurrent source of friction between Rome, Georgia, and Persia. Kings of Lazica and Iberia were known to change religions with alliances. Persia tended to support Iberian Zoroastrianism. An Iberian monastery flourished in Palestine at Bir El-Qutt from the 5th century, perhaps established by Peter the Iberian, a royal hostage sent to Constantinople who fled to Palestine to become a monk. Procopius states that "the Iberi are a Christian people and keep the ordinances of the faith as zealously as any people we know"; he explains the Iberian revolt (under Gourgenes) from Persia as a reaction to the Persian king Cavad's instructions to convert to Zoroastrianism (*Wars* 1.12.2–6).

Peter the Iberian, as bishop of Maiuma, became a leader in the Monophysite movement, and Georgian Christians, with the Armenians, rejected Chalcedon at the Council of Duin in 505 or 506. However, in the beginning of the 7th century the Georgian church separated from the Armenian church and returned to communion with Constantinople. The Georgian version of the life of Peter the Iberian removes all references to his non-Chalcedonian Christology.

BIBL.: David Braund, *Georgia in Antiquity: A History of Colchis and Transcaucasian Iberia 550 BC–AD 562* (Oxford, 1994). O. Lordkipanidse, *Archäologie in Georgien* (Wienheim, 1991). Donald Rayfield, *The Literature of Georgia: A History* (Oxford, 1994). Cyril Toumanoff, *Studies in Christian Caucasian History* (Washington, D.C., 1963).   D.C.B.

Germanic Tribes

The very phrase *Germanic tribes* is so burdened with controversy that any attempt to resolve it would lead to nothing. That being stated, herein the term will be understood to mean those political entities whom ancient and early medieval sources call *gentes* belonging to, or originating in, Germania, an area, roughly speaking, between the oceans in the north and the Danube in the south, the Rhine in the west and the Vistula in the east. This ancient Germania also included Scandinavia, which was considered to be an island in the Baltic Sea. The Latin *gens*, Greek *ethnos*, and Gothic *thiuda* refer—as do *genus/genos*, *genealogia*, and *natio*—to a community of biological descent.

The sources, however, attest to both the polyethnic character of a *gens* and equate the term with army, *exercitus,* so that its formation is not a matter of common descent but one of political decision. Consequently, Cassiodorus (*Expositio in psalmum* 95.5.7) defines *gens* as a political entity including foreigners and leaves the notion of common descent to *natio.* So long as we keep this in mind it does not make much difference whether we speak of tribes, peoples, nations, *Völker,* or *Stämme.* Even the English-French *race* could be used if it were not too close to German *Rasse,* which should be avoided under all circumstances.

The division of the region's peoples into west-Germanic, east-Germanic, and north-Germanic tribes came from linguists. Historians would rather speak of the Scandinavians and of Germanic tribes along the Elbe, the Rhine, and the Danube. In cases where it would lead to greater clarity, the artificial term "east-Germanic tribes" should be replaced by "Gothic tribes," which is true to the sources. At one time, classical ethnography had applied the name "Suebi" to so many Germanic tribes that it appeared as though in the first centuries C.E. this native name would replace the foreign name "Germans." However, in the period after the Marcomannic Wars, which were fought and lost mostly by the Suebi, the Gothic name steadily gained importance, although it did not cover all Germanic tribes except in later Scandinavian sources. Instead, around 500 C.E. the names of the Franks came to include all inhabitants of Germania, properly speaking.

The *Germania* of Tacitus and Caesar's ethnographic excurses shaped the popular image of the Germans in a way that has lasted right down to the present day. In his second chapter, Tacitus divides his description into three parts. First he speaks of the autochthonous character of the Germans. They were pure, indigenous inhabitants. To a Latin speaker this information made perfectly good sense; after all, *germanus* also meant something like "genuine." Despite, or perhaps because of, the reality of a tribal genesis, a process that had always embraced a great diversity of ethnic groups, purity of blood and native roots were highly prestigious qualities. Second, Tacitus presents an origin legend of the Germans: in their traditional songs they celebrated the earth-born god Tuisto, whose son Mannus was considered the "origin and founder of the [Germanic] tribes." Mannus ("human being" or "man") had three sons, from whom were descended the tribes of the Ingaevones, Hermiones, and Istaevones. However, outside of this ritualized genealogy, which could be found among other Indo-European peoples, there existed other Germanic tribes that also boasted divine origin, among them the Suebi and the Vandili-Vandali. Tacitus closes his second chapter with the interesting comment that the Germanic name was a relatively recent additional name that had developed from the specific name for a single tribe. The Tungri were the first to cross the Rhine pushing west-

ward and were subsequently called Germani by the Gauls. The Romans borrowed the Germanic name from the conquered Gauls and then generalized it to the point that it referred to all the tribes east of the Rhine and north of the Danube.

Though Caesar did not discover the Germans, he added solidity to the vague notions the Romans already had about them, thus helping a Germanic ethnography come into its own. Caesar placed particular emphasis on "the differences between these two nations" (i.e., the Gauls and the Germans). Most of all, he was convinced or wanted to convince his Roman audience that the Germans were far more barbaric and hostile to civilization than the Gauls (Caesar, *De bello Gallico* 6.21ff.).

Latin-Greek ethnographers of the first centuries C.E. mention a great many Germanic tribes. Two hundred years later, the overwhelming majority of those ethnic names used along the Rhine, Danube, and Elbe rivers had been replaced by new names. In Scandinavia and the eastern part of Germania, however, old names such as the Goths and the Langobards remained alive well past the migration period, and in some cases even until today (Suiones-Swedes). The tribes in this group are either Scandinavian or derive their origins from Scandinavia. Early medieval tribal sagas, *origines gentium,* are attested only for them. The Scandinavia of these sagas is a free-floating literary motif that does not reflect any past reality, and the same holds true of the motif of a primordial deed, such as the crossing of a sea like the Baltic or the North Sea or a great river, such as the Rhine, the Elbe, or the Danube, or a victorious battle against all odds and a powerful foe (e.g., the Langobards against the Vandali). These tribes are first mentioned in the first two centuries C.E. as true and old names ("*vera et antiqua nomina*"; Tacitus, *Germania* 2). They were once small peoples but not without nobility, or high prestige (this is exactly what the seemingly paradoxical sentence, "*Langobardos paucitas nobilitat,*" means (Tacitus, *Germania* 40). Among them there are composite names of the Gútthiuda (people/land of the Goths) or Saexthéod (people/land of the Saxons) type. They boast long and continuous lines of royal leadership. Consequently, there is the motif of a royal family or outstanding tribal leaders who won divine assistance in a seemingly hopeless situation, thus securing the existence of the tribe. Their kings play an important role in heroic sagas as well as in heroic poetry and are doomed to experience a tragic fate.

In contrast, the new names of the Alamanni, Franks, and Bavarians represent a recent tribal formation that reflects a historical process. There are neither tribal nor heroic sagas recorded by or for them. Their names first appear during the 3rd century C.E. and without the Gútthiuda type. Whereas the kings of the Goths, Langobards, Svear, Gauts, Vandals, Angles, and Saxons boast long genealogies headed by divine ancestors, the

Frankish king Clovis held only the fourth place in his pedigree. The leading strata of the old names, first called "kernels of tradition" by H. Munroe Chadwick in 1912, disappeared in western and southern continental Germania, a loss compensated only in part by the Merovingian creation of a Frankish monarchy. In reality both types of tribes underwent the same profound transformation of their original structures and became greater polyethnic agglomerates, even "avalanches of peoples" (Reinhard Wenskus), before and during their migration into the Roman empire. Thus the "transformation of the Roman world" was preceded by a thoroughgoing transformation of the continental Germanic tribes.

BIBL.: Patrick Geary, *Before France and Germany: The Creation and Transformation of the Merovingian World* (New York and Oxford, 1988). Herwig Wolfram, *History of the Goths* (Berkeley, 1988). Herwig Wolfram, *The Roman Empire and Its Germanic Tribes* (Berkeley, 1997). H.W.

Ghassanids

Ethnologically, the Ghassanids represent a group (traditionally called a phyle, from the Greek for "tribe") of pre-Islamic Arabs of the house of Gafna ibn Amr-Mozeiqiā that migrated from Yemen northward and supplanted the Salīḥ phyle (Zokomids) in Byzantine Syria. The Ghassanids acquired their name from some well or source of the same name around which they originally settled.

The first appearance of the Ghassanids in Syria is dated in the reign of Anastasius. At that time the leading Christian Arab phyle of Syria was the Salīḥ. Ghassanids asked the Salihids for permission to stay in Roman territory, and the Salihids obtained approval for this from the emperor Anastasius, most likely under the condition that the Ghassanids convert to Christianity. In 502 a treaty was concluded between Byzantium and Arethas Ta'alaban of the phyle of Kinda; this brought peace among the *barbaroi skēnētai*—i.e., the Kindites and Ghassanid Arabs—who were in constant conflict during all the last years of the 5th century. One of the phylarchs, according to the *Chronography* of Theophanes, was Jabala, the first Ghassanid phylarch. Thus some historians deduce that a treaty was concluded between Rome and all the *skēnētai* Ta'alabites and Ghassanids together. In all probability the conclusion of a treaty can be linked to the outbreak of the Roman-Persian hostilities, which dates back to 502 C.E.

The next period in the history of the Ghassanids is connected with the phylarch al-Harit ibn Jabala (Arethas in the Greek sources). His career began after the ascension of Justinian, with his suppression of the revolt of the pro-Persian Samaritans in 529 C.E. For that he was awarded the *axiōma basileōs* and the titles *patrikios*, *spectabilis*, and *gloriosissimus*, which signify that he was entrusted with control over the whole of Roman Arabia. While al-Harit defended Syria from the Persians, his brother Abu Karib was a Ghassanid phylarch of the Arabs in Palestina Tertia. In 531 C.E. Ghassanid Arabs took part in the battle of Callinicus, which ended in the defeat of the Roman army. In the subsequent years al-Harit contested Roman sovereignty over the important strategic road from Palmyra to Damascus, called Strata, against al-Mundhir, phylarch of the Persian Lakhmid Arabs. This conflict was settled by diplomatic means; Justinian's *Novella 102* bears witness that imperial policy was directed toward the pacification of the province of Arabia. Ghassanid Arabs then took part in the next Persian-Roman war, harassing Iranians with quick forays into their territory. In 545 peace was concluded between Constantinople and Ctesiphon, but the next year there occurred a new outbreak of hostilities between Ghassanids and Lakhmids. One of al-Harit's sons was seized by al-Mundhir and sacrificed to the Arab goddess Uzza. The Ghassanids took revenge and defeated the Lakhmids, killing al-Mundhir in 554. In the Roman-Persian peace treaty of 561, the Arabs (i.e., Ghassanids and Lakhmids) are mentioned specifically. In 563 al-Harit arrived in the capital to discuss some important topics with the emperor, among which were the problem of transmission of the power to al-Harit's son al-Mundhir-ibn-Harit, the incursions of the Lakhmids, and giving support to the Monophysites. This is the first sign of Arab adherence to the Monophysite confession.

After the death of al-Harit in 569 his son al-Mundhir-ibn-Harit became the king of the Arabs. He continued the policies of his father, especially in defending and propagating Monophysitism, and we can attribute his quite detailed biography by John of Ephesus to this fact. The beginning of his reign was again marked by conflicts with the Persian Arabs, this time led by Kabos. On 20 May 570 in the battle of Ain Ubag, "Kabos was weakened and the Cross won." After a series of victories over the Persian Arabs, the Ghassanids declined to protect the eastern borders because of discord with Emperor Justin II, who refused to pay *salaria* to the Arabs. In 577 good relations were reestablished and al-Mundhir took the Lakhmid settlement Ḥīra. In 577 a Byzantine embassy visited Ḥīra al-Harit (near Damascus) and tried without visible success to establish a religious accord with the Arabs. In 580 al-Mundhir was in Constantinople on the occasion of the Monophysite-Chalcedonian conference. There he was given a diadem (John of Ephesus uses the Syriac word *tagō*). Nevertheless during the military campaign of the same year Maurice suspected al-Mundhir of revealing to the Persians the secret of the Roman invasion. The king of the Arabs was arrested and conveyed to the capital and then to Sicily, where he lived the rest of his days with his family *en eleutheriāi*, as Evagrius says (*Hist.eccl.* 6.2, p. 223). His son Na'aman, after refusing to accept a Chalcedonian Creed, followed his father.

On Easter Sunday of 634, two years before the battle of Yarmuk, the Muslim conqueror Khālid defeated the Ghassanids at Marj Rahiṭ. This defeat turned out to be disastrous for the Ghassanids. After the disappearance of the Ghassanid state, isolated Ghassanian princes continued to reign in some oases and castles, along with Salihids and some other phylae. The Ghassanid history between 582 and 629 is quite poorly recorded in the literary sources. Some sources let us think that a single Ghassanid kingdom continued to exist even after the Persian incursion into Palestine in 614. The later Arab sources name Jabala-ibn al-Aiham as "king of all the Byzantine Arabs," which is quite unlikely, for we know of different Ghassanid chieftains of this time. In 628–629 the Muslim ambassadors Šujāʿ ibn-Vah and ʿAmmar-ibn-Yasir visited al-Ḥīrah to convert the Ghassanids to Islam. Jabala treated them well but did not accept Islam as some Muslim historians claim. The Ghassanid forces took part on the Roman side in the battle of Muta (September 629), which ended in the defeat of the Muslim troops. After this battle the Romans thought the Muslims did not represent a serious threat for them and ceased to pay *salaria* to the Ghassanids. Subsequently Arab frontier towns began to fall under Muslim protection. Then the Romans decided to proclaim Jabala king of all Arabs, but it was too late: in 632–636 the Muslims progressively took possession of Jabala's kingdom. In the summer of 636 the Roman army was defeated in the battle of Yarmuk. Soon afterward the caliph Omar began negotiations with Jabala, but they led nowhere and Jabala finally took refuge in Roman territory, where he died about 645. The remnants of the Ghassanids were dispersed in Asia Minor.

Around 510, during the last decade of the reign of Anastasius, the Ghassanids accepted Monophysitism, never confessed by Christian Arabs before. This was probably due to contact between the Ghassanids and the champions of Monophysitism, Severus, Aksenōyō (Philoxenus of Mabbug), and Symeon. Zokomids were Orthodox, but in 530 al-Hariṭ argued for the Monophysite cause against Ephrem, the Chalcedonian patriarch of Antioch. In 542 al-Hariṭ asked Empress Theodora to give him two bishops, and two Monophysites, Jacob Baradaeus (Burdʿōnō) and Theodore, were ordained for Urhōi (Edessa) and Ḥīra al-Hariṭ, respectively. In 563 al-Hariṭ ibn-Jabala pleaded the Monophysite cause during his visit to Emperor Justinian. He brought to the capital the dogmatic letter of the anti-Chalcedonian Syrian clergy. In the 560s al-Hariṭ played an important role in resolving controversy within the Monophysite clergy. A decade later al-Hariṭ protected Bishop Paul, who was condemned by the Alexandrine Monophysites on canonical grounds. In 580, during the Monophysite-Orthodox conference,

an accord was signed, but it had no future because of dissension in both camps. At the time of the Muslim conquest the Ghassanids were no longer united by faith: some of them accepted union with the Byzantine Chalcedonian church; others remained faithful to Monophysitism. Later, those who remained Christian joined Melkite Syriac communities.

BIBL.: N. Pigulevskaja, *Araby u granits Vizantii i Irana v IV–VI vv* (Moscow and Leningrad, 1964), 180–214. I. Shahīd, *Byzantium and the Arabs in the Sixth Century* (Washington, D.C., 1995). E. Key Fowden, *The Barbarian Plain: Saint Sergius between Rome and Iran* (Berkeley, 1999).   A.M.

Gifts and Gift Giving

Whether or not they are akin to systems of exchange that anthropologists have observed in nonwestern societies, in the Mediterranean area in late antiquity there existed patterns of gift giving that were constituent parts of cultures that prized munificence and recognized its utility. Legal codifications (as in Justinian's *Institutes* 2.2.7) of Roman customs in this regard tend to be archaic; more information is available in less formal documents, such as letters, dedicatory inscriptions, and the writings of early historians. Many sources refer simply to "the usual offerings." Nonetheless, this very reticence witnesses to the normality of the practice. Gifts were not only expected but assessed: Ammianus Marcellinus records that when they did not get their "regular, fixed presents," the Alamanni threw away the cheaper ones that they received and "broke through the frontiers of Germany."

Best known (because they were perennial) were the donatives paid in gold to the army and the civil service by Roman emperors on their accession, on its various anniversaries, and at triumphs. So well established were these offerings that Procopius, in his hostile *Secret History*, could plausibly impugn Justinian by claiming that the emperor abolished donatives early in his reign. No less an institution were *sportulae*, a term used for handouts to judges and other officials, monetary gifts made by private hosts to their senatorial guests, and tokens (usually of silver or ivory) offered on the occasion of births, marriages, and deaths. The well-born Ammianus resented the access to this system gained by obscure intruders, but it is clear that it eased the rapport between different classes: urban proletariats, for example, reciprocated imperial charity by financing monuments to their benefactors. Municipal *sportulae*, both cash gifts and public feasts, ensured the attendance of spectators at dedication ceremonies, as the size of the crowd enhanced the glorification of the donor. Yet convention as much as calculation may have guided such behavior. Consuls, quaestors, and praetors gave out ivory diptychs and silver bowls at the games they sponsored, and the recipients were not necessarily highly placed: according to Claudian, Stilicho's diptychs were distributed among the common people.

Presents to sometime enemies and envisaged allies were part of military and diplomatic maneuvering. This game did not always work, however. Despite an elaborate gift exchange in 357–358, Constantius II and Shāpūr were unable to arrange a peace. Yet faith in these means persisted. Maurice's *Stratēgikon* observes that gifts would persuade the Slavs, Antae, and other peoples to attack each other.

Confessional motives for some gifts are clearly indicated. Pope Boniface (619–625) sent Queen Aethelburh a silver mirror and a gold and ivory comb to help speed the conversion to Christianity of the Northumbrian king Eadwin. Later Muslim reports tell of gift-bearing Arab embassies, including one of the caliph 'Umar, who sought to attract Heraclius to Islam.

Christians were initially suspicious of offerings, even when made to the church; the gift that distinguished the new faith was that of the Holy Spirit. Yet the suasive power of older practices in this respect could not long be denied. In substitution for pagan New Year's gifts, Gregory of Nazianzus exchanged books at Easter with others of his faith, and Cyril of Alexandria sent as "blessings" to the palace in Constantinople 1,080 pounds of gold and a multitude of manufactured luxuries. Indeed, Constantine the Great had set the new example with immense oblations to his basilica in Rome, recorded in the *Liber pontificalis* along with gifts from and to successive popes. Smaller but parallel votives characterized the piety of other donors. Christian charity had replaced ancient *liberalitas,* setting a pattern for the Middle Ages.

BIBL.: Roland Delmaire, "Les largesses impériales et l'émission d'argenterie du IVe au VIe siècle," in François Baratte, ed., *Argenterie romaine et byzantine* (Paris, 1988), vol. 2, 113–122. A. Stuiber, s.v. "Geschenk," in *Reallexikon für Antike und Christentum,* vol. 10 (Stuttgart, 1977), cols. 685–703.   A.C.

Glass

The peoples of the Roman empire used more glass than any other ancient society. They invented glassblowing, made the first glazed windows, decorated buildings with glass mosaics, and produced spectacular luxury items made of glass. In late antiquity, they used every preindustrial technique of shaping and decorating glass except core forming (which had been abandoned) and staining (which had not yet been invented).

Roman glassworkers used two techniques to decorate objects before they were annealed: blobbing and trailing. Blobbing consists of picking up fragments of glass on the partly formed object and heating them until they fuse, or applying blobs of molten glass. Blobbed objects—mostly drinking vessels—came into use in the mid-3rd century C.E. In the west, production reached its peak in the early 4th century but continued on a smaller scale until the 5th century. In the east, it persisted through the 6th century. Trailing is the technique of applying threads of molten glass. Prominent among later Roman trailed vessels are late 2nd to early 4th century glasses with "snake-thread" decoration, so called because of their serpentine patterns.

Shortly after the discovery of glassblowing, glassworkers learned that objects can be formed and decorated in one operation, by inflating molten glass in a mold. Late antique mold-blown vessels include 5th to 7th century pitchers and bottles decorated with Christian or Jewish symbols, many of which were made in Jerusalem. Some of the Christian vessels depict the cross erected on Golgotha by Theodosius II in 420. Jews were banned from entering Jerusalem in 629, and it is unlikely that vessels with Jewish symbols were produced there after that date. Another group of mold-blown vessels bears the image of a person on a pillar—evidently St. Symeon (about 389–459), who was venerated at Qala'at Sem'an, Syria.

In late antiquity, the most widely practiced methods of decorating glass after it had been annealed were cutting and engraving. Wheel-cut ornamentation varied from simple, linear motifs to elaborate pictorial compositions. Cutting shops existed in many parts of the Roman world, and distinctive regional styles developed in, for example, the Rhineland and Italy. The most elaborate objects are "cage cups": vessels with open-work decoration made by cutting and grinding a thick-walled blank. Most cage cups probably date from the late 3rd and early 4th centuries. Another, much less common method of decorating glasses after annealing was by applying gold foil. Glasses with gilded decoration were made in several parts of the Roman empire in the 3rd and 4th centuries: the eastern Mediterranean, Italy, and the Rhineland. Glass objects with painted decoration are also uncommon. Some of the surviving examples appear to be decorated with vitreous enamels, some with unfired pigments, and some with fired and unfired pigments used together.

The best known of all late antique glasses are "gold-glasses," many of which were found in the catacombs of Rome. Most gold-glasses are roundels with gold foil ornament sandwiched between two fused layers of glass. Their chipped edges suggest that they were cut down from larger objects, presumably dishes or bowls. Some gold-glasses bear religious iconography, while others are decorated with secular subjects.

Buildings were decorated with glass mosaics, *opus sectile,* or mosaic-glass panels. *Opus sectile,* or "cut work," made by fitting together tiles of different shapes and colors, was employed to decorate floors, pavements, and—less frequently—walls.

BIBL.: Danièle Foy, ed., *Le verre de l'antiquité tardive et du haut Moyen Age* (Guiry-en-Vexin, 1995). Donald B. Harden, Hansgerd Hellenkemper, Kenneth Painter, and David Whitehouse, *Glass of the Caesars* (Milan, 1987). Friederike Naumann-Steckner, ed., "Glas der Caesaren: Römisches Glas des 2. bis 6. Jahrhunderts der archäologische Befund," *Kölner Jahrbuch für Vor- und Frühgeschichte* (Berlin), 22 (1989): 5–203.   D.B.W.

Gnosticism

Gnosticism is a collective term for a wide range of religious and philosophic movements that flourished primarily among Jewish and Christian circles during the 2nd century C.E. What characterizes these movements is a concern with *gnōsis* (Greek, spiritual insight), which is to be achieved by a process of introspective inquiry or by receiving an esoteric revelation, often attributed to Jesus and Paul, and sometimes to such figures as Adam or his son Seth.

Groups calling themselves Gnostic apparently were rare in antiquity; we know of only a few such cases, mentioned, for example, by Hippolytus of Rome (ca. 225 C.E.) and Clement of Alexandria (ca. 150 C.E.); most often the term was applied polemically. The Neoplatonic philosopher Plotinus wrote a polemical tract that his disciple, Porphyry, entitled *Against the Gnostics* (*Ennead* 2.9). Christian apologists such as Justin Martyr (ca. 160), Irenaeus of Lyons (180), and Tertullian (180–200) attacked Christians who claimed to have gnosis, intending to discredit teachers and groups they regarded as heretical. Irenaeus wrote a five-volume work entitled *The Refutation and Overthrow of Falsely So-called Gnosis* to refute those whom he accused of false and perverse interpretation of the Scriptures and of Christian teaching. The term *gnosis,* usually translated "knowledge," derives from the Greek verb *gignōskein,* which connotes not intellectual knowledge but the knowledge of relationship. According to a famous statement by the Christian teacher Theodotus, gnosis reveals "who we were, and what we have become; where we were; whither we hasten; from what we are being released; what birth is, and what is rebirth." For to know oneself, at the deepest level, is simultaneously to know God: this is the secret of gnosis. Another Gnostic teacher, Monoimus, said: "Abandon the search for God and the creation and other matters of a similar sort. Look for him by taking yourself as the starting point. Learn who it is within you who makes everything his own and says, 'My God, my mind, my thought, my soul, my body.' Learn the sources of sorrow, joy, love, hate . . . If you carefully investigate these matters you will find him *in yourself.*"

Although the church historian Adolf von Harnack has called Gnostic Christians "the first Christian theologians," their contemporaries among church leaders charged that they were not really Christians at all but schismatics and heretics. Those we call "Gnostics," and whom the apologists derogatorily called by the names of the various teachers they followed (Valentinians, Basilideans, Simonians, Carpocratians, and so on), were known to contemporary scholars primarily through the polemical accounts written by the heresiologists. A handful of papyrus fragments and texts associated with such esoteric Christian teaching were discovered during the 18th and 19th centuries. The text called *Pistis Sophia* ("Faith-Wisdom"), first published in the mid-1850s, for example, claimed to reveal secret conversations between Jesus and certain chosen disciples, and *P Oxy.* 1.654 and 655 contain, on the back of a property contract, a few sayings attributed to Jesus, later recognized as fragments from the *Gospel of Thomas.*

Since the late 19th century, scholars have debated whether or not Gnosticism originated as an independent, pre-Christian religion. Many scholars, taking their cue from the Christian apologists, saw Gnosticism as a phenomenon alien to Christianity, originating, as scholars variously argued, in Persian, Greek, or Egyptian religion. Hans Jonas's monograph, *Gnosis und Spätantiker Geist,* published in 1934 (later abridged and published in English as *The Gnostic Religion,* 1963), depicted the "Gnostic religion" as characterized primarily by cosmic dualism and a sense of alienation from the universe. Jonas constructed his theory on the basis of fragmentary evidence, such as the "Hymn of the Pearl" contained in the Syriac *Acts of Thomas,* and relying heavily on the anti-Gnostic writings of the church Fathers. Jonas's views remain influential among those still unfamiliar with sources now available through more recent archaeological discovery.

In 1945, however, resources for understanding Gnosticism increased enormously after a Bedouin peasant in Upper Egypt discovered thirteen codices of Coptic papyrus manuscripts hidden in a six-foot jar buried under a cliff not far from the oldest monastery in Egypt, founded by Pachomius near Nag Hammadi. The majority of the texts are religious writings containing teaching and revelations attributed to Jesus and his disciples; another group of texts show few Christianizing features and claim to reveal secret interpretations of the creation story involving Adam and his descendants. The eclectic collection of more than fifty manuscripts also includes a treatise attributed to Asclepius and a fragment of Plato's *Republic.* These books were apparently taken out of the monastery library and buried to preserve them after Athanasius, archbishop of Alexandria, sent out his Paschal letter of 367 condemning "heretics" and the "apocryphal books to which they attribute antiquity and give the names of saints."

Since the discovery of the Nag Hammadi Library, as this collection is now called, investigation of these texts is transforming our understanding of Gnosticism and, indeed, of the religions of late antiquity. Although a few of the texts are pagan, and most evince Greek and Egyptian influence, the majority focus primarily on data contained in the Hebrew Bible. Did Gnosticism originate, then, within Judaism? Scholars divide over this question. The diversity of texts suggests that the phenomenon we call Gnosticism originated among various Jewish and Christian groups as each contended, above all, with interpretations of the Hebrew Bible. Central to much discussion was the interpretation of the creation accounts of Genesis 1–3. In particular, discrepancies between Genesis 1–2:4 and 2:4f. fascinated many interpreters and evoked an enormous amount of ingenious and imaginative exegesis, often expanded by elements borrowed from Greek mythology, from philosophy perhaps (especially from Plato's *Timaeus*), or from Egyptian magical lore. Another group of texts, including the *Gospel of Truth*, the *Gospel of Philip*, and the *Tripartite Tractate*, present interpretations of Genesis in the context of the coming and the mission of Christ.

Since the 1970s, scholars investigating the texts increasingly have tended to avoid the generalizing term *Gnosticism* because it invokes a set of stereotypical—and polemical—characteristics invented by the anti-Gnostic writers. Instead, scholars speak either of specific texts, or of groups of texts classified as either Valentinian or Sethian sources. The former group of texts takes its name from Valentinus, a Christian poet and visionary who came from Egypt to Rome ca. 140. He claimed to have received divine revelation in a dream, and also to have received Paul's esoteric teaching from one of Paul's disciples. Some forty years later, Irenaeus, bishop of Lyons, characterized Valentinus as a well-meaning reformer who had inadvertently caused a schism, and whose disciples had amplified his error into "an abyss of madness and blasphemy against Christ." Tertullian described Valentinus as an ingenious and gifted teacher who, disappointed in his hope to become bishop of Rome, turned against the church.

As for Valentinus's teaching, Irenaeus attributes to him a vision of primordial being originating from the harmonious interaction of masculine and feminine divine energies, from the primordial father (called "the depth," apparently from Gen. 1:2) and from the primordial mother, the spirit (cf. Gen. 1:2). Valentinus's students, especially Ptolemy, apparently amplified the primordial cosmology into an elaborate myth in which divine Wisdom together with Christ and the Holy Spirit, participates in creating the world and redeeming God's elect. Certain versions of Valentinian theology have suggested to such scholars as Moshe Idel affinities between Valentinian Christianity and the origins of the Kabbalistic tradition among Jewish groups.

A second group of Nag Hammadi texts, including the *Apocryphon of John, Three Steles of Seth,* and *The Hypostasis of the Archons,* are called Sethian because they feature the figure of Seth, third son of Adam and Eve, as the prototype of those who are holy. In 1995 Michael Waldheim and Frederick Wisse, in their recent studies of the *Apocryphon of John,* followed the lead of Birger Pearson in describing this text (and, by implication, others in its group) as the work of Hellenistic Jewish intellectuals who used Platonic and middle-Platonic philosophy to reinterpret biblical accounts, relativizing certain anthropomorphic elements of the Hebrew Bible while affirming the transcendent God they envisioned existing beyond the confinement of those images. Originating in the milieu of Jewish wisdom and priestly schools, several Sethian texts were adapted for Christian use by identifying Jesus as a manifestation of the primordial Seth. Several others enjoyed popularity among frequenters of Plotinus's seminars in 3rd century Rome, as manuals of contemplative technique and maps of transcendental reality. Members of such groups practiced ritual prayer and techniques of contemplation as they sought spiritual enlightenment.

Fifty years after the discovery of the Nag Hammadi texts, the entire contents of the discovery have finally been published in scholarly editions, with Coptic texts, English translations, commentary, and notes, thus facilitating a new era of research.

BIBL.: *The Coptic Gnostic Library* (Leiden, 1987–1995); Eng. trans.: James M. Robinson, *The Nag Hammadi Library* (San Francisco, 1977). B. Layton, ed., *The Rediscovery of Gnosticism,* vols. 1 and 2 (Leiden, 1980, 1981). E. Pagels, *The Gnostic Gospels* (New York, 1979). M. A. Williams, *Rethinking "Gnosticism": An Argument for Dismantling a Dubious Category* (Princeton, 1996). E.P.

God

From roughly the 4th to the 8th century, we can follow deep religious transformations in the Mediterranean world and in the Near East. A grand confrontation between different conceptions of the divinity was being played out, from the Christianization of the Roman world to the establishment of the Islamic empire. One fundamental fact illustrating the centrality of ideas about the divine is that we can discern a shift in the parameters of identity, as it is phrased, more and more, in religious rather than ethnic, linguistic, or cultural terms.

As if to emphasize the centrality of religious preoccupations, this has been called an age of spirituality. Such a characterization, fit for early Byzantium, rightly emphasizes the utmost seriousness of religious arguments. However, it does not convey the fundamental importance of the complex conflict both within and between the religious communities. The history of the Christological controversies, for instance, is far from reflecting the multiple debates on the nature of God. Adherents of various polytheist, monotheist, and dualistic systems all argued against one another, and among themselves. Polemics represented a major way through which competing worldviews vied with one another. Indeed, late antiquity is characterized not only by conversion but also by the birth and establishment of religious orthodoxies, and the concomitant emergence of sects and heresies. To various degrees, this phenomenon can be observed in Judaism, Christianity, Zoroastrianism, and nascent Islam.

In a way, the emergence and victory of Islam may appear as the ultimate simplification of a highly complex web of attitudes and beliefs woven throughout late antiquity. In that sense, it is more useful to look at the various conceptions of God propounded by the different religious communities, especially in the Near East, and not to focus only, as is too often done, on the Christian transformation of the Hellenic traditions.

Beyond all religious conflicts and controversies, however, we can discern a kernel of belief and attitude common to all, or nearly all, religious groups. One such aspect is the belief in divine providence, appearing clearly in the order of the universe and on a smaller scale in the human body.

The human relationship to God (or the gods) was shaped by the increasing importance of prayer and the overgrowing recognition of the uselessness of sacrifices, since the divinity does not need anything. Together with the praise of God, the main goal of human activity toward the divine is to influence it. This is done, usually, through practices that can be defined as magical. Magic, indeed, represents in late antiquity a common religious language that cuts through various boundaries.

As to ethics, each religious community seems to be based, to a great extent, on its own conception of God's justice and goodness, two qualities sometimes seen in radical opposition to one another but usually both applicable to God. Humans are expected to model their personal and collective behavior on that of God, to imitate Him.

At the onset of the late antique period, even Hellenic intellectuals felt the need to express their beliefs as systems, to define their idea of the divinity in a way more congenial to Christian theology than to the Greek tradition. Indeed, in the 4th century "pagan" intellectuals in the Roman empire, already on the defensive, developed philosophies that reveal the influence of Christian thinkers. It is hence rather misleading to speak of "paganism," since the later Greek philosophers often propounded monotheistic—or at least monolatric—conceptions of the divine. For them, the divine world was hierarchical, with the supreme God at its top. The lower deities were perceived as being under the authority of that supreme God, representing, as it were, its various functions. A major difference remains, however, between Christian theologians (or rabbis) and the Neoplatonists: the latter's conception of God entails a link of kinship (sungeneia) between man (or more precisely his soul) and God. God is often conceived as a daimōn inside man. Such a

kinship is almost unthinkable within a system established on God's creatio ex nihilo. Thus, a different concept of God also means a new conception of the human person, made up of both body and soul. It is usually the whole of man, body and soul, that is created "in the image of God."

It is a truism to note that Christian theology not only reflects a radical reinterpretation of thought patterns inherited from Greek philosophical ideas about the divine but also is the direct heir of the biblical and postbiblical Jewish conceptions of God. This points, however, to a fundamental character of late antique conceptions of the divine: the web of influences between the theologies ensures the striking similarities of content and structure in the perception of the divine among competing religious systems. This is the case, for instance, with such major ideas about God's activity in the world as prophesy and end-time eschatology, a theme ultimately stemming from Iranian religious thought.

In many ways one of the most striking divisions between late antique conceptions of God is that between monotheists and dualists. Zoroastrians, but also Gnostics of various stripes as well as Manichaeans, seem to have been ubiquitous throughout the Near East and the Mediterranean. Everywhere, they clashed directly with Jewish rabbis and Christian theologians, and also with Greek philosophers. Eventually the radical rejection of dualist conceptions of the divinity would be one of the major themes of Islamic theology as well. And yet, on closer view, dualist theologies do not appear to have held ideas about God that were radically different from those in monotheistic or Neoplatonist systems. Rather, the various expressions of monotheism and dualism would seem to reflect different emphases of the same phenomenon. Any monotheism must deal with the inescapable problem of the existence of evil. Essentially, the various dualist theologies represented radical solutions to this problem.

The representation of God is another central problem in late antique theologies. Iconic and aniconic conceptions were in constant competition, in particular within Christianity, originally a strongly aniconic religion, which legitimated in the 4th century a vision of God through his icons. The conflict between the two opposite conceptions would not be played out until the iconoclast controversy and the emergence of Islam, with its strongly aniconic theology. In a sense, aniconic theology can be said to represent the logical conclusion of negative theology—a trend of thought adopted and developed by both "pagans" and Christians, and in a rather different way by Jews—which insists on the fundamental inapplicability of language to God.

BIBL.: H. Dörrie, "Gottesbegriff," Reallexikon für Antike und Christentum XI, 944–951. G. Madec, Le Dieu d'Augustin (Paris, 1998). L. Gardet, "Allah," Encyclopedia of Islam, 2nd ed.   G.STR.

Gold

The employment and display of rare commodities can act conveniently to mark out victors in social competition. Gold has been widely employed as a symbol and currency of wealth and prestige in ancient South America, India, the Near East, and China. Historically, western societies have held gold to be a substance of great value, and in Roman culture gold and other expensive materials were associated with both the worldly and the divine elites. Gold has a number of attributes that make it particularly suitable for such symbolism. It is scarce, brightly colored, resistant to rust, malleable, and reasonably hard-wearing, especially in alloys. Criticism of gold in antiquity and through to the Middle Ages focused on the question of the inappropriate use or overuse of gold. To deny the elite symbol was tantamount to denying the very existence of elites. People fought over who or what was "best" but did not deny that some were far "better" than others. Success in social competition was frequently marked by displays of gold in the form of medallions, jewelry, plate, textiles, foil, and book illumination. The tremendous prestige of the metal, both in religious and secular contexts, ensured that the goldsmith was foremost in status among craftsmen in the ancient world. The demand for gold was steady and was satisfied by the exploitation of reserves in Macedonia, Thrace, and Asia Minor; depletion of those sources led to reliance on importation from Armenia by the 6th century.

Gold was also at the core of the finances of the Roman state. The main coin of the late empire was the solid piece *(solidus)*. The *solidi* were issued as an important part of the payroll of the government, above all to the troops, who also received imperial accession, quinquennial, and other donatives in gold. Money changers were available to convert these coins into the smaller denominations of silver and bronze that were of practical daily use. Taxes were often offered in the same lower denominations, which would then be changed back into gold, thus ensuring the continuation of the cycle of state finances. The manufacture and issue of precious metals were the responsibility of the *comites sacrarum largitionum,* which also oversaw the manufacture and issue of ornaments, regalia, and uniform items of gold and silver. The hierarchy of the state was displayed by varying degrees of magnificence in dress and by such items as purple silk sewn with gold thread and jeweled golden brooches and belts. Thrones and gold-adorned palace apartments were especially associated with those in the upper ranks of the government and most specifically with the emperors themselves. From the 6th century in Byzantium, for example, many important ceremonies and diplomatic exchanges took place among the maximum possible display of precious objects, in a domed room of preeminent gleaming splendor called the Chrysotriclinion.

Worldly and supernatural elites were often understood as existing in close relation to one another. It is hardly surprising, therefore, that the pagan gods had often been marked out by gold in the classical world. The goldness of heavenly bodies such as the stars was closely related in classical thought to the goldness of the gods and goddesses. So, for example, in poetic convention, Helios had a gold chariot and bed; Apollo a gold cloak, lyre, and bow; Mercury a gold cloak, sandals, and wand. Adherents of cults showed their dedication by donating, in the form of treasure offerings, further markers of power. Palaces, temples, and cult statues were often adorned with splendid displays of gold and other precious substances.

These practices were replicated in the Christian churches starting in the 4th century. Constantine did honor to his God by showering the church with gifts in the form of estates, cash, buildings, and vast numbers of gold and silver objects. His example was followed down through the social ranks, and church buildings in the newly Christianized Roman empire soon became repositories of vast wealth. They were lavishly embellished with valuable "treasures," such as gold and silver fittings, furniture, vessels, and decorations. The votive cross of Justin II, now in the Vatican, is one of the few movable items to have survived, although contemporary sources, especially the *Liber pontificalis* for Rome, provide abundant testimony to what once existed. The extensive gold mosaics primarily preserved in Rome, Ravenna, Milan, and Thessalonica provide perhaps the best evidence for the golden aesthetic shared by churches and palaces in the late empire. The heavens were to be seen as a realm from which streamed the brilliant light of goodness down to the earth. Gold-glass mosaics were ideally suited for an aesthetic that valued light and brilliance so highly. These churches were described in terms of their "wonderful glitter and brilliance," which was seen as symbolic of the splendor of God and the brightness of Christian love. The fact that gold and jewels were not displaced in the great churches of much of Europe until the end of the Middle Ages testifies to the power of treasure as a positive motif in the earlier period. This potency was enough to prevent a groundswell of opinion arguing the inappropriateness of such secularly employed symbols in a Christian context that, on the evidence of the Gospels, might have been expected to have been characterized by simplicity rather than worldly exaltation.

BIBL.: S. Averincev, "L'or dans le système des symboles de la culture protobyzantine," *Studi medievali* 20 (1979): 47–67. B. Brenk, "Early Gold Mosaics in Christian Art," *Palette* 38 (1972): 16–25. J. P. Callu, "Le 'centénaire' et l'établissement monétaire au bas-empire," *Ktēma* 3 (1978). D. Janes, *God and Gold in Late Antiquity* (Cambridge, Eng., 1998).   D.J.

Goths

In the 4th century, Gothic groups were established in the northern hinterland of the Black Sea, in modern Ukraine, Romania, and Belorussia. They represented a dominating, organizing elite, rather than the entire population of those lands, and their relations with the adjacent Roman empire were close, if ambivalent. In many ways they were clients, receiving diplomatic subsidies and sending soldiers to fight against Persia. But the Goths also had their own political and cultural agendas, which they periodically asserted. They resisted the spread of Roman Christianity and supported candidates of their own choosing in Roman civil wars (Licinius and Procopius).

After ca. 375, this situation was transformed by the Huns. Some Goths were conquered by the Huns; others retreated into Roman territory, destabilizing the Roman state. In 378 Goths killed the eastern emperor Valens and two-thirds of his army at Adrianople, and in 405–406 a large Gothic force rampaged through Italy. After the collapse of the Hunnic empire in the 460s, more Goths moved into eastern Roman territory in the Balkans. The groups who fled the Huns before ca. 410 and those who remained in the Hunnic orbit until after ca. 450 coalesced into two large units: the Visigoths and Ostrogoths, respectively. These were new and unprecedentedly large Gothic political units, generated by the need to survive the dangers of contemporary political upheaval.

After 475, the military power of these new groupings underlay the creation of two major successor states to the Roman empire in western Europe. The Visigoths were originally settled as allies in Aquitaine by the Roman state in 418. As the empire lost control of its landed base, a succession of Gothic kings cultivated good relations with adjacent Roman landowners and turned the settlement into a kingdom in southern Gaul and Spain, particularly by concerted military action during the reign of Euric (467–483). The constituent groups of the Ostrogoths had at first competed with one another for "favored ally" (federate) status within the eastern empire. Once united by Theoderic the Amal, however, they formed too strong a power bloc, and a resulting political impasse was solved by sending them to Italy. There they created a second Gothic state by conquest between 489 and 493.

Ostrogothic Italy was lauded by some contemporaries as a revival of stability and prosperity. Administrative and social structures remained largely as they had been in the late 4th century, coins of good quality and fineness were issued from traditional mint cities, and diplomatic channels with Constantinople were open for both political and religious matters. However, the settlement of the Ostrogoths was no easy matter, especially when the support of the old aristocracy was still desirable. Furthermore, conflict between the bishop of Rome and the patriarch of Constantinople also produced internal factionalism. These and other factors required careful maneuvering on the part of the Ostrogothic king. Nevertheless, surviving monetary, literary, and artistic evidence of the Ostrogothic period reveal real prosperity.

In the early 6th century, the rise of the Franks destabilized the Visigothic kingdom and allowed Theoderic the Amal to bring all the Goths under his control. This superstate did not survive his death, however, and sustained Byzantine campaigns (536–562) subsequently destroyed the Ostrogothic kingdom entirely. Further west, a reemergent Visigothic kingdom was largely confined to the Iberian Peninsula by Frankish power, but redefined itself to emerge as a major force. Byzantine and Suebic enclaves within the peninsula were destroyed, local independence movements were subdued, and internal unification followed the Goths' renunciation of Arian Christianity in favor of Catholicism under King Reccared at the Third Council of Toledo in 587. In the 7th century the kingdom faced periodic political unrest, but it would probably have lasted indefinitely had it not been caught up in the rise of Islam.

BIBL.: T. Burns, *A History of the Ostrogoths* (Bloomington, 1984). P. Heather, *The Goths* (Oxford, 1996). M. Kazanski, *Les Goths (Ier–VIIe après J.-C.)* (Paris, 1991). H. Wolfram, *History of the Goths* (Berkeley, 1988). P. Amory, *People and Identity in Ostrogothic Italy, 489–554* (Cambridge, Eng., 1997).   P.H.

Greece

Most of what we would today call Greece—Crete, Achaea, Thessaly, Epirus, and Macedonia—belonged in late antiquity to the praetorian prefecture of Illyricum, while Thrace fell to the praetorian prefecture of the east. Traditionally a corridor between the east and west, northern Greece and the Via Egnatia became less secure in the late 4th and 5th centuries, and the southern land route between Patras, Corinth, and Athens probably grew in importance. The difficulty of land travel within Greece itself weakened links between north and south, and travel by sea was often preferred—in fact, Athens may have had closer contacts with Constantinople than with northern Greece.

Although it was far from the empire's frontiers, Greece fell victim to raids by Costoboci in ca. 170–171, Heruls in 267–268, Franks in ca. 280, Goths in 395–397, and Vandals in the 460s–470s. The Slavic invasions from the 580s led to their permanent settlement in much of Greece. Fortification came to take precedence over the more decorative architectural benefactions of the past. The elegant propylaea of Eleusis's sanctuary, for instance, were transformed in the mid-3rd century into a massive defensive wall with a single opening. In the wake of urban destruction, small industries sprang up in the public spaces of Athens. At the same time, archaeological surveys reveal that the rural economy was revived, or at least reorganized, in the 3rd to 6th centuries, perhaps to meet taxes in kind or in response to the foundation of Constantinople. And 5th century patrons and artists in Thessalonica and Athens, and especially in the port towns Nea Anchialos in Thessaly, and Lechaion-Corinth and Nicopolis on the west coast, advanced church architecture to a peak of refinement influenced by Italy as well as Constantinople. Monasticism seems not to have taken root before the 9th century.

Greece was home to a cultural legacy but also to a living tradition of learning. Philosophical life carried on in Sparta, Argos, and Sicyon, as well as in Athens (Julian, *Orat.* 2.119.b–c), the fountainhead of a late 4th century revival of Platonism. The author of the 4th century *Expositio totius mundi* regarded not so much the olive, or Attic honey, but education as Greece's distinctive asset. The demise of Delphi by the end of the 4th century is an often-cited milestone in the decline of public polytheism and the progress of Christianity, but the Olympic Games were held as late as 385, according to a recently discovered inscription. The old gods continued to receive private devotion, and some holy places, such as Attica's Caves of Pan, saw revived activity in the 4th century. Archaeological investigation suggests that Christians neither destroyed nor directly supplanted temples. Rather, when churches were built on or near temple sites, it was generally after the temple had been abandoned, as seems to have been the case at Olympia. Greece's greatest significance in late antiquity was not economic or strategic but ideological: for many, Christians as well as polytheists, Greece still represented the fullness of human civilization. Even in the 7th century, when Isidore of Seville wrote that the Slavs had taken Greece from the Romans, Bishop Theodore of Canterbury, a native of Tarsus, could claim to have sat at the feet of Greece's wise men.

BIBL.: Susan Alcock, *Graecia capta: The Landscapes of Roman Greece* (Cambridge, Eng., 1993). Garth Fowden, "Late Roman Achaea: Identity and Defence," *Journal of Roman Archaeology* 8 (1995): 550–567. Timothy E. Gregory, "The Survival of Paganism in Christian Greece: A Critical Essay," *American Journal of Philology* 107 (1986): 229–242. M. Jameson, T. van Andel, and C. Runnels, *A Greek Countryside: The Southern Argolid from Prehistory to the Present Day* (Stanford, 1994). Jean-Michel Spieser, "La christianisation des sanctuaries païens en Grèce," in Ulf Jantzen, ed., *Neue Forschungen in griechischen Heiligtümern* (Tübingen, 1976).   E.F.

Gregory of Nazianzus

By the 7th century Gregory Nazianzen (ca. 330–ca. 390), known as "the Theologian," was one of the most studied of all Greek authors. Admiring commentaries, painstaking scholia, and translations into Latin, Syriac, and Armenian reflect his importance in providing the standard vocabulary for discussion of God. Of chief interest for historians of late antiquity is the contrast between Gregory's posthumous fame and the apparent failure of his actual career.

Gregory's early life had promised much. Born in Nazianzus, son of a rich curial turned bishop, he studied abroad in Palestinian Caesarea and then Athens, where his contemporaries included Basil of Caesarea and Julian the Apostate, and where he won acclaim for his rhetorical prowess and Christian commitment. Back in Cappadocia, however, he lacked a congenial outlet for his talents, declining a partnership in Basil's ascetic experiments, then crying tyranny and taking flight when his father forcibly ordained him presbyter (362). His father and Basil later combined to consecrate him to the see of Sasima, provoking further complaints and another flight (372); several years as coadjutor at Nazianzus subsequently ended with another withdrawal into retirement (ca. 375). Gregory's finest hour was his three-year mission to Constantinople (379–381) to minister to the embattled Nicene congregation, culminating in his consecration to that see, acclaimed by 150 bishops and approved by the emperor Theodosius. This triumph led within weeks to his most bitter defeat, however, as the same bishops hounded him to resignation. He spent the remainder of his life in his native Cappadocia.

Gregory's orations, half of which stem from his time in Constantinople, reveal him as a superb communicator of ideas, lucid and vibrant. At another level, his whole output bears witness to remarkable communication skills. During the 360s and early 370s Gregory pioneered several subgenres—apologetic sermon (orations that followed his reluctant ordination and consecration), Christian eulogy (for his brother, sister, and father), damning obituary (his two invectives against Julian), and poetic autobiography (his poem "On His Own Affairs")—through which he at once created a platform far more intensely personal than the conventional preacher's pulpit, and attracted attention beyond the confines of his immediate audience at Nazianzus. Gregory's autobiographical focus and catalogues of misfortune easily mislead. Self-marginalization was both a literary strategy and a political choice, the basis for his ascetic self-presentation and for some devastating critiques of the ecclesiastical establishment.

Gregory's correspondence is another example of his mastery of the contemporary media. He published the collection himself (in itself an innovative step), and included letters from Basil to emphasize their long-standing friendship, thus also staking a claim to Basil's spiritual inheritance (albeit a contentious one). Furthermore, the collection is presented in the form of a schoolbook, a purpose it duly served: much of Gregory's subsequent renown derived from his presence (exceptional for a Christian author) in the curriculum. The teachers and intellectuals who figure so prominently among Gregory's correspondents were an important constituency. Gregory's relations with them further explain his willful failures as an ecclesiastical politician: he did not truly need to succeed.

BIBL.: Jean Bernardi, *Saint Grégoire de Nazianze: Le Théologien et son temps (330–390)* (Paris, 1995). F. W. Norris, *Faith Gives Fullness to Reasoning: The Five Theological Orations of Gregory Nazianzen* (Leiden, 1991). R. R. Ruether, *Gregory of Nazianzus: Rhetor and Philosopher* (Oxford, 1969).   N.M.

Gregory of Nyssa

While undoubtedly a master theologian of the Greek church, influencing certainly Maximus the Confessor and possibly Gregory Palamas, Gregory of Nyssa came to prominence as a churchman slowly, and even then followed an unusual career. Born soon after 331 C.E., he was the fourth child of his Christian parents, younger brother to Macrina and Basil of Caesarea. Ordained a reader in 355, and possibly associated briefly with Basil in his early ascetic experiments, he viewed his family's religious enthusiasms with some suspicion, married (his wife lived into the 380s), and embarked on a rhetorical career for some ten years.

He then became embroiled in his brother's episcopal ambitions, wrote his *De virginitate* against Basil's enemies, and was consecrated bishop of Nyssa (as an intended ally in the struggle against Arianism) in 372. He was deposed by the *vicarius* Demosthenes in late 375, ostensibly for financial mismanagement. After rehabilitation in the late 370s, he spent many years as an ecclesiastical envoy (in spite of Basil's judgment that he was too innocent), traveling to Arabia, intervening in disputes in Jerusalem and Nicomedia, and supervising episcopal elections in Ibora and Sebaste—indeed, in the latter he was actually elected bishop, and probably had most to do with the eventual installation there of his brother Peter. The dating of his life and works is much disputed, but he lived at least until 394.

In spite of a small collection of letters, Gregory remains the most private and inaccessible of the Cappadocian Fathers. He is most widely known, perhaps, for his *Life* of his sister, Macrina, which, like his *De virginitate* and his *Life of Moses*, focused on his favorite theme, philosophy. The biography contains useful information about the ascetic life and illustrates the value attached to virginity and the place accorded to women in the early church. It also shows how Gregory slowly emerged from under the shadow of his forceful sister and famous brother. Coming into his own at last, as both diplomat and thinker, he took up Basil's role in relation to the Antiochene schism and the last advocates of the Arian cause.

It is as a theologian that he has most claim to significance. In addition to bolstering the orthodox case against Eunomius, he constructed a theory of human dignity and divinization that lies at the root of Greek Christian thought. Because they are made in the image of God, according to Gregory's theory, human beings are called to exercise personal initiative in the cause of self-mastery. God's grace is safeguarded, because the individual's limited choices tap into a life that is made infinitely available to all. God is known as an agent, and humans come to share in his activity and thereby achieve a likeness to God. In this way Gregory added a genuinely mystical emphasis to humanity's relation to the divine (most apparent in his commentary on the *Song of Songs*), he made acceptable to orthodox Christianity the characteristic emphases of the pagan Plato and the heretical Origen, and he avoided with skill the contradictions that would later tax Augustine.

BIBL.: Margarete Altenburger, *Bibliographie zu Gregor von Nyssa: Editionen, Übersetzungen, Literatur* (Leiden, 1988). Hans Urs von Balthasar, *Présence et pensée: Essai sur la philosophie religieuse de Grégoire de Nysse* (Paris, 1942; reissued 1988). J. Daniélou, *Platonisme et théologie mystique: Essai sur la doctrine spirituelle de saint Grégoire de Nysse* (Paris, 1944; 2nd ed. 1954). Marguerite Harl, ed., *Écriture et culture philosophique dans la pensée de Grégoire de Nysse* (Leiden, 1971). Anthony Meredith, *The Cappadocians* (London, 1995). Andreas Spira, ed., *The Biographical Works of Gregory of Nyssa* (Philadelphia, 1984). W. Völker, *Gregor von Nyssa als Mystiker* (Wiesbaden, 1955).   P.R.

Gregory of Tours

During the late 5th and the 6th century the family of Gregory of Tours was one of the most prominent in central and eastern Gaul. A great-grandfather had served as count of Autun before becoming bishop of Langres, great-uncles had served as a duke and as bishops of Langres and Lyons, and an uncle had been bishop of Clermont. Gregory himself was born probably in 538, and an early patron saint for him was St. Julian, whose shrine at Brioude in the Auvergne was closely associated with his father's family. He served as a deacon at Lyons, and in 573 he became bishop of Tours, succeeding his mother's cousin. Despite his impressive pedigree, initially Gregory had to struggle to establish his authority both in Tours and throughout the ecclesiastical province in western Gaul of which he was metropolitan bishop. His most powerful supporters were his patron saints. Gregory dedicated shrines in Tours and throughout the Touraine with relics of illustrious family members. More significantly, a flash of lightning in the Church of St. Martin, where he had placed relics of St. Julian, was believed to show that the patron saint of Tours had openly allied himself with both St. Julian and Gregory, his new "foster son." During his episcopacy, having St. Martin's support helped Gregory in his dealings with subordinate clerics who resented him as an interloper, a suffragan bishop who spread malicious rumors, and various Frankish kings who were feuding over control of the city. When Gregory once presented an appeal to one king, he could even smile when he identified the "lord" who sponsored his petition as St. Martin. Toward the end of his episcopacy his friend Fortunatus noted that the ceremony rededicating the cathedral of Tours honored both St. Martin's cult and Gregory's own conspicuous reputation.

Gregory's many writings represented another way in which he promoted of his own influence, particular saints and their cults, and orthodox Christianity in general. His most familiar work is his *Histories,* often known in translations (but misleadingly so) as the *History of the Franks.* This extensive narrative begins with creation but quickly becomes an account of Christianity in Gaul. For his record of the 4th and 5th centuries Gregory focused on traditions from the two regions he knew best, the Auvergne and the Touraine, but as his episcopal prestige and contacts increased, his coverage became more extensive. Almost half of the *Histories* concerns the final decade of Gregory's episcopacy, when he had the most interaction with Frankish kings and their courts. Gregory defined his historical vision in biblical terms, writing, for example, "What David sang [in the Psalms] was true of this man." It is no surprise that one of his other works (no longer extant) was a commentary on the Psalms that was perhaps a result of or an aid for his preaching. Because he adopted a perspective on kingship based on the Hebrew Bible, Gregory was generally critical of most of his contemporary Frankish kings, because he thought they often failed to fulfill expectations about charity for Christian communities and respect for bishops; he also cast bishops such as himself in the role of prophets who admonished and advised kings. Gregory furthermore used his *Histories* to show himself in action defending orthodox theology by arguing with representatives of Arianism and Judaism. These arguments were clearly reminders to the Frankish kings of the theology they were committed to support. Gregory once even confronted a king who had issued a royal charter that denied the existence of the three persons in the Trinity by threatening him with the wrath of God and the saints.

Saints and their miracles were the subjects of the *Miracles,* an enormous collection of hundreds of stories and anecdotes about Gregory's and others' encounters with cults and shrines. Gregory composed or completed many of the books in this anthology during the 580s, after he had finally solidified his authority at Tours. Two books concerned the shrines and relics of martyrs and confessors, many of whom had lived outside Gaul during the early Christian period; one book contained short biographies of illustrious men and women in the Gallic church—most of them Gregory's contemporaries, some of them his relatives—who were honored as saints. Another book retold miracle stories about St. Julian. Originally Gregory seems to have intended to end this book with stories about the saint's assistance in establishing his protégé as bishop of Tours, but the addition of more stories blunted this self-serving goal. The four books that collected miracle

stories about St. Martin were the most introspective of Gregory's writings. After first summarizing earlier writings about St. Martin and then recording some earlier miracles, Gregory carefully collected the miracles that St. Martin had performed during his own episcopacy. Since Gregory recounted these stories in chronological order, this collection is virtually a diary up to the year before his death, which was most likely in 594. He seems to have included some of these miracle stories in his sermons as yet more proofs for his moral and theological positions. In particular, the respect for people's bodies demonstrated in miracles of healing supported the Catholic doctrine of Christ's incarnation; at the same time, miracles of healing were previews of people's bodily resurrection in the future. The miracle stories that Gregory collected in both his *Histories* and his *Miracles* were thus repeated demonstrations of God's providential intervention in ordinary life.

One of Gregory's great-grandmothers had once predicted, correctly, that she was "pregnant with a bishop." Gregory's own mother had had high expectations for him, too. She had visited him shortly after he became bishop, perhaps to remind his rivals of her family's long-standing prominence in Tours, and she had consoled him when he worried about his literary inadequacies. With her loving reassurance Gregory became a prominent bishop, and his writings, despite their oddities of grammar and style, have made him the most important, the most vivid, and, not least, the most entertaining historian of early medieval France. Gregory was successful, too, because as bishop and author he identified himself so thoroughly with St. Martin, whose cult he defended and who he hoped would represent him before the court of the king of heaven. A later tradition noted that eventually Gregory's tomb was placed, appropriately enough, next to St. Martin's.

BIBL.: A. H. B. Breukelaar, *Historiography and Episcopal Authority in Sixth-Century Gaul* (Gottingen, 1994). G. de Nie, *Views from a Many-Windowed Tower: Studies of Imagination in the Works of Gregory of Tours* (Amsterdam, 1987). W. Goffart, *The Narrators of Barbarian History* (A.D. 550–800): *Jordanes, Gregory of Tours, Bede, and Paul the Deacon* (Princeton, 1988). M. Heinzelmann, *Gregor von Tours "Zehn Bücher der Geschichte": Historiographie und Gesellschaftskonzept im 6. Jht.* (Darmstadt, 1994). R. Van Dam, *Saints and Their Miracles in Late Antique Gaul* (Princeton, 1993). K. Mitchell and I. N. Wood, eds., *Gregory of Tours* (Leiden, 1999).   R.V.

Gregory the Great

Gregory, pope from 590 to 604, marks the end of late antiquity and is considered the first medieval pope, both for his policies as an administrator and for his distinctive spirituality. Born around 540, Gregory was an urban prefect in 573 and a monk by 574. Pope Pelagius II sent him to Constantinople as *apocrisiarius* in 579 and recalled him in 585–586. Gregory returned to his family monastery, St. Andrews, and assumed the office of deacon. He was elected to succeed Pelagius in 590.

Gregory was most effective in overseeing the papal patrimony and the church of Rome itself. He aimed to free the church of secular influence and to reform and systematize the administration of papal estates. Under Gregory, the Roman church became more efficient, even keeping records of the welfare distributed. Often at odds with the imperial exarch in Ravenna, Gregory also functioned as de facto governor of Rome and southern Italy, taking responsibility for the repair of roads and aqueducts; the security of the grain supply; and the hiring, provision, and deployment of soldiers. Gregory's greatest achievements lay in his careful administration of the Roman church and patrimony, and his concern for the city of Rome. He sought ties with the Frankish church, and sent Augustine to Canterbury to evangelize the English in 596.

Gregory had less success dealing with territories within the Byzantine empire. His dispute with the patriarch of Constantinople over the latter's title, ecumenical patriarch, was largely ignored—the emperor would not support Gregory. In Africa, Gregory failed to win against the Donatists, schismatics who had rejected the papacy's acceptance of imperial condemnation of the Three Chapters. In Dalmatia he won public penance from Bishop Maximus, whom he had attempted (unsuccessfully) to depose. He attempted to intervene in Thessalonica and Prima Justiniana, but those bishops appealed to the emperor. Closer to home, Istria remained schismatic over the Three Chapters, but Gregory sent in troops, summoned a synod, and gradually won over some opponents. The bishops of other great cities had their own bases of power, and Gregory had no designs to subordinate them to a hierarchy headed by Rome. He did, however, insist on the traditional right of Rome to grant the pallium, and the right to settle disputes on certain moral issues.

Gregory's forte was moral theology. He was much influenced by Augustine, Ambrose, and Cassian. The authentic works of Gregory are the *Moralia in Iob* (579–596), which addresses the problem of suffering; the *Regula* (or *Liber*) *pastoralis* (590–591), a handbook for rectors, outlining strategies for exercising power; the *Homiliae in Hiezechelem prophetam* (591–593), which address prophecy and exegesis; and the *Homiliae in Evangelia* (593), moral lessons drawn from the Gospels. The *Dialogi de vita et miraculis patrium Italicorum* (594) was Gregory's most popular book. In it he explains the deeds of saints such as Benedict, and emphasizes the importance of the church and its sacraments. Portions of an exegesis of the *Expositio in Canticum Canticorum* (594) survive in a redaction by Claude of Ravenna. *In librum Regum expositiones* is now held to be a 12th century composition by Peter of Cava, although probably very dependent on Gregory's own work (preached 594–598). Gregory's feast day is 3 September in the west; 12 March in the east.

BIBL.: C. Dagens, *Saint Grégoire le Grand: Culture et expérience chrétiennes* (Paris, 1977). R. Markus, *Gregory the Great* (Cambridge, Eng., 1997). C. Straw, *Gregory the Great: Perfection in Imperfection* (Berkeley, 1988). C.S.

Guilds

The terms *guild* and *association* denote an organized group of persons who share a common interest or purpose. There are roughly fifty words used in Latin and Greek sources for this kind of organization, among which we will single out, for late antiquity, the expressions *collegium, corpus,* and *sodalicium/sodalitas.*

Those groups that the jurists of antiquity defined as *sodalitates* never actually achieved the status of a proper legal institution, although during the imperial era they were subjected to the same authorization and surveillance by the state that was directed toward the *collegia* and was motivated by the persistent fear that all such associations might harbor subversives. In any case, *sodalitates* were private associations. They were the expression of a cult (often concerned with salvation or health), they had a convivial and recreational character, or they were concerned with politics and patronage. Examples of *sodalitates* are found in wall inscriptions in favor of one or other of the candidates in the municipal elections at Pompeii shortly before the eruption of Vesuvius in 79 C.E.: the *Paridiani* (fans of the famous mime Paris), the *seribibi* (the late-night drinkers), the *pilicrepi* (the ball players). Associations of this sort, rather like clubs, contribute to our picture of daily life in the city.

Collegia gathered together people engaged in the same activity or profession. In some cases they were able to exercise a certain political influence. Today there seems to be no doubt that the *collegia* originally had been religious associations; there was one in each district *(vicus)* of Rome, where the inhabitants were obliged to gather in pursuance of the cult of the divinity of the *compitum* (quadrivium). Only later were they opened to voluntary membership. In the context of a city such as Rome, such neighborhood religious associations could also assume certain civic functions, serving as the basis for local defense with emergency draft powers, for example, and for the construction of public works, as is evidenced by inscriptions from the republican age. The oldest professional colleges had their roots in such *vicinitates,* because dealers and artisans of the same profession, in ancient times as in the Middle Ages, tended to settle in the same district. In the earliest inscriptions (end of the 2nd, beginning of the 1st century B.C.E.), in Rome as in Capua, Minturnae, and Praeneste, one witnesses a vigorous flourishing of colleges designated according to diverse professional activities. Nevertheless the *collegia* continued to be primarily religious and neighborhood associations:

such was the *collegium* of the *mercatores Mercuriales* in Rome, devoted to Mercury, and that of the *Hermaistai*, merchants devoted to Hermes at Delos.

It was the proletarian nature of *collegia* that, in the last decades of the republic, provided a notable mass for political maneuvers and for illegal conscription in support of demagogues such as Catiline and Clodius. *Sodalitates* and *collegia* of this kind were later suppressed by Caesar, who had had personal experience of their dangers (*lex Iulia* of 46 C.E., which was intended to break the strength of the *nobile* who had made use of them). At that time only a few *collegia* were spared, and they were among the most ancient as well as being clearly of public utility: for instance, the *fabri* (builders) and the *fictores* (sculptors). And it was from the repressive legislation of Caesar and Augustus onward that the formation of every new college, at least in theory, was subject to authorization and an evaluation of its purposes in relation to public utility ("*utilitas civitatis,*" as Asconius Pedianus was to write in the 1st century C.E., commenting on Cicero's *In Cornelium*). However, "utility" was given a wide definition and was certainly not limited to economic and professional considerations, since it was this very fragmenting of the social body into countless associative groups, each motivated by a common, nonpolitical interest, that seemed at the time to offer a possible instrument for peace (this point of view was echoed by Plutarch in *Vita Numae* 17.13, perhaps following Varro).

Initially, as a matter of fact, the state favored above all the charitable and funerary *collegia* of the *tenuiores*, that is, of the poor, whether freemen or slaves, whose social importance was slight and who presented no political threat once the links of dependence that had formerly subjugated them to the noble families had been severed. Under the Severan dynasty the meetings of the *collegia tenuiorum* (which guaranteed periodical feasts to the members and collective burial on their death) and those of the religious associations approved by the authorities were still the only ones the provincial governors could allow, together with those of the mutual aid colleges among the soldiers in the camps (Marcianus, *Digestum* 47.22, *prol.* a.1). Imperial policy at least until Trajan (Pliny, *Ep.* 10.33, 34, in 109 C.E.) was far more suspicious and illiberal in its authorizations with regard to professional associations, one exception being that of the millers of Rome *(pistores),* which at that very time was recognized as an association, having formerly been a company of free contractors in a state service; this was done to improve the supply services in the capital (Aurelius Victor 13.5, ca. 360). In short, until well into the 2nd century the public authorities seemed to have perceived in the associations a potential threat to the social harmony that the propaganda of the time advanced as the main justification for Roman imperial power.

But it is between the Antonini and the Severi that the key period in the qualitative evolution of Roman associations is to be found. It was then that the mechanism of the so-called state takeover of the associations took shape, hand-in-hand with their more accentuated and effective professionalization. Through the opinions of the jurists of the Severan age, one observes how the emperors began to grant important privileges (fiscal immunity, exemption from municipal obligations) to the members of some *collegia,* in particular the *negotiatores* of foodstuffs and the shipowners *(navicularii)* who were responsible for the provisions of the capital (*annona; Digestum* 50.6.6.3–13; 27.1.17.2–7). At the same time the terms *collegium* and *corpus* diverged semantically. *Collegium* predominated until the 1st century C.E., but even at that time the expression *corpus* (until then applied generically to organized entities) began sporadically to indicate *collegia* of varied nature, both in Italy and in the provinces, especially with reference to those associations connected with food supplies in the localities concerned. These were the large associations that tended to unite in a single *corpus* (or *ordo,* or *universitas*) all those engaged in the same activity in a town or city (or, exceptionally, in the same district, as in Ostia and Arles). From the 2nd and into the 3rd century, epigraphic sources and juridical texts converge in their more and more frequent use of *corpus* as a synonym of *collegium.* By the 4th century *corpus* is decidedly predominant, both in inscriptions and in the constitutions of the *Codex Theodosianus.*

This semantic shift is probably related to the gathering of *collegia* into larger entities. This was the case with the *navicularii marini* of Arles, employed in the transport of foodstuffs to Rome (five *corpora* as articulations of a single *corpus*: CIL 12.692; CIL 12.672 = ILS 1432; CIL 3.14165 = ILS 6987). This also happened to the *dendrophori* in 329 when Constantine decide to conflate them with the *fabri* and the *centonarii* in every city in the empire, "It being opportune that such *corpora* should increase their membership" (*C.Th.* 14.8.1)—although it is probable that this measure adopted by the first Christian emperor was also influenced by considerations of a religious nature, aimed at suppressing the autonomy of a college that had close links with the cult of Atthis and its sacred pine. Similarly in 384–385 the orator Quintus Aurelius Symmachus, then an urban prefect, pointed out the possibility of uniting the *mancipes* of the saltworks (once free contractors, as their very name recalls, but in the 4th century bound by authority to their service as *corporati*) with the *navicularii lignarii* (who transported to Rome the wood necessary for heating the thermal baths) and other *corpora,* in order that they might collectively guarantee the burdensome operation of the public baths (Symmachus, *Relatio* 44). A few years later (389) Valentinian II was to assign to the *corpus* of the *mancipes* all the suitable members of the other minor *corpora* (*C.Th.* 12.16.1).

In these same years, on the occasion of the conflict between the pro-Arian court then resident in Milan and Bishop Ambrose, who refused to give up a basilica for the "heretical" cult professed especially by members of the court and by the Palatine troops coming from the Illyrian regions, it is the bishop of Milan himself, in a letter addressed to his sister Marcellina (*Ep.* 20.6–7), who informs us that the *corpus omne* of the local merchants, which sided with him, had been threatened collectively with a very heavy fine and other repressive measures. But the compact array of the *mercatores* had shown no signs of yielding, and the punitive measures had therefore been suspended in consideration of the essential role of such a *corpus* in providing food for the court and for the armies that accompanied it. Shortly before 440 the shopkeepers of Rome put pressure on the court and obtained from the emperor the extradition from the ancient capital of the *corpus omne* of the Greek *pantapolae* (retailers), who offered them unwelcome competition (Valentinian, *Nov.* 5).

This insistent recurrence of expressions such as *corpus omne, corpus universum,* at the very time (the 4th century) when the Roman economy was most subject to state planning, seems to make explicit what must have been the constant purpose of the public authority: namely, to ensure that certain services were carried out. On a general level this was a consequence of the empire's worsening internal and external situation, which induced the state to widen its control of the associations.

In the 4th and 5th century and especially in the eastern provinces, the *corpora* seem to have enjoyed a regime of greater autonomy. In fact the Greek eastern trade associations played an active and influential part in the political, religious, and social life of the cities. In the 5th century authentic work contracts were achieved. A typical example can be found in the agreement of the builders of Sardi, stipulated in 459 and conserved in an inscription, by which the company undertook to ensure that the work agreed to was carried out so long as precise conditions were respected by the client (*CIG* 3467).

The characterization of the city associations in Asia Minor seems to confirm the belief that there, within the urban context, one absolutely should not confuse the professional categories with the trade associations. What distinguished the trade associations in the Greek-Asiatic world was their nature as elites among the professional classes. It is striking, for instance, that in references to them, epigraphs use highly honorific titles, equal to those referring to the city councils. Thus they could hardly be more different from the western *collegia,* whose origins in religion and solidarity above

all answered the need for mutual support among the weak *(tenuiores).* In the west the guilds, who safeguarded themselves mainly through emphatic demonstrations of loyalty to the emperor (epigraphically testified), assumed a character and purposes similar to those of the eastern associations only in those centers with a higher level of economic development.

In Byzantium in the 4th century, after the rebirth of the city as a "second Rome" under Constantine, there existed corporations that were controlled by the authorities to ensure indispensable services and, consequently, stability, just as in Rome in the same period. Overall functioning and structure were similar in both capitals, though in Constantinople the role of the *praefectus urbis* as controller of the civic body was consolidated and became preeminent only in the 5th century. There were, however, particular aspects that can be better understood for Constantinople if one bears in mind the associative realities of the Greek-Asian cities described above. Perhaps from the reign of Theodosius I onward, the association of the *collegiati decani* or *lecticarii* (grave diggers) was recruited in Constantinople with a member from every corporation, in as many as 950 craft workshops, and detached to the service of the church. In Rome, to the contrary, those responsible for burials always constituted an ecclesiastical organism that was officially recognized around 356 C.E. (the *fossores* or *copiatae* were members of the clergy). In Constantinople the firefighters, too, were recruited from the various corporations, while in Rome, as one reads in Symmachus (*Relatio* 14.3, of 384–385), the same activity was carried out by a single corporation of firemen *collegiati.* Again in Constantinople, the corporations also took part in maintaining public order, ensured by the city's organization into *dēmoi* (divisions of the citizens). Thus in Constantinople one may observe a growth in the public importance of the trade associations. After the middle of the 5th century the guilds even succeeded in achieving a new function, that of fixing, as a monopoly, market prices.

BIBL.: Lellia Cracco Ruggini, "Stato e associazioni professionali nell'età imperiale romana," in *Akten des VI. Internationalen Kongresses für Griechische und Lateinische Epigraphik* (Munich, 1973), 271–311, and "La vita associativa nelle città dell'Oriente greco: tradizioni locali e influenze romane," in *Assimilation et résistance à la culture gréco-romaine dans le monde ancien* (Bucharest and Paris, 1976), 463–491. Gilbert Dagron, *Constantinople: Naissance d'une capitale* (Paris, 1974). Évelyne Patlagean, *Pauvreté économique et pauvreté sociale à Byzance, 4e–7e siècles* (Paris, 1977).   L.R.

Ḥadīth

Islam possesses sacred texts of two kinds. One, the Qur'ān, is conceived as a written text (though in practice it is often recited from memory); the other, Ḥadīth, is conceived as an oral tradition—though written records of it have existed since at least the 2nd century of the Hijra (8th century C.E.). The term Ḥadīth may refer to the entire body of such orally transmitted texts, or it may refer to an individual unit of transmission (hereafter ḥadīth).

A ḥadīth is typically a short text reporting a saying or describing an action of an early Muslim, in particular the Prophet; to it is prefixed a chain of transmission. As an example of this format let us take the following: (1) "'Alī ibn 'Abdallāh related to us: Sufyān related to us: Zuhrī related to us from Sālim from his father from 'Āmir ibn Rabī'a from the Prophet, peace be upon him, that he said: 'When you see a bier, stand until it has passed you.'"

The point of the chain of transmission (isnād) is to authenticate the saying of the Prophet that follows. According to the standards developed by the Muslim scholars, a chain of transmission must meet two main criteria. First, it must be continuous. Typically, each name in the chain represents a different generation of transmitters; if Zuhrī were omitted from the chain, then it would be defective because it would have been chronologically impossible for Sufyān to transmit directly from Sālim. The most common defect in this connection is in fact failure to mention the name of the Companion (here 'Āmir ibn Rabī'a) who transmits directly from the Prophet. Second, each link in the chain must be reliable. If, for example, it was known that one of the transmitters in the chain was marked by poor memory or a tendency to conceal his sources or fabricate traditions to suit himself, this would put in doubt whether the Prophet was in fact the source of the saying attributed to him. For their examination of chains of transmission, the Muslim scholars developed an elaborate set of categories going far beyond these simple examples, and put together a vast body of data to facilitate their application.

The actual text (matn) of a ḥadīth may relate to any of the wide range of matters that were of concern to early Muslims. In the example given above, what is at issue is a point of law. The probable background to this ḥadīth is that pious Muslims had doubts about the propriety of standing as a way of showing respect for anyone but God. Could it then be right to stand for a funeral procession? In this ḥadīth, the Prophet resolves the issue by instructing Muslims that they should indeed stand. But no respectable Muslim scholar would have gone by such a ḥadīth taken in isolation. There may be many ḥadīths bearing on a given question. Some may express the same idea in different words, or perhaps develop it or qualify it in some way. An example is the following (hereafter, the chains of transmission are omitted): (2) "If one of you sees a bier and does not join the funeral procession, he should stand until it passes him, or until it is laid down if this happens first." Other ḥadīths, however, may support the other side of the question. In our case there is, for example, one which describes the conduct of the

Prophet (without quoting a saying of his) as follows: (3) "The Prophet, peace be upon him, used to stand for biers, but later he sat." In other words, the Prophet changed his practice, in which case it is his later practice that Muslims should follow. This rule, however, is not watertight: even if this last ḥadīth (3) is reliably transmitted, it might be that the Prophet sat for some special reason which the ḥadīth does not mention, so that the principle that one should stand was not thereby overridden; or it might be that he sat only to show that one is entitled to sit, for all that it is better to stand. These doubts are met by the following: (4) "The Prophet, peace be upon him, stood, and ordered people to stand; then he sat, and ordered people to sit."

This ḥadīth would be clear-cut (assuming it to be reliably transmitted). It is not, however, the last word on the question. Two Companions who were with the Prophet until the time of his death are quoted for the following ḥadīth: (5) "We never saw the Prophet, peace be upon him, ever attend a funeral and sit before the bier was laid down." To work with a given ḥadīth, it is thus necessary to collect both parallel and antithetical ḥadīths, and to compare them. The Muslim scholars did this in an extensive literature which goes back to the 2nd/8th century.

The Muslim scholars began to make collections of ḥadīths from at least the 2nd/8th century. The earliest large collections were arranged by subject. The oldest surviving collection of this kind, containing more than twenty thousand ḥadīths, is that of the Yemeni ʿAbd al-Razzāq ibn Hammām al-Ṣanʿānī (d. 211/827); the most revered are the smaller and more selective collections of Bukhārī (d. 256/870) and Muslim (d. 261/875). Thus ḥadīth (1) above is taken from Bukhārī's chapter on "standing for a bier," and (2) from his chapter on "when one should sit down when one stands for a bier." Usually a collector will include ḥadīths representing both sides in a disputed issue, but in this instance Bukhārī's selection is one-sided; (3) and (4) are taken from other sources. Collections of this kind continued to be made in the 4th/10th and even 5th/11th century. Another kind of collection was arranged not by subject but by transmitters; thus a ḥadīth like (1) would belong in a section of the collection bringing together all ḥadīths transmitted from the Prophet by the Companion ʿĀmir ibn Rabīʿa. The best-known collection of this kind is that of Ibn Ḥanbal (d. 241/855).

What has been said thus far relates to Sunnī Ḥadīth. Among the Ibāḍīs, the only surviving Khārijite group, we find a Ḥadīth literature that is similar in character to that of the Sunnīs, but on a much smaller scale. Among the Shīʿites, and particularly the Imāmī Shīʿites, there is a rich Ḥadīth literature that differs in character from that of the Sunnīs in a crucial respect: though the ḥadīths may still relate sayings or deeds of the Prophet, they are more often concerned with those of the twelve imāms, most commonly Jaʿfar al-Ṣādiq (d. 148/765). The oldest surviving Imāmī Shīʿite collections of any size date from the 4th/10th century.

A major issue regarding Ḥadīth is how much, if any of it, really goes back to the figures to whom it is attributed. The traditional Muslim scholars took it for granted that much of it was unreliable or even the product of outright fabrication, but they developed criteria that, in their view, enabled them to distinguish sound from unsound ḥadīths. An attitude of radical skepticism was also found in the early centuries of Islam, but did not survive. In modern times, western scholarship has come to be sharply divided on the question, while Muslim scholars generally but not invariably take a position in line with that of traditional Muslim scholarship. From this point of view, the ḥadīths quoted above—where judged authentic—will be taken as evidence of the actual words or deeds of the Prophet. From a skeptical viewpoint, by contrast, they are more likely to be seen as the product of a legal dispute that took place among Muslims some time after the death of the Prophet: in ḥadīths (1) and (2), those who believe that one should stand in the presence of a bier seek to support their view by ascribing it to the Prophet; in (3) and (4) their opponents seek to counter this move; and in (5) those who believe in standing strike back at these opponents. One point that impedes any definitive resolution of the question of authenticity is that we do not have written records of Ḥadīth earlier than the oldest surviving collections; another is that relatively few ḥadīths can be dated on internal grounds (the exceptions being prophecies that mention identifiable historical events).

The closest parallels to Ḥadīth are to be found in rabbinic Judaism. For example, a Talmudic statement of a legal doctrine may be preceded by a chain of authorities such as: "R. Abba said: R. Ḥiyya bar Ashi said: Rav said . . ." However, while rabbinic Judaism ascribes to Moses its oral tradition in general, cases where individual traditions are expressly traced back to him are rare, and the classical Muslim concern for complete chains of transmission is not in evidence. There is also no equivalent to the Muslim Ḥadīth collections: Jewish traditions are found scattered through juristic and other works. It is thus plausible to seek the origins of the Ḥadīth format in rabbinic Judaism, but we have to assume that this was followed by a considerable independent evolution on the Muslim side.

BIBL.: J. Robson, "Ḥadīth," in Encyclopedia of Islam, 2nd ed. Ignaz Goldziher, Muhammedanische Studien (Halle, 1889–1890); Eng. trans.: Muslim Studies (London, 1967–1971). G. H. A. Juynboll, Muslim Tradition (Cambridge, Eng., 1983). J. van Ess, Zwischen Ḥadīṯ und Theologie (Berlin and New York, 1975). M. M. Azmi, Studies in Early Ḥadīth Literature (Beirut, 1968). M. J. Kister, Studies in Jāhiliyya and Early Islam (London, 1980), and Society and Religion from Jāhiliyya to Islam (Aldershot, 1990).

H. Motzki, "The *Muṣannaf* of 'Abd al-Razzāq al-San'ānī as a Source of Authentic *aḥādīth* of the First Century A.H.," *Journal of Near Eastern Studies* 50 (1991). Iftikhar Zaman, "The Science of *rijāl* as a Method in the Study of Hadiths," *Journal of Islamic Studies* 5 (1994).　　　M.C.

Ḥallabāt

Ḥallabāt is an archaeological site located in northeastern Jordan, where the annual rainfall (about 100 mm) permits only subsistence agriculture, and only through extensive water conservation and irrigation.

The main structure is a fort (44 m square) with projecting square corner towers, and series of rooms on three sides of the internal courtyard. The northwest quadrant contains an inner structure (16.25 m square) with rooms flanking a small courtyard. Other site remains include a small mosque, domestic structures, a water reservoir, and seven cisterns. An irregular walled enclosure (approximately 270 m by 220 m)—probably horticulture related—is divided into plots irrigated by runoff water distributed through a system of sluices.

A postulated Nabataean occupation of the site was followed by the construction of a small fort, probably in the 2nd century C.E., encapsulated later by the larger fort. A Latin inscription of 213–214 mentions cohorts constructing a *castellum novum* during the governorship of Sextus Furnius Julianus. Other epigraphic finds include fragments of an edict of Anastasius (491–518) relating to the administration of Arabia. The fort's restoration in 529 under the dux Flavius Anastasius probably added the corner towers. The Umayyads transformed the fort into a rural estate with attendant structures. The residence might also have functioned as an administrative center for the Balqa region, and as a desert hunting lodge. The Umayyad-period decorations include floor mosaics, carved stucco, wall paintings, and decorative wood carvings. The site was probably abandoned after the fall of the Umayyads, in the period marked by the general decline of agricultural enterprises in marginal lands of northeastern Jordan.

BIBL.: Ghazi Bisheh, "The Second Season of Excavations at Hallabat, 1980," *Annual of the Department of Antiquities of Jordan* 26 (1982): 133–143. Ghazi Bisheh, "Qasr al-Hallabat: An Umayyad Desert Retreat or Farm-Land," in *Studies in the History and Archaeology of Jordan II*, ed. Adnan Hadidi (Amman, 1985), 263–265. David Kennedy, *Archaeological Explorations on the Roman Frontier in North-East Jordan* (Oxford, 1982), 17–68.　　　Z.F.

Harran

Also known as Karrai in Greek, Hellenopolis ("heathen city") to the Fathers of the church, and Carrhae in Latin, Harran (Harrān in Arabic), was a town in northern Mesopotamia, today in Turkey, located on one of the major east-west trade routes. According to legend, it was the birthplace of Abraham, but it is mostly known as the home of the Sabaeans and of the Moon God, Sin. It was a city of learning, with a school of medicine allegedly transferred there from Alexandria in the early 8th century and a school for translation of texts from Greek and Syriac into Arabic. The pagan Sabaeans were protected because they claimed to be the Sabians of the Qur'ān (2:58, 5:78, 22:17), who belonged to a protected religion according to Islam. The ruins of the city are quite extensive. There is an Umayyad mosque and perhaps remains of other early Islamic monuments. Excavations were carried out by D. S. Rice in the 1960s and new explorations are planned.

BIBL.: G. Fehervari, "Harran," *Encyclopedia of Islam*, 2nd ed.　　　EDS.

Heaven

Most ancient peoples imagined the sky, and all that might lie beyond it, as the dwelling place of divinity: it was the region of light, the place of the stars, the source of rain, as well as a natural symbol of the goal of human yearning, the place toward which spiritual people lifted their eyes or raised their hands in prayer. Greek mythology since Homer represented the gods as living there (so Lucian's satire, *Icaromenippus*), and Cicero somewhat tentatively spoke of heaven as the abode of the blessed, attainable for departed souls by ascending the Milky Way (*De re publica* 6.16–24; *Tusculanae Disputationes* 1.22.51). Although the most common Mediterranean conception of the human condition placed the "shades," or insubstantial images, of the dead in a dark and cheerless underworld, later Hellenistic philosophers revived the ancient Pythagorean notion that souls are made of a divine substance akin to the stars and return after death to the moon and the sun for purgation and eventual reincarnation, eventually reaching the region above the heavenly bodies when they are purified of irrational attachments (Plutarch, *De facie in orbe lunae* 28–30; Porphyry, *De antro nympharum* 29; Macrobius, *In Somnium Scipionis* 1.12.1–2).

The canonical Hebrew Scriptures generally imagine heaven, the region above the sky, as the place where Israel's God rules without rival, and conceived of the dead as permanently confined to the underworld, or Sheol; only the very last layers of the Hebrew Bible suggest the possibility of resurrection and future reward for the just, probably on a transformed earth (Dan. 12:2–3; perhaps Is. 26:14, 19; see also 2 Macc. 7:23, 12:43–45). Later apocalyptic literature, however, and the rabbinic writings took cosmological and eschatological ideas from surrounding cultures, often imagining the world as surrounded by three to seven heavens (*Testament of Levi* 2.6–3.10; *Apocalypse of Abraham* 19.3–9; b Hagigah 12b), and conceiving of the place for the just after death as a region of blessedness, even a paradise, somewhere within those heavens

(II Enoch 8; III Baruch [Greek] 10.5; b Hagigah 12b). Some later Jewish works also describe a heavenly Jerusalem in the fourth heaven, which existed before this world and which will descend to the earth as a home for God's faithful in the time of salvation (II Baruch 4; IV Ezra 7.26–35; Targ. Psalm 122.3; b Taanith 5a; compare Rev. 21).

These later Jewish notions form the background of the various conceptions of the heavens found in the New Testament and the earliest Christian writings. Most Christian writers of the 2nd and 3rd centuries C.E. assume that the fullness of reward for the just, like the fullness of punishment for the wicked, must await the end of history, when the dead will be raised with their bodies, although souls will experience some kind of awareness or anticipation of their lot immediately after death (Tertullian, Adversus Marcionem 4.34.12; De anima 7; Hippolytus [?], Adversus Graecos [PG 10.796–797]; Cyprian, Ep. 59.3). Martyrs, however, or virgins consecrated to Christ, were often understood to enter into their full reward immediately (Methodius, Symposium 8.2; later Severus of Antioch, Hom. 52, 62, 64). Although Christian preachers and theologians remained generally cautious about speculating on the details of the coming joys of the just, some 4th century poetic works—such as Ephrem the Syrian's sensuous Hymns on Paradise and a number of Prudentius's Latin hymns (Cathemerinon 5.112–124; 8.41–49)—as well as some contemporary works of ascetical hagiography, like the Bohairic Life of Pachomius (82, 114), offer strikingly concrete pictures of a garden of peace and pleasure, peopled with angels and saints and enlivened by the ineffable presence of God. Few Christian writers attempt to locate heaven precisely, except for the 6th century Alexandrian Cosmas "Indicopleustes," whose Christian Topography presents the cosmos as a two-tiered rectangular box with an arched cover, the upper part of which is "the world to come, where the Lord Christ has ascended . . . and where the just will later ascend" (Hypothesis 6). The most graphic attempt to describe the place and the features of heaven is in the Apocalypse of Paul, probably composed in Asia Minor shortly after 400, which describes the apostle's guided tour of the regions of both reward and punishment. Paul is first shown, in the third heaven, the "land of promise," a transformed version of the present earth that will descend at the end of history as the site of the millennial kingdom of Christ (21–22), and he later glimpses the still more glorious "city of Christ," where all the saints will finally reside in blessed communion with each other and with God. Most early Christian writers do not conceive of human fulfillment principally in spatial or corporeal terms, but as eternal life for the whole person in the presence of God. So for the 5th century Greek ascetical writer Diadochus of Photice, even the face-to-face "vision of God" often promised as humanity's ultimate goal should be understood not as sensible perception but as the firsthand experience of God's love and nearness, without any definite intuition of God's nature or form (Vision 13–14). At the beginning of the same century, Augustine of Hippo, whose discussion of future reward and punishment most influenced later Latin eschatology, describes heaven primarily as the community of all the faithful angels and human beings of history, united in peace by the vision and joyful praise of God: "We will be at leisure then, and we will see God as he is, and when we see him we shall praise him. And this will be the life of the saints, the activity of those at rest: we shall praise without ceasing" (Serm. 362.20.31).

Ancient Persian religion, since the time of Zarathustra (10th century B.C.E.), spoke of heaven as the Garōdemāna or "house of song," and understood it as a place full of light, the dwelling of Ahura Mazda and his holy ones. In texts of the Avestan period (4th–6th centuries C.E.), this was portrayed as the highest of four heavenly regions; the soul deemed just by Mithra and his fellow judges might reach it by crossing the lower heavens of Humata (good thoughts: the stars), Hukhta (good words: the moon), and Hvarshta (good deeds: the sun).

The Islamic understanding of heaven depends on a number of passages in the Qur'ān, especially in the suras from Muhammad's early Meccan period (610–622 C.E.)—strikingly reminiscent of Ephrem's Hymns on Paradise—which describe the place of reward for "those who have resisted evil" as a cool and lovely garden (djanna) called Eden, full of spiced fountains and streams of milk, wine, and honey, where the just will recline on couches in the company of family and friends, enjoying an endless abundance of delicious food and drink, and waited on by chaste and beautiful female companions (38:50–53; 52:17–28; 88:8–16). Later commentators drew on the verse, "There they have all that they desire, and there is still more with Us" (50:35), as grounds for suggesting that the chief reward of the just will not be the sensual pleasures of paradise but God's approval (9:72), and even the chance for an occasional glimpse of God as he is (so the 14th century commentator Ibn al-Khayyam al-Djawziyya, Hādī al-arwah 225). The central tradition of Muslim eschatological hope, however, continued to stress the rich concreteness of the Qur'ān's picture of a divinely maintained garden of delight.

BIBL.: Franz Cumont, After Life in Roman Paganism (New Haven, 1922). Brian E. Daley, The Hope of the Early Church (Cambridge, Eng., 1991). Adolf Lumpe and Hans Bietenhard, "Himmel," Reallexikon für Antike und Christentum 15 (Stuttgart, 1989): 173–212.   B.D.

Hebrew

Since the known history of the Hebrew language spans about three thousand years, the period of late antiquity constitutes only a comparatively brief interlude; however, it saw some significant developments. The replacement of Hebrew by Aramaic in the general population of Palestine and wherever else Hebrew-speaking Jews lived in the Near East had been constantly progressing during the period of the Second Temple, but Hebrew continued to thrive at least among the educated. The many discoveries of Hebrew texts and documents from the Dead Sea, including, for instance, the Bar Kochba correspondence, confirm the continued vitality of the language, as they also add greatly to our knowledge of its history.

The Hebrew language as it is known from the Bible encompassed dialectical and diachronous stages. During the period of late antiquity it underwent further noticeable changes, but without ever being altered beyond recognition or becoming difficult to understand. New features of syntax, morphology, and, above all, vocabulary entered the language, together with minor changes in orthographical usage. As in earlier periods, contacts with other languages such as closely related Aramaic and non-Semitic languages—in the first place, Greek—contributed to the changes. A subject much discussed in the scholarly literature is the language of Jesus, and this illustrates the problems involved in trying to unravel the precise linguistic situation in Palestine at the time: there can be no question that the language Jesus spoke was basically Aramaic, but his familiarity with Hebrew can hardly be doubted.

The Hebrew language of the first five centuries of the current era is known most fully from the legal discussions of Jewish religious scholars. These were codified during the period and, together with the Bible, became the basis for nearly all later Judaism. After its most important work, the Mishnah (9.V.), codified around 200 C.E., the then-current stage of the language is variously called Mishnaic Hebrew or, more comprehensively, Rabbinic Hebrew or, linguistically preferable, Middle Hebrew. The Mishnah was further explained and amplified in the culmination of the legal-religious research of the period, the Babylonian and Jerusalem Talmuds, which were codified around 500 and composed mainly in Aramaic but with an expected large admixture of Hebrew. Jewish sectarianism, that is, sects that were untouched by or that rejected rabbinic Judaism, continued to exist, but apart from the writings of the Dead Sea group, they left no authentic documents of linguistic significance for Hebrew speech, if one omits the Samaritans who developed a very distinctive form of pronunciation in their use of Hebrew.

A development in the period that had lasting consequences for our understanding of the Hebrew language was brought about by the activity of the Masoretes concerned with the Masora "transmission" of the biblical text. It was they who provided the written language that had been unvocalized or that possessed only occasional and rudimentary indications of vowels and phonetic features such as consonant doubling, with a sophisticated vocalization system that also included further reading features. Prior to their activity, Hebrew vocalization is attested only indirectly and imperfectly, mainly by Greek transliterations. The impetus for the Masoretes may have come from the Christian translators of the Bible into Syriac; their acquaintance with Greek would probably have made them aware more than the Jews of the usefulness of full and, as much as possible unambiguous, vocalization. However, the Jews clearly had an especially urgent need to fix the pronunciation of their ancient Scriptures. A number of different attempts were made, all of them relying on special marks to be placed above or underneath the preceding consonant. Three systems are known; they are designated as the Palestinian, the Babylonian Supralinear, and the Tiberian vocalizations. The last was the most successful system. It makes use of dots and small lines as well as combinations of both, placed mainly but not always underneath the consonants. A dot placed within or next to a letter was used to indicate nonvocalic features such as consonant doubling or, in the case of certain consonants, their pronunciations as either stops or spirants. Other signs were invented to indicate further reading features. The Tiberian system appears to have been developed fully only by the end of the 9th century. It is admirably detailed from the linguistic point of view but leaves some features unexplained, such as vowel quantity. It shows divergences from the other, less refined systems and whatever else is known of Hebrew vocalization. It is no safe guide, of course, to the original pronunciation of ancient Hebrew, or its dialectic pronunciations, and it represents a tradition influenced by Aramaic habits of speech. But it dominates the form of the biblical text to this day and determines how the Hebrew language in general is to be pronounced and grammatically analyzed.

Thus, the period of late antiquity witnessed the fixation of Hebrew in the form that has largely been accepted as standard Hebrew, in spite of many developments in subsequent centuries that remained minor until the creation of Israeli Hebrew in the 20th century. It has also noticeably influenced the innumerable later translations of the Bible, including those into English.

BIBL.: S. Rebenich, "Jerome: The "Vir Trilinguis" and the *Hebraica Veritas,*" *Vigiliae christianae* 47 (1993): 50–77. Angel Sáenz-Badillos, *A History of the Hebrew Language,* trans. John Elwolde (Cambridge, Eng., 1993).   F.R.

Hell

All the ancient peoples of the Mediterranean region seem to have imagined the dead as sharing a huge, dark cavern under the world—a kind of common grave, controlled by its own gods or demons and often without air, light, or water. Although the Egyptians imagined life after death in fairly full-blooded terms, most other cultures thought of this subterranean existence as scarcely constituting a continuation of life: death was not conceived of as total annihilation, but the "shade" that prolonged a living person's identity was simply a weak and colorless image of what he or she had been, lacking the power to do or experience anything except occasionally to appear as a ghost. For ancient Israel, the underworld, or Sheol, was "the Pit," a "region dark and deep" where the dead lie forever "cut off from God's hand," unremembered by their ancestral God and unable to praise him (Ps. 88:3–6; Ps. 6:5).

Under the probable influence of Egyptian thought, Greek religion began in the Homeric poems to imagine a discernment taking place among the dead, by which those specially beloved of the gods in this life would be taken to Olympus to live with them, and those who had committed outstanding crimes would receive punishment in the underworld (*Odyssey* 11.576–600). In the Greek mysteries of the 6th century B.C.E., and in Orphic and Pythagorean teaching, a judgment after death, followed by reward and punishment proportionate to one's actions, became a central feature of religious expectation and was adopted by many who reflected on human fate (see Plato, *Phaedo* 80d–82b, 107a–115a; *Republic* 10.614a–621d). In the sixth book of the *Aeneid*, Virgil reflected this later image of the underworld in a way that was to have lasting influence on the Latin west, memorably depicting both Tartarus, a region of lasting torture for egregious sinners, and the Elysian Fields, a place of earthly delight where the virtuous awaited rebirth.

Although a few passages of the Hebrew prophets suggest different places in Sheol for heroes and oppressors, the circumcised and the uncircumcised (Isa. 14:15–20; Ezek. 32:17–32), it was only in the later apocalyptic tradition that Jewish literature imagined a fiery "pit of torment" for unrepentant sinners (4 Ezra 7; 1 Enoch 18; 2 Enoch 10) and came to think of Sheol simply as a temporary place of detention for the dead, as they await resurrection and judgment (Dan. 12:2; 1 Enoch 51:1; Jubilees 24:31). By the time of Jesus, everlasting punishment in fire was commonly accepted by many faithful Jews, including those in his circle, as the fate of hardened sinners (Matt. 25:41; Luke 16:22–28; Rev. 19:20; 20:10; see also Qumran: I QS 4:12–13). Apocalyptic and rabbinic texts, as well as passages in the New Testament, often refer to this place of punishment as the "fire of Gehenna" (Apocalypse of Abraham 15; Sibylline Oracles 2.283–312; Matt. 5:22, 29; Mark 9:47; James 3:6), presumably because the Valley of Hinnom (Hebrew, Gē-Hinnom), just south of the Temple Mount in Jerusalem, was remembered as a place of fiery human sacrifice in ancient times (2 Kings 23:10; Jer. 19:1–7). Many classical rabbinic writers describe Gehenna as a vast region under the earth (b

Pesahim 94a; b Tamid 32b; Song of Songs Rabbah 6.9, 3), filled with dark smoke and fire of unparalleled heat (b Berakoth 57b; b Yebamoth 109b; Numbers Rabbah 18.20). Although the rabbis occasionally mention everlasting punishment for some extraordinary criminals—like the emperor Titus, who destroyed Jerusalem in 70 C.E. (Ecclesiastes Rabbah 5:8, 4; b Baba Metzia 58b; b Rosh ha-Shanah 16b–17a)—they tend to assume that a year's confinement in Gehenna will suffice for the punishment of most sinners (b Shabbath 33b; b Eduyoth 2.10).

Early Christian writers mainly confine their speculations about the future punishment of sinners to what can be derived from the Scriptures, although the picture of Hades from classical literature occasionally makes its influence felt. Third century western authors like Tertullian and Hippolytus imagine that both the just and sinners begin their afterlife detained in the underworld until the resurrection, judgment, and final retribution; even before the resurrection, however, they will be kept separate from each other, and will anticipate their future condition psychologically (Tertullian, *De anima* 7; Hippolytus [?], *Adversus Graecos*, PG 10.797). The Syriac Fathers of the 4th and 5th centuries developed the Hebrew picture of Sheol as the dark, airless place where the souls of all the dead must "sleep" until the resurrection, after which the damned will simply fall back into its depths with heavy, untransformed bodies, to be forgotten by God (Aphrahat, *Dem.* 22.17, 24; Narsai, *Hom.* 18; 34); in some works, however, Ephrem suggests that the souls of the just already live on the fringes of paradise (*Hymns on Paradise* 8.11). Hilary of Poiters (4th century), the first Latin Christian writer to offer a detailed picture of the underworld, imagines it also as the "prison" in which the souls of both the just and unjust will be detained until the resurrection; the damned, however, will be forced to return there in their "bodies of shame," to undergo the everlasting torture of fire, as well as the undying consciousness of guilt (*In Ps.* 68.5, 28; *In Ps.* 69.3). Augustine's depiction of the punishments of the damned, especially in book twenty-one of *De civitate Dei*, follows the biblical picture closely; he refuses to speculate on the place or details of hell, except to insist that its tortures are eternal and will involve both material fire and the guilt of fruitless repentance (see also *De civ.Dei* 20.16; *Enchiridion* 23.92). Gregory the Great, too, at the end of the 6th century, whose portraits of the condition of the dead in the fourth book of the *Dialogues* formed the later Latin religious imagination, hesitates to speculate about the location of Gehenna or the nature of its fire (*Dial.* 4.30, 41–44). He is convinced, however, that the souls of sinners go there directly at death, to suffer in the knowledge of their future bodily pains (*Dial.* 4.29), and that punishment will be carefully tailored to the various classes of sinner (*Dial.* 4.45).

Reflecting its Jewish and Christian roots, the Qur'ān also speaks of the future punishment of sinners, along with the jinns or demons, in Gehenna *(djahannam)* or simply in fire *(nār)* (7:38; 25:11–13; 70:15–16); there they will experience the extremes of both cold and heat, according to one text (38:58–59), and will sigh and wail (11:106). In some passages, it is said that sinners will abide there forever, "except those whom God wills to deliver" (6:129; 11:107), which was generally taken as a promise that sinful Muslim believers would eventually be freed from its punishments. Traditional commentators took Gehenna to be the outermost and highest of seven concentric circular stages in the underworld, all devoted to the punishment of sinners—a picture that clearly influenced Dante.

Persian religion imagined the place of punishment, the Drūjō-demāna (house of the lie), as a mirror image of heaven. Its deepest region is a place called "endless darkness" *(anaghra temah),* characterized by wailing, cold, and a foul stench; there each of the damned thinks he or she is alone, although the place is crowded with victims. After the final judgment by Mithra, all the dead must cross the bridge of Chinvot (separation), but only the just will reach the realm of light; for the wicked, the bridge will narrow to a razor's edge, and they will simply tumble from it into the depths of damnation.

BIBL.: Carsten Colpe, Ernst Dassmann, Josef Engermann, Peter Habermehl, and Karl Hoheisel, "Jenseits," *Reallexikon für Antike und Christentum* 17 (1994–95): 246–407. Brian E. Daley, *The Hope of the Early Church* (Cambridge, Eng., 1991).   B.D.

Heraclius

Heraclius was born ca. 575, probably of Armenian origin, son of the Byzantine general Heraclius and Epiphania. For approximately a decade he accompanied his father, who was exarch (governor-general) of Africa at Carthage. Together they rebelled as "consuls" against the usurping Emperor Phokas in 608. By 610 the younger Heraclius had seized Constantinople, executed Phokas, and had himself proclaimed emperor. The Persian crisis intensified because King Khosro II rejected all diplomatic overtures and ordered his generals to exploit the Byzantine civil war by overrunning upper Mesopotamia, Syria, Palestine, and Egypt. After Heraclius's first wife Fabia/Eudocia, of Africa, bore him Heraclius Constantine and then died in 612, he aroused controversy by marrying his sister's daughter Martina.

Heraclius's life in Africa and his Armenian heritage gave him unique perspectives. He broke precedent by personally but unsuccessfully campaigning against the Persians in 612 and 613. After the shocking and humiliating loss of Jerusalem and the cities and countryside and large revenues of Egypt and Syria to the Persians, he slashed expenses by canceling the grain dole at Constantinople, reducing the expensive ecclesiastical payroll, and compelling forced loans from the church. He tested the Persians and raised morale by leading his armies in successful limited clashes in Anatolia in 622 and again in 624. After confiding power at Constantinople to a regency, he marched east, allied with the Khazars, and unexpectedly arranged a détente with the Persian general Shahrbaraz, who had quarreled with Khosro II. Now free from any immediate threat from Shahrbaraz's armies, he invaded central Mesopotamia. His defeat of a Persian army east of Nineveh upset the internal Persian equilibrium. He devastated towns and countryside, and had begun to make contact with dissident elements within Persia when Khosro II fled and his son Kavad-Sheroy overthrew and slew him. Heraclius owed his victory at least as much to mastery of internal intrigue in Persia, and the use of deception, as to skills on the battlefield. He imposed peace and won restoration of former borders, prisoners, ecclesiastics, and the putative fragments of the Cross. On 21 March 630 he achieved the zenith of his fame by personally and triumphantly accompanying those relics to Jerusalem. He vainly sought a compromise formula of Monothelitism (one will) to satisfy all concerning the nature of Jesus Christ. His allies were Patriarchs Sergius and Pyrrhus of Constantinople. His order in 632 for the compulsory conversion of Jews proved divisive. Unable to check the Muslim invasions of Syria and Palestine, he withdrew in late 636 to Anatolia, where he improvised a defense. He condemned and replaced local officials in Egypt who tried to make peace with the Muslims. Late in his reign he ordered his treasurer, Philagrios, to create a new imperial census. The bitterness of the imperial succession crisis filled much of his final years, while illness intermittently impaired his effectiveness until his death in February 641. Although no great institutional reformer, he stamped his forceful yet ambiguous and torn personality on historical memories.

BIBL.: John F. Haldon, *Byzantium in the Seventh Century: The Transformation of a Culture* (Cambridge, Eng., 1990). Walter Emil Kaegi, *Byzantium and the Early Islamic Conquests* (Cambridge, Eng., 1993). Cyril Mango, "Deux études sur Byzance et la Perse Sassanide," *Travaux et memoires* 9 (1985): 91–118. D. J. Nodes, "Rhetoric and Cultural Synthesis in the *Hexaemeron* of George of Pisida," *Vigiliae christianae* 50 (1996): 274–287.   W.K.

Heresiology

Heresiology is the literary genre that lists and classifies religious heresies with the object of refuting and condemning them. In Christianity it grew up early, together with the idea of heresy (Greek *hairēsis,* or choice, hence sect) as a deviation from the truth (orthodoxy). Irenaeus, bishop of Lyons in the late 2nd century, composed a work entitled *Against Heresies*, while in North Africa Tertullian wrote against the views and followers of Marcion and Valentinian, as well as composing a general attack on Gnostic heretics. These and other such works reflected a powerful impulse within Christianity toward the prescription of correct belief, and set a pattern followed with increasing elaboration throughout late antiquity and beyond. Heresy and orthodoxy alike were thus constructs, and heresiology a tool used to control the pluralism of belief that in fact prevailed. Heresiology became progressively more important and more necessary as the church struggled to define and formulate a universally valid doctrine, especially after the First Ecumenical Council of Nicaea in 325 C.E. The statement of faith agreed to at Nicaea and finalized at Constantinople in 381 C.E. was no more successful in ending disagreement, especially on Christological issues, than were later conciliar and synodical decisions; it may indeed have exacerbated them. All sides found heresiology useful, since all parties thenceforth saw themselves as equally orthodox.

Heresiology in Syriac began early, and is represented among the works of Ephrem Syrus in the 4th century. In Greek the most remarkable writer was Epiphanius, bishop of Salamis in Cyprus, who composed a so-called *Panarion*, or "medicine chest," in the 370s: a catalogue of eighty heresies together with their "remedies," modeled on the Hellenistic poet Nicander's work listing remedies for poisons and bites. This was a more elaborate, and indeed fanciful, development of Epiphanius's earlier work, the *Ancoratus*, or "well-anchored man," and in it he drew up a "family tree" of heresies and listed them in order of chronological appearance; he derived the number eighty from the number of concubines in the biblical Song of Songs. Epiphanius applies the term *heresy* even to Hellenism and Judaism, and with him the genre has already become scholastic; many of his heresies must be imaginary. The 5th century writer Theodoret, bishop of Cyrrhus in northern Syria, continued this tradition with his *Compendium* of heretical myths; another work, the *Eranistes,* uses the technique of imaginary disputations between an orthodox and a heretical spokesman to refute the heretic. Lists of suitable quotations *(florilegia)* and an appeal to scriptural authority and earlier tradition are features of these works and subsequently become standard techniques of the genre. In the 8th century, John of Damascus composed *De Haeresibus* (On Heresies), which lists 100 heresies, including otherwise unknown and implausible examples; like Epiphanius (whose work he used), he included Judaism, and a final chapter treats Islam in a similar way. Like Theodoret, John balanced heresiology with synthesis or exposition; his *Fount of Knowledge,* or *On Orthodox Faith,* resembles Theodoret's *Exposition* in setting out the essentials of true belief.

In the period between Theodoret and John of Da-

mascus heresiology flourished. A succession of works in both Greek and Latin gave prominence to lists of alleged heresies. In the 7th century, the patriarch Germanos I of Constantinople wrote *On Heresies and Synods,* in which the denunciation of heresy was combined with lists of authoritative conciliar decisions, while the *Synodical Letter* of the patriarch Sophronius of Jerusalem (634 C.E.) anathematized all individual heretics from Simon Magus to Sophronius's own day, and then went on to condemn some thirty-odd sects. In addition, scholastic, or at least formal, condemnation of heresy often occupies space in other works, for instance the 7th century anti-Jewish treatise known as the *Trophies of Damascus,* which begins in this way. After the ending of Byzantine iconoclasm in 843 C.E., the tendency reached its logical conclusion with the so-called Synodikon of Orthodoxy, a lengthy catalogue of heresies to be formally read in the liturgical context of the annual Feast of Orthodoxy. After iconoclasm, too, heretics were frequently depicted in a stylized manner in Byzantine art. The definition of what was orthodox thus took the form of a formal denunciation of deviance. Given the persistence of heresiologies, and their formulaic character, it is often extremely difficult to know whether the heresies claimed to exist in Byzantium were real or not.

By no means were all antiheretical writings purely academic, however. Epiphanius himself was deeply involved in the Origenist controversy of the late 4th century, and the disputes over Donatism and Pelagianism that occupied Augustine in the early 5th century produced a large volume of polemical writing. The early 5th century councils held at Carthage were a major inspiration for such material. Manichaeism and Judaism also presented real targets; indeed, the large quantity of Christian literature condemning Judaism can be seen as akin to, even if not actually a part of, heresiology. Handbooks against heresy were as common in the Latin west between the 4th and 6th centuries as they were in the Greek east. Once again, during the Vandal period in North Africa (430–534 C.E.), Catholics produced quantities of tracts against their Arian rulers, in which they drew on the stereotypes of heresiology and Old Testament denunciations of tyranny.

Throughout late antique religious life, the definitions of orthodoxy and heresy were in competition. It was therefore predictable that developing Islam, too, would soon produce its "heresies"; in contrast, the world of polytheism insisted on few orthodoxies, though it developed a repertoire of arguments against Christianity. Heresiology was born of the fatal urge to prescribe the truth. It grew up in the context of the pluralism of early Christianity (revealed more clearly than ever in the Nag Hammadi texts) and flourished alongside the councils and synods that struggled with the impossible task of defining correct doctrine. It was also a product of the struggle for power within the institutional church. The longer that struggle continued (as it was to do throughout late antiquity and beyond), the more necessary it became for each side to convince itself that it was right, and the more heresiology flourished.

BIBL.: A. Pourkier, *L'hérésiologie chez Épiphane de Salamine* (Paris, 1992).   A.M.C.

Heretics, Laws on

From the 1st century onward the Christian church developed the internal procedures of penance and excommunication to punish baptized believers who strayed from the flock. However, wrong religious belief existed as a potential civil or criminal charge under Roman law only after Constantine incorporated Christianity into the structure of empire. Public prosecution for heresy was a new phenomenon in late antiquity. Between the 4th and 8th centuries a vast body of anti-heretical legislation evolved, far outnumbering the surviving laws against paganism. Orthodox religious belief became the organizing principle of society. Ecclesiastical law interacted with Roman law on a case-by-case basis, defining and categorizing heretical groups and establishing penalties that covered both this life and the next.

Imperial legislation against heretics used two strategies of definition. The first was to prescribe what constituted orthodox belief. The Edict of Thessalonica issued in 380 (*C.Th.* 16.1.2) identified the Nicene Creed as the orthodox position. It appealed to the authority of the apostles and the bishop of Rome and went on to divide those who took the name of *Christiani Catholici* from the *reliqui*, who were to be considered as demented and insane. This is no mere rhetoric: under Roman law, to be declared insane entailed disqualification from most civil legal actions. This law is often considered by modern scholars to have settled the question of orthodoxy, by linking right belief with citizenship of the Roman empire. However, it is one thing to issue blanket legislation and another to secure a legal conviction in individual cases. In 395 Aurelianus, the proconsul of Asia, was obviously at a loss as to whether to classify the Luciferian bishop Heuresius as Catholic or not. He addressed an appeal for clarification to the emperors, which resulted in *C.Th.* 16.5.28: "Those persons who may be discovered to deviate, even in a minor point of doctrine, from the tenets and path of the Catholic religion are included under the designation of heretics and must be subject to the sanctions which have been issued against them." Heuresis was thus a heretic, but a high degree of theological skill had to be employed to classify him as such.

The second strategy behind the imperial legislation was to name known heretical groups and apply both civil and criminal penalties against their adherents. Book sixteen, title five of the *Theodosian Code,* "De haereticis," details a bewildering array of heresies and

their corresponding penalties. Neither the heresies condemned nor the sanctions against them remained constant. Two factors were influential: the fluidity of Christian doctrine in deciding what was to be classified as orthodox or heretical opinion, and the personal belief of the emperor himself. In 428 Emperors Theodosius and Valentinian attempted to clarify the situation by classifying existing heretical groups in a hierarchical order with a corresponding hierarchy of punishments, "since not all should be punished with the same severity" (*C.Th.* 16.5.65). The constitution provides interesting evidence of how the relative threats from each particular heresy were perceived by the authorities at the time.

The most commonly cited penalties attacked the right of named heretical groups to worship together or to teach their doctrines. Their churches were to be confiscated, religious meetings banned, and any building or estate in which meetings were held forfeited to the crown (*C.Th.* 16.5.3, 4, 5, 22). The effectiveness of these measures is thrown into doubt by a constitution (16.5.4) that states that heretical assemblies often took place through the connivance of the judges, the very people who should have been implementing the imperial laws. In 392 a fine of ten pounds of gold was imposed on all heretical clergy, with a corresponding fine against judges who failed to enforce the law (16.5.21). In Africa this measure was extended to include any member of the Donatist church. Crushing fines were inflicted, graded according to the offender's rank (16.5.52).

Penalties affecting the civil standing of heretics were also widely invoked. The Manichaeans were declared incapable of making wills or taking inheritances in 381. In 389 the same penalty was inflicted on the Eunomians, although it was revoked in 394, reimposed and again revoked in 395, again revoked in 399 (having meanwhile been apparently reenacted), and finally reimposed in 410, clearly displaying the vicissitudes of imperial policy. Heretics were also excluded from the higher branches of public service.

In 297 the death penalty was prescribed against the Manichaeans (*Collatio* 15.3.6). For Diocletian their crime was obviously not heresy, as he was in the process of persecuting Christians en masse. The Manichaeans were, rather, a deadly threat from Persia to be associated with the crimes of *maleficium* (sorcery) and treason. The evocation of the death penalty and the association with *maleficium*, however, acted as precedents for later legislation when the Manichaeans were classified as a heretical sect. In the late 4th century Priscillianism was assimilated with Manichaeism and the death penalty applied, to the outrage of most ecclesiastics (Sulpicius Severus, *Chron.* 2.50). Similarly the more extremist heretical groups, such as the Encratites, Hydroparastatae, and Saccophori, were classified as subsections of Manichaeism and subjected to the same dire penalties as in Diocletian's earlier law (*C.Th.*

16.5.9.1; 382). In 510 the emperor Anastasius standardized the death penalty for any sect associated with the doctrines of Mani, and this remained the law under Justinian.

In general, however, the imperial legislation aimed at repentance rather than punishment. A sincere conversion to orthodox belief ensured that the accused could escape the weight of the law, even if that conversion was made during a civil or criminal prosecution (*C.Th.* 16.5.25 and 16.5.41). This clause acted as a salve to the conscience of many late antique bishops who remained unsure how much the church should rely on imperial legislation to deal with heretics. Yet this legislation itself had often been issued in response to requests from ecclesiastical authorities, who were also intimately involved in its enforcement. The laws and procedures against heretics that were established in late antiquity became the precedents for early medieval canon law.

BIBL.: L. Barnard, "The Criminalization of Heresy in the Later Roman Empire: A Sociopolitical Device?" *Journal of Legal History* 16 (1995): 121–146. J. Gaudemet, "Politique ecclésiastique et législation religieuse après l'édit de Théodose I de 380," in idem, *Droit et société aux derniers siècles de l'empire romain* (Naples, 1992), 175–196.   C.HUM.

Hieroglyphs

Hieroglyphic writing, normally used on monumental inscriptions, was the formal writing system of ancient Egypt, in use from about 3000 B.C.E., at the beginning of the dynastic period, down through the late 4th century C.E. Hieroglyphs rarely appear on papyrus, on which were used the cursive scripts known as hieratic and, after 650 B.C.E., demotic. Herodotus (2.36) first distinguished two systems at the time of his visit: "sacred writing" *(ta hira)* and popular writing *(ta dēmotika).* It was Clement of Alexandria who first distinguished the three different systems (hieroglyphic, hieratic, demotic) and used the phrase *ta hierogluphika* (*Strom.* 5.4.20–21), although the Greek phrase had already appeared in Diodorus. By the time of Egypt's incorporation into the Roman empire, hieroglyphic writing was already severely restricted, and its rapid decline may be traced at the temple in Esna, on Roman-period funerary stelae that feature predominantly Greek and demotic rather than hieroglyphic writing, and in magical texts. The end of the ancient understanding of hieroglyphic writing is clearly traced in magical texts called the "Horus-on-the-crocodile" stelae *(cippi),* dating from about the mid-Ptolemaic period down through the Roman period. Here the "pseudohieroglyphic" writing demonstrates the purely graphical, symbolic understanding of hieroglyphs.

Occasionally hieroglyphic writing was used to translate short Greek and Latin texts in the first two centuries C.E. Priests were still required to know hieroglyphic characters in the 2nd century (*P Tebtunis* 2.291.40–43; 162 C.E.), and a (small) guild of hieroglyphic carvers still functioned in the early 2nd century at Oxyrhynchus (*P Oxy.* 7.1029.24–26; 107 C.E.). From the standard repertory of around seven hundred signs, the number of signs grew to more than seven thousand by the Ptolemaic period. The use of cryptographic writing in this period enhanced the view that hieroglyphic writing recorded a symbolic rather than phonetic writing system. This view, seen already in the writing of the Egyptian priest Chairemon and in Tacitus (*Annals* 11.14) was crystallized by Horapollo, who wrote his allegorical treatise on hieroglyphics probably in the 4th century. The last certainly dated hieroglyphic inscription was recorded on the walls of the Philae temple on the twenty-fourth day of August in 394 C.E.; the last cartouche now known dates to Constantius from Armant.

BIBL.: Erik Iversen, *The Myth of Egypt and Its Hieroglyphs in European Tradition* (Princeton, 1961). Robert K. Ritner, "Hieroglyphic," in *The World's Writing Systems,* ed. Peter T. Daniels and William Bright (New York, 1996). Alessandro Roccati, "Writing Egyptian: Scripts and Speeches at the End of Pharaonic Civilization," in *Life in a Multi-cultural Society: Egypt from Cambyses to Constantine and Beyond,* ed. Janet H. Johnson (Chicago, 1992). Heike Sternberg-El Hotabi, "Der Untergang der Hieroglyphenschrift," *Chronique d'Égypte* 69 (1994): 218–245.   J.G.M.

Himerius

Born in Bithynian Prusias by ca. 320, Himerius was an accomplished Greek orator and teacher of rhetoric. He spent much of his teaching career in Athens, where he had studied. The future churchmen Gregory of Nazianzus and Basil of Caesarea numbered among his pupils there in the 350s. After Julian became sole emperor in 361, he summoned Himerius and other pagan men of learning. However, any hopes they had for a revival of polytheism or for personal advancement under the pagan emperor were dashed with Julian's death in 363. It is unclear what Himerius was doing in the years immediately after Julian's death or, for that matter, during the Apostate's brief reign. But by the middle or late 360s, after the death in Athens of his professional rival Prohaeresius, Himerius resumed his teaching there, perhaps finally winning a publicly supported chair. He died after 383.

What survives of Himerius's oratory ranges from mere titles to fragments and excerpts to complete speeches. Much of his oratory sprang from his role as a teacher. Outside of the classroom, his orations before many Roman officials and before two emperors, Constantius and Julian, are indicative of his status as a rhetor. His style is highly florid. He was heavily influenced by Greek poetry, especially lyric; he often gives the impression of being a poet "trapped" in prose. His prose rhythm is modern, favoring stress over syllabic quantity. Himerius's younger contemporary Eunapius and the Byzantine patriarch Photius were appreciative of his oratory. Modern commentators have generally not been sympathetic, though, seeing an excess of rhetorical ornament and an absence of serious content in his work.

BIBL.: T. D. Barnes, "Himerius and the Fourth Century," *Classical Philology* 82 (1987): 206–225. A. Colonna, ed., *Himerii declamationes et orationes* (Rome, 1951). H. Gärtner, "Himerios," *Reallexikon für Antike und Christentum* 15 (1991): 167–173.   R.P.

Himyar

A tribe of South Arabia, in about 110 B.C.E., Himyar formed into a kingdom and progressively unified the entire south of the Arabian Peninsula. Its capital was Zafār (130 km south of Sana'a), where the royal palace of Raydān was located. Until the 3rd century, Himyar was frequently called dhū-Raydān, after the name of the dynastic palace, in accordance with a practice common in Yemen. In the ancient languages of South Arabia, written in a consonantal alphabet, Himyar is called Hmyrm; in Ge'ez, Hamer; and in Greek, Homēritai or Ameritai. "Himyar," which is the Arabic vocalization of the noun, does not seem to be an accurate representation of the ancient pronunciation, which was probably "Humayr" or "Hamayr."

The first certified use of Himyar is found in an inscription from the Hadhramaut dating from the late 1st century B.C.E. (*Répertoire d'epigraphie sémitique* [RES] 2687). It is certain, however, that Himyarite autonomy preceded that date: a Himyarite prince bearing the name dhū-Raydān is mentioned in a Sabaic text from the 1st century B.C.E. (*RES* 4336), and in any case, the beginning of the Himyarite era was 110 B.C.E. (plus or minus a few years). During that period, Himyarite territory was confined to the southern half of western Yemen, between Aden and Dhamar.

Toward the end of the 1st century B.C.E., Himyar and Sheba joined to form a single state, whose rulers bore the title king of Sheba and dhū-Raydān. Various indications suggest that it was Himyar that annexed Sheba. For the first time, a tribe from the western Yemen mountains played a major role; prior to that, the tribes at the foot of the mountains bordering the desert basin in the interior had been ascendant. According to *Periplus of the Erythraean Sea* (paragraphs 16, 23, and 31), Himyar possessed dependencies in Africa at the time.

Sheba recovered its independence in about 100 C.E. and entered a long period of conflicts with Himyar. Himyar was finally victorious in the late 3rd century, annexing Sheba, conquering the Hadhramaut, and expelling the Abyssinians, who had occupied the Yemen coast for a century. The ruler who accomplished this military feat, Shammir Yuhar'ish, king of Sheba and dhū-Raydān, added "the Hadhramaut and Yamnat" to

his title. The meaning of *Yamnat,* which appears only in this title, is in dispute: it may refer to territories south *(ymnt)* of Himyar, between Aden and the Hadhramaut. This same Shammir is mentioned incidentally in 328 in the funerary inscription of Imru' al-Qays al-Bad', "king of all Arabs," in an-Namāmra in southern Syria.

During the 3rd century, the Sabaean and Hadramitic rulers extended their influence over the Arabian desert tribes neighboring Yemen. The Himyarites followed the same policy in the 4th century. They consolidated their authority over what is today Asir and over tribes near Yemen. Their armies ventured into Yamāma and central Arabia as far as the outskirts of modern Riyadh; altercations occurred with the tribes of Ma'add and Imru' al-Qays al-Bad'.

The Himyarite dynasty officially adopted monotheism in the late 4th century. The first two inscriptions that reflected that choice were made by King Malkīkarib Yuha'min, who reigned jointly with his sons Abīkarib As'ad and Dhara'amar Ayman; the inscriptions date from January 384. The phrasing makes it impossible to determine to what religion the dynasty converted; according to Islamic Arab tradition, however, it was Judaism, which was preponderant in western Arabia at that time.

In the 5th century, the Himyarites consolidated their domination over central and western Arabia by establishing a protectorate over Ma'add: the foundation of that principality is celebrated in an inscription engraved on the rocks of Ma'sal al-Jumh, 240 km west-southwest of Riyadh. In this undated text, which may have been written in the 440s, Himyarite rulers Abīkarib As'ad and his son Hassān Yuha'min added a new element to their title, "and Arabs of the High Country *(Tawd)* and the Coast *(Tihāma)."* "The high country" may designate Nejd, and "the coast," regions on the shore of the Red Sea across from Mecca. That episode can be linked to an event reported by Islamic Arab tradition: a Himyarite ruler named Hassān is said to have placed Hujr ibn 'Amr, nicknamed "Ākil al-murār," or "he who feeds on bitter herbs," a prince from the Kinda tribe, on the throne of Ma'add.

In June 521 another Himyarite king, Ma'dīkarib Ya'fur, engraved a new inscription on Ma'sal al-Jumh, thus declaring that Himyarite authority had been reestablished. The purpose of this second act was probably to subjugate al-Hārith ibn 'Amr, grandson of Hujr, known through Islamic tradition and through Nonnosos (Photius, *Bibl.*). Several sources, and in particular the hagiography of the Christians of Nairan, suggest that Ma'dīkarib Ya'fur was placed on the throne by Christian Abyssinians, that he was Christian, and that he acted on behalf of Byzantium.

The pro-Christian and pro-Byzantine orientation of Ma'dikarib stands in contrast to the prudent policy of his predecessors, probably Jewish or Judaized for the most part. No doubt in reaction to this Christianization, a show of force between June 521 and May 522 brought a Jew named Yūsuf As'ar Yath'ar to the throne. He bore the new title "king of all tribes," which reflected his contested legitimacy.

Yūsuf immediately massacred the Abyssinians garrisoned in Zafār and persecuted autochthonous Christians. The execution of several hundred believers, including al-Hārith ibn Ka'b (*Arethas* in Greek), in Nairan in November 523 had serious repercussions throughout the east. The consequences were immediate. The religious authorities of Alexandria in Egypt and the Byzantine emperor Justin I (518–527) asked the Abyssinian ruler Elesboas (Kaleb Ella Asbeha) to intervene militarily. A large number of ships were amassed and others were built to cross the strait of al-Mandeb. A solemn prayer for the success of the expedition was uttered in the cathedral of Axum, the Abyssinian capital, "after Holy Pentecost" in 525. The Abyssinian army set out for Arabia in seventy ships and crushed the Himyarite forces of King Yūsuf. According to several sources, the king was captured and executed; other sources relate that he died when he drove his horse into the sea. The defeat and disappearance of Yūsuf occurred between 18 May 525 and the death of Emperor Justin on 1 August 527, probably during the summer of 525. The Himyarite kingdom was replaced by an Abyssinian protectorate, and the population was converted to Christianity by force.

Himyar left relatively few architectural remains: a single monument merits mention, the famous Marib dam. In contrast, a considerable number of Himyarite inscriptions have come down to us, nearly all of them in Sabaic, no doubt to assert that Himyar was the legitimate heir of Sheba. It seems certain that the language spoken by the Himyarites was not Sabaic, as demonstrated in two texts from the federated tribes that are written in a local language. In the spoken Himyaritic language surviving in the 10th century, described by Yemenite scholar al-Hasan al-Hamdānī (893–971), some of the characteristics present in these documents were still in existence.

The Himyar tribe disappeared in the early Middle Ages, nibbled away by nomad Arab groups, most of them from Madhhij, who settled in the tribe's territory or along its periphery.

BIBL.: Jacques Briend and Christian Robin, "Sheba, I: Dans la Bible; II: Dans les inscriptions d'Arabie du Sud," *Supplément au dictionnaire de la Bible,* 70 (Paris, 1966), cols. 1043–1254. D. G. Letsios, "Die Äthiopisch-himyaratische Kriege des 6. Jarhhunderts," *Jahrbuch für Österreichische Byzantinistik* 41 (1991): 25–41. Christian Robin, ed., *L'Arabie antique de Karib'īl à Mahomet: Nouvelles données sur l'histoire des Arabes grâce aux inscriptions* (Aix-en-Provence, 1991–1993). I. Shahid, *The Martyrs of Nairan* (Brussels, 1971). J. Tubach, "Die Anfänge des Christentums in Südarabien," *Parole de l'orient* 18 (1993): 101–111.

C.J.R.

Hippodrome

A structure designed for chariot racing (Latin *circus*), the hippodrome had its origins in early Greek athletic practice. It differed in function from the stadium (which had a parallel form, but was for foot races) and in design from the semicircular theater (for dramatic and comic performances) and the elliptical amphitheater (for gladiatorial and animal exhibitions).

The standard hippodrome design was an elongated hairpin shape, with seating (stone or wood-on-stone arcading) along both sides joining in a curve at one end and interrupted at the other, straight end by the functional *carceres* (Greek *kankella, thurai*), which contained the gates from which the chariots began their race. The track itself normally measured about 450 m in length and about 70 to 80 m in width. Races were run around two goalposts (Latin *metae*; Greek *kamptēres*), set at either end of the track's interior. Between them stretched a low barrier, the *spina* (Greek *euripos*), on which stood devices to register the successive laps in each competition: particularly sets of sculpted dolphins, which could be reversed in position one by one. The *spina* customarily had other adornments, as well, appropriate to the setting. Following the example of Augustus, who erected an Egyptian obelisk on that of the Circus Maximus in Rome, Constantius II placed another there, and an obelisk that he destined for Constantinople was finally set up in its hippodrome under Theodosius I. Its *spina* was decorated with statuary and other ornaments, such as the famous bronze Serpent Column of the Athenians, brought from Delphi.

Races consisted of sets *(missus),* each of seven laps around the course. In Roman practice, by the end of the republic, ten to twelve sets were run as one event, but from the 1st century C.E. onward, these were increased to as many as twenty-four. The chariot *quadrigae* (four-horse teams) and their charioteers were sponsored by the circus factions and excited increasingly impassioned popular attachment.

Hippodromes were also used at times for gladiatorial games, special presentations, and, above all, ceremonial processions and displays. Such mass public entertainments, sponsored by the state, were the only occasions when the sovereign regularly confronted the populace face to face, and increasing use was made of them for political propaganda, ritual, and commemoration. By the late 3rd century, hippodromes were components of palace complexes, their events linked to ceremonies surrounding the emperor.

Chariot racing declined and disappeared with the disruption of Roman civilization in the 5th to 7th centuries, though it survived as late as the 12th century in Constantinople. Decaying hippodromes were treated as stone quarries. The remains of some have been excavated (Carthage, Caesarea Maritima) or their shapes can still be identified (Thessalonica). The leading specimens were Rome's Circus Maximus and the hippodrome in Constantinople, both connected to palace areas and dominated by an imperial box (Latin *pulvinar;* Greek *kathisma*). The former (only the chief of several hippodromes in Rome) could accommodate some 150,000 spectators (seated by class divisions). Its ruins were gradually pillaged and used for medieval fortifications; little but its shape now survives. Constantinople's hippodrome, first constructed by Septimius Severus, seated at least 100,000. It continued in diminished use until the Fourth Crusade (1204), when the crusaders looted it (taking, for example, the famous four bronze horses of Venice's San Marco). In its battered state it was still the site of tournaments and limited entertainments, but it was a ruin when the city fell to the Turks (1453), who maintained it partially as an arena (the Atmeydanı) for horsemanship and entertainments adjacent to the sultan's palaces. Today the two obelisks and the Serpent Column of its *spina* may still be seen.

BIBL.: Gilbert Dagron, *Naissance d'une capitale: Constantinople et ses institutions de 330 à 451* (Paris, 1974). R. Guilland, "Études sur l'hippodrome de byzance: Les courses de l'hippodrome," *Byzantinoslavica* 27 (1966): 26–40. C. Heucke, *Circus und Hippodrom als politischer Raum* (Hildesheim, 1994). J. H. Humphrey, *Roman Circuses: Arenas for Chariot Racing* (London, 1986).   J.W.B.

Holiness

Greeks and Romans shared the widespread belief in the existence of a multitude of beings that possessed numinous power and were distributed all over the world. These could be objects, trees, animals, or places, and also spirits—for instance those of the deceased—or gods as formed in man's imagination. Their beneficent or damaging activities, though mostly restricted to certain areas, were believed to determine man's well-being, both individually and socially, and man could not avoid or directly interfere with their influence. These beings and everything owned by them were conceived of as holy (Greek *hieros,* Latin *sacer*) and separate from the rest of the world *(bebēlon, profanum).* In approaching them, in particular by means of prayer or ritual, to render them benevolent, man had to be blameless *(hosios, sanctus).* Occasionally these pairs of terms and their derivatives, coined to denote the corresponding qualities in the communication between divinity and men, overlap in their meaning. Similarly *hagnos* denotes both the holiness of gods or chthonic spirits because of their awfulness (*Homeric Hymn to Demeter* 203; Hesiod, *Works and Days* 122f.) and the purity of elements, virgin goddesses, or ritually blameless persons (Pindar, *Pythians* 1.20, 9.16; Sophocles, *Antigone* 889). But mostly the two aspects of the holy are rendered by two different terms in Greek and Latin. In postclassical Greek *hagnos* was restricted to poetical usage and replaced by *hagios.*

The world was thought to be "full of gods" (Thales, *Fragmente der Vorsokratiker* A 23 Diels), and this belief eventually led to the philosophical conception of the holiness of the universe (Hippocrates, *De morbo sacro* 1). Accordingly, a person or an object could become *hieros* or *sacer* through a sacral act. Such an endowment with holiness particularly applied to priests and rulers, who had to mediate between gods and men and keep their society in harmony with the divine order of the world. But the transfer into the ownership of the gods was a curse for the sinner, whose crime his society could not cope with through legal means.

Biblical Hebrew, which mirrors the teaching of priests and prophets rather than popular beliefs, has only one word and its derivatives for the two aspects of holiness: *qadosh.* Only God the creator of everything was regarded holy (Psalm 96); the created world was profane and without its own share of holiness. The worship of created or man-made objects and the cult of the deceased were shunned accordingly. But because of his sovereignty and omnipresence, God could impart his holiness to whatever animate or inanimate being he pleased, such as, for instance, the temple where he dwells (Ps. 11) and the people of his election (Lev. 11). They were given God's holiness through the Torah, with its commandments for the religious and social life. Thus an area of holiness was being maintained in the profane rest of the world (Ps. 18). This is why the Greek Bible has *hagios* as the only equivalent of *qadosh.* It uses *hieros* and its derivatives only where the meaning of a coined term is neutral (for instance, *hiereus,* priest). Philo, without a thorough knowledge of Hebrew, used *hieros* and *hagios* as synonyms (*De virtutibus* 119).

Christian texts of the first two centuries testify to the very same conception both in Greek and Latin. *Hagios* and *sanctus* are used like *qadosh* in Hebrew, and *hieros* and *sacer* are avoided, apparently as referring to pagan religion (Tertullian, *Apologeticus* 9.3). The sanctification of the believer was no longer expected from the Torah but was regarded as the gift of the Holy Ghost, promised to those who firmly believed themselves redeemed by and attached to Christ and who tried to live according to his example (Rom. 8; Eph. 5). Baptism and the Eucharist reminded the believer of his being called to salvation and the Lord's continuous presence among his followers. This sanctification applied only to the congregation of the holy (Rom. 8), and no ritual or man-made object—as, for instance, the church building—could be called holy (Clement of Alexandria, *Stromata* 7.5; Lactantius, *Institutiones* 4.13.26).

Christian ideas of how holiness could be conveyed and its blessings attained changed along with the development of the cult, particularly in late antiquity. The cult came to include not only sacramental acts but also the worship of the tombs of martyrs and the relics of saints (*Acts of Polycarpus;* Rufinus, *Hist.eccl.* 10.7, 11.28). Thus materialized holiness became present even in everyday life in many places where one could get hold of its blessings, very much as in the pagan tradition. The longing for this presence, a pervading phenomenon in religious life, could be fulfilled by religious practice only. Thus Christians, too, came to believe that sacramental acts or physical contact with sacred objects turned the profane into the holy (*Acts of Cyprian;* Eusebius, *Hist.eccl.* 10.4). From the 3rd century onward *hieros/hagios* and *sacer/sanctus* were used in Christian and non-Christian texts without distinction.

Very early the idea of physical purity, required in all acts of ritual, had been understood in ethical terms, too (Herodotus 6.86). Under the dominant influence of dualism, both Gnostic and Platonic, philosophers and theologians in late antiquity gave a spiritual interpretation to this understanding. Ascetic life and cognition of the divine could free the soul from the bonds and pollutions of matter and eventually lead the way to man's transcendent home. A person who was considered to have reached this goal in his bodily existence owned, in the view of his fellow men, superhuman power that he was supposed to use for the benefit of the weak and suppressed, as a patron, healer, exorcist, teacher, or prophet. Thus holiness could be seen and touched not only in sacred acts and objects but also in living human beings, and it became an important factor in social and political life. This applies to the Christian saints, such as Antony and other monks and hermits, and also to the many pagan wonderworkers, like Apollonius of Tyana. To Christians this holiness was a visible gift of the Holy Ghost; to philosophers it was the ultimate goal of their striving for knowledge and illumination beyond the limitations of language. Some Neoplatonists were interested in nonverbal communication with the divine, called theurgy (Iamblichus, *De mysteriis*), and were aware of its affinity to mystery cults, where the holy was made visible to the initiated through elaborate ritual devices. Pagan intellectuals such as the emperor Julian highly valued both mystery cults and theurgy. In this context, miracle working indicated the holy life of the perfect philosopher.

Philosophy had been taught as *ars vitae* for many centuries. According to the philosophical conceptions of late antiquity, the perfect life led toward salvation (*sotēria*) beyond the physical existence through sanctification, achieved by asceticism and knowledge. This was common ground for philosophy and the Christian religion, which was called philosophy by many of the faithful. The common believer, however, both Christian and pagan, trusted in the presence of the holy in his environment, where he could get a share of its blessings through prayer and ritual. Accordingly, the holiness of rulers and priests, the guardians of social order, became increasingly important and was institutionally secured, as can be seen, in titles and ceremonies.

BIBL.: P. Brown, *The Cult of the Saints* (Chicago, 1981). C. Colpe, ed., *Die Diskussion um das Heilige* (Darmstadt, 1977). A. Dihle, "Heilig," *Reallexikon für Antike und Christentum* 14 (1988): 1–63.   A.D.

Holy Fools

The holy fool may be seen as a response to Christianity's success. By the 5th century, ascetic literature, hagiography, and historiography spoke of those who deliberately chose a spiritual vocation in the guise of madness or social disrepute. The basic components of the theme were concealment of ascetic identity, deliberate suffering of physical and social abuse, self-abasement, and moral instruction.

Some accounts described the fool as a presence that disrupted the monastic community. Palladius's account of the "nun who feigned madness" (*Lausiac History* 34) is perhaps the earliest Christian description of a holy fool. A vision revealed to St. Piteroum that the truly pious ascetic was none other than a young, nameless nun, mistreated by her community as a simple-minded fool. When Piteroum made known the nun's spiritual condition, an outcry of repentance filled her convent and honor was showered on her. Unable to bear the attention, the nun fled. Palladius narrated the episode in terms that challenged the solitary ascetic as self-righteous and the monastic life as complacent.

Most accounts present the fool as an urban figure, living as a beggar among the city's poor and outcast. Sometimes, as in the case of the famed Symeon of Emesa, the fool provoked public outrage with behavior that deliberately violated the basic tenets of the social community. Fools are portrayed as inciting others to beat, insult, and torment them. The veneer of their madness or marginality demonstrated perfect self-mastery in a context that prevented devotion or adulation from others. Again, a profound moral lesson was offered when such stories were told. The pious were challenged as vainglorious, the Christian community was admonished regarding its poor and mistreated, and the imitation of Christ was invoked in starkly didactic terms.

Admirers such as Evagrius Scholasticus (*Hist.eccl.* 1.21, 4.34) or John of Ephesus (*Lives* 12, 51, 52, 53) presented holy fools as those who had chosen a surpassingly difficult form of ascetic practice, one that required complete *apatheia*. Hagiographers frequently cited 1 Corinthians 3:18 and 4:10 to defend these saints, but the roots of the theme as a religious and civic motif run deep in biblical prophetic tradition, as well as through Graeco-Roman philosophical discussion. The anecdotes and aphorisms ascribed to Diogenes the Cynic, for example, often glorify a similar kind of behavior with similar moral implications.

However, such spiritual masters as Isaac the Syrian and Symeon the New Theologian also warned that some ascetics took the guise of a fool as an excuse to indulge their own desires, misleading the credulous, who fawned over their care.

Whether as a literary theme or an ascetic practice, holy folly overturned every achievement by which Christianity might have claimed itself triumphant. In hagiography, the motive was invariably that of rousing the world from its self-deceptive stupor for the salvation of souls. In eyewitness reports, however, the motivation was presented in humbler terms: salvation of the self through total self-annihilation.

BIBL.: Derek Krueger, *Symeon the Holy Fool: Leontius' Life and the Late Antique City* (Berkeley, 1996). Lennart Rydén, "The Holy Fool," in *The Byzantine Saint: University of Birmingham Fourteenth Spring Symposium of Byzantine Studies,* ed. Sergei Hackel (London, 1981). John Saward, *Perfect Fools: Folly for Christ's Sake in Catholic and Orthodox Spirituality* (Oxford, 1980).   S.A.H.

Homosexuality

The word *homosexuality* was unknown to antique Mediterranean peoples. There was no single term that encompassed all sexual relations between persons of the same sex. In considering three areas—desire, acts, and pleasure—we can say that (with the exception of the Jews) the ancients treated desire and pleasure indiscriminately, whether between two men, two women (few occurrences), or a man and a woman. Physicians wrote that pleasure between men was more tiring. The sexual acts themselves belonged to the realm of ethics and the law. Relations between men were classified according to the age of the partners (e.g., pederasty, the love of an adult male for a prepubescent boy), status (freeman, slave, or citizen), and privileged position (active, *pedicare, irrumare,* versus passive, *muliebria pati,* "to submit to what is done to women"; in Greek, *hubrizein,* "to exert force upon another," and *aselgainein,* "to defile oneself").

The peoples of the Mediterranean varied in their attitudes toward each of these elements. The Phoenicians allowed sexual practices such as fellatio (without discriminating between the sexes), even within a ritual framework, something that repelled the Greeks and Romans. For Jews, the general concept of homosexuality is present and the relation condemned, without ever being precisely named: "If a man also lie with mankind, as he lieth with a woman, both of them . . . shall surely be put to death" (Lev. 18:22 and 20:13). Philo used the word *allēlobainein,* "to mount one upon the other," which encompasses every status and every position. Under Justinian, the terms of the Septuagint (lying with mankind) became part of the law and sanctioned a general repression of homosexual relations.

In the 3rd century, even though the rights of Roman citizens were extended to all free persons of the empire, every new citizen kept most of his local private rights or those relating to his place of origin; hence, he kept the mores of his people. However, certain emperors wished to bring the mores of the Roman world as a whole into line with those of Rome, and, regarding sexual relations between men, they even modified Roman law. The culmination of that effort of harmonization was the *Collatio legum mosaicarum et romanarum;* book 6 is devoted to mores.

In complete opposition to a specific trait of classic Athenian civilization, Romans had a real fear of having young citizens used as partners by adults. Any man who seduced or raped a Roman boy was committing debauchery, as if he had defiled a married matron, a widow, or a divorced woman in a casual relationship (outside marriage or concubinage). Adult citizens who gave in to other men's desires and "submitted to what is done to women" (*muliebria pati,* Table of Herclea), were stripped of the right to speak on behalf of others (their defiled mouths could not speak truthfully) and denied access to municipal functions. Like criminals, they lost some of their rights as citizens.

Men of Greek culture continued to fall in love with young boys, as attested (disapprovingly) by Libanius in the late 4th century (*Orat.* 53), while Romans restated and wished to impose their horror of sexual submission in relations between men.

Slaves (even very young ones), eunuchs, and male prostitutes, often dressed as women and with their body hair removed, were frequently used in socially acceptable relations, those that placed the citizen in a position of mastery. The use of such persons in no way prevented the expression of love.

Throughout the empire, Roman law attempted to curb pederasty, calling it debauchery of a prepubescent citizen *(puer).* In the late 4th century, such efforts were unsuccessful.

Emperors wanted to limit, first, the prostitution of slaves, and second and more important, that of free persons, by those who had power over them. Septimius Severus protected slaves from the masters who prostituted them, a measure adopted by Theodosius II and Leo I. The law also attempted to prevent free citizens from selling their body. Philip the Arab banned male prostitution. In 342, then in 390, imperial constitutions, the interpretation of which is in dispute, condemned selling one's own body (in 390, being burned at the stake was the punishment). Later, repression targeted all passive homosexuals (and not just male prostitutes); a constitution of 438 condemned them to death by fire.

In the west, the Breviary of Alaric limited the condemnation to passive homosexuals, while in the east, Justinian extended it to active ones as well. Justinian hesitated between total castration, capital punishment (*Novella* of 535, reinstated in 726 in the *Eklogē*), and penance (538 and 559). The generalized repression of relations conducted by adults with young citizens, an extension of Roman law, began before the Constitution of Caracalla, by which Roman citizenship was extended to all free persons of the empire. The repression of male prostitution followed in the 3rd century. Christianity did not play a role in these measures. For centuries, the repression of passive homosexuality entailed a loss of civil rights. Beginning with Theodosius II in 438, the new punishment was a death sentence, which echoed the wording of Leviticus. Finally, it was Justinian who (under Christian influence?) condemned all types of sexual relations between men.

Christianity, even apart from Judaism, condemned certain homosexual relations among both men and women. The *Apocalypse of Peter* (2nd century) depicts hell peopled with men who pretended to be women and women who slept with other women. That punishment also appears in *The Apocalypse of Paul*, from the late 4th century. The apocryphal Epistle of Barnabas condemns fellatio and the seduction of young men; Hippolytus's *Apostolic Tradition* refuses baptism to men who are *luxuriosi;* the Council of Elvira (canon 71) definitively refuses communion to those who have debauched young boys. We learn from Augustine that men were tortured to get them to confess their passive homosexuality (*muliebria pati, De civ.Dei* 6.8).

In antiquity itself, homosexuality—especially passive homosexuality—while broadly practiced, was not only condemned morally and sometimes legally but was also considered by its opponents as a cause of general urban decadence, leading to a decline in defense capacities and slowing population growth. It was the subject of ethical debates. In discriminating between valued acts and shameful acts, these debates, whose aim was to preserve the superior status of citizens, contributed to the heinous repression practiced throughout late antiquity.

BIBL.: Eva Cantarella, *Secondo natura: La bisessualità nel mondo antico* (Rome, 1988); Eng. trans.: *Bisexuality in the Ancient World,* trans. Cormac Ó'Cuilleanáin (New Haven, 1992). James Boswell, *Christianity, Social Tolerance and Homosexuality: Gay People in Western Europe from the Beginning of the Christian Era to the Fourteenth Century* (Chicago, 1980). Aline Rousselle, *La contamination spirituelle* (Paris, 1997).   A.R.

Honestiores/Humiliores

Late Roman society was divided into two broad social categories, *honestiores,* the upper orders or privileged classes, and *humiliores,* the lower orders or common people. The *honestiores/humiliores* distinction does not appear consistently in a legal code until the *Pauli Sententiae* (ca. 300), and the words are nowhere given precise definition, but they or their variants were well understood and commonly used from the late 2nd century onward to make a broad division within the empire's free population. The root of *honestiores* is clearly *honor,* or political office, but as so often with Roman

language of social privilege, the word implies a moral and social superiority deriving from a combination of character, birth, education, political office, and wealth. Conventionally included among the *honestiores* were town councillors (*decuriones, curiales),* imperial officials, and senators. The term *humiliores* (or the variants *tenuiores, plebeii*) was used for the vast majority of the free population, who could claim no special status deriving from high birth, office, or wealth.

The distinction was important, since social status always had a bearing on legal status at Rome. Judges routinely asked litigants, "What is your social rank?" *(Cuius condicionis es?),* and the response would influence the judge's conduct of the trial and the nature of the penalties inflicted on the guilty. Litigants of low status found it harder to prevail in court and were liable to much harsher penalties than *honestiores.*

BIBL.: Peter Garnsey, *Social Status and Legal Privilege in the Roman Empire* (Oxford, 1970).   S.B.

Horapollon

Horapollon was an Egyptian pagan of the 5th century who wrote a treatise in two books on the interpretation of hieroglyphs. A Greek text of this work, entitled *Hieroglyphica,* survives, with a preface in which the author claims to have written originally in Egyptian. The manifest incompetence of Horapollon in Egyptology would suggest that this claim is no more than a pose to inspire confidence in the revelations to follow. The work is, however, important in illustrating the self-consciousness of Egyptian pagans with reference to their past in the face of an encompassing Christianity. Horapollon's family can be seen from the fragments of Damascius's *Life of Isidore* to have come from the Panopolite nome, which was an important center of 5th century Egyptian polytheism. The father of the author of the *Hieroglyphica* was an Egyptian priest by the name of Asclepiades, who wrote a history of Egypt going back more than thirty thousand years. Asclepiades's father was also called Horapollon, and his brother was the holy Heraiscus, who was likewise versed in ancient Egyptian traditions. With their names evoking both Hellenic and Egyptian divinities, the family of Horapollon well illustrates the efforts of late antique Hellenism to recover its pre-Christian past.

BIBL.: G. W. Bowersock, *Hellenism in Late Antiquity* (Ann Arbor and Cambridge, 1989), 56–61. J. Maspero, "Horapollon et la fin du paganisme égyptien," *Bulletin de l'Institut Français d'Archéologie Orientale* 11 (1914): 164–195.   G.W.B.

Horoscopes

A horoscope is, in its simplest form, a diagram showing the positions, at a given moment, of the sun, the moon, and the five planets known in antiquity: normally at the moment of birth of a particular individual, but also, in some instances, that of a city or a nation. Celestial divination of various forms was practiced in Mesopotamia in the second millennium B.C.E., and the first preserved individual horoscopes were produced there just after the middle of the first millennium. In the Hellenistic and imperial periods, diviners, often known as "Chaldaeans," began to draw up horoscopes in Greek, and then in Latin. They competed with diviners of other kinds and with medical men for the attention of clients across the Mediterranean world. By the middle of the 1st century B.C.E., L. Tarrutius of Firmum had produced a horoscope for the city of Rome itself, at the request of Varro. Not long after, Augustus turned the zodiacal sign of his birth, Capricorn, into a central image in his imperial propaganda. A vast range of individuals, from Tiberius and Domitian to many slaves, turned to astrologers for advice on a vast range of matters.

Though no surviving ancient treatise offers precise instructions on how to construct an astrological chart, a number of works provide rich information on the rules used to interpret them: especially the *Tetrabiblos* of Ptolemy (2nd century) and its commentaries and the *Mathesis* of Firmicus Maternus (4th century). A great many horoscopes survive, some on papyri, others in the preserved collection of Vettius Valens. A rich body of antiastrological polemic, the work of intellectuals as distinguished as Cicero and Augustine, also exists. But most of this material consists of attacks on practices that astrologers did not actually adopt, like the radical determinism denounced by Augustine. Hence it sheds little light on their work—though much on the way others saw them.

A few points are well established. Horoscopes ranged widely in nature and function, from detailed, luxury products aimed at rich individuals to the very brief indications of planetary positions that are normally found. The astrologer not only computed the positions of the planets but also interpreted them. On the ecliptic, with its twelve zodiacal signs, he set a second circle divided into twelve houses. Each of these determined one sector of the client's future, health, wealth, voyages, and the like, as set out by the identity and configurations of the planets found in it. A further set of doctrines—many of them Hellenistic and some ultimately Near Eastern in origin—enabled the astrologer also to take into account a vast range of further factors, from the significance of each degree of the zodiac to those of particular fixed stars.

The horoscope, in other words, could prove a very flexible instrument indeed, one into which the skilled astrologer could read anything from directions for a health regimen to predictions about the fate of the city of Rome. Its production required only a modest level of technical skill in the use of tables; but its skilled manipulation could make the astrologer into the trusted adviser of emperors and prelates. By the 4th century, both the state and the church were making

efforts, unsuccessful in the long run, to stamp out the production of these documents, whose makers supposedly claimed access to a power apparently superior to that of earthly rulers. But the horoscope survived all efforts to extirpate it. Surviving examples afford rich information about everything from the social situation of diviners and health practitioners in the late antique city to court intrigues in Persia and Byzantium.

BIBL.: T. Barton, *Ancient Astrology* (London, 1993). T. Barton, *Power and Knowledge* (Ann Arbor, 1994). A. Bouché-Leclercq, *L'astrologie grecque* (Paris, 1899; repr. Brussels, 1966). M. T. Fögen, *Die Enteignung der Wahrsager* (Frankfurt, 1993). J. North, *Horoscopes and History* (London, 1988). A.T.G.

Horses

Horses, together with ponies, mules and donkeys, played an enormous and indispensable role throughout the late antique world as riding animals, pack animals, and, to a lesser degree, draft animals. The horse's only rivals were the camel as a pack animal in the east— even camel-mounted bedouin used horses in battle— and the ox as a draft animal. The Salian Law from 8th century Francia recognizes the possibility that horses might be used for plowing, but although slower and less powerful, oxen were the overwhelming norm. Before the invention of the horse collar, which became widespread only from the 13th century onward, horses were yoked like oxen, so that the stress was on the neck rather than the shoulders, pressing the yoke against the horse's windpipe and preventing the animal from making full use of its strength.

Good horses, suitable for hunting, chariot racing, polo games, and warfare, were expensive, not only to buy but also to maintain. Such animals cannot live simply on rough grazing. They require grain or beans, and ideally specially grown fodder, such as alfalfa or lupins. Thus, high social status was always associated with their possession. Horses were appropriate gifts for emperors, kings, shahs, and khaghans. Frankish and Anglo-Saxon warriors were rewarded with horses, and the Qur'ān (sura 3:12–14; sura 16:8) echoes the sentiments of pre-Islamic poetry in regarding fine horses as something sent by God that may be a temptation for men. The papyri suggest that in 4th through 6th century Egypt, apart from bandits, horses were the preserve of high officials and the military. Most people used donkeys. The status of horse ownership is also indicated by the Roman literary genre of *Hippiatrica*, or "horse medicine." Works are known by the 4th century writers Apsyrtus, Hierocles, Pelagonius, and Vegetius (author of *De re militari*). However, horses were not exclusive to the highest elites. Bone finds in Francia suggest many villages had a horse or two. Imperial legislation in the 4th century, enacted as part of a drive to suppress banditry and restrict the ownership of horses in parts of southern Italy to the upper ranks of provincial society, shows that in these stock-breeding areas horse ownership was much more widespread. Beyond the settled world, among the nomads, fine horses were still prestige goods, but horses in general were essential to survival. Without horses a man ceased to be a nomad.

Detailed information about the breeds of horse that were available in late antiquity will have to come from zooarchaeology, and the horse burials of Asiatic Russia and central Asia hold out enormous potential. The main features, however, are already clear. Both Roman and later Muslim sources talk of two main types of horse: one smaller, lighter, more alert and active, and with a small, slightly concave head; the second larger, heavier, straight necked with a rounder, sightly convex head. Muslim sources talk of the former as Arabian, the latter as Persian. Roman sources seem to equate the former principally with Numidian or Libyan horses; the latter again with Persian horses and those breeds, such as Thessalians and Cappadocians, that appear to have included Persian blood. The larger "Persian" horses seem to have had their origin in central Asia, and from there the stock spread to Persia, China, and the Roman world. These large horses were an important part of Persian military resources, essential for the armored heavy cavalry, the *kataphraktoi,* which was originally characteristic of Sassanian armies before it was copied by their opponents. Steppe nomads prized fine Persian horses too, but they also used smaller steppe horses, which in the eyes of Roman authors, including Ammianus Marcellinus and Vegetius, constituted a separate type: ugly by Roman standards but extremely tough, capable of surviving in severe weather on open pasture. Vegetius warns his readers that "our mares are of a softer type, accustomed to the protection of roofs and used to warm stables." Turned out to winter untended on open pasture, they would suffer heavy losses.

The late antique military revolution—occurring either in the wake of the Battle of Adrianople (378), or with the adoption of stirrups around the end of the 6th century, or after the Battle of Poitiers (732)—which rendered traditional infantry forces obsolete and made cavalries the arbiters of the battlefield through to the late Middle Ages is a myth. Neither victory can be construed as one of horsemen over foot soldiers, and infantry remained the largest component of most armies and a vital battlefield force throughout the period. Stirrups, which seem to have been a steppe innovation, introduced to the Roman world by the Avars, certainly made riders more secure, particularly those wearing heavy armor and particularly in the hills, but they were not essential to an effective cavalry. At least as important was the solid saddle, used by the Roman army from the 1st century and by the Persians and steppe nomads for much longer. However, it is true that late antique armies did deploy more cavalry and did give it greater importance than had their predeces-

sors. Consequently late antique states were enormous consumers of good-quality horses. Take, for example, the figure of 150,500 cavalrymen from the *Notitia Dignitatum* for the Roman army in the east at the end of the 4th century. Each trooper would have required at least two mounts, making a total of 301,000 horses. With horses lasting about four years, the army in the east would have been looking for some 75,250 cavalry horses each year. The army would also have needed a huge number of mules. In addition, there were the needs of the *cursus publicus.* On the way to Jerusalem in 333 the Bordeaux Pilgrim passed 250 stations. Procopius's figure of forty horses at each station, with a 25 percent turnover, suggests that 2,500 horses a year were needed on this route alone. Similar numbers of horses would have been required by Sassanian Persia and by the Umayyads.

Horses could be obtained through taxation in kind, purchase, or special breeding on state stud farms. Roman imperial estates dedicated to horse breeding are attested in Cappadocia, Phrygia, and Thrace. There were equivalent Umayyad estates in Arabia. Horse breeding, particularly on this scale, requires good organization and stable conditions. Numbers and quality can rapidly fall off, and in periods of invasion or political upheaval, as for example in 7th and 8th century Byzantium or the post-Roman west, supplies would have been hard to maintain.

BIBL.: John France, "The Military History of the Carolingian Period," *Revue belge d'histoire militaire* 26 (1985): 81–99; Ann Hyland, *Equus: The Horse in the Roman World* (New Haven, 1990). M. Kretschmar, *Pferd und Reiter im Orient* (Hildesheim and New York, 1980). M.WHI.

Housing

Our knowledge regarding dwellings in late antiquity is greater than for any other premodern period. The most immediate and practical expression of the economic flourish that characterized this period was the intensive building of dwellings in city, village, and countryside. At times we find the remains of dwellings from this period in very remote areas, such as arid desert regions that after late antiquity and until the early 20th century were completely uninhabited. The preservation of the remains of these houses is, in many instances, excellent. Also, many houses continued to be occupied after the period under discussion, in the Muslim era, and in some places, such as Syria and the Hauran, one may find houses from late antiquity that are still in use.

Details about daily life in these houses may be learned from the literary sources of the period, especially rabbinic literature (the halakic and midrashic works of Jewish sages in the first centuries C.E.) and the abundance of papyri that have been discovered in Egypt and the various desert sites, such as Nessana in the Negev and Petra in Jordan. A considerable amount of complementary material may be found in various artistic forms, such as architectural depictions appearing on mosaic floors in North Africa, and illustrations found in illuminated manuscripts and on stone reliefs.

If we assert that the Roman period excelled in the public construction of various elements connected primarily with the urban landscape, such as aqueducts, bridges, and walls, as well as ritual and entertainment structures, we may also say that late antiquity was distinguished by its building activity in the private sector. In not a few instances, private construction in the city took precedence over building in public areas, whether it was for the consolidation of building blocks *(insulae)* or the expansion of dwellings into the city's streets and squares. In many cities, private houses were built outside the city walls, and in many houses, especially in the urban areas, a wealth of ornamentation was found, including the use of marble and luxurious mosaic floors—testimony to the great investment the inhabitants made in the construction of their homes.

This "building boom" created an extraordinary variety of dwelling forms that gave expression to the social stratification in late antiquity. Dwellings clearly reflect the various social strata, from the luxurious urban dwellings of the social elite to the small farm dwellings in which farmers of the remote field regions lived. Within the abundance of archaeological remains and the variety of forms, one may point to six typological groups of dwellings: homes of the urban aristocracy, regular urban dwellings, village dwellings, estate manors, farmhouses, and nomadic dwellings.

The urban aristocracy built rather well consolidated, large, and luxurious complexes. Good examples of homes of this type were found in various cities in the eastern empire, such as Antioch and Daphne in Syria, Nea Paphos in Cyprus, and Sepphoris and Tiberias in Palestine; however, the best-preserved examples have been found in North Africa (specifically in the area of modern Tunisia). These standard enormous complexes, with areas ranging between 500 and 2,500 square meters, were located in the center of the city or on its periphery. The houses boasted a symmetrical plan intended to emphasize their opulence and the social standing of the homeowners. The main entrance led into a peristyle inner courtyard, beyond which lay a reception hall or a triclinium for common meals, or both. The peristyle courtyard in the center of the house was a distinct status symbol. While the homes of the wealthy in the early Roman period contained a peristyle courtyard in the rear part of the house, in late antiquity this courtyard was to be found near the entrance. A fountain and pool (for spawning fish), and at times a flower garden, were often found in the courtyard. The reception halls and triclinia beyond the courtyard were decorated with great splendor, with mosaic floors and stucco and marble ornamentations. Next to the triclinium and in the rear of the house were the living quarters of the household members and their servants—the owner's *familia*. There were almost always private bathhouses in these complexes, which allowed the members of the upper strata to keep their distance from the masses, who frequented the public baths. Quite often, houses facing the street would incorporate a row of shops, some of which were physically independent structures and some of which were joined to the house. This is clear evidence that these homeowners were merchants, although many also owned agricultural land outside of the city. It should be noted that this type of house was found in smaller rural towns as well, such as Aphek-Antipatris on Palestine's coastal plain. Several of the structures known today were occupied until the end of the Byzantine period in the east (7th century) and even later, in the Umayyad period, such as the house in Pella in the Jordan Valley.

The private construction of regular homes for middle-class city dwellers was characterized, on the one hand, by a high standard of quality, and on the other, by congestion deriving from the building density in the urban areas. In many of these city dwellings decorated mosaic floors have been found, as well as solid walls with niches and various installations, such as private toilets. Most of these urban dwellings are of the type known as the courtyard house: houses whose rooms surround a small inner courtyard. The courtyard functioned as a source of light and ventilation. In the center of the courtyard there was usually a cistern for collecting rainwater. The average size of these urban dwellings ranges between 100 and 200 square meters, although much larger houses existed as well. Construction of two or even three stories was common, primarily in the rural towns whose inhabitants worked in agriculture. In these houses, the ground floor served as storage space for agricultural equipment and living quarters for animals, while the upper story was used for dwelling. Houses of this type continued to exist into the Muslim period.

One of the most impressive expressions of the economic prosperity of late antiquity is the village dwelling. We know of hundreds of villages from this period wherein a wide range of dwellings of a rather high quality of construction was found. Many of them exhibit preplanning and a high level of finishing, which attest to the employment of expert builders. The typical village dwelling was a simple house whose facade faced a courtyard. However, it was often the case that the original house was expanded, owing to the growth of the family, a situation that led to the creation of the courtyard house. Most of the houses had a clear internal division between the most spacious room of the house, which was used for meals and entertaining guests, and the bedrooms and the rest of the service rooms. Most of the daily activity in the household, such as cooking and laundry, would be conducted in the courtyard. In areas where the principal construction material was stone, as in the Hauran and the Negev, houses were built to a height of two stories, similar to the two-story houses in the rural towns.

The estate manors of late antiquity belong to a large category of isolated dwellings found in agricultural areas. They are an expression of the improved security conditions throughout the empire during the period, and, indeed, in the hundred years following the Muslim conquest most of these houses disappeared.

The occupants of the estate manors were large landowners or, if the owners lived in the city, their representatives, who served as estate managers. The manors were built in a plan similar to that of large courtyard houses or, at times, as a complex with wings built freely around a central courtyard. Examples of this type have been found throughout the empire, in both the east and the west. Archaeological studies have shown that many of the Roman villas in the west continued to exist in the 4th and 5th centuries. The estate manors in the east are characterized by both their fortification elements, such as a tower, thick outer walls, and compact planning, and their agricultural features, such as a combination of stables, agricultural installations, and storerooms on the ground floor and dwelling quarters on the upper story. These complexes occupied an area of about 500 square meters. A number of good examples of the estate manor have been found in the Negev and North Africa, areas that underwent intensive agricultural work in late antiquity.

Next to the large estate manors, the remains of thousands of smaller farmhouses have been found. These were rather modest dwellings (with an average area ranging between 50 and 100 square meters) built next to a courtyard. Their plan was usually rectangular, and the long facade of the house faced the courtyard. The house itself was divided into two to three rooms. Over time, many of these farmhouses were expanded by the addition of various wings around the courtyard. The occupants of these farmhouses were independent farmers or tenants who worked the tracts of land near their home. This dwelling type disappeared almost completely toward the end of the Umayyad period.

Finally, on the fringes of society in late antiquity, in the desert regions, the dwellings of nomads and seminomads were found. The massive settlement of farmers in the remote desert regions caused the nomads to move from temporary tent dwellings, such as the bedouin of today use, to houses built of stone. These houses were used for shelter in the seasons amenable to agricultural work (winter and spring) and were abandoned in the seasons when good pastureland was available (summer and fall). They had a roundish shape conforming to the topography and were built of fieldstone and roofed with branches and shrubbery indigenous to the area. In the desert areas of North Africa, the Negev, Jordan, and the Hauran, thousands of sites with this type of seasonal dwelling have been found.

Private construction in late antiquity reflected the complexity of society in this period. Economic prosperity found expression not only in the cities but also in the villages and countryside. Most of the dwellings were built to a high standard and attest to a practical and functional approach. A better quality of life was attained through a clear physical separation of the living quarters of the household members from the animals and various service areas. Especially impressive is the wide distribution of farmhouses in places that today lie desolate.

BIBL.: Yizhar Hirschfeld, *The Palestinian Dwelling in the Roman-Byzantine Period* (Jerusalem, 1995). Georges Tate, *Les compagnes de la Syrie du nord au IIe au VIIe siècles* (Paris, 1992). Yvon Thébert, "Private Life and Domestic Architecture in Roman Africa," in *A History of Private Life,* vol. 1: *From Pagan Rome to Byzantium,* ed. Paul Veyne (Cambridge, Mass., 1987), 313–409.   Y.HIR.

Huns

In the course of the tormented history of the 5th century, Attila's Hunnic empire was an episode, and his spectacular military enterprises did not result in a lasting change in the balance of power. However, they inspired fears and fantasies in his contemporaries and, even more, for posterity. In those who witnessed their appearance in ca. 375 C.E., like Ammianus Marcellinus, the Huns stirred up the worst prejudices. The Roman diplomat Priscus, who traveled to the court of Attila in 449, drew a much more favorable picture. Later, Christian writers styled Attila as the scourge of God. Germanic legends described him as a noble king, although not without ambiguity. Medieval hagiographers and Renaissance poets in France and Italy pictured the Huns as terrible enemies; Hungarian historiography claimed them as prestigious ancestors. Allied propaganda in the 20th century's World Wars applied the stereotype of the Hun invader to the Germans; postwar Germans applied it to the Soviet Union. Raphael painted Attila's encounter with Pope Leo in the Vatican Palace, Verdi made him the hero of an opera, and Anthony Quinn and Jack Palance played him in modern films. Hardly any late antique ruler has been the focus of so many widely differing projections.

Who were these awe-inspiring Huns? Even before they appeared in the European steppes, the name *Huns* had become known in central Asia. In Sogdia and Bactria, Chionites, Kidarite Huns, and Hephthalites (also called White Huns) ruled in the 4th to 6th centuries. Philologists still debate which ethnonym from Chinese, Indian, Persian, or Armenian sources is or is not identical with the Latin *Hunni* or the Greek *Chounnoi*. Since Deguignes in the 18th century identified the Huns with the H(s)iung-nu, powerful northern neighbors of the Chinese empire until the 2nd century C.E., the discussion about the central Asian ancestors of the Huns has never ceased. Recent research has, however, shown that none of the great confederations of steppe warriors was ethnically homogeneous, and the same name was used by different groups for reasons of prestige, or by outsiders to describe their lifestyle or geographic origin. Thus, the Romans often called the Huns Scythians, and the Avars Huns. It is therefore futile to speculate about identity or blood relationships between H(s)iung-nu, Hephthalites, and Attila's Huns, for instance. All we can safely say is that the name *Huns,* in late antiquity, described prestigious ruling groups of steppe warriors.

The Huns who came to Europe in ca. 375 were a confederation of warrior bands whose success was based on their willingness to integrate others. Thus, the armies of Attila eventually consisted of several more or less distinguishable Hunnic groups: Goths, Alans, Gepids, Sciri, Rugians, Sarmatians, and others. The archaeological evidence proves that these warriors, whether Germans or Huns, shared a common symbolic language and material culture, little of which was clearly of central Asian origin (such as the large bronze cauldrons). The few dozen personal names we know include Germanic, Iranian, and other elements. The latter are often regarded as Turkic, sometimes as Mongolic, but Gerhard Doerfer's view that Hunnic was not part of any known language group now seems to prevail. Ethnic and linguistic plurality, cultural synthesis, and a differentiated treatment of subjects characterized the Hun empire. It encouraged others to join the confederation, and the Huns even accepted that their subject peoples, such as Gepids and Ostrogoths, were led by their own kings. They waged war against those who refused to follow, to achieve at least symbolic submission, and they sought to deter secession, putting considerable pressure on the Romans to extradite fugitives, who then were executed.

We know little about the way in which this empire was constructed after 375 and more about its consequences. The Huns broke Gothic hegemony north of the Black Sea and the Danube, which led to a massive migration of Goths and others into the Roman empire. Throughout Roman history barbarians had never been successfully integrated, but now imperial authorities had to accept barbarian armies under their own leaders in Roman territory, for instance Alaric's Visigoths. In the meantime, the Huns extended their power over the regions north of the Danube, gradually moving into the Carpathian basin after 400. The invasions of Radagaisus (405–406) and the Vandals, Alans, and Suebi (406–407) followed this expansion of Hunnic power. But the Huns themselves did not start raiding on a similar scale, apart from a few minor expeditions, before King Ruga's death in 434. Rather, they supported the Romans against Gothic groups or supplied Roman generals, like Aetius or Constantius, with troops. Only when they had finally brought all the relevant barbarian groups along the northern frontier of the empire under their control did they turn against Rome.

This was Attila's policy: by alternating raids and treaties, he succeeded in pushing the yearly sums paid to him by the Romans to an unprecedented 2,100 pounds of gold (447). The treaty of 447, after a major raid on Balkan provinces, also forced the Romans to evacuate territories south of the Danube. Priscus's description of Attila and his residence in 449 shows the king of the Huns at the height of his power. Then he turned against the western empire, which had to endure his two largest military expeditions, both of them not fully successful. The march against Gaul was stopped by a coalition of Romans, Visigoths, and others on the Catalaunian Plains (451). In Italy, Aquileia fell and Milan opened its gates, but then diseases, logistic problems, and an exhausted army made Attila turn back (452). He suddenly died in the following year. After his impressive funeral, described by Jordanes, Attila's empire fell apart. In the battle at the Nedao (454), the Gepids and their allies won the core areas of the Hunnic empire, the Ostrogoths and others moved into the empire, and the allegiance of Hunnic elite was split between Attila's numerous sons, who soon disappeared from the political stage.

What the Huns had achieved was a massive transfer of resources from the Roman empire to the *barbaricum.* Barbarian warriors could thus enjoy the benefits of the Roman system without having to enter it. This strategy required a growing concentration of power that became harder and harder to maintain, and collapsed after Attila's death. Hunnic groups, for instance the Akatzirs, Cutrigurs, and Utigurs, continued to live in the northern steppes, but they did not achieve anything comparable. Only the Avars, who came to Europe in 558–559, successfully followed Attila's model. They assimilated the remaining Hunnic groups and were themselves, in a generic sense, often called Huns by their contemporaries. But the age in which the name *Huns* had enjoyed the highest prestige in the Eurasian steppes was over.

BIBL.: F. H. Bäuml and M. Birnbaum, eds., *Attila: The Man and His Image* (Budapest, 1993). Peter Heather, "The Huns and the End of the Roman Empire in Western Europe," *English Historical Review* 90 (1995): 4–41. Otto Maenchen-Helfen, *The World of the Huns* (Berkeley, 1973).   W.P.

Hypatia

Hypatia, ca. 355–415, Alexandrian philosopher, mathematician, and Neoplatonic teacher, was the daughter of Theon, an important Alexandrian mathematician and the last attested member of the Alexandrian Museum. She was very well educated in mathematics and philosophy, following in the footsteps of her father, who edited and produced commentaries on the works of Euclid and Ptolemy. The Suda informs us that Hypatia herself wrote commentaries on the arithmetical work of Diophantus of Alexandria and the *Conic Sections* of Apollonius of Perge, as well as a work of some sort on astronomical tables. She also worked with her father on the *Almagest* of Ptolemy, revising the third book of his commentary on this work. Nevertheless,

Hypatia's fascination with mathematics had an intrinsic connection with her philosophical predilections: mathematical knowledge was a stage along the road of Neoplatonic recognition, leading to divinity, to the One.

We do not know whether Hypatia wrote any philosophical works, but we do know—thanks to the recollections of her student Synesius of Cyrene—that she did not engage in philosophy solely for self-fulfillment, but rather shared her knowledge with others. Already in the early 390s she was a well-known and highly regarded teacher of eclectic Neoplatonism in Alexandria, continuing the metaphysical tradition of Plotinus and Porphyry. She ran something on the order of a private school of philosophy in her home, gathering around herself students not only from Alexandria and Egypt but also from Syria, Cyrenaica, and Constantinople. These students came from influential urban and manorial families (predominantly Christian); over time, they themselves came to occupy important state and ecclesiastical positions. Two of them, Synesius and his brother Evoptius, became bishops. They created around their mistress—whom they called their "genuine guide in the mysteries of philosophy," "blessed lady," or "divine lady"—a community devoted to philosophical spirituality, to mathematical and astronomical research, and to certain religious practices not connected with popular pagan ritualism. They were also bound by their commitment to the secrecy of the knowledge transmitted to them; the recognition of the supernatural reality toward which Hypatia was leading them was something that could not be communicated. In the end, it led to immersing oneself in contemplation with the highest being, to mute ecstasy in the presence of that which cannot be identified in words.

Hypatia also offered lectures for the wider public, either in her home or in municipal lecture halls. These were attended by a larger circle of students, including urban and imperial officials who exercised authority in the city.

Dressed in a modest philosophical tribon, beautiful and dignified, Hypatia attracted universal attention by her virtues, especially the virtue of self-control (sophrosunē), expressed in complete sexual purity, and in her restrained and decorous behavior. She participated in the life of the Alexandrian polis and was an adviser much valued by the ruling archons in various matters involving the city; it became a custom for newly chosen officials, on taking office, to pay her a ceremonial visit.

But it was precisely her public position that was the cause of Hypatia's violent death. She took an active role in the political struggle that began around the year 413 between Cyril, elected patriarch of Alexandria in 412, and Orestes, the imperial prefect of Egypt. Because she was a person of such prominence, with such influential students, the support she expressed for Orestes aroused consternation in ecclesiastical circles. People connected with Cyril, most likely at his prompting, began to spread gossip (as we are told by John of Nikiu) that Hypatia was an ardent, practicing pagan with mysterious powers and magical influence over the prefect, over the "people of God," and over the whole city. In the end, the quarrel between the patriarch and the prefect over the scope of the church's influence in the city led to the murder of Hypatia. In 415 retainers of Cyril (parabalanoi), under the leadership of one Peter the Reader, attacked her in the street; they pulled her from her carriage and mutilated and killed her.

The fate of Hypatia inspired European literature for centuries; in the Middle Ages, her legend shaped the hagiography of St. Catherine of Alexandria. Today she is the heroine of novels, plays, and essays, and one of the model figures of feminism.

BIBL.: Maria Dzielska, *Hypatia of Alexandria* (Cambridge, Mass., 1995). Wilbur R. Knorr, *Textual Studies in Ancient and Medieval Geometry* (Boston, 1989). D. Roques, "La famille d'Hypatie," *Revue des études grecques* 108 (1995): 128–149. J. Rougé, "La politique de Cyrille d'Alexandrie et la meurte d'Hypatie," *Cristianesimo nella storia* 11 (1990): 485–504.   M.DZI.

I

Iberia (Caucasian). *See* Georgia.

Iberia (Spain)

Diocletian administrative reforms (between 284 and 288) brought for Hispania the consequences of a new territorial division and, gradually, a change in the structure of the government of the peninsula. Hispania began to be called Diocesis Hispaniarum, and its territory was split into what were at the beginning six provinces: Baetica, Lusitania, Carthaginiensis, Gallaecia, Tarraconensis, and Mauritania Tingitana. Later, in the course of the 4th century, the province of the Balearic Insulae was added. At the head of all the diocesis was the Vicarius Hispaniarum, who claimed to represent the prefect of the Praetorium of the Galliae. His capital seat was Augusta Emerita (Merida, in the Lusitania, currently the province of Badajoz).

Each of the provinces was, in turn, governed by *praesides* of lesser rank, or by *consulares,* and capitals for these provinces were established: Corduba (and then Hispalis) was the capital of Baetica; Emerita, of Lusitania; Carthago Nova, of Carthaginiensis; Tarraco, of Tarraconensis; Bracara (Braga), of Gallaecia; Palma, of the Baleares. The capital of Tingitana was Tingis (Tangier). We know the names of some of the governors, or *vicarii,* of the Diocesis Hispaniarum during the 4th century, such as Vetius Agorius Praetextatus, Fl. Sallustius, and Volusius Venustus, many of whom were related to the highest pagan aristocracy of Rome. Hispania was for them a place of transit in their administrative careers, and it was also the site of their luxurious villas.

The Diocesis Hispaniarum remained on the margin of the great problems of the empire almost until the beginning of the 5th century. The most relevant episodes were the brief appearance of Maximian to fight against the Frankish pirates; the attempt of the usurper Maximus (388) to create a new province named after himself (Nova Provincia Maxima); and the strategic closing of the zone of the Pyrenees by the emperor Constans II (360). Hispania produced no currency, nor was it to be found along the principal routes of the empire. In the 4th century it enjoyed a period of relative prosperity both in the cities and, above all, in the rural dominions, with a self-sufficient economy. The villas of Hispania from this period were among the most spectacular of the empire, with magnificent polychrome mosaics illustrating mythological scenes and with large agricultural developments that are mentioned in the works of some authors of the period, such as Symmachus and Ausonius. Certainly Africa had replaced Hispania in the sale of oil to Rome, Italy, and the other provinces of the empire, but Hispania continued to import table china, both from Africa and from the east, and the Hispanic *garum* (fish sauce) was so renowned that it was mentioned by Ausonius and in the east by Libanius.

An event with significant consequences during the last decades of the 4th century and the first of the 5th century was the birth and subsequent move to Hispania of Theodosius, emperor from 379 to 395. Theodosius created around himself groups of relatives and friends who occupied the highest and most influential positions in the government of the empire, and many of them were of Hispanic origin. It is no coincidence that a magnificent *missorium* of silver with its central image representing an enthroned Theodosius, flanked by Valentinian II and Arcadius, in the act of delivering the codicils to a high official, probably the Vicarius Hispaniarum, has been found in the area of the capital Augusta Emerita. Theodosius's family relationships and his network of interests in the peninsula were fundamental in the arrival of the troops of the usurping Constantine III in the year 407, who took possession of Hispania and thus created under his command a new Imperium Galliarum. In turn, this episode was to give cause to the Suebi, Vandals, and Alans to enter Hispania in 409, with the result that all the provinces except Tarraconensis fell into the hands of barbarian peoples.

The relatives of Theodosius, and of his son Honorius who was at that time the legitimate emperor, attempted to defend their possessions and territory with a private army formed of colonists and slaves. But this defense failed and Hispania was, during all of the 5th century until the final arrival of the Visigoths, the stage for a series of battles, pacts, defections, and Roman expeditions. Though it is not clear how many of them there were, nor in what manner the Suebi, Vandals, and Alans were settled, we know from the sources that they first settled in Gallaecia, the Vandals in the Baetica, and the Alans in Lusitania and Carthaginiensis. The Visigoths, who after the siege of Rome were obliged to settle in the region of the Narbonensis, became allies of the Romans in order to eliminate the barbarians who had established themselves in Hispania. After some victories, and after an attempt to go to Africa, the Visigoths were obliged by Constans to return to Gallia and establish themselves as a federal people in Aquitania (418), with a capital in Toulouse. From there they would move later to Hispania.

The Vandals who had settled in Baetica defeated a Roman army sent against them in 422; probably, uneasy at the possibility of reprisals, both from the Romans and from the Visigoths, they went to Africa in 429 and there established themselves until the reconquest of Justinian. In Hispania they extended their dominance to practically all of the territory and even attempted to take possession of the Tarraconensis, in spite of local resistance.

With the rise to the throne of Theoderic II (457–466), the Visigoths began to be interested in the Iberian Peninsula. Their first step was the defeat of the Suebi and their king, Rechiarius, in 456, which included the conquest of Bracara. This meant the inevitable decline of the Suebi, who maintained their independence until 585 with a strong Visigoth influence. The year 470 marks the end of Roman control of the Tarraconensis.

The Goths' penetration of Hispania was slow and progressive and probably not numerically significant. The question of the nature of their settlements (urban? rural?) and of the nature of Visigoth control (since it was more administrative than the result of effective territorial settlement) has not been sufficiently studied. The Hispanic-Roman component continued to be strong and extensive, and the Visigoths tried to imitate the Roman world and culture.

The 6th century was for Hispania a fully Visigothic century, but it should be emphasized that the Germanic influence was not so profound. This was the period that saw the Byzantine occupation of a part of the Hispanic territory—the southeastern coast—which lasted from 551 to 621, an occupation that was not a war of conquest on the part of the Byzantines, but motivated by a request for help made by the Visigoth king Athanagild. It was the century that saw the reign of Leovigild (571–586), the most Byzantine of all the Visigoth kings, the founder of the cities of Recopolis and Victoriacum, and the one who put a final end to the kingdom of the Suebi. It was also the period of Leander of Seville and of Isidore, of splendid literature, of the creation of vivid accounts of daily life, such as the *Vitae patrum emeritensium*. The rise to the throne of Leovigild's successor, Reccared, brought the centralization of the court in Toledo and religious unification. The 7th century, on the other hand, was a dark period. Intrigues, palace conspiracies, and problems of legitimacy in power form the core of the few chronicles that refer to this period.

The arrival of the Arabs in 711 from North Africa took place first in the form of a looting expedition directed by the governor of Ifriqiyya, Musa Ibn Nusayr, and under the command of his former slave Tariq. The expedition numbered no more than 1,700 men, against whom Roderic the Visigoth king fielded some 100,000 men, according to Arab sources, although the figure seems to be exaggerated. After the death of the king early in combat, the battle turned in favor of Tariq, who decided to proceed toward the interior of the peninsula. Musa then moved a second force into Hispania to follow up on Tariq's success. Scarce resistance, as well as agreements with many noble Visigoths and with groups of urban Jews, favored the rapid Muslim expansion in Spain, which soon came under the caliphate of Damascus. The Muslims called their territory in the Iberian Peninsula "al-Andalus."

BIBL.: Ibn 'Abd Al-Ḥakam, *Conquête de l'Afrique du Nord et de l'Espagne,* 2nd rev. ed., ed. and trans. A. Gateau (Algiers, 1947). Javier Arce, *El último siglo de la España romana (284–409),* 2nd ed. (Madrid, 1994). Roger Collins, *Early Medieval Spain: Unity and Diversity, 400–1000* (London, 1983). G. Ripoll and I. Velázquez, *Hispania visigoda* (Madrid, 1996). E. A. Thompson, *The Goths in Spain* (Oxford, 1969).

J.A.

Icon

Icons in the strict sense are panel paintings of sacred subjects intended for veneration. This art historical usage of the term is therefore narrower than the ancient use of the word *eikōn*, which is the most general Greek word for image. Icon use in the Christian world is attested by Eusebius, who recognized the custom as a practice shared with the non-Christian world of late antiquity. "I have examined images of his apostles Paul and Peter, and indeed of Christ himself, preserved in color paintings; which is understandable, since the ancients used to honor saviors freely in this way fol-

lowing their pagan custom" (*Hist.eccl.* 7.18.4). Elsewhere, in a letter to Constantina, sister of Constantine the Great, Eusebius expresses his disapproval of the Christian veneration of such images, saying "these are excluded from churches all over the world" *(Ep. ad Constantinam)*. However, when a woman brought Eusebius a painting of Paul and Christ clad as philosophers, he did not destroy the icon but confiscated it and kept it in his own house to prevent its improper use by the woman. For the Christian, then, icons posed a problem of the infiltration of pagan usages into Christian worship.

For the art historian the first problem of icons is the gap in physical evidence at the outset of their development: the earliest surviving Christian icons are generally ascribed to the 6th century. In this gap historians have erected two hypotheses for the origin of icons, tracing them either to the official painted imperial image, the *lauraton*, or to Roman portraiture of the kind preserved in the Fayum portraits of Egypt. The imperial hypothesis places an archaeological burden on theologians that they should not be made to carry. Starting with Bishop Leontius of Cyprus in the 7th century, theologians justified Christian veneration of icons by citing the parallel veneration of the *lauraton,* but the parallel implies no real dependence in iconography, composition, or construction and tells us nothing about the artistic origin of Christian icons. The Fayum hypothesis also lacks archaeological conviction: as funerary portraits made for mummies, they are unframed paintings of the head and neck, while icons are independently framed pictures generally showing half-length or full-length figures.

A much more likely source for Christian icons is the class of images to which Eusebius refers, namely pagan icons. At least a dozen of these images survive, coming from Egypt and Syria; they have yet to be analyzed as a group. Two of them were found by O. Rubensohn in an archaeological context, in a house dated around 200, and others appear stylistically to belong to the 2nd and 3rd centuries. Thus a chronological gap still remains before the earliest surviving Christian icons; yet the pagan icons present much more striking parallels to their Christian counterparts than either the imperial or the portrait material. Half- and full-length figures are represented in frontal poses holding symbols of their divine power. They stare boldly at the beholder, their countenances ringed with haloes. Like Christian icons, some represent two or more sacred figures, and some assume a hinged triptych format, permitting one to activate the image by concealing and revealing the divine presence. Although public cultic images in antiquity tended to take the form of statuary, in a private domestic situation panel paintings of the gods were sometimes venerated, and it is this minor genre of antique art that Christians seized on and made into a major genre of enormous importance for the history of art.

Military god with halo, Egypt, ca. 200 C.E.

The second art historical problem is the spread of icons into the public domain of the church building. There is no reason to doubt Eusebius's testimony that in his time icons were unknown in the Christian church. In the 5th century, however, references to images in churches multiply, particularly narrative images, and by the 6th century some icons of Christ and his apostles adorned the templon barrier that surrounded the sanctuary of Hagia Sophia in Constantinople. Stone relief images of Christ and his apostles survive from the 6th century Church of St. Polyeuktos, and in the 7th century reference is made to icons on the templon barrier of a Church of St. John the Baptist in Constantinople. Icons, therefore, were being used to define the holy of holies, the most sacred space in the Christian church. Doubtless many of the surviving 6th century icons, painted to life-size proportions, were intended for this kind of public setting within the church building.

This popular development in the absence of a theological justification prompted the 8th century outbreak of iconoclasm. Although iconoclasm had important political dimensions, in that it pitted the emperor against the church, and particularly against monasteries, the movement was essentially a religious crisis. Arguing that the divine nature cannot be circumscribed in a picture and that Scripture forbade the making of images, the emperor Leo III initiated an imperial policy against icons and began by removing the image of Christ from the gate of the imperial palace in 726. The formulation of a theological defense for the use of images was the last great intellectual achievement of the patristic period. It is a doctrine of great elegance, erected on the twofold basis of the dogma of the incarnation and the Neoplatonic understanding of images. John of Damascus argued that the incarnation of the word of God in human flesh made possible the representation of the divine, and indeed that God's entry into the human condition changed humankind's relationship with the physical cosmos. Furthermore, in an extension of Neoplatonic thinking, images were interpreted as transparent windows making present the divine and transmitting human prayers heavenward. The Seventh Ecumenical Council, convened in Nicaea in 787, defined that "the honor which is paid to the image passes on to that which the image represents, and he who reveres the image reveres in it the subject represented." The death of the iconoclast policy is a sign of the power of the ingrained, popular use of icons. Once a theology of icons had been formulated, their use expanded into all contexts in Byzantine life.

Late antique icons survived iconoclasm in areas remote from Constantinople, especially in Sinai and Rome. Important examples still preserved at St. Catherine's on Mt. Sinai include icons of St. Peter (6th century), Christ Pantocrator (6th or 7th century), St. Irene (7th century), and the Madonna surrounded by angels and saints (7th century). Sixth century icons from Mt. Sinai now in Kiev include those of SS. Sergius and Baachus, St. John the Baptist, and the Madonna and Child. There are many 6th and 7th century icons in Rome, including the icon of the Madonna and Child in the Pantheon, the Salus Populi Romani icon at S. Maria Maggiore, the Madonna and Child from S. Maria Antiqua at S. Francesca Romana, and the Mandylion from S. Silvestro in Capite, now at the Vatican.

BIBL.: Hans Belting, *Likeness and Presence: A History of the Image before the Era of Art*, trans. Edmund Jephcott (Chicago, 1994). H. Maguire, *The Icons of Their Bodies* (Princeton, 1996), and *Image and Imagination: The Byzantine Epigrams as Evidence for Viewer Response* (Toronto, 1996). Jaroslav Pelikan, *Imago Dei: The Byzantine Apologia for Icons* (Princeton, 1990). K. Weitzmann, *The Monastery of Saint Catherine at Mount Sinai: The Icons,* vol. 1: *From the Sixth to the Tenth Century* (Princeton, 1976).   T.M.

Iconoclasm

Iconoclasm, in the strict sense of the word, was already a well-known phenomenon in antiquity; it often took the form of the destruction of symbols of privilege and the established order, with the religious overtones muted. In this connection, most pertinent was the destruction of images of reigning or defunct emperors in the Roman period as symbolic acts of political rebellion or of a posthumous *damnatio memoriae*. Of primary importance, however, is iconoclasm as an expression of religious sentiment. There is an essential distinction to be made, furthermore, between the obliteration of material symbols of an alien religion and the selective destruction of images connected, in some fashion, with the iconoclasts' own faith.

In Graeco-Roman religion proper, despite the trenchant criticism voiced by individual philosophers and moralists, an "internal" iconoclastic movement never came into being, though the arguments formulated by various intellectuals condemning popular image worship were put to good use in Jewish and Christian apologies against an iconophile cult. The Zoroastrian religion, originally noniconic, apparently went through a period in which the veneration of cult statues, under Hellenistic influence, was accepted; the iconophile trend was then at least partially checked by the reformist orthodoxy of the Sassanian dynasty.

The fluctuations in the attitude toward anthropomorphic images in postbiblical Judaism and the exegetical history of the Second Commandment cannot be presented in detail here, but as far as early Christianity is concerned, it would be wrong to ignore the influence of strong iconoclastic sentiments within contemporary Judaism or the scrupulous care with which rabbinical authorities evolved legislation to protect adherents of the faith from contact with idolatrous Gentiles.

In a late antique Christian context, the "external" type of iconoclasm, manifesting itself in the destruction of pagan sanctuaries and cult images—and the burning down of Jewish synagogues, for that matter—often with the encouragement or connivance of the local ecclesiastical authorities, is well attested. It is noteworthy that the veneration of imperial statues and images continued with little change both during Constantine's reign and afterward; there was no Christian polemic against this "civic" cult, the existence of which in fact was later used to justify the veneration of religious images *stricte dictu*.

The beginning of Christian art of course antedates the "establishment" of Christianity by Constantine, but literary references to the existence and religious appraisal of such an art are scant and difficult to interpret. In the succeeding period an anti-idolatry argument and the appeal to the Second Commandment were buttressed by other considerations as well, in particular those of a Christological character. Thus Eusebius of Caesarea, in his letter to the empress Constantia, emphasizes that the divine glory that invested the Savior even during his earthly incarnation precludes, ipso facto, his pictorial depiction. Epiphanius of Salamis, later in the 4th century, claims, inter alia, that the presence of images in churches and elsewhere distracts the Christian from the contemplation of purely spiritual realities. But no theological consensus for or against images emerged during the patristic era.

On the practical side, apart from isolated incidents, only in one instance—in the late 6th and early 7th century, in far-off Armenia, already firmly in the Monophysite camp—did the anti-icon protest crystallize into what one can call a short-lived iconoclastic movement that drew its strength from an ascetic ethos and a concomitant emphasis on redeemed man as the true image of God, rather than any handmade objects. But one cannot identify the battle lines of the impending iconoclastic struggle with divergent types of Christological formulations. The cult of images, though more peripheral than in the Byzantine *Reichskirche,* nevertheless was practiced by Monophysites as well as by Nestorians, both in late antiquity as well as in the medieval period.

The question of image worship was at the center of the stage, so to speak, in the Byzantine empire, during the 8th and 9th centuries. The Byzantine iconoclastic movement can be divided into three phases. The first, characterized by a relatively straightforward appeal to the biblical injunctions against idolatry, falls into the reign of the emperor Leo III (717–741) and the initial portion of the reign of his son Constantine V (741–754; 754 was the date of the iconoclastic Council of Hiereia). The second phase, stretching from this council to the death of the emperor Constantine V (775), was the apogee of the violent persecution of iconophiles, and, more generally, of attacks directed against the monastic establishment and even relic worship. Then, after a suspension of the persecution by Leo IV and the temporary restoration of image worship by his

widow, Irene, regent for Constantine VI, still a minor, came the third and final phase (815–842), the recrudescence of iconoclasm under the emperors Leo V, Michael II, and Theophilus.

On the ideological plane, iconoclasm is characterized, somewhat paradoxically, by a profound though selective traditionalism and what one could call an intellectual elitism, appealing to a sophisticated Christological argument that would convict the image worshipper of either separating or "confusing" the two natures of the God-Man, as well as to one particular patristic interpretation of the bread and wine of the Eucharist as constituting the true image of Christ. The oft-canvassed suggestion of the influence of the Islamic rejection of images of animate beings can be safely set aside: the Byzantine iconoclasts had no objection to secular art, anthropomorphic or otherwise, and in any case they wholeheartedly accepted the traditional cult of the plain cross, which, as is well known, from the very beginning proved to be a major stumbling block to Muslims. It hardly occasions surprise that it was only when the leadership of the party of the opponents of image worship was assumed by the autocratic rulers of the eastern Roman empire themselves that this movement gained momentum and attacked the popular piety of the image cult directly. Byzantine iconoclasm as an organized movement was a preeminently imperial heresy, so to speak—a late antique imperial heresy, which, with Leo III, was born in the purple, and which, with Theophilus, also died in the purple.

A special problem is posed by an alleged or assumed Islamic iconoclasm, which has been the subject of much discussion and debate for more than a century. The current fragile consensus can be summarized as follows: there is no formal rejection of representations in the Qur'ān, and the traditions about the life of the Prophet mention the occasional presence of objects, primarily textiles, with images; the Muslim leadership, however, was concerned about the impact of images on piety and decided, probably instinctively but possibly under the influence of Jewish converts, to avoid representations in anything formal and public, as on coins or in mosques; private secular art of the Umayyads and early Abbasids was replete with images of all kinds (Khirbat al-Mafjar, Amra). There may have been official instances of destructions of Christian images, as would have happened through the edict of Yazid (720–724), which would have compelled such destructions. But even though there are instances in Jordan of mosaic floors from which whole animals were removed, the authenticity of a formal iconoclastic edict is doubted by many. Some scholars prefer the term *aniconism* for the Muslim refusal to use images in official circumstances, and the theological justification for this refusal was slowly developed around the idea of God alone as a creator.

BIBL.: L.W. Barnard, "Byzantium and Islam: The Interaction of Two Worlds in the Iconoclastic Era," *Byzantinoslavica* 36 (1975). Anthony Bryer and Judith Herrin, eds., *Iconoclasm* (Birmingham, 1975). Patricia Crone, "Islam, Judeo-Christianity and Byzantine Iconoclasm," *Jerusalem Studies in Arabic and Islam* 2 (1980): 59–95. Stephen Gero, *Byzantine Iconoclasm during the Reign of Constantine V, with Particular Attention to the Oriental Sources* (Louvain, 1977). G. R. D. King, "Islam, Iconoclasm, and the Declaration of Doctrine," *Bulletin of the School of Oriental and African Studies* 48 (1985). Jaroslav Pelikan, *Imago Dei: The Byzantine Apologia for Icons* (Princeton, 1990). Daniel J. Sahas, ed., *Icon and Logos: Sources in Eighth-Century Iconoclasm: An Annotated Translation of the Sixth Session of the Seventh Ecumenical Council (Nicea 787), Containing the Definition of the Council of Constantinople (754) and Its Refutation, and The Definition of the Seventh Ecumenical Council* (Toronto, 1986).   S.G.

Images

Graeco-Roman civilization created images constantly, with themes taken from everyday life or from myths and rites. Some Mediterranean and Mesopotamian peoples had a culture that was not rich in images. Under the domination of the Greeks and Romans, most of them adopted the classical mode of figuration, primarily in the religious domain. The Jews, though they had had an early imagistic period, resisted the use of images (Lev. 26:1); after long reflection, however, they chose to accept them. The mishnaic treatise *Avodah Zarah* set the tone for that reflection. The Jews had resisted because they had a real philosophy of the image, an explicit belief. Until they, too, allowed themselves to be integrated into the world of images, the primary examples of images were the synagogue of Dura-Europus and the mosaic pavings in 4th to 6th century synagogues in Palestine.

All these peoples made use of geometric and floral decorations, which were particularly elaborate in architecture, mosaics, ceramics, and toreutics. But images depicting human beings and animals became more prevalent in their art, in portraits of princes and notables, as well as scenes from mythic and historical narratives.

After nearly a century of hesitation, 3rd century Christians, coming from dispersed Jewish communities and later from pagan areas permeated with images, entered the world of image making. At the request of Christian patrons, artists began to create a new repertoire.

In a few of the larger artistic centers (Rome, Athens, Pergamum, Aphrodisias, Thessalonica) they had before their eyes large sculpted compositions (the Trajan column, triumphal arches, ornamentation on plazas and porticoes) and ancient and recent paintings. They also had very familiar coin types with legends.

The richest site for evaluating the importance of religious iconographical paintings in the 3rd century is Dura-Europus, on the Roman Euphrates. In the first half of the 3rd century, there were decorations in a sanctuary to a god of Palmyra, a sanctuary to Mithras, a baptistery, and a synagogue. In these four religious sites, painters and sculptors pieced together works, drawing on the resources of local and regional art. These collections exemplify the new repertoire being created; the images were "rough drafts" for what would later be fixed as formulas for Christian art. Viewers could easily recognize the scenes, since the stories they told and their meanings were well known from the liturgy and the sermons. The textual referents of Christian images were episodes selected from the Hebrew Bible and the New Testament as *exempla*. Images of martyrs came later, and were associated with the beginnings of the cult of saints in the late 4th century.

The second set of artifacts that allows us to see the art form as it developed are the pre-Constantine catacombs and sarcophagi in Rome. Some of the images were taken from the environs, including very ancient models (reclining banquets, decapitations) that can be called iconographic visual referents. Objects discovered within an archaeological context sometimes make it possible to identify a real visual referent as well (scrolls, clothing, knives, bows, the attack on Daniel by a lion taken from a circus image, and so on). In iconographic elements taken from the Graeco-Roman repertoire, there is sometimes a tension between the general direction of the narrative and the direction of movement of various figures. This is true particularly in geographical areas where two opposing and hierarchically determined directions of reading—Semitic and Graeco-Roman—coexisted.

After Constantine's conversion to Christianity, images became more explicit and more numerous; documentation is augmented by mosaics and pieces of furniture. New iconographic formulas could be understood by quickly making the appropriate choice from a new vulgarized narrative repertoire.

Other late images have come down to us, including numismatic images or illustrations on imperial documents (*Notitia Dignitatum, Codex-Calendar of 354*), that give a clear idea of ceremonies and furnishings (real visual referents). The Peutinger Table suggests how space was represented.

Artists continued to copy the great classical texts and to illustrate them with copied and modified images (e.g., the Vatican Virgil, Ambrose's *Iliad*). In the 5th and 6th century east and west, notables still ordered mosaics illustrating mythical pagan narratives for their urban and rural homes. Scientific images also persisted (Dioscorides, Galen).

The power of images (linked to their meaning) was a matter for reflection by writers in classical and late antique pagan civilization, among Jews (who in the end denied that power) and among other peoples who worshipped the images of gods or powerful figures (governors, military chiefs, Hellenistic kings, Roman emperors). The image *(eidōlon, agalma, eikōn)* was considered powerful once it had been consecrated and had received prayers. Writers sought to know whether the image kept its power in reproductions, in miniatures, or in its fragments after it was broken (e.g., the Colossus of Rhodes). On this point, the reflections of the Jews were similar to those of pagan philosophers. Elaborating on Plotinus's ideas, Iamblichus attempted to produce a theory positing that the power of images was a reflection of the divine image. If images were powerful, one ought perhaps to fear them. Christians later resumed the discussion of the power of images.

BIBL.: A. Grabar, *Christian Iconography* (Princeton, 1968). H. Maguire, *Image and Imagination: The Byzantine Epigrams as Evidence for Viewer Response* (Toronto, 1996). Thomas F. Mathews, *The Clash of Gods: A Reinterpretation of Early Christian Art* (Princeton, 1993). J. Pépin, "Ut scriptura pictura," in *From Augustine to Eriugena*, ed. F. X. Martin and J. A. Richard (Washington, D.C., 1991), 168–182. P. Brown, "Images As a Substitute for Writing," in *Communication in the Early Middle Ages*, ed. E. Chrysos (Leiden, 1999), 15–34.   A.R.

Imperial Cult

Under the tetrarchy the relationship between emperor and gods was reformalized. The 3rd century emphasis on the protection of the emperor by one particular god changed with the creation of two senior and two junior emperors: the former were called "Jovius" (of Jupiter) and the latter "Herculius" (of Hercules). Contemporary panegyrics play forcefully on this type of language, and according to hostile sources, Diocletian introduced from Persia a new court ritual of obeisance. This tetrarchic world was in one sense far removed from the earlier Roman empire, in which social distance between citizens and the emperor, at least in Rome, had not been emphasized, but in another sense it merely marked the consolidation of earlier relationships between ruler and traditional gods. Such relationships were necessarily changed again with the conversion of Constantine to Christianity. In the last years of his rule, Constantine informed a grouping of towns in central Italy that they might erect a temple to his family, but that "it should not be polluted by the deceits of any contagious superstition"—that is, by pagan sacrifices (*ILS* 705.46–48). The formal apparatus of imperial temples and priests was thus allowed to continue, and imperial priests were still found in the 5th century in some provinces (and in Vandal Africa). Deceased emperors continued to be called *divus* (in the east until Anastasius in 518), but their funerals from

Constantine onward were decisively Christian and not "pagan." Constantine himself, who had probably built the Church of the Apostles in Constantinople, was buried there, with twelve coffins representing the apostles around his own. Living emperors, too, were increasingly set in a Christian context. Some aspects of court ceremonial remained untouched: the forms of obeisance toward the emperor and his image that Diocletian had introduced continued through the late empire, shedding any association they may once have had with obeisance toward pagan gods. But the creation of new emperors was, in both Byzantium and the west, a religious matter. In the east new emperors, after proclamation in the camps or elsewhere, were crowned by the church patriarch as a recognition of his status. The Christian procedures developed from the mid-5th century and took place in church from the early 7th century. In the west Christian rituals of anointing and crowning were slower to develop, but they were found among the Visigoths in the 7th century and in England and France in the 8th and 9th centuries: here the emerging religious hierarchies asserted their authority and succeeded in claiming that the anointing itself actually constituted someone as a (Christian) king.

To the east of the Roman empire, very different traditions are found. The Sassanid dynasty, though hostile to Rome, made some borrowings from the west. The Sassanids' silver vessels, for example, which display much royal imagery, are in the Greek style, but the themes and artistic conventions follow traditions of the ancient Near East going back at least to Assyrian and Achaemenid kings. The principal religions of their kingdom were Zoroastrianism and Zurvanism, and the dynasty had a varying relationship to them that seems structurally closer to the situation in Byzantium than in the west with its dominant religious hierarchy. The Umayyad successors of the Sassanids mark a clear break with earlier traditions of the area. They established their dynasty on a new ideological basis, as rulers directly on behalf of Allah. At least initially, they did not adopt many obvious symbols of kingship (throne, crown, or scepter), and court rituals were not very elaborate. Despite this seeming moderation, the dynasty was later criticized and the Umayyads regarded as mere despots and not true caliphs (successors of the Prophet).

BIBL.: David Cannadine and Simon Price, eds., *Rituals of Royalty: Power and Ceremonial in Traditional Societies* (Cambridge, Eng., 1987). L. Duchesne-Guillemin, *Cambridge History of Iran*, vol. 3 (Cambridge, Eng., 1983), 866–908. N. Duval, "Culte monarchique dans l'Afrique vandale," *Revue des études augustiniennes* 30 (1984): 269–273. Oleg Grabar, "Notes sur les cérémonies umayyades," in M. Rosen-Ayalon, ed., *Studies in Memory of Gaston Wiet* (Jerusalem, 1977), 51–60. Janet L. Nelson, "Symbols in Context: Rulers' Inauguration Rituals in Byzantium and the West in the Early Middle Ages," in *The Orthodox Churches and the West*, ed.

D. Baker (Oxford, 1976), 97–119; repr. in Janet L. Nelson, *Politics and Ritual in Early Medieval Europe* (London, 1986), 259–281.   S.P.

India

The recognition of India by the Mediterranean peoples in late antiquity used to flow from literary and mostly fictitious testimonies more than through the *realia* that western merchants and sailors might have collected from their direct or indirect knowledge of the region (e.g., Cosmas Indicopleustes). Often written about in romance, verse, and other types of literature from Philostratus to Nonnus, India was described as an idealistic country (despite countless *mirabilia*) in which a well-structured society was governed by justice and wisdom exclusively: actually, it played the role of a mirror in which the ancients were able to question their own convictions about the nation, philosophy, religion, and the nature of man, and which would reflect back the expected answers from the mouth of the Indian wisemen and Brahmans (e.g., Palladius). The fanciful descriptions of the Indian nature, landscapes, ethnography, and wonders invariably relied on the *auctoritas* of former authors from Ctesias to Strabo, without any attempt to update or substantiate the true reality of India. This unanimous picture of a "dreamlike India" (Jacques Le Goff) lasted for centuries, well into the Middle Ages.

After the end of a unified India under the Mauryas (early 2nd century B.C.E.), the historical development of the peninsula is defined as feudal by Indian scholars, although some attempts were made to revive a utopian unity. In southern India (Tamilnadu), the Cholas, Cheras, and Pandyas kingdoms survived through various dynasties, among which the Chalukyas and the Pallavas vied for supremacy from the 4th to the 9th century. Initiated in the Mauryan age, the superimposition of northern Indian cultural features (Vedic tradition, Aryanization) over the Dravidian heritage was carried out under royal patronage; Buddhism and Jainism thus declined, and the Tamils resisted through devotional cults (*Bhakti*). At the time of the Chola dynasty of Tanjore (9th century), southern India had become a blooming center of classical Indian civilization.

The Sātavāhana dynasty (= Āndhra) grew in the late 1st century B.C.E. in the Krishna and Godavari Valleys and soon extended its rule over the whole Deccan up to the Gujerat and Malwa, where it fought for decades against the "Western Satraps" (= Sakas, Pahlavas) and eventually against the Shungas in the Gangetic Valley. Sātavāhana power extended from coast to coast, and the period is characterized by the spread of writing (inscriptions) and a diversified and abundant coinage; a strong Sātavāhana involvement in Indo-Roman trade remains a topic of scholarly debate. The Sātavāhanas'

tight relation with Buddhism is evidenced by the numerous monasteries found in their realm and, in the domain of the arts, by the paintings in the Ajanta caves. The Sātavāhanas were succeeded by the Vākāṭakas dynasties allied with the Guptas (4th–5th centuries).

In northwestern India (Punjab, Sind), the "westernized" history of the Indo-Greek and Indo-Parthian (= Sakas, Scythian) dynasties ended with the Kushan (= central Asian Yüeh-chih) conquest in the mid-1st century C.E.; legend suggests that the Saka king Gondophares might have met St. Thomas in northern India. At the same time, the Gangetic Valley, including northern Deccan and the whole of Bengal, was ruled by the virtually unknown Shunga dynasty; it is clear from archaeological evidence that all the contemporary sites in the Ganges Valley and in Bengal appear wealthy, active, and well structured—one interpretation being that the post-Mauryan period would have seen the achievement of its political, economic, social, and ideological premises even under decentralized authorities. Here also the Kushan blow brought to an end the local dynasties; however, the mastery of the Kushan dynasties by the Sassanids in northwestern India did not produce any "Iranization" of the country, the only evidence of this being a few artistic expressions from northwestern India (post-Gandhara sculpture).

The major event of 4th–5th century India was the affirmation of the Gupta dynasty over most of India; the Guptas ruled directly in the Ganges Valley and northwestern Deccan, and through feudal dynasties in northwestern and peninsular India except South India. Chandra Gupta initiated a new "unified" rule in India ça. 320 C.E.; it was expanded and strengthened by his successors until the beginning of the Hun invasions (mid-5th century), which brought the northern part of the country into turmoil for more than a century. Although well attested by inscriptions, coins, archaeological evidence, and some literary sources, the blooming of the Gupta civilization expresses the ideological achievement of Brahmanical India more than a political reality—considering the continuing challenge to the central authority. The myth of a "golden age" as represented by the legend of King Vikramāditya and his companion the poet Kālidāsa is supported by the magnificence of classical Indian architecture (Amaravati, Sanchi) and the perfection of the schools of sculpture (Gandhara, Mathura): the congruity between the Gupta period and the acme of historical Indian civilization remains undisputed, although it was almost ignored by contemporary western observers.

The post-Maurya period and early centuries of the Christian era were marked all over India by major economic growth, a general increase of wealth, and the spread of urbanization. Beyond the traditional reasons for this—state centralization (which continued through most of the post-Mauryan kingdoms), the expansion of transpeninsular routes and maritime networks, and the effects of taxation—the maturation of the Indo-Roman trade is also seen as a driving force of Indian development. Accordingly, the decline of the western trade in the 3rd–4th centuries (except in Sri Lanka) led to an economic and social crisis (stabilization of the guilds and *varnas* [castes], allocations of land tenures, and stratification of the society) that affected most of India from the 5th to the 8th century. The regression of urbanization, partly balanced by the strengthening of the Brahmanical tradition (viz. the classical civilization, which reached its climax in the Gupta period) resulted in the setting of an "agrarian system" that lasted for centuries.

Such accepted theories are now challenged. H. P. Ray has convincingly argued that most of the regional and transpeninsular trade networks were developed in the late pre-Mauryan (= Megalithic) and Mauryan periods, associating mining centers (metals, precious stones) as well as producing areas of subsistence goods (especially craftsmanship) with new towns and growing villages, a large number of which were located along the most important land routes or were seaports. The basic impetus for this expansion came from the cohesive community of Buddhist traders, together with the generalization of a "monastery economy" that permitted the coalescence of an increasing number of individuals and groups into the newly organized, educated, and wealthy Buddhist communities—secondarily of Jainism. The Indo-Roman trade prospered in this milieu, strengthening and improving the existing networks and urban centers. The decline in the 3rd to the 5th century was partly due to the inability of Buddhism to resist the development of Brahmanical groups (a process known as Sanskritization, which was marked, among other features, by the incorporation of long-lived Aryan traditions, such as the recording of the *Puranas*), the progressive diverting of the Buddhist lay devotees, and the growing influence of the *bhakti* movement. These ideological changes underwent major social differentiations that eventually gave way to the "agrarian system." In the meantime, the still active trading networks reoriented themselves to the expanding political-economic organization and wealth of the Southeast Asian kingdoms, which changed the nature of the commodities traded; this process is known as the Hinduization of Southeast Asia and is seriously questioned by recent research.

BIBL.: J. André and J. Filliozat, *L'Inde vue de Rome* (Paris, 1986). A. L. Basham, *The Wonder That Was India* (1967; Delhi, 1991). M.-F. Boussac and J.-F. Salles, eds., *Athens, Aden, Arikamedu: Essays on the Interrelations between India, Arabia and the Eastern Mediterranean* (New Delhi, 1995). D. K. Chakrabarti, "Post-Mauryan States of Mainland South India (c. BC 185–AD 320)," in *The Archaeology of Early Historic South Asia: The Emergence of Cities and States*, F. R. Allchin, ed. (Cambridge, Eng., 1995), 274–326. J.-C. Carrière, E. Geny, M.-M. Mactoux, and F. Paul-Lévy, eds., *Inde, Grèce ancienne: Regards croisés en anthropologie de l'espace* (Paris, 1995). J. Le Goff, "L'Occident médiéval et l'océan Indien: Un horizon onirique" (1961), in *Pour un autre Moyen Âge: Temps, travail et culture en Occident* (Paris, 1977), 280–297.　　　　　　　　　　　　　　　　J.-F.S.

Indian Ocean

Although the name Indian Ocean was not commonly used in late antiquity, this maritime area gained a cohesion then that culminated in the Abbasid period. In the Greek or Roman sources, the traditional name of Erythra Thalassa slowly disappears; when used (by Philostratus, Aelian, Dio Cassius, Ammianus, Cosmas), it is usually in the context of information from the Hellenistic period, without a basis in actual knowledge. Through different wordings, the notion of the Indian Ocean emerges in some classical sources and is more strongly asserted in the Syriac literature; it is fully realized in the time of the early Muslim travelers and geographers.

The modern rediscovery of the ancient Indian Ocean is largely based on archaeological evidence from Madagascar and East Africa to Ceylon, not to speak of the area from the Bay of Bengal down to Indonesia, which has to be archaeologically integrated into the Indian Ocean. Many newly discovered sites around the Red Sea (Quṣayr al-Qadim, Abu Sh'ar), in South Arabia (Kana), in Africa (Axum) or the Comoros, in Oman (Suhar) or around the Persian Gulf (ed-Dur, Qala'at al-Bahrain, Siraf), in Pakistan (Banbhore), in India (Baroda, Broach, Nasik, Sopara), and in Sri Lanka (Mantai) provide striking material and cultural information on the interaction between the maritime communities of the region. The Romans and Egyptians remained active in the 4th century and later, as evidenced by the thousands of Roman coins found in Sri Lanka; they were most probably acting in cooperation with intermediaries such as the kingdoms of East Africa (Abyssinians, Axumites) and Arabia (Himyarites). The history of these peoples and their tumultuous relations is well established by epigraphical and archaeological evidence, although the classical sources often mixed up their evolution, ascribing Indian or Persian kings to East Africa or Arabia, and vice versa (e.g., Malalas of Antioch). Persian rule extended unchallenged from the mouth of the Euphrates to modern Dhofar and conquered South Arabia in the late 6th century; to the east, it fought against the Kushan dynasty for sovereignty over northwestern India until the latter submitted around 250; the Persians then established close alliances with the Gupta dynasty in India. Such long-standing relations between the Persian Gulf and India certainly favored the early Muslim conquest of Sind (712) and the intimate interconnections of the

Arab, Persian, and Indian merchants of the Abbasid period.

Maritime trade was the raison d'être of the Indian Ocean communities from the time of Augustus to Harun al-Rashid: African gold, Indian spices, Chinese silk, Arabian and Indian pearls, copper, iron, and slaves were just a few of the valuable commodities that circulated all around the Indian Ocean and often reached the Mediterranean. The paucity of written evidence is poorly balanced by archaeological discoveries. But the impact of such wealthy maritime activity can be detailed for each of the communities involved. There was also a continuous transfer of populations from one place on the Indian Ocean to another, two examples being the peopling of Madagascar and the Zānj (African) revolt in southern Iraq in the early Islamic period.

The spread of religions was a cohesive factor in the regions around the Indian Ocean. The Axumite king Ezana converted to Christianity ca. 330, and Theophilus's mission to Arabia took place ca. 350. In both areas, strong Jewish communities were also present. Eastern Arabia and the Persian Gulf were evangelized as early as the 2nd century, and Nestorianism was predominant in the ecclesiastic province of Beth Qetrayeh from Rev Ardashir (Bushir) to Mazun (Oman) as well as in western and southern India and Sri Lanka, all places where Christian communities are mentioned from the 4th–5th century onward. Buddhism did not spread westward, although a few groups are cited in the Persian Gulf; it played a major role in the integration of Southeast Asia into the trading systems of the Indian Ocean. Most of the existing Arab and Persian networks quickly became Muslim in the 7th–8th centuries, and what emerges at the dawn of the millennium is an almost fully Islamized Indian Ocean.

BIBL.: Himanshu Prabha Ray and Jean-François Salles, eds., *Tradition and Archaeology: Early Maritime Contacts in the Indian Ocean* (New Delhi, 1996). J. Reade, ed., *The Indian Ocean in Antiquity* (London, 1996). André Miquel, *La géographie humaine du monde musulman jusqu'au milieu du 11e siècle* (Paris, 1973). André Wink, *Al-Hind: The Making of the Indo-Islamic World*, vol. 1: *Early Medieval India and the Expansion of Islam* (Leiden, 1990).   J.-F.S.

Intermarriage

Late imperial legislation introduced a novel concept of marriage based on ethnic and religious disparity: a law of Valentinian I forbade marriage between provincials and "barbarians." Since both categories appear to have enjoyed Roman citizenship, the law was used as a way of controlling relations between Romans and barbarians in the empire itself, particularly at a moment of crisis. In 506 this ban was adopted by the Visigoths in Gaul, where it was applied to prevent cooperation between hostile barbarians (e.g., Franks) and the locals in areas vital to Visigothic territorial interests. Several decades later it was abrogated by the Gothic rulers of Spain, and with it disappeared the last legal barrier to full integration of Romans and barbarians in late antiquity. The limited effect of the ban can be measured by the continuing practice of intermarriage between Romans and barbarians, particularly among the military aristocracy of the later empire.

The legal ban on Jewish-Christian marriage, by contrast, had a considerably greater impact and longer life. At the beginning of the 4th century the church banned marriage between Christian women and Jewish men. However, objections to this sort of intermarriage had been raised for centuries by Jewish sources, from the very start of the Second Temple era. Throughout late antiquity rabbinic discussion affirmed the invalidity of intermarriage without conversion. At the core of the anti-intermarriage rules was the fear of conversion. In 388 the emperor Theodosius issued a law that banned Jewish-Christian marriage and pronounced such mixed marriage tantamount to adultery. Civil law thus endorsed episcopal and rabbinic efforts to control marriage and the choice of marital partners. This Theodosian law was taken into the *Justinian Code* and also adopted by the Visigoths and the Burgundians. Although the extent of Jewish-Christian intermarriage in late antiquity cannot be gauged due to the paucity of source material, the use of non-Jewish names and repeated Jewish and Christian injunctions betray an ongoing problem with keeping the boundaries of marriage as rigid as possible.

Ecclesiastical councils also introduced bans on marriage between "orthodox" Christians and "heretics." Such antagonism received further support from theological and ideological campaigns against heresy and appear to have gained success in keeping the orthodox flocks apart from their neighboring heretics. When a breach occurred, anecdotes, real or fanciful, would ensure a domestic polemic bound to be won by the "correct" or "orthodox" spouse.

BIBL.: S. J. D. Cohen, "From the Bible to the Talmud: The Prohibition on Intermarriage," *Hebrew Annual Review* 3 (1983): 23–39. P. L. Reynolds, *Marriage in the Western Church: The Christianization of Marriage during the Patristic and Early Medieval Periods* (Leiden and New York, 1994). M. L. Satlow, *Tasting the Dish: Rabbinic Rhetoric of Sexuality* (Atlanta, 1995). L. H. Silberman, "Reprobation, Prohibition, Invalidity: An Examination of the Halakhic Development concerning Intermarriage," in *Judaism and Ethics*, ed. D. J. Silver (New York, 1970). H. Sivan, "Why Not Marry a Barbarian? Marital Frontiers in Late Antiquity," in *Shifting Frontiers in Late Antiquity*, ed. R. W. Mathisen and H. Sivan (Aldershot, Eng., 1996), 136–145, and "Building Marital Boundaries in the Law: Rabbis, Bishops and Emperors on Jewish-Christian Marriage in Late Antiquity," in *Shifting Frontiers in Late Antiquity*, vol. 2: *The Transformations of Law and Society*, ed. R. W. Mathisen.   H.S.

Ireland

One of the first classical authors to discuss Ireland was the geographer Ptolemy (late 1st century C.E.). His account of the island demonstrates knowledge rather than fantasy, and includes some recognizable natural features, peoples, and places, such as the River Bououinda (Boyne) and Hisamnion (probably Emain, the royal center of the Ulaid of Ulster). Ireland was in contact with the Roman world from perhaps the beginning of the Christian era. A number of archaic loanwords from Latin into Irish suggest a context for this meeting: such words as *mil* and *long* (from *miles,* [*navis*] *longa:* soldier, ship) imply a familiarity with the Roman army, while others such as *ór, fín,* and *corcur* (from *aurum, vinum, purpureus:* gold, wine, purple cloth) imply that the native elite indulged in high-status imports. According to Tacitus, his father-in-law Agricola was convinced Ireland could easily be annexed, since merchants knew all the ports and approaches. The limited archaeological remains of the Romans in Ireland support this with evidence for a modest but continued mercantile presence.

A substantial body of early Irish law survives, much of it from the 7th and 8th centuries, providing an excellent view of the theoretical structuring of society (though it has a problematic relationship with social change and development). What it shows is that Irish society was extremely localized, strongly hierarchical, and complex. The economy was pastoral rather than agricultural, with cattle serving as the principal status markers and objects of exchange. The country was divided into about one hundred fifty *túatha,* each ruled by a king *(rí),* supported by religious specialists (first Druids, later Christian clerics), legal specialists, and poets whose main business was panegyric and the preservation of genealogies. The rights of the individual were dependent on wealth, status within the family, and gender, and existed only within the *túath:* outside his *túath,* the ordinary freeman was a nonperson. Within it, insult or injury was assessed with respect to the "honor price" of both parties. In addition to the basic categories of slave and free, the Irish added that of the *nemed* (privileged, but the root meaning is sacred/holy): in a postconversion list, the *nemed* were kings, lords, clerics, and poets. *Nemed* were the only people entitled to move freely around the country, and they enjoyed a variety of other legal privileges. Women were legally incompetent, dependent on father or husband, and there is no historical (as distinct from legendary) evidence that women ever acted as rulers or military leaders. Women's legal inability to inherit family land also explains why, though there were many women saints in Ireland, only four nunneries survived as major centers over a long period: women's communities must normally have broken up on the death of the founder.

One of the most important things to happen in Ireland in late antiquity is that it became Christian. Christianity entered Ireland through contacts with Roman Britain and Gaul. In particular, it is likely that the Irish penchant for slave raiding produced communities of Christian captives (parallel to the Greek captives among the Goths who produced Ulfilas). Our first raw date for Christianity in Ireland comes from the chronicler Prosper of Aquitaine, who records that in 431 Pope Celestine sent a bishop, Palladius, to "the Irish believing in Christ." This mission may primarily have been to such communities rather than to the Irish themselves. In any case, the legendary history of Ireland suppresses Palladius (about whom, consequently, we know nothing), and attributes Ireland's conversion entirely to one Romano-British captive, Patricius (St. Patrick), who probably flourished in the 5th century. The conversion of Ireland was certainly a more piecemeal process than the Patrick legend implies, but Ireland was Christian by the end of the 6th century, though Druids continued to survive, in an increasingly marginal position, as late as the 8th. Christianity's success in Ireland is due in part to the way it evolved to allow leading families to develop and consolidate their power. The great Irish monasteries all existed in close symbiosis with secular authority, and abbots were normally related to local rulers: St. Columba, for instance, was a scion of the Uí Néill, then the rising power of northern Ireland, as were nearly all his successors.

The intensely localized nature of Irish society led to a uniquely Irish perception of self-exile as a form of extreme asceticism described as "white martyrdom." It is not true that Ireland had no martyrs. Donnán, a would-be monastic founder, for instance, was killed with all his followers on the Scottish island of Eigg by the Picts. Rather, because the principal criterion for being culted as a saint was for the individual concerned to leave a thriving community behind him, martyrs were not canonized. But the very success of Christianity in Ireland caused the most fervent to set new goals for themselves, and self-exile commended itself to many. Thus, by the late 6th century, Irish monks began to spread across northern Europe—in most cases, clearly intending to take up a very liminal position as an introverted community of ascetics. In the event, some of them acquired a social prestige which they probably had not sought or intended, notably St. Columbanus, founder of the great monasteries of Annegray, Luxeuil, and Bobbio, and St. Fursa, the founder of Péronne. Other communities, such as the Irish monks who settled in Iceland and Shetland, perhaps remained truer to their original intentions but are now remembered only by place names such as Papay (*papar-øy,* priests island) in the Hebrides, Orkneys, and Shetland.

In addition to religious contact, represented both by the export of men such as St. Columbanus and the import of some settlers from outside, notably the Anglo-Saxon community at Mayo in Connacht, Ireland continued to have trading contacts with both Britain and the Continent throughout the early Middle Ages. The Irish were eager customers for wine, which they imported from the Loire region; *bordgal*, from *Burdigalia* (Bordeaux) became the Old Irish word for a meeting place. They also bought salt and iron, while their principal exports were probably hides, wool, and worked leather, particularly shoes. A number of 7th century royal exiles, notably the Northumbrian Aldfrith and the Merovingian Dagobert I, took refuge in Ireland during the reigns of their respective predecessors, suggesting that Ireland was in practice a less introverted society than its legal structure seems to imply.

BIBL.: T. M. Charles-Edwards, *Early Irish and Welsh Kinship* (Oxford, 1993). Donncha Ó Corráin, *Ireland before the Normans* (Dublin, 1972). K. McCone, *Pagan Past and Christian Present in Early Irish Literature* (Maynooth, 1991).

J.S.

Irish, Old

The phase of linguistic development known as Old Irish (OIr.) runs from the 6th to the 9th century C.E. However, the date of the earliest surviving Irish, known as Archaic Irish (AIr.), preserved on memorial stones in the linear script called *ogam*, may be as early as the 4th century. The earliest surviving Irish literature dates from the 6th century. A number of linguistic shifts took place between AIr. and OIr., including syncope (e.g., AIr. *Comogan* becomes OIr. *Comgan*) and the loss of most case endings other than dative plural *-ib* (cognate with Latin abl. pl. *-ibus*): the language remains inflected, but inflection is indicated only by shifts in vowel value. These changes, since they affect line length, syllable count, rhyme, and rhythm, must have created a literary watershed by making presyncope poetry unintelligible.

The earliest surviving Old Irish poetry is recognizably oral in mode. It is tightly structured, using alliteration, parallelism, rhyme, and other mnemonic "hooks"; the content, similarly, is normative and aphoristic. It survives mostly in quotations by medieval lawyers and grammarians. The Irish also evolved prose by the 7th century, on the evidence of the Cambrai Homily, a translation of a Latin homily by Gregory the Great preserved in a 7th century manuscript. Old Irish literature, both secular and Christian, continued to flourish until the Norman conquest: as early as the 9th century, virtually all original writing in Ireland is in Irish rather than Latin. A series of conquests from the 11th century onward that deliberately attacked Irish culture as a focus of potential resistance left only fragments of this once extensive literature.

BIBL.: Jane Stevenson, "The Beginnings of Literacy in Ireland," *Proceedings of the Royal Irish Academy* 89 C 6 (1989): 127–165. Rudolf Thurneysen, *A Grammar of Old Irish* (Dublin, 1946).

J.S.

Isauria

Isauria derives its name from the contentious tribe and twin settlements that were located in the rugged, isolated core of the Taurus Mountains, about 75 km from the coast of southern Turkey. Isaurian marauders created such havoc in neighboring Cilicia and Cappadocia that the emperor Probus placed a permanent fortified garrison there (ca. 278). Originally included in the Roman province of Cilicia and later in that of Galatia, Isauria became a province itself in the early 4th century during the reforms of Diocletian, who also incorporated into it most of Cilicia Tracheia and designated the Metropolis of Seleucia as the provincial capital. After the temporary success of the mid-4th century campaigns of Gallus Caesar (Amm.Marc. 14.2.1ff.), the emperor Valens responded militarily to new Isaurian raids in 370 and further gerrymandered the province by detaching the western half of Isauria (including the historic towns of Isauria Vetus and Isauria Nova) for inclusion in the new province of Lycaonia. The province of Isauria was now more southern in orientation but still extended along the coast from Korasion and Seleucia in the east to the border of Pamphylia. Despite the new boundaries the situation was so unstable that Matronianus, the *comes* (count, or military commander) of Isauria, ordered the prefect Eusebius and his first Legion of Armenians to rebuild Anamurium's defenses, which were completed about 382, and to protect other coastal settlements. In 404 Isaurian raiders are mentioned in the letters of St. John Chrysostom, who was briefly exiled to central Anatolia after the Synod of the Oak. Emperor Leo I (457–474) chose not to confront the restive Isaurians with another campaign but integrated some of their best fighters into the army and into his reorganized palace guard, the *excubitores*. Leo married his daughter Ariadne to the Isaurian chief Tarasicodissa, who took the Greek name Zeno. At this time many of the highly skilled Isaurian stonemasons were sent to the cities of the empire. On the death of Leo and his grandson (Leo II) in 474, Zeno ruled as emperor (excluding the twenty-month usurpation of Basiliscus) until 491. His successor Anastasius I (491–518) crushed the last remnants of Isaurian rebels in 498 and transferred thousands of captives to Thrace. He began the systematic construction of garrison forts throughout Isauria. In 535 a *comes* was permanently assigned there to govern the province. After the Arab consolidation of Cilicia Pedias at the end of the 7th century and the establishment of a de facto frontier at the Lamas River, the Isaurian highlands and Seleucia were included in the Byzantine theme of Anatolikon. Sometime before 732 southern Isauria was added to the coastal theme of the Kibyrrhaiotes. The Isaurian church, which had traditionally been under the authority of the patriarch of Antioch, was attached to the jurisdiction of Constantinople in the late 7th or early 8th century.

Although Isauria did not possess the wealth and large population of Cilicia, it did have a number of small cities built according to plans that were traditional in the eastern Roman provinces. Exports included tin and copper, as well as salted fish. By the 7th century an important weapons factory and mint were located in Seleucia. That city's metropolitan had twenty-four suffragan bishops when, in 359, the emperor Constantius convened a synod there on the Arian heresy.

After Seleucia, the most important harbor was Anamurium, which also controlled the coastal road. After a slow recovery from the Isaurian and Persian invasions of the 3rd and 4th centuries, Anamurium thrived in the regionwide prosperity of the 5th century. New baths were built, and probably all nine of the basilicas in the city and its *chōra* (territory) were erected at this time. Anamurium's slow decline to a village began with a devastating earthquake in 580. The decline was halted temporarily in the second quarter of the 7th century, when homes were added to the palaestra and small enterprises, such as a lamp factory, were thriving. Anamurium was defenseless when the Arabs invaded nearby Cyprus in 649; much of coastal Isauria was raided shortly thereafter. The Isaurian dynasty, the name commonly given to the family that ruled Byzantium from 717 to 802, is actually a misnomer. Its first ruler, Leo III, was mistakenly thought to have been named Konan, after Isauria's most popular indigenous saint. Leo was actually born in Syria.

BIBL.: G. Bean and T. Mitford, *Journeys in Rough Cilicia, 1962–1968* (Vienna, 1965 and 1970). Paul C. Finney, ed., *Encyclopedia of Early Christian Art and Archaeology* (forthcoming). Friedrich Hild and Hansgerd Hellenkemper, *Kilikien und Isaurien* (Vienna, 1990). R.E.

Isidore of Seville

Isidore belonged to a noble family of Spain, probably from Cartagena. After the destruction of the city by the Visigoths, the family fled to Seville, where Isidore was born ca. 560. After the early death of his father, Severianus, Isidore was raised by his brother Leander, the archbishop of Seville, which was the metropolitan see of the province of Baetica. Isidore also had a sister, the nun Florentina, and another brother, Fulgentius, who became bishop of Ecija. About the year 600 Isidore succeeded Leander as archbishop of Seville.

As bishop of a metropolitan see, Isidore took a leading role in ecclesiastical life and had a great influence over the Visigothic kings. He attended King Gundemar's council in 610, and presided over King Sisebut's Council of Seville in 619 and King Sisenand's Fourth Council of Toledo in 633. Special interests of his included education and the conversion of the Jews: the Council of 633, for example, ordered the establishment of a school in each diocese, to be modeled on that in Seville.

Isidore's primary reputation is as a scholar, and as such, he was a product of his times. He relied on what had been passed down from antiquity. Both his methods and his content tend to reflect what he had read. He possessed one of the most complete libraries of his day, and he took full advantage of it by indulging in extensive copying from earlier authors. Isidore was a compiler par excellence, and he played a preeminent role as the encyclopedist of the Middle Ages. His main sources, whom he rarely named, included Augustine, Boethius, Cassiodorus, Hyginus, Lactantius, Orosius, Pliny, Solinus, Tertullian, Varro, and Marius Victorinus.

Isidore's historical works include the *Chronicorum a principio mundi usque ad tempus suum liber* (Book of Chronicles from the Beginning of the World All the Way to His Own Time), or *Chronica maiora* (Greater Chronicle), which extended from the creation of the world to King Sisebut (615–616), and the *Historia Gothorum Wandalorum Suevorum* (History of the Goths, Vandals, and Suebi). Like Augustine, Isidore divided the history of the world into six ages.

Isidore often interpreted the Scriptures allegorically, as in his *De fide* (On Faith), *Allegoriae quaedam sanctae scripturae* (Some Allegories of Holy Scripture), and *De nominibus legis et evangeliorum liber* (Book about the Names of the Law and the Evangelists). Another interpretative work was the *Quaestionum in vetus testamentum libri duo* (Two Books of Investigations in the Old Testament), or *Mysticiorum expositiones sacramentorum* (Clarifications of the Mystical Sacraments). Isidore's *De numeris liber* (Book on Numbers), or *Liber numerorum qui in sanctis scripturis occurrunt* (Book of Numbers That Occur in the Holy Scriptures) had an important influence on later medieval numerical symbolism.

Isidore's most important theological work, the *Sententiarum libri tres* (Three Books of Opinions), was a manual of Christian faith and practices. Also in this category were *In libros veteris ac novi testamenti prooemia* (Preface on the Books of the Old and New Testament); *De ortu et obitu patrum* (On the Origin and Passing of the Fathers), or *De vita et morte sanctorum utriusque testamenti* (On the Life and Death of the Saints of Each Testament); *Officiorum libri duo,* or *De ecclesiasticis officiis libri duo* (Two Books concerning Ecclesiastical Offices); *Regula monachorum* (Rules of the Monks); and *De viris illustribus sive de scriptoribus ecclesiasticis* (On Illustrious Men, or On Ecclesiastical Writers).

Other reference works include *De ordine creaturarum* (On the Order of Created Things); *De natura rerum* (On the Nature of Things) written at the request of and dedicated to King Sisebut (612–621); *De haeresibus liber* (Book about Heresies); *Contra Iudaeos libri duo* (Two Books against the Jews), or *De fide catholica ex veteri et novo testamento contra Iudaeos* (On the Catholic Faith from the Old and New Testament, Against the Jews); and *De trinitate* (On the Trinity), which survives only in fragments.

Isidore had a particular interest in the meanings and uses of words. In his *Differentiarum libri duo* (Two Books of Differences), or *De differentiis rerum* (On the Differences of Things), Isidore examined 610 homonyms and synonyms. His *Quaestiones de veteri et novo testamento* (Investigations of the Old and New Testament) compared the Old and New Testaments. The *Synonymorum libri duo* (Two Books of Synonyms), or *Libri lamentationum* (Book of Lamentations), repeated a single thought using as many synonymous words as possible, and is perhaps Isidore's most original composition.

Isidore's love for word derivations also is seen in his most influential work, *Etymologiarum sive originum libri XX* (Twenty Books of Etymologies or Origins), also commissioned by Sisebut. It was left unfinished at Isidore's death, and the finishing touches were put on it by Isidore's protégé, Bishop Braulio of Saragossa (631–651). This encyclopedia summarized all the ecclesiastical and secular material that Isidore had gathered in his vast reading. It became one of the most popular books of the Middle Ages.

Isidore died in 636, and after his death he was accepted as an unequaled authority on matters of ecclesiastical dogma and practice. Braulio believed that Isidore had been "called by God to rescue the monuments of ancient knowledge . . . and to serve his contemporaries as tutor and protector." Isidore was formally canonized in 1598 and in 1722 was named a doctor of the church.

BIBL.: J. Fontaine, *Isidore de Séville et la culture classique dans l'Espagne wisigothique*, 2nd ed., 3 vols. (Paris, 1983). M. Reydellet, *La royauté dans la littérature latine, de Sidoine Apollinaire à Isidore de Seville* (Rome and Paris, 1981). C. M. Lawson, ed., *De ecclesiasticis officiis*, CCSL 113 (Turnholt, 1989). M. Reydellet, ed. and trans., *Etymologies, livre IX* (Paris, 1984). R.W.M.

Isis

The archaic goddess of the Egyptian royal throne, Isis proved one of the more resilient and flexible divinities in the Mediterranean world through the impact of Hellenism and the creativity of her priests. Revered as a vengeful protector of Egypt in both Egyptian and Greek texts of the Ptolemaic period and as a goddess of agrarian and maternal fertility in the crude images kept in Egyptian homes and granaries, Isis was also universalized as a goddess transcendent of any particular cult through aretalogies that extolled her many local identities and through sculpture (terra-cotta and stone) that consolidated her image according to Hellenistic style. While this universalization was certainly an indigenous Egyptian endeavor, the aretalogies and statuary themselves show the cult's diffusion throughout the Mediterranean world. Apuleius's novel *Metamorphoses* de-

scribes an extravagant Isis cult in 2nd century Rome that appealed to many non-Egyptians.

Because of their local popularity, the Egyptian cults of Isis were able to withstand the increasing weight of Christian influence, in many places through the 4th century: e.g., Kysis, in the Khargeh Oasis (through the early 4th century); Menouthis, near Alexandria (converted to a healing saint-shrine ca. 484); and Philae, at the first Nile cataract, patronized by Blemmyes as well as Egyptians and Greeks (closed in 540).

As one of the best-known goddesses of the Mediterranean world, Isis had some impact on images of the divine feminine in other religions as well: e.g., the figure of Sophia in Hellenistic Judaism and, in Christianity, the iconographic and liturgical representations of Mary.

BIBL.: Jan Bergman, *Ich bin Isis: Studien zum memphitischen Hintergrund der griechischen Isisaretalogien* (Uppsala, 1968). Françoise Dunand, *Religion populaire en Égypte romaine* (Leiden, 1979). R. E. Witt, *Isis in the Graeco-Roman World* (Ithaca, 1971). D.T.F.

Islamic Empire

The Islamic empire had its roots in the career of the Prophet Muhammad (d. 632 C.E./11 A.H.) and initially came into existence as a consequence of the extensive conquests on which Muhammad's followers embarked immediately after his death. During the empire's first two centuries, the ad hoc and sometimes tribally based governing structures of the conquest period were gradually replaced by more systematically organized bureaucratic institutions; in some cases, the Islamic empire drew on structures and traditions of the Byzantine or Sassanian empires as models for these institutions.

An empire can perhaps most simply be defined as a state that rules over a vast territory, usually including several different peoples. During the period under consideration here (up to ca. 800) Muslims were a minority in the Islamic empire's population—in the first years, only a small minority, probably no more than 5 percent of the whole; this proportion increased gradually, partly through voluntary attraction (whether for reasons of religious commitment or to secure more favorable social or economic status), and partly through the incorporation of captives into Muslim society. During the 1st century or so of the Islamic era, most converts were absorbed into the tribal structure of the original Arabian Muslims by becoming attached as clients (*mawālī*) to one of the Arab tribes; the term *mawālī* thus came to be a shorthand term for "non-Arab converts to Islam." The best estimate has Muslims becoming the majority of the population of the central regions of the empire—Egypt, Syria, Iraq, Arabia, Iran—by around 900.

The empire ruled vast areas—from Spain and northwestern Africa to eastern Iran and Afghanistan—but had to rely on rudimentary means of communication and transport to do so. Under such conditions, the state could have only weak, indirect, or intermittent control over many areas. In the absence of strong central control, various kinds of nonstate hierarchies continued to articulate power relations for many people; these included local political establishments in many cities and towns, tribal alliances and confederations in rural and pastoral areas, and non-Muslim religious hierarchies throughout the region. Sometimes these local or other hierarchies were supervised, co-opted, or manipulated in some measure by provincial governors or other agents of the empire, but at other times, when the grip of the state was weak, they operated virtually autonomously to govern life in their particular region.

It is still debated whether Muhammad's community in Medina can be characterized as a state, and how, and in what degree, the administrative and structural features of a state developed during the conquests. Muhammad's followers seem at first to have called themselves "Believers" (Arabic *mu'minūn*); after his death, they were led by rulers who called themselves *amīr al-mu'minīn,* "commander of the Believers," or "caliph" (from Arabic *khalīfa*), a Qur'ānic term that was popularized as a designation for the ruler by the Umayyads (660–750) but may have been used in this way earlier. The caliph or commander of Believers stood at the pinnacle of the imperial power structure; there was, however, no universal consensus on who was entitled to be caliph, and various contenders competed for leadership of the state during several major civil wars and in numerous smaller uprisings. This created a certain endemic instability at the top of the power structure of the empire during these years.

From its early days, the empire was organized into large provinces or governorates, known to us both from the works of the 10th century geographers and from coins and chronicles documenting the appointment of governors. The provinces were often more or less identified with their capital cities. Syria, under the Umayyads, was the metropolitan province and Damascus the seat of the empire, divided into five *ajnād* or military districts; the Abbasids, on their accession in 750, moved the imperial capital to Iraq (Baghdad, after its foundation in 762), and Syria was regularly divided either into *ajnād* or into two provinces centered on the cities of Damascus and Qinnasrīn (later, Aleppo). Provinces were sometimes combined or subdivided, and provincial borders changed over time, but relatively stable provincial units included Mecca, Medina, al-Ṭā'if (these three often combined under one governor), Yemen (capital Ṣanʿā'), Oman, Baḥrayn (= eastern Arabia), al-Kūfa, al-Baṣra (these two often combined under the later Umayyads), al-Jazīra/Mesopotamia (capital Mosul; under the Abbasids, Mosul was separated from al-Jazīra), Egypt (capital Fusṭāṭ), Ifrīqīya

(including at first all of North Africa and Spain; capital Qayrawān), Adharbayjān, Armenia, Fārs (al-Jibāl), al-Rayy, Sīstān/Sijistān, Naysābūr, and Khurāsān (capital Marv).

At the head of each province was a military governor (Arabic *wālī* or *amīr*), who ruled from the provincial capital and was backed by a garrison of troops. Although governors wielded great power, they were still under the control of the caliphs. Instances of powerful governors dominating a given province or group of provinces (especially in the east) for a long period are known, but in such cases the loyalty of these "viceroys" to the ruling dynasty appears beyond question, and the power of the governor really served the interest of the caliphs: ʿAbd al-Malik's viceroy in the east, al-Ḥajjāj ibn Yūsuf, exemplifies this pattern. Generally, the early pattern of relatively frequent caliphal appointment and dismissal of governors remained the norm through the Umayyad and the early Abbasid periods; the earliest case of a province of the caliphate becoming effectively independent under its "governor" while remaining nominally part of the empire was when the Abbasid caliph Hārūn al-Rashīd awarded Ifrīqīya (at that time, roughly equivalent to modern Tunisia) as a hereditary tax farm to Ibrāhīm ibn al-Aghlab in 800. (The seizure of Spain in 756 by an Umayyad prince who fled following the Abbasid coup was not a case of provincial autonomy but a denial of Abbasid legitimacy.)

Besides governors, the caliphs appointed other officials. In some cases, they dispatched to various provinces a financial and tax officer (Arabic *ʿāmil*) who was independent of the *amīr* or military governor. They also appointed judges (see below). The caliphs, when they did not lead the annual pilgrimage in Mecca themselves, appointed the person who performed these functions; either way, this symbolized the caliph's role as leader of the Muslim community and guardian of its religious cult.

Given the central role of the early conquests in the initial creation of the Islamic empire, and the importance of military governors in the operation of the empire, it is hardly surprising that the army was long one of the most prominent institutions of the early Islamic state. The army was probably composed at first mainly of tribal contingents led by their chiefs or notable warriors; the earliest garrisons or camp towns (Arabic *amṣār*, sing. *miṣr*), such as al-Kūfa and al-Baṣra in Iraq and Fusṭāṭ in Egypt, where these troops settled, were organized into tribal neighborhoods, probably reflecting the fact that tribes functioned as separate tactical units. The loyalty to the state of these tribally based army units, beyond the bond created in the soldiers by commitment to a common religious ideology, was sometimes enhanced by efforts of provincial governors to co-opt the tribal chiefs by forming them into a kind of advisory council, and by the distribution of patronage. An official called the *'arīf,* who was responsible for distributing the troops' pay *('aṭā'),* among other things, was attached to each tribe and served as a link between the government and the tribesmen in the army.

Under the first Umayyads, the armies of the empire resembled those of the conquest era in their reliance on a broad array of Arabian tribesmen, although the close ties of the caliph Muʿāwiya to the Syrian tribe of Kalb gave that tribe unusual influence in the state. Later Umayyad caliphs tended to rely more heavily on Syrian troops as a standing army, using them in conquest and government from Spain to eastern Iran. However, tribal factionalism in the Syrian armies complicated all Umayyad attempts to consolidate their rule. At the same time, growing numbers of *mawālī* were being drawn into the state's military operations as soldiers; Berber troops, for example, loomed large in the conquest of Spain. The last Umayyad, Marwān II, appears to have attempted to establish new military units that were not based on tribal identity and that included numerous *mawālī.* Early Abbasid armies included some tribal units, but drew more heavily on settled soldiers of both Arabian and Iranian origin hailing from the eastern provinces, particularly Khurasan. The acquisition of large contingents of slave troops by the Abbasid caliphs, which eventually led to a radical change in the character of the army, began in earnest only in the 9th century.

As the empire grew, elements of a bureaucracy to administer its affairs gradually crystallized. The nucleus of this bureaucracy formed under the earliest caliphs in Medina, who started a *dīwān,* or register of troops and others entitled to be on the state payroll. (The word *dīwān* eventually also came to be used for a government department or bureau.) The first caliphs also maintained a small chancery for the drafting of official decrees and directives to their governors and commanders; provincial governors or commanders probably also had a few clerks to handle correspondence (and, where relevant, financial matters). Until the late 7th century the tax administration consisted mainly of administrative cadres inherited by the Islamic state from its predecessors, the Byzantine and Sassanian empires, who kept their records in the traditional languages (Coptic or Greek in Egypt, Greek or Syriac in Syria, Pahlavi in Iraq and Iran). The Umayyad caliph ʿAbd al-Malik (reigned 685–705) attempted a wide-ranging reorganization of imperial institutions intended to enhance centralized control and bolster the regime's legitimacy. Although it was many years before some of these reforms were fully implemented, he initiated the issuing of a new, distinctively Islamic coinage, the establishment of more uniform weights and measures, and the use of Arabic as the official language of administrative record keeping, even in taxation. The increasing importance and pro-

fessionalism of the Arabic-speaking bureaucracy is clearly visible in the writings of the late Umayyad chief administrator ʿAbd al-Ḥamīd ibn Yaḥyā, who appears to be a forerunner of the mighty *wazīrs* (heads of the bureaucracy) of Abbasid times. By the early 9th century, the bureaucracy—particularly at the Abbasids' new imperial capital in Baghdad—had come to be staffed by legions of scribes and managers *(kuttāb),* many of them *mawālī* hailing from Iranian or Aramaean families whose ancestors had served in the Sassanian bureaucracy. This sizable class was influential in preserving, in Islamicized guise, both the administrative and the broader cultural tradition of Sassanian times.

The nature of judicial administration under the early caliphate remains unclear; later sources describe the appointment of judges (Arabic sing. *qāḍī*) by even the earliest caliphs, but the Egyptian papyri point instead to the adjudication of disputes by provincial governors or by the local pagarchs or village headmen into the late Umayyad period. Somewhat later, judges in provincial centers appear to have been appointed by the provincial governors. The judiciary was centralized by the Abbasid caliph Hārūn al-Rashīd, who appointed the noted jurist Abū Yūsuf Yaʿqūb as the first chief judge *(qāḍī al-quḍāt);* thereafter, the chief judge appointed provincial judges in the main provinces, which permitted the judiciary to function more independently of provincial governors than had hitherto been the case.

In the period under review, the Islamic empire was essentially a system of military rule, but one that served the interests of a civilian ruling elite and a religious ideology. The rationale for the empire's existence was twofold: to ensure that Believers could live in a way that allowed them open practice of their faith, and to conquer new areas for the empire. By early Abbasid times, this ideology was neatly conceptualized in terms of the "abode of Islam" *(dār al-islām),* meaning the lands of the empire, and the "abode of war" *(dār al-ḥarb),* meaning all other areas. For many subjects, the main reminders of the empire's presence were thus not only the garrison and the tax collector but the mosque and the religious judge as well. Nevertheless the Islamic system guaranteed not only Muslims but also other monotheists—particularly Christians and Jews—relative security and freedom of religious practice, showing a degree of toleration highly unusual in early medieval times.

BIBL.: Irit Irene Blay-Abramski, "From Damascus to Baghdad: The Abbasid Administrative System as a Product of the Umayyad Heritage (41/661–320/932)" (Ph.D. diss., Princeton University, 1982). Richard W. Bulliet, *Conversion to Islam in the Medieval Period* (Cambridge, Mass., 1979). Fred M. Donner, "The Formation of the Islamic State," *Journal of the American Oriental Society* 106 (1986): 283–296.

F.D.

Italy

In the five centuries between 300 and 800, Italy gradually slipped from being the center of a great empire to being a frontier area contested between rival foreign powers: the Byzantines, to the east, still laid claim to this historic part of their "Roman empire," and the Franks, to the north, marked their new imperial pretensions with the coronation in Rome of a rival western emperor on Christmas Day 800.

The decline of Italy's fortunes was, however, very gradual. In the 4th century, the western empire was wealthy, powerful, and secure, and emperors spent much time in Italy, though increasingly in Milan (which offered easier access to the frontiers), rather than in Rome. This happy state of affairs changed dramatically during the 5th century, when Italy suffered the gradual loss of the surrounding provinces of the western empire and periodic hostile incursions into its territory (most famously, the Visigothic and Vandal sacks of Rome itself, in 410 and 455, respectively). Because of the ever worsening military situation, the emperors of the 5th century generally ruled the peninsula and the rump of its empire from a new capital, Ravenna, sheltered by the marshes and watercourses of the Po delta.

In 476, after several decades in which Germanic warlords had increasingly exercised effective power, the last western emperor, Romulus Augustulus, was formally deposed by his barbarian army commander, Odoacer, who then established an independent kingdom in Italy, based in Ravenna and under the theoretical sovereignty of the eastern emperor. Under its new Germanic kings, much in Italy remained unchanged, and during the reign of the Ostrogoth Theoderic (493–526) the peninsula and its aristocracy enjoyed a long peace and considerable prestige. Theoderic even extended his power into southern Gaul, thereby reestablishing an Italy-centered empire, with its traditional praetorian prefecture at Arles, and many Roman senators served in the Ostrogothic civil service, often, like Cassiodorus, bettering their status and their purses in the process.

The tranquility of this Ostrogothic "Indian summer" was rudely shattered by the invasion in 535 of Justinian, who intended to wrest Italy from barbarian occupation and restore it to imperial (now eastern imperial) hands. The Goths resisted stoutly, and the imperial expeditions were often underresourced, so the war dragged on, inflicting considerable damage on the peninsula, until the last Gothic garrison surrendered in 562. Even then peace was short-lived: in 568 the Lombards took advantage of the weakened state of Italy to invade from Pannonia, eventually establishing a northern kingdom based in Pavia and two loosely affiliated central and southern duchies at Spoleto and Benevento.

Within the later 6th, 7th, and 8th century Byzantine empire, Italy was a remote frontier province, far from the center of power in Constantinople; furthermore, even its capital, Ravenna, was often beleaguered (eventually falling to the Lombards in 751). However, in the south and in Sicily the military situation was less disturbed, and these regions were important as a source of tax revenue for the emperors in Constantinople and a source of rents for the churches of Rome and Ravenna. During the 660s, the wealth and security of Sicily even led the emperor Constans II to experiment with transferring his residence to Syracuse, away from Constantinople and the Aegean, by now seriously threatened by Arabs, Avars, and Slavs.

The remoteness of Italy from the core of the 7th and 8th century empire meant that Italians were often able to defy imperial edicts, such as those against the use of icons. And while the absence of ready help from Constantinople (some thousand miles away) often forced Italy's inhabitants into a degree of self-help, that could lead to a habit of independent action. In particular, the bishops of Rome increasingly had to look after the feeding and defense of their city. By the mid-8th century, the popes were not only de facto rulers of a central Italian principality but were also claiming the right de jure, through possession of the (forged) Donation of Constantine.

These five centuries saw not only major political and military change but also striking alterations in the pattern of social, cultural, and economic life. Perhaps the most obvious change was the disappearance of the Senate as a political unit, and of the senatorial aristocracy as a cultural group. Despite the rise of emperors whose power base was the army and whose residences were generally far from Rome, in the 4th and 5th centuries the Senate remained a prestigious and influential body, and it flourished under the Ostrogoths, who courted its members as part of their campaign to justify alien Germanic rule in Italy. However, the Justinianic wars that followed, and the subsequent marginalization of Italy and Rome within the reestablished empire seem to have dealt a death blow to the existence of the Senate, which disappeared after enjoying almost a thousand years at the center of the historical stage. At a date shortly before 638, the abandoned Curia (the Senate House) in Rome was transformed into the Church of S. Adriano in Foro.

The death of the Senate also marked the end in Italy of traditional secular Latin high culture, once the mark of every Roman aristocrat. In Ostrogothic times, in the early 6th century, aristocrats still owned and edited the traditional classics, and indeed, in the persons of Cassiodorus and Boethius, also still produced them. But by 650 at the latest Italy was no longer dominated by a cultured civilian aristocracy of the traditional Roman type but by militarized toughs, whether Lombard or Byzantine, whose status depended on their prowess in war rather than on their understanding of Virgil's syntax. High cultural life persisted, but only within the church and, in particular, within the ever increasing number of monasteries.

Italy's period of greatest wealth was probably the late republic and early empire, long before the period under discussion here, and field surveys and other archaeological evidence suggest a gradual slide in prosperity through the subsequent centuries, down to a low point that was reached possibly in the 7th century. However, despite this general economic decline, some areas of very considerable wealth existed in late antiquity, testified to in the 4th century by some splendid villas in northern Italy and by the palatial residence at Piazza Armerina in Sicily. The new 5th century capital of Ravenna was also spectacularly rich, and in the early 6th century a single patron, the banker Julianus, was able to pay from his own private funds for the massive Church of S. Vitale. In the 7th and 8th centuries it is hard to find evidence of much wealth in Italy (outside perhaps Sicily), but already in the 8th century there are signs of renewed economic growth, with the emergence of new trading towns, such as Venice.

BIBL.: T. S. Brown, *Gentlemen and Officers: Imperial Administration and Aristocratic Power in Byzantine Italy, 554–800* (London, 1984). L. Ruggini, *Economia e società nell'Italia annonaria* (repr. Bari, 1995). C. Wickham, *Early Medieval Italy: Central Power and Local Society 400–1000* (London, 1981).   B.W.

Ivory

In late antiquity elephant ivory enjoyed a range of applications and, apparently, a degree of availability unprecedented in the ancient world and unparalleled before the Gothic era. It retained its classical reputation as an emblem of luxury even while becoming a relatively cheap commodity: in Diocletian's *Edict of Maximum Prices,* a pound of raw ivory is given a value one-fourth that of bullion silver. It cannot be proved that this low cost persisted in the 5th and 6th centuries, but the increase in the number of useful artifacts made of this material, and the size and surviving quantities of such marks of distinction as the so-called consular diptych, demonstrate at once the passion for ivory in late Roman society and the capacity of its suppliers and carvers to keep pace with the demand. In contrast, while Persia made use of elephants in warfare, the Sassanians scarcely exploited them for their tusks. Although it was worked in the Arab world, ivory did not become a major medium until the establishment of the Umayyad caliphate in Córdoba.

Entire tusks were stored in temple treasuries during the Roman republic and early empire, but small pieces of ivory were used for figurines, dolls, back scratchers and other knickknacks. By about 400, however, large slabs were being turned into diptychs, pyxides (cylindrical containers prepared from hollowed portions of tusks), and boxes, decorated with pagan and Christian subjects alike. In all cases, the amount of ivory used is remarkable when compared with the thin sections employed earlier as revetment. Ivory sheathings of this sort continued, as we know from Paul the Silentiary's description of the ambo of Hagia Sophia. But entire pieces of furniture—the cathedra of Maximian in Ravenna, and presumably the thrones sent by Cyril of Alexandria to Constantinople—were now being carved of the material.

The remains of ateliers that worked both ivory and bone have been found outside Alexandria and on the Palatine hill in Rome. Archaeologically unattested workshops are claimed for regions as far afield as Gaul and the Levant. Sites of reception, if not of manufacture, were certainly widespread. Libanius of Antioch thanks a correspondent for an ivory diptych that he had received; Augustine of Hippo requests the return of writing tablets that he had sent out; for the doorpost of a church near Oviedo, a Visigothic sculptor copied the consul, his attendants, and the games depicted on a diptych of a type current in the early 6th century.

Many consular diptychs are datable by the names they bear, together with the official's previous *cursus honorum;* in this way, they are prime documents of the relationship between family and rank in the Roman and Constantinopolitan elite. Some display inscribed dedications to the Senate, to which a law of 384 (*C.Th.* 15.9.1) was also addressed forbidding any but ordinary consuls to issue ivory diptychs. It is clear from this, as from the letters of Symmachus, that other office holders were accustomed to distribute such tokens. In fact, consular diptychs are but one class of the paired presentation plaques that were prepared for Roman aristocrats to mark important family occasions (marriages, deaths, and the like). Although these last types survive only as unica, and none issued in connection with quaestorian and praetorian games are preserved (unless these are represented by anonymous plaques showing lion and stag hunts, now in Liverpool and St. Petersburg), the extant multiples of the diptychs of Areobindus (seven, issued in 506) and Anastasius (six, issued in 517) argue for a sizable body of production responding to a widely felt urge to commemorate in this way the great events of a man's life.

Consistent with this demand is the physical evidence for the diptychs' fabrication in series. Slight variations in size, iconography, and inscriptions (where these exist) suggest the handiwork of a number of carvers, each aspiring to replicate a model. This is no less true of the scores of surviving pyxides that display well established, if eclectically chosen, incidents from mythology or equally standard scenes of Christian iconography. The uses to which "pagan" boxes of this sort were put—in fact, their literary subjects would by no means have necessarily been offensive to the new religion—cannot be inferred from their decoration. The function of Christian examples as containers for medication or the Eucharist may or may not be rightly deduced from such images as the Healing of the Blind or the Miracle of the Loaves. There is no reason to hypothesize workshops organized along confessional lines; we should, rather, suppose teams of craftsmen that gradually moved over to Christian subject matter as the faith of their members, and especially that of their customers, changed. This conversion was complete before the middle of the 6th century, when carving of all sorts went into radical decline. Although some specimens have been claimed for the 7th and 8th centuries, ivory ceased to be widely worked, returning to favor only under the Carolingians, who recycled much late antique material. There are a few ivory pieces that have been dated to early Islamic times, and a very strange one—a chess piece (?) with Indian motifs—in the Cabinet des Médailles in Paris is dated to ca. 800.

BIBL.: Anthony Cutler, "Five Lessons in Late Roman Ivory," *Journal of Roman Archaeology* 6 (1993): 167–192. Richard Delbrück, *Die Consulardiptychen und verwandte Denkmäler* (Berlin and Leipzig, 1929). E. Kühnel, *Die Islamische Elfenbeinskulpturen* (Berlin, 1971), pl. 1. H. Stern, "The Ivories on the Ambo of the Cathedral of Aix-la-Chapelle," *The Connoisseur,* July 1963. Wolfgang Fritz Volbach, *Elfenbeinarbeiten der Spätantike und des frühen Mittelalters,* 3rd ed. (Mainz, 1976). A.C.

J

Jerash

Jerash, classical Gerasa, was a major city in northern Jordan from Hellenistic times through the early Islamic period. The archaeological remains of the city are well preserved and have seen much excavation over the years, especially in the 1920s and 1930s and since the 1980s. The excavation results have been extensively published. Among the surviving monuments from the Roman period are large temples of Artemis and Jupiter, an oval plaza, colonnaded streets, including the 800 m long Cardo, two theaters, a hippodrome, and a triumphal arch.

In the Byzantine period Jerash continued to prosper. Jerash was a bishopric; the first attested bishop attended the Council of Selucia in 359. The remains of some fifteen churches have been found in the city. The cathedral is the oldest, dating from the end of the 4th century. Immediately to its west is a fountain court, where an annual festival commemorating the Wedding at Cana is mentioned by Epiphanius, writing ca. 375. The Church of the Prophets, Apostles and Martyrs (465) has a cross-in-square plan. The synagogue church was built in 530–531 above the remains of the 4th–5th century synagogue. The three churches of SS. Cosmas and Damian, St. John the Baptist, and St. George were built next to each other as a unit between 529 and 533; the central Church of St. John the Baptist has the plan of a circle set in a square. The latest dedicatory inscription, from 611, is in the Bishop Genesios church. The churches have lovely mosaic floors, most of which saw deliberate damage in the 8th century to their images of ordinary people and animals. Among other public monuments dated by inscriptions, the Baths of Flaccus were built in 454–455 and renovated in 584. Just over a kilometer to the north of the walled city was a theater and pool complex for the Maiumas festival of water spectacles, which was renewed in 535. In contrast to all the public monuments, the domestic housing from the Byzantine period has been little investigated.

Excavations since the 1980s have revealed extensive evidence for continued occupation in the early Islamic period, which was largely ignored by the earlier excavators. Of special note is a residential quarter from the 7th–8th centuries in the southern part of the city. In the 9th century those houses around the Southern Decumanus were used for the production of pottery. Other pottery kilns from the 8th–9th centuries in the former north theater and the Artemis Temple demonstrate that pottery manufacturing was a major industry in the early Islamic period. A number of terra-cotta lamps bear Arabic inscriptions that record their manufacture in Jerash in the 8th century. Jerash was also a coin mint in the early 8th century. Only one small mosque has been identified, in contrast to all the churches that continued to be used in the early Islamic period. Jerash's life as a major urban center seems to have ended in the 9th century.

BIBL.: Iain Browning, *Jerash and the Decapolis* (London, 1982). P. L. Gatier, "Nouvelles inscriptions de Gérasa: Le prison de l'évêque Paul," *Syria* 62 (1982): 297–305. Carl Kraeling, *Gerasa, City of the Decapolis* (New Haven, 1938). Fawzi Zayadine, ed., *Jerash Archaeological Project, 1981–1983* (Amman, 1986).   R.S.

Jerome

Jerome was born into a wealthy Christian family about 347 in Stridon, a frontier town between Dalmatia and Pannonia, and was later educated in Rome. In the mid-360s he moved to the imperial residence of Trier, where he converted to the ascetic life and perhaps had his famous dream wherein he accused himself of preferring pagan literature to Christian (*Ep.* 22.30: "*Ciceronianus es, non Christianus*"). After having spent some years in ascetic circles in northern Italy, especially in Aquileia, he embarked on a pilgrimage to the east but got only as far as Antioch, where he stayed in the household of his influential friend Evagrius, a rich Antiochene *curialis*. He then entered a retreat in what he described as "the desert of Syrian Chalcis," which may be located at Maronia, a village some 30 miles from Antioch, situated on an estate of Evagrius. There Jerome lived in a cenobitic community, improving his knowledge of Greek, learning Hebrew, and communicating with other Christian intellectuals. Owing to dogmatic disputes with the brethren in his neighborhood, he was expelled from his retreat; he returned to Antioch, where he was ordained a priest. About 380 he is found in Constantinople, where he promoted the case of Nicene orthodoxy and met important church politicians and theologians at the council convoked by Theodosius I (381). During his years in the east, Jerome made his debut as a Latin translator of Greek theological works and an author of the ascetic movement and Nicene orthodoxy. He wrote the *Life of Paul, the First Hermit,* began to translate into Latin the works of Origen, and translated and continued Eusebius's *Chronica.* In 382 Jerome accompanied two eastern bishops on an ecclesiastical mission to the court of Pope Damasus, who employed him as his secretary and supported his plan to revise the Latin text of the Gospels and the Psalter. In Rome, Jerome also became the intellectual center of an ascetic circle that included several aristocratic ladies whom he taught to reconcile Christian virtues with their traditional primacy. He encouraged ascetic seclusion, sexual abstinence, and scriptural reading in his letters and treatises. When Damasus, his most influential patron, passed away, a powerful opposition forced him to leave Rome in August 385. Jerome set out again for the east and, in 386, established himself in Bethlehem, where he founded a monastery and a convent financed by the Roman aristocrats Paula and Eustochium, who had followed him into exile. In Bethlehem, the erudite monk-scholar spent the last decades of his life translating the Hebrew Bible into Latin from the original languages, composing many learned commentaries on the Scripture, producing various polemical-theological pamphlets, and compiling his *De viris illustribus,* a handbook on ecclesiastical writers. His extensive collection of letters is of greatest historical importance for his life and times. As an amazingly productive exegete, he was dependent on both Greek and Latin predecessors. His ascetic manuals and monastic *Lives* combined religious edification and instruction with cultivated entertainment. Jerome intervened in all contemporary theological debates and bitterly quarreled with his former friend Rufinus of Aquileia during the Origenist controversy. He always advocated his orthodoxy and scholarly reputation as a *vir trilinguis,* promoted himself as an intermediary between western and eastern theology, and fostered an ambitious network of relations with Christian literati in Italy, Spain, and Gaul. Jerome died in 419 or 420.

BIBL.: For Jerome's complete works, see D. Vallarsi, ed. (Verona, 1734–1742), repr. in *PL* 22–30. *Chronica,* ed. R. Helm, *GCS Eus.* 7, 3rd ed. J. N. D. Kelly, *Jerome: His Life, Writings and Controversies* (London, 1975). Stefan Rebenich, *Hieronymus und sein Kreis: Prosopographische und sozialgeschichtliche Untersuchungen* (Stuttgart, 1992). M. Vessey, "Conference and Confession: Literary Pragmatics in Augustine's *Apologia contra Hieronymum, Journal of Early Christian Studies* 1 (1993): 175–213. M. Vessey, "Jerome's Origen," *Studia patristica* 28 (1993): 135–145. S.R.

Jerusalem

Sanctified as the site of the Jewish Temple and as the capital of several Jewish states, Jerusalem had been transformed into a monumental showplace by Herod the Great and the Hasmonaean dynasty. The Temple was located on an artificial platform whose walls are still preserved in the southern part of today's Haram al-Sharif. The young Jesus exercised his ministry there; he went from a glorious entry on Palm Sunday to death and resurrection west of the Herodian city; he ascended into heaven on the Mount of Olives, which is separated from the city by the Kedron Valley to the east. Jewish and Christian events were gradually transformed into memories vaguely associated with specific places, and after the wars of 70 and 132–134, the city became a Roman garrison town, Aelia Capitolina. Walls surrounded a squarish space (more or less today's Old City) that included the area of the Temple and the western hills (Golgotha, Sion), with their Christian connotations. Straight Roman streets cut across the uneven terrain, and Roman imperial and pagan monuments were built in several parts of the city. Little is known about the Jewish and Christian presence in the city at that time, but there was a Jerusalem-based church founded around the apostle James and his successors.

The conversion of Constantine and the adoption of Christianity as the religion of the empire transformed Jerusalem into the holy city of Christianity. Some (Eusebius of Caesarea, for example) argued for maintaining it as the ruined city of the Jews to illustrate God's favor for the new faith. In the short reign of Julian an attempt was made to rebuild the Jewish Temple, but he did not succeed. Under the leadership of bishops of Jerusalem like Cyril (second half of the 4th century) and Juvenal (419–458), under whom it became a patriarchate, and of imperial patrons like Constantine and Helena in the 4th century, Eudocia in the 5th, and Justinian in the 6th, Jerusalem acquired a thoroughly Christian profile within and without the Roman walls.

On the western hills of Jerusalem were found the sumptuous sanctuary of the Holy Sepulcher, with an entry from the main Roman street, a five-aisled congregational hall known as the *martyrium,* a baptistery, a circular court (later domed) with the Rotunda of the Anastasis, and various dependencies; the "new" (known as the Nea) Church of the Theotokos consecrated in 543 (as is known from an archaeologically retrieved inscription) that Justinian ordered built on the slope of Mt. Sion facing the ruined Herodian Temple, which was then already associated with Solomon; a less well known sanctuary on Mt. Sion itself, the "mother" of churches. The eastern hill was left untouched and became a quarry. There were small and large churches everywhere, and a special importance was given to sanctuaries on the Mount of Olives, to which Christ's ascension and his return became inextricably tied. This Christian transformation of the city is admirably illustrated in the Madaba map, a representation of the city from the late 6th century found on the floor of a small church in Jordan. Some seventeen churches can be identified in the peculiar code of the map, with the three great sanctuaries of the Holy Sepulcher, the Nea, and Sion dominating the city. These churches became the repository of many treasures, pious ones reflecting holy history and more secular ones as gifts brought by the believers. Holy souvenirs, like the Monza phials, were sold or distributed in the city.

Jerusalem participated in the theological and political battles of the time, but it was most particularly a city of pilgrims, many of whom have left accounts of their visits that offer glimpses into the piety and behavior of various social classes from many regions. It was probably to accommodate these pilgrims that the empress Eudocia enlarged the city toward the south through a curtain wall, sections of which are still visible today. The area around the city became a place for monastic settlements, as many *lavras* were formed there. It was a place of theological learning, liturgical inventions, and exchanges of ideas. Its ecclesiastical policies were affected by the aftermath of the Council of Chalcedon and the religious politics of Justinian's court. Its language was primarily Greek, but Aramaic was present as well, and there is now evidence for the existence of Arabic-speaking Christians.

The last decade of the 6th century and the first three decades of the 7th were turbulent years. In 614 the city fell to the Persians, considerable massacres and destructions ensued (although some doubt can be expressed about the accuracy of sources), the True Cross was taken away, and the patriarch went into exile. There may have been a Jewish attempt at recapturing the area of the Temple, but it did not last and, under the abbot (later patriarch) Modestus, part of the city was reconstructed to permit Heraclius's triumphant return with the Cross in 630. These events were accompanied by an increase in eschatological pronouncements among Christians and Jews that was to continue throughout the century.

In 638 Jerusalem fell peacefully to the Muslim Arabs in ways that are shrouded in myth. The main immediate consequence of the takeover was the transformation of the Herodian platform into a Muslim sanctuary, eventually to be called the Haram al-Sharif. A mosque was built first and the access points to the platform were restored, especially the southern ones that led to Muslim settlements (these have recently been excavated). In 691–692 the Dome of the Rock was erected, making fully visible the new holiness of the eastern hill of Jerusalem facing the Christian western ones. The shape, inscriptions, and mosaics of the Dome of the Rock have ideological as well as pious purposes and deal especially with the significance of its presence as a sign of the last revelation in a city associated with the previous ones and as a demonstration of Umayyad power. At a more popular level, the themes of the Prophet Muhammad's Night Journey and Ascension, as well as all sorts of Muslim accounts of Jewish prophets, began to acquire their own spaces in the city. Around 700 the old mosque was replaced with a large new one, more or less on the spot of the present Aqsa Mosque, and the Hellenistic space of the Jewish Temple had become a Muslim sanctuary, the *masjid bayt al-maqdis,* "the mosque of the Holy House." These Umayyad creations are all remarkable for the quality of their art, inspired by classical and Christian monuments.

The Christian population of the city came to reflect the ethnic and linguistic breadth of the whole Christian world, a significant Jewish population moved to Jerusalem, and Arabic began to replace Greek as the common language for the city's diverse people.

BIBL.: M. Van Berchem, *Matériaux pour un corpus des inscriptions: Syrie du Sud: Jérusalem* (Cairo, 1922–1927). M. Ben-Dov, *In the Shadow of the Temple* (Jerusalem, 1985). K. Bieberstein and H. Bloedhorn, *Jerusalem, Grundzüge der Baugeschichte,* 3 vols. (Wiesbaden, 1994). O. Grabar, *The Shape of the Holy* (Princeton, 1996). B. Kuhnel, *From the Earthly to the Heavenly Jerusalem* (Rome, 1987). F. E. Peters, *Jerusalem and Mecca* (New York, 1988). M. Rosen-Ayalon, *The Early Islamic Monuments of al-Haram al-Sharif* (Jerusalem, 1989). R. L. Wilken, *The Land Called Holy* (New Haven, 1992). O.G.

John Chrysostom

Patriarch of Constantinople from 398 to 404, John Chrysostom was born in Antioch between 340 and 350 to a family headed by a military officer. He was given a traditional classical education and studied for a time under Libanius, the leading rhetorician of Antioch. Although as a young man John turned his attention away from the possibility of a secular career and toward a life in the church, his training in rhetoric was not wasted: he was to become one of the most famous and eloquent Christian orators of late antiquity, so much so that later Christian writers gave him the name Chrysostom, "golden mouth" in Greek. Soon after he began his life in the church, he ventured out to live among the monks of the Syrian desert. He returned to the city after two years because of the toll that extreme asceticism was taking on his health. As a deacon for the next five years, he was responsible for much of the administration of the church's charity.

He was ordained a priest in 386, and in the following year he faced one of the greatest civic upheavals of his time, the Riot of the Statues, in which large numbers of Antiochenes rioted and destroyed imperial statues on account of new taxes. A series of sermons survive in which John both rebukes his congregation for their rebellious behavior and consoles them in the face of the possibility of stern imperial punishment for their acts. He continued to preach to them for the next twelve years, explaining the meaning of the Gospels and Paul's epistles, especially their implications for ideal Christian behavior.

John came onto the stage of high-level ecclesiastical and imperial politics and controversy after the leaders of Constantinople chose him as their new bishop in 398. From the start, John had enemies. Theophilus, bishop of Alexandria, viewed the new bishop with suspicion because he was worried that Alexandria's status among the bishoprics was threatened by the prestige of the new imperial capital. As bishop, John immediately began to reform the church's administration and finances. Rather than wooing ecclesiastic and imperial leaders with flattery, hospitality and gifts, he dined alone and used his funds to support hospitals. He spoke out against clerics who lived with women and deposed bishops guilty of simony. Because of these reforms, the higher clerics and the monks of the city, accustomed to more independence, also turned against the new bishop. Especially disastrous to his career were his remarks against the empress Eudocia's love of luxury. At the same time, John won the favor of his congregation through his reforms as well as his sermons, in which he criticized the powerful and defended the weak.

John's widespread popularity did not prevent his powerful enemies from conspiring against him. After John received a group of Egyptian monks who were reputed to be heretics, Theophilus used this as a pretext for a strike against him, hoping to brand John as a heretic by association. Theophilus came to Constantinople, along with other Egyptian bishops, and in early 403 summoned the Council of the Oak, which John refused to attend. The council deposed him, and the emperor Arcadius approved its action. The next day,

when the populace learned what had transpired, they refused to let the emperor's men into the church complex to take their bishop into exile. After John had slipped out of town to avoid further conflict, the populace continued to protest until the empress ordered John's return.

A happy crowd met John's return, but he was soon in trouble again. Shortly before Easter in 404, Arcadius had the bishop confined to the episcopal residence, and the church was closed to John's clerics. The bishop's followers responded by gathering outside the walls to celebrate Easter until they were attacked by armed soldiers. Two months later, John was taken to Cucusa, a town in Armenia, where he was to remain until he died in 407. When his supporters again protested his forced departure, soldiers attacked them. In the shuffle, the Hagia Sophia burned, as did the Senate House. The Johannites (as John's supporters came to be known) refused to acknowledge John's successors until 415, when the bishop Atticus added John's name to the diptychs (lists of people to be honored in prayer).

John's influence on other Christian writers was apparent soon after his death. Between 415 and 421, a selection of the sermons of Chrysostom were translated into Latin by Anianus of Celeda, a Pelagian who found John's combination of moral rigor and emphasis on human freedom congenial. In his debate with Julian of Eclanum, Augustine appealed (somewhat tendentiously and with little understanding of the Greek) to other Chrysostom sermons. An extensive body of sermons circulated under Chrysostom's name, some of which inspired the *kontakia* of Romanos Melodes (J. Grosdidier de Matons, *Romanos le Mélode*, Paris 1977, 250–252). In Byzantium from the 9th century onward, his memory remained especially prominent because it was attached to the Constantinopolitan liturgy.

BIBL.: J. A. de Aldama, *Repertorium pseudochrysostomicum* (Paris, 1965). P. Allen and W. Mayer, "Tradition of Constantinopolitan Preaching," *Byzantinische Forschungen* 24 (1997): 93–114. J.-P. Bouhot, "Version inédite du sermon 'ad neophytos' de Saint Jean Chrysostome," *Revue des études augustiniennes* 17 (1971): 27–41. K. Cooper, "An(n)ianus of Celeda and the Latin Readers of John Chrysostom," *Studia patristica* 27 (1993): 249–255. J. N. D. Kelly, *Golden Mouth* (London, 1995). J. H. W. G. Liebeschuetz, *Barbarians and Bishops* (Oxford, 1990). Robert Louis Wilken, *John Chrysostom and the Jews: Rhetoric and Reality in the Late Fourth Century* (Berkeley, 1983). J.M.

John of Ephesus

John of Ephesus, also known as John of Amida, was the leading Monophysite church historian and hagiographer of the 6th century. His life reflects the vicissitudes of the Monophysite church. He was born in northern Mesopotamia under the tolerant Anastasius, shortly after peace had been restored on the eastern frontier in 506. At the age of two he fell critically ill but was restored to health after being brought to the local stylite Maro, whose prescription of cooked lentils effected a cure; in exchange John was committed to Maro's care and prepared for a monastic life. In the 520s John joined the Amidan monastery of John Urtaya and shared in the tribulations and exile during the Chalcedonian persecution of the 520s and 530s. By 540 John had reached Constantinople, where he was among the group of monks protected by the empress Theodora; there he probably witnessed the arrival of the plague in 542, since his *History* includes a vivid account of its impact. Also in 542 John was commissioned by Justinian to organize the conversion of pagans and heretics in southwestern Asia Minor, an initiative that resulted (on John's own account) in eighty thousand conversions and the construction of more than one hundred churches and monasteries. Thereafter, although now titular bishop of Ephesus, he was based near the capital of Sycae on the Golden Horn, where the imperial eunuch Callinicus had provided him with a suburban property that was transformed into a monastery. After Justin II's accession in 565, John was recognized as the leading Monophysite at Constantinople and a representative of his coreligionaries in attempts to devise a formula for Christological reunion; although John was amenable to reconciliation and twice even celebrated communion with Chalcedonians, after discussions broke down he was subjected to more persecution and imprisonment in the 570s. He died in about 589.

John's major works were composed during the last part of his life. *The Lives of the Eastern Saints* is a collection of fifty-eight chapters devoted to Monophysite ascetics from Syria and Mesopotamia, many of whom were known personally to John. Writing when the Monophysite church was rent by schisms and threatened by persecution, John's intention in this work was to urge the benefits of unity by recalling the heroes of his youth and their endurance during the persecution of Abraham bar Khaili of Amida. John deliberately denigrated the competitive overachievers of the ascetic world and instead promoted a quietist ideal in which religious harmony was stressed and social engagement played down. His *Church History* is only partially preserved. The first part extended from Julius Caesar to the death of Theodosius II, and the second part continued the narrative to the early years of Justin II (about 570); it is believed to have influenced the narratives of subsequent Syriac historians, e.g., Pseudo-Dionysius of Tel-Mahre and Michael the Syrian. Most of the third part survives, providing a jumbled and sometimes repetitive account of persecutions, Monophysite divisions, and warfare, especially on the eastern frontier. John was a much better raconteur than historian.

BIBL.: Susan Ashbrook Harvey, *Asceticism and Society in Crisis: John of Ephesus and the Lives of the Eastern Saints* (Berkeley, 1990). Jan van Ginkel, "A Monophysite Historian in Sixth-Century Byzantium" (Ph.D. diss., University of Groningen, 1995). A. Witakowski, *John of Ephesus: The Book of the Plague* (Liverpool, 1996). Witold Witakowski, *Pseudo-Dionysius of Tel-Mahre, Chronicle Part III* (Liverpool, 1996).   L.M.W.

John of Nikiu

Egypt's only native historiographer of the 7th century, John served as Monophysite bishop of Nikiu, a fortified island in the Nile delta. John also acted as "director" (Ethiopic *madabber;* Arabic *mudabbir*) of the monasteries of Upper Egypt. According to the 10th century Arabic *History of the Patriarchs of Alexandria,* John was elected as *apotritēs,* or administrator, of these monasteries by the Monophysite Simeon, forty-second patriarch of Egypt, but he ended his career in disgrace, deposed after having beaten a monk to death. Already elderly during the height of his ecclesiastical career (ca. 686–694), it is unlikely that John survived much beyond the beginning of the 8th century.

At some point John composed a chronicle, probably in Greek. He depended heavily on three Greek sources: John Malalas, John of Antioch, and the unknown author of the *Chronicon paschale.* As Greek fell into disuse in Egypt, his chronicle was translated into Arabic and, much later, into Ethiopic, the language of the only two extant manuscripts. A substantial portion of the original text was lost in transmission.

John's *Chronicle* remains important as a vital historiographical source for the otherwise poorly documented 7th century Egypt. As a Monophysite, John included in his *Chronicle* apocalyptic passages that view the Arab invasions of that century as the direct consequence of the Chalcedonian division of Christ into two natures. John's *Chronicle* thus presents us with the historical vision of an ecclesiastic who was grappling with the tumultuous events of his own time.

BIBL.: A. Carile, "Giovanni di Nikius, Cronista Bizantino-Copto del VII Secolo," *Felix Ravenna* 4 (1981): 103–155. R. H. Charles, *The Chronicle of John, Coptic Bishop of Nikiu* (London, 1916; repr. Amsterdam, 1966). Hermann Zotenberg, *Chronique de Jean, evêque de Nikiou: Texte éthiopien publié et traduit* (Paris, 1883).   N.D.

Jordanes

The chronicler Jordanes, once referred to as "Jornandes," was of Gothic origin. He is first attested in the early 6th century as a *notarius* (secretary) in the service of the Ostrogothic general Gunthigis *qui et* Baza. He eventually converted from Arian to Nicene Christianity, and he seems to have become a cleric. Some historians identify him with the contemporary bishop Jordanes of Croton. Around the year 550 he composed his *On the Origin and History of the Goths,* usually called the *Getica,* which summarized the now lost

Gothic History written by the Roman senator Cassiodorus.

Jordanes also wrote *A Survey of the Times, or, On the Origin and History of the Roman People*, usually referred to as the *Romana*. This work is actually in two parts, the first of which covers the history of the world up to the beginning of the Roman empire, and the second of which covers the Roman empire. It was based in part on another lost history, that of the Roman senator Aurelius Memmius Symmachus, although not nearly to such an extent as once was thought.

It has been suggested that Jordanes's works, both in Latin, were written in Constantinople. Jordanes's underlying intention was to justify the Gothic domination of the Romans. He gives the earliest extant account of barbarian history written from the barbarian viewpoint, and his works include much material that is found nowhere else.

BIBL.: Theodor Mommsen, ed., *Monumenta Germaniae historica, Auctores antiquissimi.* vol. 5, pt. 1 (Berlin, 1882). Charles Christopher Mierow, trans., *The Gothic History of Jordanes in English Version* (Princeton, 1915). Brian Croke, "A.D. 476: The Manufacture of a Turning Point," *Chiron* 13(1983): 81–119. Walter Goffart, *The Narrators of Barbarian History (A.D. 550–800): Jordanes, Gregory of Tours, Bede, and Paul the Deacon* (Princeton, 1988). R.W.M.

Judaism

The evidence for Judaism in late antiquity is primarily of two sorts, literary and archaeological. The literary evidence consists of rabbinic literature and various references to Jews and Judaism scattered throughout Greek, Latin, and Syriac texts. The archaeological evidence consists of synagogues, cemeteries, catacombs, and inscriptions, as well as various other remains. The central problem for the historian is how to put all these bits of evidence together to create a coherent picture.

Rabbinic texts reveal a vigorous and creative society of Jews in Palestine and Babylonia. This society produced several enormous and enormously difficult books in Hebrew and Aramaic, not only the Mishnah and the Talmud but also books of biblical exegesis and biblical translation (from the original Hebrew into Aramaic), synagogal poetry and prayers, moral exhortation, and compendia of rabbinic law. The virtuosos of this society were men who studied God's Torah, disputed with each other the details of its interpretation, and served as teachers to would-be virtuosos. This was a coherent society with clearly marked boundaries, but it was not closed to outsiders; indeed, the degree of cultural interaction between rabbinic Jews and their non-Jewish neighbors remains the subject of ongoing scholarly controversy. The presence of Greek (and some Latin and Pahlavi) words and phrases, of Hellenistic and Byzantine literary and rhetorical forms, of motifs drawn from Greek literature, of dispute stories involving Gentiles, "philosophers,"

and "heretics," reveals that the creators of rabbinic literature were not cut off from the world around them, even if they were not fully part of it.

The literary evidence produced by outsiders reveals a Jewish society that is distinctively Jewish, but whose distinctiveness is different from that of rabbinic society. There are few references here to masters of Torah, rabbinic judges, or talmudic dialectic. We see here plain Jews, from shopkeepers to ship captains. We see Jews who observe the basic laws of the Torah (circumcision, Sabbath and festivals, abstention from pork and other prohibited foods, avoidance of worship of idolatry, and so on) as well as Jews who are expert in medicine and magic, blessings and curses. In his *Against the Jews* (available in English translation as *Against the Judaizing Christians*), John Chrysostom, bishop of Antioch in the 380s, fulminates against those of his flock who seek out Jews to bless their crops. Similarly, the Egyptian magical papyri invoke the God of Abraham, Isaac, and Jacob to enhance the efficacy of various spells, and several Greek inscriptions of Asia Minor invoke the curses of the book of Deuteronomy. The boundary between these Jews and their non-Jewish neighbors seems to have been more blurred than that which is assumed by the rabbinic texts.

Rabbinic literature itself reveals that at the margins of rabbinic society, in both Palestine and Babylonia, were Jews who did not live by or endorse the rabbinic program. They attended synagogue, observed the Sabbath, and honored the Torah, but did not always respect and honor the rabbinic virtuosos and did not always lead a life consonant with the ways of the Torah as defined by the rabbis. Perhaps these Jews of Palestine and Babylonia are of a piece with the Diaspora Jews envisioned by the non-Jewish literary evidence.

The most puzzling part of the literary evidence is the absence of nonrabbinic Jewish literature. There is no Philo or Josephus in late antiquity; in the Hellenistic and early Roman periods Greek-speaking Jews produced a luxuriant literature, but after 100 C.E. they appear to have become illiterate. A few shards remain: some poems in the *Sibylline Oracles;* some Christian prayers and apocryphal texts of the 2nd and 3rd centuries that seem to be based on Jewish Greek originals; a few Latin texts, mostly dealing with the Hebrew Bible, that have been ascribed by some modern scholars to Jewish origins. These bits and pieces are interesting and important but do not add up to much. Greek-speaking Jews lived in all the large cities of the eastern Roman empire (Alexandria, Antioch, Byzantium) as well as throughout Palestine, Syria, Asia Minor, and the Italian Peninsula. Latin-speaking Jews lived in North Africa. But no substantial literature is extant from any of these communities. Greek-speaking Jews read the Bible in Greek (apparently preferring the version of Aquila to the Septuagint, which had been taken over by the church) but were not inspired thereby to write. Why, we do not know.

The archaeological evidence is rich but uneven. The Jewish catacombs of Rome reveal a community secure in its Jewish identity, with numerous synagogues. In death the Jews wanted to be together, separate from their Gentile neighbors. At the same time, the epitaphs (most of them written in Greek), the artwork, and the mode of burial reveal a community that was part of its urban environment. No rabbis are mentioned. The catacombs of Beth Shearim, a small town on the edge of lower Galilee, were the burial grounds for Jews not only from Palestine but also from all over the Near East; many of the epitaphs memorialize people from Palmyra. Some of the artwork, however, suggests not insular Jewish communities but ones that were integrated into the common Semitic culture of Syria. A series of burial chambers were set aside for people called "rabbis," although the identities of these rabbis, and the degree of their connection with the society that produced the Mishnah and the Talmud, are not clear.

The synagogue remains are more impressive and more significant. The inscriptions show that a culture of public benefaction ("euergetism") flourished among the Jewish communities of late antiquity, just as it flourished in late antique society generally. Wealthy donors would endow the construction of all or part of a synagogue, thereby displaying their power and gaining the gratitude of the community. We may assume that the workings of the community were influenced, if not controlled, by such individuals (among whom are several women). The synagogues of Byzantine Palestine also reveal a comfortable cultural interaction with their environment. The architecture and more especially the artwork (mosaics, carvings) often followed standard models that were also used in contemporary churches. The liturgy that was recited in these synagogues is not known. We may assume that by the 7th or 8th century most synagogues, certainly in the land of Israel and Babylonia and perhaps even in the Diaspora, followed a rabbinic regimen, but before that point such an assumption is not warranted.

All of this evidence, of course, suggests a great deal of diversity within the Jewish communities of late antiquity. But the single most important development in late antique Judaism was the emergence of a single Jewish culture unifying the Jewish world. In the 3rd century this culture is attested only in its cultural homelands, Palestine and Babylonia, but by the 10th century it is attested from Spain in the west to Iran in the east, from Egypt and Yemen in the south to France and Germany in the north. Talmudic culture and rabbinic hegemony kept the diverse Jewish communities attached to each other throughout the Middle Ages.

BIBL.: S. Fine, *This Holy Place: On the Sanctity of the Synagogue during the Greco-Roman Period* (Notre Dame, 1998). W. J. Van Bekkum, "Anti-Christian Polemic in Hebrew Liturgical Poetry (Piyyut) of the Sixth and Seventh Centuries," in *Early Christian Poetry* (Leiden, 1993), 297–308. Beat Brenk, "Die Unwandlung der Synagoge von Apamea in eine Kirche. Eine mentalitätsgeschichtliche Studie," in *Tesserae: Festschrift Josef Engemann* (Münster in Westfalen, 1991), 1–25. *Severus of Minorca: Letter on the Conversion of the Jews,* ed. S. Bradbury (Oxford, 1996). L. V. Rutgers, *The Jews of Late Ancient Rome* (Leiden, 1995).   S.J.C.

Julian the Apostate

Flavius Claudius Julianus (ca. 331–363), known as the Apostate, ruled as sole emperor for only nineteen months (November 361–June 363), yet he passed into history as one of the most controversial of Roman rulers. His historical notoriety derives largely from his religious policies, but his ability as military commander, administrator, and man of letters made an equally strong impression on his contemporaries. His life and reign are unusually well documented. The chief sources are Ammianus Marcellinus, books 16–25; eight orations of Libanius on Julianic themes; and Julian's own remarkable literary output: three panegyrics, two polemics against philosophical opponents, two prose hymns, the tract *Against the Galilaeans,* a satire on the city of Antioch *(Misopogon),* a satire on his imperial predecessors *(Caesars),* and numerous letters.

Julian's father and uncles were murdered in the palace massacre following the death of Constantine in 337. Spared because of his youth, he grew to manhood in Asia Minor, relegated from 342 to 348 to a remote estate in Cappadocia but later permitted to move about freely and to study with excellent teachers. The fierce love he conceived for Greek *paideia* in all its aspects had a profound impact on his beliefs and conduct, both public and private. His adolescent encounter with the Neoplatonist successors of Iamblichus proved decisive, leading in 351 to a secret "conversion" to traditional polytheism and a strong interest in theurgy. Summoned from his studies in Athens in 355, he was appointed caesar by Constantius II and dispatched to Gaul, which was overrun by Franks and Alamanni. Although unprepared for public life, he demonstrated exceptional skill as a general and succeeded, over the next five years, in restoring the Gallic provinces and amassing a formidable record of victories. When Constantius II requested legions for a Persian campaign in 360, Julian's Gallic troops mutinied and proclaimed him Augustus. Constantius's sudden death averted civil war.

Julian sought to impose a fundamental shift in the course of late Roman society. Hostile to the "big government" of the late empire, he drastically reduced palace personnel and simplified court ceremonial, affecting the *civilitas* of early emperors. He sought to reinvigorate traditional civic life by restoring the cities' finances and by compelling city councillors to fulfill their civic duties. He made vigorous efforts to restore the fabric of traditional polytheism, repairing shrines and altars, promoting the revival of traditional cult practices, particularly blood sacrifice, and making pagan priesthoods once again prestigious. Simultaneously, he sought to undermine and marginalize Christianity within the governing classes. Religious toleration was proclaimed in the hope that Christians would weaken themselves through schism, and although he deplored physical persecution, he came to advocate openly the political promotion of polytheists. The most notorious of his anti-Christian acts, however, was the issue of an edict forbidding Christians to teach classical literature or philosophy. His premature death while on a campaign against the Persians in June 363 nullified any long-term effects of these initiatives, but his fame was ensured by his clear enunciation, in word and deed, of a radical alternative to the social and religious developments of his day.

BIBL.: G. W. Bowersock, *Julian the Apostate* (London and Cambridge, Mass., 1978). Polymnia Athanassidi, *Julian: An Intellectual Biography*, 2nd ed. (London and New York, 1992). Rowland Smith, *Julian's Gods: Religion and Philosophy in the Thought and Action of Julian the Apostate* (London and New York, 1995).   S.B.

Justice

Justice in the later Roman world was neither universally available nor uniformly applied. Many who attempted to resolve disputes through the official judicial system found the courts inaccessible, the expense of litigation (court costs and advocate's fees) prohibitive, the archaic technicalities of the law difficult to comprehend, and the outcome of any action uncertain.

These "inefficiencies" in the delivery of justice were to some extent deliberate. The imperial government did not maintain a legal system as a form of public service. Rather, it was part of a pattern of rule. The disputes that mattered were those that threatened the security of a province, its financial stability, or the social and economic dominance of the local notables on whom the central government significantly depended for the collection of taxes and the maintenance of good order.

From that point of view, it is perhaps unsurprising that the central government sought to limit the number of cases heard in its courts by doing little to relieve either judicial delays or the distances parties and witnesses had to travel to a hearing. In 382 an imperial constitution reminded litigants "that they should convey to our sacred ears those matters which are most suitably litigated before emperors, and they should not assume that Our Everlastingness should be taken up with superfluous legal actions" (*C.Th.* 12.12.9.1). Monetary thresholds were also imposed, particularly to prevent appeals. In 536, for example, the emperor Justinian ruled that only actions worth more than 720 *solidi* could be brought in the highest appellate courts in Constantinople (*Nov.* 103.1). As a further complication to any action, if the litigation involved a soldier or an imperial official (as defendent or plaintiff) that

party could exercise a right of *praescriptio fori* to have the case removed to the court of one of their own superiors.

Court fees imposed a further disincentive to litigate. A detailed schedule of fees issued sometime between 361 and 363 to the provincial governor of Numidia (the so-called *Ordo Salutationis*) laid down the amounts to be paid to each court official for each stage of litigation (*CIL* 8.17896; *L'année épigraphique* [1978]: 892). The fees were not great—perhaps in all 2 to 3 *solidi* for a successful action—but when added to all the other expenses, they would in practice have prevented a peasant farmer from litigating in the governor's court except in the most serious of cases. Higher courts imposed greater charges. According to John Lydus, a senior bureaucrat on the judicial staff of the praetorian prefect, in the early 6th century the cost in fees alone of the documentation to commence an action before a prefect was 37 *solidi* (*Mag.* 3.25).

Faced with the costs, risks, and difficulties of litigation, many turned to the official judicial system only as a last resort. At a local level, rather than litigating before the governor, it might be possible to bring an action before the *defensor civitatis*, given jurisdiction by Justinian in 535 to decide cases worth up to 300 *solidi* (*Nov.* 15.3.2), or before the local bishop (*episcopalis audientia*). These were seemingly popular alternatives. Like the emperors in Constantinople, Augustine, bishop in the small North African town of Hippo at the turn of the 4th century, is said to have found his judicial duties frustratingly time consuming (Possidius, *Vita Augustini* 19).

But—as is still the case in modern western society—those disputes that resulted in some formal legal proceeding represented only a small fraction of the total number of disagreements. Some instead sought arbitration or mediation; others relied on self-help or direct action; many had no option but to bear a loss. Of course, in any one dispute, a combination of these mechanisms might be used to force a resolution, or to keep in play what for one party could be a profitable disagreement. In this context, too, it is important to recognize that formal petitions requesting a court hearing might sometimes have less to do with a desire to litigate than with a series of threats or bargaining positions in the face of what one party (at least) was keen to present as the unwelcome risks of going to court.

Undoubtedly such a system tended to reinforce the position of the powerful. Not only were they in the best position to bear the risks and costs of litigation, but they also could hope to bring pressure to bear on judges, who were not professional experts but administrators (governors, treasury officials, praetorian prefects) sitting in a judicial capacity. In late 4th century Antioch, Libanius, the famous teacher and orator—and on occasion an unsuccessful litigant—complained that some of his fellow local notables exercised their right to sit with the governor in court only to protect their own interests. "There they are, sitting beside him on the tribunal, whispering in the ears of those judging, paying more attention to cases which concern them, rather than listening to those brought on behalf of the state" (*Orat.* 52.4). But in other circumstances even Libanius was prepared to write on behalf of others, openly seeking to influence the outcome of a case by commending them to an official (often a friend or a former pupil) and asking that he act "on behalf of justice and for my sake" (*Letters* 83.2).

Under such circumstances, the poor, the powerless, and those without influential connections had little hope of justice. Their claims, whatever the merits, had to wait. Preaching on the apocalypse, John Chrysostom, a contemporary of Libanius in Antioch, imagined the last judgment in a heavenly court where the accused finally stood alone: "Who will stand by us when we are brought to trial at the dread tribunal of Christ? Who will dare speak out? Who will have the power to deliver those led away to unbearable punishments?" (*Homilies on the Statues* 13.2). But such visions of judicial equity belonged firmly to the next world. In late antique society, too many were too greatly advantaged by the uncertainty, opacity, and difficulty of formal litigation—and its resulting inequalities—to permit any significant move toward a more accessible and evenhanded system of justice.

BIBL.: A. H. M. Jones, *The Later Roman Empire 284–602: A Social, Economic, and Administrative Survey,* 3 vols. (Oxford, 1964; repr. in 2 vols., 1973), vol. 1, ch. 14. J. H. W. G. Liebeschuetz, *Antioch: City and Imperial Administration in the Later Roman Empire* (Oxford, 1972). R. MacMullen, "Judicial Savagery in the Roman Empire," *Chiron* 16 (1986): 147–166; repr. in R. MacMullen, *Changes in the Roman Empire: Essays in the Ordinary* (Princeton, 1990), 204–217.

C.K.

Justinian

Born Flavius Petrus Sabbatius, of Thracian-Illyrian peasant stock, Justinian (ca. 482–565) took the name Justinianus in tribute to his uncle, who had sponsored his education and advancement in Constantinople.

When his uncle, commander of the palace guard, unexpectedly took the throne as Justin I in 518, Justinian became his adviser and right-hand man, then heir-designate and colleague, and finally successor in 527. During those nine years, Justinian began to formulate ambitious policies and to surround himself with the most important associates of his reign, such as the jurist Tribonian, the general Belisarius, the historian Procopius, and, above all, his wife and empress, Theodora, who had a scandalous background and an imperious will.

Freeing himself from the long-festering war with the neighboring kingdom of Sassanian Persia, Justinian only barely averted being overthrown by the destructive Nika Riots of 532, but he emerged with new resolve and opportunity. During the next decade he launched his boldest initiatives in both internal and external policy. A massive building program was undertaken throughout the empire, the triumphant cathedral of Hagia Sophia in the capital (dedicated 537) being only one of its enduring products. The landmark legislative codification produced the massive *Corpus juris civilis* (*Codex* 529/534; *Digest/Pandects* and *Institutes* 533; *Novellae* 534ff.) as the definitive distillation of Roman law. Campaigns of reconquest recovered for the empire North Africa from the Vandals (533–534), Italy from the Ostrogoths (535–540), and even a bit of Visigothic Spain (550).

The spread of plague in 542–543 that devastated the whole Mediterranean world and nearly carried off the emperor himself signaled a tide of reversal, further marked by the death of Theodora in 548. The seemingly quick reconquests developed unexpected extensions, with mutinies and local resistance in North Africa (537–548), and a bloody, destructive renewal of the Ostrogothic War in Italy (541–554). The unwanted resumption of war with Persia (540–562) further added to the endless hemorrhaging of manpower and treasure, and prompted neglect of other sectors, such as the Balkans, where barbarian attacks increased and the way was paved for massive intrusions and losses later in the century.

Justinian's growing exhaustion and disillusionment as his long reign continued were exacerbated by constant religious controversy. A passionate theologian himself, Justinian persecuted various dissenting groups while trying every means (conciliation, coercion, compromises) to heal the major breach between Chalcedonian orthodoxy and Monophysite regional dissent (strongest in Syria-Palestine and Egypt). Justinian's often high-handed "caesaropapism," including even an abduction of the pope, availed little, and he left these problems—perhaps insoluble anyway in terms of unity—even more aggravated than he found them. After his reign of thirty-eight years, his death in 565 was viewed as a relief by his subjects.

Historians continue to debate whether Justinian's reign merely represented an anachronistic effort to restore the pan-Mediterranean Roman world of the past or introduced innovations that contributed to the empire's continuing evolution; whether his great initiatives, especially his reconquests, were part of a coherent "program" or simply impulsive pursuits of random opportunity; whether he gave the world of late antiquity one last burst of glory or accelerated its vulnerability and demise—or, perhaps all of the above.

BIBL.: Robert Browning, *Justinian and Theodora* (London, 1971; rev. ed., 1987). A. Honoré, *Tribonian* (London, 1978). John Moorhead, *Justinian* (London, 1994). Ernest Stein, *Histoire du bas-empire,* vol. 2 (Paris, 1949; repr. Amsterdam, 1968).

J.W.B.

Kalends of January

A festival of Janus marking the inception of the Roman New Year, the *kalendae Ianuariae* was a public holiday celebrated over several days. It was associated with the inauguration of the ordinary consuls and public pledges of loyalty to the emperor. Among the high political elite, the *commercium strenarum,* exchange of gifts, affirmed the established hierarchy and strengthened bonds of loyalty. Commoners also gave and received *strenae* that became increasingly monetary in nature. The Kalends came to represent a rite of transition and cosmic renewal on which depended the prosperity and welfare of the city and of the empire. Already attested outside of Rome in the 3rd century, it became a universally celebrated festival in the late 4th. Acknowledging its close connections with consular and imperial rituals of power, Christian emperors counted the Kalends among the recognized holidays even as they removed many traditional "pagan" religious festivals from the official calendar. Still, the character of the Kalends was fundamentally altered as a result of the official ban on public sacrifice, since the customary animal offerings to Jupiter Optimus Maximus on the Capitol could no longer take place. Instead, the festival became increasingly an occasion for popular carnivalesque celebrations. While staunchly defended by the likes of Libanius, the desacralized festival continued to attract jeremiads from ecclesiastical authors, notably Augustine, John Chrysostom, and Asterius of Amaseia, who castigated it for encouraging, among other vices, the ostentatious display of wealth, immoral and excessive behavior, idolatry, and gross insensitivity to the lot of the poor. Interestingly, the Kalends clashed with the Christian celebration of Epiphany (6 January), a fact that may explain the vehemence of certain Christian attacks. Justinian's abolition of the consulship in 541 (later revived under Justin) spelled the end of the Kalends as an occasion for traditional state celebrations featuring large-scale public spectacles. But as a festive event of the people that inherited many merrymaking aspects of the Saturnalia, the Kalends survived the fall of Roman political power in the west; in the east it was banned, probably ineffectually, at the Trullan Synod in 691–692. The feast continued to be celebrated as far away as Celtic northern Britain (Aneirin, *Y Gododdin* 27.286) and throughout the southern Mediterranean, where it became known to Muslims as "a great feast of the Christians."

BIBL.: H. R. Idris, "Fêtes chrétiennes en Ifriqiya," *Revue africaine* 98 (1954): 261–276. M. Meslin, *La fête des Kalendes de Janvier dans l'empire romain* (Brussels, 1970). R.L.

Kellia

Known as "the Cells" and referred to descriptively as "the innermost desert," Kellia was a 4th century Egyptian monastic foundation located about 12 miles south of Nitria on the road leading toward Scetis. It was founded in 338 C.E. by Amoun of Nitria, with the guidance of Antony, for those who had begun their training in the cenobitic life in Nitria and were ready to advance to the semi-anchoritic monasticism practiced at Kellia. Both Palladius and Evagrius followed this pattern, spending time in training in Nitria before going to Kellia. In his description of Nitria, Palladius mentions bread being baked there for the 600 anchorites living at Kellia (*Lausiac History* 7.2).

Rufinus described the practice of the monks at Kellia in his translation of the *Historia monachorum* (20.8). The cells were arranged so that they were far enough apart that a monk could not see or hear his neighbor. The monks joined together on Saturdays and Sundays to celebrate the liturgy and to share a meal (the *agapē*), some journeying a distance of three or four miles from their cell to the church. If a monk failed to appear at this weekly meeting, the others would know he had fallen sick or died, and individually they would go to see him, bringing whatever might be needed.

There was division among the monks concerning the Council of Chalcedon (451), and since those who supported the council and those who rejected it refused to communicate with each other, a second church was built. Evagrius's cell is reported to have survived into the 6th century, according to John Moschus (*Pratum spirituale* 177), and was supposed to be still inhabited by the demon that had seduced Evagrius into heresy. Kellia is referred to as al-Muna in Arabic sources and was inhabited until the 9th century.

Kellia was identified in 1964 by A. Guillaumont and was extensively excavated over the next twenty-five years by French and Swiss archaeological teams. The excavation has uncovered many churches and *koms* (living quarters) covered with inscriptions and wall decorations. Many of the *koms* accommodated several monks, although there are examples of the earlier single-occupancy cells described by the literary sources. Kellia is the best excavated early monastic site in Egypt, although the construction of a railway from Tanta to Alexandria in 1977 damaged one section, and the site is now under threat from the natural hazards of wind and sand, as well as encroaching agriculture.

BIBL.: Hugh G. Evelyn-White, *The Monasteries of the Wadi 'n Natrun* (New York, 1932). *Les Kellia: Ermitages coptes en Basse-Egypte* (Geneva, 1989). Pierre Miguel, *Déserts chrétiens d'Egypte* (Nice, 1993). *Survey archéologique des Kellia (Basse-Egypte)* (Louvain, 1983).　J.H.-H.

Kharana

Probably used for political conferences or reunions of local tribes to strengthen their allegiance to the Umayyads, the isolated Kharana *qaṣr* is located in eastern Jordan about 55 km southeast of Amman, where the annual rainfall rate is less than 100 mm. The building is approximately 35 m square and two stories high. The southern wall features two quarter-round buttresses flanking the only entrance. Elsewhere, round and semicircular buttresses are located in the corners and centers of curtain walls, respectively. The rooms around the central courtyard are arranged in discrete

clusters *(bayts),* isolated from each other on the ground floor (three *bayts* = twenty-five rooms) but interconnected on the upper floor (five *bayts* = thirty-six rooms). Shallow barrel vaulting supported by transverse arches predominates, but semidomes on squinches are also evidenced. The decoration includes stucco mouldings, blind and open arcades, brick bands on the facades, and uncommonly designed windows.

The suggested Sassanian origins of the *qaṣr* remain unconfirmed. Byzantine ceramics at the site and reused fragmentary Greek inscriptions imply an earlier occupation nearby. Shards in one of the plaster floors are all Umayyad. The occupation is estimated for ca. mid–7th to ca. mid-8th century C.E. A painted inscription that dates to the equivalent of 24 November 710 and other epigraphic finds confirm the Umayyad occupation and later casual visits.

The lack of a permanent water supply, the ambiguous fortified character of the *qaṣr,* and the absence of attendant structures largely exclude economic, administrative, or military significance. Kharana was never finished, and its political utility did not survive the fall of the Umayyads.

BIBL.: H. Gaube, "Amman, Harane und Qastal: Vier frühislamische Bauwerke in Mitteljordanien," *Zeitschrift für Deutschen Palästina-Vereins* 93 (1977): 52–86. Frédéric Imbert, "Inscriptions et espaces d'écriture au Palais d'al-Kharrana en Jordanie, *Studies in the History and Archaeology of Jordan V* (Amman, 1995), 403–416. Stephen K. Urice, *Qasr Kharana in the Transjordan* (Durham, N.C., 1987).

Z.F.

Khosro

Khosro (Persian Xosrow, derived from the Avestan Haosrauua) is the name of several members of the late Sassanid royal dynasty, signifying their descent from the Kayan kings mentioned in the *Avesta*. A descendant of Ardashīr I called Khosro was enthroned briefly at Ctesiphon in 420, but abdicated in favor of Bahram V.

Khosro I (531–579), called Anushirvan (of immortal soul), was famous for his justice, his support of the Mazdaean form of Zoroastrianism, and his love of literature and philosophy. He suppressed the Mazdakites and completed the administrative and military reforms that restored the power of the Sassanid state. A new class of military landlords was created; the state was divided into four quarters, each under a military governor; the agricultural tax as a proportion of the harvest was replaced by a tax per unit of area under cultivation according to the crop; and an annual poll tax was imposed on the male population between the ages of twenty and fifty. The central administration, with hierarchies reaching down into the provinces, was divided into seven departments: the chancellery, the registry, finance, the royal domains, the judiciary, the priesthood, and the army. He had literature translated from Greek, Syriac, and Sanskrit into Middle Persian; a set of royal astronomical tables were produced for him; and philosophical discussions were held at his court, where he welcomed the philosophers exiled from Athens.

Khosro I made peace with the Byzantines in 532 but resumed war with them from 540 to 561 over Armenia and Lazica. He invaded Syria in 540, destroyed Antioch, and deported the survivors to a new city he built for them near Ctesiphon. He invaded Lazica in 541, Syria in 542, Armenia in 543, and Mesopotamia in 544. He conquered the Hephthalite territory south of the Oxus in about 557–558 and concluded a fifty-year peace with the Byzantines in 561. An Armenian revolt in 571 led to renewed war with the Byzantines from 572 to 582. Between 575 and 577 a naval expedition conquered Yemen, taking it from the Ethiopians.

Khosro II was enthroned at Ctesiphon in 590 by rebellious nobles who deposed his father, but he fled from the rebellion of Bahrām Chobīn and took refuge with the Byzantines, who restored him with military aid sent by Maurice, in return for territorial concessions. His reign (591–628) was the most extreme expression of late Sassanid political absolutism and imperial ambition. He was called Aparwēz (the triumphant), and he eliminated all rival sources of power. The deposition and death of Maurice in 602 gave Khosro II the opportunity to regain territory he had ceded to the Byzantines by posing as his avenger. Between 604 and 610 Sassanid armies conquered Armenia and Mesopotamia and invaded Syria and Anatolia. With the accession of Heraclius in 610, Khosro II extended his ambition to the conquest of the entire Byzantine empire. From 611 to 614 Syria was conquered and Jerusalem sacked, and from 616 to 620 Egypt was conquered as far as Ethiopia in the south and Libya in the west. In 622 and 624 Heraclius invaded Armenia and ravaged Adharbayjan (Azerbaijan), driving Khosro back to Iraq. The joint Sassanid-Avar siege of Constantinople failed in 626, as did the Byzantine-Khazar siege of Tiflis (Tbilisi). In 627 Heraclius invaded Armenia again and entered Iraq, but withdrew to Adharbayjan. With the war going badly, Khosro suspected and feared everyone, imprisoned thousands of people, and ordered his officers executed. Enfuriated by his behavior and his rejection of peace proposals, a group of generals and high officials deposed him in February 628 and had him executed.

A descendent of Ardashīr I was briefly enthroned as Khosro III in about 632; his coins are known.

The Arabic *Kisra* refers to the rulers of the Sassanian dynasty and especially to Khosro I or II, both of whom acquired legendary qualities in medieval Arabic literature. But the term also came to mean royal qualities in the Persian manner. It was often used together with *qaysar* (caesar) to refer to a way of life practiced by kings and abhorrent to true Islam. The great palace of Khosro in Ctesiphon, in ruins already in the Middle Ages, became a symbol of the vanity of princes.

BIBL.: *Cambridge History of Iran*, vol. 3 (Cambridge, Eng., 1983). Richard N. Frye, *The History of Ancient Iran* (Munich, 1984). Ferdinand Justi, *Iranisches Namenbuch* (Marburg, 1895), 134–139. M.G.M.

Kuṣāṇa

The Kuṣāṇa (Kushans), descendants of a nomadic central Asian people, the Yuezhi, first rose to power in Transoxiana. The Great Kuṣāṇa ruled an area that stretched from central Asia to northern India, from the 1st through the 3rd or 4th century C.E. Due to its central geographic position, this vast empire served as the economic and cultural link between China and India.

Under the fourth king of the dynasty, Kaniṣka I, the empire reached its greatest extent, including Pāṭaliputra (modern Patna) in the east, Sāñcī (Sanchi) to the south, and Kyzil to the north. Huviṣka, son of Kaniṣka I, preserved this extensive empire. According to the recently discovered Bactrian inscription from Rabatak, the first four kings were Kujula Kadphises, Wima I Tak(to), Wima II Kadphises, and Kaniṣka I. They were followed by Huviṣka and Vasudeva I. Proponents of the "dropped 100" argument begin the second century of the Kaniṣka era with Kaniṣka II. From this period the empire lost more territory and entered a decline. The last kings of the dynasty were Vasiṣka, Vasudeva II, Shaka, and Kipunadha.

The Kuṣāṇa lost their northern provinces to the Sassanians in the 3rd century. The Kuṣāṇa-Sassanian empire ended with the Hephthalite invasions of the 5th century. In the subcontinent the Kuṣāṇa were succeeded by the Kidarites (an early group of Huns), or the so-called lesser Kuṣāṇa. The Kidarites ruled until ca. 460. South of the Punjab the empire was gradually eroded by the Gupta empire.

Four different eras are used in the Kuṣāṇa inscriptions, the Azes era, the Kaniṣka era, and two unknown eras. The dating of all of these eras is debated. The era initiated by Kaniṣka I is particularly important for establishing an absolute chronology. Numerous dates for the Kaniṣka era have been proposed: 78 C.E., 100–110, 128, 132, 144, 232, and 278. Due to the absence of contemporary sources, our understanding of Kuṣāṇa culture is derived primarily from archaeological, numismatic, epigraphic, and art historical evidence.

Political stability over long periods facilitated rapid development in agriculture, trade, and urban civilization: Sirkap at Taxila, Shaikan Dheri at Charsada, Begram in Kāpiśa north of Kabul, Dalverzin Tepe in Bactria (modern Uzbekistan), Toprak Kala in Chorasmia. These developments were linked with the extensive growth in intraregional and long-distance international trade.

Both Indian and Iranian languages were used for administrative and cultural life, depending on the time and location. Bactrian is an Iranian language written in the Greek alphabet. In the eastern province the population spoke Indian languages: Sanskrit and different Prakrits were written in two scripts—Kharoṣṭhi and Brāhmī. Kharoṣṭhi was used in the northwest and Mathurā and Brāhmī elsewhere. Ghandhāri Prakrit, written in Kharoṣṭhi, was the language of Gandhāra, used for official and economic purposes.

Based on the literary sources, Mahāyāna Buddhism developed significantly during the Kuṣāṇa period. At this time the most important Buddhist texts in Buddhist Hybrid Sanskrit were either written or compiled.

A large corpus of sacred art from throughout the Kuṣāṇa empire has survived. The majority of this is dedicated to Buddhism, but in the eastern regions images have been found that were associated with Jaina, Hindu, and nature cults. From the supposed Jaina stupa at Kankali Tila have come images of Jaina Tirthankara and square plaques, known as *ayagapatas.* Less numerous are Hindu cult images, for example *liṅga,* and nature deities, such as those that come from the Naga temple (all in the Government Museum in Mathurā). Most of the surviving sculptures were used within the context of the decoration of monumental religious architecture; even the isolated images were placed within niches, where they served as the focus of worship.

The two Kuṣāṇa temples, *devakula* at Surkh Kotal (north of the Hindu Kush) and Mat near Mathurā have long been considered dynastic shrines. In these temples were found large-scale images of the kings (identified by inscription as *devaputra*), represented in a hieratic style, together with smaller images of different deities. Fussman concluded that in the shrines the king, his family, and high officials worshiped the deity who protected them. This hypothesis appears to be supported by the text of the Rabatak inscription.

At the end of the 1st century C.E., the Buddha image emerged in both the northwest part of the realm, Gandhāra, and in Mathurā, south of modern Delhi. These images have quite different formal characteristics, though their iconographic features are basically the same, as is the ideological content of the images.

In Mathurā an important cult image took the form of the seated Buddha stele representing a Buddha of the so-called Karpadin type (referring to the snail-shaped *uṣṇīṣa*). An example is the figure made in Mathurā but found in Ahicchatra (now in the National Museum in New Delhi); it bears an inscribed date of 32. A stylistic development of the Buddha image in Mathurā and Gandhāra can be defined on the basis of a comparative stylistic analysis integrated with dated inscriptions. The chronological development of the Bodhisattva image is not so easily defined.

Fragments of painting, architectural decoration of religious structures, have survived. Stylistically they belong to the Graeco-Buddhist tradition: Kara-Tepe in Uzbekistan, Dilbirdin-Tepe north of the Hind Kush, and Haḍḍa south of the Hindu Kush in Afghanistan. The latest objects from the approximately 20,000 recovered from the royal tombs at Tillya Tepe in southern Bactria (Afghanistan) may date to the early Kuṣāṇ period. The extraordinary gold jewelry, often set with precious stones, is worked in a style related to the art of the steppe but also integrating Hellenistic iconography.

BIBL.: Stanislaw J. Czuma, *Kushan Sculpture: Images from Early India* (Cleveland, 1985). N. Sims-Williams and J. Cribb, "A New Bactrian Inscription of Kanishka the Great," in *Silk Road Art and Archaeology,* vol. 4 (Kamakura, Japan, 1996), 75–142. B. J. Stavisky, *La Bactriane sous les Kushans: Problèmes d'historie et de culture* (Paris, 1986).   D.K.-S.

Lakhmids

Founded in the late 3rd century by 'Amr ibn 'Adī, the Lakhmid dynasty was for three centuries under the control of the Persians in Arabia and the Syro-Mesopotamian desert. Despite chronological uncertainties and the difficulties of documentation, it is relatively easy to make out the Persians' role in this area.

'Amar ibn 'Adī seems to have taken advantage of the decline of Palmyra and the Tanūkh to assert his own authority and, in choosing Hira as a permanent installation, placed himself in the Sassanid camp. Our knowledge of him comes from legendary or unverifiable accounts. In contrast, the epitaph for his son Imru' al-Qais al-Bad', "King of all Arabs," who died in Nemara in 328, is a firsthand account: it presents serious difficulties of interpretation because of variants in the classical sources, among which it is not possible to choose. Imru' al-Qais al-Bad' subdued most of peninsular Arabia, but his presence in Nemara at the time of his death remains a mystery. Was he joining an alliance with Rome? Conducting a raid on behalf of the Persians? Taking action against the bedouins in concert with Rome, after the accord between Shapur and Constantine (Eusebius, *Vit.Const.* 4.8)? After his death, the history of the Lakhmids sinks into obscurity until the early 5th century.

After the reign of al-Nu'mān I, who built the castle of Khawarnak, al-Mundhir I (about 418–452) consolidated the Lakhmids' takeover of Arabia for the Persians' benefit and participated in the Roman-Persian war of 421–422. We know nothing of his two successors, but al-Nu'mān II seems to have been particularly active in the wars against Byzantium. Defeated in 498, he marched against Harran in 502 and died shortly thereafter. The apogee of the dynasty occurred under the reign of al-Mundhir III (502–554), who dominated all Arabia. He was active as far as Yemen, where he fought the Ethiopians and Byzantines. Lakhmid governors administered Bahrain and 'Uman for the Sassanids. At the same time, al-Mundhir launched raids in Syria against the Byzantines (520, 531) and their allies, the Ghassanids (539); it was during such a raid that he was killed in northern Syria, near Qennishrin. His three sons, 'Amr ibn Hind (554–569), Qābūs (569–573), and al-Mundhir IV (ca. 574–ca. 580) followed the same policy, even though the peace treaty of 561 between Byzantium and the Persians barred the allied Arabs from fighting. As a result, Hira was threatened in 570, then burned in 578 by the Ghassanids. Despite these difficulties, the Lakhmid court attracted the most famous Arab poets, including Adi ibn Zayd and al-Nabigha al-Dhubyani. The palace of Khawarnaq, built by a Lakhmid ruler, became over the centuries a symbol of royal magnificence. Even though the Lakhmid kings were not Christians (with the exception of the last one), a number of Christian princesses and a strong Nestorian community built churches and a convent. Hira played the role of urban metropolis to the Arab world; Christianity, writing, and various borrowings from the Byzantines and Persians spread outward from it to the tribes. The last king, al-Nu'mān III (580–602), after an unlucky expedition in Arabia, fell out of favor with Khosro II, who had him executed. Thus, the

Sassanids' allies disappeared: although sometimes disobedient and judged too independent, they had been effective in maintaining the authority of the Sassanids on the Arabian Peninsula and in protecting the Syro-Mesopotamian desert.

BIBL.: Irfan Shahid, *Byzantium and the Arabs in the Fourth Century* (Washington, D.C., 1984); *Byzantium and the Arabs in the Fifth Century* (Washington, 1989); *Byzantium and the Arabs in the Sixth Century* (Washington, 1995). C. E. Bosworth, "Iran and the Arabs before Islam," *Cambridge History of Iran,* vol. 3 (Cambridge, Eng., 1982).　　M.S.

Landscape

No single ancient or medieval term corresponds fully to the English *landscape,* encompassing as it does an unmediated view of the natural world as well as its depiction in both literature and the visual arts. In ancient rhetoric, the closest terms are *ekphrasis topou* or *topographia,* both conceived as smaller sections of a larger work. The lack of a single term is significant in itself, and it is notable that in both literature and the visual arts, landscapes are rarely represented for their own sake. Representations of the natural environment tend rather to be used as backdrops to human action, or as a complement to the manmade environment of the city.

In the visual arts, the decorated surface is rarely conceived as an illusionistic window into nature, offering a glimpse of a coherent landscape. Instead, fragmented elements are arranged all over the picture field emphasizing its nature as a surface. Often, the inclusion of isolated landscape motifs is the only suggestion of a natural setting. In representations of hunting scenes on floor mosaics, such as those of the Great Palace of Constantinople or at Piazza Armerina, trees are placed next to individual figures or groups of figures that are disposed over the whole surface with no unified ground line or perspective. In floor mosaics of Orpheus or the Good Shepherd, the animals are similarly scattered around the central figure. An exception is the mosaic lunette in the mausoleum of Galla Placidia in Ravenna, showing Christ and his flock against a unified backdrop of rocks and plants. In North African villa mosaics, like that depicting the estate of Dominus Iulius (in Tunis, in the Bardo Museum), the expression of a symbolic order takes precedence over the depiction of a realistically coherent representation. Here, figures alternating with trees are arranged in registers around the central depiction of the villa. The estate is not represented as a physical entity but is suggested instead by the figures offering its fruits to the master of the estate. Human activity here stands for the landscape.

In secular rhetoric it is the human landscape of the city that is most frequently described, although handbooks recommend the use of elements of landscape such as groves and springs to enliven epideictic speeches. The late 3rd century treatises attributed to Menander Rhetor recommend that speeches of invitation or farewell should include scenes of land, mountains, and sea that might be seen by the addressee on his journey. Here the natural world is conceived as the space between the cities. It is these intervals that form the significant points in the rhetorician's conceptual map. The model *ekphrasis* of spring by Libanius describes the season in terms of its effects on the land and sea, but above all through its effects on human activities and emotions. Libanius's Eleventh Oration in praise of Antioch includes a lyrical description of the natural beauties of the city's suburb, Daphne. As the site of Apollo's rape of the eponymous nymph, Daphne is also a place of mythological allusion for Libanius.

Literary evocations of generic landscapes, rather than specific sites, may appeal to memory of a different kind. Allusions to the literary tradition of descriptions of gardens or natural settings take precedence, drawing attention to the surface of the text and the artistry of the author. Most influential among the earlier models are the description of the garden of Alcinous in the *Odyssey* and the opening scene of shady plane trees and the cool water of the River Ilissus in Plato's *Phaedrus,* the ideal locus of literary and philosophical composition. Procopius of Gaza, for example, returns to Plato's Ilissus in his evocation of a meadow (*Declamatio* 2). Here the density of allusion accumulated by elements of literary landscape is clear: in enumerating the plants he sees—the hyacinth, the narcissus—the narrator appeals to mythological rather than botanical knowledge, treating and responding to each not as as a plant but as the symbol of a myth. Choricius likewise weaves allusions to Homeric and pastoral landscapes into his account of the decoration of the Church of St. Sergius in Gaza and, in the very act of praising the artist for omitting the nightingale and cicada as unsuitable to a holy place, exploits the still active mythical connotations of these "poetic" creatures.

In the context of church decoration, scenes such as those described by Choricius may have had a symbolic significance as representations of God's creation. The beauty and wonder of the natural world are the subject of Gregory Nazianzen's second Theological Oration (*PG* 36) and Basil's *Hexaemeron* 5 on the creation of the earth (*PG* 29). Gregory's Homily 44 (*PG* 36) on New Sunday ends with an *ekphrasis* of spring, closely modeled on Libanius. Gregory adapts the subject to its new Christian context by emphasizing the renewal of human activity and introducing the image of bees and their hive as a metaphor for the church.

In the new conceptual map of Christianity, specific sites also drew symbolic significance from the events associated with them. The pilgrim Egeria says little about the desert landscape of Sinai but concentrates on its role in both the Hebrew Bible and the New Testament. In the Church of St. Catherine on Sinai, the apse mosaic of the transfiguration shows the figures against a plain gold background with no indication of a natural setting: in this case landscape is entirely eclipsed by event.

BIBL.: K. Dunbabin, *The Mosaics of Roman North Africa* (Oxford, 1978). H. Maguire, *Earth and Ocean: The Terrestrial World in Early Byzantine Art* (University Park, Pa., 1987).   R.W.

Latin

The Latin language had two histories, local and imperial. By late antiquity, the local history of Latin in its land of origin was of little interest, as it had been swamped by the imperial history. We know too little of the process by which Latin became the language of the western Roman world to a degree sufficient to remain in place as the foundation of the "Romance" languages, but the main outline is clear. Not so much governors as soldiers, especially those old soldiers planted in colonies on their retirement, provided the seed corn for *latinitas* across the Mediterranean world.

The corpus of Latin inscriptions built up by Theodor Mommsen in the 19th century still offers the best rough-and-ready map of the language's penetration of the Roman world. Latin did not take root equally everywhere. The outer boundaries of empire provided one unsurprising limit to expansion: on the fringes of the African desert have been found ostraca bearing scraps of military Latin, a mix of official formalese and the vulgar errors of those whose native language may have been some strand of Punic. And in one direction an inner limit prevailed as well. Greek had so far generalized itself as the common tongue of the Hellenistic eastern Mediterranean that Latin never supplanted it.

The line separating Greek from Latin speakers matched roughly the modern boundary between Bulgaria and the former Yugoslavia. East of that line, Latin was most palpably present in Constantinople through the 6th century as an official court language, and it made a curious further outpost in Beirut, the center of Latin legal education for the eastern empire; but even in both those cities, the plantation was ultimately unsuccessful. With Greek as a barrier, other languages to the east and south (Syriac, Hebrew, Coptic) had greater persistence and longer lives. (In the western Mediterranean, moreover, Greek was commonly encountered in cities: in the Christian church of the city of Rome, Greek remained the liturgical language until almost the end of the 4th century.)

But the Roman world was always multilingual. Latin in turn was never a "national" language, and there was little nationalistic language patriotism. Persons from a wide variety of geographic locations acquired the language, adapted it, and took some sense of ownership. Strikingly, Latin's fate matches that of modern English or Spanish, taken over and spoken, sometimes in surprising ways, by the descendants of those whom the tongue's native speakers had once conquered, and to an extent that ultimately undermined the authority of the conquering native speakers over their own tongue.

What made Latin such a consistent cultural artifact was its attachment to a writing system. Writing systems freeze and universalize language, preserving it against the normal diversity and ebullient transformation of usage. The advantage of such a system is that it makes culture a transportable artifact not only over space but also over time. Education can inflict the pleasant agonies of endless repetition on generations of students, who can genuinely believe that they are speaking and learning as their fathers did. "Literature" in the Roman world was palpably an instrument of cultural hegemony in a way that only popular film and music are in our times. What a writing system so consistently imposed masks is the evolution of language. On the evidence of written texts, the long-vexed question of when Latin died out as a spoken language, giving way to Romance, answers itself by pointing to the 9th century. But the internal evidence of the development of languages pushes the points of palpable divergence back much further—some would say to the age of Augustus. Over a long period the sounds of Latin, mostly irretrievable for us, would have begun to take on a distinctly post-Latin character, even as the makers of texts were carefully adhering to Latin rules of diction, spelling, and forms. On that argument, the remarkable event of the 9th century was not a change in practice but the sudden awareness of a change in practice made possible by the importation of the educational reformer Alcuin from beyond the boundaries of Romance speech. Roger Wright has credited Alcuin with "inventing" medieval Latin (that is, a form of Latin spoken as it was written, against the norms of writing he knew and reinforced) and thus creating a separate consciousness of what his time would call "lingua Romana"—Romance.

The great and instructive anomaly in late antique Latin was "Christian Latin." An earlier generation argued whether Christian Latin was a separate language in any useful sense. The answer today is clearly no, but distinctive features need to be observed. First, Christianity in the Latin realms consciously used a written literature in the official language of the empire to create the self-consciousness of a community not defined by place or ancestry. The Latin Bible was an artificially created substitute for the school classics that drove education and fostered upper-class self-consciousness. Second, and more remarkably, Christian Latin offers one of few examples in premodern times of the written word's power to shape speech. Grecisms and Hebraisms from the Bible and particularly from liturgy did succeed, by power of repetition and divine authority, in becoming part of the spoken language. Church ritual did what schooling often fails to do.

Latin survives today in its Romance children in obvious and not so obvious places. Four great Romance languages have been pieced together in modern times (with the help of national governments, the printing press, and compulsory schooling): French, Spanish, Portuguese, and Italian. The boundary between Romance and German (which is a zone—consider Alsace-Lorraine—not a line in the sand) still marks the extent of Julius Caesar's military successes and the ambiguous borderlands in which that military success petered out. But outposts within the Roman world, like Sardinian and the Rhaeto-Romance of isolated Swiss cantons, give lingering evidence of the diversity that was once the norm. And then the great exception of Romanian looms to the east. Modern Romania was only briefly (as such things go) under Roman rule, through most of the 2nd century C.E. On all sides, other more persistent invaders (Greek, Turkish, Slavic) have defined the linguistic map, but Romania and its dialects continue to be markedly Romance in form. Modern nationalist scholarship has fought fierce battles to determine, inconclusively, how much the language's presence depends on an uninterrupted tradition on or adjacent to Romanian soil, and how much depends on later importation. The latter seems the more likely force, but the lack of historical documentation for when and how such penetration occurred is a sobering reminder that large and powerful historical processes can be invisible to the eye of the narrative historian.

BIBL.: J. N. Adams, "British Latin: Text, Interpretation and Language in the Bath Curse Tablets," *Britannia* 23 (1992): 1–26. M. Banniard, *Viva voce: Communication écrite et communication orale du IVe au IXe siècle en Occident latin* (Paris, 1992). S. Lancel, "La fin et la survie de la latinité en Afrique du Nord," *Revue des études latines* 59 (1981): 269–297. E. Löfstedt, *Late Latin* (Oslo, 1959). C. Mohrmann, *Études sur le latin des chrétiens*, 4 vols. (Rome, 1958–1977). R. Wright, ed., *Latin and the Romance Languages in the Early Middle Ages* (London and New York, 1991).   J.J.O.

Law Codes

The law codes of the Roman empire were works of reference made possible by a technical advance, the codex. This was a method of book production by which leaves of writing material, such as parchment, were bound together in a volume rather than rolled up, as previously. The work was then easier for readers to consult. Bound volumes were first used for keeping accounts and (by Christians) for preaching.

The first known law codes appeared in the reign and at the prompting of the emperor Diocletian (284–305 C.E.). The earliest was the *Codex Gregorianus* of 291. It collected rulings of Roman emperors from Hadrian (119–138) to the date of issue. Most of these were private rescripts: replies on points of law given to petitioners who had written to the emperor to ask for legal advice. A second collection along the same lines, the

Codex Hermogenianus, covered the years 293 to 295 and went into several editions.

Though officially sponsored, these codes were published in the names of their editors, Gregorius and Hermogenianus. The latter at least had been legal adviser to the emperor Diocletian and was partly responsible for drafting the rescripts included in his collection. The codes were convenient works of reference, but since both were private documents, there was nothing to stop litigants from relying in court on laws not included in them.

The next code, that of Theodosius II (402–450), was innovative. It covered the period of the Christian empire from 312 to 438 and differed from the earlier codes in several ways. Though the detailed work of compilation owed a great deal to a powerful lawyer-minister, Antiochus Chuzon, it was published not privately but in the emperor's name, as a law in its own right. It contained only general laws, most of them approved by the emperor's council (the Consistory), and excluded rescripts. It was comprehensive, so that no law of the period that was left out of the code could in future be cited in court. The *Theodosian Code* took nine years to compile (429–438). The work was undertaken by a group of officials and lawyers based in Constantinople, but the code, which contained a roughly equal number of eastern and western laws, was promulgated in Rome as well. Indeed one of its aims was to unify the law in the eastern and western halves of the Roman empire, which had often been at loggerheads in recent years. But it wisely did not try to harmonize laws that conflicted. Instead, all the laws included in the code had to be dated, and in case of conflict, the later law was to prevail over the earlier.

The *Theodosian Code* had a different fate in west and east. When it was issued, the western Roman empire was already disintegrating. In the part taken over by the Visigoths, including Spain, Alaric II in 506 issued a law for his Roman subjects. This *Breviarium Alaricianum* was largely made up of extracts from the Theodosian and the two earlier codes. The handbook issued by King Gundobad of the Burgundians for his Roman subjects about 535 *(lex Romana Burgundionum)* was also largely drawn from the three codes. After Charlemagne (712–814), however, Justinian's eastern codification gradually displaced the *Theodosian Code* and came to be regarded in western and central Europe as a source of law on which to fall back when there was a gap in the local law.

In the east the ambitious emperor Justinian (527–565) pursued the idea of embodying law in a set of codes. He relied for success on Tribonian, a learned and ingenious lawyer, along with other ministers, law professors, and practitioners. Between 528 and 534 Justinian sponsored three works, each of which was enacted as a law in its own right. The first, rapidly produced in 528–529, updated and superseded the previous three codes. Only the second edition of this work (Codex Iustinianus), issued in 534, survives. The second work was a first-year teaching manual (the Institutes), issued in 533. It expanded and updated a similar work by the 2nd century law teacher, Gaius. The third volume was even more innovative. It collected those extracts from the private writings of Roman lawyers between 100 B.C.E. and 300 C.E. that the lawyers of Justinian's age regarded as still having practical value. Theodosius II had planned this enterprise but had lacked the resources to pursue it. Justinian's editors carried it through, astonishingly, in three years (530–533). They selected only about a twentieth of the material available to them. Even so the resulting volume, Justinian's Digest, or Pandects, runs to about 700,000 words. It was promulgated in December 533.

The three volumes together make up Justinian's codification (the Corpus Iuris). Since they are so bulky, they were treated in practice as works of reference rather than concise codes of the modern sort. All the same, Tribonian and his helpers, in contrast with the Theodosian codifiers, made an effort to eliminate conflicting laws. To achieve this, Justinian gave them power to shorten and alter the texts. Out of respect for antiquity, however, he allowed them to attribute the altered text to the emperor or private lawyer who had originally laid it down. The existence of these hidden changes, called interpolations, presents difficult textual and historical problems.

Justinian briefly reconquered Italy, and his codification was brought into force there in 554. Justinian's laws became the foundation of legal education in the universities that grew up from the 11th century onward. Long after the Roman armies had disappeared, Justinian's legal treasure house left its mark on the history and politics of western and central Europe.

BIBL.: F. Schulz, History of Roman Legal Science (Oxford, 1952). Jill Harries and Ian Wood, eds., The Theodosian Code (London, 1993). T. Honoré, Tribonian (London, 1978). P. Wormald, "Lex Scripta and Verbum Regis: Legislation and Germanic Kingship from Euric to Cnut," in Early Medieval Kingship, ed. P. Sawyer and I. N. Wood (Leeds, 1977), 105–138.   T.M.H.

Law Courts

Roman law offered two alternatives for pursuing a dispute: private arbitration undertaken by a third person agreeable to both parties and recourse to a court of law.

The organization of the law courts was tied to the administrative structure of the empire; almost all of the higher imperial functionaries had judicial as well as administrative functions. In 294 the emperor Diocletian overhauled the court system by separating civil courts from those of the military. Between the 3rd and 6th centuries a complex structure of appeal from lower to higher courts of civil jurisdiction evolved. Petitions against judgments could be made by either the plaintiff

or the defendant, in person or through the judge who had presided over the disputed case. This system was, however, complicated by the increase in courts of special jurisdictions, which handled particular categories of cases (such as the imperial fiscal courts) or cases in which one or both of the parties belonged to a privileged group (privilegium fori). The emperor himself was theoretically the final court of appeal.

In the early 4th century the court of first instance for most private litigation was that of the provincial governor (iudex ordinarius). Once legal proceedings had been initiated the case would be heard in the secretarium of his official residence. Each governor retained a substantial legal staff and was held legally responsible for its official conduct; the staff included exceptores to deliver the legal summons, heralds to announce the arrival of the parties, advocates to defend them, assessores to advise on the legal points of the case, and notarii to transcribe the proceedings and issue the record of the trial (editio gestorum). Both the plaintiff and defendant could expect to pay each of these court officials for his services, in the form of sportulae. In criminal trials the accused and the witnesses could also expect torture to be applied as a credible means of establishing the truth behind the case, unless their legal status precluded it. The magistrates themselves were ordered to receive the parties gratis, judge publicly, and conclude the processes in audience (C.Th. 1.16.6–7, 331; 1.16.9, 364). Justinian also set strict time limits for the duration of proceedings, "to prevent lawsuits being almost immortal and exceeding the term of human life" (C.Just. 3.1.13).

The heavy workload of the provincial courts was eased by the gradual introduction of the defensor civitatis as judge in minor civil and criminal cases. Each city thus had access to its own court of law (C.Th. 1.29 and Nov.Just. 15.3). Another local court was that of the bishops. The episcopalis audientia proved such a popular institution that in the 6th century bishops also employed professional legal staffs to help ease their workload (Vita Sabae 75 and Vita Euthymii 3).

Papyri from late antique Egypt refer almost exclusively to private settlements outside of court, although evidence for the presence of law courts (mega dikastērion) testifies that they were still in use. The early Arabic papyri include citations to court, petitions, and requests for legal advice in forms that suggest that the organization of early Islamic law courts was modeled on that of the Roman period.   C.HUM.

Law Schools

During the late republic and early empire, education in substantive Roman law was provided for informal groups of pupils by individual juris consulti. In the later empire this loose arrangement was replaced by the formal establishment of schools of law.

The late rhetorical schools provided the model for

the organization of the law schools; students who wished to specialize in legal science would proceed from the former to the latter. Those who taught in the law schools (termed *professores iuris, magistri, doctores,* and, in the early Byzantine period, *antecessores*) were themselves experts in the *ius civile,* with practical experience as imperial functionaries. The Christian epitaph of Floridus, master of the school at Rome (d. 427) provides an example of this career structure: advocate and assessor (legal adviser) of the Vicarius Urbi, then assessor at the prestigious court of the Praefectus Urbis, and finally public teaching of Roman law. During the 4th and 5th centuries the duration of the course of study varied between two and four years. The method of teaching was for professors to establish comparisons between the opinions of the studied author and other classical jurists *(iura),* or with the imperial constitutions *(leges).* On completion of their studies most students followed careers in the imperial bureaucracy.

Between the 4th and 7th centuries the administration of the legal schools was regulated by imperial constitutions, with official state salaried chairs established in Rome, Beirut, and Constantinople (*C.Th.* 14.9.3, dated 425). In 533 the emperor Justinian restricted the teaching of civil law to these three legal centers and specified the courses of study to be undertaken (*Digest., Omnem* 7). These measures were enacted by Justinian as an integral part of his ambitious plan for the *renovatio* of all aspects of Roman law. The school in Beirut was given eminent status as a result of its involvement in Justinian's project of compilation and codification. The professors were actively engaged in fusing together Roman law with provincial laws; thus the school played an important role in the formation of a new Byzantine society.

The *Vita* of Severus by Zacharius the Scholasticus paints a vivid picture of cosmopolitan cultural life at the school of Beirut. Students came from all over the eastern provinces, including Egypt, to study law. Zacharius also recounts the Christian students' extracurricular activities, which included destroying pagan temples and advising on the prosecution of heretics.

Despite the reputation of Beirut and Constantinople, Libanius states that there was a preference among eastern students to study law in Rome (*Orat.* 48.22). Rome also acted as a center for legal study in the western provinces. Augustine's lifelong friend Alypius traveled from North Africa to Rome for his legal education. Rutilius Namatianus, Symmachus, and many ecclesiastical writers testify to students who came from all over Gaul.

Between the 4th and the early 6th century epigraphic evidence suggests that law schools existed in Alexandria, Caesarea, Carthage, Marseilles, Autun, Narbonne, and Toulouse. Extensive postclassical revisions of classical juridical writings also indicate that legal activity was widespread. Modern research has attempted to tie this activity to specific legal schools, but this approach has attracted much criticism.

BIBL.: Paul Collinet, *Histoire de l'école de droit de Beyrouth* (Paris, 1925). W. Selb, *Sententiae Syriacae* (Vienna, 1990). Edoardo Volterra, "Appunti sulle scuole postclassiche occidentali," *Annali di storia del diritto* 1 (1957): 51–65.

C.HUM.

Leo I

A native of Tuscany, Leo served first as a deacon under Pope Celestine, and then as archdeacon for Pope Sixtus. In 440, while in Gaul attempting to patch up a quarrel between Albinus, the prefect of Italy, and Aetius, the master of soldiers, he was notified that he had been chosen to be pope.

Leo struggled to expand, consolidate, and enforce the authority of the bishop of Rome. His methods included the effective use of church councils and the timely assistance of powerful *saeculares.* He eventually was able to bring the weight of the imperial government to bear against any opposition. He spoke out on issues ranging from the date of Easter to the importance of charity to the administration of church property.

Leo was particularly interested in increasing papal authority outside Italy. In Africa, he renewed attempts to establish papal authority over the independently minded bishops there. He increased his authority in Illyricum, arguing that the primacy of Peter gave him the care of all the churches. An appeal from some disgruntled Spanish bishops gave him the opportunity to intervene there as well. Leo's most difficult challenge, however, came from Gaul, where a well-organized group of bishops was led by Hilary of Arles. Once again, Leo's opportunity came in the form of an appeal from a disaffected bishop. Claiming the authority of St. Peter, Leo summoned Hilary to a council in Rome. Hilary responded by excommunicating Leo. Leo, in turn, declared Hilary to be divested of his metropolitan status and obtained from Valentinian III a rescript entitled "On the Ordination of Bishops" that not only confirmed Leo's judgments but also promoted the primacy of the see of Rome.

Leo continued the papal policy of persecuting schismatic and heretical sects, such as the Novatianist and Pelagians. He especially opposed the use of apocryphal Scriptures, "through which the Manichees and Priscillianists attempt to justify their entire heresy." In 444 Leo attacked the so-called New Manichees, who actually seem to have been Priscillianists. They were condemned by a council of ecclesiastics and influential laymen, and in 445 Leo obtained from Valentinian III a rescript condemning the Manichees throughout the empire.

In the east, Leo faced other difficulties with heterodoxy. Eutyches, a proponent of Monophysitism, was acquitted at the Council of Ephesus (the Robber Council) in 488, over Leo's objections. Only in 451, at the Council of Chalcedon, was Eutyches convicted, largely on the basis of Leo's "Tome," a definitive statement on the nature of the incarnation. The resultant Nicene-Chalcedonian faith became a Christian orthodoxy that survives essentially to the modern day.

In 452 Italy was invaded by Attila and the Huns, who, some said, were turned back by Leo's appeals. In 455, when Rome was captured by the Vandals, Leo was said to have obtained their agreement not to burn the city. Leo died on 10 November 461. His surviving literary efforts, written in a cultivated style, include ninety-six sermons and many letters. Leo I was declared a doctor of the church in 1754.

BIBL.: C. Bartik, "L'interpretation théologique de la crise de l'empire romain par Léon le Grand," *Revue d'histoire ecclésiastique* 63 (1968): 745–784. Edmund Hunt, *St. Leo the Great: Letters* (New York, 1957). Trevor O. Jalland, *The Life and Times of St. Leo the Great* (London and New York, 1941). N. W. James, "Leo the Great and Prosper of Aquitaine," *Journal of Theological Studies* n.s. 44 (1993): 554–583.　　　　R.W.M.

Limes

Limes (plural *limites*) in the Roman empire never meant a military frontier in the modern sense and was probably never used as an official term for boundary. But even in the earlier empire, it carried the informal sense of borderland, and by the 4th century, in Africa at least, it became the official term on the *Notitia Dignitatum* for a frontier sector administered by a military commander, not unlike the modern "command." Originally a surveyor's expression for a road, and subsequently a military road, it inevitably gave rise to the notion of a borderline. But a 5th century manual prefers the term *finis* to *limes* for the frontier road line (*viae militares finem faciunt*, Ps.-Boethius, *Gromatici veteres* 401.8, Lachmann) and Justinian's decree ordered the restitution of the African *fines* in the 6th century, in contrast to maintaining the *limites*, which appeared as structures within a geographic zone (*C.Just.* 1.27.4).

Ideologically and strategically the concept of a limit to power was foreign to Romans, and this may account for the relative rarity of the word. In the cosmographies circulating in the later empire, *limites* and frontiers were not listed and the provinces of the empire had undefined boundaries, while a 6th century author refers to two *limites* on the Saracen border, one of which was "towards the Indias" (Malalas, *Chronographia,* p. 448, Dindorf). Imperial propaganda was contradictory, traditionally divided between boosting the protection offered by defenses and proclaiming unlimited dominion. Inscriptions declared the protection of *praesidia* and *propugnacula* of fortifications, while simultaneously claiming power beyond them. Con-

stantine's sons claimed to have stopped the attack of the Goths *in parte limitis* on the Danube (*CIL* 3.12483), but Constantine inscribed the "subjection and control of the Franks" on his Rhine fortress of Deutz (*CIL* 13.8501). Although nature provided rivers to protect the provinces "by that *limes*," the emperor, whose presence extended beyond the "*termini* of nature" (*Pan.Lat.* 2[12] 22.2), proved that "there was no *terminus imperii*" (*Pan.Lat.* 10[2] 7). No emperor could admit the loss of territory or accommodation of barbarians without a dangerous loss of prestige, as exemplified in the anger of Ammianus (25.9.9) at Jovian's cession of Nisibis to the enemy, and in the unpopularity of Constantius's leniency toward the Alamans. Conservative Roman dislike for Stilicho's reliance on foreign federates contrasted with Claudian's praise for the order he imposed on the Chauci and Suebi beyond the frontiers. The much cited passage of Zosimus (2.4) that praised Diocletian for restoring frontiers but attacked Constantine for withdrawing troops to interior cities was less concerned with reality than with the political correctness of good and bad emperors by exploiting the ideology of frontiers.

The ideology had strategic implications. The notion of the *limes* depending on a line of road, such as the strata Diocletiana in the east, never disappeared, since the strategy of the Arabian and Syrian desert frontiers depended largely on roads to link forts and cities, with little else besides. Malalas, for instance, in the 6th century declared that "on the *limites* [Diocletian] built *castra* from Egypt to the Persian borders" (*Chronographia* 12.308, Dindorf). Apart from this, a recently found inscription uses the term *praetensio* for a road that ran like an antenna from Bostra to control the approaches from the desert oases; this in turn evokes the description of the Mesopotamian districts as guarded by *praetenturae* and *stationes* (Amm.Marc. 14.3.2). The roads were not frontiers in themselves but lines of communication; they were paralleled by the great rivers of the European frontiers, along which the major camps of the *limites* were placed to receive supplies. Inevitably the banks of the rivers *(ripae)* and the roads came to be regarded in a general sense as boundaries, but they were neither the *limites* themselves, nor military lines of defense. The image of Julian sailing down the Danube, receiving the acknowledgment of kneeling barbarians on the far bank *(Pan.Lat.* 3[11] 7.2) was a picturesque, if idealized, reminder that both banks had to be controlled for rivers to be viable for transport. But there were nevertheless administrative borders, and it is arguably mainly for commercial and legal motives, not defense, that visible frontiers were important. The Romans used frontiers from time to time as commercial weapons, as, for instance, in 369, when the Goths were limited to two trading sites on the Danube. Legal rights of *postliminium* were available for prisoners of war to reclaim their property when they returned home (*C.Th.* 5.7). Clearly for these purposes the *limes* was not a zone but a frontier line of Roman jurisdiction, even if not the military frontier.

There is little evidence that Roman frontiers were ever defensive lines, or that defense in depth was a strategy developed by Constantine's mobile field army. Zosimus (2.4), who gave rise to the theory, when attacking Constantine's corruption of military discipline through use of city garrisons, was circumstantially wrong and ideologically biased. Constantine, as much as Diocletian, developed the perimeter defenses of the Rhine and Danube through such massive fortifications as Cologne-Deutz and proved his aggressive intentions with such projects as the famous bridge crossing the Danube at Daphne. Julian penetrated deeply into barbarian territory, and Valentinian was noted for the construction of forward posts and double camps at river bridgeheads, such as those at Altrip-Neckerau on the Rhine. Although walls on frontiers were more characteristic of the 2nd century than the later empire, Hadrian's Wall and the African *fossatum* were still maintained until the end of Roman rule, and there are records of walls constructed in the Balkans and the Caucasus. Most archaeologists, however, agree that Hadrian's Wall was unsuitable as a military barrier, and it is never documented as such in the later empire. The *fossatum Africae* was manifestly not a line of defense, since most forts of the *limites* bore no relation to the *fossatum*'s ditches and walls, which were probably used to control southern pastoral transhumance. Some walls in the Caucasus may have been intended to block invaders, but constructions in the Balkan and Alpine passes look more like tactical battle defenses against political rivals than means of excluding barbarians.

BIBL.: B. Isaac, *The Limits of Empire* (Oxford, 1990). P. Trousset, "La frontière romaine: Concepts et représentations," in *Frontières d'empire: Nature et signification des frontières romaines*, ed. P. Brun, S. van der Leeuw, and C. R. Whittaker (Nemours, 1993), 115–120. C. R. Whittaker, *Frontiers of the Roman Empire: A Social and Economic Study* (Baltimore and London, 1994).   C.W.

Literacy

Research on the topic of literacy in the ancient and medieval worlds has opened up a range of questions and approaches to be applied to late antiquity. Against a presumed decline in literacy, cautious historians are more likely to highlight regional diversity and sometimes surprising continuity in the uses of the written word. The profound upheavals in social and economic structures wrought by the disintegration of imperial power, the cultural changes associated with barbarian settlement, the spread of Christianity, and the breakdown of the network of ruling elites who were defined by an urban, literate cultural milieu—all these developments created new societies with new attitudes toward literacy and different methods of using it. The questions should not be, "How literate was the society of late antiquity?" nor "How many people were literate?" but rather, "What was produced in literate form?" "What were the linguistic barriers of the written material to the intended audience?" and "What are the indications that such barriers were faced, and how were they dealt with?" Such an approach provides an understanding of many types of "literacies" specific to their time and location, from the "functional" literacy of understanding a document to the composition of a philosophical text.

The dramatic fall in the number of private inscriptions produced from the late 3rd century onward has been seen as symptomatic of a decline in literacy, but it may instead be due to a diminishing of their importance in a changing political system in which such public display was deemed irrelevant to the advancement of an individual's career, rather than to any decline in the ability to read them. The status of the individuals commemorated in inscriptions became increasingly elite: the epigraphy of the 3rd century shows a severe decline in the number of prosperous bourgeois and freedmen who are attested. Epigraphic production continued to decline after a short revival under the tetrarchs.

The evidence of documents can be misleading, owing to the capricious pattern of their survival. The Oxyrynchus Papyri of Egypt constitute our main source evidence for the use of documents at the provincial level, often leaving us to speculate about other regions of the empire. Quantitative analysis provides no evidence of a chronological decline in the number of surviving documents until they cease in the 7th century. Qualitative analysis reveals a substantial decline in the number of different types of business documents used in the 4th century in comparison with the 3rd, especially those involving building and land sales. Some types, like written contracts for wet-nursing, disappear altogether; others, such as labor and service contracts, disappear after the year 200, only to return in considerable quantities during and after the reign of Justinian. Writing signatures and a short formula for witnessing may not be evidence of a high level of literate skill; nonetheless they testify to an awareness of the importance of written proofs and written law. Not until 439 did any legislation attempt to make concessions for those incapable of subscribing.

To function, the inflated bureaucracy of the Dominate required high numbers of literate employees. By drawing recruits from the army and lower provincial offices, it possibly expanded the range of social classes that participated in the literate workings of the government, thereby broadening the social base for reading and writing skills. Yet it is far from clear whether this expanded bureaucracy generated more paperwork that directly impinged on the life of the empire's subjects. Although the tetrarchic government increased the use of writing to administer the fiscal system, it is impossible to ascertain a substantial increase in widespread base literacy of the empire's inhabitants.

Systematic compilations of written Roman law, beginning with the *Codex Gregorianus* (291) and *Codex Hermogenianus* (294), and continuing with the *Theodosian Code* (439), culminated in the legal corpus of Justinian (533–565). Legal compilations can also be seen in the barbarian successor kingdoms of the west. Although the army always needed literate recruits for its bureaucratic administration (cf. Vegetius, *De re militari* 2.4), military records on papyrus such as those from Dura-Europus and Egypt cease after 260 to be so numerous or so detailed. The increasing convergence of military and civilian society in the late empire, and the eventual predominance of the former in provincial administration, probably reduced the importance of the local curiae and their record offices *(gesta municipalia)*.

There continued to be specialists of various social ranks who used writing in their work (notaries, jurists, court officials, craftsmen, epigraphers, and so on), but a new social location for the written word was to be found among the more professional and enthusiastically pious of the officially Christian society. The spread of Christianity, a religion of the book, was of great importance for changes in literate activity and attitudes toward the written word. The impact of Christianity was characterized by a complex dualism. On the one hand, Christ was the word, the beginning of all things, so that holy Scripture, the record of his sayings and actions, written by divinely inspired individuals, acquired sacredness. Thus, the authority of the Scriptures became the supreme justification for belief and practices, generating interpretation and translation: by the 3rd century Scripture began to be the subject of learned commentaries. The early Christians' need for a more efficient textual reference system encouraged the transition from papyrus roll to parchment codex. On the other hand, the tradition that St. Peter and the other apostles were uneducated and illiterate, therefore pure of heart and unsullied by the theology of false creeds enshrined in written doctrine or by subservience to philosophic rationalism, denied the idea that literacy could bring one closer to God. Christianity suggested that knowledge of the sacred texts was necessary for knowledge of the way to salvation, yet it removed the necessity of being able to read the sacred texts for oneself. Illiterate heroes, such as the monk St. Antony, could be role models for piety and holiness.

Nevertheless, missionary activity and the need to translate the message of Christ into vernacular idioms stimulated the diffusion of literate languages other than Greek or Latin within the empire, as can be seen by the development of Coptic, Syriac, Gothic, and Armenian as written languages. In the west, Latin was to predominate as the written form of communication until the 9th and 10th centuries. Most organized monastic communities stipulated compulsory reading of at least the Scriptures and some patristic works, as can be seen by the admonitions of the more popular founders of monasticism, Pachomius, Basil of Caesarea, Athanasius, and, for the west, Benedict, though some of a more solitary, ascetic vein remained happily illiterate. Monasteries provided elementary education toward literacy for their young novices, and this extended in some cases to the instruction of lay children. Despite regional and chronological variance, monasteries in late antiquity increasingly assumed the role of the guardian of literate culture by combining several functions—school, library, center of studies, scriptorium—that had more often in the past been separate institutions.

Arabian society at the time of Muhammad was predominantly illiterate. Pre-Islamic poetry was orally transmitted and was written down only in Islamic times, when written culture began to spread. However, two occupations confirm the continued priority of the oral transmission of texts and knowledge in early Islamic society, those of the Qur'ān reciter (Arabic *qārī*) and the religious storyteller (Arabic *qāṣṣ*).

BIBL.: Alan K. Bowman and Greg Woolf, eds., *Literacy and Power in the Ancient World* (Cambridge, Eng., 1994). Guglielmo Cavallo, "Scrittura, alfabetismo, e produzione libraria nel tardo antico," *La cultura in Italia fra tardo antico e alto medioevo* (Rome, 1981), vol. 2, 523–538. William V. Harris, *Ancient Literacy* (Cambridge, Mass., 1989). P. Kahle, "The Arabic Readers of the Koran," *Journal of Near Eastern Studies* 8 (1949): 65–71. Charles Pellat, "Ḳāṣṣ," *Encyclopaedia of Islam,* 2nd ed. Gregor Schoeler, "Writing and Publishing: On the Use and Function of Writing in the First Centuries of Islam," *Arabica* 44, no. 3 (1997).   N.E.

Liturgy

In classical Greece, the term *liturgy (leitourgia)* was used to indicate a public service imposed on a rich citizen, who was expected to spend money of his own to meet the cost of the job he had been nominated to carry out. In the course of time, the meaning of liturgy was broadened, and during the Hellenistic period it indicated a public work of any kind. A new meaning was added to liturgy in the Greek translation of the Hebrew Bible (Septuagint). There, the term *liturgy* was used to translate the Hebrew word *avoda* whenever it designated a religious service. This use of the term was later borrowed by the New Testament, and subsequently by the Greek Church Fathers. Thus liturgy has come to be applied to any religious service, and more particularly to the eucharistic rite. In the Latin-speaking church, the terms *officium* and *ministerium* were used to indicate religious rites. Only from the 17th century onward was the Latin word *liturgia* used in the west to mean a religious service.

The sources for the study of early Christian liturgy are extremely sparse, and nothing except fragments survive prior to the 3rd century. Although there are a number of New Testament allusions to the existence of the eucharistic rite, the New Testament, in sharp contrast to the Hebrew Bible, contains no instructions or detailed account of the celebration of any rite. Nevertheless, from the little evidence that does exist, it is obvious that Jewish liturgy played a large part in the rites and ceremonies of the Christians. Jewish cleansing rites inspired the concept and development of baptism, and Jewish meal customs on solemn occasions were followed in the development of the eucharistic rite. On a broader level, the Jewish concept of communal worship influenced the emergence of Christian worship. Christ and, subsequently, his disciples associated themselves with the synagogue for as long as they could. It is highly probable, therefore, that those churches that first separated themselves from the synagogue shaped their communities on the model of the synagogue, and even regarded themselves as a synagogue. Thus, many characteristics of the synagogue service, such as the reading and exposition of the Scriptures, as well as the communal worship on Sabbath and holy days, are also to be found in the communal service of the early Christians.

Many more shared themes, perspectives, symbols, and metaphors can be identified, but no direct line of influence can be traced. One has to be extremely cautious not to read too much into these similarities. Our knowledge of Jewish rites and ceremonies of the 1st century is based on patchy evidence, and might be misleading. Furthermore, the breach between the church and the synagogue that took place around the end of the 1st century C.E., and the antagonism that emerged from it, limited the Jewish influence on Christian liturgy after the close of the 1st century. The influence of pagan rites and customs on the development of early Christian liturgy is much less obvious than the Jewish influence. The pagan influence, if it exists at all, is more likely to have been marginal, and it is very difficult to trace.

The core of the Christian rite is the sacramental celebration of the Eucharist, which was originally a common meal to commemorate Jesus's last supper. Already by the time of Paul (1 Cor. 11:23–26) some mystical and sacramental meanings were attached to it. The Eucharist was celebrated with fixed symbolic gestures, accompanied by prescribed prayers and benedictions. Several readings from the Scriptures and various supplementary prayers were added, to form what is known as canon in the western church and *anaphora* in the eastern church. This, however, must not be taken to imply that a single, uniform way of celebrating the Eucharist existed, or that a standard text was available. No liturgical uniformity was forced on the Christian communities, and the celebrants were free to choose the prayers they deemed appropriate. Consequently, several liturgical traditions emerged during the first five centuries of Christianity, mainly in influential Christian centers such as Alexandria, Antioch, and Rome, and in response to efforts made by charismatic Christian patriarchs. These traditions developed in their own particular ways, influenced by various local customs, and embedded with many local elements. It is customary to divide the liturgical traditions of late antiquity and the early Middle Ages into two groups, following historically determined geopolitical and geocultural divisions: that is, into the eastern liturgy and the western liturgy.

Eastern liturgy is usually characterized by a huge range of *anaphorai,* which, although sharing the same basic structure, are extremely diverse. The various traditions that belong to this group are: the Jerusalem tradition, usually attributed to Jacob, Jesus's nephew and the first bishop of Jerusalem; the Syrian tradition, which is divided into the East Syrian tradition (also known as the Nestorian tradition), attributed to Addai and Mari, and the West Syrian tradition (also known as the Antiochean tradition), from which the Byzantine liturgy probably emerged and which is still preserved by the Maronites of Lebanon; and the Alexandrian tradition, which developed in both Greek and Coptic, and which is known to us mainly through Hippolytus's *Apostolic Tradition* and through Sarapion's *Euchologion.* This tradition was also the basis for the Ethiopian liturgy.

The Byzantine tradition (also known as the Constantinople tradition) has two branches, one attributed to Basil of Caesarea and the other to John Chrysostom. The former became the most widespread rite in the Byzantine world, and it spread farther with the Christian mission to the Slavs and the Russians, whence it was translated into those native tongues at a fairly early stage. Subsequently it was accepted with minor changes and variations by the Armenian and Georgian churches.

Among the western traditions, the most important and influential was the liturgical rite of Rome, whose first stages of development are documented by Hippolytus of Rome in his *Apostolic Tradition.* The gradual formation of the Roman tradition was strongly influenced by the activities of Roman bishops, such as Pope Damasus (366–384) who, according to the *Liber pontificalis,* instituted Latin as the liturgical language of the west. The defining characteristic of the western Roman tradition, as opposed to eastern traditions, is the fact that a single canon was used for all eucharistic celebrations.

Although the liturgy of Rome influenced the emergence of local liturgical traditions in the west, one should not overemphasize its influence. There is ample evidence to demonstrate that liturgical traditions in the west, although based on Roman traditions, developed in their own peculiar ways. Among these western traditions are: the African tradition, which developed in North Africa (west of Cyrenaica) at least from the time of Cyprian of Carthage, but following the Vandal invasion and the Arab conquest ceased to be practiced; the Ambrosian tradition (also known as the Milanese tradition), developed in Milan under Bishop Ambrose and practiced throughout northern Italy, apart from the region of Venice, which had its own tradition known as the Aquileian tradition; the Mozarabic tradition, the liturgical practice of Visigothic Spain; the Gallican tradition, which developed in Merovingian Gaul; and finally the traditions that emerged in Ireland and Anglo-Saxon England. Although in the past scholars were accustomed to evaluating these independent traditions as mere derivatives of the Roman rite, modern scholars tend to acknowledge greater creativity and individuality in each of these subdivisions of the western rite, although it is obvious that all of them made ample use of Roman material. This diversity in western liturgical traditions was gradually limited by various church councils that demanded uniformity and compliance with the Roman rite, such as the Council of Clovesho (747) in Anglo-Saxon England and the Carolingian reform councils. The uniformity these councils aimed at was still far away, but the first steps toward it had been taken.

The importance of the study of the Christian liturgy goes far beyond the simple fact that it elucidates the way people celebrated their solemn rites and festivals. As the anthropologist Clifford Geertz has pointed out, "It is primarily . . . out of the context of concrete acts of religious observance that religious conviction emerges on the human plane." In other words, liturgy is an indispensable tool for the study of any Christian society in its historical, cultural, and spiritual context. It gives us a rare glimpse of the actual rites people performed, and it provides a great deal of information about the perceptions and ideas of the society in question.

BIBL.: George Dix, *The Shape of Liturgy,* 2nd ed. (London, 1945). Cheslyn Jones, Geoffrey Wainwright, Edward Yarnold, and Paul Bradshaw, eds., *The Study of Liturgy,* 2nd ed. (London, 1992). Cyrille Vogel, *Medieval Liturgy: An Introduction to the Sources,* rev. and trans. William G. Storey and Niels K. Rasmussen (Washington, D.C., 1986).   Y.H.

Lombards

The Lombards (Latin *Langobardi,* from Old High German, "Long-beards") shifted from their settlement in the Roman province of Pannonia to enter Italy in 568–569 and established a kingdom that lasted until their conquest by the Franks under Charlemagne in 774.

They are first attested in Tacitus's *Germania* (40) as inhabiting the regions of the lower Elbe. Except for the brief notices of other classical authors (Strabo, Vellius Paterculus, Ptolemy) we hear no more of them until 6th century writers inform us of their settlement in Rugiland (lower Austria, 488–489) and their defeat of the Heruli (507–508). Moving farther south across the Danube to settle in Pannonia and Noricum, they were made confederates of the empire (546–547) and under their king Audoin (547–560) engaged in intermittent warfare with the Gepids for the next two decades until the Gepids' destruction in 567 by Audoin's son, King Alboin, who led the Lombards into Italy in 568–569. Their reputation for warfare persuaded the emperor Justin to use them as mercenary troops for the empire on the Danube frontier and as auxiliary troops against the Persians in Phosis (Poti, Georgia) and Mesopotamia. They were also used by Justinian to fight the Ostrogoths in General Narses's reconquest of Italy (535–554).

The exact nature of Lombard origins, identity, and social structure in the pre-Italian period are obscured by lack of sources. In texts of the 7th–8th centuries the Lombards themselves promoted the idea of Scandinavian origin, though this smacks of Graeco-Roman ethnographic *topoi.* Archaeological research in tracing the geographic descent of a distinctly identifiable group to Italy often panders to these spurious origin myths, but has revealed settled, pastoral societies along the proposed trajectory. At the time of their arrival in Italy, the Lombards were supposedly a conglomeration of different ethnic groups—Suebi, Heruls, Gepids, Bavarians, Bulgars, Avars, Saxons, Goths, and Thuringians, as well as Romanized Pannonians—under a military elite who adhered to a core of traditions, law, and customs. Traces of tribal organization and institutions still remained in a society already well adapted to the imperial military system, in which a hierarchy of dukes, counts, and gastalds (local officers) commanded warrior bands formed from kinship groups called *farae.* What is identified as Lombard language, from the meager and problematic evidence of juridical terms, place names in Italy, and loan-words in the Italian dialects, was of the "high" western Germanic variety, probably akin to that of the Alamanni and not too far removed from the "low" western Germanic tongues of the Angles, Saxons, and Franks.

Crossing the Julian Alps in 568–569, the Lombards swiftly conquered most of northern Italy north of the Po River and took the major cities almost unopposed except for Pavia, which endured under siege until 572. A number of Lombard duchies were established in the north, such as Friuli (Cividale), Trento, Brescia, Bergamo, Turin, and Pavia; it is uncertain how many others. Immediately pushing farther south, they then took Tuscany and established the two duchies of Spoleto and Benevento in central and southern Italy, leaving a corridor of Byzantine-held territory across the middle of the peninsula from Rome to Ravenna, the imperial capital, along the Via Amerina. These, along with Venetia, Calabria, Sardinia, Sicily, Naples, and coastal Campania, were to remain in Byzantine possession. Yet advances by ambitious Lombard kings and dukes, particularly the kings Rothari, Liutprand, and Aistulf, continually encroached on imperial territories, eventually taking Liguria, Corsica, and Apulia throughout the course of the 7th and 8th centuries. Benevento continued as an independent duchy after the fall of the kingdom until the Norman invasions of the 11th century.

The main narrative source for the Lombards is the unfinished *Historia Langobardorum* (History of the Lombards) written at the end of the 8th century by Paul the Deacon, a monk from Monte Cassino who was of noble Lombard origin and who later was a major literary luminary at the Frankish royal court of Charlemagne. Information on Lombard political and diplomatic history can be cautiously gleaned from hostile Byzantine, Frankish, and papal sources of chronicles and letters, particularly the *Liber pontificalis* and papal correspondence. The Lombard law code, written in Latin and first promulgated by Rothari in 643—then it contained 388 laws, which were subsequently added to by later kings, most notably Liutprand (155 laws)—provides much information on Lombard society and customs and had a continual influence on Italian law to the 12th century and beyond. More than 290 private charters survive that reveal the continuity of late Roman legal norms for landholding and administrative practices. The Lombard period also saw important developments in art, church architecture, sculpture, and epigraphy; a range of various influences—Byzantine, Frankish, Germanic, native Italian—combined to create a discernible "Lombard style."

The Lombard political system was based on a hierarchy with the king and his court officials at the top, controlling the local power of the dukes by a range of other royally appointed officials—gastalds, mayors, judges—among whom exact relationships are difficult to ascertain, though they probably varied regionally, particularly in the southern duchies. At the foundation of the Lombard state was the concept of the "freeman," synonymously called an *arimmanus* or *exercitalis,* the respective Lombard and Latin words for soldier, who conducted military service in the national army, carried out at the summons of either the duke or the king, and held public responsibilities according to rank, wealth, and influence.

Historians have long debated how unified the Lombard kingdom was, though there is a general consensus as to the importance of Italian towns in providing a network of administrative centers for relations among the royal courts, the dukes, and local officials. The splintering of power seen in the interregnum period (574–584) demonstrated what would be a continual problem of ducal insurrection: rebellious dukes and powerful magnates were sometimes autonomous enough to oppose the king and his royal army, or were bribed with Byzantine gold into defecting. As testimony to the strength of the state, however, the rebels rarely aimed at independence; they sought the throne. The duchies of Spoleto and Benevento were to remain quasi-independent and presented a perpetual problem of diplomatic chicanery with their Byzantine and papal alliances and opposition to the centralizing policies of the royal court at Pavia.

The geopolitical logic of unifying the peninsula meant the Lombards were a continual threat to papal territory and the duchy of Rome. The failure of alliances with the Lombard duchies, the territorial isolation of the exarchate, and the religious alienation from Constantinople over the iconoclastic controversy encouraged Rome to look elsewhere for protection. The pope pleaded with his Frankish allies to invade Italy in defense of papal territorial rights. The Franks defeated the Lombards three times (under Pippin in 754 and 756, and finally under Charlemagne in 773–774), thereby incorporating the Lombard kingdom into the Carolingian realm.

BIBL.: Neil Christie, *The Lombards* (Oxford, 1995). Paolo Delogu, "Lombard and Carolingian Italy," in *The New Cambridge Medieval History,* ed. R. McKitterick (Cambridge, Eng., 1995), vol. 2, 290–319. Chris Wickham, *Early Medieval Italy: Central Power and Local Society 400–1000* (London and Basingstoke, 1981). N.E.

Lyons

Situated at the confluence of the Rivers Rhône and Saône, Lyons had long been a city of considerable importance for the Gauls. As such it was also an important center for the imperial cult, and it housed a significant mint as well. Its riverine communications capabilities made it a major economic center. Not surprisingly Lyons also attracted an early Christian community, whose fate is well known from records of its persecution in 177: the forty-eight martyrs of Lyons were to become the focus for a significant Christian cult in the city. More important than those martyrs, however, was their contemporary Irenaeus, a native of Asia Minor, who became bishop of Lyons ca. 178, and who suffered martyrdom in 202.

From the period of the tetrarchy onward, Lyons was the metropolitan city of the province of Lugdunensis Prima, and despite the subsequent reduction of its province, it remained an important city throughout the later empire and then under the Burgundians, whose kings used it as one of their chief residences. During the period of the Burgundian kingdom, secular laws were issued from Lyons, which was also the site of a church council (518–523). Although it did not retain its political importance under the Merovingians, it remained a major ecclesiastical center, being a metropolitan see, and as such it hosted at least two other church councils (in 567–570 and 583).

The cultural and social life of the city in the mid- to late 5th century is well known from the letters of Sidonius Apollinaris, who was a native of Lyons, and who acted as the city's spokesman when the emperor Majorian took umbrage at the welcome given the Burgundians by the senatorial aristocracy. For the opening decades of the 6th century, there are the letters of Avitus, metropolitan bishop of the neighboring metropolitan diocese of Vienne. Both authors reveal the continuance of secular literary traditions.

Equally important were the religious authors of the city. Already in the mid-5th century Lyons could boast of having as its bishop Eucherius, the author of the *De laude heremi* among other ascetic works. Among his successors was Patiens, who gained a notable reputation for his pastoral care, and who also commissioned works from Sidonius Apollinaris and from the priest Constantius, who wrote the *Life of Germanus of Auxerre* for him. Although the bishops of the 6th century were not of such literary or religious eminence, manuscript evidence suggests that the city continued to be a center for book production. Moreover, two 6th century bishops, Nicetius, the uncle of the historian Gregory of Tours, and Nicetius's bitter rival Priscus, both came to be remembered as saints (and were buried next to each other).

Eucherius's ascetic interests were echoed by a number of monastic foundations, most notably that of the Insula Barbara, and the city was famous for its churches, some of which were thought of as forming a ring around it. Although little remains from this period, excavations have revealed the foundations of some of these late antique churches.

BIBL.: A. Coville, *Récherches sur l'histoire de Lyon du Ve siècle au IXe siècle (450–800)* (Paris, 1928). *Topographie chrétienne des cités de la Gaule des origines au milieu du VIII siècle*, vol. 4: *Province ecclésiastique de Lyon*, ed. N. Gauthier and J.-C. Picard (Paris, 1986).   I.W.

Macedonia

The Macedonian landscape presents an often inhospitable sequence of mountains and basins that, to the south and east, open onto the Aegean coastal plain. With the exception of the Haliacmon, which rises in the Pindus Mountains, the many rivers that traverse Macedonia (most notably the Axius, Strymon, and Nestus) follow a roughly north-south direction. An important road that linked the city of Stobi with Thessalonica and its port followed the Axius. The river valleys served as channels for trade and passages for raiders and settlers from the north.

Broadly speaking, the linguistic boundary between Latin and Greek ran north of the province of Macedonia, although Latin inscriptions turn up in the larger urban centers, especially along the Via Egnatia, and in Roman colonies, such as Philippi, and occasionally among people of Roman origin. To the chagrin of the patriarch of Constantinople, the church of Rome, via the papal vicar of Illyricum based in Thessalonica, closely guarded its jurisdiction over Macedonia and all of Illyricum until 732–733.

Administrative boundaries shifted frequently to meet changing political and military circumstances. Reorganization begun by Diocletian made Macedonia one of ten provinces in the diocese of Moesia. Constantine split Moesia into the dioceses of Dacia and Macedonia, making the province of Macedonia one of seven provinces in the diocese of Macedonia, all of which was under the praetorian prefect of Illyricum. Although the exact dates are still unclear, between the late 4th and the mid-6th centuries the province of Macedonia was bisected and called Macedonia Prima, with its capital and metropolitan see at Thessalonica, and Macedonia Secunda, with a capital at Stobi. The latter province was briefly called Macedonia Salutaris in the late 4th century, though this probably did not cover precisely the same territory as the later Secunda. Macedonia's provincial borders can now be only roughly reconstituted, but it seems that by the 330s Lychnidus (Ochrid) belonged to Epirus, just west of its frontier with Macedonia; from the 5th century, Macedonia's northern boundary included Bargala, while the border with Thessaly ran just south of Dium. In the east, the River Nestus divided Macedonia from Thrace.

Macedonia's importance as a bridge between east and west was underlined by the Via Egnatia, but from the late 4th century the road frequently became a freeway for plunder and its security was seriously threatened. For more than two decades after the battle of Adrianople in 378, Goths became a thorn in Macedonia's side. Alaric's spree along the Via Egnatia in 395 was a notable example of Gothic disruption of the region. In 473–483, Ostrogoths devastated Stobi, Pella, Edessa, and Heraclea Lyncestis, and threatened Philippi and Thessalonica.

The fortification of cities was stepped up: in the 3rd century the inhabitants of Dium at the foot of Mt. Olympus girded their city with a *spolia*-studded wall that incorporated old altars, statues, and architectural fragments. The partially intact city walls of Thessalonica still show how, in the late 5th and the 6th century, walls were transformed into majestic symbols of imperial control. Manmade defenses were buttressed by divine support: in the mid-5th century, one of the main gates at Philippi was inscribed with the famous pair of letters purportedly written by King Abgar the Black (of Osrhoëne) and Christ, which acted as a talisman for the city against its enemies. At Thessalonica the role of city protector, once performed by the Cabiri, gradually fell to the local Christian saint, Demetrius, who eased the inhabitants through famine and siege in the 7th century, appearing on the battlements as a fully armed soldier. In the 7th century mosaics of the St. Demetrius Basilica near Thessalonica's public center, the miracle-working saint poses with benefactors in front of the city walls.

Travel by sea grew in importance, and the harbor of Thessalonica, enlarged by Constantine, became a busy center for international commerce. Archaeological investigation reveals an economic revival from the 4th century until the onslaught of the Slavic invasions in the 580s. Ecclesiastical complexes on the cutting edge of architectural development, luxurious villas encrusted with mosaics, large-scale fortifications, and small industrial installations reflect the booming atmosphere based primarily on trade, agriculture and cattle breeding, and mining and marble quarrying. The commercial links of the marble quarries on Thasos stretched as far as Italy and Syria.

Macedonia's prosperity was cut short by a combination of invasion and natural disaster, earthquakes in particular, which in 619–620 wreaked havoc in Thessalonica, Philippi, and Thasos. The Avar and Slav invasions led to widespread abandonment of the countryside by the former Greek-speaking inhabitants and its resettlement by nomadic Slavic tribes. Between 620 and 680 we lose trace of the praetorian prefecture of Illyricum, whose responsibilities were taken over by local authorities. The *Miracles* of St. Demetrius, an invaluable witness to conditions in Macedonia under Slavic occupation, suggests that by 615 the prefect of Illyricum had become de facto the urban prefect of Thessalonica. Sirmium, capital of the praetorian prefecture of Illyricum until 441, became the seat of the Avar Khagan. Coexistence was eventually fostered by commercial relations between the two groups and by the adoption of Greek cultural trappings by Slavic chieftains, such as Perbundus, whose integration into Thessalonica society and ultimate downfall in Constantinople distills the many tensions and jealousies that energized the relations of Greeks and non-Greeks in the late empire.

During the migrations of the late 6th and early 7th century, confrontation with Iran handicapped Roman efforts to repulse the Slavs in the Balkans. In the late 8th century, after nearly two centuries of virtual Slavic control of Greece, the long process of reconquering Greece for the Roman empire began. This major administrative feat included the re-Hellenization and re-Christianization of the region, since with the exception of a few resilient pockets, particularly in urban centers and coastal settlements, what evidence exists suggests that Macedonia, like the rest of Greece, had lapsed into Slavic polytheism. Gradually the southern Balkan Peninsula was incorporated into the theme system: Thrace by 680–685, Hellas in 695, but Macedonia not until ca. 801–802. The establishment of the theme of Thessaloniki in 836 finally betokened internal calm.

BIBL.: Paul Lemerle, *Les plus anciens recueils des miracles de saint Démétrius et la pénétration des Slaves dans les Balkans* (Paris, 1979 [texte], 1981 [commentaire]). *Villes et peuplement dans l'Illyricum protobyzantin* (Rome, 1984).

E.F.

Madaba

Madaba, located in Jordan, was one of the city-states of the province of Arabia, having been elevated to that rank in the 2nd century. It possesses ruins that date back to the Bronze Age. The oldest known bishop of Madaba was Gaianos, who attended the Council of Chalcedon (451). First Roman, then proto-Byzantine, the city spread over a hill bordering a fertile plain, growing outward from a street that ran east to west. Four churches were built along this street, including the Church of the Virgin, which had a circular plan and was constructed on the remains of a Roman building, and the Church of the Prophet Elijah, which had a crypt dedicated to the martyr Elianos. The remains of at least seven other basilica are known, including an edifice with a baptistery that is believed to have been the cathedral.

Of Madaba's churches, the most famous is the so-called Church of the Map, discovered in the late 19th century. It is decorated with a floor mosaic representing a map of Palestine and northern Egypt, with elements of physical geography—rivers, mountains, seas—and locales, including Jerusalem, identified with inscriptions. Cities, villages, and buildings are illustrated with vignettes, some reduced to a symbolic element and others very detailed, as in the cases of Gaza and, especially, Jerusalem. Emphasis was placed on the religious meaning of the Holy Land. Numerous pilgrim sanctuaries appear on the map, and the territories of the tribes of Israel are noted. However, several sites without religious traditions are also represented, and they situate the map within the proto-Byzantine Near East. Apart from the Bible, a road map and Eusebius of Caesarea's *Onomasticon* were the primary sources used in constructing the map. The presence of the Nea of Justinian on the map of Jerusalem allows us to date the mosaic after 542, probably in the second half of the 6th century.

Madaba is known for many other mosaics that were laid in its churches; the oldest of them date from the

6th century and the most recent from 767, in the Church of the Virgin. In 6th century private residences, several mosaics with mythological subjects have been discovered.

Madaba spread out over a vast *chōra*. Large towns, such as Castron Mefaa, and a large pilgrimage site, the Moses Memorial on Mount Nebo (one of the rare biblical relics still in existence in the province of Arabia), were located there. Several mosaics have been found in the territory of Madaba: inscribed in Greek, they attest to the restoration of the mosaic pavings—but not the construction of churches—up until the 8th century, under Bishops Job (in 756 and 762) and Theophanes (in 767).

BIBL.: H. Donner, *The Mosaic Map of Madaba* (Kampen, 1992). M. Piccirillo, *Chiese e mosaici di Madaba* (Jerusalem, 1989). P.-L.G.

Mafjar

Khirbat al-Mafjar, a palace located in the Jordan Valley a few miles north of the modern town of Jericho, belongs to a series of Umayyad establishments located in or near large agricultural enterprises. The main features of the Mafjar latifundia are visible from surveys and aerial photographs. The palace itself consists of a square residential building with a monumental entrance and rooms on two floors (the upper ones have not been preserved) around a porticoed courtyard, a small mosque, a bath with a huge and heavily decorated main hall next to minuscule bathing and resting rooms, and a long porticoed court (perhaps an afterthought), with a fountain pavilion in front of the whole establishment. Fragments of writing give the name of the caliph Hishām, under whose reign (724–743) Mafjar is assumed to have been built.

The architectural decorations at Khirbat al-Mafjar include frescoes (only fragments), mosaics (including the floor of the bath's main hall—mostly geometric designs and several representations), and especially stone and stucco sculptures. Thousands of fragments remain unstudied in the Rockefeller Museum in Jerusalem, where the most telling ensembles have been reconstructed. The techniques of decoration represent part of the variety available in the late antique world, from the Roman empire to central Asia. The same variety exists in the topics represented, from geometry to almost full-size animals and personages, and in the stylistic origins of the motifs.

The architecture of the bath's main hall and the fountain contains many examples of otherwise unknown late antique and classical secular building traditions. Robert Hamilton, the excavator of the palace, has convincingly related it to the life and character of Walid ibn Yazid, an eccentric and libertine Umayyad prince who ruled briefly in 744.

BIBL.: R. Ettinghausen, *From Byzantium to Sasanian Iran and the Islamic World* (Leiden, 1972). R. W. Hamilton, *Khirbat al-Mafjar* (Oxford, 1959). R. W. Hamilton, *Al-Walid and His Friends* (Oxford, 1988). R. Hillenbrand, "La Dolce Vita in Early Islamic Syria," *Art History* 5 (1982). O.G.

Magi

Magos, or plural *magi*, the Old Persian term for the Zoroastrian priestly order devoted to fire rites, had evolved in Greek from well before the Hellenistic period into a euphemism for an extravagant (and potentially fraudulent) foreign performer of bizarre rituals and holder of esoteric ritual knowledge. Attempts to derive this "magical" sense of *magos* from the actual cultic practices of Zoroastrian priests, including dream interpretation (Dan. 2:2, 10), astrology, and efficacious ritual speech (Plutarch, *De Iside et Osiride* 46 [369E]), are probably to be disregarded, as these practices were typical to traditional priesthoods throughout the Mediterranean and Near Eastern world.

More basic to the aura of the magi as these figures developed in Hellenistic and late antique culture were their exoticism, an aspect clearly central in the Gospel of Matthew's infancy narrative (2:1), their professional affiliation with one of the archaic priesthoods of the Near East, and their general repertoire of ritual services, overtly drawn from ancient priestly tradition. In fact, members of various Near Eastern priesthoods were circulating through the Mediterranean world during the Hellenistic and Roman periods (and probably earlier), either individually or as leaders of expatriate communities. Such priests gained a particular cachet as Greeks and Romans began to crave the romanticized "wisdom of the Orient," a cultural trend evident in the *Alexander Romance*, Lucian's *Lover of Lies*, and the Pseudo-Clementine *Recognitions*. But in the new environment a foreign priest or ritual specialist would lack native cultural significance as a religious authority, and the value of his ritual services within a community's tradition would go unrecognized. Thus Graeco-Roman authors used the term *magos* and its cognates to designate alien priests, legendary sages (Zoroaster, Moses), and anyone else appearing in this mold of foreignness (Jesus, Apollonius of Tyana) as bearers of uniquely efficacious spells from an unfamiliar, exotic culture. A stereotype also developed of the *magos* as a guru who went beyond the dispensing of spells to initiate clients into mysteries.

But the same reputation for exotic powers might be construed as sorcery, particularly as *magos* in popular usage came to designate anyone associated with the typically magical rite of "binding" a victim to unintended love or to failure (an activity for which much evidence exists from the Graeco-Roman world). An identification as *magos*—a practitioner of *mageia*—could, moreover, be grounds for legal or mob action in many parts of the Roman empire when that *mageia* was supposed to consist of harmful or disruptive rituals. Thus Apuleius of Madaura stood trial in a North African city for successfully wooing a well-connected heiress *(Apology)*. While *magos* seems to have carried far more dangerous implications in the Latin west (as Latin *magus*) than the Greek east, such accusations occurred anywhere and at any time societies or officials in the Roman empire held a particular terror of the covert use of the supernatural for political or social advantage. Likewise, *magos* came to serve as a derogatory term (in the sense of sorcerer) for any local or itinerant ritual specialist working outside Christian authority and with whom the apostles and saints of early Christian legend were often represented in competition.

BIBL.: Toufic Fahd, "Le monde du sorcier en Islam," in *Le monde du sorcier,* ed. S. Sauneron and G. Condominas (Paris, 1966). Fritz Graf, *Magic in the Ancient World* (Cambridge, Mass., 1997). Arthur Darby Nock, "Paul and the Magus," *Essays on Religion and the Ancient World,* ed. Zeph Stewart (Oxford, 1972), vol. 1, 308–324. Jonathan Z. Smith, "The Temple and the Magician," in *Map Is Not Territory: Studies in the History of Religions* (Leiden, 1978), 172–189.

D.T.F.

Magic

Practices that modern observers would classify as "magical" are very well attested in many parts of the Roman empire throughout its history and provide an important opportunity for the understanding of ancient religious life. The evidence includes spells and magical formulas preserved on papyri; curses inscribed on lead sheets *(defixiones)*; objects, such as amulets and other protective devices; literary references, including a quite probably fictional defense against a charge of magical practices by Apuleius of Madaura *(Apology)*; historical accounts of accusations against leading citizens; and much philosophical discussion for and against magic and wonder-working. All these would meet a generalizing modern definition of magic, such as the manipulation of supernatural powers for practical objectives by persons not officially sanctioned. So, as a matter of fact, would early Christian miracles.

Four main types of well-attested activity in late antiquity seem to fall within this arena. First, ritual actions of many kinds, most notoriously the sacrifice of human victims; second, the use of special words, often words in written form, as a means of binding and obliging unseen powers; third, the use of various natural objects, especially plants and herbs but also parts of human bodies and animals; fourth, the use of artifacts such as dolls and whirling tops. Of course, the pursuit of a particular objective might involve using more than one of these techniques; all of them imply special access to superhuman knowledge or powers. It is also

not uncommon for further religious activities to be brought under the description of magical practices, such as forms of divination and astrology, which might seem not characteristically magical at all.

The services that practitioners of magical arts were supposed to offer were manifold, but prominent among them were the destruction of the client's enemies by poison or other means, the attraction of the client's beloved, and the protection of the client from any forms of supernatural or demonic harm. Such activities are well attested for all periods of the empire, not least from the 3rd century C.E. onward. It is still sometimes assumed that magic was an archaic practice gradually declining in the face of rational forms of science or religion, but little in the late Roman evidence supports this.

A problem for all theories of ancient magic is that it is contestable whether "magic" constitutes a definable category of ancient activity at all or is simply a rhetorical device. There is never a hard boundary between what is religious and what is magical; rather, the term is regularly used to discredit religious claims of which the speaker disapproves: my achievements are miracles, yours are only magic. It is also far from clear that magical practices constituted a legal charge as such, rather than an accusation within a murder or treason charge, or that the Roman authorities ever attempted to repress magic methodically. Wherever an accusation is found, therefore, it is essential to examine its social and adversarial context. But however proper a skeptical attitude may be, the Romans apparently did have the idea of a magical tradition that had its own founder (Zoroaster) and its own pseudohistory (see Pliny, *Nat.Hist.* 30.1–18).

There are without question important changes in the pattern of the evidence that survives from late antiquity compared with earlier periods. First, the papyri show that magical practice was operating in a syncretistic religious context, with pagan, Jewish, and some Christian elements all contributing to the rich vocabulary of powers and conceptions. This tradition may well have had its origins in Graeco-Egyptian culture, but it must be, as we have it, a phenomenon of the 4th century and later. Second, curse tablets (frequently written on lead, rolled up and hidden in wells, rivers, or tombs), which have a history from classical Greece onward, show an increasing tendency toward elaboration in the course of the imperial period: the invocations become more complex, more and more of the text seems to be taken up with incomprehensible formulas (incomprehensible to us, not to the powers to whom they were addressed), drawings become more frequent. Third, accusations of involvement in magical activities become far more prominent between the republican period, in which they are virtually unknown, and the late empire, when they appear as high-profile events, for instance in the *Histories* of Ammianus Marcellinus (29.1–2), where magical divination figures among the crimes of prominent alleged conspirators in the reign of Valens (364–378).

Finally, magical practices under the name of "theurgy" became the topic of pagan elite debate in such contexts as the Hermetic writings and Neoplatonic philosophy. In terms of metaphysical theory, the claims of magic might be justified as expressions of the sympathy that existed between the physical world and the higher, divine sphere. The earliest Neoplatonists did not develop this potential, but Iamblichus of Chalcis *(On the Mysteries)* debated the issues raised by various pagan traditions of magic and divination and was interpreted, perhaps wrongly, by his successors as a ritualist, holding that union with the divine could be achieved only through theurgic contact with the gods. In any case, this view came to be established in later Neoplatonist thought. So magical practice and pagan philosophy ultimately came into close contact.

These arguments suggest that we can at least indicate a style of magical practice characteristic of late imperial as opposed to early imperial Roman culture. To put it crudely, magic seems to move up market in the course of the Roman empire's history: it seems to become more elaborated, more acceptable to philosophers, more prominent in the calculations of the elite. It could be said that a similar process in Christianity reconciled philosophic thought with belief in the efficacy of the relics of saints. At any rate, magic as such never achieved recognition within Christianity but instead provided Christians with an adversarial weapon that could be used to condemn as demonic either pagan survivals or objectionable practices by other Christians.

BIBL.: H. D. Betz, *The Greek Magical Papyri in Translation Including the Demotic Spells* (Chicago, 1986). G. Fowden, *The Egyptian Hermes: A Historical Approach to the Late Pagan Mind* (Princeton, 1993), 75–94. J. Gager, *Curse Tablets and Binding Spells from the Ancient World* (New York and Oxford, 1992). Fritz Graf, *Magic in the Ancient World* (Cambridge, Mass., 1997). C. R. Phillips, "Nullum crimen sine lege: Socioreligious Sanctions on Magic," in *Magika Hiera: Ancient Greek Religion and Magic*, ed. C. A. Faraone and D. Obbink (New York, 1991), 260–276. J.N.

Maioumas

The Maioumas was a popular aquatic festival in the late antique and early Byzantine world. Its name is formed from the Semitic word for water *(may)*, and Gaza, with a port bearing the same name, would appear to have been one of the obvious places for the celebration of the festival. John Chrysostom's vivid account of naked women swimming in a shameful display *(Homily on Matt. 7:6)* is usually thought to refer to the Maioumas. But there is no reason to infer from Malalas's allusion to the entertainments (12.284–5)

that the festival was normally held at night. The aquatic character of the Maioumas has recently been confirmed by the discovery of a vast shallow pool at Aphrodisias in Caria together with an inscription honoring a Maioumarch, who was obviously the festival's leader. It is clear from the inscription that this official was a Christian, and so we may deduce that this event was, like the stage performances of mimes and pantomimes, among the lubricious entertainments that Christians enjoyed. A celebration of the festival by Leo IV in baths at Constantinople in 778 (Theophanes 451.26, De Boor) shows the longevity of the Maioumas. In middle Byzantine Greek the word *maioumas* takes on the meaning of "largesse," but it is unlikely to have that sense in Theophanes's allusion to Leo's celebration.

BIBL.: K. Mentzu-Meimare, "Der *chariestatos Maïoumas,*" *Byzantinische Zeitschrift* 89 (1996): 58–73. C. Rouché, *Performers and Partisans at Aphrodisias in the Roman and Late Roman Periods* (London, 1993), 188–189, no. 65 (with G. W. Bowersock, *Gnomon* 69 [1997]: 49). G.W.B.

Malalas

John Malalas (ca. 490–ca. 570) was the author of a chronicle in eighteen books on world history to the reign of Justinian. He was from Antioch and probably of Syrian background, and he was a rhetor (the root *mll* has connotations of eloquence and learning) and thus had some legal training. He was also a Christian with an interest in Gnostic Hermeticism. From the chronicle's Antiochene focus and the interest demonstrated in provincial administration and military maneuvres, it is possible that Malalas worked in the office of the *comes Orientis*, which was based in Antioch until the 530s. The chronicle survives in Greek in one manuscript (Oxford, Barocc. 182, 11th–12th century) in a slightly abbreviated form, as can be seen by comparison with later excerptors (such as in the *Chronicon Paschale* and Theophanes) and translations (the Slavonic version is particularly significant). The chronicle circulated in at least two editions, though the point at which the first edition ended is disputed (at 528 or 532?); in Book 18 the emphasis shifts to Constantinople, and it is possible that this continuation may have been written by a different author: Malalas himself urged others to continue his work. According to the preface Malalas's chronicle had two purposes: to narrate sacred history according to the Greek chronographic tradition, and to give a summary account of events from Adam to the author's own time. The first objective is met in Books 1–8, which cover biblical and early Greek and Roman history, with attention to Egypt, Assyria, and Persia; the second was addressed in Books 9–15, which deal with Roman republican history, culminating in Christ's incarnation (Book 9) and the Roman emperors (Books 10–14), while Books

15–18, each treating one emperor apiece (Zeno, Anastasius, Justin I, and Justinian), cover events from Malalas's lifetime. Greek legendary history is recounted anachronistically with 6th century constitutional practices implied, while Greek mythology is fitted into the overall chronological framework and euhemerized. Malalas frequently displays an idiosyncratic stance, which has caused his chronicle to be regarded slightingly: his narrative, for example, on Trajan's Parthian Wars, cannot be reconciled with any other account. This may in part be due to insensitive blending of a multiplicity of sources: many authorities are cited, though most seem to be known secondhand, while analysis based on the chronicles' cross-references indicates that for Books 1–14 Malalas was probably drawing on perhaps four previous, and no longer extant, compilers of Antiochene history. For Books 15–18 Malalas claimed to have access to oral informants, who may have included Hermogenes, *magister officiorum* 529–533; he also makes largely unacknowledged use of near contemporary historians such as Eustathius of Epiphaneia (d. ca. 505). Antioch is the focus of Malalas's interest. Many anecdotes are introduced largely, it seems, to explain Antiochene civic rituals: for example, the annual door-knocking commemoration of Io and the use of antimosquito charms at the June horse races. The work as a whole is the product of a culturally complex environment and can be taken as an index of attitudes and historical perspectives that were probably widespread in the 6th century.

BIBL.: L. Dindorf, *Ioannis Malalae Chronographia* (Bonn, 1831). E. M. Jeffreys, M. J. Jeffreys, and R. Scott, eds., *The Chronicles of John Malalas: A Translation* (Melbourne, 1986). E. M. Jeffreys, B. Croke, and R. Scott, eds., *Studies in John Malalas* (Sydney, 1990). E.J.

Malchus of Philadelphia

Malchus of Philadelphia (late 5th century), a sophist, was probably of Syrian origin and almost certainly Christian. He was the author of a seven-book *Byzantine History (Buzantiaka)*, according to Photius, that ran from 473–474, the seventeenth year of Leo I, to 480, the death of Nepos, but apparently formed part of a longer work that began with Constantine I. It survives independently only in the Suda and the Constantinian *Excerpta;* these extracts probably overemphasize Malchus's interest in the Ostrogoths and certainly underreport internal affairs, to judge from Photius's summary. Focusing on the reigns of Basiliscus and the Isaurian Zeno, Malchus is persistently hostile to the Isaurians and to Zeno and so was probably writing under Zeno's successor, Anastasius. Though it is not clear what his sources were, he appears well informed, with access perhaps to Constantinoplitan officials. A classicizing historian, he makes use of set speeches, some of which have an air of authenticity

that survives condensation in the *Excerpta*. While he did not avoid technical terminology, his style is praised by Photius for its clarity and well-ordered narrative, and the work is described, with some justice, as "a paradigm of historical writing."

BIBL.: R. C. Blockley, *The Fragmentary Classicising Historians of the Later Roman Empire: Eunapius, Olympiodorus, Priscus and Malchus*, vols. 1 and 2 (Liverpool, 1981, 1983). B. Baldwin, "Malchus of Philadelphia," *Dumbarton Oaks Papers* 31 (1977): 91–107. E.J.

Mandaeism

Mandaeism was a religion in Mesopotamia (Iraq) and southwestern Iran during late antiquity. It is named after the Mandaean word for knowledge *(manda),* reflecting Gnosticism's centrality to the faith. Mandaeism probably originated among Gnostics dwelling along the River Jordan's banks around the 2nd or 3rd century C.E. Persecution by Jews and Christians forced the community to relocate, first to Harran (now in southeastern Turkey) and later to Mesopotamia (which they reached during the final century of Parthian rule), where they settled near river and canal embankments, owing to the overriding importance of water in their cultic practices.

Most Mandaean Scriptures were compiled in their extant form around the 7th century. However, the earliest extant *qulasta* (hymnal) dates from four centuries earlier and is one of many prayers. The major corpus of Mandaean beliefs is the *Ginza,* which consists of two parts—the *Right Ginza,* dealing with cosmogony and cosmology, and the *Left Ginza,* describing the afterlife and eschatology. Other canonical works include a *Book of John,* the illustrated *Scroll of the Rivers,* and the *Book of the Zodiac.* All these ecclesiastic materials drew on older sources and were written in Mandaean, an East Aramaic language that preserves West Syrian features from the devotees' original homeland. Because of constant fear of pollution, lay persons often were not permitted to have contact with the sacred books, lest the holy words be defiled. At a popular level, incantation bowls were produced with spells to ward off evil and harm. The priestly hierarchy included the positions of *tarmida* (disciple), *ganzibra* (treasurer), and *rishama* (communal leader). Clergy symbolically represented the spiritual, or right, world; laity the material, or left, world.

A dualism between good and evil, embodied by light or spirit and darkness or matter, respectively, was central to Mandaean belief. So was the notion of a universal conflict between these two opposing forces. As in the case of many other Gnostic sects, Mandaean sacred cosmology postulated a heaven of light inhabited by a supreme being known as the Great Life, his female companion, the Treasure of Life, and lesser *utria,* or light spirits. Next came purgatory or *matarata,* where human souls were reckoned, punished, and purified after death by fallen *utria,* the leader of whom was Abatur, the underworld spirit of justice. At the lowest level in this religious universe stood the earth, which had been fashioned by a light spirit named Ptahil. Central to Ptahil's ill-fated creation was the first man, Adam, who came to be infused by a soul *(ruha)* from heaven. This soul's role was to direct Adam, his wife, Eve (Hawwa), and all generations of their descendants toward *nasiruta,* "gnosis." Only through knowledge of its true origin could each human soul, averse to being trapped in matter, return to the realm of light. Supposedly also involved in the creation of the first human couple, and consequently all other people, was an underworld female spirit: Ruha. This Ruha and her evil companions were thought to control time and space, thus seeking to keep the light imprisoned beyond the reach of *manda.* However, several light spirits, such as Hibil and Shitil (Seth), serve as messengers, carrying gnosis to humans. The creation of matter and the entrapment of the light spirit in Adam having occurred, the ages of the world were believed to pass until the fourth or current evil age, at the end of which human history would draw to a close. Within their limited time and space Mandaeans were required to strive toward the ultimate goal of releasing all the light or spirit back to heaven.

Rituals played a fundamental role in this quest for salvation. Basic to Mandaean communal life was baptism *(masbuta).* It served as both a rite of passage and a means of purification, being undergone frequently on Sundays and in conjunction with particular events such as marriage or accouchement, and prior to death. Men clad in white and women in white with black shawls would gather at the banks of a river. To the chanting of prayers, each devotee thrice immersed himself or herself in the water, then underwent three reimmersions by the officiating cleric. While kneeling in the river, each initiate had a symbol of water drawn on his or her forehead, drank three handfuls of water, and obtained a small myrtle wreath denoting spiritual rebirth. Back on the bank, the newly baptized person would be anointed with oil. He or she then consumed bread during a communal repast at the conclusion of which the officiating priest shook *(kushta)* each devotee's hand. Lesser ritual ablutions such as the *tamasha* and *rishama* could be performed without the oversight of a priest. Tending to the deceased was another important aspect of Mandaean religiosity, for it was believed that the soul had to be assisted in passing safely via purgatory to the heaven of light. On the third day after death, a *masiqta,* or funeral mass, was celebrated in which food offerings were consecrated for nourishing the freed light entity that was seeking to rejoin those of other Mandaeans already in heaven.

After the advent of Islam, once Mandaeans fell under Muslim rule they sought a de facto protected status (Arabic *dhimma*) alongside Jews, Christians, and Zoroastrians by claiming that their faith had been founded by John the Baptist and that the *Ginza* was their Scripture. Sporadic persecutions occurred during the caliphate, not only at the hands of Muslims but also more frequently by Christians, who resented Mandaean claims that Jesus had been an apostate and that Mirjai (Mary) had converted to Mandaeism. Consequently, the community sought to ensure its survival by withdrawing from extensive contact with others.

BIBL.: Ethel S. Drower, *The Mandaeans of Iraq and Iran* (Leiden, 1962). Mark Lidzbarski, *Ginza, Der Schatz oder Das grosse Buch der Mandäer* (Göttingen, 1925; repr. 1978). Kurt Rudolph, *Die Mandäer,* 2 vols. (Göttingen, 1960–1961).

J.K.C.

Manichaeism

Manichaeism came into the mainstream of late Roman religious life through the missionary vision of Mani (216–276), the prophetic founder of the sect, and the evangelistic endeavors of his disciples. According to the *Cologne Mani-Codex,* Mani grew up in a Jewish Christian baptizing sect in southern Babylonia whose members acknowledged Elchasaios—a well-known Jewish Christian leader—as one of its founders. Patronized by Shapur I, Mani disseminated his teaching both within the Sassanian empire and in the frontier regions of the Roman empire and central Asia. A mission led by Adda was active along the Syrian frontier at the time of the ascendancy of Odaenathus at Palmyra (ca. 262–266). The mission later reached Egypt, especially Alexandria, and established a number of "communities." It appears that a separate mission to Egypt, probably via Eilat and the Red Sea ports, was also dispatched, and Lycopolis became its center. Persecution against the sect, instigated probably by Diocletian or Galerius, was probably instrumental in the establishment of a major Manichaean community at Kellis in the Dakhleh Oasis. The sect had reached North Africa, Asia Minor, the Balkans, and Italy by the end of the 3rd century.

A religion of the book par excellence, Manichaean missionaries first disseminated the sect's literature in Syriac, using a distinctive Estrangela script that was also widely used by Manichaean communities in central Asia. The texts were soon translated into both Greek and Coptic, as evidenced by the discovery of Syriac-Coptic bilinguals at Kellis, and later into Latin. The spread of the religion was assisted by trade between Rome and Sassanian Iran and by the conversion of the empire to Christianity, which opened many missionary possibilities for a religion that claimed to be a superior form of Christianity proclaimed by a prophet who styled himself the Apostle of Jesus Christ and the promised Paraclete.

At the heart of Manichaean teaching was a radical dualism that stemmed from an extreme interpretation of the dichotomy between Body and Flesh in Pauline teaching. A cosmogonic myth based on Two Principles and Three Epochs was developed to account for the basic evil nature of the human body and of much of the visible creation. The Two Principles, Light and Darkness, were originally separate and distinct. However, an invasion of the Kingdom of Light by the covetous forces of the Prince of Darkness in the Middle Epoch necessitated the sending of a Redeemer Figure—the Primal Man—to repel the incursion. He was drugged and overwhelmed by the forces of Darkness, though he was recalled to consciousness by a divine Call, and his protective armor of Light Elements, or Particles, was partially devoured by the Archons of Darkness. An elaborate and horrific myth involving cannibalism and incest was woven around the theme of the redemption of these captive Light Particles and the attempts by the forces of Darkness to forestall such a scheme through the creation of plant, animal, and human life. Plant life, especially melons, were alleged to hold more Light Particles than flesh. The Particles were released through the digestive system of the Manichaean Elect, and the Sun and the Moon were celestial receiving vessels for the liberated Particles. The human soul was regarded as an element of divine nature held captive in the flesh, and the recognition of this distinction is an important element of the Manichaean gnosis. In the final epoch, the two primeval elements, light and darkness, will become separate again after the visible creation has been purified by a final conflagration lasting 1,468 years.

The gnosis of Mani is expected to be understood literally, as it constitutes the raison d'être for the hierarchical structure of the sect, in which the Elect were forbidden to marry or to prepare food. Their daily needs had to be tended to by the Hearers, who were permitted to live a more normal life. In the Roman empire, the strict asceticism of the Elect, the rejection of the Jewish Scriptures as essential for salvation, and the solution offered by dualism to the perennial problem of the origin of evil made the religion attractive to some members of the late Roman intellectual class; Augustine of Hippo—a Hearer for nine years—was the best known example.

A cache of genuine Manichaean texts, consisting of seven codices, including didactic, historical, and liturgical texts as well as the letters of Mani, was recovered at Medinet Madi in 1929 and divided between the Chester Beatty Collection in England and the Staatsbibliothek of Berlin. The texts, though written in Sub-Achmimic B, were found in an area where the predominant dialect of Coptic would have been Fayummic. This might indicate that the texts were imported into the region by Manichaean missionaries from farther south. The Manichaean settlement at Kellis possessed older versions of some of the same texts in the same dialect. At Kellis, relatively untroubled by persecution, the Manichaeans were able to regard themselves openly as true Christians, and private documents reveal a complex pastoral structure. The site was aban-

doned ca. 400, possibly because the underground water supply for the oasis was drying up.

The Manichaean religion was heavily persecuted by the Christian Roman state from Theodosius I onward and was the target of vehement polemics by orthodox-minded churchmen. These polemical writings constituted our main source on the history of the sect until the beginning of this century and were also used regularly by the Byzantine and Catholic churches in the Middle Ages against "Neo-Manichaean" sects, such as Paulicianism, Bogomilism, and Catharism. The Manichaeans were also persecuted by the Muslim establishment and were the main examples of a category of nonbelievers known as *zindīq*, i.e., intellectual, evil, and immoral, but not necessarily pagan. Mani is remembered mythically as the creator of Persian painting.

BIBL.: A. van Tongerloo, S. N. C. Lieu, and J. Van Oort, eds., *Corpus Fontium Manichaeorum, Series Coptica*, vol. 1: *Liber Psalmorum, Pars II. Fasc. 1, Die Bema-Psalmen* (Turnhout, 1996). I. Gardner, "The Manichaean Community at Kellis," in *Emerging from Darkness*, ed. P. Mirecki and J. BeDuhn (Leiden, 1997), 161–175. James E. Goehring, "Monastic Diversity and Ideological Boundaries in Fourth-Century Christian Egypt," *Journal of Early Christian Studies* 5 (1997): 61–83. S. N. C. Lieu, *Manichaeism in the Later Roman Empire and Medieval China*, 2nd ed. (Tübingen, 1992). S. Stroumsa and G. G. Stroumsa, "Anti-Manichaean Polemics in Late Antiquity and under Early Islam," *Harvard Theological Review* 81 (1988): 37–58. Michel Tardieu, "La diffusion du Bouddhisme dans l'empire kouchan, l'Iran et la Chine, d'après un Kephalaion manichéen inédit," *Studia Iranica* 17 (1988): 153–182. A. Villey, *Alexandre de Lycopolis contre la doctrine de Mani* (Paris, 1985). S.L.

Manumission

In the early 5th century a young Roman woman named Melanie decided to give up her luxurious lifestyle, donate her huge property to the poor and the churches, and pursue the life of a saint. One of her generous deeds was "to free 8,000 of her slaves with their consent, while all the other slaves prefered to become the slaves of Melanie's relative" (Palladius, *Hist.Laus.* 61). To be or not to be a slave was a difficult and risky choice, certainly for those men and women who had no property *(peculium)* at all and were no longer young and strong.

From the end of the Roman republic on, manumissions were frequent and had many different motives. It was an old and noble Roman tradition to free one's slave in return for his or her long-lasting services and merits. The lawyer Julian (2nd century), for example, reports that physicians "commonly" freed their slaves if they were also trained in medicine (Justinian, *Digest* 38.1.25.2). A less generous motive for manumission was profit: the master granted freedom to his slave under the condition that the latter would pay a kind of ransom. So long as the total sum had not been paid to the master or his heir, the slave remained a so-called *statuliber*. Last but not least, manumissions served senatorial families as a way of displaying their wealth and generosity.

Though we have no statistics, the number of manumissions in the late antique era was obviously considerable. The emperor Augustus had already issued two laws that restricted manumissions. The *lex Fufia Caninia*, 2 B.C.E., limited the number allowed: those who had up to 10 slaves were allowed to liberate no more than half of them, those who had up to 500, no more than one-fifth, 100 being the maximum in any case. The *lex Aelia Sentia*, 4 C.E., required that the slave had to be at least thirty years old and the master at least twenty. It had been presumed that Augustus thereby wanted to prevent Rome's becoming overcrowded with foreign and disgraceful freedmen. Manumissions seemed ambivalent with respect to the freedman's future and economic security, on the one hand (as the case of Melanie's slaves shows), and with respect to the social structure especially in the cities, on the other. Augustus's laws were formally abrogated only in the 6th century by the emperor Justinian.

The legal means to free a slave were several. The classical method, according to Roman civil law, was either by testament or in front of the magistracy, called *manumissio vindicta*, because one of the officials, the lictor, had to touch the slave with a rod. The lawyer Gaius, though, tells us in the 2nd century that it had become common to free slaves "in transition, for example if the praetor passes by on his way to the bath or the theatre" (*Inst.* 1.20). According to the law established by the praetor, manumission was also performed in the presence of friends as witnesses *(manumissio inter amicos)* or by a written document *(manumissio per epistulam)*. From Constantine the Great on, the "pious intention to grant freedom to one's favorite slaves" could also be realized in churches, under the eye of the bishop (*C.Th.* 4.7.1). It has been debated whether the so-called *manumissio in ecclesia* was just a Christian development of the older *manumissio inter amicos* or whether the new ceremony was inspired and influenced by an ancient Greek rite called *hierodoulia*, a solemn form of manumission by which the slave bought his own freedom, sacrificing the money to his master and himself to the deities.

The legal effect of manumission was that the slave became a freedman *(libertus)*. As such he was "free" only in a certain sense, however. Only in the case of the *manumissio vindicta* did he become a Roman citizen right away. In the other cases of manumission, the freedmen were *Latini Iuniani*, with limited political and civil rights but many duties with respect to their former masters, their "patrons."

In the 6th century Justinian reconsidered the problem of slavery and manumission. In his *Institutes* (1.5) he explained and confirmed the Roman concept of slavery: natural law *(ius naturale)* makes no difference between free or unfree men; the law of all people *(ius gentium)*, however, knows three classes: freeborn men, freedmen, and slaves. So far as the political status of freedmen was concerned, Justinian granted them full citizenship. But the rights of the patrons to demand certain services and grateful obedience were corroborated and even extended to the patrons' successors. Only in certain cases did freedmen become free also from patronage, e.g., if the master had prostituted or mistreated the former slave, or if the freedman could pay off his duties (*C.Just.* 6.4.4).

The Christian emperors slightly reformed the law of manumission, but they did not touch on the institute of slavery and patronage as such.

BIBL.: Robert Brunschvig, "'Abd," *Encyclopaedia of Islam*, 2nd ed. J. A. Harrill, *The Manumission of Slaves in Early Christianity* (Tübingen, 1995). H. Langenfeld, *Christianisierungspolitik und Sklavengesetzgebung* (Bonn, 1977). Joseph Schacht, *An Introduction to Islamic Law* (Oxford, 1964).   M.F.

Maps

For us, maps are the most familiar representation of—and tool for orientation in—space. They require the acquisition of exact geographical data, the conversion of these data into a scale drawing, and the reproduction of this image. None of these three preconditions could be met in late antiquity. Since longitudes could not be measured with reasonable precision, exact coordinates were difficult to get; the concept of scale was not developed; and while multiple copies of texts could be produced through dictation and copying, it remained difficult to reproduce images correctly.

Instead, space was sometimes represented in symbols: simple globes or unspecific images of the land and the sea stood for the world, personifications for provinces or regions. Far more frequently used, however, were texts. Even the "Map of Agrippa," produced under Augustus, may have been a long inscription listing place names and distances, although it may equally have consisted of a prototype of the Peutinger Table. It was utilized in the 1st century by Pliny the Elder for the geographical books of his *Nat.Hist.* (3–6), and again in the late antique anonymous treatises *De mensuratio provinciarum* and *Divisio orbis terrarum*, which were used in turn by Dicuil in the 8th century. There also were lists of toponyms in itineraries like the late 3rd century *Itinerarium Antonini* and in lists of provinces and regions like the 5th century *Notitia dignitatum*. And even the massive 2nd century Greek geography by Claudius Ptolemaeus contained just lists with the raw data for maps: toponyms and their coordinates. Later these were used for drawing maps that were to become the foundation both of early Islamic geography and of the early modern western view of the world.

Most common were literary geographies like Pom-

Section of the *Tabula Peutingeriana* showing Italy. Rome is central; the Adriatic Sea is above Italy and the Tyrrhenian Sea below.

ponius Mela's *De chorographia* and Pliny's books mentioned above; these were repeatedly excerpted and widely read in late antiquity, as was the 2nd century Greek geography by Dionysius Periegetes, which by 500 had twice been translated into Latin.

Representations of space in the form of recognizable maps were relatively rare. Two surviving artifacts are schematic route diagrams comparable to the metro diagrams displayed in many cities today: the "shield" from Dura-Europus, a 3rd century diagram of stations along the coast of the Black Sea, and the "Tabula Peutingeriana," a 12th century world "route map" based on a late antique original. A 6th century mosaic from Madaba is a schematic graphical representation of many place names in Eusebius's *Onomasticon* and other lists. An unpublished papyrus now in Milan appears also to show some kind of map.

The display of world maps was part of an ideology

of extended rule, used both by the emperor Theodosius II at Constantinople, in the 5th century, and by Pope Zachary II in the Lateran Palace at Rome, in the 8th.

BIBL.: K. Brodersen, *Terra Cognita* (Hildesheim, Zurich, and New York, 1995). O. A. W. Dilke, *Greek and Roman Maps* (London, 1985). I. Kretschmer, J. Doerflinger, and F. Wawrik, eds., *Lexikon zur Geschichte der Kartographie* (Vienna, 1986). J. B. Harley and D. Woodward, eds., *The History of Cartography* (Chicago, 1987–). Y. Tsafrir, "The Maps Used by Theodosia: Pilgrimage Maps of the Holy Land and Jerusalem in the Sixth Century C.E.," *Dumbarton Oaks Papers* 40 (1986): 129–145.   K.B.

Marble

Imperial exploitation of the most important quarries of high-quality white and colored marbles, started by the emperor Tiberius (14–37 C.E.), reached its zenith after it had been submitted to very tight imperial control during the second quarter of the 2nd century. The mass production of architectural elements and sculpture that resulted continued throughout the century into the Severan period (193–235). Whereas the large building programs of the first Severan emperors revived the quarrying and use of marble on a large scale (e.g., the red granite from Assuan), the assassination of Alexander Severus (235) started a period of upheaval and disruption in the Roman order that continued during the largest part of the century and led to a decline in the availability of and trade in freshly quarried marbles. The presence of enormous stocks of (mainly colored) marbles in the *statio marmorum* at Rome and a sharp reduction in building activity in the capital also caused a saturated market and declining quarry activities. The *ratio marmorum,* or department for the imperial marble exploitation and trade, may even have ceased to function, as there are no imperial quarry inscriptions found from later than 236. Whereas some quarries in modern Turkey (Proconnesus [Island of Marmara], Ezine in the Troad, Docimium-Iscehisar) still remained productive, the activity of Luni (Carrara) diminished considerably. In Rome marble was mainly replaced in official constructions by Proconnesian and Thasian imports. At the same time, combining white marbles from different origins in the same building became a common practice. In Asia Minor, the Milesian quarries seem to have been abandoned shortly after the invasions of the Goths during the third quarter of the 3rd century, whereas in Attica the decline of the Pentelic and the Hymettan quarries was as much the result of a precarious economic situation as of the Herulian raids of 267. By that time, the use of colored marbles, such as green and red porphyry from Greece and Egypt, respectively, had also become rare. Even if colored marbles from Teos *(africano)* and Chios *(portasanta)* were still used as late as the reign of Diocletian, their production had declined or ceased al-

together shortly after the Antonine period. During the later part of the 3rd century, the export to Italy of yellow-to-orange Numidian marble *(giallo antico,* from Simitthus) also stopped.

However, the tetrarchs who ruled the empire in the last quarter of the 3rd century, and especially the emperors Diocletian and Maxentius, were responsible for a last revival of monumental building, both in Rome and in some provincial capitals, that may have exhausted the stocks of white building marble. These building programs also resulted in a resumption of important quarrying activities at Simitthus *(giallo antico)* in Tunisia and at Mons Porphyrites in Egypt (productive until the 5th century). The Egyptian red porphyry would become particularly popular for imperial statuary and sarcophagi in late antiquity. Similarly, the *"granito del foro"* (from Mons Claudianus, Egypt, active until the middle of the 4th century) remained more or less restricted to imperial constructions but was replaced elsewhere by other types of granites, especially the "marble from the Troad" (Ezine, Turkey), which was exploited until the Byzantine period.

Despite this renewed activity, the availability of freshly quarried marble for the tetrarchic constructions was still so limited that a lot of older architectural elements had to be reused, and marble-faced brick entablatures sometimes took the place of solid marble elements. On the whole, the demand for white and colored marbles was so pronounced that in 301 Diocletian fixed a price limit for nineteen types of them in his famous Price Edict. (Some of the cheaper marbles still available on the market may not have been included in this list.)

As a result of the foundation of Constantinople in 324–330, marble exports to Rome became much rarer. On a limited scale, half-worked (columns, bases, Ionic capitals) and half-finished building elements (Corinthian capitals) from the Proconnesus and the Troad still were shipped to Italy during the later 4th century and the first half of the 5th. But in most cases they represented specific orders from members of the imperial household or personalities affiliated with it. Similarly, during the 6th century the import of "eastern" marbles and products was mainly restricted to seats of the Byzantine government, such as Ravenna. The recapturing of North Africa by Justinian explains why eastern marble elements reached that continent. At the same time, the difficulties in obtaining "eastern" marbles for private use in Italy and Gaul may explain why during the later 4th and early 5th centuries there was an increased use of Luni marble (Carrara) by private workshops in Rome and Ostia. These shops specialized in the production of Christian sarcophagi and architectural elements, such as composite capitals with smooth leaves, for smaller churches and private houses. Luni marble most probably was quarried then on a largely reduced scale by private entrepreneurs beyond direct imperial control. Elsewhere, a number of quarries with a previously local or regional importance now increased their production to meet the increased demand. This was the case with a number of quarries of white and colored marbles located on the French side of the Pyrenees that between the later 4th and the 6th centuries exported to southern Gaul, Rome, the Adriatic, and even Constantinople.

In the east, some quarries located in a favorable position to provide the new capital with its much needed building materials flourished again in the 5th and 6th centuries. These sites include Proconnesus (white marble), the Troad (granite from Ezine), Docimium (purple-veined *pavonazzetto*), and Hierapolis (colored onyx from Gölemezli near Pamukkale, quarried as late as the 6th century) in Anatolia, and the quarries of Larisa (green *verde antico* from Thessaly), Karystos (green *cipollino* from Euboea), and Thasos (white marble from Aliki) in Greece. The latter were abandoned only after the Slavic invasions of the 6th century. For about two hundred fifty years, starting around 320, it was Proconnesian white marble that became the main building stone for the construction projects in Constantinople. Thereafter, even if there was a resumption of activity on the island during the Ottoman period, the production of prefabricated architectural elements in the quarries on the island seems not to have extended beyond the 6th century. This does not mean, however, that all activities must have ceased, only that the workshops for shaping building elements had been transferred to Constantinople. Even in Docimium there was still some minor activity in the quarries as late as the 10th century. Yet on the whole, most other quarry operations may not have survived the end of the 6th century. At this point, *spolia* replaced freshly quarried material.

Before the end of the 1st century C.E. most major quarries had become imperial property and were administered from the *statio marmorum* in Rome. As mentioned, this system may not have survived the political upheaval and economic decline following the murder of Alexander Severus, so that the output of most quarries decreased sharply or even ceased completely. To meet the increased demand for freshly quarried material during the 4th century, some emperors found themselves obliged to take measures to stimulate exploitation by private entrepreneurs. In 320 Constantine the Great thus allowed the private exploitation of quarries that were not state property in North Africa (*C.Th.* 10.19.1). In 363 the emperor Julian did the same in the eastern provinces (*C.Th.* 10.19.2). These measures seem to have had such success that Julian was forced to promulgate a law forbidding senators and other officials to make use of the *cursus publicus* for transporting their marble products (*C.Th.* 8.15). Other laws stimulating marble exploitation by private people in exchange for fiscal advantages were issued in

365 (*C.Th.* 10.19.3) and 376 (*C.Th.* 10.19.8). At least some of these entrepreneurs were Roman senators or high officials. Some entrepreneurs may have owned their quarries, others may have leased them. Eventually this system seems to have become so popular that it was a threat to the direct imperial exploitation that apparently still continued in some of the larger quarries. As a result, new laws were issued to reduce private quarrying activities. Laws from 382 (*C.Th.* 10.19.10) and 384 (*C.Th.* 10.19.11) stated that whoever leased a quarry had to present one-tenth of its output to the state and another tenth to the legal owner of the quarry. In 393 the emperor Arcadius even forbade private quarrying altogether (*C.Th.* 10.19.14), which led to a new shortage of architectural marble during the first decade of the 5th century. Consequently, with the exception of Proconnesus, the Troad, and Docimium quarries, which remained owned and exploited by the emperor himself, in 414 all quarries were reopened for private exploitation, and the leasing of quarries was once more stimulated through fiscal reductions (*C.Th.* 11.28.9). It certainly is no coincidence that the three quarries that remained under direct imperial control were exactly those that provided the emperors with material for their building projects in the capital. Granite columns from the Troad were very popular in combination with Proconnesian white marble capitals and bases, while Docimian marble remained popular for wall veneering (*pavonazetto*) and sculpture.

The fact that the emperor Justinian issued a law condemning prisoners to work in the Proconnesian quarries proves that at least these quarries were still controlled by the state during the 6th century (*Collatio legum mosaicarum et romanarum* 15.2). Thus far there is no evidence that this system continued into the next centuries. When, during the 10th century, a bishop of Constantinople needed people capable of sawing marble blocks into slabs for veneering, he addressed himself to the bishop of Synnada, where the imperial administration of the Docimian quarries had been established during the Roman imperial period. This shows that by that time activities in the quarries had slipped beyond state control. Traces in various quarries indicate that from the early Byzantine period onward, the practice of sawing marble must have been lost in many provincial cities, so that thenceforth slabs were sawn directly from quarry faces.

From the late 2nd and especially the 3rd century onward, the practice of ordering specific architectural elements directly from the quarries had become widespread. In Rome and in Italy this resulted in an increasing import of half-completed columns and completely finished capitals in Proconnesian marble during the 3rd century and particularly during the following tetrarchic and Constantinian times. The transfer of the seat of power to Constantinople in 324–330 interrupted the import of eastern building materials (from the Proconnesus and Thasos) in Italy and the western provinces (Gaul, Spain). The larger elements (column shafts, octagonal plinths, Corinthian capitals) that still reached the west were mainly gifts from emperors or higher officials for the construction of prestigious Christian basilicas. As a result of this shortage of imported elements, a new type of capital (mostly in Luna marble)—a composite capital with smooth leaves—was developed in Rome during the later 4th and the first half of the 5th century. Nevertheless, the import of smaller half-finished products from Thasos, the Pentelic quarries, and the Proconnesus to Ostia during the third quarter of the 4th century indicates that even by that time there still existed trading mechanisms that could bring such items on the western markets.

The practice of producing standardized marble elements in the quarries themselves may have been first developed in the Proconnesian quarries, where it became common practice in the production of sarcophagi (2nd to 3rd centuries) and column capitals, bases, and shafts (middle of the 2nd until the 6th century). Whereas many other important quarries mainly exported marble blocks, the Proconnesian quarries were more inclined to shape the marble on site. During the 2nd and 3rd centuries these elements had been exported either roughly shaped or in a half-finished form. During late antiquity Proconnesian workshops started to produce completely finished items as well. During the reign of Theodosius I (379–395) workshops located right within the quarries thus finished or nearly finished specific column shafts or drums of an unusual type for the emperor's building projects in the capital. This implies that during the early Christian period, the Proconnesus had become an open work yard for workshops cooperating with the building yards in Constantinople. During the reign of Theodosius II (408–450), completely finished bell-shaped, Ionic, and mainly Corinthian capitals were also shipped from the island. These did not represent real mass production but must have been prepared for specific buildings in Constantinople. More common capital types of the same period (composite capitals, Ionic impost capitals, impost blocks) probably were completely shaped in Constantinople. Judging from the elements discovered in the quarries, workshops for completely finished building elements seem to have ceased activity by the 6th century.

However, there still existed the mass production of half-finished capitals in the late antique Proconnesian quarries. In fact, during the 5th and 6th centuries Proconnesian workshops produced two types of roughed-out capitals that received their final decoration after shipment to Constantinople or elsewhere: the quarry-state Corinthian capital with finished abacus and uncut torus, and the quarry-state basket capital, an impost capital characteristic of the 6th century and composed of a cylindrical lower part, a kettle-shaped

or conical body, and a square top. The basket capital was also produced in the quarries of the "Hierapolitan marble," as this material was convenient for finishing various types of capitals and was therefore exported in huge quantities to meet the architectural demands of the early Byzantine empire. During late antiquity elements for the upper parts of buildings (e.g., arches) apparently were shipped only in a half-finished form. As illustrated by the shipwreck from Marzamemi, other workshops of the 6th century exported half-finished elements for the decoration of churches (capitals, columns, bases, and an altar in Proconnesian marble) as far away as Sicily. The same ship also contained ambon plates in *verde antico* from Larisa in Thessaly. This seems to suggest that the workshop that had prepared these elements may have been located in Constantinople rather than on Proconnesus. Most probably it was involved in Justinian's policy of imperial propaganda, carrying building materials for new churches in the reconquered parts of the empire. After the 6th century all evidence for a systematic prefabrication of marble elements disappears.

As a result of the declining activity in most quarries and thus the shortage of freshly quarried marbles, especially colored ones, a systematic exploitation of ancient monuments had begun by the 4th century. The tone was set by the construction in 303–304 on the Via Lata of Diocletian's *arcus novus,* which incorporated a relief from an arch dedicated to Antoninus Pius, and by Constantine's arch in 315, built with reused sculpture from Trajanic, Hadrianic, and Antonine monuments. This reuse of specific and well-selected reliefs also reflected political purposes, producing links with some of the "good" emperors and with Rome's glorious past. In other cases, the use of *spolia* by the authorities not only was caused by a shortage of building materials but also reflected an effort to preserve precious older monuments.

Following the reign of Constantine and throughout the 4th century, innumerable older materials, and in particular colored marbles, were reused to build the large Christian basilicas of Rome (St. John Lateran, St. Peter's in the Vatican, St. Paul's outside the walls). However, the limited number of ruined buildings that could be looted made it necessary to combine columns and capitals of different shapes and materials in a single building. This disadvantage sometimes was turned into an advantage, when the different materials were used to better emphasize the various parts of a church. Even later, when more material became available, this last practice would not be abandoned. During the 4th century the phenomenon of reusing older marbles took root in some other large cities with important Christian communities, both in the west (Milan, Trier) and the east (Thessalonica, Ephesus, Palestine). Elsewhere in the empire, innumerable monuments were dismantled to be reused in the building projects of the new capital at Constantinople. The whole phenomenon of reusing older elements, in particular bronzes and marbles, was also greatly accelerated as the result of the suppression of pagan cults by Theodosius I in 391–392, as this led to a looting of many pagan temples.

In particular, decorated marble elements, called *ornamenta,* were sought after. To avoid a systematic dismantling of many of the still well preserved older monuments, laws protecting them were promulgated in 349 (*C.Th.* 9.17.2), 356 (*C.Th.* 9.17.4), 357 (*C.Th.* 15.1.1), 363 (*C.Th.* 9.17.5), 398 (*C.Th.* 15.1.37 = *Corpus Justiniani* 8.11.13.1), 399 (*C.Th.* 16.10.15 and 16.10.18), 405 (*C.Th.* 15.1.43), 408 (*Sirmondianus* 12), 447 (*Nov.Val.* 23), and 458 (*Nov.Maior.* 4.1). Other laws issued in 376 (*C.Th.* 15.1.19) and 389 (*C.Th.* 15.1.25) prevented private parties from tearing down public monuments.

On a different level, the sack of many of the Roman cities by foreign tribes, starting with Alaric's sack of Rome in 410, inaugurated the practice of reusing marble objects of smaller dimensions, previously stored in treasuries, for the benefit of the raiders and their offspring.

Later, especially during the 7th and 8th centuries, elements in precious materials or marble were systematically reused in churches as containers for the relics of saints and martyrs, or as thrones. When Charlemagne eventually imported Roman workers and materials for his own building projects, he was only continuing an already well established practice; at the same time, he set a model for later generations of church and palace builders.

Umayyad builders in Syria and Palestine also reused many marble elements from earlier constructions and at times recut them for their own purposes (Mosque of Damascus, Dome of the Rock and Aqṣā Mosque in Jerusalem, palace of Khirbat al-Mafjar).

BIBL.: Nuşin Asgarı, "The Proconnesian Production of Architectural Elements in Late Antiquity, Based upon Evidence from the Marble Quarries," in *Constantinople and Its Hinterland,* ed. Cyril Mango and Gilbert Dagron (Aldershot, Eng., 1995), 263–287. Antonio Giuliano, "Colored Marble from Constantine to Napoleon," in *Radiance in Stone: Sculptures in Colored Marble from the Museo Nazionale Romano,* ed. Maxwell L. Anderson and Leila Nista (Rome, 1989), 23–34. Patricio Pensabene, "Amministrazione dei marmi e sistema distributivo nel mondo romano," in *Marmi antichi,* ed. Gabriele Borghini (Rome, 1989), 45–53.   M.W.

Marib

Capital of the kingdom of Sheba in southwestern Arabia, Marib is located 120 km east of San'a. In Sabaic inscriptions, the city is called "Maryab" (first attestation in the 8th century B.C.E.), then "Marib" beginning in the late 2nd century C.E. The name became "Mar'ib" in Arabic, after its root was reinterpreted; today it designates a township in eastern Yemen.

Marib sits at the foot of the mountains in the Yemenite chain, at an altitude of 1,150 m, at the point where the Wadi Dhana, an intermittent river that collects the waters from the mountains, feeds into the desert basin of Ramlat as-Sab'atayn. In addition to the ruins of a vast city (a stone wall encloses an area of 110 to 120 hectares) there is an irrigated perimeter that includes an enormous dam, canals, and floodgates, and there are two temples located outside the city and devoted to Almaqah, the Sabaean national god. Several buildings mentioned in inscriptions, such as the palace of the kings of Sheba (Salhīn) and a 6th century church, have not been located.

The most famous monument of Marib is the dam on the Dhana River, 7 km upstream from the city. It provided irrigation for 9,000 to 10,000 hectares. In its last state, which dates from the 5th to 6th century, it was made up of a thick earthen retaining wall 650 m long and 15 m high, with two stone locks anchored in the rocks on the north and south banks. Between the mid-4th century and 558, inscriptions mention four reconstructions of the dam. It finally collapsed between 558 and the era of Muhammad, who died in 632 (Qur'ān, sura 34:15–16). As a symbol of the collapse of Himyarite supremacy in Arabia, this disaster had enormous repercussions throughout the peninsula.

The ruins of Marib, visited for the first time by the Frenchman T. J. Arnaud in July 1843, have as yet hardly been excavated. In 1951–1952 an American archaeological mission had to interrupt prematurely its removal of propylaea from the large temple of Almaqah. Since 1980, a German mission has resumed archaeological exploration of the site, recovering a small sanctuary about 10 km west of the ancient city, then the second temple of Almaqah.

Marib played a key role in the history of South Arabia as long as the kingdom of Sheba remained independent—that is, until about 275. At that time, the city came under Himyarite domination and rapidly declined. The pagan temples were abandoned in the third quarter of the 4th century, when the Himyarite dynasty converted to Judaism.

BIBL.: Walter W. Müller, "Mārib," *The Encyclopaedia of Islam,* 2nd ed.   C.J.R.

Marketplace

The economy of late antiquity in the eastern Mediterranean was a monetary one. Coins in a variety of denominations were generally circulated, and trade goods like African red-slip ware were widely distributed throughout the region. However, our knowledge of the markets, the physical enviroment in which transactions took place, is very limited. Ancient cities had often had marketplaces (forums, agoras), but while some of these were maintained in late antiquity, as at Ephesus, where the Lower Agora seems to have been repaired ca. 400, there is no evidence for the construction of new marketplaces.

The typical commercial area of a late antique city was the linear market, a street flanked by rectangular, one-room stores. Many classical cities had regularly planned shops opening onto the sidewalks of the main colonnaded streets, which must have given them a commercial character. From the writings of Libanius and other sources it is clear that even in the 4th century, these streets were less orderly that the archaeological evidence at first suggests, with goods often piled up between the pillars.

In many cases late antique markets occupied the same places, and sometimes the same structures, as their classical predecessors. The best documented examples, the shops at Sardis, were laid out as a line of rooms opening onto a colonnaded street. Probably built in the 5th century, they remained in use until their sudden destruction at the beginning of the 7th century. Although the basic plan remained that of the classical period, the excavators noted a number of differences. The construction was poorer, and many of the materials, including the columns, had been reused. The measurements were less regular than in classical examples. In some cases the shops had been allowed to expand onto the sidewalk of the street. These differences suggest that the shops were built by individuals rather than by city authorities, which accords with what we know from other sources about the disappearance of local city governments in this period. The developments at Sardis can be paralleled with examples from sites like Gerasa, Scythopolis, and Apamea.

Much commercial activity probably did not take place in cities at all but at rural fairs. These may have coincided with the celebration of a saint's day, such as St. Demetrius's day at Thessalonica or the panegyris of St. Thecla at Seleucia in Isauria. The celebration of St. Sergius at Sergiopolis (Rusafa) certainly attracted visitors from all over the northern Syria desert and must have been the scene of much buying and selling. The shops whose ruins can still be seen at the bottom of the processional way to the shrine of St. Simeon at Qal'at Sim'an show that the pilgrimage center had its commercial side. Probably the best known and best documented annual fair in the late 6th century was the fair at Ukaz, near Makkah, described in detail in the early Muslim tradition. None of these temporary fairs would have left any archaeological evidence.

The early Islamic period saw the further development of linear markets, and in sites like Scythopolis and Palmyra we can see how the Arab *sūq* developed from the late antique market street. In both Jerusalem and Aleppo, the modern *sūq*s stand directly on the sites of late antique commercial centers.   H.K.

Marriage

Marriage was an institution fundamental to Graeco-Roman society. Only in a legal marriage could legitimate children be born who would take their father's name and inherit his property. The production of children, the primary purpose of marriage, was necessary for continuation of both the individual family and the state. Before the Christian era, it was generally assumed that all freeborn women and most freeborn men would marry at least once. Christianity offered both men and women an alternative, lifelong celibacy in the service of God, and some ascetic Christians questioned the value of marriage and procreation altogether. The ascetic movement brought an ideological shift of enormous significance in attitudes toward marriage, but its impact on late antique demography is unclear. Marriage and childbearing continued to be the lot of most women and men; however, remarriage, which the church discouraged, may have become less common when the cloister or church resources offered an alternative.

Sources for marriage in the Mediterranean world, as for other aspects of ancient social history, are disparate, scattered, tendentious, and often intractable. Literary sources, ranging from highly stylized *epithalamia* to juristic texts that detail rules of succession and restrictions on the choice of partner, present the views of urbanized, educated males. Special ceremonies and religious rites accompanied the transfer of the bride to the groom's home (the most common locus for the married couple in Graeco-Roman society, though residence with the family of the bride is attested), but these are known through visual representations, literary allusions, and later scholia rather than contemporary descriptions by participants. Private letters describing marriage preparations are rare; a few are known from Egyptian papyri and elite men like Libanius and Sidonius, but the emotions of those most closely involved, particularly women, remains opaque. Funerary epitaphs represent a broader section of society than do the literary and legal sources, and can provide evidence on age at marriage, family relationships, and the marital ideals of those below the elite strata. However, virtually all sources, from the emperor's edict to the freedman's tombstone, are heavily laden with ideology and the desire to impress and exhort rather than to provide "facts" for historians two millennia later.

Unlike women, young men were permitted premarital sexual experiences, but they, too, were expected eventually to marry and produce children. Marriage age varied according to class, region, and sex. Twelve was the minimum age for marriage for girls in Roman law (*Digest* 23.2.4); boys had to have reached puberty (Justinian, *Inst.* 1.10), and most were well beyond it. Most women married in their teens (early teens for upper-class Roman women, a few years later for those outside the elite); most men by the age of thirty (with, again, a somewhat lower age for men of the Roman senatorial class). Thus a husband was on average about ten years older than his wife. Exceptions are known: the senatorial couple Melania the Younger and Pinianus were married when she was fourteen and he was about three years older (*Vita Melaniae* 1). This may in part account for her evident dominance in the marital relationship, contrary to the dictates of ancient society, which held that the husband should be the superior partner. Funerary inscriptions from Christian Rome indicate a somewhat later age at marriage for women than does the pre-Christian epigraphic evidence, but this need not reflect the impact of Christianity; Brent Shaw has suggested that the Christian material may be more representative of lower-class practices in both the earlier and late empire (*Journal of Roman Studies* [1987]: 30–46).

First marriages were generally arranged by the parents of the prospective partners, primarily the *paterfamilias* (the father or the paternal grandfather, if still alive); young men usually had some say in choice of partner, though not necessarily the final word. Augustine's account of his own marital arrangements demonstrates the influence a strong-minded mother could wield with a son of quite mature age (*Confessions* 6.13; cf. 6.15). Less weight was given to the preferences of a young woman, who was expected to have little experience of mixed society and none at all of sex (though repugnance for her future mate was inadvisable, as it would hamper successful reproduction). For a marriage to be valid, Roman law required the consent of all parties—bride, groom, and the *paterfamilias* of each (*Dig.* 23.2.2)—but consent was interpreted broadly and paternal pressures no doubt often outweighed legal rules. Late Roman laws stress the necessity of paternal consent for a woman's marriage, even in the case of widowed daughters no longer under paternal power, and express little confidence in the preferences of the young women themselves. In the absence of a *paterfamilias,* mothers or other relatives could make the decision, and the laws suggest that family conflicts over the choice of suitor were likely to arise when property or powerful connections were at stake (*C.Th.* 3.5.12, 3.7.1; *C.Just.* 5.4.20). It was essential that there be a proper betrothal agreement between families and that the young people themselves not take matters into their own hands; criminal penalties were enacted for abduction marriages (which were often disguised elopements), for they not only subverted paternal authority but also could lead to interfamily violence (*C.Th.* 9.24; *C.Just.* 9.13).

In law, a marriage's existence was demonstrated by intent to be married *(affectio maritalis)* on the part of both parties, rather than cohabitation or dowry (*Dig.* 50.17.30; *C.Just.* 5.17.11, dated 533); if intent was present and there were no legal impediments, the union was a marriage in the eyes of law and society. Cohabitation without evidence of marital intent suggested *concubinatus* rather than *coniugium.* Until the 5th century, Roman law required neither document nor dowry for a valid marriage, and late imperial attempts to require proof of marriage appear to have been short-lived and aimed at the propertied elite (*C.Th.* 4.6.7; Majorian, *Nov.* 6.9; Justinian, *Nov.* 74.4). However, even in the earlier empire, when there was property at stake, families would want a record of the dowry transfer and other financial arrangements. Many marriage documents on papyri have been found in Egypt and a few elsewhere in the Near East, and their use in Italy and North Africa is also well attested. Late Roman legislation also devotes considerable attention to the exchange of gifts between the betrothed before marriage, particularly the groom's bestowing of a prenuptial gift on his bride as a concomitant to her dowry, indicating the increased importance of such gifts in late antiquity (*C.Th.* 3.5; *C.Just.* 5.3; Theodosius II, *Nov.* 14; Valentinian III, *Nov.* 35.8; Majorian, *Nov.* 6.9).

Impediments to valid marriage might arise from close kinship ties between the partners or disparity in their legal and social status. Slaves did not have the legal ability to marry; their de facto unions were termed *contubernia,* and their children were illegitimate. If both partners became free, however, the union became a marriage, and children born after that point were legitimate. Roman law had always prohibited certain types of close-kin marriage (brother and sister; paternal uncle and niece), but had not interfered with the arrangements of noncitizens, and papyrological evidence from Egypt suggests that as many as 20 percent of all marriages were between close relations. After the *Constitutio Antoniniana* of 212 granted Roman citizenship to virtually all free subjects, such marriages became illegal, but the practice continued in some parts of the east despite repeated legal sanctions (*C.Th.* 3.12.1; *C.Just.* 5.4.17, 5.5.6, 5.8.2, 5.5.9).

The ideal of the harmonious, lifelong marriage appears frequently in imperial literature and especially in funerary epitaphs, both pre-Christian and Christian. The most famous example is the long commemoration of the great pagan aristocrat Praetextatus by his wife Paulina, in which she credits him with guiding her through various religious initiation rites and he praises her *pudor, castitas,* and *fides* (*CIL* 6.1779 = *ILS* 1259). The same expressions and ideals of marital behavior can be found in contemporary Christian dedications (*ILCV* 81, 333, 404, 3343, 4311, 4346). Despite this ideal (or perhaps because of it), divorce in the pre-Constantinian empire was apparently not uncommon. In the later empire, emperors and ecclesiastical leaders alike expressed strong disapproval of unilateral divorce and remarriage after divorce, and enacted sanctions against divorcés, especially women, though the sanctions' actual effect on contemporary society is unclear.

Christians by and large inherited the marital practices and ideology of their predecessors, whether Jewish or Gentile. In two important respects, however, exponents of the Christian view of marriage broke with both Jewish and Graeco-Roman traditions: they condemned divorce and remarriage after divorce (and regarded remarriage after widowhood with suspicion), and they esteemed the refusal to marry and lifelong virginity more highly than marriage. Some Christian groups went so far as to condemn marriage altogether; they were considered extremist but were simply taking the exaltation of celibacy over marriage to its full length. Nevertheless, mainstream Christian spokesmen from Paul to Augustine stressed that marriage itself was not evil and was indeed advisable for those Christians who were unable to maintain complete sexual abstinence. Not until Augustine's *De bono coniugali,* however, was Christian marriage given a full theoretical treatment, and Augustine, like earlier Christian apologists for marriage, was writing to counteract extreme antimarriage views expressed by other Christians (in this case, Jerome's *contra Jovinianum*).

Legal sources devote much attention to the beginning and ending of marriage (betrothal and divorce) but shed no light on the day-to-day realities of the married state itself. The bearing and rearing of children was then, as always in the premodern period, the main duty of the married woman, and household management was also her responsibility. Women in the upper classes could delegate the physical labor of childcare and housekeeping to slaves. Men were expected to provide for their wives and children; the wife's dowry was supposed to contribute toward household expenses and become part of her children's settlement after her death. Material conditions of married life varied with the wealth and social level of the couple; as always in antiquity, our evidence centers on the urban elite.

Perhaps our most intimate account of married life is Augustine's portrait of his mother Monica, married for many years to an unbeliever whom she eventually converted (*Confessions* 9.9). Monica advised her married women friends that *tabulae matrimoniales* were the legal instruments by which women became slaves *(ancillae)* to their husbands. Her intelligence and tactfulness enabled her to endear herself to an initially hostile mother-in-law and avoid physical abuse from her volatile spouse, to the amazement of her less fortunate friends. (Evidence for wife beating emerges from other Christian sources and was evidently a fact of marital life.) As the wife of one man, she exemplified the traditional Roman ideal of the *univira;* she did her duty by her parents, governed her household responsibly and religiously, and her care and anxiety for her children

(primarily for Augustine himself) did not cease as they grew older. Her son's literary epitaph for her recalls contemporary inscriptions, such as this one dated 376 for a Christian wife from Volsinii (Bolsena): "To Mettia Navigia, a good wife, a very sweet daughter, a most obedient daughter-in-law, whose fidelity, modesty and dutifulness could never be conquered" (*ILCV* 365 = *CIL* 11.2834).

BIBL.: Antti Arjava, *Women and Law in Late Antiquity* (Oxford, 1996). Judith Evans Grubbs, *Law and Family in Late Antiquity: The Emperor Constantine's Marriage Legislation* (Oxford, 1995). Aḥmad Ibn Ḥanbal, *Chapters on Marriage and Divorce: Responses of Ibn Ḥanbal and Ibn Rāḥwayh,* trans. Susan Spectorsky (Austin, 1993). P. L. Reynolds, *Marriage in the Western Church: The Christianization of Marriage* (Leiden, 1994). Susan Treggiari, *Roman Marriage: Iusti Coniuges from the Time of Cicero to the Time of Ulpian* (Oxford, 1991).　　　　J.E.G.

Marseilles

Despite its importance as a Greek colony, Marseilles was surprisingly unimportant during the high empire, when the neighboring port of Fos was at its peak. By contrast, under the later empire and in the 6th and early 7th centuries the city flourished and Fos declined in importance. The two ports thus seem to have been rivals competing for control of shipping at the mouth of the Rhône. The prosperity of Marseilles from the 4th to the 7th century is clear both from the evidence of growth in the extramural suburbs, which has been revealed by rescue excavations, and from the importance of the city's mint. The fact that the city produced quasi-imperial coinage, unlike the design of that of most other Merovingian coinage in the late 6th century, suggests that Marseilles played an important role in Mediterranean trade. This point can be supported by written evidence, which emphasizes the interest of the Merovingians in controlling the revenues of the port, and by the finds of 6th century African pottery. The decline of Marseilles, which is apparent in the archaeology from the later 7th century onward, may reflect Arab dominance in the southern Mediterranean.

Apart from its economic importance, Marseilles was also a notable religious center. Its bishops were usually subordinate to the metropolitan of the province of Viennensis (based in either Vienne or Arles), but in the late 4th century Proculus established himself as metropolitan of Narbonnensis II. In addition to a distinguished line of bishops, 5th century Marseilles could also boast the presence of the priest Salvian, and perhaps that of the monastic author John Cassian. Christianity is well represented by archaeological finds from the Church of St. Victor.

BIBL.: S. T. Loseby, "Marseille: A Late Antique Success Story?" *Journal of Roman Studies* 82 (1992): 165–185.

Topographie chrétienne des cités de la Gaule des origines au milieu du VIII siècle, ed. N. Gauthier and J.-Ch. Picard, vol. 3: *Provinces ecclésiastiques de Vienne et d'Arles* (Paris, 1986).

I.W.

Martianus Capella

Martianus Minneius Felix Capella, perhaps a lawyer, lived under the Vandals in later 5th century Carthage and wrote both a prosimetrical allegorical encyclopedia (usually known as *On the Marriage of Mercury and Philology*, but called the *Philologia* by its author) and a short Latin metrical treatise. The *Philologia* is an original Neoplatonic myth describing the ascent to heaven of Philology, her apotheosis, and her wedding to Mercury, at which each of the seven bridesmaids (the personified liberal arts) presents her discipline to the assembled gods. While the encyclopedic material is largely pedestrian and derivative, the myth shows fantasy and imagination. A nostalgic pagan, Martianus used his resounding and hermetic periodic style to good effect to promulgate Neoplatonic doctrines on the ascent of the soul and Chaldaean theurgy, and to voice his regret for the silence of the oracles. He was a learned squirrel, enamored of archaic words, abstruse Etruscan lore, cosmology, the iconography of the gods, all arcane fragments that he shored against his ruin. But he also exhibits a heavy-handed humorous bent derived from the parodic tradition of Menippean satire that poked fun at councils of the gods and the pretentious futilities of philosophers. While the *Philologia* had an immediate influence on Boethius's *Consolation of Philosophy* and had reached Merovingian Gaul by the time of Gregory of Tours, it was most popular during the Carolingian period and the 12th century Platonic revival, both as a textbook and as a literary source. There are 241 manuscripts of the *Philologia* extant.

BIBL.: L. Lenaz, *Martiani Capellae De Nuptiis Philologiae et Mercurii Liber Secundus* (Padua, 1975). D. R. Shanzer, *A Philosophical and Literary Commentary on Martianus Capella's De Nuptiis Philologiae et Mercurii Liber 1* (Berkeley, 1986). W. H. Stahl and R. W. Johnson, with E. L. Burge, *Martianus Capella and the Seven Liberal Arts*, 2 vols. (New York, 1971 and 1977).

D.S.

Martin of Tours

A Pannonian who served in the Roman army in Gaul for almost twenty-five years, Martin of Tours then became an itinerant monk before returning to Gaul with Hilary, bishop of Poitiers, and founding a monastery at Ligugé in the Poitou. In 371 the citizens of Tours proclaimed him their bishop. Martin's behavior as bishop was confrontational and a bit outrageous. As he traveled throughout central Gaul he apparently demolished pagan shrines, and during visits to Trier he challenged the emperors Valentinian I and Magnus Maximus. Although his promotion of ascetic values annoyed other bishops, he founded a monastery at Marmoutier, across the Loire River from Tours. In 397 he died in his monastery in Candes and was buried in Tours.

Already during his lifetime people were transforming Martin into a saint by treasuring threads from his clothes as protective relics and collecting stories about his miracles. The writings of Sulpicius Severus, in particular his *Life* of Martin, are the primary historical sources for Martin's life and career; they were also early attempts to reconfigure him as a model bishop comparable to emperors and local rhetoricians. Even as the imperial court was abandoning northern Gaul in the late 4th century, Sulpicius compared Martin's initial reception in Tours to the ceremony of an imperial arrival and his funeral to an imperial triumph; and even though Martin was uneducated and left no writings of his own, Sulpicius nevertheless compared him to a teacher who enacted biblical teachings in his miracles of healing. He also corrected some of Martin's extemporaneous remarks about the possibility of forgiveness for the devil, once this theological position was proscribed; later copyists of Sulpicius's treaties sanitized Martin's millenarian outlook even further by simply omitting his apocalyptic prophecies.

Despite the popularity of the *Life* throughout the Mediterranean world, in Gaul Martin's reputation initially suffered. Although Marmoutier became a memorial shrine at which pilgrims venerated Martin's cell, his stool, and his bed, other monastic communities, especially those associated with Lérins that spread into eastern Gaul, were critical of Martin's use of miracles and his unregulated monasticism. In Tours itself Bishop Brictio even accused his predecessor of senility. But after facing accusations of adultery himself, Brictio constructed a small church over Martin's tomb. The cult of St. Martin then became a unifying force in Tours, and subsequent bishops enhanced their prestige by acting as its guardians. In the later 5th century Bishop Perpetuus expanded the saint's cult by constructing a larger church over the tomb, commissioning a series of murals for the church's walls that depicted scenes from Martin's life, promoting the saint's annual festivals on 4 July (commemorating Martin's consecration as bishop) and 11 November (commemorating his death), and collecting an anthology of the saint's posthumous miracles. On his own initiative the poet Paulinus of Périgueux had already versified Sulpicius's *Life* of Martin; Perpetuus now invited him to versify Sulpicius's other writings about Martin's episcopacy, as well as his own anthology. As he rewrote Sulpicius's treatises Paulinus also updated the myth of St. Martin, in particular by toning down the earlier confrontations between Martin and other bishops in order to acknowledge the increasing prominence of local bishops in Gallia.

The Church of St. Martin, containing his tomb, was

about a mile west of the walls of Tours, and it gradually became the center of a small settlement that included other churches, monasteries, oratories, courtyards, and shrines. Even though during the later 5th century the expansion of various saints' cults was common throughout Gaul, the cult of St. Martin became the most prominent. In 508 the Frankish king Clovis visited the Church of St. Martin and distributed gifts. Yet subsequent Frankish kings were intimidated by the saint's power and most kept their distance; rather than visiting Tours, one king tried to consult St. Martin by sending a letter to his tomb. Instead, various aristocratic families and bishops came to dominate many saints' cults in Gaul, including the cult of St. Martin. In the late 6th century the poet Fortunatus again versified Sulpicius's *Life* and other writings about Martin. By stressing that Martin, the nondescript veteran who had become a bishop, was now a "senator in the heavenly abode" seated next to the King of Heaven, Fortunatus again revamped the myth of St. Martin so that it now appeared to legitimate the continuing domination of episcopal sees by old aristocratic families.

One such pedigreed aristocrat was Gregory, who served as bishop of Tours until 594. Gregory followed Perpetuus's lead in promoting St. Martin's cult. He rebuilt the ruined cathedral, restored the smudged murals in the Church of St. Martin, and diligently recorded the saint's miracles during the two decades of his episcopacy. Gregory's huge collection of miracle stories provides extraordinary evidence for the working of a saint's cult. The saint's church was the central focus, since miracles of healing happened repeatedly at a specific place, near the saint's tomb, and at a specific time, during the celebration of the saint's festival days: "while the miracle stories were being read from Martin's *Life*, a flash similar to a lightning bolt flared over the blind men." Tours soon became an attractive destination for pilgrims, especially from central and northern Gaul, many of whom came looking for relief from their ailments but all of whom wanted to demonstrate their devotion to St. Martin. Upon departing, pilgrims took away stories about their experiences (that they might later confide to Gregory) as well as relics, the most common of which was dust from the saint's tomb. Some constructed shrines or dedicated churches with their relics; these shrines to St. Martin outside the Touraine were most common, again, in central and northern Gaul.

Because of their extensive writings, Sulpicius Severus, Paulinus of Périgueux, Fortunatus, and Gregory of Tours were eventually considered to be the "four evangelists" of St. Martin. Thereafter information about the saint's cult becomes more scarce. Frankish kings increasingly honored St. Martin, and by the middle of the 7th century they finally acquired their own special relic, the saint's cloak, that they apparently kept at their court in Paris. According to Sulpicius's *Life*, Martin had once cut his military cloak in half to share it with a beggar; throughout the Middle Ages this story defined one of the most durable images of selfless generosity.

BIBL.: J. Fontaine, *Sulpice Sévère, Vie de saint Martin. Sources chrétiennes* 133–135 (Paris, 1967–1969). R. Van Dam, "Images of Saint Martin in Late Roman and Early Merovingian Gaul," *Viator* 19 (1988): 1–27. R. Van Dam, *Saints and Their Miracles in Late Antique Gaul* (Princeton, 1993). R.V.

Martyrs

Etymologically, "martyrs" are "witnesses" to the Christian faith. But the term particularly designates Christians who heroically confess their faith before persecutors, not only through their words but also through their death. They are thus to be distinguished from "confessors," who remained alive. During the time when the Roman empire was persecuting Christians (1st to early 4th century), martyrs, through the key role they played in strengthening the church and spreading the faith, acquired an exceptional status. At the same time, a spirituality of martyrdom developed, which marked Christianity in a lasting way. With the reign of Constantine and peace with the church, martyrs became more rare, but it was then that the cult of martyrs appeared openly.

Martyrs appeared very early. Stephen was the first, then James, son of Zebedee; James, "the Lord's brother," and certain apostles followed. At the time, Christians were the object of hostility from Jews and from pagans. They were also persecuted by Roman authorities, who recognized that the new religion, with its universalist pretensions, its rejection of traditional gods and of the cult of the emperor, represented a danger for the established order. After sporadic persecutions under Nero and Domitian, the legal framework for prosecuting Christians came into being. This is clear from correspondence between Pliny the Younger and Emperor Trajan in about 111. Christians denounced as such were to be punished if they refused to make sacrifices to the gods; but they were not to be sought out. The persecutions of the 2nd and early 3rd centuries made their victims famous (Polycarp of Smyrna in 156; the Lyons martyrs in 177; the Scillitan martyrs in Carthage in 180, Felicitas and Perpetua in 202–203) but remained sporadic. They became systematic with Decius in 249–250 and Valentinian in 257–258: every citizen of the empire had to prove his loyalty by making sacrifices. Among the martyrs of the time, let us note Pionios in Smyrna, known through a contemporary text.

The great persecution (303–324) inaugurated by Diocletian and Galerius had four decrees of 303–304 as its legal framework: the Christian cult was forbidden; the property of the churches was confiscated; the clergy or influential church members were prosecuted; and the obligation to make sacrifices was reaffirmed.

The number of martyrs was high, but their distribution uneven: the west was spared while persecutions wreaked havoc in the east, in particular in Egypt and Palestine, under Diocletian, Galerius, Maximinus Daia, and Licinius. Eusebius of Caesarea, a contemporary, gives an account of this persecution in his *Historia ecclesiastica* and in a treatise on the martyrs of Palestine. New documents have recently been published: the martyrdom of St. Athenogenes of Pedachthoe, and the Coptic acts of the priest Stephanos. The victory of Constantine (324) marked the end of persecutions in the empire. All the same, new martyrs appeared during the pagan reaction under Julian and, as a new phenomenon, during Christian persecutions of other Christians (victims of Arianism or Monophysite martyrs). The persecutions in neighboring countries (Persia and, in rare instances, South Arabia) also produced martyrs, who were honored in the imperial church.

Contemporary texts explain what martyrdom meant at the time of the persecutions: "baptism by blood" redeemed every previous sin and brought about a new spiritual life. The martyr who confessed his faith ("I am a Christian") before his judge and rejected all compromise with traditional religions reproduced the Passion of Christ through his suffering and death. Moreover, Christ lived again in him and suffered with him, conferring on his deeds and words a value similar to Christ's own. The martyr who submitted to torture and went to his death giving thanks to God escaped the human condition. His body was transfigured. Visions and wonders were produced. The Christian community stood firm with the martyr, visiting him in prison, looking on during his torment. When it could, it collected his body after death and celebrated his memory. The church was thus vitalized by the blood of martyrs, which rekindled faith and reinforced cohesiveness. For their part, pagans reacted with hostility or indifference, but the spectacular heroism of the saints also brought about conversions. After death, the martyr's soul, escaping the common fate, did not go to hell but to paradise.

Very early on, martyrs received special honors. Local churches commemorated them, compiling Acts relating their trial, or Passions or Martyrdoms, which recounted their ordeals at greater length. The Christians of Smyrna, beginning in the 2nd century, collected the bones of Polycarp and arranged to celebrate the day of his death. Liturgical celebrations, accompanied by funeral meals (*agapai, refrigeria*), were held on martyrs' tombs on the day of their birth to God *(dies natalis)*. With the reign of Constantine, this cult became public and spectacular; the emperor and the church organized it. The first extant martyrologies (lists of martyrs, with the date of their death) were composed in the 4th century. The graves of certain martyrs were adorned with constructions, the *martyria*, some of them quite splendid. Thus, the authorities did nothing more than join

a spontaneous, powerful, and widespread current. As relics were created and moved about, religious sites multiplied.

The cult of martyrs had its origin in Jewish practices, but it was also somewhat related to paganism (funeral rites, cult of heroes and gods), as was seen in certain customs (meals, incubation, consulting oracles). This contamination did not escape contemporaries: Vigliantius was troubled by it, but Jerome replied by defending the cult of saints. The Church Fathers did not hesitate to encourage the cult of relics: "Anyone who touches the bones of martyrs is partaking in the holiness and grace that reside in them" (St. Basil). Conversely, certain pagans were outraged that Christians, through their contact with the dead, were disrupting the purity and order of the city-state and of the cosmos. This underscores how the concepts of the body and death had changed with Christianity.

As the cult of the martyr developed, the figure of the martyr changed. The historical Passions moved away from "epic" Passions (Delehaye) that, listing the many torments from which the martyr emerged triumphant thanks to his constancy, made him into a superhuman being. The ordeals he went through during his lifetime earned him the right to be a powerful protector and thaumaturge after his death. The martyr's soul was with God, but his body, his relics, and, later, his images were in the grave, hence with men. "A very special dead man," the martyr was the intercessor par excellence to be invoked.

Attempts were made to subject popular practices connected with the cult of the martyrs to clerical control. The efforts of Augustine of Hippo in this respect are revealing. He wished to deprive the festivals of their euphoric character, so as to avoid disorder and immorality but also, more significantly, to emphasize the fact that the heroism of the martyrs was not exceptional and so inimitable: God's grace was still at work when average Christians faced the "daily martyrdom" of illness, and especially when they rejected the use of healing remedies of pagan origin (e.g., Augustine, *Sermo Dolbeau* 18.6–7). He also expressed a distinct preference for the reading of the original *gesta*: they moved him "more intimately" than did modern rewritings of the *Passiones* (Augustine, *Ep. 29**).

BIBL.: A. A. R. Bastiaensen et al., *Atti e passioni dei martiri* (Milan, 1987). G. W. Bowersock, *Martyrdom and Rome* (Cambridge, Eng., 1995). C. Butterwerck, *"Martyriumsucht" in der alten Kirche? Studien zur Darstellung und Deutung frühchristlicher Martyrien* (Tübingen, 1995). H. Delehaye, *Les origines du culte des martyrs*, 2nd ed. (Brussels, 1966). P.-A. Février, "Martyre et sainteté," in *Les fonctions des saints* (Rome, 1991), 51–80. J. M. W. Salomonson, *Voluptatem spectandi non perdat sed mutet* (Amsterdam, 1979). V. Saxer, *Morts, martyrs et reliques en Afrique chrétienne* (Paris, 1980).

B.F.

Mauri

The origin of the Mauri (Greek *Maurousii*) was northern Morocco, opposite Gibraltar, according to the Elder Pliny and Ptolemy. But the name lost its geographic identity when the kingdoms of western Mauretania spread their influence to the borders of Roman Africa. By the later empire, "Maurus" denoted an inhabitant of Mauretania, but by the 3rd century, in many military inscriptions dedicated to "*Dii Mauri*," the term also signified any African. The military context was important, since in Africa recruiting continued unimpeded during the crisis of the 3rd century, when so many other provinces had seceded. Integration of Mauri cavalry and infantry auxiliary units into the army, many of which served as corps d'elite, played a crucial role in holding the empire together, as their numbers and distribution in the *Notitia Dignitatum* testify. Doubtless this accounts for the influential role played by Mauri leaders in the 4th and 5th centuries, who served on the *limites* of Caesariensis and Tripolitania as prefects, *tribuni*, and *principes* of either *comitatenses* or *gentiles* units. Many were prominent in building *castella* and *centenaria*, often indistinguishable from private fortified farms and estates, like those at Petra in the Soummam Valley (*ILS* 9351) and Ghirza in the Wadi Soffegin. Their power as local warlords, when Roman rule disintegrated, kept alive the Roman and Christian name, and accounts for the "kingdoms" of the 5th and 6th centuries in the Mauretanian highlands, the Aures Mountains, and the Tripolitanian valleys, such as that of Masuna, "king of Mauri and Romans," who built a *castrum* at Altava in 508 (*CIL* 8.9835).

It is ironic, therefore, that the name Mauri was regularly associated with barbaric savagery in literary sources. Early writers had always regarded Mauri as outside the empire, a focus for stories of monsters and savages (Strabo 17.3.8), and this ideological strain appeared again in Gallic panegyricists who talked of fierce Mauri tribes in the same breath as other barbarian invaders (*Pan.Lat.* II(XII) 5.2). Probably the rebellions of Firmus and Gildo, from the house of Nubel in Caesariensis in the latter part of the 4th century, provoked the most virulent racist attacks, despite—or because of—the fact that Gildo had risen to the rank of *comes et magister militum per Africam*, which made him all the more dangerous. In the late 4th century and the 5th and 6th centuries, the authors of the Augustan histories, Claudian, Salvian, Procopius, and Corripus, had few good words for Mauri, who were associated with the past treachery of Syphax, Jugurtha, and Tacfarinas. Augustine and Claudian contrasted warlike Mauri with peaceful Afri. The stereotype of Mauri as outsiders, montagnards, and shifting nomads was deeply set in Roman historiography.

These sentiments were encouraged by events of the 5th and 6th centuries. Mauri supported the Vandals' attack on Rome in 455, took part in several rebellions in Byzacium and Numidia, and helped make up the federation of the Tripolitanian Laguatan in a fierce war against the Byzantines in 545–546. But despite the clichés about perfidious savages in Corripus, final word should go to Masties, "*dux* and *imperator*" in the Aures during the 5th or 6th century, who "never forswore or broke his trust with either Romans or Mauri" (*AE* (1945), 97).

BIBL.: G. Camps, "De Masuna à Koceila: Les destinées de la Maurétanie aux VIe et VIIe siècles," *Bulletin du Comité du Travaux Historiques* 19B (1985): 307–325. C. Courtois, *Les Vandales et L'Afrique* (Paris, 1955; repr. Aalen, 1964). P.-A. Fevrier, "Différences et conflits: Maures et barbares," in *Approches du Maghreb romain*, 2 vols. (Aix-en-Provence, 1990). H. Sivan, "Why Not Marry a Barbarian? Marital Frontiers in Late Antiquity," in *Shifting Frontiers in Late Antiquity*, ed. H. Sivan and R. W. Mathisen (London, 1996), 136–145.   C.W.

Mavia

Mavia was queen of a 4th century confederation of seminomadic Arabs in southern Syria. The royal title is found elsewhere in this confederation and is not to be confused with the title of phylarch given to Arab rulers in later centuries. Mavia's ancestors belonged to the Tanūkh, who migrated northward from the Arabian Peninsula in the previous century in consequence of the growing Sassanian power in Iran. She was the most powerful woman in the late antique Arab world after Zenobia. What we know of her derives largely from a lost account by Gelasius of Caesarea, which served as a source both for Rufinus's continuation of his translation of Eusebius and for several 5th century Greek ecclesiastical histories. Later tradition turned Mavia into a Christian of Roman stock, but she was evidently Arab and initially pagan. Her Arab name was Māwiyya, not (as sometimes asserted) Mu'awiyya, which is a man's name.

At the time of Valens's withdrawal from Antioch in the spring of 378 Mavia appears to have undertaken a massive revolt against the central government, much as Zenobia had done a century earlier. Her forces swept down into Arabia and Palestine, advancing to the confines of Egypt. But in the process she was converted to orthodox Christianity by an ascetic hermit called Moses. Her revolt came swiftly to an end when, at her demand, Moses was ordained bishop of her people with the express authorization of Valens. As an Arian, Valens acted undoubtedly under duress. Mavia took as her husband a certain Victor, *magister militum*, later *magister equitum*, and she quickly returned to the imperial fold. Later in 378 Mavia appears in the Gelasian tradition with her tribesmen as *foederati* (*hupospondoi*) of the Byzantine empire. They came to the empire's aid in protecting Constantinople after the Battle of Adrianople. The sight of the queen's shrieking and nearly naked Arabs on the city's ramparts left a terrifying impression in the tradition represented by Ammianus. The Arab-Byzantine alliance appears to have been broken subsequently, to judge from a reference in a panegyric of 389 to a *pollutum foedus*.

BIBL.: G. W. Bowersock, "Mavia, Queen of the Saracens," *Studien zur antiken Sozialgeschichte: Festschrift Friedrich Vittinghoff* (Cologne, 1980), 477–495, repr. in G. W. Bowersock, *Studies on the Eastern Roman Empire* (Goldbach, 1994), 127–140. P. Mayerson, "Mauia, Queen of the Saracens—A Cautionary Note," *Israel Exploration Journal* 30 (1980): 123–131. I. Shahīd, *Byzantium and the Arabs in the Fourth Century* (Washington, D.C., 1984), 138–202.

G.W.B.

Mazdakism

Mazdakism may have arisen from a Manichaean subject under Bundos, an Iranian who preached in Rome during the 3rd century C.E., or a Zoroastrian reform movement led by the magus Zardusht i Khurragan two centuries later. But the faith is named after its major Iranian missionary, Mazdak i Bamdad, who lived during the late 5th century. Followers called it the *drist* (correct) or *khurram* (happy) religion.

Since no scriptures are extent, the religion's tenets must be reconstructed from Iranian, Syrian, Arab, and Greek records. Presenting a dualistic worldview, Mazdakism proposed two primal spirits embodying goodness or light and evil or darkness, respectively. The mixture of these two forces produced the material world, with its three light elements: earth, water, and fire. The god of light's four powers—discernment, understanding, memory, and joy—became embodied in humans. That deity's seven regents and twelve helper spirits regulated the world. The role of each human was to liberate the light trapped inside him or her. That could be accomplished through asceticism and strict moral conduct, it was believed. To prevent light from becoming further entangled in matter, the consumption of meat was forbidden. To detach themselves from corporeal desires, followers were encouraged to share property and women.

Mazdak preached to King Kavad I at the Sassanian royal court. Social reforms were promulgated on the basis of Mazdakism. It is unclear whether Kavad believed Mazdak's message or was using the faith to break the aristocracy's power through land redistribution. Magi considered Mazdakism a heresy and feared the proposed restructuring of Iran's class-based society. Nobles and clergy united to depose Kavad, who fled to central Asia from whence he returned with Hephthalite troops to quash the upper-class rebellion. Seeking to reestablish the social hierarchy and win over aristocrats and clerics, Kavad's son Khosro I had Mazdak executed. Despite ensuing persecution, Mazdakites

transmitted their faith into Islamic times, when it influenced the Khurramiyya and other movements. Orthodox Muslims, like Zoroastrians before them, regarded Mazdakites as heretics (Arabic *zindīg* from Pahlavi *zandig*, "one who distorts exegesis").

BIBL.: Patricia Crone, "Kavad's Heresy and Mazdak's Revolt," *Iran* (London), 29 (1991): 21–42. Heinz Gaube, "Mazdak: Historical Reality or Invention?" *Studia Iranica* 11 (1982): 111–122. Zeev Rubin, "Mass Movements in Late Antiquity—Appearances and Realities," in *Leaders and Masses in the Roman World*, ed. I. Malkin and Z. W. Rubinsohn (Leiden, 1995), esp. pp. 179–187. Ehsan Yarshater, "Mazdakism," in *The Cambridge History of Iran*, vol. 3, pt. 2, ed. Ehsan Yarshater (Cambridge, Eng., 1983), 991–1024.

J.K.C.

Mecca

The city of Mecca is in the Ḥijāz, a province of western Arabia located some 50 miles east of the Red Sea and more or less halfway between Yemen to the south and the province of Arabia to the north. It is in a narrow and relatively inhospitable valley surrounded by high hills that are cut up by narrow gulleys that occasionally create violent flash floods. There are a few wells in Mecca, and it gets almost no rain. As a result, no significant agriculture can develop in its immediate vicinity.

Mecca's claim to historical fame is that it was the birthplace of the Prophet Muhammad (ca. 570), the place where he grew up, where the new faith of Islam was first revealed to him, where he was rejected by most of the local population, and from which he escaped in 622, the year of his migration, or *hijra* (hegira). Its earlier sanctuary, the Ka'ba, became the holist shrine in Islam and the *qibla*, or direction, in which all Muslims are to pray. The city and its environs are the place of the hajj, the pilgrimage imposed on all able-bodied Muslims, to be made at least once in their lifetime.

Little is known about the actual history of Mecca. Known in classical antiquity as Macroba and locally as Bakka as well as Makka, it may not have been permanently or significantly settled until the 4th century, although it had been, probably for a long time, the site of some sort of local sanctuary, either a constructed one or simply a marked enclosure within a much wider sacred area, as exist in almost all primarily nomadic areas. Control over access to and use of this space was deemed important, and local Arab tribes, through struggles about which we know next to nothing, exercised that control, which was held for a long time by the Jurhum, then the Khuza'a, and finally the Quraysh in the late 5th century or thereabouts. There certainly was a settled community in the 6th century, as there is no reason to doubt a major effort by Ethiopian-inspired Yemeni invaders under the leadership of the probably historical King Abraha to occupy, if not destroy, Mecca in the second half of that century. The attempt failed, thanks to all sorts of miraculous events much expanded in later literature, and thereby strengthened the importance of Mecca and of the Ka'ba, by then a squarish low enclosure with a black stone in one of its corners, usually covered with textiles. Seasonal gatherings of tribes may have been accompanied by religious rituals, but it is more likely that they were primarily periods of peacemaking and other negotiations among frequently feuding clans. The Ka'ba grew as a collective treasure house for relics, valuable objects, and perhaps tribal insignia.

The inhabitants of Mecca rejected the message brought by the Prophet Muhammad and revealed to him in and around the city. They also persecuted his followers, some of whom emigrated before he did so in 622. It was in his new city, Yathrib, soon to become Medina, or Madīna al-nabī (City of the Prophet), that he established the Ka'ba of Mecca as the direction for prayer. After several failures, his forces reentered Mecca triumphantly in 629, but he himself returned to Medina for the last three years of his life. After Muhammad's death, Mecca, by then no longer accessible to non-Muslims, became a place where his followers and successors, recent converts, gathered and transmitted information about his life, and to which elderly Muslims from elsewhere retired. It played a political role, and a local tribal leader, 'Abd Allāh ibn al-Zubayr, occupied the city as part of a major revolt against the Umayyads. The Ka'ba, which had been damaged by fire, was rebuilt in allegedly ancient ways. In 693 Mecca was taken back by the Umayyads and the Ka'ba rebuilt as it had been at the time of the Prophet. Some of the area around the Ka'ba was cleared away to allow for increased numbers of pilgrims. Rituals required a more unified space, in as much as, in early times, caliphs or their very official representatives often led the yearly pilgrimage. Eventually, in the early 8th century, a colonnade was built around a relatively empty area, and the first steps were taken toward the practical and symbolic monumentalization of the Masjid al-Ḥarām, the Sacred Mosque, as it became known.

Alongside this chronological and reasonably secure scheme of a historical Mecca between the 4th and 8th centuries, a mythical Mecca exists on two levels. First there is a holy history of Mecca that is the vision of the place found in Muslim belief and piety. In it, the Ka'ba is the "sacred house" built by Abraham and his son Isma'il, who had been brought there by his mother, Hagar. It was the first sanctuary built on earth and the well nearby, the Zemzem well, had sprung miraculously to life so that Hagar could feed her infant child. At a later date, as the Ka'ba had to be rebuilt, it was the child Muhammad who came at the right moment to set the Black Stone in its right place without antagonizing local tribal leaders. As the pious and mystical meanings of Mecca grew, more and more such stories

became associated with it. In the 9th century, the chronicler al-Azraqi finds a mythical explanation for every space and every peculiarity of the city and for the practices carried out in it.

A second mythical level for Mecca lies in the scholarship that has surrounded it. The focus of study was to find out how this peculiar tribal-Arabian pagan city nurtured the beliefs and ethics of Islam. For much of the 20th century the prevailing western theory was that Mecca had become a major financial and commercial center involving much of the Levant and India in its far-flung operations and thereby acquiring a sophistication that was no longer satisfied with traditional ways. In the past decade this theory has been laid to rest on practically all counts. However, the problem of the sources for the emergence of Muslim beliefs in the Meccan context remains. In ways yet to be discovered or hypothesized, its solution requires an understanding of the interregional connections of Arabia. A few archaeological investigations, like the one at al-Faw in central Arabia, may contain parts of the answer.

BIBL.: A. R. Al-Ansary, *Qaryat al-Fau* (London, 1982). Al-Azraqi, *Akhbar Makkah*, vol. 1 of F. Wüstenfeld, *Die Chroniken der Stadt Mekka* (Leipzig, 1857–1861). P. Crone, *Meccan Trade and the Rise of Islam* (Princeton, 1987). P. Crone, "Sergeant and Meccan Trade," *Arabica* 29 (1992). M. J. Kister, *Studies in Jahiliyah and Early Islam* (London, 1980). W. M. Watt, *Muhammad at Mecca* (Oxford, 1953). Entries "Ka'ba," "Makka," "Kuraysh," in *Encyclopaedia of Islam*, 2nd ed.   O.G.

Medallions

The term *medallion* is used to describe a piece that is larger than ordinary coins, but it also refers to its intended role as a presentation piece. There is no direct ancient reference to the presentation of a medallion, but Toynbee marshalled convincing links between the Roman new year's custom of presenting *strenae* and the imperial consulship, which began on January 1. The special character of medallions is further indicated by the ambition of their motifs, their higher quality of execution, and the occasions they commemorate.

No republican medallions are known, and only a very few medallions of any kind are known before the 2nd century C.E. The gold medallions of Augustus might well be seen as successors to occasional massive pieces struck by Hellenistic kings (notably Alexander and Eucratides of Bactria), but the real flowering of the art began in the time of Hadrian and reached its zenith in the period of his Antonine successors. These early medallions are of copper or orichalcum (or occasionally both, with a collar of one metal enclosing the types struck on a flan of the other). Presentation occasions, in addition to consulships, included imperial marriages and births, military campaigns, the 900th anniversary of the foundation of Rome (celebrated by an ambitious series), and many others. The high value attached to

Medallion of Honorius. On one side is the bust of Honorius; on the reverse, the emperor standing in military garb, with a captive crouched below to his left.

dies created by the most skilled engravers is attested by their reuse, sometimes with slight modifications, year after year.

The tradition of base-metal medallions continued into the 4th century, albeit ever more tenuously. The most frequently struck type was the three Monetae, personifications of the metals in which coinage was nominally produced, even as the quality of the coinage was declining. From the time of Claudius II (268–270) "money medallions"—pieces struck in silver (or, more commonly, gold) were produced; they conformed to multiples of existing denominations and, like coins, were hoarded. The Arras hoard, among others, permits the inference that imperial *donativa* provided the occasion for many distributions of medallions. Many later medallions and crude imitations of them have been found outside the empire, suggesting that they were presented to foreign rulers or their ambassadors.

Our record of later imperial medallions is imperfect; most types are known in very few examples, and new discoveries often bring to light previously unknown types. The tradition seems to have died out gradually beginning with the house of Valentinian, though occasional later pieces are known.

This decline of medallic production coincides chronologically with the emergence of *contorniates,* which are similar in diameter, though not in thickness or weight, to medallions. Of them Toynbee remarked, "Inasmuch as they are coin-like pieces not issued to circulate as currency, the Roman contorniates may be associated with the study of Roman medallions. But whereas medallions were essentially works of art of a high order, executed by the best artists Rome could produce, with selected individuals, highly placed and highly cultured, as recipients in mind, the contorniates were obviously mass-produced by inferior, somewhat illiterate, designers for persons themselves devoid, for the most part, of high education and cultured tastes." In the 1940s Alföldi produced a synthetic study arguing that these objects were the pagan successors to a tradition suppressed by Christian emperors. His view has not found wide acceptance.

BIBL.: A. Alföldi and E. Alföldi, *Die Kontorniat-Medaillons* (Berlin and New York, 1974–1986). J. M. C. Toynbee, *Roman Medallions* (New York, 1944; repr. with additions by W. E. Metcalf, New York, 1986).

W.M.

Mediterranean Sea

The Mediterranean was at the heart of the political, economic, and cultural world until the mid-5th century. All the big cities were established either on or near its shores (Rome, Constantinople, Antioch, Alexandria, and Carthage), or along the rivers flowing into it (Milan, Arles, Lyons). The city of Rome was everywhere considered the model and point of reference. It held sway in institutions, which Germanic kingdoms first maintained and then gradually adapted; in fashion, regarding clothing, housing (the large noble villas), written documents (the preponderance of papyrus), and food (the consumption of oil in addition to butter); and in the noble ideal, which remained relatively stable from the Roman republic on.

As independent states asserted themselves over the course of the 6th century, the sea was slowly transformed into a frontier. Capital cities such as Paris, Toledo, and Pavia were located in the interior, and sovereigns minted coins bearing their own portraits. Beginning in the early 7th century, local nobilities merged into a larger nobility, e.g., the one that defined itself as "Frankish."

In the east, the end of the Mediterranean world's domination came about with the Arab invasion. The Byzantine empire was reorganized around the Aegean and the Black Sea. As for the Muslim world, it established its large cities away from dangerous zones—in Damascus, then in Baghdad, Cairo, Kairouan, and Cordova. The shattering of the Muslim world was a result, because relations were difficult among the various groups.

In about 800, the three large cultural groups of the Roman empire were cut off from one another, and the Mediterranean lost its role as convenient and omnipresent mode of social contact and commercial exchange. Local nobilities gave precedence to relations with their sovereigns, on whom they depended for the acquisition of high posts and the revenues associated with them, and contacts between elites became rare. The key factors in this process of change were social. Fourth-century senators from Rome and Constantinople had traveled from one end of the empire to the other and met with local elites; these elites had emulated them because they aspired to join their assembly.

In the 5th century, in contrast, western nobles had established closer ties with their own sovereigns, and very few knew the rest of the world. Gregory the Great (590–604) had maintained relations with the court of Constantinople, but had written to the Franks and Visigoths as if to foreigners, though he still had friends —such as Leander of Seville—in Spain. During the same period, the important men of Egypt, like the Apions, had lived in Constantinople. In 700, however, the senators of Constantinople knew little more than their own city and Asia Minor; Egyptians went to the court of Damascus; and the Franks had almost no contact with foreign countries but frequented the courts established in Neustria or Austrasia.

In becoming a frontier, the Mediterranean lost the preeminent role it had played in contacts among all the regions bordering it. Westerners were less likely to know Greek; Greeks did not speak the western languages; and few Germanic and Byzantine people made the effort to learn Arabic. As Germans gradually prepared to create a new culture, the Byzantines focused on their own ancient heritage. Thus two original systems of thought began to blossom in the 9th century: a Carolingian culture and a properly Byzantine culture. This phenomenon becomes clear when we consider the progressive distance between western and eastern churches, whose members rarely had any occasion to meet one another.

This social evolution also explains developments in commerce. Given the absence of war fleets, naval wars were of limited importance: first the Vandals, then Justinian (at the time of his reconquest), and finally the Arabs mobilized civilian boats for their expeditions. They did not curb trade, which brought in large sums of money through customs duties. Nonetheless commerce, though it had never been very developed (overland transportation was very expensive), felt the effects of the shattered Roman world. Only luxury products moved beyond the coastal zones (this is attested in the distribution of shards along the coasts), with weak penetration into the interior. Until the 7th century, large quantities of grain circulated, but it was only public grain from tax granaries, destined for the cities. The Persian conquest, followed by the Arab conquest, relieved the tax burden only on the Nile Valley and, to a lesser extent, on Africa. These conquests completed Rome's decline and led to that of Constantinople. High-quality wine and oil, marble, papyrus, spices, silk, and incense still circulated, and popes could always find a boat to send a letter to any Christian country they wished. In 716, the Corbie monastery, for example, was still receiving some of these products from the granaries of the Fos customs house, provided as payment of taxes in kind. But the volume of commerce decreased, because the nobles and the rest of the population now preferred such local products as butter for cooking, tallow for light, parchment for writing, and wood for construction. Almost the only products still giving rise to trade were spices and silk in one direction, and timber and iron in the other. This trade was handled primarily by Jews, who were united by their religion, until the Venetians, officially subjects of the Byzantine empire and located at the gateway to the west, took over. In playing on the price differences between different countries, these merchants established the foundations for commercial capitalism, which flourished beginning in the 11th century.

Between the 4th and the 8th century, then, the role of the Mediterranean changed profoundly. It remained the best means of communication between the countries that bordered it, but these countries no longer felt the need to use it so extensively. This was the result of political and social changes, which came about because the empire could no longer defend its land borders. The *mare nostrum* was transformed into a zone of contact between new civilizations, but it took several centuries for exchanges to develop among them.

BIBL.: Richard Hodges and D. Whitehouse, *Mohammed, Charlemagne and the Origins of Europe* (London, 1983). *Hommes et richesses dans l'empire byzantin*, vol. 1: *IVe–VIIe siècle* (Paris, 1989). *Società romana e impero tardoantico*, vol. 3: *Le merci: Gli insediamenti*, ed. Andrea Giardina (Rome and Bari, 1986).   J.D.

Mefaa

Umm er-Rasas in Jordan, 30 km southeast of Madaba, in the steppe, has been identified as Castron Mefaa, cited in Eusebius of Caesarea's *Onomasticon*. The name is mentioned in the Bible, and the most ancient discoveries from the site date from the Iron Age. Castron Mefaa is an example of a military site that developed into one of the large towns of the Madaba *chōra*.

Mefaa was made up of a fortress and large installations outside the walls. According to the *Notitia Dignitatum*, the fortress (late 3rd century to early 4th century) housed the *Equites Promoti Indigenae*. It was a quadrilateral (158 m by 139 m) enclosed by a wall reinforced by quadrangular towers and with a single gate on the east side. In the 5th and early 6th centuries, the civilian population moved into the enclosure. Two orthogonal streets crossed at the city's center, joining the three gates that existed at that time. Houses encroached on courtyards, and also on streets, which were transformed into winding pathways. Four churches were built in the enclosure; two identical ones, dating from the 6th century, have been excavated. Houses within the fortress were abandoned in the late 8th or early 9th century.

About ten churches have been identified outside the walls. Four of them form a complex, including a church turned toward the west, and a Church of St. Stephen with large mosaics. The sanctuary *(presby-*

terium) of St. Stephen was covered with a geometrical mosaic in 756; the nave was adorned with another mosaic depicting cities and monuments in Palestine, Arabia, and Egypt. The date of the "geographical" mosaic is a matter of debate. The most visible monument in Castron Mefaa was a tower 14 m high, flanked by a church called Church of the Lions. That tower, probably built for a recluse, is depicted in the mosaics of the Church of St. Stephen and of the Church of the Lions, in vignettes of Castron Mefaa.

BIBL.: J. Bujard et al., "Les églises géminées d'Umm er-Rasas," *Annual of the Department of Antiquities of Jordan* 36 (1992): 291–306. M. Piccirillo and E. Alliata, *Umm ar-Rasas Mayfa 'ah,* vol. 1: *Gli scavi del complesso di Santo Stefano* (Jerusalem, 1994).   P.-L.G.

Mesopotamia

Mesopotamia today suggests to us the cradle of civilization. The term "Land of Two Rivers" was coined by Strabo (1st century C.E.) for the northern, steppe section between the Tigris and Euphrates, lying partly in modern Syria, partly in Iraq, and it is synonymous with the Arab al-Jazira, "the Island." The area "where civilization began" is actually the southern part of modern Iraq, the land of 3rd millennium B.C.E. Sumer and Akkad, later Babylonia, and Arab al-'Iraq. The 19th century Ottoman Turks broke the area into five provinces (cf. *vilayet* of Baghdad); it was the British military campaign in 1914 that reintroduced the name Mesopotamia, applied especially to the southern part of the region. Mesopotamia is defined here as stretching from the Anti-Taurus foothills in Turkey to the Persian/Arab Gulf, and between the Syrian desert and the Zagros Mountains of Iran, encompassing 130,000 square miles. The Iranian province of Khuzistan is excluded, because technically the separate river systems there place this region beyond the Land of Two Rivers.

The considerable environmental difference between northern and southern Mesopotamia is in strict contrast to the unity of cultural expression that was fostered with extraordinary homogeneity, from the 3rd millennium B.C.E., by a succession of peoples of diverse ethnic and linguistic backgrounds. Many of these elements survived until Islam in the 7th century. This heritage is relevant to an understanding of the area in the late antique period.

Unity of belief and expression was based on the concept of a theocratic state, dominated by a temple hierarchy and a god-king. Alexander the Great naturally relished the notion and envisaged Babylon as the center of the civilized world. Greek gods were merged in identity with local ones, such as Zeus and Bel; Greek replaced Semitic Aramaic as the language of administration; and royal coin denominations followed Greek standards for many years. Cities such as Seleucia-on-the-Tigris and Dura-Europus issued their own autonomous bronze coins and enjoyed layouts reflecting west-

ern concepts of urban life. Yet there was also a conscious, official effort to preserve aspects of Mesopotamian culture. At the indigenous level, conservatism ensured the survival of many ancient traditions, including the use of cuneiform writing until the 1st century C.E. Macedonian conquerors transmitted the principles of Babylonian mathematics and astronomy to the western world. Eventually Aramaic would enjoy a revival, evolving into different dialects, such as Syriac, and effecting various Persian permutations, such as Parthian/Sassanian Pahlavi.

The 141 B.C.E. expulsion of the Macedonian Seleucids by the Arsacid (Parthian) dynasty marks the political domination of Mesopotamia by Iranians, with the indigenous inhabitants now reduced to minority status. The Iranian political capital was founded across the Tigris from Seleucia, at Ctesiphon. Yet, apart from minor lapses when persecutions occurred, the Parthians were generally tolerant of minorities. Jews resident since the early days of the Diaspora preserved old religious identities; Mandaeans and Manichaeans established new ones. Rulers of the area's marginal provinces, such as Osrhoëne (around Edessa) and Adiabene (around Arbela) established independent principalities, affiliated with the nominal "king of kings" in a loose system of confederacy. Josephus records an interlude in the 1st century C.E. when two Jewish weavers turned robbers were given de facto authority over territory in the south, an apparent indication of weakness on the part of the monarchy. Yet other examples can be cited, such as the right to issue coins, where accommodations made to local figures resulted in stability and can be judged more effective than rigid authoritarianism.

The 1st century B.C.E. burgeoning of international trade furnished wealth that allowed small political entities (like the kingdom of Hatra) to flourish for a time. Rome became envious of the east's riches. Crassus had dreamed of a lucrative campaign, only to be thwarted in 54 B.C.E. by the infamous mobile Parthian archers. Lured in turn by dreams of eastern conquest, Emperor Trajan invaded Mesopotamia in 116 C.E. by way of Armenia, and then Babylonia (confusingly called Asuristan at this time, not to be confused with ancient Assyria), crossing all the way to the Gulf. He overextended himself, however, and called a retreat. For the most part, the boundary between Rome and Parthia lay along the Euphrates. In other words, Mesopotamia in both its broad and narrow senses was subjected to brief moments of military conquest but was never administered by the Romans. The 164 C.E. Roman occupation of Dura-Europus reflects a military strategy based on economic concerns, and underlines continuing Roman interest in Mesopotamia, though it was confined to the western bank of the Euphrates. Farther north, a milestone reported near Sinjar attests to the Romans' physical presence in northern Mesopotamia, along the 2nd century Khabur frontier line.

Under the more authoritarian Sassanians (3rd century successors to the Parthians), Iranian control over the Euphrates was reasserted. The state religion of Zoroastrianism was aggressively promulgated, and the Magi inherited and modified the ancient Chaldaean (Babylonian) traditions. Conflict with Rome (later Byzantium) reached an apogee. At first the Christians in Mesopotamia were victims of these power plays. Their lot improved only in 484, when they declared officially heretical Nestorianism as their faith. Successful campaigns to the west established a pattern of bringing back imprisoned Roman engineers, who were conscripted into various building projects. Procopius records how, after the sack of Antioch in 540, Khosro I built a new city for the deportees near the capital of Ctesiphon, complete with baths and hippodrome, a magnanimous gesture to his captives. He is said also to have brought back marble from Antioch to adorn the Taq-I Kisra Palace at Ctesiphon.

The 3rd century witnessed the increasing settlement of Arab tribes that either infiltrated the region from the arid southwest, seeking land, or were encouraged to do so by the two imperial powers seeking to extend their respective spheres of influence through mercenary services. Charismatic leaders were able to turn this license into opportunities to form affiliated or even independent principalities, such as that of the Lakhmid kingdom of al-Hira. By the 7th century this separate ethnic identity, as distinct from an Iranian one, combined with common Semitic language and Mesopotamian cultural tradition, may have contributed to the comparative ease with which the Islamic conquests occurred, and the rapid assimilation of the conquered territories into Islam. Nestorius (d. 451) was the single most important transmitter of the ancient Mesopotamian traditions into Islam.

BIBL.: R. M. Adams, *Heartland of Cities: Surveys of Ancient Settlement and Land Use on the Central Floodplain of the Euphrates* (Chicago, 1981). C. Hopkins, ed., *Topography and Architecture of Seleucia on the Tigris* (Ann Arbor, 1972). C. Hopkins, *The Discovery of Dura-Europos* (New Haven, 1979). G. J. P. McEwan, *Priest and Temple in Hellenistic Babylonia* (Wiesbaden, 1981). D. Oates, *Studies in the Ancient History of Northern Iraq* (London, 1968).   E.K.

Messalians

The Messalians, a group of ascetic Christians originating in Mesopotamia, emphasized the indwelling Holy Spirit. Their name comes from a Syriac word meaning "those who pray" (Greek Euchitai). Since there is no evidence for any Christians calling themselves Messalians, historians must rely on descriptions of those who opposed "Messalian" behavior. The earliest references to Messalians appear in the 370s in the anti-heretical writings of Ephrem (*Contra haereses* 22) and Epiphanius (*Ancoratus* 13; *Panarion* 80), neither of whom seems to have had much information about the beliefs of the new group. Epiphanius criticizes their social behavior: they do not separate men and women, nor do they fast, nor do they engage in manual labor, he said, instead they support themselves by begging, pretending to pray unceasingly. Epiphanius is unable to connect them with a specific leader and laments that they have neither head nor root.

Theodoret (ca. 393–ca. 466) and Photius (b. ca. 810, d. after 893) provide evidence for the expansion of the Messalians from Syria into Asia Minor in the late 4th or early 5th century, as well as the measures taken to repress the sect. A synod in Antioch (ca. 390) led by the archbishop Flavian condemned the Messalian leader Adelphius from Edessa. The same year, a council at Side in Pamphilia confirmed this decision. Letoïs of Melitene and Amphilochius of Iconium also took measures against the Messalians. Severus of Antioch (ca. 465–538) and Philoxenos of Mabbug (ca. 440–523) also attest the proceedings against Adelphius.

In the first part of the 5th century, the reaction against Messalian views was centered in Asia Minor. The Synod of Constantinople in 426 condemned the Messalians. The imperial decree of 428 against heretics mentioned the Messalians by name as a group that was forbidden to assemble and pray inside Roman territory. The Third Ecumenical Council, which met at Ephesus in 431, decreed that any cleric or layman suspected of being a Messalian would be required to anathematize the heresy. Those who refused would lose their rank and be prohibited from participating in communion or exercising leadership in the monasteries. The council also condemned a Messalian book called the *Asceticon*.

Information about the doctrines and practices of the Messalians has been preserved in the lists used by church historians and heresiologists including Theodoret, Severus of Antioch, Timothy of Constantinople, and John of Damascus. The writings of Pseudo-Macarius are another source for beliefs of the Messalians. The fifty anonymous Greek homilies on spiritual discipline circulated under the name of Macarius or Symeon probably reflect the teaching of the Messalians and are thought to be linked with the condemned *Asceticon*. They contain a distinctive vocabulary that, although unusual in Greek literature, has parallels in Syrian spirituality. The Messalians believed that sin or a demon dwelled within each human soul. Baptism alone could not expel this evil; only prayer was sufficient. They emphasized the coming of the Holy Spirit to dwell within the soul, once the demon had been expelled. The Holy Spirit granted the Christian freedom from the passions that had previously tormented him.

The Messalians emphasized prophecy and visions, inviting the criticism that they slept excessively. Their vows of poverty and refusal to work precluded them from giving alms. Their emphasis on unceasing prayer as a means of being cleansed from sin decreased the salvific value of communion and baptism, which in turn devalued the authority of the ecclesiastical hierarchy. The anti-Messalian sources frequently accuse them of perjury, because they refused to admit their heresy.

The Messalians do not appear to have formed a separate organized sect. Recent scholarship (Stewart) suggests that the term *Messalian* became a general pejorative that could be applied to a variety of ascetic groups that emphasized prayer over ecclesiastical hierarchy. The Pseudo-Macarian material, associated with heresy, was also used by writers whose orthodoxy was well established, including Gregory of Nyssa. These homilies have been associated as well with the monasticism of Eustathius of Sebaste and Basil. The Pseudo-Macarian writings were translated into Syriac, Georgian, Latin, Arabic, and Church Slavonic and remained popular for devotional purposes among eastern Christians. In the 14th century Russian Hesychasts not only drew on Pseudo-Macarian spirituality but also were derogatorily called Messalians. The Pseudo-Macarian homilies survived in the western tradition as well, inspiring a wide diversity of later groups, including the Jesuits and Methodists.

BIBL.: A. Louth, "Messalianism and Pelagianism," *Studia patristica* 17, no. 1 (1982): 127–135. John Meyendorff, "St. Basil, Messalianism and Byzantine Christianity," *St. Vladimir's Seminary Quarterly* 24 (1980): 219–234. Reinhart Staats, "Messalianism and Antimessalianism in Gregory of Nyssa's De Virginitate," *Patristic and Byzantine Review* 2, no. 1 (1983): 27–44. Columba Stewart, *"Working the Earth of the Heart": The Messalian Controversy in History, Texts and Language to AD 431* (Oxford, 1991). K. Fitscher, *Messalianismus und Antimessalianismus* (Göttingen, 1998). J.H.-H.

Metalware

The metals most used for metalware in the later Roman empire include gold, silver, copper, lead, and tin; iron was used for tools and weapons. Mining in late antiquity is less well studied than in other periods. However, mines in Spain, the Balkans, and the Taurus Mountains have been the subject of recent scholarship. Late antique texts, supported by archaeological evidence, attest to the trade of Cornish tin in the Mediterranean as late as the 7th century. Compositional analyses have revealed the use of very pure (up to 99 percent) gold for coins and jewelry, pure silver (92–98 percent), and various types of copper. Unalloyed copper was used for sheet metal; for other uses there was a shift from bronze to brass and quaternary alloys (copper, tin, zinc, lead). A system of state factories producing armor, shields, and weapons, installed in strategic locations in both the western and eastern empires and listed in the *Notitia Dignitatum,* would have helped to ensure universal standards of metalworking in this period. Names of gold- and coppersmiths are recorded in city and village alike, while only urban silversmiths are

documented. Silver production and stamping in mints, or *thesauri,* under the control of the *comes sacrarum largitionum* may also have encouraged standardization of plate throughout large parts of the empire.

Gold was largely reserved for coins, jewelry, and imperial plate, while silver was used more for plate than for coins (400–615 C.E.) or jewelry. Cast pewter made in the 4th century in Britain and Gaul from local tin combined with lead was used to imitate late Roman silver services. Copper and its alloys bronze and brass were put to a wide variety of uses. In large-scale production, these included doors (those in the Lateran Baptistery in Rome, in Hagia Sophia in Constantinople, and in the monastery church at Mt. Sinai survive), fountains, and the revetment of public monuments, such as the Anemodoulion in Constantinople (379–395). Bronze statues continued to be cast, of which the Colossus of Barletta, now identified as a portrait of Leo I from Constantinople, is a unique late surviving example; the latest recorded example is the equestrian statue of Nicetas the patrician, also set up in Constantinople (615). Bronze ceremonial armor encrusted with gold and silver was made in state workshops in Constantinople and Antioch.

Three grades of copper vessels can be identified. Prestige objects include the head-shaped ewer in the Esquiline Treasure and the silver- and copper-inlaid bronze bowl (now in Paris) that illustrates a foundation myth of Caesarea in Palestine. A series of 6th century brass buckets, most decorated with punched hunting scenes and Greek inscriptions, have been found widely scattered from Britain to Mesopotamia. Also elaborately decorated is a brazier with various possibly Dionysiac figures in relief and griffin-shaped feet; excavated at Mafraq in Jordan, it is of classical inspiration and may be Byzantine or Umayyad. Samovars *(authepsae)* with a wide body and narrow neck have been excavated at Sardis and in Nubia. Tripods, some incorporating large figures, have been found in Egypt and were probably exported from there to Nubia; from elsewhere come tripods with cross-shaped terminals.

From a second, less pretentious level of mass production came numerous cast copper-alloy household vessels (basins and ewers) typologically influenced by contemporary silver vessels; some were ornamented with punched Greek inscriptions and figural decoration. More than 100 such vessels have been discovered in European burials dated to the late 6th and early 7th centuries, and another 170 were discovered in tombs in Nubia. Once mistakenly called Coptic rather than Byzantine, they in fact represent part of a thriving but unlocated industry that also mass produced a wide range of lamps, many of which also recall contemporary examples in silver. A common type of lighting device in late antiquity was a lamp supported on a baluster tripod. Both standing and hanging lamps took various forms. Some were zoomorphic in body or handle (in the shape of a horse, griffin, bird, or lion), and the cross-shaped handle became very popular. Used to illuminate a larger space was the circular, oblong, or cruciform openwork *polycandelon,* which held a series of stemmed glass lamps and was suspended by three or four chains or straps. Sets made of silver form part of the Sion treasure from Asia Minor, and another set in bronze was excavated within a church in Israel. Early Byzantine openwork, bowl-shaped, hanging lamps of silver probably influenced the form of later lamps of tinned copper, such as the one, possibly of the 8th century, from a church near Bursa, and the very similar "mosque lamps" of the Islamic world. *Polycandela* continued to be made into and throughout the Byzantine Middle Ages, while few are known in the Islamic world other than the set in the mosque at Kairouan. In addition to sets of lamps, church equipment made in bronze rather than the preferred silver included suspended censers (without lid) and crosses, such as that incised with figures of Moses and preserved in the monastery on Mt. Sinai. Standing censers are known from Egypt, where a wide variety of bronze objects has survived.

The third level of production was that of metal kitchen equipment, much of it made of sheet copper. These include pitchers, jugs, and cauldrons that have been excavated in several parts of the empire. Cauldrons, usually of two types—low and broad vessels, and compact and tall ones—have been found in shipwrecks, for example at Dor off the coast of Israel and at Yassi Ada off of Asia Minor, and excavated at various sites, including Sardis, where a wide range of beaten copper household vessels datable to the early 7th century were recovered inside shops. Late antique iron frying pans with folding handles were also preserved. The shapes of many cooking equipment utensils were retained into the Middle Ages.

In small-scale production, copper was used for navigational and surgical instruments, weighing and locking devices, commercial stamps, various fittings and trappings, and jewelry (sometimes gilded).

BIBL.: H. Maryon, *Metalwork and Enameling* (New York, 1971). O. Minaeva, *From Paganism to Christianity* (Frankfurt am Main, 1996). *Metalkunst von der Spätantike bis zum ausgehenden Mittelalter* (Berlin, 1982).   M.M.M.

Metropolis

The term *metropolis,* mother city, evolved in the centuries of Greek colonization to describe the relationship between the city that had sent out the colonists and the new foundations. By the Roman imperial period it had become a term of honor, indicating the age and distinction of a city, and therefore it was among the titles for which the cities of the Roman empire competed with notorious jealousy. By the mid 2nd century cities could

be ranked, and a single province could have more than one metropolis. "Metropolis" denoted the most important cities, followed by those with assize centers, followed by the rest (Modestinus, *Digest* 27.1.6.2).

Rank was increasingly associated with a city's position within the Roman imperial administrative system. Even though several ancient cities—such as Miletus—used the title without being a center of imperial government, to be the capital of a province entailed the rank of metropolis. The increase in the number of provinces from the late 3rd century therefore meant that many more cities were entitled to call themselves "metropolis" in this sense. For a while, the two usages—honorary and administrative—survived together: the city of Hierapolis in Phrygia used the title in the 350s, and Tralles, in Asia, used it in the early 5th century, although neither was a capital. In 449–450 Theodosius II bestowed the rank of metropolis on Beirut, while making it clear that this did not reduce the authority of Tyre, the administrative capital of the province.

Over the same period the rank of metropolis gained even more importance because it also applied to the church hierarchy. Because the church was organized in provincial units that followed the structures of the civil administration, a city that was made metropolis of a province also became the seat of a metropolitan bishop, who had authority over the bishoprics of that province. Cities with special secular status, such as Miletus, also retained special ecclesiastical status as metropolitan bishoprics; Beirut, made a secular metropolis in the 5th century, almost immediately started contending with Tyre for authority over subordinate bishoprics. All of this served to increase the sense of the title as one solely describing official standing, rather than one with historical origins; and all such "mother cities" were eventually overshadowed by the preeminent mother city, Constantinople.

BIBL.: C. Roueché, "Floreat Perge," in *Images of Authority,* ed. M. M. Mackenzie and C. Roueché (Cambridge, Eng., 1989), 206–228.   C.R.

Milan

Geopolitics thrust sudden greatness upon 3rd century Milan's dowdy respectability, as emperors and their armies made it their regular northern Italian base. The tetrarch Maximian supplied a palace and a circus (the indispensable focus for imperial display), vast new baths, and, to compensate for inadequate natural defenses, a formidable defensive circuit. Duly equipped for a dual military and political role, Milan offered 4th century emperors a convenient headquarters from which to monitor the Danube (Gratian), Gaul (Valentinian II), or Constantinople (Maximus, Eugenius), or, conversely, to consolidate a newly acquired grip on the west (Constantius II, Valentinian I, Theodosius I).

Milan's 4th century imperial apogee is celebrated by Ausonius, whose *Order of Noble Cities,* noting Milan's lavish buildings and imposing walls, proclaims everything "wonderful." Corroborating Ausonius's further emphasis on the excellence of Milan's inhabitants is Augustine's conversion experience, a series of encounters with inspirational men, notably Bishop Ambrose. Augustine was a typical court figure in the brevity of his residence in Milan (his three years surpass the totals of either Gratian or Theodosius); Ambrose, however, owed his remarkable influence over resident emperors largely to his being a fixture there. The bishop's adventures abroad—at Sirmium, Trier, and Rome—meanwhile reflect the effective horizons of the western court; neither Ambrose nor Gratian is known ever to have traveled by sea.

Gothic invasion (and the abandonment of imperial commitments to the Rhine) occasioned the transfer of the court to the seaport of Ravenna (402). Milan's past luster subsequently attracted Attila, who occupied—and allegedly redecorated—the palace (452), and Belisarius, whose premature efforts to regain this "bulwark of the whole Roman empire" (538) led to a disastrous sack. The Ostrogoths had kept the circus functioning and imperial symbolism alive; the Lombard king Agilulf crowned his son there in 604. But such occasions were exceptional: Milan had become something of a white elephant, the resources of the post-Roman state being inadequate to defend its vast perimeter.

The Lombard invasion (569) had occasioned an eighty-year removal of the Milanese clergy to Genoa. Their return saw a series of episcopal burials and restoration projects at Ambrose's churches, heralding a new civic identity. A brother of King Liutprand was "dragged to his cathedra" by popular acclaim and duly "adorned the city," to recreate in a minor key the Ambrosian partnership between bishop and ruler. Our source on this Bishop Theodore, the *Versum de Mediolano civitate* (739), conveniently summarizes the continuities and changes since Ausonius's poem. The massive walls again receive prominent attention, but the chief architectural splendor is now the Church of San Lorenzo, founded (symbolically) on spoils from the demolished amphitheater. The most impressive secular amenities are infrastructural: the forum, the network of paved streets, and a functioning aqueduct. The poet acknowledges (as had Ausonius) Milan's rich hinterland but now measures the city's superiority over Italian rivals by its saints' graves. He also shows the populace devoted not to theater and circus but to the city's distinctive liturgy; visitors are attracted by generous alms, not the political and social ambitions that had drawn Augustine, while the "chiefs of Italy" who flock there are not imperial governors, like Ambrose, but provincial bishops.

BIBL.: Richard Krautheimer, *Three Christian Capitals: Topography and Politics* (Berkeley, 1983), 68–92. *Milano: Capitale dell'impero romano, 286–402 d.C.* (Milan, 1990). F. Monfrin, "A propos de Milan chrétien," *Cahiers archéologiques* 39 (1991): 7–46. C. Violante, *La società milanese nell'età precomunale,* 2nd ed. (Milan and Bari, 1974). N.M.

Millenarianism

Earliest Christianity drew deeply on the biblical wellsprings of Jewish apocalyptic hope: the belief that God would speedily redeem his people, liberating the living and raising the dead; bring them home from exile to Jerusalem; end foreign domination, evil, and death; establish his kingdom of righteousness and peace. With Jesus's death and the belief in his bodily resurrection, the younger community added to these themes the expectation of his imminent return—the Parousia, or second coming—which would itself inaugurate the establishment of the Kingdom (e.g., 1 Cor. 15; Mark 13, esp. 26–27). By the end of the 1st century, John of Patmos contributed a further refinement: that the martyrs would rise bodily at Christ's second coming to reign with him for a thousand years on earth (Rev. 20:1–6).

With this last formulation we touch on the formal definition of millenarianism as the belief in this thousand-year terrestrial reign. In the 2nd century, the idea became virtually definitive, against various dualist and Gnostic forms of Christianity, of proto-orthodox eschatology. The roll call of defining figures within this community—Papias, Ireneaus, Justin Martyr, Tertullian—all championed this conviction. Indeed, in its emphasis on bodily resurrection and historical, communal redemption, specifically focused on Jerusalem, millenarianism cohered effortlessly with the chief touchstones of orthodox doctrine: incarnation Christologies, Jesus's own resurrection in the flesh, the essential relevance of the Septuagint to Christian revelation.

When would the Kingdom come? When would Christ return? Throughout antiquity, despite the arguments of the erudite who sought to allegorize millenarian traditions, various social, political, and natural disasters stimulated popular expectations of the end in both clergy and laity. In part to allay these disruptive hopes, some learned Christians undertook to calculate the age of the world, hence the date of Christ's return. These chronologies conflated the creational week of Genesis 1 (God making the world in six days and resting on the seventh), the line in Ps. 90:4 (quoted in 2 Pet. 3:8) that a day is as a thousand years in the sight of the Lord, and a thousand years one day, and the tradition in Rev. 20 of the thousand-year reign of the saints. According to the millennial week, Christ would return in the 6000th year since the creation to begin the millenarian sabbath rest of his saints: their reign would constitute the seventh "day" of 1000 years. When Hippolytus and Julius Africanus devised this scheme in the early 3rd century, they calculated that the year 6000 would fall sometime around the equivalent year 500. The Parousia was thus pushed well beyond their own lifetime. For Augustine's contemporary the bishop Hilarianus, reiterating this chronological calculation c. 397, the end loomed considerably closer.

The fall of Rome in 410 occasioned a huge wave of millennial panic. "Behold," some Christians exclaimed, "from Adam all the years have passed, and behold, the 6000 years are completed, and now comes the Day of Judgment!" (Augustine, *Serm.* 113.8). Against this conviction, Augustine brought to bear the full weight of his prestige and exegetical virtuosity in Book 20 of the *City of God*. Numbers such as 1000, he argued, symbolized spiritual truths, not quantifiable periods; and postbiblical history is opaque, so that one could never match the signs of the times with sacred Scripture to know what time it was on history's clock. His arguments have certainly persuaded most modern historians, who often hold that Christian millenarianism received its deathblow from him. In fact, evidence of active and vivid millenarian expectation continues from Augustine's time throughout the Middle Ages in the west, occasioning three major shifts in western universal chronologies (Hippolytus, Eusebius/Jerome, Bede) that sought thereby to redate the age of the world, hence the hour of its end.

BIBL.: P. Fredriksen, "Apocalypse and Redemption in Early Christianity, from John of Patmos to Augustine of Hippo," *Vigiliae christianae* 45 (1991): 151–183. L. Gry, *Le millenarisme* (Paris, 1904). R. Landes, "'Lest the millennium be fulfilled': Apocalyptic expectations and the pattern of Western chronography, 100–800 C.E.," in *The Use and Abuse of Eschatology in the Middle Ages*, ed. W. Verbeke, D. Verhelst, and A. Welkenhuysen (Leuven, 1988).   P.F.

Mining

The mines of the Roman empire were exploited most intensively and extensively from the late 1st century B.C.E. until the early 3rd century C.E. The main mining regions were Spain (with numerous gold, silver, copper, tin, and lead mines); Gaul (gold, silver, and iron); Britain (iron, lead, tin, and some gold and silver); the Danubian provinces of Noricum, Dalmatia, Pannonia, Moesia, and Dacia (gold and iron); Macedonia and Thrace (gold and silver); and Asia Minor (gold, silver, iron, and tin). Three main types of mining were practiced: the exploitation of alluvial deposits; open-cast mining of rock deposits found near the surface; and underground mining of deeper deposits by means of shafts and connecting galleries. The last type of mine required quite elaborate drainage works, and a number of waterwheels and pumping devices, including Archimedean screws, have been discovered in Roman mines in southern Spain.

While private individuals and occasionally cities continued to own and operate some mines, most gold and silver mines and many other mines became imperial property. The emperor leased out the right to exploit the mines to individual contractors or associations (as at the Vipasca mines in southern Portugal: *Fontes Iuris Romani AnteIustiniani* I 104 and 105), but in some cases organized production directly, as in the rich gold-mining region of northwestern Spain. The most productive mining regions were supervised by mining procurators, who were imperial freedmen or, later, of equestrian rank. Slaves made up a sizable part of the labor force, but convicts, prisoners of war, and freeborn wage laborers also worked as miners. Detachments of the Roman army were stationed at the larger mines to watch over the workforce, the mined ore, and the processed metals, and also to provide technical help in mining, smelting, and drainage operations.

The instability of the mid- to late 3rd century appears to have led to reduced production in many parts of the empire, with some mines being closed down at least temporarily. The Gothic invasions under Gordian III caused the temporary loss of the mines of the central Danubian provinces. The incursions of the Franks and Moors in 260 forced production to halt at the silver and copper mines of southwestern Spain. The important gold mines of Dacia were lost after Rome gave up control of that province in 271. The political problems of the later 3rd century exacerbated a decline in production that had already started to occur in some regions in the later 2nd century: e.g., at the silver, copper, and gold mines at Rio Tinto in southern Spain. However, despite the troubles some mines did remain open; we hear of Christians being condemned to the mines of Numidia in 257–258 (Cyprian, *Ep.* 76.2) and to the mines of Cyprus, Palestine, and Cilicia ca. 310 (Eusebius, *Martyrs of Palestine* 8.13, 13.2).

The generally more favorable political conditions of the 4th century allowed some mines to resume production, although the very patchy and scattered nature of the evidence (literary, archaeological, and legal) makes it difficult to assess either its nature or scale with any confidence. Many important mines have provided some archaeological traces of occupation, and hence possibly exploitation, in the 4th century: e.g., Rio Tinto and Tharsis (southern Spain), Vipasca (southern Portugal), Dolaucothi (Wales), and a number of mines in Bosnia and Serbia. In the 4th and 5th centuries some activity even resumed at the silver mines of the Laureion region of Attica, which had been dormant since the 2nd century C.E. The discovery of late imperial and Byzantine lamps in mining shafts at Thorikos corroborates the remark of Paul the Silentiary (Descriptio—Sancta Sophia 679–680) that the Church of Hagia Sophia in Constantinople, rebuilt after the Nika Riots of 532 and reconsecrated in 537, was decorated with silver from Sounion (i.e., the Laureion) and Mt. Pangaion in Thrace. In short, although large-scale mining operations were no longer feasible in the later empire, exploitation of mines did continue, if often on a smaller scale.

Various statutes in the *Theodosian Code* show that several emperors attempted to revitalize mining in the later 4th and early 5th centuries, and they provide us with glimpses of the administrative regime under which mining took place. Gold (and probably silver) mines were the responsibility of the *comes sacrarum largitionum,* while various regional *comites metallorum* oversaw local production. The *Notitia Dignitatum* ([*or.*] 13.11) mentions the *comes metallorum per Illyricum.* Members of the curial class were required to serve as procurators of individual mines at least in Macedonia, Dacia Mediterranea, Moesia, and Dardania (*C.Th.* 1.32.5). The epitaph of a 4th century procurator of gold mines survives from Appia, Phrygia (*SEG* 6.166). However, by 386 such procurators were shirking their duty in the face of Gothic invasions, since in that year Gratian, Valentinian, and Theodosius attempted to force them back to their duties (*C.Th.* 1.32.5).

In the later 4th century, various emperors tried to revitalize gold mining by allowing individuals to exploit state-owned gold mines in return for the payment of an annual fee: eight *scripuli* of gold dust in 365 (*C.Th.* 10.19.3), reduced to seven *scripuli* in 392, at least for the dioceses of Pontus and Asia (*C.Th.* 10.19.12). Taxes were also levied on other types of mines. In 372 Bishop Basil of Caesarea wrote to the praetorian prefect Modestus to request some relief of the tax on iron production in the Taurus Mountains (*Ep.* 110). In 377 a number of gold miners from Thrace fled to join the Goths, "unable any longer to support the taxes" (Amm.Marc. 31.6.6). Various emperors also made frequent (and hence presumably futile) attempts to tie miners *(metallarii)* to their profession on a hereditary basis (*C.Th.* 10.19.5–6, of 369; 10.19.7, of 370; 10.19.9, of 378; 10.19.15, of 424). These measures suggest that the fresh bullion (especially gold) being produced was not sufficient to meet the state's needs.

Following the loss of Roman control of the west, there is evidence that some Gothic kings attempted to stimulate mining. The Ostrogothic king Theoderic sought to expand iron mining in Dalmatia ca. 510, while in Italy, following the discovery of gold in Bruttium, King Athalaric ordered its immediate exploitation (Cassiodorus *Variae* 3.25–26; 9.3). Evidence for mining in Visigothic and Suebic Spain is scant, but some mining probably continued. Some North African mines were operational under the Vandals in the 5th century (Victor Vitensis, *Historia persecutionis Africanae provinciae* 3.68). In Gaul a number of Merovingian coins of the late 6th century have been discovered at tin mines in Brittany, while the gold mines of the Massif Central and the Loire Valley were exploited under the Franks. The important silver mines at Melle that later supplied much of the metal for Carolingian coinage were already being worked in the 7th century, as were the gold and silver mines at Kremnitz and Schemnitz in Saxony, where production was revived and expanded under Charlemagne in the early 9th century.

Under the Byzantine empire there is evidence for considerable mining of gold, silver, and tin in the Taurus Mountains in Anatolia. And recent archaeological work has revealed some gold-mining settlements of the 5th and 6th centuries in the eastern desert of Egypt. However, Byzantine emperors had to import some gold from outside the frontiers of the empire. In the 5th century the Romans and the Sassanian Persians cooperated in the exploitation of Armenian gold. Relations soured in 421, when the Persians refused to hand back the gold workers hired out by the Romans (Socrates, *Hist.eccl.* 7.18). The gold mines of Pharangium in the Caucasus became a cause of dispute in 530 during the wars between the Romans and the Persians (Procopius, *Bell.Pers.* 1.15.18, 15.27, 22.3, 22.18). Byzantine emperors also imported some gold from Nubia and Ethiopia.

Following their conquests of the 7th and early 8th centuries, the Arabs were active in seeking out fresh sources of gold, especially in Egypt, Nubia, and Ethiopia. They were the first to exploit the silver resources of North Africa in a systematic fashion. Arab geographers, such as Edrisi, refer frequently to important mining sites in Spain, which may hint at renewed production there. Some archaeological evidence suggests that they reactivated mining at Rio Tinto.

BIBL.: O. Davies, *Roman Mines in Europe* (Oxford, 1935). C. Domergue, *Les mines de la péninsule ibérique dans l'antiquité romaine* (Rome, 1990). J. C. Edmondson, "Mining in the Later Roman Empire and Beyond: Continuity or Disruption?" *Journal of Roman Studies* 79 (1989): 84–102.   J.E.

Miracles

The miracle, an exceptional intervention by God in the world, has held an important place in Christianity since New Testament times. As in other religions, a miracle is a paradoxical event that interrupts the ordinary course of things and may take a wondrous form. It is a manifestation of a superhuman power and produces astonishment (hence its name, *thauma* or *miraculum*), often combined with the fear elicited by an encounter with the sacred. In addition, the Christian miracle is a sign that the kingdom to come is already present. It presupposes or produces faith in Christ. While theoretically open to all forms of wonders, it is limited by the concern to reproduce the miracles attested in the Hebrew Bible and the New Testament.

In a society that widely accepts the possibility of miracles and expects help from them, such supernatural phenomena have the value of proof: for Jews, proof of the messianic character of Jesus; for pagans, proof of the truth of Christianity. Later, miracles were also the distinctive sign of the true faith in relation to heresy. Miracles' function as plerophory gives them a special role in evangelizing. Hence they were performed by the apostles on their missions, and the charisma of miracles seems to be particularly associated with apostolic times. In the history of the church or of the Christian empire, which was conceived on the model of holy history, miracles occupied a place similar to that which they had in the historical books of the Bible. Above all, miracles had come to be associated with evolving forms of holiness, and hagiography used them to prove that a particular person was a saint. The privileged agents of miracles were the ascetic, a living saint, and also the dead saint, or martyr.

The ascetic, who turns away from the world and is victorious over the flesh, over passions, and over demons, receives miraculous help from God and returns to the state of nature; that is how Athanasius describes Antony, as a new Adam in a new paradise. The ascetic's body is transformed, the world changes around him, beasts obey him, demons flee him. Speaking freely (parrhēsia) with God, he becomes an intercessor; he bestows exceptional blessings on others, spreading the charismata acquired in the desert. Visitors flocked to the ascetic, asking for his prayers or simply seeking contact with him. In this way, they obtained spiritual and material favors: counsel, comfort, prophesies, exorcisms, healings, protection in all areas of daily life, and even resurrection. The ascetic's miracles were the most spectacular aspect of his acts of apostolate, of catechism, and of patronage; he also acted through apparently natural means, but his miracles revealed that they, too, were the effect of charismata.

Beneficiaries of the acts of the holy thaumaturge could be from the most humble social strata or the ruling classes; they could even include the emperor and those close to him. There is evidence of disbelief and resistance, but the sources show above all the degree to which miracles were integrated into daily life. Symeon Stylites the Elder, for example, attracted crowds who came to see a wondrous ascetic and to benefit from the miracles he was performing. Such cases show that in the eyes of a whole society and even among non-Christians, the saint, through his ordeals, had acquired a superhuman stature. Supernatural powers were associated with him, and people expected to benefit from them.

Among the beneficiaries of these miracles, the saint's disciples formed a privileged group. The community that gathered around an ascetic was organized according to laws, which the founding miracles sanctified. It inherited the founder's charismata, and the miracle, at first the prerogative of an isolated saint, thus became the property of a social group—a monastery, and, more broadly, monasticism as a whole—and the specific way it acted in the world.

The saint's miracles did not end with his earthly life. Those produced at his death were the decisive sign of his holiness. After he died, the ascetic could be the object of a cult; these cults were identical to cults of martyrs, which were more widespread and better documented. Believers attempted to profit from the miracles of a dead saint by means of various practices: invocation and prayer, worship of images and relics. These miracles were most spectacular in the martyries around the saint's tomb or near some of his relics. A *Life* of a saint often included a section devoted to miracles post mortem, which were also the subject of special works: collections of miracles, written to the glory of a saint or a sanctuary. In the west, Augustine himself made every effort to have contemporary miracles, gathered firsthand, written down in *libelli*. He devoted a chapter of *De civ.Dei* to saints' miracles; in addition, two books of miracles performed by St. Stephen in Uzalum (Africa) were composed within Augustine's entourage. In the late 6th century, Gregory of Tours, historian of the Franks, collected the miracles of St. Julian and St. Martin. In the east, there are a greater number of ancient collections: e.g., the miracles of St. Thecla (5th century, Cilicia), of St. Cyrus, and of St. John by Sophronius of Jerusalem (7th century Egypt); of SS. Cosmas and Damian (6th century Constantinople); and of St. Artemius (7th century Constantinople). The eastern collections shed light on the beliefs and practices of believers. After their death, saints continued to inhabit their sanctuary. They appeared to believers who had come to practice incubation—that is, to stay and sleep near the saint's tomb. Saints healed believers free of charge (but the person who had received the miracle could show his gratitude with a return gift), either through classic medical procedures or through unusual and paradoxical remedies. Believers, to obtain the miraculous favors they were soliciting, sought to enter into intimate contact with the saint's body, which was permeated with a particular virtue: they touched the tomb and relics, or used objects or liquids that had been in contact with them. Some of these practices were of pagan origin and similar to magical procedures. Augustine, who knew that saints' miracles were reminiscent of those of the ancient gods, invoked the example of Moses facing the Pharaoh's magicians, and proclaimed the superiority of martyrs. Sometimes, accounts of miracles echo actual dream narratives and allow us to glimpse a link between the mechanism of miracles and dream logic. As for miracles performed by ascetics, the clientele of sanctuaries was not limited to the lower classes. The church and the Christian intelligentsia shared with the common people faith in miracles. They were simply careful to make sure that such miracles were attributed not to the saint's own power but to God's action through the saint.

BIBL.: G. Dagron, *Vie et miracles de sainte Thècle* (Brussels, 1978). H. Delehaye, "Les recueils antiques de miracles des saints," *Analecta Bollandiana* 43 (1925): 5–85, 305–325.

B. Flusin, *Miracle et histoire dans l'oeuvre de Cyrille de Scythopolis* (Paris, 1983). W. D. McCready, *Signs of Sanctity: Miracles in the Thought of Gregory the Great* (Toronto, 1989). W. D. McCready, *Miracles and the Venerable Bede* (Toronto, 1994). G. de Nie, *Views from a Many Windowed Tower: Studies of Imagination in the Works of Gregory of Tours* (Amsterdam, 1987). R. Van Dam, *Saints and Their Miracles in Late Antique Gaul* (Princeton, 1993).   B.F.

Mishnah

The Mishnah (meaning repetition, or teaching) is the first rabbinic book, written in Hebrew and edited around 200 C.E. The work is anonymous and lacks a preface; nowhere does the author, who is assumed by both the Palestinian and the Babylonian Talmud and by all subsequent scholarship to have been Rabbi Judah the Patriarch (Yehudah ha Nasi), address his readership or explain the purpose or setting of the work. The Mishnah contains primarily material of a legal character: anonymous rulings, rulings ascribed to named sages, and debates between sages. The Mishnah also contains anecdotes, maxims, exhortations, scriptural exegesis, and descriptions of the rituals of the Jerusalem Temple. The sages named in the Mishnah, generally known as *tanna'im* (teachers), are customarily assigned by modern scholars to distinct generations; the bulk of the sages named in the Mishnah belong to either the generation of Yavneh (ca. 80–120 C.E.) or the generation of Usha (ca. 140–180). Relatively little material is ascribed to named figures who lived before the destruction of the Jerusalem Temple in 70.

The Mishnah covers a broad range of topics and is divided into six sections known as orders; each order, in turn, is divided into tractates. There are sixty-three tractates in all. The six orders are: *Zera'im* (Seeds), on the disposition of the agricultural products of the land of Israel; *Mo'ed* (Feasts or Appointed Times), on the festivals and pilgrimage to the Jerusalem Temple; *Nashim* (Women), on marriage, divorce, and family law; *Neziqin* (Damages), on civil and criminal law, and judicial procedure; *Qodashim* (Holy Things), on Temple sacrifices and rituals; and *Toharot* (Purities), on the maintenance of ritual purity and the removal of ritual impurity.

The Mishnah clearly was not meant to be a law book. It omits too many topics to have functioned as a legal code, and even the topics that it contains are treated only in part. Further, many legal questions are not resolved but are left in the form of a debate between rival authorities. In subsequent Jewish tradition the Mishnah has functioned as a source of law, an authoritative book from which normative law can be deduced, but it is debatable whether this was the Mishnah's original purpose.

In two respects the Mishnah marks a radical break with the Hebrew literature that came before it. First, it does not appeal to Scripture for its authority; the Mish-

nah is not written in biblical idiom, and nowhere does it claim to be an exposition of the written Torah. As a literary artifice the Mishnah is independent of Scripture (even if a close knowledge of the Torah is often essential for understanding a given line of the Mishnah, and even if the Mishnah contains occasional bits of scriptural exegesis). The Talmud later attempted to tame this intellectual arrogance by asserting that the Mishnah is identical with the Oral Torah, a set of traditions that were revealed by God to Moses on Mt. Sinai alongside the written Torah. Second, the Mishnah is the earliest Jewish book to attribute conflicting legal opinions to individuals who, in spite of their disagreements, remain members of the same group. The rabbinic penchant for vigorous debate and argument begins with the first rabbinic book.

BIBL.: *The Mishnah,* trans. H. Danby (Oxford, 1933).
S.J.C.

Mithraism

Long before Franz Cumont, Ernest Renan raised the specter of a late antique world that might have become Mithraist rather than Christian. The legacy of such speculation has been two common convictions, that Mithraism was especially important both to Julian and to the senatorial "pagan reaction," and that, among pagan cults, it was particularly obnoxious to Christians. Both convictions gain some color from Jerome's allusion to the destruction of a Roman mithraeum by Furius Maecius Gracchus as a gauge of his Christian fervor before his baptism (*Ep.* 107.2). Some nuancing, however, is in order.

There is little doubt that Mithraism came to the notice of the Roman elite mainly through service in the army. Many of the twenty-four certain or probable

An image of Mithras on a relief dedicated by a late antique pagan, Appius Claudius Tarronius Dexter.

Roman mithraea, mostly on higher ground and therefore in more expensive dwelling areas, were established in the later 3rd century and continued well into the 4th. The absence of Mithraic inscriptions between that of the first civilian senatorial dedication, in 313 (PLRE 1, Severianus 9), and the bulk of the inscriptions, which cluster between 370 and 388, prevents us from tracing senatorial engagement in detail. At least sixteen senators of Rome were dedicated to Mithras, or are known to have been *patres,* between 357 and 388—fewer than those dedicated to Cybele/Attis but more than to Isis/Sarapis. Of these, only four are known to have had careers in imperial service; almost all the others are known solely from their Mithraic dedications. It was surely the mysteries' openness to reinterpretation that made them now "Roman" and respectable—above all, the Platonization of Mithras known to us from Porphyry, by which Mithras became a demiurge, along with the cult's extensive invocation of Aratean astronomy. The inscriptions from St. Silvestro in Capite provide unique evidence of the ritual activity of a senatorial family over three generations to the 380s (PLRE 1, Olympius 18). By contrast, the temple beneath 128 Via Giovanni Lanza suggests that Mithras might have been merely one of many emblems of private pagan religiosity, perhaps even indicative of a tacit rapprochement with the ineffable God of the opposition.

Mithraism remained marginal to the culture of *paideia.* Only two works devoted to Mithras are known to have been written in antiquity: those by Euboulos and Pallas, cited solely by Porphyry (De antro nympharum 6; De abstinentia 2.56, 4.16). There was thus no common knowledge wreathing the secret "mystery" to serve either Christian apologetic or late pagan erudition. Mithras is, for example, simply ignored by Tertullian in his *Apologeticus* and *Ad nationes* (even though Tertullian himself knew specific ritual details, De cor. 15,3), and by Arnobius *(Adversus nationes)* and Lactantius *(Divinae institutiones).* (But at midcentury note Firmicus Maternus, De errore 1.5, 19.) There is hardly a trace of Mithras in the elevated pagan solar theology of the 3rd and 4th centuries, even in Julian's *Oratio* 4, and he is ignored completely in Macrobius's summary of this tradition in *Saturnalia* (1.17–26).

Moreover, the archaeology of sites, such as it is, hardly supports the view that mithraea were the special target of Christians. On the Rhine-Danube frontier and also at Dura-Europus, violent destructions were evidently due to barbarian incursion (pace Sauer, 1996). Elsewhere, for example in Italy, the majority of mithraea—particularly those on private property, as in Marino, Capua, or Palazzo Barberini, but also many in public buildings, such as the Baths of Titus on the Carinae—were not destroyed but were simply abandoned in the 4th century. Although the erosion of Mithraism was probably continuous, we can point to

two moments in particular. First is the closure of many mainly military mithraea (Lambaesis, Carrawburgh, Carnuntum III) that seems to have been due to the Constantinian legislation of 324 (Eusebius, *Vit.Const.* 4.25). Whereas the tetrarchs had named Mithras *fautor imperii sui* at Carnuntum in 307 under military influence (ILS 659), the nominal religious allegiance of the soldiery, at any rate, was directly subject to imperial will. The second is the period of increasingly insistent interdiction of sacrifice, from 370 to 373 (C.Th. 9.16.8). A few temples in public spaces, such as Terme di Mitra in Ostia and Castra Peregrinorum on the Caelian, were indeed violently destroyed then, but St. Clemente, for example, located in a private house, seems to have continued to be used into the 5th century. Mithraism's urban constituency, and its elective status, meant that it was vulnerable to such legislation, supported by delation, in a way that rural cults, genuinely ancestral, were not (compare Libanius, *Orat.* 30.9–10).

BIBL.: W. M. Braeshear, "A Mithraic Catechism from Egypt (P. Berol. 21196)," supplement to *Tyche* (Vienna), 1992. Manfred Clauss, "Mithras und Christus," *Historische Zeitschrift* 243 (1986): 265–285. Eberhard Sauer, *The End of Paganism in the North-Western Provinces of the Roman Empire: The Example of the Mithras Cult* (Oxford, 1996). Roger Beck, "The Mysteries of Mithras: A New Account of Their Genesis," *Journal of Roman Studies* 88 (1998): 115–128. N. McLynn, "The Fourth-Century *Taurobolium,*" *Phoenix* 50 (1996): 213–330.   R.G.

Monasticism

In the early 4th century, Egyptian papyri begin to record the existence of *monachoi*—literally, "singular people"—who had abandoned their homes for the sake of a new life in the desert, free of sexual and financial entanglements. Barely one hundred years later, these localized groups were famed across the Roman empire as the pioneers of the monastic life, which had come to be seen as the surest path to moral perfection. Wealthy Christian elites had begun to support (and themselves to adopt) this way of life, a material and spiritual commitment that made monasticism a foundation stone for Byzantine and European civilization over the next millennium. This development is often regarded by scholars in a positive light—although for Edward Gibbon, notoriously, the success of monasticism was the signal emblem of the superstition that sapped the civic spirit of the Roman empire.

A problem of definition has attended Christian monasticism since its inception. *Monachoi* did not profess to be following a new way of life; they merely wanted, they claimed, to live out Christian precepts to the full. The range of their mortificatory practices did not differentiate them from earlier ascetics, pagan, Jewish, or Christian. Generations of commentators debated the nature of monastic "singularity": was it based in physical solitude, or singleness of heart, or solidarity as a group? What these suggestions have in common is a conviction that *monachoi* were separate, physically or imaginatively, from other human beings. An awareness of the social tensions that might arise from such separatism underpins much of the monastic literature produced in the period.

Clarity of definition eluded the earliest desert fathers and mothers. We should beware the simplified account of monastic origins that accords to the hermit St. Antony (d. 356) the invention of the anchoretic or eremitic life lived alone, and to Pachomius (d. 346) the subsequent institution of the cenobitic life lived in community. In fact, Antony and Pachomius were contemporaries of each other and of other monastic leaders, both male and female, and their respective activities are not accurately described by a distinction between the hermit and the cenobite. This binary classification was the invention of later visitors to Egypt. The withdrawal *(anachorēsis)* into the desert (or to another village) that characterized the original monastic movement seems to have had its roots in nonreligious strategies of communal farming. While monastics were not illiterate peasants incapable of speaking for themselves—witness the letters of Antony, the *Rule* of Pachomius, and the *Sayings of the Desert Fathers*—the immensely influential *Life* of Antony by the controversialist Bishop Athanasius of Alexandria (d. 373) shows how quickly monasticism could be adopted for causes other than those first intended.

The monastic life in the desert attracted extraordinary attention from the urban intelligentsia around the Mediterranean. Two broadly contrasting views emerged: one group of writers, exemplified by Evagrius Ponticus (d. 399), Jerome (d. 420), and John Cassian (d. ca. 435) saw monasticism primarily as a framework for ascetic achievement. As publicly professed monastics, Christians could school themselves in virtue as an example to the world they had renounced. Others, such as Basil of Caesarea (d. 379) and Augustine of Hippo (d. 430), were wary of the pitfalls of any absolute claim to moral superiority, and accordingly sought the meaning of monasticism in its communal aspect. It was Basil who offered the first systematic discussion of monasticism in terms of the eremitic and cenobitic lives, in order to argue for the superior value of the latter. Basil's taxonomy became standard, although not all agreed with his ranking of the two ways of life. In the decades around 400, these divergent visions of the monastery as a theater of purity, on the one hand, and an instrument of social integration, on the other, contributed to the violence of the feuds among learned Christians, in particular the Origenist and Pelagian controversies.

Whatever their divisions, Christian intellectuals of the late empire shared an interest in bringing desert monasticism into the purview of city dwellers and, above all, the clergy. Urban monasteries and monk-bishops assumed a central role in the future development of both the eastern and the western empire. In Byzantium, the institutional weight and complexity of monasticism in town and country underwrote the continuing vigor of the imperial state and local civic society. Monks and nuns were key protagonists in the doctrinal disputes that were the medium of imperial politics in Constantinople, and in the provinces, above all in Syria and Palestine, monastic foundations lent energy to the internal colonization of hitherto uncultivated land. In the west, by contrast, the disintegration of the Roman state made for a less certain politics of monasticism. By the turn of the 7th century, rule-based cenobitic traditions for men and women had developed in Italy, Gaul, Ireland, and Spain—but despite the rhetorical élan and later success of some of these Rules (notably that of Benedict of Nursia (d. ca. 540), this was a heterogeneous and ephemeral body of ad hoc prescriptions, in a state of flux and continuous adaptation. In England and in Saxony, as in Syria and Palestine, monasteries were vehicles for economic and cultural expansion, notwithstanding an intense competition among the parties investing in monastic foundations (lay nobles, bishops, abbots, and abbesses).

By the time of Charlemagne's imperial coronation, the contrast between the stately monastic culture of the east and the volatile west had, to some extent, been reversed. As a result of the Arab conquests, mosques, not monasteries, now flourished in the Judaean desert, while in Asia Minor, iconoclasm threatened the very basis of the monastic claim to spiritual expertise. In the west, the rise of the Carolingians saw the concerted articulation of monastic authority. In the last decades of the 8th century, a Frank from Aniane in Provence, styling himself a "second Benedict," began the task of compiling a dossier and a concordance of all existing monastic rules in Latin. It was the conclusion of his researches that the 6th century Rule of St. Benedict best summed up the entire tradition—a judgment that took on the force of imperial edict in 817, when Charlemagne's son Louis the Pious decreed that all monasteries in the Frankish empire should observe the Benedictine Rule. Whether or not we assent to Gibbon's view of the contribution of the desert fathers to the decline of the Roman empire, it is clear that the Carolingian reinvention of Rome owed not a little to their early medieval heirs.

BIBL.: G. Jenal, *Italia ascetica: Das Asketen- und Mönchtum in Italien (ca. 150/250–604),* 2 vols. (Sigmaringen, 1995). Robert Markus, *The End of Ancient Christianity* (Cambridge, Eng., 1990). G. Muschiol, *Famula Dei: Zur Liturgie in merowingischen Frauenklöster* (Münster, 1994). F. Prinz, *Frühes Mönchtum im Frankenreich,* 2nd ed. (Darmstadt, 1988). Philip Rousseau, *Pachomius: The Making of a Community in Fourth-Century Egypt* (Berkeley, 1985).

C.L.

Monks, Image of

Early admiration for monks and the monastic life was revealed in four stages: the attraction of disciples and local villagers, the anxious attention of bishops, the visits of pilgrims, and the proliferation of ascetic texts. None of these should be taken at face value, however. Disciples did not always stay, bishops were intent on orthodoxy and canonical discipline, pilgrims came to marvel as much as imitate, and texts are deceptive in their propaganda.

The "outsider's view" of monasticism could be critical as well as admiring. Eunapius of Sardis and Rutilius Namatianus expressed disgust and resentment (*Vitae sophistarum* 6.11; *De reditu suo* 1.439f., 515f.). Emperors legislated against monks' privilege and disorder (*C.Th.* 9.40.16, 16.3.1f.). Popes deplored their clerical ambition (Siricius, *Ep.* 13 (17); Celestine, *Ep.* 4.2, 7).

The Arian controversy, which coincided with the first monastic developments, forged a fateful link between ascetics and church authorities. In Egypt, and later in Palestine (in connection with the Christological controversies of the 5th century), bishops wished to harness to both their theological causes and their pastoral endeavors the prestige and growing population of ascetic settlements and communities. Large crowds of monks could rally, often with violence, in defense of theories or reputations: thus Athanasius attempted to co-opt Antony and Pachomius, Theophilus the ascetics of Nitria and Scetis, Cyril his henchmen against Orestes in 415 and Nestorius in 431. The pattern was repeated in Jerusalem, vis-à-vis Sabas, and in Antioch under Severus. Jacob Baradaeus rallied Monophysites in the 540s very largely with monastic followers.

Admirers brought wealth. Generosity, like that of the two Melaniae in the 370s and 420s, while viewed with some suspicion, fostered the growth of extensive foundations, many of them urban, and exposed monks to the accusation of greed and pride. Ascetic literature adopted, on that account, a tone of both fear and anxiety: fear that property would undermine virtue; anxiety that opportunities to help others might be squandered by indiscriminate rejection.

Once monasteries in the fullest sense became more common, lay patrons and imperial officials displayed increasing interest. Here was a way to enhance one's reputation, impede the alienation caused by wealth, and secure the profitable and orderly development of rural estates. Those ambitious for ecclesiastical advancement learned that a display of ascetic virtue, combined with more practical qualities, might strengthen their candidacy for episcopal office.

Monastic texts were part of this development. They were designed to be read by the elite, frequently urban and lay. The world they described—particularly its remoteness and extravagance—reflected literary convention as much as informed travel. While learning about desert "athletes," the reader was surrounded by urban establishments, or by moral enthusiasts who continued to live alongside their more measured fellow citizens. An act of the imagination was demanded, more than literal imitation. Only when the structures of erudite and established classicism began to decline did ascetics take more literally, in the days of Gregory of Tours or Columbanus, and more rarely in the east, the remote settings and vigorous self-denial of spiritual classics like those of Cassian.

BIBL.: Derwas J. Chitty, *The Desert a City* (Oxford, 1966; repr. London, 1977). Gilbert Dagron, "L'ombre d'un doute," *Dumbarton Oaks Papers* 46 (1992): 59–68. E. D. Hunt, *Holy Land Pilgrimage in the Later Roman Empire* (Oxford, 1982; repr. 1984). E. A. Judge, "The Earliest Use of Monachos for 'Monk' (P. Coll. Youtie 77) and the Origins of Monasticism," *Jahrbuch für Antike und Christentum* 20 (1977): 72–89. Evelyne Patlagean, "Ancienne hagiographie byzantine et histoire sociale," *Annales* 23 (1968): 106–126; Eng. trans.: "Ancient Byzantine Hagiography and Social History," in *Saints and Their Cults,* ed. Stephen Wilson, trans. Jane Hodgkin (Cambridge, Eng., 1983), 101–121.   P.R.

Monks, Status of

Monks were at first lay persons who chose an ascetic lifestyle, living either alone, in a small group, or in communities, and who applied words such as *monachos* to themselves. One of the first monks, the Egyptian Antony (ca. 251–356), was praised by the bishop of Alexandria, Athanasius, for his devotion to asceticism and to fighting with demons. Thus the church of Alexandria not only recognized this Christian way of life but it also publicized it via a biography of Antony, soon translated from Greek into Latin.

Unlike consecrated virgins, who received a veil and a blessing from the bishop and who had a special status in the church as members of the *ordo virginum,* monks had no official ceremony to mark their adoption of a monastic lifestyle. It was a private choice. Vows did not exist, yet being a monk required chastity and ascetic practices to achieve some control over the body's appetites. Ascetic practices were up to them, as were their poverty and association with a monastic group. Marriage, however, was forbidden by church authorities. Civil law condemned those who ravished consecrated maidens (*C.Th.* 9.25.1–3) and tried to marry them.

The first civil laws mentioning monks were not very favorable to their lifestyle. In the east, around the 270s, the emperor Valens condemned the "devotees of idleness" who had deserted their civic duties to join a band of monks (*C.Th.* 12.1.61). In the west, at the same time, the emperor Valentinian condemned both clerics and monks *(continentes)* who had visited widows and orphans hoping for gifts or legacies, and nullified any such transactions (*C.Th.* 16.2.20). Civil law especially was aimed at preventing monastic dwellings from becoming refuges for criminals and fugitive slaves. Monastic regulators such as Pachomius and Basil of Caesarea also insisted that no one be accepted in a monastic community if he was fleeing from tax collectors, judges, or a master.

Monks came from different social and cultural backgrounds, but in many regions of the eastern Roman empire, they were mostly peasants. Their growing number and their involvement with church politics created troubles in some cities. They were sent back to their "deserts" by the emperor Theodosius in 390 and by the Council of Chalcedon in 451. They were also placed under the control of bishops. In the west, monasticism was adopted by members of aristocratic families, or by clerics who modeled their ascetic lifestyle on what they knew of the Desert Fathers' experience. In the 4th century, monasticism came under harsh criticism for taking away members of the aristocracy who thus did not produce heirs for their family or take part in administering the cities or provinces. The aristocrats' sale of their properties at the time of their monastic conversion was also seen as disruptive. Paulinus of Nola and Melania the Younger, to cite just two cases, were criticized for adopting a monastic lifestyle. The Council of Saragossa in 380 criticized clerics who left their duties to become monks; this criticism, however, gave way to a recognition of the spiritual value of a life devoted to prayer and asceticism. In the 5th century, Christian families started giving some of their children to monastic institutions or promised them to a virginal life to ensure their salvation and attract God's blessings to the whole family. This practice was controversial, especially because the children had no freedom of choice, and in 458 Emperor Majorian forbade maidens to receive the veil of consecrated virgins before the age of forty (*Nov.Major.* 6).

Christians of the 5th and 6th centuries tended to grant a high value to monastic life among all the possible Christian lifestyles. Many monks were venerated as saints. Some monks became bishops and maintained their attachment to monastic practices throughout their life. Monks evolved from a marginal status to playing a central role in many areas. In the 6th and 7th centuries, monks were sent as missionaries, for example to Britain and central Asia. Major monastic centers, such as those of the stylites Symeon the Elder and Symeon the Younger attracted many visitors, not only Christians but also pagans and, later, Muslims. Hermits' cells, convents, and monasteries dotted the landscape. In cities, monks were taking care of houses for the poor and for the pilgrims. The figure of the monk and nun was a familiar and respected one in Christian societies of the early Middle Ages. In the Byzantine empire, some monks still came under attack for their attachment to one or the other Christian theology, but their status was not challenged, except during the period of the first iconoclasm, when some Byzantine monks were persecuted for their veneration of images.

This persecution, however, reinforced the position of monasticism in the post-iconoclasm Byzantine society, for monks and nuns had been the true keepers of orthodoxy. In the west, monks and nuns suffered from wars and warlords. Their status in society, however, was greatly enhanced by the support of aristocratic families who wished to have some of their children pray for their kin, supervise family properties offered to the monastery, and rule over a large community. As literate and learned figures, monks and nuns gained respect and some prominence in early medieval societies, including in the Muslim empire, where they played a major role in translating Greek medical and philosophical texts into Syriac and Arabic.

BIBL.: Jean Gaudemet, *L'eglise dans l'empire romain (IVe-Ve siècles)* (Paris, 1958). S. Hackel, *The Byzantine Saint* (London, 1981). Adalbert de Vogüé, *Histoire littéraire du mouvement monastique dans l'antiquité*, 3 vols. (Paris, 1991-1996).

B.C.

Monophysites

Monophysitism (from *monos* and *phusis*) is the doctrine of the one and single nature of Christ. It emerged from the theological problem of expressing in linguistic terms the mystery of the unity of divinity and humanity in Christ.

Those who opposed the terminological teachings of the Council of Chalcedon (451) and held to the *mia phusis* formula of Cyril of Alexandria were called Monophysites only from the 7th century. But in this context the term is technically incorrect and misleading. These are four possible ways of understanding Christ in terms of one principle of nature: (1) divinity and humanity are mixed into a third nature; (2) humanity is the principle of union, and divinity is absorbed into it; (3) divinity is the principle of union, and humanity is absorbed into it; (4) there is one united nature with a dynamic continued existence of divinity and humanity. Usually the third version is labeled as Monophysitism, although technically the first two models also follow the same logic. From a theological point of view the fourth version may not be called Monophysitism. Thus, current research differentiates real Monophysites from Miaphysites. Real Monophysites follow one of the first three possibilities indicated above; for them (Arius, Apollinarius), the union creates a *tertium quid*. Eutyches is the representative of the third model, classical Monophysitism. Miaphysites follow the fourth view, which expresses the unity of Christ with the *mia physus* Christology of Cyril and not with the Chalcedonian theology. Since G. S. Assemani (1687–1768), theologians have tried to distinguish Miaphysites from the Eutychians. They are also called verbal Monophysites, Diplophysites (C. D. G. Müller), or Henophysites (S. P. Brock).

In 428–431, in the course of his arguments against Nestorius, who was accused of separating the divine and human natures of Christ, Cyril (412–444) used texts that circulated under the names of Athanasius and the popes Julius and Felix but were Apollinarianist forgeries. Therefore the terminology employed in them could only evoke misunderstanding and disturb theologians like Nestorius, who struggled against Apollinarianism. But Cyril used the main Apollinarianist formula, "one incarnate nature of the Word of God," in an orthodox way. Further, he realized that the incarnation was not merely an apparent unity of divinity and humanity but a real and ontological, physical or hypostatic union.

Theodosius II (408–450) was concerned about peace in the empire and convoked a Council at Ephesus (431). In tumultuous circumstances Nestorius was excommunicated, and the second letter of Cyril to Nestorius was regarded as the true expression of the Christian faith according to the Creed of Nicaea (325). This council resulted in a schism between the patriarchates of Antioch and Alexandria.

Discussions in following years led to a Christological agreement, the so-called Formula of Union (433). But the terminology was still not precise enough to avoid misinterpretations of the faith in Christ. The attitude of defensiveness against Nestorianism led to the teachings of the archimandrite Eutyches, rightly called "Monophysitism," although his Christology is not entirely clear. Eutyches simplifies Cyril's doctrine. For him, Cyril's understanding of unity seems to mean the absorption of humanity into divinity.

Both Patriarch Flavian of Constantinople (446–449) and Pope Leo the Great (440–461) condemned Eutyches. Because of the influence of the archimandrite at the emperor's court, another council was convoked by Theodosius II at Ephesus (449). With Dioscorus of Alexandria (444–457) in the chair, Eutyches was rehabilitated and Flavian excommunicated. Further, Dioscorus did not proclaim the Christological teachings of Leo (Tomus Leonis). This caused the pope to call this council a "Robber Council" (Latrocinium).

After the death of Theodosius, his sister Pulcheria and her husband, Marcian, convoked the Council at Chalcedon (451). Dioscorus, the successor of Cyril, was deposed but not condemned as a heretic, and Flavian was reinstalled. The deposition of the most powerful patriarch in the east was a scandalous act for the Alexandrine party. Since the deposition took place on the initiative of the papal legate Paschasinus, it seems to have been revenge for ignoring the Tome of Leo at the synod of 449. The rivalries between the patriarchates of Rome, Constantinople, and Alexandria constitute the background of the theological controversy.

Originally it was not planned to formulate another symbolum alongside those of Nicaea (325) and Constantinople (381). But at the urgent request of the imperial couple, the council fathers tried to draft a new and clearer formula of faith. "Two natures in one person and hypostasis" was the Chalcedonian attempt to express the unity and the distinction of the perfect divinity and perfect humanity of Christ. One group of bishops, those from the Alexandrine and Antiochene patriarchate in particular, saw the true faith endangered by formula. For them, it betrayed the Christology of Cyril. Furthermore, the council did not clarify the important but controversial terms phusis and hupostasis. This was accomplished only in the post-Chalcedonian period.

After the council the anti-Chalcedonian theology was elaborated by Philoxenus of Mabbug, Jacob of Sarug, Peter the Iberian, Timothy Aelurus, Theodosius of Alexandria, and especially Severus of Antioch. For more than half a century, it was not clear whether the Chalcedonian or the anti-Chalcedonian movement would predominate.

Imperial political policy strove to restore the unity of the church but employed insufficient means: the Encyclion of the usurper Basiliscos (475), the Henoticon of Emperor Zeno (476), and the Typos of Emperor Anastasius (511–512), which was created under the influence of Severus. At the end of the 5th and the beginning of the 6th century the Christian east was dominated by the Miaphysites. Characteristics of the anti-Chalcedonian movement were the rejection of the Council of Chalcedon and the Tome of Leo and adherence to the Henoticon. During this period, extreme Monophysite positions—Eutychians/Phantasiasts, Akephaloi/Aposchistai, Aphtartodocetae (Julian of Halicarnassus)—split from the Miaphysite movement.

After 518, under the emperors Justin and Justinian, a Chalcedonian restoration took place, and opponents of the council were persecuted. The tumultuous theological struggle, the rivalries of the patriarchates, and the imperial political policy led to the schism. Even the early 6th century theology of mediation, the so-called Neo-Chalcedonianism (Scythian monks, Nephalius, John Grammaticus, John of Skythopolis, Leontius of Jerusalem), and the Council of Constantinople (553) failed to reconcile the dogmatic conflicts.

Severus had already given impulse to the ordination of Miaphysite clergy (Jōhannàn von Tellā). Under the protection of Empress Theodora, the exiled Patriarch Theodosius of Alexandria (535–566) ordained two bishops: Theodore of Arabia, who worked among the Ghassanids in the Syrian desert and the Transjordan territory, and Jacob Baradaeus, who ordained many priests and bishops on his way from Syria to Isauria. This became the basis for an anti-Chalcedonian church organization.

Today the five Miaphysite churches are called the Oriental Orthodox churches: Coptic Orthodox, Syrian Orthodox, Armenian Apostolic, Ethiopian Orthodox, and Malankara Orthodox Syrian.

BIBL.: Pauline Allen, "Monophysiten," *Theologische Realenzyklopädie,* vol. 23 (Berlin, 1994), 219–233. Alois Grillmeier, *Christ in Christian Tradition,* vol. 1, 2nd rev. ed. (London, 1975); vol. 2, pt. 1 (London, 1987); vol. 2, pt. 2 (London and Louisville, 1995); vol. 2, pt. 4 (London and Louisville, 1996). Dietmar W. Winkler, *Koptische Kirche und Reichskirche: Analyse des Schismas und gegenwärtiger ökumenischer Dialog* (Innsbruck and Vienna, 1997). D.W.W.

Monopolies

In the 19th century, liberal historians gave credence to the planned, monopolistic character that the Dominate, consistent with its political authoritarianism, imposed on economic life. They thus dramatized the importance of state factories and the level of professional connections to guilds. Guilds were believed to constitute two forms of monopolization, in production and in trade. Depending on the particular case, this view needs to be either nuanced or substantially revised.

Like the minting of money (a royal prerogative), commercial monopolies were not new. Some, such as the monopoly on salt, went back to the origins of the Roman state; others, such as those on alum and saltpeter and on papyrus, preexisted the Roman conquest of the provinces that produced them. In the 4th century, the state established the monopoly on purple dye by extending the system already in place in Egypt. At the same time, in 338–339, the monopoly's artisans of and dealers in purple clothing *qui devotioni nostrae deserviunt* coexisted with those working on their own behalf. The former enjoyed exemptions of *munera*, as did "state transporters" of the civic *annona (navicularii qui annonae urbis serviunt).* That duality was also found later among those who fished for the purple-yielding murex shellfish, though the tax bureau exerted its control even on independent fishermen and artisans.

The clearest development of a monopoly was in silk, but that was an important product, subject to the particular system of foreign trade. In fact, the late imperial state, wishing to ban individual access to the borders and to draw an optimal profit from customs duties, progressively acquired tools that allowed it to exert exclusive control over international trade (though without any protectionist intention). The state set in place an extremely limited number of *commercia*, points through which entering and departing merchandise had to pass. It was within this framework that the monopoly on the purchase of silk was established under the Valentinians; the silk monopoly was therefore unrelated to the economic centralism commonly attributed to the tetrarchy. In addition, domestic and foreign policy were important economic considerations: domestically, the imperial authorities wanted exclusive rights over the distribution of largesse; externally, they faced a confrontation with Persia. The *comes commerciorum*, civil servants who centralized the purchasing system, were in a strong position to negotiate favorable prices. In the 6th century, the *kommerkiarioi* (apparently monopoly farmers) took their place. The system

then fragmented into regional jurisdictions, and the *kommerkia* were taken over by the state in 730. In the meantime, the activities of the *kommerkiarioi* had probably been transferred to silk produced within the empire. The silk monopoly thus no longer operated solely to exact customs duties but was still used to raise revenues.

As for domestic commerce, the monopolies denounced by Leo in a law of 473 are described as agreements between merchants to impose minimum prices, with the complicity of provincial authorities. They resembled agreements among workers in certain trades to impose a minimum wage. Procopius accused Justinian of systematically violating the law: even if we give due allowance to exaggeration, it seems that Peter Barsymes, then in charge of imperial finances, systematically used this type of monopoly to increase state revenues, perhaps by charging licensing fees on commercial transactions.

The theory of the "monopolistic late empire" would seem to be more solidly supported in the realm of public factories, the creation of which has been vaguely attributed to the tetrarchy. Yet in the case of weapons factories *(fabricae),* far from replacing private artisanal production, as was believed, they in fact took the place of another form of state production: the workshop that was part of the classical legion, and which did not survive after the legions were dismantled. A monopoly on weapons fabrication was not established before Justinian *(Nov.* 85). The sources also demonstrate the high number of employees in the public textile shops *(gynaecea, linyphia),* which catered to official needs but never succeeded in satisfying them. These shops were probably created over a long period of time, becoming more visible under the tetrarchy because of the growing number of capital cities. Another production sector believed to have been incorporated into the state economy, the sector in charge of fabricating silver objects to be distributed by imperial largesse—as gifts or supplementary wages—may in fact have functioned primarily through public orders passed on to private silversmiths. And although there were court goldsmiths, they were not new for the period (Delmaire). All in all, the state's interest in this area of production was more financial than economic. Moreover, production did not even cover all the state's needs or extend beyond areas of state consumption (army supplies, public construction, imperial largesse). It was only in a few sectors that goods were sold back to the public: traditional "monopoly products" (noted above), silk, certain mineral products, and, above all, the share of *annona* goods not distributed free of charge.

In what is in fact a metaphorical use of the phrase, some have claimed that by vastly extending the realm of public property *(res privata),* the state exercised a quasi monopoly on production and redistribution in such sectors as Spanish or African oil. One should not imagine, however, that this public domain functioned as a state-run sector of production, since its management was linked to private patrimonies. Hence, the growth of olive production was due to state *conductores*, more and more often emphyteutic quasi owners without the title, seeking to increase the benefits of exploitation by marketing products. Another sector of the *res privata* was mines and quarries: here, the late empire seems to have retained the previous system under which mines belonging to the state coexisted with mines that were the property of individuals. The same was true for quarries, though imperial lands continued to exploit the most prestigious of them, directly or as concessions. Private quarries had to pay a *vectigal*, which should be understood as a production tax and not as rent paid to the owner state. Among imperial quarries, Fant distinguishes between those where production was monopolized by the emperor and those that, from the beginning, were exploited principally for commercial ends (Euboean cipolin and Proconnesus marble). A third category might be added: those that were worked both for the emperor's unique needs (sarcophagi and porphyry statues) and for the free market (the other uses of porphyry). All in all, then, there is practically no economic area about which one can say that state monopolies occasioned the disappearance of private activities.

BIBL.: Roland Delmaire, *Largesses sacrées et res privata: L'aerarium impérial et son administration du IVe au VIe siècle* (Rome, 1989). Clayton Fant, "Ideology, Gift, and Trade: A Distribution Model for the Roman Imperial Marbles," in *The Inscribed Economy: Production and Distribution in the Roman Empire in the Light of instrumentum domesticum*, ed. W. V. Harris (Ann Arbor, 1993), 45–170.   J.C.

Montanists

The term *Montanists* denotes a 2nd century movement whose founders Montanus, Prisc(ill)a, and Maximilla proclaimed prophetic revelations received from the Holy Spirit. They demanded the renewal of existing Christian practices through asceticism, celibacy, martyrdom, and penitence. Accordingly, the movement, which originated ca. 170 in Ardabau in Phrygia (Asia Minor), called itself the New Prophecy; its detractors referred to it as the Phrygian Prophecy. The term *Montanists* is a 4th century creation first used by Cyril of Jerusalem in ca. 350 (*Catechesis* 16), following the tradition of denoting heresies by the name of their founder.

One of our main sources concerning the Montanists is Eusebius's *Ecclesiastical History*. Eusebius attests that early opposition to the movement was caused principally by the form in which prophecy was experienced. Its earliest opponent, Bishop Apollinarius of Hierapolis, took action when it became clear that Montanus "was carried away as by the spirit, and suddenly experienced some kind of possession, and spurious ecstasy . . . and began to speak" (Eusebius,

Hist.eccl. 5.16.7). As other 2nd and 3rd century authors, such as Tertullian, reveal, the nature of prophecy—whether or not it should occur in ecstasy, and whether or not it should occur at all—was widely debated at the time. The geographical distribution of Montanist tendencies during the period, from Phrygia to Rome (Can. *Mur.*; Eusebius, *Hist.eccl.* 2.25.5–7), Gaul (Eusebius, *Hist.eccl.* 5.3.3–4), Africa (Tertullian [after 207], *Passio Perpetuae*), and Alexandria (Clement *Strom.* 4.13.93.1 and 7.17.108), attests to strong sentiments in favor of continuing ecstatic prophecy, even though it was ultimately condemned as heretical.

Some of Montanus, Maximilla, and Prisc(ill)a's prophetic utterings have been preserved. The content of these oracles was eschatological and apocalyptic, drawing on the Johannine tradition, especially the Book of Revelation. They predicted the imminent coming of the bridegroom and demanded personal rigor appropriate to the severity of the situation while also stressing the role of the prophet as a mere vessel transmitting divine revelations.

The 4th and 5th century notices regarding Montanists confirm the continuity of these theological tendencies, and indicate an increase in the literal interpretation of passages from Revelation. Thus, followers of the later prophetess Quintilla considered the Phrygian village Pepuza as the site of the second coming. Epiphanius (*Panarion* 48.49), Pacian of Barcelona (*Ep.* 1.1, *PL* 13.1053), and Sozomen (*Hist.eccl.* 7.18–19) describe variations in the liturgy, the calendar, and penitentiary practices reflecting a concretization of Revelation's millenarian expectations.

At the same time, writings attacking the Montanists increased in severity. Thus, beginning again with Cyril of Jerusalem, Montanists are accused of ritual child murder, sometimes by "pierc[ing] a child, just an infant, throughout its whole body with bronze needles" (Epiphanius, *Panarion* 48.15), and pagan associations.

However, despite their long history of being accused of heresy, Montanists persevered. By the 4th century their hierarchy was well developed and included a patriarch, male and female bishops, presbyters, deacons and *koinōnoi*, or companions (of the Lord) (Jerome, *Ep.* 41.3; Epiphanius, *Panarion* 49.2; Sozomen, *Hist.eccl.* 7.19.2). A sizable number of 3rd through 5th century inscriptions from western central Anatolia (Apameia, Sebaste, Temenothyrai, Appia, Pepouza [?], and Hierapolis; the Phrygian highlands, the territory of Dionysopolis, the Upper Tembris Valley [?]; and Lydian Philadelphia and surroundings, with a slight majority of them in urban settings versus rural) confirm their continuity. Notices grow faint after Justinian; the last significant testimony is by John of Ephesus (*Hist.eccl.* 3.20.32, ca. 580).

BIBL.: S. Gero, "Montanus and Montanism according to a Medieval Syriac Source," *Journal of Theological Studies* n.s. 28 (1977): 520–524. R. E. Heine, *The Montanist Oracles and Testimonia* (Macon, Ga., 1989). W. Tabbernee, "Remnants of the New Prophecy: Literary and Epigraphical Sources of the Montanist Movement," *Studia patristica* 21 (1989): 193–201. A. Strobel, *Das heilige Land der Montanisten* (Berlin, 1980). C. Trevett, *Montanism: Gender, Authority, and the New Prophecy* (Cambridge, Eng., 1996).   S.E.

Mosaics, Ecclesiastical

The great church-building era that started in post-Constantinian times launched the mosaic technique as a choice means for creating a highly polychrome, versatile, and sturdy frame for large gatherings.

Early Christian mosaics on floors have survived in much greater numbers and better condition than those on walls, of which relatively complete series have been preserved only in Italy. Pavement mosaics are set in different layers of mortar, the finest being the top one, which is the setting bed of the mostly square tesserae, cut out of mainly stone and some pottery or glass paste for certain less natural colors, such as bright blues, greens, reds, and orange.

The relatively new Roman technique of wall and vault mosaics used a much greater quantity of glass cubes, of smaller dimensions, set in plaster mortar. Each of them could be differently tilted so as to catch the light. Wall panels could be prepared in the workshop and then installed.

In 4th and early 5th century mosaics, gold (in fact a sandwich of gold leaf between two unequal layers of protective glass) was used mainly to heighten special details and zones. The gold background that situated all figures in an abstract, spiritual, otherworldly space of pure brightness would not be used systematically until the 7th century. In the meantime backgrounds remained a classical white or were superpositions of bands of landscape or color, such as the intense harmony of blues around the figures of the enthroned Christ, the two churches, and the apostles in the mosaic in the apse of S. Pudenziana in Rome.

The main apse of a church was reserved for the representation of Christ, God, and Man, and the axial image was a theophany. This central iconographical theme, common to the whole early Christian world, was adapted to local circumstances. Thus in the Church of St. Catherine in Sinai (Justinianic period), a building that commemorates Moses' local encounters with God, the apse carries the only New Testament theophany in which Moses plays a part: the transfiguration scene. The apse of Ravenna's S. Vitale (546–548) is a different type of witness to local history: a model of this round church is presented by its founder, the bishop of the city, to the enthroned apocalyptic Christ, who, with his right hand, crowns the local martyr saint, Vitalis. Jesus' movement can be read as extending down to the panel where Justinian is shown with the victorious army that has just reconquered Italy and with those that assisted him in the building of the monument. On the opposite wall of the sanctuary

he and his wife, the empress Theodora, carry offerings of costly golden vessels: their gift to the church treasury—and, beyond it, to God—is thus commemorated. On the hem of Theodora's cloak are pictured the offerings of the three Magi to the child Jesus; they represent a typological reference, the prefiguration of all gifts to the Christian authority. Thus, the meaning of the figured wall and vault mosaics in a church is not only in the scene featured; it is generated by the interaction between a local message and the general iconographical system, and by both the structural function of each surface and the liturgical function of each space.

The longitudinal perspective of the prevailing basilican architecture conditioned the layout of floor and wall decorations. Either long, rectangular compositions or series of more or less square panels were used to accompany worshipers in their progress toward the sanctuary. The encompassing character of a conch or dome gave a cosmic meaning to the vertex figures, embracing both the viewer and the universe. Bishops or Church Fathers illustrated on narrow strips of wall, as though standing between or under arches or windows, acted as true "pillars" of the Christian community, their frontality establishing a direct spatial relation with the beholder.

The liturgical function of a specific area inside the church is most obvious in the space around the altar. This is the place where, during each mass celebration, both the institution of the Eucharist, with the offering of bread and wine at Jesus' and his disciples' Last Supper, and the sacrifice of his death on the Cross are commemorated. In S. Maria Maggiore in Rome the nave wall panel (432–440) that has survived nearest the altar represents the offering of loaves and wine by Abraham and Melchisedech (scenes from the lives of Abraham and Jacob on the left wall, facing the apse; on the right wall: lives of Moses and Joshua; triumphal arch with majestic glorification of Mary and Jesus in scenes of Christ's childhood). In S. Apollinare Nuovo in Ravenna, near the altar, the Cana wedding is shown, where the water was turned into wine (lefthand cycle, of Jesus' public life) opposite the Last Supper (right wall, Passion cycle). S. Vitale's sanctuary walls are covered, on both sides of the altar, with sacrificial prefigurations: the offerings of Abel and Melchisdech, brought together in a strikingly symbolic anachronism, Abraham and Sarah offering their hospitality to their three visiting messengers, and Abraham raising his knife over his only son, Isaac. The Ravenna mosaics may be qualified as Byzantine in their style—their solemn frontality, ample gestures, tension of captive movement, majestic monumentality of figures—but they are western and Roman in their iconography and their liturgical inspiration.

The growing use of mosaics for large church pavements promoted carpetlike compositions and tackled such different layout challenges as semicircular apse spaces and series of symmetrical intercolumnar panels.

The layout evolved from the 4th century design of numerous "carpets" containing many-paneled, small-scale systems with geometric filling or one animal or flower to large-scale carpets and scenes and a final profusion of interlacing and interlooping designs.

In church mosaics, epigraphy and ornament share the surface with figures. Of the great number of inscriptions, most, in east and west, are commemorative of the setting and are of a votive character; they give precious information on church and clerical organization, dimensions and costs of surfaces donated, architectural vocabulary, and some liturgical formulas. The holiness of the church or sanctuary space may be signaled by crosses, Solomon's knots, or an appropriate biblical quotation on a threshold or bay panel.

The basic repertoire of profuse geometrical and vegetal ornament (fruit, vegetables, trees, and flowers in garlands and bouquets, found especially in North Africa) may be enlivened by other iconographical motifs: innumerable vases and baskets, personified seasons and months, shown with their produce (Aquileia [south basilica], Delphi, Qabr Hiram, Deir es-Sleib, Gerasa), birds, animals, and scenes of country life (mainly in the eastern Mediterranean) that never lose the lively, naturalistic character of their Graeco-Roman antecedents. Such biblical themes as Jonas (Beit Jibrin, Khirbet Beit Loya, Furna, Aquileia), the Golden Age according to Isaiah 11:7 (Ma'in, Khirbet el-Mekhayet, Korykos, Ayash, Karlik), Noah (Apollonia [east church], Misis), Adam in paradise (northern Syria [Huarte], Copenhagen Museum, Cleveland Museum), and the ram caught in the bush near Isaac's sacrifice (Madaba, Masouh), all inspired by the Hebrew Bible, never the New Testament, owe their presence to their link with the animal world. The four rivers of paradise, though particularly adequate for decorating baptisteries, also mark the four directions of certain church floors (Tegea, Madaba, Sobata, Qaṣr el-Lebia).

Nowhere is the choice of figures as broad and rich as in the Near East, where large "animated landscape" mosaic carpets became fashionable in the mid-5th century. Occasionally fragmented into smaller panels or set inside vegetal scrolls, some of their scenes of everyday life are set on the banks of the Nile (Cyrene Cathedral). Examples of such landscapes in the west, such as in Catania, St. Maria des Ports on Majorca, or in Aquileia's southern basilica, are isolated and are possibly eastern imports.

A group of Transjordanian floors, characterized by their large images of cities and conspicuous buildings (Gerasa: St. Peter and Paul and St. John the Baptist; Ma'in, Umm er-Rasas/Kastron Mephaa: St. Stephen and Church of the Lions; Khirbet Samra: Large Church) seem quite specifically to picture the world of Christian faith, "the Holy Land," sanctified through time by events from biblical and church history.

This iconography is to be understood in relation to eastern Christian mystical symbolism, according to which each church is a microcosm. The church pavement figures the terrestrial world, more or less organically consistent but perfectly clear in the Madaba church pavement map, where Jerusalem is in its center. From this ground level rises an ordered hierarchy up to the higher zones of the church building. In the main apses of the Cyprus churches of Kiti and Lythrankomi (6th–7th century) are early mosaic examples of the theophany that will gradually impose itself in the system of mature Byzantine architectural decoration, dominated by the central dome: they carry a glorious Mary, "Mother of God," the perfect intermediary, in whom indeed the earthly and the heavenly meet.

BIBL.: Elisabeth Alföldi-Rosenbaum and John Ward-Perkins, *Justinianic Mosaic Pavements in Cyrenaican Churches* (Rome, 1980). Pauline Donceel-Voûte, *Les pavements des églises byzantines de la Syrie et du Liban: Décor, archéologie et liturgie* (Louvain-la-Neuve, 1988). Milagros Guardia Pons, *Los mosaicos de la antigüedad tardía en Hispania* (Barcelona, 1992). Walter Oakeshott, *The Mosaics of Rome from the Third to the Fourteenth Centuries* (London, 1967). Michele Piccirillo, *The Mosaics of Jordan* (Amman, 1993). Marie Spiro, *Critical Corpus of the Mosaic Pavements on the Greek Mainland, 4th–6th Centuries* (New York, 1978). P.D.V.

Mosaics, Secular

The process of administrative partition and economic reforms initiated by Diocletian and continued by his successors coincided, paradoxically, with some new artistic phenomena of quite the opposite nature. In many of the arts of this period, and in mosaics in particular, there is perceptible the beginning of a gradual abandonment of regional styles and the emergence of what can be called a new style that, in the course of successive centuries, would characterize in ever stronger ways the art of late antiquity and the Byzantine period. In this crucial period of change, the east of the empire (Syria, Cyprus, Asia Minor) was still strongly permeated by the Hellenistic mosaic tradition of pictures in the floor, that is, considering the floor as a space to be decorated in an illusionistic way by placing emblemata panels within a geometric "carpet." The subjects were predominantly mythological. In the west, regional styles were more pronounced. In central Italy there continued, though to a much lesser degree, black and white mosaics either with a wide range of subjects set on a neutral background and arranged in free compositions encompassing the whole surface of the floor or with geometric patterns. Mosaics in the north of Italy as well as the northern provinces (Gaul, Germany, Britain) are characterized by the predominance of polychrome geometric compositions favoring rigid division of the floor design into regular compartments filled (or not) with figure insets. The Iberian Peninsula was exposed to these two styles, the Italian and the northern, and to a third, from North Africa. Economically more prosperous than the rest of the empire, the North African provinces developed their own regional style that may be characterized by a preference for strong polychromy and specific subjects, such as scenes of country life on large estates (latifundia cycles), hunts, amphitheaters, genre scenes, animals, and marine scenes, without, however, rejecting mythological subjects. Also, specific compositions were favored: in registers, in circular patterns, or with free distribution of large-scale figures in all-over designs, the figures being conceived as independent decorative elements. The concept of the floor, which was considered as a unified whole, was purely decorative (e.g., the mosaics in Smirat, amphitheater scenes; Batten Zammour, athletic games; Althiburos, hunting scenes; Carthage, Dominus Iulius mosaic; El Djem, Dionysus and beasts; Tina, Arion mosaic; Hippo Regius, hunting scenes). There is also perceptible a gradual abandonment of space and depth and a plastic style in the rendering of figures in favor of a more linear one. After the Vandal conquest and in the following period of Byzantine reconquest in the 6th century, only a few floors, generally of lower quality, testify to this. Sporadic mosaics executed in the Roman tradition are also known from the early Arab period, for instance in the Aghlabit Palace at Raqqada.

In the east, taking Antioch mosaics as the most characteristic, the 4th and most of the 5th century floor decorations are dominated by abstract geometric designs with a strong emphasis on the unity of the floor. Polychrome "carpets" were created that might also include flat figure motifs. Later they also included animals, birds, or floral ornaments arranged in repeated patterns, or flowers replaced geometric elements, creating instead a floral framework. These are genuinely local inventions of Syrian ateliers. Geometric floors with animal and bird insets (or, more rarely, human insets) in the form of small panels spread over the whole surface characterized for long centuries mosaics in Greece and the Balkans, both in sacral and secular buildings.

In the second half of the 5th century and in the 6th century and later, there appeared in Syria, Palestine, and Asia Minor new types of mosaic compositions and subjects. The latter are well exemplified by the hunting and animal pavements in Antioch, Apamea, and, especially, Constantinople (Great Palace). These are free-figure compositions in which figures and elements of landscape are disposed without special depth over the whole surface, against a flat neutral background and according to compositional schemes known already from North Africa (registers, long friezes, circular compositions). In the east, however, such compositions are not mere replicas of North African designs. They are more carefully arranged, more balanced. The figures are not copies of earlier, often awkward models but are rendered according to the Hellenistic tradition, more elegant and better proportioned. Another phe-

nomenon is the reappearance in the late 5th and in the 6th century in Syria and Asia Minor (earlier in Nea Paphos in Cyprus: Villa of Theseus, House of Aion) of large pictures, sort of pseudo-emblemata within rich vegetal or geometric frames, or both. They are deprived of true illusionistic settings, and often become two-dimensional (mosaic of Meleager and Atalante in Apamea; mosaic from the Hippolytos Hall in Madaba). As much as mosaic floors become rare in Syria, from the end of the sixth century, they continued in the south, in the area of modern Jordan. Mosaics with hunting scenes and animal subjects freely spread or set within geometric frameworks are found in houses of the wealthy well into the Arab period (Madaba, Qaṣr al-Hallabat, and elsewhere).

The abandonment of illusionistic settings in space and a stress on ornamental aspects of design and strong polychromy, relatively free compositions, and the symbolic value of the representation, as well as a preference for specific realistic subjects, are expressions of a style that eventually was used throughout the late empire. Many aspects of the style spreading in the east were found earlier (4th century) in other areas of the empire besides North Africa, in Rome for instance (hunting mosaics from Esquiline); in Piazza Armerina; in Ravenna (the so-called Palace of Theoderic); gladiatorial scenes from Torre Nuova); in the Balkans (hunting scenes in Gamzigrad). Sporadically they appear in Gaul (Lillebone, mythological and hunting scenes; Blanzy-les-Fismes, Orpheus; Avenches, hunting scenes and Orpheus mosaic) and in Germany (Cologne, amphitheater scenes). They reveal either the direct influence of or inspiration by the North African style. In Italy just as in Gaul, such mosaics coexist with traditional ones made along old local schemes but often with new subject matter. Especially rich in examples of the new style are Spanish mosaics of the 4th and 5th centuries, for example in Merida (El Hinojal, hunting scenes; Calle Masona, circus scenes; Holguin, symposion, circus scenes); Toledo (port and maritime scenes). Perhaps the most outstanding are the hunting and mythological mosaics in Villa de la Olmeda. All these floors coexist with pavements decorated along traditional lines influenced by earlier schemes from Italy and Gaul. However, the taste for free compositions, strong polychromy, megalographic representations, and specific subject matter is documented until the period of Visigothic domination.

The new style is not just an expression of close links between the Iberian Peninsula and North Africa or the activity of African mosaicists in Spain. As in the east, it reflects deep social changes, and the aspirations and interests of the ever richer and more powerful landowners, who favored the new style in their country and town residences. It became a sort of "class style" that found appreciation in Byzantine and medieval palaces as well.

BIBL.: K. M. D. Dunbabin, *The Mosaics of Roman North*

Africa (Oxford, 1978). J. Balty, *Mosaïques antiques de Syrie* (Brussels, 1977). W. A. Daszewski and D. Michaelides, *Mosaic Floors in Cyprus* (Ravenna, 1988). D. Levi, *Antioch Mosaic Pavements* (Princeton, 1947). K. Parlasca, *Die Römischen Mosaiken in Deutschland* (Berlin, 1959).   W.D.

Moses Khorenats'i

Nothing certain is known about Moses Khorenats'i, author of the most important work in a long tradition of Armenian historical writing. His *History of Armenia* is the most learned Armenian history, in that it draws on the widest range of written sources, and it is important for numerous quotations of ancient poetry and song otherwise lost. First quoted in the early 10th century, it remained unchallenged as a reliable document until the end of the 19th century.

Taking the *Chronicle* of Eusebius of Caesarea as a model and source, in Book 1 Moses linked the descendants of Hayk (the eponymous ancestor of the Armenians) to the sovereigns of the ancient empires and the offspring of Japheth, thus creating an honorable niche for Armenia in world history. In Book 2 he traced the fortunes of Armenia from Alexander the Great down to Trdat (Tiridates IV), the first Christian king of Armenia. Here one of his sources was a now lost Armenian version of the *Jewish War* by Josephus, whose information about Armenia Moses embellished in patriotic fashion. Parallels between Armenians and the Maccabees had been brought out by earlier writers, but Moses postulated an actual Jewish origin for the Bagratuni noble family. Their origin and fame are the real theme of his *History.*

Moses elaborated the earlier account of Trdat's conversion found in Agathangelos by adapting the *Ecclesiastical History* of Socrates and the legendary *Acts of Silvester.* He also emphasized legendary Christian missions to Armenia and made Abgar, the king of Edessa who had supposedly corresponded with Jesus Christ, an Armenian. Bagratid nobles were then given the status of first Christians in Armenia. This emphasis on the Bagratids is pursued more subtly in Book 3, which deals with the 4th and early 5th centuries. Reworking several earlier Armenian sources, Moses downplayed the roles of the Bagratids' rivals. He ends with an account of his own travels to Alexandria and a lament for the death of Mashtots', inventor of the Armenian script.

The claim of Moses Khorenats'i to have been himself a pupil of Mashtots', which would thus place him in the 5th century, conflicts with his use of texts only available much later in Armenian versions, for he did not use the originals. His clear effort to provide a splendid origin for the Bagratids, and the subtle alteration of earlier texts in their favor, point to a time when that family needed antiquarian justification for their new preeminence in the 8th century. The broad sweep of Moses's *History,* its link with Mashtots', the most

famous name in Armenian literature, its interweaving of ancient oral traditions with a wealth of written sources (including Armenian "archives" of dubious authenticity), and the development of legends concerning its author, all ensured it a preeminent place in the annals of Armenian historiography.

A *Geography* of the early 7th century (now ascribed to Ananias of Shirak), a book of rhetoric based on Aphthonius and other Greek sources, and some theological homilies have also been attributed to Moses Khorenats'i.

BIBL.: *Movses Khorenats'i: Patmut'iwn Hayots'*, ed. M. Abeghean and S. Yarut'iwnean (Tbilisi, 1913; repr. with further collations, Erevan, 1991); French trans.: *Histoire de l'Arménie par Moïse de Khoréne,* trans. Annie and Jean-Pierre Mahé (Paris, 1993); Eng. trans.: *Moses Khorenats'i: History of the Armenians,* trans. and commentary by Robert W. Thomson (Cambridge, Mass., 1978).   R.T.

Mosque

Perhaps the only original building type introduced by the Muslims, the mosque reflects in its development the transformation of Islam from a minor reform movement in early 7th century Arabia to a full-fledged empire that influenced and was influenced by the several civilizations it encountered. The word *mosque* is a latinized form of the Arabic word *masjid,* itself borrowed from the Aramaic *msgd'* (place of worship). Etymologically, *masjid* is a place for *sujud* (prostration), an important component of the prayer required of every Muslim five times a day, whether alone or in a group. But *masjid* is also used in the Qur'ān to signify a pre-Islamic place of worship such as a church or a mausoleum, and, with qualifiers, the sacred sanctuaries of Mecca (al-Masjid al-Ḥaram) and Jerusalem (al-Masjid al-Aqṣā).

We know very little about the early mosques. Their model was the House of the Prophet in Medina, built in 622 (1 A.H.), which became known as the Mosque of the Prophet after Muhammad's death. It was an enclosure surrounded by walls made of sun-baked brick on three sides and a series of rooms built for the Prophet's wives on the fourth. Palm trunks were used on the northern side to support a makeshift roof under which the Prophet's followers stood in rows for prayer. When the Prophet changed the direction of prayer *(qibla)* from the north (toward Jerusalem) to the south (toward Mecca) almost a year later, thereby symbolically abandoning the Mosaic *qibla* in favor of the traditional Arabic one, a new prayer area with a hypostyle arrangement of tree trunks was added to the south side of the structure, and the northern portico became a shelter for the poor. The *miḥrāb* and the *minbar,* which came to be considered essential to any mosque, first appeared in simple forms here: the former merely a staff indicating the place in the middle of the *qibla* wall where the Prophet led the prayer, the latter a three-step pulpit where he stood to deliver his sermons.

The House of the Prophet was also the center of social life. People rested there, discussed their daily affairs, settled their disputes, and gathered to listen to the Prophet's teaching. It was also the center of government: tribal delegations were received and alliances concluded in it, and occasionally warriors paraded in its courtyard before military campaigns.

In the conquered territories, the Muslims either converted churches to mosques by rearranging their interiors to be oriented toward Mecca or built new mosques in the newly founded garrison towns—Basra and Kufa in Iraq, Fustat in Egypt, and Qayrawan in Tunisia—using crude materials and spolia from ancient buildings. Like their prototype in Medina, these mosques also functioned as civic centers; they were built next to the governor's residence, from which he had direct access through a special door to the prayer hall.

Surprisingly, the first Islamic monument, the Dome of the Rock in Jerusalem, was not a mosque, though special prayers may have been said there. Built in 692 by the Umayyad caliph ʿAbd al-Malik (685–705) on a site revered by both Muslims and Jews, it is a classical *martyrium* with a high gilded dome above that mysterious object of veneration, the Rock. This monument preceded the construction of a series of imperial mosques all over the Umayyad dominion by caliph al-Walid I (705–715), probably as part of the plan initiated by his father, ʿAbd al-Malik, to organize and integrate the caliphate, which included arabizing the administration and Islamizing the coinage. Most prominent were the Great Mosque in Damascus, the capital of the caliphate, the Mosque of the Prophet in Medina (where the concave *miḥrāb* was reportedly first introduced in 707), and al-Aqṣā Mosque in Jerusalem. These mosques appropriated elements from the Hellenistic, Roman, Byzantine, Sassanian, and local Syrian arts and synthesized them to create a new Umayyad style, while still retaining the flexibility of their archetype in Medina. But only the Great Mosque of Damascus today preserves its original plan and some of its decoration.

The Great Mosque occupies the entire area where the Roman Temple of Jupiter Damascenus once stood, and it incorporates some of the walls of its temenos. It consists of a triple-arcaded hypostyle hall extending along the southern temenos wall, intersected in the middle by a high gabled and domed transversal aisle, and fronted by a large courtyard surrounded by porticoes on the other three sides. The courtyard facade distinctly resembles the *palatium* of Theoderic represented in mosaic on the wall of the 5th century basilica of St. Apollinare Nuovo in Ravenna, suggesting a deliberate, if perplexing, link between the Umayyad mosque and Byzantine imperial palaces, which Theoderic's *palatium* was supposed to have imitated.

The mosque was connected to the palace of government *(dār al-imāra)* and had a treasury *(al-khazna),* consisting of a cupola on columns, in its courtyard. This arrangement effectively assembled the religious, political, and administrative functions in the center of the city.

Two new architectural elements first appeared in the Damascus mosque: the minaret, which may have been adopted from the towers flanking the northern side of the earlier Roman temenos, and the *maqsura,* which was an enclosure intended to protect the caliph and his entourage. The mosque was richly decorated with mosaic scenes of buildings in fanciful but unpopulated landscapes. Several examples can be matched up with a classical prototype, but none of them is completely realistic. Their origin, the identity of their makers, and their meaning are still matters of debate. Scholars have either referred to Qurʾānic texts to find paradisiac connotations in them or have adduced cosmographical explanations.

After the fall of the Umayyads in 750, congregational mosques continued to act as civic centers. In Dar al-Salām (Baghdad), the new Abbasid capital founded in 762 by al-Manṣūr (754–775), the congregational mosque was still attached to the caliphal palace. But with the gradual withdrawal of the caliph from public life under the influence of Persian traditions, the connection between palace and mosque was broken. This development, first seen in Samarra, the new capital established by caliph al-Muʿtasim in 836, ultimately resulted in the mosque's relinquishing its political character and retaining only its religious one.

BIBL.: Afif Bahnassi, *The Great Omayyad Mosque of Damascus: The First Masterpieces of Islamic Art* (Damascus, 1989). Oleg Grabar, *The Formation of Islamic Art,* rev. ed. (New Haven, 1987). N.R.

Muʿallaqāt

The *Muʿallaqāt,* the most famous anthology of Arabic verse, consists of seven odes (the canon), or sometimes ten. They are all pre-Islamic compositions of 6th century vintage, but the anthology itself was made in Islamic times and is traditionally ascribed to a rhapsodist and transmitter of early Arabic poetry, a certain Hammād, who lived in the 8th century. The authenticity that sometimes haunts single verses or fragments of pre-Islamic poetry does not apply to these odes; it applies only to the identity of the anthologist and the circumstances that occasioned their compilation. The anthology has been given many names: *Tiwāl* (the long ones); *Mudhhabāt* or *Mudhahhabāt* (the gilded ones); *Sumūt* (necklaces); but the most common has been *Muʿallaqāt,* plural of *muʿallaqa* (the suspended ones), with reference to the fiction that they were suspended at the walls of Kaʿba in Mecca in pre-Islamic times.

These odes represent some of the finest specimens

of pre-Islamic Arabic poetry, each being the best poem of the seven or ten poets represented. All are monorhymed, monometered, longish, and polythematic. Each poet opens his ode with an elegiac-amatory prelude on the deserted encampment of his departed mistress; he then describes his mount, horse or camel, and the wastes he traversed, together with their plants and animals; finally he indulges in some meditations, reflects on his self-image, and lauds his own tribal group. Thus, in its content, each *mu'allaqa* presents a panoramic view of the desert and desert life, while artistically it represents the achievement of its pre-Islamic author in going beyond the narrow confines of the short monothematic poem to a complex and layered structure.

Although these odes have many features in common, each of them is utterly individualistic, breathing a different spirit from all the others. The earliest of them and the most celebrated, that of Imru' al-Qays, the vagabond prince of the tribe of Kinda, expresses his passionate and tempestuous life and personality. The second, that of Tarafa, is reflective, anguished, and pessimistic. The third, that of 'Antar, the "black knight," breathes the spirit of chivalrous love and tells of heroic encounters on the intertribal battlefield. The fourth, that of Zuhayr, is striking in its praising of peace among the tribes and its denunciation of war, almost Horace's *bellaque matribus detestata*. The fifth is that of Labīd, the perfect Arab *sayyid* (tribal chief), the paragon of Arab *murū'a*, or manliness, whose ode architectonically is the best of the seven. The sixth, that of Hārith, is a spirited panegyric on his tribe, Bakr, and its claims on the attention of the Lakhmid king of Hīra. The seventh is that of 'Amr, who sings the praises of the sister but rival tribe of Taghlib. His abhorrence of Lakhmid control and love of freedom is crowned with a regicide, none other than that of the king to whom his rival Hārith had appealed.

Like all pre-Islamic poetry, the *mu'allaqāt* are important aesthetically and historically. As literary art, these poems of pre-Islamic Arabia depict desert scenes from that fabled region that had attracted the attention of the Greek geographers. They give vivid pictures of its natural phenomena, difficult terrain, terrible landscapes, sand dunes, flora, and fauna. For pre-Islamic Arab history, these odes are invaluable documents, especially because, unlike the prose accounts of later Islamic times, they are contemporary and primary records of a period, the history of which we must reconstruct from exiguous non-Arab contemporary sources and from a few inscriptions.

The *Mu'allaqāt* still constitutes standard reading in the *paideia*, the Arab-Muslim educational system, in spite of the odes' pre-Islamic provenance. Through his *sīra*, the prose romance that carries his name, one of the poets, the half-Arab half-Abyssinian manumitted slave 'Antar, has remained alive in the consciousness of the Arabs in Islamic times—and so has he in Europe through translations of his romance and through Opus 9 of Rimsky-Korsakov, the 'Antar Symphony.

BIBL.: A. J. Arberry, *The Seven Odes* (New York, 1957). F. Sezgin, *Geschichte des arabischen Schrifttums* (Leiden, 1975), vol. 2, 109–132.   I.A.S.

Mu'āwiyya

Mu'āwiyya ibn Abi Sufyān, fifth caliph after Muhammad and founder of the Umayyad dynasty (661–750). His prominent family led the opposition to Muhammad and did not accept Islam until the Prophet conquered Mecca in 630. Mu'āwiyya thereafter served as a scribe under the Prophet, an army commander in Syria under Abu Bakr, governor of Damascus under 'Umar, and finally governor of all of Syria and Jezira under 'Uthmān. After 'Uthmān's assassination in 656, Mu'āwiyya resisted 'Alī ibn Abī Tālib's caliphate on the grounds that 'Alī was harboring the killers of 'Uthmān. The ensuing indecisive battle of Siffin (657) weakened 'Alī's position; he became entangled in fighting the dissenting Kharijites in his camp. Meanwhile, the versatile and energetic Mu'āwiyya strengthened his hold on Syria and Jezira, took Egypt, and, in a ceremony in Jerusalem around 660, assumed the throne without acknowledging 'Alī's suzerainty. After 'Alī's assassination in 661, Mu'āwiyya won universal recognition as the sole caliph. During his long, prosperous, and relatively calm reign (661–680), he created a centralized authority dependent on the military support of Arabic tribes in Syria and Palestine and expanded the Islamic conquests in Africa, the east, and the Mediterranean.

Most Islamic sources present Mu'āwiyya in a negative light, as having craftily maneuvered his way to the caliphate only to turn it into a hereditary succession by forcing all Muslim notables to take an oath of allegiance to his son Yazīd. His reign is depicted as marking the end of the idealized Medinese period and the beginning of a Roman-like kingship (*mulk*). But all sources emphasize his proverbial personal qualities, chief among them his cunning (*daha'*) and forbearance (*hilm*), which effectively allowed him to stay in power with little recourse to force.

BIBL.: Salah al-Din al-Munnajid, *Mu'jam Banu Umayya* (Beirut, 1970). Erling Ladewig Petersen, *Ali and Muawiya in Early Arabic Tradition*, trans. P. Lampe Christensen (Odense, Denmark, 1974). G. R. Hawting, *The First Dynasty of Islam: The Umayyad Caliphate A.D. 661–750* (Carbondale, Ill., 1987).   N.R.

Muhammad

Muhammad, the Prophet of Islam, was born in Mecca ca. 570 A.D. and died in Medina in 632 (11 A.H.).

The Ḥijāz, the region of western Arabia that was the scene of his career, is largely desert. Its scattered oases are neither as numerous as those of Najd nor as large as those of eastern Arabia, and it lacks the mountainous terrain that attracts the relatively abundant rainfall of Yemen and Oman.

The population of the region was Arab with a significant Jewish presence, and almost entirely tribal. Outside the oases the tribes were primarily nomadic and pastoral; within the oases, agriculture was generally predominant. Of the five major oases of the Ḥijāz, the two northernmost, Khaybar and Fadak, were inhabited by Jews; each of the two southernmost oases, Mecca and Ṭā'if, was in the hands of a single Arab tribe, Quraysh in the case of Mecca and Thaqīf in that of Ṭā'if. The central oasis, Yathrib (later known as Medina), had a mixed population of two Arab and three Jewish tribes. Mecca was unusual in that its agricultural resources were poor; the Qurashīs made their living from trade.

In political terms, this region lay outside the limits of direct or indirect Byzantine or Persian rule, though the southern Ḥijāz had been the object of a campaign by a ruler of Yemen around the time that Muḥammad was born. None of the nomadic tribes of the Ḥijāz exercised a regional hegemony, nor did any of the oases; Yathrib, geographically the most plausible hegemon, was disabled by the high level of conflict within its heterogeneous population. So far as we know, none of the other oases possessed even a local ruler. Thus Mecca had no supreme authority, and its day-to-day politics were a matter of relations between and within its clans. With this absence of state structures went the absence of professional armies: warfare, like politics, was the business of every adult male tribesman.

The Arabs of the Ḥijāz, like much of the population of Arabia, adhered to pagan cults that were in some cases very ancient. Despite the dramatic rise of Christianity in the Mediterranean world since the 4th century, the main monotheist presence in the Ḥijāz was Jewish, and some Arabs had converted to Judaism. The southern Ḥijāz was virtually untouched by this influence, and both Mecca and Ṭā'if were associated with pagan sanctuaries.

All in all, the Ḥijāz was arid and remote. It had no major economic resources, no political structure deserving of the name of a state, and almost nothing of interest to outsiders. No events of any great significance to the wider world had taken place there in the past; and the colorful but intermittent and petty warfare that characterized the Ḥijāz at the beginning of the 7th century gave no indication that this was likely to change.

Muḥammad was born into the Banū Hāshim, one of the clans of Quraysh, and various miracles are reported in connection with his birth. His childhood was unsettled: first his father and then his mother died, and eventually he came into the care of his uncle Abū Ṭālib, who at one point took him on a trading voyage to Syria. He was later fortunate enough to catch the eye of a rich widow, Khadīja, whose agent he became in

the trade with Syria; she later married him. But it was not until the age of forty that he was called to his prophetic mission. He received this call while in retreat on a hill near Mecca. The angel Gabriel came to him in his sleep and taught him to recite a short passage from what would come to be known as the Qur'ān. Muḥammad was at first suspicious but was eventually satisfied that the source of his supernatural experience was not demonic. After receiving his call, he resided in Mecca for a further ten to fifteen years. During this period, he continued to receive revelations through Gabriel, and these established the rudiments of the new religion. It was also in this period that Gabriel took him on his famous "night journey" to Jerusalem, from whence he briefly ascended to heaven.

Meanwhile, Muḥammad had been making converts in Mecca. At first these were limited to his immediate family, but after three years he was instructed to make his religion public. However, the existence of a Muslim community among the pagan Meccans began to cause trouble, not because the pagans were intolerant but because Muḥammad as a monotheist prophet was obliged to speak ill of their gods. In the celebrated incident of the Satanic verses, Satan is said to have taken advantage of Muḥammad's wish to extend an olive branch to the pagans, and to have prevailed on him to insert into the text of the revelation a statement referring in favorable terms to three of their deities. This interpolation was, of course, soon removed, and relations with the pagan majority again deteriorated.

Muḥammad's problem was thus to find a way to secure protection for his followers against their pagan enemies. One measure he took was to send some of them to take refuge with the ruler of Abyssinia, who was sympathetic to his cause. Another was to seek a protector within the Ḥijāz; in this connection he made an unsuccessful visit to Ṭā'if, and set about making contacts with tribes at fairs. Eventually these efforts paid off. He was able to make a deal with some Arab tribesmen from Yathrib, whose hope it was that Muḥammad would be able to draw together the quarrelsome people of their oasis. Muḥammad then sent his Meccan followers to Yathrib, and in due course joined them there in 1/622. This was his "emigration," or *hijra,* and those of his Meccan followers who made the journey were known as the Muhājirūn, while his local adherents were termed the Anṣār. The year in which the *hijra* took place was later adopted as the first of the Muslim era.

Muḥammad spent the remaining ten years of his life in Yathrib, or Medina as it was now increasingly called. During this period, he continued to receive the revelations that were to be put together as a book after his death; of particular importance for the later elaboration of Islam were those concerned with legal questions. He also continued to give the inspired guidance on legal and other matters that was to be transmitted by his followers in the form of oral accounts of his sayings and doings (the hadith). The political history of this decade is dominated by two themes. One is the establishment of Muḥammad's political power in Medina, the process that brought the Islamic state into being. The other is the extension of the power of this state to other parts of Arabia through military and diplomatic activity.

The first process is reflected in a document that western scholars have dubbed the "Constitution of Medina." It proclaims the existence of a community ('umma) of Muḥammad's followers, including both those of Quraysh (that is to say, the Muhājirūn) and those of Yathrib (that is to say, the Anṣār). It also states that the Jews belong to this community, and that they fight external enemies as part of it, while retaining their own religion. A vital stipulation is that any dispute among the parties to the agreement is to be referred to God and Muḥammad; this is as far as the document goes toward establishing Muḥammad as the ruler of a state. If this document suggests an arrangement in which the Arabs and Jews of Medina were united in a single political community, this was not how matters fell out. Muḥammad did succeed in unifying the Arab tribes of Medina; paganism disappeared, despite the persistence of much political dissidence below the surface. But his relations with the Jewish tribes turned sour. Two of them were expelled; when the turn of the third came, instead the men were killed and the women and children enslaved.

The main engine of the expansion of the Islamic state was holy war, or jihad. At first, however, its energies were mostly taken up by the struggle against the pagans of Mecca. An unsuccessful attempt to capture a Meccan caravan led to the battle of Badr in 2/624, in which a Meccan force was defeated by Muḥammad and some three hundred of his followers, assisted by angels, it was said. However, this early victory was followed by a defeat at Uḥud, near Medina, in 3/625, and a siege of Medina by the Meccans in 5/627. In 6/628 Muḥammad was strong enough to negotiate a truce, but no more, when he reached Ḥudaybiyya near Mecca. It was not until 8/630, two and a half years before his death, that Mecca submitted to Muḥammad; this was followed by the battle of Ḥunayn and the surrender of Ṭā'if. Meanwhile, in the northern Ḥijāz he had taken Khaybar and Fadak in 7/628. His successes in his last years, and above all the conquest of Mecca, encouraged Arab tribes much further afield to submit to his authority. But he never invaded the territory of either of the empires. His expedition to Tabūk in northwestern Arabia in 9/630 did not lead to a confrontation with the Byzantines, and a planned expedition to Syria in 11/632 was overtaken by his death.

Muḥammad died in 11/632 at an age given variously as sixty, sixty-three, and sixty-five. He was sur-

vived by nine wives and four daughters. Of his wives, 'Ā'isha played the most important role after his death and was a major protagonist in the opening events of the first civil war. Of his daughters, Fāṭima is important by virtue of her marriage to Muḥammad's cousin 'Alī, reinforcing the claims of his descendants by her to political authority. Muḥammad had no surviving sons; one born to him by an Egyptian concubine died in infancy.

The account of Muḥammad's life given above is taken from the Muslim biographies, and in particular from that of Ibn Isḥāq (d. 150/767) in the recension of Ibn Hishām (d. 218/833). These biographies are rich in detail, and despite the presence of miraculous elements, they have a texture very different from that of Christian hagiography. Overwhelmingly they are Sunnī works; we possess no comparable literature from the Khārijites or Shī'ites.

These sources are nevertheless problematic in certain respects, the most important of which is that they represent a tradition of living narrative that is likely to have developed orally for a considerable period before it was given even a relatively fixed written form. Ideally, one would like to be able to check such accounts against contemporary evidence, or at least evidence not subject to the process of transmission through which the Muslim material has passed. In fact, however, there is no relevant archaeological, epigraphic, or numismatic evidence dating from the time of Muḥammad, nor are there any references to him in non-Muslim sources dating from the period before 632. Non-Muslim sources written in the following decades give only very scrappy information and are subject to problems of their own. One point of interest is that they suggest that Muḥammad was still alive when the Muslim expansion outside Arabia began. In key respects they give a strikingly different picture of his career and teaching, but only in a fragmentary way.

Most Islamicists ignore these sources and work exclusively with the Muslim literary tradition. Here there are perhaps three main lines of research that are relevant to the attempt to assess the historical reliability of the tradition. The first is research that seeks to work back to the sources behind our earliest written sources. If we could show that it is possible to reconstruct what was said about the biography of Muḥammad in, say, the late 1st/7th century, then we would have eliminated some of the problem. The second is research that makes a point of bringing together material from diverse Muslim sources, particularly those not directly concerned with the biography of Muḥammad: if the results of such work yield a consistent and convincing picture, this is an argument for its historicity. The third is research that probes the contradictory elements found in the tradition: if it can be shown that our choices between divergent accounts of significant facts or events are essentially arbitrary, this will limit the use of the material for historical reconstruction. It is too early to assess where these lines of research will take us, but whatever the outcome, it is unlikely that the problem of historical reliability will ever entirely go away.

Despite the problems with the sources, a major historical issue stands out with regard to the formation of the Islamic state: why did it take place when it did? Although our knowledge of the history of pre-Islamic Arabia is very imperfect, it is likely to be significant that we know of no case of religious state formation in the earlier history of the peninsula that could be compared with Muḥammad's. By contrast, the Muslim tradition describes a minor epidemic of such ventures in the period immediately following his death, such as that of the false prophet Musaylima in eastern Arabia; and religious state formation within the Islamic tradition is a familiar feature of the history of Arabia thereafter.

To the question of what might have been different about conditions in Arabia at the time of Muḥammad, two main answers have been given. One is the rise of Meccan trade, leading to the disruption of Meccan society through commercialization. This, however, has been shown to have little or no foundation in the Islamic sources, and in any case it would fail to explain why Muḥammad achieved his success in Medina, not Mecca, and why this success should have resonated so widely in Arabia. The other answer sees Muḥammad's venture and doctrine as a response to increasing pressure on Arabia from the neighboring empires. Though considerably more plausible as an approach, this would lead us to expect the rise of Islam to have taken place in 6th century eastern Arabia, the time and place when imperial influence, in this case Persian, was at its height—rather than in western Arabia in the 7th century, a context in which Byzantine influence seems to have been negligible. In the end, the innovative role of Muḥammad himself remains a key element in the picture.

BIBL.: F. Buhl and A. T. Welch, "Muḥammad," section 1, "The Prophet's Life and Career," in *The Encyclopedia of Islam,* 2nd ed. W. M. Watt, *Muhammad: Prophet and Statesman* (London, 1961). M. Rodinson, *Mohammed* (London, 1971). Ibn Ishaq, *The Life of Muhammad,* trans. A. Guillaume (London, 1955). E. Yarshater, ed., *The History of al-Tabari* (Albany, 1987–1997), vols. 6–9. P. Crone, *Meccan Trade and the Rise of Islam* (Princeton, 1987). M. Lecker, *Muslims, Jews and Pagans: Studies on Early Islamic Medina* (Leiden, 1995). G. Schoeler, *Charakter und Authentie der muslimischen Überlieferung über das Leben Mohammeds* (Berlin and New York, 1996). M.C.

Music

The late antique world was filled with music. Secular music was heard in theater and circus, marketplace and tavern, field and family home. None of it was given a written record, however, and all has vanished. Sacred music was heard day and night in churches and monasteries, and some of this is reclaimable from later written sources.

Augustine knew the attractions of secular music ("the lust of the ear caught me in its mesh and enslaved me") and also of sacred music ("I fear not, surrendering myself to the delights of sound, uttered by a pleasant and well-trained voice, so long as Thy word gives life to them"). Some features of the secular are known from denunciations by church fathers. Instrumental music was excluded from most churches (John Chrysostom: "Where the *aulos* is, there Christ is not"), along with dancing and hand clapping. Clement of Alexandria disapproved of the chromatic gender, with its small intervals; he preferred the diatonic gender, whose echoes are in our major and minor scales. There are representations of secular music making in paintings, mosaics, and sculpture, showing instruments and the gestures made in playing, but they are sometimes too stylized to be believed.

Music was a focus of liberal learning. Theorists sustained the ancient Greek view of music as an aspect of number, in archaizing discusssions that paid little attention to the artful manifestation of sound. They saw in its proportions the counterparts of the proportions in which the universe was framed. The late 3rd century grammarian Censorinus put musical matter into his collection of birthday lore, *De die natali,* including the classic definition, "scientia bene modulandi" (the science of fine tuning), which may reach back to Varro. Augustine's six books entitled *De musica* (the first five were written before his baptism in 387) deal with rhythmics; he planned a complementary six books, *De melo,* as part of a general coverage of liberal arts, but they were never written. Martianus Capella's *De nuptiis Philologiae et Mercurii* (before 439?) includes an amateur's treatment of Harmony as the wedding's seventh bridesmaid; the theoretical notions are filtered down from Aristides Quintilianus. Boethius composed treatises on all four of the mathematical disciplines of antiquity—arithmetic, geometry, astronomy, and music. His *De institutione musica,* partly preserved, drew on Nichomachus and Ptolemy. It launched the popular threefold division of *musica mundana* (harmonious relationships of the heavenly spheres) *musica humana* (relationship of soul and corporeal body), and *musica instrumentalis* (pitch relationships on which heard music is based, as measured on the monochord).

Cassiodorus's *Institutiones (Saecularium litterarum)* contain a brief coverage of music as part of the quadrivium; the work became a major authority for monastic learning in the 7th through 10th centuries. In a more original treatment, Isidore of Seville's *Etymologiae* discards some baggage of ancient musical theory and recognizes music as something that "moves the feelings and changes emotions." He speaks of particular instruments, and of the antiphons and responsories used in the divine office.

Music had a major place in worship, adding its special persuasions to the liturgy's other appeals. St. Paul, in a memorable phrase, urged congregations to express themselves in "psalms, hymns, and spiritual songs" (*Eph.* 5:19, *Col.* 3:16). Early Christian music likely concentrated on simple, vocal psalm singing, reflecting synagogue practice rather than the more elaborate musical ritual of the Temple, with its choirs and instruments. The full assembly—men and women, children and elders—was involved in the chanting. Egeria mentions boys' choirs *(pisinni)* in 4th century Jerusalem, and St. Basil approves of children's readiness for church singing.

Early Christian musical style was vocal and monophonic. A single melodic line was its whole substance; there were no differentiated voice parts and no chordal harmonic supports; there probably were no simple drone accompaniments. And the music was sung, not played. Instruments were unsuitable because of their secular associations, and their absence helped distinguish Christian from pagan cult. The ban on instruments continued in the west until the appearance of organs in Carolingian-Ottonian times; in the east it went on much longer.

The music's more elaborate forms must have begun in spontaneous, improvised deliveries that were generated fresh on each occasion. Some soloists' chants would have used formulaic techniques, typical of oral transmissions. Through regular liturgical repetitions, much of the music, while still oral, acquired the fixity of remembered melody. The transmission seems to have remained oral throughout late antiquity, although a Greek hymn survives, noted on a late 3rd century papyrus (*P. Oxy.* 1786), with Hellenistic alphabetic pitch and rhythmic signs. Addressed to the Trinity, it is cast in a high G-mode, with a musical stylization otherwise unknown in Christian hymnody. Some of the vast, unrecorded oral repertory may be recoverable by working backward from the eventual noted states. By such means, the musical core of the 4th century Eucharist—the recitatives of the Anaphora and Sanctus (Is. 6:3)—can be tentatively traced.

In the east, the main musical centers were in Jerusalem and Constantinople, and the emphasis was on hymns for the divine office. Thousands of hymnic troparia, stichera, kontakia, kanons, and the like were produced during the 5th through 8th centuries by Greek "melodes"—among them Romanos, Andrew of Crete, and John of Damascus—who combined the functions of poet and composer. The Latin west had writers of hymns (St. Ambrose, Hilary of Poitiers, Caelius Sedulius, Venantius Fortunatus), but its main emphasis was on settings of biblical, and above all psalmic, texts for the Mass. Rome was a major factor,

but there were considerable accumulations of Bible-based chants in Spain, Gaul, Lombardy, and southern Italy (the Beneventan zone) during the 6th through 8th centuries. When Gregory the Great oversaw a reorganization of the Roman liturgical-musical repertory ca. 600, he was content to let those other musical rites flourish. Later, under Pepin and Charlemagne, a single, ostensibly Roman musical repertory was imposed throughout Carolingian domains, and much of the older regional practice was lost.

The melodies in both east and west were eventually written down in neumes, but the origins and rationales of the early neumings are obscure. "Ekphonetic" neumes, which regulate the formulaic musical recitations of bible lessons at Byzantium, may reach well back in time; so too may the neumatic notations that are used for Byzantine hymns; but for neither of those notational species are there surviving traces before the 9th or 10th century. In the west, Isidore of Seville remarks ca. 600 that "unless sounds are retained by memory they vanish, as they can't be written down." Yet there were letter notations at the time, and Isidore may mean only that notators using letters—or staffless neumes—as memory aids could not aspire to verbatim recall. Neumes surface in the west during the middle decades of the 9th century, and their beginnings there likely reach no further back than the middle 8th century. For the music those neumes describe, the basic question is, how well do the noted versions reflect the prior oral deliveries? The answer varies depending on the region, the liturgical category, and the individual chant. The late antique phase of sacred music can be seen to end in the turn from oral to written transmission—in the codifications of Roman-Carolingian and Constantinopolitan liturgical-musical repertories during the later 8th and the 9th century.

BIBL.: James McKinnon, *Music in Early Christian Literature* (Cambridge, Eng., 1987). James McKinnon, "Christian Antiquity" and "The Emergence of Gregorian Chant," in *Music and Society: Antiquity and the Middle Ages,* ed. McKinnon (Englewood Cliffs, N.J., 1990), 68–119. Johannes Quasten, *Music and Worship in Pagan and Christian Antiquity* (Washington, D.C., 1973).   K.L.

Mysticism

In the context of the late antique world, this rather vague term may be taken to refer chiefly to those dimensions of philosophical speculation (the philosophy of the time being almost exclusively Neoplatonism) that transcend the normal processes of reasoning and intellection. Theorists of mysticism, such as R. C. Zaehner, have made a distinction between "monistic" and "theistic" mysticism, which is of some use in this connection. The mystic may have a sense of complete blending into unity with the absolute, or however the object of his contemplation is characterized (monistic);

or he may rather have the sensation of intimate union with the deity, while retaining a sense of his own identity (theistic). Like any such simple dichotomy, this distinction does not quite answer to phenomena that we observe; however, the mystical element in the thought of Plotinus and his Platonist successors may broadly be characterized as "theistic," in contradistinction to, for example, the mysticism characteristic of much Indian thought.

There is another distinction needing to be made, that between "practicing" and "theoretical" mystics. A problem arises because, in the Platonist tradition, there is much terminology borrowed from the "mystery" religions and stimulated by the language of Plato himself (in such dialogues as the *Phaedrus* and the *Symposium*) that an author might use without himself undergoing a properly "mystical" experience. Hence, while Plotinus certainly was and Iamblichus probably was a "practicing" mystic, it is more likely that such men as Porphyry, Proclus, and even Damascius were merely theoretical.

In any case, all these men are broadly in the "theistic" tradition of mysticism. Plotinus speaks repeatedly of union with the One (e.g., *Enneads* 1.6.9, 5.3.17, 6.7.34–36, 6.8.15, 6.9.11), but rather than the individual losing itself in the absolute, it seems to be the case that Plotinus's individual consciousness expands to take in the absolute. Plotinus does this by penetrating into the core of himself. Despite the language of "the ascent of the soul" that he has inherited from his tradition, it is the image of "turning inward" that is dominant for him. What he finds there is an element corresponding to the One in the universe, which he terms "the One in us" (6.5.1 and 6.9.7 are good passages in this connection). His aim is to unite "the One in us" with the One in the universe. This aim might be seen as monistic, were it not for Plotinus's startling view that the One is to be united to us, rather than we to the One.

Such union cannot be attained, of course, by normal intellective processes. Passage 6.7.35 is an important explication of this: "Intellect," he says, "has one power for thinking, by which it looks at the things in itself, and one by which it looks at what transcends it, by a sort of direct awareness and receptivity." He distinguishes these functions of intellect as "intellect sober" and "intellect drunk"—"but it is better for it to be drunk with a drunkenness like this than to be more respectably sober."

Plotinus certainly sets the agenda for late antique Platonist mysticism, but later Platonists, such as Iamblichus, followed by Damascius, discerned a contradiction within Plotinus's doctrine of the One, which serves both as the utterly transcendent first principle and also, somehow, as the first cause of all things. For Iamblichus these two functions are incompatible, and he

postulates, above the One, an "utterly ineffable" first principle, which cannot be directly cognized even by the highest element in the intellect (cf. *In Parmenidem* frg. 2A Dillon). Damascius elaborates on this conception in his *Problems and Solutions,* in chapters 1–9. For him, the "utterly ineffable" can be sensed only by indirection, though it underlies all cognition. The question arises as to whether this notion is the product of practical or merely theoretical mysticism, but Damascius's discussion of it seems to embody real experience.

A peculiarity of the late Hellenic tradition, however, by contrast with the Indian, is the general lack of any practical instruction as to how to attain mystical vision. We have no handbooks on the subject, nor any suggested exercises or recommended mantras. Some of Plotinus's more powerful images (such as the images of the hand carrying the piece of wood and of the light in the lamp in 6.4.7) have been seen as "spiritual exercises" of a sort, and indeed may well be, but they are not presented as such. Plotinus, nonetheless, comes across as a man for whom what we would term "mystical experience" is central to his being. The man who penned the beginning of passage 4.8 is thoroughly familiar with another plane of reality than ours: "Often I have woken up out of the body to myself, and have come to be within myself, and outside of all else; and then I have seen a beauty wonderfully great, and felt assurance that then most of all I belonged to a greater destiny."

However, mysticism in the Platonist tradition is always subordinated to philosophic reason. This is not so clearly the case with the late antique Christian tradition, of whom the chief representatives are Gregory of Nyssa and the adventurous 6th century Christian Platonist who shelters behind the pseudonym of Dionysius the Areopagite. Gregory's most strikingly mystical utterances come in his commentary on the Song of Songs, and in particular in his description of the ascent to the third heaven. Of course, for a Christian there is no question of the identification of the soul with God, but Gregory's great insight is that the third heaven is not a state but an ever-developing process of nearer approach to God and deeper understanding of him. Dionysius's use of language is striking, but he gives the impression, for instance in the *Mystical Theology,* of using negations and *hyper-* compounds on occasion with a rather reckless exuberance (see, for instance, chapter 5, 1045Dff.), as if he is taking over the terminology of a thinker such as Damascius without fully appreciating the rationale behind it.

BIBL.: A. H. Armstrong, ed., *The Cambridge History of Later Greek and Early Mediaeval Philosophy* (Cambridge, Eng., 1970), pts. 3, 4, and 6. J. M. Rist, *Plotinus: The Road to Reality* (Cambridge, Eng., 1967), ch. 16. R. C. Zaehner, *Mysticism, Sacred and Profane* (Oxford, 1957).   J.DIL.

Nessana

Nessana was a large village in the western part of the central Negev (modern Nitzana; in Arabic, Auja el Hafir). The ancient name was ascertained from the papyri found at the site, which mention the village of Nessana in the district of the polis of Elusa.

Like other major sites in the central Negev traditionally known as the "Negev towns," such as Oboda (Avdat), Rehovot-in-the-Negev, Mampsis (Kurnub), Obata (Shivta), and Elusa (Halutza), Nessana started its history in the Hellenistic and early Roman period as a Nabataean road station on the branch of the Petra-Gaza road that runs from Elusa to Rhinocorura (El Arish) and Egypt. It reached its peak in the Byzantine period in the 4th to 7th centuries, when the region, formerly part of the Provincia Arabia, belonged to Palaestina Tertia. The Christian church played a crucial role in the development of the area and the conversion of the neighboring nomadic tribes to Christianity and Byzantine civilization.

Though the overall size of the village was about 17 hectares, there were large open spaces between the houses; thus we can estimate the population of the site as no more than two to three thousand at its peak. In the middle of the village was a natural hill that served as an acropolis, on top of which were built a fortress and two churches. The northern church (dedicated to SS. Sergius and Bacchus), probably of the late 4th century, was part of a monastery. The southern church, a triapsidal basilica (founded in 601 C.E.), was dedicated to St. Mary. The fortress served as a military garrison but primarily as a shelter for the citizens in time of

danger. Two more churches were built in the plain below the acropolis; one of them has been recently excavated and partially restored.

The economy depended on typical desert agriculture, based on the use of runoff water and floods. The valleys around the site were terraced, and runoff water was conducted to them by a network of channels. Apart from wheat and barley, other crops included fruits and grapes. There is also evidence of local commerce and facilities for caravans and other travelers, including Christian pilgrims on their way to Mt. Sinai.

Many Greek inscriptions, including dedications on buildings and tombstones, were found at the site, but the most important discovery was the archive of papyri, discovered mainly in rooms around the northern church. In addition to fragments of literary texts (including Virgil's *Aeneid*), the archive is made up of 195 major and minor documents. Their contents are both personal and of a legal nature: marriage contracts, divorces, accounts and contracts for purchase of goods and land, wills, records of sales, financial reports of merchants, documents relating to church administration, lists of donors. The papyri shed light on private and community life in the Christian Negev in the 6th–7th centuries. The leaders of the village were the abbots of the monastery (which was probably attached to the northern church). Some of them had families but retreated to the monastery in later life.

A large part of the archive (in Greek and Arabic) belongs to the period after the Muslim conquest, up to 689. In addition to the legal documents, they include administrative orders concerning taxes and levies. In this period Nessana seems to have been in decline. The archaeological finds show that Nessana was almost totally abandoned not much later than the early 8th century.

BIBL.: H. D. Colt, ed., *Excavations at Nessana,* vol. 1 (London, 1962). C. J. Kraemer, *Excavations at Nessana,* vol. 3: *Non-Literary Papyri* (Princeton, 1958). J. Shershevski, *Byzantine Urban Settlements in the Negev Desert* (Beer-Sheva, 1991).   Y.T.

Nestorians

The Nestorians, or as they called themselves, the "Church of the East," were the largest and most influential Christian community of the Sassanian and early Islamic Near East. At the time of the Arab conquest in the mid-7th century, the Nestorian patriarch based in Ctesiphon (later in Baghdad) oversaw ten metropolitan sees and ninety-six bishoprics spread throughout Mesopotamia, around the Persian Gulf, and on the Iranian plateau. Nestorian dioceses were most densely clustered in northern and eastern Iraq (especially on the upper Tigris, in Adiabene and Beth Garmai), where Christianity had spread during the 3rd century along trade routes leading from Roman Syria. Converts from the substantial Jewish communities of this region were numerous and influential. Further centers of Christianity developed in southern Mesopotamia (especially Khuzistan) and southwestern Iran (Fars), where resettled captives from Roman Syria intermarried with the local Aramaic and Persian populations. The Christianity of Iraq and Iran thus became from an early stage a multilingual and multiethnic phenomenon.

Under Sassanian rule (224–651), the Church of the East developed many of the enduring features of its institutional, doctrinal, and cultural identity. Political factors played an important role in shaping the general course of these developments. The execution of hundreds of clergy and ascetics during the great persecution (ca. 340–378) under Shapur II seems to have had the unintended effect of consolidating the Christian community within the empire. The persecution generated an extensive martyr literature in Syriac (some of it later translated into Greek and Armenian) that constitutes our best source of evidence for the social and cultural conditions of the 4th century church. From the early 5th century, synodical documents supplement the evidence of the *passiones.* The *Synodicon orientale,* which preserves the acts of thirteen synods convoked by the Nestorian patriarchs between 410 and 775, charts the steady improvement of church-state relations in the middle and late Sassanian periods. The bishops assembled in 410 at Seleucia, across the river from Ctesiphon, offered their thanks to King Yazdegird I (399–420), who gave "deliverance and repose to the assemblies of Christ" (Persian tradition remembers the same king as "Yazdegird the sinner"). There were further outbreaks of persecution later in Yazdegird's reign and also under his successors Bahram

V (420–438) and Yazdegird II (438–457), but they were more limited in scale and duration. Persecution focused on the court, or was carried out against Christians who had defiled Zoroastrian sacred spaces. Accusations of complicity with the Romans could also cause problems, particularly for the *katholikos,* who as titular head of the Church of the East was expected to keep his flock in line.

By the late Sassanian period, Christianity was the dominant religion of the Aramaic territories of the western Sassanian empire, and the royal court played an active and often the decisive role in the selection of each new *katholikos.* Persecution was restricted to the rare prosecution of Persian apostates from Zoroastrianism, usually at the instigation of local Zoroastrian magi, or of the rival Jacobite (Monophysite) church, which had powerful patrons in the court of Khosro II (591–628). This modus vivendi between the church and its non-Christian rulers continued under Islamic rule. As S. Brock observes, it appears that "most of the rights of, and restrictions laid upon, the 'peoples of the book' under the new Arab rulers were simply formulations of what had already been general practice under the later Sasanids" (p. 12).

This pattern of political reconciliation was facilitated by the doctrinal schism between the Church of the East and Byzantium that developed in the late 5th century and hardened during the reign of the emperor Justinian (527–565) and his successors. In crude terms, the schism grew out of a debate over the orthodoxy of the leading exponents of Antiochene Christology. Sassanian Christians, many of them trained at the school of Edessa before 489, tended to accept the orthodoxy of Nestorius (condemned by the Council of Ephesus in 431 and again at Chalcedon in 451), and revered Theodore of Mopsuestia (ca. 350–428) as an authoritative interpreter of Scripture. The famous School of Nisibis (founded ca. 489 after the enforced closure of the School of the Persians at Edessa) trained more than five generations of Nestorian teachers, monks, and clergy, including many future bishops and several patriarchs, in a rigorous curriculum of Antiochene theology, exegesis, and Aristotelian logic. Although the name *Nestorian* was first used as a polemical epithet used against them, many Christians in the east later accepted the name as a self-designation. By the early 7th century, Babai the Great and other teachers associated with the School of Nisibis had produced a definitive exposition of Nestorian theology. By the early 9th century, the *katholikos* Timothy I could argue for the primacy of his see over the patriarchates of Rome, Antioch, Alexandria, and Constantinople.

Political toleration and theological conviction laid the foundation for the remarkable cultural florescence in the Nestorian church during late Sassanian and early Islamic periods. A monastic revival movement that began at Mt. Izla near Nisibis during the 6th century and continued into the early Abbasid period, inspired the foundation of hundreds of small monasteries scattered throughout Iraq (a few of which remain to this day). Nestorian literature in Syriac blossomed: hagiography (much of it still untranslated); theology and exegesis; ecclesiastical and secular law. Syriac translations of Greek works (primarily medical and philosophical) and Middle Persian literature (mostly secular court works, including the Sassanian version of the *Alexander Romance* and the Indian animal fables known as *Kalilah wa Dimnah*) created a major conduit for cultural interchange between Byzantium and its eastern neighbors.

This cultural florescence was accompanied by a dramatic geographic expansion of the church into Asia. The development of Christian literature in Middle Persian facilitated the expansion of the church into the Persian Gulf and along the trade routes to the coasts of southern India, where one Christian donor left a half dozen crosses inscribed in Middle Persian. From northeastern Iran (where Christian dioceses are attested as early as 424), Christian merchants and teachers also moved into central Asia and even China where they proselytized among the Turks, Sogdians, and other ethnic groups. Literary fragments discovered in the ruins of a Nestorian monastery in Chinese Turkestan attest to the complex process of interaction and assimilation that accompanied this expansion into Asia.

The fortunes of the Nestorian church began to wane in the 9th century, as conversion to Islam severely eroded its population base first in Iran and then in Mesopotamia, although Christian villages remained much longer in mountainous and remote areas, as well as in southern India.

BIBL.: J. P. Asmussen, "Christians in Iran," in *The Cambridge History of Iran*, vol. 3: *The Seleucid, Parthian and Sasanian Periods*, ed. Ehsan Yarshater (Cambridge, Eng., 1983), 924–948. Sebastien Brock, "A Case of Divided Loyalties: Christians in the Sasanian Empire," in *Religion and National Identity*, ed. S. Mews (Oxford, 1982), 1–19. S. Gero, *Barsauma of Nisibis* (Louvain, 1981). J. Labourt, *Le christianisme dans l'empire perse sous la dynastie Sassanide (224–632)*, 2nd ed. (Paris, 1904). W. Stewart McCullough, *A Short History of Syriac Christianity to the Rise of Islam* (Philadelphia, 1982). M. A. L. Comneno, "Cristianesimo nestoriano in Asia Centrale nel primio millennio: Testimonianze archeologiche," *Orientalia Christiana Periodica* 61 (1995): 495–535.   J.W.

Nestorius

Nestorius (ca. 381–ca. 451) was bishop of Constantinople from 428 to 431. Theological controversy and political conflict led to his condemnation at the First Council of Ephesus (431) and his eventual exile.

Nestorius came originally from Germanicea in Syria, and he studied in Antioch at the same school that produced such luminaries as Diodorus of Tarsus, John Chrysostom, Theodore of Mopsuestia (who may have been Nestorius's teacher) and Theodoret of Cyrrhus. He spent some time in the monastery of Euprepius, and then served as a presbyter in Antioch, where he became known as a skillful preacher. In 428 he was chosen by Emperor Theodosius II, who decided that an eloquent outsider would reconcile the different factions within the local church. But Nestorius did not bring peace to the church. His very first public sermon as bishop set the tone for his tenure: "Give me, O emperor, the earth purged of heretics, and I will give you heaven. Help me destroy the heretics and I will help you destroy the Persians." Just four days later, his threat to demolish an Arian church caused the Arians to set it on fire themselves, and the resulting conflagration earned Nestorius the nickname "firebrand." His harsh persecution of Novatianists, Quartodecimans, Macedonians, and other sectarians in Constantinople and nearby Asia Minor led to much disorder and bloodshed.

Theological controversy soon erupted when Nestorius came out in support of a presbyter who had said, "Let no one call Mary Theotokos." Nestorius, in the tradition of Antiochene Christology, insisted on a careful conceptual distinction between the divine and human elements in Christ, and he felt that calling Mary "Mother of God" rather than simply "Mother of Christ" would introduce unacceptable confusion. His position offended many, both in Constantinople and elsewhere in the east, where the cult of the Virgin had become a focus of intense popular piety. Nestorius had already made several very powerful enemies. One of them, Cyril of Alexandria, quickly saw an opportunity to pursue Alexandria's longstanding vendettas against the patriarchate of Constantinople and the Antiochene school of Christology. Nestorius had in a rare display of tolerance harbored some suspected Pelagians fleeing from Rome, and this angered Pope Celestine, who was then more willing to hear Cyril's side of the story. Nestorius had already irritated the formidable Augusta Pulcheria when he blocked her from taking communion in the sanctuary of the church, and insisted that she stay back in the women's gallery; she was not in any mood to tolerate his attacks on the cult of Mary, which served as the model for Pulcheria's own personal devotion and public self-presentation as a dedicated virgin. Like John Chrysostom before him, Nestorius made the mistake of clashing with a strong-willed empress.

An increasingly hostile exchange of letters between Nestorius and Cyril culminated in the latter's demand, endorsed by Pope Celestine, that Nestorius renounce his earlier teachings and accept Cyril's controversial Twelve Anathemas or be deposed. Finally, late in 430, the emperor called for an ecumenical council to meet in June 431 at Ephesus. As the council began, Nestorius still enjoyed the favor of the emperor and some of the powerful people at the imperial court, including Candidian, *comes domesticorum,* and the count Irenaeus (later bishop of Tyre) who accompanied Nestorius to Ephesus with a military escort. At the first session of the council, dominated by Cyril's supporters, Nestorius (who chose not to attend) was declared heretical, condemned, and deposed. Months of intrigue then followed as the supporters of Cyril struggled with those of John of Antioch (who had met separately and declared Cyril's council invalid) for influence at the imperial court. Through diplomacy, popular agitation, lavish bribery, and the public intervention of the revered Constantinopolitan archimandrite Dalmatius, the Cyrillian party eventually persuaded the emperor to back away from his initial support for Nestorius. Late in 431, Nestorius yielded, asking only to be allowed to return to his old monastery near Antioch. When the Cyrillian and Antiochene parties finally reached an agreement and restored formal unity to the church in the spring of 433, both sides had had to give up something: Cyril withdrew his Twelve Anathemas, and the Antiochenes assented to the condemnation of Nestorius. The emperor's change of heart concerning his former favorite bishop was extreme: "Let no one speak of this man to me," he said. By 435 he ordered Nestorius's works burned, and Nestorius himself was sent into exile, first to Petra and then to the remote Great Oasis (modern Kharga) in the Egyptian desert, where he spent the remainder of his life. At one point he was captured by barbarians, who then released him—no doubt to the consternation of the imperial authorities, who later marched him from place to place under increasingly harsh conditions until his health finally gave out. The same treatment had killed John Chrysostom and would later finish off Flavian, two other patriarchs of Constantinople also overthrown by patriarchs of Alexandria.

Despite the harsh conditions of his exile (his plaintive petitions to the governor of the Thebaid are preserved in Evagrius, *Hist.eccl.* 1.7) Nestorius managed to keep in touch with the outside world. The apologetic work that has survived in Syriac translation under the pseudonym Heracleides shows that even after fifteen years in remote exile, Nestorius had access to a variety of official documents such as the Acta of the Council of Ephesus, letters of Cyril, and the *Tome* of Leo. The *Book of Heracleides* can be fairly closely dated by the author's awareness of the death of Theodosius II and the accession of Marcian, and the preparations for the upcoming Council of Chalcedon in 451, but not of the events of the council itself. Heracleides alternates between lengthy exposition and explanation of Nestorius's Christology and bitter denunciations of Theodosius II, Pulcheria, and, especially, Cyril. Nestorius grudgingly accepts the term *Theotokos* but continues to warn of the dangers of confusing the human and divine in Christ. Twenty years after Ephesus I, Nestorius sees the greatest theological danger in the more extreme representatives of the tradition later called "Monophysite," who would implicate the almighty divinity in birth, suffering, and death, and some of whom

would literally say "God died." For his part, he vehemently denied the charge of preaching "two sons" that was commonly brought against him by his opponents. Commenting on the events of 448–451, he saw the fate of Flavian as a repetition of his own downfall. Once he had yielded on the matter of the *Theotokos*, it seemed to him that his views were identical with those expressed in the *Tome* of Leo, which formed the basis for the declaration of faith adopted at Chalcedon. Opponents of Chalcedon, ironically, felt the same way: to them, the Chalcedonian position was thinly disguised Nestorianism. Despite the dire predictions of Monophysite propagandists, however, the new regime of Marcian and Pulcheria had no intention of recalling or rehabilitating Nestorius, by this time universally reviled as a heresiarch every bit as infamous as Mani or Arius. The heresy commonly denounced as Nestorianism was an extremely distorted version of his actual teaching, falsely crediting him with beliefs, such as "two sons" or "Christ was a mere man," that were explicitly rejected in his own writings. Within the Roman empire, even adherents of the Antiochene school, such as Theodoret of Cyrrhus, were forced to anathematize him, and only in the church of Persia would he be accepted and revered as a great orthodox teacher.

BIBL.: Paul Bedjan, ed., *Le livre d'Héraclide de Damas* (Leipzig and Paris, 1910); Eng. trans.: *Nestorius: The Bazaar of Heracleides,* ed. and trans. G. R. Driver and Leonard Hodgson (Oxford, 1925). *Cyril of Alexandria: Letters,* trans. John I. McEnerney (Washington, D.C., 1987), 2 vols. C. E. Braaten, "Modern Interpretations of Nestorius," *Church History* 32 (1963): 251–267. M. Brière, "La légende syriaque de Nestorius," *Revue de l'Orient chrétien,* 2nd ser. 5 (1910): 1–25. F. Loofs, ed., *Nestoriana: Die Fragmente des Nestorius* (Halle, 1905). H. E. W. Turner, "Nestorius Reconsidered," *Studia patristica* 13, no. 2 (1975): 306–321.   J.M.G.

Nicaea, Council of

The First Ecumenical Council, or Council of Nicaea, was believed to have produced the creed that became a significant part of the Christian liturgy. The council was summoned by Constantine to meet first in Ancyra, then in Nicaea, not long after Constantine defeated Licinius and became sole ruler of the empire in late 324. The council convened to settle a variety of issues. In addition to the Arian controversy, these included matters of discipline and practice, and disputes over hierarchy that had been put on hold for several years while Licinius had forbidden Christian assemblies.

Two hundred fifty to 300 bishops (the tradition of 318 bishops emerged later as a reference to the 318 companions of Abraham in Genesis 14:14), the vast majority from the east, traveled to Nicaea on the imperial *cursus publicus* and met in the audience hall of the palace between May and July 325, at which time they celebrated the emperor's *vicennalia*.

Although there had previously been significant regional councils (e.g., Elvira ca. 305, Neocaesarea ca. 314–325, Ancyra ca. 314–319), this was the first time that such a large group of bishops had assembled under imperial patronage and claimed to speak for the entire Christian world. We have very limited information about the actual proceedings of the council. There is no strong evidence that the sort of official transcripts characteristic of the 5th century councils were ever made at Nicaea. Eusebius presents an image of an enlightened emperor carefully guiding the discussion and bringing the bishops to consensus through reasoned persuasion, but many scholars have expressed doubt (citing, among other reasons, Constantine's imperfect command of Greek) and assign a leading role to Bishop Ossius of Córdoba, Constantine's companion and influential adviser, or to Alexander of Alexandria. Eusebius is maddeningly vague as to what was actually debated and discussed. Church historians of the early 5th century tend to present the council in terms of a straightforward conflict between clearly defined homoousian and Arian "parties" (which could scarcely yet be said to exist in 325), or focus on edifying if sometimes dubious anecdotes about pious confessors and unlettered ascetics confounding clever pagan sophists with a simple profession of faith.

The council attempted to resolve a variety of problems and conflicts that had arisen during the previous decades, setting out penances for those who had lapsed during the persecutions and conditions for their readmission to communion, and attempting to reconcile rigorist groups such as Novatianists and Melitians (as Constantine had already attempted with the Donatists in the west) who had split from the larger church over the treatment of the lapsed. Canons attempted to regularize and tighten disciplinary standards, especially for clergy, and explicit legislation formalized existing "traditions" concerning episcopal hierarchy and precedence (e.g., the primacy of Alexandria over all Egypt and Libya, and the general rule that no bishop be ordained without the consent of the metropolitan of the province). Ritual worship practice was to be standardized: Christians were directed to pray standing rather than kneeling (as was the custom in some areas), and Easter was thenceforward to be celebrated on the date calculated by Alexandrian usage, rather than with reference to the Jewish calendar, because it seemed wrong to the bishops, and especially to Constantine, that Christians should worship differently merely because they lived in different provinces. The date of Easter was particularly important because it was widely believed that Christ would return on that day.

It was Constantine's concern for unity and consensus, as much as actual theological consideration, that guided his response to the controversy over the teachings of Arius. The Nicene Creed anathematized such statements as, "the Son was created" and "there was a time when he was not," and the word "consubstantial" (*homoousios*) was coined specifically to express the relation between God the Father and God the Son in such a way as to disallow any Arian interpretation that might liken the Son's status to that of any other created being. Constantine quickly seized upon *homoousios* and demanded that all agree to it. Under strong pressure, nearly all the bishops put their signatures to the creed, though many did so grudgingly and with reservations, and went home with very different ideas about what the word actually meant. Only two Libyan bishops, Secundus and Theonas, refused to sign; the council deposed them and Constantine then exiled them along with Arius. It seems that Constantine was angered less by their beliefs than by their stubbornness. In the next few years, Constantine readmitted various Arians once they had made a profession of faith satisfactory to him, and when hardline homoousians such as Athanasius refused to accept the former Arians, Constantine's wrath turned against them as the new obstacles to unity.

Far from creating the desired consensus, Nicaea was for the following several decades a source of unending controversy. Many were uncomfortable with *homoousios* for a variety of reasons (it did not appear in Scripture, it seemed to recall the 3rd century Sabellian heresy that had denied the individuality of the different persons in the Trinity), even if some of them also rejected the ideas of Arius. By the late 4th century, however, the homoousian party had begun to view Nicaea as a unique and holy gathering distinct from the numerous other councils of the intervening decades. Nicaea became a touchstone of orthodoxy: people defined and professed their faith in terms of its agreement with "the faith established by the 318 Fathers at Nicaea." The status of Nicaea as a fundamental basis of orthodox faith, rather than simply another gathering of bishops, was formally ratified by the Council of Constantinople in 381 and the accompanying legislation of the emperor Theodosius. Bishops at 5th century and later councils accepted without question the idea that the faith had been laid down by the Fathers at Nicaea for all time, and they themselves had only to reaffirm and clarify it.

BIBL.: J. Stevenson, ed., *A New Eusebius: Documents Illustrating the History of the Church to AD 337* (London, 1987), 338–355. R. P. C. Hanson, *The Search for the Christian Doctrine of God: The Arian Controversy, 318–381* (Edinburgh, 1988), esp. 129–180. Ernest Honigmann, "The Original Lists of the Members of the Council of Nicaea, the Robber Synod and the Council of Chalcedon," *Byzantion* 16 (1944): 20–80. Richard Lim, *Public Disputation, Power, and Social Order in Late Antiquity* (Berkeley, 1995), esp. 182–216. Colm Luibheid, *The Council of Nicaea* (Galway, 1982).   J.M.G.

Nile

The longest river in the world, the Nile facilitated communication, travel, and commerce between the Axumite Ethiopian and Meroitic Nubian kingdoms, and

Egypt of the later Roman and early Byzantine empires. From Lake Tana in the lush Ethiopian highlands, the Blue Nile flows down to the desert steppes of Nubia, where it joins the White Nile from Lake Victoria to follow a meandering northward route, rushing in rapids across granite cataracts, then north through the arid length of Egypt before fanning out across the delta and emptying out into the Mediterranean Sea. Each summer, rainfall in the highlands would flood the lands downriver, depositing the fertile sediments that allowed for Egypt's famed agricultural prosperity (until modern constructions of dams at the first cataract). Throughout late antiquity in Egypt, Nilometers, strategically positioned measuring devices, allowed predictions of the height of the floodwaters, and thus the thickness of the soil deposits and the richness of the crops to be harvested. Religious significance was seen in this recurring cycle. Late antique Egyptian descriptions emphasize the Nile's relation to the land it "embraces" in its flooding, and the ensuing generation of vegetable and animal life. The two figures of Nilos and his companion Ge may be accompanied by erotes who signify, in part, the "watery marriage" of these two chthonic divinities (Nonnos, *Dionysiaca*, Book 26). Religious rituals intended to ensure high floods continued long into Christian times.

BIBL.: D. Bonneau, *La crue du Nil: Divinités égyptiennes à travers mille ans d'histoire, 332 av.–641 ap. J.C., d'après les auteurs grecs et latins, et les documents des époques ptolémaïque, romaine et byzantine* (Paris, 1964). L. Kakosy, "Nile, Euthenia, and the Nymphs," *Journal of Egyptian Archaeology* 68 (1982): 290–298.   T.T.

Nisibis

Nisibis (modern Nusaybin in eastern Turkey) was a military, mercantile, and religious center located in the desert on the western bank of the Mygdonius (modern Jaghjaghah) River, which feeds into the upper Euphrates River. After Trajan's troops entered the city in 116, Nisibis became an important frontier of the Roman empire. Authority over Nisibis changed hands several times. The Sassanians under Ardashir I gained control of it in 238. Odenaethus, ruler of Palmyra, which was then a Roman client state, seized Nisibis for a few years around 260.

During the 4th century Nisibis suffered repeated Sassanian attacks. In 338 the Persian king Shapur I laid siege to the town of Nisibis for sixty-three days. Later tradition would remember the bishop Jacob miraculously saving the city through his prayers. After Jacob's death, Babu succeeded as bishop. In 345 Constantius, embarking on an eastern campaign, visited Nisibis but was forced to turn west when Julian declared himself Augustus. Shapur laid siege to Nisibis for three months the following year but did not succeed in taking the city. The third siege of Nisibis occurred four years later, in 350. Shapur, determined not to repeat his earlier failures, diverted the Mygdonius, which flowed past the city, and used ships carrying siege engines in an attempt to overwhelm the city walls. The people of Nisibis defended themselves by hurling fiery missiles at the ships and repairing the walls. Shapur's plan backfired as first the Persian cavalry and then the elephant brigade got stuck in the mud. This siege is described both by Julian and by Ephrem, who was an eyewitness to the events. While Julian's account (*Orat.* 2) lauds the bravery of the inhabitants, Ephrem's *Carmina Nisibena*, poems written during and after this traumatic siege, were intended to remind the Christian inhabitants of Nisibis of God's salvific purposes.

After withstanding three sieges, Nisibis was surrendered by Jovian during peace negotiations in 363, in the aftermath of Julian's defeat by the Persians. Ephrem continues to be an important contemporary source for these events (*Hymns against Julian*) and was among those inhabitants of Nisibis who were forced to evacuate the city and move westward into Roman territory. The shocking surrender of the city and the forced exodus of its citizens troubled Roman observers.

In 543–544 Byzantine forces under Belisarius sacked the countryside surrounding Nisibis, and the emperor Justin II unsuccessfully besieged the city in 572. The city's inhabitants capitulated to advancing Arab Muslim forces in 639 or 640. Despite being devastated by an earthquake in 717, Nisibis endured as a Muslim city under the Abbasids and subsequent Islamic dynasties.

Nisibis became the main trading post between Sassanians and Romans under a treaty between Narseh and Diocletian in 298. Silk was transported by caravan from China across Iran to Nisibis for sale to western merchants. This trade continued irrespective of which empire controlled the city.

The inhabitants of Nisibis in late antiquity included pagans, Jews, and Christians. The prophet Mani preached to its residents during the middle of the 3rd century. After 410 Nisibis became the seat of a Christian metropolitan. In 489 the School of Edessa, persecuted by Zeno for its Nestorian Christology, moved to Nisibis. The School of Nisibis ensured that the theological writings of Theodore of Mopsuestia were translated from Syriac into Pahlavi. Greek philosophical and scientific texts were also rendered into Iranian languages. As conversion to Islam occurred, Muslims constructed a congregational mosque (Arabic *masjid al-jami'*).

BIBL.: Jean M. Fiey, *Nisibe: Métropole syriaque orientale et ses suffragants des origines à jours* (Louvain, 1977). Richard N. Frye, *The History of Ancient Iran* (Munich, 1984). Stephen Gero, *Barsauma of Nisibis and Persian Christianity in the Fifth Century* (Louvain, 1981). Robert Turcan, "L'abandon de Nisibe et l'opinion publique (363 ap. J.-C.)," in *Mélanges d'archéologie et d'histoire offerts à André Piganiol*, ed. R. Chevallier (Paris, 1966), vol. 2, 875–890. Pierre

Yousif, "Histoire et temps dans la pensée de saint Ephrem de Nisibe," *Parole de l'Orient* 10 (1981–1982): 3–35.   EDS.

Nitria

Nitria (modern El Barnūgi) was a monastic settlement 65 km southeast of Alexandria, 30 km south of the old Hermopolis Parva (modern Damanhūr). Closely associated with the settlement were the Cells (Kellia) 15–20 km farther south in more remote desert.

The ascetic settlements of Nitria itself were placed on the rough escarpment above the westernmost streams of the Nile delta. They were founded by Amoun, who in the earliest years of the 4th century had adopted with his wife a life of continence and hard work. She eventually allowed him to withdraw, and he spent twenty-two years in the desert. In founding the remoter offshoot of the Cells, he was aided by Antony. Pambo and Macarius of Alexandria were the other most famous first-generation inhabitants, Evagrius and Palladius were in the second generation.

Nitria illustrates the fundamental characteristics of Egyptian asceticism: the gradual accretion of a community of disciples, the close relations between all Egyptian ascetics (there was considerable traffic between Nitria and the Pachomian settlements farther south), the proximity of ascetics to village life and to centers of population (here, in the delta), and their constant involvement in church controversy.

Nitria began to decline under the impact of Arian persecution and the curiosity of pilgrims. Palestine acquired greater ascetic significance from the end of the 4th century. Monks from Nitria were involved in the murder of Hypatia in 415, were deeply divided by controversy over the Council of Chalcedon of 451, and were gradually eclipsed by the increasingly prestigious and better organized monasteries of Scetis (the Wādi 'n Natrūn).

BIBL.: Derwas J. Chitty, *The Desert a City* (Oxford, 1966; repr. London, 1977). Hugh G. Evelyn White, *The Monasteries of the Wādi 'n Natrūn,* pt. 2: *The History of the Monasteries of Nitria* (New York, 1932). See also the *Apoph.patr.;* Rufinus, *Hist.eccl.* 2 3f.; *Historia monachorum* 21, 22, 30; Palladius, *Hist.Laus.* 7, 8, 10, 18; Socrates, *Hist.eccl.* 4.23.

P.R.

Nomads (Near East). *See* Ghassanids; Lakhmids; Saracens

Nomads (North Africa)

Evidence of the existence of nomadism in Roman North Africa is circumstantial, and therefore controversial. For example, a 3rd century custom's tariff from Zarai (*CIL* 8.4508) on the southern border of Numidia proves regular traffic of livestock through the post, almost certainly from southern predesert land; another 3rd century inscription from Maktar in Tunisia (*CIL* 8.11824) records the career of a traveling reaper, probably a seasonal laborer known from southern regions; a tribe called Ba(r)bari Transtagnenses are recorded in the later 3rd century (*CIL* 9324), probably people who crossed to the north from the southern Mauretanian *chotts* (salt marshes). In the late empire the Circumcellions, often linked to southern Donatists, are thought to have derived their name from the markets they toured as traveling harvesters. The Arzuges of the southeast Tunisian border, from whom an oath of allegiance was demanded, traveled north as baggage escorts and to guard the harvest (Augustine, *Ep.* 46), and the predesert Austuriani apparently frequented Tripolitanian territory (Amm.Marc. 26.4.5, 28.6.2–3).

Historiographically nomads have fared badly, with a reputation as wreckers. For what it is worth, Ibn-Kaldūn (*Hist.* 2.365, Slane) in the 14th century believed that their cattle culture proved that Berbers had followed a nomadic life "for centuries." The debate, however, is not about the existence of seminomadism before or after the Romans, but whether the Romans transformed the seasonal ebb and flow of populations, some of them from beyond the frontiers, through an active policy of containment and forcible sedentarization. Without invoking geographic determinism, one can properly see in the regular, seasonal migration of populations an explanation of the phenomena of Roman-African history. Although "grand nomadism" probably never existed, seminomadism or transhumance of flocks is not incompatible with sedentarism and leads frequently to symbiotic alliances among tribal groups between the desert and the sown. Provided that controls are maintained to prevent incursions while crops are growing, the labor of harvesters assists northern farmers, shepherds value the field stubble after the climate has dried up southern pastures, and meat is exchanged for grain.

Current archaeology illustrates how forts, *clausurae* (walls), and *fossatum* (wall and ditch) on the Tripolitanian and Numidian frontiers—many of them constructed in the later empire—seem located for controlled passage through the *limites* rather than for exclusion. The same tribal names of Roman Africa, such as the Nicives, Suburbures, Numidae, and Musulamii, appear in widely separated regions, often on nomadic routes known in more recent history, and look like fractions of symbiotically related tribes. Some market inscriptions show how the Roman administration regulated the function of exchange and labor between farmers and outsiders, and come from points where tribal groups were in contact with great estates. Inclusion of border tribes such as the Arzuges within the orbit of Roman control was probably designed to assist such seasonal movements of labor. The eventual formation of the hostile Laguatan confederation and the wars described by Procopius and Corippus in the 6th century almost certainly incorporated some of these former transhumant groups, whose power was unleashed when Roman authority crumbled.

BIBL.: D. J. Mattingly, *Tripolitania* (London, 1995). R. Rebuffat, "Nomadisme et archéologie," in *Atti del colloquio: L'Afrique dans l'Occident romain* (Rome, 1990), 231–247. B. D. Shaw, *Rulers, Nomads, and Christians in Roman North Africa* (Aldershot, Eng., 1995).   C.W.

Nomads (Northern Empire)

The vast steppes that stretched beyond the Danube, the Black Sea, and the Caucasus remained a distinctively alien and little-known space throughout antiquity. Many late antique authors still turned to Herodotus for information about the region's barbarian inhabitants, for whom the traditional name Scythian continued to be used. Others mixed old stereotypes with recent observation (e.g., Ammianus Marcellinus in his descriptions of Alans and Huns). Most texts draw a frightening picture of these "abnormally savage" barbarians. But there was also a literary tradition of positive perceptions of the Scythians, from Pompeius Trogus to Justin's *Skythika* and on to Orose and Jordanes. Few authors made use of firsthand information collected by Roman ambassadors such as Priscus—who knew the court of Attila from a diplomatic mission—Menander Protector, and Theophylactus Simocatta. It was in the later 6th century that most reliable news from the steppe reached Constantinople, a time when Byzantine diplomats traveled as far as central Asia to draw the Turks into an alliance against Persians and Avars. But that did not change the general outlook of the late Romans toward the northern peoples.

Thus, most late antique texts about the life of the nomads are colored by prejudice. Nomads are usually described as ugly and dirty, dressed in animal skins (even the skins of field mice stitched together, as in Ammianus); they were thought to eat raw meat and drink fresh blood; they did not live in houses and spent most of their time on horseback, wherefore they were almost unable to walk properly. They were described as being greedy and brutal, perjured and quarrelsome, as not obeying laws but being governed only by fear, which led to either anarchy or tyranny. But they were most able warriors who seemed to become one with their horses, sending showers of deadly arrows against their enemies and confusing them with pretended flight and sudden turns.

Not all of this was mere invention, of course; but it is a generalized image that leaves little space for acknowledging the widely different forms of life in the northern steppes. The very notion of nomadism has often been misleading, both in late antiquity and modern historiography. It tends to be confused with pastoralism—a stock-raising economy common in many parts of ancient Europe—and with a specialized cavalry warfare of the steppe that often, but not necessarily, coincided with mobile stock raising. Three fundamental mistakes have often distorted perceptions of nomadism. First, ancient observers frequently describe nomads as hunters and gatherers, tending to forget their differentiated stock breeding. Second, nomadism was—and still is sometimes—regarded as a more primitive form of life than sedentary agriculture, although it often requires very sophisticated strategies of survival in an extremely difficult ecological niche. And third, life in the Eurasian steppes was always more varied than the label "nomadism" suggests. Apart from different types of nomadic stock raising (seasonal or constant migration of part or all of the population), cooperation between nomads and sedentary economies was essential for life in the steppe. Herodotus distinguished farming, nomadic, and "royal" Scythians. Nomadic warriors' becoming sedentary after a while was a phenomenon not unknown in central Asia, but under the ecological conditions in central and eastern Europe, it was the norm. Priscus visited regular Hunnic villages. Excavations in the Carpathian basin have shown that only a few decades after their invasion, many Avars lived in villages and started to bury their dead in cemeteries that would be maintained for generations. Horse breeding, however, remained essential for all the empires of the Eurasian steppe. The *Strategikon* of Maurice notes that Avar armies had large numbers of spare horses at their disposal. This required careful coordination of their movements but gave the steppe riders unparalleled speed and mobility.

Warfare on horseback was the most obvious feature of the nomads that late Romans perceived. There were two basic types of mounted warriors: one was the Scythian type, with light armor, who mainly relied on bow and arrow, and the other was the heavily armored *kataphraktarios*, who often used a long lance, the *contus*, for which Sarmatians, Parthians, or Ostrogoths were known. Both types were successfully employed in late Roman armies, although the steppe riders remained masters of these tactics. The Avars introduced the metal stirrup in Europe, which gradually changed mounted combat in the west, whereas the reflex bow with three-sided arrowheads remained a feature of nomadic weaponry. Their cavalry attacks made Huns, Avars, and later, Magyars formidable enemies, although they were by no means invincible; the speed with which they could appear and disappear contributed to the awe they inspired. But the construction of steppe empires was by no means a purely military achievement. The success of the Huns and Avars in Europe, and that of the Hiung-nu, the Hephthalites, the Juan-Juan, and the Turks in central Asia, lay in their enormous potential to integrate very heterogeneous groups of warriors, to coordinate their movements, and to gain control of vast spaces very quickly. Although nomadism had created their potential, a tribute economy maintained these empires, and we know that

Attila and the later khagans of the Avars and Khazars had already abandoned a nomadic lifestyle for definite residences (a wooden palace in Attila's case). These enormous concentrations of power, however, survived only so long as they could expand and often could not be maintained for more than two generations.

Thus, the late Romans had to deal with several "Scythian" peoples beyond, and increasingly within, their northern frontiers. Sometimes there was a multitude of them, which allowed Roman diplomats to establish some balance. This was the case in the later 3rd and 4th centuries, when Goths dominated most of the European steppes, although never under a single ruler. Alans in southern Russia and Sarmatians on the middle Danube had already lost most of their horror. After 375 the Huns established their empire, which lasted for about eighty years and reached its peak under Attila. When the impressive tribal coalition commanded by him crumbled after his death in 453, smaller units of Huns, Goths, Bulgars, Cutrigurs, and Utigurs competed for more profitable raids in, and treaties with, the Roman empire—until the Avars appeared in 558. The Avar empire controlled the steppes along the northern frontiers of the Roman empire until their siege of Constantinople failed in 626. After that, the Avars preserved some of their power until about 800 by adapting to their Slavic environment. But the initiative in the still-profitable game of wars and treaties with Byzantium passed to the Bulgars, especially when Asparuch established a Bulgar empire on the lower Danube that was even more successful in its synthesis of nomadic and Slavic ways of life, and was therefore destined to last. Bulgars and, later, Magyars were steppe riders who successfully entered the post-Roman world, but they did so at the expense of nomadism. Nomads were to live in the Russian steppes for much of the second millennium, but only occasionally did they spill over into the grasslands along the Danube, where sedentary agriculture prevailed.

BIBL.: W. Irons and N. Dyson-Hudson, eds., *Perspectives on Nomadism* (Leiden, 1972). Otto Maenchen-Helfen, *The World of the Huns* (Berkeley, 1973). Walter Pohl, *Die Awaren* (Munich, 1988). W.P.

Noricum

Noricum, with its rich iron mines, conquered under Augustus and established as a province under Claudius, covered roughly the eastern Alps up to the Danube, east of the River Inn, between Raetia and Pannonia. Diocletian divided the province into Noricum Mediterraneum and Noricum Ripense, both governed by *praesides*; the administrative centers were Virunum, later Teurnia, and Ovilava, later Lauriacum. Along the Danube numerous fortresses were reinforced in the 4th century. This was a period of relative prosperity in which Christianity spread. Lauriacum,

Poetovio, Celeia, Teurnia, Virunum, and Aguntum are attested as late antique bishoprics.

A vivid picture of Noricum in the 5th century emerges from Eugippius's *Vita Severini*. Severinus came to Noricum after the death of Attila and established a monastery at Favianis. The population was under pressure from several groups of barbarians, especially Rugians and Heruls north of the Danube, Goths in Pannonia, and Alamans in Raetia. Although several *castra* were plundered and abandoned, Severinus organized relief and negotiated Rugian protection. Soon after the saint's death in 482, Odoacer's armies destroyed the Rugian kingdom in 487–488 and withdrew the provincials of Noricum Ripense to Italy. Thus, Heruls (until ca. 508) and Lombards (until 568) lacked the basis for a stable barbarian kingdom. Noricum became a thinly populated border zone between Avars and Bavarians. In Noricum Mediterraneum, late Roman life went on until ca. 600 under Ostrogothic and, later, Frankish dominion, as excavations at Teurnia and the Hemmaberg show. Then the Avars conquered and Slavs settled what became Carantania, whereas the name Noricum was later used for the region that would become Bavaria.

BIBL.: Geza Alföldy, *Noricum* (London, 1974). Herwig Wolfram, *Grenzen und Räume: Geschichte Österreichs vor seiner Entstehung* (Vienna, 1995). W.P.

North Africa

Late Roman Africa was more stable than most other provinces of the west, despite sporadic disturbances. Tribal coalitions in the mountains of Mauretanian Caesariensis revolted in the late 3rd century; the *vicarius* of Africa, Domitius Alexander, attempted to usurp power between 308 and 311; the southern Austuriani raided the Tripolitanian cities in 363; and there were two attempted usurpations by Firmus in 372–376, followed by the more serious revolt of Gildo in 397–398, both in the central highlands of Caesariensis. The end of Roman rule came in the early 5th century amid court intrigues of ambitious Roman officials. After 410, Alaric threatened to cross to Africa, provoking the opposition of Heraclian, the *comes Africae*, who himself crossed to Italy but was defeated. Boniface, *comes Africae* in the 420s, invited the aid of the Vandals, who crossed from Spain in 429, swept away Boniface, and overran the north. The fall of Carthage in 439 ushered in a hundred years of Vandal rule.

The North African frontiers underwent little physical change, although they were radically reorganized. The eastern sector under the *dux Tripolitaniae* was subordinate to the *comes Africae*, commanding a small field army and frontier troops on the Numidian and Mauretanian frontiers. The distinctive features, recorded on the *Notitia Dignitatum*, although begun under Diocletian (*CIL* 8.9025, dated 301), were the di-

North African mosaic depicting a prosperous Vandal leaving his villa.

vision of the *limites* into sectors under separate *praepositi,* and the heavy employment of *gentiles* units made up of southern natives under local *tribuni.* As is clear from legislation concerning the *fossatum Africae,* such *gentiles* were serving *milites.* In the western zone the sector's headquarters was located on the inland road running from the Babors to the Chelif Valley. In the far west Mauretania Tingitana was reduced to two enclaves around Sala (Rabat) and Tingis (Tangiers), protected by a *comes* within the Spanish *dioecesis.*

The civil administration was also radically restructured from three to seven (later six) provinces within the diocesis of Africa: Proconsularis, Byzacena, Tripolitania, Numidia Cirtensis and Numidia Militiana (subsequently reunited), Mauretania Sitifensis, and Mauretania Caesariensis. Unusually for a single diocesis, there was sporadically a praetorian prefect of Africa, while the governor of Proconsularis, who was technically outside his jurisdiction, sometimes doubled up as *vicarius.* There was also a prefect of the *annona* in Africa, directly responsible to the Italian prefect, showing the central importance of Africa to Rome's food supply.

The economy of Africa flourished. Material evidence of exports, amphorae (for oil and *garum*) and red-slip ware, is ubiquitous in the Mediterranean, increasingly in the east as the trade in the west declined in the 5th and 6th centuries. The effects were manifested in the cities and on rural estates of the rich. After a period of stagnation during the tetrarchy, many monumental buildings were constructed and repaired from the reign of Constantius II, most spectacularly under the house of Valentinian, stimulated and sometimes paid for by governors (often themselves African estate owners) or by rich local benefactors. Despite difficulties in finding

curiales (C.Th. 12.4), it was an "age of gold" *(AE* [1911],217) that sustained civic and ecclesiastic life until the end of Roman, Vandal, and Byzantine rule. Augustine makes repeated references to urban prosperity, and the fine mosaics of cities such as Thuburbo Maius in the late 5th and early 6th century demonstrate that Vandals did not always destroy. This municipal spirit exhibited itself in the vigor of urban institutions. Unusually for this period in the empire, Africans continued to value urban titles of status, and popular acclamations were recorded for urban magistrates. The celebrated Album of Timgad, dating to the mid-4th century, records the active magistrates of one city, while Africa has preserved the names of many *curatores,* men charged with the care of buildings and public spaces. The agricultural base from which this wealth derived is attested by the unusually numerous references to rich landlords, vast imperial estates, *conductores* encouraged by emphyteutic leases, and the depressed conditions of coloni and rural workers who augmented the profitability of the land. Augustine in the early 5th century, however, proves that one cannot generalize. While debt slavery, indentured labor, slave raiding, and abject poverty appear to have been almost everyday phenomena, some tenants were virtually free farmers. Although the Donatists made violent use of itinerant harvesters, perhaps from the south, there was little rural unrest elsewhere.

The history of the church in North Africa is almost entirely that of the struggle between the Catholic church and Donatism, suppressed under Arian Vandals but given a new twist by Monophysites under Byzantium. Donatists built as prolifically as Catholics in every city, and penalties assessed against Donatists in 412 *(C.Th.* 16.5.52) show that they were represented throughout the social strata. The penetrating influence of the church is illustrated by its perpetuation in the western territories—e.g., in the princely burials of the Djeddars—long after the end of Roman rule.

The Vandal occupation of Africa was formally recognized by Rome in 442 (and of Tripolitania in 455). It evidently was not a period of great upheaval, since Vandals often simply replaced Romano-African landlords and Roman law was applied, judging by the celebrated Albertini Tablets. Weak control, however, allowed the south and west to fall into tribal hands, illustrated by the large, fortified, and nucleated farms, such as at Ghirza in Tripolitania, belonging to local chiefs. In Tripolitania the chiefs combined to form the Laguatan confederacy, which fought the Byzantine army, while the Aures and highlands of Mauretania were effectively independent. The rapid Byzantine reconquest in 533 showed the frailty of Vandal rule but was not much more firmly rooted, depending as it did on campaigns and a chain of massive forts quarried from former city monuments. The wealth of Africa, plus a vicious tax regime, financed new building at the expense of internal revolts that left Africa prey to southern invaders. By 548 peace was established by John Troglita, and it held for a century. But continued peripheral pressure racked the exarchate of Africa, and in 647 Islamic forces broke upon the Maghreb, which finally succumbed to Arab intrusions along the southern marches in the late 7th century.

BIBL.: C. Courtois, *Les Vandales et l'Afrique* (Paris, 1955; repr. Aalen, 1964). Yvette Duval, *Loca sanctorum Africae: Le culte des martyrs en Afrique du IVe au VIIe siècle,* 2 vols. (Rome, 1982). C. Lepelley, *Les cités de l'Afrique romaine au bas-empire* (Paris, 1981). David J. Mattingly and R. Bruce Hitchner, "Roman Africa: An Archaeological Review," *Journal of Roman Studies* 85 (1995): 165–213. D. Pringle, *The Defence of Byzantine Africa from Justinian to the Arab Conquest* (Oxford, 1981). Susan Raven, *Rome in Africa,* 3rd ed. (London and New York, 1993). Brent D. Shaw, *Environment and Society in Roman North Africa: Studies in History and Archaeology* (London, 1995). Brent D. Shaw, *Rulers, Nomads, and Christians in Roman North Africa* (London, 1995).   C.W.

Notarii

In the strict sense of the term, *notarii* were stenographers (also called *exceptores* or *amanuenses*) who served rich individuals as well as the central state, the provincial administration, and the imperial army. The profession had servile connotations from its beginnings and well into the 4th century, even though at that time some imperial notaries reached the highest levels of power and social position, in areas unrelated to their initial technical competence. High-ranking imperial stenographers obtained the title of tribune (*tribuni et notarii;* those of lower rank were *domestici et notarii*) and constituted a *schola.* The latter term has naturally led people to believe that the corps had a military origin—to be precise, that it emerged from the palace *protectores* and praetorian tribunes. But just as the *notarii* were in close contact with emperors long before the oldest known attestation of them (386), we may suppose that they were recruited from the ranks of the educated bourgeoisie beginning in the 3rd century. These new *notarii* then gradually replaced the servile and emancipated staff (still largely attested under Diocletian). We need not suppose, however, that there was a transitional phase when the bureaucracy was militarized (Teitler, adopting the traditional explanation).

The *schola* of *notarii* may have been created in the age of Constantine and Licinius (Teitler), along with the *magister officiorum* to which it was attached but which never did more than keep its enrollment records.

Moreover, the *tribuni* and *notarii* answered only to the emperor, whom their commander attended directly; he was in charge of the *laterculum malus,* or list of all holders of civilian and military posts. Under Constantius, there was a sudden expansion of the role of *tribuni* and *notarii,* and the number of their missions multiplied. Given access to state secrets, they were to use their vocation to be the emperor's representatives; they were charged with special missions, and this has led some commentators to associate them with the *agentes in rebus.* Like the latter, *notarii* have been called a "secret service agency." Such an association should not be exaggerated (notaries were more visible than the *agentes in rebus*), and the use the authorities made of *notarii* had a visibility that is difficult to reconcile with the idea of secrecy. In fact, might the term *tribune* not be an allusion to the tribunician power the emperor delegated to them? One can only be struck by the extent of their powers, which they freely exercised on governors and dukes, and which included the right to put persons to death without a judgment. They were in all respects their masters' eyes and hands, in political and legal missions as well as military, ecclesiastic, and diplomatic ones.

At first, the position of *notarius* was a social springboard only for secretaries of the Consistory; the key was to move through the ranks and duties of consistorial *comes.* But soon all *tribuni et notarii* followed. The highest careers opened up to them: Ablabius, a notary who came to Constantine's attention, was praetorian prefect under Constantius; Flavius Taurus was by turns palace quaestor, praetorian prefect in Africa, then in Italy and Africa, and finally consul. Procopius was the first usurper to have come from the notary corps. It took a few decades to carve out this new type of political career, which the senatorial aristocracy itself finally had to accommodate, after having looked down on these parvenus. Their level of recruitment rose very rapidly, as did their cultural profile. Some held their positions as sinecures, and many of these were distinguished in letters (Claudian, John Lydus). The importance of their role did not change in later eras, as attested in Justinian's *Novella* 8.

Exceptores were still to be found in the *officia* of governors, particularly to take down the minutes of judicial hearings. Like any administration, the churches also acquired *notarii* (e.g., Paulinus, Ambrose's biographer), who assumed their full importance in the Middle Ages. City-states continued to use them, under the name *symbolaiographoi, nomikoi, notarioi,* or *advocati,* in their *archivum* or *grammatophylakion.* This was the case for even the smallest city-states, such as Thubursicu Numidarum, where *notarii* refused to work overtime to record the public doctrinal controversy between Augustine and local Donatists. In 316 their social rank was lower than that of the curials, but the profession's role, status, and honoraria continued to grow. Notaries' access to curial duties, which required that an old legal prohibition be sidestepped, attests to their relentless social ascent, itself a metaphor for the power of the written word in that late antique civilization.

Finally, more modestly, another branch of the *notarii* developed as a liberal profession in the service of individuals, to compile and guarantee their transactions. In an Egyptian "notarial" document of 319 the term *tabellio* appeared for the first time, a word that in some sense marked the birth of the modern notary corps. However, it was only with medieval communal law that the notary was recognized as a public officer. Notaries recorded the most important contracts *(insinuatio apud acta gesta municipalia),* and under Leo the concept of *instrumentum publice confectum* developed. It was these private *notarii* whose practices Justinian *(Nov.* 44 and 73, for 536–538) sought to reform; he licensed them, it seems, and imposed standards of form and substance for writing materials ("paper protocol"), guaranteeing in exchange the "efficacy" of the documents compiled by the *notarii.* Even under these conditions, their legal knowledge remained elementary and their professional conscientiousness unremarkable. They were primarily concerned with the external presentation and bombastic formularies of their documents, since they were paid by the line for their longueurs and redundancies. As a relic of the origins of the profession, some of these private *notarii* were still slaves, as shown in a law of 530, which also suggests opening the profession to women.

BIBL.: Mario Amelotti, "Alle origini del notariato romano," in *Studi storici sul notariato italiano,* ed. Mario Amelotti and Giorgio Costamagna (Rome, 1975). Hans C. Teitler, *Notarii and Exceptores: An Enquiry into the Role and Significance of Shorthand Writers in the Imperial and Ecclesiastical Bureaucracy of the Roman Empire* (Amsterdam, 1985). J.C.

Notitiae

Notitiae were lists or catalogues, also referred to as *latercula.* Such lists were typical of the systematization that characterized the late Roman bureaucracy. The variety of extant *notitiae* (most published in the *Notitia Dignitatum* as edited by Seeck [1876]) can be broken down into four categories: provincial lists, urban catalogues, episcopal lists, and the *Notitia Dignitatum.*

Provincial lists include the *Notitia Galliarum* (late 4th century), which lists provinces in Gaul together with their capitals and cities; it was later readapted as an episcopal list; the *Laterculus Veronensis* (revised ca. 314 but reflecting earlier redactions) lists dioceses and provinces of the empire and barbarian peoples; the *Laterculus Polemii Silvii* (448–449) lists dioceses and provinces, mixed with a hodgepodge of further cata-

logues ranging from calendars to animal sounds (ed. Mommsen *MGH.AA* 9.1.511–551). These, together with conciliar lists of bishops and their sees, are crucial for charting late Roman provincial divisions.

Among urban catalogues, the *Notitia urbis constantinopolitanae* (ca. 425–430) lists the fourteen regions of Constantinople, along with their most notable buildings and local officials. The *Notitia urbis regionum XIV* (preserved in two manuscript traditions, one before 357, the second before 403) lists the fourteen regions of Rome and their monuments, officials, and facilities. These documents are central to understanding the topography and demography of 4th century Rome and 5th century Constantinople.

The extant episcopal lists *(taxeis)* of eastern ecclesiastical dioceses are referred to by modern scholars as *notitiae.* The oldest surviving Constantinopolitan list dates to the early 7th century but was probably built on a late 4th century original; the Antiochene list originated in the 6th century.

The *Notitia Dignitatum omnium tam civilium quam militarium*—the "*notitiae* of all offices, both civil and military," also called the *laterculum maius*—lists all civil officers and their subordinates together with all military officers, their subordinates, and the units under their command. Most of the *notitiae* mentioned have been transmitted from copies of a now lost manuscript, a fragment of which indicates a 10th century date. The manuscript included illustrations that are especially abundant for the *Notitia Dignitatum* and that are accurately reproduced in their late Roman style in a copy of 1551. The lists of civil officers include illustrations with the insignia of their office; the lists of limitanean officers illustrate their forts; those of the *magistri militum* show the shield emblems of their units.

The *Notitia Dignitatum* is divided into eastern *(orientalis = Or.)* and western *(occidentalis = Oc.)* halves, which were maintained as ranked personnel rosters by the *primicerius notariorum* (or. 18.4; Oc. 16.5). Attempts at dating are complicated because each half was revised piecemeal after its initial composition; particular confusion arises in the western military sections, which reflect several phases of alteration: Clemente argues for an original ca. 395 with revisions ca. 401–408 and ca. 425–429; Hoffmann supports 394 for the eastern military sections (except Illyricum) and ca. 425 for the western. The entire document is crucial for establishing the size and shape of the late Roman bureaucracy and army.

BIBL.: G. Clemente, La "Notitia Dignitatum" (Cagliari, 1968). R. Goodburn and P. Bartholomew, eds., Aspects of the Notitia Dignitatum (Oxford, 1976). D. Hoffmann, Das spätrömische Bewegungsheer und die Notitia Dignitatum, 2 vols. (Düsseldorf, 1969–70). Jordan, ed., Topographie der Stadt Rom im Altertum (Berlin, 1871). Darrouzès, ed., Notitiae episcopatuum ecclesiae constantinopolitanae (Paris, 1981). N.L.

Novatianists

The history of the Novatianists stands paradigmatic for rigorist movements within late antique Christianity: their followers were either lauded as paragons of the perfect Christian life or condemned as misguided schismatics or heretics.

Novatian, the personality whose name would become associated with the schismatic church, entered history in the context of a fundamental debate: how to deal with the *lapsi,* persons who had recanted during periods of persecution.

Novatian's origins are unknown. According to Eusebius's *Historia ecclesiastica* (6.43.17), he became presbyter of the Roman church before 250, whereby his uncommon erudition counterbalanced reservations caused by his sick-bed baptism. He first appeared in public when the martyrdom of Bishop Fabian during the Decian persecutions had left the Roman see vacant: Novatian exchanged letters with Carthage on behalf of the Roman clergy, confirming that—until Fabian's successor had been nominated and a binding synodal agreement reached—*lapsi* (those who had sacrificed) had to do penitence, and could be readmitted into the community only if death was imminent (Cyprian, *Ep.* 30.8 and 8.3.1; 20.3.2).

When persecutions ceased in 251, the majority of the Roman clergy elected Cornelius as bishop. Novatian, supported not only by other clerics and bishops but also by the influential confessors, became counterbishop. Subsequently both bishops sharpened their position: Cornelius (and Cyprian) favored a more lenient stance, whereas Novatian, as speaker of the "pure" (*katharoi*), maintained that all cooperation, whether through purchase of a *libellum* or actual sacrifice, required penitence (Cyprian, *Ep.* 45; 55; 57; 59; Eusebius, *Hist.eccl.* 6.43.5–22).

Since these issues concerned all of Christianity, both bishops sought churchwide support. By 253 Cornelius's conciliatory position had found acceptance in Antioch and Alexandria as well as Carthage. Novatian, despite his official condemnation, organized his own, oppositional church (Cyprian, *Ep.* 55; 59; Socrates, *Hist.eccl.* 4.28). One of the most prominent Roman Christians, Novatian must have died around 258, under Valerian; his designation as martyr incited long-lasting controversy (Vogt, *Coetus* 24–26).

Novatian was the first Roman Christian to write in Latin. Four works preserved under the names of Tertullian and Cyprian (in addition to Cyprian, *Ep.* 30, 31, 36; for the remainder cf. Jerome, *De vir.ill.* 70) emphasize the purity of the church and a rigorist attitude toward "sexual sins" derived as much from Stoic ethics as New Testament precepts, an indication that this characteristic of later Novatianists had a long tradition (Vogt, *Coetus,* 136–153).

Novatianist congregations survived opposition in all major Christian centers and even flourished in several areas. In 325, Nicaea supported the receiving of Novatianist clergy into the Catholic hierarchy under preservation of rank if they admitted penitent apostates and those who had married again, that is, renounced Novatianism (*can.* 8). In 326, Constantine recognized Novatianist churches (*C.Th.* 16.5.2).

A number of mostly oppositional 4th and 5th century sources affirm the widespread influence and high praise elicited by the Novatianists in east and west. The *Quaestiones* attributed to Ambrosiaster and works by Ambrose, Pacian of Barcelona, and Recticius in Gaul illustrate that the Novatianist version of a pure Christianity required constant refutation (Ps.-Aug., *Qu. test.* 102; Ambrose, *De paen.* 1.3; Pacian, *Epp. tres;* Jerome, *De vir.ill.* 82). Socrates (*Hist.eccl.* 4.28, 5.21, 7.6 and passim; Sozomen, *Hist.eccl.* 2.22) confirms a strong Novatianist presence in Asia Minor and Constantinople (perhaps a revitalization of Montanist tendencies). He saw them as formidable Christians worthy of emulation, not as heretics. Eusebius of Emesa noted growing support of Novatianists in Syria (Jerome, *De vir.ill.* 91). In Africa, the Donatists seem to have become their successors. A 7th century refutation by Eulogius of Alexandria (Photius, cod. 182, 208, 280) attests to the continuing vigor of rigorist movements subsumed under the label Novatianism, which might have influenced Bogomils and Cathars.

BIBL.: G. F. Diercks, ed., *Novatiani Opera, Corpus Christianorum, Series Latina,* vol. 4, 1972. H. J. Vogt, *Coetus Sanctorum: Der Kirchenbegriff des Novatian und die Geschichte seiner Sonderkirche* (Bonn, 1968). S.E.

Nubia

The modern concept of Nubia roughly corresponds to what Greek and Roman authors refer to as Aithiopia, the middle Nile region from Aswân in the north to south of Khartoum. Our detailed knowledge of its northern part, lower Nubia, largely derives from surveys and excavations necessitated by the successive dam constructions in southern Egypt, culminating in the United Nations (UNESCO) salvaging campaign of 1959–1969. Upper Nubia, the heartland of ancient Nubian civilization, has only recently begun to attract systematic archaeological attention, and our picture of its history is consequently in a state of flux.

The beginning of late antiquity was a turbulent period in Nubian history. Allegedly on the order of Diocletian (Procopius, *Wars* 1.19), the Romans left their garrisons in the Dodecaschoenus, which since Augustus had served as a buffer between Egypt and Nubia—that is, between the Roman empire and sub-Saharan Africa. The kingdom of Meroe, more specifically its lower Nubian province, filled the vacuum and inherited the struggle against the ferocious desert tribes, the Blemmyes (identified with modern Beja). Meanwhile, the Meroitic state itself, with its splendid capital of Meroe, had great problems closer to home. Its history in the 3rd and 4th centuries has been described in terms of the classic paradigm of decline and fall: its economy was weakened through a decrease in trade; the desert nomads west of the Nile, in particular the Noba, occupied parts of its territory; its neighbor to the southeast, the kingdom of Axum (modern Ethiopia), outdid it commercially and invaded it by military force (testified by Axumite inscriptions in Greek found at Meroe; *Fontes historiae nubiorum* 3.285f.).

Recent scholarship stresses the continuity between the Meroitic kingdom and the succeeding local dynasties, which left rich burials at Ballana and Qustul in lower Nubia and el Hobagi in upper Nubia. A fascinating glimpse of the internal strife that seems to have characterized the period is provided by the Greek inscription of Silko, "*basiliskos* of the Nobades and all the Aithiopians," who in colorful language claims to have triumphed repeatedly over the Blemmyes (mid-5th century; *Fontes historiae nubiorum* 3.317); it has been suggested that Silko acquired the status of a federate to the Roman emperor. Another intriguing document is the papyrus letter of the Blemmyan king Phonen to his Nobadian counterpart (*Fontes historiae nubiorum* 3.319), written in a kind of pidgin Greek that obscures its allusions to historical events.

Nubia emerges again in our historical sources in the 6th century, divided into three kingdoms that were all converted to Christianity, though allegedly in different forms: Nobadia in the north and Alodia (Alwa) in the south received Monophysite missionaries, whereas Makuria in the middle region became orthodox; John of Ephesus tells the picturesque story of the rivalry between Justinian and Theodora that was behind this. Christianity had in fact entered Nubia earlier, as archaeological finds show. At least by the late 7th century, when Nobadia and Makuria merge into one powerful kingdom with Old Dongola as its capital, Monophysitism seems in sole control.

Christian Nubia kept a kind of Byzantine identity for centuries after the Arab conquest of its northern neighbors. While Coptic influence was strong in Nubian monasteries where religious refugees from Egypt were received, elaborate epitaphs discovered all over Nubia of bishops and worldly dignitaries show that Greek remained the official church language. The style of the delicate 8th century wall paintings of the Cathedral of Faras, as well as the titles of Nubian officials, are further indications of a persisting Hellenism.

BIBL.: William Y. Adams, *Nubia: Corridor to Africa* (London, 1977). J. Cuoq, *L'islamisation de la Nubie chrétienne* (Paris, 1986). Tormod Eide, Tomas Hägg, Richard H. Pierce, and László Török, eds., *Fontes Historiae Nubiorum*, vol. 3 (Bergen, 1998). László Török, *Late Antique Nubia* (Budapest, 1988).   T.H.

Nubian Language

In late antiquity and the Middle Ages, Nubian was the principal language of the kingdoms of Nobadia, Makuria, and Alodia, a region covering roughly the area of modern Sudan and southern Egypt, and it is the direct ancestor of the Nubian still spoken in that area. Belonging to the Nilo-Saharan family, Nubian is the only native African language whose development can be traced for more than a millennium.

The written remains of Old Nubian—so called to distinguish it from the contemporary language—extend from the 8th to the 15th century, though most of the texts come from the 10th to the 12th. The language is written in a modified form of the Greek uncial alphabet, with extra letters drawn from the Coptic and Meroitic scripts. If printed in a modern edition, the corpus of Old Nubian would occupy fewer than one hundred pages of continuous text. Of the material preserved, about half is of religious content, consisting of translations of the Greek New Testament, the Septuagint, and other Christian writings, while the remainder is documentary, made up of public contracts, private letters, and similarly ephemeral material.

Until recently, all research on Old Nubian was based on the collection assembled by F. L. Griffith in *The Nubian Texts of the Christian Period* (Abhandlungen der Königlich Preussischen Akademie der Wissenschaften, 1913). But the material available to Griffith amounted to only about twenty pages of continuously printed text. Now, thanks in large part to excavations undertaken in response to the United Nations (UNESCO) campaign to save the monuments threatened by the Aswân Dam, many new texts have come to light, and the corpus has more than quadrupled. The new material has also allowed significant improvement in understanding the language, and consequently many of the interpretations proposed by Griffith must now be abandoned. The recent works listed in the bibliography at the end of this article build on the information now available.

Of the new texts, particularly important is the Old Nubian translation of Ps.-Chrysostom, *In venerabilem crucem sermo*, discovered by the University of Chicago in the course of its excavations at Serra East. It is by far the longest Old Nubian text extant, and direct comparison with the surviving Greek model has permitted us greatly to enhance our understanding of the language. In addition, a substantial body of material—both literary and documentary—has been uncovered at Qaṣr Ibrīm by the Egypt Exploration Society.

The general characteristics of Nubian are: the word order is subject-object-verb; the language employs postpositions instead of prepositions; and the genitive tends to precede its noun, while the adjective follows it.

BIBL.: G. M. Browne, *Introduction to Old Nubian* (Berlin, 1989). Browne, *Literary Texts in Old Nubian* (Vienna, 1989).

Browne, *Old Nubian Dictionary* (Louvain, 1996). *Old Nubian Texts from Qaṣr Ibrīm* (London: Egypt Exploration Society), vol. 1 by J. M. Plumley and G. M. Browne (1988); vols. 2 and 3 by G. M. Browne (1989 and 1991).   G.M.B.

Nudity

The period of late antiquity saw broad changes in conceptions of nudity as a result of religious teachings about the body in Christianity and later in Islam. These changes, visible in dress and art, in public spectacles and religious rituals, reflect the accommodation of new cultural concerns and social values. At the beginning of the period, nudity was accepted in Roman culture in a variety of contexts. Naked female dancers and theatrical performers of both sexes entertained spectators in mimes and at festivals. An early 4th century mosaic at Piazza Armerina in Sicily depicts young women exercising and sporting. Men competed unclothed in athletic games, and public baths were a cherished site of social activity around the late Roman world, although there were probably separate bathing times for women and men. Wealthy Romans who owned slaves felt no unease at being naked before them, regardless of their sex.

Public nudity, however, had always been moderated by Roman social values, and it was accepted in contexts in which the social status of the person was obvious to everyone. Modesty was seen as largely unnecessary for the lower classes, while strict standards of dress for elite women had long been upheld. Thus, in 203 C.E., when Perpetua was stripped for martyrdom in the arena at Carthage, the crowd recognized the shocking humiliation of a well-to-do woman. Ammianus Marcellinus records that in 368 when Flaviana, an accused adulteress, was brought out naked for her execution, the executioner himself was subsequently burned alive for his crime against a Roman of high birth. There were fewer constraints on the bodies of men. The nude of the soldier, a common subject in Roman art, exemplified the honored status of the male body in Roman culture. The Romans viewed heroic nudity in other cultures similarly. Their historians described the Celts sending a vanguard of naked soldiers into battle who wore only a neck torque for magical protection. Ferocious, strange, and impractical as this custom was, it was also impressive. The strength and vigor of the body in its natural state was something the Romans could understand.

Yet by the 4th century, monks had become acutely aware of the dangers of not only women but also the bodies of their brethren and even their own genitalia. In Egypt, Pachomius (d. 347) cautioned monks against lifting their tunics too high while working, lest they inspire temptation among their companions. In the 5th century they were instructed to avoid looking at their own body. The late antique world, where it was touched by Christianity, gradually adopted new standards of dress and sexuality. Clothing became a protection against desire, and as dress codes began to reflect this, the slightest show of hidden parts, even the hair of a woman, yielded a glimpse of nakedness. Local customs sometimes had to be explicitly addressed by the church: bishops in Ireland in the late 5th century dictated that clerics must wear long tunics and conceal their private parts and that their wives should cover their heads. In late Roman statuary, the ideal male and female forms of ancient Greece continued to be invoked, but now they were draped in clothing. The scale of the nude dwindled: female mythological characters, such as the Nereids, once widely diffused in Roman public art as figures of sensuality and abundance, survived in smaller form on sarcophagi and in Coptic needlework.

There was a growing concern in the church with not only the purposes of sexuality but with its management as well. Early Christian authors who promoted the ideal of celibacy and approved of intercourse solely for the purpose of procreation were writing against the pervasive Roman conception of sexuality and desire as natural and good. The effect of Christian teachings was not just that the sexes were separated, for this had existed in pagan society as well, but that the standard of modesty could not be mitigated by lower social status. If the end result of modesty in the Christian world appears uniform, the process by which this occurred was full of debate about the meaning of the flesh. Christian writers differed in the degree of optimism or pessimism with which they saw the ability to shut out occasions for and even thoughts of sexuality. Jerome (d. 420), among others, tried to devise ways of conquering sexual urges; his contemporary Augustine (d. 430) saw the pudenda as beyond the control of the will, a consequence of the expulsion from paradise. Hence human flesh was inextricably bound to the notion of permanent shame for all humanity.

Judaism had preceded Christianity in its concern with shame, as was evident in the Maccabaean dislike of the gymnasia in the 2nd century B.C.E. But the shame of public nudity, in Judaism, was not predominantly sexual. An anonymous opinion in the *Sifre to Deuteronomy*, a midrashic collection of the 3rd or 4th century C.E., interprets the "nation of fools" referred to in Deuteronomy 32:21 as meaning "those who come from Barbary and Mauretania and walk about naked in the marketplace." This was an image of contemptible and uncivilized behavior, evidence even of barbarity.

The emergence of Islam in the early 7th century wrought a less dramatic change in the social practices of Arabia, where there existed few occasions for public nudity. Arabian styles of dress were already modest; Tertullian, writing four centuries before the Prophet Muhammad, reported that Arabian women left only one eye uncovered by their long mantle. Men customarily wore a long outer garment as well. However, one important event demonstrated clearly the assertion of Islamic standards over a pagan practice of nudity. In pre-Islamic Mecca, the sanctuary around the Ka'ba had long been the site of pluralistic pagan worship, and the circumambulation *(ṭawāf)* of the Ka'ba was a ritual that predated Islam. Etiquette at the sanctuary was dictated by prominent tribes who had strict ideas regarding the Ka'ba's holiness. They required that special garments be worn at the sacred precincts; men who did not have the proper clothing, usually those from visiting bedouin tribes, performed the *ṭawāf* naked. By 630 Muhammad had gained enough political support to dictate the customs of the Ka'ba, and he prohibited both nudity and pagan worship there.

The Qur'ānic portrayal of Adam and Eve's nudity (e.g., 7:22–27) mirrors the equation of clothing and shame in the book of Genesis. The Qur'ān tightened the parameters of permissible behavior and dress, advising both men and women to keep their glance cast down and to cover their private parts (24:30–31). One verse seems to restrict visual contact between the head of a household and his slaves and children: "Let those who are in your possession and those who have not yet reached puberty ask leave of you before the morning prayer, and when you put off your clothing at noontime, and after the evening prayer: these are three times of nakedness for you" (24:58). The verse thus indicates not a proscription of nudity but rather the delineation of social boundaries in specific contexts and between different categories of people.

The teachings and exemplary practices of Muhammad, as contained in the hadith literature, provide examples of how local customs were corrected: during the rebuilding of the Ka'ba, Muhammad had hitched up his loincloth to make it easier to carry stones, but afterward he declared that this constituted nudity. Islamic dress codes came to require that a specific amount of the body be covered by clothing; the private area *('awra)* included a zone that extended well beyond the genitals and was defined according to gender, status, and context. During prayer, for example, legal scholars asserted that the *'awra* of a free woman included her body and her hair; on a man it extended from his navel to his knees. The *'awra* of the slave woman was the same as for a man, though some legal traditions added that her front and back should be covered as well, and this was more than likely the normal practice.

Nudity was thus imbued with various meanings over the course of late antiquity. The heroic nude, which had slowly vanished from late Roman life, was nowhere to be found in the Islamic world. When the historian al-Masūdī described a rebellion in Baghdad in 812, he enlivened his account with a description of a group of riffraff who attacked the army naked but for their loincloths, riding naked human mounts who were decorated as horses. To some degree, Roman cultural values survived the onset of both Christianity and Islam, as evident in the fresco paintings of nude women and men in the Umayyad bathhouse at Quṣayr 'Amra in Jordan. But nudity was hardly a vital part of public life in any of the lands that came under Muslim rule in the 7th century. Unclothed bodies had retreated to the household and to the private hours of domestic life.

BIBL.: Peter Brown, *The Body and Society: Men, Women, and Sexual Renunciation in Early Christianity* (New York, 1988). Henri-Irénée Marrou, "Sur deux mosaïques de la villa romaine de Piazza Armerina," in *Christiana Tempora* (Rome, 1978), 253–295. F. E. Peters, *The Hajj: The Muslim Pilgrimage to Mecca and the Holy Places* (Princeton, 1994). Aline Rousselle, *Porneia: On Desire and the Body in Antiquity,* trans. Felicia Pheasant (Oxford, 1988). Georg Schöllgen, "Balnea Mixta: Entwicklungen der spätantiken Bademoral im Spiegel der Textüberlieferung der Syrischen Didaskalie," in *Panchaia: Festschrift für Klaus Thraede,* ed. Manfred Wacht (Münster in Westfalen, 1995). M.R.

Ocean

The traditional Graeco-Roman personification of Oceanus shows a full-length figure standing or reclining, often accompanied by his consort Tethys or Thalassa. A more striking image, whose origins go back to the early empire but which is particularly common on monuments from the 3rd century C.E. onward represents the god as a huge bearded mask from which water streams. It is frequently crowned with lobster claws or antennae, has fish entwined in the hair, dolphins issuing from the mouth, and a beard or hair ending in scrolls of seaweed. This image of the source of all waters occurs especially on mosaics in fountains, where water may literally pour from the mouth, or in baths; other marine figures and deities may be associated with it in a subordinate position. The image is found throughout the western Mediterranean, but is especially frequent in the North African provinces and in Spain; outstanding examples come from Themetra in Byzacena, Aïn Témouchent near Sitifis in Mauretania Sitifensis, and Dueñas near Palantia in Hispania Tarraconensis. A similar image occurs in silver at the center of the Great Plate of the Mildenhall treasure, surrounded by marine and bacchic friezes. Alternatively, four such heads may be depicted, for instance at the corners of a mosaic, in allusion to the streams of Ocean encircling the world.

The role of Ocean in baths was not only a straightforward allusion to the watery element; it also served as metaphor for the profusion of pleasures and blessings. In a similar metaphorical sense "Ocean" could be used (like "Nile") as an acclamation to applaud a benefactor's liberality. Moreover there are signs that in North Africa the image, which often has huge staring eyes, could be credited with magical or apotropaic powers and used for protective purposes; thus on the mosaic from Aïn Témouchent, which probably dates to the 4th or 5th century, the image is accompanied by an inscription that implies that it is powerful against the force of envy or the evil eye.

Ocean could also be used, like other personifications of natural and cosmic forces, in a Christian context. The mosaics of a church in Petra show a full-length figure holding a rudder and ship, identified by name as Okeanos, among other images of the earth under God's rule. In the transept of the 6th century Basilica of Dometios at Nicopolis, a panel shows a border of marine creatures and fish surrounding a landscape of trees and birds; the accompanying inscription explains it as an image of "the famous boundless Ocean containing the earth in its midst . . ." The traditional personification has been replaced here by a more literal symbol, but the basic sense is unchanged.

BIBL.: K. Dunbabin, "*Baiarum grata voluptas:* Pleasures and Dangers of the Baths," *Papers of the British School at Rome* 57 (1989): 26–27. H. Maguire, *Earth and Ocean: The Terrestrial World in Early Byzantine Art* (University Park, Pa., 1987). Pauline Voûte, "Notes sur l'iconographie d'Océan: À propos d'une fontaine à mosaïques découverte à Nole (Campanie)," *Mélanges de l'École Française de Rome, Antiquité* 84 (1972): 639–673. K.D.

Officials

Later Roman imperial bureaucracy was a small organization. By the 6th century, there were perhaps somewhere around 35,000 salaried imperial officials—a tiny number compared with the area and population of the empire; insignificant compared with the public service bureaucracies of modern industrialized states. That said, the imperial bureaucracy in late antiquity was significantly larger than its counterpart of the first three centuries C.E., an increase that was most marked in the growth of a more sophisticated and more highly centralized court-based administration.

The most convenient guide to the formal structure and duties of late Roman officialdom is the *Notitia Dignitatum,* a dossier of official positions, given in strict rank order by administrative department. The copy that survives is a composite of a number of separate lists, each updated at different times. But it is reasonably certain that it provides a fairly comprehensive picture of the imperial bureaucracy in the eastern half of the empire at the end of the 4th century.

At court, the *Notitia* catalogues an intricate and highly centralized structure dominated by six high-ranking officials: the *praepositus sacri cubiculi,* who organized the imperial household; the *magister officiorum,* who supervised the secretariats *(scrinia)* dealing with petitions, reports, and embassies, as well as exercising some responsibility for the imperial postal system *(cursus publicus)*, the palace guard *(scholae palatinae)*, and the *agentes in rebus;* two senior officials who headed the imperial treasury; the *quaestor sacri palatii,* who was responsible for drafting imperial legislation; and the *primicerius notariorum,* who supervised the *notarii* and drew up the *Notitia Dignitatum.*

An equally complex hierarchy of administration enforced imperial rule in the provinces. At its apex were four prefectures—Gaul (which included Britain and Spain), Italy (which included Africa), Illyricum, and the East—each in the charge of a praetorian prefect, one of the most powerful civil officials in later Roman government, with overall responsibility for judicial, financial, and taxation matters. At its base, each provincial governor (114 are listed in the *Notitia*) headed a permanent administrative department *(officium)*, with its officials carefully graded from the departmental head *(princeps officii)* down to the basic administrative officers *(exceptores)* and financial staff *(scriniarii)*.

Of course in practice the pristine clarity of the *Notitia*'s meticulous classification of rank and function was rarely realized. Rather, the bureaucracy often presented a set of confusing complexities—areas of administrative responsibility frequently overlapped or shifted between departments; rules and regulations were sometimes inconsistent or contradictory; the arcane "burcaucratese" in which they were written was difficult to comprehend. Dealing with bureaucrats was both time consuming and costly. At the very least, those seeking administrative action were expected to pay fees to an official to ensure his cooperation in the performance of his duty.

Officeholders, too, could find their own organization complex and unrewarding. With no clear set of criteria for promotion, some remained for years in junior positions or as part of the corps of unsalaried, nonestablished officials *(supernumerarii)* who worked for each department in the hope of promotion when a vacancy arose through death, retirement, or the resignation of an official who no longer enjoyed the support (or protection) of his superiors. Others were more successful, perhaps combining talent with advantageous connections or with the resources to purchase a good position in a strong department able to protect—or better expand—its administrative responsibilities.

Some insight into the institutional culture of later Roman bureaucracy and the attitudes of its personnel is provided by John Lydus, for forty years an official on the judicial staff of the eastern praetorian prefecture. In his *On the Magistracies of the Roman State,* written in the early 550s, he included a partly autobiographical account of the prefecture's history. John's appointment as an *exceptor* and early rapid promotion were due principally to the support of the praetorian prefect Zoticus, a fellow provincial, and to the strength of the judicial side of the department, which had expanded its duties at the expense of the rival financial branch. In such favorable circumstances, John enjoyed "a not insubstantial income from fees and a most eminent honour coupled with effective power" (*Mag.* 3.10).

For John, the charging of fees for his official services was morally unproblematic. Fees were a necessary and expected supplement to a small salary. In the absence of any state pension or superannuation, fees provided funds for his retirement, and they allowed him to recoup the expenses he had incurred in acquiring his position. But the good times of John's early career did not last. The financial side was advantaged by a series of reforms that deprived the judicial branch of much of its fee income, "and those who were nearing the end of their service lamented and wept, sinking as they were into an old age of poverty" (*Mag.* 3.66). John, forced to abandon his career, retained a lasting and bitter hatred of his financial colleagues and of the praetorian prefect John the Cappadocian, who had favored them. Writing *On the Magistracies* was, in part, John Lydus's fantasy revenge on a superior whom, alongside administrative incompetence, he graphically accused of avarice, luxury, gluttony, cruelty, sexual depravity, and physical deformity.

The colorful invective of the disappointed John Lydus, and his account of self-seeking interdepartmental rivalries, provides a version of late antique officialdom at some difficult distance from the impersonal, serried ranks of the *Notitia.* These conflicting pictures are not easily reconciled. It has been argued that, on balance, the administrative blockages and inefficiencies caused by bureaucrats concerned to pursue their own best interests and maximize their fee income hindered rather than helped imperial rule. In some circumstances, that was undoubtedly the case. But overall, without some kind of reasonably effective administrative organization, it is difficult to see how later Roman government would have been able to operate in so many new areas or to raise the funds to finance its armies, support a new religion, and build a second imperial capital. In that sense—despite a clear failure in practice to realize the kind of streamlined organization set out in the *Notitia Dignitatum*—the marked increase in the number of officials in late antiquity, and in the range and complexity of their administrative tasks, can be seen as contributing to a pattern of rule aimed at consolidating and strengthening the power of central government.

BIBL.: T. F. Carney, *Bureaucracy in Traditional Society: Romano-Byzantine Bureaucracies Viewed from Within* (Lawrence, Kans., 1971). A. H. M. Jones, *The Later Roman Empire 284–602: A Social, Economic, and Administrative Survey,* 3 vols. (Oxford, 1964; repr. in 2 vols., 1973), vol. 1, chs. 12 and 16. R. MacMullen, "Roman Bureaucratese," *Traditio* 18 (1962): 364–378; repr. in R. MacMullen, *Changes in the Roman Empire: Essays in the Ordinary* (Princeton, 1990).   C.K.

Olives

Cultivated olives are a basic food in the Mediterranean diet. They were known in Palestine as early as the sixth millennium; olive oil has been known since the fourth millennium. Olives came to the west only slowly. In Provence, cultivated olive trees appeared in about the 4th century B.C.E., spread by the Phocaeans. The olive can be consumed as is or in various preparations. Above all, it produces an oil that can be used not only as food but also in the care of the body, in medicine, and in industry (lighting, lubrication). Olive press residues have been used for heating and for animal feed.

There were many religious uses for olive oil in late antiquity: in addition to providing light in sanctuaries (a very important function), consecrated oil served as an unction during baptism and was a beneficent and healing substance when it came into contact with relics. In northern Syria, reliquaries provided sanctified oil on demand. The reliquaries, several of which were established in an annex located north or south of the altar or joined to the chancel, offered a service distinct from the mass. Pilgrims could carry away holy oil in glass flasks, metal vials (such as those conserved in the Bobbio monastery), or clay vials.

Oil was produced in two basic phases. First, the olives were crushed to separate out the oil-gorged pulp and to drain off the bitter liquid called *amurca*. Through crushing, a homogeneous paste composed of pulp and pits was obtained. In several regions, water was added during this operation to avoid fermentation, which could give the oil a bad taste. In late antiquity, the crushing was done with a single millstone that pivoted around a central column inserted into a stationary tank. In northern Syria, another system was also used in which olives were thrown into a shallow tank and crushed under stone rollers that moved about in it.

In the second phase, the olives were pressed. The paste obtained from the first operation was placed in frails *(fiscinae)*, flat, round baskets whose diameter varied from .5 m to 1 m. Frails were made of vegetable fiber or goat hair. Paste was piled into the frail and gradually pressed. Oil seeped out of the paste and was gathered in a collecting vat and purified. In the purification process, water was added to separate the oil from the lees, and the liquid was drawn off. The pressing operation was frequently done with a beam: one end was secured in a recess in the wall or between two *arbores* (plain or slotted press piers), while the other end was slowly lowered. The pile of lees was gradually pressed on a press bed near the secured end of the beam. A wooden frame was sometimes placed between the lees and the moving end of the beam, to prevent the latter from shifting under heavy pressure.

In the west, the great olive oil–producing regions were the Iberian Peninsula of North Africa (including the Tripolitana), and, in the *pars orientis*, Palestine and northern Syria. Excavators have discovered several hundred complete olive press installations in Syria. Although olive oil production in the west declined somewhat in the second half of the 3rd century (the region continued to export oil, however), in the east it increased greatly between the 4th and 6th centuries. Other regions, such as Cyprus, Asia Minor, Greece, the Aegean Islands, and Provence also produced oil, but little is known about the size of those operations.

Every region developed technical variations. Curiously, Judaea (and the lower Galilee) preferred a system without a beam, using a direct frame press installed between two *arbores*. In the rest of Palestine, the beam was used consistently and was lowered with the help of a weight, sometimes simply suspended from the beam. Sometimes the weight was maneuvered by a windlass. Beginning in the 3rd and 4th centuries, however, a more advanced technology, the screw, was most often used. Depending on the type of brace used, the screw could be fixed, surmounted on a moving nut (a technique rarely attested elsewhere), or moved with a fixed nut. Palestine had another particularity: in the south, the vat into which the pressed oil ran was under the press bed, but in northern Palestine the vat was next to it. In northern Syria, all sorts of procedures were used to lower the lever (windlass mounted on a frame or on a parallelepiped weight) but, as in Palestine, the screw-type lever was more widespread, with cylindrical, parallelepiped, or (rarely) truncated weights. The vat was located in the press column. Cyprus has a few good examples of 6th and 7th century oil works where the use of the screw was widespread. Weights, most often of the screw type, are being discovered in great numbers in the Aegean basin (on Lesbos and Amorgos, in the Pontus, and also in Bithynia and Phrygia).

In Spain and Portugal, early Christian presses had one end of the beam secured by two *arbores,* and the weights were of the screw type. There is a good example of such a press in the villa of Vilauba. In North Africa and Tripolitana, presses from the early Christian era generally had one end of the beam secured by *arbores,* and the weights were generally parallelepipeds with a windlass. The absence of a screw may indicate a certain technological backwardness. In Carthage, however, several cylindrical weights with screws have been found, apparently indicating eastern influences. The round central mortise and screw heads may indicate this was a fixed screw (as in Palestine). In southern Gaul, the use of the screw spread in the 4th century. Ten percent of windlass weights were modified at that time to accommodate a screw.

One phenomenon characteristic of the time was the presence of presses beside other farm equipment in the outbuildings of churches, as has been found in Dalmatia, Salona (an episcopal complex, the churches of Monastirine and of Kapljuc), Greece (Brauron and Gortyna), Cyprus (Agia Varvara in Amathus and Chrysopolitissa in Kato Paphos), Syria (monastery of Ed Deir), and Palestine (Horvat Beit Loya and Ain el-Jedide).

Thus the Mediterranean production of olive oil continued to be significant during late antiquity. No doubt the concentration of the means of production was not as high as it had been in the 2nd century and the first half of the 3rd. There were no longer four or even six presses together, as in Roman North Africa. Production seems to have been broken down into smaller units (most often two presses), but there were also more of them. Thus we cannot exclude the possibility that in certain regions (northern Syria, Palestine) there was an exportable surplus that may have played a role in trade (primarily sea trade), which was very active until the 7th century. All the same, the containers have yet to be identified. Many late amphorae now appear to have been designed for wine (the inside is coated with resin), but other containers (such as casks and perhaps wineskins) must have existed as well.

BIBL.: O. Callot, *Huileries antiques de Syrie du Nord* (Paris, 1984). J. P. Brun, *L'oléiculture antique en Provence, les huileries du département du Var* (Paris, 1986). M. C. Amouretti, J. P. Brun, and D. Eitam, eds., *La production du vin et de l'huile en Méditerranée* (Paris, 1993). W. Gessel, "Das Öl der Märtyrer," *Oriens christianus* 72 (1988): 183–202.

J.-P.S.

Olympiodorus of Thebes

Olympiodorus, from Egyptian Thebes, was a Greek poet and historian of the early 5th century. He traveled widely, both on his own (e.g., to the Blemmyes of Upper Egypt) and as a Roman ambassador (to the Huns north of the Danube, among others). We can be confident that he visited Italy and Rome at least once, and he may have spent considerable time in the west, which is the main focus of his *History,* over the course of his life.

Of his poetry, we have only one line, unless a fragmentary *Blemmyomachia* preserved on a Berlin papyrus has been rightly ascribed to him. We know something of his *History* from the Byzantine patriarch Photius's summary and from the use made of it by the church historian Sozomen and the pagan historian Zosimus. Dedicated to the eastern emperor Theodosius II, it covered in detail the period from 407 or 408 to 425. The story of the dismemberment of the west by northerners, mainly Germanic peoples, begins in this period, which was also a time of considerable internal disorder for the west. Olympiodorus began with the fall of the western generalissimo Stilicho (408), to whom he was sympathetic, and with the low point of the Visigothic ruler Alaric's sack of Rome (410) and ended on a note of hope with Theodosius II's installation of Valentinian III as western emperor. He appears to have been generally well informed, interested in detail, and a man of independent judgment. His *History* contained a good amount of personal information and a variety of digressions. Not aiming to produce a work in the high historiographical style, Olympiodorus used Latin terminology in Greek transliteration. His *History* clearly revealed his pagan views, despite its Christian addressee.

BIBL.: R. C. Blockley, *The Fragmentary Classicising Historians of the Later Roman Empire,* 2 vols. (Liverpool, 1981–1983). J. F. Matthews, "Olympiodorus of Thebes and the History of the West (A.D. 407–425)," *Journal of Roman Studies* 60 (1970): 79–97. F. Paschoud, "Le début de l'ouvrage historique d'Olympiodore," *Studia in honorem Iiro Kajanto = Arctos Supplementum* 2 (1985).

R.P.

Origenism

Origenist heresy takes its name from Origen, an Alexandrine theologian whose theses, though condemned in the 3rd century, spread and developed in the 4th, especially when espoused by Evagrius Ponticus.

In the late 4th century, a group of Origenist monks settled in Lower Egypt in Nitria and Kellia (the Cells), near Ammonius and his three brothers (the "Tall Brothers"). Evagrius joined them in 383. These influential monks were acquainted with Rufinus of Aquileia and Melania the Elder, who were then living in Jerusalem.

The first crisis for Origenism was triggered by Epiphanius of Salamis, who in 374 attacked Origen and contemporary Origenists. In Palestine in 393, he took action against Bishop John of Jerusalem, who was suspected of Origenism. St. Jerome, a monk in Bethlehem and once a great admirer of Origen, rallied behind Epiphanius and attacked John of Jerusalem and Rufinus. He succeeded in having Origen condemned by Pope Anastasius. In Egypt, Theophilus of Alexandria, until then having favored the Origenists, severed all ties with them. In 400 he convened a synod that condemned Origen's writings and their readers. A police operation was mounted against the monks of Nitria, and the Tall Brothers left Egypt. The bishop of Constantinople, John Chrysostom, welcomed them; Theophilus then fought against him and won (403). He reconciled with the surviving Tall Brothers in 404. Jerome was now alone in battling Origenism, but his attacks on John of Jerusalem thenceforth had to do with Pelagianism.

During that first period of crisis, the Origenists were criticized for their doctrine of the preexistence of souls: that intellects, which once existed with God, had become separated from him; joined to bodies, they were transformed into stars and planets, angels, men, or demons. After a complex cycle of resurrections, they again assumed their initial place and their bodies were destroyed. Origenist Christology subordinated the Son to the Father and distinguished between Christ and God as Logos.

After a century of calm, Origenism resurfaced in Palestine. In 514 the superior of the New Lavra, a monastery founded by Saba, discovered Origenist monks in his ranks. Their leader, Nonnos, remained the soul of the movement until his death. These monks were expelled, but they returned. In 530 Saba, now in Constantinople, exposed another Origenist, Leontius of Byzantium, in his own entourage. He expelled him, but Leontius became influential in the capital city. From then on, the Origenists had two bases of operation at their disposal: the monasteries of Palestine, where they made inroads after the death of Saba in 523; and Constantinople. In 536 two Origenists were named to important bishoprics by Emperor Justinian: Domitian in Ancyra (Galatia), and Theodore Ascidas in Caesarea (Cappadocia). In 537 orthodox leaders reacted. Led by Gelasius, superior of the Great Lavra of St. Saba, they expelled the Origenist monks, who took refuge in the New Lavra. Most important, with the help of the Roman deacon Pelagius, they obtained a decree from Emperor Justinian condemning Origen (543).

The Origenists did not relent. One of them became superior of the New Lavra (547); another, Macarius, was bishop of Jerusalem (552). However, at the death of Nonnos (547), they divided: the "Isochrists" of the New Lavra, along with Ascida, attacked the "Tetradites," so called because they were accused of introducing a fourth personage (the "Christ") into the Trinity. The Tetradites, whose Christology was more orthodox (for them, Christ's intellect was the first to be created, hence their other name, "Protoctists") changed camps. In 552, Conon, orthodox superior of the Great Lavra, and Isidore, head of the Protoctists, obtained the emperor's intervention. Macarius of Jerusalem was replaced. In 553 the bishops, gathered in Constantinople for the Fifth Ecumenical Council, subscribed to the fifteen anti-Origenist anathemas the emperor had submitted to them and put an end to the crisis.

Just as the condemnation of 543 was directed at errors committed in the 4th century, the anathemas of 553 targeted the Christology the Isochrists had borrowed from Evagrius: Christ was the only intellect that had not experienced the Fall; it was he, not God, who had created the world, and he also who incarnated himself. At the final restoration, every intellect would be Christ's equal (hence the name "Isochrist") and would be able to create worlds.

BIBL.: Elizabeth A. Clark, *The Origenist Controversy: The Cultural Construction of an Early Christian Debate* (Princeton, 1992). A. Guillaumont, *Les Képhalaia gnostiques d'Evagre le Pontique et l'histoire de l'Origénisme chez les Grecs and chez les Syriens* (Paris, 1962).   B.F.

Ostrogoths

The nature and causes of the long-term survival of the Goths as a people have been hotly debated in recent years. Few now accept that there are many points of genetic, let alone cultural, similarity between the Gotones described in the late 1st century C.E. in Tacitus's *Germania* and the Gothi, whose rulers established kingdoms in Italy and Spain four hundred or more years later. The traditional view of Gothic history derives almost exclusively from the *Getica,* written around 551 in Constantinople by Jordanes, himself a Goth, who was drawing on the lost twelve-book history of the Goths by Cassiodorus. On the basis of Jordanes's account, it has been thought that the Goths migrated southeastward from an original homeland in southern Scandinavia in the 1st century C.E., arriving in the region between the lower Danube and the River Don in the mid-3rd century. Thence they were pushed westward by the Huns about a hundred years later, and in consequence came to enter Roman territory in a series of waves. It is now accepted that early Gothic history is more complex than Jordanes's version would indicate. Some scholars, though not all, dismiss the account of the Scandinavian origins and most accept that the Goths formed just one of the several elements of a Germanic-speaking population that shared a common material culture and set of distinctive burial practices. Archaeologists have labeled this the Wielbark culture. It appears to have been centered initially in the north of modern Poland and to have gradually extended its influence southward toward the Carpathians in the later 2nd and 3rd centuries. Its burial practices also link the Wielbark culture to the subsequent Černjachov/Sîntana de Mureş culture, the main find sites of which are farther to the southeast, along the edge of the Carpathians and down to the Black Sea, and date from the later 3rd century to the early 5th. This seems to have represented the Germanic domination of a larger subject population of mixed origins that included Slavic and Sarmatian elements and that corresponds with Ammianus Marcellinus's account of the Gothic kingdoms of the Tervingi and the Greuthungi, often taken as the immediate ancestors of the subsequent Visigoths and Ostrogoths. Reality was probably more complex, with numerous different Gothic and other Germanic groups being established across a wide area from the Don to the Danube. Their ascendancy was disrupted by the cultural changes associated with the establishment of Hunnic hegemony over a wide range of subject populations north of the Danube. In consequence various Gothic groups began to be admitted into Roman territory from 376 onward, and as the result of complex, changing relationships with successive imperial governments, varying from economic dependence to open warfare, they then came to be widely distributed across the empire, from Anatolia to Gaul.

The real origins of the Ostrogoths as a clearly distinguishable component of the larger Gothic population probably lie in the mid-5th century. The first stage can be identified as the creation of a following by a certain Valamer during the troubled period preceding and following the collapse of the Hunnic hegemony north of the Danube around 453–454. Despite Valamer's death in battle against the Gepids, leadership of this group was retained by his family, in the person, first, of his brother Theodemer, and then of his son Theoderic. Under pressure from the Gepids, Heruls, and Avars, they and their followers crossed the Danube into imperial territory in 473, where they came into rivalry and occasional conflict with another large confederacy of mixed origin but under Gothic leadership. This group was ruled by another Theoderic, known as Strabo or "Squinter," and then, after his accidental death in 481, by his son Rechitach. The two Theoderics sought to succeed to the military and political role once exercised by Aspar, and to institutionalize the position of their followers within the empire by securing office for themselves and annual supplies and subsidies for their troops. The emperor Zeno (474–491) played off the two confederacies and their leaders until the younger Theoderic was able to murder Rechitach in 484 and take over most of his following. Unwilling to concede to Theoderic's demands, but unable to face him militarily, Zeno came to an agreement with the Gothic leader in 488. This led to Theoderic's invasion of Italy in 489 and, after some hard fighting and the siege of Ravenna, the overthrow of its ruler, Odoacer, in 493. Theoderic was accompanied to Italy by remnants of the Rugi, who had been defeated by Odoacer in the 480s and who retained their own separate ethnic identity under the rule of the Gothic kings. The new emperor, Anastasius I (491–518), was initially unwilling to ratify his predecessor's treaty with Theoderic, who

was proclaimed king of Italy by his followers after he murdered Odoacer. Not until 498 was a new agreement with the empire reached, and very few of its details are known for certain. In practice Theoderic and his successors ruled unopposed from Ravenna until Justinian's army, fresh from victory over the Vandal kingdom in Africa, invaded Italy in 535. The ensuing war lasted for nearly twenty years, with a brief pause in 539–540 following the surrender of the Ostrogothic king Vitigis (536–539). Renewed fighting broke out the following year under new Gothic leaders, the most successful of whom was Baduila, or Totila (541–552). His defeat by Justinian's general Narses at the battle of Busta Gallorum in June 552, and that of his short-lived successor Theia at Mons Lactarius in October of the same year, put an end to large-scale Gothic resistance, and the surviving Goths began to be shipped out of Italy to serve in imperial armies in the east. There, broken up into small units, they lost their sense of ethnic and cultural distinctiveness, and they are not heard of again. However, in Italy some local Gothic communities continued to resist in the north, and Verona fell only in 562. Any remaining Goths in Italy are likely to have been absorbed into the ranks of the Lombards following their invasion in 568.

The nature of the settlement that followed the conquest of Italy in 493 is not clear, in that there is still scholarly disagreement over the meaning of the procedures of *hospitalitas*, the method whereby Germanic populations were integrated into Roman fiscal and administrative structures. Traditionally, it was taken that references to Gothic "thirds" implied that Roman estates were divided up, with a fixed proportion of the lands, slaves, and movable goods being redistributed to the barbarian "guests." However, it has been strongly argued that what was reassigned was tax liability, with the Roman taxpayer being made directly responsible for the financial support of specified Germanic soldiers. The older view would imply a rapid establishment of Goths as landed proprietors throughout Italy, while the latter could leave them functioning as no more than urban military garrisons. Archaeologically, the evidence for the Ostrogothic presence in Italy is very limited, but what there is indicates that the greatest concentration was to be found north of the Po. This was reflected in the proposal made in negotiations in 540 that Italy should be divided, with a much reduced Ostrogothic kingdom continuing to exist north of the river.

Relations between Goths and Romans in Italy were normally harmonious, until the later phases of the war of reconquest. Theoderic (493–526) appointed senators to the major posts in the civil administration, and very occasionally to important army commands. In general, however, a distinction was maintained between the civilian character of Roman society and the military function of that of the Goths. This ideology was articulated not least in Cassiodorus's official correspondence, which also stressed the king's aims of restoring the cultural splendors of the former Roman state. Several Goths, notably Theoderic's nephew and short-lived successor Theodehad (534–536), embraced Roman intellectual as well as material culture. Although, like most of the Goths, Theoderic was an Arian, his intervention in 506 to end the long-running schism in the see of Rome was warmly welcomed. Bishop Ennodius of Pavia (d. 517), a partisan of the victorious Pope Symmachus, was a vocal supporter of Theoderic's regime, and composed a panegyric on him. It was long thought that harmonious relations between the court at Ravenna and the Roman Senate broke down late in Theoderic's reign, because of the trials and executions of Boethius in 523 and his father-in-law, Symmachus, in 525, and the death in prison of Pope John I (523–526). Recent arguments modify such a view, denying that Boethius and his circle wanted an imperial restoration and placing greater weight on factional conflicts within the Senate. Several monuments of the Ostrogothic period still survive in Ravenna and its port of Classis, notably the two churches dedicated to St. Apollinaris and a baptistery, all built for Gothic Arian congregations. Although altered after the imperial conquest, they retain traces of their original mosaic decoration, including a possible portrait of Theoderic relabeled in the name of Justinian. The king's mausoleum and sarcophagus also survive.

BIBL.: Patrick Amory, *People and Identity in Ostrogothic Italy, 489–554* (Cambridge, Eng., 1997). Peter Heather, *The Goths* (Oxford, 1996). Michel Kazanski, *Les Goths (Ie–VIIe après J.-C.)* (Paris, 1991). R.C.

P

Pachomius

Born ca. 292 in southern Egypt to a pagan family, Pachomius, at the age of twenty, was conscripted into the army of Maximinus Daia during his war against Licinius. One night the soldiers were shut up in a prison in Thebes and some Christians brought them food. Impressed by their charity, Pachomius prayed to their God, promising to serve him. When Maximinus was defeated a few months later, Pachomius returned to the area where he had met the Christians. He was instructed in the Christian faith and baptized in Chenoboskion. For a few years Pachomius practiced asceticism with the anchorite Palamon. After Palamon's death, Pachomius was joined by his brother John, who disagreed with Pachomius's plan to invite others to join their life of asceticism. After his brother's death, Pachomius began to build a monastic community around himself.

Regarded by posterity as the founder of communal or cenobitic asceticism in 4th century Egypt, Pachomius was in that sense "the father of monasticism." By the time he died in 346, at least seven monasteries for men and two for women had been established under his influence and command along the Nile between Latopolis and Panopolis. His first foundations, at Tabennesi and Chenoboskion, were not far from the famous Coptic "library" of Nag Hammadi. Although they varied surprisingly in size and structure, each developing its own relationship to a loose federation, these communities bore the mark of his genius for order and efficiency.

Tradition has been ambiguous in safeguarding Pachomius's memory. Detailed hagiographies in both Coptic and Greek (the Bohairic *Life* and the Greek *Vita prima,* in particular) encourage us to construct a moderate portrait, in which a degree of self-doubt is balanced by spiritual insight and the encouragement of mutual regard and support. Such accounts appear to spring from the monastic communities themselves, and their later devotion and their vigorous attachment to orthodoxy may disguise the realities of their past. Other witnesses, such as the letter of Ammon and the *Paralipomena,* create an impression at once harsher and less stable. However, their present forms, which are as late as the hagiographies, are frequently marred by animus, ignorance, or falsification. It may be wisest in the end to fall back on what we know from other types of sources—indirectly related papyri, in particular—about ascetics in Egypt during Pachomius's lifetime.

Those who wish to underpin a secure heritage and an orthodox disposition, therefore, or who—like Palladius—admired the size and discipline of later foundations, should not obscure for us the figure of a pioneer less certain and successful in his own lifetime, and more closely allied both to the eremetical tradition represented by Antony and to the often turbulent life of church and community in the towns and villages of Upper Egypt.

BIBL.: David Brakke, *Athanasius and the Politics of Asceticism* (Oxford, 1995). Derwas J. Chitty, *The Desert a City: An Introduction to the Study of Egyptian and Palestinian Monasticism under the Christian Empire* (Oxford, 1966; repr. Crestwood, N.Y., 1995). J. E. Goehring, *The Letter of Ammon and Pachomian Monasticism* (Berlin and New York, 1986). James

E. Goehring, "New Frontiers in Pachomian Studies," in *The Roots of Egyptian Christianity,* ed. Birger A. Pearson and James E. Goehring (Philadelphia, 1986), 236–257. Philip Rousseau, *Pachomius: The Making of a Community in Fourth-Century Egypt* (Berkeley, 1985). Armand Veilleux, *La liturgie dans le cénobitisme pachômien au quatrième siècle* (Rome, 1968). *Pachomian Koinonia,* ed. Armand Veilleux (Kalamazoo, Mich., 1980).   P.R. AND EDS.

Pagan

Pagan derives from the Latin *paganus;* in classical Latin, the term referred to a nonparticipant, one excluded from a more professional or more distinguished group. It could mean no more than "private" as against "public" or "official." The implications of inferior status became clear as the term spread throughout the later empire. *Paganos, pgn,* or *pgn'* was a Latin loanword common to Greek, Hebrew, Aramaic, and Syriac. It stood for "civilian" as distinct from "soldier" or "official," for "commoner" as distinct from "civic notable." The adoption of *paganus* by Latin Christians as an all-embracing, pejorative term for polytheists represents an unforeseen and singularly long-lasting victory, within a religious group, of a word of Latin slang originally devoid of religious meaning. The evolution occurred only in the Latin west, and in connection with the Latin church. Elsewhere, "Hellene" or "gentile" *(ethnikos)* remained the word for "pagan"; and *paganos* continued as a purely secular term, with overtones of the inferior and the commonplace—in 19th century Egyptian Arabic, *baghanūs* still meant "stupid" or "unrefined."

The use of *paganus* in Latin Christianity echoed a widespread need to see the world in strictly religious categories. Persons, such as the framers of curses, who had an interest in descriptions that left no human group unaccounted for, added religious categories to the usual social categories (male/female, slave/free): *christianus/gentilis* appear on a 4th century curse tablet at Bath; Jew/gentile on a magic bowl in Iraq; ". . . *ani*" (pagans or Romans), Jews, and Christians on a 4th century gravestone at Salona. Used by Tertullian in its old sense of "civilian," *paganus* occurs on Christian inscriptions of the early 4th century in clear distinction to the baptized *fidelis.* Up to the end of the 4th century, Christian writers tended to employ *paganus* as a self-conscious "vulgarism," a word of common Christian parlance adduced to define the more traditional *gentilis.* In the 5th century, such reserves vanished: *pagan,* even *paganism—paganitas—*became universal terms in Christian Latin. In 417, in his *Histories against the Pagans,* Orosius deliberately identified the cultivated Roman defenders of the old gods as men of the *pagus,* peasants (*pagus* > *pays* > *paysans, paesanos*), excluded by their "earthy" ignorance from participation in the true city—the City of God. Orosius's etymology of *paganus* was further elaborated in the early Middle Ages. Originally a learned jibe, the identification of polytheists with the *pagus* was not meant to describe the actual distribution of paganism between town and country, but it has continued to play a role in fostering the assumption that paganism, as a religion of the peasantry, must have survived longer in the countryside than in the cities of the west. The religious connotations of the word *paganus* did not affect the Byzantine world until the conversion of the Balkans in the 9th century. But the Old Slavonic *pogan',* for "pagan," represents the reemergence of *paganus* in its western, religious meaning, as it had continued to be used among the surviving Latin speakers of the Balkans. Describing Croatia, the emperor Constantine VII Porphyrogenitus wrote: "For *Pagani* means 'unbaptized' in the Slavonic tongue."

BIBL.: Constantine Porphyrogenitus, *De administrando imperio* 29, ed. G. Moravcsik and R. Jenkins (Budapest, 1949), 126. E. Demougeot, "Remarques sur l'emploi de paganus," *Studi in onore di A. Calderini* (Milan, 1956), vol. 1, 337–350. E. A. Sophocles, *Greek Lexikon of the Roman and Byzantine Periods* (Leipzig, 1914; repr. Hildesheim, 1992), 829. S. Krauss, *Griechische und lateinische Lehnwörter in Talmud, Midrash und Targum* (Berlin, 1899), 421. J. Zeiller, *Paganus* (Paris, 1917). B. Altaner, *Zeitschrift für Kirchengeschichte* 58 (1939): 130–141, and C. Mohrmann, *Vigiliae christianae* 6 (1952): 109–121.   P.B.

Paganism

The populations of the Roman world (apart from the Jews), whether living under city jurisdictions or in ethnic communities, had many cults and worshiped many deities without structuring their beliefs into a religion. In the 1st century of the Christian era, the Jew Philo gave a name to that set of beliefs: polytheism. Beginning in the 4th century, Christians in the west spoke of pagans *(pagani),* and those in the east of "Hellenic" cults, adopting a term already used by the pagans themselves. Between the 3rd and 7th centuries, though remaining robust, these cults without question experienced a decline in numbers and political influence in Mediterranean regions, to the advantage of Christianity and Islam.

Since the local components of cults are known to us primarily through inscriptions, and since inscriptions as a whole (religious or not) declined sharply beginning in the mid-3rd century, it is difficult to follow this evolution. One cannot infer from the gap in documentation that the cults grew weaker, and Christian sources, such as Augustine, Macrobius, Firmicus Maternus, Theodoret of Cyrrhus, and John of Ephesus, must be used with circumspection.

While Christianity was seeking its own path, pagan gods and their rites persisted everywhere. The cults were primarily local (civic or not) and worshiped local (city or ethnic) deities. These gods were sometimes associated with Graeco-Roman deities, more by their powers than by the myths. The cults, which remained local even under Graeco-Roman influence in iconography and language, did not weaken in the 3rd century. In Dura-Europus on the Euphrates and in Ostia, the cults continued. In Rome, the cult of the Arval brothers, which flourished in the early 3rd century with the construction of the *thermae*, elected a new magister in 304. All the same, in regions affected by invasions, such as northern Gaul, sanctuaries suffered along with residences, and buildings were not maintained to the same degree everywhere. After a period of pillaging in the 4th century, reconstruction of pagan sanctuaries again occurred.

One public cult united the various peoples of the empire, as declared in the edict of Caracalla, which in 212 gave citizenship to all free residents of the empire. This was the cult of the emperor. In the 3rd century few temples to the imperial cult were still being built, but emperors granted *neocoria* (a function of this cult) to cities in Asia. Until the great persecutions by Diocletian (303–304), animal and plant sacrifices made to the emperor, to his *genius*, his *numen*, or his statue, served as a test that true Christians would refuse to carry out. Deceased emperors were believed to join the ranks of the gods (in the Greek world) or of divine personages, or *divi* (in the Latin).

Certain local pagan cults in Greece and in the east had followers in the west. The cult of Cybele (an official cult in Rome in 204 B.C.E.) and of Attis persisted in the upper strata of society until the late 4th century. Initiations in the cult of Isis continued, and the temple of Portus Romae was restored. Mithras, rarely attested in the east, though he originated in Persia, was popular in the northwestern Mediterranean in the 2nd century. In the 3rd century, new places to worship Mithras appeared: in the east in Dura-Europus, and in the west in Bordeaux, for example. Rooms dedicated to Mithras were built or restored on the ruins of Gallic sanctuaries in the late 4th century.

Cults did evolve, however. Although the rites persisted, Christian criticisms produced a new phase of myth interpretation in the 3rd century. In general, we must deduce the pagan beliefs based on practices described in these texts. It was never necessary within pagan practice itself to make beliefs (faith) explicit, except within mystery cults, where the elaboration of myths and rites was an essential component of the ritual. But there was no universal, normative pronouncement of faith. Since the classical Greek era, the question of belief had appeared within the context of philosophical discussions. Porphyry and Emperor Julian felt they had to give new interpretations of myths and rites, moving beyond the explanations already offered in the ritual practices of Mithras (Porphyry, *On the Cave of the Nymphs in the Odyssey*) or Cybele (Julian, *On the Great Mother*). Statues of gods or emperors were sacred, as practices attest, and pagan philosophers sought justifications for them. Iamblichus produced reflections on statues, sacrifices, and supernatural phenomena. There were never unified or fixed beliefs, however.

Extraordinary (paradoxical) events, which the Romans called wonders, were carefully recorded. These could be ecological events (in zoology, botany, meteorology) as well as healings. Interpretations of these events were advanced and recorded as well, particularly regarding the future of rulers, as seen in the *Historia Augusta* and in Ammianus Marcellinus.

When Christian emperors restricted and then banned pagan cults, they were targeting sacrificial rituals in particular. Constantine allowed a temple to be built to his *gens* (*CIL* 11.5265), provided that it not be a place for criminal superstition—that is, for sacrifices. New converts to Christianity had attempted to link the religious slaughter of animals to Christian celebrations. In 6th century Byzantium, pagans were still making sacrifices. Feasts, banquets, and even games were allowed by Christian emperors, provided sacrifices and gladiators were excluded. It is believed that pagan rites persisted as "relics" in certain Christian practices. They had a new spirit, however, inasmuch as monotheism focused the expectations of believers on a single god.

In the 3rd and early 4th centuries, paganism manifested its vitality and, above all, its concerns about those who refused to respect its rites, by demanding the death of Christians. That situation changed when political power fell into the hands of Christian emperors. There was no systematic reverse persecution, but pagan cults were attacked at their foundations. Civic cults were denied public funds, and temple property was confiscated. Gratian, for example, refused to be *pontifex maximus* and had the altar of Victory removed from the Senate. Pagans were not allowed to teach, and sacrifices were forbidden.

BIBL.: P. Brown, "Christianization and Religious Conflict," *Cambridge Ancient History* 13, ed. A. Cameron and P. Garnsey (Cambridge, Eng., 1998), 601–631. G. W. Bowersock, *Hellenism in Late Antiquity* (Cambridge, Eng., 1990). Pierre Chuvin, *Chronicle of the Last Pagans* (Cambridge, Mass., 1990). Toufic Fahd, *Le panthéon de l'Arabie central à la veille de l'Hégire* (Paris, 1968). J. Teixidor, *The Pagan God: Popular Religion in the Greco-Roman Near East* (Princeton, 1977).

A.R.

Pahlavi

Pahlavi, the major dialect of Middle Persian—one of the West Middle Iranian languages—was used between the 3rd and the 11th century. Attested in cursive-book and inscriptional forms, it served as both the official language of the Sassanian empire and as the medium in which Zoroastrian exegesis, theology, and mythology were elaborated.

Despite being an Indo-European language, Pahlavi

was written using a modified Aramaic script in which short vowels were not recorded. The script displayed a considerable degree of ambiguity, with several letters having multiple consonantal values and no distinguishing diacritical marks. The cursive-book Pahlavi script possessed fourteen letters, the inscriptional script nineteen. A lesser variant, used to write Psalter, had eighteen letters. The corpus of surviving Pahlavi language materials includes the *Psalms of David* discovered in Chinese Turkestan, graffiti, official and personal rock inscriptions from the Sassanian era, legends on Sassanian coins and seals, legends on coins of the Dabuyid Ispahbads of Tabaristan, and a fairly large number of Zoroastrian texts mainly dating from 800 to 1000. Pahlavi was eventually replaced by New Persian, which developed from the former but came to be written in a modified Arabic script.

Pahlavi inscriptions from Sassanian times include those by Shapur I at Naqsh-i Rostam and Marseh at Paikuli. Sassanian coin obverse legends often read: "The Mazdean lord . . . [king's name] . . . king of kings of Iran [later adding: 'and non-Iran'])) who is from the lineage of the gods." The reverse usually mentioned the ruler's regnal flame: "The fire of . . . [king's name] . . ." Zoroastrian Pahlavi books include a *Zand* "commentary" on the *Avesta;* the *Bundahishn* ([Book of] Primal Creation), preserving the Magian creation myth; the *Denkard* (Acts of the Religion), providing in synoptic form a compendium of knowledge available to persons living in late antiquity; and the *Arda Wiraz Namag* (Book of the Righteous Wiraz), describing a journey through heaven, limbo, and hell—an account that may have influenced similar sagas in Islam and medieval Christianity.

BIBL.: Jean P. De Menasce, "Zoroastrian Pahlavi Writings," in *The Cambridge History of Iran*, vol. 3, pt. 2, ed. Ehsan Yarshater (Cambridge, Eng., 1983), 1166–1195. Robert C. Zaehner, *The Teachings of the Magi: A Compendium of Zoroastrian Beliefs* (New York, 1976). J.K.C.

Painting

The main categories of surviving late antique painting are three—mural, manuscript, and panel—and they yield interesting results when analyzed historically, both individually and in conjunction. Alongside continuity with the Roman tradition of painting, the works demonstrate innovation in the new functional contexts of the church, the liturgical book, and the icon. Painting on any surface, by its very nature, is fragile. No late antique Pompeii has yet come to light, and this should be borne in mind with regard to generalizations about painting.

Ancient painters were creative in devising wall systems for interior decoration, one of the most popular of which involved illusionistic elements: architecture, landscape, and marble revetment. All of these elements appear in late antique wall painting, though recon-

figured to reflect the taste of the time, with a preference for precious materials and dark, rich colors (purple, often in imitation of porphyry, and gold). Colored floor mosaics played an increasingly important role in interior decoration in both private and public spaces (Ostia; Theodosian Basilica at Aquileia), and the coordination of painted walls and colored floors (or lack thereof) is exemplified by the Villa at Piazza Armerina, with its bold and simple mural schemes in dark red, dark yellow, and purple adjoining brilliant, multicolored floors filled with figures and scenes. The room that once held the painted ceiling at Trier, with its rows of staring heads and *putti* in fictive coffers (one of the rare examples of painted ceiling decoration from this period) may also have been outfitted with dark walls and colored floors, resulting in an overall impression that would have been ponderous indeed. The visual pleasure of gold, and the difficulty of rendering its glistening effect in paint, however, must be considered one of the reasons why mosaic supplanted painting as the preferred form of mural decoration. Thus large-scale painted landscapes, in the tradition of the garden room of the Villa of Livia at Prima Porta, become mosaic murals as in the Great Mosque at Damascus and in the churches of the Byzantine iconoclasts.

Christian buildings, such as churches, baptisteries, and *martyria,* offered great scope for narrative art in painting. How many of these narrative compositions were originally achieved may be argued from the evidence of the Quedlinburg *Itala,* a painted Christian manuscript of the 5th century. The painted surface on some of the miniatures has flaked off to reveal the inscriptions written underneath directing the artist to take the stock figures of his (non-Christian) repertory and deploy them to illustrate the narrative from the Hebrew Bible. The same procedure must have held for the lengthy narrative cycles of Paulinus's basilica at Nola and Roman basilicas like St. Maria Maggiore, to which, stylistically, the Quedlinburg *Itala* itself has been related. The visual vocabulary of these painted narratives comes from classical antiquity: the mise-en-scène is established by landscapes and architectural forms that seek to fix the moment in time and establish the amplitude of space. As ecclesiastical pictorial narrative became yoked to the liturgy in the following centuries, however, these elements were diminished in favor of simple monochrome backdrops of blue or gold.

The great future of manuscript painting in the Middle Ages, in both Christian and Muslim worlds, is only dimly prefigured in late antiquity. Wealthy patrons of the 5th and 6th centuries had the classics issued in luxury editions with painted illustrations (Vatican Virgil; Roman Virgil; Milan *Iliad*). Interestingly enough, at least one of these examples relates closely to a painted Christian text of the same period (Vatican Virgil to the Quedlinburg *Itala*), but the manuscripts otherwise bear little or no resemblance to one another in the form and placement of miniatures. Similarly, the Christian painted manuscripts of late antiquity are a heterogeneous lot—even more so than the literary texts—embracing books from the Hebrew Bible (Vienna and Cotton Genesis; Quedlinburg *Itala* [Kings]) and the Gospels (Rossano; Rabbula), with no obvious interrelations among them. It is difficult to believe that they reflect a common heritage in Hellenistic book illustration (as has been argued) or were created other than on an ad hoc basis. That high-ranking patrons took pride in owning the beautiful books is illustrated by the portrait miniature of Anicia Juliana and its accompanying inscription in the Vienna Dioscurides.

Between the end of the reign of Justinian and the outbreak of iconoclasm in the 8th century, panel painting emerged as a major art form. The greatest collection of paintings from this period is now to be found in the Monastery of St. Catherine on Mt. Sinai, a Justinianic foundation of the mid-6th century. In paintings such as the Christ Pantokrator, the Virgin and Child with SS. Theodore and George, and St. Peter, one senses the persistence of the past in the tradition of Roman portraiture in encaustic. In the compositions of these works, which resemble those typically found in other art forms, such as the consular diptychs, one feels the impact of the present. And one also sees the future: these paintings are icons, not simply *pro memoria* but holy images, endowed by their audience with the capacity of response to the devotion (or disrespect) paid to them. The activities of such empowered images are abundantly attested in the sources.

The influence of monumental painting on manuscript illustration may be detected in the Pilate miniatures in the Rossano Gospels, which have been argued to reflect large-scale compositions in the Domus Pilati in Jerusalem. Conversely, the biblical narrative in the Church of St. Maria Maggiore in Rome may well owe its "bookish" quality to the desire on the part of its creators to render the decoration of the nave an open book, in the most modern manner of the time. But perhaps the most potent source of new visual ideas came from the icon, under whose influence monumental church decoration was fundamentally reconfigured in the 7th to 9th centuries. The decorations of churches such as St. Maria Antiqua in Rome and St. Demetrios in Thessalonica are not unified narrative programs in the early Christian mode, but concatenations of icons, arranged in separate devotional loci, not on the upper reaches of the church wall, but lower down so that they can stand in a more direct and intimate relationship to the viewer.

BIBL.: Hans Belting, *Likeness and Presence* (Chicago, 1994). H. L. Kessler, *Studies in Pictorial Narrative* (London, 1994). Irving Lavin, "The Ceiling Frescoes in Trier and Illusionism in Constantinian Painting," *Dumbarton Oaks Papers*, 21 (1967): 97–113. K. Weitzmann and H. L. Kessler, *The Frescoes of the Dura Synagogue and Christian Art* (Wash-

ington, D.C., 1990). David Wright, *The Vatican Vergil: A Masterpiece of Late Antique Art* (Berkeley, 1993).　　W.T.

Palaces

Palaces *(palatia)* served as urban residences for emperors, imperial dignitaries, governors, military commanders, and church officials. Exhibiting no standardized disposition of elements in late antiquity, they consisted of public and private parts, with ceremonial chambers (including audience hall and banqueting hall), private residential quarters, courtyards, gardens, statuary, stables, service quarters, and usually a bath suite.

Establishment of the tetrarchy led to the creation of half a dozen new capitals—at Antioch in Syria, Nicomedia, Thessalonica, Sirmium, Milan, and Trier. Each of these cities was provided with circuit walls and featured an imperial palace that was either built anew or enlarged. Scattered archaeological vestiges of tetrarchic palaces are visible in Thessalonica, Sirmium, and Trier. The palace Diocletian built in Antioch must be visualized from *Oration* 11 by Libanius.

In Thessalonica Galerius erected for himself a palace between the hippodrome and the recently discovered stadium, in a new sector he added to the southeastern edge of the city. To the north of the ceremonial and private chambers he erected a triumphal arch connected by a broad colonnaded avenue to a sacred walled *temenos*. In the midst of this towered a large domed rotunda intended to serve as his mausoleum, or perhaps for the use of his imperial cult. Later the rotunda was converted into a church now known as Hagios Georgios. The location of part of the palace alongside the hippodrome is a relationship initially established by the Flavian Palace in Rome, and such a juxtaposition was a regular feature of late antique imperial palaces (Antioch, Constantinople, Sirmium, Milan, Trier). The imperial palace in the old capital probably also influenced other elements of late antique palaces. At Thessalonica a peristyle courtyard is surrounded by small chambers on three sides and an enveloping corridor, a rectangular hall terminates in a spacious apse (perhaps an audience hall) along the east side, and there is a domed octagonal hall almost exactly the size of Hagios Georgios, and a thermal establishment.

Diocletian built a "palace" sometime before 305 for his years of retirement at Spalato (Split) on the Dalmatian coast. Covering some 7.56 acres and enclosed by fortified walls accessible by four gates, this palace was an independent, self-contained country residence divided into four quadrants by two main streets intersecting at right angles, revealing the influence of the traditional Roman *castrum*. The imperial residential suite took up the terraced southern half of the two southern quadrants, overlooking the Adriatic Sea through a long galleried facade. The partially excavated substructures of the imperial apartments have revealed a series of rectangular halls separated by straight corridors, a circular vestibule, and a bath suite.

At Trier Constantine I altered an earlier imperial palace complex by erecting a ceremonial apsed audience hall known as the Basilica (29 m by 58 m), which is well preserved. A spacious porticoed forecourt led to a transverse forehall giving access to the Basilica, which was flanked along the sides by low, porticoed courtyards. At the south extremity of this palace Constantine launched construction of the Imperial Baths (Kaiser-thermen), which were completed on a reduced scale by the emperor Valentinian I.

Constantine later established the Great Palace in Constantinople as the new principal residence of the emperors, on a site at the southeastern edge of the peninsula on which his new capital city was located, and the palace was remodeled and enlarged by various emperors throughout late antiquity. Its site was partly determined by the location of the earlier hippodrome. Known from literary sources and meager archaeological remains, the Great Palace was erected on a grand scale, initially covering possibly some 100 hectares, and rose on a walled-off, terraced site as did the Flavian Palace in Rome. Its monumental entrance, known as the Chalke, stood at the end of a ceremonial porticoed street (the Regia) that was flanked by the large public Baths of Zeuxippos, the porticoed and walled Augustaion, and the Senate House. Some of the principal component parts of the late antique complex included a huge court called the Tribunal or Delphax, with meeting chambers; a formal banqueting hall (Triklinos of the Nineteen Couches) where foreign ambassadors were feasted; an apsed basilican reception hall called the Magnaura that was accessible to the public; two nearby Consistoriums; a private residential suite (the Daphne) that communicated with the imperial box in the hippodrome via a spiral staircase; courtyards, pleasure gardens, fountains, statuary, and elevated passageways; and a number of Christian chapels. Some of the palace buildings were of two or three stories. There were also staff quarters, stables, barracks for the palace guards (whose number grew to 5,500 under Justinian), and an armory. Excavations have brought to light a peristyle courtyard (66 m by 55 m) paved

An interior view of the audience hall in the Basilica of Constantine at Trier.

with splendid mosaics (probably 6th century), off of which projected an apsed hall, and standing above the onetime artificial harbor of Boukoleon are remnants of a galleried seaward facade that enjoyed a commanding view of the Sea of Marmara. The emperor Justinian enlarged the Great Palace by incorporating the earlier Palace of Hormisdas and its adjoining Church of SS. Sergius and Bacchus, and he also built a granary and a cistern. His successor, Justin II, erected the Chrysotrik-linos (Golden Throne Room), a domed and niched octagonal structure that became the hub of palace ceremonial until the 12th century. Justin II's successor, Tiberius, (578–582) erected a bath suite in the northern sector of the palace.

Rather than the compact, tightly coordinated, and largely symmetrical ensemble of suites and halls seen in Diocletian's residence at Split (and possibly his palace at Antioch), the overall layout of the Great Palace may have resembled elements of the sprawling, opulent country villa that an aristocrat or wealthy magnate built at Piazza Armerina in Sicily ca. 310–325. Consisting of a loosely arranged aggregate of quasi-independent, nonaxially aligned suites, this villa included a peristyle courtyard giving access to a long forehall set at right angles to an imposing apsidal audience hall, a bath suite, and a triconch preceded by an oval colonnaded forecourt.

By the year 425 Constantinople boasted five imperial palaces, and others appeared in the following centuries. Justin II, for example, is said to have built a palace called the Deuteron inside the 5th century landwalls of the city, and it incorporated a circus, gardens, and pleasure grounds punctuated with statuary. A few nonimperial palaces of late antiquity have come to light in Constantinople. Early in the 5th century the wealthy Antiochus, *praepositus sacri cubiculi*, built a luxurious palace adjacent to the northwest side of the hippodrome that consisted of a number of circular and polygonal multilobed halls disposed fanlike around a semicircular portico 52 m in diameter. Later, probably in the 6th century, the central hexagonal hall of this palace was converted into a church, in which the relics of St. Euphemia were deposited in the early 7th century. Lausos, the successor to Antiochus as *praepositus*, erected nearby a dazzling palace that included a domed rotunda (22 m in diameter) leading into a banquet hall that was 52 m long, with seven apses. (A heptaconch triclinium also existed in the above-mentioned Palace of Hormisdas.) The palace of Lausos also housed a celebrated collection of classical sculpture that burned in a fire in 476. Ceremonial in character, the palaces of Antiochus and Lausos echoed the grandeur and other aspects of the Great Palace.

Between about 410 and 425 a vast but never finished "Palace of the Giants" was constructed alongside the venerable Street of the Panathenaia in the center of the ancient agora in Athens. The grounds of this complex covered about 13,500 square m, surrounded by a wall for privacy. A pretentious facade of reused statues of Triton and Giants gave access to a monumental colonnaded courtyard, two smaller courtyards, a two-story grouping of residential apartments, a small bath suite, an octagonal tower at the southeast corner, and extensive gardens. In overall planning this palace displays a disregard of precise axial symmetry and a striking dissimilarity to other late antique palaces. It was erected for official use or perhaps built as a private urban residence for a wealthy senatorial landowner of Attica.

At Qaṣr ibn Wardān in the desert *limes* of Syria, a complex with a two-story palace, a church, and barracks was constructed, most probably by a military commander, in 561–564. The palace included a triconch audience hall similar to that of other Syrian palaces (e.g., at Bostra), and elements of its planning are echoed in the early 8th century Umayyad palace at Mschatta. Several other Umayyad and early Abbasid palaces have been preserved or are described in written sources.

BIBL.: Noël Duval, "Existe-t-il une 'structure palatiale' propre à l'antiquité tardive?" in *Le système palatial en Orient, en Grèce et à Rome,* ed. E. Lévy (Strasbourg, 1987), 463–490. Irving Lavin, "The House of the Lord: Aspects of the Role of Palace Triclinia in the Architecture of Late Antiquity and the Early Middle Ages," *Art Bulletin* 44 (1962): 1–27. John Bryan Ward-Perkins, *Roman Imperial Architecture* (New Haven, 1981), 415–466.   W.E.K.

Palestine

The province of Palaestina (sometimes called Syria-Palaestina) was founded by Hadrian on the eastern coast of the Mediterranean, in the area of the former province of Judaea, after the suppression of the Bar Kokhba Revolt (135 C.E.). The name Palestine was used in antiquity specifically for the region of the southern coastal plain (Philistia) but was sometimes applied to other parts of the country. The change of name was part of Hadrian's anti-Jewish policy.

Palestine in the 2nd century extended on both sides of the Jordan, partially reflecting the former area of Judaea. The northern border in the coastal plain, dividing Palestine from Phoenicia, passed north of Caesarea Maritima, the capital city of the province, toward the Carmel ridge, and crossed Galilee toward the northeast. In the east, Palestine included the Golan Heights, the Jordan Valley, and the western slopes of Gilead, leaving the Transjordanian plateau in Arabia. Southern Transjordan, the Negev south of Beer Sheva, and southern Sinai belonged to Arabia. The border between Palestine and Egypt in the southwest passed between Raphia and Rhinocorura (El Arish). Under the reforms of Diocletian, Palestine was considerably enlarged: southern Transjordan, the Negev, and southern Sinai were transferred from Arabia to Palestine.

Further administrative changes took place during the 4th and early 5th centuries. The south became a separate province named Palaestina Salutaris. At the end of the 4th century (or at any rate no later than 409) Palestine was divided into three provinces. Palaestina Prima included the coastal plain, Judaea and Samaria, and the Jordan Valley on both sides of the Jordan up to the borders of Arabia on the western edge of the Transjordanian plateau. Among the many prominent cities of the province were Caesarea (the metropolis), Jerusalem-Aelia Capitolina, Gaza, Ascalon, Samaria-Sebaste, Neapolis, Lod-Diospolis, Emmaus-Nicopolis, and Eleutheropolis. Palaestina Secunda comprised the northern regions: the Jezreel Valley, the Galilee, the Golan Heights, and northern Gilead east of the Jordan. Scythopolis (Beth Shean) was the metropolis; among the important cities were Gaba and Legio-Maximianopolis in the Jezreel Valley, Sepphoris-Diocaesarea and Tiberias in the lower Galilee, and Hippos, Gadara, and Pella east of the Jordan. Palaestina Tertia (also called Salutaris in the 4th century) was the largest in size but sparsely populated. It spread over southern Transjordan, the Negev, and southern and central Sinai. The metropolis was Petra, east of the Arava Valley; Elusa in the Negev served as the regional capital of the western part of the province. Among the important settlements (without the status of polis) were Aila, Beer Sheva, and the Negev settlements Nessana, Sobata, Rehovot, Mampsis, and Eboda. The region between the settled country and the Negev, from Raphia in the west along the Beer Sheva Valley, was settled by *limitanei* as part of the fortified strip of the *limes Palaestinae;* its northern part, *limes Arabiae,* stretched along the Transjordanian heights from Aila to the north.

Palestine was ruled by a governor of consular or proconsular rank. From the days of Diocletian the military command was taken by the *dux Palaestinae.* After the division of Palestine into three provinces the governors continued to have the consular rank of *clarissimus.* From 536 the governor of Palaestina Prima was of proconsular rank *(spectabilis).* Recent excavations at Caesarea have revealed parts of the province's administrative quarters, including the governor's residence as well as the main court, tax collection office, and archives.

During the suppression of the Bar Kokhba Revolt, the Jews, who formerly had been a majority, suffered heavy losses, and the pagans apparently became a majority in the country. The Judaean hills, the central area of the revolt, were emptied of Jews, who were either killed or sold into slavery. Jews were not permitted to live in Jerusalem, newly built as Aelia Capitolina, but were concentrated in the Galilee, mostly in the areas of Sepphoris and Tiberias, where the patriarchs and the Jewish supreme court were located. Judaea was occupied by pagans, except for its southern eastern and western parts, where Jewish villages continued to exist. The Samaria Hills were settled in large part by Samaritans. In the Negev and on the borders of the desert there were pagan nomadic tribes of Arab origin. Christian communities were scattered throughout the country.

A radical change took place from the time of Constantine the Great. His victory over Licinius in 324 was followed by an intensive process of Christianization, which included the discovery of Jesus' tomb by Helena, the emperor's mother, and the foundation of the Church of the Holy Sepulcher and other churches on the Mount of Olives and in Bethlehem and Mamre. Palestine became the destination of large-scale Christian pilgrimages, stimulating the building of churches and monasteries and the invention of more holy sites and relics. At the end of the 4th century the triumph of Christianity (marked by the destruction of the Temple of Marnas in Gaza and the building of a new church in

its place) was completed. Most pagans converted to Christianity, and Christians became the majority. Following the Council of Chalcedon, Jerusalem, site of the Mother of All Churches, was appointed as the fifth patriarchate, which dominated Palestine and Arabia. Unlike Egypt and Syria, which embraced Monophysitism, the Palestinian church remained orthodox, in large part due to the influence of the monks of the Judaean Desert, led by Euthymius. Nevertheless a large and aggressive Monophysite minority, led by Peter the Iberian (a Georgian by origin), existed throughout the Byzantine and early Islamic periods. Today, remains of more than four hundred churches have been discovered in some three hundred fifty sites in the area of the three *Palaestinae.* For comparison, remains of only about one hundred twenty synagogues, some ten of which are Samaritan, have been found. These figures probably reflect the proportions of Christians, Jews, and Samaritans in Palestine in the later Byzantine age. The Samaritans suffered severe losses and lost much power during the suppression of their revolts against the Byzantine regime in 488 and, especially, in 529 and 536.

The economy of Palestine depended mostly on agriculture, although we have evidence of the existence of industry and some international commerce. Pilgrimage was also a major factor in the economy of parts of Palestine. Archaeology reveals a high standard of living in the cities, villages, and farms. During the 4th century a process of demographic growth began that reached its peak in the first half of the 6th century. An estimation of some one million inhabitants in Palestine seems reasonable. Building inscriptions and literary sources indicate intensive building activity in the days of Anastasius, Justin I, and Justinian. Archaeology and the Madaba mosaic map show that the large cities preserved much of the grandeur of the Roman past, boasting colonnaded streets, porticoes, nymphaea, and theaters. The best evidence for demographic growth are the numerous large and small settlements in the arid Negev area, settled in part by members of nomadic tribes of Arab origin who converted to Christianity. Cultural life was of a high quality, as demonstrated by local authors and spiritual leaders, among them Origen, Eusebius, Jerome, Cyril of Jerusalem, Cyril of Scythopolis, and Choricius of Gaza, as well as by the marvelous mosaic pavements and other arts and crafts. The final composition of the Mishnah, the Palestinian Talmud, and other compositions of Talmudic literature are the peaks of Jewish spiritual activity in the Palestines.

The prosperity of Palestine was impaired by the Samaritan revolts and mainly by the bubonic plague, which broke out in 541–542; a gradual process of decline is discerned in the second half of the 6th century. However, the country was most seriously affected by the general decline of Byzantine power in the capital.

The conquest of Palestine by the Sassanians in 614 had a great impact on Palestine. Many thousands of Christians were massacred in Jerusalem and others were expelled to Ctesiphon (together with the patriarch and the Life-Giving Cross), and churches in Jerusalem and the area were destroyed. We have no clear indications of damage in other parts of the country, but the disconnection with the imperial court in Constantinople and the collapse of the provincial administration weakened individual settlements. The reconquest by Heraclius in 628 left no time for reconstruction of the Byzantine regime, as the Muslims started to attack Byzantine Arabia and Palestine in 629. The loss of the south (632–634), the defeat of the Byzantines in the battle of the Yarmuk (636), the surrender of Jerusalem (638), and the fall of Caesarea (ca. 640) marked the main stages of the Arab victory.

During the first period of Muslim rule Christians remained a majority of the population; Byzantine coins (or Muslim coins imitating Byzantine coinage), as well as the administrative and fiscal system, remained in use. Sometime after the conquest a new provincial division took place that partially reflected the Byzantine division. Palaestina Prima was replaced by the Jund Filastin; its capital was moved from Caesarea to the new city of Ramla around 718. The north, including Palaestina Secunda and parts of Phoenicia, was replaced by the Jund al-Urdunn and its capital moved to Tiberias. Parts of the Jordan Valley and Transjordan, including areas of Palaestina Tertia, were divided between Filastin and al-Urdunn, or belonged to the region of Damascus. Altogether the area was part of Syria (el Shām). During the years 661–750, the country was ruled by the Umayyad dynasty. Although there was a process of change and gradual decline (indicated, for example, by the abandonment of the large settlements in the Negev no later than the early 8th century), the Muslim rulers maintained a prosperous economy and much building activity. Remains of palaces, marketplaces, irrigated farms, and mosques have been found all over the country. Most magnificent were the Dome of the Rock, al-Aqṣā Mosque, the decorative gates of the Temple Mount and the palaces in Jerusalem. In 696 'Abd al-Malik started a reform that emphasized religious and nationalistic aspects of Islam. The transfer of rule, in 750, from the Umayyad dynasty, whose capital was Damascus, to the Abbasid dynasty, which was based in far away Baghdad, accelerated the economic and demographic decline in the general state of Filastin and al-Urdunn.

BIBL.: M. Avi-Yonah, "Palaestina," *RE*, supp. 13 (1974), 322–354. M. Gil, *A History of Palestine, 634–1099* (Cambridge, Eng., 1992). R. Schick, *The Christian Communities of Palestine from Byzantine to Islamic Rule: A Historical and Archaeological Study* (Princeton, 1997). Y. Tsafrir, L. Di Segni, and J. Green, *Tabula Imperii Romani Iudaea-Palaestina: Maps and Gazetteer* (Jerusalem, 1994).   Y.T.

Pannonia

Pannonia was the region southwest of the middle Danube bend. In the early 4th century it was divided into four provinces: Pannonia I, Savia, Valeria, and Pannonia II, with capitals in Savaria, Siscia, Sopianae, and Sirmium, respectively. Because it was located at the nexus between the eastern and western empires, control over Pannonia shifted constantly between east and west and became a point of serious contention after 395.

Archaeological evidence indicates underdeveloped manufacturing in the region, which derived its wealth rather from agricultural produce. Its reputation for fertility (*Expositio totius mundi* 57) is supported by the excavation of numerous large-scale 4th century villa estates like that at Fenékpuszta, near Lake Pelso. Numismatic evidence confirms extensive trade with the eastern empire, apparently in grain, wool, and livestock. The wealth produced in the region is attested by the recent discovery of a hoard of fourteen grandiose silver vessels owned by a certain Seuso.

The urban centers that had thrived along the Danube in 2nd and 3rd century Pannonia (Carnuntum, Aquincum) failed to maintain their prosperity beginning in the 4th century. In their place, the cities of central Pannonia, particularly the provincial capitals, flourished: Sopianae was rebuilt on a new street grid, and a palace with a bath complex was added; Savaria was expanded and outfitted with an imperial treasury, a palace, and a pair of grain warehouses; Sirmium, which housed the Praetorian Prefecture of Italy, Africa, and Illyricum, gained an arms factory, a cloth works, and a mint, and boasted a new hippodrome and palace, new grain warehouses, and new bath complexes. Urban prosperity in 4th century Pannonia was due, however, to imperial rather than local initiative. Indeed, Pannonia, like all of Illyricum, produced a number of emperors in the 3rd and 4th centuries and hosted many more for lengthy stays, particularly in Sirmium. The benefits of this imperial contact can be seen even in the massive villa estates, many of which belonged to the imperial *res privata*. When infusions of imperial money dried up after the mid-4th century, prosperity declined.

Pannonia bordered directly on barbarian territory and was therefore subject to frequent attack. Extensive fortification efforts along the Danube, particularly well attested in the 360s and 370s, were only marginally effective in controlling the problem. Early in the 4th century barbarian peoples were often settled inside Pannonia under imperial auspices (Carpi, Sarmatians); beginning with a settlement of Gothic *foederati* in 378, the area began to be occupied by groups not subject to Roman control. Between 401 and 408 it became a corridor for various tribal peoples who forced the departure of most Roman inhabitants. In treaties struck in

425 and 433 the empire acquiesced to the occupation of the region by Hunnic *foederati*. Despite efforts by Avitus to reclaim the territory in 455, it was soon occupied by Ostrogoths (late 5th century) and later Avars (mid-6th century). Archaeological evidence confirms that, despite the continuation of Roman customs in some areas down to the 6th century, Roman influence largely gave way. Even Sirmium, controlled by Constantinople until 582 and regained from the Avars in 600, saw almost no new building after the mid-4th century and witnessed the transformation of public spaces into cemeteries and middens.

BIBL.: J. Fritz, *L'administration des provinces pannoniennes sous le bas-empire romain* (Brussels, 1983). A. Mócsy, *Pannonia and Upper Moesia: A History of the Middle Danube Provinces of the Roman Empire* (London, 1974). M. Mundell-Mango, *The Seuso Treasure* (Ann Arbor, 1994). A. G. Poulter, "The Use and Abuse of Urbanism in the Danubian Provinces during the Later Roman Empire," in *The City in Late Antiquity*, ed. J. Rich (London, 1992), 99–135. S. Soproni, *Die Letzten Jahrzehnte des pannonischen Limes* (Munich, 1985). N.L.

Papa

The term *papa*, from the Greek *pappas*, which was used to denote colloquially the natural father or, in its Latin transliteration, the guardian as well, became widespread among Christians who used it to express, with loving respect, the notion of a spiritual father embodied by their bishop. It was first used in this sense in texts that date back to the early 3rd century. Since these texts mainly related to the bishops of Alexandria, Carthage, and Rome, it was thought that the term *papa* at the time was only used for the most important bishoprics. However, in 253, Gregorius of Neocaesarea called *hiere papa* an anonymous correspondent who was certainly holding a bishopric in the Pontus. Origen used it in relation to Alexander of Jerusalem, and in a number of papyri the title was also used for simple presbyters.

In the following centuries the term *papa* was applied to all bishops, together with *antistes, pontifex*, and *episcopus*. Its specific use in relation to church figures becomes evident if compared with *abba* and *apa*, which start to occur very frequently in papyri as of the second quarter of the 4th century. These terms expressed the same concept of spiritual fatherhood implicit in *papa*. In a set of ostraca from the late 4th and the 5th century, *abba/apa* seem to be interchangeable with *patēr*. However, while the original meaning was the same, they became differentiated in usage. *Abba* occurs almost always in monastic contexts, also in relation to bishops but, usually, to those who had been monks before being ordained. *Apa*, usually a less prestigious title than *abba*, is used in a more diversified manner: in papyri it refers to members of the clergy as

well as to men who were neither priests nor monks, whereas *papa* was only used for bishops. For this reason, it came to be perceived as denoting a function, not as an honorific title.

Although the word *papa* was applied to the bishops of Rome, such expressions as *meus, suus, noster, papa Urbis, Romae, urbicus,* and *urbis Romae* also appear in older sources. Only in the 6th century did this title start to be used solely in relation to the bishops of Rome, and such usage did not become generalized until the end of the century. There are late occurrences of *papa* in relation to bishops other than those of Rome until the 10th century; they are, however, rare. A major exception was Alexandria, whose bishops were called *papa* throughout the period. To this day, the head of the Coptic church is commonly called "pope." *Papa* became the customary title that the bishops of Rome used in relation to themselves as of the late 7th century. In the *Liber Pontificalis, papa* becomes the final substitute for *episcopus* starting with Agapitus.

BIBL.: Tomasz Derda and Ewa Wipszycka, "L'emploi des titres *abba, apa* et *papas* dans l'Egypte byzantine," *The Journal of Juristic Papyrology* 24 (1994): 23–56. R.LIZ.

Papacy

The late antique papacy invented itself as an institution and as an idea. After the Constantinian "Peace of the Church," the papacy was able to function publicly and to assume a wide range of responsibilities. Although there were inheritances from the 3rd and earlier centuries, the popes between ca. 300 and 700 built two fundamentally new structures. One was the framework from which all later generations of popes drew in defining their office and its mission. The other was the institutional structure upon which virtually all elements of the later papal government were eventually erected. The papacy began as a product of the Mediterranean world and slowly reoriented itself toward western Europe.

The papacy reveals itself to scholars through sources that also display the papacy's emerging sense of identity and self-definition. The *Liber Pontificalis* is a collection of papal biographies beginning with St. Peter. The surviving version was begun in the 6th century but draws on nonextant materials that were older. These biographies provide both valuable details and a clear sense of the papacy's institutional memory. The *Liber Pontificalis* is, thus, more the collective biography of an institution than an assemblage of individual lives. Several thousand papal letters, containing everything from routine administrative matters to lofty ideological and ecclesiological pronouncements, represent a second great source of information about events and what contemporaries thought about them. A third source is the physical topography of papal Rome, ranging from the sites of papal burials to the complex of buildings that constituted the Sancta Romana Ecclesia as a visible institution.

The papal government had two distinct components: the liturgical and the administrative. Religious life in Rome, as in other cities, centered on the bishop. Rome's size and large population necessitated considerable delegation. By the end of the 8th century, and although Rome had some two hundred churches, the pope's church consisted of five "patriarchal" basilicas, twenty-eight "title" churches, and a set of basilican monasteries. The pope himself celebrated in Rome's cathedral, St. John Lateran, where he was assisted by the suburbicarian bishops (the bishops, whose numbers changed over time, who presided in the churches in Italia Suburbicaria, the region immediately around Rome). The senior priests in the title churches exhibited their ties to the central Roman church by celebrating, in turns, at the other four patriarchal basilicas. Gradually the title priests came to be called cardinals. As a body the title priests advised the pope, and one of them, the archpriest, headed the Roman ecclesiastical personnel.

The administration of the papal government had charitable, financial, and archival branches. Rome was divided into seven regions, each with a regional deacon who oversaw charitable distributions of food and money to the poor, to orphans and widows, to consecrated virgins, and to pilgrims. The seven regional deacons also came to be called cardinals. As secular Roman administration diminished, the charitable functions of the papacy grew in scope and significance and made the popes the great patrons of the local populace. The resources necessary to provide charitable services and to maintain the fabric of the Roman churches and the expenses of the clergy came from papal patrimonies. These were estates scattered all over Italy and Sicily, with a few in North Africa and southern Gaul. Papal letters are particularly rich sources for the management of the patrimonies. As early as the 3rd century there were papal notaries in the regions of Rome, ostensibly to keep records of the martyrs. In time, the notaries kept routine ecclesiastical records and, under the *primicerius* of the notaries, who was headquartered in the Lateran, managed the papal correspondence, archives, and library. Alongside the pope, the archpriest, the *primicerius* of the notaries, and the senior deacon constituted the great officers of the church. They ruled the church *sede vacante* and supervised papal elections. Popes were in principal elected "by the clergy and people," but in the 6th century the clergy began trying, without uniform success, to exclude the laity. The papacy's prestige, power, and patronage made elections contentious and often violent.

Already in the 4th century popes began to claim a unique place for themselves in the Christian world. To the amorphous but widely shared idea of "apostolic succession"—the theory that the church was a colle-

gial body of bishops who jointly inherited the teaching authority of the apostles—Rome added a special claim on the basis of its "double apostolicity," its descent from Peter and Paul, and another claim grounded in the Roman bishop's succession to Peter, the "Prince of the Apostles." To this day the pope succeeds St. Peter and not the pope's immediate predecessor. The great proponent of the Petrine Theory of papal primacy was Leo I (440–461).

Gelasius I (492–496) added to the papacy's claims. In a famous letter to Anastasius I rejecting the emperor's right to interfere in dogmatic issues, Gelasius asserted that the world was governed by the *potestas* of kings and the *auctoritas* of priests. He was drawing a distinction between raw power and legitimate authority. Ordinarily priests and kings had distinct spheres of action, but in case of conflict priests had the last word because they were concerned with immortal souls not mortal bodies.

Precedence in the church and moral superiority in society were lofty claims, and they were contested at every turn by Roman rulers in Constantinople and by churchmen who rejected papal doctrinal formulations and jurisdictional claims. When the imperial administration definitively abandoned Rome in the 5th century and the Arab conquest cut off eastern centers of Christian life and thought in Antioch and Alexandria, papal Rome and imperial-patriarchal Constantinople were left in a tense confrontation. Emperors and patriarchs sought but failed to attain papal assent to their views on Monophysitism, Monothelitism, and iconoclasm. The decisions of eastern church councils were unenforceable in Rome.

If the papacy could not succeed in advancing worldwide claims, it did build a potent local organization in Rome and central Italy. Threats to its local interests by the Lombards eventually led the popes to turn to the Franks for protection. By the middle of the 8th century the popes had effectively reoriented their larger interests away from the Mediterranean. This momentous shift was prepared by the opening of a mission to the Anglo-Saxons by Gregory I (590–604), by increasing correspondence between papal Rome and the Visigothic and Frankish kingdoms, and by papal promotion of missionary work in Germany. Important, too, was papal leadership in Italy against Byzantine tax and administrative policies. With the elimination of Byzantine authority in central Italy, the Roman nobility entered the clergy in large numbers and refashioned its local leadership through ecclesiastical channels.

Popes were not as a rule impressive intellectual figures. From Leo I to Gregory I individual popes made important contributions to the church's liturgy. Leo, who sent a *Tome* to the Council of Chalcedon (451) was a competent theologian. Gregory I's *Pastoral Rule* was influential for centuries as a set of guidelines on the episcopal office, and his theological reflections, as in the *Moralia in Iob* and his exegetical works, were widely admired. Popes saw themselves as defenders of the traditional faith, not as original theologians. Their most impressive achievements came in the area of local administration.

BIBL.: C. Pietri, *Roma Christiana,* 2 vols. (Paris, 1976). E. Caspar, *Geschichte des Papsttums,* 2 vols. (Tübingen, 1933). Walter Ullmann, "Leo I and the Theory of Papal Primacy," *Journal of Theological Studies* 11 (1960): 25–51.   T.N.

Papyrus

Papyrus was the most important writing material of the ancient Mediterranean world. It was produced in Egypt from the fibers of a reedlike plant and sold in rolls of varying height. Until the 4th century, most books and all official records used the roll format, but the codex gained ground steadily from then on. Even in Egypt papyrus coexisted with other writing materials, including parchment, potsherds (ostraca), and wooden tablets, and in some regions papyrus was much less dominant. Finds of papyrus from Greece, Italy, Palestine, Arabia, and Syria, however, show that its use there was both widespread and similar to that in Egypt.

Numerous documentary papyri survive from the late antique east. Among the most prominent sources for this period are Oxyrhynchus, Hermopolis, Panopolis, Syene, Aphrodito, and the Arsinoite nome (Fayum) in Egypt, and recently Petra in Arabia. Papyri have also turned up along the Euphrates at an unidentified site in Syria or Mesopotamia. The 4th and 6th centuries are particularly heavily documented, with several thousand papyri known and published so far. These texts, although often fragmentary and difficult to interpret, provide abundant evidence for matters of provincial and local administration, the economy, taxation, social structure, religion, language, literacy, culture, and private life. Most of the published papyri are written in Greek, but many in Coptic and Arabic (most still unpublished) also survive, along with smaller numbers in Persian (mostly from the Persian rule in Egypt, 619–629). Although more than nine-tenths of all papyri are documentary, the literary finds have had a dramatic impact particularly on the study of religion, with the Oxyrhynchus papyri, the Nag Hammadi library, the Tura finds, and the ancient collection now mainly in the Chester Beatty and Bodmer libraries only the most prominent examples.

BIBL.: Roger S. Bagnall, *Reading Papyri, Writing Ancient History* (London, 1995). D. Feissel, J. Gascon, J. Teixidor, "Documents d'archives romains inédits du Moyen-Euphrate," *Journal des Savants* (Jan./June 1997): 1–57 (with bibliography of earlier publications). Hans-Albert Rupprecht, *Kleine Einführung in die Papyruskunde* (Darmstadt, 1994). Eric G. Turner, *Greek Papyri: An Introduction* (Oxford, 1968; 2nd ed. 1980).   R.S.B.

Paradise

Paradise was, for people in late antiquity, an idyllic abode of joy, bountifulness, and tranquility. It had three basic manifestations in religious beliefs: as a primordial region of perfection, as an intermediate locale where virtuous souls awaited resurrection, and as heaven, or the final dwelling place of the righteous. In many respects, and not accidentally, paradise came to be envisioned as a beautiful garden. The term originated in Old Iranian languages, e.g., Avestan *pairidaeza* (from *pairi,* round, plus *diz,* form), in which it designated a park surrounded by a wall. This Iranian word entered Greek as *paradeisos* (park, pleasure grounds), then became the Latin *paradis(us),* and the Old and Middle English *paradis,* or paradise.

In Iran, Zoroastrians referred to the abode of righteous souls by two other terms—"house of song" (Avestan *garodemana,* Pahlavi *garodman*) and the "best place" (Pahlavi *wahisht*). According to the Avestan *Hadhokht Nask* and especially the Pahlavi *Arda Wiraz Namag,* each soul faced judgment after death based on its deeds while alive, then crossed a bridge to enjoy heaven, fell into a cold hell for punishment, or lay motionless in limbo until the final renovation of the universe, at which time all souls would be purified and given a renovated earth on which to dwell for eternity. Heaven and the final earth were certainly described as pleasant and serene locations, but not as verdant gardens. Even the primordial earth was simply a series of flat lands surrounded by water and enclosed by the sky.

Gardens may have first been associated with heavenly places in Sumerian thought, according to which a lush island called Dilmun was supposedly frequented by deities. The biblical notion of the garden of Eden "delight" could have been influenced by this Mesopotamian precursor. Eden, according to Genesis 2–3, was watered by a river and inhabited by Adam, plants, animals, birds, and, finally, Eve. When Judaism developed beliefs in afterlife, messianism, and resurrection (Is. 11:6–8, Ez. 47:1–12), perhaps under Zoroastrian influence around the 6th to 3rd century B.C.E., souls of the righteous were said to enjoy a blissful existence until the end of time, when they would enter the garden of Eden. In contrast to this spiritual paradise there emerged a fiery realm, Gehenna (Hebrew *gehinnom*), where wicked human souls received punishment. Paradise, although occasionally regarded as earthly, was often thought of as located in the heavens; hell reputedly lay in the netherworld. When the Septuagint was prepared, the concept of Eden as a garden was conveyed through the Greek word *paradeisos*—thus linking paradise to the garden created by God. With the advent of Christianity, Eden came to be associated not only with exile but also with a spiritual consequence of the Fall—original sin. Paradise for the dead was assigned to the third heaven (2 Cor. 12:2–3), where virtuous souls resided in joy (Luke 23:43). The eschatological paradise, again linked to a rejuvenated garden of Eden, was said to await believers, together with a new heaven, earth, and Jerusalem (Rev. 2:7, 21:1–3). It was in the Qur'ān (2:25, 25:15, 47:15, 56:36–37) that heaven saw its fullest development as a garden of paradise (Arabic *jannāt al-firdaws*) and a garden of eternity (Arabic *jannāt al-khuld*). The souls of righteous Muslim men were promised a paradise filled with rivers of cool water, milk, wine, and honey; fruit-bearing trees; and immortal virgins, or *ḥūrīs*. Later Islamic theologians suggested that Eden was just one part of this heavenly garden. For the damned there awaited, under the cosmic bridge, the scorching torments of hell (Arabic *jahannam*). Muslims in late antiquity and the early Middle Ages expressed their desire for the fecundity of paradise through numerous gardens laid out for Iranian nobles.

In the 4th century Ephrem (ca. 306–373) wrote a series of hymns in Syriac on paradise. These hymns described paradise as a holy mountain. The Tree of Life was located at the mountain's summit, but the Tree of the Knowledge of Good and Evil obscured Adam and Eve's view of it. It was only after they had eaten the forbidden fruit that they saw the Tree of Life at the summit that had been prepared for them as a reward for obedience. The zones of paradise corresponded with the divisions in the Temple: the summit represented the divine presence, the Tree of Life the Holy of Holies, and the Tree of Knowledge the Sanctuary Veil.

BIBL.: Ephrem, *Hymns on Paradise,* trans. Sebastian Brock (Crestwood, N.Y., 1990). Colleen McDannell and Bernhard Lang, *Heaven: A History* (New Haven, 1988). Elizabeth B. Moynihan, *Paradise as a Garden: In Persia and Mughal India* (New York, 1979).　　J.K.C.

Parchment

Parchment is the term generally used for writing material made from the skins of animals, through a process of drying the pelt (wet, unhaired, and limed skin) under tension. The hair and flesh sides can be distinguished. Parchment was already in use in the second millennium B.C. but few early examples are preserved, because in Egypt it could not compete with papyrus and elsewhere the preservation of organic material is less common. The finds from Dura-Europus, Bactria, and elsewhere show that it was a standard material for legal documents in much of the Hellenistic world, being replaced by papyrus only when the Romans took control (at Dura, in the 3rd century C.E.), and it may have retained a similar role in many areas of the Near East outside the Roman orbit. Parchment sheets could be stitched together, in a manner similar to the gluing together of papyrus sheets, to form products like the composite rolls used for official archives.

It is in the codex and in late antiquity that parchment came into its own. Parchment is generally considered superior to papyrus for durability in codex form, but there are far fewer parchment codices than papyrus before the 4th century, and there is no clear evidence for parchment's priority in the history of the codex. Parchment became a popular luxury medium for book production in late antiquity; the codices usually had a squarer shape than their papyrus counterparts and more readily allowed larger formats (with multiple columns on a page). The greatest of surviving late antique Bibles (Codex Sinaiticus and Codex Vaticanus) were written on parchment. Although papyrus remained in use in the west until the 11th century or even later, it was largely displaced by parchment (as it was in the east by paper) in the early medieval period.

BIBL.: N. Lewis, *Papyrus in Classical Antiquity* (Oxford, 1974). R. Reed, *Ancient Skins, Parchments and Leathers* (London, 1972). E. G. Turner, *The Typology of the Early Codex* (Philadelphia, 1977).　　R.S.B.

Paris

Although Paris in late antiquity was the site of the elevation of Julian to the position of Augustus, the tradition that it boasted a palace seems to be a later invention. In fact Paris was of little importance under the Roman empire, as it was subordinate to Sens within the province of Lugdunensis Senonia, despite having been the center of the tribe of the Parisii.

The importance of Paris changed dramatically in the course of the 5th century. First, the role of the virgin Geneviève (Genovefa) under Childeric I in defending the city against the Franks gave Paris a saint of considerable renown, who was honored by a church built in the early 6th century by Childeric's son Clovis I. Further, Geneviève herself helped to develop the cult of the martyr Denis, which was subsequently to be promoted by the Merovingian kings, notably by Dagobert I. By the reign of Dagobert a major trading fair was also associated with the community of St. Denis. Other significant cults developed in the 6th century, notably those of Marcellus, who may have been bishop of the city in the 4th century, and the Spanish saint Vincent of Saragossa.

Apart from building the Church of St. Geneviève, Clovis also decided ca. 508 to treat Paris as his capital. After the division of the Frankish kingdom in 511, the city served as capital for one of Clovis's sons, Childebert I. He must have built the massive new cathedral, whose scale is known from excavation. Subsequently the city, which was surrounded by royal *villae,* was treated as a capital of the Frankish kingdom regardless of whether any king resided there. Its importance can be seen in the numerous royal burials in the city itself, at St. Denis and other monasteries of the hinterland.

BIBL.: P. Périn, "Paris mérovingien," *Klio* 71 (1989): 487–502. *Topographie chrétienne des cités de la Gaule des origines au milieu du VIII siècle,* ed. N. Gauthier and J.-Ch. Picard, vol. 8: *Province ecclésiastique de Sens* (Paris, 1992).　　I.W.

Patronage

Late antique society was significantly shaped by a complex web of personal relationships between patrons and clients. These ties, between individuals of often greatly differing social status, were important factors in the allocation of political and economic resources, in securing preferment in office (civil, military, or ecclesiastical), and in obtaining access to—or protection from—those in power. Moreover, in a vast empire whose emperor must to many have seemed a far-off and awe-inspiring figure, a patron-client relationship offered the possibility of attachment to local "big men" who might stand between a client and those whose very power often made them seem inaccessible and unconcerned. In a steeply hierarchical society a patron-client relationship made many feel less helpless and less vulnerable.

Those promoted by a well-placed individual were commonly linked to their patron and to each other by a set of mutually reinforcing ties. The accession to the imperial throne of the Pannonians Valentinian I and Valens in 364, or of the Spanish Theodosius I in 379, resulted in a perceptible rise in the number of office-holders recruited from their native provinces. More narrowly, in the late 4th century, the consecration of Basil, a member of the local aristocracy, as bishop of Caesarea in Cappadocia provided the opportunity for a steady campaign that saw, over the next fifteen years, the elevation to nearby sees of Basil's kin, school friends, and religious sympathizers.

The successes of patronage networks can be matched by failures. In 396, the rival court faction that deprived the praetorian prefect and consul Flavius Tatianus of his office also had his son executed, and secured a law removing his fellow provincials from their posts in the imperial administration (*C.Th.* 9.38.9). More dramatically, in 361 the emperor Julian (who had avoided civil war with his predecessor Constantius II only because of the latter's death), on entering Constantinople, ordered the dismissal of all the palace staff and their connections—down to the cooks and barbers (Amm.Marc. 22.4).

As these stories neatly emphasize, patronage was a mutual relationship; its advantages and disadvantages—although always unequal—were in some measure always reciprocal. In an uncertain and highly competitive society whose government did not aim at providing protection or services to all citizens on the basis of universal or impersonal criteria, clients needed patrons for the benefits they might be able to provide. Patrons, in turn, needed clients as loyal supporters, reliable subordinates, and as tangible evidence of their own position and influence.

Both parties expected that their relationship would be publicly advertised. Patrons might appear attended by their clients, like "mini-emperors" surrounded by their courtiers. Clients might commemorate their patron, in an inscription or by erecting a statue, for the benefits they had received. Similarly, in churches, wealthy civic benefactors recorded their gifts or charitable donations. Their splendid monuments both celebrated their position in their own community and suggested an equally exclusive relationship with God—or at least with his episcopal representatives on earth.

Even those Christians without wealth or position might hope for some special protection. When Christ—more distant and more powerful even than a Roman emperor—came to judge the world, many hoped that the intercessions of a local saint might advantage those who had prayed to him and supported his cult. Like a good patron, an effective saint would shield his faithful clients from the stark terrors of the Apocalypse. The number of worshipers and pilgrims, and the magnificence of a saint's shrine, were public testaments to his influence and power.

The idea that the same kind of relationship that offered protection in this world might also work in the next was attractive for many Christians. In the face of a distant and powerful divinity, it made ordinary mortals seem less helpless and less vulnerable. But there was never any guarantee of success. God, as St. Augustine argued at the beginning of the 5th century, could not be constrained to act (wrathfully or mercifully) by either prayers or good works. There was nothing predictable or contractual about this relationship. Rather, in its dealings with the divine, humanity had to rely on hope, perseverance, and the chance of clemency. "Let us hold on to what we have all just sung," Augustine advised his congregation, "'Have mercy on me, O Lord, have mercy on me'" (*Sermon* 165.9).

In this world, too, relationships between patrons and clients were often delicate and difficult. Again, there was never any guarantee of success. Something of that uncertainty is captured in the model letters of recommendation that were included in the published collections of such notables as Quintus Aurelius Symmachus (urban prefect of Rome in 384), Libanius (one of the most famous orators in the mid-4th century), and Basil, bishop of Caesarea. The correct language for requesting hospitality, administrative office, taxation immunity, or preferential treatment in a court case was one of a studied but polite intimacy that suggested a cordial exchange of favors as between distant friends. In recommending a client, Symmachus noted in a letter to one of his most powerful peers: "It is part of your customary good nature to regard as worthy of your affection those whom others have found agreeable. I ask you, then, if nothing stands in the way of satisfying the wishes of those who make this request, to allow Sexio to profit from my words and the hopes of many" (*Letters* 2.43).

Patrons, like clients, were under constant pressure to succeed. For a client, a patron was only as good as the benefits he could deliver or the new contacts he could make with other powerful individuals. Conversely, a client requesting a favor relied on his ability to convince his patron of benefits often yet to be provided. Each individual was continually testing his relationship with others above and below him. The historian Ammianus Marcellinus, in attempting to explain the unparalleled career of Petronius Probus, consul in 371 and four times praetorian prefect, suggested that, among other motives, he was compelled to seek power to satisfy the demands of his many connections (Amm.Marc. 27.11.3).

In such a volatile and high-risk social game, both patrons and clients attempted to construct a relationship to their own particular advantage and, by spreading both their risks and opportunities, to minimize the consequences of the other party's failing to deliver. For example, some peasant farmers were prepared to pay local magnates for protection. Around 390, Libanius complained that his tenants had abandoned their traditional obligation to regard their landlord as a patron. They had instead offered "barley, corn, ducks, and fodder" to secure the protection of a local military commander whose troops forcibly ejected rent collectors from their village (Oration 47.13). Libanius was outraged at the loss of revenue and prestige his tenants' decision involved. But alongside the benefits to smallholders able to exploit the rivalries of those competing for clients, there were also risks involved in a change of patron and in changing the currency regulating the relationship. By the 5th century, on many great estates, payments had become standardized. Successful patrons, to whom peasants once attached themselves as a matter of some choice and mutual advantage, gradually came to dominate an increasingly lopsided relationship. Under an arrangement sometimes known as *patrocinium,* "patrons" demanded ownership of the peasants' land before offering their "clients" any protection at all (*C.Th.* 11.24).

This spectrum of possibilities is important. Above all, it emphasizes that patronage was not the only social practice regulating access to power, protection, or advancement. Some opted to pay or receive money, preferring an impersonal, one-time transaction to the longer-term benefits of a more personal relationship. Of course, in many cases, these strategies overlapped, each carrying its own particular set of risks and benefits. It is unsurprising that by the end of the 4th century, *suffragium*—which had once referred to the influence exercised by a patron on behalf of a client—had also come to mean the sum paid in return for a favor. So far as they were able, both patrons and clients sought to keep in play whatever options they could, to their own best advantage. Basil of Caesarea, seeking immunity from civic duties for an important member of his congregation, wrote to a nearby colleague with tellingly shrewd advice on how best to proceed: "So that we may set about asking this favor from each of our friends in power, either as a gift or for some moder-

ate price, however the Lord may help us forward" (*Letters* 190.2).

BIBL.: P. Brown, *The Cult of the Saints, Its Use and Function in Latin Christianity* (London, 1981). B. E. Daly, "Position and Patronage in the Early Church," *Journal of Theological Studies,* n.s. 44 (1993): 529–553. G. E. M. de Ste. Croix, "Suffragium: From Vote to Patronage," *British Journal of Sociology* 5 (1954): 33–48. A. Wallace-Hadrill, ed., *Patronage in Ancient Society* (London, 1989).   C.K.

Paulinus of Nola

Landowning aristocrat, imperial magistrate, and then ascetic recluse, classicizing poet and also bishop and monk, protégé of powerful notables and officials and then guardian of a saint's cult, Paulinus of Nola seemed already to his contemporaries to personify many of the transformations characteristic of late Roman society in Gaul and Italy. Born into a notable family of Aquitaine, he became a student of the distinguished Ausonius in Bordeaux. In Italy he held a suffect consulship before serving as governor of Campania, probably in 381. While governor he patronized the tomb of St. Felix outside Nola, a small town near Naples; he then visited Bishop Ambrose of Milan before returning to his family's estates. There he married and enjoyed a conventional aristocratic life focused on literary culture and friendships; he also began to link biblical teachings about the final judgment with exhortations about "contempt for this world." The example of Martin, the confrontational bishop of Tours whom he met in Vienne, may have enhanced the attractions of worldly renunciation and ascetic detachment. In 389 Paulinus and his wife abruptly abandoned Aquitaine to live as ascetics in northern Spain.

Paulinus subsequently considered this secular renunciation to have been more important than his baptism. His aged mentor Ausonius, however, was baffled and angered by his sudden silence and repeatedly chided him for ignoring his friendships and social expectations. Paulinus's replies were anguished but still sensitive attempts at refashioning his past life to conform to his current commitments. Even as he candidly acknowledged his enormous gratitude to Ausonius as his "patron, teacher, and father," he indicated his intention of "living for Christ" in order to avoid God's "fearsome anger" at the coming final judgment. His new patron, and the new focus of his identity, was St. Felix, in whose honor he composed the first of a series of poems, known as the *Natalicia,* commemorating the saint on his festival day.

Despite having been ordained a priest in Barcelona, in 395 Paulinus and his wife left for Italy to settle at the shrine of St. Felix, where he founded a community of monks. Eventually he became bishop of Nola, and his patronage and financial support led to an expansion of the saint's cult. A new courtyard linked a new church with the church containing the saint's tomb; paintings of biblical scenes decorated the churches, and portraits of martyrs were displayed in the porticoes surrounding one courtyard. The annual celebration of the saint's festival in January encouraged the participation of the local rural population. Paulinus also developed a wider network of friends and notable acquaintances throughout the Roman empire. His correspondents included Ambrose, Augustine, Jerome, and Sulpicius Severus, all of whom contributed to the rather misleading representation of Paulinus's life as an exemplary paradigm of radical conversion and complete disengagement from worldly possessions. The priest Uranius memorialized Paulinus's virtues in an account of his death in 431.

BIBL.: P. Fabre, *Saint Paulin de Nole et l'amitié chrétienne* (Paris, 1949). J. T. Lienhard, *Paulinus of Nola and Early Western Monasticism* (Cologne and Bonn, 1977). D. Trout, *Paulinus of Nola* (Berkeley, 1999)   R.V.

Pelagianism

Pelagianism, a 5th century movement of Christian perfectionism and theological dissent, takes its name from Pelagius, a British-born teacher and ascetic who settled in Rome in the mid-380s, where he enjoyed the patronage of the Christian aristocracy. Pelagius expected much of the Christian. He held that, if one wished, one could do what God required—for God does not command the impossible—and that, with a fresh beginning in baptism and with the teaching and example of Christ, the Christian could and should avoid all sin. Pelagius's associates in Rome included Rufinus "the Syrian" and Caelestius. Rufinus opposed the notion that the entire human race is guilty of the sin of Adam and Eve and that consequently unbaptized infants are destined for everlasting punishment; rather, he believed that all would be judged by their own conduct, since all possess freedom of choice. These views contributed to a larger debate about human origins in the wake of the Origenist controversy, and about the value of asceticism, which had been questioned recently by Jovinian and others in Rome.

Although Pelagius was obliged in the early 400s to explain how he did not eliminate the need for divine assistance in Christian faith and practice, it was not until Pelagius and Caelestius fled Rome after the sack of 409 that their views came under official scrutiny. North African Christians, who had long held that infants were baptized for the remission of Adam's sin, were particularly inhospitable. Caelestius, seeking ordination to the priesthood there, was accused of heresy by Paulinus, a deacon from Milan, for views akin to Rufinus's and was condemned by a synod in Carthage in 411. The proceedings were reported in the east by Orosius, an emissary of Augustine, who, together with Jerome, brought charges against Pelagius, now settled in Palestine. Pelagius explained his position to the satisfaction of synods in Jerusalem and Diospolis in 415,

reconciling the possibility of sinlessness with the need for divine grace. The African church, in reaction, condemned Caelestius and Pelagius at synods in Carthage and Milevis in 416, and appealed to Pope Innocent I to do likewise. The Africans charged that the Pelagians endangered orthodoxy on original sin, infant baptism, and divine grace. Innocent, while silent on the African doctrine of original sin, condemned Caelestius and Pelagius in 417. They appealed to his successor, Zosimus, an easterner, who absolved them both. In 418, however, the emperor Honorius, acting on petitions from Africa and reacting to violence associated with the controversy in Rome, condemned Caelestius and Pelagius and ordered them expelled from Rome. Zosimus subsequently reversed his decision, advising the major sees of the empire by a circular letter (tractoria).

By now there was a growing body of writing against the Pelagians, chiefly from Augustine, who had come to believe that the human will was so disordered that only God, working secretly within, could restore its love for God. A second phase of the controversy unfolded after Julian, bishop of Aeclanum, and eighteen other Italian bishops refused to subscribe to the pope's *Tractoria*. In their view the African church had imposed a Manichaean notion of hereditary sin on the Roman church, thereby compromising Christian teaching on divine justice, human freedom, the goodness of creation, and marriage. The dissenting bishops were condemned and deposed by Zosimus; their bid to refer the question to an ecumenical council failed. Augustine, apprised of Julian's allegations, was obliged to explain how his view of sexual desire (disordered by lust after the fall) did not impugn the value of creation or marriage. A decade of writing ensued, in which Julian relentlessly pursued the implications of Augustine's teachings on the consequences of the fall, while Augustine defended the imputation of the guilt of original sin to infants.

Condemned in the west, Pelagians took refuge in the east, where theological traditions did not posit so sharp an antithesis between human initiative and divine grace. Augustine found it necessary to warn Cyril of Alexandria against harboring Pelagians. Julian and other exiles were received by Theodore of Mopsuestia, himself an opponent of the notion of inherited sin, though Theodore later condemned Julian's teachings. Julian appealed to Nestorius, the newly consecrated patriarch of Constantinople, and the emperor Theodosius II in 428. Nestorius was unwilling merely to reiterate Rome's condemnation, but the westerner Marius Mercator forced the issue with his dossier against the Pelagians. Theodosius expelled Julian and his associates and then Caelestius in 429. In 431 the Council of Ephesus dispensed with the Pelagian error in a summary condemnation, identifying it (as Cyril of Alexandria now argued, unfairly) with the error of Nestorius (who had by now also rejected Pelagianism).

Pelagian teachings did not sustain interest in the east, but debate continued in the west, largely in reaction to Augustine's view of grace and predestination. In 426–427 Augustine responded to monks at Hadrumentum who felt that, by attributing to divine grace any inclination of the human will toward good, Augustine vitiated ascetic endeavor. Augustine's reply prompted further queries from monks around Marseilles, eliciting from Augustine an exposition of his mature doctrine of predestination. Prosper of Aquitaine became a resolute defender of this doctrine against monastic luminaries in south-central Gaul—John Cassian, Vincent of Lerins, and others—whose spirituality, indebted to the east, eschewed both Pelagian and Augustinian extremes (a position misnamed "semi-Pelagianism" in the 17th century). At the same time, Germanus of Auxerre was summoned to secure Augustinian orthodoxy in Britain. The Gallic controversy subsided in the 440s but revived in the 470s, moving Faustus of Riez to articulate a view of divine grace that was both anti-Pelagian and antipredestinarian. Faustus was posthumously denounced by Fulgentius of Ruspe, a radical Augustinian writing for the African church at the behest of Scythian monks in Constantinople. Under popes Gelasius I (492–496) and Hormisdas (514–523) Rome inclined toward the African position but stopped short of affirming the Augustinian doctrine of predestination. A moderate Augustinianism was declared catholic teaching by the Gallic Synod of Orange under Caesarius of Arles in 529 and ratified by Pope Boniface II in 531. Nevertheless, anti-Augustinian and anti-Pelagian debates periodically convulsed the western church during the medieval and early modern periods.

Fragments of Pelagian writings are preserved in the anti-Pelagian literature of Augustine, Jerome, Marius Mercator, and others. Some works, chiefly biblical commentaries and letters of ascetic counsel, have survived intact through anonymous or pseudonymous transmission. Several letters originating in Sicily are exacting in their ascetic demands and severe in their social criticisms. The biblical commentaries were generally well regarded; Pelagius's commentary on the Pauline epistles, for example, circulated in Ireland, England, and the Continent from the 6th to the 9th century.

BIBL.: Flavio G. Nuvolone and Aimé Solignac, "Pélage et pélagianisme," *Dictionnaire de Spiritualité* 12:2 (1986): 2889–2942. T. de Bruyn, trans., *Pelagius' Commentary on St. Paul's Epistle to the Romans* (Oxford, 1993). D. Dumville, "Late Seventh–Eighth Century Evidence of the British Transmission of Pelagius," *Cambridge Medieval Celtic Studies* 10 (1985): 39–52. R. Markus, "Pelagianism: Britain and the Continent," *Journal of Theological Studies* n.s. 37 (1986): 191–204. B. R. Rees, *Pelagius: A Reluctant Heretic* (Woodbridge, Eng., 1988), and *The Letters of Pelagius and His Followers* (Woodbridge, Eng., 1991). J. Tauer, "Neue Orientierungen zur Paulusexegese des Pelagius," *Augustinianum* 34 (1994): 313–358. R. H. Weaver, *Divine Grace and Human Agency: A Study of the Semi-Pelagian Controversy* (Macon, Ga., 1996).   T.D.

Penalties

Late Roman jurists and judges inherited the dual-penalty system of the early empire, whereby the judicial penalty imposed on a defendant depended on his social rank. The privileged orders (*honestiores*)—town councillors and those superior to them—were, in the 2nd and 3rd centuries, legally immune from corporal punishment. In capital cases, fines, confiscation of property, and exile were the normal punishments, the death penalty being reserved for extraordinary crimes such as treason or parricide. By contrast, citizens of low rank (*humiliores*) were liable to torture during judicial inquiries and execution in capital cases. Decapitation by the sword was the most common form of execution, but *humiliores* were also subject to crueler punishments—the *summa supplicia*—of which the most common were crucifixion (*crux*), burning the victim alive (*crematio*), and exposure to wild beasts (*ad bestias*). Common secondary penalties were hard labor in the mines or public works, or, in less serious cases, flogging. In actual practice, governors exercised considerable discretion in devising and meting out punishments, and instances of arbitrary conduct are well attested, but corporal punishment of *honestiores* is almost invariably regarded as an outrage against legal norms.

The 4th century witnessed the steady erosion of the legal safeguards enjoyed by *honestiores* and a general exacerbation of the legal penalties inflicted on all levels of society. The language of late Roman law is often fiercely moralizing, with threats of savage reprisals for misconduct—amputation of a hand or worse tortures for a corrupt government official (*C.Th.* 1.16.7), molten lead down the throat of a nurse who misleads her young charge (*C.Th.* 9.24.1). Such laws attest the unprecedented desire of the imperial government to discipline society with a military-style rigor and to exact social conformity. Dozens of new crimes appear in the later codes, and these often involve activities that had drawn far less judicial attention in the past, for example, magic, divination, and participation in pagan cults. Many more crimes carry the death penalty. In the *Theodosian Code,* crucifixion and exposure to wild beasts disappear as capital punishments, replaced almost invariably by burning the victim alive. The dual-penalty system did not disappear, but it is seldom mentioned in the later codes, and judges were far less likely to honor it. *Honestiores,* particularly the weaker members of the group, became more and more exposed, both de iure and de facto, to savage and degrading penalties. Nothing illustrates so graphically the changed conditions of the late empire as the public flogging of city councillors, who were responsible for tax collection and were increasingly imperiled when they failed in their duty. Flogging could disfigure, cripple, or kill the victim (whips had lead tips), but equally horrifying for civic notables was the social degradation. The elite of the city councils, the *principales*, tenaciously guarded their social and legal prerogatives through imperial service and cooperation with imperial officials, while rank and file councillors sank in social status. In the steeply hierarchical society of the later empire, imperial service was the best safeguard of one's physical safety before the law.

BIBL.: D. Baker, ed., *Du châtiment dans la cité: Supplices corporels et peine de mort dans le monde antique, Rome 9–11 novembre 1982* (Paris, 1984). Peter Garnsey, "Why Penal Laws Became Harsher: The Roman Case," *Natural Law Forum* 13 (1968): 141–162. Ramsay MacMullen, "Judicial Savagery in the Roman Empire," *Chiron* 16 (1986): 147–166.

S.B.

Petra

Petra, former capital of the Nabataeans, became part of the Roman province of Arabia in 106 C.E. It was united with Palestine under Diocletian, then became capital of the province of Palaestina Salutaris, created in the mid-4th century and transformed subsequently into Third Palestine. In the 6th century, Petra still had its ancient title as *Augustocolonia Antoniana*, Mother of Colonies, and metropolis of the Tertia Palaestina Salutaris.

Four churches from proto-Byzantine Petra are known. One is located on the Jabal Hārūn; converted into a Muslim sanctuary, it may have been the Church of the High Priest Aaron known through a papyrus. Two other churches have recently been discovered. One is called the Ridge Church, the other the Papyrus Church. The latter is characterized by large adjoining offices, a baptistery, and exceptional decorations in *opus sectile* on the central nave. A fire that destroyed the church in the early 7th century carbonized a collection of papyri, and these are now being studied. A fourth church was converted into a "Doric urn tomb" in 446; it was wrongly taken to be the late antique cathedral. Papyri mention the Church of the Theotokos and the hospice of the martyred saint Cyrikos.

Christianity does not seem to have come to Petra later than it did to the rest of the region, and accounts of pagan resistance in the late 4th and early 5th century are nothing out of the ordinary. We know of several bishops of Petra, including Asterius in 343 and Theodore, author of a life of St. Theodosius.

It was long thought that Petra fell into extreme decadence during late antiquity. The city was a place of exile, in particular for the heresiarch Nestorius. However, archaeological discoveries, including 4th century houses (destroyed in 419) and churches, show that this view has been exaggerated. The installations above the collapsed porticoes of the main street attest to its con-

version into a *sūq*. We do not know when this occurred. The earthquake of 363 can no longer be considered responsible for the city's destruction.

The newly discovered papyri belong to a set of 152 scrolls, 42 of them well preserved. They make up a collection of family archives dating from between 528 and 583–586. Their last owner was Theodoros the archdeacon, son of Obodianos. That set of contracts, receipts, donations, and partitions lists the possessions of a family of landowners living in villages, some at a distance of 30 km from the city; they had vineyards, cultivated fields, and gardens or orchards. Municipal institutions were still functioning in the city in the 6th century, and the question of a bouleuteria was raised. Petra must therefore have been abandoned at a later date, most likely during the 7th century, when the Papyrus Church was destroyed and the seat of the metropolitan moved to Areopolis.

BIBL.: Z. T. et al., "The Petra Church Project: Interim Report, 1992–94," in *The Roman and Byzantine Near East: Some Recent Archaeological Research*, ed. J. H. Humphrey (Ann Arbor, 1995), 293–303. L. Koenen, "The Carbonized Archive from Petra," *Journal of Roman Archaeology* 9 (1996): 177–188. M. Sartre, *Inscriptions de la Jordanie*, vol. 4 (Paris, 1933).

P.-L.G.

Pharmacy

In late antiquity, more than one thousand substances of vegetable, animal, and mineral origin were employed medicinally, but it is likely that there was a working pharmacy of about two hundred core drugs that accounted for most usages. Drugs were an important trade item and accounted for much of the trade between regions within the Roman empire and between Rome and east Asia and southeastern Africa. The medicinal substances, materia medica, were roughly 80 percent herbal (such as belladonna, cinnamon, ginger, parsley, pennyroyal) or plant (cherry syrup, juniper, galls, buckthorn). Minerals (copper oxide, calamine, calcium hydrate, lead acetate, sulfur, mercury) and animal products (burned mussels, viper meat, castoreum from the beaver, eggs, milk, various fats) account for the remainder. These drugs acted in much the same way as many modern analgesics, anodynes, antiseptics, and laxatives.

Physicians dispensed medicines, but most medicines were either gathered at home or purchased in the streets and shops from specialists called (in Greek with Latin equivalents) *pharmakopōlai* (druggists), *rhizotomoi* (root cutters), *migmatopōlai* (mixture sellers), *myropōlai* (dealers in scented oils), *murephoi* (unguent makers), and from a variety of sellers of cosmetics who often plied medicines, especially for the eyes. Scribonius Largus (fl. 14–54 C.E.), a writer on medical recipes, admonished physicians to consult with such vendors. The Romans extolled the virtues of household remedies, known through the customs of their forebears, in contrast to the foreign drugs that filled their marketplaces. In the republic Cato the Elder spoke of the medicinal usages of Roman farm and field herbs, cabbage being his favorite, and reminded people that the garden cured as well as nourished. Gargilius Martialis (fl. 220–260), a retired soldier in North Africa, wrote a treatise on the medicines that an estate manager should know.

The greatest authority on pharmacy was Dioscorides, who wrote in Greek, around 65 C.E., a comprehensive, five-book guide to materia medica in which he classified drugs first by general category (e.g., aromatics, roots, pot herbs, trees, animals and animal products, minerals) and then, within these categories, according to their physiological effects. Thus, his method was to classify drugs by medicinal affinities. Galen (129–post 210), author of a number of pharmacy treatises, employed an alphabetical arrangement, thereby negating Dioscorides's influence. Galen supplied a pharmacological theory for drug administration that closely connected pharmacy with the so-called Hippocratic humoral thesis and Empedocles's elements thesis: a drug, being various combinations of the four elements, had two possible actions on the body, either a warming or a cooling action (active faculty) and either a drying or a moistening action (passive faculty). Galen postulated that the action (properties, or *dynameis*) of each drug was determinable through experience to four degrees of intensity. Thus an extremely powerful drug might be cooling to the fourth degree and drying to the second degree. If drying were not a desired therapeutic approach, a drug that was moistening to a third degree of intensity would be required to balance the other's drying effect. Ultimately Galen's theoretical approach would prevail throughout the Middle Ages. Generally most drugs were administered empirically on the basis of what seemed to work, with a broad theoretical approach of opposites—thus a cooling drug was used to combat a fever. An older, more primitive approach known as the doctrine of signatures was occasionally invoked whereby a quality embodied in a drug was thought to engender the same quality in the body (e.g., using bulls' testicles as an aphrodisiac).

During the first four centuries of the Roman empire there was a trend toward more magic and superstitious practices. During the early Middle Ages late Roman medical writings on medicine and pharmacy by Quintus Serenus Sammonicus (fl. 212), Pseudo-Pliny *(De medicina)*, Pseudo-Apuleius *(Herbal)*, Marcellus Empiricus (fl. 410), Theodorus Priscianus (fl. 450), Cassius Felix (fl. 450), Caelius Aurelianus (fl. 450), and Anthimus (fl. 500) were a bridge between classical and medieval pharmacy. Comprehensive medical authorities, such as Oribasius and Paul of Aegina, describe medicines extensively as part of their work.

BIBL.: Georg Harig, *Bestimmung der Intensität im medizinischen System Galens: Ein Beiträg zur theoretische Pharmakologie, Nosologie und Therapie in der Galenischen Medizin* (Berlin, 1974). John M. Riddle, *Dioscorides on Pharmacy and Medicine* (Austin, 1985).   J.R.

Philosophy

In the context of late antiquity, "philosophy" is almost exclusively Platonism, or rather the variety of Platonism that emerged from the synthesis of the Platonic tradition with that of Aristotle and the Stoics, coming from the school of Plotinus toward the end of the 3rd century. This "fortified" Platonism came to seem the true repository of ancient wisdom, with Aristotelianism being accepted only in the sphere of logic, as a suitable introduction to the higher levels of wisdom.

A significant image of the way in which philosophy was regarded in this period is provided by the appearance of Philosophia to Boethius in his *Consolatio* (1.1). She is a stately dame, appearing both young and ancient, and of a bewildering stature; at one moment she seems no more than of human dimensions, but at another the crown of her head appears to penetrate the heavens and become lost to view. Her garments are fine, but they are obscured by the grime of many centuries and had been torn in places by violent hands (these being the various sects who had deviated from Platonic truth through the ages).

Philosophia's dress is adorned on its lower border with the Greek letter pi, for *praktikē,* and on its upper border with theta, for *theoretikē,* representing the two main areas into which philosophy was divided. *Praktikē* comprised logic (when this was not regarded as a preliminary to philosophy proper) and ethics (including politics and economics, or household management), while *theoretikē* comprised physics and theology—all this, save for logic, which was conceded to Aristotle, being thoroughly Platonist (though the Stoics had left their mark on late antique ethics).

Boethius dramatizes most effectively the view of philosophy that prevailed throughout late antiquity. It can thus be seen why Platonism constituted a serious rival to Christianity, whereas Aristotelianism did not. For the Platonists, philosophy comprised an accumulated deposit of truth, already visible in the inspired poetry of such figures as Orpheus, Homer, and Hesiod, but also presented, in remote antiquity in Egypt, by Thoth, or "Thrice-Greatest Hermes," and in later times by the gods themselves, through the so-called Chaldaean Oracles. These documents, of course, require allegorical exegesis to unlock their wisdom, but the deposit of truth was presented in a more straightforward (though still by no means perspicuous) manner in ancient times by Pythagoras and Plato, and with various degrees of distortion by their successors, from Aristotle on, until restored to something like its pristine purity by Plotinus. This is the view of the history of philosophy that we find presented by Proclus in the preface of his *Platonic Theology,* and it accurately represents the consensus of Hellenic late antiquity.

Educated Christians, from Clement of Alexandria on, gave a different twist to this tradition by borrowing from Philo of Alexandria the ingenious notion that Pythagoras had himself learned whatever was valid in his philosophy from the followers of Moses, so that the true wisdom was "barbarian," and not Hellenic—a nice piece of one-upmanship. The teaching of Christ was thus seen as completing and validating all previous intimations of the truth, including those provided by Platonism.

Both sides, however, concurred in the notion of the work of philosophy as the exposition of an ancient deposit of truth, rather than as the development of ever new insights, and thus the most characteristic and appropriate form of philosophical text becomes the commentary. The late antique commentary, in turn, became the means by which original work in philosophy might be covertly accomplished.

What was the content of this philosophical consensus, at least in the Hellenic tradition? In metaphysics, the primary issue was seen as the derivation of all things, and of multiplicity and variety in general, from a single, absolutely simple, and transcendent first principle, superior even to intellection and cognizable, if at all, only by indirection; second was the means by which all things seek to maximize their unity, and realize their essence, by turning back toward their common source. Physical speculation was based on interpretations of Plato's *Timaeus*, with some help from such Aristotelian works as the *Physics*, the *De caelo*, and the *De generatione et corruptione*. It envisaged a universe permeated by divine providence and held together by *logoi* emanating from the system of Forms which comprised the intelligible realm.

Ethical doctrine tended to Stoic-style austerity, though permeated by a transcendental perspective proper to Platonism, but rejecting any Aristotelian hospitality to the concept that "bodily" or "external" goods can make any contribution to happiness. The aim of life was agreed to be "assimilation to God" (a formula derived from Plato, *Theaetetus* 176), and the means to that was the acquisition and exercise of the virtues. To resolve a tension between the practice of virtue as a social and civic function and its practice as a means of escape from this world and all social ties, Plotinus, in *Ennead* 1.2, propounded a distinction between the "civic" and the "purificatory" virtues, the former being featured in the *Republic,* the latter in the *Phaedo,* and his successors, Porphyry and Iamblichus, elaborated on this theory, Iamblichus arriving at a system of fully seven grades of virtue.

Logic, as has been indicated above, was taken over from Aristotle, with some later Peripatetic accretions, and Porphyry's interpretation of Aristotle's *Categories* formed the basis for later arguments about nominalism and realism. Logic, however, was generally held to be an "instrument" *(organon)* rather than an integral part of philosophy.

The emperor Justinian's famous closing of the Platonic Academy in 529 may well not have been as definitive an act as has been traditionally presented, but the date will do as signifying the approximate end of philosophy as a force independent of Christian (or, later, Muslim) theology. For a man like Proclus, "revealed" theology (as represented by the Orphic poems or the Chaldaean Oracles), though greatly honored, was always the handmaid of philosophy; thenceforth philosophy, even for a man like Boethius, was to be the handmaid of theology.

BIBL.: A. H. Armstrong, ed., *The Cambridge History of Later Greek and Early Medieval Philosophy* (Cambridge, Eng., 1970). A. Badawi, *La transmission de la philosophie grecque au monde arabe* (Paris, 1987). J. Geffken, *The Last Days of Greco-Roman Paganism,* trans. S. MacCormack (Amsterdam, 1978). P. Hadot, *Exercices spirituels et philosophie antique* (Paris, 1981); trans., with additions, as *Philosophy as a Way of Life,* ed. A. I. Davidson (Oxford, 1995).

J.DIL.

Philostorgius

Philostorgius's ecclesiastical history began with the theological dispute between the Alexandrian priest Arius and his bishop Alexander and ended in 425. The patriarch Photius characterized Philostorgius as an Arian or Eunomian, and his work as a panegyric of heretics and denigration of the orthodox rather than a history. Although the original text is lost, much of Philostorgius's *History* can be reconstructed in outline, and sometimes in detail, for in addition to and separate from the brief notice in his *Bibliotheca,* Photius wrote a long and detailed summary that permits the identification of Philostorgian material in a wide variety of later authors. Substantial borrowings are especially evident in the *Passion of Artemius* by one John, who is now plausibly identified as John of Damascus. Joseph Bidez produced a magisterial reconstruction of Philostorgius's lost history that superseded all earlier editions; it has been reprinted with extensive addenda and corrigenda by F. Winkelmann, incorporating additional fragments.

It is hard to make a general assessment of Philostorgius. He gives a consistently different perspective on events and personalities from the orthodox ecclesiastical historians, and preserves much of value that they omit, yet his narrative is frequently tendentious and sometimes demonstrably false. Philostorgius is of value for secular as well as ecclesiastical events. For the 4th century he drew on Eunapius, while the concluding section of his work is greatly indebted to the lost history of Olympiodorus. This latter fact implies that Philostorgius was writing in the 440s (though a date as early as 433 has often been argued).

BIBL.: J. Bidez, *Philostorgius Kirchengeschichte mit dem Leben des Lucian von Antiochien und den Fragmenten eines arianischen Historiographen* (Leipzig, 1913); 2nd and 3rd eds., rev. F. Winkelmann (Berlin, 1972, 1981). A. E. Nobbs, "Philostorgius' View of the Past," in *Reading the Past in Late Antiquity*, ed. G. W. Clarke (Rushcutters Bay, Australia, 1989), 251–264. G. Zecchini, "Filostorgio," in *Metodologie della ricerca sulla tarda antichità*, ed. A. Garzya (Naples, 1991), 579–598.   T.D.B.

Pilgrimage

Pilgrimage essentially involves movement from a local cult and sphere of piety to one that embraces a broad region; as such pilgrimage is to be found in many indigenous cultures. Regional cults and shrines serve as ultimate courts of appeal in circumstances of particular misfortune, as defining religious centers for a wide area of local cults, or simply as supplementary cults, conveying a sense of universality to visitors that neither threatens nor guarantees the local cults. As described by Victor Turner, the dynamics of pilgrimage lie in the transformation undergone by the individual and the group while, first, disengaging from local society to become a marginal "pilgrims' society"; second, at the goal, merging with other pilgrims' societies; and, third, reintegrating with the local society. The final stage usually involves bringing back tokens, souvenirs, or "blessings" in some concrete form; these often incorporated pieces of the relic or dust from the holy site, sometimes enclosed within an iconographic representation of the pilgrim shrine's divinity (an ampulla or a decorative reliquary) that could serve as an amulet in the subsequent life of the pilgrim. The supplying of such souvenirs and blessings, as well as travelers' necessities, usually gave rise to extensive trade in the vicinity of the shrine.

What attracted pilgrims in late antiquity, as in earlier and subsequent eras, was the direct encounter with a god or saint that could be gained in a specific place. Thus pilgrimage times often corresponded with scheduled festivals, when the god or saint was believed to be the more immanent because of the holy day and during which an image of the god or saint might emerge in procession. Another popular way of receiving the culminative encounter with the divine figure, common to native and Christian shrines, was the practice of incubation: pilgrims would spend the night in the temple or saint-shrine and receive revelations from the god or saint in their dreams. But in many cases the very experience of reaching the pilgrimage goal after long mental preparation and an arduous journey could prompt epiphanies of gods, saints, or sacred events.

A pilgrimage could serve as the apex of one's religious life, or it could constitute one's regular religious duty as part of a festival calendar: "Travel in homage to each temple," advises an Egyptian pilgrim to the Temple of Talmis in the 2nd or 3rd century (*CIG* 3.5041). Pilgrimage also could be indistinguishable from tourism, inasmuch as ancient tourism was based on a profound reverence for archaic and exotic holy places. The sounds emitting from the dilapidated statue of Memnon in Thebes, a popular sight on the Roman tourist route, became for many the oracular voice of a god, and many visitors to Thebes seem to have expected to find a guru among the dwindling priesthood. In the 4th century, tours to see ascetics in Syria, Egypt, and Palestine, according to "guidebooks" like Palladius's *Lausiac History* and Theodoret's *History of the Monks of Syria*, likewise combined pilgrimage with the tourist's penchant for the exotic.

Through the pious tourism of Greeks and Romans, many native regional cults became major pilgrimage shrines in the Mediterranean world, serving to anchor the native religions of late antiquity (as well as an ideological "paganism") in a sacred geography of monumental temples. The conversion of these same shrines to places of Christian or Muslim pilgrimage does not seem to have stopped the flow of pilgrims, and the new religions were able to tap into the regional authority of a place with continual visitors from throughout a region. Christianization of pilgrimage sites usually involved the importation (translation) or feigned discovery (invention) of a martyr's relics, with the resulting cult often offering services (e.g., incubation and healing) similar to those of earlier times. In the person of desert holy men like Symeon Stylites, Christianity also developed new regional pilgrimage cults in areas of exclusively local cults. Here, however, the new regional cults stood in tension rather than in reciprocity with the traditional local cults.

By the 5th century the Mediterranean world was a network of international and regional pilgrimage centers, including Apa Mena in the desert west of Alexandria; Telneshe, the site and eventually basilica of Symeon Stylites's pillar, east of Antioch; Seleucia, the sprawling shrine of St. Thecla in southern Asia Minor; and the Holy Land itself.

The rise of Christian Holy Land pilgrimage in the 4th century followed a long tradition of Jewish veneration of sites and tombs in Palestine. The earliest Christian testimonies to a sacred geography show reverence for sites of biblical rather than Christian legend (Matt. 23:29, 27:52–53; Bordeaux Pilgrim). But among literate visitors like Helena, mother of Constantine, or Egeria, arriving from Gallaecia in the 380s, the Holy Land pilgrimage became an opportunity to participate in the Gospel text itself. Written accounts of these pilgrimages became guides in their own right during the 4th and later centuries, sparking the "identification" of many more sites of Gospel events. By the end of the 4th century, Christian Holy Land pilgrimage combined biblical with Gospel sites, and a large number of local anchorites and monasteries were visited as well.

Where for Christians, Holy Land pilgrimage involved primarily the mental recapturing of scriptural events, for Jews it involved ritual mourning over the ruined Temple of Jerusalem and messianic anticipation of its reconstitution. For both religions, and subsequently for Muslims as well, Jerusalem and its environs were traditionally the "center" of the sacred geography (in Islam, second to Mecca and Medina).

In Islam the pilgrimage to Mecca, the hajj, was a duty imposed on Muslims by the Qur'ān (e.g., 2:196, 3:97). Islamic law dictates that Muslims who are able both physically and financially should perform the hajj once during their life, but in the early Islamic period, it was often a yearly event for those who lived within a manageable distance of Mecca. The hajj must be undertaken in a state of ritual purity, symbolized by the wearing of special garments. It takes place during the second week of the Islamic lunar month of Dhū'l-Ḥijja and consists of a series of events that lead the pilgrims from the Ka'ba at Mecca to Minā and 'Arafāt, which lies 15 miles (25 km) to the east of Mecca.

Pilgrimage had been important in the social and religious life of the pre-Islamic Arabs, and the hajj retained certain elements of their practices, such as the circumambulation of the Ka'ba. Yet the hajj is a distinctly Islamic ritual in its prayers, its objectives, and its religious meaning. Its geographical course and some of the ritual activities commemorate Muhammad's actions during his "farewell" pilgrimage in 632. A Muslim may perform some part of the hajj rituals at other times during the year, and this type of pilgrimage to Mecca is called the 'umra (Qur'ān 2:158). The act of visiting shrines, grave sites, or the holy cities of Jerusalem and Medina is known by the term ziyāra; such undertakings are voluntary and have no canonical rituals, but they have grown to be an important component in Islamic piety.

BIBL.: J. Elsner, *Art and the Roman Viewer* (Oxford, 1996). Pierre Maraval, *Lieux saints et pèlerinages d'orient* (Paris, 1985). Arthur Darby Nock, "A Vision of Mandulis Aion," *Essays on Religion and the Ancient World* (Oxford, 1972), vol. 1, 356–400. Robert Ousterhout, ed., *The Blessings of Pilgrimage* (Urbana, 1990). M. E. Stone, "Holy Land Pilgrimage of Armenians before the Arab Conquest," *Revue Biblique* 93 (1986): 93–110. F. E. Peters, *The Hajj: The Muslim Pilgrimage to Mecca and the Holy Places* (Princeton, 1994). Victor Turner and Edith Turner, *Image and Pilgrimage in Christian Culture: Anthropological Perspectives* (New York, 1978). *Pilgrimage and Holy Space in Late Antique Egypt*, ed. D. Frankfurter (Leiden, 1998). C. Hahn, "Seeing and Believing," *Speculum* 72 (1997): 1070–1106.   D.T.F.

Plotinus

The Platonist philosopher Plotinus, perhaps the most original philosophic mind of late antiquity, never aspired to be more than a faithful interpreter of Plato. He was born and grew up in Lycopolis, in Upper Egypt, probably the scion of a well-to-do and well-connected Greek family (the name is actually Roman), but we know very little of his early life, despite having a remarkable memoir of him written by his pupil Porphyry (prefixed to Porphyry's edition of Plotinus's philo-

sophical essays), since he was extremely reticent about this. We do know, however, that he came to Alexandria in 232, at the late age of twenty-seven, and, after rejecting the established teachers of philosophy, enrolled with the maverick and charismatic Pythagoreanizing Platonist Ammonius Saccas, with whom he remained eleven years (probably until Ammonius's death). He then got himself taken onto the personal staff of the emperor Gordian III on his expedition against Persia, with the aim of visiting the sages of Persia and India. The expedition was aborted after the murder of Gordian by Philip the Arab, and Plotinus escaped, first to Antioch, and then to Rome, where, at the age of forty, he set up a philosophical school.

He remained based in Rome for the rest of his life, gathering round him a circle of pupils and noble patrons, including even the emperor Gallienus and his wife. His senior pupil, Amelius, was eclipsed later by Porphyry of Tyre, who arrived from the Platonic school in Athens in 262–263 and became Plotinus's chief pupil and literary executor. It was he (by his own account) who persuaded Plotinus to commit his views to writing, which he only began to do at the age of fifty, and who gathered them into their present form, the *Enneads,* six groups of nine essays arranged broadly according to topic, from ethics through the physical world (enneads I–III), the soul (IV), the intellect (V), and, finally, the first principle (VI). These were published long after his death, in around 305.

Plotinus's innovations in Platonism are mainly two: first, above the traditional supreme principle of earlier Platonism (and Aristotelianism), a self-thinking intellect, which was also regarded as true being, he postulated a principle superior to intellect and being, something totally unitary and simple ("the One"); second, he saw reality as a series of levels (One, Intellect, Soul), each higher one flowing or radiating into the next lower, while still remaining unaffected in itself, and the lower ones fixing themselves in being by somehow "reflecting back" on the prior levels. This eternal process gives the universe its existence and character. Intelligence operates in a state of nontemporal simultaneity, holding within itself the "forms" of all things. Soul, in turn, generates time, and receives the forms into itself as "reason-principles" *(logoi).* Our physical, three-dimensional world is the result of the lower aspect of Soul (nature) projecting itself on a kind of negative field of force, "matter." Matter has no positive existence but is simply the receptacle for the projection of forms. This system, known in modern times as Neoplatonism, came to be the dominant philosophy in late antiquity.

BIBL.: D. J. O'Meara, *Plotinus: An Introduction to the Enneads* (Oxford, 1993). J. M. Rist, *Plotinus: The Road to Reality* (Cambridge, Eng., 1967).   J.DIL.

Police

In the Roman empire, policing operations were traditionally shared between the state and city-states. Against local bandits—shepherds were the archetype of antique delinquents—cities mobilized citizens *(iuvenes, neaniskoi)* under the orders of the *paraphulakes* or *irenarchs.* As soon as a situation became serious, the army was brought in. Thus, in areas with endemic security problems, such as Isauria, military units were sometimes stationed with the express purpose of ensuring order. Some critics have even proposed that the placement of military forces on the eastern border was more a police operation than a strategic decision. The language of the time, in fact, used the same term *latrones* (pillagers) to designate both domestic delinquents and barbarians who crossed the border to carry out raids.

Another tradition was to link policing operations with justice duties; this occurred both among city magistrates and among agents exercising direct public authority. Thus, the *stationarii,* under the governor's orders, were military personnel on special duty. The same individuals maintained law and order, received denunciations and complaints, led investigations, arrested and summoned the accused, and sent files to tribunals. Many commentators have attributed a long-term militarization of the police to the Severi. This thesis cannot be sustained even for the 3rd century, when territorial centurions and decurions *(benephikiarioi, statizōntes)* were indistinguishable from their counterparts in previous centuries. They had no relation to the *frumentarii,* special government agents suppressed by the tetrarchy and soon replaced by the civilian *agentes in rebus.* The thesis is even more suspect for later centuries, when military police and justice officers had disappeared, completely abandoning the field to civilian staff, either municipal or of municipal extraction. It is significant that, in 556, the distant successors of 3rd century *stationarii,* given the mission of "repressing violence" *(biokōlutai)* or "pursuing bandits" *(lēstodiōktai),* were civilians delegated by the governors *(Nov.* 134, which forbade the practice).

The late empire thus allotted the better part of its *liturgi,* designated by the city-states but responsible to the provincial authorities, to serve public policing and justice missions. In the east the post of *irenarch,* a magistrate who held office for one year only, seems to have been eliminated in 409 but was later reestablished. In Egypt it was replaced in 346 by the collegial *riparii.* In Rome itself, where urban cohorts had been demilitarized, the urban prefect, stripped of policing powers, had at most his *apparitores;* similarly, provincial governors had their personal guard of *spathiarioi* and *doryphoroi.* Also in Rome, the *vicomagistri et priores regionum* manned a kind of medieval lookout before the fact, like the *nuctostrategoi* in eastern cities (despite their name, they stood watch both day and night).

Generally, the Roman-Byzantine state limited the armaments local police could use and continued the ban on *usus equorum,* which left them unequipped for operations of any significant size. In serious cases, the army was called in directly: in Constantinople, where troops were permanently stationed; in Alexandria, where troops intervened constantly in religious uprisings; and also in Rome (e.g., in 419, during the eventful election of Boniface). In cases of actual political agitation, the emperor sent a personal representative to follow developments on the scene.

Beginning in the 5th century, the insecurity of the populations, who had been abandoned by the central powers, led to the rebirth of local militias of *iuvenes* or *neaniskoi,* a practice that had declined in the previous century. In Cyrenaica, Synesius even tried to mobilize a civilian army, flouting the legal ban on carrying weapons. As for the private guards who surrounded *potentes* in the 5th and 6th centuries, they were less a manifestation of a privatized police force than the instrument of usurped local power, civil disobedience, and tax revolt.

BIBL.: Keith Hopwood, "Policing the Hinterland: Rough Cilicia and Isauria," in *Armies and Frontiers in Roman and Byzantine Anatolia,* ed. Stephen Mitchell (Oxford, 1983), 173–187. James G. Keenan, "Village Shepherds and Social Tension in Byzantine Egypt," *Yale Classical Studies* 28 (1985): 245–259. Brent D. Shaw, "Il bandito," in *L'uomo romano,* ed. A. Giardina (Rome and Bari, 1989).   J.C.

Population

Population has two fundamental but distinct aspects: size and distribution, and process. The size of a population in a preindustrial empire is a primary index of its power: the greater the population, the larger the central government's potential revenues, the larger the army that can be supported, and so forth. Its distribution by region, and between town and country, is an index of the empire's economic productivity. Population process, the cycle from birth to death, is a basic determinant of life chances.

Unfortunately, we possess very little reliable information about population size or process from the later Roman empire. We have to rely instead on speculation, bounded on one side by fragmentary evidence and on the other by comparative statistics. Standard estimates or guesses about the total population of the Roman empire in the first century C.E. center on 50–60 million people. Any sizeable, sustained growth above that number would have made the Roman empire invincible. The total population of the later Roman empire was probably similar. There is no convincing evidence of a sustained long-term decline in total population before the 5th century.

Postmedieval European populations before the 18th century demographic revolution showed significant century-long population swings. It is likely that the population of the whole Roman empire underwent similar long-term fluctuations. The bubonic plague of 542, graphically described by Procopius (*Bell.Pers.* 2.22–23), with its subsequent reappearances may have heralded one such long-term decline.

The total population of the more urbanized, eastern Mediterranean was larger than that of the western Mediterranean. This imbalance was reinforced by the foundation of Constantinople in 324, and by the effective disuse of Rome as a capital city (inhabited by emperors for only three years in the 4th century, sacked by Goths in 410). By the 6th century, Constantinople probably had a population of more than 500,000, helped (as Rome had been throughout the 4th century) by distributions of free wheat. The mobility of the imperial court between temporary capitals, mainly in the 4th century (Arles, Trier, Sirmium, Ravenna, Nicomedia, Antioch) affected local economies and the lines of trade. By the 5th century, the barbarian invasions reduced trade and, thus, town sizes in the western empire.

Comparative evidence suggests that the proportion of the population living in towns (with a minimum size arbitrarily set at 2,000 people) was unlikely to have been above 15 percent (perhaps 20 percent in the east and 10 percent in the west; lower in the 5th century). Local estimates of urbanization in Roman Egypt, based on multiplying figures from one or two not necessarily representative towns, are difficult to believe if they exceed these base figures significantly.

Comparative evidence suggests that the average life expectancy at birth was probably in the region of twenty to thirty years, so fertility had to be high to balance the high mortality. Women had to have, on average, five to six live births if population was to be maintained. Marriage was nearly universal, which throws into relief the prominent celibacy of Christian ascetics, male and female. Infant mortality was high, but deaths also occurred throughout the normal life cycle. On average, one-fourth of the males surviving to age twenty-five died by the age of forty, and one-half of the males surviving to age forty died by the age of sixty. Female mortality was similar; death rates in childbirth, though traumatic, did not exceed 1.5 percent per birth.

The pervasiveness of unexpected deaths is fundamental to our understanding of Roman institutions and social life. Wealth usually came via inheritance. Deaths eased promotion prospects in the army and the bureaucracy, children were released from paternal control by their father's early death, and wives were often widowed young (given the common age gap between husband and wife).

BIBL.: R. S. Bagnall and B .W. Frier, *The Demography of Roman Egypt* (Cambridge, Eng., 1994). K. J. Beloch, *Die Bevölkerung der griechisch-römischen Welt* (Leipzig, 1886). T. G. Parkin, *Demography and Roman Society* (Baltimore, 1996). K.H.

Pork

The hunting of boar and the raising of domesticated pigs have been known to humanity from prehistoric times, and the hunting, sacrifice, and consumption of pork are documented from the earliest periods of Greek literature (e.g., *Iliad* 19.250–275, *Odyssey* 19.428–454). In later periods pork was a common staple of Greeks and Romans alike, though it was occasionally prohibited for certain sacrifices (especially for Aphrodite, a taboo commonly explained by her hatred of the animal that had killed Adonis). Outside the Greek and Roman worlds, however, pork was not as universally accepted. In Cappadocian Comana, for example, no pork was eaten in the temple of Ma-Enyo, nor in the town itself (Strabo, *Geography* 12.8.9), and similar taboos are recorded for the cult of Cybele (Julian, *Orat.* 8.17) and others. Prohibitions against sacrificing or eating pork are also attested among Syrians and Phoenicians, but the exact details as to who observed which taboo vary greatly from one ancient author to the next. Among the Egyptians, the pig was considered impure (Herodotus 2.47), but there was no universal prohibition against its consumption, outside the priestly caste, and the literary and papyrological evidence demonstrates the vitality of the country's swineherds. The Jews' avoidance of pork, based on biblical injunction (Lev. 11:7; Deut. 14:8), was a subject of much ancient speculation and occasional derision (e.g., Philo, *Legatio* 361; Plutarch, *Cicero* 7.5, *Quaest.conv.* 4.5; Macrobius, *Sat.* 2.4.11). Jewish literature records several attempts of non-Jews to force Jews to eat pork (e.g., 2 Macc. 6–7; Philo, *In Flaccum* 96), attempts that made the observance of this taboo a symbol of Jewish steadfastness in the face of religious persecution. The Jews' persistence on this score was noted even by Juvenal (*Sat.* 14.98–99), Sextus Empiricus (who attributed to Jews and Egyptian priests the willingness to die rather than eat pork, *Pyr.* 3.223), and Porphyry (who also attributed similar traits to Phoenicians, Egyptians, and Syrians; *De abstin.* 2.61). It should be noted, however, that although rabbinic literature maintained the strict taboo with regard to the consumption of pork, and prohibited even the raising of pigs (m Bava Kama 7.7), archaeological evidence suggests that pig farming was not unknown even in those regions of early Byzantine Palestine where Jews predominated.

The generally antinomian position on matters of dietary regulations adopted by the early Christians applied also to the biblical prohibition against pork, which was interpreted as spiritual and anagogic rather than literal. Nonetheless, Christian leaders occasionally had to remind their followers that this indeed was the case, a sure sign that in some circles, at least, the ancient taboo remained in force. In the Muslim world, pork was strictly forbidden. This prohibition is repeated on several occasions in the Qur'ān (2:173,

6:146, 16:116) and apparently went back to pre-Islamic practices among the Arabs (as recorded, e.g., by Sozomen, *Hist.eccl.* 6.38.10).

Although pork was a prohibited food in many regions and for the adherents of many religions, and although the keeping of pigs was considered a sign of exceptional poverty in other areas (Palladius, *Hist.Laus.* 32.10, on Middle Egypt), pork was an essential part of the diet in most of western Europe. Pork was a carefully maintained item in military rations and in the *annona* given to the people of Rome. Until at least the middle of the 5th century, arrangements were made for the delivery of 3,629,000 pounds per year from southern Italy (*C.Th.* 14.4.1–9 and Valentinian, *Nov.* 3.36).

BIBL.: S. Barnish, "Pigs, Plebeians and *Potentes*," *Papers of the British School of Rome* 55 (1987): 157–185. W. Helck, "Schwein," in *Lexikon der Ägyptologie,* ed. W. Helck and E. Otto, vol. 5 (Wiesbaden, 1984). M. Rodinson, "Ghidha'," in B. Lewis et al., eds., *Encyclopaedia of Islam,* 2nd ed., vol. 2 (Leiden, 1965). T. Wächter, *Reinheitsvorschriften im griechischen Kult* (Giessen, 1910), 82–87.   G.B.

Pornography

Pornography is a modern concept embellished with a Greek name; the rarely attested ancient word *pornographos* basically means just "painter of prostitutes" *(pornai)* (Athenaeus 13.567b). Applying the concept to late antique material thus runs the usual risk of distorting the picture or emasculating the term, but it is legitimate at least to discuss what kind of texts and objects might have had, in their historical context, a function similar to pornography, understood as the exploitation of nakedness and sexual acts for commercial, ideological, or otherwise nonpersonal uses. If, as Alexander Kazhdan suggests, the "sexy stories" of Byzantine hagiography, exhibiting sex without love, are included simply to capture readers for Christian edification, would this function perhaps make a description like that of Andrew the Fool being fondled by prostitutes pornographic also in the nonliteral sense?

"Thecla was stripped, and seized a cloth to cover herself. She was thrown into the arena, and lions and bears were let loose on her." This scene from the apocryphal *Acts of Paul and Thecla* exemplifies how martyrologies tend to emphasize the enforced nakedness of the victim. Whether destined for the stake or for combat in the arena, the martyr is "unnecessarily" naked (in the later *Life of Thecla* her nudity is explained as arousing the *animals!*), and this public, degrading nakedness, in combination with violent physical abuse and an erotically exciting virginity, would perhaps qualify for the status of (soft) pornography. If so, it was conveyed by widespread texts, by pictorial representations (cf. the half-naked Thecla between beasts and flames in a 6th century Coptic relief)—and, of course, in pre-Constantinian times, by the spectacles themselves. Now, Thecla had asked her persecutors to

be allowed to die a virgin; if we add Apuleius's description of public rape (here executed by an animal) as a spectator-friendly form of punishment (*Metamorphoses* 10.34), staged after a mythological tableau performed by boys and girls in titillating nakedness (30–31), we may imagine a hard-core variety of martyrdom presented before the pagan gaze.

When persecution was over and gladiatorial games gradually ebbed away following their prohibition in 325, this peculiar mix of naked (male or female) bodies, violence, and sex disappears. Theatrical performances with pornographic potential lived on, however, even if vigorously denounced by the church—witness Empress Theodora, the former mime actress. If patristic homilies, our usual index of late antique vice, do not seem to specify any coarser forms of pornography besides general references to lewdness and obscenity, this may just be due to decorous reticence. After all, Tertullian, with a memorable phrase, "Rather omit than recall" (*"malo non implere quam meminisse,"* De spectaculis 19), had declined to report his most disgusting experiences at the public spectacles. The description of pornography easily becomes pornography.

As for representations of sexual acts in mosaics and paintings, sometimes in mythological guise, it is difficult to tell, in the absence of verbal testimony, if there was a pornographic aspect involved; located in bedrooms or where symposia took place, they will at least have had an erotically stimulating function. Smaller, portable objects of art may be more relevant, for example, painted pictures *(tabellae)*, relief-decorated pottery, and mirrors with erotic motifs. A case in point are the Roman lamps bearing scenes of copulating dwarfs, perhaps reflecting public sex shows of that nature. At the same time, in a culture accustomed to the cult of Priapus and replete with phallic symbolism, the mere depiction of genitalia (for instance, to advertise or decorate brothels) can hardly count as pornography; that some images have posthumously achieved that status when reproduced on modern postcards is another matter. With the spread of Christianity, erotic art and artifacts gradually disappeared, along with other pagan motifs; it is only when they reappear, in a Victorian or later cultural context, that we may more properly apply the term *pornography* to some of their uses.

BIBL.: Catherine Johns, *Sex or Symbol: Erotic Images of Greece and Rome* (London, 1982). Alexander Kazhdan, "Byzantine Hagiography and Sex in the Fifth to Twelfth Centuries," *Dumbarton Oaks Papers* 44 (1990): 131–143. Amy Richlin, ed., *Pornography and Representation in Greece and Rome* (New York, 1992).   T.H.

Prayer

Prayer, timelessly close to the essence of religious belief and practice, also raises timelessly persistent questions, some philosophical, others unsophisticated but elemental. In classical times difficulty was felt when petitions to the gods were left unanswered. Were they unheard? Or was it rather that the petitioner had not pleased the divine powers, or that the actual benefit asked for was not in accord with the will of the gods? In ancient Greek tragedy the pain felt by unanswered prayer was already being wrestled with. Pre-Socratic philosophers (Xenophanes and Heraclitus, in particular) were long remembered for their critical sayings concerning the crude notions of the divine presupposed by simple petitions for prosperity. In postclassical times the pseudo-Platonic dialogue *Alcibiades II* (141–143) observes that prayers for power may be harmful to the petitioner if actually answered—for how many who have aspired to high political or military power have lost their lives; how many have prayed to have children and then found them to create dreadful problems and disasters. In such cases, it was observed, the prayer turned out to seem nothing but a curse, and then people blamed the gods for what was merely their own folly.

The philosophical argument revolves largely around the interpretation of providence and questions about freedom and determinism. In the tenth book of *Laws*, Plato debates providential care with those who regard the gods as negligent, or who find it easier to accept providential care in general for the ordering of very large matters than to suppose that a divine being could take the trouble to be interested in small things. The Platonic tradition stems from *Phaedo* (108b, 113d): belief in a guardian daemon guiding the soul, a belief that presupposed providential care for particulars as well as generalities.

Prayers for material goods and worldly success were closely associated with divination and astrology, and therefore were always close to magic. Plotinus (4.4.40–41) regarded all petitions for this world's benefits as a form of magic that, when successful, could be explained by the principle of inner cosmic sympathy, for when people pray to the sun or the stars, the heavenly bodies have no memory and no organs for hearing the words of the petitioner. The inner harmony of all elements in the universe explained how one's prayers had been answered. Plotinus was sharply critical of the idea that people guilty of wrongdoing could look to someone else to be their saviour and to answer their prayers by offering themselves in sacrifice (3.2,9,10–12, possibly a sharp reference to his notion of Christianity). Prayers for forgiveness appear to have been more biblical than classical, but instances occur outside the Judaic or Christian sphere of influence, and a basic theme of concepts of sacrifice was the need to keep the celestial or (closer at hand) daemonic powers friendly and propitious.

Plotinus's aspiration for the soul's ascent to union not merely with Intellect (Nous) but even with the One, "alone to the alone," involved detachment from the material world and images of it. It required a "stretching out" of the soul in prayer to God (5.1,6,9–

11). More than one text of Plotinus speaks of "alone to the alone" (1.6,7,8; 6.7,34,7; 6.9,11,51).

The philosophic ascent to the One is to attain "an inspired dance" (6.9,8,45). The One (or God) is the locus of goodness for humanity, as the soul is 'in love with God and longs to be united with him" (6.9,9,34). If one does not long remain at the summit, that is because one has not entirely emerged from the world. The ultimate vision is beyond reason (6.9,10,9). The vision of God, or union with the One, will finally be complete rest, calm, and solitude.

Plotinus defended a belief in providence but qualified it so as not to deny freedom and responsibility. His discussion of the power of the stars presupposes that a deterministic fate controls inferior things in the material world but not incorporeal realities in the intelligible world. Nemesius of Emesa (*On the Nature of Man* 35, p. 289 Matthaei) commented that if everything were to be ruled by the stars, then all prayer would be useless. And the work of law courts would be equally futile. Iamblichus allowed astral determinism, but held that prayers and aversion sacrifices could propitiate the planetary powers to make them favorable. Nemesius knew of Platonists who held that while initial decisions lie in our power, the consequences are determined by fate, so that once our choice has been made, further prayer for a good outcome is futile (38, p. 306 f.).

The determinist view was congenial to those whose thinking about prayer did not really distinguish it from magic. In Latin the normal word for a prayer, *prex*, was also the regular term for a spell (e.g., Ovid, *Met.* 7.251). A prayer might also carry the content of a curse. That at the popular level both pagans and marginal Christians thought of prayers in this lowly manner is clearly attested. Petronius (*Satyricon* 88) scathingly writes of prayers to gods to grant wealth, and offerings in temples to achieve the early death of a rich relative. Augustine (*Serm.* 90.9) had to admonish his people not to think that at the Eucharist, at the commemoration of the faithful departed, they could invoke God's power to bring about the death of an enemy.

Magical spells were normally muttered almost inaudibly. Justinian (*Nov.* 137.6) forbade Christian clergy to be inaudible, for example in the eucharistic *anaphora*.

In antiquity prayers were normally said aloud. One might not wish one's enemies to overhear, however, and those enemies might include malevolent spirits. Likewise, if one were praying for success in getting someone else's spouse to bed, one might keep quiet about it, and the same would apply if one's petition were for someone's violent death. So there were risks involved in prayers for potentially embarrassing objectives. One of the consequences of imperial legislation prohibiting pagan sacrifices was that polytheists had to practice their cultic rites in private, a move that fortified the Christian thesis that pagan rituals were a form of black magic. The late Platonist thesis that the old religious rituals offered a method of preparatory purification, elevating the soul for higher philosophic flights, was present, with some blushes, in the writings of Porphyry and became full-blown in Iamblichus and Proclus, where theurgy, or the practice of old rituals to make the gods propitious and to purify the soul, is a potent form of prayer. For Christians like Augustine (*Confessions* 10.42.67) theurgy was sorcery and hobnobbing with wicked demons. Christian writers on prayer took it for granted that prayers should be audible, even though the wisdom of God was able to hear silent petitions. Although God heard the innermost longing of the heart—"One who longs for something, even if his tongue is silent, is singing in his heart" (Augustine, *Enarr. in Ps.* 86.1)—silence and solitude were necessary for Christian meditation (Augustine, *In Evangelium Johannis* 17.11).

According to Christian thought, God can will a change without changing his will. Prayers are not said to persuade him to take a more benevolent view, and certainly not to inform him about matters of which he is ignorant (Augustine, *Ep.* 130, 17 and 21). Prayer's purpose is or should be not to get God to agree with you but to bring your will into line with his (Augustine, *Confessions*, 10.26.37). All Christian prayer is answered, not necessarily at the time or in the way that the person praying expects, with the proviso that our prayers should be for nothing wicked, and should be for moral strength rather than for power or wealth (Augustine, *De ordine* 2.20,52).

In the Greek east an ascetic theology of the spiritual life was developed late in the 2nd century by Clement of Alexandria (*Stromateis* 7), then by Origen *(On Prayer),* and by Origen's speculative follower Evagrius of Pontus, whose themes were brought to the Latin west by John Cassian. But the west appears less interested in the theology of prayer than in practical questions such as whether one should pray facing the east, kneeling, sitting, or standing, with uplifted head and hands, and so on.

Among all religious groups of late antiquity, the physical gestures of prayer conveyed specific messages. A strong sense of geographical orientation toward a distant sacred center determined the prayers of Jews and Christians long before the establishment of the Islamic *qibla*. Jews turned toward Jerusalem—as Muhammad would do in the early years of his preaching. Christians turned to the east, reminding themselves, thereby, either of their exile from paradise, which lay to the east, or of the imminent return of Christ from the east. Even in private prayer, the Christian believer would turn to the east; indeed, many preferred to have a clear view in that direction through a door or a window (Origen, *De oratione* 31.1). An overriding sense of the priority of a distant sacred center effectively relativized other forms of holy space within the churches themselves. In North Africa, where few

churches faced east, the exhortation at the end of the sermon, *"Conversi ad Dominum"* ("Turned to the Lord"), was a signal for the entire congregation to turn its back on the preacher, the altar, and the benches of the clergy in the apse so as to face, together, the Lord of the east. Only in the early Middle Ages did this sharp sense of place weaken in western Europe. Carolingian liturgical commentators bypassed late antique practice for a learned reappropriation of the Hebrew Bible, where prayer to the Temple from the royal palace took place toward the west. Also, a growing sense of the sacrality of the church itself, even when churches came to be oriented to the east, subsumed and eclipsed the ancient geographical sense of the Christian's true goal: the present altar replaced the distant east.

Among Christians, as among other groups, the gestures of prayer were expected to be melodramatic and noisy. Prayers were accompanied by upstretched arms and acclamations. Such highly demonstrative practices assumed two possible states in the believer—either as redeemed, standing upright, with raised eyes and open face before the Lord (Ps.-Chrysostom Latinus, *Hom.* 17: *PL Supp.* 4.707), or as a penitent supplicant, visibly weeping, with "knees ground down" by full prostrations, performed by throwing oneself from the standing position onto the floor (Augustine, *Serm.* 90.97, 311.13; *Confessions* 8.6.14; Prudentius *Peristephanon* 9.99–100). When Augustine preached, a rumble of chest beating—like the hammers of mosaic craftsmen tapping on a pavement—accompanied his use of the word *confession* (Augustine, *Serm.* 332.4). Thus, when Shenoute of Atripe likened the behavior of hypocritical converts to Christianity to the gestures of the decorative peacocks who strutted, flapped, and squawked in the courtyards of the churches, he implied that such persons repeated, without understanding, the expansive arm movements and exclamatory prayers that characterized normal Christian worship (Shenoute, *Ep.* 18, trans. Wiessmann, *Corpus Scriptorum Christianorum Orientalium* 96: *Scriptores Coptici* 8.22). As in the case of unveiled women or the enthusiastic leaps and "shadowboxing" gestures ascribed to the Messalians (the "praying ones" of Syria), heresy lay in the exaggeration of demonstrative gestures that indicated the saved state of Christians and their daily battle with invisible enemies. In the closed space of monasteries, deviations in gesture attracted notice: a monk might even be uncertain whether he should close his eyes to meditate during the liturgy (Barsanuphius, *Correspondance* 325). Benedict reminded his monks that the correct manner in which to pray was to be subdued and to the point, according to the ceremonious norms of late Roman social etiquette: "For if we wish to make a request of men of power in this world we would not dare to do so other than with reverence and humble gestures" (Benedict, *Regula* 20.1).

Despite the yearning of mystics to be alone with the Alone, in normal practice prayer to God and conflict with everpresent invisible beings went together. Hence prayer and imprecation merged. John Chrysostom recommended the renunciation of Satan as a prayer before leaving the house (*Catechesis ad illuminandos* 2.5). The monks of Egypt favored short, exclamatory prayers so as to hold at bay the demons who constantly threatened to infiltrate the flow of thought, as unduly prolonged prayer exposed the believer to his or her own fantasies (Augustine, *Ep.* 130.10.20). In such a world, the "Jesus Prayer" developed—it served both as a protection against demons and as a means to the state of unceasing prayer that was the true end of every human soul. In the words of Apa Macarius, perpetual repetition of the name of Jesus sweetened the mind, as the perpetual chewing of mastic sweetened the mouths of village girls.

Prayer in Islam is of two kinds: ṣalāt (ritual prayer) and du'ā' (individual supplication). The ṣalāt, performed five times daily facing the direction of Mecca, was from the beginning of Islam the main ritual obligation that framed the daily life of Muslims, and its main intent is the glorification of God. Ṣalāt is preceded by a public call to prayer and by ritual ablution. Its performance consists of a series of ritual movements and the recitation of Qur'ānic phrases and other formulas. These are said either aloud or silently, according to the time of prayer. While the Qur'ān does not require that the daily prayers be performed in a mosque, Muslim tradition supports the idea of communal worship led by a prayer leader or imām. The one obligatory communal prayer falls at noon on Friday, the "day of assembly," and includes a sermon. Communal prayers may be performed on other occasions; Muhammad, for example, led a prayer appealing for rain.

Du'ā', a word used in the Qur'ān for the activity of invoking God, is not a formal ritual, though it can have a place in the ṣalāt. It usually takes the form of a request for blessing but can also be an invocation of God against one's enemies. The du'ā' can be uttered on many occasions; according to one early tradition, Muslims are assured of the efficacy of a son's du'ā' on behalf of his dead father. It might also be uttered at the beginning of a journey, when donning new clothing, or while entering or leaving a mosque. For examples in the Qur'ān, see Suras 10:130–132, 62:9, and 4:43 for ṣalāt, Sura 3:38 for du'ā', and Sura 14:40 for both.

BIBL.: Barsanuphius, *Correspondance,* trans. L. Regnault (Solesmes, France, 1971), 236. Richard Bell and W. Montgomery Watt, *Introduction to the Qur'ān* (Edinburgh, 1970). F. Dölger, *Sol Salutis Gebet und Gesang im christlichen Altertum* (Münster in Westfalen, 1925). L. Gardet, "Du'ā'," and G. Monnot, "Ṣalāt," in *Encyclopaedia of Islam,* new ed. (Leiden, 1954-). "Gebet," *Jahrbuch für Antike und Christentum* 8 (Stuttgart, 1972), 1134-1258. E. Peterson, "Die geschichtliche Bedeutung der jüdischen Gebetsrichtung," *Frühkirche, Judentum und Gnosis* (Rome, 1959), 1-14. P. W. Van der Horst, "Silent Prayer in Antiquity," *Vigiliae christianae* 41 (1994): 1-25. H.C., P.B.

Priesthood

Despite a host of exotic images of the "pagan priest" conjured by ancient novelists and modern historians, one finds little uniformity in the organization of ritual expertise in the ancient Mediterranean world. Taking "priest" to represent ritual expertise as a recognizable social status (often implying a certain purity and numinosity in the person) and "priesthood" as implying some kind of institution or set of traditions dictating the comportment and interaction of priests, one is met with such extreme contrast among the cultures of antiquity as Israel (pre–70 C.E.), whose complex ranks of hereditary priests were professionally committed (according to biblical law) to ritual purity and the performance of a central temple cult, and Greece, where "priest" could designate any high-ranking person temporarily purified to perform a sacrifice. In Rome a complex of priestly "colleges" and extensive ritual texts reflected not a caste or clan of religious specialists but an institutional means by which the economic elite might maintain additional political authority, gain the weight of established tradition, and involve themselves in the ritual maintenance of Rome and its empire. Membership in the Egyptian priesthood, composed of a great number of hierarchical and peripheral roles (of which only the "pure" could enter the temple sanctuaries) was inherited and required specialized training in an archaic writing system. Yet in most places cultic service represented only a fraction of one's overall professional life. Thus in many ancient Mediterranean cultures there were indeed clans, societies, or castes that carried the traditional status of ritual experts: for example, in Persia, Carthage, Syria (Hierapolis, Palmyra), Asia Minor (Edessa), and Celtic Europe, as well as in Egypt and in Judaism. But the degree to which "priestly" status actually distinguished an individual from other elite groups in the culture or implied a strong affiliation with others of similar status varied considerably among and within these cultures.

Priestly status and function depends on "cult," by which is meant a localized ritual complex consisting of a sacred place and usually a rudimentary calendar. Priests' cultic functions consequently include a range of activities, including the vocalizing of liturgies, the slaughter of sacrificial animals, the adornment of holy images, and the interpretation of omens or ecstatic utterances. From texts and iconography one can infer the participation of priests in temple festivals: carrying images, consecrating animals, and directing processions. Traditional processional oracles in Egypt and Hierapolis (Syria), still attested in the 3rd century, required priestly image bearers. Papyri of the 2nd century record the festal visits of priestly "circuit riders" to open unstaffed shrines and preside over their ceremonies. Festivals sometimes required the assistance of religious confraternities dedicated to the service of particular gods and often headed by priests. Such groups constituted a kind of occasional priesthood and represented an important dimension of local self-determination in religious activity in late antiquity.

As holders of religious tradition, whether of the broader culture or merely of single communities, priests held a variety of additional ritual functions within the mundane world: the many blessings (apotropaic and productive) made over house, flock, children, fields; healing and exorcistic rituals; curse rituals; amulet preparation; and the delivery or interpretation of mantic revelations. These more mundane realms of priestly activity may be said to extend from priests' main cultic roles, as interpretations or adaptations of cultic tradition. By such means the priest encompassed much of the ritual territory often ascribed to the "magician."

In Egypt and probably in other cultures whose priesthoods held a high degree of literacy, this popular priestly role of wielding supernatural power and efficacious words stemmed specifically from the priesthoods' control of sacred scripts, since writing held intrinsic power, not just a semantic function, in the ancient world. Many priesthoods in world religions are responsible for the literary systematization of cultic practice and belief, and in late antiquity these literary tendencies also led to the development of esoteric intellectual cultures among priesthoods, combining a nostalgic conservatism with striking endeavors at synthesis, translation, and even exoteric self-promotion in the Hellenistic idiom: the Egyptian *Corpus hermeticum,* the Greek Chaldaean Oracles, the Jewish Enoch writings, and the diverse Greek pseudepigrapha of Persian origin.

An affiliation between priestly hierarchy and the upper echelons of the social order tends to characterize ancient priesthoods. People acting in the position of priest in Greece came largely from the local magistracy, for any position of social authority gave one the ability to preside over a community cult. By virtue of their biblical charter and control of the one Temple's practices and politics, Jewish priests of the Sadducee line constituted the social elite in Palestine up to the Temple's destruction in 70 C.E. (thereafter the little evidence for priestly status suggests a crushing reversal, with rabbis and "sages" in the ascendancy).

In Egypt the temple priesthoods functioned traditionally as extensions of the king in their ritual activities, and many temples held great regional authority in influencing royal policy. The high social status of some Egyptian priestly families continued into the 4th and 5th centuries C.E., and priests included such figures as Aurelius Petearbeschinis, patriarch of a well-connected priestly family in 4th century Panopolis (*P Duke* inv. G 176–178); the anonymous priests of a village in 5th century Panopolis who succeeded in bringing Abbot Shenoute of Athribis to court for plundering their temple; and Horapollo, author of the *Hieroglyphica,* who

turned a diminished ritual expertise into a hybrid native intellectual piety (Maspero, 1914). So also the elite, the dignitaries, could assume some types of quasi-priestly authority: a gold crown discovered at Kysis (Khargeh Oasis) and associated with the Sarapis temple there was evidently meant to be worn by such a dignitary in procession. By the 5th century it may have been that such committed dignitaries alone maintained festival life in some Egyptian communities.

Priests' affiliations with elite culture were not by any means uniform within ancient cultures, however, and in many regions priesthoods represented the instruments of popular resistance, first to Roman imperial authority and then to Christian authority. One can attribute these insurgent tendencies both to the ideological conservatism typical of priestly tradition and to the profoundly local affiliations and "charisma" held by many priests. As proponents and instigators of popular sentiment, priests had access to a battery of media for mobilizing communities, including oracles, augury, ritual cursing, and the sheer force of the office.

But Roman rule and its administration of native religions went far in putting religious authority in the hands of the political elite, the beneficiaries of the imperium, and ensuring that no sacred elite might exist in opposition to the Roman order. As the administration of Egyptian religion was placed under the secular office of the Idios Logos, so in Carthage priestly offices long associated with specific families became, as in Rome, the natural functions of the civic magistrates. In some areas (among Celts, Jews) Roman intervention effectively removed the priesthood from society. In others, despite the growing repression of native religions under Christian imperial rule, priesthoods and priestly rituals continued through late antiquity: in Menouthis (Egyptian delta) and Panopolis (Upper Egypt) through the 5th century, in Philae (first cataract, Egypt) through the 6th century, in Persia beyond the Islamic conquest, and in rural pockets throughout Byzantium into medieval times.

BIBL.: Mary Beard and John North, eds., *Pagan Priests* (Ithaca, N.Y., 1990). Glen W. Bowersock, "The Mechanics of Subversion in the Roman Provinces," in *Opposition et résistances à l'empire d'Auguste à Trajan,* Entretiens Hardt (Geneva, 1986), 291–317. Jean Maspero, "Horapollon et la fin du paganisme égyptien," *Bulletin de l'institut français d'archéologie orientale* (Cairo) 11 (1914): 163–195.   D.T.F.

Priscillianism

The term *Priscillianism* first surfaces in 414 in the writings of Orosius, who may be responsible for its later usage by both Augustine and his correspondent Consentius. The label—and its association with Gnosticism, Manichaeism, astrology, and Trinitarian errors—had become commonplace by the mid-5th century. A heresiological category produced in the struggle to impose a "catholic orthodoxy" on the resistant Christian communities of Spanish Galicia, Priscillianism was subsequently exported into the language of theological debate elsewhere.

In 5th century texts, Priscillianism associates opponents with the influence of a man who was briefly bishop of Avila in the early 380s. Sulpicius Severus's *Chronicle* constitutes the most important source for the life and teachings of Priscillian, who is depicted as a learned and charismatic teacher whose ascetic practices and "gnosticizing" doctrines won him a large following in Spain and Gaul among both clerics and laity, and particularly among women. By 380 Priscillian had been made the subject of attacks at the Council of Saragossa. His subsequent election to the episcopacy heightened the opposition of local bishops, led by Hydatius of Merida, who appealed to the emperor Gratian for a rescript against "Manichaeans and pseudo-bishops." Dodging threats of deposition and exile, Priscillian and two other bishops journeyed with their followers to Italy to argue their orthodoxy both at the imperial court of Milan and before Bishop Damasus of Rome. Denied an audience with Damasus, the supplicants fared better at Gratian's court, and Priscillian returned to his Avilan see. The defeat of Gratian in 383 by the usurper Magnus Maximus, however, ushered in an imperial regime characterized by a more aggressive politics of orthodoxy that shifted the advantage toward Priscillian's opponents. By the mid-380s, Priscillian had been charged with heresy before a council in Bordeaux, appealed his case to the emperor Maximus, and been tried and found guilty of sorcery, for which he was executed ca. 386, along with the Aquitanian noblewoman Euchrotia and several others.

Two major questions continue to preoccupy interpreters. First, what was the controversy over Priscillian himself really about? Since the late 19th century rediscovery at Würzburg of texts stemming from Priscillian and his circle, it no longer seems likely that opposition to Priscillian derived solely from his propagation of self-evidently "heretical" doctrines. Doctrinal issues were clearly at stake, but these appear closely intertwined with issues of authority, played out in the tensions between "ascetic" and "accommodating" stances to the social and cosmological order. The controversy surrounding Priscillian can thus be placed within the context of widespread late ancient debates over asceticism, the body, gender, episcopacy, orthodoxy, and exegetical practices.

The second question concerns the aftereffects of Priscillian's life and death. Although his execution was directly linked to subsequent factional struggles in both Gaul and Spain, whether anything emerged resembling a Priscillianist sect remains debatable, especially for the period after 400. Also therefore debatable is whether and how the category of Priscillianism serves the purposes of contemporary historiography.

BIBL.: Virginia Burrus, *The Making of a Heretic: Gender, Authority, and the Priscillianist Controversy* (Berkeley, 1995). Henry Chadwick, *Priscillian of Avila: The Occult and the Charismatic in the Early Church* (Oxford, 1976). Raymond Van Dam, *Leadership and Community in Late Antique Gaul* (Berkeley, 1985). Georg Schepss, "Würzburg Tractates," rev. ed., *Patrologia Latina*, supp. 2 (1961), cols. 1413–1483.

V.B.

Proclus

Proclus (412–485), Neoplatonist philosopher and chief figure of the so-called Athenian school, was born in Constantinople to a prosperous Lycian family from Xanthos. His father, Patricius, a lawyer, was in Constantinople on business at the time, but the family returned shortly afterward to Xanthos, where Proclus received his basic education. His parents were staunch pagans but nonetheless flourished in the empire of Theodosius II. To complete his education, Proclus was sent to study rhetoric and philosophy in Alexandria, where he was introduced into the ruling circles of Byzantine Egypt by his teacher, the sophist Leonas. Around 430, Leonas was sent by the governor on a mission to Constantinople, and he took Proclus with him. While there, Proclus experienced a conversion to philosophy, and this led him to Athens, to study with the Platonists Plutarchus and Syrianus. He became the star pupil of the latter, and succeeded him as head of the school in Athens on Syrianus's death ca. 437.

He became a most prolific author and the great synthesizer of later Neoplatonism, though Syrianus may have been the more original mind. By the age of twenty-seven, Proclus had already composed his major commentary on Plato's *Timaeus*, and he followed this with commentaries on most of the other dialogues of Plato, of which those on *Alcibiades*, *Cratylus* (in abbreviated form), and *Parmenides* survive, as well as a series of essays on the *Republic*. He also composed a commentary on the first book of Euclid and some important systematic treatises, notably *Elements of Physics*, *Elements of Theology*, and *Platonic Theology* (in six books). We know, as well, of lost commentaries on *Phaedo*, *Gorgias*, *Phaedrus*, *Theaetetus*, and *Philebus*, as well as one on the Chaldaean Oracles. He continued lecturing, composing, and taking an active part in the civic affairs of Athens until shortly before his death in 485. It is indeed notable that, despite an obscure setback in the 450s that led to his having to leave town for a year and return to Xanthos, he managed to maintain the position of the Platonic Academy as a seat of Hellenic learning throughout the 5th century.

His philosophical position involves a considerable elaboration of the relatively simple metaphysical scheme propounded by Plotinus, building on the developments already proposed by Iamblichus, in which, first of all, the realm of the One suffers much complexity, the One itself being split into a higher and a lower aspect, with the whole being enriched by a system of "henads" (seen as archetypes of forms). The realms of both Intellect and Soul are divided triadically (and even into triads of triads) to a remarkable degree. In general, we can observe a proliferation of levels of reality and a tendency to objectify concepts. Proclus's philosophy is governed by certain overall dynamic principles, such as the derivation of multiplicity from unity, and the cycle of procession and return, which are set out succinctly in *Elements of Theology.*

BIBL.: W. Beierwaltes, *Proklos, Grundzüge seiner Metaphysik* (Frankfurt am Main, 1965). Marinus, *Vita Procli,* ed. R. Masullo (Naples, 1985); Eng. trans.: Kenneth S. Guthrie, *Marinus: Life of Proclus* (Grand Rapids, Mich., 1986). L. J. Rosán, *The Philosophy of Proclus* (New York, 1949). R. T. Wallis, *Neoplatonism* (London, 1972).

J.DIL.

Procopius

Procopius, the greatest of the secular historians, was born in Caesarea in Palestine about 500. He received a traditional education in the Greek classics and became an attorney-at-law *(rhetor).* In 527 he became legal adviser *(assessor)* to Belisarius, and he remained with him at least until the capture of Ravenna in 540. He witnessed the plague in Constantinople in 542, and probably the connection with Belisarius ended with his fall from favor that year. His disillusion with Belisarius, and Justinian's regime generally, intensified thereafter. At some point, however, he received the rank of *illustris,* and in 562 a Procopius was urban prefect of Constantinople (but we cannot definitely identify him with the historian).

Procopius's chief work was the *History of the Wars of Justinian* in seven books, the first two on the Persian wars, followed by two on the African campaign and three on the Gothic War. It was published in 550–551; the volumes on the Gothic War continue to the completion of the 550 campaigning season and conclude on a pessimistic note. Procopius later added an eighth book, which extends to the Ostrogothic defeat, and his disenchantment is even clearer. Internal evidence (*Bell.Goth.* 8.15.17) dates this book to 557.

Procopius's remaining works, *On Buildings (Peri Ktismaton)* and *Secret History (Anecdota)* are difficult to date. The first is a panegyric on Justinian's building program, and since it refers (4.9.9–12, 5.3.8–11) to two projects dated to 559 and 560, respectively, it belongs in its present form to the early 560s. However, Book 1 describes Hagia Sophia's construction without reference to the dome's collapse in 558. Probably, therefore, Procopius wrote this book before the collapse as an encomium on Justinian's projects in Constantinople, and added five books later on the rest of the empire. *On Buildings* may be unfinished, but one

argument in support of that hypothesis, the omission of Italy, is weak, for Justinian built little there.

The *Secret History,* first mentioned in the Suda, was discovered in the Vatican Library and published in 1623. Its authenticity is now accepted. It purports to be an underground commentary on *Wars* 1–7, written in 550, and there can be little doubt that 550 is the artistic if not the actual date of composition. It is an invective, no less literary than Procopius's other works, containing information too defamatory for publication in *Wars.*

Procopius, like other secular historians, found his models in the classical past. His idiom was Attic and his subject war. Procopius's disengaged attitude toward Christianity once aroused suspicion that he was a pagan, but his disengagement is only a literary mask. He twice (*SH* 1.14, 26.18) promises to write an ecclesiastical history, but the promise is not kept. His debt to Thucydides and, to a lesser extent, Herodotus, is obvious, but there are other possible influences as well, such as Arrian. His attitude progressed from cautious optimism and partisanship for Belisarius to hostility, and his *Secret History,* which vents his rancor, portrays Justinian as a prince of demons. However, his *Buildings* presents the conventional view that he was an ideal emperor who served God and defended and nurtured his people. The date of Procopius's death is unknown.

BIBL.: Averil Cameron, *Procopius and the Sixth Century* (London and Berkeley, 1985). J. A. S. Evans, *Procopius* (New York, 1972). Geoffrey Greatrex, "The Dates of Procopius' Works," *Byzantine and Modern Greek Studies* (Oxford) 18 (1994): 101–114.

A.E.

Prostitution

In the ancient Mediterranean world, prostitution existed in an organized form. Sacred prostitution occurred in certain pagan sanctuaries. In Rome, prostitution had an official character, and male and female prostitutes had a two-day holiday devoted to them (25–26 April). Panders and prostitutes of both sexes were subject to restrictions on their civil rights (eligibility for office, *conubium* with legitimacy of children and paternal powers, the right to inherit goods and land).

Pressed by poverty, some mothers and fathers sold their children, and enterprising men and women bought women, and especially children (boys or girls, free or slave), and took in babies who had been abandoned to die of exposure. They then raised them as slaves and prostituted the children at a very young age. The prostitution of children met the general demand in the Roman world for prepubescent partners.

Under Roman law, women who served in taverns were assumed to be prostituting themselves, while the proprietress of the tavern, depending on the period, was sometimes accepted as an honorable woman. Free prostitutes (men or women) had to be registered; they paid a tax and held an inferior, nonhonorable status, visibly marked by their clothing. Female prostitutes wore togas and not *stolae;* males wore a loose girdle and left their shoulder exposed. Their physical bearing suggested approachability. Free prostitutes could never regain their respectability, but male or female slaves who had been prostituted by someone else could gain both freedom and respectability through emancipation.

Beginning in the 3rd century, emperors took measures to limit certain aspects of prostitution. Emperors forbade parents and masters from benefiting from the earnings of their dependents, under threat of being considered panders. They banned male prostitution and castration. They refused to integrate the prostitution tax into the treasury, but earmarked it for urban development projects. They protected slaves against their purchasers; they supported a legal clause that returned slaves to vendors or gave them their freedom if the purchaser broke the law. Constantine ordered the destruction of a sanctuary where sacred prostitution was practiced (Eusebius, *Vit.Const.* 2.55). In making laws against abduction and the overseas transport of children purchased from the poor, emperors tried to prevent an international traffic across the empire. Although they granted women the freedom to prostitute themselves, emperors increased the penalties for those who forced women under their power (daughters or slaves) to become prostitutes: exile and the mines in 428, flogging and expulsion from Constantinople, loss of official duties, confiscation of property. The slave prostituted by his master was emancipated, according to a law made by Justinian in 531. Justinian allowed prostitutes to repent and change their lives. Leo I attempted to ban prostitution in 460.

In making civic sanctions a reason to exclude persons from being baptized or from receiving communion (Hippolytus, *Apostolic Tradition* 16), the church marginalized prostitutes of both sexes. It raised the question of reconciling women with the church (Council of Elvira, canons 44 and 12). Augustine was against suppressing prostitution, because it lowered the number of assaults on respectable women.

Judaism forbade men to prostitute their daughters (Gen. 19:4–9; Lev. 19:29). Flavius Josephus reminded Jews that they were forbidden to marry prostitutes. The prostitute became the metaphor for all who appeared doomed. Prophets compared faithless people to a prostitute. Jesus told the Jews that prostitutes would enter the Kingdom of God before they did (Matt. 21:31–32). Revelation predicts the ruin of the great whore of Babylon (Rev. 14:8 and 17:1, 2, and 4), a city that itself became the metaphor for sinful civilizations.

BIBL.: Joëlle Beaucamp, *Le statut de la femme à Byzance (4e–7e siècle),* 2 vols. (Paris, 1992). James A. Brundage, *Sex, Law and Christian Society in Medieval Europe* (Chicago,

1987). Eva Cantarella, *Secondo natura: La bisessualità nel mondo antico* (Rome, 1988); Eng. trans.: *Bisexuality in the Ancient World* (New Haven, 1992).   A.R.

Provinces

The Roman empire had evolved as a series of provinces—areas under the authority of an official appointed from Rome. The shape of these provinces was partly determined by how they had been acquired. Many of them, for historical reasons, covered the same territory as preexisting political units, but some with a much stronger historical tradition than others: Egypt, for example, was an ancient kingdom inherited by the Romans in its Ptolemaic form; Asia simply represented the extent of the rule of Pergamum at the end of the 2nd century B.C.E. The two aspects of what constituted a province are reflected in the Greek terminology used to describe them—*eparchia,* meaning "area under authority," and *ethnos,* "people." But for most inhabitants of the empire, the significant institution was not the province but the city in whose territory they lived. The governors of civil provinces were largely taken up with adjudication—between citizens dissatisfied with a local judgment, and between communities. The provinces did have provincial councils, made up of delegates from the cities of the province, whose main responsibility was to assert loyalty to Rome by ensuring the proper celebration of the imperial cult.

During the first three centuries of the empire there were frequent adjustments to the divisions of the provinces, most often in the areas where military considerations were of particular importance; the peaceful province of Asia retained its Hellenistic form for several centuries. From the middle of the 3rd century, however, there seems to have been a developing interest in creating smaller provinces. While many of these changes can be seen as responding to increasing military problems, even in the peaceful area of Asia Minor a new province of Caria and Phrygia was created from the southeastern part of the province of Asia in the 250s.

This tendency toward subdivision reached a peak under the tetrarchs. Diocletian was criticized by a hostile commentator for "cutting up the provinces into little pieces" (Lactantius, *De mort.pers.* 7.4). By the reign of Constantine, the Severan province of Thrace was replaced by four provinces; the three provinces of southern Gaul had become seven; the single province of Asia had been replaced by eight smaller units. This was the most dramatic moment of change, but provinces continued to be subdivided well into the 5th century.

Interestingly, there is no agreed explanation—ancient or modern—for this policy. Lactantius describes it as "imposing many governors and bureaus on each region," which A. H. M. Jones interpreted as meaning increasing central control; but ancient government was never very good at controlling, tending more often to be reactive. It can be argued that what Diocletian undertook—and Lactantius described—was the creation of comfortable, profitable posts for large numbers of people. Not only were governors and their *officia* of staff provided for each city, but the provinces themselves were also grouped in dioceses, each under a *vicarius* who reported to the praetorian prefect, creating a further layer of posts.

It is easier to describe the consequences of this reform. It brought imperial government much closer to the inhabitants of the empire—a citizen seeking adjudication now had a much better chance of being heard by an imperial official. It had the effect of shifting local identities. The new provinces each had provincial assemblies, which continued to celebrate the power of the emperors at provincial festivals; in Africa men continued to be appointed to priesthoods of the imperial cult well into the 5th century. The membership of these assemblies was, however, changed: they now were made up of not a series of delegates from the constituent cities of the province but all the citizens of curial status. Such arrangements meant that the province as an institution must have become more important in the life of its inhabitants—just as the influence of cities was dwindling. By the 6th century, we find successful men described in terms of their province—"John the Lydian" or "John the Cappadocian"—rather than their city.

It also seems, in the longer term, to have diminished the relative status of the governor vis-à-vis powerful local citizens. While provincial governors appear prominent and active in the 4th and early 5th century, far fewer of them are mentioned in the later 5th and the 6th century, when local citizens appear more often as benefactors. The next major reform of the imperial administration, undertaken by Justinian, seems to have been intended to redress the balance. He combined various provinces and various offices, suppressing the intermediate administrative tier of the dioceses and aiming to appoint fewer, better paid officials to the provincial administration. But this was apparently not sufficient. In 554 Justinian, in legislating for the administration of Italy, ordered that the provincial governors be elected from the areas to be administered by "the bishops and primates of each region" (*Appendix Constitutionum* 7.12). In 569 Justin II legislated to prevent provincial governors from buying their office. His solution, instead of enhancing the status of the representative of central government, was to entrust to the bishops, and to the most prominent among the *possessores* and the residents of the province, the task of nominating candidates for the office of governor (*Nov.* 49.1). Although this particular arrangement seems not to have lasted, the implication is that the system of provincial government was in rapid decline. It was from the ruins of this system that, during the 7th

century, the *thēmata* of the Byzantine empire were to emerge.

The Umayyads preserved, more or less, the late antique structure of provinces in Syria and Palestine, only creating a special province *(jund)* for the frontier with Byzantium *(al-thughūr),* modifying the structure of northern Mesopotamia into several districts of the Jazirah, and transforming southern Syria into the new province of Qinnashrin. A governor in each province represented the caliphs, and allegiance was sworn to him. The governor was responsible for taxation and military levies.

BIBL.: A. H. M. Jones, *The Later Roman Empire* (Oxford, 1964), app. 3. Fred Donner, *The Early Islamic Conquests* (Princeton, 1981). C.R.

Punic

When Augustine speaks of *lingua punica,* is he speaking about Punic or Berber? Debate about this question arose when W. H. C. Frend and C. Courtois compared the literary evidence from Augustine with the epigraphical evidence of thousands of Libyan inscriptions. Courtois noted that the region where *lingua punica* was spoken is precisely the one where Berber was written (Camps, 1994). Libyan inscriptions are dated earlier (mainly from the 1st and the 2nd centuries). It is impossible to imagine a linguistic revolution that in the 3rd century would have resulted in people speaking Punic instead of Berber. Given the present state of knowledge, it seems, therefore, difficult to reconcile Augustine's references to Punic with the archaeological evidence for Berber or Libyan.

In several texts Augustine attests that *lingua punica* is the spoken language in the countryside around Hippo. Macrobius, the Donatist bishop of Hippo, spoke to the Circumcellions through a Punic interpreter (Augustine, *Ep.* 108.5) as did the Catholic bishop of Fussala to his flock (Augustine, *Ep.* 209.3; see also *Ep.* 20*, 21, and 66.2). For Augustine, *lingua punica* is the *lingua afra* per se, as he once said (*In Iohannis epistulam* 2.3), and he attests that it was strongly associated both with Numidia (in texts where he denounced the nationalism of Donatists: *In Io.ep.* 2.3; *Serm.* 162A [= Denis 19], 10; *Ep.* 66.2) and with the countryside (in a letter against a pagan who despised Christian martyrs because they had Punic names: *Ep.* 17.2; in *De haeresibus* 87 and in *Epistulae ad Romanos inchoata expositio,* Punic is spoken by *rustici*).

Does Augustine know any Punic himself? He mentions a Punic proverb in one sermon but relates it in Latin, "as not everybody knows Punic" (*Serm.* 167). He also knows several Punic words, which he mentions in exegetical commentaries when he encounters an untranslated Hebrew word in the Bible: mammon (*Serm.* 113; *De sermone Domini in monte* 2.47; *Serm.* 359A), Messias (*Contra litteras Petiliani,* 2.104, 239; *In Io-*

hannes evangelium 15.27), Edom (*Enarr. in Ps.* 136.18). In these cases, he usually emphasizes that Punic is a language from the same family as Hebrew, a fact that is well known and beyond any doubt for historical linguistics. In more than one case, however, he makes clear that his knowledge is indirect and not sufficiently secure (*De magistro* 13; cf. *Enarr. in Ps.* 136.18).

Augustine's interest in Punic was twofold. On the one hand, Punic was the language spoken by the *rustici* of his diocese. It was important for him to be sure that Christian doctrine could be taught either through an interpreter or by a Punic-speaking priest, as in the case of the bishop of Fussala, who was chosen precisely for this ability (*Ep.* 209.3). On the other hand, Augustine had a learned interest in Punic because of its relation to Hebrew. The common point of these two perspectives is, as once suggested by Peter Brown, the conversion of people: by underscoring the affinity of the Punic language with the language of the Bible, Augustine was trying to convince the population of his diocese of its congenial affinity with Christianity (Brown, 1968).

BIBL.: Peter Brown, "Christianity and Local Culture in Late Roman Africa," *Journal of Roman Studies* 58 (1968): 85–95. Gabriel Camps, "Punica lingua et épigraphie lybique dans la Numidie d'Hippone," *Bulletin archéologique du Comité des travaux historiques et scientifiques,* n.s., Afrique du Nord 23 (1994): 33–49. C. Courtois, "S. Augustin et la survivance de la punique," *Revue africaine* 94 (1950): 239–282. "*Serm. Dolbeau* 3.8.126," *Revue des études augustiniennes* 39 (1993): 389 = F. Dolbeau, *Augustin: Vingt-six sermons au peuple d'Afrique* (Paris, 1996), 489 (*ylim* for God).

E.R.

Qāḍī

In early Islamic society, the *qāḍī,* or judge, was a salaried local official who was responsible for deciding fact and rendering judgment in legal cases brought before him. Although the first *qāḍī*s were appointed by the caliphs in Medina beginning in the 630s, during the Umayyad caliphate (661–750 C.E.) most *qāḍī*s were appointed by governors. The *qāḍī* represented, in theory, the delegated judicial authority of the caliph; as there was no juridical hierarchy, he acted alone, hearing cases in the local mosque or even in his home. However, the role of the *qāḍī* was chiefly developed in the context of Umayyad provincial administration, where governors had broad political autonomy. The *qāḍī* was in practice the legal secretary of the governor, and his duties usually included a range of administrative as well as judicial tasks.

Until the 2nd century of Islam, when the roots of Islamic jurisprudence were established in a systematic way by scholars, there was no corpus of Islamic legal doctrine on the basis of which to render a decision. Some *qāḍī*s were themselves learned in the Qur'ān and knowledgeable about the exemplary practices of Muhammad; others sought out the opinions of pious men before making their judgments. In cases not directly addressed by the Qur'ān, they relied on local customary law and personal reasoning. It was also common for men to be appointed as judges because they were already key figures in the provincial administration, and thus not all *qāḍī*s were known for their piety or religious knowledge. Some held multiple posts, including the offices of treasurer, chief of police, or tax collec-tor. Toward the end of the Umayyad period, however, judges often came into conflict with the secular authority of the governors as their role became more specifically identified with religious law.

When the Abbasids took power in 750, they claimed to implement Islamic religious law (the *sharī'a*), though it was still in formation, throughout the empire. Beginning with Hārūn al-Rashīd, the appointment of local judges was taken over by the central administration, and the position of chief *qāḍī (qāḍī al-quḍāt)* was established in Baghdad. The *qāḍī*s were now only to hear cases of Islamic law, while the government assumed responsibility for a wider range of administrative and criminal cases. Both Umayyad and Abbasid sources record the reluctance of pious men to accept the role of *qāḍī.* Their fears—of divine punishment for wrongful verdicts, of being perceived as seeking worldly reward, or of reprisals by governors unhappy with decisions—highlight the heavy responsibility of applying sacred law and the exigencies of its worldly context.

BIBL.: Irit Bligh-Abramski, "The Judiciary *(Qāḍī*s) as a Governmental-Administrative Tool in Early Islam," *Journal of the Social and Economic History of the Orient* 35 (1997): 40–71. N. J. Coulson, "Doctrine and Practice in Islamic Law: One Aspect of the Problem," *Bulletin of the School of Oriental and African Studies* 18, no. 2 (1956): 211–226. A. Kevin Reinhart, "Transcendence and Social Practice: *Muftī*s and *Qāḍī*s as Religious Interpreters," *Annales islamologiques* 27 (1993): 5–28. Joseph Schacht, *An Introduction to Islamic Law* (Oxford, 1964). Emile Tyan, *Histoire de l'organisation judiciaire en pays d'Islam,* 2nd ed. (Leiden, 1960). M.R.

Qaṣr al-Hayr

Two early Islamic sites in the Syrian steppe bear the name Qaṣr al-Hayr. One, Qaṣr al-Hayr West, is located 37 miles southwest of Palmyra. A dam in the mountains served to distribute water for its gardens and agriculture. A Ghassanid monastery had been located there, and an early watchtower is still preserved. The palace built there at the time of Hishām (the date 727 is in one of the buildings) had two stories, set around a courtyard. It was most remarkable for its decoration, which is now kept in the Damascus National Museum, where the whole facade has been reconstructed. Two complete painted floors had classical and Iranian motifs, respectively. Many painted fragments, some with unusual central Asian features, have recently been published but not studied. Thousands of fragments of stucco sculpture exhibit an astounding variety of stylistic origins, ranging from archaic Greek to Palmyrene or Sogdian and, like Khirbat al-Mafjar and Quṣayr ʿAmra, they illustrate the juxtaposition of forms from many sources that was typical of the Umayyad period. A similar range is found in the representations of personages and animals.

Qaṣr al-Hayr East is located 70 miles to the northeast of Palmyra, at the crossroad of major routes across the Syrian Desert. It consists of two large walled enclosures and an extensive hydraulic system for the irrigation of a vast area. It is dated by an inscription to 728–729 and is identified as a "city" (madīna). Its builders reused older materials, since a Greek and a Palmyrene inscription were found in its ruins. Excavations show that it was a settlement for several families, next to a fancy caravanserai and a small bath; a mosque and oil presses were also located there. The settlement continued to be used until the 13th century.

BIBL.: K. A. C. Creswell, *Early Muslim Architecture* (Oxford, 1969). O. Grabar et al., *City in the Desert, Qasr al-Hayr East* (Cambridge, 1978). D. Schlumberger, "Les Fouilles de Qasr el-Heir el-Gharbi," *Syria* 20 (1939). D. Schlumberger, "Deux Fresques Omeyyades," *Syria* 25 (1946–1948). D. Schlumberger et al., *Qasr el-Heir el-Gharbi* (Paris, 1986).

O.G.

Qur'ān

The Islamic Scripture, the Qur'ān, contains revelations that the Prophet Muhammad recited to his followers over a period of about twenty years, up to the time of his death in 632 C.E. During his lifetime most of the units of revelation, later called sūras, had no set form but were revised and expanded as he recited them on different occasions. A distinctive characteristic of the Qur'ān is that it responds frequently and often explicitly to Muhammad's changing historical circumstances. The revelations offered him encouragement in times of persecution and doubt, refuted accusations made against him by his opponents who claimed that

he was a soothsayer or a poet inspired by the jinn, and responded to questions raised by his followers. The Qur'ān reflects developing events in the life of Muhammad and his followers, and in a fascinating way it became a historical event in itself, influencing the nascent Muslim community. God is the "speaker" throughout the Qur'ān (usually indicated by the first person plural, "We"), while Muhammad is frequently the "addressee" (indicated by second person singular verbs, often in the imperative mood). Other passages are addressed to specific groups of Muhammad's contemporaries, such as his opponents in Mecca, the Jewish clans in Medina, his followers in general, and occasionally even his wives. The Qur'ān mentions by name Muhammad (in sūras 3:144, 33:40, and 47:2), his servant Zayd (33:37), and current events such as the battles of Badr (3:123) and Ḥunayn (9:25).

A large part of Meccan portions of the Qur'ān consists of stories that have parallels in the Bible, but they often contain details that occur only in Jewish and Christian noncanonical writings and oral tradition. Stories involving Adam, Noah (Nūḥ), Abraham (Ibrāhīm), Moses (Mūsā), and Jesus (ʿĪsā, almost always called ʿĪsā ibn Maryam, Jesus, Son of Mary) are among the most prominent. These biblical characters and a number of others appear in the Qur'ān as prophets, all said to have brought the same message of "submission" (islām, in Arabic) to the one true God. Each is said to have brought a version of the Book of God in the language of his people. The most prominent are the Torah (Tawrāt), the Gospel (Injīl), and the Recitation (Qur'ān), delivered to the Jews, the Christians, and the Arabs by the prophets Moses, Jesus, and Muhammad. The later Islamic teaching is that the angel Gabriel "brought down" portions of the heavenly Book of God to these prophets, that the Jews and Christians later changed or added to the Scriptures their prophets brought, and that only the Qur'ān remains an exact copy of the heavenly book. Parts of the Qur'ān that date from the last ten years of Muhammad's life, when he was actively establishing a new religious community in Medina independent from the Jews and the Christians, institute distinctively Islamic practices, such as daily performance of the prayer ritual called the salat (ṣalāt), fasting during the month of Ramadan, and the pilgrimage to Mecca. Qur'ānic credal statements dating from this same period (e.g., in 4:136) require belief in God, his angels, his Scriptures, his prophets, and the Last Day.

Muhammad's followers memorized parts of the Qur'ān and some had their own private collections, but no complete, official text was compiled and edited until about twenty years after his death, during the reign of the third caliph, ʿUthmān. This so-called ʿUthmānic text contains 114 suras arranged roughly in order of descending length, except for sura 1 (a short prayer that serves, according to its title, as "The Opening") and several groups (10–15, 29–32, 40–46, 57–

64, and 113–114) that are kept together for a variety of reasons. Early Qur'ān manuscripts were written in a *scriptio defectiva,* consisting of consonants only, without the diacritical marks that came to be used later to indicate vowels and to distinguish two or more consonantal sounds that share the same written form. Even after the 'Uthmānic consonantal text came to be accepted by the vast majority of Muslims, it continued to be interpreted and recited in a variety of ways, by reading different short vowels and by taking certain forms to represent different consonants—for instance, the same set of consonantal signs could be read *kabīr* (great) or *kathīr* (numerous) in sura 2:219, and another could be read *ḥadab* (mound) or *jadath* (tomb) in 21:96. The famous governor of Iraq al-Ḥajjāj (694–714) attempted to stabilize the 'Uthmānic text by establishing a standard system of signs for indicating short vowels and dots for distinguishing consonantal sounds.

This *scriptio plena* came to be accepted only very slowly, and even then it did not prevent the 'Uthmānic text from continuing to be read in more and more diverse ways. Also, scholars continued to use versions of the Qur'ān that had been collected by Companions of the Prophet before the 'Uthmānic text was established. Those by one of Muhammad's secretaries, Ubayy ibn Ka'b (containing two short sūras not found in other collections), and by Muhammad's servant 'Abdallāh ibn Mus'ūd, whom the Prophet recommended to others as an authority on the Qur'ān (his had 111 sūras), are the best known of these so-called Companion codices. Three centuries after the death of Muhammad, Ibn Mujāhid (d. 936) made a major contribution toward establishing a uniform text of the Qur'ān by asserting that only the 'Uthmānic consonantal text was authentic (thus rejecting the Companion codices), while accepting as equally valid the "readings" *(qirā'āt)* of seven famous 8th century Qur'ān scholars, three from Kufa and one each from Medina, Mecca, Damascus, and Basra. Eventually one version of one of the Kufan readings came to be accepted throughout the Muslim world except in parts of North Africa.

For Muslims the Qur'ān has been from the beginning much more than a book, the Islamic equivalent of the Scriptures of other religious communities. It is unique in several ways. The vast majority of Muslims throughout history have experienced the Qur'ān primarily in its oral form, memorized and recited in worship, and in its visual form, as Arabic calligraphy, a major decorative motif in Islamic architecture and art. It has only been in modern times, and even then among only a minority of Muslims throughout the world, that the Qur'ān has had significance as a book to be read and studied for devotional or academic purposes. During the formative years of Islam, when orthodoxy and orthopraxy were being established, the Qur'ān became the first source for Islamic theology and law. The belief that the Qur'ān is the eternal Speech of God became a cornerstone of Islamic doctrine. This led to belief in its perfection and "inimitability" *(i'jāz)* as the highest form of Arabic expression, thus influencing the development of classical Arabic grammar and lexicography during the period of late antiquity.

Christian comments on the Qur'ān were, understandably, unflattering. Christian apologists claimed that its message was derivative. But they also showed a clear awareness of its importance in the Muslim community and sought to defend their own reverence for Jesus as Word of God and, even, for icons, by analogy to the Muslim reverence for the Qur'ān.

The earliest dated fragments that seem to be from the Qur'ān occur in the inscriptions of the Dome of the Rock (completed 691–692). There are thousands of undated parchments with Qur'ānic fragments for which a date in the 8th or 9th century has been proposed. Among the most spectacular groups of such pages are the 40,000 pages found in Yemen; they have never been published in their entirety, and some of them contain rather striking illuminations through architecture that have been dated in the 8th century, even though a later date may be more likely.

BIBL.: A. J. Arberry, *The Koran Interpreted,* 2 vols. (London and New York, 1955). Richard Bell, *The Qur'ān: Translated, with a Critical Re-arrangement of the Surahs,* 2 vols. (Edinburgh, 1937, 1939); rev. and enl. by W. M. Watt (Edinburgh, 1970). S. H. Griffith, "Muhammad's Scripture and Message according to Christian Apologists in Arabic and Syriac," *La vie du Prophète Muhammad* (Strasbourg, 1980), 114–118. R. S. Hoyland, *Seeing Islam as Others Saw It* (Princeton, 1997). Muhammad Marmaduke Pickthall, *The Glorious Koran: A Bi-Lingual Edition with* [the 1923–24 Egyptian Standard Edition of the Arabic text and] *English Translation, Introduction and Notes* (Albany, 1976). J. Sahas, *John of Damascus on Islam* (Leiden, 1972). K. Verstegh, "Greek Translations of the Qur'ān in Christian Polemics," *Zeitschrift der deutschen morgenländischen Gesellschaft* 141 (1991): 52–68.   A.T.W.

Rationality

Reason, or the principle of rationality *(logos, ratio),* may in a broad sense be described as the a priori human capacity for grasping important truths about the world; it normally presupposes the fundamental rationality both of the world and of man. As the Graeco-Roman intellectual elite continuously debated the nature of human perception, language, and logic and their usefulness as tools for attaining certain knowledge from which to derive metaphysical and ethical constructs, it is not possible to document a linear development of rational thought through antiquity. Stoics based their theory of cosmic sympathy on the *logoi spermatikoi,* through which all individuals participated in the Logos, the Divine Reason that ordered the world, and based their ethics on the imperative to live virtuously—in harmony with nature and hence in accordance with reason. Certain Christians, such as Clement of Alexandria, accepted these Stoic precepts but equated the Divine Reason with God, thereby concluding that all men possessed an innate knowledge of the divine and the ability to be virtuous: here rationality connotes the ability to recognize and live according to the dictates of both the immanent and the revealed Logos. While the Stoic categories influenced Middle Platonists and Neoplatonists, Albinus, Plotinus, and Porphyry of Gaza, among others, also incorporated Aristotelian philosophical tools with their Platonist tradition. These philosophers aimed at anchoring their metaphysical speculations on a rigorously rational method through the application of the categories—dialectic and logic—that Aristotle outlined in works that

later made up the late antique compilation of his logical treatises, entitled the *Organon.* Many philosophers considered the exercise of reason a protreptic device, a starting point in the quest for wisdom, as any would-be philosopher must first purify his soul by learning how to discern truth from falsehood and mere opinion. But for them, neither the particularistic knowledge of reality nor discursive thinking constituted the final end of the philosophical life. To reach the highest truths, according to Plotinus, the philosophical man must seek spiritual union *(henōsis)* with "the One," a superior, ineffable experience. Development of the rational faculties using Aristotelian methods thus remained ancillary to the rarer attainment of mystical ecstasy. The subordination of dialectic and logic to more sublime forms of philosophical *gnōsis* was even more strongly asserted by the later (especially Athenian) Neoplatonists, who put Aristotelian learning beneath Platonist philosophy and theurgy in the hierarchy of knowledge that became a part of the Late Platonist curriculum. The belief that the higher truths were by nature ineffable—that is, beyond the capacity of human language to describe precisely and accurately—or even ungraspable—beyond the ability of the human mind to understand properly at all—gave an important impetus to the development of a counterpoint to rational philosophy. Apophaticism, which proposes the *via negativa* as a nondiscursive form of knowledge, became a feature of the Middle and, especially, Later Platonist traditions that heavily influenced Christian theological formulations and culminated in the early Byzantine mystical theology of Pseudo-Dionysius the Areopagite.

Christians in the first few centuries of the religion

were often accused of perpetrating deception among women, children, and old men—people whose rational capacities were thought to be, respectively, undeveloped, not yet developed, and no longer developed. Thus Celsus the philosopher and Galen denounced as irrational the talk of miracles and the use of parables in attempts at proselytism. Certain Christian apologists responded by boasting of the simplicity and paradoxical nature of a religious message that rendered the knowledge of God accessible even to the unlettered through revelation and the coming of Christ into the world. This *via universalis*, a more "democratic" path to knowledge regarding the divine compared to the elite philosophers' de facto monopoly on divine speculation, was itself asserted as a central virtue of Christianity. But even as this debate continued, converts who were well versed in philosophy began to engage in their own discussions about the nature and extent of human rationality as it related to divine revelation. In theory, at least, rationality is not necessarily incompatible with either revelation or traditional authority: the latter could become an important source of axioms or premises from which the rational faculty could draw its conclusions; in practice, however, those among both philosophers and Christians who championed a form of rational skepticism in their search for knowledge often had to contend against the insistent claims of traditional, textual, or social authority. Questions about the nature of the divine (e.g., the divinity of Christ) often occasioned disagreements regarding the ability of unaided human reason to comprehend such sublime matters. Consequently, some Christians sought to qualify the *via universalis* that had vouchsafed divine knowledge even to the lowly: while all Christians could know God through what he had chosen to reveal of himself, they could not (all) know his being or essence with perspicuity, for such knowledge was denied to mere created beings. But others instead insisted on proceeding from scriptural premises, through a chain of necessary philosophical arguments, to arrive at true and exact knowledge of the divine nature. In the mid- to late 4th century, some Christians, as represented by Aetius the Syrian and Eunomius of Cappadocia, argued that a precise understanding of the relationship between God the Father and God the Son—one of the most vexing theological questions of the time—could be reached through applying the Aristotelian categories, dialectic, and syllogistic reasoning to scriptural premises. Their claims and methods were opposed by other Christians, such as Basil of Caesarea, Gregory of Nazianzus, and Gregory of Nyssa, who proposed a more restricted scope for human rationality and who labeled their rivals "Aristotelians" and "dialecticians," suggesting that they were "hair-splitting rationalists." Yet the dispute—the so-called Anomoean controversy—was not merely a contest between those who championed Christian knowledge and those who embraced Greek *paideia*, for given the eclecticism of

the age, both sides incorporated elements of the latter. Meanwhile, the adjudication of these issues had profound implications for the constitution of religious and social authority within the churches and the definition of the Christian community. The Anomoeans' arguments were commonly framed in the form of challenging dialectical questions and were much feared by those Christian leaders who, not being adept in this philosophical technique, saw their positions undermined by their inability to respond in kind. However, in ideological terms (as seen from within the orthodox tradition), the Cappadocians eventually triumphed, and their victory helped enshrine the doctrine of an "incomprehensible" God who should remain beyond the grasp of human reason (which nonetheless remained capable of recognizing the divinely ordained order made manifest in physical creation). The theological debate over human rationality and, specifically, the value of the Greek (Aristotelian) philosophical tradition as an autonomous method for arriving at true and certain divine knowledge within the context of a biblical religion continued. It even occurred under Islam, as the Mu'tazilites, who favored the interpretation of the Qur'ān using established philosophical methods, were opposed by more "traditionalist" Muslims, who accused their adversaries of being "rationalists," one of those terms that historically has been used more frequently in polemic and abuse than in neutral description.

BIBL.: Averil Cameron, *Christianity and the Rhetoric of Empire: The Development of Christian Discourse* (Berkeley, 1991). R. Lim, *Public Disputation, Power, and Social Order in Late Antiquity* (Berkeley, 1995). R. A. Mortley, *From Word to Silence*, 2 vols. (Bonn, 1986). R.L.

Ravenna

A prosperous provincial city amid the marshes along the upper Adriatic coast, Ravenna was the important commercial center for northeastern Italy, and it drew added significance from its port suburb of Classis, a major Roman naval base. A belated elevation in status came in 402, when the diffident young Emperor Honorius chose Ravenna as a quieter and more secure alternative to Milan, then the imperial seat in the west. Ravenna's isolation in the marshes and its water routes to the sea were augmented by new fortifications, and the city became a center of building activity at a pivotal era in the development of early Christian architecture and art.

Though Rome continued to retain certain ceremonial and cultural significance down to the end of the western imperial succession in 476, Ravenna was the working capital of Italy; it remained so under the regime of the barbarian generalissimo Odoacer, and was then made the seat of the Ostrogothic kingdom. With Justinian I's reconquest of Italy in the second quarter of the 6th century, and thanks to the astute politics of its bishops, Ravenna entered a plateau of importance as the imperial administrative seat for Italy.

The Lombards' entry into Italy in the late 560s only partially isolated Ravenna, whose commander was, by the 580s, elevated to the special rank of exarch, or viceroy. Through their exarchs, the emperors in Constantinople attempted to direct Italian affairs and even to control the Roman popes, but unrest and occasional local revolts brought instability; around 709 the vindictive Emperor Justinian II sent a force to suppress savagely Ravenna's disloyalty. Renewed Lombard aggressions further threatened the city's safety, while the iconoclastic policies of the 9th century emperors, unpopular in Italy, undermined Ravenna's tenuous position in the peninsula's politics. In 751, the Lombard king Aistulf finally succeeded in capturing the city, ending the exarchate, and restricting Byzantine power in Italy to southern territories only. The deterioration of the port at Classis, the challenge of Venice's rise in the north, and its annexation by the papacy reduced Ravenna to a minor city, though its past traditions and its surviving monuments of imperial glory preserved for it a special aura in its medieval somnolence. The visiting Charlemagne was greatly impressed and influenced, while much later the exile Dante, who was to die and be buried there, is said to have drawn inspiration from Ravenna's mosaics.

Though now only a fragment of its late imperial self, the historical center of Ravenna, within its surviving circuit of Roman walls, still preserves remarkable monuments and glorious works of art. The ensemble of 5th century mosaics in the St. Lawrence Chapel—which is popularly, but almost surely incorrectly, known as the Mausoleum of Galla Placidia—is perhaps the most stunning masterpiece of early Christian decoration, seconded by the contemporaneous decoration of the Orthodox (Neonian) Baptistery. Several churches begun by the Ostrogoths in the early 6th century and completed under Justinian I's regime (S. Vitale, S. Apollinare Nuovo, S. Apollinare in Classe), together with the Ostrogothic (Arian) Baptistery and the Archbishop's Chapel, contain dazzling constellations of Byzantine mosaic works. An architectural marvel, too, is the extraordinary mausoleum of the first Ostrogothic king, Theoderic the Great (493–526); there also survives a fragment of the Palace of the Exarchs (erroneously called the Palace of Theoderic).

BIBL.: F. W. Deichmann, *Ravenna*, 6 vols. (Wiesbaden,

The Mausoleum of Theoderic at Ravenna, early 6th century.

1958–1989). Thomas Hodgkin, *Italy and Her Invaders, 376–814*, 8 vols. (Oxford, 1880–1889; 2nd ed. 1896; repr. 1967). Edward Hutton, *The Story of Ravenna* (London, 1926). Mark Johnson, "Towards a History of Theodoric's Building Program," *Dumbarton Oaks Papers* 42 (1988): 73–96. Otto G. von Simson, *Sacred Fortress: Byzantine Art and Statecraft in Ravenna* (Chicago, 1948; repr. 1976). Chris Wickham, *Early Medieval Italy: Central Power and Local Society, 400–1000* (London, 1981; Ann Arbor, 1989). J.W.B.

Reading

Most reading in late antiquity that was not merely utilitarian—undertaken, say, for business or bureaucracy—was in the nature of a performance: this is the most immediate difference between the ancient and the modern ways of reading. It is not that reading a text silently to oneself, for pleasure or edification, was unknown or eccentric (an inference sometimes drawn, incorrectly, from Augustine, *Confessions* 6.3.3). Rather, the basic aims and methods of education ensured that the reading of any text valued by the high literary culture would engage the ear as well as the eye and be undertaken for others as well as oneself, as an act more overtly communal and more directly interpretive than the typical reading performed by the user of this book.

Once a child had mastered the elementary sign system of the alphabet and was able to sound out individual letters, syllables, whole words, and simple complete thoughts, most effort was spent on making him (most readers were male) an effective *expressive* reader. To that end the schools taught reading as a blend of several skills with a strongly aural dimension. Attention had to be paid first to accent and tone—to ensure that the sound of each syllable was represented "purely," with no suggestion of the servile or the foreign—and the sound of one word or phrase had to be distinguished correctly from the next. The student was then required to create the proper persona (or set of personae) for the text being read, with decorous representation of the conventions governing differences in age, gender, and social status. Finally, the student had to avoid monotony or jarring harshness both by modulating his voice (but not too much, lest he be thought effeminate), and by being alert to the demands of poetic meter and prose rhythms.

Such skills were attained through no small effort (and at no small price, if one wished to buy a slave who had them); they also demanded that the reader, even as a young child, actively and audibly participate in producing the text's meaning. For example, distinguishing one word or phrase correctly from the next, in a text written with no punctuation and little or no separation between words, required one to think about the meaning at an almost atomic level and, in some sense, to create the text one was reading. (At *Aeneid* 8.83, for example, was one to say *conspicit ursus*—"the bear espies"—or *conspicitur sus*—"the pig is spied"?) Similarly, the impersonation expected of the skilled reader required a fair degree of prior acculturation (how else to know the properly nuanced way to distinguish old man from young or free man from slave?) and would affect the listener's reception of the text in obvious ways.

Reading demanded that the reader "create" the text in another way that is, in practical terms, unknown to the modern reader: by correcting any errors. The ancient world knew nothing of standard editions, of books that passed through a series of quality controls before publication and that, once published, were identical from one copy to the next. Each book was a handmade artifact, individually (and, often, idiosyncratically) copied, with many more quirks and blemishes than even the most slovenly product of today's print culture. Errors could range from missing, added, or transposed words to the omission of whole lines or groups of lines, and such errors occurred frequently enough to make reading an uncorrected manuscript book a chore, or worse. (Of course, uncorrected errors in one book tended to be copied by the next scribe who came along, so that successive "generations" of books could quickly become ever more corrupt.) It was therefore common for readers sedulously to correct the books they read, by comparing them with another copy (often the book from which their own copy was made) and by relying on their own sense of language and context. Some of this correction was no more challenging than the correction of the occasional typographical error in a printed book, but much of it was more consequential. The best fate a book could find was to be read by a reader who was careful and well schooled (and therefore inclined to take correction seriously) but not overconfident in his skills or memory (and therefore apt to introduce as many errors as he removed).

The schools determined not only the methods of reading but also, to a great extent, what was read. The literary texts that were commonly known to educated men largely overlapped with the canon of texts read in the schools; and that canon, in turn, largely determined which texts would be copied in sufficient number to survive into the Middle Ages and beyond. In Latin, Virgil, Terence, Horace, Cicero, Sallust, and (some) Livy never went out of fashion; their Greek counterparts—Homer, Menander, Aristophanes, the three great tragedians, Pindar, Demosthenes, Thucydides, Xenophon—enjoyed a similarly consistent vogue. (The Greek authors just named account for 78, or 72 percent, of the 108 identifiable literary papyri to survive in fragmentary form from Hermopolis, a major Egyptian town, and its territory; Homer alone accounts for half of those 78.) Not that tastes remained entirely unchanged: it is clear, for example, that in the late 4th century and into the 5th some Latin poets who had been out of favor for generations—especially Lucan, Statius, and Juvenal—came to be regarded as "suitable authors" and displaced other, earlier authors (e.g., Plautus) who had long had a place in the scholastic canon. The reasons for such shifts in taste are now beyond recovery. Less obscure are the causes of other shifts revealed by the palimpsested manuscripts in which magnificent texts of Cicero's *De republica* or Sallust's *Histories* have been scraped away and overwritten with texts of Augustine and Jerome. Such decisions, which resulted less from hostility toward the old texts than from the greater utility of the new, exemplified and sustained the larger changes that brought reading, with the rest of late antique culture, into the Middle Ages.

BIBL.: Stanley F. Bonner, *Education in Ancient Rome* (Berkeley, 1977), chaps. 13, 16. Martin Levine, *The Making of Textual Culture: "Grammatica" and Literary Theory 350–1100* (Cambridge, Eng., 1994).   R.K.

Red Sea

Dotted with ports of call along its African shore during the Ptolemaic dynasty, the Red Sea became the gateway to commerce with India in the Graeco-Roman world, as soon as Mediterranean sailors learned to harness the monsoons to make crossings on the high seas of the Indian Ocean (about 115 B.C.E.). It also continued to be a passageway to the banks of Azania (African coast of the Indian Ocean). After Egypt became part of the Roman empire (30 B.C.E.), traffic in spices, precious stones, ivory, cotton, and silk, which were traded for metal tools, glass jewelry, and inexpensive clothing, greatly increased over the course of the next two centuries. During the long period of military anarchy that weakened the Roman empire in the 3rd century (ca. 235–285), Rome's influence in the Red Sea vacillated. Nomads, the Blemmyes, controlled the routes joining the Egyptian ports of call along the sea (Myos Hormos = Qoseir el-Qadim, and Berenice of the Troglodytes = Medinet el-Haras, south of Ras Benes) to Upper Egypt, while the Arabs (Homerites and Sabaeans of Yemen, Adramites of Hadramaut) and the Axumites of Eritrea, on the African shore, controlled most maritime commerce. Trade does not seem to have been affected, however: most spices and aromatics were sold at a lower cost in the empire under Diocletian than during the reign of the Julio-Claudian line.

The tetrarchy reestablished Roman power in the Red Sea zone by restoring order in Egypt and reducing the Persian threat (297). In the 4th century and, more precisely, during the age of Constantine and his son Constantius II, commerce was almost equally shared among the Mediterraneans, Axumites, and Homerites. The Axumites and Homerites, having become dominant on both shores of the Red Sea, began to convert to Christianity (owing to the missions of Frumentius and Theophilus). In about 360 Alexandria was rich with aromatics and other merchandise from the "barbarian" (that is, the Somalian) coast, according to the *Expositio totius mundi et gentium*. Thousands of 4th century Roman and Indo-Roman coins have been discovered in Sri Lanka, the center of trade between India, Persia, and Ethiopia at the time. On the Egyptian side, boats reached Clysma (Qolzum) at the far end of the Gulf of Suez; cargo could also reach the Syro-Palestinian cities via Aela, at the far end of the Gulf of Aqaba. In contrast, routes in Upper Egypt were still threatened by Blemmyes plunderers; all the same, Berenice of the Troglodytes, where excavations have recently been undertaken, was able to maintain limited activities until the early 6th century. It seems that the empire's boats did not venture far beyond Axum on the African coast and perhaps traveled to Ocelis (on the peninsula of Cheikh-Saïd in Yemen, at the tip of Bab el-Mandab). Between these cities and Sri Lanka, commerce was now dominated by the Axumites and Persians.

After another period of decline (late 5th century), commercial exchanges in the Red Sea region recovered their vigor, thanks to the alliance between Byzantium and Axum. In the expedition of Ela Atzbeha/Kaleb, king of Axum, to Yemen in 525, he fought against the sovereign of Himyar, who had converted to Judaism and allied himself with Sassanid Persia; Abyssinian power was reestablished in Yemen. But Justinian was unable to divert the Silk Route to the Red Sea and Axum and thus remove it from Persian control. The situation was reversed when, in about 572, the Persians seized South Arabia. That region fell into profound decadence after nomadic Arab tribes from the north infiltrated it; these tribes showed no interest in navigation. Axum's power was gone. In 632, shortly before the death of the Prophet, the great tribes of Yemen rallied behind nascent Islam and emancipated themselves from Persian suzerainty. Ten years later, Byzantium was cut off from the Red Sea by the Arab conquest of Egypt. In the early 8th century, the Arabs of Hejaz occupied the Dahlak Archipelago, and Adulis, port of Axum, was destroyed. From then on, the Red Sea became the exclusive domain of Arab navigation.

BIBL.: Jehan Desanges, *Recherches sur l'activité des Méditerranéens aux confins de l'Afrique (VIe siècle avant J.-C.–IVe siècle après J.-C.)* (Rome, 1978). George F. Hourani, *Arab Seafaring in the Indian Ocean in Ancient and Early Medieval Times*, rev. and exp. by John Carswell (Princeton, 1995). Stuart Munro-Hay, *Aksum: An African Civilisation of Late Antiquity* (Edinburgh, 1991). J.DES.

Refugees

In many ways, late antiquity was a time of disruption, and one result of this was that refugees of various kinds virtually covered the landscape. Many became such as a result of the arrival and settlement of the barbarians. Indeed, some refugees were barbarians themselves, such as Ulfila and the "lesser Goths," who fled across the Danube in the 340s as a result of a Visigothic persecution. They were followed in 376 by a much larger body of Goths who were fleeing the Huns. This marked the beginning of the so-called barbarian invasions, which engendered great disruptions among the Roman population in subsequent years.

The Spanish priest Orosius advised those who were affected, "When you are persecuted in one city, flee to another." Many followed his advice. Roman flight from Spain, Italy, Africa, Britain, Illyricum, and elsewhere is attested in the early 5th century. Many refugees merely moved to more secure areas of the same region. In the 410s, for example, several aristocrats of northern and central Gaul took refuge in the southern monastery of Lérins; some soon returned home when the threat turned out to be less serious than anticipated. During the 470s, four clerics of Bishop Polichronius of Verdun, who was himself already a refugee, fled to Chartres and plaintively wrote to him, "We have been compelled by grave necessity to leave home, and the misfortune which has made you an exile from our homeland also has compelled us to go into exile." In North Africa, some Romans fled westward to Numidia and Mauretania.

Other refugees went farther afield. Rutilius Namatianus described Victorinus, a native of Toulouse and a former vicar of Britain, as "a wanderer, whom the capture of Toulouse compelled to settle in the Tuscan lands and worship foreign gods." Avitus of Braga wrote of his inability to return home from a pilgrimage to the Holy Land: "But my desire is impeded by the enemy now dispersed throughout all of Spain." North Africans escaped the Vandal onslaught by fleeing to Italy and the east; in Syria they strained the resources of the ecclesiastical relief system.

Some refugees were able to maintain their standard of living better than others. Placidia, the daughter of the emperor Valentinian III (425–455), was taken captive during the Vandal sack of Rome in 455 and carried off to Carthage. Her husband, Olybrius, meanwhile, fled to Constantinople. Eventually she was released and joined her husband. Their daughter Anicia Juliana never returned home but remained in the east and eventually married the general Areobindus. Other aristocrats, however, were not quite so fortunate. Rutilius said of the Gallic refugee Protadius, "He exchanged his paternal inheritance for middling estates in Umbria . . . his unconquered spirit oversees small things in place of great."

Political disruption created more pitiable refugees among the less privileged. In the 470s, a deacon abandoned his property in the Visigothic kingdom, became a wanderer *(peregrinus)*, and fled to Auxerre, "avoiding the whirlwind of the Gothic depredation." Shortly thereafter, Ruricius of Limoges told of the presbyter Possessor, who, "In order that he not lose his life through a most cruel death, himself has been made an exile from his homeland."

For all of these individuals, the choice of whether to remain or leave must have been a difficult one. Some aristocrats simply made bad choices. Paulinus of Pella considered leaving Gaul to escape the barbarians, "whose many repeated hostilities, which I endured while I delayed, convinced me that I must leave my homeland as quickly as possible." But he eventually chose to remain, blaming his wife for her refusal to leave. As a result he entered what he called "perpetual . . . poverty-stricken exile." His daughter, however, was more resolute: "Departing her homeland, she avoided the common ruin."

And as for why some did not flee, Salvian of Marseilles explained, "And, indeed, I can only marvel that all dependent and impoverished paupers do not do this together, unless there is only one reason why they do not do so, because they are unable to transfer thence their possessions and little habitations and families." Salvian even went so far as to claim that some Romans fled to the barbarians to escape Roman oppression: "And should we marvel if the Goths are not defeated by our side, when Romans prefer to live among them rather than among us?" A Greek from Viminacum in Moesia explained to the historian Priscus in 448 why he had fled to the Huns: "The exaction of taxes is very severe, and unprincipled men inflict injuries on others, because the laws are not imposed equally upon all classes."

Some legislation, however, did attempt to ease the lot of those whose lives had been disrupted. A western law of 408 made it illegal to hold against their will "persons of diverse provinces, of any sex, status, and age, whom the spread of barbarian savagery has displaced." North African refugees were granted a moratorium on debts and allocated imperial lands in Numidia and Mauretania to make up for those they had lost, and refugee lawyers were granted special licenses to allow them to practice in Italy. Moreover, the laws of *postliminium* protected the property of those who had been displaced but later returned. Two of the sons of the senator Gordianus, who had fled North Africa in 442, did in fact later return and successfully reclaim part of the family property.

For those unable to depart physically from troubled areas, there always was the option of becoming a metaphorical refugee. Spiritual escape was recommended by Faustus of Riez, who preached, "I therefore urge each of you men of our time to flee eagerly from these whirlwinds of the world to the house of God." And the anonymous author of the *Poem of a Husband to His Wife* sought solace in religion, saying, "If I am shut up in a dark prison, and bound in chains, I will turn to God, freed through the release of my spirit . . . I do not fear exile; the world as a whole is a home for everyone." Such individuals would have seen themselves as "refugees" no matter where they were.

The Muslim takeover of western Asia led to several different groups of refugees: Christians who left Syria and Palestine (probably a relatively small number); Persian elites who left Iraq and settled in northern and northeastern Iran; Buddhists who escaped in the secluded valley of Afghanistan; Sogdians and Manichaeans who moved eastward. Each one of these forced movements of people may well have had significant cultural results, but they have never been fully investigated, singly or as a group.

BIBL.: E. Doblhofer, *Exil und Emigration: Zum Erlebnis der Heimatferne in der römischen Literatur* (Darmstadt, 1987). W. Klingshirn, "Charity and Power: Caesarius of Arles and the Ransoming of Captives in Sub-Roman Gaul," *Journal of Roman Studies* 75 (1985): 183–203. R. W. Mathisen, "Emigrants, Exiles, and Survivors: Aristocratic Options in Visigothic Aquitania," *Phoenix* 38 (1984): 159–170. G. Walser, "Flüchtling und Exil im klassischen Altertum," in *Der Flüchtling in der Weltgeschichte,* ed. A. Mercier (Bern and Frankfurt, 1974), 67–93.   R.W.M.

Relics

The Mediterranean world under Roman rule was littered with relics. The city of Rome was so cluttered with statues that eventually it required a *tribunus rerum nitentium,* a municipal magistrate responsible for the "shiny stuff." Monuments and tokens commemorating memorable people, significant events, and sacred sites also blanketed the provinces; during the 2nd century Pausanias wrote a detailed guidebook for travelers visiting the antiquities in ancient Greece. Even a guidebook for Christian pilgrims took note of the tombs of the playwright Euripides and the general Hannibal.

From the beginning Christians venerated mementos of martyrs. During the 2nd century Christians in Smyrna carefully collected the remains of the martyr Polycarp and celebrated an annual festival at his tomb, while in Lyons the magistrates burned the bodies of martyrs and swept the ashes into the river to prevent the collection of relics. In the later Roman empire many theological controversies focused on aspects of the body of Jesus Christ, such as its essence or its divine and human natures. Not surprisingly, relics associated with Christ were specially venerated. Later traditions credited Helena, the mother of the emperor Constantine, with the discovery of the True Cross in Jerusalem; Constantine himself funded the construction of a church over Christ's tomb. Relics of the True Cross were so prized that in Jerusalem deacons stood guard to prevent the pilgrims who came to kiss the holy wood from biting off a sliver. Fragments of the True Cross nevertheless circulated throughout the Mediterranean world, and bishops of Jerusalem as well as eastern emperors sometimes used them as diplomatic gifts. In the early 7th century the Persians sacked Jerusalem and carried off the True Cross; when the emperor Heraclius finally restored the relic, he was acclaimed as a new Constantine.

Doctrines about Christ's incarnation and resurrection provided the theological foundations for beliefs in the mediation of the saints and the efficacy of their relics, and objections that Christians were simply perpetuating pagan ceremonies or turning into "ashmongers" were brushed aside. Christian relics took many forms. Some were manufactured almost as inexpensive souvenirs, such as the small flasks embossed with depictions of shrines that held oil from the lamps in the Church of Christ's Tomb. Other relics were mementos that commemorated events from saints' lives or tokens that had come into contact with their tombs; at various shrines in Gaul one popular relic was the dust scratched from a saint's sarcophagus. Body parts or bodily effusions were also common, although the trade in them was open to abuse; the cache of one relic peddler in fact included roots, mouse bones, and bear claws. The most valuable relics were the bodies of saints. Many saints' bodies remained remarkably well preserved, seemingly more healthy than the ill people who clustered at their shrines; when people opened saints' tombs, they were amazed at the sweet scent and the robust blush on the saint's face. Since ideas about relics derived primarily from a language of the body, they readily provided justification for various theological teachings. The veneration of relics thus offered a powerful and accessible idiom for articulating to ordinary believers sophisticated doctrines about the implications of Christ's life, the value of their own body, and the hope for a future bodily resurrection.

Some saints and their relics became associated with specific cities, in particular the two imperial capitals. In Rome the enhancement of the dual cult of St. Peter and St. Paul seemingly compensated for the decline of the city as an imperial residence. These martyrs were hailed as the new founders of the city, and the Spanish poet Prudentius even claimed that their blood had purified Rome of its long and disgraceful pagan past. The cult of St. Peter and St. Paul also promoted the standing of the bishops of Rome, and the spread or absence of these saints' relics during the early medieval period was a measure of the fluctuating prominence of the papacy in western Europe. Constantinople was a belated interloper among the great cities of the eastern empire. One way it demonstrated its accelerating preeminence was through a form of sacred imperialism, since among the resources that it siphoned from the eastern provinces were important relics, such as the nails from Jesus's crucifixion, the remains of the prophet Samuel, a hand of the protomartyr Stephen, and the body of Symeon the Stylite. During the 5th century the cult of the Virgin Mary became prominent, and her sobriquet Theotokos, "Bearer of God" or "Mother of God," became a rallying cry of doctrinal disputes. Because theologians eventually acknowledged her direct assumption into heaven, there were few bodily relics of the Virgin Mary, and shrines in Constantinople instead commemorated her robe and her girdle. In the early 7th century her protection was credited with saving Constantinople from the Avars and Persians.

Various shrines became the favored goals of pilgrimages. The most attractive destinations were biblical sites in the east, and especially in Egypt and Palestine, to which pilgrims such as Egeria during the late 4th century traveled with Bible in hand, diligently reading the passages appropriate to each site or monument. Actually seeing the sacred topography provided historical verification for the biblical narratives and effectively transformed distant events into compellingly present realities. The inverse of pilgrimages was the circulation of relics. One particularly attractive relic was dirt from Palestine, since it allowed people to recreate, literally, the Holy Land in their homeland; in North Africa one man kept dirt from Christ's tomb in his bedroom. Imperial legislation may have continued to repeat the traditional restrictions on tampering with tombs, but increasing demand simply disarmed any misgivings, even about the dismemberment of saints' bodies.

The most intimate relics that pilgrims took away were the stories of their own experiences. Many of the huge collections of miracle stories from late antiquity consist of tales that the authors had heard from others. In their own stories people were no longer mere observers but participants, the direct beneficiaries of the saints' miracles. Listening to the reading of a saint's life, admiring an icon at home or the frescoes in a church, or fingering a sacred memento were all means of expressing devotion to a saint, but retelling the story of one's own healing conjured up, over and over, the warm emotions of a deeply personal encounter.

Relics certainly did not exist in the early Islamic world with the complexity of meanings present in Christianity or Buddhism. But actions were accomplished around objects which could, and sometimes did, lead to a certain kind of veneration. Such objects are the Black Stone on the Ka'ba in Mecca, the marble and staff of the Prophet, the pages of the Qur'ān with the blood of the caliph 'Uthmān on them, and remains from the martyred Shī'ite imāms 'Alī and Ḥusain.

BIBL.: P. Brown, *The Cult of the Saints: Its Rise and Function in Latin Christianity* (Chicago, 1981). Y. Duval, *Loca sanctorum: Le culte des martyrs en Afrique du Ive au VIIe siècle*, 2 vols. (Rome, 1982). E. D. Hunt, *Holy Land Pilgrimage in the Later Roman Empire AD 312–460* (Oxford, 1982). Raymond Van Dam, *Saints and Their Miracles in Late Antique Gaul* (Princeton, 1993). S. Wilson, ed., *Saints and Their Cults: Studies in Religious Sociology, Folklore and History* (Cambridge, Eng., 1983).   R.V.

Rent

Rent is the amount paid, whether in money or in produce, by the tenant of a property to its owner or possessor, in return for its use for a period of time. In the late antique economy, rent meant, above all, payments to an owner of agricultural land who had leased it to a tenant farmer, and as such was central both to the flexibility of agriculture and to the maintenance of elite individuals and institutions. But there was also a lively rental market in residential quarters and commercial space, particularly in the cities.

Agricultural tenancy occurred at every level of the Roman world. Apart from smallholders' direct farming of their own land, leasing was the principal means of exploiting land. Those who could not farm their land themselves, including those who owned large amounts, usually preferred leasing it to hiring or owning large numbers of workers. Leasing provided a steadier, more reliable income with less bother and minimal managerial staff. In some settings it may also have been more profitable than direct operation, and

tenants sometimes brought equipment or other capital into the relationship. Rents on such leases were commonly paid in produce (especially cereal grains), but rents on properties that produced cash crops such as oil or wine were often due in cash. Both fixed rents and rents proportional to the harvest are attested.

Leasing and rents were the main foundation of large private incomes among the elites of Rome, Constantinople, and virtually all provincial cities of any size. Although some wealthy landowners spent considerable time on their estates, many preferred rent to revenues from direct exploitation precisely because renting enabled their absence from the land. Late antiquity shows little difference from the earlier Roman imperial period in this respect, except to the degree that the increased concentration of wealth made absentee rent collection all the more attractive. The rental system also made it feasible to give lands as endowments to pious foundations, especially enabling the church and its related institutions to draw sizable incomes without direct involvement in agriculture.

How burdensome rents were for the tenants is difficult to say and must have varied considerably; hardly ever is the total productivity of a parcel of land known. On very poor land rent might have been only a tenth of the meager produce; on the best land (particularly in the most productive parts of Egypt), perhaps as much as half. Most surviving Egyptian leases specify that the landlord pays the taxes; net after-tax rents to the landlord were thus much lower than gross rents.

A substantial portion of the urban population of almost all classes rented living space, ranging from well-to-do tenants of spacious apartments in Rome to lodgers occupying a room or two in someone's house in a provincial city. The rental market made spatial mobility possible and accommodated the substantial number of unattached people living in the cities. There is also considerable evidence for the rental of shops and workshops; both renters and proprietors often lived and worked in the same space.

Modern observers have sometimes looked on the widespread pattern of rental relationships in ancient and late antique society as a sign of economic and social distress. Many tenants were certainly among the poorest members of this society, but others were not; and even for the poor the rental market made possible a flexibility in place of residence and work that may have been better than inflexibility. Reliable farm tenants were a desirable item in short supply in many times and places, and the terms they secured were by no means always to their disadvantage. Rent was not only the way in which the late antique social and institutional world was supported, but it was a major contributor to the dynamism of the economy.

BIBL.: B. W. Frier, *Landlords and Tenants in Imperial Rome* (Princeton, 1980). M. Kaplan, "L'économie paysanne dans l'empire byzantin du Vème au Xème siècle," *Klio* 68 (1986): 198–232. E. Patlagean, *Pauvreté économique et pauvreté so-*

ciale à Byzance (Paris, 1977). J. L. Rowlandson, *Landowners and Tenants in Roman Egypt* (Oxford, 1996).   R.S.B.

Rhetoric

In the matter of rhetorical technique, late antiquity was an age of compilation and interpretation. In the Greek east, the treatises of Hermogenes (2nd to 3rd century) and Aphthonios (4th century) were collected into a canonical corpus, probably at the turn of the 6th century, and were the object of unflagging commentaries. Once again, rhetoric encountered philosophy, in this case Neoplatonism as represented by Syrianus. Head of the Platonic Academy of Athens, Syrianus was also a commentator on Plato, Aristotle, and Hermogenes, and the master of Proclus. At the same time in the Latin world, *artes* and *compendia* proliferated. Because of the linguistic rift between the east and the west, Greek manuals were increasingly replaced by Latin ones. Commentaries on Cicero were produced by Marius Victorinus (4th century) and Boethius (6th century); Boethius's commentary on the *Topica* was a turning point in the relation between dialectic and rhetoric. The encyclopedists of the 5th to 7th centuries—Martianus Capella, Cassiodorus, and Isidore of Seville—all grant a place to rhetoric. Although these theoretical writings of late antiquity were often lacking in inventiveness, they looked toward the future, since they were destined to exert a major influence on medieval rhetoric. They selected and consecrated doctrines—Aphthonian and Hermogenian in Byzantium, Ciceronian and pseudo-Ciceronian in the Latin west—that would become dominant.

A rich oratorical practice developed in concert with the theoretical work. The tradition of the second sophistic, which went back to the high empire, was perpetuated in the exemplary figure of Libanius, who lived in Antioch, Syria, in the 4th century. He was at once a scholar, a professor of rhetoric, a popular lecturer, an orator involved in municipal and provincial policy, and an interlocutor of governors and emperors. The same sophistic tradition can be observed in the 4th century, with Themistius and Himerius, and in the 6th, with the representatives of the school of Gaza (Procopius of Gaza and Choricius). The west provided a rich collection, the *Latin Panegyrics,* composed in Gaul in the late 3rd to 4th century. Those wide-ranging oratorical texts, which have recently attracted new scholarly interest, followed an evolution that had begun in the previous centuries by highlighting the "epideictic" genre (ceremonial eloquence based on the panegyric); harangues and appeals were assigned a less important role. One characteristic was the insistent use of the empire and the emperor as subject matter in speeches (in addition to the names already cited, see the panegyrics of Constantius and Eusebius by the future emperor Julian, Eusebius of Caesarea's *Life of Constantine,* and Ennodius's panegyric of Theoderic). The royal or imperial panegyric is probably the most representative oratorical form of late antiquity, because its eloquence is always linked to politics. That period, more than any other, required a reflection on monarchic power, given the transformations under way with the partition, fall, and recomposition of empires. Late antiquity exploited all the tools of rhetoric and applied them to contemporary questions.

The primary question raised in this period was the relation between rhetoric and Christianity. In the eyes of Christians, Graeco-Roman rhetoric was suspect, as was the entire tradition of pagan culture to which it belonged. The very idea of rhetorical technique was questionable for believers, whose aim was to express the word of God in its truth and in the plainest manner possible. In any case, there was a need for a new, sui generis rhetoric to express the most difficult aspects of the divine message, its paradox, mystery, and revelation. And yet, pagan rhetoric had proven itself as a method of education, as a technique of persuasion, and as an art of culture and beauty. The result was a complex problematic: some wished to repudiate the Graeco-Roman heritage or tried to circumvent it, while the majority set out to recuperate, rework, and transform it. The most significant theoretical text to delineate a Christian eloquence, distinguished from pagan traditions but not severed from them, is book four of St. Augustine's *De doctrina christiana.* The works of Ambrose of Milan and the Greek writings of the Cappadocian Fathers (Basil of Caesarea, Gregory of Nyssa, Gregory of Nazianzus) and of John Chrysostom illustrate the implementation of that eloquence. Their speeches date from the 4th century, which was decidedly one of the most brilliant moments in the entire history of classical rhetoric. Christian eloquence continued to develop, particularly in preaching (sermons, homilies) and within ecclesiastical institutions.

The world of late antiquity was splintered and pluralistic. No one city—Athens or Rome, for example—set the tone as in the past; no one structure guaranteed cohesion in the provinces. Rhetoric was everywhere and nowhere, from Gaul to the Middle East, from the Black Sea to Egypt. The borderlands or margins had great importance. As significant examples of the cultural and disciplinary mix of the era, one should note: in the 5th century, a version of Theon's *Progymnasmata* (more complete than the text of the Greek tradition); at the turn of the 6th century, the figure of Priscianus, a grammarian born in Mauritania, teacher of Latin in Byzantium with many contacts in Rome, who translated Hermogenes into Latin; in 529, the Persian teachers' exile from the Neoplatonic Academy of Athens—seven philosophers who also taught rhetoric; and in the 6th century, the library of Dioscorus of Aphrodito in Egypt, recovered with the aid of papyrology, which combined the Coptic and the Greek works, notarized acts, and a poetry steeped in rhetoric.

It is unlikely that the early Islamic period had already developed a theory of rhetoric, although this did occur later. But the preservation of particularly effective speeches (like the one al-Hajjaj dramatically made in the mosque of Kufah) and endless queries about the most effective poetry, past or present, suggest the existence very early in Islamic culture of a concern for the best ways to make a verbal impact.

BIBL.: K. Abu Deeb, *Al-Jurjani's Theory of Poetic Imagery* (Warminster, 1979). Averil Cameron, *Christianity and the Rhetoric of Empire* (Berkeley, 1991). George A. Kennedy, *Greek Rhetoric under Christian Emperors* (Princeton, 1983). J. W. Watt, "Syriac Panegyric in Theory and Practice," *Le mouséon* 102 (1989): 271–298. C. E. V. Nixon and B. S. Rodgers, eds., *In Praise of Later Roman Emperors* (Berkeley, 1994). *The Propaganda of Power,* ed. Mary Whitby (Leiden, 1998). L.P.

Ritual

Ritual is a term developed from the Latin *ritus,* "religious ceremony." It finds no exact equivalent in ancient Greek; words such as *ergon* (work), *praxis* (business), or the substantive use of the adjective *hieros* (sacred) stand in. In its contemporary scholarly use, ritual may be defined as the performance of actions that create, re-create, or symbolize a relationship between two parties, typically mortal and divine. Often it refers to actions that are repeated periodically, such as those associated with an annual festival, but it may also be applied to those that are performed only as needed, such as rituals of healing. Typically, the actor believes that the actions he performs are effective not only for himself but also for others in some group to which he belongs.

Although rituals were central to ancient Greek and Roman religious practice, they were not accepted without question. From earliest times, the Greeks took care to explain the origin and specific form of a ritual through an etiological myth; the explanation usually reiterated the need to continue practicing the ritual as well. Ovid plays with the power of such *aitia* to explain and validate ritual in his *Fasti,* a poem about Roman festivals. In later antiquity, however, the meaning, effectiveness, and appropriateness of ritual began to be challenged in new and more serious ways. Philosophers, particularly Neoplatonists, rejected or reinterpreted many traditional rituals. Most famously, Plotinus regarded ascesis and contemplation—as opposed to ritual action—as the only means by which the mortal could be unified with the divine. His pupil Porphyry countered that, for the average man, ritual might provide a first step toward this goal (cf. Augustine, *De civ.Dei* 10.9). Iamblichus embraced ritual even more enthusiastically, defending its role in worship at length in the *De mysteriis* and denying that thought alone could unite a mortal with god (*Myst.* 2.11, 95.15–99.10). Rituals of various kinds were central to theurgy (literally, divine work), the soteriologically oriented cult practiced by Iamblichus and many other

Neoplatonists, who believed that its rituals had been taught to them by the very gods to whom they would be directed (cf. Chaldaean Oracles frg. 147, 148, 149); ritual lay, therefore, at the very center of any relationship between mortals and gods.

Nonetheless, specific rituals came under fire even from ritual's advocates; the battles were grounded in interpretations of the nature of divinity and the human soul and the value (positive or negative) of the material world, as well as the details of the actual rituals themselves. Porphyry *(De abstin., Letter to Anebo)* rejected animal sacrifice as misguided—true gods would not desire the smoke of burning meat—and disparaged many traditional means of divination. Iamblichus *(Myst.)* countered that sacrifice facilitated the individual soul's participation in the cosmic order by reminding it of the gods' beneficence and by symbolizing the eventual dissolution of the individual's own corporality; to defend divination he offered a revision of the Stoic doctrine that true divination was based on the perceptions of the ecstatic soul, released from the body through god-given ritual. Sallustius (*De diis et mundo* 16.2) somewhat similarly justified sacrificial ritual by arguing that the soul of the animal formed a bridge between the mortal and divine souls. Essentially the same arguments that we find among the Neoplatonists went on in the early Christian church as well, where there was disagreement, for instance, over the role that sacramentalism and the veneration of divine images could play in uniting the individual with God.

In other contexts, existing rituals were modified to suit new situations in which they were practiced or were replaced by symbolic actions that were understood to replicate their effects. In Judaism of later antiquity, for example, especially following the destruction of the Temple and the relocation of ritual into domestic space, actual sacrifice gave way to discourse about sacrifice. Discourse about ritual, in turn, could become a new ritual, as J. Z. Smith notes, citing the requirement that the story of the paschal lamb be retold every year on Passover. He identifies an analogous phenomenon in the creation of magical texts, where ritual is partially replaced by writing about ritual. Similarly, the increasing domestication of ritual in many Mediterranean traditions led to the "miniaturization" or "abbreviation" of what originally were grander civic or temple-based rituals. This demanded that the rituals carry a value more intensely symbolic than real; they became, as Smith puts it, "rituals of rituals," honoring the god through the fact of the ritual's performance itself rather than through any goods the ritual might deliver.

Especially interesting for the student of late antique ritual are the Graeco-Egyptian magical papyri, in part because they provide rare, detailed descriptions of ritual but also because they demonstrate the flexibility that ritual had acquired by this time. Among the notable features are the ease with which ritual acts could be "fine-tuned" to serve different purposes (*PGM* 4.2871–76 and 4.2145–2240) and modified or supplemented if at first unsuccessful (*PGM* 2.1–64), which suggest that the practitioner felt himself to be a "craftsman" of ritual, with a variety of tools at his disposal that he could use as he thought best and as the situation demanded. Although the rituals of these papyri still work to establish relationships between mortal and divine and share many features with earlier, traditional Greek, Roman, and Egyptian rituals, the approach is more blatantly functional, and this reflects, in a different way, one of the issues over which the philosophers were arguing: were rituals gifts of the gods, provided primarily for mortals' benefit?

A final illustration of late antiquity's challenge to traditional ritual is provided by the creation of the imperial cult, for although ritual was always liable to alteration as times and physical circumstances demanded, in few other cases did this occur with such deliberateness, or to serve such consciously recognized goals. As Simon Price shows, the careful combining of elements from existing funeral cults and divine cults was intended to articulate a complex picture of the ideal emperor, who was, in his mortal essence, no different from any other member of the noble class, but who, by his very practice of noble virtues, had risen out of the mortal realm. Modifications *within* the imperial cult, once it was established, were also deliberate and reflected such things as the changing relationship between the emperor and the elite class. In the imperial cult, we find the practitioners of ritual consciously using it for what contemporary scholars have repeatedly argued it really is: a means of communication between not mortals and gods but mortals and other mortals.

BIBL.: Simon Price, "From Noble Funerals to Divine Cult: The Consecration of Roman Emperors," in *Rituals of Royalty: Power and Ceremonial in Traditional Societies*, ed. D. Cannadine and S. Price (Cambridge, Eng., 1987), 56–105. Gregory Shaw, *Theurgy and the Soul: The Neoplatonism of Iamblichus* (University Park, Pa., 1995). J. Z. Smith, "Trading Places," in *Ancient Magic and Ritual Power*, ed. M. Meyer and P. Mirecki (Leiden, New York, and Cologne, 1995), 13–28.   S.I.J.

Roads

Roads in the Roman and Byzantine era were essentially of three different types: state or public highways, regional or vicinal roads, and private roads on local estates. The terminology in literary sources is not always precise, and the categories are frequently confusing. The thousands of regional and private roads supplementing the major imperial arteries remain largely undocumented. In contrast, the official imperial system is known from a few ancient cartographic documents, the itineraries of travelers and pilgrims, and more than eight thousand inscribed milestones. The state postal or transport system of the early Roman era (*vehicula-*

tio) became known in the 4th century as the *cursus publicus* (Greek *dēmosios dromos*). These roads were generally restricted to imperial officials or state couriers and were frequently used in military expeditions. The major routes in the west included the Via Appia between Rome and Capua, the Via Egnatia across the Balkan Peninsula from the Adriatic to the Aegean (eventually extended across Thrace to Contantinople), and the northern route from the Danube near Belgrade to Constantinople. From Constantinople, across Asia Minor, other major arteries led eastward to Melitene on the Euphrates or through the Cilician Gates to Antioch in Syria. From Antioch, two major routes led south, one along the coast to Egypt and the other inland through Syria to Damascus and finally Aqaba on the Red Sea. These administrative and military roads were the responsibility of the praetorian prefect and later the *magister officiorum*, who alone issued official permits for use of the imperial highways. Other roads were maintained by the state for transporting agricultural goods, building materials, and other products to the cities by ox cart (Greek *hamaxēgē*; Latin *plaustrum* or *sarracum*). Smaller and lighter vehicles pulled by mules and sometimes horses were used for regular travel. Eventually the official public roads became the responsibility of liturgies of citizens from the various cities who were also occasionally responsible for providing transport, provisions, and hospitality for expeditionary armies. Abuses of the system were common and resulted in a flood of imperial legislation from the reign of Constantine to Justinian.

The most detailed account of the earlier Roman imperial road system is represented in the *Antonine Itinerary* and *Tabula Peutingeriana*. The latter document is known only from a medieval copy that reflects additions and editing until at least the reign of Theodosius II. The later elements include the name of Constantinople for Byzantium, the pictorial representation of the Church of St. Peter in Rome, and the inclusion of Ravenna on the map. Distances and stops along the major routes are indicated throughout, reflecting major cities, road stations, and inns. Guard stations and watchtowers also lined the official roads for security reasons and to facilitate travel. A few official travel documents provide further insight into the system. Papyri from the archive of Theophanes, a *scholasticus* on the staff of the prefect of Egypt, record his official journey between Alexandria in Egypt and Antioch in Syria between 317 and 323, listing some twenty-five stations (*P Rylands* 627–639). Another less colorful but more detailed itinerary papyrus of the 5th or 6th century (*P Leiden* G 110) lists some sixty-two towns and stations between Alexandria and Constantinople. Christian pilgrims also provided descriptions of travel along the major routes. The earliest of these is the *Itinerarium Burdigalense*, recording a pilgrimage in 333 from Bordeaux in Gaul across the Alps and through the Balkans to Constantinople and then across Asia

Minor to Palestine, a journey of more than 2,000 miles that took almost six months. The *Itinerarium Egeriae* records a pilgrimage in 381–384 that lists some twenty-five *mansiones* along the coastal road between Syria and Jerusalem. By this time the *cursus publicus* was being extended to bishops and their entourages. The Madaba mosaic map of the 7th century in Transjordan is probably based on a road map for the Levant similar to that used earlier by Eusebius in compiling his biblical topography preserved in the *Onomasticon.*

In spite of the impression given by well-preserved paved roads throughout the empire, not all routes were paved, particularly in frontier regions and over difficult terrain. In fact, none of the roads in North Africa and Egypt were paved except for the great military road between Carthage and Theveste. The paved roads elsewhere required constant repair and have mostly eroded over time. They would be basically unknown without the milestones that were placed at regular intervals of approximately 1.4–1.5 m, marking the Roman mile. These cylindrical stone columns with a square base were originally 2–3 m high, and they frequently bear inscriptions indicating the distance from the nearest major city. More than two thousand are known from North Africa, almost a thousand from Europe and the west, and the rest are from the provinces in the eastern Mediterranean. These milestones were often associated with specific military campaigns and with the collection of the *annona*. The names and titularies of emperors and governors provide the dating mechanism, but inscriptions do not necessarily denote road construction or repairs, as milestones were convenient kiosks for purely imperial propaganda.

Milestones with dated inscriptions appear rather late in the west. A milestone of 435 is known from Arles in Gaul (*CIL* 12.5494) and even the Ostrogoth king Theoderic (471–526) erected a milestone inscription near Terracina on the Via Appia in Italy (*CIL* 10.6850–52 = *ILS* 827). In western Turkey, there are milestones with dated texts extending from the reign of Arcadius and Honorius (in 402) to the reign of Anastasius (491–518), but most of these later texts are of secondary nature, inscribed over or appearing with earlier inscriptions. In contrast, the use of inscribed milestones ceased in the Near East by the 4th century, in Syria as early as the reign of Constantine, in Arabia as early as that of Julian, and in Palestine as early as Arcadius. No milestones are known at all in Egypt, except on its Nubian, Libyan, and Palestinian frontiers. The end of the epigraphic habit in the region is perhaps signaled by the "Constantine habit" of merely painting texts over plastered inscribed milestones. It is also possible that the more numerous anepigraphic milestones were erected after the 4th century and bore painted texts, but this can at present remain only a hypothesis. Although Justinian's road building projects are known from Procopius, no milestones are dated to

his reign or afterward in the east; the earlier erected milestones must have retained their usefulness for travelers, judging from the tendency of Eusebius to mark many sites and settlements in Palestine according to the adjacent numbered milestones. The *Itinerarium Egeriae* also refers to using milestones as guides to locate Mt. Nebo and Zoar in Transjordan. Their existence in the region after the Islamic invasions of the Near East perhaps stimulated the Umayyad caliph ʿAbd al-Malik ibn Marwan (685–705) to erect milestones inscribed in Kufic on the road between Damascus and Jerusalem, indicating repairs and maintenance of the route under his rule. The Abassid rulers followed the practice, using milestone slabs to mark stations on the Darb Zubayda pilgrim road between Kufa and Mecca in the Hijaz.

In contrast, R. W. Bulliet (in *The Camel and the Wheel,* 1975) has argued that the Roman imperial road system fell into decline in the east between the 4th and 6th centuries in different regions and at various times. In the Near East, this is based on the assumption that camels replaced the more expensive wagon transport and decreased any need to maintain the paved roads for wheeled traffic. The evidence fails to support such a transition, however. Maintenance of the state road system after the 4th century is reflected by the imperial rescripts preserved in the *Theodosian Code* and the *Justinianic Code*. Regulations include limitations on travel permits, restrictions on vehicles and animals, and prohibitions of travel on secondary roads. It is evident that both the swift courier horse service and the heavy transport system by carriage or wagons are involved in the injunctions. Although the preserved rescripts for the *cursus publicus* cease by 423 in the *Theodosian Code,* subsequent legislation is preserved into the early 6th century in the later *Justinianic Code.* By this time supervision of the roads is assigned to the local decurions of the municipal councils. The indications of the "immense ruin of the highways" at the end of the 4th century (*C.Th.* 15.3.4) is matched in the 5th century by legislation invalidating all exemptions from *angariae* (state and private corvée and purchases) previously extended to members of the imperial household, dignitaries, and churchmen. The compulsory taxes for the "repair of the roads" after 441 is now without "distinction of any honors, persons or privileges" (Valentinian, *Nov.* 10.3)

Even if the more inexpensive use of camels and donkeys dominated long-distance transport, it never replaced regional wagon traffic. According to Procopius, the wagon was still the measuring stick for roads built in Italy, Thrace, Asia Minor, North Africa, and Syria throughout the reign of Justinian. Papyri from Egypt also indicate that wagons were still utilized in traditional fashion in the 7th century. Procopius (*SH* 30) does indicate that Justinian dismantled the postal system in Thrace, forcing couriers to use ships to communicate with Constantinople, but the courier route to

Persia in the east was left intact, with only the number of road stations in Syria-Palestine reduced as far as the limits of Egypt, where donkeys replaced horses. Elsewhere Procopius indicates Justinian was responsible for paving roads in Thrace and refurbishing the couriers' quarters in road stations in Asia Minor. The armies and administration of the empire continued to be dependent on an efficient communication system. Even state wagon roads in Byzantium are still mentioned in the early medieval period.

BIBL.: R. Chevallier, *Roman Roads*, trans. N. H. Field (Berkeley, 1976). David French, *Roman Roads and Milestones of Asia Minor* (Oxford, 1981–1988).   D.G.

Rome

"Rome" denotes a place, an institution, and a politicocultural symbol. The survival of the ancient city in all three capacities was a determining fact of medieval European history, as were the definitive transformations that began around 300.

The city centered topographically and symbolically on the Roman and Imperial Forums, and on the Capitoline and Palatine hills that overlooked them. On the other side of the Capitoline hill was the Field of Mars, filled with temples, theaters, stadia, and commemorative monuments; and at the other foot of the Palatine stood the Circus Maximus. The extensive periphery within the 19 km Wall of Aurelian (begun 271) was occupied by gardens and residential, commercial, military, and recreational buildings. Outside the wall, along the roads leading to its nineteen gates, were suburban estates, monumental tombs, and several types of underground cemeteries, including catacombs.

Around 300 Rome was at its physical acme and also, therefore, at the beginning of its long decline. At least two of its characteristic building types achieved their greatest realizations at this moment: the Baths of Diocletian, dedicated in 305/6 (*CIL* 6.1, 1130) and the Basilica Nova in the Roman Forum, sponsored by Maxentius (306–312). Maxentius also repaired the Temple of Venus and Rome (founded 121), probably the city's largest temple. But repair and replacement ceased to keep pace with decay. Ruin would be accelerated by the practice of taking architectural *spolia*—marble ornaments, including columns and figural reliefs—for reuse on new buildings, such as the tetrarchic Arcus Novus (293–294).

The Senate celebrated Constantine as its "liberator" from Maxentius with a *spolia*-laden triumphal arch dedicated in 315/6 (*CIL* 6.1, 1139). Constantine himself sponsored mostly ecclesiastical structures, including two that changed the course of architectural history. On the southeast rim of the city he erected the vast Basilica Constantiniana (later called S. Giovanni in Laterano) for use by the bishop. To the northwest, outside the wall, he is credited with leveling a cemetery at the Mons Vaticanus, where tradition located the

tomb of St. Peter, to build an even larger basilica over the tomb. These churches took up the colonnaded, wooden-roofed design of Trajan's Basilica Ulpia, which they rivaled in size and magnificence. They also canonized the use of *spolia*, as all of their columns (80 in the Basilica Constantiniana and 100 in St. Peter's) were reused.

Though its grandeur had peaked, Rome remained the showpiece of western civilization until the Gothic War (535–554). In the 4th century its immensely wealthy, culturally conservative aristocracy maintained its buildings, its rituals, and its public services, including the grain dole and the lavish spectacles, such as hunts and circuses. As these families converted to Christianity, the church adapted to their values and bishops became builders, replacing the pre-Constantinian house churches *(tituli)* with basilicas and similarly monumentalizing the cemeteries. Imperial women were entombed in grandiose mausoleums: Helena (d. 327) in a building possibly made for Constantine on the Via Labicana, Constantina (d. 354) in what is now S. Costanza, and Honorius's wife, Maria (d. 404/7), in a rotunda attached to St. Peter's. The splendorous impression of the city is conveyed at midcentury by Ammianus Marcellinus (16.10) and at its climax by Prudentius (*Crowns of Martyrdom*, 11.215–224, 12.31–54) and Claudian (*On the Sixth Consulship of the Emperor Honorius* [404]).

The three-day sack of Rome by the Goths in 410 shocked the world. Notable buildings were burned, including the Basilica Iulia in the Forum and palatial urban villas like that of Pinianus and Melania the Younger, and churches were looted. Despite its epoch-making symbolism, the damage was quickly overcome. Public buildings were repaired, and the popes recompensed the pillaged churches and constructed lavish new ones, including S. Maria Maggiore. Recent opinion holds that the great circular Basilica of S. Stefano may also date from the vigorous decades before 455.

In 455 the Vandals looted the city for two weeks. According to Procopius, their plunder included the treasure of the imperial palace, the gilded roof tiles of the Capitoline Temple of Jupiter, and an entire shipload of statues that later sank en route to Carthage (*Bell.Van.*, 1.5.1–5, 2.9.5). Despite this depredation, the city immediately resumed its role as a stage for traditional imperial ceremonial (Sidonius Apollinaris, *Carmina* 7 [456], 2 [468]; *Ep.* 1.5.9–11, 9.5–6), and the pope was once again able to replace the looted silver of the *tituli (Liber pontificalis, vita Leonis)*.

The succession of Gothic kings to power after 476 fostered a final revival. For ideological reasons Theoderic (493–526) was committed to the symbolism of *invicta Roma,* and his efforts ensured that life, albeit impoverished, went on as in the past. The imperial baths, the Circus Maximus, and theaters all continued to function; aqueducts, the Wall of Aurelian, public buildings, and statues were maintained by all available means (Cassiodorus, *Variae*, esp. 3.30, 31, 51; 4.30; 7.6, 13, 15, 17; *CIL* 6.1, 1716; 15.1, 1663–1670). Theoderic's urban policy is reflected in two significant milestones: the last known instance of a privately sponsored repair of a public building (Symmachus repaired the Theater of Pompey in 507–511; *Variae* 4.51), and the first known alienation of a public building for use as a church (the structure on the Roman Forum consecrated as Santi Cosma e Damiano, 526–530; *Liber pontificalis, vita Felicis* 4).

Theoderic's efforts were annulled by Justinian's war on his successors, despite the fact that Byzantines, too, waxed eloquent over Rome as a cultural symbol (Procopius, *Bell.Goth.* 3.22.6–17). Unlike the 5th century calamities, the Byzantine war destroyed the social and political infrastructure that had sustained the ancient city into its dotage. Long sieges in 537–538 and 546–547 beggared the senatorial aristocracy, which was then exiled or massacred, and finally dispersed. Absent the wealth and civic piety of this traditional class of patrons, secular amenities and memorials would not be restored. The aqueducts, broken by Vitigis and blocked by Belisarius in 537, remained so except for one or two; the imperial baths were never used again; the last races in the Circus Maximus were staged by Totila in 549 (*Bell.Goth.* 3.37.4). Secular education disappeared.

The Rome that emerged after the Gothic War was a militarized hierocracy, with dual governments centered on the pope in the Lateran Palace and the representatives of a Byzantine colonial administration on the Palatine. For the next two hundred years, papal building initiatives were principally directed toward three functions: charity, dispensed in complexes called *diaconiae;* monasteries; and pilgrimage. The tomb of St. Peter was embellished by nearly every pope, and gemlike new churches were erected over the tombs of other martyrs (S. Lorenzo Fuori le Mura, 579–590; S. Agnese Fuori le Mura and S. Pancrazio, 625–638). Secular spectacles were replaced by increasingly elaborate clerical displays, staged within the churches and also in frequent liturgical processions in the streets. The demise of ancient institutions was confirmed by the conversion of a conspicuous temple (the Pantheon) and the Senate House into churches (609 and 625–638, respectively). In rhetoric, the symbolism of Rome changed antipodally, from the persistence of a great civilization to its definitive ruination (e.g., Gregory the Great, *Homiliae in Hiezecihelem prophetam* 2.6.22; *Dialogues* 2.15.3).

In the 5th century, the ecclesiastical primacy of Rome was defined by popes Leo I (440–461) and Gelasius I (492–496) in terms of its particular relation to St. Peter. These arguments did not avail vis-à-vis Byzantium, but in the west Peter was the basis of a remarkable theory of government developed in the 8th century, as popes from Gregory II (715–731) onward assumed the military and civil powers of the disintegrating Byzantine exarchy. The church of St. Peter was reconfigured practically as a civil bureaucracy, and rhetorically as a republic, an eponymous state to which Christian kings owed spiritual submission. The physical city remained an emblem of past glory (Alcuin, *Carmina* 9.37–40), but its political symbolism was renewed in the vision of a Christian empire headed by St. Peter and the Franks.

BIBL.: Richard Krautheimer, *Rome: Profile of a City, 312–1308* (Princeton, 1980). Thomas F. X. Noble, *The Republic of St. Peter: The Birth of the Papal State, 680–825* (Philadelphia, 1984). C. Pietri, *Roma Christiana,* 2 vols. (Paris, 1976), and *Christiana Respublica,* 3 vols. (Rome, 1997). L. Richardson, Jr., *A New Topographical Dictionary of Ancient Rome* (Baltimore and London, 1992). G. W. Bowersock, "Peter and Constantine," in *St. Peter's in the Vatican: Memory and Art* (Cambridge, forthcoming).   D.K.

Rufinus

Born ca. 345 in Concordia, Rufinus of Aquileia was educated there and in Rome. He was baptized in Aquileia ca. 370. In Egypt, he weathered a persecution by Arians, studied with Didymus the Blind, and met various Desert Fathers. Around 380 he took up monastic residence in Jerusalem with his friend Melania the Elder. In the 390s, Rufinus became embroiled in the Origenist controversy in Palestine. In 397, Rufinus returned to Italy, where he first translated Basil of Caesarea's Rule, Pamphilus's *Apology for Origen* (adding his own *On the Adulteration of the Works of Origen*), and Origen's *On First Principles*. This project prompted a bitter literary controversy with Jerome. After Pope Siricius died in 399, Rufinus fell out of favor and moved to northern Italy. Sometime after 403, Rufinus moved southward again. Having fled Rome with relatives of Melania the Elder in advance of the Gothic invasion, he died in Sicily in 410 or 411.

Rufinus is best known for his translations into Latin of Greek theological writings. In addition to the works noted above, he translated Origen's *Homilies* on Genesis, Exodus, Leviticus, Numbers, Joshua, Judges, 1 Samuel, and Psalms 36–38, and had begun those on Deuteronomy shortly before his death. He also made an abridged translation of Origen's *Commentary on Romans* and an incomplete version of his *Commentary on the Song of Songs*. Rufinus translated some sermons of Basil and Gregory Nazianzen, an anonymous *Dialogue with Adamantius*, the *Sentences of Sextus*, Eusebius of Caesarea's *Ecclesiastical History* (which he updated to 395), the *History of the Monks of Egypt*, the Pseudo-Clementine *Recognitions*, and some works of Evagrius Ponticus. He himself composed a *Commentary on the Apostles' Creed* and a treatise entitled *The Benedictions of the Patriarchs*, but his *Apology against Jerome* remains his most masterful original composition. Twentieth-century scholars have debated whether Rufinus doctored his translations of Origen's writings to make them seem more "orthodox." Although

Rufinus appears to have tamed Origen's views and deleted some incriminating passages, many scholars now think that Rufinus conveyed the sense of Origen, if not always his words.

Another notable feature of Rufinus's life was his circle of famous Christian intellectuals and aristocrats, including several distinguished women; his own corpus of letters, no longer extant, would probably have further illumined the workings of late ancient patronage and social networks. It is also worth noting that the copying of manuscripts at Rufinus's monastery encouraged the development of monastic scriptoria elsewhere, as Caroline Hammond Bammel has shown.

Rufinus's own theology centered on points of earlier Christian and Trinitarian doctrine. Like Origen, he believed that those matters on which the church had not made a pronouncement were open for discussion. Despite his quarrel with Jerome, both men judged that much in Origen's biblical scholarship was valuable and should be made available to Latin audiences. Recently, Rufinus's links with the more radical Origenist Evagrius Ponticus, and with Melania the Elder's circle, have prompted a reassessment of him as a more theologically interesting and historically important character than earlier scholars had assumed.

BIBL: Elizabeth A. Clark, *The Origenist Controversy: The Cultural Construction of an Early Christian Debate* (Princeton, 1992), ch. 4. Francis X. Murphy, *Rufinus of Aquileia (345–411): His Life and Works* (Washington, D.C., 1945). F. Thelamon, *Païens et chrétiens au IVe siècle: L'apport de l'"Histoire ecclésiastique" de Rufin d'Aquilée* (Paris, 1981). P. R. Amidon, *Rufinus: The Ecclesiastical History* (Oxford, 1996).   E.C.

Runes

By runes we understand the characters of the system of writing used by the early Germanic nations (except the Goths), from the 2nd century C.E. until roughly 1350. In shape, runes have rectilinear forms that make them easy to carve in wood and other materials. They were used for short epigraphic inscriptions, which are usually difficult to read and interpret owing not only to their brevity and lack of context but also to the decay of the material in which they were carved. The most commonly known form of inscription was done on raised stones, but these are late, and runes are also found in large numbers on jewelry, bracteates, coins, weapons, and tools. It is widely agreed that the earliest inscriptions, which are all found in Norway and Denmark, belong to the 2nd century. Yet it is also understood that the source or model of the script must be found in the south. Two theories are current, one seeking the origin of runes in North-Italic, Etruscan writing and the other, in Latin majuscules, the latter theory now being the favored one.

Runic script never developed a cursive style, which suggests that little need was seen for it to serve practical and utilitarian ends. The ordering of the characters is different from alphabetic order. It is known as the fuþark, from the first six characters of the accepted order. There is an older fuþark of twenty-four characters, which was in use until about 750, and a more recent fuþark of sixteen characters that was standard in Scandinavia after 800. Presumably the change occurred to adjust to phonological changes for which the older fuþark offered no solution. In England, by contrast, the fuþark (as it was known in accordance with English phonology) was for similar reasons expanded to twenty-eight, and in one case even to thirty-three characters. Runes were especially associated with the god Woden, and in teachings of the sages they are often invested with magical powers, but there is no reason to believe that they were always linked with magic. In the early Germanic languages the word for rune also means secret, hidden lore, mystery. This may have led 17th century antiquarians to reintroduce the word *rune* in the sense of runic character, for they believed that runes held quasi-cabbalistical lore and derived the runes from Hebrew letters.

The study of runes is full of excitement and surprises. In excavations that followed a fire at the old Hanseatic wharf in Bergen, Norway, in the 1960s, no fewer than some 550 new inscriptions were found, dating mostly from the 13th century. They are all written on wooden sticks or tablets, and are in the nature of letters, commercial records, legal issues, and the like.

BIBL.: Lucien Musset, *Introduction à la runologie, en partie d'après les notes to Fernand Mossé* (Paris, 1965). R. I. Page, *An Introduction to English Runes* (London, 1973).   H.A.

Rusafa

Thirty kilometers south of the Euphrates, on the road between Palmyra and Sura in the Syrian steppe, lies Rusafa, a Roman *castellum* that has been known since the 1st century C.E. The Christian soldier Sergius, martyred with Bacchus, was buried there ca. 300 C.E. His relics became an important pilgrimage site. Rusafa became a see in about 454 and an ecclesiastical metropolis under Emperor Anastasius, who changed the name of the city to Sergiopolis, "city of Sergius."

The growth and fortification of the city, which Procopius attributed to Justinian, date from the early 6th century. The rectangular wall (400 by 500 m), equipped with fifty towers and four monumental gates (the north gate is richly ornamented), is still well preserved. Gigantic cisterns with sophisticated hydraulic mechanisms were installed. A hospice for pilgrims is known to us, and four large Christian sanctuaries are still visible, one in the form of a Greek cross on a central plan, plus three basilicas, designated A, B, and C. Basilica A, with numerous outbuildings and a large central platform (in Syriac, *bema*), is a church dedicated to the Holy Cross. It later held the relics of St.

Sergius. These relics seem to have been moved, first from the original tomb to a brick building—replaced in 518 by a basilica B—then to basilica A.

Pilgrims flocked to Rusafa from Italy and from the east as a whole. The Sassanid king Khosro II returned a gold cross, taken when the city was plundered by Khosro I in 540, to the sanctuary of St. Sergius, and added a second, ex-voto cross. Pilgrimages seem to have transformed the city into a gathering place for Arabs from the steppe. The Ghassanids venerated Sergius, and al-Mundhir is acclaimed on the inscription of a building outside the walls that is believed to have been his audience hall. It is obvious why the Umayyad caliph Hishām (724–742) made Rusafa, known by the name Rusafat-Hishām, his residence. Vast palaces were built outside the ramparts. A mosque was established north of basilica A, encroaching on and communicating with the large courtyard designed to receive pilgrims. A *sūq* was established west of the basilica. Christians continued to make pilgrimages to basilica A, which was reinforced with enormous buttresses. It was the last of the churches to survive, and remained in operation until the Mongol invasions.

BIBL.: P.-L. Gatier and T. Ulbert, "Eine Türsturzinschrift aus Resafa-Sergiupolis," *Damaszener Mitteilungen* 5 (1991): 169–182. T. Ulbert, *Resafa II: Die Basilika des Heiligen Kreuzes in Resafa-Sergiupolis* (Mainz am Rhein, 1986). T. Ulbert, "Resafa-Sergiupolis, archäologische Forschungen in der nordsyrischen Pilgerstadt," in *Syrien: Von den Aposteln bis zu den Kalifen,* ed. E. M. Ruprechtsberger (Linz, 1993), 112–127. E. Key Fowden, *The Barbarian Plain: Saint Sergius between Rome and Iran* (Berkeley, 1999).   P.-L.G.

S

Sacred Space

The expression "sacred space" refers to places associated with the divine, or at least with the superhuman, in whatever form that might take. Such places are granted certain privileges; access to them is regulated, or prohibitions are attached to them. In any case these spaces are monumentalized, built up as theaters for religious rites and practices, judged to be seats of power or manifestations of the divine. Thus the definition of such places cannot be separated from the persons and cultures that consider them sacred nor, especially, from the notion of the sacred and the view of the divine in its ever-changing relation to humanity. This means that there are no sacred spaces per se, but only spaces institutionalized and recognized by humans. Springs, woods, and caves can be favorable places for hierophanies, kratophanies, and epiphanies. A single inlet on the upper Yarmuk, amid numerous gorges, was identified as the site where the waters of the Styx flowed: in the late 5th century, full of fear and trembling, the pagan philosophers Isidore and Damascius paid tribute to it (Damascius, *Life of Isidore* 199). Similarly, the Coptic *Asclepius* (*Nag Hammadi Codices* 6.8, p. 70, lines 3–10) celebrated Egypt as the "mirror image of heaven," "dwelling of all the energies that are in heaven," "the temple of the world." Nonetheless, however contagious the notion of the sacred might be, the lands born of the gift of the Nile were not all sacred lands, as demonstrated by the *proskunēmata*, marks of adoration engraved in precise locales to mark a pilgrimage and leave a lasting memorial of "presence." It is clear that the very notion of

sacred place can be charged with different meanings, depending on the religious context—polytheistic, Jewish, Christian, or Muslim. And in fact, polytheism itself was not homogeneous: a harem in pre-Islamic Arabia did not follow the same logic of the sacred as a fire temple in Mazdean Persia. A harem was a delimited, inviolable area, located around a sanctuary, often founded by a charismatic person and linked to his family. They were established on the borders of territories belonging to rival tribes and formed a neutral zone for exchanging goods or settling disputes. A Persian temple of fire, in contrast, was a sanctuary where the sacred fire burned eternally in a strictly monitored room to which only priests had access. Believers gathered in surrounding rooms. We must thus understand sacred spaces in all their variety, especially since certain legal and religious traditions differentiate between various forms of sacredness. Thus, at least in principle, the Romans distinguished between the *locus religiosus*, a tomb, for example, object of a private dedication, and a *locus sacer*, which was given an official consecration. We must also distinguish between various degrees of sacredness in the topography itself. For example, in the 3rd century the sanctuary *ad deam Diam* on Monte delle Piche near Rome had three zones, arranged hierarchically from the bottom to the top of the hill: first, a space reserved for pavilions and *thermae* of priests associated with a circus; above it, the *Caesareum*, a consecrated place for deified emperors; and finally, at the very top, the sacred wood surrounding the temple of the goddess, which was accessible only to other gods or priests, and then solely for religious ends.

That tripartition of the sanctuary is reminiscent of

the complex hierarchization of the sacred space of the Temple of Jerusalem in Herod's time. The differences are key, however: the Temple was the unique dwelling of the only God in his glory. In addition, it was less a "sacred place" than a "holy place" and entailed an original relation between the living God and his sanctuary. Finally, the Temple was destroyed in 70 C.E., and its ruins haunted Jewish memory. Rabbis worked out a scale of ten degrees of holiness, based on the Halakhic criteria of "pure" and "impure," culminating in the Holy of Holies (Mishnah 6; Kodashim 1; Kelim 1:6–9). Over the course of centuries, synagogues were increasingly designated as "holy" or as "holy places," because they housed the scrolls of the Torah. Even so, that gradual sanctification was completely different from polytheistic sacralization and defined a completely different geography. It was also very different from the Christian notion of "holy place."

The Christian concept seems to have emerged only in the second half of the 3rd century. At a site in Rome called *ad catacumbas*, associated with the memory of Peter and Paul, visitors left several hundred graffiti invoking the intercession of the two apostles. In 295, the corpse of Maximilian, who was tortured to death in Tebassa, was transported to Carthage to be buried near the martyr Cyprian. The cult of martyrs and, more broadly, of Christian saints, with the pilgrimages it inspired and the practice of burial *ad sanctos*, led to the partial eclipse of a deep-seated tradition that opposed any sacralization of space (see John 4:20–24). It also brought about the gradual formation of a network of Christian holy places, to which the venerated sites of biblical lands were added, mostly after 324. Jewish traditions, Christian memories, and local fables competed to produce, to the great joy of pilgrims, an inventory of holy places, which continued to grow. Such places were associated with characters or episodes from the New Testament or the Hebrew Bible, particularly with Christ. The "Holy Land" was born. As relics spread, sanctuaries proliferated; in basilicas, they were often near the altar, theater of Eucharistic sacrifice. The very status of Christian religious sites underwent a transformation: from simple liturgical meeting halls— before the 6th century, consecrated species were not ordinarily kept in churches—they became true sanctuaries celebrated by a discourse with biblical overtones. They were protected by provisions often inspired by regulations relating to the sacred spaces of paganism, even as that ancient sacred geography was collapsing.

In the 7th century, a time of intense, generally topographical confrontations between different logics of the sacred, Islam made its own contribution: Mecca, Medina, and Jerusalem acquired a new sacredness. While Jerusalem witnessed an adaptation of Islam to older spaces, Mecca with its small Ka'bah and open space slowly carved out of the city transformed into an urban order old and traditional forms of the holy in nomadic Arabia. Medina, on the other hand, was a totally new kind of space based on the new form of the mosque adapted to the site of the Prophet's house. Mecca and Medina also became sacred cities, whose boundaries could not be crossed by nonbelievers, thus extending to the whole urban ensemble the holiness of one of its parts.

BIBL.: Robert A. Markus, "How on Earth Could Places Become Holy? Origins of the Christian Idea of Holy Places," *Journal of Early Christian Studies* (Baltimore) 2, no. 3 (1994): 257–271. M. Raoss, "*Locus nel diritto sacrale,*" *Dizionario epigrafico di antichità romane,* vol. 4, ed. E. De Ruggiero (Rome, 1946–1985), 1649–1716. John Scheid and Olivier de Cazanove, eds., *Les bois sacrés* (Naples, 1993).　　M.P.

Sallustius

Sallustius (in Greek, Saloustios) was the author of an extant Greek treatise, *On the Gods and the Universe,* that was an introduction to what he viewed as the fundamentals of pagan belief, aimed at an educated but theologically untutored audience. The treatise gives instruction on the First Cause and the classes of gods subordinated to it; the nature of the universe; mind and soul; Providence, Fate, and Chance; virtue, vice, and the nature of evil. Sallustius accepts the traditional myths only if they are given a proper allegorical interpretation. He encourages prayer and animal sacrifice, which benefit the worshipers, not the impassive gods, who are unaffected by humankind. He upholds the doctrine of metempsychosis. He teaches that evil has no objective existence but is merely the absence of good; that fate and the heavenly bodies affect humans but do not determine moral behavior; that the universe is uncreated and imperishable.

Although a number of religious and philosophical streams fed into Sallustius's treatise, it is most immediately indebted to Iamblichan Neoplatonism. Scholarly consensus puts its composition in the reign of Iamblichus's admirer Julian the Apostate, who also seems to have influenced Sallustius intellectually. The treatise would have contributed to the emperor's project of reviving polytheism. Although Sallustius engages in no explicit polemic against the Christians, it is they whom he mainly has in mind when he allays his readers' concerns about the rise of "atheism." He is probably to be identified with Saturninius Secundus Salutius, Julian's close friend and praetorian prefect of the east.

BIBL.: A. D. Nock, ed. and trans., *Concerning the Gods and the Universe* (Cambridge, Eng., 1926). G. Rinaldi, "Sull'identificazione dell'autore del *Peri theōn kai kosmou,*" *Koinonia,* 2 (Naples, 1978): 117–152. G. Rochefort, ed. and trans., *Des dieux et du monde* (Paris, 1960).　　R.P.

Sanctity

Disputes about the meaning and location of holiness had long been components of larger dialogues in ancient society. Some of these dialogues had concerned the distribution and working of power and influence among magistrates and aristocrats, others had involved attempts by individuals to define themselves and their roles in communities. Pagan intellectuals, for instance, associated holiness with philosophical learning, spiritual insight, ascetic detachment, and virtuous piety, and they wrote Lives to commemorate their heroes, some of whom had served as envoys to emperors and confronted various other notables. The rise of cults of Christian saints in the later Roman empire both incorporated and modified these characteristics. The early church had venerated martyrs as the true imitators of the suffering of Jesus Christ; once persecution ended with the establishment of Christian emperors, many Christians honored a "bloodless martyrdom" that was most apparent in lives of renunciation (for instance, through the adoption of chastity) or of extraordinary, often self-imposed ascetic torments. Christians considered the lives of earlier martyrs and notable contemporaries as exemplary paradigms of virtue, and they established numerous cults in their honor. Theologians reinterpreted biblical passages to justify the veneration of saints, and they linked it with doctrines of mediation, intercession, and the communication of God's grace. Hence, as a coda to his extended demonstration of God's providence in history in the *City of God*, Augustine included a catalogue of miracles attributed to the power of the relics of the protomartyr St. Stephen that had only recently arrived in North Africa.

Although prominent local aristocrats and their families often took the lead in patronizing saints' cults, in many communities bishops tried to establish themselves as the arbiters of holiness. They presided at the annual festivals, constructed churches and shrines, and often wrote or commissioned the Lives of the saints. Sometimes they also debunked existing cults or discovered new saints' relics. In Tours, Bishop Martin compelled the ghost of a presumed martyr to admit that he had been only a thief. In Milan Bishop Ambrose thwarted the opposition of an emperor through the timely unearthing of the remains of the martyrs Gervasius and Protasius, who then served as his "bodyguards." Since their functions could vary greatly over time and among different regions, saints' cults showed enormous diversity. Once established, however, they served to reinforce the values of small communities by imposing norms of behavior. Failure to demonstrate proper respect for the possessions of shrines or the demands of the liturgical schedule often left people blinded or lame, unable to participate in ecclesiastical festivals with the other members of the community. Bishops also sometimes threatened adulterers and murderers with the wrath of saints and expulsion from the celebration of the sacraments.

Despite the central role of the bishops, several factors prevented the rise of the cult of saints from becoming simply another enhancement of episcopal power in late antique cities. First, there was still no formal process for creating a cult. All that was required was some combination of a relic (often the saint's body), a shrine (often including the saint's tomb), a *Life,* and the endorsement of other people. Like an emperor's prestige or an aristocrat's reputation, the acknowledgment of sanctity clearly reflected the estimation of popular opinion, which did not always correspond with bishops' preferences. The establishment and maintenance of every saint's cult thus represented repeated acts of negotiation, whether explicit or unspoken, among bishops, local elites, and ordinary believers.

An even greater challenge to episcopal control was the recognition of some people, usually solitary ascetics and sometimes monks, as living holy men or holy women who might therefore also act as powerful patrons in secular affairs. One notorious example was Symeon the Stylite, who stood impassively atop a tall column for decades, until his death in 459. Locals in Syria were so impressed by his transformation into a "bodiless being" suspended between heaven and earth that they requested his intervention in disputes; Roman emperors took his advice; even Armenians, Persians, and Arabs consulted him. Symeon's paradigm of detached devotion inspired Daniel to live on a pillar outside Constantinople. There, a dispute between a usurping emperor and the patriarch of the city ended with both men stretched at the holy man's feet. Immediately after Daniel's death his body was strapped to a plank and displayed "like an icon." In the east the holiness associated with ascetics and monks posed a challenge to bishops and even emperors that eventually culminated in the controversy over iconoclasm. In the west bishops were more successful in confining the location of holiness to the relics of dead saints whose cults they could usually dominate. Bishops in northern Gaul during the 6th century, for instance, were so dismayed by an ascetic who decided to imitate Symeon's example that they demolished his pillar and forced him into a monastery. During the early medieval period, aristocratic pedigree, wealth, and ecclesiastical prominence soon overwhelmed ascetic ideals as the important factors in acknowledging new saints.

Finally, the creeds issued by councils had defined the "communion of the saints" as another object of orthodox faith. Ordinary people could share in this communion through the celebration of sacraments such as the Eucharist, which commemorated Christ's suffering. Bishops and clerics may have presided over these sacraments, but the saints themselves were among the congregation, sometimes even joining in the antiphons from their tombs. Furthermore, often people were first healed at a saint's shrine before they felt worthy to participate: in Tours a mute woman began to chant the Lord's Prayer with the other worshipers only after she recovered her voice at St. Martin's tomb. A miracle of individual healing by a saint validated, and even permitted, a person's membership in that community. Many Christians thus found their true identity and defined their true self in terms of their private relationship with a particular saint. In Cappadocia, for instance, Macrina justified her ascetic life through her "secret name" acquired from St. Thecla, a patron saint for virgins. Definitions of sanctity may well have always been deeply implicated in the maneuvering for power, status, and legitimacy and in enforcing communal norms, but for many people saints and their cults represented, most of all, heartfelt attachments and a loving intimacy.

BIBL.: P. Brown, *Society and the Holy in Late Antiquity* (Berkeley, 1982), and "The Rise and Function of the Holy Man, 1971–1997," *Journal of Early Christian Studies* 6 (1998): 353–376. G. Fowden, "The Pagan Holy Man in Late Antique Society," *Journal of Hellenic Studies* 102 (1982): 33–59. R. Van Dam, *Saints and Their Miracles in Late Antique Gaul* (Princeton, 1993).   R.V.

Sanctuary

In the *City of God,* Augustine recalls on several occasions that in August 410, during the sack of Rome by Alaric's Goths, the city's population sought sanctuary in Christian places of worship. He underscores the fact that the pagans abandoned their temples for the churches (3.31), and that the barbarians respected the refuge thus procured. This was certainly not the first time such buildings had been considered possible sanctuaries: such events were already attested in the mid-4th century. The new development, at least if Augustine is telling the truth, was that the churches' status as zones of refuge was now universally acknowledged. This reflects a decisive shift in the history of sanctuaries.

Traditionally, spaces dedicated to the gods in the Hellenistic Roman world were recognized as inviolable by virtue of their sacred character. This began to change, however, probably as the result of the measures successive Christian emperors took to limit the practice of polytheistic cults, before finally banning them altogether. Until that time, particularly in the Greek east, every supplicant who entrusted his salvation to a deity by embracing the altar devoted to him or her became one with that God and as such, beyond reach, since everything found in a sanctuary was considered the property of the deity and therefore protected from theft or assault. Obviously there were countless times when this general principle was not respected. In addition, there was an institutionalized form of inviolability, the strict sense of the Greek term *asulia.* Recognized by the emperors for certain prestigious sanctuaries, it prohibited all violence against persons and their possessions within the confines of a defined space surrounding consecrated places, particularly during festivals.

Under the Christian empire, nothing remained of the old asylum except a very regulated system linked to imperial statues and images, stemming from provisions related to lèse-majesté (see *C.Th.* 9.44 for year 386; adapted in the 6th century, *C.Just.* 1.25.1). The basis for the new form of sanctuary was entirely different and original: it stemmed, first, from the capacity of intercession attributed to bishops, clerics, and even monks, rather than to some acknowledged sacred character of the churches themselves. It was to these new mediators that refugees appealed. Yet they could be sure neither of the success of these mediators' intervention nor of their capacity to protect refugees from their pursuers, especially if such pursuers were representative of the state. A first legal recognition of the inviolability of Christian places of worship was attested in the early 5th century. Two laws—in 419 and 431 (*Sirmond Constitution* 13 and *C.Th.* 9.45.4)—defined precise topographical boundaries, on the model of the ancients, who had pronounced in favor of pagan sanctuaries. Soon, milestones were placed at the borders of sanctuaries (see *Bulletin épigraphique* 1992, 619), monasteries reaped the benefits of their newly protected state, and the old name *asulia* was given them. This development resulted primarily from the repeated interventions of bishops, and even more, perhaps, from the growing sacralization of Christian meeting places. Now it was the powerful intercessor whose relics were found near the altar who tended to be the refugee's acknowledged protector. Such was also the case in Mecca, whose Haram was a protected place for men and even certain animals, but it is a moot question whether other early Islamic sanctuaries or mosques had the same function. Whatever limitations government authorities set on sanctuaries in the east and west, and despite the many real violations recorded here and there, a new geography of the sanctuary had come into being.

BIBL.: A. Ducloux, *Ad ecclesiam confugere: Naissance du droit d'asile dans les églises (IVe–milieu du Ve s.)* (Paris, 1994). Philippe Gauthier, *Symbola: Les étrangers et la justice dans les cités grecques* (Nancy, 1972), 210–284. Hans Langenfeld, *Christianisierungspolitik und Sklavengesetzgebung der römischen Kaiser von Konstantin bis Theodosius II (Bonn, 1977),* 107–209. Kent J. Rigsby, *Asylia: Territorial Inviolability in the Hellenistic World* (Berkeley, 1996).

                M.P.

Saracens

The late 4th century historian Ammianus Marcellinus twice (22.15.2; 23.6.13) explains the name *Saracens* as a designation for nomadic Arabs, the *Scenitae Arabes* ("Arabs who live under tents"). The earliest attestation of the word *Saracen* in this sense occurs in a panegyric of the year 291. But in a more restricted sense it appears as a name for Arabs in the Ḥijāz as early as Ptolemy's *Geography* in the 2nd century and Bar Daisān's *Book of the Laws of Countries* in the early

3rd. Pliny's *Araceni* (*Nat.Hist.* 6.32, 157) appear to refer to the same people in the first century.

It is therefore likely that a word that had once referred to a specific group of Arabs was extended in the 3rd century to designate nomadic Arabs in general. The etymology of the word in both its restricted and its general application is still controversial. Some have seen Saracen (*Sarakēnos* in Greek) as an adjective from a place name, Saraka. Others have postulated a connection with the Semitic root for "east" *(šrq)*, whereas more recently a derivation from the word *šrkt*, understood to mean a confederation, has found favor. But this meaning for *škrt* has now been soundly demolished by Michael MacDonald. The problem remains unsolved.

The development of Saracen confederations in late antiquity, notably those of the Lakhmids and Ghassanids, is well documented in Procopius, and the fortunes of both may be surveyed in entries under their names in the present volume.

BIBL.: D. F. Graf and M. O'Connor, "The Origin of the Term Saracen and the Rawwāfa Inscriptions," *Byzantinische Studien* 4 (1977), 52–66. G. W. Bowersock, "Arabs and Saracens in the Historia Augusta," *Bonner Historia-Augusta-Colloquium* 1984–85 (Bonn, 1987), 71–80. M. MacDonald, "Quelques réflexions sur les Saracènes: L'inscription de Rawwāfa et l'armée romaine," in *Présence arabe dans le Croissant fertile avant l'Hégire*, ed. H. Lozachmeur (Paris, 1995), 93–101.   G.W.B.

Sarapis

A synthetic god associated in legend (Tacitus 4.83) with the foundation of Alexandria, the Sarapis image drew on both the Egyptian funerary god Osiris in his avatar as the Apis bull (an ancient cult based in Memphis) and a Greek iconography and ideology probably inherited from the god Asclepius. Asclepian traits include, for example, the representation of Sarapis as a bearded and enthroned male figure and a traditional association with healing cults. The particularly resilient (through the late 4th century) cult of Sarapis in Canopus, near Alexandria, claimed healing powers through incubation almost from its inception (Strabo 17.1.17).

If Sarapis originally appealed only to elite Greeks, the god had become largely indigenized by the Roman period, above all through his consortship with the popular goddess Isis. Thus 2nd and 3rd century temples that focus on Isis as an agrarian goddess might be designated as temples of both deities, or simply of Sarapis. Egyptian festivals of the Roman period show Sarapis in various forms, representing in Greek communities imperial power and in more Egyptian or Egyptianized communities an agrarian force like Osiris.

Through the spread of this ecumenical image and cult throughout the Mediterranean world during the Graeco-Roman period, the Sarapis Temple of Alexandria became by the 4th century an ideological center of traditional religious observance in the Roman world and a bulwark against encroaching Christian authority. In the late 4th century social tensions and the machinations of church leaders in Alexandria and Constantinople came to a head, and in 391 a combined force of monks, Christian confraternities, soldiers, and a sympathetic mob, all under the Alexandrian bishop Theophilus, demolished the Sarapeum and its images. For Christian writers (Rufinus, Sozomen, Theodoret) and some of their opponents (e.g., Eunapius, *VS* 471–72) this destruction signified a decisive victory of Christianity over the established native cults.

BIBL.: P. M. Fraser, "Two Studies on the Cult of Sarapis in the Hellenistic World," *Opuscula atheniensia* 3 (1960): 1–54. Wilhelm Hornstable, *Sarapis* (Leiden, 1973). G. J. F. Kater-Sibbes, *Preliminary Catalogue of Sarapis Monuments* (Leiden, 1973). Françoise Thelamon, *Païens et chrétiens au IVe siècle: L'apport de l'"Histoire ecclésiastique" de Rufin d'Aquilée* (Paris, 1981).   D.T.F.

Sarcophagi

The sarcophagus, the coffinlike container for the body of the deceased, usually oblong in shape, was popular for the burial of well-to-do citizens from the 2nd century on (after the change from cremation to inhumation). In late antiquity, sarcophagi were fashioned from materials as diverse as porphyry, marble, lead, or plaster, and they took a variety of forms (with reliefs on one or more sides, with a curved or pitched lid, with or without acroteria, and so forth). Late antique sarcophagi are usually classified, and hence studied, according to the reliefs that they bear, which itself is interesting. Like the decorated clothing of late antiquity, the sarcophagus ornamented with reliefs brought imagery into a direct relationship to the body, but in perpetuity. The main centers of the production of sarcophagi in late antiquity included Rome, Constantinople, southern Gaul, and Asia Minor. After the 5th century, sarcophagi become rare.

The preponderance of surviving sarcophagi are carved in marble, and unfinished examples indicate that the form was first roughed out at the quarry. This rough carving may have taken into account the size and position of reliefs that were ultimately intended for the piece, but those intentions may not always have been fulfilled. One such case is an exquisite 3rd century fragment from Acilia, now in the Museo Nazionale delle Terme in Rome, on which the hands of several figures have been brought together and pulled forward from the main surface of the relief by the sculptor, who clearly took advantage of a projecting block of rough marble left in place at the side of the piece, probably for a lion's head. An industrial production of sarcophagi is indicated by the unfinished heads on many pieces, which would have been completed with the portrait features of the deceased, perhaps in wax or paint. Mass production seems to have reached a peak in Rome in the late 3rd century through the first half of the 4th. Thereafter stands a series of singular examples, such as the great sarcophagus of Junius Bassus (359) recovered from Old St. Peter's, which suggests a fundamental shift in patronage.

Themes on late antique sarcophagi include stories from mythology (Dionysius, Hercules, Meleager), garden images (vintaging *putti,* vine scrolls), apotropaic devices (lions' heads, griffins), and battle scenes. Christian subjects on sarcophagi of the 3rd and early 4th century closely parallel those found in catacomb paintings (signitive images from the Old and New Testaments), as do the Jewish sarcophagi from Rome (menorahs). As one moves through the 4th and into the 5th century, however, the influence of the monumental public art of the Christian basilica is detectable in scenes such as the *Traditio legis* and the assembly of the apostles around Christ. What was presumably Constantine's sarcophagus in Rome (now called the sarcophagus of Helena) shows a battle scene; that of his daughter, Constantia, is decorated with vintaging *putti.* Both of these pieces are massive and are carved from porphyry, as are many of the later imperial sarcophagi, from Constantinople, with their simpler decoration of wreaths and garlands.

BIBL.: Giuseppe Bovini and Hugo Brandenburg, eds., *Repertorium der christlich-antiken Sarkophage,* vol. 1 (Wiesbaden, 1967). Philip Grierson, "The Tombs and Obits of the Byzantine Emperors, 337–1042," *Dumbarton Oaks Papers* 16 (1962): 1–63. Adia Konikoff, *Sarcophagi from the Jewish Catacombs of Ancient Rome: A Catalogue Raisonné,* rev. ed. (Stuttgart, 1990).   W.T.

Sassanians

The Sassanian dynasty ruled Iran from the 3rd to the 7th century C.E. The Sassanians claimed descent, probably spuriously, from the Achaemenian royal family. The Sassanian period witnessed a transformation of Iranian society into the dominant culture east of the Tigris River.

The dynasty began in 224 when troops of the last Parthian (Arsacid) monarch Ardawan (Artabanus) V failed to crush a rebellion that had broken out in Fars (Persia). The rebel leader Ardashir, whose clansmen were governors at the city of Istakhr, took over. Ardashir I had a sacred fire lit at Ctesiphon to commemorate his investiture as the first King of Kings of the Sassanian dynasty (named after one of his ancestors, Sasan) and to signal that Zoroastrianism was the regime's official faith.

During the late Parthian period the Roman empire had extended its reach into Mesopotamia. Ardashir attacked the Romans, capturing the trading center of Hatra in 239. He also brought the eastern Iranian provinces of Kirman, Sistan, Makran, and Khurasan

(Abarshahr) firmly under Sassanian control. In administrative matters, however, much of what was attributed to Ardashir appears to have been merely an attempt to extol the virtues of a dynastic founder. Actual restructuring of the state took place after his time. A case in point is that various provinces were still governed not by Persian lords but by Parthian nobles. Yet Ardashir did appoint a chief of scribes, a head of protocol, a chief justice, and a leader of the Zoroastrian clergy. In 240, his health failing, Ardashir abdicated in favor of his son Shapur.

Shapur I left behind an inscription at the site of Naqsh-i Rostam. This inscription, written three times in different languages—Pahlavi (Middle Persian), Middle Parthian, and Greek—recorded the king's genealogy, accomplishments, beliefs, family, and courtiers. Names and titles of Shapur's queens reveal that he had consolidated his power largely through matrimonial alliances, and attached to his harem were the daughters of many regional noblemen, such as the Saka (Scythian) leader. Shortly after he gained power, Shapur was confronted by a Roman invasion led by the emperor Gordian III. Gordian lost his life to Sassanian troops in 244. Philip the Arab took over the Roman forces and made peace, but a few years later, he led the Romans into Armenia. After repelling that incursion, the Sassanian monarch sought revenge. Shapur commanded Iranian soldiers to invade the Roman province of Syria, sacking Antioch in 258. The new Roman emperor, Valerian, was captured and taken to Iran, where he died. Shapur erected rock reliefs to commemorate his victories, including one of Valerian kneeling. Captured Roman senators and soldiers who were resettled in Khuzistan, near Jewish communities, brought Christianity with them. Shapur incorporated lands along the southern shore of the Persian Gulf, including Bahrain and Oman, into the Sassanian empire and then awarded himself the title "Mazda-worshiping lord, king of kings of Iran and non-Iran" *(mazdesn bay shahan shah eran ud aneran).*

Shapur began a reorganization of the state bureaucracy, which had been Hellenized under the Seleucids and early Parthians. Pahlavi became the spoken language of the royal court and upper classes, and slowly spread throughout the land. Aramaic served as the scribal language. The position of satrap (provincial governor) persisted, with the king's sons being appointed to these posts. So did another position, that of the margrave or *marzban* (frontier governor) who oversaw border regions. A Zoroastrian chief magus *(mowbedan mowbed)* was permanently attached to the royal court, although Shapur also provided the prophet Mani with royal patronage, much to the magi's dismay. The 3rd century witnessed the beginning of a standardized coinage—gold *(denar),* silver *(drahm),* and copper/bronze *(pashiz),* in multiple denominations. Sassanian silver became the medium of exchange, even in international trade—amber, fur, gems, and walrus ivory from the steppe were paid for with silver coins and vessels, for example. Sassanian craftsmen and -women produced a range of silver objects bearing high relief images on the exteriors and interiors. Hunting and banqueting scenes were especially popular, as were images of young women.

The period immediately following Shapur I's reign was entwined with the expansion and persecution of Manichaeism, culminating in Mani's execution (ca. 277) during Bahram II's reign. In 309 Shapur II was appointed king of kings, prior to his birth. His mother acted as regent for the first sixteen years of his life. Politically, Shapur II's reign saw tussles over Armenia with the Roman-Byzantine emperor Constantius (Constantine), the invasion of Mesopotamia by Julian the Apostate (363), and incursions by Arab tribes into the agriculturally vital southern region of Mesopotamia—attacks that Shapur attempted to halt by constructing long, heavily defended walls (limes). To shore up his support inside Iran, Shapur reorganized the magi into a rigid hierarchy

Silver plate with image of Peroz or Kavad I hunting rams. Iran, late 5th to early 6th century.

that attempted to spread an orthodox version of Zoroastrianism throughout the kingdom. A class system that had existed for several centuries was institutionalized and given added legitimacy by the Zoroastrian faith, recognizing it as divinely ordained. In that social structure the king of kings stood at the apex, followed by the great feudal families (waspuhragan) and the magi (mowbedan). Next came members of the high nobility (wuzurgan), followed by free men and women (azadan) and then scribes (dibiran). Thereafter stood merchants (wazaraganan), artisans (hutukhshan), farmers (dahigan), herdsmen (wastaryoshan), and finally slaves (anshahrigan).

Conversion to the official religion of the empire usually did not free a slave but merely protected him or her from being sold to a non-Zoroastrian master or mistress. Only if a slave who converted to Zoroastrianism had a non-Zoroastrian owner could he or she purchase freedom. An owner could, however, manumit a slave. Slaves were also owned by temple foundations, in which case they were governed by the laws of the religion that the particular temple served.

In the late 5th century Iran was invaded from the northeast by a tribe known as the Hephthalites, or "White Huns." Those nomads defeated the Sassanian ruler Peroz and took his son Kavad captive. Kavad was raised among the Hephthalites and returned to Iran to claim the throne with their support in 488. While these political events were transpiring, heavy taxes were extracted from peasants and merchants to finance battles, support the upper classes, and pay tribute to the nomads. Disenchanted portions of the population united in rebellion behind an individual named Mazdak. Mazdak and his followers were eventually defeated; many were executed and others were persecuted.

Administrative and social changes aimed at preventing future uprisings were initiated by Kavad's son, Khosro I, known as anoshagruwan/anushirvan, "he of the immortal soul." Tax reform was instituted once a population census had been taken, and all land was allocated to specific tax brackets based on water rights and average annual productivity. Revenues that had formerly gone to local nobles were channeled into a central government treasury. Taxes on earnings and land were collected in three installments each year. The reforms of Diocletian seem to have been the prototype for Khosro's. Professional tax collectors and scribes were placed in charge of the system's administration, and this bureaucratic elite gradually replaced the older noble ranks. Dams and irrigation channels conducting water from the Euphrates and the Tigris to the fields of Mesopotamia were repaired. Salination in that region, the empire's breadbasket, was held at bay by this swift-flowing water. As a result, the agrarian productivity of Mesopotamia reached its peak during the 6th century. Next, the military was overhauled by disbanding feudal regiments and creating a conscripted army. Commanders of each unit were granted landholdings by the state as part of their salary, creating a class of petty landlords *(dehgans/dehkans)*. Defense of the empire from external foes was handled by placing the new military units under the command of four generals *(spahbeds)*, each of whom was responsible for guarding the border at one corner of the empire.

With the empire in order, Khosro turned on Byzantium, invading Syria in 540 and sacking Antioch, then bringing the rebellious Armenians—who had become Christians—back under Sassanian political control. Next, Sassanian troops drove off the Hephthalites. Finally, between the years 575 and 598, the Sassanian navy landed troops in Yemen and installed an Iranian viceroy there.

Propelled by military superiority, the Sassanians were able to seize maritime trade in the Persian Gulf and the Arabian Sea from the Indians. Expansion of the empire's territory and influence facilitated not only water-borne business, for overland commerce thrived too. One trade route led eastward from Ctesiphon to Hamadān, then to Ray, on to Nishapur and Merv, from there to Balkh or else Kashgar, and eventually to central Asia and China. Silk, ceramics, and silver flowed along this route. Another route branched off from Nishapur to Herāt, then Peshawar, and onward to northern India, bringing spices to Iran. A third route went to the southeast, from Ctesiphon, via Istakhr and the city of Kirman, to the lower Indus Valley, where gold was traded for cotton. To the south a route connected Ctesiphon to Hira and then ran down along the northern coast of Arabia to Oman. And to the west, trade flowed between Ctesiphon, Damascus, and Jerusalem, carrying goods from China and India. So, although often disrupted by warfare, trade linked the people of Sassanian Iran with the Roman, Byzantine, Indian, and Chinese societies—forming ties that withstood the fiercest of conflicts in the name of profit. These trade routes also facilitated the transfer of another vital commodity—knowledge, via scholars and texts.

The Sassanian judicial system was reorganized, with magi becoming the judges not only in the Zoroastrian community but in intercommunal disputes. Archaeological excavations have turned up stamp seals, ostraca, and parchments that, together with law books written in Pahlavi and Syriac during the 6th century, facilitate reconstruction of the Sassanian legal system. Several aspects of Iranian law were finely developed—marriage, commerce, and religious status are three instances. Unlike men, women could not ordinarily arrange their own marriages. Only if a close male relative was not available to make the arrangements or the woman was a widow or had been divorced could she choose her husband. A woman was not permitted more than one husband at a time, although men could take as many wives as they could support. Sassanian secular law followed Zoroastrian practice in assigning the wives of a single man differential standing within the family unit, based on the women's legal status prior

to marriage, the nature of their marriage contracts, and whether they had borne children. Divorce could be initiated by either the husband or the wife, but usually both parties had to consent to it. A wife's consent was not required if she was infertile or had committed adultery and that charge had been proved in a court of law. A woman could divorce her husband if he was infertile or if he changed religion. A man could divorce his wife on any one of four grounds: adultery, sterility, sorcery, and concealing that she was menstruating—this fourth stipulation was related to a belief, shared by many of Iran's religious communities, that having sex with one's wife while she was in menses stripped a man of his ritual purity. When divorce was granted, the husband was required to provide financial support for his ex-wife and all their children, even if the wife had initiated the divorce or had committed adultery. In the area of commerce, major dealings had to be recorded, witnessed, signed, and sealed. Copies of contracts were provided to all parties involved. One copy of each contract involving long-term or high-value transactions had to be deposited in a local archive. Loans could be given with or without interest, and with or without a cosigner or other type of security. Disputes that could not be resolved through arbitration were referred to the courts, where attorneys presented the competing positions to a judge, the judge examined written documents, interrogated witnesses, and passed verdicts. A judge's ruling could be appealed to a superior justice. Each religious community—of which Zoroastrians, Christians, and Jews were the major ones—was permitted to administer its own internal affairs and report to the royal court through a chief cleric. Non-Zoroastrian adult men did, however, have to pay an annual poll tax *(gazidag)*. This levy was collected within each sect semiannually and forwarded to the state department of revenue.

Secular and religious literature flourished in 5th and 6th century Iran. Under royal patronage the Iranian national epic, *Khwaday Namag,* from which the New Persian *Shahnama* (Book of Kings) derives, was codified in Pahlavi. At the same time, the text of the *Avesta* was fixed. Literature in the genre of advice *(andarz)* manuals for princes, so popular later in Islamic times, also began to develop. Within the Jewish community, the Babylonian Talmud was compiled.

When Khosro I died in 579, his son through a Turkish queen, the prince Hormizd IV, became king. The Byzantines, sensing weakness, attacked Iran. The Sassanian state was defended by forces following a general named Bahram Chobin, who claimed descent from Parthian nobility. After turning back the invaders, this commander rebelled against Hormizd. At the same time, other nobles at Ctesiphon seized Hormizd, blinded him, and placed his son Khosro II on the throne. Bahram Chobin marched against the new king of kings, who fled to Constantinople, supposedly married a daughter of the Byzantine emperor Maurice, and, with assistance from the Byzantine army, regained the Sassanian throne. Khosro II now took the title *parwez/parviz*, "the victorious." He ceded territory west of the Tigris River to the Byzantines in thanks for the help they had extended, and for a time cordial relations ensued between the two empires. But when Maurice was assassinated, Khosro II turned against Byzantium, capturing Damascus in 613 and Jerusalem in 614. Legend has it that he attacked Jerusalem to find and present the relics of the True Cross to his Christian wife Shirin. Soon the new emperor of the west, Heraclius, retaliated. Heraclius and his troops sailed across the Black Sea, drove Sassanian forces out of Armenia, then moved into Azerbaijan and sacked an important Zoroastrian fire temple center at Ganzak (modern Takht-i Sulayman) before continuing southward to pillage the area east of Ctesiphon. Members of the Sassanian royalty sought to placate the Byzantines by deposing and slaying Khosro II in 628. His son Shiroy (Kavad II) made peace with Heraclius, restoring Jerusalem and the Christian relics to the Byzantines.

During the political turbulence that followed, a time made worse by an epidemic of bubonic plague, a daughter of Khosro II named Boran (Borandukht) was installed as ruler and minted her own coinage. But she fell ill and died after little more than a year. As in earlier times, again an Iranian dynasty was collapsing due to internal strife, poor socioeconomic management, and external attacks. On-again, off-again wars with the Byzantines had laid waste the lowlands of Mesopotamia, exposing the southwestern frontier to Arab tribes. Arab Muslim soldiers began invading the Sassanian empire in 632. In 651 the king Yazdegird III was slain by a miller while taking refuge from the invaders, ending the Sassanian dynasty. Sassanian cultural forms persisted for many centuries, however, combining with the mores and beliefs of the Muslim newcomers to create the society of Islamic Iran.

BIBL.: Averil Cameron, "Agathias on the Sasanians," *Dumbarton Oaks Papers* 23 (1969). N. N. Chegini and Alexander V. Nikitin, "Sasanian Iran—Economy, Society, Arts, and Crafts," in *History of Civilizations of Central Asia*, vol. 3, ed. Boris A. Litvinsky et al. (Paris, 1996), 35–77. Arthur Christensen, *L'Iran sous les Sassanides*, 2nd ed. (Copenhagen, 1944). P. Crone, "Kavad's Heresy and Mazdak's Revolt," *Iran* 29 (1991): 21–42. J. Howard-Johnson, "The Two Great Powers in Late Antiquity: A Comparison," in *States, Resources and Armies*, ed. Averil Cameron (Princeton, 1996), 125–155. Ahmad Tafazzoli and Albert L. Khromov, "Sasanian Iran—Intellectual Life," in *History of Civilizations of Central Asia*, vol. 3, ed. B. A. Litvinsky et al. (Paris, 1996), 79–102. J.K.C.

Scetis

Situated in the Wadi 'n Natrun, the monastic center of Scetis was more remote from the Nile Delta than the centers in Nitria and Kellia. Its name comes from the Coptic *shi hēt*, "to weight the heart," fitting for a place devoted to ascetic practice. A little more than 20 miles long, the wadi is an area of low elevation where water can be found. In antiquity it was known for its rich deposits of natron. Monasticism in Scetis was founded by Macarius the Great (ca. 300–390). A confused biographical tradition links him with other individuals, not least St. Antony and Macarius the Alexandrian (from whom he is distinguished by the epithet "the Egyptian"). At the same time, his reputation encouraged biographers to appropriate his achievements to the advantage of their own heroes. The portrait presented by Palladius has a reasonably firm basis (*Hist.Laus.* 17).

Colonized initially because of its remoteness and tranquillity, Scetis quickly became both crowded and organized. The *Apophthegmata patrum* probably originated in Scetis and features many of its prominent inhabitants, including Paphnutius and Arsenius. By the end of the 4th century, there were four distinct communities there, each with churches and priests of their own. Of these four monasteries, three have remained active until the present day: St. Bishoi, St. Macarius, and Baramus (from the Coptic: of the Romans). The fourth, the Monastery of John the Little, was deserted in the 14th century. Another, the Syrian Monastery, or the Monastery of the Holy Virgin and St. John Kame, which stands near St. Bishoi, was established in the 8th century, although tradition provides a 4th century pedigree linking it with St. Ephrem.

Internal turmoil erupted among the monks in the late 4th century in conflicts over Origenism and anthropomorphism. Many Greek-speaking monks adhered to the allegorical interpretation of the Bible taught by Origen of Alexandria (d. 254), while some Coptic-speaking monks preferred a more literal reading of Scripture. In 399 Theophilus, archbishop of Alexandria, condemned anthropomorphism, a literal understanding of God's having human attributes. In the subsequent uproar, Theophilus reversed his position, condemning Origenism. Many monks fled Egypt for Constantinople and Palestine.

A few years later the communities in Scetis came under threat from an external enemy, the destructive raiding of desert tribes. Scetis was attacked three times in the 5th century (407, 410, and 434) and once in the 6th (ca. 570). Between the Council of Chalcedon and the reign of Justinian it recovered remarkably, especially under the leadership of Daniel (b. 485). The 6th century devastation left a deeper wound, which remained unhealed for nearly a hundred years: John Moschus had almost nothing to report when he visited Scetis ca. 578. In the earlier period, however, imperial patronage and theological division contributed to an extensive building program, and economic self-sufficiency in agricultural produce and marketable craftwork was a feature of the late 5th century in particular. At that time, the communities reflected the doctrinal conflicts of the empire at large, but under the influence of Justinian's more forceful policies, Scetis became a stronghold of Monophysite sentiment and practice, for several decades standing as an alternative patriarchate to the Chalcedonians of Alexandria.

BIBL.: Derwas J. Chitty, *The Desert a City* (Oxford, 1966; repr. London, 1977). W. H. C. Frend, *The Rise of the Monophysite Movement* (Cambridge, Eng., 1972). Otto F. A. Meinardus, *Monks and Monasteries of the Egyptian Deserts* (Cairo, 1961). Tim Vivian, "The Monasteries of the Wadi Natrun, Egypt: A Monastic and Personal Journey," *American Benedictine Review* 49, no. 2 (June 1998). Hugh G. Evelyn White, *The Monasteries of the Wādi 'n Natrūn,* part 2: *The History of the Monasteries of Nitria and of Scetis;* part 3: *The Architecture and Archaeology* (New York, 1932, 1933).

P.R.

Sculpture

The transformation of Nicomedia into a tetrarchic residence, then the creation of Constantinople and the progressive displacement toward the east of the government's vitality, did not result in major modifications in the activities of sculptors and stonecutters. The quarries of Proconnesus became active again after a decline in the second half of the 3rd century, but even in the 2nd century they were the most important quarries of the empire, supplying stone for all types of sculpture, including statuary, sarcophagi, and architectural sculpture. The extremely Hellenized tastes of the 4th century aristocracy were indistinguishable from those of the Antonii and the Severi. The sculptors of Aphrodisias were already in Rome and were appreciated in the western and eastern capitals. The use of marble in the development of capital cities had become commonplace, thanks to a meticulously organized process of extraction and transport.

Nascent Christianity rejected the use of statuary to express its conception of the divine, but the educated elites appreciated its beauty. The destruction of "idols" or their desecration (crosses were cut in them) was far from systematic. Statuary in marble, bronze, and ivory from pagan temples was collected in repositories or reused in public spaces such as the Baths of Zeuxippos in Constantinople and the hippodromes (Plataean offering of Delphi, bronze horses of the Sphendone). Wealthy citizens, who often remained attached to pagan culture even after they had become Christians, kept diverse collections of statues in their homes, as the excavations of residences in Athens, Carthage, Antioch, Silaterga (near Constantinople), Rome (the famous Esquiline complex), and even Chiragan in Aquitaine have shown. These statues, often small in size, were maintained, reworked, refurbished, or sculpted de novo. Hence, in Rome, the statues of the Via delle Sette Sale, attributed to the Antonine age, were signed by 4th century sculptors from Aphrodisias. The Ara Pacis was restored in the early 4th century; the Arch of

Constantine was constructed from a "patchwork" of fragments, new and recycled. Naturally this taste for classical statuary explains the conservatism and technical virtuosity of works from the 4th century and the first half of the 5th. Emperors, their family members, and local governors placed statues of themselves in public squares and along avenues (there are good examples in Ephesus) until the early 7th century. The chariot driver Porphyrius was honored with several gilded statues at the hippodrome of Constantinople.

After a marked drop-off in the second half of the 3rd century, the production of sarcophagi resumed and remained strong. Quality remained high in the 4th century and the first decades of the 5th. Until 410 Rome was one of the principal centers of production and exportation of sarcophagi, including exceptional items such as the sarcophagus of Junius Bassus (d. 359). Other centers were also created, either under Rome's influence or independently; sarcophagi were produced using marble (Aquitaine), marble and local stone (Milan, Arles), and local stone alone (Spain, Salona, Carthage). Constantinople created its own style and iconography, which spread to the Aegean basin and Asia Minor, and also to Ravenna. In the second half of the 5th century and throughout the 6th, human figures became less common and the Cross and plant motifs more prominent.

Architecture was the primary consumer of stone and marble sculpture. With the resumption of urban construction and the building of luxurious residences for magnates, there was a renewal of architectural splendor. A characteristic style developed alongside a thoughtful use of architectural *spolia*. Colonnades proliferated along the *cardines* and *decumani* of large and midsize cities (Constantinople, Jerusalem, Sardes); in Antioch and Palmyra, preexisting colonnades were consistently maintained despite earthquakes and fires. New types of constructions sprang up, primarily churches. Whether built on a central plan or with basilicas, churches required a large quantity of molded and sculpted pieces for thresholds, doorjambs and lintels, cornices, free-standing supports (columns, mullions), and secondary furnishings (parapets, liturgical articles). This huge output led to "mass produced" foundations and capitals. A Constantinopolitan style gradually took root. In the manufacture of Corinthian capitals, the number of leaves per wreath dropped, and leaves were made to cling more closely to the abacus. The capitals could thus be more easily transported with less risk of breakage, and above all, they could bear the weight of arches, which were rapidly replacing architraves. The Severan Baroque or other early forms were also borrowed: for example, capitals were divided into two zones, and the upper zone was decorated with doves, griffin protomas, or rams. Grandiose works were produced in the 6th century. The Church of St. Polyeuctos (ca. 524–527), built by Julia Anicia, was truly revolutionary. The first truncated or "basket" capitals made their appearance, sumptuously decorated with oriental motifs, which often imitated gold plate (openwork sculpture imitating *interasile* silver). Very thick architraves were recessed with niches or with arches sporting peacocks with their tails spread. Marble pavings and carved plaques added to the brilliance of the building. Justinian used the same type of ornament for Hagia Sophia, the Church of SS. Sergius and Bacchus, and the reconstruction of the Church of the Holy Apostles.

Altar tables, either rectangular or in the form of a Greek sigma, copied from the tables of the *stibadia* (semicircular seats for guests), were produced in great number, as were low pillars and *colonnettes* to enclose altars. Two specific types of furnishings made their appearance, the pulpit or rostrum and the ciborium.

The works of the capital city spread widely to the Aegean basin, as attested by the Church of St. John of Ephesus, the churches of Ravenna (and Porec) and Cyrenaica, renovations in the mosques of Cairo and Tunisia, and the shipwrecked cargo of Marzamemi. Other quarries in the region (Thasos, Phrygia, and Aphrodisias, as well as Thessalia and Sangarios) imitated these works and exported them in turn. The workshops of Attica, while sometimes adopting the style of the capital city, kept their own ornamentation for a long time. Of the regions that used local stone, Lycia, northern Syria, and Egypt were prolific in their production of sculpture. Depictions of human and animal figures were particularly splendid.

The west was not as rich in architectural sculpture, and the reuse of old materials was often more prominent there. Sbeitla and Brevigliera (El-Khadra) were the exceptions in North Africa and the Tripolitana, as were the marble capitals of Aquitaine in western Europe.

The last glimmer of late antique sculpture shone among the Umayyads. All the same, the sculpted and molded capitals and ornamentation in the large palaces (Qaṣr el Heir el Gharbi, Mshatta, and Khirbat al-Mafjar) seem to have taken their model more from Persia than from the Graeco-Roman world.

BIBL.: S. G. Bassett, "Sculpture and Tradition in the Baths of Zeuxippus," *American Journal of Archaeology* 100 (1996): 631–669. N. Hannestad, *Tradition in Late Antique Sculpture* (Aarhus, 1994). B. Kiilerich, *Late Fourth-Century Classicism in the Plastic Arts* (Odense, 1993). C. Strube, *Baudekoration in Nordsyrischen Kalksteinmassiv* (Mainz, 1993). A. Cutler, "The Righthand's Cunning: Craftsmanship and Demand for Art in Late Antiquity and the Early middle Ages," *Speculum* 72 (1997): 971–994.   J.-P.S.

Scythopolis

The city of Scythopolis (biblical and modern Beth Shean), in the Jordan Valley, was situated in a fertile region with abundant water, at the junction of the international roads running east from the seacoast (via Caesarea) toward Syria and Arabia and from the Galilee and Syria to Jerusalem. Settlement began in the fifth millennium B.C.E. and continued in the Bronze and Iron Ages. The Greek and Roman polis was called Nysa-Scythopolis, commonly known in the abbreviated form Scythopolis. The Hebrew and Aramaic name Beth Shean, or Beishan, continued to exist, and the city survived in Arabic as Baysan.

Scythopolis was a major Roman city; in the 1st century it was a prominent member of the league of the Decapolis. Local tradition, known from Pliny and Solinus, told that it was founded by Dionysus, who buried his nurse Nysa and settled his Scythian companions here. Massive building activity reshaped the city during the *pax Romana*, mostly during the 2nd and 3rd centuries. Extensive archaeological excavations have been carried out in the city center and in some suburbs, revealing a large and lavish urban area. In the center was the acropolis (originally the biblical mound, or *tell*), at the summit of which was the temple of Zeus Akraios. In the civic center below the acropolis were temples and cult places, colonnaded streets, squares and porticoes, a theater, an odeon, bathhouses, nymphaea, basilica, and other public monuments. A hippodrome (later transformed into an amphitheater) was erected in the south suburb. Roman Scythopolis was ornamented by architectural decoration and statues. Greek inscriptions mention the contribution of the city *boulē*, various officials, and many private donors.

The city economy of late antique Scythopolis was based on the agricultural produce of the region; most famous were its linen products, classified as most costly in the price edict of Diocletian and praised in other 4th century sources. The population of the city was mixed: pagans were the majority, though there were also large Jewish and Samaritan communities. A Christian congregation existed there no later than the 3rd century; Eusebius praises Procopius, a reader, translator, and exorcist in the church of Scythopolis, who suffered martyrdom in Caesarea in 303. During the 4th century, Christians, who according to Epiphanius were Arians, became the majority. The Arian bishop Patrophilus acted in Scythopolis in the mid-4th century, but there is no mention of Arians in later periods. All the city temples were apparently abandoned during the late 4th century.

An earthquake damaged Scythopolis in 363, followed by extensive building activity that continued during the 5th and early 6th century. Before 409 Scythopolis was chosen as the capital of the new province of Palaestina Secunda. Many of the (previously unknown) provincial governors (archons) are mentioned in building inscriptions. The general demographic and economic prosperity of Palestine also influenced Scythopolis, which reached its peak in size and population in the first half of the 6th century. The city was encircled by a wall with gates (mentioned in the Halakhic inscription found in the synagogue at

Rehov, south of Beth Shean). Its area (including the extramural suburbs) was some 150 hectares; the population probably reached thirty to forty thousand. The excavations reveal a rich and lively city furnished with bathhouses, commercial streets and plazas, marketplaces, and the like. The theater (the exact nature of which is unknown) probably remained in use up to the 6th century. The amphitheater remained in use (probably for sport and entertainment rather than bloody spectacles) during the 5th century.

Social and cultural life in Scythopolis concentrated in and around the churches. Several churches have been discovered, the most important of which is a circular-plan church built on the acropolis; additional churches and monasteries have been found mostly in the northern suburb. Others, including a church of a certain martyr Basilius, are mentioned in sources and inscriptions. Excavations have also revealed two synagogues, Jewish and Samaritan. The most famous native of the city was Cyril of Scythopolis, the hagiographer of the Judaean Desert Fathers.

The Samaritan revolts of 529 caused some damage to the city, and they were followed by the bubonic plague of 541–542. These events appear to mark a turning point and the beginning of a slow decline noted in other sites in Palestine as well. The Sassanian conquest of Palestine, while not damaging Scythopolis in particular, ended the Byzantine rule of Palestine and hastened the decline of the city. Scythopolis was taken by the Muslims around 635, following their victory near Pella (Fihl). No violence seems to have followed the conquest, but the gradual decline continued, augmented by the selection of another city, Tiberias, as the capital of Jund al-Urdunn. Some revival is discerned from the days of the Umayyad caliph Hishām (724–743), who built a new market in the town center, but it survived for only a short period. A strong earthquake completely destroyed the town on 18 January 749. A settlement of rural character, built on top of the ruins, existed through the Crusader and Mamluk periods. The medieval settlement of Baysan was concentrated on the plateau south of the Roman-Byzantine city center but never reached the size and importance of Scythopolis.

BIBL.: See archaeological reports by G. Foerster and Y. Tsafrir (Hebrew University excavations) and G. Mazor and R. Bar-Nathan (Israel Antiquities Authority excavations) in various issues of *Excavations and Surveys in Israel*, from vol. 6 (1987–1988) on. M. Avi-Yonah, "Scythopolis," *Israel Exploration Journal* (Jerusalem) 12 (1962): 123–134. G. M. Fitzgerald, *Bet-Shan Excavations 1921–1923: The Arab and Byzantine Levels* (Philadelphia, 1931). G. M. Fitzgerald, *A Sixth Century Monastery at Bet-Shan* (Philadelphia, 1939). A. Rowe, *The Topography and History of Beth-Shan* (Philadelphia, 1930). Y. Tsafrir and G. Foerster, "Urbanism at Scythopolis in the Fourth–Seventh Centuries," *Dumbarton Oaks Papers* 51 (1997). Y.T.

Seleuceia-Ctesiphon

The metropolitan area of Seleuceia-Ctesiphon, known to the Arabs as Mada'in, included two different settlements on either side of the Tigris, just below the Diyala confluence. Old Seleucia on the right bank, founded by Seleucus I in the late 4th century B.C.E., had by the 3rd century C.E. lost its former importance. The site had become a suburb of the late Sassanian capital of Ctesiphon, though much of it had been reduced to archaeological ground. However, occupational traces of a nonurban nature survived, and there were even some large buildings standing in isolation. At Tell 'Umar, Khosro II built an imposing elliptical tower incorporating the ruins of the old theater of Seleuceia. In early Islamic times handicrafts were established in the area, as is shown by the existence of kilns that supplied glass vessels to nearby settlements or remoter markets.

Seleuceia's successor as the main urban center was the circular city of Veh-Ardashir, also known as New Seleuceia, or Kokhe. This city was founded by Ardashir I on the left bank of the river, opposite Seleuceia; remains from the Parthian period are also attested here. Fieldwork has unearthed near the massive walls a large residential and handicraft quarter consisting of large blocks separated by streets. The house style shows some architectural pretensions, with an *iwan* opening on to a courtyard. Individual dwellings lay inside the blocks, with access provided by narrow lanes; the main streets were lined with shops. In addition to houses and shops, these were numerous metalwork and glass production facilities. Several locally produced bronze objects of Roman type (fibulae, statuettes) and a Gandharan relief reflect the Sassanids' wars in the east and west.

The circular town was not only a place of residence and work. A large late Sassanian building constructed of baked bricks with fine stucco decoration has been identified as a Christian church. There is no direct evidence linking it with the *katholikos* of Seleuceia attested by the written sources, but it is certain that Christians and Jews lived in the town. The inhabitation of Veh-Ardashir continued down to the 12th or 13th century, though it was by then mainly restricted to Tell Baruda.

The precise position of Parthian Ctesiphon has not yet been located, but successive rulers, from Shapur to Khosro, established royal foundations on the northeastern outskirts of Veh-Ardashir, so that Sassanian Ctesiphon had various centers. The royal palace was later used as a mine of building materials for the construction of Baghdad, but the baked-brick remains of Khosro I's palace are still standing: we have the impressive parabolic vault of the Taq-e Kisra and half of the grand facade that flanked it. Various residential buildings of the Sassanian period, with sumptuous stucco decoration, have been investigated at Umm Za'atir and

Ma'ridh. Other structures show that the same building techniques and ornamental patterns remained popular in early Islamic times. The Bustan-Kisra was perhaps a walled hunting park, while the small walled settlement of Tell Dheheb has been identified as Veh-Antioch-e Khusro.

BIBL.: Giorgio Gullini, "Undici campagne di scavo a Seleucia e Ctesifonte," *Quaderni de "La Ricerca Scientifica"* (Rome), 100 (1978): 477–512. A. Invernizzi, R. Venco Ricciardi, and M. M. Negro Ponzi Mancini, "Al-Mada'in," *La terra tra i due fiumi* (Alexandria, 1985), 87–110. Jens Kröger, *Sasanidischer Stuckdekor* (Mainz, 1982). A.I.

Senate

During the principate (27 B.C.E.–284 C.E.), the Senate was comprised of those who either by officeholding or adlection (that is, appointment) had become members of the Senate of Rome. Initially, such individuals often moved to Italy and became part of the Italian aristocracy, even though they maintained ties and property elsewhere in the empire. The actual number of senators was relatively small, rather less than one thousand. At least in theory, moreover, the Senate shared the ruling power with the emperor, and new emperors were legitimized by receiving recognition from the Senate. But as the years went by, the authority of the Senate declined.

By the time of Diocletian (284–305), who remodeled the Senate House, or Curia, into the form we see today, the Senate had been stripped of virtually all of its political authority. In theory its decrees still may have had the force of law, but this theory was never practiced. Even its right to issue bronze coinage was lost. Recognition of new emperors by the Senate, although still granted, was no longer needed. The Senate continued to meet, presided over by the *praefectus urbi* (prefect of the city), but its jurisdiction was restricted almost exclusively to the city of Rome, where its members still had the right to stage and pay for circus games and public works projects.

Senate business sometimes consisted merely of shouted congratulatory acclamations that the senators hoped would reach the ears of the emperors; the body also sent delegations to the emperor bearing adulatory messages or self-serving entreaties. One of its few remaining privileges was the right to try senators accused of crimes. The *indicium quinquevirale*, a tribunal consisting of five senators chosen by lot and presided over by the prefect of the city, oversaw such proceedings, which could even include trials for high treason, as in the case of Arvandus in 468.

One could become a member of the Senate by several routes. Sons of senators were eligible to hold the praetorship, a financially onerous position that generated funds for the aforementioned circus games and public works. Greater numbers of senators were adlected by the emperor, either as a result of actual office-

holding or the bestowal of honorary titles and offices. Junior senators held the entry-level rank of *clarissimus* (most distinguished). More senior members held higher ranks, such as *spectabilis* (respectable) or *inlustris* (illustrious), which were gained either by officeholding or, increasingly, by honorary grants.

As offices, ranks, and honors proliferated, the number of persons who qualified to be senators increased by leaps and bounds. At the same time, even persons who were senators increasingly preferred to remain in the provinces and focus their interests there. More and more, the Senate of Rome came to represent only Italian interests. By the middle of the 4th century, fifty members served as a quorum.

The foundation of Constantinople in the early 4th century brought another change. Under Constantine, the city had a "senate of the second order," but the emperor Constantius II (337–361) gave the senate of Constantinople a status equal to that of Rome. This meant that thenceforward, senators of the west would congregate at Rome, whereas those of the east looked to Constantinople. There remained, however, the problem of membership. In the late 350s, Constantius assigned the orator Themistius, who also served on several senatorial delegations, the task of drumming up members for the new Senate, and Themistius soon claimed that there were 2,000 members. Initially there were two senate houses in Constantinople, although by the 6th century the body met in the imperial palace.

By the middle of the 5th century, the number of senators had become so large and so geographically dispersed that even the imperial government accepted the impossibility of continuing the two Senates under the old terms. As a result, the *clarissimi* and *spectabiles* were officially cut off from membership in the Senate and retained only the right to pay senatorial taxes. Thereafter only *inlustres* could be true senators, the size of the Senate would have plunged to not much more than a hundred, if even that.

As a result the Senate, whether east or west, became an elite body of the highest-ranking, most influential aristocrats in the empire. A Senate of this nature was worth cultivating, and the emperors consulted with it, as well as with their own imperial council (*consistorium*), before issuing new legislation. The emperor Valentinian III also courteously issued *Orationes ad senatum* in which he officially announced his resolutions. In neither case, of course, did the Senate exercise independent action.

In general, the Senate of Constantinople was under closer scrutiny and much more beholden to the emperors than that of the west, and it lacked the history, the wealth, the privilege, and the esprit de corps of its more exalted and haughty counterpart. In the mid-6th century, Procopius noted that "the sessions of the senate were a mere form . . . it was convened only for the sake of appearances and custom." Nevertheless, the

Senate sometimes did conduct real business, usually because it was to the emperor's advantage for it to do so. In 378, after Adrianople, the Senate was convened to approve the massacre of Goths in the Roman army. In the 390s it was obliged to declare Stilicho a public enemy (the western Senate did the same for Gildo). The emperor Leo (457–474) publicly accused the general Ardaburius of treason during a meeting of the Senate. And in 478, when Zeno asked it to resolve the claims of two barbarians for huge subsidies, the Senate replied that the government could not afford it.

As for the Senate of Rome, it did have the opportunity to take independent action, especially when it felt that its interests were threatened, because the emperors rarely resided there any longer. During the 380s, for example, as the last bastion of Roman paganism, the Senate sent several delegations to the emperor Gratian to plead fervently, but unsuccessfully, for the restoration of the Altar of Victory to the Curia in Rome. In 408, the Roman Senate was consulted on the issue of paying ransom to Alaric, and in this instance one bold senator even went so far as to vote in the negative—and then immediately took sanctuary in a church. Subsequently, the Senate attempted to treat with Alaric on its own authority.

The Senate of Rome enjoyed a momentary resurgence at the end of the 5th century and the beginning of the 6th, when it collaborated with the barbarian rulers Odoacer and Theoderic in the administration of the city. Once again, coins bearing the legend *SC (Senatus consulto)* were issued. The Senate oversaw the refurbishment of the Colosseum, in which seats were engraved with the names of influential senators. But during and after the Byzantine reconquest of Italy, the Senate of Rome again lapsed into obscurity. The Senate of Constantinople, however, continued to serve as a "sounding board" for imperial policy and participated enthusiastically in imperial ceremony.

BIBL.: M. T. W. Arnheim, *The Senatorial Aristocracy in the Later Roman Empire* (Oxford, 1972). S. Barnish, "Transformation and Survival in the Western Senatorial Aristocracy," *Papers of the British School of Rome 66* (1988): 120–155. A. Chastagnol, "La fin du Sénat de Rome," in *La fin de la cité antique et le début de la cité médiévale,* ed. C. Lepelley (Bari, 1996). A. Chastagnol, *Le sénat romain sous le régne d'Odoacre* (Bonn, 1966). B. Näf, *Senatorisches Standesbewusstsein in spätrömischer Zeit* (Fribourg-en-Suisse, 1995). Richard J. A. Talbert, *The Senate of Imperial Rome* (Princeton, 1984). R.W.M.

Sergius

Nomads, farmers, merchants, and kings invoked the soldier-martyr Sergius, whose cult had its roots in Syria-Mesopotamia. Numerous churches and monasteries dedicated to the saint, and the increased use of the personal name Sergius, reflect the cult's spread in the Greek-, Syriac-, and Arabic-speaking east. A *passio,* composed in Greek in the early 5th century and translated into Syriac and Latin, describes how Sergius and Bacchus, both high-ranking officers and confessed Christians, were exiled to the empire's eastern frontier by Maximinus Daia (scholarly consensus emends the texts' "Maximinianus"). Sergius was beheaded outside the walls of the castrum of Rusafa, later Sergiopolis, where the miracle-working martyr began to attract pilgrims. During the 5th and 6th centuries, Rusafa became one of the east's most vibrant religious centers: the circuit wall was rebuilt and three major churches were erected. Offerings ranged from cheap metal trinkets to curtains of Hunnish silk. Gregory of Tours relates the humiliation inflicted by Sergius on a man who stole a chicken dedicated to the martyr, only to find it petrified in his cooking pot. Royal benefactors included Anastasius and Justinian, and even the Sassanian Khosro II, who sent offerings in thanksgiving for a victory and the birth of a child. Justinian also dedicated a major church to Sergius in Constantinople. Images of Sergius portray him either as a rider saint or as an imperial bodyguard, wearing the *maniakion* and sometimes accompanied by Bacchus. The cult's prosperity owed much to Rusafa's location in the frontier zone between the two empires, and to growing interest in soldier-saints like George and Demetrius as divine defenders in moments of crisis.

BIBL.: Elizabeth Key Fowden, *The Barbarian Plain: Saint Sergius between Rome and Iran* (Berkeley, 1999). Irfan Shahīd, *Byzantium and the Arabs in the Sixth Century* (Washington, D.C., 1995). Thilo Ulbert, *Resafa 2. Die Basilika des Heiligen Kreuzes in Resafa-Sergiupolis* (Mainz, 1986). E.F.

Shenoute

The charismatic abbot of a large monastery near the ancient town of Atripe (Panopolis) from the 380s until his death in 466, Shenoute is best known for the size of his oeuvre (primarily sermons), the idiosyncrasies of his Coptic expression, the ferocity of his crusades against local religion and heterodox Christianity, and the daunting personality that fills his *Life,* written by his disciple and successor Besa.

If the age Shenoute reputedly reached (118 years) belongs to legend, there is evidence that he did in fact first join the monastery in which he spent the duration of his life ca. 371. His charisma as abbot gained him a reputation as a prophet second only to Elijah. He was a visionary whose very words carried supernatural efficacy, and he had a public presence of such force that Archbishop Cyril of Alexandria brought Shenoute along to the Council of Ephesus (431) to oppose Nestorius. By such personal force and conviction Shenoute was able to expand the population of his monastery during his tenure to perhaps five thousand monks and nuns (if we can believe an Arabic *Life* given to some hyperbole).

In his interests and reputation Shenoute carried many of the attributes of the desert hermit as this figure had achieved prominence in 4th century Egyptian Christianity. A reputation for visionary and prophetic powers like that of other holy men carried beyond Shenoute's death into a series of pseudepigraphic apocalypses. Also, Shenoute's concerted interest in the devil in his sermons reflects the typical demonological focus of Egyptian ascetic culture. Shenoute saw the devil's wiles behind heterodoxy, behind the native gods still actively celebrated in his region, and behind the various quasi-demonic beings (like snakes) that plagued peasant culture. But the argument he made to his audience in these sermons was one of encouragement, revealing the devil's activities, true nature, and even impotence so that people could withstand him and even "trample down" his demons.

It was native religion in Atripe, and Panopolis more generally, that bore the brunt of this dualistic worldview, as we find illustrated repeatedly in Shenoute's *Life* and in a number of his sermons. He marched into villages to plunder temples and destroy cultic images, and inveighed against popular religious practices as simple as the lighting of celebratory lamps. Shenoute reserved his most vehement attacks for a local patron of native religious cult in Panopolis named Gesios, whose domestic shrine he ransacked and whom he then castigated directly in several sermons. In these sermons Shenoute sets himself up as a protector of the poor against Gesios, a wealthy landowner, whom he describes as oppressive. Shenoute thus promotes himself as a new, Christian patron in opposition to Gesios's traditional economic role as keeper of cultic traditions and perhaps sponsor of festivals. It is not apparent, however, that most others shared Shenoute's view of Gesios as oppressor.

In his repeated criticisms of local religion Shenoute provides important evidence for the continuity of traditional Egyptian piety at the village level and even of some Egyptian priesthoods' political influence as late as the 5th century. While admitting a considerable degree of polemical topoi in his presentation, one can find references to the gods Min and Petbe (otherwise hardly documented for the Roman period), to domestic celebrations of an Egyptian spirit of supernatural beneficence ("Shai"), and to the common use of archaic execration rituals to protect a village from Shenoute's monks. Other sermons give witness to the conversion of local temples to Christian shrines and to the "magical" services of some local monks.

Shenoute's rhetorical promotion in many of his sermons of poverty, Coptic culture, and Christianity over landholding, Greek culture, and adherence to native religion once prompted scholars like J. Leipoldt to see a real social and economic context for the rise of Coptic Christianity, even an incipient nationalism, in the abbot's thought. But subsequent examination of, for example, Shenoute's own Greek cultural inheritance and the strong adherence to traditional religion among many Egyptian peasant communities of the time has rendered the actual circumstances of Shenoute's conflicts far more complex.

BIBL.: E. C. Amelineau, *Oeuvres de Schenoudi*, 2 vols. (Paris, 1907–1914). David N. Bell, *Besa: The Life of Shenoute* (Kalamazoo, Mich., 1983). Johannes Leipoldt, *Schenute von Atripe und die Enstehung des national ägyptischen Christentums* (Leipzig, 1903). Jacques van der Vliet, "Spätantikes Heidentum in Ägypten im Spiegel der koptischen Literatur," *Begegnung von Heidentum und Christentum im spätantiken Ägypten* (Riggisberg, 1993), 99–130.

D.T.F.

Shi'ism

The major heterodox movement of Islam in the late antique world, Shi'ism tenaciously upheld the rights of Muhammad's family *(ahl al-bayt)* to political and religious leadership and developed the central doctrine of the imām as the charismatic leader and authoritative teacher of the Muslim community. The movement split into many subdivisions and sects, with the principal branches known as Twelver (Imāmī), Sevener (Ismā'īlī), and Fiver (Zaydī) Shi'ism, named after the number of imāms recognized, respectively, in succession.

After the murder of the third caliph, 'Uthmān, in 656, Shi'ism appeared during the First Muslim Civil War as the *shī'at 'Alī*, the "party" of 'Alī, husband of Muhammad's daughter Fātima and his cousin. The Shī'ites, however, trace their origins to the Prophet's explicit choice of 'Alī as his rightful successor, reportedly made at the oasis of Ghadīr Khumm in the last years of Muhammad (d. 632). This claim is rejected by Sunnism, the sect that represents the majority of Muslims; Sunnism recognizes Abū Bakr (d. 634), 'Umar (d. 644), and 'Uthmān as the first three caliphs and 'Alī as the fourth.

After 'Alī's murder in 661 and the slaying of 'Alī's son Husayn at Karbalā' in 680, the Shī'a emerged from their center at Kūfa in militant opposition to the Umayyad caliphs ruling the Arab empire from Damascus. During this Kūfan revolt in 685, al-Mukhtār proclaimed 'Alī's son, Muhammad ibn al-Hanafiyya (d. 700), to be the messianic restorer of Islam *(mahdī)*. Arising from this revolt, the radical Kaysāniyya, made up of Arabs and non-Arab neoconverts to Islam, or "clients" *(mawālī)*, expected the *mahdī*'s imminent return in glory from hiding, rather than death, to begin a reign of justice. The more politically oriented Hāshimiyya found in Muhammad ibn al-Hanafiyya's son Abū Hāshim a fulcrum of their organized opposition, and after his death in about 717 they recognized Muhammad ibn ʿAlī (d. 743), the great-grandson of the Prophet's uncle ʿAbbās, as the imām. After the unsuccessful Kūfan revolt in 740 of Zayd, another scion of ʿAlid descent, and his son Yaḥyā ibn Zayd's execution in Khurasān in 743, the supporters of Muhammad ibn ʿAlī and his sons, relying substantially on Iranian clients led by Abū Muslim, organized a revolutionary movement in Khurasan that overthrew the Umayyads and established the Abbasid dynasty in 750. In their effort to gain wider support in the Muslim community, the early Abbasids, ruling from Baghdad, abandoned the extreme Shīʿī claims and suppressed the rebellions of the client Abū al-Khaṭṭāb at Kūfa in 754 and the ʿAlid Muhammad al-Nafs al-Zakiyya at Medina in 762.

With the rapid disintegration of the radical Shīʿa, labeled as *ghulāt* (extremists), the moderate Shīʿa of Kūfa took decisive lead of the movement, developing, however, as two different groups. The followers of Zayd, known as the Zaydiyya, advocated armed uprising against illegitimate rule and deemphasized the religious claims made about their imāms. Tracing the line of imāms as descending through Ḥusayn and his grandson Muhammad al-Bāqir (d. 735), and shifting the emphasis from the imām as charismatic leader to that of authoritative teacher, the Imāmiyya remained aloof from political strife. Nevertheless, through the teachings on law and religion that are traced back to the sixth imām, Jaʿfar al-Ṣādiq (d. 765), they became the most influential branch of Shīʿī thought. The core of Shīʿī doctrine is the belief in an enduring prophetic mission *(wilāya)* that survives the death of Muhammad, the final prophet, and is entrusted to the chain of explicitly designated imāms who, divinely protected against sin and error *(ʿiṣma)*, continue to provide humanity with inspired leadership and authoritative teaching. The imāms neither bring new revelation nor convey another Scripture; rather, they offer normative and binding interpretation *(tawīl)* of revealed Scripture (Qurʾān) and divine law *(sharīʿa)* for all circumstances of life. Extracting a level of esoteric meaning *(bāṭin)* from the Qurʾān, Jaʿfar al-Ṣādiq's mystical thought focused on the preexistential covenant *(mīthāq)* and the Logos-like "light of Muhammad" *(nūr Muḥammad)*, while other more extreme thinkers advocated antinomianism *(ibāḥa)* as well as ideas of incarnation *(ḥulūl)* and metempsychosis *(tanāsukh)* that had their roots in the Gnostic speculations of late antiquity.

The dispute about Jaʿfar's succession led to a major schism between the Imāmiyya and the Ismāʿīliyya, prompted by the rival claims to the imamate, raised either on behalf of Jaʿfar's son Mūsā (d. 799) or his son Ismāʿīl (d. 765) and grandson Muhammad ibn Ismāʿīl. In 819, moreover, the Imāmiyya saw its resurgent political expectations thwarted with the death, apparently by poison, of ʿAlī al-Riḍā, Mūsā's son, who, two years earlier, had been appointed by the Abbasid al-Maʾmūn as successor to the caliphate. Eventually the Imāmiyya came to recognize twelve imāms and professed the occultation and eschatological return of the twelfth imām, Muhammad, the purported offspring of the eleventh imām, Ḥasan al-ʿAskarī (d. 874). The Ismāʿīliyya, adhering to seven imāms and incorporating Gnostic and Neoplatonic influences in their philosophy, developed two major branches by the end of the 9th century: the intellectually active movement of the Qarāmiṭa in Iraq, Bahrayn, and Iran, and the politically powerful Fatimid dynasty that flourished into the 12th century in North Africa and Egypt.

BIBL.: Heinz Halm, *Die islamische Gnosis* (Zurich, 1982); *Kosmologie und Heilslehre der frühen Ismāʿīlīya* (Wiesbaden, 1978); *Shiism* (Edinburgh, 1991). S. Husain and M. Jafri, *Origins and Early Development of Shīʿa Islam* (London, 1979). Henri Laoust, *Les schismes dans l'Islam* (Paris, 1965).

G.H.B.

Ships

The later Roman empire saw great changes in the nature and construction of ships, both men-of-war and merchantmen. For well-nigh a millennium, from the 5th century B.C.E. to the 5th C.E., the ancient ship of the line had been the trireme, a decked galley driven by three levels of one-man oars. Its prow at the waterline had a ram, a massive bronze-plated projection that ended in a blunt point, for smashing into an enemy hull; this was its distinctive weapon. In the 4th century B.C.E. and subsequent centuries, the trireme was joined by larger types of ships driven by one, two, or three levels of oars that were pulled by more than one man. For cruising, the main drive was supplied by a large square mainsail mounted amidships.

By the 6th century C.E. all these types of ships had vanished. The ship of the line was now the *dromōn,* or runner, a galley that, as the name indicates, was designed particularly for speed. It was still decked and fitted with a ram, but it was low and light, with just one level of one-man oars. By the 10th century the standard *dromōn* had increased in size and become more complex. It usually had two levels of oars, 25 to a side on each level for a total of 100, while some versions were even larger, powered by as many as 200 men: 50 rowed on the lower level and the others rowed on the upper level or served as marines or did both. For cruising and carrying dispatches and the like, there was a smaller, lighter type of ship with only one level of oars; its name, *galea,* is the source of the word *galley.*

The warships of late antiquity were no longer fitted with rams. Their chief weapon was "Greek fire," an inflammable mixture whose key ingredient was crude oil (available at various areas in the Near East, where it oozed out of the ground). *Dromōnes* had mounted in the bow a *siphōn,* a cannonlike tube of wood sheathed with bronze; the oil mixture was loaded into it, and

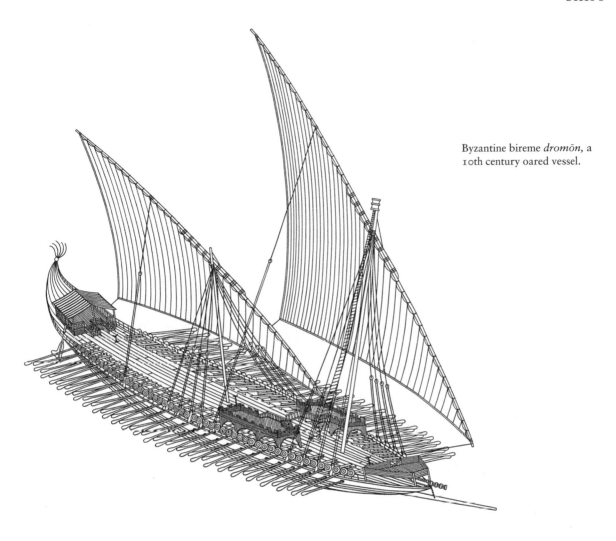

Byzantine bireme *dromōn*, a
10th century oared vessel.

when ignited, a sheet of flame would flare forth from
its muzzle, much like from a modern flamethrower.
Large *dromōnes* mounted a *siphōn* amidships as well
as forward. The ships' rig, too, saw a radical change. It
now consisted of two masts carrying lateen sails.

In merchantmen a major change took place in the
method of construction. From the Bronze Age on,
ships had been built "shell first," i.e., shipwrights created a hull by building up a shell of planking, joining
each plank not to an inner framework but to its neighbors above and below; this was done by means of
multiple mortise-and-tenon joints, thousands of them
in a well-built craft. They then inserted a number of
frames to stiffen the shell. The framing was auxiliary;
the ship's major strength lay in its tightly knit shell of
planking. Shell-first construction produced a very
sturdy hull but was costly in terms of both materials
and labor. By the 4th century C.E., a shift away from
this method is clearly visible: the joints holding plank

to plank are smaller and fewer, and the framing is increasingly stronger. By the 10th century, the transition
has been completed. From this shell-first construction
gives way to skeleton-first construction, the method
that was to be favored by European shipwrights beginning in the Middle Ages. In this method, a skeleton of
keel and frames is erected and the planking is fastened
to this skeleton, which provides the vessel's strength.
The change in construction is attested by a series of
wrecks of merchantmen that have been excavated and
studied; it very likely took place in war galleys too, but
proof is lacking.

Another important change was in rig. The standard
sail of the ancient world had been the squaresail. The
lateen rig had been known at least as early as the 2nd
century C.E. but was used chiefly for small craft. In the
later Roman empire it began its ascent to become the
sail par excellence of the Mediterranean for both merchantmen and men-of-war.

BIBL.: S. McGrail, *Ancient Boats in N.W. Europe: The Archaeology of Water Transport to AD 1500* (London and New York, 1987). J. Pryor, "From Dromōn to Galea: Mediterranean Bireme Galleys AD 500–1300," in *The Age of the Galley*, ed. R. Gardiner (London, 1995), 101–116. J. R. Steffy, *Wooden Ship Building and the Interpretation of Wrecks* (College Station, Tex., 1994; 2nd ed., London, 1999).   L.C.

Sidonius

Senatorial officeholder, bishop, and man of letters, the noble Gallo-Roman Sidonius Apollinaris (ca. 430–ca. 484) was one of the principal witnesses of the political disintegration of the western Roman empire in the 5th century.

Born in Lyons into a family that had been implicated in a usurpation some twenty years before, Sidonius also boasted a lifelong connection with the Aviti of Clermont, to whom he was related on his mother's side. Through his marriage to Papianilla he became the son-in-law of Eparchius Avitus, whose reign as western Augustus (455–456), supported by the Gothic settlers in Toulouse, gave the young Sidonius his first taste of imperial politics and literary fame. After Avitus's overthrow by Majorian in October 456, Sidonius returned to Gaul. In late 458 he benefited from the new emperor's policy of conciliation and became an active—but occasionally controversial—figure among the literary glitterati of Majorian's court in Gaul and Italy.

On Majorian's fall in 461, Sidonius again returned home. His social circle now included some of the foremost Gallic Christian thinkers of his day, notably the priest Claudianus Mamertus, of Vienne, at whose theological seminars Sidonius was by no means the slowest of students, and his own bishop, Patiens of Lyons. Patiens's predecessor, Eucherius (bishop 434–449), was closely associated with the monastic island of Lérins, as was Faustus of Riez (bishop 461–477), the great Gallic theologian, who baptized Sidonius, an occasion commemorated in Sidonius's *Poem 16*, which, in part, follows the structure of the catechism.

During the early 460s Sidonius continued the contacts with the Gothic court at Toulouse previously fostered by Avitus, a policy not accepted by all Gallo-Romans, some of whom made common cause with Majorian's former general, Aegidius, who, in alliance with the Franks, warred against the Goths. Sidonius's description of a day in the life of Theoderic II (*Letters* 1.2) was designed to make the "barbarian" king acceptable in Roman eyes as a moderate ruler who spent his time giving judgments (seated on his magisterial *sella*), hunting, playing games of dice—although it was important for a petitioner to combine losing with a convincing show of annoyance—and enjoying civilized evening parties, while his "skin-clad" guards were kept tactfully in the background. Sidonius's discreet support for the Goths was further demonstrated in his belated reaction to the highly controversial cession of Narbonne to the Goths in 461; writing in 463, Sidonius celebrated Theoderic's affection for his prize, describing the king as the "support and pillar of the Roman name" (*Poem 23*).

Sidonius had not yet given up his ambitions for a career in the Roman imperial service. In Rome late in 467, Sidonius, through his Roman contacts, won the privilege of delivering a public panegyric of the new emperor. Keen to win support where he could, Anthemius responded to the gesture by offering Sidonius the prefecture of the city of Rome. But Sidonius had not left the problems and divisions in Gaul behind him. In 469 the former prefect of the Gauls, Arvandus, was accused by the Gallic provincial council of extortion—and treason, because he had corresponded with Euric, seeking to engineer a division of what remained of Roman Gaul between the Goths and the Burgundians, "and other such lunacies" (*Letter* 1.7). Sidonius's attempts to warn his headstrong friend proved ineffectual, and in the aftermath of Arvandus's condemnation, his own position, as a friend of the Goths, may have appeared suspect. A few months later he returned to Gaul, to be consecrated bishop of Clermont.

Roman Clermont of the Arverni was poised uneasily between the expanding realms of the Goths and the Burgundians. Sidonius's task as bishop was to preserve its independence of both, if he could, through negotiation, where possible, and armed resistance. From 471 to 475 Clermont resisted repeated assaults from the Goths, while its bishop boosted morale through attention-grabbing liturgical innovations and well-timed material support and military interventions by his friends. Clermont was finally handed over, by treaty, to Euric in 475, an outcome bitterly denounced by Sidonius, who had not been consulted.

Unlike some, Sidonius survived the end of his world. After a brief stint in exile, he was recalled to Clermont as its bishop and served amicably alongside Euric's commander in the city. His last years were devoted to literature and his pastoral work. His book of twenty-four *Poems* had been published in 469. As bishop he wrote *Missae*, perhaps linked to the liturgy of saints' days, which do not survive, and from 477 to 481 he edited and produced nine books of *Letters*. These contain correspondence going back to the early 460s and provide a unique perspective on the aristocratic, literary, and Christian society of late Roman Gaul. Despite their ornate verbiage, both *Poems* and *Letters* reveal the confusion of loyalties among the Gallo-Roman elite. Not all shared Sidonius's determination to cling to an empire that, as even he partly saw, had outlived its usefulness to him and his kind. Naturally he defined the empire in his own terms, as office in the imperial service, laws, and the Latin literary heritage. By the end, he recognized that all but the last of these were no more.

BIBL.: John Drinkwater and Hugh Elton, eds., *Fifth Century Gaul: A Crisis of Identity?* (Cambridge, Eng., 1992). Jill Harries, *Sidonius Apollinaris and the Fall of Rome* (Oxford, 1994). C. E. Stevens, *Sidonius Apollinaris and His Age* (Oxford, 1933).   J.H.

Silk

Silk *(serikon, metaxa)* yarn was produced in China from filaments of the cocoons of moths that feed on mulberry leaves. Silk textiles from the Far East appear in the west as early as the 5th century B.C.E., in tombs in the Kerameikos of Athens and near Stuttgart in Germany. In the early Roman imperial era, as shown by discoveries of imported silk fabrics in the tower tombs at Palmyra that have Far Eastern designs and Chinese characters, there is little doubt that silk was transported as intact textiles and not just as raw silk. The collapse of the Han dynasty and the 3rd century crisis in the Roman empire appear to have disrupted the trade, but by the 4th century it was again gaining momentum. The famous Silk Route led from China across the southern Russian steppes to Persia, the main supplier of silk to the west. Ammianus Marcellinus depicts the market town of Batnae in northern Syria as filled with wealthy traders dealing in merchandise from India and China (14.3.3). Silk was widely used in the imperial court and in ecclesiastical settings for vestments, embroidered costumes, tapestry hangings, curtains, altar cloths, and other coverings. Purple silk *(blattion)* was eventually exclusively for the use of the imperial court and was often given as an imperial gift in diplomacy.

By the 4th century, officials known as the *comes commerciorum* were placed at the head of the markets of frontier towns and given exclusive rights in purchasing silk from foreign merchants. The raw silk was then sold to imperial weaving workshops *(gynaikeia)* at Berytus and Tyre for producing purple silk garments for the court in Constantinople. Under Justinian, the purchasing and wearing of silk was restricted to the imperial family and court and became a state monopoly (Procopius, *SH* 25). The *comes commerciorum* were then replaced by official contract agents called *kommerkiarkoi* who were appointed over specific districts, called *apothekai,* to purchase silk and other goods for the imperial authorities. The prices for acquiring raw silk from merchants *(metaxarii)* and reselling it to the workshops of silk spinners *(katartorioi)* were strictly regulated (*C.Just.* 4.40.2; Justinian, *Nov.App.* 5). The activities of the *kommerkiarkoi* in Antioch, Tyre, and Mesopotamia are known from literary sources and from 6th century lead seals inscribed with their names and the emperor's effigy, evidently used to validate garments that had been produced in the imperial workshops. Some fragments of silk textiles and tunic decorations of the late 6th or early 7th century have been discovered at Nessana and 'Avdat (Oboda) in the Negev of Palestine and Egypt. After the Islamic conquests, the Byzantine silk industry shifted to Asia Minor, Constantinople, Greece, and Italy.

In late antiquity Persia monopolized the export of silk to the west, making it available, at exorbitant custom duties, only at designated frontier stations in Syria (Nisibis, Dara, Callinicum) and Armenia (Artaxata). Byzantium attempted in various ways to bypass Persian control of silk. By diplomatic efforts with the Hephthalites, or "White Huns," an effort was made to develop a land route across the Russian steppes north of the Caspian Sea. The southern sea route was the other way in which Far Eastern goods made available in Ceylon could be shipped, through the Red Sea to the ports of Clysma and Aila. During the 6th century, Byzantium encouraged the Christian Abyssinian kingdom in Axum (Ethiopia) to seize control of the Straits of Aden and occupy South Arabia. In spite of these efforts, Persia retained its position as the intermediary for the luxury goods of the Far East until 554, when missionaries or Indian monks smuggled to the west some silkworms in a hollowed-out cane (Procopius, *Wars* 8.17.1–8). By the reign of Justin II (565–578), the indigenous production of silk in Byzantium was under full sway. Efforts were still made to secure silk from the Far East in 568 by diplomacy with the Turks of Sogdiana, but they were as futile as the earlier efforts.

With the embassies of Chang Ch'ien to Sogdiana and Bactria in 128–122 B.C.E. and Kan Ying to the Persian Gulf in 97 C.E., the Han dynasty had become familiar indirectly with the west. The initial name of Li-kan for the west (probably referring to Rekem, the Semitic name of Petra, the capital of the Nabataean kingdom in Arabia rather than Alexandria) was replaced with Ta-ch'in (greater *Ch'in*) after the latter expedition. By the 5th century, the terms P'u-lan and, later, Fu-Lin were used (transcriptions into Chinese of the word *Rome*). According to the Chinese annals, embassies from Rome (P'u-lan) were sent to the northern Wei court during the reigns of Marcian (450–457) and Leo I (457–474). In 643 another embassy from Fu-Lin was sent to China with gifts for the T'ang dynast T'ai-tsung and received silk garments in exchange. By 661 the same Chinese sources indicate that the Arabs have defeated the Persians and Fu-Lin.

Very soon after the Arab conquest, the central authority of the caliphate took over control of silk manufacture through an institution known as the *tiraz.* Dozens of different types of silks are recognized in texts, but the few remaining fragments from early Islamic types are difficult to match with the textual evidence.

BIBL.: A. Baginski and A. Tidhar, "A Dated Silk Fragment from 'Avdat (Eboda)," *Israel Exploration Journal* 28 (1978):

113–115. N. Oikonomidès, "Silk Trade and Production in Byzantium from the Sixth to the Ninth Century: The Seals of Kommerkiarioi," *Dumbarton Oaks Papers* 40 (1986): 33–53. R. B. Serjeant, "Materials for a History of Islamic Textiles," *Ars Islamica* 9–16 (1942–1951).   D.G.

Silver

In the Roman empire, silver was little coined from 300 to 615 C.E. but was made into a variety of secular and cult objects that circulated at several levels of society, from the court to village churches. State control stamps were applied to some silver. From a simple mark, used in the early 4th century, these had evolved by the end of the fifth into a more complicated set of five stamps incorporating imperial and other official monograms, images, and names. Applied between shaping and final decoration, the stamps provide a means of dating objects to a particular emperor's reign. The stamps thus confirm the production of silver plate, often with mythological decoration, at least until ca. 661. The same type of silver, unstamped, reappears by the 9th and 10th centuries, as attested by an ink pot in Padua that is decorated in repoussé with a Medusa head, Apollo, and other classical figures.

Sets of silver were acquired by families (the Esquiline treasure), perhaps over several generations (the Lampsacus treasure), while cult plate accumulated in churches through prestige donations by imperial and other important figures (the Sion treasure) or numerous small offerings (the Kaper Koraon treasure). Plate of regulated weight was produced by the state for imperial largesse *(largitio)* distributed on regnal anniversaries and other specified occasions. Silver was used as well as displayed; hoards that had been left concealed for safekeeping have been rediscovered in modern times. Earlier Roman laws covering legacies of silver plate were reissued by Justinian.

Silver vessels were mostly shaped by hammering, and attachments such as handles were cast from copper-strengthened silver. Compositional analyses have established that nearly all late antique plate is 92 to 98 percent pure. Decorative techniques were varied and included traditional repoussé, chased relief work, appliqués, openwork, incised images and gouged patterns, niello inlay, and gilding, as well as cast solid ornaments. While many shapes and types of decorative layout derived from earlier times, other forms (angled handles, convex moldings, faceted surfaces, beaded rims) were innovations of the late 3rd or the 4th century.

Domestic plate continued to include types known from earlier centuries, namely plates, bowls, cups, spoons and other small utensils, ewers, amphorae, situlae, washbasins, lamps, caskets, mirrors, furniture attachments, and animal trappings. Some objects, such as plates and spoons, became increasingly larger and heavier. Between them, the Esquiline and Sevso hoards include the widest variety of object types and represent the sumptuous end of the market, while the Mytilene treasure, with seventeen simple objects (plates, ewers, basins, spoons, lamps) all made and stamped between 605 and 630, was probably acquired as a ready-made set at the more modest end. The Kaiseraugst treasure has several elaborate objects (display plates, a lampstand, a statuette), plainer plates, bowls, a washbasin, and a large series of spoons. The Mildenhall treasure has a set of three Dionysiac display plates, serving dishes, and utensils. The Lampsacus treasure, with objects stamped between 527 and 613, has elegant spoons engraved in Greek and Latin, lamps, a plate with a personification identified as India, bowls, a goblet, a mirror, and furniture. A treasure found at ancient Lapethus in Cyprus includes a set of nine display plates illustrating events in the life of King David (stamped 613–630), other serving plates, large spoons, a censer, and a bowl decorated with a military saint, together with gold jewelry and imperial medallions. Today, the largest museum collections of late antique domestic plate are held by the British Museum and the Hermitage in St. Petersburg.

Seen as cultural documents, decorated domestic silver pieces display the mix of pagan and Christian elements that characterizes the period. While overtly pagan subjects with cultic overtones appear on some pieces (the Parabiago plate), on others, Graeco-Roman mythological scenes may merely illustrate literary texts (the Kaiseraugst Achilles plate) or express in classical guise human pursuits and emotions (hunting, bathing, love) rather than religious beliefs. Human pursuits are also rendered in the direct mode of genre scenes (the Sevso treasure hunting plate). On a few objects, Christian inscriptions or symbols accompany neutral or mythological subjects (the Esquiline casket). Eventually the Cross and Christian legends came to ornament domestic plate.

Items for church use (such as chalices, patens, censers, and crosses) were introduced by the 4th century (Water Newton treasure). Large amounts of silver were deposited in churches: Constantine donated more than 11,720 Roman pounds of silver (in addition to gold) to his cathedral in Rome, while Justinian embellished Hagia Sophia with 40,000 pounds. Heaviest among these donations were the silver sheets used to revet liturgical furniture, such as the altar, chancel screen, ambo, and synthronon. Some recorded silver ciboria weighed 2,000 pounds. In addition to important cathedrals and pilgrimage churches, villages, too, received local offerings of silver; these often took the form of liturgical objects inscribed with the names of donor and church. One large treasure, perhaps numbering more than fifty objects, dedicated to the Church of St. Sergius at Kaper Koraon in Syria between 550 and 650 by about three generations of four or five families, included chalices, patens, a ewer, a bowl, a flask, crosses, a pair of liturgical fans, book covers, spoons, a ladle, strainers, and lamps. Even more impressive is the Kumluca treasure from Asia Minor, dedicated to the rural shrine of Sion. Many of its fifty-some objects were stamped in ca. 560; they include the largest silver plate from late antiquity (77 cm across) and several other large patens, chalices, a ewer, amphorae, censers, book covers, extensive sets of lamps (many of open-work), and sheets of silver furniture revetment.

In Sassanian Persia silver provided both abundant coin and plate, which was also controlled, as reflected in the subject matter chosen for the decoration of plate. Only the king's image appeared on objects made in the 4th century, and the dancing figures introduced on objects of the 5th century may have been restricted to court or cult use. Other more incidental subjects introduced on objects of the 6th century may have been been intended for the new feudal lesser nobility. In contrast to the purity of Roman/Byzantine silver, this last category of Sassanian plate can have a copper content reaching as high as 10 to 20 percent.

Silver similar to both late Roman and Sasanian plate was produced in central Asia before and after the Arab conquest of the Near East.

BIBL.: Alan Cameron, "Observations on the Distribution and Ownership of Late Roman Silver Plate," *Journal of Roman Archaeology* 5 (1992): 178–185. P. Harper, *Silver Vessels of the Sasanian Period* (New York, 1981). C. Johns, "Research on Roman Silver Plate," *Journal of Roman Archaeology* 3 (1990): 28–44. K. Painter, "Late Roman Silver Plate: A Reply to Alan Cameron," *Journal of Roman Archaeology* 6 (1993): 109–115.   M.M.M.

Sinai

A triangular peninsula of about 60,000 square km lying between Egypt and what was ancient Palestine, the Sinai is bordered on the north by the Mediterranean, on the west by the Gulf of Suez and the Suez Canal, and on the east by the Gulf of 'Aqaba and Israel. Geologically, the Sinai is part of the Arabian Desert, between the plateaus of Galata and al-Tih. Three large regions are to be distinguished. They are, from north to south: a sandy zone about 20 km wide; a limestone plateau about 220 km across and 1,620 m high; and, finally, after a low-lying zone, a granitic massif reaching heights of more than 2,000 m. The coastal and desert plain consists of, in the west, the Wadi al-'Arīsh; in the center, the Sebhat Bardawil (Sirobnis for the Greeks), a lagoon 80 km long that includes Jabal Jelsa (Ras Kasrun); and, in the east, the Isthmus of Suez (formed as a result of silt buildup and human labor) and the Bay of Pelusium. A road lined with wells and towns crosses the plain. In the center, the al-Tih Desert and the Egma Plateau, with sparse pasture lands and a small oasis, were once occupied by Bedouin tribes. A few stock farms and gardens allowed caravans and herds to travel from one water hole to the next. Two of the southern mountains are particularly famous, the

Jabal Mūsā (2,285 m) and the Jabal Katrinah (2,637 m). On the first, Moses received the Ten Commandments; angels placed the martyred body of Catherine of Alexandria on the second. The famous Monastery of St. Catherine was established at the foot of the twin peaks. The Bible speaks of a road cutting through the granitic massif via Paran (the modern oasis of Feiran). Other roads known in antiquity belonged to the "land of the Philistines" (Ex. 13:17) north of the land of "Shur," where Moses led his people after crossing the Red Sea (Ex. 15:22).

At the intersection between Africa and Asia, Sinai was one of the most important crossroads of remote antiquity. The pharaohs had the road to Shur built, joining Beersheba and Jerusalem. Sinai has been inhabited since paleolithic times (there were numerous protohistorical settlements in the northern region); its history has been closely linked to that of Egypt since the Middle Kingdom (about 2000 B.C.E.). The northern route, or "Ways of Horus," was taken by armies until the 7th century B.C.E., and Pelusium became one of the gateways to Egypt. In 525 Cambyses defeated the Greeks and Egyptians there; in 342, Artaxerxes lost part of his army at the same site. Alexander established a garrison there in 332, before leaving for Memphis. Very early on, the pharaohs took an interest in the copper, turquoise, and galena mines. The Maghara mines were exploited during the Thinite era (3000 B.C.E.). Greeks and Romans left numerous remains on the coast (Ptolemaic village of Tell Mufarig, theater and Roman baths in Tell el-Kanaïs). At the dawn of the 4th century, anchorites and monastic communities settled nearly everywhere (remains in Raithu, Farān, Wadi 'Aleiyāt). But the triumph of Christianity was marked especially by constructions on Jabal Mūsā and Jabal Katrinah and the famous Monastery of St. Catherine. The Arab conquest stabilized the lives of monks and Bedouin populations for a time.

For a long time, "Sinai" and "Monastery of St. Catherine" were synonymous: along with all the adjoining religious buildings (the hermitage of St. Stephen on Jabal Mūsā, the Monastery of the Holy Apostles, and the Convent of the Forty Martyrs on Jabal Katrinah), the Monastery of St. Catherine attests to the continual importance of Christianity beginning in the 5th and 6th centuries, and to remarkable artistic currents. Icons produced there were one of the high points. A wall dating back to Emperor Justinian (527) encloses buildings from different eras, separated by small courtyards. There is a church with three naves, a mosque (built in the 10th century), a museum, a very rich library (its collection of manuscripts is one of the largest in the world), a refectory with beautiful paintings from the 16th century, and chapels representing the various denominations.

Certain sites to the north, such as Pelusium, have long attracted attention, but it was during the Israeli occupation following the Six Day War in 1967 that a geological survey was finally conducted (by the University of Negev). Since 1983, the Organization of Egyptian Antiquities (OEA) has conducted regular operations. For example, in 1985, in collaboration with the Université de Lille III, the OEA undertook excavations in Tell el-Herr. In November 1992 the OEA was able to report the results of its work at Tell Kedua (a necropolis from the thirty-sixth dynasty), Tell Mufarig (a Ptolemaic village), Tell el-Luly (a Roman and Byzantine site), Tell el-Aḥmar (Roman and Islamic residences), Tell el-Makhzan (a church with three naves, with baptistery, crypts, and sepulchers), and Tell el-Kanaïs (a Graeco-Roman bath). It also reported on work conducted in collaboration with the German Institute at Tell Hebua (remains from the second intermediate period and the new kingdom) and Tell el-Kanaïs (Roman tombs); with the Université de Lille III in Tell el-Kanaïs (a Roman theater); with the Institut Français d'Archéologie Orientale in Tell el-Fadda (a late Roman site); on the "embankment" and in the western part (a Greek and Roman quarter, including a "theater") of Tell Farāma (Pelusium); and, finally, with both institutes in southern Tell Farāma (Byzantine and Islamic remains). Since then, every year has brought new discoveries (a 6th century basilica with three naves in Gezira el-Fir'aun), new prospecting (mining sites in the southern Sinai, remains from the Neolithic and Bronze Ages on Jabal al-Tih, Roman and Coptic necropolis in Abu Oruq), or more precise information on chronology (in Tell al-Herr, there are traces of occupation from the 5th century B.C.E. to the 4th century C.E.). Since 1991, aid from foreign institutes has consistently grown: the University of Toronto joined the OEA in Tell Qedwa (fortresses from the 7th and 6th centuries B.C.E.); the Austrian Archaeological Institute of Cairo has concentrated on sector four in Tell Hebua; and Franco-Egyptian expeditions working in Pelusium have been joined by delegations from the Royal Ontario Museum of Toronto, the Swiss Institute of Architectural and Archaeological Research of Ancient Egypt, and the Egypt Exploration Society (four operations in the southern sector).

BIBL.: J. Daumas, *La péninsule du Sinaï* (Cairo, 1951). G. Gerster, *Sinaï: Terre de la Révélation* (Paris, 1961). G. Sotiriou and M. Sotiriou, *Icōnes du Mont Sinai*, 2 vols. (in Greek, with summary in French; Athens, 1956–1958). G. Viaud (text) and A. S. Taher (illustrations), *Sinaï: Guide de la péninsule et de la mer Rouge* (Glyka Nera Attikis, 1992). K. Weitzmann, *The Monastery of Saint Catherine at Mount Sinai: The Icons, I: From the Sixth to the Tenth Century* (Princeton, 1976). D. Valbelle and C. Bonnet, *Le Sinaï durant l'Antiquité et le Moyen Age* (Paris, 1998). M.R.-D.

Slavery

There are four overlapping questions that concern slavery in the later empire: the terminology for slaves; the extent of slavery; the conditions of slaves; and how

far slavery merged into the colonate and both merged into medieval serfdom. There is no dispute that chattel slavery continued after Roman rule, since in Euric's Code slaves were sold by the same *forma venditionis* as cattle.

The ambiguity of vocabulary for slavery and freedom is a reflection of their partial assimilation. In the *hospitalitas* legislation of the Burgundian Code a proportion of *mancipia* was allocated to new settlers that could not possibly refer to slaves alone. Symmachus (*Relatio* 28) referred to the *mancipia* on an Italian estate that almost certainly included both slaves and free, while *mancipia* in the *Theodosian Code* (*C.Th.* 11.3.2 [327]) were listed on the tax rolls (*adscripta censibus*) like coloni. Bagaudae supporters in Gaul, described as *servitia,* were not all slaves, and when Salvian attacked landlords for turning free refugees into *servi* (*De gub.Dei* 5.9), it is uncertain whether he meant slaves or coloni *inquilini.* Similarly, the language of the laws concerning the fiscal status of tenants may have been metaphorical, not literal. Constantine demanded that runaway coloni be reduced to *servilis condicio* (*C.Th.* 5.17.1 [332]). By the late 4th century a law in the *Justinianic Code* called them slaves of the land (*servi terrae: C.Just.* 9.52.1 [393]), and Justinian later denied the difference between *adscripticii* and slaves (*C.Just.* 11.48.21). There was, however, a spectrum of statuses of slaves, just as of coloni. Debt slavery and indentured labor, both in theory redeemable, were common in the rural African world described by Augustine, and records tell of the sale of children into slavery at the fair of St. Marceḷḷiana in Italy. Whether such transactions were legal or not, they illustrate the fluidity of status frontiers.

Slavery, like most statistical problems in ancient history, is impossible to quantify, since the evidence is anecdotal. Many historians now are less inclined than in the past to accept a priori arguments that slave numbers had declined from the earlier empire, whether due to contradictions in the slave mode of production, as Marxists argued, or because of reorganization of the republican "villa system," or because of fewer wars of conquest. Since rural slavery was never an empire-wide phenomenon, the arguments are valid only in limited regions of Italy and a few older provinces, where tenancy probably increased. On the supply side, even if the huge numbers of prisoners of war cited during the republican wars are unparalleled, there are many references to slaves from the frontiers, such as the stable boys Symmachus purchased through a friend (*Ep.* 2.78) or the many starving Goths who sold themselves to soldiers in return for food (Amm.Marc. 31.4.11). Augustine (Ep. 10*) provides a vivid picture of slave traders (conventionally called "Galatians") illegally kidnapping African villagers by night, with the connivance of Roman officials, quite apart from captives brought from beyond the frontiers, who formed a rich export commodity from Pannonia and Africa. The number of slaves born in captivity probably increased, as the state encouraged owners to keep slave families together.

On the demand side, although Palladius did not write of gang slave labor at his model villa, he was inconclusive about the status of the workers organized by the central farm office (*praetorium*). Numerous sources refer to rural slaves, such as those who lived in the sixty-two villages of Melania's estates in 4th century Italy and the *pueri* recorded by Gregory on church estates in 6th century Sicily, who may have worked either on a domanial farm or as quasi coloni on plots. The latter was probably true of the slaves belonging to a Jew at Luni, whom Gregory the Great instructed to manumit but to leave on the land "they have been accustomed to cultivate" (*Ep.* 6.21). Legislation assumed that rural and urban slaves were registered on properties, where "cottagers" (*casarii:* probably quasi coloni) and coloni worked together (*C.Th.* 9.42.7 [369]). The largest number cited is 8,000 slaves manumitted by Melania (Palladius, *Hist.Laus.* 61.5); if not necessarily all rural, those freed were only those willing to accept freedom. To arrive at firm conclusions about numbers of slaves is impossible. In Italy, since slaves had originally served as substitutes for peasants who had been recruited into the army, when land was at a premium, it is logical that their numbers would have diminished in the later empire, when the army was largely provincial and marginal land became deserted after Diocletian imposed taxation. This supports sources that give the impression of an increase in tenancy and a decline in the commodity market. But the constant fear of slave revolts in Symmachus's letters suggests slaves were still common in the countryside. In provinces like Africa and Gaul, where slavery had never been the main form of labor, most rural chattel slaves were *vilici* and *actores* of the rich, and Augustine makes no reference to them working as field hands. Domestic slaves, by contrast, were ubiquitous, and they were owned, according to varied sources, by even the very poor.

The condition of slaves in general probably improved in late antiquity, if only because of the state's determination not to break up the unity of its estates by splitting resident slave families (*C.Th.* 2.25.1 [325]). Some of Melania's slaves demanded to be sold rather than be manumitted, and quasi coloni or *casarii* must have closely resembled the tied tenants with whom they were often grouped. One should not, however, exaggerate the pleasantness of slavery: rural slaves could still be sold as chattels, and urban slaves were sometimes treated with great cruelty (Amm.Marc. 28.4.16). Despite claims that Christianity introduced more humane treatment, the church accepted slavery as part of the moral order and acquiesced in their savage punishment. The law never confused the rights of coloni and slaves, who always remained without a legal *persona*.

The direct line of descent from coloni and slaves of the later empire to the serfs of the Middle Ages was challenged strongly by Bloch, on the grounds that "servitude of the soil" did not define the medieval serf and had nothing to do with feudalism. The dependency of rural workers, both slave and free, on their *patroni* inevitably increased as central political power disintegrated. But the serf was essentially an *homme de corps* whose ancestry may be traced in the personal entourages acquired by rich landlords and warlords in the twilight of the empire.

There were slaves in pre-Islamic Arabia, probably non-Arabs for the most part, but very little is known about them or their activities. The Qur'ān rarely uses the ordinary Arabic word for "slave," *'abd,* but prefers terms like *raqaba* ("neck") or *ma malakt aymānukum* ("what your right hand possesses"), thereby emphasizing a symbolic act of enslavement and the special juridical status of slaves as property with certain rights. Quite early, much legal discussion was devoted to these rights, especially with regard to Muslim slaves (usually born to slaves) or to children of slaves. The freeing of slaves was always considered a particularly good deed (Qur'ān 2:177, among many places). Industrial work forces of slaves, especially in southern Iraq, and military slaves made their appearance in the 9th century.

BIBL.: Peter Garnsey, *Ideas of Slavery from Aristotle to Augustine* (Cambridge, Eng., 1996). R. MacMullen, "Late Roman Slavery," *Historia* 36 (1987): 359–382. C. R. Whittaker, "Circe's Pigs: From Slavery to Serfdom in the Later Roman World," in *Classical Slavery,* ed. M. I. Finley (London and Totowa, N.J., 1987). R. Brunschvig, "'abd," in *Encyclopaedia of Islam.*   C.W. AND O.G.

Slaves

"The elemental, daily demonstration of the power of man over man is that of master over slave. Almost every household has a display of power of this kind" (Augustine). A slave was property; he was completely in this master's power; and he was without kin, stripped of an old social identity and denied access to a new one. These are the three basic components of chattel slavery. There have been other types of "unfree" (and dependent free) labor. Slave societies, in which slaves make a vital contribution to the production of wealth, as distinct from societies with slaves, have been historically uncommon, but the ancient world furnishes examples of this relatively rare phenomenon. Slavery was everywhere in the household, as Augustine writing in the early 5th century asserts for North African society; it maintained a significant presence in the urban and rural economies of the Mediterranean world from archaic Greece to late antique Rome.

Was slavery still important in late antiquity? By the conventional view, it was not: slavery was in decline and perhaps had been since the principate. The characteristic mode of dependent labor was now the colonate, a system of tied tenancy bearing some similarity to medieval serfdom; the colonate evolved at the expense of slavery, as slaves became coloni.

This traditional account has recently come under scrutiny, as have other aspects of the "decline" of the ancient world. Slavery was not as important in its apogee as has been assumed. Though dominant in some areas, over the Roman empire as a whole it was one of a number of systems of dependent labor, free and unfree, with which it coexisted, sometimes side by side. Slaves had never made up more than a minority of the workforce in the most significant wealth-creating sector of the economy, agriculture. In North Africa, where slaves (at least in Augustine's time) were ubiquitous in the household, in the rural economy they existed only in some areas (in the 2nd century notably in Tripolitania, for example, on the estates of Pudentilla, wife of Apuleius), being heavily outnumbered by free coloni (who, also in the 2nd century, are known from inscriptions to have worked the huge imperial properties, or *saltus,* of Africa Proconsularis). The workers whom Augustine sought to protect against being kidnapped and sold abroad by marauding "Galatian" slave-traders were coloni, not slaves. A similar picture, so far as we can tell (and the evidence is thin), could be painted for many other parts of the Roman empire. Domestic slavery was a regular feature of urban society, and it probably flowed over into the rural sector on some of the properties owned by the leaders of that society, perhaps those that lay near the city. In ancient society as in other societies, there was no sharp divide between domestic and agricultural, urban and rural, employment. Slavery was probably less significant in areas where the cultural influence of Rome, as signaled in the first place by a high degree of urbanization, was less marked, such as Celtic Gaul and Britain. On the other side, slavery had long been a structural feature of the society and economy of the city of Rome, its home provinces, and Sicily.

One consequence of scaling down the incidence of slavery is that a "decline" of slavery and "growth" of the colonate cannot be reduced to two aspects of one and the same process. The ambit of slavery was more circumscribed than that of the colonate, and it survived as a distinct phenomenon. A letter written by Augustine to Eustochius suggests there was a real risk of a leakage from the ranks of (free) coloni into those of slaves, rather than vice versa. It is still open to debate (the evidence is inconclusive) whether slaves on farms—for example, the 400 *servi agricultores* on the *villulae* of Melania—were now predominantly operating as quasi coloni rather than, as in the past, working directly under the supervision of the owner or his agent or manager. This would have involved a significant change in the structure and functions of agricultural slavery.

Were there developments in the manner or scale of enslavement—or manumission—in late antiquity? This is germane to the issue of decline. The main entry points into slavery were capture in war and birth to a slave mother. Warfare and other forms of capture continued to make a contribution to the slave population, in numbers unknown. The inheritance of slave status was probably at least as common as the infusion of "new stock," and had been so ever since the major wars of expansion had ceased (in the Augustan principate). The question is whether, in late antiquity, presumably under Christian influence, manumissions significantly increased, correspondingly reducing the reproductive potential of the slave population. The answer is to be sought not in the laws of Christian emperors, who did not press manumission on slave owners and strongly upheld the existing social divisions, but in the attitudes of bishops and the slave owners in their congregations. We may suspect but cannot demonstrate that the new and convenient procedure of *manumissio in ecclesia* stimulated manumission rates. However, instructions to masters to manumit do not appear in sermons, whereas injunctions to slaves along lines laid down by St. Paul—to stay put and serve their master, good or bad, as serving Christ—do. In general the leaders of the church (slave owners themselves, as was the church) accepted and sometimes justified slavery. Gregory of Nyssa was unusual in denouncing slave owning as an aspect of the sin of pride.

Men and women of an ascetic inclination, like Melania the Younger, did free their slaves or, like Macrina, Gregory's sister, try to treat them more as equals. There is no sign or likelihood that their example was followed by ordinary pious Christians, let alone slave owners in society at large.
P.D.G.

Slavs

The first writers to notice the Slavs—or Sclavinians, as they were often called—were Jordanes and Procopius, in the middle of the 6th century. The Slavs seem to have appeared north of the lower and middle Danube in the beginning of the century. Little can be said about their origin and earlier history on the basis of the written evidence. The scarcity of the sources has stimulated a variety of historical reconstructions, many of which trace the history of the Slavs back to pre-Christian times. These claims of continuity are often based on the Venethi, a people Tacitus had located to the east of the Germans; this name was later used for the Slavs by their Latin- and German-speaking neighbors. But the use of the name does not prove ethnic continuity, just as in the case of the people the Greeks called Scythians, or those the Germans called Welsh. Many scholars also use archaeological evidence to clarify Slavic prehistory. But any definition of archaeological regions as Slavic before the 6th century is purely hypothetical. There is a lot of evidence to suggest that in the first centuries of our era, the cultures northeast of the Carpathian Mountains enjoyed a relatively steady development;

but there is little proof that any of them were exclusively Slavic. Baltic, Finnic, and Germanic peoples, Dacians, Goths, and Sarmatians contributed to a cultural universe between the "Scythian" steppes and the forests of the Germania from whence the early 6th century saw the emergence of the Slavs into the light of history.

In the middle of the 6th century, Slavic groups lived north of the Danube, and from there they raided the countryside in Roman provinces. They were closely related to the Antae, who seem to have been more centrally organized. In central Europe, Slavs lived on both sides of the Carpathians, where the Lombard pretender Hildigis went into exile and found their support. After 567, Slavs moved into the spaces conquered by the Avars: the Carpathian Basin, the eastern Alps, Moravia and Bohemia, and the northwestern Balkans. As subjects of the Avars, they fought in Avar armies, as foot soldiers or in their dug-out boats *(monoxyla)*, for instance in the siege of Constantinople in 626. But their scattered settlements, often in wetlands, were hard to control, a problem Byzantine armies had to face as well. Slavs also attacked on their own. To curb the constant Slavic raids in the Balkan provinces, the emperor Maurice repeatedly launched offensives against Slavic settlements north of the lower Danube that were so unpopular with the soldiers that they rebelled in 602, resulting in the usurpation of Phocas, and soon in the collapse of the Roman order in most of the Balkan provinces. Slavic groups settled in most of the peninsula, from the Danube to the Peloponnesus, and the empire only gradually drew most of them more or less into its orbit and organized them into federate "Sklaviniai." Others became part of the Bulgar khanate after 680. Meanwhile, many Slavic groups in the periphery of the Avar empire had acquired some independence. Between 625 and 660, the Frankish leader Samo reigned over Bohemia and some neighboring regions as king of the Slavs. Much of the eastern Alps was ruled by Carantanian princes, who came under Bavarian dominion in ca. 740. This was the beginning of the first successful Slavic mission in the west. Earlier missionaries, like Columbanus or Amandus, had failed or abandoned their plans. Farther north, Slavs had moved into the lands along the Elbe, where they are well attested from the 7th century onward (for instance, the Sorbs).

Only in the ninth century do Slavic peoples regularly begin to appear in the sources, and their names are often geographical designations. The Antae, the Carantanians, the Sorbs, and a number of smaller groups in the Balkans are among the few ethnic units attested before 800; even some who later claimed ancient origins, such as the Serbs, the Croats, the Bohemians, and the Moravians, are not mentioned before the 9th century. Even more remarkable is that hardly any early Slavic rulers appear in the sources. The Antae had a king, at least until they were subjected by the Avars. In the later 6th century, the Byzantines had to deal with "*archontes*" of smaller groups (whom they mostly sought to eliminate). In the 7th, Slavic regional kings recognized by the emperor are known in the region around Thessalonica. Again the Carantanians and the Sorbs are exceptions; for instance, there was the *dux Surbiorum* Dervan (ca. 630) mentioned by Fredegar. However, there are several instances in which Slavs followed leaders from abroad: for example, the Greek impostor Chilbudios and the Lombard pretender Hildigis (Procopius), and the Frankish merchant Samo (Fredegar).

The expansion of the early Slavs does not fit neatly into the models that contemporaries, and modern scholars, use to describe Germanic barbarians and steppe warriors. What is striking about it is its success as a decentralized movement that was not led by monarchic rulers and a conspicuous warrior aristocracy. Many Slavic scholars have argued that the social differentiation among the early Slavs was comparable to that of Germanic peoples, only our witnesses did not notice. But the sources repeatedly contradict such a model. Others have maintained that Slavic groups spread only in the service of others, for instance as slaves of the Germans or, in Omeljan Pritsak's hypothesis, as the military retinue of the steppe aristocracy. That "Slav" meant "slave" both in the medieval west and in Arabic seems to support such a notion, although this is due, rather, to developments in the slave trade. But neither model can explain the apparent success of the early Slavic communities. They survived defeats and foreign rule not *although* they had not developed ambitious warrior elites and strong rulers, but *because* they had not. They seem to have had a strong sense of identity, expressed in the common Slavic language. It is not as easy to find common archaeological traits. Many, but not all, Slavs practiced cremation, lived in sunk huts, and used simple, hand-formed pottery of the "Prague type." But in many areas where Slavs are attested in written sources, archaeological evidence is still more or less lacking. This is partly due to lacunae in research but is also characteristic of the way in which the Slavs changed the landscape of large parts of late Roman Europe. Along most of the Danube and as far south as the Aegean, the appearance of the Slavs marks a disruption of the Roman order, much more than in the cases of the Germans in the western empire and the steppe warriors or the Arabs in the east. All of these groups had more or less tried to profit from existing systems of distribution and dominion. The Slavs usually settled as peasants and did not maintain the remnants of the Roman order they encountered. Only centuries later did they build their own Christian states in the region.

BIBL.: John V. A. Fine, Jr., *The Early Medieval Balkans: A Critical Survey from the Sixth to the Late Twelfth Century* (Ann Arbor, 1983). Joachim Herrmann, ed., *Die Welt der Slawen* (Munich, 1986). Walter Pohl, *Die Awaren* (Munich,

1988). Omeljan Pritsak, "The Slavs and the Avars," *Settimane di studio* 30 (Spoleto, 1982): 353–432.   W.P.

Sogdian

Sogdian, a major East Middle Iranian language, was used between the 4th and the 10th century C.E. Attested in two main forms—ancient (early) and cursive (formal)—it served as the administrative, mercantile, and religious medium of the Sogdians, who lived in central Asia during late antiquity.

An Indo-European language, like its West Middle Iranian counterpart Pahlavi, Sogdian was written using modifications of the Aramaic script. The early form of Sogdian is attested from fragmentary inscriptions found along the Upper Indus Valley and in the so-called Ancient Letters found within a ruined watchtower between Dunhuang and Loulan (in Chinese Turkistan). The cursive form is best known from an archive at Mt. Mugh (in modern Tajikistan) and from Buddhist, Manichaean, and Christian manuscripts. The scripts have approximately twenty to twenty-three letters each. Sogdian was eventually replaced by Yaghnobi, a language still spoken and written by people living in the Yaghnob River valley east of Samarkand. The Sogdian cursive script was also adapted for recording the Uighur language around the eighth century, remaining in use into the seventeenth century.

Secular Sogdian documents include the aforementioned Ancient Letters, which describe political and economic events along the Silk Road, and ostraca from a palace at the site of Varakhsha near Bukhara—all dating to the 4th century—legends on coins and graffiti from 8th century Panjikent, textual fragments of the Rostam epic, and the records of Prince Dewastich written as he held off Arab Muslim invaders at the fortress on Mt. Mugh around the year 722. Since the Sogdian language was used by religious sects in central Asia, a much larger corpus of devotional materials has survived. Buddhist Sogdian texts of the Mahayana tradition include the ever popular *Vessantara Jataka,* "(Birth) Story of (the Buddha) as (Prince) Vessantara," and the didactic "Sutra of the Causes and Effects of Action." Manichaean Sogdian writings include the canonical "Book of Giants," with its myth of fallen angels; "epistles" to guide the elect and hearers; and dozens of exquisitely illustrated fragments. Nestorian Christians translated Syriac materials into Sogdian, generally between the 5th and 8th centuries—including the Gospels of Matthew, Mark, and John, the book of Daniel, and hymns such as *Gloria in excelsis Deo.*

BIBL.: Mark Dresden, "Sogdian Language and Literature," in *The Cambridge History of Iran,* vol. 3, pt. 2, ed. Ehsan Yarshater (Cambridge, Eng., 1983), 1216–1229. Rüdiger Schmitt, ed., *Compendium Linguarum Iranicarum* (Wiesbaden, 1989). P. Oktor Skjaervø, "Aramaic Scripts for Iranian Languages," in *The World's Writing Systems,* ed. Peter T. Daniels and William Bright (New York, 1996), 529–530.   J.K.C.

Soghd

Soghd, Sogdia, or Sogdiana was a region of central Asia, located between the upper to middle reaches of the Oxus River (Amu Darya) and the Jaxartes River (Syr Darya) and also extending eastward into the Ferghana Valley (a total area roughly corresponding to modern Uzbekistan and southeastern Kazakhstan). By around 1000 B.C.E. it had been settled by east Iranians, people who eventually spoke the Sogdian language in late antiquity. The major cities of Soghd were Bukhara and Samarkand.

The *Avesta* designated this region as Sughdha. Called Sugda and Suguda by the Achaemenians, it was listed as a satrapy, or province, of their empire in inscriptions commissioned by Darius I and Xerxes I. Alexander the Great's forces conquered the region in the 4th century B.C.E., after which it became part of the Graeco-Bactrian kingdom, and then was held by the Saka or Scythian and Yueh-chih tribes. Han Chinese forces penetrated the area in the 2nd century B.C.E. It is unclear if the Parthian empire ever exerted much control or even influence here. The Kushans, however, did both. Herodotus, Strabo, and Ptolemy commented on the area's Iranian culture and on its large mercantile cities. By the 3rd century C.E., Soghd (*Pahlavi* Sulig, later Sogdestan; Parthian Sugd, Sugud) had become a northeastern province of the Sassanian empire. As Sassanian political control waned, Hephthalites and Turks entered the region between the 4th and 6th centuries. On the eve of the Arab Muslim conquest in the 8th century, al-Sugdh as it came to be called in medieval Arabic sources, was a semi-independent territory whose city rulers fell loosely within the Sassanian empire's sociopolitical sphere of influence. The population was still largely Iranian, but its rulers were of Irano-Turkish backgrounds—such as the *khatun,* or queen, of Bukhara. Muslim troops pillaged Sogdian cities from 674 to 676, before finally subjugating the region a little more than twenty-five years later. Arab settlers then joined the ethnic mix in al-Sugdh, a term which for Muslims usually denoted the territory between Bukhara and Samarkand. Sporadic strife persisted between the newcomers and the older communities for about two hundred years.

During all these periods, the region's economic base lay in trade that flowed between east and west through the highly urbanized Sogdian oases located along the Silk Road. In addition to a large merchant class, the region possessed a powerful, well-entrenched landlord class that dwelled in villas on the outskirts of the main cities. Workers and slaves were also an intrinsic part of the society. Due to its relative political independence and the constant presence of travelers, Soghd during late antiquity became a center for several religions, commencing with Zoroastrianism and followed by Hinduism, Buddhism, Nestorian Christianity, and Manichaeism—all of which developed local syncretic forms. Wall paintings at Panjikent and Varakhsha attest to this confluence. Later, at the end of late antiquity and during the Middle Ages, Islamization of Sogdiana occurred under the Abbasids, when Muslim missionaries preached in the cities and wandered the backroads seeking converts. The region then developed a flourishing Islamic culture.

BIBL.: G. Azarpay et al., *Sogdian Painting* (Berkeley, 1981). B. Gharib, "Source Materials on Sogdiana," *Bulletin of the Iranian Culture Foundation* (Tehran) 1 (1969): 66–81. Richard N. Frye, *The Heritage of Central Asia: From Antiquity to the Turkish Expansion* (Princeton, 1996).   J.K.C.

South Arabian

The phrase *South Arabian* was created in the early 20th century to designate languages of South Arabia other than Arabic. It is preferred over South Arabic, since these languages were not a southern branch of the Arabic family.

There are four South Arabian languages known through ancient inscriptions. From west to east, these are Minaic, in Jawf; Sabaic, in the region of Ma'rib; Qatabanic, in Wadis Bayhan and Markha; and Hadramitic, in the Hadhramaut. Sabaic is fairly close to classical Arabic and Ethiopic (Ge'ez), while the others, especially Hadramitic, are more distantly related.

The first known documents written in these languages (primarily from northeastern Yemen, between Jawf and Shabwa) date from the second half of the 8th century and the early 7th century B.C.E. The most recent are from the end of the 2nd century B.C.E. (Minaic), the 2nd century C.E. (Qatabanic), and the 3rd century (Hadramitic). These dates mark the end of independence for the kingdoms that used these languages. Only Sabaic was still being written at the end of South Arabian civilization, shortly after the mid-6th century. Moreover, a few indications suggest that, at that time, it had already been supplanted by Arabic for 200 years and was no longer spoken. That hypothesis would explain the rapid collapse of South Arabian civilization shortly after the conquest of Yemen by the Christian Abyssinians (in 525). The massacre of (Jewish) elites and the plague epidemic in the 550s may have eliminated all those still conversant in Sabaic. Thus, the works written in that language could no longer be understood.

The South Arabian epigraphic languages belong to the Semitic family of languages, such as Akkadian (in Mesopotamia), Hebrew, Arabic, and Semitic Ethiopic. They are distinguished by two original characteristics. First, they have three nonemphatic sibilants, notated s^1, s^2, and s^3 so as not to prejudice pronunciation. In comparing words of similar meaning in the various Semitic languages, linguists have hypothesized that the sibilants were pronounced /š/, /ś/, and /s/ (š is pronounced like the English "sh" as in *shoe*; ś is a lateral, articulated by passing air through one side of the mouth only, and has no equivalent in Arabic or in European languages). Second, the article, -*n* or -*hn*, is always positioned at the end of the word.

Three of these languages (Minaic, Qatabanic, and Hadramitic) form the factitive verb with the prefix s^1- (schema $s^1f'l$) and the third-person suffix pronouns with the s^1 element; Sabaic uses an -*h* in the place of s^1.

Given the available documentation, we are unable to assert that the South Arabian epigraphic language constituted a true family within Southern Semitic (a branch of Western Semitic). The similarities (such as the existence of three sibilants) are obvious, but differences are noted as well. To make the case, we would have to know the phonetics and, especially, the vowels and double consonants.

Several non-Arabic languages, called modern South Arabian, are still spoken in various regions of Yemen (Mahra and the Island of Socotra) and Oman (Zafār). They are distinguished from Arabic primarily by their phonetics: they include lateral consonants; their sibilants are distributed differently; and the emphatics are glottalized rather than velarized, as in Arabic. The lexicon and morphology are also very different. A speaker of modern South Arabian cannot be understood by a speaker of Arabic, and vice versa. It is believed that these modern South Arabian languages are derived from ancient languages that are not attested epigraphically, but that were no doubt closely related to those on inscriptions.

As a linguistic term, *South Arabian* is the opposite of *North Arabian*, a term that encompasses all the languages with some relation to Arabic that, in antiquity, were spoken on the rest of the peninsula, and also on the northern fringes of Yemen and perhaps in Tihama.

South Arabian, originally a linguistic notion, is also applied to the writing system of antique South Arabia. That system, exemplified in nearly ten thousand inscriptions, counting the fragments, has two forms. The first, called monumental, is particularly elegant, with regular, geometrical letters. It is found on inscriptions cut into stone or bronze and designed to last. The second, called cursive or minuscule, is a smaller version of the basic form, with appendages linking the letters. It is the system that was commonly used for handwritten documents of everyday life: letters, contracts, and inventories, superficially carved on small wooden cylinders. It has no aesthetic pretensions. Although cursive writing was derived from monumental, it was a different writing system, just as our minuscule letters differ from majuscules.

The South Arabian alphabet has twenty-nine consonants. As a general rule, doubled consonants are not notated. Certain vowels are notated by the consonants *w, y,* and *h,* especially when they are long vowels appearing at the end of words. This alphabet is perfectly suited to the notation of South Arabian languages, possessing letters in a sufficient number to transcribe all the consonants. Every character has a form easily distinguishable from the others, at least in the monumental inscriptions. A hyphen separates words.

The alphabetic order of South Arabian is specific to the southern Semitic writing systems, South Arabian and Ge'ez. It originated in Syria but was abandoned in that country in favor of the Ugaritic order, from which the order of the Latin alphabet was derived. Seven numeric symbols (for 1, 5, 10, 50, 100, and 1,000) complement the alphabet. Used before the Christian era, these were later replaced by spelled-out numbers.

South Arabian is written from right to left. However, during the ancient period, texts of several lines sometimes began in the normal direction (right to left), then changed direction with each succeeding line. That system, which suggests the movement of an ox plowing its field, is for that reason called *boustrophedon*. It makes it easier to read texts composed of very long lines, as seen on certain monuments. Arabic, Syriac, and Hebrew are also written from right to left, but Ethiopic is not, even though it is derived from South Arabian.

Although the letters are formed in the same way throughout South Arabia, modes of execution may have varied slightly from one kingdom to another and over the course of time. These differences help us determine the origin and date of the documents.

South Arabian writing was not invented in Yemen. It was derived from writing systems that appeared toward the middle of the second millennium B.C.E., between Sinai and northern Syria. That genesis has not been completely clarified. In Yemen, the most ancient written documents—pottery fragments with a few painted or carved letters—appeared between the 13th and the 10th centuries B.C.E. Because they are so sparse, it is not possible to identify the language used. Identification becomes possible with the first monumental inscriptions, which may date from the mid-8th century B.C.E.

The writing today called Arabic is not attested in pre-Islamic Arabia. It came from the Arabs of the Syrian desert, who borrowed it from the Christians of Syria and Iraq in the early 6th century.

South Arabian is, finally, the term by which one designates in a general way the civilization created by the South Arabian populations and languages and, as a result, those populations themselves.

BIBL.: A. F. L. Beeston, *Sabaic Grammar* (Manchester, Eng., 1984). John H. Healey, *The Early Alphabet (Reading the Past)* (London, 1993).   C.J.R.

Spiritual Direction

Spiritual direction was a prominent feature of late antique religious practice. From the aristocratic society of Rome and Constantinople to the cells of the Egyptian desert, Christian men and women sought spiritual directors to guide their ascetic discipline. In Neoplatonic circles, philosophers revered as much for their personal piety as for the intellectual content of their teaching attracted groups of disciples eager for instruction in philosophical mysticism.

The disciples of men such as Plotinus (205–270), Iamblichus (ca. 250–ca. 324), and Aedesius (d. ca. 353) sought intimacy with their individual instructors rather than identification with a particular philosophical "school." The philosopher's circle included both a large group of "hearers" and a smaller group of more dedicated followers who often shared in the instruction of the others. Philosophic instruction was combined with shared ascetic practice and, occasionally, communal living. In addition to the teachings of the "divine Plato," the Neoplatonic masters also revived and reinterpreted Pythagorean beliefs and experimented with theurgy. Because of the value placed on close personal association with an individual teacher, these groups usually disbanded following the teacher's death.

In Christian literature two genres of sources document the process of spiritual direction: collections of sayings and collections of letters. The most widely known collections of sayings on the spiritual life are the 4th century *Apophthegmata patrum*. These sayings from Egypt, Palestine, and Syria reveal the intimate relationships between the Desert Fathers (and Mothers) and their spiritual offspring. The Greek *Apophthegmata patrum* spread quickly and were translated into Latin, Coptic, Syriac, Armenian, Georgian, Ethiopic, and Arabic. The spirituality of the *Apophthegmata patrum* was based on a radical understanding of the Gospel that inspired dramatic renunciation of worldly goods, obligations, and family ties. Men and women gifted in personal holiness and discernment *(diakrisis)* undertook the instruction of disciples who gathered near their cells. The spiritual director taught by example, living out the ideal of holiness, as well as through verbal instruction. He taught lessons through dramatic visual parables. Abba Moses the Black instructed his brothers on humility. Summoned to a council to pass judgment on another, he arrived carrying with him a leaking jug filled with water. To the others who wanted to know the meaning of his action, Abba Moses replied, "My sins run out behind me, and I do not see them, and today I am coming to judge the errors of another" *(Moses 2)*. John the Dwarf learned obedience by following his spiritual director's command to water a dead stick stuck in the sand every day for a year, although the water source was at considerable distance *(John the Dwarf 1)*.

In the *Apophthegmata patrum,* teaching is often introduced by a disciple's approaching his instructor and saying, "Give me a word, Abba." The responses were collected from a rich oral tradition that passed from generation to generation. Spiritual direction entailed more than teaching; prayer was also a fundamental component of the spiritual director–disciple relationship, as attested in the common refrain, "Abba, pray for me."

The oral tradition of the Desert Fathers was transformed in later generations into a separate genre for a more literate group of ascetics. In the 6th century the prolific spiritual director Barsanuphius and his colleague John, living as anchorites outside of Gaza, together wrote 850 letters to monks, clergy, and laymen seeking guidance. They addressed concerns ranging from individual struggles with temptation to the evaluation of candidates for the episcopacy. Their letters merged the wisdom of the Desert Fathers with the genre of letter writing, which was already an established tool for spiritual direction.

Letters addressed by spiritual fathers to their protégés appear to record the progress of individuals within an intimate relationship, but they were also intended for a wider circulation. Chrysostom's letters to Olympias and Jerome's letters to a group of aristocratic women in Rome are examples of letters written for a dual audience. Jerome's letter to Laeta, the daughter-in-law of his own protégée Paula, counseling her on how to raise her own daughter as a dedicated virgin, was clearly meant to serve as a model for early training in the ascetic life. His advice is quite similar to that offered in an anonymous Greek homily written in Syria in the early 4th century that emphasized the important role of biological parents in the spiritual direction of their child.

The practice of ascetic spiritual direction pervasive among eastern Christians also gained popularity in the west. John Cassian (ca. 360–ca. 433), trained as a monk in Palestine and Egypt, collected the wisdom of great Egyptian spiritual directors and presented it to Latin audiences in his *Institutes* and *Conferences*. His writings influenced Benedict of Nursia (ca. 480–ca. 547), who recommended that they be read to the monks when they assembled in the evening (*Rule of St. Benedict* 42). Spiritual direction was a principal theme in the Benedictine Rule (*Rule of St. Benedict* 4–7), as in many other contemporary western rules. The abbot of the monastery assumed the oversight of the souls in his charge, preserving the reciprocal nature of obedience and obligation characteristic of the spiritual director–disciple relationship that had emerged from the earlier, informal setting of the desert.

BIBL.: Douglas Burton-Christie, *The Word in the Desert: Scripture and the Quest for Holiness in Early Christian Monasticism* (Oxford, 1993). Garth Fowden, "The Pagan Holy Man in Late Antiquity," *Journal of Hellenic Studies* 102 (1982): 33–59. Garth Fowden, "The Platonic Philosopher and His Circle in Late Antiquity," *Philosophia* 7 (1977): 359–383. Irénée Hausherr, *Spiritual Direction in the Early Christian East* (Kalamazoo, 1990).　J.H.-H.

Stilicho

Son of a Vandal, Stilicho rose quickly under Theodosius I, becoming *magister militum* in 392–393. In 393 he accompanied Theodosius on the campaign against the western usurper Eugenius. On Theodosius's death in January 395, Stilicho took control of the western empire in the name of Theodosius's son Honorius (age eleven). He also claimed the right to act as regent for Theodosius's other son, Arcadius, and to rule the entire empire. In this capacity Stilicho intervened twice in eastern territories in the Balkans, in 395 and 397, notionally to subdue Alaric's Goths but with the real aim of attracting political support in Constantinople.

After ca. 400, circumstances became increasingly difficult. First, Alaric and his Goths invaded Italy in 401–402 but were forced to withdraw. In 404–405 Stilicho made an alliance with them to wrest control of part of the Balkans from Constantinople, perhaps because Alaric's Goths were settled in the area and he needed their support. The planned campaign was postponed, however, when Italy was invaded by the Goths of Radagaisus in 405–406. Stilicho successfully defeated Radagaisus, but on 31 December 406 the Rhine frontier was crossed by Vandals, Alans, and Suebi. This prompted the usurpation of Constantine III, whose power spread across Gaul in 407. These events undermined Stilicho's control of Honorius, who broke from Stilicho entirely in 408, when Stilicho was forced to pay off Alaric with 4,000 pounds of gold and the two disagreed over how to respond to the death of Arcadius. In August of that year Stilicho accepted his own overthrow and death rather than provoke civil war.

BIBL.: A. D. E. Cameron, *Claudian: Poetry and Propaganda at the Court of Honorius* (Oxford, 1970). J. F. Matthews, *Western Aristocracies and Imperial Court AD 364–425* (Oxford, 1975). S. Mazzarino, *Stilicone: La crisi imperiale dopo Teodosio* (Rome, 1942).　P.H.

Stylites

Symeon, called Symeon Stylites the Elder, was born in about 390 in Sisa, a village of the *chora* of Nicopolis in Cilicia; he died on 2 September 459. He was the founder of an original type of ascetic life, stylitism. His biography comes to us from three sources, the account of Theodoret in his *Religious History;* the Greek *Life of Symeon Stylites* written by a certain Antony, who gives accounts of Antiochene traditions, and the Syriac *Life,* which comes from the Convent of Telanissos (Qal'at Sem'an).

The life of Symeon, son of well-off peasants, perfectly illustrates the progress of a "holy man" toward sainthood—and power—in the Syria of late antiquity. Symeon came to the monastery of Teleda in the territory of Antioch when still very young, in about 402, having already spent two years pursuing ascetic experiences. He imposed exceptional ordeals on himself, which earned him the hostility of other monks. Subsequently he left the convent, then moved to a nearby village, Telanissos, and eventually climbed to a peak overlooking the village that was surrounded by a wall, or *mandra*. To escape the throngs of pilgrims attracted by his reputation of holiness and his miracles, he isolated himself on a high rock; then, for forty-five years, he occupied a series of three or four pillars of increasing height. The last pillar, of which there are still remains, measured 40 cubits in height, that is, 18 to 20 m. It was constructed of three drums—in honor of the Holy Trinity—fixed on a pedestal. During his lifetime, Symeon attracted throngs of people from throughout the empire, including far-off Brittany, and from the entire east, including Iberia (Georgia) and South Arabia. At his death, his body was taken back to Antioch by a troop led by the *magister militum* Ardaburius, to ensure control over his relics. Symeon's success was the result of his extreme ascetic practices: fasting, standing up or squatting for prolonged periods of time, praying, bowing repeatedly, and exposing himself to the air, rain, snow, and sun. His success lay also in his capacity to intervene, sometimes through miracles, in rural conflicts or situations of distress—female sterility, drought, illness—or even in important public matters. He corresponded with emperors and met the sisters of Theodosius II. A vast pilgrims' sanctuary formed around the last pillar, with a monastery, a baptistery, and inns, built for the most part in the second half of the 5th century, after the saint's death. Pilgrimages to the site declined beginning in the 7th century.

Symeon's example inspired many stylites. Daniel, a native of Maratha, near Samosata, was a monk in Syria, then a hermit near Constantinople. He went on to live the life of a stylite for thirty-three years, until 493. Symeon the Younger settled on Wondrous Mountain near Seleucia Pieria; he died in 592. The stylite Alypius of Adrianopolis, from Paphlagonia, died during the reign of Heraclius. Both Symeon the Younger and Alypius are known through the hagiography of late antiquity. They, too, attracted crowds, spoke with emperors and the powerful, and performed many miracles. As late as the 11th century, figures such as St. Luke the Stylite or St. Lazarus the Galesiote exemplified this monastic mode of life, which continued even after that time. It was in Syria, above all, and primarily around Antioch, that numerous stylites lived between the 5th and 7th centuries. Their pillars, made of three drums placed on a pedestal, imitated that of Symeon. They were set up in convents, according to the almost universal practice of stylites. Their number seems to demonstrate that the practice became rather commonplace in the region.

From the beginning, however, the eccentric nature of the stylites' asceticism led to condemnations because of the pride and excess associated with it. Hence, a stylite who established himself in the Ardennes in the 6th century was forced to come down from his pillar by bishops who asked: "Who are you to compare yourself to Symeon of Antioch?" He was sent to a community of cenobites.

Though originally associated with Syria, stylites lived in widely distant regions: in Egypt (*P Turner* 54), on the outskirts of Trier (Gregory of Tours, *Hist.* 8.15), and in the Zagros Mountains, perched "like a carrion vulture" above hostile Nestorian villages (Thomas of Marga, *Book of the Governors* 3.8, trans. E. A. W. Budge, London, 1883). During the last civil wars of the Umayyad dynasty, a stylite was consulted by a Muslim general: his pillar was overthrown and he was burned for giving an unacceptable answer (*History of the Patriarchs of Alexandria* 1.8: *PO* 5.156).

BIBL.: H. Delehaye, *Les saints stylites* (Brussels, 1923). D. Frankfurter, "Stylites and *Phallobates*," *Vigiliae christianae* 44 (1990): 168–198. *The Lives of Symeon Stylites,* trans. R. Doran (Kalamazoo, 1992). P. Van den Ven, ed. *La vie ancienne de saint Syméon Stylite le Jeune,* 2 vols. (Brussels, 1962–1970). S. A. Harvey, "The Stylite's Liturgy," *Journal of Early Christian Studies* 6 (1998): 523–539.   P.-L.G.

Sufism

The term *Sufism (taṣawwuf)* designates a type of piety that began to emerge in the Islamic world in the 8th century. Sufism combined elements of asceticism found in early Islam, such as fasting, voluntary poverty, and renunciation of the world, with a firmer doctrinal base regarding spiritual experience and the worshiper's relationship with God. In this period it is difficult to distinguish between Sufism and various strands of asceticism; in the earliest biographical sources, it is clear that one could be both a Sufi and an ascetic (*'ābid, zāhid,* or *nāsik*). However, Sufis generally saw ascetic practices as devices to be used on the path toward union with God, whereas in the devotional piety of the ascetics these practices were undertaken for the sake of heavenly reward and as a way of embodying certain social values.

The origin of the term *ṣūfī* is unknown, but early authors frequently connect it to the word *ṣūf,* meaning wool; the wearing of a simple woolen cloak became a distinguishing feature of the Sufi. The term was first applied to contemporary figures in the late 8th century, but as Sufism began to take shape in the 9th and 10th centuries Sufi writers often claimed earlier ascetics as their forebears. While rejection of the world and solitude typifies the Sufi experience presented in literature, many early ascetics and Sufis were active as teachers, transmitters of hadith, fighters at the frontiers, or judges. Similarities in Christian and Islamic asceticism may be a result of the contiguity of these two communities; the famous ascetic Ibrāhīm ibn Adham (d. 777 or 778) even studied with a monk named

Abū Simʿān (Simeon) in Syria. However, it is impossible to isolate the effects of such contacts. Islamic asceticism and especially Sufism are marked by a distinct corpus of beliefs and practices that fully reflect the Islamic tradition.

BIBL.: A. J. Arberry, *Sufism: An Account of the Mystics of Islam* (London, 1965). Michael Bonner, *Aristocratic Violence and Holy War: Studies in the Jihad and the Arab-Byzantine Frontier* (New Haven, 1996). Louis Massignon, *Essai sur les origines du lexique technique de la mystique musulmane*, 2nd ed. (Paris, 1954). Annemarie Schimmel, *Mystical Dimensions of Islam* (Chapel Hill, N.C., 1975).   M.R.

Sulpicius Severus

In the late 4th century Sulpicius Severus became a successful legal advocate, married into a consular family, and seemed poised to become yet another young Gallic aristocrat to serve in the imperial administration. Then a meeting with Martin, the influential bishop of Tours, transformed his life: "I was overwhelmed by the man's authority." Sulpicius's response to Martin's challenge to abandon worldly attractions was to build two new churches and establish a monastic community on an estate in Primuliacum, somewhere in the vicinity of Toulouse and Narbonne. His father was dismayed at his son's rejection of his ancestral inheritance, and other Gallic bishops had already opposed Martin and his austere asceticism; so to explain his new lifestyle Sulpicius now also became an author.

Sulpicius's extant writings include an account of "sacred history," known as the *Chronicle*, that began with the Creation, summarized Old Testament events at length, and continued with a short survey of the history of early Christianity. This *Chronicle* concluded with an account of Martin's role in the controversy over the alleged heretic Priscillian. Sulpicius's other writings focused on the meaning of Martin's life and career. After his pilgrimage to Tours he published a *Life* of Martin, even before the bishop's death in 397. In it Sulpicius minimized Martin's earlier career as a Roman soldier and wandering ascetic in favor of a portrait of Martin as the ideal bishop who confronted emperors and propagated Christianity by performing miracles of healing, but never reneged on his "vow of a monk." In two subsequent letters he described Martin's death and funeral. This *Life* became very popular, especially after Sulpicius sent a copy to his friend Paulinus of Nola in Italy. It was also so controversial that in another letter Sulpicius contradicted skeptics of Martin's ability to revive dead people, and in his *Dialogues* he recounted at length more anecdotes about Martin's episcopal career and insisted that the bishop's asceticism was comparable to that of the illustrious monks in the Egyptian desert.

Despite his own conversion to asceticism Sulpicius was never able to lay aside his love of classical culture. With his writings he tried to recast biblical stories,

ecclesiastical history, and the life of an ascetic bishop into traditional literary genres and a classical style. In his monastic community a new baptistery displayed, in telling juxtaposition, portraits of both Martin of Tours, an uneducated bishop, and Paulinus of Nola, a distinguished Gallic aristocrat before his retirement to a saint's shrine in Italy. Sulpicius also commemorated the tomb of St. Clarus, another of Martin's disciples, whose most attractive feature was perhaps that before becoming an ascetic he had been, like Sulpicius, "a most distinguished young man."

A later tradition recorded by the Gallic priest Gennadius claimed that Sulpicius eventually became a priest, was interested in the controversy over Origenism, and maintained a vow of silence after being deceived by Pelagian heretics in his old age.

BIBL.: G. K. van Aandel, *The Christian Concept of History in the Chronicle of Sulpicius Severus* (Amsterdam, 1976). C. Stancliffe, *St. Martin and His Hagiographer: History and Miracle in Sulpicius Severus* (Oxford, 1983). R. Van Dam, *Leadership and Community in Late Antique Gaul* (Berkeley, 1985).   R.V.

Symmachus

Q. Aurelius Symmachus, who had the *signum* Eusebius, was born around 340 and died in 402; he was prefect of Rome (384–385), consul (391), *princeps senatus*. The antiquity of his family is debated, but it is possible that the Symmachi were already senators under Septimius Severus. Along with Vettius Agorius Praetextatus and Virius Nicomachus Flavianus, Symmachus was one of the leaders of the pagan contingent of the Senate who asked the Christian emperors for a tolerant policy toward paganism and preservation of the traditional religious institutions of the Roman state. In 382, he unsuccessfully led a delegation to Milan to ask Gratian, who had been the first among the emperors to reject the title *pontifex maximus*, to return the statue of the goddess Victory to the Senate hall. In 384, as the prefect of Rome, he wrote a long petition (*Relatio* 3) to young Valentinian II to request return of the statue, reestablishment of public funding to the Roman schools for priests, in particular to the vestals, and return of the lands confiscated by the tax office to the temples and the schools for priests. The response was negative, in part because of the fierce opposition of Ambrose, bishop of Milan, who threatened to excommunicate the emperor. Subsequent attempts by Symmachus with Theodosius and Honorius are remembered by Prudentius (*Contra Symmachum*), but the credibility of this source is uncertain. Among the ancients, Symmachus was noted, above all, as an orator and imperial panegyrist (*CIL*, 6.1699; *Olympiodorus* frg. 44), but only eight orations, published around 376, have come down to us. Today his fame is tied to the forty-nine *Relationes*, written to the emperors while he was prefect, and to his private correspondence (902 letters); these constitute two fundamental sources for knowledge of the political, social, and cultural history of the 4th century.

BIBL.: Jean Pierre Callu, *"Symmaque: Lettres"* (Paris, 1972, 1982, 1995). R. H. Barrow, *Prefect and Emperor: The Relationes of Symmachus, A.D. 384* (Oxford, 1973). J. F. Matthews, "The Letters of Symmachus," in *Latin Literature of the Fourth Century,* ed. J. W. Binns (London, 1974). *Symmaque,* ed. F. Paschoud (Paris, 1986).   D.V.

Synagogue

The ancient synagogue was the central Jewish communal institution in the Graeco-Roman and Byzantine worlds. In fact, we know of no other communal framework within the Jewish community from this era. From its inception, the synagogue fulfilled a myriad of functions, from the social and political to the religious and educational, as required by each Jewish community. Ordinarily, the synagogue served as the site for classes for children, study sessions for adults, and court proceedings; it was a communal meeting place, a depository for funds to be used locally as well as for funds to be sent abroad, the site of the community archives and library, a hostel for travelers and, of course, a place for communal religious worship. This multipurpose aspect of the synagogue building is clearly evident from the complex of rooms that often accompanied the synagogue hall. In the Diaspora, remains from Stobi, Ostia, and Dura-Europus are particularly relevant in this regard, as are those from Ḥammat Tiberias, Kefar Naḥum, ʿEin Gedi and Meroth in Roman-Byzantine Palestine.

The origins of the synagogue are shrouded in mystery. It emerges into the full light of history only in the 1st century C.E., although earlier traces are in evidence from Hellenistic Egypt and from the island of Delos. The synagogue evolved as a center for public activities that were once held in the city-gate complex. It was in this setting that almost all the functions attested for the synagogue in the 1st century C.E. onward had taken place in earlier periods. The transition occurred in the Hellenistic period, and the appearance of the synagogue in Palestine and the Diaspora was thus more or less simultaneous, as Jewish communities everywhere looked for an alternative to the changed city-gate structure.

Beginning in the 1st century, synagogues are mentioned in a variety of sources—Josephus, Philo, the New Testament, and rabbinic literature—and later on, in the words of pagan authors, church fathers, Roman imperial legislation, and later rabbinic traditions. While archaeological material is relatively sparse for the first few centuries C.E., it becomes far more abundant from the 3rd century onward. To date, thirteen buildings in the Diaspora have been identified as synagogues, while well over one hundred have been found in Roman-Byzantine Palestine. In all, some 350 in-

Mosaic in the synagogue at Hammath-Tiberias. Below a section with menorahs and the Ark of the Torah is one depicting Helios encircled by the signs of the zodiac.

scriptions relating to the synagogue or its officials have been discovered.

The prevailing Hellenistic-Roman culture was a decisive factor in the physical appearance of the synagogue. Synagogue buildings in the Diaspora were invariably built in the regnant styles of the particular locale, following the models of either local domestic or public architecture. Many buildings in Palestine, especially in the Galilee and Golan, were patterned after Roman civic buildings or perhaps Nabataean temple courtyards, while others drew on the Christian basilical model, featuring a central nave, two aisles, an apse or *bima,* narthex, and atrium, as, for example, in the synagogues in Beth Alpha, Ḥammat Gader, and Maʿon (Nirim). Moreover, these synagogues reflected many of the prevalent art forms of the times. The stone carvings found in many Galilean synagogues are imitations of motifs widespread in antiquity; the designs on mosaic floors often drew on Byzantine models found in churches, palaces, and villas. An example of one such popular mosaic design is an amphora with extended vines forming medallions that encircle depictions of animals, baskets, and fruit; it can be found in Beth Shean, Maʿon (Nirim), and Gaza.

Acculturation is further expressed by the ubiquitousness of Greek language and terminology within the synagogue. Some 95 percent of synagogue inscriptions appear in Greek, Aramaic, and Latin—the linguae francae in Palestine and the Diaspora at the time—of which the overwhelming majority are in Greek. Similarly, the official titles of synagogue functionaries (such as the archisynagogue, archon, and others) were drawn from the larger Graeco-Roman cultural context.

Synagogues were located in diverse settings and designed in a variety of ways—monumental and modest, with single and multiple entrances, ornate and simple, and in central and peripheral locations within a city, to mention but a few. Diversity is likewise evident in synagogal art. Some synagogues were conservative in nature and featured almost no figural art, others were more acculturated and represented animal, human, and even mythological motifs. Many of the boldest representations are found not in the Diaspora but within Palestine itself (see below). Given this pattern of widespread diversity—both architectural and artistic—there is little justification today for the once dominant theory that assigned a different synagogue typology to different historical periods. Rather, various types of synagogues were built at one and the same time, and even in the same places. Ancient Beth Shean (Scythopolis), where five strikingly different synagogue buildings were found, is an excellent example of this diversity.

Artistic depictions in synagogues were also the result of changing norms over time. In the late Second Temple period, figural art had been almost universally eschewed by the Jews; by later antiquity, the pendulum had swung back considerably and figural art was being employed in the majority of synagogues in Palestine. The most remarkable expression of this newly discovered openness is the central place accorded depictions of Helios and the zodiac signs in five synagogues of Palestine (Hammat Tiberias, Huseifa, Beth Alpha, Sepphoris, and Naʿaran), and possibly in two others (Susiya and Yafia). At the same time, the synagogue in ʿEin Gedi named the zodiac months but without figural representation. Clearly, this last-mentioned community was much more conservative than many others in the country.

While the synagogue remained the central communal institution of each Jewish community throughout antiquity, its religious component gained more prominence in the course of late antiquity. This trend finds expression archaeologically in the orientation of synagogue buildings; Diaspora synagogues focused their worship toward Eretz Israel, those in Palestine toward Jerusalem. This emphasis on a Jerusalem orientation for worship finds expression in rabbinic literature as well (Tosefta, Berakhot 3:15–16, and parallels). Excep-

tions to this rule are few. The focus of the building—the wall facing Jerusalem—was almost always highlighted by a *bima*, apse, or niche, or a combination of these elements. Moreover, synagogue interiors were increasingly decorated with Jewish symbols, particularly the menorah, shofar (ram's horn), and Torah shrine. At times the decoration was quite lavish, as attested by the walls of Dura-Europus or the impressive mosaic pavements in Hammat Tiberias and Beth Alpha. In many cases, the highlighting of a cluster of the above-noted Jewish symbols takes precedence; on occasion biblical scenes or figures are featured. Such scenes include the Binding of Isaac (*ʿAqedah*) story (Beth Alpha, Dura-Europus, and Sepphoris), the Noah story (Gerasa), Daniel (Susiya, Naʿaran), and David (Gaza, Meroth?), not to speak of the forty or fifty panels of biblical scenes that once graced the Dura synagogue. Moreover, inscriptions in both Palestine and the Diaspora now begin to refer to the synagogue building as a "holy place" and to the congregation as a "holy community."

The increasingly religious dimension of the synagogue is likewise evident in the expanding liturgy from late antiquity. The central liturgical component of the pre-70 synagogue was the reading of the Torah, along with its ancillary activities (translating the Torah into the vernacular, reciting the *haftarah,* and delivering a sermon). This was certainly true of the ordinary Judaean synagogue (although it should be noted that the sectarian community at Qumran had already developed a fixed prayer liturgy from the late Hellenistic period). The situation in the Diaspora was probably somewhat different. While we have no traces of prayers from this early period, the very fact that the Diaspora synagogue was often called a *proseuche* (house of prayer) seems to bear witness to the importance of this component in such settings. Following the destruction of the Temple in 70, daily, Sabbath, and festival prayers developed among the sages of Yavneh, and with this addition came a greater formalization and institutionalization of already existing components of the liturgy. How quickly the rabbinic model became normative in the average synagogue is difficult to say, but it was probably a matter of only decades or, at most, generations rather than centuries. Later on, in the Byzantine period, the recitation of sacred poetry (*piyyut*) was added to the synagogue liturgy. This practice undoubtedly has much to do with the *poetes* being recited concurrently in Byzantine churches.

By late antiquity the character of the synagogue had undergone considerable change. While it continued to serve as a community center, the synagogue had acquired a distinctly sacred status. Religious symbols were often depicted prominently, the Jerusalem orientation of the entire building was emphasized, and the building was frequently referred to as a "holy place." One sage refers to the synagogue as a "lesser (or diminished) Temple" (Babylonian Talmud, Megillah 29a).

Thus, even if only partially, the synagogue had come to replace the Temple in the religious life of the Jewish community.

BIBL.: Ismar Elbogen, *Jewish Liturgy: A Comprehensive History*, trans. Raymond Scheindlin (Philadelphia, 1993). S. Fine, *This Holy Place: On the Sanctity of the Synagogue in the Greco-Roman Period* (Notre Dame, 1997). Rachel Hachlili, *Ancient Jewish Art and Archaeology in the Land of Israel* (Leiden, 1987). Lee I. Levine, "The Nature and Origin of the Palestinian Synagogue Reconsidered," *Journal of Biblical Literature* 115 (1996): 425–448.   L.L.

Synesius

Synesius's literary work reflects the intellectual atmosphere of the eastern empire in the 4th and 5th centuries and expresses a very interesting personality. Synesius was passionately fond of philosophy, but he also loved hunting parties, which he organized for his friends on his estate. He held the highest political offices of his town and, as ambassador in Constantinople, he was an eyewitness to important political events. When he was near the end of his life, Synesius became the bishop of Ptolemais. In continual contact with friends and relatives, this philosopher-bishop wrote letters to many military and civilian officials, to the Pentapolis priests, and to his much adored philosophy teacher, Hypatia.

Synesius was born in Cyrene around 370 C.E. The date of his move to Alexandria is uncertain, but he remained there until 395 or 398 at the school of Hypatia, the daughter of the mathematician and astronomer Theon. Then he made a journey to Athens, a town that very much disappointed him. Athens was probably a quick stop on the way to Constantinople. He went to the capital to bring *aurum coronarium* to the emperor and deliver a speech. The date and interpretation of his *Peri basileias* and *Peri pronoias* are linked to the correct date of this journey. It is not clear whether he was in Constantinople between 399 and 402 or from 397 to 400 C.E. In the latter case, the *Peri basileias,* written in 397, should show Synesius's hostility to Eutropius's policy in that year with respect to Alaric and the Illyricum. On the other hand, a broader program for a general political renewal could fit well with the work if it was written in January of 400, after Rufinus's fall (395), Alaric's invasion, and especially after Eutropius's end (399). Equally uncertain is the dating, and so the significance, of the *Peri pronoias.*

Many letters written before or after the Constantinople journey also continue to have unsure dates, nor is it easy to understand the chronology of the other letters. In total there are 156 authentic epistles addressed to about forty people, distributed over about twenty years (390–413). Although undated, the letters have great value because of the variety and elegance of their style. We also learn from them the central events of Synesius's life: his wedding in Alexandria to a Christian woman; the births (and deaths in adolescence) of his three sons; the actions taken in defending the Pentapolis region from barbarian raids with local and irregular troops; the difficult relationships with the military governors, who were weak and unfamiliar with the localities; the strong fight against the corrupt and inauspicious *praeses* Andronicus; and especially his election as bishop in Ptolemais.

Whether his bishopric lasted just over a year (ordination on 1 January 412, death at the beginning of 413) or more than two years (acclamation during the summer of 410 and consecration at the beginning of 411), this period was extraordinarily intensive. His letters were filled with pain, but it was not over the choice between paganism and Christianity. Indeed, he was born to a Christian family and it is now difficult to believe that he converted only formally at the time of his ordination. Rather, his doubts concerned the accession to an ecclesiastical post, which required renunciations (including that of a full conjugal life) and imposed the preaching of the central Christian dogmas. For him, these were nothing more than popular myths in comparison with his Neoplatonic views.

BIBL.: T. D. Barnes, "Synesius in Constantinople," *Greek, Roman, and Byzantine Studies* 27 (1986): 93–112. A. J. Bregman, *Synesius of Cyrene, Philosopher-Bishop* (Berkeley, 1982). A. Cameron and J. Long, *Barbarians and Politics at the Court of Arcadius* (Berkeley, 1993). J. H. W. G. Liebeschuetz, *Barbarians and Bishops: Army, Church and State in the Age of Arcadius and Chrysostom* (Oxford, 1990). D. Roques, *Etudes sur la correspondance de Synésios de Cyrène* (Brussels, 1989). D. Roques, "Synésios à Constantinople: 399–402," *Byzantion* 65 (1995): 405–439. S. Vollenweider, *Neuplatonische und christliche Theologie bei Synesios von Kyrene* (Göttingen, 1985).   R.LIZ.

Syria

In classical antiquity, Syria designated, first, the vast zone extending from the Amanus to Sinai, bounded on the east by deserts and on the west by the Mediterranean Sea. The concept is related to populations: Syria is the land of the Syrians, that is, the settled Semites; it can extend far to the north, toward Mesopotamia. Arabs of the Middle Ages called the zone we know as Greater Syria "al-Sham," "the country on the left." But although people living in late antiquity knew that meaning of the word *Syria,* they also used it in another way. Syria could refer to the patriarchate of Antioch, including Cilicia and Isauria, then minus Palestine after the creation of the patriarchate of Jerusalem in the mid-5th century. Syria could also be applied to more restricted zones in the interior of Greater Syria, with, at minimum, the provinces of Syria Prima and Syria Secunda around Antioch and Apamea, or, more broadly, those two provinces plus the two Phoenicias and the Euphratensis. In that case, it was no longer the populations that produced the geographical language, but rather administrative decisions. The texts of late antiquity used these various systems, sometimes even combining them. Contemporary scholars hesitate between the broad study of Greater Syria during late antiquity, as a prefiguration of the central kernel of the Umayyad empire, and that of a less vast region ranging north to south from Cyrrhus to Damascus, and east to west from the Mediterranean to the Euphrates. We shall adopt the latter definition, leaving aside Osrhoëne, Mesopotamia, the Palestines, and Arabia.

The region thus defined is about 350 km long north to south, and 150 to 350 km west to east, depending on the course of the Euphrates. Late antiquity was characterized by unprecedented economic development in the region. The main aspect of that development was continuous demographic expansion between the 4th and 6th centuries, which led to the growth of villages, as seen in the limestone massif of northern Syria shared by the territory of Antioch and Apamea. Thanks to recent research, we are beginning to understand that, farther to the east, in Chalcidice, for example, or near the Euphrates, new villages appeared, particularly in the territories of cities founded near military posts, such as Rusāfa or Anasartha. In the steppe, archaeological prospecting has revealed a high level of land development, which included the use of sophisticated hydraulic systems, generally employing the qanat technique. The limestone massif and the steppe were marginal zones, however, preserved by chance by medieval depopulation. We can only imagine the agricultural activity of the most developed zones, such as the Antioch plain and the coastal regions. The overpopulation of Syria is also illustrated by numerous inscriptions mentioning Syrians in the west—in Italy, in particular—and by accounts, especially those of Gregory of Tours and Salvianus, noting the presence of Syrian merchants in Gaul.

One important activity in the cities, especially at such ports as Tyre, Sidon, Berytos, Tripolis, Laodicea, and Seleucia, was the manufacturing of artisanal goods. Glass, silk, purple dye, and textiles were produced there and established the cities' renown. We have the impression that other cities in the interior also had significant artisanal activity, as was the case in Antioch, Emesa, and Damascus. Large-scale commerce was still unknown for the most part. Populations had almost no knowledge of the Euphrates route after Palmyra disappeared in the 3rd century; relations with the western Mediterranean are attested for men more often than for products, but certain "Antioch-style" amphorae are being uncovered at western sites. Before the advent of Islam, contacts with Ḥijāz concerned primarily Bostra and Gaza, outside the zone we have delimited.

The prolonged peace in Syria until the end of the 5th century allowed economic growth to accompany demographic growth. Wars occurred farther to the east and north. However, between the 520s and the 640s, a series of raids, invasions, and demolitions touched Syria, culminating in the Persian occupation of 613 and 629, then with the Islamic conquest of 635 to 640. Not all war operations were equally destructive, but they were accompanied by two major epidemics, one in the 540s, the other, called the Amwas plague, beginning in 639. They had catastrophic effects on the Syrian population. Current historical researchers have been inclined to posit the beginning or middle of the 6th century as the turning point. At that time, it is believed, expansion stopped, the villages of the limestone massif, now saturated, began their decline, and Antioch, plundered by the Persians and destroyed by earthquakes, lost its importance. One aspect of the crisis was no doubt regional: beginning in the early 6th century, it seems that Arabia and the Palestines, farther from the war zones, more closely linked to prosperous Egypt, and better suited for large-scale international trade, did not experience the same decline. They continued to be prosperous until the mid-7th century. It is also possible that the pioneer zones of the Syrian steppe better resisted the tendency toward decline than did the traditional farming zones. Nonetheless, the decline during the Umayyad period was not arrested by the royal installations, called "Umayyad castles," built in this same steppe.

Late antiquity brought the Christianization of Syria, which occurred for the most part between the mid-4th and the mid-5th century, an astonishingly short period of time. It took place despite the well-known pagan resistance, which has been largely overestimated by modern authors. It is accurate to say that Syria was entirely Christianized, but not homogenized. Doctrinal disputes were very intense, dividing Chalcedonians and Monophysites in particular. It would be wrong to locate Syria as a whole within the Monophysite zone, like Egypt. Regional differences were firmly rooted, and though Monophysites were numerous in Antiochene and near the Euphrates, they were much less common in Apamea, Emesa, Damascus, and along the coast. It would also be overly simplistic to contrast rural zones where the Syriac language was spoken and Hellenized cities, or to oppose Hellenized Chalcedonians and Syriac Monophysites. In reality, we can distinguish between those who used Syriac as a written language—a habit that disappeared near the coasts and south of Emesa—and those who wrote only in Greek. In both cases, however, people may have had a knowledge of the other language.

Was Syria's conquest by the Muslims favored by these divisions or, as Kaegi believes, is there a strictly techno-military explanation? The conquest, in any case, placed Syria at the center of a world empire whose capital was Damascus. The advent of the Abbasids later led to Syria's marginalization.

BIBL.: F. M. Donner, *The Early Islamic Conquests* (Princeton, 1981). G. R. Hawting, *The First Dynasty of Islam* (London, 1986). W. E. Kaegi, *Byzantium and the Early Islamic Conquests* (Cambridge, Eng., 1992). G. Tate, "La Syrie à l'époque byzantine: Essai de synthése," in J. M. Dentzer, W. Orthmann, eds., *Archéologie et histoire de la Syrie* (Saarbück, 1989), II, 97–116. G. Tate, *Les campagnes de la Syrie du Nord du IIe au VIIe siècle,* vol. 1 (Paris, 1992).   P.-L.G.

Syriac

Syriac is the designation in general use for the Aramaic dialect of the city of Edessa that became the principal indigenous vehicle of linguistic expression for Semitophone Near Eastern Christianity. The Graeco-Latin form *Syriac* has been retained in western scholarship to distinguish the language from polysemous *Syrian,* but neither Syriac nor Syrian is fully justified by linguistic or geographical criteria, since Syriac belongs to the Eastern Mesopotamian group of Aramaic dialects. The language is rather conservative in its written appearance. Among its characteristic Eastern Aramaic features are the loss of the determinative force of the postpositive definite article -*ā* and the use of the preformative *n-* for the third person masculine imperfect. In general, the dialect of Edessa was certainly not much different from dialects spoken in other cities of the region. Its ultimate predominance was due to the fortunate combination of the political independence enjoyed by Edessa (through about the first third of the 3rd century C.E.) with the early official status of Christianity in the city. A famous legend speaks of one of its rulers, named Abgar, who sent an embassy to Jesus; it brought back not only a helpful letter but also a painting of Jesus, which became the prototype of miraculous portraits of Christ "not made by human hands." However, the actual conversion of the ruling house and the majority of the population is assumed to date only from the late 2nd century. Still, the city's language became the predominant literary medium of the Christian Near East for many centuries. A large literature was produced in it and served for the expression of a highly developed culture. Above all, it is a basic source for the religious history of late antiquity. Missionary activity carried it far into eastern Asia. Among the old Syriac inscriptions discovered in the region, the most noteworthy are those forming part of colorful and instructive mosaics. Among its early literary remnants, the works connected with the name of Bar-Daisān (Bardesanes, 154 to ca. 222) are valuable examples of the philosophical and religious crosscurrents within the Near Eastern Hellenistic (and Persian) civilization.

A Syriac book hand is attested by a vast store of preserved manuscripts dating from the 5th century on. Three different types of script were developed. The oldest is known as *esṭrangelā* (from Greek *stroggylē,* round). A quite similar ductus with, however, much less clean-cut forms of the letters is known as "Nestorian," implying its use in the eastern, Persian-dominated region where Nestorianism predominated, while a widely employed more cursive ductus was called *serṭō* "script" (*ō* corresponds in the west to eastern *ā,*

this being one of the phonetic features that distinguish the western pronunciation of Syriac from that in the east). As in older Aramaic, no vocalization system existed in Syriac originally. The need for an indication of phonetic and also certain grammatical features led to the invention of a system mainly consisting of dots that became eventually quite complicated and was most fully developed for Nestorian writing. In the west, the Greek vowels were taken over. They were written small, either above or underneath the consonant preceding the vowel; attempts to insert vowel signs between the consonants were unsuccessful. The Syriac vocalization activity appears to antedate that of the Hebrew Masoretes and to have inspired them.

Syriac has remained in use as a church language to the present. Its use as a spoken language declined after the Muslim conquest. Modern Aramaic dialects spoken by Christians and Jews in Kurdistan did not develop directly from Edessan Syriac. As a literary language, Syriac continued to be kept alive and even achieved a quite productive resurgence in the Middle Ages and later. The works composed in Syriac have preserved for us the most extensive vocabulary known so far of any Aramaic dialect. They have also preserved many loanwords (as well as transliterations) from the Greek and, more important linguistically, from various stages of Iranian. Being primarily a religious and monastic literature, Syriac contains fundamental information on the Christological struggles, on Bible interpretation, and on matters of liturgy and theology in its many manifestations, as it has also preserved occasional data on paganism and Gnosticism as well as mysticism. Among Bible translations, the one generally known and accepted as the *Peshiṭṭā* or "simple one" occupies a deserved place in Bible criticism.

A particularly noteworthy trait of Syriac literature is its admirable quality of artistic expression. Poetry, especially, which uses strictly syllable-counting meters, was intensively cultivated and often achieved a high degree of emotional effectiveness. Among its many representatives, the most lasting fame fell to Ephrem of Edessa (Ephraem Syrus, d. 373). The numerous lives of martyrs and saints are often written in vivid prose and show literary skill and imagination in addition to providing historical and typological information. Secular subjects, such as philosophy, history, and science, were no doubt cultivated to a much larger extent than the surviving texts suggest. For the history of linguistic theory, it is important that the grammar of Dionysius Thrax found its way into Syriac. From Muslim times, but probably continuing earlier interests, a handbook of rhetoric by Antonius of Takrit and dictionaries like that of Bar Bahlūl, who was much concerned with Greek loanwords, suggest further aspects of Syriac participation in the surrounding civilization. Preserved translations from Greek into Syriac include some of the works of Aristotle and Hippocrates and Galen. Essays from Plutarch's *Moralia,* as well as moral treatises by

Themistios and others, are represented in Syriac. The Syriac "two books of Homer," however, are known only from bibliographical reference but may have served as a conduit into Arabic. The translation methods employed by speakers of Syriac, which eased the flow of the Greek cultural heritage into Arabic, is particularly well documented in the Arabic *Risālah* "epis-tle" of the 9th century Ḥunayn ibn Isḥāq, on "what he knew about the works of Galen that were translated (into Syriac and Arabic) and some that were not." As a means of transmission of Hellenistic civilization into Arabic, and from there, later, to medieval Europe, Syriac played a prominent role. F.R.

Tabari

Abū Jaʿfar Muhammad ibn Jarīr al-Tabarī (b. ca. 839 in Amol, the capital of Tabaristan, Iran), was the most authoritative Qurʾānic commentator and historian of the classical Islamic period. His prodigious scholarly output included exegetical, legal, historical, ethical, and theological treatises, several of which have been preserved and published. His gigantic Qurʾānic exegesis *Jamiʿ al-Bayan ʿan Taʾwil Ay al-Qurʾān* (known as *Tafsīr,* 30 vols., Cairo, 1905–1911) and his universal history *Taʾrīkh al-Rusul waʾl-Mulūk* (15 vols., Leiden, 1879–1901) established the methodologies followed for many centuries after him in these two fields, which are considered fundamental for Islamic learning until today. Al-Tabarī was also the founder of a *madhhab* (school of jurisprudence), called al-Jaririyya after his father, but it does not seem to have long survived his death.

Al-Tabarī, who appears never to have married, devoted all of his long life to scholarship. He was a precocious learner. He memorized the Qurʾān by the age of seven, left home at fourteen, and traveled to the major centers of learning in Iran, Iraq, Syria, Ḥijāz, and Egypt in *talab al-ʿilm* (the pursuit of knowledge). Around 870 he settled in Baghdad, where he studied, taught, and wrote until his death in 923. He was a prolific and highly disciplined writer (some reports state that he produced fourteen folios every day for forty years), a witty and diplomatic interlocutor, and a proud and idealistic scholar who revered solid and pure scholarship and declined the patronage of many powerful politicians on moral grounds. He was no doubt helped in that respect by the financial independence provided by income from properties in Tabaristan that he drew on until his death.

In his writing, al-Tabarī was more of a compiler than a composer: he collected, sifted through, and arranged an enormous amount of oral and written material that would otherwise have been lost to us. In the *Commentary,* he followed the Qurʾān text word by word, supplying all the explanations transmitted in reports from the Prophet Muhammad, his Companions, and their followers. In the *History,* he used, in addition, written monographs on genealogy, poetry, tribal affairs, and specific events, recorded by earlier Muslim scholars (many of which monographs are known only through his work). His narrative begins with the creation, followed by the history of the patriarchs, prophets, rulers of antiquity, and the Sassanian shahs. This part is arranged by periods. The second part, beginning with the life of the Prophet, followed by the rule of the four caliphs, the Umayyads and Abbasids, is arranged by years. It stops in July 915. The work is universal only in a theocentric sense. It presents the development of human history as a divinely inspired succession of prophecies culminating in the career of the Prophet Muhammad, and, from that point on, it treats the progress of the Islamic community as a continuous manifestation of God's purpose.

In approach, al-Tabarī was a strict traditionalist. His method, developed for the study of ḥadīth, centered on examining the probability and authority of the *isnad* (chain of transmission) for every report. He was, on principle, not critical of the content of the reports themselves, and thus permitted competing versions with varying degrees of veracity to stand side by side. He sometimes, however, especially in the Qurʾānic commentary, allowed himself as a true *mujtahid* (a legist formulating independent opinions) to judge the content of the account at hand. His achievements nonetheless were crucial for the development of both Qurʾānic and the historical sciences.

BIBL.: *Al-Imam al-Tabari fi dhikra murur ahada ashara qarnan ala wafatih, 310 H–1410 H*, 2 vols. (Rabat, 1992). *Yadnamah-i Tabari: Shaykh al-Muʾarrikhin Abu Jafar Muhammad Ibn Jarir Tabari, 225–310 Hijri Qamari* (Tehran, 1991). Claude Gilliot, *Exégèse, langue, et théologie en Islam: L'exégèse coranique de Tabari (m. 311/923)* (Paris, 1990). Muhammad Mustafa Zuhayli, *Al-Imam al-Tabari: Shaykh al-Mufassirin, wa-ʿUmdat al-Muʾarrikhin wa-Muqaddim al-Fuqaha al-Muhaddithin, Sahib al-Madhhab al-Jariri: 224 H–310 H* (Damascus, 1990). Franz Rosenthal, "The Life and Works of al-Tabari," in *The History of al-Tabari*, vol. 1: *General Introduction* and *From the Creation to the Flood*, ed. and trans. F. Rosenthal (Albany, N.Y., 1989), 5–134.   N.R.

Tablettes Albertini

In 1928 natives living in the region of Djebel Mrata on the Algerian-Tunisian border brought to light forty-five complete and incomplete documents written in ink on square or oblong pieces of cedar wood. The texts deal with a variety of matters—one records a portion of the dowry of a young woman, another the sale of a slave, and yet another what seems to be the accounts of the *fundus tuletianus,* a local estate. This fundus is the concern of most of the documents, which also register sales of olive trees and small plots of land that were under cultivation by peasants. In their present condition most transactions bear a date in the form of the regnal year of the Vandal king Gunthamund (ruled 484–496 C.E.); all surviving dates extend from 17 September 493 to 21 April 496. In several of the texts the vendors indicate that the plots of land they are selling are part of their *culturae Mancianae* (Mancian cultivations)—that is, lands whose disposition is governed by the Mancian agrarian law of the 1st century C.E.—and that the owner of these lands is one Flavius Geminius Catullinus, Perpetual Priest. The sellers reckon prices in *solidi* (the imperial gold currency) and *folles* (bronze pieces valued in multiples of *nummi,* the *nummus* being the basic unit of bronze coinage). With the purchases went guarantees—against vendor fraud and third-party intervention. Occasionally the vendors themselves drew up the deed (signed before local witnesses), but more often village officials or priests performed this function.

The great specialist Eugène Albertini took on the task of reporting the discovery of these tablets to the Paris Académie des Inscriptions et Belles-Lettres (1928) and offering a preliminary publication of two of the texts (*Journal des savants,* 1930). In the definitive edition of all the documents, achieved in 1952

under the auspices of the government of Algeria, the editors named the tablets after their first distinguished student.

The ancient literary sources for the Vandal sojourn in Africa portray the intruders as barbarians who shattered the Christianized civilization of Roman Africa. The Tablettes Albertini offer a fascinating corrective to this depiction. A land tenure system set forth in the great days of the Roman empire is still alive and well, and the landowner holds a traditional priesthood. Some recently discovered documents support further the image of continuity in Vandal Africa. In 1965 local nomads discovered ostraca at and around Bir Trouch, located near the Oued el Mitta in Algeria. These ostraca, dated also by regnal years of King Gunthamund, record, frequently in measured units, the produce from an estate. The common date of these texts and the Tablettes Albertini, together with the fact that Gunthamund was the first Vandal monarch to issue silver coinage in his own name, bring to view the interesting possibility that Gunthamund made a systematic attempt to organize the economy of his kingdom. If so, he had no hesitation to accept procedures handed down from the Roman past.

BIBL.: C. Courtois et al., ed., *Tablettes Albertini: Actes privés de l'époque vandale* (Paris, 1952). P. Grierson, "The Tablettes Albertini and the Value of the *Solidus* in the Fifth and Sixth Centuries C.E.," *Journal of Roman Studies* 49 (1959): 73–80. J.-P. Bonnal and P.-A. Février, "Ostraka de la région de Bir Trouch," *Bulletin d'archéologie algérienne* 2 (1966–1967): 239–249.   F.C.

Talmud

The Talmud, or "study" (plural, Talmudim) is a massive commentary on the Mishnah extant in two forms: one produced in the land of Israel, known as the Yerushalmi (the Jerusalem Talmud, or Palestinian Talmud), and the other produced in Babylonia, known as the Bavli (the Babylonian Talmud). The named sages who appear in the Talmudim are known collectively as amoraim (commentators) and are conventionally assigned by modern scholars to distinct generations. Both Talmudim are written in a combination of Hebrew and Aramaic. The two Talmudim cite many of the same authorities (Babylonian amoraim are cited frequently in the Yerushalmi, and amoraim of the land of Israel are cited frequently in the Bavli), share much material in common, and exhibit many common traits. Each is nominally a commentary on the Mishnah, although neither is a commentary on the entire Mishnah, and each is so discursive, so elaborate, so prone to digression, and so prepared to pursue its own agenda, that at some point the label "commentary" no longer is appropriate. The Talmudim attempt to clarify the Mishnah's obscurities, resolve contradictions both within the Mishnah itself and between the Mishnah and related documents, find sources in Scripture for the Mishnah's rulings, and extend the Mishnah's rulings to areas that the Mishnah itself did not consider. Both Talmudim advance the theory that Moses at Mt. Sinai received from God two Torahs, a written Torah and an oral Torah, and that the Mishnah is the repository of the oral Torah. Like the Mishnah, the Talmudim are primarily interested in legal questions, but each contains large amounts of nonlegal material (homilies, sermons, anecdotes, tall tales, fanciful scriptural exegesis, magic, medicine, and so on).

Each Talmud reflects its own setting. The Yerushalmi has many references to Roman governors, emperors, judges, taxes, festivals, soldiers, and the like. The Bavli has many parallel references to things Parthian. Both Talmudim are surprisingly reticent about the triumph of Christianity. The Yerushalmi is much shorter and less polished than the Bavli, apparently because it was shaped over a shorter period. The Yerushalmi seems to have reached completion in the late 4th century; the amoraic generations in the Yerushalmi stretch from ca. 220 to ca. 375. The Bavli, in contrast, went through a protracted process that lasted centuries; the amoraic generations, which stretch from ca. 220 to ca. 500, were followed by several generations of anonymous *tradents* who polished the text, expanded it, and gave it many of its defining characteristics, especially its most distinctive casuistic and hair-splitting passages.

With the decline of the Jewish community of the land of Israel and the growth of the Jewish community of Babylonia after the Muslim conquest, the Bavli gradually eclipsed the Yerushalmi in rabbinic culture; in time the Bavli became *the* canonical document of rabbinic Judaism. All of later rabbinic law and much of later rabbinic theology derives, or claims to derive, from the Bavli.   S.J.C.

Taxation

The fiscal policy of the imperial government in the late Roman empire contributed in a significant way to the transformations in society that led to the bound colonate. Although there is still much uncertainty about many of the details, the ample documentation in the law codes and the papyri from Egypt provides enough information for us to understand the basic principles of taxation in the late Roman empire.

By far the most important source of revenue for the state was the *annona*, which was administered by the praetorian prefect. Collected in kind but sometimes commuted in the form of money, this tax funded imperial civil servants and the army, and it also provided grain and other foodstuffs for Rome and Constantinople. When Diocletian became emperor, the *annona* consisted of ad hoc assessments in kind imposed on communities. Diocletian undertook to reform it with a more centrally organized and, in theory at least, more equitable system of taxing land and individuals. Central to Diocletian's reforms were regular censuses, which counted the rural population and recorded holdings in land and livestock. The censuses allowed for a more complete assessment of the empire's financial resources than was available in the early empire, and they soon evolved into the indiction, a fifteen-year cycle of tax assessment administered by the praetorian prefect. The manifest intention of Diocletian's reforms, to achieve a more equitable system of taxing the empire's population, is revealed in a decree by Aristius Optatus, prefect of Egypt in 297 C.E.

At the heart of Diocletian's system were the two methods of assessing tax liability known as *iugatio,* based on notional units of productive land, *iuga,* and *capitatio,* based on notional human and animal units, *capita.* In the early empire, methods of taxing had varied considerably by province, but they generally involved some combination of land taxes and poll taxes. The development of *iugatio* secured a more uniform system of assessment that took into consideration local agricultural conditions and the varying productivity of different categories of land. Accordingly, vineyards were taxed at a higher rate than grain land, which in turn was taxed at a higher rate than pasture land. Diocletian also sought to tax individuals independently of their property, so that wealthy individuals who did not own land would not escape tax liability, and landowners would not shoulder a disproportionate share of the tax burden. Under this reform, taxpayers would be liable for *capita* representing themselves, adult members of their family, their slaves, livestock, and even tenants. However, *capitatio* was abolished in some provinces as a basis for taxation in the late 4th century.

Under the fiscal system set in place by Diocletian, the praetorian prefects established a tax schedule for each province based on its declared *iuga* and *capita.* It would then be the responsibility of the administration in each province to collect the taxes. Taxes were generally collected, as in the early empire, by the individual city or village, with the chief responsibility for collecting taxes and delivering them to the appropriate governmental authorities falling on liturgists, that is, private citizens performing compulsory public services.

To some extent, the task of collecting taxes devolved onto large landowners. They assumed the tax liability for people registered on their estates, the coloni. This institution of *autopragia* is closely connected with the emergence of the colonate. As in the early empire, individuals were liable, for tax purposes, to their city or village of origin, that is, their *origo* or *idia;* the city or village, for its part, was collectively liable for the taxes of all of its residents. In the late empire, the imperial government began to recognize an estate as a possible *origo.* The colonate was, therefore, in some sense a fiscal institution, and the status of colonus did not in and of itself reveal much about a person's economic status or even his or her profession. It only denoted that the individual was registered on a landowner's estate for tax purposes. With time, however, it became state policy to bind coloni to their land in much the same way that all people were bound to their inherited professions. In this way, the state restricted the movement of the rural population. One result of this policy was the emergence of very powerful landowners over whom the imperial government exercised little control. In some circumstances, persons placed themselves under the protection of large landowners to avoid tax liability in their village or town. It remains a controversy whether the imperial government fostered the development of this institution or merely tolerated it.

The responsibility of collecting taxes was shared by two other branches of the imperial government, namely the *res privata* and the *sacrae largitiones*. The *res privata* collected revenues from imperial properties, as well as occasional charges imposed on holders of land grants. The *sacrae largitiones*, whose revenues paid for clothing the imperial court, the army, and the imperial service, collected a number of taxes, paid mostly in cash. These included indirect taxes, such as tolls and customs duties, as well as a number of other levies. Among the most important of these was the *annona militaris*, which paid for clothing for the army. The *annona militaris* was originally a system of mandatory sales of clothing at a price fixed by the government, and then, in Egypt at least, a tax collected in gold. The *sacrae largitiones* also collected other taxes in gold and silver, such as those imposed at the time of an emperor's accession and at the quinquennial celebrations of an emperor's rule. These taxes included the *aurum coronarium,* imposed on cities, the *aurum oblaticum,* paid by members of the Senate, and the *collatio lustralis,* or *chrusarguron,* collected from businessmen. Other taxes included the *collatio glebalis* or *follis,* a land tax paid by senators; the *aurum tironicum,* a levy in gold, assessed as a commutation for army recruits; and the *siliquatum,* a sales tax instituted by Valentinian III in the west.

Taxation under Islam varied in the different geographical areas that came under Muslim rule during the 7th century. Although special taxes were collected from Muslims, the bulk of state revenue was derived from taxes paid by non-Muslims living under Muslim rule. The earliest agreements with the non-Muslim populations in the lands previously governed by Byzantium and the Sassanians allowed the local population to keep practicing their own religion in exchange for the payment of a tribute (*jizya*). The tribute was generally collected by local landowners or notables. Soon the Muslims began to build a system of provincial administration, and the *jizya* evolved into a poll tax. The basis of determining tax liability, and the process of collection, differed in each province, since the Muslims tended to utilize parts of the tax systems they found already in place. In Mesopotamia and Syria taxes were assessed according to the projected produc-

tivity of the land and the amount of work required to farm it, following the Roman system of *iugatio*. A poll tax was levied on the residents of the cities and on merchants. In Iraq, the Muslims adopted the Sassanian system of collecting both a land tax and a poll tax. Egypt was governed as a single area, thus breaking down the old system of *autopragia*. Village populations were communally responsible for paying both a land tax and a poll tax.

The taxes that Muslims were required to pay are known by several terms: *zakāt, ṣadaqa,* and *'ushr.* The *zakāt* is an obligatory gift of alms that was paid toward the support of the Muslim poor. *Ṣadaqa* generally has the same meaning as *zakāt,* and both are described in the Qur'ān. Muslims who derived their income from landed property were subject to the payment of *'ushr,* or tithe tax, at the rate of 10 percent. In some sources this is described as one load of produce out of every ten harvested being set aside and given to the government. Customs duties, which were not considered Islamic, were nevertheless collected at borders and ports. Beginning in 685, Muslim merchants paid 2.5 percent on their merchandise, non-Muslims residing in Islamic lands (known as *dhimmīs*) paid 5 percent, and foreign non-Muslims paid 10 percent.

BIBL.: Jean-Michel Carrié, "Un roman des origines: Les généalogies du 'colonat du bas-empire,'" *Opus* 2 (1983): 205–251. J. M. Carrié, "Dioclétien et la fiscalité," *Antiquité tardive* 2 (1994): 33–64. Daniel C. Dennett, *Conversion and the Poll Tax in Early Islam* (Cambridge, Mass., 1950). A. H. M. Jones, *The Later Roman Empire 284–602: A Social, Economic and Administrative Survey,* 2 vols. (repr. Baltimore, 1986). Walter Goffart, *Caput and Colonate: Towards a History of Late Roman Taxation* (Toronto, 1974).   D.P.K.

Temples

The Roman *templum* was an area ritually identified by an augur as a place for taking auspices; often it contained an *aedes,* or house of one or more divinities, who might be represented there by statues. Roman temples were state property, and they were maintained by public monies at least until 408 (*C.Th.* 16.10.19). Until Gratian refused the office in 382, the emperor was *pontifex maximus,* head of the priestly colleges charged with performing temple rites. The fate of the temples in the late empire was therefore determined, on the one hand, by the policies of the Christian emperors and, on the other, by the impersonal social, economic, and physical forces that affected the Roman state. Temples were officially closed, dismantled, or converted to other uses (including use as churches), and they also were unofficially sacked and burned; many simply fell down from disuse.

The evidence for the end of the temples is difficult to work with. Except for recently excavated sites such as Aphrodisias, the archaeological record has not been consistently preserved. About the temples in Constantinople, Milan, and Ravenna, for example, we know little more than that they disappeared. Beyond inscriptions, the written sources are tendentious. The most important Christian testimonies include Eusebius's *Life of Constantine* (337–339); the *Ecclesiastical Histories* of Rufinus (to 395), Sozomen (to 425), and Socrates (to 439); Sulpicius Severus's *Life of St. Martin of Tours* (397); Mark the Deacon's *Life of Porphyry of Gaza* (d. 420); Theodoret's *History of the Monks of Syria* (ca. 444); and the writings of Shenoute of Atripe (d. 466). Speaking for the pagans are Symmachus (*Relatio* 3 [384]), Libanius (*Orat.* 30, *Pro templis:* [386?]), and Zosimus (*New History* [to 410]). The *Codex Calendar of 354,* though made for a Christian, contains important information about the vitality of temple rites in mid-4th century Rome. By far the most neutral source is the *Codex Theodosianus* (438), but the reader must bear in mind that the laws collected in it are often ad hoc responses to localized situations, rather than products of a consistent legislative program intended to be applied across the empire.

Pace the Christian assertion that Constantinople had neither temples nor cult images (Augustine, *De Civ.Dei* 5.25), Constantine's capital preserved a number of pre-4th century temples (John Malalas, *Chronicle* 324), and Constantine himself seems to have made some sort of structure in honor of the Fortune *(Tyche)* of the city (Zosimus 2.31). He did deprive the old temples of their revenue (Malalas; Libanius 5–6), and he ordered the demolition of selected shrines that offended or impeded Christian worship, notably the temple of Aphrodite that had been erected over the cave of Christ's sepulcher in Jerusalem (Eusebius, *Hist.eccl.* 3.26–27; cf. 54–58).

The legislation collected in the last book of the *Codex Theodosianus* (16.10, "On Pagans, Sacrifices, and Temples") spans the period from Constantine and his sons to 435. From it, modern scholars have deduced an initial hardening of opposition to the old cults under Constantius II (confirmed by Libanius 38), followed by the brief pagan restoration under Julian (361–363), a period of tolerance under Valentinian I and the early Gratian (to 382), and a decisive, fatal turn under Theodosius I in 391–392 (16.10.10–12). From the same laws one can also infer an appreciation of the temples' cultural value, expressed at first in attempts to keep them open for nonsacrificial purposes (16.10.3, 7, 8, 10–12) and subsequently in decrees protecting their buildings and ornaments (16.10.15, 18). By the beginning of the 5th century, however, the edicts show a progressive acquiescence in the temples' demolition (15.1.40; 16.10.19, 25).

Contrary to the spirit of the laws are the vivid accounts of popular assaults on temples, which seem to have been common in the last decades of the 4th century. In the 380s Libanius protested the destruction of temples by marauding monks in the countryside around Antioch; Archbishop Marcellus of Apamea,

backed by soldiers, brought down that city's temple of Zeus (Theodoret, *Hist.eccl.* 5); and Martin of Tours burned and dismembered temples in the countryside of Gaul (Sulpicius Severus 13–15). Some of this zealotry may have been inspired by biblical exemplars (e.g., 2 Kings 10:25–27, 11:18), while in other cases it may have been part of a calculated effort to convert pagans by intimidation. The most shocking act of violence in this period was against the Serapeum in Alexandria, which went up in flames in 391 along with the ancient world's greatest library (Rufinus 11). Other disasters befell temples around the same time, such as during the incursion of Alaric into Greece, which brought an end to the sanctuary at Eleusis in 396, and the sack of Rome in 410, which seems to have caused the ruin and dismemberment of at least some temples there.

The afterlife of temples in the 5th century and later differed regionally, depending on such factors as the strength and longevity of non-Christian cults, the rate of Christianization of the governing classes, and the fanaticism or tolerance of bishops and abbots. In Gaza (Palestine) in 402, Christians were still a weak minority, so Bishop Porphyry obtained an imperial decree to destroy its temples (Mark the Deacon, 50–51). Temple cults seem to have been especially resilient in Egypt. In the mid-5th century Abbot Shenoute was still leading temple-smashing expeditions, and he met legal and physical opposition from their priests. The temple of Isis at Philae on the Upper Nile was used by pagans until the reign of Justinian, who destroyed it (Procopius, *Wars* 1.19.36).

In the 4th and 5th centuries, antagonism between pagans and Christians exacerbated a general tendency to pillage disused buildings for *spolia* (*C.Th.* 9.17.1–5; 15.1.14, 19, 37), and churches all over the empire were constructed with pieces of destroyed temples. However, in the strongholds of traditional culture, Greece and Italy, attempts to preserve temples as civic ornaments were partly successful. In Athens, Phidias's famous cult statue of Athena remained in the Parthenon until the 480s, and the building was later consecrated as a church with only minimal remodeling. The first such temple conversion recorded in Rome was of the Pantheon, which was ceded to Pope Boniface IV (608–615) by the Byzantine emperor Phocas (*Liber pontificalis*). By the 8th century, the relatively few surviving temples had become objects of cultural nostalgia in parts of Italy. The best witness to this trend is the so-called Tempietto del Clitunno, a small church near Spoleto built by an unknown Lombard (or early Carolingian) patron in nearly perfect imitation of a Corinthian temple of the early empire.

BIBL.: J. P. Caillet, "La transformation en églises d'édifices publics et des temples à la fin de l'antiquité," in *La fin de la cité antique et le début de la cité médiévale,* ed. C. Lepelley (Bari, 1996), 191–211. Garth Fowden, "Bishops and Temples in the Eastern Roman Empire," *Journal of Theological Studies* n.s. 29 (1978): 53–78. Alison Frantz, "From Paganism to

Christianity in the Temples of Athens," *Dumbarton Oaks Papers* 19 (1965): 187–205. R. P. C. Hanson, "The Transformation of Pagan Temples into Churches in the Early Christian Centuries," in Hanson, *Studies in Christian Antiquity* (Edinburgh, 1985), 347–358. Eberhard Sauer, *The End of Paganism in the North-Western Provinces of the Roman Empire* (Oxford, 1996). Frank R. Trombley, *Hellenic Religion and Christianization 370–529,* 2 vols. (Leiden, New York, and Cologne, 1993–1994). J. Vaes, "Christliche Wiederverwendung antiker Bauten," *Ancient Society* 15/17 (1984/1986): 305–443. Bryan Ward-Perkins, *From Classical Antiquity to the Middle Ages: Urban Public Building in Northern and Central Italy* A.D. *300–850* (Oxford, 1984).   D.K.

Textiles

In late antiquity, textiles played an important role in both pubic and private life. They are one of the most interesting phenomena from an economic point of view as well as from a social-historical one. Within the confines of the Roman empire, an eastern and a western textile tradition are clearly distinguishable. In both cases written sources, weaving implements, and original textiles give reliable information, the most important source being the large quantity of textiles found in Egypt, dating from the 3rd to the 10th century C.E. However, these finds from Egypt should not mislead us to think that Egypt was the only region producing textiles in large quantities. Precious textiles were produced in abundance in the neighboring regions, namely Syria, Palestine, and Asia Minor. Finds from Dura-Europus, Palmyra, and Masadah have brought to light the importance of those regions for textile production and underlined what we know from representations on wall paintings and mosaics of those regions. From an imperial decree, the *Notitia Dignitatum* (about 300 C.E.), we learn that state-supervised textile factories *(gynaecea/gynaikeia)* and dying workshops were spread over the whole empire from southern France to Tunisia. Some workshops in the northern provinces produced textiles with silver decoration *(barbaricariorum sive argentariorum).* Little is known about how these *gynaecea* were run or what fabrics they produced.

Until the decline of the Roman empire Egypt produced garments—short tunics and cloaks—for nearly the entire Roman army. In medium-size cities such as Oxyrhynchus, about 60 percent of the working population was involved in textile production. During the 4th century the number of independent workshops in Egypt increased. We hear of specialists producing different types of goods, such as garments, looped textiles, cushion covers, textiles in the "Tarsian" style, and many more.

One of the most important branches of late antique textile production in the east was the manufacture of large wall decorations. Such hangings played an important role in the upper-class houses and took the place of the colorful wall paintings of Roman villas. Preserved hangings and fragments of hangings reflect popular iconographical motifs. Genre motifs such as gardens with fruit trees; maritime scenes with fish, sea monsters, and Nereids; the Four Seasons with their bounties; and mythological themes—Dionysus with his *thiasos,* Artemis hunting, Meleager and Atalante—were widespread before the 6th and 7th centuries. Thereafter Sassanian motifs, such as winged animals, palmettes, and hunting riders, become fashionable. Although all these fragments of hangings are found in Egypt, there is evidence that some of them were imported. One example is a hanging with an inwoven inscription naming its provenance from Heraclea in Asia Minor. Other hangings with patterns dyed red or blue were probably produced in Alexandria and Antioch. These hangings show mythological as well as Christian scenes, which is also the case for a series of hangings painted with tempera colors. In the course of the 5th and 6th centuries such large wall decorations must have been used in churches as well. The extensive need for textiles in liturgical contexts from the 4th century onward is testified by the inventory of a small church at Tivoli near Rome, the so-called *charta Cornutiana (Liber pontificalis,* ed. L. Duchesne, vol. 1, Paris, 1886). Finally, silk textiles start to play a prominant role during the 7th century in all the eastern Mediterranean regions. The manufacturing centers for silk fabrics were Baghdad, Antioch, probably Alexandria, and Byzantium.

BIBL.: R. B. Serjeant, "Materials for a History of Islamic Textiles," *Ars Islamica* 9–16 (1942–1951). Annemarie Stauffer, *Textiles of Late Antiquity* (New York, 1995). Peter van Minnen, "Urban Craftsmen in Roman Egypt," in *Münstersche Beiträge zur antiken Handelsgeschichte,* vol. 6 (Münster, 1986), 31–88. J. P. Wild, *Textile Manufacture in Northern Roman Provinces* (Cambridge, Eng., 1970).   A.S.

Theater

For the still largely oral society of late antiquity, the stage served as a principal medium for civic communication and education as well as popular entertainment. In late Roman cities, the theater provided a place where the citizens could assemble to welcome governors and other potentates or to produce acclamations to exhibit their communal consensus. More important, it was where they could view the ubiquitous pantomime and mime shows that had then superseded the earlier scripted performances of tragedies and comedies.

The mostly male pantomime actors were masked and costumed virtuosos who danced to instrumental music and choral singing while acting out librettos inspired by traditional mythological themes. Libanius of Antioch regarded their improvised acting as a worthy successor to classical tragic performances. Adored by theatergoers throughout the empire, the actors were known to have prompted, often with the active in-volvement of claqueurs, violent partisan riots in the theaters. To their many critics, however, their per-formances were detrimental to the moral sensibilities of the citizen-spectators. Considerably less well re-garded in social terms, though no less popular in ap-peal, *mimi* and *mimae* were maskless performers who acted out unscripted slapstick burlesque and who also sometimes sang. The roles they played were adapted from comedy and daily life in a tradition dating back to the republic. Their lowbrow buffoonery formed the staple of the celebrations of many traditional Roman festivals, including the Floralia, when naked *mimae* were featured.

In the Greek east, stage actors, or *technitai*, were grouped into troupes as well as synods, professional organizations designed to protect the common inter-ests of the members. In the Roman west, we also find troupes, or *greges*, of pantomimes and mimes that plied their trade in one city or region after the next. They performed in a variety of contexts: while they often occupied the civic stage, many also performed for wealthy private individuals, including emperors, at their homes, sometimes as part of dinner entertain-ment. Under Roman civil law, stage performers who acted before the general public were regarded as "infa-mous" persons and subject to a range of legal disabili-ties; their legal status was comparable to that of gladi-ators, charioteers, and prostitutes. Indeed, female actresses were often classed with prostitutes in legal discourse and in elite social attitudes, as evidenced by Procopius's discussion of the former career of Empress Theodora. By the late 4th century, a perceived shortage of performers for the theater in certain localities had caused their métier to be classified by the emperors as an obligatory and hereditary service, or *munus*. As a result, stage performers, especially in the west where they were mostly slaves or freedmen, appear to have lost their customary social and geographical mobility and instead became attached to a particular city.

In this period, the Christian church, which viewed the theater generally in a disapproving manner, consid-ered stage performers as degraded persons who were to be refused baptism unless they first abandoned their profession. At the same time, the application to receive this sacrament also became virtually the only means for the performers to escape their profession. Partly using established pagan arguments against the theater, Tertullian and Cyprian of Carthage were among the first Christian writers to denounce the stage. Soon nu-merous followers expressed their objection to its al-leged celebration of pagan idolatry (e.g., its repre-sentation of the mythological deeds of gods and goddesses) and also against the performers' ability to excite lascivious passions in the spectators through their sinuous movements. But this antagonism toward the theater was also spurred on by the envy of its broad appeal among the Christian population and by anger

at the occasional mockery on stage of Christian rites and beliefs. Accompanying this polemic were a number of Christian saints' lives that narrate the conversion and rehabilitation of former stage performers, the most famous one being that of St. Pelagia of Antioch.

Despite being condemned by pagan moralists and Christian authors alike, large-scale public theatrical shows remained a staple of late Roman urban life: the *Codex-Calendar of 354* lists 101 days of theatrical *ludi* a year for the city of Rome, where, in 353, three thou-sand female dancers served. Other cities put on as many shows as they could. Even as Christianization proceeded apace, the appetites of commoners and elites for stage shows, which they regarded as relaxing and diverting entertainment, continued unabated. In the 6th century, Choricius of Gaza, a Christian sophist, defended mimes against their critics by claiming that the mimetic art remained the basis of poetry and rheto-ric, art and dance, and that, echoing Libanius, it was indeed the heir to Attic comedy. Official attitudes fa-vored the continuation of the shows, even though on several occasions civic unruliness, such as pantomime riots, caused the emperors to impose temporary local bans to punish the offending community. To judge by the archaeological evidence, theaters long remained important sites both for civic gatherings and for the staging of spectacles.

With some significant regional variation, permanent stone theaters began to be abandoned toward the end of the 7th century. But even this last process did not signal the demise of the late Roman stage as such. While pantomime shows seem to have disappeared af-ter the 6th century, mimes were still counted on to perform between races at the circus, at festivals, and at private and imperial functions (such as banquets) well into the Byzantine period. Despite occasional imperial bans and repeated conciliar condemnations (culminat-ing in the ban against mimes at the Trullan Synod in 691–692), these performances continued, though in in-creasingly diminished circumstances and frequency. While many Christian Fathers condemned the "pro-fane" theater as a den of sin and Satan's workplace, some of them came to dramatize the portions of their homilies devoted to historical narrative in an attempt to achieve a similar hold on the audience's attention. However, whether liturgical dramas were actually per-formed in the early Byzantine church is uncertain and remains a matter of scholarly dispute.

BIBL.: H. Jürgens, *Pompa Diaboli: Die lateinischen Kirchenväter und das antike Theater* (Stuttgart, 1972). R. Lim, "Consensus and Dissensus in Public Spectacles in Early Byzantium," *Byzantinische Forschungen* 24 (1997): 159–179. O. Pasquato, *Gli spettacoli in S. Giovanni Crisostomo: Paganesimo e cristianesimo ad Antiochia e Costantinopoli nel IV secolo*, Orientalia Christiana Analecta 201 (Rome, 1976). *Theater und Gesellschaft im Imperium Romanum*, ed. J. Blansdorf (Tübingen, 1990). W. Weissmann, *Kirche und Schauspiele: Die Schauspiele im Urteil der lateinischen*

Kirchenväter unter besonderer Berücksichtigung von Augustin (Würzburg, 1972). R.L.

Theodora

Much of the interest Empress Theodora has attracted throughout history is the product not only of her indisputably eventful life but also of the embroideries that were worked on it by both admirers and detractors, making it difficult to distinguish the historical individual from her various personae. The writing of a contemporary observer, Procopius of Caesarea, which furnishes much of her lore, is a case in point. Different moments in his works present particular facets of Theodora, who reigned with her husband, Justinian, from his succession in 527 until her death in 548.

From Procopius's pen flowed a notorious account, in the *Secret History,* of her wanton childhood amid the carnival atmosphere of the circus factions and her subsequent career as an actress and a prostitute; a famous scene in his *Wars,* in which Theodora stood firm in the face of insurrection, stilling the emperor's preparations for flight and rallying his loyalists behind him; and testimony, in *On Buildings,* to her many charitable works. Hers is at once a striking rags-to-riches story, a tale of palace intrigue and ruthless machinations, and yet also a record of her own genuine convictions and nuanced participation in the work of government.

Although later accretions of legend attempted to whitewash her past, Theodora's disreputable background obliged Justinian to obtain special legislation to permit their union. The two were married in 525. She had already borne a daughter, who would give her two grandsons; possibly she had a son as well. Neither child belonged to Justinian, who would die without producing an heir. It would appear that the emperor was devoted to her and that her influence over him was substantial. He described Theodora in his legislation (*Nov.Just.* 8.1, anno 535) as a partner in his counsels. She reportedly dealt harshly with rivals, and in matters of ecclesiastical policy took a particularly independent line. Though Justinian was a Chalcedonian, Theodora remained a convinced Monophysite. Without straying into outright opposition, she furnished crucial support for the Monophysites' cause, which earned her the undying admiration and veneration of their clergy.

BIBL.: R. Browning, *Justinian and Theodora,* rev. ed. (London, 1987). A. Cameron, *Procopius and the Sixth Century* (London, 1985). C. Pazdernik, "Our Most Pious Consort Given Us by God: Dissident Reactions to the Partnership of Justinian and Theodora, AD 525–548," *Classical Antiquity* 13 (1994): 256–281. C.P.

Theodosian Code

The *Theodosian Code* is a collection of imperial constitutions dating from Constantine to 437, divided into sixteen books and compiled by a commission established by the emperor Theodosius II in 429. Theodosius promulgated the code named after him in Constantinople, shortly after he gave his daughter Eudoxia in marriage to the western emperor Valentinian III on 29 October 437, and he proclaimed that after 1 January 438 no law of Constantine and his successors, including himself, issued before the end of 437, was to have legal force unless it was included in the *Code.* A copy of the *Code* was brought to Rome and officially received by the Roman Senate on 25 December 438: from this copy ultimately derive all surviving manuscripts of the *Theodosian Code,* all extracts in later Latin law codes, and all later quotations in Latin sources.

The *Theodosian Code* replicated the format of the codes compiled by the Diocletianic lawyers Gregorius and Hermogenianus, being arranged in books and titles (for example, "On Holidays," "On Decurions"), and, within each title, in strict chronological order. Like the earlier codes, the *Theodosian Code* was designed for practical use by magistrates in deciding cases in court, and as a supplement to existing law and the writings of the classical jurists, whose authority Theodosius had expressly confirmed in 426. Internal consistency was not attempted: contradictory rulings were allowed to stand, since Theodosius recognized that law changed over the course of time (for example on such questions as whether heretics were entitled to bequeath and inherit property). But whereas the documents in the two Diocletianic codes were predominantly imperial replies to private petitions, though they also included rescripts to governors, when Theodosius established his commission in 429, he ordered them to include only edicts and general laws. Thus the *Theodosian Code* has an entirely different character from its apparent predecessors. For whereas rescripts were short, simple, and usually on a single topic, edicts and general pronouncements tended to be long, rhetorically elaborate, and complex documents that often dealt with a variety of topics: the incomplete texts of two early 4th century edicts, for example, which are preserved on stone at Lyttus in Crete, are fifty and forty-six lines long, respectively. Hence the compilers were instructed to divide constitutions and include only the relevant extracts in each title. Although Theodosius does not state this clearly and explicitly, the intended starting point was 312, the year when Constantine proclaimed himself a Christian. This date can only have been chosen on ideological grounds, not for legal reasons.

The commission appears to have taken six years to collect the material from which it selected the texts that are reproduced in the *Code.* Analysis of the addressees of the edicts, letters, and rescripts contained in the *Code* (for a substantial number of extracts were included from documents other than edicts and general laws) shows that the commission had no access to any central archive that had systematically preserved imperial legislation since 312, except possibly an archive in Constantinople that contained constitutions addressed to praetorian prefects of the east after the eastern imperial court took up permanent residence there toward the end of the 4th century. For the most part, however, and especially for the period before 380, the commission was compelled to assemble documents laboriously from dispersed nonimperial collections: these seem to have comprised principally the personal files of individual officials who had kept papers from the whole of their career and passed them on to their heirs, and perhaps also the archives of certain provincial governors (such as the proconsul of Africa).

The conditions under which the commission searched out imperial constitutions had a profound effect on the content of the code that they compiled. Although the commission was eastern, and completed its work in Constantinople, the majority of imperial constitutions earlier than 380 are western. More important, the coverage of the early period, especially of the legislation of Constantine, is very uneven, so that it is a mistake to assign the *Code* a priority of regard in any investigation of the political, social, economic, and religious structure of the early and middle 4th century.

Theodosius issued a second set of instructions in 435. By this time, it is presumed, the commissioners had collected all the material that they could use and were about to begin the process of excerpting and editing. Theodosius instructed them to provide indexes, to include only the legal point at issue when dividing documents between different titles, and to emend the wording, where necessary, to make the meaning clear.

Constantine had ruled that imperial constitutions lacking an exact date were legally invalid, and Theodosius specified that, in case of conflict, the later law took precedence over the earlier. Hence the commissioners were required to provide each extract in their compilation with a precise and easily recognizable date. Being human, they could not avoid mistakes in performing this task, and they frequently fell into three types of error. First, they often confused different consular dates that looked similar, especially imperial consulates. Second, when they affixed a date to documents that lacked one, of necessity they proceeded by inference and conjecture, both of which are fallible guides. And third, errors inevitably crept in as they emended anomalous consular dates in original documents to conform to an official list of consuls recognized each year since 312.

The existence of all three types of error is abundantly proved by contradictions within the *Code,* by mistakes concerning addressees who are attested by contemporary evidence, and by modern attempts to construct imperial itineraries. A great deal of scholarly labor has been expended in correcting the transmitted dates and places of issue, especially by prosopographers and scholars interested in the institutional his-

tory of the late Roman empire. The most significant systematic attempts to rectify the errors committed by the compilers have been by Godefroy in his pioneering edition (Lyons, 1665), by Theodor Mommsen, and by Otto Seeck in 1919, but their cumulative results have been refined still further in recent studies of imperial chronology in the 4th century. The process of correction is continuous, cumulative, and unlikely to cease: a rough estimate suggests that at least 35 percent of the subscriptions in the *Code* contain some error, large or small.

The original text of the *Theodosian Code* has not survived entire: in particular, many titles from books 1–5 and the start of 6 are preserved only because they were included in the breviary of Alaric, which was compiled in 506. The manuscripts are fully described in Mommsen's standard critical edition of the full text, published after his death by P. M. Meyer (Berlin, 1905). There is a superior edition of books 1–8 by Paul Krüger (Berlin, 1923–1926), which appears to be something of a bibliographical rarity. The English translation produced under the supervision of Clyde Pharr (Princeton, 1952), though widely used in recent decades, often misrepresents both the tenor and the precise meaning of the original Latin.

BIBL.: T. Honoré, "The Making of the Theodosian Code," *Zeitschrift der Savigny Stiftung für Rechtsgeschichte,* Romanistische Abteilung 103 (1986): 133–222. W. Turpin, "The Law Codes and Late Roman Law," *Revue internationale des droits de l'antiquité* 32 (1985): 339–353. J. Harries and I. Wood, eds., *The Theodosian Code* (London, 1993).

T.D.B.

Theology

It would be possible to define late antiquity as the period during which theology completed the move, anticipated in such Hellenistic writers as Philo and Origen, from being seen as the antithesis to official religion to being regarded as its servant, if also sometimes its uneasy partner. In substantial measure, the change was the consequence of the change of the official religion to Christianity under Constantine, but it was brought about also by the development of the several genres and methods of theology, together with the evolution of the several theological styles or schools of thought.

Statistically the most dominant, and at least theoretically the most important, among those methods and genres was the interpretation of sacred texts. The Christian appropriation of Jewish Scripture, largely in Bible translations (Septuagint, Vulgate, Peshitta), was made possible by the application of allegorical and typological exegesis, which was able to find anticipations of the New Testament in Old Testament history, as Basil and others did in Genesis. Commentaries on the Gospels, of which those on John and on the harmony of the Gospels by Augustine are outstanding representatives, shaped both the doctrinal and the ethical emphases of the church.

In practice, biblical exegesis often blended with polemics against heretics that had already, in such writers of the 2nd and early 3rd century as Irenaeus, Tertullian, and Hippolytus, articulated and expanded orthodox theology against its gainsayers, in the process preserving for later centuries substantial portions of the writings of Gnosticism that would otherwise have perished. During the 4th century it was, above all, Arianism; during the 5th century, Nestorianism; and during the 6th century, the Monophysites and Origenism evoked the orthodox formulations of Christian doctrine that went on to become normative for all the centuries to follow.

Although the adoption of Catholic Christianity as the state religion might have seemed to make *apologetics* appear moot, the effort to "justify the ways of God to man" through the use of reason and philosophy nevertheless continued to be part of the job description of theology to the end of the period covered by this volume—and well beyond it into the Middle Ages, as the works of the Christian philosopher-theologians Anselm of Canterbury in the west and Michael Psellos in the east, the Jewish philosopher-theologian Maimonides, and the Muslim philosopher-theologian Averroës would document. Pagan as well as Christian thought engaged the attention of such Greek theologians as Athanasius and Gregory of Nyssa and such Latin theologians as Augustine, notably in his *City of God*. The most intriguing sample of this genre is the *Consolation of Philosophy* of Boethius.

As theology evolved into officially legislated dogma under the guidance of bishops, councils, and emperors, the genre of systematic theology, brilliantly pioneered by Origen's *De principiis*, became increasingly necessary and increasingly possible. The most influential of such works was *The Fount of Wisdom* by John of Damascus, which has shaped eastern Christian theology into modern times and which was also of substantial significance for Thomas Aquinas and other medieval theologians in the west. More modest systematic works, sometimes in the form of catechisms or oral discourses, communicated theology and dogma to clergy and laity.

In addition to full-length treatises and expositions, each of these genres took the form of anthologies or florilegia, often compiled for a particular purpose or controversy. As is evident from the *Sentences* of Isidore of Seville, such a florilegium could in turn become the basis for further glosses or commentaries, until, in works like the *Sacra Parallela* of John of Damascus and above all the *Sentences* of Peter Lombard (on which there are more than two thousand commentaries), it was not the original work but the compilation that later generations knew best.

The most persistent issues for theology in all of these forms during late antiquity were the doctrine of God as Trinity and Christology, both of which at the end of this period were once again the focus of the exchanges of Christian theologians with the followers of Muhammad over the oneness of God and the identity of his prophet. Especially in the west, the relation between grace and nature, and thus the doctrine of sin, often became central, particularly in the tradition of Augustinianism.

Such controversies as those over Christology illustrate the differences among theological schools of thought. Many of the most celebrated works of theology were associated with the school of Alexandria, which had been since the Hellenistic period the venue for the interaction of Jewish and Christian theologians with Neoplatonic philosophy. Its propensity for the allegorical interpretation of the Bible and for speculative metaphysics made the Alexandrian school fruitful soil for both heresy and orthodoxy. It was often in conflict with the school of Antioch, whose theologians—for example, Theodore of Mopsuestia—tended to a more literal-grammatical method of exegesis and thus to a relatively greater emphasis on the concrete events of sacred history.

When Alexandrian and Antiochene styles of theologizing collided, it often fell to the west, above all to Rome, to propose a third way beyond the alternatives and hence to point to an orthodox resolution of the conflict. Thus in 449 Pope Leo I of Old Rome, in an epistle to Patriarch Flavian of Constantinople, articulated formulas with ancestry in Ambrose and Augustine that would carry the day at the Council of Chalcedon in 451—even though Antioch and Alexandria and their adherents would go on with the dispute for another three centuries and more. In Syria, meanwhile, the theological methodology represented by Aphrahat also transcended (or avoided) many of the divisive tendencies of the Greek east and Latin west, providing asylum and a forum for various exiled and condemned groups, both Nestorian and Monophysite, to the end of late antiquity and even beyond it.

BIBL.: Jaroslav Pelikan, *The Christian Tradition: A History of the Development of Doctrine*, vols. 1–3 (Chicago, 1971–1978). Johannes Quasten, *Patrology*, 4 vols. (Westminster, Md., 1951–1986). H. D. Saffrey, "Les débuts de la théologie comme science," *Revue des sciences philosophiques et théologiques* 80 (1996): 201–220.   J.P.

Theotokos

Theotokos, a title given to the Virgin Mary, literally means in Greek "the one who bore God" but is commonly translated as "Mother of God." Although it may have been used in the 3rd century by Hippolytus of Rome, the first undisputed use of this title was by Alexander, bishop of Alexandria, in his encyclical of 319 against the Arians (*Epistle to Alexander of Con-*

stantinople 12). The term is in some manuscripts of Athanasius's *Against the Arians* (2.29) and was probably used widely in the popular devotion of 4th century Alexandria. A 3rd or 4th century papyrus fragment contains a Greek version of the *Sub Tuum,* which had previously been considered a medieval prayer. The Theotokos is invoked in the vocative case to deliver the supplicant from danger. Julian mocks Christians for calling Mary Theotokos (*Against the Galileans* 262). In addition to being used against Arians, the title Theotokos was used to combat various forms of Docetic teaching that argued that the Logos passed through Mary as a channel, without taking flesh from her. The Cappadocian Fathers considered the title Theotokos crucial for affirming the divinity and humanity of Christ.

The term *Theotokos* became a flashpoint for controversy in the 5th century debates between the Antiochene and Alexandrian schools of Christology. Theodore of Mopsuestia, a theologian of the Antiochene school, first objected to the appellation, but it was not until one of his disciples, Nestorius, became bishop of Constantinople that conflict escalated. Nestorius became involved in a controversy already in progress: one of his priests preached a sermon condemning the use of the title Theotokos for Mary and insisting that Mary could be called only Anthropotokos, "Bearer of Man," since the divine Logos was preexistent, and Mary, a creature, could bear only the man Jesus. Nestorius tried to reach a compromise, suggesting that Mary be called Christotokos, "Mother of the Christ," but this failed to satisfy a large part of the church that was accustomed to using Theotokos in its daily devotion.

Cyril of Alexandria led the opposition to Nestorius, who was deposed at the Council of Ephesus in 431. This council, which met in a church dedicated to the Virgin, affirmed the title Theotokos for Mary, as did a Roman synod under Celestine I (430) and the Council of Chalcedon (451). In response to the Council of Ephesus's granting of the title Theotokos to Mary, Pope Sixtus III built the Basilica of St. Maria Maggiore in Rome. The debates over the title Theotokos were instrumental in the development of the doctrine of *communicatio idiomatum.* This doctrine states that attributes predicated of Christ's humanity could be predicated of his divinity, and vice versa: Mary was the mother of God, although the divine Logos was eternal, because she had given birth to Christ, who was both human and divine.

While the 4th and 5th century debates over the title Theotokos were largely Christological, the cult of the Theotokos grew in the 6th century. Theotokos was the primary epithet for the Virgin Mary in the Byzantine empire, and she came to be very closely associated with Constantinople. Her relics, including her girdle and veil, were venerated in the city, and her feasts celebrated, especially the Feast of the Annunciation (25 March), the Feast of the Presentation (14 February), and the Feast of the Dormition (15 August). In 626 the inhabitants of Constantinople credited her with protecting the city from Persian and Avar attack when Patriarch Sergios carried her icon around the walls of the besieged city.

Theotokos was sometimes translated into Latin as Deipara, but more commonly as Dei Genitrix or Mater Dei. In the west, Vincent of Lerins (d. 450) expounded the significance of Mary's title Theotokos (*Commonitorium* 1.15). The Marian feasts, first established in the east, also spread to the west. Gregory of Tours formulated the doctrine of the Assumption of Mary (*Glory of the Martyrs* 4), which had previously been found in apocryphal works.

BIBL.: Averil Cameron, "The Theotokos in Sixth-Century Constantinople," *Journal of Theological Studies* 29 (1978): 79–108. Aloys Grillmeier, *Christ in Christian Tradition,* trans. J. S. Bowden (New York, 1965; rev. 1975). G. Giamberardini, "Il 'Sub tuum praesidium' e il titolo 'Theotokos' nella tradizione egiziana," *Marianum* (Rome) 31 (1969): 324–362. Michael O'Carroll, *Theotokos: A Theological Encyclopedia of the Blessed Virgin Mary* (Wilmington, Del., 1982). Jaroslav Pelikan, *Mary through the Centuries: Her Place in the History of Culture* (New Haven, 1996).   J.H.-H.

Thessalonica

A port city at the head of the Thermaic Gulf, east of the Vardar River's mouth, Thessalonica was the most important stop on the Via Egnatia, between Dyrrhachium/Apollonia and Constantinople. Of Hellenistic origin, it became the administrative capital of Roman Macedonia, maintaining important municipal privileges while serving as the southern focus of Balkan trade and traffic. The apostle Paul visited its Jewish community early in his missionary work, and converts resulting from his two stays there (50 and 56 C.E.) made the city an important center of early Christianity.

The beginnings of barbarian attacks in the 3rd century amplified Thessalonica's strategic importance. Under Diocletian's tetrarchy it became the regional mint and served as residence for the emperor Galerius (293–305). Of his proud buildings, there survive some remains of his palace, his massive triumphal arch, and a great rotunda assumed to be his intended mausoleum. Under Galerius also occurred the martyrdom of St. Demetrius, who would become the city's great medieval patron. Constantine I expanded the city's harbor while using it as a naval base during his war with his rival, Licinius, who was exiled there after his defeat. Theodosius I (379–395) made Thessalonica the official capital of the prefecture of Illyricum. It was his base during his struggle with the Visigoths, and it was there that he issued his decrees in 380 establishing orthodox Christianity as the Roman empire's state religion. Ten years later, however, when its populace rioted against his Gothic soldiers, Theodosius furiously ordered their massacre by the thousands in Thessalonica's hippodrome.

Despite distant menaces in the Balkans, Thessalonica enjoyed relative tranquility and prosperity during the ensuing centuries. From this period date monuments testifying to its early emergence as the second city of the surviving eastern Roman, or early Byzantine, empire. Galerius's Rotunda was converted into a Christian church; the great basilican Acheiropoiïtos (either 4th or 5th century) is reputed to be one of the oldest churches still in Christian use; also from the 4th century dates the beginning of the church commemorating the martyr Demetrius. Replacing Hellenistic antecedents, the city's walls—eventually a major example of late Roman and Byzantine urban fortification—began to take shape: lower sections were begun in the 3rd century, and they were given fuller definition in the 5th.

The walls proved essential when the barbarian incursions into the Balkans reached Thessalonica by the late 6th century. Recurrent Slavic attacks menaced the city through the 7th century—repulsed, the inhabitants believed, through miraculous interventions by St. Demetrius. Decisive relief from these assaults came only in 688, when Emperor Justinian II cleared his way through "Sclavenia" and entered the city in triumph. During the 8th century the metropolitan archbishopric of Thessalonica, previously under the jurisdiction of Rome, was part of a massive transfer to the see of Constantinople. By the 9th century, Thessalonica was capital of one of the new European themes, or military-administrative provinces, of the Byzantine empire. From Thessalonica came the 9th century brothers Constantine-Cyril and Methodius, who initiated the decisive conversion of the Slavs to Christianity. Late antiquity for Thessalonica might be seen as ending with its devastating capture and sack in 904 at the hands of Saracen pirates led by Leo of Tripoli. But the city's fortunes revived, and it was again the Byzantine empire's second city in the centuries to follow.

BIBL.: G. Gounaris, *The Walls of Thessaloniki* (Thessaloniki, 1982). J.-M. Speiser, *Thessalonique et ses monuments du IVe au VIe siècle* (Paris, 1984). Apostolos E. Vakalopoulos, *A History of Thessaloniki*, trans. T. F. Carney (Thessaloniki, 1972). P. Lemerle, *Les plus anciens recueils des miracles de Saint Démétrius et la pénétration des Slaves dans les Balkans* (Paris, 1979–1981). J.W.B.

Theurgy

The term *theurgy*, meaning "divine work," eventually came to be used in very late antiquity for almost any form of worship that combined philosophic study and magical ritual. It first was applied, however, to an esoteric religious system that developed in the late 2nd or early 3rd century. This system took as its authoritative basis dactylic-hexameter Greek poems collectively known as the Chaldaean Oracles, which the theurgists claimed had been recited by Apollo and Hecate either during epiphanies or through the mouths of entranced mediums. We now possess only fragments of the Oracles, which were quoted by later exegetes and critics of theurgy such as Proclus and Michael Psellus, but a substantial body of longer Oracle texts once circulated widely, attracting significant interest among philosophers and mystics as early as Porphyry and as late as the Renaissance. Several writers of late antiquity wrote lengthy commentaries on the Oracles and their doctrines, seeking to interpret them both in their own right and in comparison with similar religious systems such as the Orphic. Like most esoteric religious systems, theurgy passed its doctrines and rites from individual to individual, guarding them from hoi polloi. Transmission often is portrayed as taking place within families: Asclepigenia was initiated by her father, Plutarch, who was himself initiated by his father Nestorius. Theurgy's most famous follower was the emperor Julian, who was initiated by Maximus of Ephesus (for all of these figures, see Eunapius, *Vitae Sophistarum* 461–475).

Theurgy was said to have been founded by Julian the Chaldaean and his son, Julian the Theurgist, to whom the Oracles were supposed to have been spoken. The two Julians also were credited with the authorship of other theurgical works, including a book describing techniques for animating statues. To what extent these men were real and to what extent legendary is open to debate. Ancient sources describe the younger Julian as accompanying Marcus Aurelius on campaigns, aiding him in battle by creating masks that threw thunderbolts, by splitting rocks in half by magical commands, and by bringing on a rainstorm that saved the army from dying of thirst (Psellus, *Scripta Minora* 1.446.28; Sozomen, *Hist.eccl.* 1.18; Suidas, see *Ioulianos* [434 Adler]). He also was credited with ending a plague in the city of Rome (St. Anastasius Sinai, *PG* 89, col. 525a). Such stories typically gather around charismatic religious leaders, suggesting that whoever the real founders of theurgy were, they had a commanding personal presence.

For its philosophical basis, theurgy adopted many popular Middle Platonic doctrines of the time, including transcendence of the highest god, who is often referred to in theurgy as the Father. This Father was characterized as pure Intellect *(Nous)*. Out of the Father sprang various nontranscendent emanations, or *hypostases,* including the Paternal Power *(Dunamis),* the Second or Demiurgic Intellect, the Cosmic Soul *(Psuchē),* and numerous lesser entities such as the *Iunges* and the Connectors *(Sunocheis),* all of whom had cosmogonic and soteriological roles. The theurgist's goal was to learn how the universe functioned and then to put that knowledge to work on his own behalf, particularly with an eye toward the purification of his soul and its temporary ascent *(anagōgē)* into the heavenly (or "noetic") realm while he was still alive. As in some other Middle Platonic systems, matter *(hulē)* was situated at the bottom of the ontological scale and was understood to reflect the pure intellectual ideals found in the heavenly realm, only imperfectly. Because of this defectiveness, matter induced corporeal passions that might distract the theurgist from his psychic and intellectual labors. The passions were personified in the Oracles as demons referred to as "dogs" and were understood to be under the supervision of the goddess Nature *(Physis)*. Both philosophical training and religious rituals helped the theurgist to overcome them.

In terms of ritual, theurgy largely resembled mainstream Greek and Roman religions. It included purifications and initiations as well as various magical rites, such as the invocation of gods by their secret names; the use of natural materials, such as plants and stones; and the manipulation of a tool called the iynx-wheel. The deity most intimately involved with the theurgist in his daily work was Hecate, who was identified with the Platonic Cosmic Soul. As such, she was imagined to exist between the earthly and heavenly worlds, dividing the two and yet facilitating the passage between them both of the individual mortal soul as it ascended to the heavenly realm and of various divine benefits as they descended into the earthly realm. She was credited with teaching the theurgist his ritual techniques. She also had important cosmogonic functions, as did the Greek god Eros.

There was disagreement even in antiquity as to how a theurgist could best achieve psychic ascension; choice of method may have depended on both the individual's interpretation of theurgic texts and the individual's perception of his own abilities. It is possible that some theurgists believed ascent could be accomplished through contemplation and ascesis alone, although most advocated the use of appropriate ritual techniques as well. Some of these techniques are referred to in fragments of the Oracles or in the discussions of their exegetes; the most notable is the inhalation of sunlight. Iamblichus and others emphasized that, in addition to anything the theurgist himself might do, divine grace and the presence of divine love (Eros) were necessary before ascension could occur. Under this interpretation, the term *theurgy* should be understood to mean the work of the gods on mortals rather than the work of mortals on the gods. Upon ascension, the soul of the theurgist was imagined to learn more about the workings of the cosmos and to enjoy a beneficial communion *(sustasis)* with divinity. The fate of the theurgist's soul after death is not clearly described in our texts, although there are indications that the theurgist expected it to enjoy advantages.

The issue as to whether theurgic magic could produce "light-filled" and reliable visions remained an issue of dispute throughout the Byzantine period, emerging in 15th century criticisms of the visions of the Uncreated Light associated with Hesychast mysticism.

BIBL.: Sarah Iles Johnston, *Hekate Soteira* (Atlanta, 1990). Ruth Majercik, trans. and comm. *The Chaldean Oracles* (Leiden, 1989). G. Shaw, *Theurgy and the Soul* (University Park, Pa., 1995). B. Tambrun-Krasker, "Allusions anti-palamites dans le *Commentaire* de Pléthon sur les *Oracles Chaldaïques*," *Revue des études augustiniennes* 38 (1992): 168–179. S.I.J.

Thrace

As a geographical concept, Thrace is essentially the fertile plain bounded on the north by the Haemus Mountains, on the south by the Rhodope Mountains, and extending eastward as far as the Bosphoros. By the 8th century B.C.E. the region was already dominated by the Thracian people, and although heavily Romanized from the 1st century C.E., a Thracian identity and language still survived in the 6th century—especially away from the more urbanized areas on the edge of the Sea of Marmara and along the main military roads. John Chrysostom states that the Scriptures had been translated into Thracian.

Late antique Thrace owed its strategic significance to its proximity to Constantinople. In general the Balkans were of secondary importance compared with the empire's eastern front, but since the Thracian plain formed the capital's western approaches, its security could not be ignored. The main routes linking the capital to Italy, central and western Europe, and the steppe world converged on Thrace. Regularly used by imperial soldiers and messengers, they also brought a succession of invaders: Goths, Huns, Kutrigurs, Slavs, Antes, Avars, and Bulgars. Repeated invasion meant that Thrace did not benefit as much as Bithynia from the growth of Constantinople, but the region's agricultural output, partly exploited through estates owned by the emperor and the Constantinopolitan establishment, was an important source of supply for the city, particularly after the loss of Egyptian grain supplies in the 7th century. Thrace was also a major source of recruits for the Roman army.

In the late 3rd century Diocletian divided the Severan province of Thrace into four provinces south of the Haemus range (Europa, Haemimontus, Rhodopa, and Thracia), and added two to the north along the Danube (Moesia II and Scythia) to create the diocese of Thracia. The reorganization reflected the fact that up to the Gothic war of 377–378, the defense of Thrace rested on the Danube, and to support this frontier a section of the eastern field army was based in the diocese, commanded by the *magister militum per Thraciam*. The crises of the late 4th and the 5th century forced a new approach, culminating in Anastasius's building of the formidable Long Walls, a frequently underestimated defensive barrier that crosses Thrace from the Black Sea to the Sea of Marmara just 65 km from Constantinople. A further retreat came in 621–622, when Persian victories forced Heraclius to move the army of the *magister militum* to Asia Minor, where they formed the core of the new Thrakesion theme, leaving Constantinople to rely on the Theodosian walls.

A theme of Thrace covering the eastern section of the plain was created in ca. 680, probably as a response to the establishment of the Bulgar state on the lower Danube. In the 8th century, taking advantage of waning Arab pressure in the east, imperial rule was expanded into western Thrace. The Slav tribes who controlled the area were easily subdued, but the advance also provoked intervention by the Bulgars, who would occupy western Thrace from the early 9th century.

BIBL.: James Crow, "The Long Walls of Thrace," in *Constantinople and Its Hinterland,* ed. Cyril Mango and Gilbert Dagron (Aldershot, 1995), 109–124. Ralph-Johannes Lilie, "'Thrakien' und 'Thrakesion': Zur byzantinischen Provinzorganisation am Ende des 7. Jh.," *Jahrbuch der Österreichischen Byzantinistik* 26 (1977): 7–47. Peter Soustal, *Thrakien (Thrakē, Rhodopē und Haimimontos)* (Vienna, 1991).

M.WHI.

Thrones

A naively positivist survey of late antique art, in contrast to earlier Graeco-Roman and postmedieval art, would reveal a strong disposition to sitting. Far from reflecting a characteristic sedentary lifestyle, this distinction reflects a preference for a particular mode of representation. Significant (and novel) classes of late antique art, such as consular diptychs, commonly show seated figures, while important state formulas feature the One Seated, first the emperor and later Christ. Certain genres or classes of representation appear to shift in form, for example author portraits that before late antiquity were likely standing figures or *imagines clipeatae* become seated portrayals, most numerously in the large group of evangelist portraits. Indeed the seat itself becomes the focal element of many important large ensembles, whether as an actual object, such as the episcopal cathedra that gives its name to the greatest Christian churches, or the royal and imperial thrones whose elaborate settings can to some degree be reconstructed from literary sources (the famous throne room or Chrysotriklinos of Theophilus in the early 9th century imperial palace in Constantinople, with its golden organs and warbling birds perched in a golden tree). Late antique art even prominently featured the image of an empty throne, as in the *hetoimasia* that appeared as a focal element of mosaic decorations (St. Maria Maggiore in Rome).

This discussion lumps together a disparate collection under the modern term *throne,* including objects that late antiquity often distinguished with narrower terms (e.g., Latin *solium, sella, cathedra, sedes, faldistorium*), using the term to denote a genre of seats of power. That power may be judicial, expository, or apocalyptic, and may be conveyed by a particular context (in an apse), material (ivory or gold), iconography (lions or other animals depicted on supports), allusion (having six steps, like the throne of Solomon), construction (a folding mechanism), or a combination of such elements. Surviving examples of thrones that may be dated (at least in part) to late antiquity are rare and include the ivory throne of Archbishop Maximian from Ravenna, the stone Frith Stool of Wilfrid at Hexham, the stone Sedia di San Marco from Grado (now in Venice), and the bronze folding throne known as the Throne of Dagobert now in Paris, but representations of such elaborate "power seats" are legion and by no means limited to imperial or Christian iconography. The central axial images above the Torah Shrine in the Dura-Europus synagogue displayed David enthroned, while the silver-gilt toiletry box of the aristocratic 4th century Roman lady Projecta showed her on an elaborate seat framed by an arch and attendants, beneath an image of Venus enthroned on a seashell. The Umayyad desert châteaux made consistent and elaborate arrangements for reception halls and throne rooms, which may owe a considerable debt to Sassanian as well as Roman forerunners. At Quṣayr 'Amra and Qaṣr al-Hayr West, these complexes displayed, respectively, painted and sculpted images of enthroned rulers.

Roman imperial iconography often employed the image of the ruler (or his representatives, such as consuls or judges) seated and facing his people (two examples among many being found on the Arch of Constantine and the base of Theodosius's obelisk), and from an early period Christian art utilized similar compositions for Christ (or his representatives, such as his mother or his bishops). Thomas Mathews has recently suggested that such throne imagery encodes an imitation of or reference to teachers rather than rulers, to Socrates rather than Constantine, as it were. Yet by proposing one specific (and reductive) allegorical reading for another one, his theory perhaps misses the broader issue presented by a semiological reading of these objects and images. That is, a distinctive feature of late antique art and ceremonial was its predilection for themes of majesty, and the utilization of varying symbolic modes of conveying that majesty, including immobilized symmetrical and generally frontal compositions framing a central seated figure. One particularly rich example may illustrate the phenomenon. The Basilica Euphrasiana at Poreč (Parenzo) displays behind its altar a triple representation of enthroned majesty: at the top, above the triumphal arch, is Christ enthroned on the world, surrounded by his apostles; in the center, in the conch of the apse, is the Virgin seated on a bejeweled and bepillowed backless throne, holding her son on her lap, flanked by angels and local martyrs and donors; on the ground level is the raised marble throne of the bishop (reached by six steps) flanked by benches for the clergy, now empty but conceived as a living tableau arranged for the viewing of the congregation. Each of the three thrones has its own character and symbolism, to be sure, and these may be analyzed separately, but of overriding importance is their construction of a theme in the mind of the viewing audience.

BIBL.: J. Elsner, *Art and the Roman Viewer: The Transformation of Art from the Pagan World to Christianity* (Cambridge, Eng., 1995). Galienne Francastel, *Le droit au trône* (Paris, 1973). André Grabar, *L'empereur dans l'art byzantin* (Strasbourg, 1936). Thomas F. Mathews, *The Clash of Gods: A Reinterpretation of Early Christian Art* (Princeton, 1993), 92–114.   L.N.

Tiberias

A city on the western shore of the Sea of Galilee, Tiberias was founded by Herod Antipas around 20 C.E. and was settled by Jews. From the 2nd century the city was under direct Roman rule, becoming a colony under Elagabalus (218–222). Much of its fame was due to the nearby hot springs that became an important medical center. After the suppression of the Bar Kokhba Revolt (135) in Judaea and the transfer of the center of the Jewish community to Galilee, Tiberias gradually became the most important Jewish city in Palestine. In the 3rd century the Jewish patriarchs, as well as the supreme court and educational and scholarly centers, were located there. A large part of the Palestinian Talmud was composed and edited in Tiberias. Tiberias continued to be the center of the Jewish community in Palestine during the Byzantine period, as it was after the Muslim conquest and in the medieval period. It is mentioned frequently in the talmudic literature, which informs us about its rich culture and many urban, religious, and national institutions, such as bathhouses, porticoes, synagogues, and schools *(batei midrash)*. The Christianization of the holy sites near the Sea of Galilee in the region of Tiberias was rather slow. The first Christian congregation of Tiberias is attested in the 4th century, and Tiberian bishops are listed among the participants of the various councils from the 5th century on. Procopius mentions the building of a wall there by Justinian. At its peak the city extended from the Sea of Galilee to the mountains in the west, an area of about 75 hectares. Under the Muslims, Tiberias became the capital city of Jund al-Urdunn and flourished in the 8th and 9th centuries, despite suffering severe damage in the earthquake of 749. In the medieval period the city gradually declined, though occupation has continued uninterrupted up to today. South of the city is the suburb of Hammath Tiberias (the Hot Springs of Tiberias).

Archaeological excavations have revealed various parts of the city from the Roman to medieval periods. In the south was found the Roman city gate, to which a city wall was attached in the Byzantine period. Along the main street running north-south (the *cardo*) several buildings were uncovered, among them a marketplace and a bathhouse. A basilica was discovered on the shore in the east. A Byzantine church with a basilical ground plan (rebuilt in the medieval period) was unearthed on the spur of Mt. Berenice, in the westernmost part of Tiberias. Remains of a synagogue were discovered in the northern part of the town, and two others were excavated in Hammath Tiberias. Most important is the 4th–5th century synagogue in which there is a depiction of the zodiac and a Torah shrine. Many tombs, some of them monumental, were located around Tiberias.

BIBL.: M. Dothan, *Hammath Tiberias* (Jerusalem, 1983). Y. Hirschfeld, *A Guide for the Antiquity Sites in Tiberias* (Jerusalem, 1992). Y. Hirschfeld, ed., *Tiberias from Its Foundation to the Muslim Conquest* (Jerusalem, 1988).   Y.T.

Tigris-Euphrates

With headwaters remarkably close to one another in historical Armenia (now eastern Turkey), but with quite different courses, these two rivers proverbially define Mesopotamia. In Genesis, they are two of four rivers emanating from Eden. In the northern half of Mesopotamia (historical Assyria), the land is little affected by the rivers, for this region either receives adequate rain for agriculture or cannot be artificially watered. But in its southern half (historical al-'Iraq), the Euphrates deposits vast quantities of silt, forming the fertile alluvial soil for which Mesopotamia is famous. From its source near Mt. Ararat where it is fed by melting snows as late as May, the Euphrates (ancient Sippar and Arabic Furat) appears headed for the Mediterranean, but it turns near Aleppo and skirts the Syrian steppe in its 1,480-mile course to the Persian/Arab Gulf. The tributaries al-Balikh and al-Khabur are more important for the settlement they sustain than the water they supply to the Euphrates. Rising with a southern exposure south of Lake Van, the 1,150-mile-long Tigris (biblical Hiddekel, Arabic Diglah) receives its melting snows earlier than the Euphrates, and is joined as well in April by rain-fed, flood-prone tributaries from the flanking Zagros Mountains.

Lying 250 miles apart below the Anti-Taurus range, the two rivers come within 25 miles of each other near modern Baghdad. To this point they follow almost exactly their ancient courses, apart from frequent meanders. Today they widen again before merging completely to form the Shatt al-Arab tidal estuary. In antiquity, both rivers may have constantly bifurcated into numerous separate streams that reached a coastline then as much as 100 miles inland of its position today. Constant sediment deposition by the Euphrates eventually forced the Tigris eastward into its own channel.

Beginning in Parthian times, and exacerbated by a great flood in 629 when the Tigris shifted temporarily back to the west, former settled land became engulfed by a great marsh, the Haur al-Hammar. It is argued the plain was sinking under the weight of its own rising alluvium.

From its raised height, since early historical times, the Euphrates had a tendency to break away to the west at a point above Babylon, so that engineers were forced to battle the river's natural inclination. But the raised water level also allowed canals to be drawn out onto the central alluvium, in contrast to the capricious and down-cut Tigris, which was not nearly so suitable for these purposes. It was only in the late antique period that irrigation projects were initiated along the Tigris, possibly in an attempt to start the irrigation season earlier. A huge Nahrawan canal project was engineered by the Sassanians to supplement water drawn initially from the Diyala, a tributary of the Tigris, which watered the area east of Baghdad.

Since early historical times it was possible to navigate both rivers using shallow craft. With the development of the eastern caravan trade, the Tigris provided a convenient land route because of the position of Charax, a port city founded by Alexander. With the emergence of Palmyra as a caravan center in the 2nd century, merchants crossed to the Euphrates to avoid Parthia and made the journey across the Syrian Desert from the region of 'Ana.

BIBL.: R. M. Adams, *Heartland of Cities: Surveys of Ancient Settlement and Land Use on the Central Floodplain of the Euphrates* (Chicago, 1981). J. Hansman, "Charax and the Karkheh," *Iranica antiqua* 7 (1967): 21–58. A. Northedge, A. Bamber, and M. Roaf, *Excavations at 'Ana* (Warminster, 1988). W. H. Schoff, ed., *The Parthian Stations by Isidore of Charax: The Greek Text, with a Translation and Commentary* (London, 1914; repr. Chicago, 1989). E.K.

Torture

The Mediterranean peoples of antiquity had institutionalized torture, both as part of interrogations and as a method of execution for capital crimes. Beginning in the 3rd century the uses of torture were broadened, both in legislation and in practice.

In principle, Greek and Roman citizens of classical times were protected from torture, which was reserved for noncitizens and was required in Rome for the interrogation of slaves.

Torture was applied as part of interrogations either to extract the confession of a slave suspected of a crime, or to obtain information from him in conjunction with his master's interrogation. The ban on using torture when interrogating witnesses of free status was renewed in the 3rd century. In 314, a law of Constantine admitted that torture procured confessions that were true or that, when added to other testimony, contributed toward ascertaining the truth (*C.Th.* 9.40.1;

n. 36.1 and 4). Forms of torture used during interrogations involved primarily whips, canes, and iron nails.

In the 2nd century, citizens were subjected to torture as punishment, but the decurions and upper classes were exempted by Marcus Aurelius. This already represented an escalation of the use of torture compared with classical times. These tortures were not designed to kill.

Christians arrested during persecutions could confess (as *confessores*) without torture. In Carthage in 250, some of them, generally tortured after their confessions to force them to adopt pagan practices, recanted or died under torture.

In most capital trials, the magistrate in charge of justice (the governor of the province) adapted the punishment to the status of the condemned person: decapitation, burning at the stake, or more spectacular punishments. The severe and sometimes inventive methods used to execute prisoners may also be considered as forms of torture. Some of these original and lethal torments were stagings of cruel mythological episodes and were carried out during intermissions in public games. Certain punishments were inspired by the unusual torments of pagan hell (*Odyssey* 11; *Aeneid* 6, paintings of Lesches of Delphi). The fourth book of the Maccabees, known to Christian authors in the 3rd and 4th centuries, provided an assortment of torments, designed to induce religious acts, that became lethal if prolonged. Between the 2nd and 4th centuries, the Apocalypses (of Peter and Paul) described the eternal torments of Christian hell.

Constantine made the interrogatory torture of slaves and free persons in capital cases obligatory for the most serious crimes (adultery, homicide, magic, divination, falsifying of documents), crimes whose definition became wider in the 4th century. The overall number of crimes defined as capital increased consistently (there were fourteen or so in about 200, twenty-five in about 300, sixty at the end of Constantine's reign).

The number of reasons for torturing a condemned man or woman to death increased in late antiquity, as did the number of persons subjected to interrogatory, punitive, and capital torture, with no privilege granted because of status. There was also an escalation in the types of torments. Capital punishment was abandoned at times in favor of mutilations. Truth was to be obtained by tormenting the body; the soul was to be corrected by marking the body. Various reasons for the escalation of torture have been proposed: the internalization of sin; the influence of the mores of peoples ruled by Rome; the treatment of defeated peoples, criminal soldiers, and slaves; and the desire of a weak power to prove itself powerful. The ruthlessness Roman authorities displayed between 250 and 304, as they forced Christians to make sacrifices to the gods, may have made torture commonplace and given it meaning.

BIBL.: Laurent Angliviel de la Beaumelle, "La torture dans

les *res gestae* d'Ammien Marcellin," in *Institutions, société et vie politique dans l'empire romain au IVe siècle ap. J.-C.* (Rome, 1992). *Du châtiment dans la cité* (Rome, 1984): articles by J.-P. Callu, D. Grodzinski, and E. Patlagean. B. Johansen, "Verité et torture: *Ius commune* et droit musulman," *Séminaire Françoise Héritière* (Paris, 1996), 125–168. R. MacMullen, "Judicial Savagery in the Roman Empire," *Chiron* 16 (1986): 147–166. Y. Thomas, "*Confessus pro iudicato:* L'aveu civil et l'aveu pénal à Rome," in *L'aveu: Antiquité et Moyen Age* (Rome, 1986), 89–117.   A.R.

Tosefta

The Tosefta (addition or supplement) is a rabbinic book that supplements the Mishnah. Written in Hebrew, it seems to have been edited not long after the Mishnah itself and contains little material that is explicitly attributed to figures who flourished after the production of the Mishnah. The work is anonymous. The Tosefta's organization as a whole mirrors that of the Mishnah almost exactly: the same six orders, the same tractates in more or less the same sequence. In fact, the two texts should be regarded as having a "synoptic" relationship, akin to that of the synoptic gospels. The Tosefta's material relates to the Mishnah's in five different ways: (1) the Tosefta repeats verbatim what is in the Mishnah; (2) the Tosefta repeats more or less what is in the Mishnah, but in different language; (3) the Tosefta modifies what the Mishnah has, perhaps even contradicting it; (4) the Tosefta comments on, augments, or discusses what the Mishnah says, even if the underlying Mishnaic statement does not actually appear in the Tosefta; (5) the Tosefta adds new material that is thematically related to what is in the Mishnah but otherwise has no parallel in the Mishnah. The Tosefta's relationship with the Mishnah varies from tractate to tractate, and sometimes even within a single tractate. Because of these complex variations, the synoptic relationship between the Mishnah and the Tosefta resists any simple explanation.

The Tosefta is immensely useful for reconstructing the sources of the Mishnah and Talmud. Material of the second and third types may contain traces of the sources out of which the Mishnah was constructed. Material of fourth and fifth types represents the earliest stages of what eventually would become the Talmud, even though it is not known whether the editors of the Talmud had access to the Tosefta as we know it.

S.J.C.

Tours

Situated on the River Loire, the city of Tours lies on two great axes of communication: one uses the river itself and runs east-west, and the other comes from the south (from the direction of both Bourges and Poitiers) and runs north to Le Mans. Despite its significance in the network of communication, it was only in the 4th century that the city came to prominence, first as the second city of Lugdunensis Secunda, and subsequently, at the end of the century, as the metropolitan city of the newly created Lugdunensis Tertia. It was also only in the course of the 4th century that the city received its walls. Tours's importance was thus relatively new at the time of the election of Martin as the city's bishop in 371. Indeed Martin may have been only the second bishop of the *civitas*.

The city's subsequent importance seems to have depended entirely on the cult of Martin (d. 397). This cult was promoted initially by his hagiographer, Sulpicius Severus, and then by a number of bishops, notably Perpetuus (460–490), working with the poet Paulinus of Perigueux, and Gregory of Tours (573–594), who commissioned works from the poet Venantius Fortunatus. It may be significant that the majority of the bishops of Tours came from Gregory's family.

The cult of Martin dramatically altered the topography of the town, leading to the creation of a separate *suburbium* around the burial place of the confessor. At the center of this was the Church of St. Martin, built initially by Bishop Brictius (Brice), and then rebuilt by Perpetuus and restored by Bishop Euphronius. Despite the significance of the cult, however, the city was never anything other than a religious center.

BIBL.: *Grégoire de Tours et l'espace gaulois*, ed. N. Gauthier and H. Galinié (Tours, 1997). L. Pietri, *La ville de Tours au IVe au VIe siècle: Naissance d'une cité chrétienne* (Rome, 1983). *Topographie chrétienne des cités de la Gaule des origines au milieu du VIII siècle*, ed. N. Gauthier and J.-C. Picard, vol. 5: *Province ecclésiastique Tours* (Paris, 1987).   I.W.

Transport

Modes of transportation remained remarkably stable between the 4th and 8th centuries, but the considerable geographical differences among regions led to marked differences in these modes and explains why transporting men and, especially, products was more difficult in some places than in others.

For shorter trips, barks were used to transport merchandise and men, particularly troops, on the Mediterranean Sea. For greater distances, bigger boats were used; their usual capacity seems to have been slightly less than 200 hectoliters—150 quintals in the case of grain. They often traveled in convoys with other boats that belonged to the same captain. Captains sometimes borrowed money to build their boats or to undertake trips, since lending at interest was legal and even regulated. Contracts stipulating the sharing of losses and profits had apparently been known for a long time. Called *commenda* in the later Middle Ages, they are attested in the Rhodian Law, which dates from the 7th century.

The cost of sea transport was relatively low since, in

the case of grain—the least expensive foodstuff—the price in Alexandria was increased by 12 percent for Constantinople, by 16 percent for Rome, and by 26 percent for Lusitania. But, lacking even the most rudimentary banking system, merchants were unable to establish large companies or organize commercial routes that could influence client demand. Guilds, which seem to have survived in the German west, existed purely for tax purposes. They no doubt facilitated contacts but not the concentration of capital. There was no marketing process. Sources give no examples of merchants, or companies of merchants, seeking out prospective new markets. They always frequented the same ports, where they met traders whom they knew well and who guaranteed them a return freight. Merchants from Alexandria or Constantinople were called *gallodromoi,* because they traveled regularly, or exclusively, to Gaul; easterners came every year to Merida. As a result of these regular contacts, some merchants became notables or bishops in the regions where they did business, such as Naples and Paris. However, the nobility's prejudice against productive activities and the church's distrust of the profits earned by playing on the difference between purchasing price and selling price required that merchants leave their trade before they could accede to public or ecclesiastical offices. St. Augustine did not understand the argument of a merchant who tried to demonstrate the social utility of bringing items found elsewhere in abundance to regions lacking them.

These little private enterprises could not ensure the provisioning of the large cities and, in the first place, of the capitals. Rome (until the 5th century), then Constantinople (until the early 7th century), consumed some 150,000 tons of grain. Beginning with the Roman republic, the state had organized supply fleets run by the curiae, which had boats built and chartered. The grain came primarily from Egypt, since large barks traveled easily on the Nile. The states possessed a few war ships but also requisitioned a large number of private boats for their expeditions and for transport, both civilian and military.

Beginning in the 7th century, the sources provide information on commerce in the North Sea and the Baltic that extended to all the rivers feeding into them. Trade was in the hands of the Frisians, and, to a lesser extent, the Saxons, who went to London or to the fairs of St. Denis, for example. On the English Channel, they met up with a few eastern merchants who came for Cornwall tin, which was indispensable in the fabrication of tin implements, at least until the Arab conquest.

All the rivers were used by small craft adapted to local conditions: the Po and the Seine were navigated quite regularly; the Loire was traveled only when it was not dry or flooding. Even the smaller tributaries carried flat-bottomed barks. Transportation in Mesopotamia was similar to that in Egypt, thanks to the Tigris and Euphrates. It was river transport on the Tigris and Euphrates that allowed the Abbasids to establish their new capital at Baghdad.

In contrast, overland travel was extremely slow, whether by camel (camels could carry about 200 kilograms), mule, donkey, horse, or cart (carts had a capacity of 400 kilograms). Oxen traveled at a rate of 3 km an hour, and the routes or trails, set up for military convoys, were of very poor quality, as were the many roads. This type of transportation was suited only for trade in luxury products or for local use. This explains how people could be starving in the cities while abundance reigned elsewhere: the absence of waterways precluded any other form of transportation. Merchants generally owned their animal or cart and often traveled in convoys. Their businesses were necessarily small and stagnant, though some were able to set up actual companies and rise in the social hierarchy. Eventually some were even able to live like nobles, though they could not hold municipal office.

There was thus an enormous contrast in the Roman empire between regions close to the sea and those inland. Luxury products, such as spices and silk, or semi-luxury items, such as oils and high-quality wine, fine ceramics, and Proconnesus marble, circulated freely to seaport cities. In inland regions, however, only the richest people could buy products from afar, and then only in small quantities.

The idea that trade declined abruptly after the Germans moved into the area must be nuanced. Classical sources focus on the situation existing in large cities and among the nobles, giving the impression that transportation was easy everywhere. The sources from the western kingdoms reveal what had always existed in their regions: difficult trade, limited to certain products, and concentrated around impractical commercial routes. Loads frequently had to be transshiped when moved from one river valley to another, for example from the Saône to the Rhine. Sources rarely mention commerce with other Mediterranean countries, though it had not disappeared. Egyptian papyri give a fairly similar picture of transportation between the 4th and 8th centuries.

BIBL.: Dietrich Claude, *Der Handel im westlichen Mittelmeer während des Frühmittelalters,* vol. 3: *Der Handel des frühen Mittelalters,* ed. Klaus Düwel, Herbert Jahnkuhn, Harald Siems, and Dieter Timpe (Göttingen, 1985).　J.D.

Travelers

Travel was an important component in all of the cultures of late antiquity: Roman, Persian, Byzantine, and Arabic. Travelers journeyed for a variety of reasons, including commerce, official government business, education, religion, migration, and forced displacement.

Sea travel provided the fastest means of transportation, yet passenger vessels were rare, and the journeys were difficult. Most maritime travelers booked deck passage on commercial vessels, especially the huge ships that provided Rome with grain from Egypt and Africa. Since sailors navigated by sight, sea travel was restricted to the predominantly clear months from April to October. Piracy and shipwreck were ever-present dangers.

Most travelers instead journeyed overland. The Roman road system remained largely intact, and was heavily used. The Roman postal service, the *cursus publicus,* was used not only for communication but also by people traveling on official business. Evidence from the *Theodosian Code,* however, reveals that frequently bribes were paid by unauthorized travelers using the service. Several alternatives to pedestrian travel were available. Egeria traveled on mules during her 4th century journey through Egypt, Palestine, and Syria. Wagons and two-wheeled carts pulled by mules were also used by travelers but were exceedingly uncomfortable. Travelers were guided by milestones inscribed with distances to and from various destinations. Guidebooks and maps for travelers, such as the famous Peutinger road map, were commonly used. A normal day's travel covered around 12 miles by foot or 20 by mule. Weary travelers could stop at hostels or monasteries to rest during their journey. In the west, precepts concerning monastic hospitality appear in monastic rules. In the east, *xenodochia,* monastic guest houses, were set up to deal with the volume of visitors to the holy places.

Some travelers were merchants and traders on the commercial sea routes of the Mediterranean or overland caravan traders moving through the Arabian Desert and dependent on the camel. Students traveled to the important centers of learning, such as Constantinople, Beirut, Athens, and later Damascus and Baghdad. Messengers, too, filled the roadways and ships, carrying letters and official documents throughout the Mediterranean basin.

Pilgrimage was popular in both the Christian and Islamic worlds, but it was not the only form of religious travel. Bishops and priests attended distant church councils. Some Christians practiced a wandering lifestyle based on an asceticism of *instabilitas.* Orosius's 5th century journey defies classification: fleeing his Spanish homeland at the time of the Germanic invasions, he embarked on a long journey throughout the Mediterranean. It was a pilgrimage and a letter-carrying mission, as well as a journey to a church council.

Beginning with the Visigoths' long journey through the Roman world, the western Mediterranean was forever changed by the migrations of Germanic peoples. In turn, the movement of these tribes forced many Romans to flee, causing refugees to crowd the cities of Africa and the eastern Mediterranean. In the east, displacement also followed the Persian invasions of the

early 7th century. And a new wave of migration followed the birth of Islam and its spread though Syria, Palestine, Africa, and Spain.

BIBL.: O. Perler, *Les voyages de saint Augustin* (Paris, 1969). E. D. Hunt, *Holy Land Pilgrimage in the Later Roman Empire, A.D. 312–460* (Oxford, 1982).   M.D.

Treasure

The term *treasure* here refers to items made of rich materials that suggest social eminence—in Rome, these included especially gold, silver, and gems, but also purple silk and ivory, among other materials. Typically such items were accumulated for the purpose of display, or they were given as gifts from a leader to subordinates, between friends, or from an individual and to a divinity. The Roman empire went some distance toward development of a market economy; nevertheless, it must be emphasized that Roman gold coinage was itself a "special purpose" money, associated with the state and military organization, being of far too great a value for everyday transactions. Gold coins, along with jewelry and dishes, were given by the state as gifts to servants and soldiers, according to rank. Decorations represented a buying of troops' favor, much as a Germanic war lord might reward his retinue with booty.

Personal gifts were a common aspect of social interaction among the elite. This can be seen in the letters of Sidonius Apollinaris, for example, when Euodius asks the bishop of Clermont to write a poem to be inscribed on a silver vessel to be sent to the Visigothic queen (*Letters* 4.8). Gift giving was a part not only of life but also of death. Grave goods represent offerings to the dead, and treasure was also received from the dead, via the agency of wills. Treasures were also offered as votives to saints, as they had been to pagan deities. Donated silverware typically bore the name of the donor, the name of the recipient, and the reason for the gift. Offerings were made for the repose of a soul, for the donor's salvation, as atonement for sins, as in an act of worship, and in thanksgiving (for benefits received or desired). Such gifts could be used as a way of displaying personal eminence and private wealth; reusing or selling such items was a socially significant act. Ambrose drew fire for melting down silverware, even though he had the justification that it was given by supporters of his Arian predecessor.

Goods of this kind have occasionally been preserved through their deliberate burial, often in time of danger, and subsequent nonretrieval. In the later Roman empire, laws gave rights both to the finder of a treasure and to the one on whose land it had come to light. From the late antique period of the Roman east alone, some thirty treasures have been preserved, half of which are domestic silver and the rest ecclesiastical vessels; this is without taking into account the evidence of coin hoards. However, the very finest accumulations of treasure have long since been dispersed, and their nature must be reconstructed from inventories such as those found in the *Liber pontificalis*.

BIBL.: D. Janes, *God and Gold in Late Antiquity* (Cambridge, Eng., 1998). M. M. Mango, *Silver from Early Byzantium: The Kaper Koraon and Related Treasures* (Baltimore, 1986). C. Morrisson, "La découverte des trésors à l'époque byzantine: Théorie et pratique de l'heuresis thesaurou," *Travaux et mémoires* 8 (1981): 321–343.   D.J.

Treasure Hoards

Treasure hoards contain articles of precious metal concealed for safekeeping and never recovered, presumably because of a catastrophe. In hoards, such as that from Traprain in Scotland, preserved uniquely for their bullion value, plate had been cut into pieces (*Hacksilber*) for storage; in others, objects had been carefully packed and survived in good condition. Because of their value and recyclability, precious metal coins and silver plate were rarely abandoned in an inhabited context and seldom deposited as part of a burial within the empire. Consequently, they are infrequently found during scientific excavation. Exceptions include domestic silver unearthed in houses at Antioch and ecclesiastical silver found outside a church at Luxor, as well as plate uncovered in burials at Kertch in the Crimea, at Taranesh in the Balkans, and in the tomb of Maria, wife of Honorius, in Rome.

Nonetheless, several treasure hoards of late antique silver plate have been recovered, most in unrecorded circumstances, from many parts of the empire. Two of *largitio* silver issued by Licinius have been found: one at Niš (ancient Naissus, where it had been made and stamped) and the other, the Munich treasure, apparently near Istanbul. Notable hoards of domestic silver have been unearthed in Rome on the Esquiline Hill, in Switzerland at Kaiseraugst, in Britain at Mildenhall, in Sicily near Syracuse, in North Africa at Carthage, in Egypt at Bubastis, in Syria near Laodicea, in Cyprus at Lambousa, in Asia Minor at Lambsacus, and in the Aegean at Mytilene.

Compared with domestic plate, church silver has been found at relatively fewer sites, and these, with one exception (Malaya Pereshchepina in the Ukraine), were within the empire. The hoards contain objects inscribed with the name of the donor and, often, the church to which it was offered, and these churches were in villages, not cities. The earliest such hoard (4th century) was unearthed in a field at Water Newton in Britain; another find from the western empire came from ancient Gallunianu in Italy. Objects recovered in Syria were donated to churches in the ancient villages of Kaper Koraon, Attarouthi, Phela, Beth Misona, and Sarabaon. The largest hoard of church plate—fifty-five objects, weighing about 500 Roman pounds—was discovered at Korydalla (Kumluca) in Lycia. In addition to some of the largest dishes surviving from antiquity

and other elaborate objects, this important hoard contains silver furniture revetments.

Outside the empire, late Roman and early Byzantine silver has been found in the Caucasus, and in barbarian contexts in Nubia and in Europe at Petrossa, Concesti, Bolshoi Kamenets, Apahida, Martynovka, Sutton Hoo, Kuczurmare, Malaya Pereshchepina, Vrap, and Erseke. Barbarian imitations of plate from the empire have been found in some of these sites and at Zalesiye, Zeminaksy Vrbovok, Kunagota, and Bosca. Farther north, in the Kama Valley west of the Urals, approximately 170 Byzantine, Sassanian, post-Sassanian, and central Asian silver objects of the 6th to the 13th century have been discovered together in mixed hoards at thirty-two sites. Here, ritualistic figures had been scratched onto several late antique items that were pierced for attachment for upright display, possibly in the 9th and 10th centuries; central Asian inscriptions on some objects suggest an earlier destination for the silver before it was taken north.

BIBL.: C. Johns and R. Bland, "The Great Hoxne Treasure," *Journal of Roman Studies* 6 (1993): 493–496. Marlia M. Mango, "The Sevso Treasure," *Apollo* 1990.   M.M.M.

Trier

From the 2nd century, Trier was the capital of the province of Belgica, and subsequently of Belgica Prima. Controlling a significant stretch of the Moselle, it was an important economic center whose wine trade is reflected in numerous grandiose funerary monuments. Its economy also incorporated the manufacture of imperial clothes and armament factories. Not surprisingly, Trier housed an important imperial mint from the period of the Gallic emperors onward.

Beginning in the late 3rd century the city was often an imperial residence. The presence of Valentinian I's court is recorded in the writings of Ausonius, especially in his *Mosella*, and it was while he was at the imperial court at Trier that Jerome was converted. The city's imperial importance is illustrated by a magnificent Constantinian ceiling, now restored and housed in the diocesan museum. Among other remnants of the late Roman period, the most striking is the city gate, the so-called Porta Nigra.

The city may have been besieged by barbarians in 406–407, and this may have prompted the transfer of the praetorian prefect of the Gauls from Trier to Arles, perhaps as early as 407 and certainly by 418. Trier was probably taken by the Franks in 411, and it seems to have been sacked on two further occasions, although after the last of these the population continued to attend the circus, according to Salvian of Marseilles. Salvian himself was one of a number of Gallo-Romans who abandoned the Trier region to begin an ascetic life in Provence.

The city's economic survival is known from the production of coins under Valentinian III, and even after the Frankish takeover it seems to have retained some economic importance: coin production was resumed in the late 6th century. Under the Franks, however, Trier never quite regained its political importance.

BIBL.: E. Ewig, *Trier im Merowingerreich, Civitas, Stadt, Bistum* (Trier, 1954). *Topographie chrétienne des cités de la Gaule des origines au milieu du VIII siècle*, ed. N. Gauthier and J.-C. Picard, vol. 1: *Province ecclésiastique de Trèves* (Paris, 1986).   I.W.

Turks

"Türk" is the name of the founding tribe or tribal confederation of the Türk qaghanate in Mongolia from which many of the more important Turkic political formations of medieval Eurasia derive. The origins of the Turks are unclear, as is the question of the original homeland of the earliest Turkic-speaking groupings. Presumably they were located in the western zone of the Altaic linguistic community, in contact with Indo-European and Uralic in southern Siberia. Chinese sources, which report a number of ethnogenetic legends, trace them to a branch of the Hsiung-nu. These same accounts place their ruling clan, the A-shih-na, in eastern Turkestan, or Kansu, a region that was at that time predominantly Tokharian and East Iranian, both of which provide possible etymologies for this name. In the mid-5th century C.E., the A-shih-na fled to the Altai region, where they became vassals of the Jou-jan, or Avars, specializing in metallurgy. In 552 they revolted against their overlords and overthrew their state, replacing it with their own rapidly expanding empire.

Their first qaghan was Bumïn (in Chinese, T'u-men, d. 552), who shared power with his brother Ishtemi (552 to 575–576), the Yabghu Qaghan (Silziboulos of the Byzantine sources, Sinjibū of the Arabo-Persian accounts), producing an at first nominal division in the state, with the supreme power residing in the eastern qaghanate. While Mughan Qaghan (Chinese Mu-han) (553–572) solidified Türk power in the east, his uncle, Ishtemi, was charged with conquering the lands to the west and assuring an outlet for the silk that the Türks had been accumulating. A Türk military and marital alliance with Sassanid Iran led to the destruction of their common foe, the Hephthalites, in 557 and brought Türk authority to the Pontic steppes, driving the War-Hun/European Avars into Pannonia (567–568).

The Türk-Sassanid alliance soon ended, because of a conflict of mercantile interests, and in 568 Ishtemi initiated contacts with the Byzantine empire, calling for trading and military agreements largely aimed against Iran. A Türk embassy (perhaps not the first, if the mission noted by Theophanes as sent in 563 by "Askel, king of the Ermikhions" is, indeed, to be identified as Türk) was led by Maniakh from the recently conquered Sogdian city-states of central Asia. An important subject people in both the eastern and western halves of the empire, the Sogdians were major figures in the east-west trade along the Silk Route, and their language served as a language of commerce and diplomacy in Eurasia. The earliest Türk inscription (Bugut) is in Sogdian, and the Turkic scripts that subsequently developed were based on Aramaic/Syriac alphabets spread through inner Asia by the Sogdians. A reciprocal Byzantine embassy led by Zemarkhos went to Sogdia (August 569) and thence to the camp of the Yabghu Qaghan at "Ektag" (*Aq Tagh, or White Mountain, translated into Greek as Golden Mountain, perhaps located in eastern Turkestan but not to be confused with the Altai, the Chin shan, or Golden Mountain, of the Chinese sources), where the Byzantine ambassadors were duly impressed with the enormous wealth of their "barbarian" hosts (see Menander). As relations worsened with Iran, another Türk embassy, under Taghma Tarkhan, was dispatched, reaching Constantinople in 571. Hostilities with Iran had begun, and the Türks were anxious to have the emperor Justin II "show his friendship." Additional embassies followed from different peoples under Türk rule, so that when Valentinos led a new Byzantine embassy in 576, he took with him 106 "Türks" who had accumulated in Constantinople. Valentinos found a hostile reception in which the Türk ruler Tourksanthos (*Türk-shad?), who had recently buried the Yabghu Qaghan, berated the Byzantines for their inactivity against Iran, for treaty making with "our slaves" the War-Hun/Avars, and for speaking "with ten tongues and lying with all of them" (Menander, frg. 19). A Türk army was sent to Byzantine Crimea, where Bosporos was taken (579). The Türk-Byzantine alliance was shaken but not broken.

Far more disruptive was Türk internecine strife. Taspar Qaghan (572–581), who extorted enormous quantities of silk from China while promoting Buddhism in the eastern qaghanate, was the last qaghan to enjoy more or less untroubled rule over a united realm. A throne struggle, encouraged by a revived China under the Sui, weakened Taspar's successor, Ishbara Qaghan (581–587) and provided the backdrop for the spectacular revolt of the western qaghan, Tardu, Ishtemi's son, in 582 (a murky reflection of which is found in Theophylaktos Simokattes, 7.7–8). He was sufficiently strong to withstand a serious defeat at Herat (589) at the hands of the Sassanids and become master of the Türk empire ca. 600. His collapse in 603, due to tribal revolts and Sui intrigues, was the prelude to the fall of the eastern qaghanate in 630 to China. The weakening of Türk rule was felt in the Pontic steppes, where the Avars reasserted their authority for a time over the Bulgar tribes which, ca. 631–635, achieved their independence under Qubrat. Western Türk power, especially in Central Asia, revived under Tardu's brother Tong Yabghu Qaghan (618 or 619? to 630). He was also the ally of the Byzantine emperor Heraclios (610–641) against the Sassanids, playing a key role in Constantinople's victories in Transcaucasia that set the stage for the Sassanid collapse. Internal disputes led to his assassination, which ushered in a new round of civil strife and the de facto division of the western qaghanate into the rival tribal coalitions (five tribes each) of the Tu-lu and Nu-shih-pi of the On Oq (Ten Arrows). They, too, succumbed to the T'ang in 659, while some groupings acknowledged Tibetan overlordship.

In the late 680s, the eastern qaghanate revived and, under Qapaghan Qaghan (691–716), extended its authority to the western Türk lands in eentral Asia. However, the far western territories (the Volga-Pontic steppes), were now under the control of the Khazar qaghans, of Türk origin but independent of their kinsmen in the east. Qapaghan and his successor, Bilge Qaghan (716–734), from whose reign we have the remarkable Orkhon inscriptions in Turkic runiform script, engaged in constant campaigning against their subject peoples, China, and the advancing Arabs in Transoxiana. The eastern qaghans were toppled in 742 by their subjects the Basmïls and Uighurs. The latter supplanted the Basmïls in 744 and founded an important empire largely limited to Mongolia, southern Siberia, and eastern Turkestan (744–840) that played an important role in T'ang history. The western Türks, when not quarreling among themselves, were engaged in conflict with the advancing forces of Islam and the Tibetan empire. For a time, the Türgesh union came to dominate the On Oq and led the resistance to the Arab conquests (until 737). The T'ang then reasserted themselves in the On Oq lands, which were coming under the control of the Qarluqs (ca. 745),

who had aided the Uighurs in their defeat of the Basmïls and now, disenchanted with the new qaghans in Mongolia, had migrated westward. This was the background to the Battle of the Talas (751), in which the Qarluqs defected from the T'ang army to gain the victory for the Arabs, thereby ensuring that Islam would triumph in the Sogdian lands and beyond.

Meanwhile, the Qarluqs took over Suyab/Ordukent (near Tokmak in Kyrgyzstan), the western Türk capital in 766. This marked the end of the Türk empire. Its successor states were the Khazar realm (ca. 650–965) in the west, the Qarakhanids (mid-10th–early 13th century) in Transoxiana, and the Uighurs in inner Asia. The former two were ruled by dynasties of probable A-shih-na origins. Through Arabo-Persian and, to a lesser extent, Greek and Latin usage, *Turk,* a political and later a cultural designation also used by peoples of the Türk qaghanate, became a generic term for the largely, but not exclusively, Turkic-speaking nomads of Eurasia.

BIBL.: T. J. Barfield, *The Perilous Frontier: Nomadic Empires and China* (Oxford, 1989). C. Beckwith, *The Tibetan Empire in Central Asia: A History of the Struggle for Great Power among Tibetans, Turks, Arabs, and Chinese during the Early Middle Ages* (Princeton, 1987). R. C. Blockley, ed. and trans., *The History of Menander the Guardsman* (Liverpool, 1985). P. B. Golden, *An Introduction to the History of the Turkic Peoples: Ethnogenesis and State-Formation in Medieval and Early Modern Eurasia and the Middle East* (Wiesbaden, 1992). *Theophylacti simocattae historiae,* ed. C. de Boor, re-ed. P. Wirth (1887; repr. Stuttgart, 1972); Eng. trans.: *The History of Theophylact Simocatta,* trans. M. and M. Whitby (Oxford, 1986). P.B.G.

Umayyads

Under the Umayyads, the first Muslim dynasty (661–750), the new Islamic world reached India and central Asia to the east and the Atlantic and southern Gaul to the west. It was also the only time in history when all of Islamdom was ruled from a single center, in what is modern Syria.

The founder of the dynasty was Muʿāwiyah ibn Abi Sufyān. He came from a prominent and wealthy Meccan family that had opposed the Prophet Muhammad. Like most of his relatives, he accepted Islam relatively late in life, a few years before the death of the Prophet in 632. The first caliph, Abū Bakr, sent Muʿāwiyah to lead the vanguard of the Arab army in Syria, and his successors appointed him governor of that rich and highly Hellenized province, as well as of the newly formed province of the Jazirah in the middle Mesopotamian area. Muʿāwiyah established there a firm political base among the many old or newly migrated Arab tribes, fought successfully against the Byzantines, and withstood the competition of ʿAlī ibn Abī Tālib, the son-in-law of the Prophet and the fourth caliph, with his Iraqi power base. After ʿAlī's assassination in 661, Muʿāwiyah was sworn in as caliph, possibly in Jerusalem, moved the capital of the state from Medina in Arabia to Damascus in Syria, and spent the rest of his life consolidating his power against various tribal or Meccan rivals by fostering the expansion of Muslim power eastward and westward, checking Byzantine incursions, and developing a new Muslim navy.

Allegiance was sworn during Muʿāwiyah's lifetime to his son Yazid (680–683), who, like his own son

Muʿāwiyah II (683–684), failed to keep control over the traditional rivalries among Arab tribes and the new rivalries, especially in Iraq, among new Muslim sectarian divisions. The result was a series of internal civil wars that lasted many years. In 684, the caliphate was given to an older and astutely wise member of the Umayyad family, Marwan ibn al-Hakam, who was succeeded by his son ʿAbd al-Malik (ruled 685–705), undoubtedly the most brilliant organizer of the dynasty, under whose rule Arabic replaced Greek and Pahlavi as the administrative language of the empire and a clearly identifiable Muslim coinage was created. Furthermore, he appointed brilliant governors in Iraq, Egypt, and North Africa who not only succeeded in maintaining a relative peace within the lands they controlled but also supervised the lucrative conquests that led Arab armies to the Atlantic Ocean and to the frontiers of China. Under ʿAbd al-Malik's eldest son, al-Walīd (705–715), Spain was taken over. While the brief reign of Omar ibn ʿAbd al-Aziz (717–720) was hailed as a return to a more traditional Muslim type of leadership, the other sons of ʿAbd al-Malik who ruled in succession—Sulaiman (715–717), Yazid (720–724), and especially Hishām (724–743)—honed the administrative organization created by their father; established through marriages and an adroit distribution of funds a reasonable equilibrium between competing tribal and sectarian groups; transformed through urbanization the landscape of the Tigris and Euphrates Valley; presided over the permanent settlements of formally nomadic Arabs; adopted into their system the populations of conquered areas (converted or not); gave a boost to trans-Asian trade and to the cultivation of new plants imported from the east; permitted the elaboration, mostly in Iraq, of nearly all the major religious, social, and intellectual movements that would become the mainstream as well as the heterodoxies of Islam; formalized the pattern of the congregational mosque as a consistent feature of Muslim life; sponsored the construction of major public mosques in Damascus (still extant), Jerusalem (partly redone), and Medina (totally redone); and fixed the approximate frontiers of Islam for some four hundred years. Under their rule, the battle of Poitiers (732) marked the farthest advance of Islam in the west, and it was shortly after the fall of the dynasty that the battle of Talas (751) brought the Arabs to a victorious clash with a Chinese army—and led, incidentally, to the introduction of paper to western Asia and, eventually, Europe.

All this was made possible for many reasons that have been debated by scholars for nearly a century and that already puzzled medieval chroniclers, who often considered the Umayyads as reprobates and, with an occasional exception, unworthy Muslims who introduced the ways of ancient empires, particularly those of the Romano-Byzantine Caesar and the Persian and Iranian Khosro, instead of acting like true believers. There is no doubt that much in the success of the dynasty was the result of the enormous wealth brought by the conquests east and west, and it is probably true that, by maintaining their capital in Syria (primarily Damascus, but, under Hishām, also Rusafah in the northern Syrian steppe), the Umayyads revealed their reliance on the administrative and cultural patterns of the eastern Roman empire.

The Umayyads were not only a hierarchical dynasty but also a complex network of family members and allied chieftains who were involved in large economic ventures in trade and agriculture, many of which have been discovered through archaeological investigations. Many of their living establishments, some remarkably luxurious, have been uncovered as well, and they demonstrate, as do the religious monuments in Jerusalem and Damascus, their patronage of the most expensive artisans and techniques available in the late antique world. At the same time, traditional Arabic poetry continued to flourish under their rule, as did the early stages of a prose literature in Arabic. Recent investigations have also shown that Christian patronage was very active under the Umayyads, especially in Jordan and in the Jazirah.

In short, the Umayyads were a lively, vibrant, and creative Arab dynasty which supervised, by will or by accident, the transformation of half of the old Roman empire and of the whole Sassanian empire in Iran and central Asia into a new medieval Muslim world.

But the structure they built was based on a complex equilibrium of forces that could not continue to be controlled from Syria by descendants of Arab clan and tribe leaders. A new urban society with different expectations grew up in Iraq, too many sectarian movements went unchecked, and the successor of Hishām, al-Walīd II, turned out to be a libertine poet and drinker who was hardly up to the rule of a huge empire. A series of revolts began in the eastern provinces and, in spite of the caliph Marwan II's efforts, overwhelmed Umayyad forces in 750. Most male members of the family were massacred. The one survivor fled to al-Andalus and founded there the Umayyad dynasty of Spain.

BIBL.: P. Crone and M. Hinds, *God's Caliph* (Cambridge, Eng., 1986). H. Kennedy, *The Prophet and the Age of the Caliphate* (London, 1986). G. R. Hawting, *The First Dynasty of Islam* (Carbondale, Ill., 1987). F. Donner, "The Formation of the Islamic State," *Journal of the American Oriental Society* 106 (1986). G. Rotter, *Die Umayyaden und die zweite Bürgerkrieg* (Wiesbaden, 1982). A. Cameron, ed., *The Byzantine and Early Islamic Near East* (Princeton, 1980–).

O.G.

Urbanism

The city had been the center of the social and political life of antiquity. The ordered magnificence of the classical city, with its emphasis on regular street plans and the embellishment of public open spaces and monuments, was the product of a society in which civic values were central. Important cities had their own temples and cults, their own city councils, their baths, theaters, and public water supply. This was a society in which the rich sought prestige in this world and immortality after death by lavishing resources on the embellishment of their hometown.

In late antiquity in the eastern Mediterranean, the city remained the center of political life and government. Unlike in the contemporary west, the wealthy did not, on the whole, desert the cities for rural villas and monasteries. Nonetheless, the cities evolved and developed in response to wider changes in society.

The social and political status of the cities began to change from the middle of the 3rd century. The emperors of the second half of the century put an end to municipal fiscal autonomy, city treasuries were abolished, and local bronze coinage, which had often carried city emblems, was no longer minted. It is likely, too, that the disappearance of local treasuries and town councils led to the abandonment of many of the great bathhouses of antiquity. The coming of Christianity meant further important changes in urban life. The temples, which had been the centerpieces of much urban planning, were either destroyed or gradually allowed to fall into decay. The *temenē* that surrounded them and the processional ways that led to them became useless and were often built over or turned into sites for pottery kilns. In addition, some early Christians were fiercely critical of theatrical performances, and slowly, from the 4th to the 6th century, the massive theaters that had been so imposing a feature of most large towns fell into disuse.

As in western Europe at the same time, the unsettled conditions of the 3rd century meant that almost all large cities were provided with walls. In contrast to the west, where these fortifications generally enclosed a much reduced urban area, the walls of such eastern cities as Antioch, Apamea, and Gerasa, not to speak of Constantinople itself, were many kilometers long and enclosed the whole of the built-up area of the city. The fortification of the cities may have put pressure on urban open spaces, since new development and expansion had to be carried on within the perimeter rather than by expanding into the surrounding country. This pressure, coupled with the gradual abandonment of wheeled traffic in late antiquity and the early Islamic period, meant that wide paved streets were increasingly built over.

Because of these changes, the city of late antiquity lost much of its classical aspect. By the year 500, few if any temples survived. Prominent citizens spent their money on the endowment of churches, whose often modest exteriors concealed an interior rich and vibrant with mosaics, marbles, and icons. The porticoes of the old colonnaded streets were built up with small shops, and the main pavements were increasingly invaded by secondary structures.

The pace of these changes varied. In provincial capitals until the mid-6th century, the emperor and his representatives were still prepared to invest money in maintaining streets, as is shown by Procopius's account of the rebuilding of Antioch after 540. In Ephesus a major new colonnaded street leading to the port was constructed in the early 5th century. Archaeological evidence from Jerusalem, where the main colonnaded street was lengthened in the early part of Justinian's reign, and from Scythopolis, where the provincial governors spent money on new roads and baths, shows that the authorities still considered the maintenance of civic structures a government responsibility. In contrast, in nearby Gerasa, not a provincial capital, only churches were built in the 6th century. Private patronage for civic improvements was virtually unknown by this time.

Evidence suggests that the numbers of cities, and probably the numbers of their inhabitants, remained buoyant throughout the 4th and 5th centuries. In the second half of the 6th and the early 7th century, however, many cities disappeared altogether. Anemurium, on the south coast of Anatolia, provides a well-documented example of a thriving commercial center that became impoverished and was finally deserted during this period.

In Syria, by contrast, a significant number of new quasi-urban centers developed in the 5th and 6th centuries. It was a time of expansion for the cities of the Negev in southern Palestine, the Hawran, and for many of the small towns in the limestone massif of northern Syria, all areas from which the archaeological record is particularly rich. However, these towns were very different from the planned cities of antiquity. Their streets were no more than narrow winding lanes, and there were no public buildings except churches. At the same time, the domestic architecture of these areas shows large and well-built houses, suggesting an emphasis on family rather than civic life.

The coming of Islam intensified some of these developments: streets tended to become more built up, as is shown at Palmyra, where the recently excavated Umayyad *sūq* was built in the center of the great Roman colonnaded street. In other cities—Jerusalem, Damascus, and Aleppo, for example—the *sūq*s continued to follow the lines of the main streets of the classical period. The coming of Islam also meant the building of mosques. In small towns these were often unobtrusive buildings, as in Gerasa, where the mosque occupies a small plot by the main street, and Subeita (Shivta) in the Negev, where, surprisingly, it is built into the narthex of a church. In larger centers of government the mosques occupied more prestigious sites. In Jerusalem and Damascus they were built over the old cult sites of the Temple platform and the temenos of the ancient temple of Haddad/Zeus, respectively. In Aleppo, it seems as if the mosque was built on the site of the ancient agora.

BIBL.: G. Bühl, *Constantinoplis und Rom: Stadtpersonifikationen in der Spätantike* (Zurich, 1995). L. Di Segni, "The Involvement of Local, Municipal and Provincial Authorities in Urban Building in Late Antique Palestine and Arabia," *Journal of Roman Archaeology: Supplementary Series* 14 (1995): 313–332. C. Saliou, *Le traité d'urbanisme de Julien d'Ascalon: Droit et architecture en Palestine au VIe siècle* (Paris, 1996). H.K.

Usury

As in the previous centuries of the empire, the interest loan was widely used in all social strata in late antiquity and in different sectors of economic life. Imperial legislation from the 4th to the 6th century continued the previous legal tradition: interest was not to exceed the traditional rate of 12 percent per year *(centesima)*. Senators were prohibited from demanding interest higher than 6 percent (C.Th. 2.33.4). In 325 (C.Th. 2.33.1) Constantine ruled that the annual interest on loans to farmers—a widespread practice in the agricultural world—could not exceed half of the amount received as a loan *(hemiolion)*. Influenced by Christianity, perhaps, in 528 (C.Just. 4.32.26–27) Justinian reduced all legal interest rates for humanitarian reasons, to 6 percent for the ordinary loan, 4 percent for the *viri illustres,* 8 percent for the commercial and artisan loan, 12 percent for the naval loan *(fenus nauticum)*. Subsequently, in 535 (Nov. 32, 34), the emperor decreed a marked decrease in the maximum interest on loans to poor farmers: 4 percent for all loans in money, one-eighth of the amount received for agricultural products.

Christian thinking was completely different. The church fathers condemned interest received on a loan, continuing the position expressed in the Hebrew Bible that allowed loans but not interest: "descendants of vipers are the result of interest" (Basil of Cesarea). A considerable number of treatises and sermons were produced on this subject. In the east, Basil, Gregory of Nyssa, and John Chrysostom were among those who condemned interest on monetary loans. Among the westerners, Ambrose, Jerome, and Pope Leo the Great stand out: in their writings, the legal argument is more detailed and the moral condemnation extends to every type of interest, even those in kind. Jerome explicitly condemns the *hemiolion,* which, in 325, Constantine had declared legal. Church councils—from Elvira (Spain, in 305) until the 7th century—took a more accommodating position, however. *Foenus* and *usura* were forbidden only to the clergy, not to all the faithful.

BIBL.: A. Laiou, "The Church, Economic Thought, and Economic Practice," in *The Christian East,* ed. R. F. Taft, Orientalia Christiana Analecta 251 (Rome, 1996), 435–464.

D.V.

Vandals

In ca. 300 C.E., the Vandals occupied land in central Europe but were not in direct contact with the Roman frontier. This changed when, probably in the face of Hunnic pressure, two Vandal groups—the Hasdings and Silings—participated, with Suebi and Alans, in the famous Rhine crossing of 406. The invaders eventually crossed into Spain in 409, and in 411 they divided it: the Hasding Vandals and Suebi shared Gallaecia, the Silings took Baetica, and the Alans Lusitania and Carthaginiensis. Between 416 and 418 a joint force of Romans and Goths destroyed the Siling Vandals and many Alans. The survivors joined the Hasding Vandals, whose rulers thenceforth styled themselves "kings of the Vandals and Alans."

In the 420s, first King Gunderic and then, from 428, his half-brother Gaiseric raided widely in Spain and the Balearic Islands, before moving their followers into North Africa in 429. A first treaty with the empire in 436 recognized their domination of Numidia and Mauretania. In 439, Gaiseric broke this agreement to seize Carthage and the richer provinces of Proconsularis and Byzacena. The new conquests were recognized by treaty in 442.

After the death of Valentinian III in 455, Gaiseric wanted the Vandals, like the Goths and Burgundians, to be included in the new political order. His forces sacked Rome in 455 because a usurper, Petronius Maximus, married his own son to Valentinian's daughter Eudocia, who had previously been betrothed to Gaiseric's son Huneric. But successive western regimes, particularly those of Majorian in 461 and Anthemius in 468, with the backing of Constantinople, saw the reconquest of the rich North African provinces as the best means of revivifying the western empire. When these attempts failed, peace was finally made between Gaiseric and the eastern empire in 474.

Huneric, his son and successor, was much more concerned with internal affairs. The Vandals adhered to non-Nicene—so-called Arian—Christianity, and the last year of Huneric's reign, 484, was marked by fierce persecution of Catholics. His ambitious aim was to create uniformity of belief throughout his kingdom, but he died before the policy could have substantial effect.

From the 490s, the Vandal kingdom, led by Thrasamund, was faced with the rise of the Ostrogothic empire of Theoderic. Thrasamund eventually married Amalafrida, Theoderic's sister, accepted a Gothic military presence in Carthage, and had to make a humiliating public apology for briefly aiding Gesalic, one of Theoderic's enemies. Thrasamund's successor, Hilderic, exploited Theoderic's old age to put Amalafrida in prison (where she died) and kill her attendants. This was part of a rapprochement with Constantinople, which also saw Hilderic recall exiled Catholic bishops and convene a church council in Carthage in 522. Hilderic was eventually overthrown by Gelimer in 530, who reversed some of Hilderic's religious policies. This gave the eastern emperor Justinian a pretext for invading North Africa in 533. The Vandal army was defeated within two years, and with it, the kingdom. Adult male survivors of the fighting were shipped to the Persian front, which destroyed the Vandals as a sociopolitical entity.

BIBL.: F. M. Clover, *The Late Roman West and the Vandals* (London, 1993). C. Courtois, *Les Vandals et l'Afrique* (Paris, 1955). Y. Modéran, "La chronologie de la vie de S. Fulgence de Ruspe," *Mélanges de l'école française de Rome: Antiquité* 105 (1993): 135–183. J. Moorhead, *Victor of Vita: History of the Vandal Persecution*, Translated Texts for Historians (Liverpool, 1992). "La renaissance des cités de l'Afrique au VIe siècle," in *La fin de la cité antique et le début de la cité médiévale*, ed. C. Lepelley (Bari, 1996), 85–114.   P.H.

Victor of Vita

The manuscripts that preserve a *History of the Persecution of the Province of Africa in the Time of Gaiseric and Huneric, Kings of the Vandals* (hereafter *HP*) also provide virtually all that is known about its author. He was a bishop named Victor, and his home was the city of Vita. The *HP* is a stirring record of the Maccabaean determination of Africa's orthodox (or "catholic") Christians in the face of persecution by the Vandals, who subscribed to the faith set forth by the prelate Arius. The *HP* contains not only Victor's purple prose but also some quoted documents—three edicts of Huneric (two with precise dates), a letter of Eugenius (orthodox bishop of Carthage under Huneric), and the *Book of the Catholic Faith*, a statement of belief composed for a colloquium held on 1 February 484. One of the Victor manuscripts, the 9th century *Codex Laudunensis* number 113, preserves this last text together with a parallel record, the *Register of the Provinces and Cities of Africa*—ostensibly a roster of Catholic bishops who attended the colloquium of 484. From this source one learns that Victor's home city was located in the province of Byzacena.

The *HP* betrays Victor's intimate knowledge of the ecclesiastical affairs of Carthage, especially during the reign of Huneric (477–484). Just when Victor penned his reflections on the persecutions is a matter of uncertainty. Most modern critics believe that the *HP* reached a reading public late in Huneric's reign. The text itself tells against this interpretation, however. Early in the second book (*HP* 2.12–17) Victor describes Huneric's dynastic butcheries, all aimed at eliminating collateral members of his family and thereby assuring the succession of his own offspring. In this passage Victor twice emphasizes that this did not come to pass (*HP* 2.12 and 17). Evidently Victor published the *HP* during the reign of Gunthamund or Thrasamund (484–496 and 496–523, respectively)—Huneric's nephews, who survived the slaughter—and before the accession of Huneric's son Hilderic (523).

For the historian of the late Roman empire and Christianity, the *HP* is replete with useful information. The Arianizing Councils of Ariminum and Seleucia-in-Isauria, of evil repute among orthodox Christians, receive commendation in one of the edicts of Huneric (*HP* 3.5). Huneric, to judge from the *HP* and other evidence, was the first Vandal monarch to employ the elaborate title "king of the Vandals and Alans" (*HP* 2.39 and 3.3–14). A passage describing the persecution of 484 suggests that Huneric also used the title *dominus noster rex* (our master the king; *HP* 3.19). He was therefore the first Vandal monarch to appropriate a title reserved for the emperor. The *HP*, even with its evident biases and rhetorical flourishes, is a precious record of the Vandal sojourn in Africa.

BIBL.: C. Courtois, *Victor de Vita et son oeuvre: Étude critique* (Algiers, 1954). J. Moorhead, trans., *Victor of Vita: History of the Vandal Persecution* (Liverpool, 1992). M. Petschenig, ed., *Victoris episcopi vitensis Historia persecutionis africanae provinciae*, in *CSEL* 7 (1881): 1–107.   F.C.

Villas

The Roman villa was a central feature within the social, economic, and cultural structure of the Roman empire; it is illustrative of that structure, and its history is in this sense the history of the empire itself. Its emergence in Italy was the result of imperial expansion, and in the provinces it was one of the more striking examples of Romanization. Its heyday was the "high" empire; it encountered the pressures common to the empire in the 3rd century; and for the remaining two hundred or more years it underwent a process of change that for the empire as a whole was once characterized as a decline and fall, but which for it and the empire alike can now be seen, rather, as a positive, even productive, phase in a continuing history.

However one characterizes the 3rd century "crisis" in general terms, there can be no doubt that for the villa the central years of the century represent at best a standstill and at worst a serious decline. Some villas, without doubt, were destroyed by invaders. Many, if not actually destroyed, were abandoned to lie derelict, and by no means were all of these rebuilt later. Many more were run down and functioned at a reduced level. It is extremely difficult to find a site at which there was expansion or there were building improvements, or at which new amenities such as baths or mosaic pavements were installed. The impression one gets is of owners hanging on and hoping for better times. On the continent of Europe, the period of prosperity under the Severan and Antonine emperors that saw the development of such palatial houses as Chiragan and Montmaurin in southwestern France, and Haccourt in Belgium, as well as a host of less spectacular but still prosperous and successful establishments, had clearly come to an end. In Britain, which had begun the process a century or so later, the slower but steady growth of a villa culture was temporarily halted.

The recovery of that culture, as of the empire itself, in the 4th century was not everywhere uniform, and what emerged as a result of the reconstruction from Diocletian onward was in many ways strikingly different from what had existed earlier. Some areas did better than others: the appearance of large and splendid villas in Britain during this period, and indeed the establishment there of the most prosperous and successful phase of its villa history, is a particularly striking development and one that is even now not fully understood. The area around the late imperial capital at Trier experienced a similar revival, as did southern and southwestern Gaul, and provinces such as Pannonia and Dalmatia. Even in such successful areas, however, there were signs that times had changed: standards of workmanship were not always what they had been; on many sites there is evidence of haste in the construction of buildings; and on many, again, a greater concentration on the working aspects and rather less on the luxury apartments. Here, no doubt, are the observable effects of the complex social and economic changes of the period. There remained a rural aristocracy, prosperous still and perhaps locally more powerful than before, but it was less underpinned by political and administrative structures, more dependent on its own initiatives for power and status, and rather less willing than in previous generations to take a role in the wider community. While some still sought to uphold the traditional culture and values, many no doubt adopted a narrower perspective and become more local, more inward-looking, more self-sufficient. The villas of this period reflect a concentration of wealth and power, but one can see in many of them a greater emphasis on their role as estate centers, and perhaps a loosening to some degree of the economic and social ties between them and the towns that had once been one of their defining characteristics.

The 4th century development, therefore, is one of change rather than decline. In some respects, of course, and certainly in some parts of the empire, the villa had effectively come to the end of its history by the last years of the 4th century or at the latest by the first decade or so of the 5th. In Britain, for example, where 5th century material on villa sites is rare and insubstantial, and where the evidence for late occupation is essentially confined to the appearance of the occasional primitive hut, it would be difficult at present to argue for survival on any but a minimal level. On the Continent, on the other hand, where the "end" of the empire was in many respects more gradual, a long-held view that the life of villas may have extended significantly into the 5th century has recently received archaeological support. Mosaics at a number of larger sites in southwestern Gaul, and at one or two other sites farther afield, have now been assigned to the 5th and, in some cases, even the 6th century; the assignment of similar dates to some types of pottery that appear fairly widely in villa contexts is also suggestive. The nature of the survival this represents is not entirely clear: the rather monumental appearance of the villas, and the tendency of their late mosaics to appear in more public areas such as corridors and colonnades, may suggest that the villas themselves were becoming in some sense more public and less private, perhaps that they were no longer simply the residences of landowners but were the seats of secular or religious officials. This could, if correct, give greater meaning to the changes that seemed to be occurring in the 4th century, though more work is needed before firm conclusions may be drawn. There is also the problem of linking this fairly recent evidence to the contemporary literary descriptions of villas, most notably in the poems and letters of Sidonius Apollinaris, and although the two kinds of material are to some extent mutually supportive, it may well be that the end result will be to point up a need for greater caution, or greater subtlety, in the use of Sidonius's text.

The background to this later phase, after all, is one of increasing insecurity, linked to the steady shrinkage of the Roman area and the growth within the empire of increasingly independent and competing Germanic kingdoms. The effects on the villa of such radical developments can no longer be categorized simply in terms of change but must be seen, rather, as a transformation into something utterly different from what had existed before. Fortunatus in the 6th century writes of villas as Sidonius had done in the 5th, but they strike one as a curiosity, an antiquarian attempt to recall what by now was something from the past. Significantly, what now appears most frequently in the written record is not the living villa but the dead one, the ruin which has been reused, often as a religious site and therefore a new focus of settlement. The word itself continues, to be further transformed in later centuries, but what it had once denoted is no more.

The Roman villa has been considered the model behind the establishment of Umayyad palaces in the countryside and even in semideserted areas. Many of them used the infrastructure provided by Roman engineering and, like the villa, brought amenities of life to the countryside.

BIBL.: O. Grabar, *The Formation of Islamic Art,* 2nd ed. (New Haven, 1987), chap. 5. John Percival, *The Roman Villa: An Historical Introduction* (London, 1976). Peter Salway, *Roman Britain* (Oxford, 1981). Edith Mary Wightman, *Gallia Belgica* (London, 1985).   J.PER.

Villages

Villages were the essential component of the eastern Mediterranean during late antiquity. It is estimated that, in Egypt, they numbered between 2,000 and 2,500 and occupied about 75 percent of arable land. Archaeological studies in Lycia, Cilicia, Antiochene, and Apamenea, in the northern part of the Arabian province (Hawran), and in Third Palestine (the Negev) have made it possible to understand how they were organized.

The first striking characteristic is the differences that existed among villages. Some were very small, such as Bsilla or Qirkbiza in northern Syria, but there were also very large villages, sometimes called *metrokōmia*, *kōmopolis,* or simply *kōme megistē.* These towns, such as Umm el-Jimal in Arabia, could sometimes occupy an area of more than 700 m by 500 m, with an enclosing wall and fifteen churches. Fairs, as in Tarutia in eastern Syria, or baths, gave an urban character to large villages, which sometimes attained the status of city-states.

The absence of straight streets built by design, combined with the chaos of village constructions, which grew organically, tended to make even the largest villages profoundly different from cities. Villages were entirely devoted to farming and, apart from the building trades, seem to have had little or no artisanal activity. The production of ceramics, known in Egypt but not in Syria, may have been an exception. Here and there goldsmiths and moneylenders could also be found. Despite regional specialization, village agriculture was diversified, combining vineyards, gardens, orchards, and livestock; crops included cereals, dry beans, and olives. The idea that olives were the only crop grown in northern Syria must be abandoned.

Apart from religious buildings and sometimes a bathhouse or, more rarely, an inn, villages had only houses, farms, granaries, Egyptian dovecotes, mills, and oil presses. The large houses of Cilicia had courtyards, sometimes with a peristyle, as did the houses of northern Syria. Residents lived upstairs and reserved the ground floor for cattle, supplies, and farming activities. Porticoes on facades were much less common in Arabia than in northern Syria, and most of the houses of Hawran used arches to support floors and roofs made of basalt slabs.

It is difficult to assess the exact proportion of property held by peasant farmers, broadly attested in Nessana in the Negev or in Karanis, Egypt, compared with that held by urban nonresidents. Independent peasant owners seem to have been typical in the vast majority of villages. Inequities in wealth between residents of a single village were the general rule. Houses in northern Syria differ greatly in size and ornamentation. Solidarity based on the rhythms of farming life, the use of vast communal cisterns in Hawran—but not in northern Syria, where cisterns were private—and, especially, collective tax responsibilities did not lead to any real autonomy on the part of villages. Apart from tax obligations, it is difficult to discern real village institutions. Sometimes the local clergy seem to have embodied authority in the villages.

BIBL.: G. Dagron, "Entre village et cité: La bourgade rurale des IVe–VIe siècles en Orient," *Koinōnia* 3 (1979): 29–52. *Das Dorf der Eisenzeit und des frühen Mittelalters,* ed. H. Jahnkuhn, et al. (Göttingen, 1977). P.-L. Gatier, "Villages du Proche-Orient protobyzantin (4ème–7ème s.): Etude régionale," in *The Byzantine and Early Islamic Near East,* vol. 2: *Land Use and Settlement Patterns,* ed. G. D. R. King and A. Cameron (Princeton, 1995), 17–48. G. Tate, *Les campagnes de la Syrie du Nord du IIe au VIIe siècles,* vol. 1 (Paris, 1992).
P. L.G.

Virginity

In the classical world, the virgin (Greek *parthenos,* Latin *virgo*) was a woman in the unmarried state. The virgin goddess of the hearth, Hestia (Vesta), stood for the stability and enclosure of the household, in opposition to her brother, the messenger god, Hermes (Mercury), who left the hearth to serve as a bearer of tidings. In Rome, Vesta's fire was tended by thirty virgins, priestesses whose symbolic and political importance endured to the end of antiquity. Though it was her aptness as an icon of purity that gave the virgin her importance, it was the unmarried state, not the sexual inexperience that might accompany it, that constituted her "virginity."

The Christians, however, redefined virginity to mean perpetual abstinence from sexual intercourse, a change that struck at the root of the ancient notion of the temperate, legitimate sexual union of husband and wife as the symbol and medium of social cohesion in a society based on clan and dynasty. Though paganism and Judaism were not without ascetic currents (such as those exemplified by the Essene community documented in the Dead Sea Scrolls), in the main their adherents, and, later, those of Islam, conceived of virginity as a transient state. Its benefits visited each household in the uncompromised loyalty of unmarried daughters but were destined, ideally, for impermanence as the daughters married and established binding ties to other families. There, as fertile and faithful wives, they would demonstrate their chastity (Greek *sophrosunē,* Latin *castitas*) by shunning the vice of fornication and by bearing offspring of unquestioned legitimacy. This in turn would cement the dynastic alliance for the sake of which the marriage had been contracted.

With Christianity, virginity became a virtue to be preserved by both women and men, though the nubile maiden remained its personification. No longer a symbol of the fleeting innocence of youth, it became, precisely, the virtue that stood for permanence. The unchanged and unchanging quality of the sexually untouched body emerged as a powerful sign of the Christian's exchange of transient earthly ties for the security of eternal life. The idea had its beginnings in the exhortation of St. Paul to the believers at Corinth to "remain in the condition in which you were called" (1 Cor. 7:20) on account of the imminent end of the world. As early as the 1st century, this was understood by some to mean that the virgin's refusal to marry represented a form of Christian commitment superior to that of those who were already married at the time of their conversion. Yet the failure of the expected end to arrive encouraged the view of others that Christians did well to marry and beget legitimate children.

In the 2nd century, controversy raged between Encratites such as the followers of Marcion (d. ca. 160), who believed that sexual abstinence was incumbent on the entire Christian population, and traditionalists, such as the author of the New Testament's first letter to Timothy, who believed, with their pagan and Jewish contemporaries, that the most reliable religious leader would be a married man, "above reproach, married only once, temperate, sensible, respectable, hospitable" (1 Tim. 3:2). The controversial 2nd century Christian novel, the *Acts of Paul and Thecla*, chronicles the adventures of the pagan Thecla, who jilts her fiancé in order to convert to Christianity, devotes herself to virginity, and follows the apostle Paul on his travels. By the end of the 2nd century, unmarried women enrolled formally as virgins by the Christian churches lived in organized communities in at least some parts of the empire; the emergence of similar communities for men seems to have taken place in the following century.

Across the 2nd and 3rd centuries, the majority of Christians came to accept a compromise. The Christian rank and file might continue to marry and beget children, but a particular authority would accrue to those who pursued the life of perfection, who would "neither marry nor [be] given in marriage" (Mark 12:25), in imitation of the angels. The theology of virginity as a lifelong commitment to purification of the soul through the discipline of the body, leading to union with the divine, finds its most vivid expression in the 3rd century writings of Origen of Caesarea (d. ca. 254).

It was in the 4th century, however, that the ideal of virginity gained a broad audience among the empire's cultural elite. While the *Symposium* of Methodius, bishop of Olympus (d. 311), recast Plato's celebrated debate on desire as a dispute among Christian virgins, it was the treatises on virginity by such figures as Ambrose of Milan (d. 397) and Gregory of Nyssa (d. 395), written during the intense competition for ascendancy between paganism and Christianity of the late 4th century, that established the praise of virginity as a central element of the Christian claim to moral superiority. The virgin as literary heroine reemerges at this juncture: Gregory of Nyssa's *Life* of his sister Macrina (d. 379), a female counterpart to the immensely popular *Life of Antony* by Athanasius of Alexandria (d. 373), was particularly influential. A few voices, such as that of Jovinian (d. ca. 405), were raised to challenge the intrinsic superiority of virginity over marriage; while Jerome (d. 420) wrote a passionate refutation of this view, Augustine (d. 430) adopted a more moderate position, arguing that although virginity was in theory superior to marriage, for a virgin to dwell on this point was a sign of moral failure.

It is in this period that the cult of Mary began to gain importance, along with the assertion of her virginity during and after the birth of Jesus. Writing in Rome in the 380s, Helvidius argued that the Virgin had maintained a respectable and fertile sexual union with her husband, Joseph, after giving birth to the Son of God, bearing the siblings of Jesus referred to in the New Testament (e.g., Mark 6:3), a view held by earlier writers such as Tertullian but now resoundingly silenced by Jerome. The assertion of Mary as Theotokos, "God-bearer," at the Council of Ephesus in 431 was seen to honor the spiritual achievement of virgins among the Christian faithful.

By the end of antiquity, the virginal ideal was firmly entrenched. An increasingly celibate clergy was central to the success of the early medieval church, as were countless male and female ascetics across Europe and Byzantium. By unyoking the Christian imagination from the household-based civic ideal of antiquity, the proponents of the virginal ideal had, perhaps unwittingly, solved the great institutional problem of antiquity: the challenge of maintaining a legacy intact across generations, in the face of the instability of biological kinship as a medium of transmission. By dissociating themselves from ties based on marriage and procreation and establishing a network of relationships that were ideally (though not always in practice) voluntary and based on shared values, the proponents of virginity were able to secure fierce and enduring loyalty for substitute "kin-groups" such as ascetic communities, a handful of which have survived from antiquity to the present day.

BIBL.: Peter Brown, *The Body and Society: Men, Women, and Sexual Renunciation in Early Christianity* (New York, 1988), and "Asceticism: Pagan and Christian," *Cambridge Ancient History* 13, ed. A. Cameron and P. Garnsey (Cambridge, Eng., 1998), 601–631. Kate Cooper, *The Virgin and the Bride: Idealized Womanhood in Late Antiquity* (Cambridge, Mass., 1996). Susanna Elm, *Virgins of God: The Making of Asceticism in Late Antiquity* (Oxford, 1994).

K.C.

Water

Water was a pressing necessity of life in the ancient Mediterranean and Middle East, and the Byzantine, Sassanian, and Umayyad cultures built on earlier Roman, Nabataean, and Achaemenid achievements in hydraulic technology. The applications of water, however, remained much the same in late antiquity: it was used for human and animal consumption, irrigation, bathing, washing and craft processes, cooling, fire extinguishing, canal transport, the driving of mills, and display (as in nymphaea and fountains). The ritual value of water was enhanced by the importance of baptism in the Christian Byzantine culture and by a Zoroastrian reverence for the natural world that reflected earlier Achaemenid attitudes (see Herodotus, *Histories* 1.138, 188; Pliny, *Nat.Hist.* 31.21.35). The desert environment of Mecca and the influence of biblical symbolism ensured water an important role in the imagery of the Qur'ān (see, e.g., Jonah 10:25, The Cave 18:30–40, The Light 24:39) and thus in Islamic art, for example in the mosaics of the Dome of the Rock and the Great Mosque of Damascus.

Climate, geology, and topography naturally determined the local applications of water, its sources, and the techniques developed to collect, lift, transport, or store it. Despite the typical summer drought, there was sufficient winter rainfall around the north and east coasts of the Mediterranean and on the steppes above Mesopotamia to allow drought farming and dependence on springs, wells, and occasional streams for drinking. In Arabia Petraea, however, the Edomites and Nabataeans developed techniques of harvesting the exiguous precipitation by diverting it from catchment fields in the rocky landscape to small agricultural fields, cisterns, or reservoirs. The occasional spring fed by a distant aquifer enjoyed regional importance, as at ʻAin Musa above Petra. These techniques remained in use by the Byzantine and Islamic successors in this region and were applied around urban centers in the Negev: Eboda, Eleusa, and Subeita. To the east and south, precipitation diminishes to near insignificance, and only springs and deep wells—such as those at Palmyra—made habitation possible outside the great river valleys.

The Nile, Tigris, and Euphrates Rivers carried copious runoff from distant mountains through low alluvial plains virtually devoid of rainfall, fostering the early development of complex societies dependent on sophisticated techniques of irrigation agriculture. The elaborate regime of irrigation canals and basins and mechanical water lifting devices developed during the Hellenistic period to maximize agricultural production in the Nile Valley was extended by its Roman, Byzantine, and Islamic administrators. Harnessing of the Tigris and Euphrates presented more problems (see Strabo, *Geography* 16.1.9–10), but the Parthians maintained the arrangement of dams, canals, dikes, and basins that had taken shape under the Achaemenid kings. In Zoroastrian belief, any action that promoted cultivation of the soil was meritorious, and the Sassanian kings energetically expanded the irrigation system, bringing more land under cultivation than has been seen since. Shapur I made use of the engineering skills of Roman prisoners of war to build dams and to rework the irrigation system at Shushtar and Ahwaz, and Shapur II carried on similar work at Dizful. Khosro I constructed diversion dams across the Tigris and its tributaries at Dur and Beldai and expanded the great Nahrawan canal system above Ctesiphon. The dams were built with clamped stone blocks facing a rubble and concrete core, like late Roman prototypes at Harbaka and Homs in Syria, and the great canals fed networks of delivery channels. The rivers and canals of Egypt and Mesopotamia were also important routes of transport, trade, and communication.

In the more moist climate of the Mediterranean world, hydraulic technology focused on the problems of urban water supply and drainage (summarized well in Pliny, *Nat.Hist.* 36.123–125). No new aqueducts were added to the fourteen in the water system of Rome after Severus Alexander, and Belisarius had to rebuild the conduits after they were cut by the Goths in 534. An impressive system, however, was constructed in Constantinople in the 4th century, fed by streams diverted or impounded by large masonry dams—one of which had the earliest known intentionally arched plan to resist the water (Procopius, *Aed.* 2.3.16–21). The 4th century line from Vize, which included more than forty raised sections in its 242 km course, is the longest ancient aqueduct known. Because of the vulnerability of such conduits to intentional or accidental damage, the water was delivered to enormous cisterns in Constantinople for storage. More than eighty open and roofed cisterns were built within the city walls between the late 4th and early 7th centuries, with a total capacity of more than 1,000,000 cubic meters. The covered Basilike cistern has 336 columns and a capacity of 78,000 cubic meters. The water system fed by these cisterns serviced public fountains and numerous baths. Few public baths were constructed in the Byzantine world after the 6th century, but the technology and liturgy of Roman communal bathing was taken up enthusiastically in the Umayyad world, and elaborate baths survive at sites such as Quṣayr ʿAmra and Khirbat al-Mafjar.

While aqueducts survived and were maintained, the urban center might be better served than the countryside, and Cassiodorus (*Variae* 3.53.1, 6) describes an emergency situation near Rome in 507/511 that required both a water diviner (*aquilegus*) and a water-lifting engineer (*mechanicus*). In Persia, long-distance water supplies were more often provided by *qanats*, subterranean channels that tapped deep aquifers beneath the alluvium at the base of mountain ranges. The earthen channels were planned, leveled, excavated, and maintained by means of vertical access shafts placed at convenient intervals, often surrounded by circular mounds of excavated soil. Described as typical of this region as early as 210 B.C.E. (Polybius, *History* 10.28.2), *qanats* spread south to Oman and Yemen

under Sassanian rule, and west as far as the Wadi Arabah during the Byzantine period. They have continued to be used throughout this region until the present.

Water mills with either horizontal or vertical paddle wheels were used throughout the Byzantine and Sassanian realms and the western kingdoms to grind grain, and related devices were used to lift water. In the late 4th century, Ausonius (*Mosella* 359–364) provides the only premedieval record of a different industrial application: water-driven stone-cutting saws on the Kyll and Ruwar Rivers. Both the flow of aqueduct water and the outflow from baths were used to drive water mills for grinding grain. The mills built along the course of the Aqua Traiana down the Janiculum Hill in Rome were still critical to the food supply of Rome in the 6th century (Procopius, *Wars* 5.19.8–9, 19–22), and grain mills were built into the basement of the Baths of Caracalla in Rome and driven by the stream of waste water, in an efficient arrangement recommended by Palladius (*Agriculture* 1.41).

The *shaduf*, or counterbalanced tip beam, was used to lift water for irrigation in Mesopotamia and the Nile Valley from the Middle Bronze Age. More complex water-lifting devices propelled by human or animal labor or water power were invented in Hellenistic Egypt and spread throughout the Roman empire. There is rich liturgical, archaeological, and papyrological testimony for the use of these devices in the Byzantine world for agricultural and industrial purposes (see Oleson, 1984), and many survived in the Islamic world virtually unchanged until the recent past: compartmented wheels driven by water (*naʿura*) or by animals working a gear system (*saqiya*), bucket chains (*qadus*), and the water screw. The relevant works by Ktesibios, Philon of Alexandria, and Heron were known in Arabic translations and provided inspiration for imitators, such as the 9th century *Book of Ingenious Devices* of the Banu Musa of Baghdad.

BIBL.: Mohammed El Faïz, *L'agronomie de la Mésopotamie antique: Analyse du 'Livre de l'architecture nabatéenne de Qûtâmâ* (Leiden, 1995). John P. Oleson, *Greek and Roman Mechanical Water-Lifting Devices* (Toronto, 1984). Norman Smith, *A History of Dams* (London, 1971).   J.O.

Weaving

Although a large number of fragments from late antique textiles survive, and although many written sources talk about textile production, there is little reliable evidence about the appearance and function of different late antique looms. Having been constructed of wood, ancient looms completely disappeared, and only a few weaving implements survive. However, we know that there were two main types of looms: upright looms with vertical warp and horizontal looms with horizontal warp. Among upright looms there are again two main models. The first is the warp-weighted loom, where the single warp threads are kept in parallel vertical position by weights made of stone or clay. Weaving is started at the top, and the weft is forced upward. The second model is the two-beam upright loom, where the warp threads are fixed between two wooden beams. Weaving starts at the bottom, and the weft is forced downward.

The warp-weighted loom was used throughout the Roman empire, as testified by the many finds of warp weights. This type of loom was used for the production of large pieces (240–300 cm). For large pieces such as cloaks or tunics, two or more people worked together. A source from Egypt even talks about four weavers working at one time on one piece of cloth. The warp-weighted loom allowed weavers to produce tabby fabrics as well as self-patterned twills. A special type of weaving executed on warp-weighted looms is the so-called tabular weave, used for seamless garments. The two-beam upright loom is depicted on a relief in the Forum of Nerva (96–98 C.E.) and in the Hypogeum of the Aurelii (about 220 C.E.), both in Rome. It was used for tapestry weaving, among other things.

For more sophisticated patterns the only appropriate medium was the horizontal loom. No weights or other parts from these looms survive. However, their existence is proven by technical analyses of late antique textiles. With this type of loom the warp threads could be manipulated with the help of rods called heddle rods. The technique of weaving with heddle rods was improved constantly. The width of fabrics made on the horizontal loom was between 45 and 150 cm. Typical weaves were so-called weft-faced compound tabbies, made with two different warps, and twill damasks. Compound tabbies were woven in many different places in the eastern Mediterranean. The earliest examples found in Masadah can be dated to the 1st century C.E. A large number of two-color compound tabbies have been found dating from late antique Egypt. They are mainly made of wool. Popular patterns included animals, such as lions and deer, and animals and hunters.

Damasks were a specialty of Syria. They were mainly made of silk. The pattern was realized by a special binding system. The earliest damasks, found in Palmyra (2nd century C.E.), have merely geometrical patterns. Later silk damasks have figured patterns, such as animals and hunters. The most important innovation in the further development of pattern weaving was the weft-faced compound twill, worked with a two-warp system as the compound tabby. The use of two warps allowed the execution of very sophisticated, multicolored patterns. It is not clear where this weaving technique originated, nor how it entered the Near Eastern world. The earliest compound twill, found in Dura-Europus on the Euphrates (from before 257 C.E.), shows a central Asian pattern. As early as the 4th century compound twills with entirely Graeco-Roman

decorations were woven to the highest perfection. This weaving technique, executed on the horizontal loom, is decisive for determining later imperial Byzantine silks. Although we know a lot of compound twills from the 4th to the 15th century, we do not know precisely what the loom for such excellent weavings looked like.

BIBL.: N. P. Constas, "Weaving the Body of God," *Journal of Early Christian Studies* 3 (1995): 169–194. Daniel De Jonghe and Marcel Tavernier, "Les damassés de la Proche-Antiquité," *Bulletin du Centre International d'Etudes des Textiles Anciens* 47–48 (1978): 24ff. Marta Hoffmann, *The Warp-Weighted Loom* (Oslo, 1974). R. B. Serjeant, "Materials for a History of Islamic Textiles," *Ars Islamica* 9–16 (1942–1951). John Peter Wild, "The Roman Horizontal Loom," *American Journal of Archaeology* 91 (1987): 459ff.

A.S.

Wheat

Wheat was the most important staple in the Roman agrarian economy; together with other grains, it accounted for as much as 75 percent of the ancient diet. Wheat was consumed either as a porridge, *puls*, or as bread. The chief varieties grown were *Triticum durum* and *Triticum turgidum* from the emmer group, and *Triticum vulgare* from the spelt group, which produced *siligo*, the fine flour from which white bread was made. Wheat yields were modest, on the order of 500 kg per hectare in areas where Mediterranean dry farming was practiced, and approximately 1,500 kg per hectare in Egypt. Landowners in virtually all parts of the Roman empire derived income from selling wheat to supply urban markets, while wheat provided a basis for taxation in several provinces, most notably Egypt. The Roman government made a great effort to supply its capital cities, Rome and later Constantinople, with wheat and other foodstuffs.

At the heart of this effort were the government's free distributions of wheat, which represented more a privilege of citizenship than relief to the urban poor. In the early empire, a select group of 200,000 adult male Roman citizens domiciled in Rome received monthly allocations for 5 *modii*, or 33 kg, of wheat, which represented somewhat more than the nutritional requirements of an individual adult male. In the later empire, bread was distributed on a daily basis to some 120,000 recipients in Rome; the ration was at first 50 ounces of coarse bread, and later 36 ounces of better-quality bread. The distributions in the later empire included other staples as well, especially olive oil and pork. Wine was sold by the state at subsidized prices. Constantine established a food program in Constantinople based on the Roman model, and set the number of recipients at 80,000. Other major cities, including Alexandria, Antioch, and possibly Carthage, imitated the imperial capitals in establishing their own programs of wheat distribution. So, too, did smaller cities on occasion, such as Oxyrhynchus in Egypt.

The free distributions of staples covered only a portion of the nutritional requirements of those who lived in the imperial capitals. There was also a lively free market in foodstuffs, and the state was concerned to keep this market adequately supplied. The principal wheat producing regions in the empire were in Egypt, which supplied Constantinople principally, and Africa, which exported grain to Rome. The task of provisioning Rome and Constantinople from these regions required the state to intervene in key areas of the economy, and the official charged with supervising this effort was the equestrian *praefectus annonae*. In the early empire, the state provided legal incentives for shippers to import grain into Rome, and the emperors Claudius and Trajan undertook substantial improvements at the ports of Ostia to facilitate shipping. In the later empire, shipping grain to the imperial capitals became a hereditary liturgy, as did the responsibilities of grinding grain and baking bread. The Roman government created professional associations responsible to oversee the performance of these liturgies.

BIBL.: Lin Foxhall and H. A. Forbes, "Sitometreia: The Role of Grain as a Staple Food in Classical Antiquity," *Chiron* 12 (1982): 41–90. Geoffrey Rickman, *The Corn Supply of Ancient Rome* (Oxford, 1980). Boudewijn Sirks, *Food for Rome: The Legal Structure of the Transportation and Processing of Supplies for the Imperial Distributions in Rome and Constantinople* (Amsterdam, 1991). D.P.K.

Wills

Wills *(testamenta)* in late Roman society transferred property to heirs after the death of the testator. Imperial constitutions about wills in the *Codex Justinianus* and the *Codex Theodosianus* treated fundamental issues of validity, formality, and secrecy. They came to define and accept four types of wills: the nuncupated or oral will (*Nov.* of Theodosius 16.6 = *C.Just.* 6.23.21.4), witnessed by seven witnesses; the will "read" into city archives (*C.Just.* 6.23.19.pr.1); the "tripartite" will, subscribed by the testator and seven witnesses, who also had to seal the will (*Nov.Theod.* 16.2 = *C.Just.* 6.23.21; *Inst.* 2.10.3); and the testator-written or "holograph" will (*Nov.* Valentiniani 21.2). In all but the nuncupatory will, the use of writing was greater than it had been in Roman wills of the classical period, for writing had gradually come to incorporate and transform the ceremonial and oral aspects of earlier acts of testation, including statements by the testator and acts of witnessing.

Imperial efforts to ensure the validity of wills, while also permitting testators to express their final wishes fearlessly, reflected a traditional concern for the orderly but relatively unrestricted transfer of wealth and a respect for the authoritative (and vivid) social judgments such transfers had always conveyed. Constitutions that attempt to limit improperly vigorous legacy hunting by Christian clerics and excessive bequests to the church are probably also a response to the preoccupations of the rich (e.g., *C.Th.* 16.2.20). Yet late imperial constitutions also demonstrate an awareness, imperceptible in the classical jurists, that the testamentary habit now extended far beyond the wealthy. They make accommodation not only for soldiers, non-Latin-speakers, and the deaf, mute, and blind—whose special needs had been of concern to the classical jurists as well—but also for *rustici*, for whom the high level of writing now required might pose some difficulty (*C.Just.* 6.23.31); the withdrawal of *factio testamenti* from heretics, many of them also country dwellers, is employed as a form of punishment (*C.Th.* 16.5, 16.7).

Late antique wills or quoted will fragments (usually from inscriptions, or will openings recorded in archives) survive from Spain, Gaul, Italy, Asia Minor, and Egypt. All are characterized by the regular repetition of certain phrases (e.g., *do lego dari*). The persistence of these formulas despite imperial reassurance that they were not needed (*C.Just.* 6.23.15) points to the existence of formularies, the use of notaries, and centuries-old traditions of will making that made certain phrases extremely familiar to a wide public. Such phrases were perhaps also learned through parodies such as the "Will of the Piglet" (ed. N. Bott, Zurich, 1972), mentioned, sourly, as a favorite among schoolchildren by Jerome (*Commentarius in Isaiam* 12 pref., *Contra Rufinum* 1.17).

Roman testamentary formulas and conceptualizations survived despite the disappearance of Roman authority in the west. The Germanic societies that produced late legal compilations almost certainly practiced no testation before their contact with Rome (cf. Tacitus, *Germ.* 20), but they rapidly incorporated aspects of Roman usage into their law codes (e.g., *Burgundian Code* 115). As a vehicle for the free disposition of property that overrode fixed succession within the family, the Roman will was of clear value to the treasuries of kings and the church, but Roman will making also survived and prospered in post-Roman society because the habit was traditional, well known, widespread, socially distinguished, economically useful, and Roman. The will's continued prominence is, finally, reflected in the use, by the eighth century, of *testamentum* to refer to any witnessed legal document.

BIBL.: M. Kaser, *Das Römische Privatrecht*, vol. 2: *Die nachklassischen Entwicklungen* (Handbuch der Altertumswissenschaft 10.3.3.2; Munich, 1959), 334–398. U. Nonn, "Merowingische Testamente: Studien zum Fortleben einer römischen Urkundenform im Frankenreich," *Archiv für Diplomatik* 18 (1972): 1–129. E.A.M.

Windmills

The origins of the practical windmill capable of significant work remain obscure. Hero of Alexandria

(*Pneumatica* 1.43, mid-1st century), describes an air-pump for a water organ worked by a "disk with blades like the so-called *anemouria*," which itself was turned by the wind. Related forms of *anemourion*, derived from the Greek for "wind," may occur in two Byzantine texts that involve oscillating and rotating fans (*P Rylands* 4.627.165, 4th century; Olympiodorus, *In Aristotelis meteora commentaria* 200.19, 6th century). Manuscript illustrations for Hero's text, derived from a Byzantine archetype, depict the drive as a vertical disk with radial blades set at an angle.

Although Hero understood the principle of wind power, his device was impractical, and there is no further literary or archaeological evidence for attempts to harness the wind in the Roman or Byzantine world—other than the use of sails on ships. The 10th century historians al-Tabarī and al-Mas'udi report that a Persian slave named Abu Lulua promised to build a "mill worked by the wind" for the caliph 'Umar I but then assassinated him in 644 C.E. This story, often cited as the earliest evidence for the existence of the famous windmills of Sistan province in eastern Iran, is in fact not conclusive. The Banu Musa in their *Book of Ingenious Devices* (Baghdad, 9th century) provide the first credible reference to such a mill, using the term *anburia* borrowed from the Greek. The Persian mills consisted of paddlelike sails turning around a vertical axle, framed by walls that directed the wind. They resemble neither Hero's windmill nor the postmills that appeared in northern Europe in the 12th century, both of which incorporated horizontal axles and could be turned toward the wind. Independent invention is likely for all three traditions.

BIBL.: A. G. Drachmann, "Heron's Windmill," *Centaurus* 7 (1961): 145–151. Michael J. T. Lewis, "The Greeks and the Early Windmill," *History of Technology* 15 (1993): 141–189.

J.O.

Wine

Cassiodorus (*Variae* 12.22.1) classifies wine among the three "excellent products" (*egregii fructus*) of agriculture, along with grain and oil. Without doubt this triad represents the basis of food production for the majority of the Mediterranean provinces. For Rome, an annual consumption per person of 146–182 liters has been hypothesized. Irregularly beginning with Aurelianus, and then consistently from the 4th century on, wine was distributed (along with bread, oil, and meat) to the Roman population as part of the public *annona*, at a price 25 percent lower than market prices. The wine regions of Italy were delegated to contribute these wines. In Constantinople, however, the *annona* distributed only bread.

The hegemony of Italian wines in Mediterranean commerce ceased with the late Antonine age, and new wines of the Narbonne region and Asia Minor became more common. From the 4th to the 7th century there was a preponderance, even in the west, of the eastern wines that had wide circulation. Terracotta wine vessels identify the areas of production: Asia Minor (the valleys of Hermus and of Maeander), the Aegean, Cilicia, Cyprus, northern Syria, Palestine, and Egypt. There is evidence of diffusion of Italian wines from Abruzzi (Calabria) and Sicily (Naxos) in Italy, Sicily, and Mediterranean Gaul and Spain. In late antiquity, the terracotta vessel remained the dominant container, but in the west use of the barrel (*cupa*) spread, becoming the prevalent container in some regions and for some types of transport. This fact modifies the evidence, since the wooden barrel rarely leaves traces. In Christian art and literature wine frequently assumes the symbolic equivalence of blood—that is, of life—together with representations of vines and grapes.

BIBL.: Clementina Panella, "Merci e scambi nel Mediterraneo tardoantico," in *Storia di Roma*, vol. 3.2 (Turin, 1993), 613–697. André Tchernia, *Le vin de l'Italie romaine* (Rome, 1986).

D.V.

Women

In the history of late antiquity, few women are known individually. They are either known as members of imperial or royal families, having been born (Pulcheria, Amalasuntha) or married into them (Athenais-Eudocia, Theodora); rare scholars (Hypatia); aristocrats, who became famous through the churchmen they showered with gifts (Paula, Olympias, Melania the Younger); or elite women from the provinces, remembered only through the writings of male relatives (Macrina). Texts or speeches emanating from women are extremely rare (a few letters or poems, apothegms from the "Desert Mothers," Egeria's travel journal). Of the most-mentioned woman in papyri, Charite, we know only that she was daughter and wife of a curial, mother of at least three children, landowner near Hermopolis, and that she could write.

The life of women can be grasped from information rather unsuitable for statistics and from comparisons with preindustrial Mediterranean societies. Life expectancy seems to have been twenty-two years at birth and forty-five at five years of age. Biological factors and the traditional reproductive role weighed heavily. Women were married between sixteen and nineteen (in the Roman upper class, at puberty). The hazards of childbirth were considerable. The wealthy seem to have had wet nurses, but the impact of this on the fecundity rate is unknown, as is that of abortion and contraception. From the 4th century on, the spread of the Christian ascetic and monastic ideal offered women a choice outside marriage, which had been their only fate until then. Even if this new option remained theoretical for many, a new type of social behavior became possible.

Differences in legal and social status counted as much as gender in determining one's place in the world. A status acquired at birth could rarely be changed: even if rising socially through marriage was looked on rather favorably, homogamy was extensive from the lower to the upper classes. A vast majority of the female population escapes our scrutiny, for even hagiography, which focuses less on urban elites, hardly speaks of peasant women, whose role in agriculture remains unknown. Literary sources show interest in actresses and prostitutes in the cities. Inscriptions and papyri mention numerous urban trades exercised by women in crafts and retailing: in some cases wives would help their husband and take over the family business after his death; other women were on the brink of enslavement. Domestic slavery remained widespread, however varied the situations (ranging from nurses mentioned in testaments to slaves reserved for sexual needs). Narratives about servants who followed their mistress en masse into a monastery confirm the absolute nature of their dependence. Concubinage must also be taken into account in the Byzantine empire and in the west, where it appears to have flourished among the Merovingians. Whether a slave or free woman, the concubine was deprived of all rights, as is shown in Augustine's biography. According to 4th century papyri, women of the propertied classes owned much less land than men did, and their education level was lower. They would stay at home, managing property under the control of an absentee husband or transforming goods he bought outside (such as by cooking or weaving), in accordance with traditional attitudes.

Those attitudes are better known to us, for there are many records of men's reflections on women. The discourse on the greater weakness of the female sex, seen as more inclined to passion and prone to error, is to be found everywhere. The inferiority of women's nature, at times described in an extremely deprecating manner (women embodied matter, sexuality, evil) justified their subordination, especially in couples. The force of that social norm is seen in the indignation provoked by its reversal (as in the cases of Eudoxia and Arcadius, Antonina and Belisarius). And the division of roles (and space) attributed indispensable but inferior work to women: keeping the home and managing the household, with the emblematic task of making clothing. The rare affirmation that gender differences concerned only the body and not the soul, and that there was a spiritual equality between men and women, met two limits: spiritual equality in no way affected social subordination, and, above all, women could attain it only in abandoning their sex, as in Perpetua's martyrdom.

Pagans and Christians shared this system of representation. But the Christian discourse hardened it, grounding it in an original myth, a sign of divine will: the narratives of the creation and fall justified man's superiority over woman, who was the primary cause of sin and disgrace. The sin of Eve still determined the feminine condition, in spite of Mary, through whom

salvation was reached. The Christian church thus shaped the female figures of medieval thought: woman as the Devil's door, the submissive wife, and the asexual virgin.

The legal status of women is well known, thanks to the abundant legislation of late antiquity. Imperial law perpetuated their exclusion from public functions and, in a more general fashion, from all responsibility for others. Their political role was due to family connections or dynastic attachment, as when Pulcheria or Ariadne legitimated the transmission of imperial power. It was only on the fringes of the empire that Mavia and Amalasuntha attained sovereignty. Another legacy from classical law was the double standard of morality according to gender, which led to the division of women into two groups. One group (prostitutes, actresses, barmaids, slaves), not subject to rules of sexual morality and thus available without penal risk to men, had to endure infamy and disabilities in return for that freedom. The honorability of other women required, in exchange, respect for moral demands and the rules of propriety, which became stricter—or breaches were punished more rigorously—from the 4th century on. The double standard was loosened in the east (under Justinian) but grew stronger in western kingdoms.

The family status of women changed as paternal power and agnatic ties declined in favor of the nuclear family: relatives other than the father received authority over young girls; husbands obtained more power regarding their wife's affairs; widows could become guardians of their own children. The husband seems to have controlled all family estates, in spite of the theoretical property separation that prevailed in Roman law; the widow, who recovered power over her fortune on her husband's death, would take over his role. Comparable changes affected property transmission. Classical law had treated daughters and sisters, on intestacy, as sons and brothers but given only partial recognition to the ties between mother and child. Now the mother's rights of inheritance were reinforced at the agnates' detriment, and, under Justinian, successoral equality was extended to all levels of kinship.

The status of Visigothic (and, to a lesser degree, Burgundian) women was quite similar to that under Roman law regarding the husband's role, the widow's status, and inheritance rights. But the Langobardic woman remained her entire life under the authority of a man, who exercised *mundium*: father, husband, son, or other kinsman. Other Germanic laws seem to present intermediate characteristics. Most important, life became more difficult for women in the west, where state authority was fading and could not protect them against the surrounding violence.

BIBL.: R. Bagnall, "Women, Law and Social Realities in Late Antiquity," *Bulletin of the American Society of Papyrologists* 32 (1995): 65–86. Joëlle Beaucamp, *Le statut de la* femme à Byzance (4e–7e siècle), vols. 1 and 2 (Paris, 1990–1992). Gillian Clark, *Women in Late Antiquity: Pagan and Christian Life-styles* (Oxford, 1993). Georges Duby and Michelle Perrot, eds., *A History of Women in the West,* vols. 1–2 (Cambridge, Mass., 1992). U.-W. Krause, *Witwen und Waisen im römischen Reich,* 3 vols. (Stuttgart, 1995). Denise Spellberg, *Politics, Gender and the Islamic Past: The Legacy of 'A'isha bint Abi Bakr* (New York, 1994). Barbara Freyer Stowasser, *Women in the Qur'ān: Traditions and Interpretation* (New York and Oxford, 1994).   J.B.

Yemen

A noun derived from the Arabic *al-Yaman,* the name Yemen designates the southern part of the Arabian Peninsula. Etymologically, *al-Yaman* means "south" and is the opposite of *ash-shām,* "north." (These two words are themselves derived from Arabic terms designating right and left.) Yemen's name in the ancient languages of South Arabia is unknown.

Among Arab geographers, the boundaries of Yemen are fairly loose. For the Yemenite al-Hasan al-Hamdānī (893–971), for example, Yemen included all territories south of a line beginning in Qatar and ending at the Red Sea, midway between Mecca and Nairan.

The history of South Arabia until the Arab and Muslim conquest of 632 C.E. has been reconstructed by comparing eastern sources (the Bible, Assyrian historical texts, hagiographies of eastern Christianity, and Arab traditions from the Islamic era) and classical sources with local inscriptions, which number in the thousands. They are written in four languages (Sabaic, Qatabanic, Hadramitic, and Minaic). These languages differ from Arabic but are related to it, since they all belong to the Southern Semitic family.

Until about 300 C.E., political disunity prevailed in South Arabia: each of the large valleys leading into the desert basin of Ramlat as-Sabʿatayn was home to a different nation. From east to west, these were the Hadramaut, Awsān, Qatabān, and Sheba. Jawf, the northernmost of these valleys, was divided between Sheba and several small kingdoms. In the western mountains, the division was no less significant: it was

there that Himyar had appeared, separating from Qatabān in about 110 B.C.E. Himyar progressively unified all of South Arabia, annexing the last independent kingdoms, Sheba and the Hadhramaut, in the last quarter of the 3rd century C.E.

The kingdom of Himyar, which dominated South Arabia for two centuries, disappeared in the summer of 525 after a violent religious crisis. The persecution of Christians undertaken by its Jewish ruler led Kaleb, king of Christian Abyssinia, to intervene. Himyar was conquered and converted to Christianity by force. A Christian Himyarite, Sumuyafaʾ Ashwaʾ (Esimiphaios in Procopius), was placed on the throne. Before returning to Abyssinia, Kaleb requested a bishop and established a number of churches.

Abraha, an Abyssinian general, soon seized power, hastily broke off from Abyssinia, and transferred the capital of Zafār to Sanʿa, where he built a superb cathedral. Abraha attempted to control the tribes of the Arabian Desert, who had previously been under Himyar's administration. In 662 of the Himyarite era (552 C.E.), he launched a great expedition toward northern Arabia, which reached Hulubān (300 km southwest of Riyadh) and Turabān (130 km east of at-Tāʾif). It is possible that this expedition was the famous so-called elephant expedition, reported to have failed at Mecca. It is recorded in the Qurʾān (sura 105) and commemorated in Islamic Arab tradition.

In the 570s, to rid the country of Abyssinian occupiers, a Jewish Yemenite aristocrat, Sayf ibn dhī-Yazʾan, appealed to Sassanid Persia. Persia sent troops who settled permanently in Yemen. The last Persian governor of Yemen rallied behind the Islamic powers in 632 or slightly before, during the lifetime of Muhammad, Prophet of Islam. As a result, Yemen became merely a peripheral province of the vast Islamic empire, whose capital was Medina (northwestern Arabia), then Damascus (Syria), and finally Baghdad (Iraq).

The history of ancient South Arabia is relatively well known up to and including the reign of Abraha, thanks to epigraphic texts; after that, this source dries up completely and the only data come from the Arab tradition of the Islamic era, which is littered with legendary and often contradictory accounts. The end of inscriptions is not the only sign of decline: the architecture, which had previously been splendid, was no longer distinguished by any monuments whatsoever; and, finally, the Yemenites, usually the most populous people of Arabia, were almost nonexistent in the armies that conquered the Islamic empire. The crisis into which the country fell lasted for several centuries. Its causes have not been entirely elucidated, though one may have been the depopulation brought about by the religious wars and epidemics of the 6th century.

Only a few inscriptions remain from Christian Yemen: they usually begin with an invocation to the Trinity. One of these, which dates from Abraha's reign, mentions the dedication of a church in Marib. The cathedral of San'a, built by this same Abraha and called al-Qalīs by authors who described it in Arabic, passed for the most beautiful monument of pre-Islamic Arabia. According to al-Azraqī, the building measured approximately 150 cubits by 40 cubits. The walls were made of multicolored stones and surmounted by a frieze of alabaster blocks. The copper door opened on a nave measuring 80 cubits by 40 cubits, its ceiling supported by wooden columns decorated with gold and silver nails. Next came a room to the right measuring 40 cubits and the same to the left, decorated with mosaics with plant and gold star motifs. Finally, there was the ebony and ivory throne, under a cupola measuring 30 cubits square, covered in gold and silver and decorated with mosaics depicting crosses. Abraha is reported to have received help from Byzantine artisans in the sculpting of the marble and the laying of the mosaics (al-Tabarī). The monument was made so magnificent because Abraha, a foreigner who had taken the throne by force, needed to legitimate his power. Moreover, according to al-Azraqī, he wanted Arabs to abandon their traditional pilgrimages and come to San'a. That cathedral was destroyed in the third quarter of the 8th century by a governor of Yemen who wanted to reuse the materials. A few capitals with crosses still remain, now part of the city's great mosque.

Yemenite Christianity barely survived the Islamic conquest, except in the oasis of Nairan and on the island of Socotra. In Nairan, the Christian community still had considerable political influence in the late 9th century: according to a Yemenite Arab source, an agreement was reached with Christians and Jews of the oasis in 897, when the Zaidi principality was founded. In the early 8th century, Nairan was still one-third Christian and one-third Jewish, according to Ibn al-Mujāwir. The last pocket of Christianity was the Yemenite island of Socotra, which was Islamized only after the Portuguese arrived in the Indian Ocean in the 16th century.

In contrast, Judaism remained robust in Islamic Yemen, especially in the mountain regions. It was characterized by a strong tendency toward messianism. The three population movements known to us occurred, first, in the 12th century, then between 1499–1500 and 1666 (after the unrest in the Ottoman empire brought on by Shabbetai Tzevi), and finally in 1860 and 1870 (under Kuhayl I and II). Most of the community emigrated to Israel, and since that time Judaism has been represented in Yemen by only a few hundred believers.

BIBL.: Jacques Briend and Christian Robin, "Sheba, I: Dans la Bible; II: Dans les inscriptions d'Arabie du Sud," *Supplément au dictionnaire de la Bible* 70 (Paris, 1996), cols. 1043–1254. Christian Robin, ed., *L'Arabie antique de Karib'îl à Mahomet: Nouvelles données sur l'histoire des Arabes grâce aux inscriptions* (Aix-en-Provence, 1991–1993).

C.J.R.

Zoology

In antiquity scientific zoology had reached its apogee with Aristotle. In individual areas further research using his methods superseded his work—for example, the inquiries of Alexander of Myndos in ornithology and of Sostratus (fl. Alexandria ca. 25 B.C.E.) in the study of insects and snakes. The Alexandrian lexicographers summarized the fruits of earlier investigations.

New concerns began to emerge under the aegis of the general debate between Stoics and Skeptics. Whereas the Stoics Chrysippus and Posidonius stressed providence and anthropocentrism, the Skeptic philosopher Carneades emphasized rationality and virtue in animals. Both sides of this argument saw animal behavior as illustrative of larger cosmological and ethical questions. In the early Roman imperial period, Philo of Alexandria (d. 45), Pliny the Elder (d. 79), Plutarch (d. ca. 121), and Aelian (d. ca. 235) addressed these issues; each in turn gleaned materials from previous writers.

In his *De animalibus* (preserved only in Armenian) Philo adopted animal lore collected by others to illuminate Stoic and biblical convictions about the centrality of human beings in the world. Assuming the notions of *imago dei,* understood as human dominion over animals, and of an original harmony upset by human disobedience to the Creator, Philo portrayed the use of animals for clothing, food, and sacrifice as the necessary and acceptable consequence of these protohistorical events. In books 7–11 of his *Natural History* Pliny attempted a systematic treatment of animals under the Aristotelian categories of habitat (land, sea, and air). At the end he undertook a general discussion of the entire animal kingdom, including humans, on the basis of bodily parts and systems.

In three treatises *(Whether Land or Sea Animals Are More Intelligent; Gryllus, or the Rationality of Animals; On Eating Flesh)* Plutarch set forth with witty aplomb arguments for the rationality and moral superiority of brute beasts. Under the images of crocodile and ibis in his *On Isis and Osiris* Plutarch brought together animal lore with the Middle Platonic stress on the ineffability and invisibility of God. Finally, under the patronage of the empress Julia Domna, Aelian produced his *On the Characteristics of Animals,* a Stoic miscellany of strange and paradoxical animal behavior presented more for the intellectually pretentious entertainment characteristic of the Deipnosophists than for ethical instruction.

Beginning with Paul (Rom. 1:20) and the Epistle to the Hebrews and building on Philo and the earlier Alexandrian Jewish tradition, 2nd century Christian writers elaborated notions of the divine presence in the world, a presence made evident through material things sometimes also mirrored in a spiritual plane. Origen and especially the anonymous *Physiologus* brought animals into this new world of Neoplatonic and Christian symbols. Probably written in Alexandria ca. 200–375, the *Physiologus* describes a hodgepodge of animals, both real and imaginary, with the fig tree and a few stones with remarkable properties thrown in. Explicit Christological interpretations of the lion, pelican, and adamant stone, among others, dispel the apparent resemblance of the *Physiologus* to Aelian's collection. Many patristic and early medieval writers used the *Physiologus* to compose works on natural history. A plethora of versions—both truncated and expanded—began to appear by the 8th century.

In expounding on the "Six Days of Creation" in his *Homilies in Hexaemeron,* Basil gives a more structured and systematic treatment to animals and the theological and ethical lessons to be gleaned from them. True to his general purpose to show that "the world is a work of art displayed for the beholding of all people" *(Hom.* 1.7), he presents an array of animals of the sea, air, and land, drawing a variety of ethical instructions from them and admiring the craftsmanship of the Creator. A hierarchy of creatures, from nonliving to plant to sea creature to land animal, culminates in the uniquely rational human being on whom God has conferred dominion even over the huge elephant *(Hom.* 9.5 and passim). This work, too, was widely translated, admired, and occasionally emulated in later antiquity.

BIBL.: Monique Alexandre, *Le commencement du livre Genèse I–V: La version grecque de la Septente et sa réception* (Paris, 1988). Michael J. Curley, trans., *Physiologus* (Austin, 1979). Maureen A. Tilley, "Martyrs, Monks, Insects, and

Animals," in *The Medieval World of Nature: A Book of Essays,* ed. Joyce E. Salisbury (New York, 1993), 93–107.

K.M.

Zoroaster

Zoroaster founded the religion called Zoroastrianism, or Mazdaism. Evidence from comparative linguistics suggests he preached around the 14th to 12th century B.C.E., probably in the region between northern Afghanistan and the Aral Sea. An alternative chronology, followed by Iranians during late antiquity, placed Zoroaster at the town of Rhages (Ray, now a suburb of Tehran) 300 to 258 years before Alexander the Great. A third date was also followed during antiquity (one having even less historical basis) whereby, according to Greek sources, Zoroaster lived 6,000 years before Plato or 600 years before Xerxes. His Avestan name, Zarathushtra, is a compound word perhaps meaning "possessor of golden camels." The name Zoroaster, by which the prophet is commonly identified, derives from the Greek form, *Zoroastrēs.*

Very little is actually known about Zoroaster. He authored the five *Gathas,* or songs, in the Avestan language, calling himself a *zaotar,* "libation offerer." Other sections of the *Avesta* refer to him as an *athravan,* or fire priest. The society described in the *Gathas* was a pastoral one organized around family, clans, and tribes. Many deities were worshiped by Iranian tribesfolk during Zoroaster's lifetime. Some of these supernatural beings, like the *ahuras* (Sanskrit *asuras*) and *daevas* (Sanskrit *devas*), shared a common devotional heritage with early Indian beliefs. A ritual called the *yasna* (sacrifice, worship service) was performed by tribal priests each dawn. Animal sacrifice seems to have been part of this daily service. Zoroaster reformulated the beliefs and practices of his time by removing animal sacrifice from the *yasna* ritual, condemning the *daevas* as demons, and elevating the divinity of wisdom, Ahura Mazda, to the stature of high god and creator. As part of his new pantheon, Zoroaster spoke of a holy spirit, or Spenta Mainyu, the hypostasis of Ahura Mazda, in perpetual opposition to Angra Mainyu, the evil spirit. In this manner, the prophet established an ethical dualism. The *Gathas* indicate that Zoroaster faced opposition to his ministry from two groups, the *kavis* (princes) and the *karapans* (priests). But with support from the kavi Vishtaspa and other noblemen, such as Jamaspa and Frashaoshtra, whose daughter Hvovi he married, Zoroaster was able to preach successfully.

Because so little was known about the prophet, a detailed but spurious hagiography developed in late antiquity under the Sassanian magi. It has been preserved in Pahlavi language texts, including the *Denkard* (Acts of the Religion), books 5 and 7, and the *Wizidagiha* (Selections) of Zadspram. This tradition recast the image of Zoroaster, bringing him in line with

Near Eastern religious leaders like Moses, Jesus, and Muhammad. According to these sources, Zarathushtra left home at the age of twenty. After a decade of wandering and contemplation in the wilderness he received revelation, then returned home to spread the message of Ahura Mazda. Zarathushtra was persecuted by clergy of the older cults in his native lands and had to seek refuge at the court of the Khorasmian ruler Vishtaspa, who accepted the religion. There, it was written, Zarathushtra preached and gained many followers until he was assassinated by a rival priest at the age of seventy-seven. Another change in Zoroaster's image had occurred even earlier, when the magi included him among the ranks of their ancestors. Magian claims proved to be so highly effective that, by late antiquity, Greeks and Romans referred to Zoroaster as a magus. For Hellenistic scholars, Zoroaster eventually came to represent the archetype of a sage and magician (a term that, like the Latin *magus,* derives from Old Iranian *magupaiti*).

BIBL.: Mary Boyce, "Zoroaster the Priest," *Bulletin of the School of Oriental and African Studies* (London), 33 (1970): 22–38. Jacques Duchesne-Guillemin, *The Western Response to Zoroaster* (Oxford, 1958). Helmut Humbach and Pallan Ichaporia, trans., *The Heritage of Zarathushtra: A New Translation of His* Gathas (Heidelberg, 1994).　　J.K.C.

Zoroastrianism

Zoroastrianism, or Mazdaism, was a major religion in Iran and Transoxania during late antiquity. The prophet Zoroaster (Zarathushtra) preached some time between the 14th and the 12th centuries B.C.E. or, according to other sources, the 7th and 6th centuries B.C.E. Later, his preachings were adopted by a sacerdotal class known as the magi. The religion's Scriptures, the *Avesta,* include the *Gathas* of Zoroaster. Prayers, such as the Ashem Vohu, recited by the laity during daily religious observances, were gathered together into the *Khorde Avesta,* "shorter Avesta." Next in importance are religious exegeses written in Pahlavi. Among these is the *Zand* (Commentary) on the *Avesta,* compiled during Sassanian times.

By the end of the Sassanian period, the religion was structured around a rigid dualism between righteousness *(asha)* and evil *(drug),* personified by a pair of primal spirits: Ahura Mazda, the lord wisdom, or god, and Angra Mainyu, the evil spirit, or devil. Ahura Mazda supposedly created six *amesha-spentas,* "beneficent spiritual beings," representing aspects of material creation—Ameretāt (plants), Haurvatāt (water), Spenta Armaiti (earth), Asha Vahishta (fire), Khshathra Vairya (metal), and Vohu Manah (animals)—plus other minor spirits, such as Anahita (fertility) and Verethraghna or Wahram (victory), to assist him. In response, Angra Mainyu produced numerous *daevas,* or demons, including Azi (avarice), Nasush (pollution), and Asto Vidhatu (death). Because they

worshiped Ahura Mazda, Zoroastrians in late antiquity called themselves *Mazda-yasni,* "Mazdeans"—the designation Zoroastrian is a western one.

Zoroastrian sacred history is divided into two periods. The first period is that of creation. Its initial 3,000 years were marked by the first encounter between Ahura Mazda and Angra Mainyu, the genesis of lesser beneficent and malevolent spiritual beings, and an offer of peaceful coexistence in a state of purity. After Angra Mainyu spurned Ahura Mazda's overture of peace, he was temporarily overcome when the lord wisdom chanted the Ahuna Vairya prayer. Another 3,000 years passed while Angra Mainyu lay in a stupor, during which time Ahura Mazda transformed the spiritual creations into corporeal ones. The sphere of the sky was made of stone, enclosing oceans, seven continents, and a firmament with sun, moon, planets, and stars. In the central continent Ahura Mazda placed the first human being—an androgyne named Gayo-Maretan (mortal life)—the primordial bull, and the first plant. The second period of religious history is the ongoing age, in which good and evil mix together; it will also last 6,000 years. At its start, Angra Mainyu was aroused from his daze by lesser demons, invaded the world with them, and destroyed Gayo-Maretan, the primordial bull, and the first plant. Humanity arose from the semen of the androgyne, animals and cereals from the body of the first bull, and other plants from the seed of the initial plant. Human history passed, with the rise and fall of legendary dynasties, until the prophet Zoroaster was born in the religious year 8970. According to this sacred history, the era of Zarathushtra was followed by those of the Achaemenians, Parthians, and Sassanians. Thereafter, the Arabs conquered Iran. This conquest, and the reduction of Zoroastrians to the status of a religious minority, was rationalized in terms of a steady increase in evil heralding the final days of existence.

Zoroastrianism claims that human beings were created by Ahura Mazda as allies in his cosmic struggle against Angra Mainyu, and that humans consented to assume physical form to further this battle. Ahura Mazda, in turn, promised to resurrect all humans and grant them immortality once Angra Mainyu had been defeated. Trapped in the material world—which cannot be exited by evil—Angra Mainyu and his pandemonium will gradually be vanquished by divine beings and devotees acting in unison, it is believed. The rewards of heaven, after death, are offered to the souls of believers who have upheld righteousness and combated evil during their lifetime. Zoroastrians hold that when an individual dies, his or her soul stays by the corpse for three days. On the fourth day, Sraosha, the divinity of obedience and prayer, approaches the righteous soul, wards off the demon of death, the Shaker of Bones, and other ghouls, and leads the soul to the bridge of the separator (Pahlavi *chinwad puhl*). Here the soul encounters its conscience in the form of a

Rock relief from the site of Taq-i Bostan in Iran depicting the creator deity Ahura Mazda granting the Sassanian king Ardashir II (379–383 C.E.) a diadem of sovereignty, while Mithra protects the king's back.

beautiful maiden. Sraosha does not approach the soul of a sinner, however. An impure soul is fettered by the demons and led to the bridge, where it encounters its conscience in the form of an ugly hag. Each soul undergoes individual judgment, presided over by a triad of divine beings—Mithra, the deity of covenants; Rashnu, the judge; and Sraosha—at the base of the bridge. If the soul's good deeds are greater than its evil deeds, it is then led across the bridge into paradise. If its evil deeds outweigh the good ones, the impure soul is cast by the demons into hell. In cases where a soul's good and evil deeds are equal, it is consigned to limbo, or the "place of the motionless ones." During late antiquity, Islam absorbed not only Zoroastrian notions of heaven, hell, and limbo but also the entire scheme involving individual judgment at a bridge of separation. Christianity also assimilated the Zoroastrian belief in the soul's afterlife.

Years of evil, pollution, and suffering will, in the Zoroastrian belief of late antiquity, be followed by two millennia during which three saviors will be born. Eventually, in the religious year 11,973, the final savior, Saoshyant, will resurrect the dead. Ahura Mazda and other deities will descend to earth, and righteous individuals will be separated from evil ones. Each sinner, having already suffered in hell or limbo after death, will be purified of his or her transgressions by means of an ordeal involving molten metal. Immortality of body and soul will be granted to all humans. Ahura Mazda, the beneficent immortals, and other divine beings will then annihilate all the minor demons. Angra Mainyu will be forced back into hell, which will

be sealed shut with molten metal. Thus human history will end, eternity will recommence in absolute perfection, and humanity will dwell happily on a refurbished earth from the religious year 12,000 onward.

Between the ages of seven and fifteen, each Zoroastrian boy or girl would undergo initiation into the religion. After initiation, each believer became fully responsible for his or her own moral and communal life. During the ceremony, the initiate—having learned basic prayers—donned a white undershirt (Pahlavi *shabig*, New Persian *sudra, sedra*) and tied a sacred cord (Pahlavi *kustig*, New Persian *kusti*) around his or her waist. The sacred cord had to be untied and retied with the recitation of prayers, at the beginning of each division of the day, and prior to worshiping at a fire temple.

Once performed outdoors, by the Sassanian era most Zoroastrian rituals came to conducted within complexes known as fire temples. Fire was one of the seven sacred creations, the others being water, earth, metal, plants, animals, and human beings. In addition, fire was believed to be capable of vanquishing evil. Consequently, it became the faith's icon. A sacred fire (*atakhsh i Wahram*) was kept constantly burning in an altar at each of the major fire temples (*dar i Mihr*) in Iran—such as Adur Farrobay in Fars, Adur Gushnasp in Media, Adur Burzenmihr in Khurasan, and the Sassanian family flame Adur Anahid at the city of Istakhr. Smaller temples (*dadgah, gumbad*) also existed in most towns throughout Iran and Transoxania. The central devotional ceremony performed in fire temples was termed the *yasna*, in which, among other rites, the *haoma*, or ephedra plant, was pounded for sacrifice to Ahura Mazda and other divinities. *Jashan* (thanksgiving) services would also be celebrated at fire temples; so too the *gahanbars* (feasts). Zoroastrians in late antiquity exposed their dead to animals and birds of prey. This practice appears to have been introduced by the magi to prevent pollution of the sacred earth, fire, and water by decaying corpses. Each corpse would be washed, carried to a *dakhma* (funerary tower), and placed within this circular enclosure open to the sky. Once a corpse's flesh had been eaten away, the bones were deposited in an ossuary.

Conversion to Islam of Zoroastrians occurred after the Arab conquest of Iran in the 7th century C.E., reaching its zenith in the 9th century. For an apostate who had embraced Islam, reconversion back to Zoroastrianism was possible, but this happened infrequently. Children raised within an Islamic context lost contact with Zoroastrianism. The threat of absorption into an increasingly large Muslim community forced persons who remained Zoroastrian to seek refuge in the thinly populated regions of central Iran, in places like Yazd. Others immigrated to India in the 10th century, where they became known as Parsis, or "Persians."

BIBL.: Jamsheed Choksy, *Purity and Pollution in Zoroastrianism: Triumph over Evil* (Austin, 1989). Shaul Shaked, *Dualism in Transformation: Varieties of Religion in Sasanian Iran* (London, 1994). Robert C. Zaehner, *The Dawn and Twilight of Zoroastrianism* (London, 1961). J.K.C.

Zosimus

Zosimus wrote his *New History* shortly after 498. (The precise significance of the title is disputed.) Apart from an introduction, the work comprises three main sections that differ in scope, attitude, and accuracy. In compiling his work, Zosimus condensed three earlier histories one after another, sometimes adding material from other sources into their narratives, which he often abbreviated drastically. For the period from 238 to 270, Zosimus appears to base himself on Dexippus; from 270 to 404 he follows the vague, highly rhetorical, and violently anti-Christian Eunapius; then from 407, after a gap caused by the transition between sources, he reproduces the far more exact and dispassionate Olympiodorus, whose transliterated Latin he faithfully transcribed in many passages. Zosimus's text breaks off abruptly in the summer of 410, shortly after the beginning of book 6. It seems probable that both Zosimus's pagan account of Alaric's sack of Rome and his account of the reign of Diocletian and the Diocletianic persecution, which is missing at the end of book 1 and start of book 2, were deliberately removed by Christian readers or scribes who were offended by their polemical tone.

Zosimus defines his main theme as the antithesis of Polybius's account of how the Romans rapidly acquired their empire: he states that he will tell "how they destroyed it in no long period 'by their own presumptuous sins'" (quoting *Odyssey* 1.34). The crucial verb in this passage has often been mistranslated (it means "corrupted" or "ruined," not "lost"), and on this basis Zosimus has been interpreted as a spiritual forerunner of Gibbon. But all the pessimistic passages adduced to support this interpretation occur in the Eunapian section of Zosimus: hence they reflect the mediated voice of Eunapius presenting the defeat at Adrianople and the decline of the Roman empire as the inevitable outcome of Constantine's conversion to Christianity.

BIBL.: W. A. Goffart, "Zosimus, the First Historian of Rome's Fall," *American Historical Review* 76 (1971): 412–441, repr. in his *Rome's Fall and After* (London and Ron-

ceverte, W. V., 1989), 81–110. F. Paschoud, trans., *Zosime: Histoire nouvelle* (Paris, 1971–1989). R. T. Ridley, trans., *Zosimus: New History* (Sydney, 1982). T.D.B.

Zurvan

Zurvan, a divinity of time and fate, is attested both as a minor entity in Zoroastrianism and as the high god of Zurvanism. It is, however, unclear whether Zurvanism was an independent religion, a monist movement within Zoroastrianism, or a manner of contemplating the nature and passage of time. Zurvanite ideas are attested in Iran, even in Zoroastrian doctrine, from Achaemenian through early Islamic times, and may have gained the following of leading members within the Sassanian royal court.

Zoroastrian theology in the Pahlavi language mentions Zurvan in two broad contexts—*zurwan i akaranag* (Avestan *zrvan akarana*), "infinite time," and *zurwan i drang-khwaday* (Avestan *zrvan dareghokhvadhata*), "time of the long dominion" or *zurwan i kanaragomand* (alternately *zurwan i brinomand*), "finite time." Traces of Zurvanite ideas may be present in the 9th century *Wizidagiha* (Selections) of Zadspram the magus. The chief extant sources for Zurvan and his worship are, however, Christian and Muslim, including the Cappadocian bishop Theodore of Mopsuestia, the Armenian writers Enzik of Kolb and Elishe Vardapet, the Syriac authors Theodore bar Konai and Yohannan bar Penkaye, and the Iranian heresiographer al-Shahrastani.

Zurvanite mythology claims that Ohrmazd (Ahura Mazda) and Ahriman (Angra Mainyu) were twin spirits born from a paternal deity, Zurvan. Ohrmazd was conceived as a result of a thousand-year sacrifice by Zurvan for a son who would create the universe. Ahriman was conceived because Zurvan doubted that his sacrifice would prove effective. Zurvan, realizing that twins had been conceived, vowed to grant dominion to the firstborn. Ahriman, perceiving this, emerged first and claimed the universe. Zurvan, seeking to limit the evil twin's power, established a finite period of 9,000 years during which Ahriman would be in charge. Thereafter, Ohrmazd would gain power and righteously determine the trajectory of events forever. Through this creation story Zurvan, although playing no major role after the beginning of time, emerged as the singular source of all existence.

BIBL.: Mary Boyce, "Some Further Reflections on Zurvanism," in *Iranica Varia: Papers in Honor of Professor Ehsan Yarshater* (Leiden, 1990), 20–29. Richard N. Frye, "Zurvanism Again," *Harvard Theological Review* 52 (1959): 63–73. Robert C. Zaehner, *Zurvan: A Zoroastrian Dilemma* (New York, 1972). J.K.C.

ABBREVIATIONS

Adv.Haer.	Irenaeus, *Adversus Haereses*	*Against Heresies*
AE	*Année épigraphique*	
Aed.	Procopius, *De aedificiis*	*On Buildings*
Aen.	Virgil, *Aeneis*	*Aeneid*
Amm.Marc.	Ammianus Marcellinus, *Res Gestae*	*History*
ANRW	*Aufstieg und Niedergang der römischen Welt*	*Rise and Fall of the Roman World*
Anth.Pal.	*Anthologia Palatina*	*Palatine Anthology*
Apoph.patr.	*Apophthegmata patrum*	*Sayings of the Desert Fathers*
Bell.Goth.	Claudian, *De bello gothico;* Procopius, *Wars,* Books 5–7: *De bello gothico*	*On the Gothic War*
Bell.Iug.	Sallust, *Bellum Iugurthinum*	*The Jugurthine War*
Bell.Pers.	Procopius, *Wars,* Books 1–2: *De bello persico*	*On the Persian War*
Bell.Van.	Procopius, *Wars,* Books 3–4: *De bello vandalico*	*On the Vandal War*
Bibl.	Photius, *Bibliotheca*	*Library*
C.Cels.	Origen, *Contra Celsum*	*Against Celsus*
C.Just.	*Codex Justinianeus*	*Justinianic Code*
C.Th.	*Codex Theodosianus*	*Theodosian Code*
Carm.	*Carmen; Carmina*	Poem; Poems
Carm.min.	Claudian, *Carmina minora*	*Minor Poems*
CCSL	*Corpus Christianorum, Series Latina*	*Corpus of Christian Writers, Latin Series*
CH	*Corpus Hermeticum*	*Corpus of Hermetic Writings*
Chron.	*Chronicon*	*Chronicle*
CIG	*Corpus Inscriptionum Graecarum*	*Corpus of Greek Inscriptions*
CIL	*Corpus Inscriptionum Latinarum*	*Corpus of Latin Inscriptions*
Clem.	Seneca, *De clementia*	*On Clemency*
CSEL	*Corpus Scriptorum Ecclesiasticorum Latinorum*	*Corpus of Latin Ecclesiastical Writers*
De abstin.	Porphyry, *De abstinentia*	*On Abstinence*
De civ.Dei	Augustine, *De civitate Dei*	*City of God*
De fac.	Plutarch, *De facie in orbe lunae*	*On the Face in the Lunar Orb*
De mort.pers.	Lactantius, *De mortibus persecutorum*	*On the Deaths of the Persecutors*
De vir.ill.	Jerome, *De viris illustribus*	*Lives of Illustrious Men*
Dem evang.	Eusebius, *Demonstratio Evangelica*	*Proof of the Gospel*
Enarr. in Ps.	Augustine, *Enarrationes in Psalmos*	*Commentaries on the Psalms*
Ep.	*Epistula*	*Epistle*
Ep. ad Eph.	Ignatius, *Epistula ad Ephesios*	*Letter to the Ephesians*
Etym.	Isidore of Seville, *Etymologiarum libri*	*Etymologies*
GCS	*Die griechischen christlichen Schriftsteller*	*The Greek Christian Writers*
Gen. c. Manich.	Augustine, *De Genesi contra Manichaeos*	*On Genesis against the Manichaeans*
Germ.	Tacitus, *Germania*	*Germania*
Gramm.Lat.	*Grammatici Latini*	*Latin Grammarians*
HGM	*Historici Graeci Minores*	*Minor Greek Historians*
Hist.	Gregory of Tours, *Historia Francorum*	*History of the Franks*
Hist.Ar.	Athanasius, *Historia Arianorum*	*History of the Arians*

Hist.eccl.	Historia ecclesiastica	Ecclesiastical History
Hist.Lang.	Paulus Diaconus, Historia Langobardorum	History of the Longobards
Hist.Laus.	Palladius, Historia Lausiaca	Lausiac History
Hom.	Homilia	Homily
IG	Inscriptiones Graecae	Greek Inscriptions
IGUR	Inscriptiones Graecae Urbis Romae	Greek Inscriptions of the City of Rome
ILCV	Inscriptiones Latinae Christianae Veteres	Ancient Christian Latin Inscriptions
ILS	Inscriptiones Latinae Selectae	Selected Latin Inscriptions
In Ruf.	Claudian, In Rufinum	Against Rufinus
In Tim.	Proclus, In Timaeum	On the Timaeus
Inst.	Institutiones	Institutes
Itin.Anton.	Itinerarium Antoninianum	Antonine Itinerary
Ling.	Varro, De lingua latina	On the Latin Language
Mag.	John Lydus, De magistratibus	On Magistracies
Mens.	John Lydus, De mensibus	On the Months
Met.	Ovid, Metamorphoses	
MGH	Monumenta Germaniae Historica	
Myst.	Iamblichus, Abammonis responsio = De mysteriis	On the Mysteries
Nat.Hist.	Pliny, Naturalis Historia	Natural History
Not.Dig. (oc.) (or.)	Notitia Dignitatum	List of Offices (West) (East)
Nov.	Novella	Novel
Orat.	Oratio	Oration
P	Papyrus	
P Oxy.	Oxyrhynchus Papyri	
Paed.	Clement of Alexandria, Paedagogus	The Schoolmaster
Pan.Lat.	XII Panegyrici Latini	Twelve Latin Panegyrics
Peri strat.	Peri strategias	On Strategy
PG	Patrologia Graeca	Writings of the Greek Fathers
PGM	Papyri Graecae Magicae	Greek Magical Papyri
Phil.	Cicero, Orationes philippicae	Philippics
PL	Patrologia Latina	Writings of the Latin Fathers
PLRE	Prosopography of the Later Roman Empire	
PO	Patrologia Orientalis	Writings of the Eastern Fathers
Praep.evang.	Eusebius, Praeparatio evangelica	Preparation for the Gospel
Prin.	Origen, De principiis	On First Principles
Quaest.conv.	Plutarch, Quaestiones conviviales	Table Talk
RE	Paulys Realenzyklopädie der classischen Altertumswissenschaft	Pauly-Wissowa, Encyclopedia of Classical Antiquity
Rep.	Cicero, De re publica	Republic
RLM	Rhetores Latini Minores	Minor Latin Rhetoricians
Sat.	Macrobius, Saturnalia	Saturnalia
SEG	Supplementum epigraphicum graecum	
Serm.	Sermo	Sermon
SH	Procopius, Anecdota	Secret History
SHA	Historia Augusta	Augustan History
Strom.	Clement of Alexandria, Stromateis	Miscellanies
Tact.	Arrian, Tactica	Tactics
Theol.Platon.	Proclus, Theologia platonica	Platonic Theology
Trin.	Augustine, De Trinitate	On the Trinity
Tusc.	Cicero, Disputationes tusculanae	Tusculan Disputations
VA	Philostratus, Vita Apollonii	Life of Apollonius of Tyana
Vera Relig.	Augustine, De vera religione	On True Religion
Verr.	Cicero, Orationes in Verrem	Verrines

760

Vit.Ant.	Athanasius, *Vita Antonii*	*Life of Antony*
Vit.Const.	Eusebius, *Vita Constantini*	*Life of Constantine*
VS	Eunapius, *Vitae philosophorum et sophistarum*	*Lives of the Philosophers and Sophists*

Contributors

A.C.	Anthony Cutler, Department of Art History, Pennsylvania State University
A.D.	Albrecht Dihle, Klassische Philologie, Ruprecht-Karls-Universität Heidelberg
A.E.	J. Allan S. Evans, Department of Classics, University of British Columbia
A.I.	Antonio Invernizzi, Dipartimento di Scienze Archeologiche, University of Turin
A.J.	Alexander Jones, Department of Classics, University of Toronto
A.J.W.	Annabel J. Wharton, Department of Art and Art History, Duke University
A.L.	Ariel Lewin, Department of History of Science, Linguistics, and Anthrolopology, Università degli Studi della Basilicata, Potenza, Italy
A.M.	Alexei Muraviev, Russian Academy of Sciences, Moscow
A.M.C.	Averil M. Cameron, Keble College, University of Oxford
A.Mar.	Arnaldo Marcone, Dipartimento di Storia, Università degli Studi di Parma
A.P.	Andrew Palmer, Department of the Study of Religions/School of Oriental and African Studies, University of London
A.R.	Aline Rousselle, Faculté des Lettres et Sciences Humaines, Université de Perpignan
A.Ric.	Alessandra Ricci, Department of Archaeology and History of Art, Bilkent University, Ankara
A.S.	Annemarie Stauffer, Department of Textiles, University of Applied Sciences, Cologne
A.T.G.	Anthony Grafton, Department of History, Princeton University
A.T.W.	Alford T. Welch, Department of Religious Studies, Michigan State University
A.W.	Andrew Watson, Department of Economics, University of Toronto
B.A.	Birgit Arrhenius, The Archaeological Research Laboratory, Djurksholm
B.C.	Béatrice Caseau, Collège de France, CNRS, and Université de Paris IV–Sorbonne
B.D.	Brian E. Daley, S.J., Department of Theology, University of Notre Dame
B.E.	Bonnie Effros, Department of Historical Studies, Southern Illinois University
B.F.	Bernard Flusin, Collège de France
B.J.	Baber Johansen, Ecole des Hautes Etudes en Sciences Sociales, Paris
B.M.	Bruce Metzger, Princeton Theological Seminary
B.S.	Brent D. Shaw, Department of Classical Studies, University of Pennsylvania
B.W.	Bryan Ward-Perkins, Trinity College, University of Oxford
C.C.	Carolyn L. Connor, Department of Classics, University of North Carolina, Chapel Hill
C.F.	Clive Foss, Department of History, University of Massachusetts, Boston
C.H.	Christopher Haas, Department of History, Villanova University
C.Hum.	Caroline Humfress, St. Catherine's College, University of Oxford
C.J.	Christopher Jones, Department of the Classics and Department of History, Harvard University
C.J.R.	Christian Julien Robin, Institut de Recherches et d'Etudes sur le Monde Arabe et Musulman, Maison de la Méditerranée, Aix-en-Provence
C.K.	Christopher Kelly, Corpus Christi College, Cambridge University
C.L.	Conrad Leyser, Department of History, University of Manchester
C.P.	Charles Pazdernik, Department of Classics, Emory University
C.R.	Charlotte Roueché, Department of Classics and Department of Byzantine and Modern Greek Studies, King's College London
C.S.	Carole Straw, Department of History, Mt. Holyoke College
C.W.	C. R. Whittaker, Churchill College, Cambridge University
D.B.	David Brakke, Department of Religious Studies, Indiana University
D.B.W.	David B. Whitehouse, The Corning Museum of Glass, Corning, New York

D.C.B.	David C. Braund, Department of Classics and Ancient History, Exeter University
D.D.L.	Donald D. Leslie, Research School of Pacific and Asian Studies, Australian National University, Canberra
D.F.	Denis Feissel, Centre d'Histoire et Civilisation de Byzance, CNRS, Collège de France
D.G.	David Graf, Department of History, University of Miami, Florida
D.J.	Dominic Janes, Pembroke College, Cambridge University
D.K.	Dale Kinney, Department of History of Art, Bryn Mawr College
D.K.-S.	Deborah Klimburg-Salter, Institut für Kunstgeschichte, Universität Wien
D.L.	A. D. Lee, Department of Classics, University of Wales, Lampeter
D.P.K.	Dennis P. Kehoe, Department of Classical Studies, Tulane University
D.S.	Danuta Shanzer, Department of Classics, Cornell University
D.T.F.	David T. Frankfurter, Department of History, University of New Hampshire
D.V.	Domenico Vera, Dipartimento di Storia, Università di Parma
D.W.	Donald Whitcomb, The Oriental Institute, University of Chicago
D.W.W.	Dietmar W. Winkler, Institute of Liturgiology, Christian Art, and Hymnology, University of Graz
E.A.M.	Elizabeth A. Meyer, Department of History, University of Virginia
E.C.	Elizabeth Clark, Department of Religion, Duke University
E.F.	Elizabeth Key Fowden, National Hellenic Research Foundation, Research Centre for Greek and Roman Antiquity, Athens
E.J.	E. M. Jeffreys, Exeter College, University of Oxford
E.K.	Edward J. Keall, Royal Ontario Museum, Toronto
E.P.	Elaine Pagels, Department of Religion, Princeton University
E.R.	Eric Rebillard, CNRS, Paris
E.S.	Erkki Sironen, Institutum Classicum, University of Helsinki
E.S.-S.	Emilie Savage-Smith, Oriental Institute, University of Oxford
F.C.	Frank M. Clover, Department of History, University of Wisconsin
F.D.	Fred M. Donner, The Oriental Institute and Department of Near Eastern Languages and Civilizations, University of Chicago
F.G.	Frantz Grenet, CNRS, Paris
F.R.	Franz Rosenthal, Department of Near Eastern Languages and Civilizations, Yale University
F.Y.	Fikret Yeğül, Department of History of Art and Architecture, University of California, Santa Barbara
G.B.	Gideon Bohak, Department of Jewish Philosophy, Tel Aviv University
G.D.	Giselle de Nie, Department of History, University of Utrecht
G.F.	Garth Fowden, National Hellenic Research Foundation, Research Centre for Greek and Roman Antiquity, Athens
G.F.-M.	Gladys Frantz-Murphy, Department of History, Regis University, Denver
G.H.	Georgina Hermann, Institute of Archaeology, University College London
G.H.B.	Gerhard H. Böwering, Department of Religious Studies, Yale University
G.K.	Genevra Kornbluth, Department of Art History and Archaeology, University of Maryland, College Park
G.M.B.	Gerald M. Browne, Department of Classics, University of Illinois at Urbana-Champaign
G.P.	Glenn Peers, Department of Art and Art History, University of Texas, Austin
G.R.	Giesela Ripoll López, Departmente de Prehistoria, University of Barcelona
G.S.	Georg Scheibelreiter, Institut für österreichische Geschichtsforschung, Universität Wien
G.Str.	Guy G. Stroumsa, Department of Comparative Religion, Hebrew University of Jerusalem
G.T.	Gocha Tsetskhladze, Department of Classics, Royal Holloway and Bedford New College, University of London
G.W.B.	G. W. Bowersock, School of Historical Studies, Institute for Advanced Study, Princeton
H.A.	Hans Aarsleff, Department of English, Princeton University
H.C.	Henry Chadwick, Christ Church, University of Oxford
H.D.	Harold Drake, Department of History, University of California, Santa Barbara
H.J.D.	Han J. W. Drijvers, Department of Languages and Cultures of the Middle East, Rijksuniversiteit, Groningen
H.K.	Hugh Kennedy, Department of Mediaeval History, University of St. Andrews
H.M.	Henry Maguire, School of Art and Design, University of Illinois at Urbana-Champaign
H.S.	Hagith Sivan, Department of History, University of Kansas

H.W.	Herwig Wolfram, Institut für österreichische Geschichtsforschung, Universität Wien
I.A.S.	Irfan A. Shahîd, Department of Arabic, Georgetown University
I.W.	Ian N. Wood, School of History, University of Leeds
J.A.	Javier Arce, Departamento de Historia Antigua y Arqueología del CSIC, Madrid
J.B.	Joëlle Beaucamp, CNRS Centre Camille Jullian, Aix-en-Provence
J.Ban.	Jairus Banaji, University of Oxford
J.C.	Jean-Michel Carrié, Ecole des Hautes Etudes en Sciences Sociales, Paris
J.D.	Jean Durliat, Université de Toulouse II (Le Mirail)
J.Des.	Jehan Desanges, Ecole Pratique des Hautes Etudes, Sciences historiques et philologiques, Sorbonne
J.Dil.	John Dillon, School of Classics, Trinity College, Dublin
J.E.	Jonathan Edmondson, Department of History, York University, Toronto
J.E.G.	Judith Evans Grubbs, Department of Classical Studies, Sweet Briar College
J.-F.S.	Jean-François Salles, Maison de l'Orient Méditerranéen, CNRS, Université Lyon 2
J.G.C.	James G. Crow, Museum of Antiquities, University of Newcastle Upon Tyne
J.G.M.	Joseph G. Manning, Department of Classics, Stanford University
J.H.	Jill Harries, Department of Ancient History, University of St. Andrews
J.H.-H.	Jennifer Hevelone-Harper, Department of History, Gordon College
J.J.O.	James J. O'Donnell, Department of Classics, University of Pennsylvania
J.K.C.	Jamsheed K. Choksy, Department of Near Eastern Languages and Cultures, Indiana University
J.M.	Jaclyn Maxwell, Department of History, Princeton University
J.M.D.	John M. Duffy, Department of the Classics, Harvard University
J.M.G.	Michael Gaddis, Department of History, Syracuse University
J.N.	John North, Department of History, University College London
J.O.	John Peter Oleson, Department of Greek and Roman Studies, University of Victoria
J.P.	Jaroslav Pelikan, Department of History, Yale University
J.Per.	John Percival, School of History and Archaeology, University of Wales, Cardiff
J.-P.S.	Jean-Pierre Sodini, U.F.R. d'Histoire de l'Art et Archéologie, Université de Paris I, Institut Universitaire de France
J.R.	John Riddle, Department of History, North Carolina State University
J.R.R.	James R. Russell, Department of Near Eastern Languages and Civilizations, Harvard University
J.S.	Jane Stevenson, Centre for British and Comparative Cultural Studies, University of Warwick
J.W.	Joel Walker, Department of History, University of Washington at Seattle
J.W.B.	John W. Barker, Department of History, University of Wisconsin
K.B.	Kai Brodersen, Alte Geschichte, Universität Mannheim
K.C.	Kate Cooper, Department of Religions and Theology, University of Manchester
K.D.	Katherine Dunbabin, Department of Classics, McMaster University
K.G.H.	Kenneth G. Holum, Department of History, University of Maryland
K.H.	Keith Hopkins, Faculty Board of Classics, Cambridge University
K.L.	Kenneth Levy, Department of Music, Princeton University
K.M.	Kathleen McVey, History Department, Princeton Theological Seminary
K.U.	Kevin Uhalde, Department of History, Princeton University
L.C.	Lionel Casson, Department of Classics, New York University
L.D.	Luuk de Ligt, Department of Law, Utrecht University
L.L.	Lee Levine, Department of Jewish History and Department of Archaeology, Hebrew University of Jerusalem
L.M.W.	L. Michael Whitby, Department of Classics and Ancient History, University of Warwick
L.N.	Lawrence Nees, Department of Art History, University of Delaware
L.P.	Laurent Pernot, University of Strasbourg II
L.R.	Lellia Cracco Ruggini, Faculty of Letters, University of Turin
M.C.	Michael Cook, Department of Near Eastern Studies, Princeton University
M.D.	Maribel Dietz, Department of History, Louisiana State University
M.Dzi.	Maria Dzielska, Department of Byzantine History, Jagiellonian University, Krakow
M.F.	Marie Theres Fögen, Rechtswissenschaftliches Institut, University of Zurich
M.G.	Michal Gawlikowski, Institute of Archaeology, University of Warsaw

M.G.M.	Michael G. Morony, Department of History, University of California, Los Angeles
M.J.R.	Michael J. Roberts, Department of Classical Studies, Wesleyan University
M.K.	Michaela Konrad, Kommission zur archäologischen Erforschung des spätrömischen Raetien, Bayerischen Akademie der Wissenschaften, Munich
M.M.	Michael Maas, Department of History, Rice University
M.M.M.	Marlia Mundell Mango, Institute of Archaeology, University of Oxford
M.P.	Michel-Yves Perrin, Paris, France
M.P.S.	Michael P. Speidel, Department of History, University of Hawaii at Manoa
M.R.	Megan Reid, Department of Religion, Princeton University
M.R.-D.	Marguerite Rassart-Debergh, Brussels, Belgium
M.R.S.	Michèle Renée Salzman, Department of History, University of California, Riverside
M.S.	Maurice Sartre, Département d'Histoire, Université François-Rabelais, Tours, and Institut Universitaire de France
M.W.	Marc Waelkens, Department of Archaeology and Art History, Katholieke Universiteit Leuven
M.Whi.	Mark Whittow, Oriel College, University of Oxford
N.D.	Nicola Denzey, Department of Philosophy and Religion, Skidmore College
N.E.	Nicholas Everett, Clare Hall, Cambridge University
N.J.	Naomi Janowitz, Department of Religion, University of California, Davis
N.L.	Noel Lenski, Department of Classics, University of Colorado
N.M.	Neil McLynn, Keio University, Japan
N.R.	Nasser Rabbat, Department of Architecture, Massachusetts Institute of Technology
O.G.	Oleg Grabar, School of Historical Studies, Institute for Advanced Study, Princeton
P.B.	Peter Brown, Department of History, Princeton University
P.B.G.	Peter B. Golden, Department of History, Rutgers University
P.C.	Paavo Castrén, Institutum Classicum, University of Helsinki
P.D.G.	Peter D. Garnsey, Jesus College, Cambridge University
P.D.V.	Pauline Donceel-Voûte, Department of Archaeology, Université de Louvain at Louvain la Nueve
P.E.R.	Paul E. Rorem, Princeton Theological Seminary
P.F.	Paula Fredriksen, Department of Religion, Boston University
P.G.	Patrick Geary, Director, Medieval Institute, University of Notre Dame
P.H.	Peter Heather, Department of History, University College London
P.J.	Peter Jeffery, Department of Music, Princeton University
P.-L.G.	Pierre-Louis Gatier, Department of Archaeology, Université Saint Joseph, Beirut
P.R.	Philip Rousseau, Department of History, University of Auckland
R.A.L.	Richard A. Landes, Department of History, Boston University
R.B.	Richard Bulliet, Department of History, Columbia University
R.C.	Roger Collins, Institute for Advanced Studies in the Humanities, University of Edinburgh
R.E.	Robert W. Edwards, Armenian Educational Council, Troy, N.Y.
R.F.T.	Robert F. Taft, S.J., Pontificio Istituto Orientale, Rome
R.G.	Richard Gordon, Ilmmünster, Germany
R.K.	Robert Kaster, Department of Classics, Princeton University
R.L.	Richard Lim, Department of History, Smith College
R.Liz.	Rita Lizzi, Turin, Italy
R.M.	Richard Miles, Churchill College, Cambridge University
R.P.	Robert Penella, Department of Classics, Fordham University
R.S.	Robert Schick, Albright Institute, Jerusalem
R.S.B.	Roger S. Bagnall, Department of Classics and Department of History, Columbia University
R.T.	Robert Thomson, Faculty of Oriental Studies, University of Oxford
R.V.	Raymond Van Dam, Department of History, University of Michigan
R.W.	Ruth Webb, Department of Classics, Princeton University
R.W.M.	Ralph W. Mathisen, Department of History, University of South Carolina
S.A.H.	Susan Ashbrook Harvey, Department of Religious Studies, Brown University
S.B.	Scott Bradbury, Department of Classics, Smith College
S.C.	Sarah Currie, London, England

S.E.	Susanna Elm, Department of History, University of California, Berkeley
S.G.	Stephen Gero, Orientalisches Seminar, Universität Tübingen
S.I.J.	Sarah Iles Johnston, Department of Greek and Latin, The Ohio State University
S.J.C.	Shaye J. Cohen, Department of Judaic Studies, Brown University
S.L.	Sam Lieu, Department of Ancient History, Macquarie University
S.P.	Simon Price, Lady Margaret Hall, University of Oxford
S.R.	Stefan Rebenich, Seminar für Alte Geschichte, Universität Mannheim
S.S.	Suzanne Saïd, Department of Classics, Columbia University
S.T.S.	Susan T. Stevens, Department of Classics, Randolph-Macon Woman's College
S.Z.	Stephen Zwirn, Byzantine Collection, Dumbarton Oaks, Washington, D.C.
T.D.	Theodore de Bruyn, Ottawa, Canada
T.D.B.	Timothy D. Barnes, Department of Classics, University of Toronto
T.H.	Tomas Hägg, Department of Greek, Latin, and Egyptology, University of Bergen
T.M.	Thomas F. Mathews, Institute of Fine Arts, New York University
T.M.H.	Tony Honoré, All Souls College, University of Oxford
T.N.	Thomas F. X. Noble, Department of History, University of Virginia
T.P.	S. Thomas Parker, Department of History, North Carolina State University
T.T.	Thelma K. Thomas, Department of the History of Art, University of Michigan
V.B.	Virginia Burrus, The Theological School, Drew University
W.D.	Wiktor Daszewski, Klassische Archäologie, Universität Trier
W.E.K.	W. Eugene Kleinbauer, Department of Art History, Indiana University at Bloomington
W.F.	William Frend, Gonville and Caius College, Cambridge University
W.K.	Walter Kaegi, Department of History, University of Chicago
W.Kli.	William Klingshirn, Department of Greek and Latin, Catholic University of America
W.M.	William E. Metcalf, American Numismatic Society, New York
W.P.	Walter Pohl, Forschungsstelle für Geschichte des Mittelalters, Österreichische Akademie der Wissenschaften
W.T.	William Tronzo, Newcomb Department of Art, Tulane University
Y.H.	Yitzhak Hen, Department of General History, University of Haifa
Y.Hir.	Yizhar Hirschfeld, Institute of Archaeology, Hebrew University of Jerusalem
Y.T.	Yoram Tsafrir, Institute of Archaeology, Hebrew University
Z.F.	Zbigniew Fiema, Dumbarton Oaks Research Library, Washington, D.C.

ILLUSTRATION CREDITS

INDEX